The Grove Encyclopedia
of Decorative Arts

The Grove Encyclopedia of

Decorative Arts

Volume I

Aalto to Kyoto Pottery

Edited by
GORDON CAMPBELL

Oxford University Press, Inc., publishes works that further
Oxford University's objective of excellence
in research, scholarship, and education.

Oxford   New York
Auckland   Cape Town   Dar es Salaam   Hong Kong   Karachi
Kuala Lumpur   Madrid   Melbourne   Mexico City   Nairobi
New Delhi   Shanghai   Taipei   Toronto

With offices in
Argentina   Austria   Brazil   Chile   Czech Republic   France   Greece
Guatemala   Hungary   Italy   Japan   Poland   Portugal   Singapore
South Korea   Switzerland   Thailand   Turkey   Ukraine   Vietnam

Published by Oxford University Press, Inc.
198 Madison Avenue, New York, New York 10016
www.oup.com

Library of Congress Cataloging-in-Publication Data

The Grove encyclopedia of decorative arts / edited by Gordon Campbell.
p. cm.
Includes bibliographical references.
ISBN-13: 978-0-19-518948-3 (hardcover : alk. paper)
1. Decorative arts—Encyclopedias. I. Campbell, Gordon, 1944- II. Title: Encyclopedia of
decorative arts.
NK28.G76 2006
745.03—dc22
2006009866

Printing number: 9 8 7 6 5 4 3 2 1

Printed in the United States of America
on acid-free paper

Contents

Preface

The Grove Encyclopedia of Decorative Arts offers an expansive collection of more than 3000 articles covering all aspects of decorative arts from Acanthus to Zebra wood. In recent years the decorative arts have risen in importance—an increasing number of exhibitions and dissertations focus on the subject, and it has become part of most core art history curricula. Its elevated place in academia and growing devotion among general collectors reaffirms the integral role the decorative arts have had in the history and development of world art.

Gordon Campbell, a highly experienced editor and a true Renaissance man, has accomplished the Herculean task of distilling the vast corpus of information on the decorative arts in Grove Art Online, nearly 4 million words, into a cohesive and remarkable reference work. Gordon has also written more than 1000 new entries to cover many areas that were not discussed in Grove Art Online. Indeed without the abundant talents and knowledge of Gordon and the scholarly community, major projects such as this could never come to exist.

This is the first in a series of print reference works from Oxford University Press to draw upon the wealth of material in Grove Art Online and fully update and illustrate this information for scholars, collectors, curators, students, researchers and general readers. Grove Art Online has its roots in *The Dictionary of Art* (1996, ed. Jane Turner), the landmark 34-volume encyclopedia containing 45,000 entries written by more than 6700 contributors from 120 countries. Today Grove Art Online is the foremost electronic visual arts resource; it is updated quarterly and, in our digital age, has become the indispensable online publication for thousands of researchers worldwide.

We hope that these subject-based print reference works will provide greater access to the highly specialized and diverse art historical material so many of us need. Publications such as this remind us that the pleasures and possibilities afforded by the printed book—the irreplaceable experience of leafing through pages of text, images and graphic design—remain valuable to the processes of learning and discovery, even in the 21st century.

Christine Kuan
Senior Editor
Grove Art Online
New York, 2006

Introduction

The distinction between the fine arts and the decorative arts first emerged in the 18th century. Until that time, artists had been members of craft guilds, and the terms 'artist' and 'artisan' were used interchangeably. From the mid-18th century, however, a distinction was drawn according to the criterion of purpose: the fine arts were intended to give pleasure, while the mechanical arts, which were later known as the decorative arts, were merely useful. The five fine arts were deemed to be painting, sculpture, architecture, music (i.e. composition) and poetry; sometimes this list was extended to include performing arts (rhetoric, dance, drama). The mechanical arts, which were variously known as *Handwerk* (German), *métier* (French), *artisanat* (French) and *mestiere* (Italian), included crafts such as ceramics, glassware, metalwork, weaving, furniture-making and interior decoration, all of which are represented at length in this book. The distinction between art and craft also created hierarchies within the fine arts, and at the bottom of these hierarchies, certain crafts were deemed to be merely decorative: easel painting was a fine art, but the painting of figures on pottery was decorative; the exteriors of buildings (including their gardens) were the product of the fine art of architecture, but the interiors (including layout as well as fittings and furnishings) were decorative art; sculpting in marble was a fine art, but ivory-carving and wood-carving were crafts. These excluded subjects are all included in this book in the defiant conviction that they are as important as the fine arts.

Such distinctions between arts and crafts may now seem untenable, but they have been institutionalized by museums such as the Victoria and Albert Museum in London and the Musée des Arts Décoratifs in Paris. It is the collecting principles of such museums that have largely determined what is included in this book. I have followed the lead of the V&A (which was initially known as the Museum of Manufactures) in including entries on designers and manufacturers as well as craftsmen. Fashion is sometimes considered as a distinct field (hence the Musée des Arts de la Mode in Paris), and has not been included here, but I have included an abundance of material on textiles, even though they are often the subject of separate museums, such as the Musée Historique des Tissus in Lyon. All crafted objects are designed and most are decorated, but most are not accommodated in museums of decorative arts, and so are not to be found in this book. I have, for example, included very little material relating to the design of transport, even though I am aware that cars, trains, ships, pogo sticks and shoes could have been included; the exclusion is not complete, however, in that decorative features such as figureheads are included in the entry on ship decoration. In the case of engravers, I have concentrated on those who specialized in ornamental rather than figurative subjects. I have cast my net widely, and so have included domestic arts (e.g. quilting and patchwork) and arts associated with death (e.g. taxidermy and head-shrinking), as well as arts of higher cultural status. In the case of large subjects, I have sometimes provided an overview (e.g. ceramics and furniture in China, toys, wallpaper) as well as entries on individual makers and types. In short, I have provided entries on subjects that one might reasonably expect to find in a book with this title. Within the limits that I have described, I have exercised my own judgement and indulged scores of personal enthusiasms, mostly stimulated by the labours of those who choose objects for display in museums. I have been fortunate in being able to visit museums all over the world, and so have been delighted to be able to include material on collections in Europe, the Middle East, Africa, Asia, the Americas, Australasia and the Pacific Islands. Collections typically range from antiquity to the present, and I have aspired to a similar chronological range, albeit with an emphasis on the period from the Middle Ages to the present.

I have also attempted to provide material that is not accessible to Anglophone users of electronic search engines. It is possible to Google one's way to facts, though as medical doctors complain when presented with pre-emptive diagnoses by patients, the facts may be inaccurate or out-of-date. What electronic resources (especially free ones) cannot at present provide is comprehensive access to material based on the most recent scholarship, or translations of much of the material in languages not understood by the reader. In the entries that I have written I have drawn on material in a score of languages, and in the entries that I have edited the writers have drawn on material in a vast number of languages. The entries therefore mediate this material for our intended readers, who are not only specialists in the decorative arts but also a miscellaneous group that includes collectors, practitioners of the crafts, university and high-school students and individuals who may have bought a crafted object and simply want to know more about it.

The fine arts are widely studied in universities and so generate a vast secondary literature. Many of the decorative arts, such as arms and armour or clocks and watches, are not much studied in the universities, and the responsibility for scholarly investigation falls on museum curators, whose meticulous scholarship is sometimes confined to local publications. The bibliographies attached to many entries often contain such items, most of which can be secured through inter-library loan systems. The bibliographies also include one type of book not normally found in reference publications, which is that of manuals intended for readers who wish to practise the crafts that are described in the entries.

GC
Leicester, 2006

Acknowledgements

Projects of this magnitude always rely on the talents of numerous individuals who help to conceptualize, plan and create the final publication. This publication began when Christine Kuan, Senior Editor of Grove Art Online, decided to commission a *Grove Encyclopedia of Decorative Arts*. On the recommendation of Pam Coote, who had been my editor for previous projects at Oxford University Press, I was asked to undertake the task; I am grateful to Pam for trusting me once again. Many of the articles in this book are edited and updated versions of nearly four million words on the decorative arts in Grove Art Online; the names of the original authors are listed at the end of volume two. More than 1000 articles in this book are not to be found in *The Dictionary of Art*, but in drafting them I have sometimes pillaged Grove entries.

Throughout the process of writing and editing I have been supported by a multitude of scholars and colleagues. Christine Kuan has been the best of all possible editors, responding quickly and efficiently to my daily e-mails and always eager to assist despite a heavy range of editorial commitments. Eleanor Graff-Baker has worked creatively and tirelessly both as bibliographer and as picture editor; in the former capacity she often tactfully drew attention to discrepancies between what I had written and what the secondary literature said, and so raised the scholarly standard of the enterprise, and in the latter she sometimes produced images that made me adjust the balance of an entry. Gerald Ward (Museum of Fine Arts, Boston) put his formidable expertise at my disposal, and greatly strengthened the American coverage. Christopher Rowell (The National Trust, London) read hundreds of entries, and his learned comments have enriched the entries on European (including English) furniture. I have also availed myself of the expertise of Pascale Aebischer (University of Exeter), David Cathers, Christian De Cock (University of Wales, Swansea), Piotr Kuhivchak (University of Warwick), Lois Stoehr (Winterthur Museum and Country Estate), Warren Roberts (SUNY, Albany) and Barbara McLean Ward (Tufts University). My institutional debts include University of Leicester, where my colleagues have tolerated the considerable extent to which this book has taken over my working hours, and the Victoria and Albert Museum, which rightly describes itself as the world's greatest museum of art and design, and through its exhibits, its website and its willingness to answer enquiries has contributed substantially to this encyclopedia.

At the production stage, the manuscript was ably copy edited by Gillian Northcott, who has been the copy editor for Grove Art Online for several years and had served as indexer to *The Dictionary of Art*; she cheerfully exceeded her brief, suggesting new entries and even drafting several. Last-minute queries were adeptly answered by John-Paul Stonard. The highly skilled team of development and production editors who helped bring this project to fruition included Martin Coleman, Tim DeWerff, Katherine Henderson, Georgia Maas, Carol Holmes, Dorothy Bauhoff, Caitlin Campbell, and Katharyn Dunham. Finally, I should like to thank my wife Mary, who has once again seen domestic life squeezed by a large book.

GC
Leicester, 2006

Abbreviations

Aab. Nord. Oldknd. Hist.
Aarbøger for nordisk oldkyndighed og historie [Yearbooks for Nordic antiquities and history]
Aachen, Domschatzkam.
Aachen, Domschatzkammer
Aachen, Suermondt-Ludwig Mus.
Aachen, Suermondt-Ludwig Museum
A. Afrique Noire
Arts d'Afrique noire
A. & Ant.
Art and Antiques
A. & Artists
Art and Artists
A. Asia
Arts of Asia
A. Asiatiques
Arts asiatiques
A. & Auction
Art and Auction
A. Bull.
Art Bulletin
Acad. Anlct. Kl. Wetsch.
Academiae analecta: Klasse der wetenschappen
ACT
Australian Capital Territory
AD
Anno Domini
Adelaide, A. G. S. Australia
Adelaide, Art Gallery of South Australia
Afr. A.
African Arts
Afrik.
Afrikaans
AH
Anno Hagirae
Ahmadabad, Calico Mus. Textiles
Ahmadabad, Calico Museum of Textiles
A. Inst. Chicago Mus. Stud.
Art Institute of Chicago Museum Studies
A. Islam.
Ars Islamica
Aix-en-Provence, Bishop's Pal.
Aix-en-Provence, Bishop's Palace
Aix-en-Provence, Mus. Tap.
Aix-en-Provence, Musée des Tapisseries
A. J. [London]
Art Journal
AK
Alaska (USA)
Akron, OH, A. Mus.
Akron, OH, Akron Art Museum
AL
Alabama (USA)

Alençon, Mus. B.-A. & Dentelle
Alençon, Musée des Beaux-Arts et de la Dentelle
Alès, Mus.-Bib. Pierre-André Benoît
Alès Musée-Bibliothèque Pierre-André Benoît
Allentown, PA, A. Mus.
Allentown, PA, Art Museum
Altenburg, Staatl. Lindenau-Mus.
Altenburg, Staatliches Lindenau-Museum
Altötting, SS Philipp und Jacob, Schatzkam.
Altötting, SS Philipp und Jacob, Schatzkammer
A. Med.
Arte medievale
Amer.
American
Amer. A. J.
American Art Journal
Amer. A. Rev.
American Art Review
Amer. Cer.
American Ceramics
Amer. Craft
American Craft
Amer. Furn.
American Furniture
Amer. Ind. A.
American Indian Art
Amer. Ind. A. Mag.
American Indian Art Magazine
Amherst, MA, Amherst Coll., Mead A. Mus.
Amherst, MA, Amherst College, Mead Art Museum
Amsterdam, Hist. Mus.
Amsterdam, Historisch Museum
Amsterdam, Rijksmus.
Amsterdam, Rijksmuseum
Amsterdam, Rijksmus. van Gogh
Amsterdam, Rijksmuseum Vincent van Gogh
Amsterdam, Stedel. Mus.
Amsterdam, Stedelijk Museum
Anchorage, AK, Hist. & F.A. Mus.
Anchorage, AK, Historical and Fine Arts Museum
Angers, Château, Col. Tap.
Angers, Château et Galerie de l'Apocalypse, Collection des Tapisseries
Angers, Mus., B.-A.
Angers, Musée des Beaux-Arts
Angers, Mus. Lurçat
Angers, Musée Jean Lurçat
Ann Arbor, U. MI
Ann Arbor, MI, University of Michigan

Ann Arbor, U. MI, Kelsey Mus.
  Ann Arbor, MI, University of Michigan, Kelsey
  Museum of Ancient and Medieval Archaeology
Ann Arbor, U. MI, Mus. A.
  Ann Arbor, MI, University of Michigan, Museum
  of Art
Annu. Rep. & Bull., Walker A.G., Liverpool
  Annual Report and Bulletin, Walker Art Gallery,
  Liverpool
Annu. Scu. Archeol. Atene & Miss. It. Oriente
  Annuario della Scuola archeologica di Atene e
  delle missioni italiane in oriente
An. S. Afr. Mus.
  Annals of the South African Museum
An. Sci.
  Annals of Science
Ant. Colr
  Antique Collector
Ant. Dealer & Colr's Guide
  Antique Dealer and Collector's Guide
Antibes, Mus. Picasso
  Antibes, Musée Picasso
Antiqua. Horology
  Antiquarian Horology
Ant. J.
  Antiques Journal
Antol. B.A.
  Antologia di belli arti
Ant. Viva
  Antichità viva: Rassegna d'arte
Antwerp, Mus. Vleeshuis
  Antwerp, Museum Vleeshuis
Anz. Ger. Nmus.
  Anzeiger der Germanischen Nationalmuseums
A. Q.,
  Art Quarterly
Arab.
  Arabic
Arca Lovan.
  Arca Lovaniensis
Archaeol.
  Archaeology
Archit.
  Architecture, Architectural
  Archit. Aujourd'hui
    L'Architecture d'aujourd'hui
Archit. Des.
  Architectural Design
Archit. Dig.
  Architectural Digest
Archit. Hist.
  Architectural History [Society of Architectural
  Historians of Great Britain]
Archit. J.
  Architecture Journal
Archit. Rev. [London]
  Architectural Review
Archv Asian A.
  Archives of Asian Art
Archv Esp. A.
  Archivo español de arte
Archv Kultgesch.
  Archiv für Kultgeschichte

Archv Stor. Lombardo
  Archivio storico lombardo
Arkhangel'sk, Reg. Mus. F.A.
  Arkhangel'sk, Regional Museum of Fine Arts
Arms Collect.
  Arms Collecting
Arnhem, Gemeentemus.
  Arnhem, Gemeentemuseum
Arras, Mus. B.-A.
  Arras, Musée des Beaux-Arts
Artibus & Hist.
  Artibus et historiae
Aschaffenburg, Schloss Johannisburg, Hof-& Stifts-
bib.
  Aschaffenburg, Schloss Johannisburg, Hof-und
  Stiftsbibliothek
Assoc.
  Association
Atami, MOA Mus. A.
  Atami, MOA Museum Art (MOA Bijutsukan)
Athens, Benaki Mus.
  Athens, Benaki Museum
Atlanta, GA, High Mus. A.
  Atlanta, GA, High Museum of Art
Atti & Mem. Accad. Agric., Sci. & Lett. Verona
  Atti e memorie dell'Accademia di agricoltura,
  scienze e letter di Verona
Atti Soc. Ligure Stor. Patria
  Atti della Società ligure di storia patria
Atti Soc. Piemont. Archeol. & B.A.
  Atti della Società piemontese di archeologia e
  belle arti
Atti Soc. Savon. Stor. Patria
  Atti della Società savonese di storia patria attrib.
  attributed
Augsburg, Maximilianmus.
  Augsburg, Maximilianmuseum
Augsburg, Städt. Kstsamml.
  Augsburg, Städtische Kunstsammlungen
Autun, Mus. Rolin
  Autun, Musée Rolin
A. VA
  Arts in Virginia
A. Ven.
  Arte veneta
A. & Vie
  L'Art et la vie
Avignon, Mus. Calvet
  Avignon, Musée Calvet
Avignon, Mus. Petit Pal.
  Avignon, Musée du Petit Palais
AZ
  Arizona (USA)
b
  born
Baghdad, Iraq Mus.
  Baghdad, Iraq Museum
Bagnères-de-Bigorre, Mus. A.
  Bagnères-de-Bigorre, Musée d'art
Baltimore, MD Hist. Soc. Mus.
  Baltimore, MD, Maryland Historical Society Mu-
  seum

Baltimore, MD, Mus. A.
  Baltimore, MD, Baltimore Museum of Art
Baltimore, MD, Walters A.G.
  Baltimore, MD, Walters Art Gallery
Bamberg, Domschatzkam.
  Bamberg, Domschatzkammer
Bangkok, N. Mus.
  Bangkok, National Museum
bapt
  baptized
Barcelona, Inst. Mun. Hist.
  Barcelona, Institut Municipal d'Història
Barcelona, Mus. Picasso
  Barcelona, Museu Picasso
Barlaston, Wedgwood Mus.
  Barlaston, Wedgwood Museum
Barnard Castle, Bowes Mus.
  Barnard Castle, Bowes Museum
Basle, Hist. Mus.
  Basle, Historisches Museum
Basle, Kstmus.
  Basle, Kunstmuseum
Basle, Mus. Vlkerknd.
  Basle, Museum für Völkerkunde und Schweitz-
  erisches Museum für Volkskunde
Basle, Öff. Kstsamml.
  Basle, Öffentliche Kunstsammlung
Bayeux, Mus. Tap.
  Bayeux, Musée de la Tapisserie de la Reine Math-
  ilde
BC
  Before Christ
BC
  British Columbia (Canada)
Beauvais, Archvs Dépt.
  Beauvais, Archives Départementales
Beauvais, Gal. N. Tapisserie
  Beauvais, Galerie nationale de la tapisserie
Beaux-A.
  Beaux-arts
Beaux A. Mag.
  Beaux Arts Magazine
Bedford, Cecil Higgins A.G.
  Bedford, The Cecil Higgins Art Gallery
Beds
  Bedfordshire (UK)
Beijing, Hist. Mus.
  Beijing, Historical Museum
Belfast, Ulster Mus.
  Belfast, Ulster Museum
Belg. Tijdschr. Oudhdknde & Kstgesch.
  Belgisch tijdschrift voor oudheidkunde en kun-
  stgeschiedenis [Belgian journal for archaeology
  and art history]
Belluno, Mus. Civ.
  Belluno, Museo Civico
Bergamo, Gal. Accad. Carrara
  Bergamo, Galleria dell'Accademia Carrara
Bergen, Vestlandske Kstindustms.
  Bergen, Vestlandske Kunstindustrimuseum
Berichte Musver. Judenburg
  Berichte des Museumsverein Judenburg

Berkeley, U. CA, A. Mus.
  Berkeley, CA, University of California, University
  Art Museum
Berkeley, U. CA, Hearst Mus. Anthropol.
  Berkeley, CA, University of California, Phoebe A.
  Hearst Museum of Anthropology
Berks
  Berkshire (UK)
Berlin, Altes Mus.
  Berlin, Altes Museum
Berlin, Antikenmus.
  Berlin, Antikenmuseum
Berlin, Bauhaus-Archv
  Berlin, Bauhaus-Archiv
Berlin, Bodemus.
  Berlin, Bodemuseum
Berlin, Freie U.
  Berlin, Freie Universität
Berlin, Kstbib. & Mus.
  Berlin, Kunstbibliothek Berlin mit Museum für
  Architektur, Modebild und Grafik-Design
Berlin, Kupferstichkab.
  Berlin, Kupferstichkabinett
Berlin, Märk. Mus.
  Berlin, Märkisches Museum
Berlin, Mus. Islam. Kst
  Museum für Islamische Kunst
Berlin, Pergamonmus.
  Berlin, Pergamonmuseum
Berlin, Skulpgal.
  Berlin, Skulpturengalerie mit Frühchristlich-By-
  zantinischer Sammlung
Berlin, Staat. Mus.
  Berlin, Staatliche Museen
Berlin, Tiergarten, Kstgewmus.
  Berlin, Kunstgewerbemuseum
Berne, Hist. Mus.
  Berne, Historisches Museum [Musée d'Histoire]
Besançon, Mus. B.-A. & Archéol.
  Besançon,   Musée   des   Beaux-Arts   et
  d'Archéologie
Besançon, Mus. Hist.
  Besançon, Musée Historique
Birmingham, Mus. & A.G.
  Birmingham, City of Birmingham Museum and
  Art Gallery
Birmingham, W. Midlands A.
  Birmingham, West Midlands Arts
Bloomfield Hills, MI, Cranbrook Acad. A. Mus.
  Bloomfield Hills, MI, Cranbrook Academy of Art
  Museum
Bloomington, IN U.
  Bloomington, IN, Indiana University
Bloomington, IN, U. A. Mus.
  Bloomington, IN, Indiana University Art Mu-
  seum
Bol. Cult. Assembl. Distr. Lisboa
  Boletim cultural da Assembléia distrital de Lisboa
Boll. A.
  Bollettino d'arte
Bol. Mus. Arqueol. N. Madrid
  Boletín del Museo arqueológio nacional de Ma-
  drid,

Bologna, Gal. Com. A. Mod.
  Bologna, Galleria Comunale d'Arte Moderna
Bologna, Mus. Civ. Archeol.
  Bologna, Museo Civico Archeologico
Bologna, Mus. Civ. Med.
  Bologna, Museo Civico Medievale e del Rinascimento
Bologna, Musei Civ.
  Bologna, Musei Civici
Bologna, Mus. S Domenico
  Bologna, Museo di S Domenico
Bologna, Pin. N.
  Bologna, Pinacoteca Nazionale
Bonn. Jb. Rhein. Landesmus. Bonn & Ver. Altertfreund. Rheinlande
  Bonn Jahrbücher des Rheinischen Landesmuseums in Bonn und des Vereins von Altertumsfreunden im Rheinlande
Boston, MA, Isabella Stewart Gardner Mus.
  Boston, MA, Isabella Stewart Gardner Museum
Boston, MA, Mus. F.A.
  Boston, MA, Museum of Fine Arts
Bouwknd. Wkbld
  Bouwkundig weekblad
BP
  Before Present (1950)
Brecon, Brecknock Mus.
  Brecon, Brecknock Museum
Bremen, Focke-Mus.
  Bremen, Focke-Museum [Bremen Landesmuseum für Kunst-und Kulturgeschichte]
Brescia, Musei Civ.
  Brescia, Musei Civici
Brighton, A.G. & Mus.
  Brighton, Art Gallery and Museum
Brighton, Royal Pav.
  Brighton, Royal Pavilion
Bristol, Mus. & A.G.
  Bristol, City of Bristol Museum and Art Gallery
Brit.
  British
Brit. A. J.
  British Art Journal
Brooklyn Mus. Bull.
  Brooklyn Museum Bulletin
Brookville, NY, Hillwood A. Mus.
  Brookville, NY, Hillwood Art Museum
Bros
  Brothers
Bruges, Memlingmus.
  Bruges, Memlingmuseum
Bruges, Stedel. Musea
  Bruges, Stedelijke Musea
Brunwick, Herzog Anton-Ulrich Mus.
  Brunswick, Herzog Anton-Ulrich Museum
Brunswick, Städt. Mus.
  Brunswick, Städtisches Museum
Brunswick, ME, Bowdoin Coll. Mus. A.
  Brunswick, ME, Bowdoin College Museum of Art
Brussels, Bib. Royale Albert ler
  Brussels, Bibliothèque Royale Albert ler

Brussels, Inst. Cervantes
  Brussels, Instituto Cervantes de Bruselas
Brussels, Mus. A. Anc.
  Brussels, Musée d'Art Ancien
Brussels, Mus. Hôtel Bellevue
  Brussels, Musée de l'Hôtel Bellevue
Brussels, Musées Royaux A. & Hist.
  Brussels, Musées Royaux d'Art et d'Histoire [Koninklijke Musea voor Kunst en Geschiedenis]
Bucharest, Acad. Socialist Repub. Romania
  Bucharest, Academy of the Socialist Republic of Romania (Academia Republicii Socialiste României)
Bucharest, N. Mus. A.
  Bucharest, National Museum of Art of Romania (Muzeu National de Artă a României)
Bucharest, Roman. Acad.
  Bucharest, Romanian Academy
Bucks
  Buckinghamshire (UK)
Budapest, Mus. Applied A.
  Budapest, Museum of Applied Art
Budapest, N.G.
  Budapest, Hungarian National Gallery (Magyar Nemzéti Galéria)
Budapest, N. Mus.
  Budapest, Hungarian National Museum (Magyar Nemzéti Múzeum)
Buffalo, NY, Albright-Knox A.G.
  Buffalo, NY, Albright-Knox Art Gallery
Bull. Amis Mnmts Rouen.
  Bulletin des amis des monuments rouennais
Bull. Asia Inst.
  Bulletin of the Asia Institute
Bull. Cleveland Mus. A.
  Bulletin of the Cleveland Museum of Art
Bull. Club Fr. Médaille
  Bulletin du Club français de la médaille
Bull. Liaison Cent. Int. Etud. Textiles Anc.
  Bulletin de liaison du Centre internationales d'étude des textiles anciens
Bull. Met.
  Bulletin of the Metropolitan Museum of Art
Bull. Mnmtl
  Bulletin monumental
Bull. Mus. Far E. Ant.
  Bulletin of the Museum of Far Eastern Antiquities
Bull. Needle & Bobbin Club
  Bulletin of the Needle and Bobbin Club
Bull. Orient. Cer. Soc. Hong Kong
  Bulletin of the Oriental Ceramic Society of Hong Kong
Bull. Rijksmus.
  Bulletin van het Rijksmuseum
Bull. Soc. Archéol. & Hist. Limousin
  Bulletin de la Société archéologique et historique du Limousin
Bull. Soc. Hist. A. Fr.
  Bulletin de la Société de l'histoire de l'art français
Bull. Soc. Hist. Paris & Ile-de-France
  Bulletin de la Société de l'histoire de Paris et de l'Ile-de-France

Bull. Soc. Indust. Mulhouse
   Bulletin de la Société industrielle de Mulhouse
bur
   buried
Burgos, Real Monasterio de las Huelgas, Mus. Telas & Preseas
   Burgos, Real Monasterio de las Huelgas, Museo de Telas y Preseas
Burl. Mag.
   Burlington Magazine
Bury St Edmunds, Manor House Mus.
   Bury St Edmunds, Manor House Museum
c.
   circa [about]
CA
   California (USA)
Cah. Cér., Verre & A. Feu
   Cahier de la céramique, du verre et des arts du feu
Cairo, Egyp. Mus.
   Cairo, Egyptian Museum
Cairo, Mus. Islam. A.
   Cairo, Museum of Islamic Art
Cairo, N. Lib.
   Cairo, National Library
   Caldas da Rainha, Osíris-Gal. Mun.
Caldas da Rainha, Osíris-Galeria Municipal das Caldas da Rainha
   Calgary, Glenbow–Alta Inst.
   Calgary, Glenbow–Alta Institute
   Cambridge, Fitzwilliam
   Cambridge, Fitzwilliam Museum
Cambridge U.
   Cambridge, Cambridge University
Cambridge, MA, Busch-Reisinger Mus.
   Cambridge, MA, Busch-Reisinger Museum
Cambridge, MA, Fogg
   Cambridge, MA, Fogg Art Museum
Cambridge, MA, Harvard U., Peabody Mus.
   Cambridge, MA, Harvard University, Peabody Museum of Archaeology and Ethnology
Cambridge, MA, MIT
   Cambridge, MA, Massachusetts Institute of Technology
Cambridge, MA, Sackler Mus.
   Cambridge, MA, Arthur M. Sackler Museum
Cambs
   Cambridgeshire (UK)
can
   canonized
Can. Colr
   Canadian Collector
Cardiff, N. Mus.
   Cardiff, National Museum of Wales
Carson City, NV, State Mus.
   Carson City, NV, Nevada State Museum
Caserta, Pal. Reale
   Caserta, Palazzo Reale
Castelli, Mus. Cer.
   Castelli, Museo della Ceramica
cat.
   catalogue

Cer. Mthly
   Ceramics Monthly
Cer. Rev.
   Ceramic Review
   Certaldo, Pal. Pretorio
   Certaldo, Museo del Palazzo Pretorio Vicariale
Cer. Tech.
   Ceramics Technica
Cer. Technical
   Ceramics Technical
Cer. Today
   Ceramics Today
Chanoyu Q.
   Chanoyu Quarterly
Chantilly, Mus. Condé
   Chantilly, Musée Condé
Chapel Hill, U. NC
   Chapel Hill, NC, University of North Carolina
Charleroi, Mus. Verre A. & Tech.
   Charleroi, Musée du Verre, Art et Technique
Charlottesville, NC, Mint Mus. Craft & Des.
   Charlottesville, NC, Mint Museum of Craft and Design
Chartres, Mus. B.-A.
   Chartres, Musée des Beaux-Arts
Chelles, Mus. Alfred Bonno
   Chelles, Musée Alfred Bonno
Cheltenham, A.G. & Mus.
   Cheltenham, Cheltenham Art Gallery & Museum
Ches
   Cheshire (UK)
Chicago, IL, A. Inst.
   Chicago, IL, Art Institute of Chicago
Chicago, IL, Field Mus. Nat. Hist.
   Chicago, IL, Field Museum of Natural History
Chicago, IL, Terra Mus. Amer. A.
   Chicago, IL, Terra Museum of American Art
Chicago, IL, Ukrainian Inst. Mod. A.
   Chicago, IL, Ukrainian Institute of Modern Art
Chicago, U. Chicago, IL, Orient. Inst. Mus.
   Chicago, IL, University of Chicago, Oriental Institute Museum
Chicago, U. Chicago, IL, Smart Mus. A.
   Chicago, IL, University of Chicago, David and Alfred Smart Museum of Art
Chin.
   Chinese
Christies Rev. Season
   Christie's Review of the Season
Ciba Z.
   Ciba Zeitschrift
Cie
   Compagnie [French]
Cincinnati, OH, A. Mus.
   Cincinnati, OH, Cincinnati Art Museum
Cincinnati, OH, Treadway Gall.
   Cincinnati, OH, Treadway Gallery
Cleve, Städt. Mus. Haus Koekkoek
   Cleve, Städtisches Museum Haus Koekkoek
Cleveland, OH, Mus. A.
   Cleveland, OH, Cleveland Museum of Art
CO
   Colorado (USA)

Co.
  Company
Coburg, Veste Coburg
  Coburg, Kupferstichkabinettder Kunstsammlungen der Veste Coburg
Col., Cols
  Collection
Colmar, Mus. Unterlinden
  Colmar, Musée d'Unterlinden
Cologne, Gal. Ulrich Fiedler
  Cologne, Galerie Ulrich Fiedler
Cologne, Josef-Haubrich-Ksthalle
  Cologne, Josef-Haubrich-Kunsthalle
Cologne, Kstgewmus.
  Cologne, Kunstgewerbemuseum [name changed in 1989 to Museum für Angewandte Kunst]
Cologne, Mus. Ostasiat. Kst
  Cologne, Museum für Ostasiatische Kunst der Stadt Köln
Cologne, Röm.–Ger.-Mus
  Cologne, Römisch–Germanisches-Museum
Cologne, Schnütgen-Mus.
  Cologne, Schnütgen-Museum
Columbia, MO, U. Missouri-Columbia
  Columbia, MO, University of Missouri-Columbia
Columbus, GA, Mus.
  Columbus, GA, Columbus Museum
Columbus, OH State U.
  Columbus, OH, Ohio State University
Conn. A.
  Connaissance des arts
Copenhagen, Davids Saml.
  Copenhagen, Davids Samling
Copenhagen, Jensen Mus.
  Copenhagen, George Jensen Museum
Copenhagen, Kon. Bib.
  Copenhagen, Kongelige Bibliotek
Copenhagen, Kon. Saml.
  Copenhagen, Kongelige Samling
Copenhagen, Kstindustmus.
  Copenhagen, Danske Kunstindustrimuseum
Copenhagen, Ny Carlsberg Glyp.
  Copenhagen, Ny Carlsberg Glyptothek
Coral Gables, FL, U. Miami, Lowe A. Mus.
  Coral Gables, FL, University of Miami, Lowe Art Museum
Corning, NY, Mus. Glass
  Corning, NY, Museum of Glass
Corp.
  Corporation
Corriere Cer.
  Corriere dei ceramisti
Coventry, Herbert A.G. & Mus.
  Coventry, Herbert Art Gallery and Museum
Cremona, Mus. Civ.
  Cremona, Museo Civico
CT
  Connecticut (USA)
Cuenca, Mus. Dioc.-Catedralicio
  Cuenca, Museo Diocesano-Catedralicio
Cult. & Hist.
  Culture and History

Current Archaeol.
  Current Archaeology
$
  dollars
d
  died
Dallas, TX, Pillsbury & Peters F.A.
  Dallas, TX, Pillsbury & Peters Fine Art
Damascus, N. Mus.
  Damascus, National Museum of Damascus
Darmstadt, Hess. Landesmus.
  Darmstadt, Hessisches Landesmuseum
Dayton, OH, A. Inst.
  Dayton, OH, Dayton Art Institute
DC
  District of Columbia (USA)
DE
  Delaware (USA)
Dec
  December
Decatur, IL, Millkin U., Dept. F.A.
  Decatur, IL, Millikin University, Department of Fine Art
Derby, Mus. & A.G.
  Derby, Museum and Art Gallery
Derby, U. Derby
  Derby, University of Derby
Derbys
  Derbyshire
Dertua, Mus. Reg. Cer.
  Deruta, Museo regionale della ceramica
Des. Issues
  Design Issues
destr.
  destroyed
Detroit, MI, Inst. A.
  Detroit, MI, Detroit Institute of Arts
Deurne, Prov. Mus. Sterckshof
  Deurne, Proviniciaal Museum Sterckshof
Devon
  Devonshire (UK)
diam.
  diameter
Dijon, Mus. B.-A.
  Dijon, Musée des Beaux-Arts
diss.
  dissertation
Donaueschingen, Fürstenberg-Samml.
  Donaueschingen, Fürstenberg-Sammlungen
Dr
  Doctor
Dresden, Gal. Richter
  Dresden, Galerie Richter
Dresden, Hist. Mus.
  Dresden, Historisches Museum [in Zwinger]
Dresden, Kupferstichkab.
  Dresden, Kupferstichkabinett
Dresden, Kstgewmus. Staatl. Kstsamml.
  Dresden, Kunstgewerbe-Museum der Staatlichen Kunstsammlungen
Dresden, Porzellansamml.
  Dresden, Porzellansammlung [in Zwinger]

Dresden, Staatl. Kstsammlungen
   Dresden, Staatliche Kunstsammlungen
Dresden, Staatsarchv
   Dresden, Staatsarchiv
Dublin, Chester Beatty Lib.
   Dublin, Chester Beatty Library and Gallery of Oriental Art
Dublin, N. Coll. A. & Des.
   Dublin, National College of Art and Design
Dublin, N.G.
   Dublin, National Gallery of Ireland
Dublin, N. Mus.
   Dublin, National Museum of Ireland
Dublin, U. Coll.
   Dublin, University of Dublin, University College
Dumbarton, Scot. Pott. Soc.
   Dumbarton, Scottish Pottery Society
Dumbarton Oaks Pap.
   Dumbarton Oaks Papers
Durham, U. Durham
   Durham, University of Durham
Düsseldorf, Hejtens-Mus.
   Düsseldorf, Hejtens-Museum [Deutsches Keramikmuseum]
Düsseldorf, Kstmus.
   Düsseldorf, Kunstmuseum
Düsseldorf, Mus. Kst Pal.
   Düsseldorf, Museum Kunst Palast
Dut.
   Dutch
Duxbury, MA, A. Complex Mus.
   Duxbury, MA, Art Complex Museum
E.
   East
Eastbourne, Towner A.G. & Local Hist. Mus.
   Eastbourne, Towner Art Gallery and Local History Museum
East Lansing, MI State U., Kresge A. Mus.
   East Lansing, MI, Michigan State University, Kresge Art Museum
Ecouen, Mus. Ren.
   Ecouen, Musée de la Renaissance, Château
ed.
   editor
Edinburgh, N.G.
   Edinburgh, National Gallery of Scotland
Edinburgh, N.G. Mod. A.
   Edinburgh, National Gallery of Modern Art
Edinburgh, N. Mus. Ant.
   Edinburgh, National Museum of Antiquities
Edinburgh, N.P.G.
   Edinburgh, National Portrait Gallery
Edinburgh, Royal Mus. Scotland
   Edinburgh, Royal Museum of Scotland
Edinburgh, Scot. A.C.
   Edinburgh, Scottish Arts Council
Edinburgh, Scot. Min. Mus.
   Edinburgh, Scottish Mining Museum
edn
   edition
eds
   editors

e.g.
   exempli gratia [for example]
Eichenzell, Schloss Fasanerie, Mus.
   Eichenzell, Schloss Fasanerie, Museum
Enna, Mus. Alessi
   Enna, Museo Alessi
Eng.
   English
Erie, PA, A. Mus.
   Erie, PA, Erie Art Museum
Essex Inst. Hist. Coll.
   Essex Institute Historical Collections
est.
   established
etc
   etcetera [and so on]
Évora, Mus. Évora
   Évora, Museu Évora [Museu Regional]
exh.
   exhibition
Faenza, Mus. Int. Cer.
   Faenza, Museo Internazionale delle Ceramiche
Fairbanks, U. AK Mus.
   Fairbanks, AK, University of Alaska,Museum
Farnham, W. Surrey Coll. A. & Des.
   Farnham, West Surrey College of Art and Design
Feb
   February
ff
   following pages
fig.
   figure (illustration)
FL
   Florida (USA)
fl
   floruit [he/she flourished]
Flem.
   Flemish
Flensburg, Städt. Mus.
   Flensburg, Städtisches Museum
Florence, Accad.
   Florence, Galleria dell'Accademia
Florence, Bargello
   Florence, Museo Nazionale del Bargello
Florence, Bib. Medicea–Laurenziana
   Florence, Biblioteca Medicea–Laurenziana
Florence, Mus. Horne
   Florence, Museo Horne
Florence, Mus. Opera Duomo
   Florence, Museo dell'Opera del Duomo
Florence, Mus. Opificio Pietre Dure
   Florence, Museo dell'Opificio delle Pietre Dure [e Laboratori di Restauro d'Opere d'Arte]
Florence, Mus. Stibbert
   Florence, Museo Stibbert
Florence, Pal. Davanzati
   Florence, Palazzo Davanzati
Florence, Pal. Medici – Riccardi
   Florence, Palazzo Medici – Riccardi
Florence, Pal. Vecchio
   Florence, Palazzo Vecchio
Florence, Pitti
   Florence, Palazzo Pitti

Florence, Sopr. B.A. & Stor. Col.
  Florence, Soprintendenza de Belle Artistiche e Storiche Collezioni
Florence, Uffizi
  Florence, Galleria degli Uffizi
F.M.R. Mag.
  F.M.R. Magazine
Folk A.
  Folk Art
Forsch. & Ber.: Staatl. Mus. Berlin
  Forschungen und Berichte: Staatliche Museen zu Berlin
Forsch. & Fortschr.
  Forschungen und Fortshritte
Fort Worth, TX, Kimbell A. Mus.
  Fort Worth, TX, Kimbell Art Museum
Fr.
  French
Frankfurt am Main, Mus. Ksthandwerk
  Frankfurt am Main, Museum für Kunsthandwerk
Frankfurt am Main, Städel. Kstinst. & Städt. Gal.
  Frankfurt am Main, Städelsches Kunstinstitut und Städtische Galerie
Fränk. Lebensbild.
  Fränkische Lebensbilder
Franschhoek, Huguenot Mem. Mus.
  Franschhoek, Huguenot Memorial Museum
Frederick, MD, Delaplaine Visual A. Cent.
  Frederick, MD, Delaplaine Visual Arts Center
Freiburg im Breisgau, Augustinmus.
  Freiburg im Breisgau, Augustinmuseum
Freiburg im Breisgau, U. Freiburg im Breisgau
  Freiburg im Breisgau, Albert-Ludwigs Universität
Furn. Hist.
  Furniture History
g
  gram(s)
GA
  Georgia (USA)
Gal., Gals.
  Gallery, Galleries
Gaz. B.-A.
  Gazette des beaux-arts
Geneva, Mus. A. & Hist.
  Geneva, Musée d'Art et d'Histoire
Geneva, Mus. Ariana
  Geneva, Musée Ariana
Gent. Bijdr. Kstgesch. & Oudhdknd
  Gentse bijdragen tot de kunstgeschiedenis en de oudheidkunde [Ghent contributions to art history and archaeology]
Genoa, Col. Pallavicino
  Genoa, Collezione Pallavicino
Genoa, Pal. Ducale
  Genoa, Palazzo Ducale
Genoa, Pal. Reale
  Genoa, Palazzo Reale
Genoa, Pal. S Giorgio
  Genoa, Palazzo S Giorgio
Genoa, Teat. Carlo Felice
  Genoa, Teatro Carlo Felice,

Ger.
  German
Gera, Mus. Stadt
  Gera, Museen der Stadt
Getty Mus. J.
  J. Paul Getty Museum Journal
Ghent, Mus. Sierkst
  Ghent, Museum voor Sierkunst
Ghent, Mus. S. Kst
  Ghent, Museum voor Schone Kunst
Ghent, Provgebouw
  Ghent, Provinciegebouw
Glasgow, A.G. & Mus.
  Glasgow, Art Gallery and Museum [Kelvingrove]
Glasgow, Burrell Col.
  Glasgow, Burrell Collection
Glasgow, Mus. Mod. A.
  Glasgow, Museum of Modern Art
Glasgow, School A., A. Col.
  Glasgow, School of Art, Art Collection
Glasgow, U. Glasgow, Hunterian A.G.
  Glasgow, University of Glasgow, Hunterian Art Gallery
Glass Circ.
  Glass Circle
Glass Club Bull.
  The Glass Club Bulletin
Glass Rev.
  Glass Review
Glass Technol.
  Glass Technology
Glens Falls, NY, Hyde Col.
  Glens Falls, NY, Hyde Collection
Glos
  Gloucestershire (UK)
Golfe-Juan Vallauris, Mus. Magnelli
  Golfe-Juan Vallauris, Musée Magnelli
Göttingen , U. Göttingen, Kstsamml.
  Göttingen, Georg-August-Universität, Kunstsammlungen
Gr.
  Greek
Graz, Karl-Franzens U.
  Graz, Karl-Franzens Universität
Grenoble, Mus. Grenoble
  Grenoble, Musée de Grenoble
Gressenhall, Norfolk Rural Life Mus.
  Gressenhall, Norfolk Rural Life Museum
Guangzhou, Guangdong Prov. Mus.
  Guangzhou, Guangdong Provincial Museum
Guardia Sanframondi, Mus.
  Guardia Sanframondi, Museo di Guardia Sanframondi
Guéret, Mus. Guéret
  Guéret, Musée de Guéret
Guildhall Misc.
  Guildhall Miscellany
Guizhou, Batik A. Acad.
  Guizhou, Batik Art Academy
h.
  height
Hadassah Mag.
  Hadassah Magazine

The Hague, Gemeentemus.
　The Hague, Haags Gemeentesmuseum
The Hague, Kon. Bib.
　The Hague, Koninklijke Bibliotheek [Nationale Bibliotheek]
The Hague, Kon. Huisarchf
　The Hague, Koninklijke Huisarchief
The Hague, Nouv. Images
　The Hague, Nouvelles Images
The Hague, Rijksmus. Meermanno–Westreenianum
　The Hague, Rijksmuseum Meermanno–Westreenianum
Halifax, Dean Clough Gals
　Halifax, Dean Clough Galleries
Halle, Kstgewmus.
　Halle, Kunstgewerbemuseum
Hamamatsu, Mun. Mus.
　Hamamatsu, Municipal Museum
Hamburg, Altonaer Mus.
　Hamburg, Altonaer Museum [Norddeutsches Landesmuseum]
Hamburg, Kst-& Gewsch.
　Hamburg, Kunst-und Gewerbeschule
Hamburg, Ksthalle
　Hamburg, Kunsthalle
Hamburg, Mus. Kst & Gew.
　Hamburg, Museum für Kunste und Gewerbe
Hamburg. Mittel-& Ostdt. Forsch.
　Hamburger mittel-und ostdeutsche Forschungen
Hannover, Kestner-Mus.
　Hannover, Kestner-Museum
Hants
　Hampshire (UK)
Harvard J. Asiat. Stud.
　Harvard Journal of Asiatic Studies
Heb.
　Hebrew
Heidelberg, Ruprecht-Karls-U.
　Heidelberg, Ruprecht-Karls-Universität Heidelberg
Heimatbl. Siegkreises
　Heimatblätter des Siegkreises
Helsinki, Athenaeum A. Mus.
　Helsinki, Athenaeum Art Museum
Helsinki, Mus. Applied A.
　Helsinki, Museum of Applied Arts (Taideteollisuusmuseo)
Helsinki, Mus. Fin. Archit.
　Helsinki, Museum of Finnish Architecture (Suomen Rakennustaiteen Museo)
Hereford & Worcs
　Hereford & Worcester (UK)
Herts
　Hertfordshire
HI
　Hawaii (USA)
Hildesheim, Diözmus. & Domschatzkam.
　Hildesheim, Diözsanmuseum mit Domschatzkammer
Hist.
　History, Historical

Hist. Archaeol.
　Historical Archaeology: The Annual Publication of the Society for Historical Archaeology
Hist. Preserv.
　Historic Preservation
Hist. & Soc.
　História e sociedade
Hist. Today
　History Today
Hohenberg an der Eger, Mus. Dt. Porzellanindust.
　Hohenberg an der Eger, Museum der Deutschen Porzellanindustrie
Holland. Rev.
　Hollandsche revue
Hong Kong, Chin. U., A.G.
　Hong Kong, Chinese University, Art Gallery
Hong Kong, Chin. U., A. Mus.
　Hong Kong, Chinese University, Art Museum
Hong Kong, Flagstaff House Mus. Teaware
　Hong Kong, Flagstaff House Museum of Teaware
Hong Kong, Mus. A
　Hong Kong, Museum of Art
Hong Kong, Tsui Mus. A.
　Hong Kong, Tsui Museum of Art
Houston, TX, Mus. F. A.
　Houston, TX, Museum of Fine Arts
HRH
　His/Her Royal Highness
Hull, Ferens A.G.
　Hull, Ferens Art Gallery
Hung.
　Hungarian
IA
　Iowa (USA)
Ibiza, Mus. Arqueol.
　Ibiza, Museo Arqueológico
i.e.
　id est [that is]
IL
　Illinois (USA)
IN
　Indiana (USA)
Inc.
　Incorporated
incl.
　includes, including
India Int. Cent. Q.
　India International Centre Quarterly
Indianapolis, IN, Mus. A.
　Indianapolis, IN, Museum of Art
Indon.
　Indonesian
Innsbruck, Tirol. Landesmus.
　Innsbruck, Tiroler Landesmuseum
Interior Des.
　Interior Design
intro.
　introduction
Ipswich Mus.
　Ipswich, Ipswich Museum
Irish A. Rev.
　Irish Arts Review

Irish A. Rev. Yb.
    Irish Arts Review Yearbook
Istanbul, Mus. Turk. & Islam. A.
    Istanbul, Museum of Turkish and Islamic Art
Istanbul, Topkapı Pal. Mus.
    Istanbul, Topkapı Palace Museum (Topkapı Sarayı Müzesi)
It.
    Italian
Ithaca, NY, Cornell U.
    Ithaca, NY, Cornell University
J. Aesth. & A. Crit.
    Journal of Aesthetics and Art Criticism
Jaipur, Maharaja Sawai Man Singh II Mus.
    Jaipur, Maharaja Sawai Man Singh II Museum
J. Amer. Port. Soc.
    Journal of the American Portuguese Society
Jan
    January
Jap.
    Japanese
J. Archaeol. Sci.
    Journal of Archaeological Science
Jb. Berlin. Mus.
    Jahrbuch der Berliner Museen
Jb. Ksthist. Mus. Wien
    Jahrbuch des kunsthistorischen Museums Wien
Jb. Ksthist. Samml. Wien
    Jahrbuch des kunsthistorischen Sammlungen in Wien
Jb. Mus. Vlkrknde. Leipzig
    Jahrbuch des Museums für Völkerkunde zu Leipzig
Jb. Staatl. Kstsamml. Dresden
    Jahrbuch der staatlichen Kunstsammlungen Dresden
Jb. Ver. Christ. Kst München
    Jahrbuch des Vereins für christliche Kunst in München
J. Dec. A. Soc.
    Journal of the Decorative Arts Society
J. Des. Hist.
    Journal of Design History
J. Early S. Dec. A.
    Journal of Early Southern Decorative Arts
Jewel. Stud.
    Jewellery Studies
Jever, Schlossmus.
    Jever, Schlossmuseum Jever
J. Glass Assoc.
    Journal of the Glass Association
J. Glass Stud.
    Journal of Glass Studies
J. Hist. Col.
    Journal of the History of Collections
J. Intl. Snuff Bottle Soc.
    Journal of the International Snuff Bottle Society
J. Jew. A.
    Journal of Jewish Art
J. Mus. Ethnog.
    Journal of Museum Ethnography

J. Mus. F. A., Boston
    Journal of the Museum of Fine Arts, Boston
J. N. Cer. Soc.
    Journal of the Northern Ceramics Society
J. Northampton Mus. & A.G.
    Journal of the Northampton Museums and Art Gallery
Jouy-en-Josas, Mus. Oberkampf,
    Jouy-en-Josas, Musée Oberkampf
J. Pre-Raphaelite Stud.
    Journal of Pre-Raphaelite Studies
jr
    junior
J. Royal Soc. Antiqua. Ireland
    Journal of the Royal Society of Antiquaries of Ireland
Jschr. Salzburg. Mus. Carolino Augusteum
    Jahresschrift des Salzburger Museums Carolino Augusteum
J. Soc. Archit. Hist.
    Journal of the Society of Architectural Historians
J. Stained Glass
    Journal of Stained Glass
J.: Tiles & Archit. Cer. Soc.
    Journal: Tiles and Architectural Ceramics Society
Jud. Boh.
    Judaica Bohemiae
Juneau, AK State Mus.
    Juneau, AK, Alaska State Museum
J. Walters A.G.
    Journal of the Walters Art Gallery
J. Warb. & Court. Inst.
    Journal of the Warburg and Courtauld Institutes
J. Weavers, Spinners & Dyers
    Journal for Weavers, Spinners & Dyers
Kansas City, MO, Nelson–Atkins Mus. A.
    Kansas City, MO, Nelson–Atkins Museum of Art
Karlsruhe, Bad. Landesmus.
    Karlsruhe, Badisches Landesmuseum
Karlsruhe, Staatl. Ksthalle
    Karlsruhe, Staatliche Kunsthalle
Kassel, Dt. Tapetenmus.
    Kassel, Deutsches Tapetenmuseum
Kassel, Hess. Landesmus.
    Kassel, Hessisches Landesmuseum
Kassel, Staatl. Museen
    Kassel, Staatliche Museen Kassel
Kellinghusen, Mus.
    Kellinghusen, Museum Kellinghusen
Kendal, Abbot Hall A.G.
    Kendal, Abbot Hall Art Gallery
Ker.-Freunde Schweiz
    Keramik-Freunde der Schweiz
kg
    kilogram(s)
Kingston, Ont., Queen's U.
    Kingston, Ont., Queen's University
Kingswinford, Broadfield House Glass Mus.
    Kingswinford, Broadfield House Glass Museum
Kirkwall, Orkney, Tankerness House Mus.
    Kirkwall, Orkney, Tankerness House Museum
km
    kilometre(s)

Kraków, N.A. Cols
  Kraków, National Art Collections (Państwowe Zbiory Sztuki na Wawelu) [Wawel Castle]
Kraków, N. Mus.
  Kraków, National Museum (Muzeum Narodowe w Krakowie)
Kremsmünster, Stiftsgal.
  Kremsmünster, Stiftsgalerie
KS
  Kansas (USA)
Kst & Ant.
  Kunst und Antiquitäten
Ksthist. Tidskr.
  Konsthistorisk tidskrift [Art historical magazine]
Kstjb. Stadt Linz
  Kunstjahrbuch der Stadt Linz
Kuwait City, Mus. Islam. A.
  Kuwait City, Museum of Islamic Art
Kuwait City, N. Mus.
  Kuwait City, National Museum
KY
  Kentucky (USA)
Kyoto, N. Mus. Mod. A.
  Kyoto, National Museum of Modern Art (Kyoto Kokuritsu Kindai Bijutsukan)
Kyoto, Raku Cer. Mus.
  Kyoto, Raku Ceramics Museum (Raku Tōjoki Hakubutsukan)
Kyoto, Yugi A. Mus.
  Kyoto, Yugi Art Museum
£
  libra, librae [pound, pounds sterling]
l.
  length
LA
  Louisiana (USA)
Lagos, N. Mus.
  Lagos, National Museum [Nigerian Museum]
La Granja de San Ildefonso, Fund. Cent. N. Vidrio
  La Granja de San Ildefonso, Fundación Centro Nacional del Vidrio
La Granja de San Ildefonso, Mus. Vidrio
  La Granja de San Ildefonso, Museo del Vidrio
Lancs
  Lancashire (UK)
Laon, Mus.
  Laon, Musée de Laon
La Rochelle, Mus. Orbigny-Bernon
  La Rochelle, Musée d'Orbigny-Bernon
Lat.
  Latin
lb, lbs
  pound(s) weight
Leeds, C.A.G.
  Leeds, City Art Gallery
Leeds, U. Leeds
  Leeds, University of Leeds
Leeuwarden, Fries Mus.
  Leeuwarden, Fries Museum
Leicester, De Montfort U.
  Leicester, De Montfort University
Leicester, Jewry Wall Mus.
  Leicester, Jewry Wall Museum

Leics
  Leicestershire (UK)
Leiden, Rijksmus. Kon. Penningkab.
  Leiden, Rijksmuseum Het Koninklijk Penningkabinet
Leiden, Rijksmus. Oudhd.
  Leiden, Rijksmuseum van Oudheden
Leiden U.
  Leiden, Universiteit Leiden
Leids Ksthist. Jb.
  Leids kunsthistorisch jaarboek
Leipzig, Mus. Bild. Kst.
  Leipzig, Museum der Bildenden Künste
Leipzig, Mus. Gesch.
  Leipzing, Museum für Geschichte der Stadt Leipzig
Leipzig, Mus. Ksthandwks
  Leipzig, Museum der Kunsthandwerks
Le Mans, Mus. Tessé
  Le Mans, Musée de Tessé
Lexington, MA, Scot. Rite Mason. Mus. N. Her.
  Lexington, MA, Scottish Rite Masonic Museum of Our National Heritage
Liège, Mus. Verre
  Liège, Musée du Verre
Lille, Mus. Hosp. Comtesse
  Lille, Musée de l'Hospice Comtesse
Limoges, Dir. Rég. Affaires Cult. Limousin
  Limoges, Direction Régionale des Affaires Culturelles du Limousin
Limoges, Mus. N. Adrien-Dubouché
  Limoges, Musée National Adrien-Dubouché
Lincs
  Lincolnshire (UK)
Lisbon, Mus. Azulejo
  Lisbon, Museu do Azulejo
Lisbon, Mus. Gulbenkian
  Lisbon, Museu Calouste Gulbenkian
Lisbon, Mus. N. A. Ant.
  Lisbon, Museu Nacional de Arte Antiga
Lisbon, Mus. S Roque
  Lisbon, Museu de Arte Sacra de São Roque
Lisbon, Pal. N. Ajuda
  Lisbon, Palácio Nacional da Ajuda
Liverpool Mus.
  Liverpool, Liverpool Museum
Liverpool, Sudley A.G.
  Liverpool, Sudley Art Gallery
Liverpool, Walker A.G.
  Liverpool, Walker Art Gallery
Logan, UT State U., Nora Eccles Harrison Mus. A.
  Logan, UT, Utah State University, Nora Eccles Harrison Museum of Art
London, ACGB
  London, Arts Council of Great Britain
London, Anthony d'Offay Gal.
  London, Anthony d'Offay Gallery
London, Barbican A.G.
  London, Barbican Art Gallery
London, Barbican Cent.
  London, Barbican Centre
London, Bethnal Green Mus. Childhood
  London, Bethnal Green Museum of Childhood

London, BM
London, British Museum
London, Buckingham Pal., Royal Col.
London, Buckingham Palace, Royal Collection
London, Cent. Sch. A. & Crafts
London, Central School of Arts and Crafts
London, Clockmakers' Co.
London, Worshipful Company of Clockmakers
London, Crafts Council Gal.
London, Crafts Council Gallery
London, Crane Gal.
London, Crane Gallery
London, Des. Mus.
London, Design Museum
London, F.A. Soc.
London, The Fine Art Society plc
London, Fan Mus.
London, Fan Museum
London, Girdlers' Co,
London, Worshipful Company of Girdlers
London, Goldsmiths' Co.
London, Worshipful Company of Goldsmiths
London, Hayward Gal.
London, Hayward Gallery
London, Jew. Mus
London, Jewish Museum
London, Laurent Delaye Gal.
London, Laurent Delaye Gallery
London, Mus. London
London, Museum of London
London, Nat. Hist. Mus.
London, Natural History Museum
London, N.G.
London, National Gallery
London, N. Mar. Mus.
London, National Maritime Museum [Greenwich]
London, N.P.G.
London, National Portrait Gallery
London, Queen's Gal.
London, Queen's Gallery
London, RA
London, Royal Academy of Arts
London, RIBA
London, Royal Institute of British Architects
London, S. Bank Cent.
London, South Bank Centre
London, Sci. Mus.
London, Science Museum
London, Soane Mus.
London, Sir John Soane's Museum
London, Tower
London, Tower of London
London, U. Coll., Strang Print Room
London, University of London, University College, Strang Print Room
London, U. London, Courtauld Inst. Gals
London, University of London, Courtauld Institute Galleries
London, U. London, SOAS, Percival David Found.
London, University of London, School of Ori-

ental and African Studies, Percival David Foundation of Chinese Art
London, V&A
London, Victoria and Albert Museum
London, Wallace
London, Wallace Collection
London, Whitechapel A.G.
London, Whitechapel Art Gallery
London, William Morris Gal.
London, William Morris Gallery and Brangwyn Gift [Walthamstow]
Long Beach, CA, Mus. A.
Long Beach, CA, Museum of Art
Los Angeles, CA, Co. Mus. A.
Los Angeles, CA, County Museum of Art
Los Angeles, CA, Getty Mus.
Los Angeles, CA, J. Paul Getty Museum
Los Angeles, CA, MAK Cent. A. & Archit.
Los Angeles, CA, MAK Center for Art and Architecture
Los Angeles, UCLA
Los Angeles, CA, University of California
Los Angeles, UCLA, Fowler Mus. Cult. Hist.
Los Angeles, CA, University of California, Fowler Museum of Cultural History
Los Angeles, UCLA, Res. Lib.
Los Angeles, CA, University of California, Research Library
Los Angeles, USC
Los Angeles, CA, University of Southern California
Louisville, KY, Speed A. Mus.
Louisville, KY, J.B. Speed Art Museum
Ltd
Limited
Lugano, Col. Thyssen-Bornemisza
Lugano, Collection Baron Thyssen-Bornemisza
Luxembourg, Gal. A. Ville
Luxembourg, Galerie d'art de la Ville de Luxembourg
Lyon, Mus. B.-A.
Lyon, Musée des Beaux-Arts
Lyon, Mus. Hist. Tissus
Lyon, Musée Historiques des Tissus
Lyon, Mus. Hospices
Lyon, Musée des Hospices Civils de Lyon
m
metre(s)
MA
Master of Arts; Massachusetts (USA)
Madison, U. WI
Madison, WI, University of Wisconsin
Madrid, Escorial
Madrid, El Escorial
Madrid, Inst. Valencia Don Juan
Madrid, Instituto de Valencia de Don Juan
Madrid, Mus. Arqueol. N.
Madrid, Museo Arqueológico Nacional
Madrid, Mus. Ejército
Madrid, Museo del Ejército
Madrid, Mus.-Monasterio Descalzas Reales
Madrid, Museo-Monasterio Descalzas Reales

Madrid, Pal. Real
    Madrid, Palacio Real de Madrid
Madrid, Patrm. N.
    Madrid, Patrimonio Nacional
Madrid, Prado
    Madrid, Museo del Prado
Mag. Ant.
    The Magazine Antiques
Malibu, CA, Getty Mus.
    Malibu, CA, J. Paul Getty Museum
Malmaison, Château N.
    Malmaison, Château National de Malmaison
Manchester, C.A.G.
    Manchester, City Art Gallery
Manchester, Met. U.
    Manchester, Metropolitan University
Manchester, U. Manchester, Whitworth A.G
    Manchester, University of Manchester, Whitworth Art Gallery
Manchester, NH, Cent. High School
    Manchester, NH, Manchester Central High School
Manchester, NH, Currier Gal. A.
    Manchester, NH, Currier Gallery of Art
Man NE
    Man in the Northeast
Mannheim, Städt. Reiss-Mus.
    Mannheim, Städtisches Reiss-Museum
Mantua, Pal. Ducale
    Mantua, Palazzo Ducale
Marietta, GA, Marietta/Cobb Mus. A.
    Marietta, GA, Marietta/Cobb Museum of Art
Marseille, Mus. A. & Trad. Pop. Terroir Marseill.
    Marseille, Musée des Arts et Traditions Populaires du Terroir Marseillais
Marseille, Mus. Cantini
    Marseille, Musée Cantini
Marseille, Mus. Faïence
    Marseille, Musée de la Faïence
Marseille, Mus. Grobet-Labadié
    Marseille, Musée Grobet-Labadié
Martinsville, VA, Piedmont A. Assoc.
    Martinsville, VA, Piedmont Arts Association
Master Drgs
    Master Drawings
MD
    Maryland (USA)
ME
    Maine (USA)
Meissen, Porzellanmus.
    Meissen, Porzellanmuseum
Melbourne, U. Melbourne
    Melbourne, University of Melbourne
Mem. Amer. Mus. Nat. Hist.
    Memoirs of the American Museum of Natural History
Mem. Comm. Ant. Dépt Côte-d'Or
    Mémoires de la Commission des antiquités du départment de la Côte-d'Or
Mém. Comm. Dépt. Mnmts Hist. Pas de Calais
    Mémoires de la Commission départmentales des monuments historiques du Pas-de-Calais

Memphis, TN, Dixon Gal.
    Memphis, TN, Dixon Gallery and Gardens
Mém. Soc. N. Antiqua. France
    Mémoires de la Société nationale des antiquaires de France
Met. Mus. A. Bull.
    Metropolitan Museum of Art Bulletin
Met. Mus. J.
    Metropolitan Museum Journal
Mexico City, Mus. N. Antropol.
    Mexico City, Museo Nacional de Antropología
Mexico City, Mus. Soumaya
    Mexico City, Museo Soumaya
MI
    Michigan (USA)
Miami, FL, Cent. F.A.
    Miami, FL, Center for the Fine Arts
Miami, FL, Lowe A. Mus.
    Miami, FL, Lowe Art Museum
Middx
    Middlesex (UK)
Miho Mus.
    Miho Museum
Milan, Brera
    Milan, Pinacoteca di Brera
Milan, Gal. Caviglia
    Milan, Galleria Caviglia
Milan, Mus. Poldi Pezzoli
    Milan, Museo Poldi Pezzoli
Milan, Mus. Teat. alla Scala
    Milan, Museo Teatrale alla Scala
Millville, NJ, Wheaton Village, Amer. Glass Mus.
    Millville, NJ, Wheaton Village, American Glass Museum
Milton Q.
    Milton Quarterly
Milwaukee, WI, A. Mus
    Milwaukee, WI., Milwaukee Art Museum
Milwaukee, WI. Villa Terrace Dec. A. Mus.
    Milwaukee, WI, Villa Terrace Decorative Arts Museum
Minneapolis, MN, Inst. A.
    Minneapolis, MN, Minneapolis Institute of Arts
Minneapolis, U. Minnesota
    Minneapolis, MN, University of Minnesota
Mitt. Ksthist. Inst. Florenz
    Mitteilungen des Kunsthistorischen Instituts in Florenz
Mitt. Ver. Gesch. Stadt Nürnberg
    Mitteilungen des Vereins für Geschichte der Stadt Nürnberg
Mlle
    Mademoiselle
mm
    millimetre(s)
Mme
    Madame
MN
    Minnesota (USA)
MO
    Missouri (USA)
mod.
    modern

Modena, Gal. & Mus. Estense
    Modena, Galleria e Museo Estense
Mons
    Monmouthshire (UK)
Monterey, CA, Peninsula Mus. A.
    Monterey, CA, Monterey Peninsula Museum of
    Art
Monticello, VA, Jefferson Found.
    Monticello, VA, Thomas Jefferson Foundation
Montpellier, Mus. Fabre
    Montpellier, Musée Fabre [Musée des Beaux-
    Arts]
Montreal, McGill U.
    Montreal, McGill University
Montreal, Mus. F.A.
    Montreal, Museum of Fine Arts [Musée des
    Beaux-Arts]
Moritzburg, Barockmus. Schloss Moritzburg
    Moritzburg, Barockmuseum Schloss Moritzburg
Moscow, All-Rus. Mus. Dec.-Applied & Folk A.
    Moscow, All-Russian Museum of Decorative-
    Applied and Folk Art
Moscow, Hist. Mus.
    Moscow, Historical Museum (Istoricheskiy
    Muzey)
Moscow, Mus. Cer. & Kuskovo Estate
    Moscow, Museum of Ceramics and Kuskovo Es-
    tate (Muzey Keramiki i ?Usad?ba Kuskovo XVIII
    Veka')
Moscow, N.E. Zhukovsky Mem. Mus.
    Moscow, N.E. Zhukovsky Memorial Museum
    (Nauchno-Memorialnyy Muzey N.E. Zhukovsky)
Moscow, Pushkin Mus. F.A.
    Moscow, Pushkin Museum of Fine Arts (Muzey
    Isobrazitelnykh Iskusstv Imeni A.S. Pushkina)
Moscow, Tret'yakov Gal.
    Moscow, Tret'yakov Gallery
MS., MSS
    manuscript(s)
Mt
    Mount
Mulhouse, Mus. Impression Etoffes
    Mulhouse, Musée de l'Impression sur Etoffes
Münchn. Jb. Bild. Kst
    Münchner Jahrbuch der bildenden Kunst
Munich, Alte Pin.
    Munich, Alte Pinakothek
Munich, Bayer. Nmus.
    Munich, Bayerisches Nationalmuseum
Munich, Bayer. Staatsbib.
    Munich, Bayerisches Staatsbibliothek
Munich, Bayer. Verwalt. Staatl. Schlösser, Gärten &
Seen
    Munich, Bayerische Verwaltung der Staatlichen
    Schlösser, Gärten und Seen
Munich, Kstver.
    Munich, Kunstverein
Munich, Ludwig-Maximilians-U.
    Munich, Ludwig-Maximilians-Universität
Munich, Pin. Mod.
    Munich, Pinakothek der Moderne

Munich, Residenzmus.
    Munich, Residenzmuseum
Munich, Stadtmus.
    Munich, Münchener Stadtmuseum
Münster, Stadtmus.
    Münster, Stadtmuseum
Münster, Westfäl. Landesmus.
    Münster, Westfälisches Landesmuseum für
    Kunst und Kulturgeschichte
Murano, Mus. Vetrario
    Murano, Museo Vetrario
Muscatine, IA, A. Cent.
    Muscatine, IA, Muscatine Art Center
Mus. J.
    Museum Journal
Mus. Management & Curatorship
    Museum Management and Curatorship
Mus. Stud.
    Museum Studies [Art Institute of Chicago]
N.
    North, National
Nancy, Mus. B.-A.
    Nancy, Musée des Beaux-Arts
Nancy, Mus. Ecole Nancy
    Nancy, Musée de l'Ecole de Nancy
Nanjing, Jiangsu Prov. Mus.
    Nanjing, Jiangsu Provincial Museum [Nanjing
    Museum]
Naples, Capodimonte
    Naples, Museo e Gallerie Nazionali di Capodi-
    monte [Museo Borbonico]
Naples, Mus. Archeol. N.
    Naples, Museo Archeologico Nazionale
Naples, Mus. N. Cer.
    Naples, Museo Nazionale della Ceramica Duca di
    Martina
Naples, Mus. N. S Martino
    Naples, Museo Nazionale di San Martino
Naples, Pal. Reale
    Naples, Palazzo Reale
NC
    North Carolina (USA)
n.d.
    no date
NE
    Nebraska (USA)
Ned. Ksthist. Jb.
    Nederlands(ch) kunsthistorisch jaarboek
Neu-Affoltern, Glaubtern Church Cent.
    Neu-Affoltern, Glaubtern Church Centre
Neuenstein, Hohenlohe-Mus.
    Neuenstein, Hohenlohe-Museum
Nevers, Mus. Mun.
    Nevers, Musée Municipal de Nevers
Newark, NJ, Mus.
    Newark, NJ, Newark Museum
Newark, U. DE
    Newark, DE, University of Delaware
New Brunswick, NJ, Rutgers U.
    New Brunswick, NJ, Rutgers University
New Delhi, N. Mus.
    New Delhi, National Museum

New Haven, CT, Yale Cent. Brit A.
New Haven, CT, Yale Center for British Art
New Haven, CT, Yale U. A.G.
New Haven, CT, Yale University Art Gallery
New Hung. Q.
New Hungarian Quarterly
New Orleans, LA, Mus. A.
New Orleans, LA, New Orleans Museum of Art
New Port, RI, William Vareika F.A.
Newport, RI, William Vareika Fine Arts
Newport News, VA, Mar. Mus.
Newport News, VA, Mariners Museum
New York, Amer. Craft Mus.
New York, American Craft Museum
New York, Amer. Mus. Nat. Hist.
New York, American Museum of Natural History
New York, Amer. Numi. Soc.
New York, American Numismatic Society
New York, Austria Inst.
New York, Austrian Institute
New York, Barbara Mathes Gal.
New York, Barbara Mathes Gallery
New York, Bard Cent. Stud. Dec. A.
New York, Bard Graduate Center for Studies in the Decorative Arts
New York, Brooklyn Mus.
New York, The Brooklyn Museum
New York, Cloisters
New York, The Cloisters
New York, Columbia U.
New York, Columbia University
New York, Cooper-Hewitt Mus.
New York, Cooper-Hewitt Museum, Smithsonian Institution; National Museum of Design
New York, Delorenzo Gal.
New York, Delorenzo Gallery
New York, Forbes Mag. Col.
New York, Forbes Magazine Collection
New York, Frick
New York, Frick Collection
New York, Hebrew Un. Coll., Jew. Inst. Relig.
New York, Hebrew Union College, Jewish Institute of Religion
New York, Heller Gal.
New York, Heller Gallery
New York, Japan House Gal.
New York, Japan House Gallery
New York, Met.
New York, Metropolitan Museum of Art
New York, MOMA
New York, Museum of Modern Art
New York, Mus. A. & Des.
New York, Museum of Arts and Design
New York, Mus. Amer. Ind.
New York, Museum of the American Indian
New York, Mus. City NY
New York, Museum of the City of New York
New York, N. Acad. Des.
New York, National Academy of Design
New York, Neuhoff Gal.
New York, Neuhoff Gallery

New York, NY Hist. Soc.
New York, New-York Historical Society
New York, Paolo Baldacci Gal.
New York, Paolo Baldacci Gallery
New York, Pierpont Morgan Lib.
New York, Pierpont Morgan Library
New York, Pub. Lib.
New York, Public Library
New York U.
New York, New York University
New York, Van Cortlandt House Mus.
New York, Van Cortlandt House Museum
New York, Washburn Gal.
New York, Washburn Gallery
New York Gen. & Biog. Rec.
New York Genealogical and Biographical Record
N. G. Tech. Bull.
National Gallery Technical Bulletin
NH
New Hampshire (USA)
Nice, Mus. N. Chagall
Nice, Musée National Marc Chagall
Nicosia, Cyprus Mus.
Nicosia, Cyprus Museum
Niederdt. Beitr. Kstgesch.
Niederdeutsche Beiträge zur Kunstgeschichte
Nikkō, Tōshōgū Col.
Nikkō, Tōshōgū Collection
19th C.
Nineteenth Century [New York]
19th C. A. Worldwide
Nineteenth-Century Art Worldwide
NJ
New Jersey (USA)
N. Knife Mag.
The National Knife Magazine
NM
New Mexico (USA)
no., nos
number(s)
Norfolk, VA, Chrysler Mus.
Norfolk, VA, Chrysler Museum
Northampton, Central Mus. & A.G.
Northampton, Central Museum and Art Gallery
Northants
Northamptonshire (UK)
Northumb.
Northumberland (UK)
Norwich, Castle Mus.
Norwich, Castle Museum
Norwich, Strangers Hall Mus.
Norwich, Strangers Hall Museum
Norwich, U. E. Anglia
Norwich, University of East Anglia
Not. Pal. Albani
Notizie del Palazzo Albani: Rivista quadrimestrale di storia dell'Arte [Università degli studi di Urbino]
Nottingham, Castle Mus.
Nottingham, Castle Museum
Notts
Nottinghamshire (UK)

Nov
  November
n.p.
  no place (of publication)
nr
  near
N. S.
  Nossa Senhora
NSW
  New South Wales (Australia)
NT
  National Trust (UK)
Nuremberg, Ger. Nmus.
  Nuremberg, Germanisches Nationalmuseum
NV
  Nevada (USA)
NY
  New York (USA)
Oakland, CA, Mus.
  Oakland, CA, Oakland Museum
Oct
  October
ODNB
  Oxford Dictionary of National Biography
OH
  Ohio (USA)
Ohara, Mus. A.
  Ohara, Museum of Art [Chiba Prefecture]
Old Furn.
  Old Furniture
Ont.
  Ontario (Canada)
OR
  Oregon (USA)
Orient. A.
  Oriental Art
Orient. Carpet & Textile Stud.
  Oriental Carpet and Textile Studies
Orrefors, Glasbruk Mus.
  Orrefors, Glasbruk Museum
Orvieto, Pal. Sette
  Orvieto, Palazzo dei Sette
Osaka, Fujita Mus. A.
  Osaka, Fujita Museum of Art
Osaka, Mus. Oriental Cer.
  Osaka, Museum of Oriental Ceramics
Osaka, N. Mus. Ethnol.
  Osaka, National Museum of Ethnology
Oshkosh, WI, Paine A. Cent.
  Oshkosh, WI, Paine Art Center
Oslo, Kstindustmus.
  Oslo, Kunstindustrimuseum
Oslo, Riksarkv
  Oslo, Riksarkiv
Österreich Z. Kst & Dkmlpf.
  Österreichesche Zeitschrift für Kunst und Denk-
  malpflege
Oswego, SUNY, Tyler A.G.
  Oswego, NY, State University of New York, Ty-
  ler Art Gallery
Ott.
  Ottoman

Otterlo, Tegelmus.
  Otterlo, Nederlands Tegelmuseum
Oxford, All Souls Coll.
  Oxford, All Souls College
Oxford, Ashmolean
  Oxford, Ashmolean Museum
Oxford, Bodleian Lib.
  Oxford, Bodleian Library
Oxford, New Coll.
  Oxford, New College
Oxford, St John's Coll.
  Oxford, St John's College
Oxon
  Oxfordshire (UK)
p., pp
  page(s)
PA
  Pennsylvania (USA)
PACT
  PACT: Revue du groupe européen d'études pour
  les techniques physiques, chimiques et mathé-
  mathiques appliquées à l'archéologie
Paderborn, Diözms. & Domschatzkam.
  Paderborn, Erzbischöfliches Diözesanmuseum
  und Domschatzkammer
Padova & Territ.
  Padova e il suo territorio
Padua, Mus. Civ.
  Padua, Museo Civico
Palermo, Gal. Reg. Sicilia
  Palermo, Galleria Regionale della Sicilia [Galleria
  Nazionale della Sicilia]
Palermo, Pal. Cinese
  Palermo, Palazzina Cinese
Paris, Bib. A. Déc.
  Paris, Bibliothèque des Arts Décoratifs
Paris, Bib. Forney
  Paris, Bibliothèque Forney
Paris, Bib. N.
  Paris, Bibliothèque Nationale
Paris, Bib. N., Cab. Est.
  Paris, Bibliothèque Nationale, Cabinet des Es-
  tampes
Paris, Bib. N., Cab. Médailles
  Paris, Bibliothèque Nationale, Cabinet des Mé-
  dailles
Paris, Ecole B.-A.
  Paris, Ecole des Beaux-Arts
Paris, Ecole N. Sup. B.-A.
  Paris, Ecole Nationale Supérieure des Beaux-Arts
Paris, Gal. B.-A.
  Paris, Galerie Beaux-Arts
Paris, Gal. Dario Boccara
  Paris, Galerie Dario Boccara
Paris, Gal. Luxembourg
  Paris, Galerie du Luxembourg
Paris, Gal. Vallois
  Paris, Galerie Vallois
Paris, Grand Pal.
  Paris, Grand Palais [Galeries Nationales
  d'Exposition du Grand Palais]
Paris, Inst. Fr. Archit.
  Paris, Institut Français d'Architecture

Paris, Inst. Géog. N.
  Paris, Institut Géographique National
Paris, Invalides
  Paris, Hôtel National des Invalides
Paris, Louvre
  Paris, Musée du Louvre
Paris, Mobilier N.
  Paris, Mobilier National
Paris, Mus. A. Déc.
  Paris, Musée des Arts Décoratifs
Paris, Mus. A. Mod. Ville Paris
  Paris, Musée d'Art Moderne de la Ville de Paris
  [Musée de la Ville de Paris]
Paris, Mus. Armée
  Paris, Musée de l'Armée
Paris, Mus. Carnavalet
  Paris, Musée Carnavalet
Paris, Mus. Cluny
  Paris, Musée de Cluny
Paris, Mus. Dapper
  Paris, Musée Dapper
Paris, Mus. Guimet
  Paris, Musée Guimet
Paris, Mus. Jacquemart-André
  Paris, Musée Jacquemart-André
Paris, Mus. Mode & Cost.
  Paris, Musée de la Mode et du Costume
Paris, Mus. Nissim de Camondo
  Paris, Musée Nissim de Camondo
Paris, Mus. Orsay
  Paris, Musée d'Orsay
Paris, Mus. Rodin
  Paris, Musée Auguste Rodin
Paris, Mus. Vie Romantique
  Paris, Musée de la Vie Romantique
Paris, Myrna Myers Gal.
  Paris, Myrna Myers Gallery
Paris, Pal. Luxembourg
  Paris, Palais du Luxembourg
Paris, Pal. Tokyo
  Paris, Palais de Tokyo
Paris, Petit Pal.
  Paris, Musée du Petit Palais
Paris, Pompidou
  Paris, Centres Georges Pompidou
Pavlovsk Pal.
  Pavlovsk, Pavlovsk Palace (Pavloskiy Dvorets)
Pensacola, FL, Mus. A.
  Pensacola, FL, Pensacola Museum of Art
Pers.
  Persian
Perugia, G.N. Umbria
  Perugia, Galleria Nazaionel dell'Umbria
Pesaro, Mus. Civ.
  Pesaro, Museo Civico
PhD
  Doctor of Philosophy
Philadelphia, PA, Mus. A.
  Philadelphia, PA, Museum of Art
Philadelphia, PA, U. A., Rosenwald-Wolf Gal.
  Philadephia, PA, University of the Arts, Rosen-
  wald-Wolf Gallery

Philadelphia, U. PA, Mus.
  Philadelphia, PA, University of Pennsylvania,
  University Museum [of Archaeology & Anthro-
  pology]
Philadelphia Mus. A.: Bull.
  Philadelphia Museum of Art: Bulletin
Piacenza, Coll. Alberoni
  Piacenza, Collegio Alberoni
Pisa, Mus. N. S. Matteo
  Pisa, Museo Nazionale di S Matteo
Pittsburgh, PA, Carnegie Mus. A.
  Pittsburgh, PA, Carnegie Museum of Art
pl.
  plural
Plymouth, MA, Pilgrim Hall Mus.
  Plymouth, MA, Pilgrim Hall Museum
Poggio a Caiano, Mus. Villa Medicea
  Poggio a Caiano, Museo Villa Medicea
Poitiers, Mus. Sainte-Croix
  Poitiers, Musée Sainte-Croix
Port Elizabeth, Nelson Mandela Met. Mus. A.
  Port Elizabeth, Nelson Mandela Metropolitan
  Museum of Art
Portsmouth, City Mus. & A.G.
  Portsmouth, City Museum & Art Gallery
Portsmouth, Mary Rose Mus.
  Portsmouth, Mary Rose Museum
Prague, Hist. Mus.
  Prague, Historical Museum (Národni Muzeum v
  Praze, Historické Muzeum)
Prague, Mus. Dec. A.
  Prague, Museum of Decorative Arts (Umelecko-
  Prǐmyslové Muzeum v Praze)
Prague, N.G., Convent of St George
  Prague, National Gallery (Národnie Galerie),
  Convent of St George
Prefect.
  Prefecture, Prefectural
Princeton U., NJ
  Princeton, NJ, Princeton University
Prt Q.
  Print Quarterly
priv.
  private
Proc. Brit. Acad.
  Proceedings of the British Academy
Proc. Huguenot Soc. London
  Proceedings of the Huguenot Society of London
Proc. Royal Irish Acad.
  Proceedings of the Royal Irish Academy
Proc. Soc. Silver Colrs
  Proceedings of the Society of Silver Collectors
Prov.
  Province(s), Provincial
Providence, RI, Haffenraffer Mus. Anthropol.
  Providence, RI, Haffenraffer Museum of Anthro-
  pology
Providence, RI, Sch. Des., Mus. A.
  Providence, RI, Rhode Island School of Design,
  Museum of Art
pseud.
  pseudonym

pt, pts
> part(s)

pubd
> published

Purchase, SUNY, Neuberger Mus.
> Purchase, NY, State University of New York, Neuberger Museum

PVC
> polyvinyl chloride

Quebec, Mus. Civilis.
> Quebec, Musée de la Civilisation

R
> reprint

Rabat, Mus. A. Maroc
> Rabat, Musée des Arts Marocains

Rangoon, N. Mus.
> Rangoon, National Museum

Readings Glass Hist.
> Readings in Glass History

Rec. A. Mus., Princeton U.
> Record of the Art Museum, Princeton University

reg
> *regit* [ruled]

Reg. Furn. Soc. J.
> Regional Furniture Society Journal

Reims, Mus. St-Rémi
> Reims, Musée St-Rémi

Rennes, Mus. B.-A. & Archéol.
> Rennes, Musée des Beaux-Arts et d'Archéologie

Rep.
> Report(s)

Res.
> Research

rev.
> revision, revised

Rev. A.
> Revue de l'art

Rev. A. Anc. & Mod.
> Revue de l'art ancien et moderne

Rev. Belge Archéol. & Hist. A.
> Revue belge d'archéologie et d'histoire de l'art

Rev. Louvre
> *Revue du Louvre et des musées de France*

Rev. Vieux Genève
> La Revue du vieux Genève

RI
> Rhode Island (USA)

Richmond, VA Mus. F.A.
> Richmond, VA, Virginia Museum of Fine Arts

Rio de Janeiro, Mus. N.
> Rio de Janeiro, Museu Nacional

Riv. A.
> Rivista d'arte

Rixheim, Mus. Pap. Peint
> Rixheim, Musée du Paper Peint

Rochester, NY, Strong Mus.
> Rochester, NY, Strong Museum [Margaret Woodbury Strong Museum]

Rochester, U. Rochester, NY, Mem. A.G.
> Rochester, NY, University of Rochester, Memorial Art Gallery

Rome, Accad. N. S Luca
> Rome, Accademia Nazionale di S Luca

Rome, Dt. Archäol. Inst.
> Rome, Deutsches Archäologisches Institut

Rome, Fond. Camillo Caetani
> Rome, Fondazione Camillo Caetani

Rome, Gab. N. Stampe
> Rome, Gabinetto Nazionale delle Stampe

Rome, Gal. Borghese
> Rome, Galleria Borghese

Rome, Gal. Doria-Pamphili
> Rome, Galleria Doria-Pamphili

Rome, G.N.A. Mod.
> Rome, Galleria Nazionale d'Arte Moderna [e Arte Contemporanea]

Rome, Mus. Capitolino
> Rome, Museo Capitolino

Rome, Mus. Cent. Ris.
> Rome, Museo Centrale del Risorgimento

Rome, Mus. Napoleonico
> Rome, Museo Napoleonico

Rome, Pal. Braschi
> Rome, Palazzo Braschi

Rome, Pal. Madama
> Rome, Palazzo Madama

Rome, Pal. Quirinale
> Rome, Palazzo del Quirinale

Rome, Pal. Venezia
> Rome, Palazzo Venezia

Rome, Vatican, Bib. Apostolica
> Rome, Vatican, Biblioteca Apostolica Vaticana [Vatican Library]

Rome, Vatican, Mnmt., Musei & Gal. Pont.
> Rome, Vatican, Monumenti, Musei e Gallerie Pontificie

Rome, Vatican, Mus. Pio-Clementino
> Rome, Vatican, Museo Pio-Clementino

Rome, Vatican, Mus. Profano Bib. Apostolica
> Rome, Vatican, Museo Profano della Biblioteca Apostolica

Rome, Vatican, Mus. Stor. A. Tesoro S Pietro
> Rome, Vatican, Museo Storico Artistico Tesoro di S Pietro

Rotterdam, Mus. Boymans–van Beuningen
> Rotterdam, Museum Boymans–van Beuningen

Rouen, Mus. B.-A.
> Rouen, Musée des Beaux-Arts

Rouen, Mus. Le Secq des Tournelles
> Rouen, Musée Le Secq des Tournelles

Rudolstadt, Mus.
> Rudolstadt, Museum

Rus.
> Russian

Rye, NY, Rye Hist. Soc.
> Rye, NY, Rye Historical Society

S
> San, Santa, Santo, Sant', São [Saint]

S.
> South, Southern

Saffron Walden, Fry A.G.
> Saffron Walden, Fry Art Gallery

Saggi & Mem. Stor. A.
> Saggi e memorie di storia dell'arte

Sahagún, Ayuntamiento, Mus.
    Sahagún, Ayuntamiento, Museo
Saint-Denis, Mus. A. & Hist.
    Saint-Denis, Musée d'Art et d'Histoire
Saint-Denis, Mus. Bouilhet-Christofle
    Saint-Denis, Musée Bouilhet-Christofle
Saint-Etienne, Mus. A. & Indust.
    Saint-Etienne, Musée d'art et d'industrie
St Fagans, Welsh Flk Mus.
    St Fagans, Welsh Folk Museum
St John's, Mem. U. Nfld, A.G.
    St John's, Memorial University of Newfoundland,
    Art Gallery
St Louis, MO, A. Mus.
    St Louis, MO, Art Museum
St Petersburg, Hermitage
    St Petersburg, Hermitage Museum
St Petersburg, Inst. Archaeol.
    St Petersburg, Institute of Archaeology (Institut
    Arkheologii)
St Petersburg, Lomonosov Porcelain Factory Mus.
    St Petersburg, Lomonosov Porcelain Factory
    Museum
St Petersburg, Peter's Pal.
    St Petersburg, Peter's Palace (Petrodvorets)
St Petersburg, Rus. Mus.
    St Petersburg, Russian Museum (Russkiy Muzey)
St Petersburg, FL, Mus. F.A.
    St Petersburg, FL, Museum of Fine Arts
Salem, MA, Peabody Essex Mus.
    Salem, MA, Peabody Essex Museum
Salt Lake City, U. UT, Mus. Nat. Hist.
    Salt Lake City, UT, Uuniversity of Utah, Museum
    of Natural History
Salzburg, Gal. Mozartplatz
    Salzburg, Galerie am Mozartplatz
San Bernardino, CA State U., Fullerton A. Mus.
    San Bernardino, CA, California State University,
    Robert V. Fullerton Art Museum
San Francisco, CA, Craft & Folk Mus.
    San Francisco, CA, Craft and Folk Museum
San Francisco, CA, de Young Mem. Mus.
    San Francisco, CA, M. H. de Young Memorial
    Museum
San Francisco, CA Pal. Legion of Honor
    San Francisca, CA, California Palace of the Le-
    gion of Honor
San Marino, CA, Huntington Lib. & A.G.
    San Marino, CA, Huntington Library and Art
    Gallery
Santa Barbara, U. CA, A. Gals
    Santa Barbara, CA, University of California, Uni-
    versity of California Art Galleries
Santa Barbara, U. CA, A. Mus.
    Santa Barbara, CA, University of California, Uni-
    versity Art Museum
Santa Cruz, CA, Mus. A. & Hist.
    Santa Cruz, CA, Museum of Art and History
Santa Fe, NM, Mus. Int. Flk A.
    Santa Fe, NM, Museum of International Folk Art
SC
    South Carolina (USA)

Scand. J. Des. Hist.
    Scandinavian Journal of Design History
Schwerin, Staatl. Mus.
    Schwerin, Staatliches Museum
Sculp. Rev.
    Sculpture Review
Seattle, WA, A. Mus.
    Seattle, WA, Seattle Art Museum
Seattle, U. Washington
    Seattle, WA, University of Washington
Sebago, ME, Jones Mus. Glass & Cer.
    Sebago, ME, Jones Museum of Glass and Ceram-
    ics
Sendai, Tohoku Fukushi U., Serizawa Keisuke A. &
Craft Mus.
    Sendai, Tohoku Fukushi University, Serizawa
    Keisuke Art and Craft Museum
Sept
    September
Ser.
    Series
Sèvres, Mus. N. Cér.
    Sèvres, Musée National de Céramiques
Sharon, MA, Kendall Whaling Mus.
    Sharon, MA, Kendall Whaling Museum
Sheboygan, WI, John Michael Kohler A. Cent.
    Sheboygan, WI, John Michael Kohler Arts Center
Sheffield, Mappin A.G.
    Sheffield, Mappin Art Gallery
Shreveport, LA, Norton A.G.
    Shreveport, LA, W. R. Norton Art Gallery
Shrewsbury, Clive House Mus.
    Shrewsbury, Clive House Museum
Siena, Pal. Piccolomini, Archv Stato
    Siena, Palazzo Piccolomini, Archivio di Stato
Siena, Pal. Pub.
    Siena, Palazzo Pubblico
Siena, Pal. Reale
    Siena, Palazzo Reale
Sinaia, Peles N. Mus.
    Sinaia, Peles National Museum
Sion, Mus. Cant. Valère
    Sion, Musée Cantonal de Valère
16th C. J.
    Sixteenth Century Journal
Skt
    Sanskrit
Soc.
    Society
Sofia, N. Archaeol. Mus.
    Sofia, National Archaeological Museum of the
    Bulgarian Academy of Sciences (Nacionalen Ar-
    chaeologičeski Muzej na Balgarskara Akademija
    na Nankite)
Sonneberg, Dt. Spielzeugmus.
    Sonneberg, Deutsches Spielzeugmuseum
Sp.
    Spanish
Space Des.
    Space Design
Springfield, MA, Smith A. Mus.
    Springfield, MA, George Walter Vincent Smith
    Art Museum

sq.
    square
SS
    Saints, Santi, Santissima, Santissimo; Steamship
St
    Saint, Sankt, Sint, Szent
Staffs
    Staffordshire
Stanford U., CA, Cantor Cent. Visual A.
    Stanford, CA, Stanford University, Iris and B. Gerald Cantor Center for Visual Arts
Ste
    Sainte
Stockholm, Kun. Husgerådskam.
    Stockholm, Kungliga Husgerådskammar med Skattkammar och Bernadotte-Bibliothek [Royal collections]
Stockholm, Kun. Slott
    Stockholm, Kungliga Slott
Stockholm, Livrustkam.
    Stockholm, Livrustkammern [Royal Armoury]
Stockholm, Mod. Mus.
    Stockholm, Moderna Museum
Stockholm, Nmus.
    Stockholm, Nationalmuseum
Stockholm, Nordiska Mus.
    Stockholm, Nordiska Museum
Stockholm, Östasiat. Mus.
    Stockholm, Östasiatiska Museum
Stockholm, Stat. Hist. Mus.
    Stockholm, Statens Historiska Museum
Stoke-on-Trent, City Mus. & A.G.
    Stok-on-Trent, City Museum and Art Gallery
Stor. A.
    Storia dell'arte
Storrs, U. CT, Benton Mus. A.
    Storrs, CT, University of Connecticut, William Benton Museum of Art
Strasbourg, Mus. A. Déc.
    Strasbourg, Musée des Arts Décoratifs
Strasbourg, Mus. B.-A.
    Strasbourg, Musée des Beaux-Arts
Strasbourg, Mus. Hist.
    Strasbourg, Musée Historique
Strasbourg, Mus. Oeuvre Notre-Dame
    Strasbourg, Musée de l'Oeuvre Notre-Dame
Stud. Conserv.
    Studies in Conservation: The Journal of the International Institute for Conservation of Historic and Artistic Works
Stud. Dec. A.
    Studies in the Decorative Arts
Stud. Hist. A.
    Studies in the History of Art
Stud, Iconog.
    Studies in Iconography
Stud. Textile Hist.
    Studies in Textile History
Stuttgart, Standort Schlossmus.
    Stuttgart, Standort Schlossmuseum
Stuttgart, Staatsgal.
    Stuttgart, Staatsgalerie

Stuttgart, Württemberg. Landesmus.
    Stuttgart, Württembergisches Landesmuseum
Sudhoffs Archv Ges. Mediz. & Natwiss
    Sudhoffs Archiv für Geschichte der Medizin und der Naturwissenschaften
suppl.
    supplement(s), supplementary
Surface Des. J.
    Surface Design Journal
Suzhou Mus.
    Suzhou, Suzhou Museum
Svensk. Orientsällskapets Åb.
    Svenska Orientsällskapets årsbok
Swansea, Vivian A.G. & Mus.
    Swansea, Glynn Vivian Art Gallery and Museum
Swed.
    Swedish
Sydney, Mus. Applied A. & Sci.
    Sydney, Museum of Applied Arts and Sciences
Tahit.
    Tahitian
Talavera de la Reina, Mus. Cer. Ruiz de Luna
    Talavera de la Reina, Museo de Cerámica Ruiz de Luna
Tarnów, Dist. Mus.
    Tarnów, District Museum (Muzeum Okregowe)
Tehran, Archaeol. Mus.
    Tehran, Archaeological Museum
Teruel, Mus.
    Teruel, Museo de Teruel
Textile Hist.
    Textile History
Textile Mus. J.
    Textile Museum Journal
Thessaloniki, Mus. Byz. Cult.
    Thessaloniki, Museum of Byzantine Culture
TN
    Tennessee (USA)
Tokyo, Idemitsu Mus. A.
    Tokyo, Idemitsu Museum of Art
Tokyo, Met. Teien A. Mus.
    Tokyo, Metropolitan Teien Art Museum
Tokyo, N. Mus.
    Tokyo, National Museum (Kokuritsu Hakubutsukan)
Tokyo, N. Mus. Mod. A.
    Tokyo, National Museum of Modern Art [Metropolitan Museum of Modern Art]
Tokyo, Sezon Mus. A.
    Tokyo, Sezon Museum of Art
Toledo, Mus. S Cruz
    Toldeo, Museo de S Cruz
Toledo, OH, Mus. A.
    Toledo, OH, Museum of Art
Toledo, OH, Owens − Illinois A. Cent.
    Toledo, OH, Owens − Illinois Arts Center
Tønder, Sonderjyllands Kstmus.
    Tønder, Sonderjyllands Kunstmuseum [Kulturhistorisches Museum & Kunstsammlung]
Toronto, Gardiner Mus. Cer. A.
    Toronto, Gardiner Museum of Ceramic Art

Toronto, A.G. Ont.
  Toronto, Art Gallery of Ontario
Toronto, Royal Ont. Mus.
  Toronto, Royal Ontario Museum
Toronto, U. Toronto A. Cent.
  Toronto, University of Toronto Art Center
Tournai, Mus. Hist. & Archéol. & A. Déc.
  Tournai, Musée d'Histoire et d'Archéologie et des Arts Décoratifs
trans.
  translation, translated by
Trans. Eng. Cer. Circ.
  Transactions of the English Ceramic Circle
Trans. London & Middl. Archaeol. Soc.
  Transactions of the London and Middlesex Archaeological Society
Trans. Orient. Cer. Soc.,
  Transactions of the Oriental Ceramic Society
Trans. Soc. Glass Technol.
  Transactions of the Society of Glass Technology
Trapani, Mus. Reg.
  Trapani, Museo Regionale Pepoli
Trenton, NJ State Mus.
  Trenton, NJ, New Jersey State Museum
Turin, Arm. Reale
  Turin, Armeria Reale
Turin, Gal. Sabauda
  Turin, Galleria Sabauda
Turin, Mus. Civ. A. Ant.
  Turin, Museo Civico d'Arte Antica
Turin, Pal. Madama
  Turin, Palazzo Madama
Turin, Pal. Reale
  Turin, Palazzo Reale
Turk.
  Turkish
TX
  Texas (USA)
Udaipur, Batik A. Res. & Training Cent.
  Udaipur, Batik Art Research and Training Centre
UK
  United Kingdom of Great Britain and Northern Ireland
Ulm, Ulm. Mus.
  Ulm, Ulmer Museum
unpubd
  unpublished
Unsere Kstdkml.
  Unsere Kunstdenkmäler
Urbino, Mus. Duomo
  Urbino, Museo del Duomo
Urbino, Pal. Ducale
  Urbino, Palazzo Ducale
US
  United States
USA
  United States of America
USS
  United States Ship
USSR
  Union of Soviet Socialist Republics

Utica, NY, Munson—Williams—Proctor Inst.
  Utica, NY, Munson—Williams—Proctor Institute
Utrecht, Cent. Mus.
  Utrecht, Centraal Museum
VA
  Virginia (USA)
Valladolid, Mus. N. Escul.
  Valladolid, Museo Nacional de Escultura
V&A Mus. Bull.
  Victoria and Albert Museum Bulletin
V&A Mus. Yb.
  Victoria and Albert Museum Yearbook
Växjö, Smålands Mus.
  Växjö, Smålands Museum
Venice, Col. Cini
  Venice, Collezione Cini
Venice, Correr
  Venice, Museo Correr
Venice, Fond. Cini
  Venice, Fondazione Giorgio Cini, Istituto di Storia dell'Arte
Venice, Gal. Rossella Junck
  Venice, Galleria Rossella Junck
Venice, Pal. Rota
  Venice, Palazzo Rota
Verona, Musei Civ.
  Verona, Musei Civici di Verona
Versailles, Château
  Versailles, Musée National du Château der Versailles et Trianon
Versailles, Musées N.
  Versailles, Musées Nationaux
Vic, Mus. Episc.
  Vic, Museu Arqueologic Artistic Episcopal
Victoria, BC, A.G. Gtr Victoria
  Victoria, BC, Art Gallery of Greater Victoria
Victoria, Royal BC Mus.
  Victoria, BC, Royal British Columbia Museum
Vienna, Albertina
  Vienna, Graphische Sammlung Albertina
Vienna, Bundesmobiliensamml.
  Vienna, Bundesmobiliensammlung
Vienna, Dom-& Diözmus.
  Vienna, Dom-und Diözesanmuseum
Vienna, Glass Gal. Michael Kovacek
  Vienna, Glass Galerie Michael Kovacek
Vienna, Hochsch. Angewandte Kst
  Vienna, Hochschule für Angewandte Kunst in Wien
Vienna, Ksthist. Mus.
  Vienna, Kunsthistorisches Museum
Vienna, Mus. Vlkerknd
  Vienna, Museum für Völkerkunde
Vienna, Österreich. Mus. Angewandte Kst
  Vienna, Österreichisches Museum für Angewandte Kunst
Vienna, Schatzkam.
  Vienna, Schatzkammer
Vienna, Schatzkam. Dt. Ordens
  Vienna, Schatzkammer des Deutschen Ordens

Vrienden Ned. Cer.: Medebl.
    Vrienden van de Nederlandse ceramiek: Mede-
    delingenblad [Friends of Dutch ceramics: Re-
    ports]
VT
    Vermont (USA)
w.
    width
WA
    Washington (USA)
Waf.-& Kostknd.
    Waffen-und Kostümkunde
W. Afr. J. Archaeol.
    West African Journal of Archaeology
Wallraf-Richartz-Jb.
    Wallraf-Richartz-Jahrbuch
Walpole Soc.
    Walpole Society
Warrington, Mus. & A.G.
    Warrington, Museum and Art Gallery
Warsaw, Mus. Pol. Army
    Warsaw, Museum of the Polish Army (Muzeum
    Wojska Polskiego)
Warsaw, N. Mus.
    Warsaw, National Museum (Muzeum Narodowe)
Warsaw, U. Warsaw, Lib.
    Warsaw, University of Warsaw Library
Warsaw, Zachea Gal.
    Warsaw, Zachea Gallery
Warwicks
    Warwickshire (UK)
Washington, DC, Corcoran Gal. A.
    Washington, DC, Corcoran Gallery of Art
Washington, DC, Freer
    Washington, DC, Freer Gallery of Art [Smith-
    sonian Inst.]
Washington, DC, Hillwood Mus.
    Washington, DC, Hillwood Museum
Washington, DC, Lib. Congr.
    Washington, DC, Library of Congress
Washington, DC, N. Bldg Mus.
    Washington, DC, National Building Museum
Washington, DC, N.G.A.
    Washington, DC, National Gallery of Art
Washington, DC, N. Mus. Amer. Hist.
    Washington, DC, National Museum of American
    History [Smithsonian Inst.]
Washington, DC, N. Mus. Nat. Hist.
    Washington, DC, National Museum of Natural
    History [Smithsonian Inst.]
Washington, DC, Renwick Gal.
    Washington, DC, Renwick Gallery [Smithsonian
    Inst.]
Washington, DC, Smithsonian Inst.
    Washington, DC, Smithsonian Institution
Washington, DC, Textile Mus.
    Washington, DC, Textile Museum
Waterford, Mus. Treasures
    Waterford, Museum of Treasures
Whitehaven, Mus.
    Whitehaven, Whitehaven Museum

WI
    Wisconsin (USA)
Williamstown, MA, Clark Art Inst.
    Williamstown, MA, Sterling and Francine Clark
    Art Institute
Wilts
    Wiltshire (UK)
Windsor Castle, Berks, Royal Col.
    Windsor, Berks, Windsor Castle, Royal Collection
Winter Park, FL, Morse Gal. A.
    Winter Park, FL, Morse Gallery of Art
Winterthur, DE, Du Pont Winterthur Mus.
    Winterthur, DE, H.F. Du Pont Winterthur Mu-
    seum
Winterthur Port.
    Winterthur Portfolio
W. Midlands
    West Midlands
W. Midlands Archaeol.
    West Midlands Archaeology
Wolfenbüttel, Herzog-August Bib.
    Wolfenbüttel, Herzog August Bibliothek
Wolverhampton, U. Wolverhampton
    Wolverhampton, University of Wolverhampton
Woman's A. J.
    Woman's Art Journal
Worcester, MA, A. Mus.
    Worcester, MA, Worcester Art Museum
World Int.
    World of Interiors
Würzburg, Mainfränk Mus.
    Würzburg, Mainfränkisches Museum
Würzburg , U. Würzburg, Wagner-Mus.
    Würzburg, Universität Würzburg, Martin von
    Wagner-Museum
WV
    West Virginia (USA)
W. Yorks
    West Yorkshire (UK)
Xi'an, Shaanxi Hist. Mus.
    Xi'an, Shaanxi History Museum
Yale U. A. G. Bull.
    Yale University Art Gallery Bulletin
Yangzhou Mus.
    Yangzhou, Yangzhou Museum
Yogyakarta, Batik Res. Cent.
    Yogyakarta, Batik Research Centre
York A.G. Q.
    City of York Art Gallery Quarterly
York, C.A.G.
    York, City Art Gallery
Yorktown, VA, Col. N. Hist. Park
    Yorktown, VA, Colonial National Historical Park
Z. Dt. Ver. Kstwiss.
    Zeitschrift der deutschen Vereins für Kunstwis-
    senschaft
Zerbst, Mus. Stadt
    Zerbst, Museum der Stadt Zerbst
Z. Kstgesch.
    Zeitschrift für Kunstgeschichte

Zöfingen, Stadtbib.
    Zöfingen, Stadtbibliothek
Zurich, Kstgewmus.
    Zurich, Kunstgewerbemuseum
Zurich, Mus. Bellerive
    Zurich, Museum Bellerive

Zurich, Mus. Rietberg
    Zurich, Museum Rietberg
Zurich, Schweiz. Landesmus.
    Zurich, Schweizerisches Landesmuseum
Zweisel, Waldmus.
    Zweisel, Waldmuseum

A Note on the Use of the Encyclopedia

Abbreviations used in the encyclopedia are listed on pp. xi–xxxiii of Volume 1.

Alphabetization of headings, which are distinguished in bold typeface, is letter by letter up to the first comma (ignoring spaces, hyphens, accents and any parenthesized or bracketed matter); the same principle applies thereafter. Abbreviations of 'Saint' and its foreign equivalents are alphabetized as if spelt out, and headings with the prefix 'Mc' appear under 'Mac'.

Authors of every article are included in the Contributors list on pp. 583–586 of Volume 2. Author names are not listed beneath each article because the editor revised the articles and wrote many of them himself.

Bibliographies are arranged chronologically (within section, where divided) by order of year of first publication and, within years, alphabetically by authors' names. Abbreviations have been used for some standard reference books. Abbreviated references to alphabetically arranged dictionaries and encyclopedias appear at the beginning of the bibliography (or section).

Biographical dates when cited in parentheses in running text at the first mention of a personal name indicate that the individual does not have an entry in the encyclopedia. Where no dates are provided for an artist or patron, the reader may assume that there is a biography of that individual in the encyclopedia (or, more rarely, that the person is so obscure that dates are not readily available).

Cross-references are distinguished by the use of small capital letters, with a large capital to indicate the initial letter of the entry to which the reader is directed; for example 'Dürer collaborated with WENZEL JAMNITZER . . .' means that the entry is alphabetized under 'J'.

The Grove Encyclopedia
of Decorative Arts

A

Aalto, **Hugo Alvar Henrik** (*b* Kuortane, 3 Feb 1898; *d* Helsinki, 11 May 1976). Finnish architect and designer. He collaborated with his wife Aino Marsio-Aalto (1894–1949) in the design of Artek furniture, which was first designed in 1928 for Paimio Sanatorium. His furniture was typically made from sheets of birch plywood, which were bent into shape and supported with solid wood or thick laminates. His designs included stacking furniture (e.g. stacking stools, *c*. 1930; London, V&A).

Á. Ólafsdóttir: *Le mobilier d'Alvar Aalto dans l'espace et dans le temps: La diffusion internationale du design, 1920–1940* (Paris, 1998)
E. Ottillinger: *Alvar Aalto: Möbel: Die Sammlung Kossdorff* (Vienna, 2002)
P. Tuukkanen: *Alvar Aalto, Designer* (Helsinki, 2002)

Abaquesne, **Masséot** (before 1520–before 1564). French potter based in Rouen. Nothing is known of his work prior to the ornamental tiles and tiled pav-

Alvar Aalto: stacking stools, *c.* 1930 (London, Victoria and Albert Museum)

ings at the château of Ecouen, which are in the style of the Fontainebleau school (1542–59; Ecouen, Mus. Ren.). His best-known works are the tiles ordered by Claude d'Urfé (1502–58) in 1551 for the Château de la Bastie d'Urfé (now Paris, Louvre) and the 4152 albarelli ordered in 1545 by the Rouen apothecary Pierre Dubosc (see colour pl. I, fig. 1).

P. Oliver: *Masseot Abaquesne et les origines de la faïence de Rouen* (Rouen, 1952)
C. Leroy: 'Avers et revers des pavements du château d'Ecouen' [a reconstruction of the original floor design], *Rev. A.*, cxvi (1997), pp. 27–41

Abbotsford period. Late 19th-century term for the heavy mock-Gothic furniture of the 1820s and 1830s, so-called from the name of Sir Walter Scott's house; the style is now called 'Scottish Baronial', a term otherwise used to denote an architectural style.

Abildgaard, **Nicolai Abraham** (*b* Copenhagen, 11 Sept 1743; *d* Frederiksdal, Copenhagen, 4 June 1809). Danish painter, designer and architect. From 1794 he worked for the heir-presumptive, Prince Frederick (1753–1805), on the decorations of the latter's apartments at the Amalienborg Palace in Copenhagen. The State Room is a work of great integrity and originality, one of the first in the Neo-classicist style in Denmark. The originally yellow walls were divided by white and gilt Ionic pilasters resting on a violet–blue panel base. The frieze, with gilt garlands on a royal blue ground, corresponded to the colouring of the furniture and curtains. In niches flanking the main door there were sculptures of the muses *Euterpe* and *Terpsichore*, probably modelled by the young Bertel Thorvaldsen (1768/70–1844) after Abildgaard's design. In the Throne Room the walls were decorated with allegorical oval paintings and overdoors by Abildgaard himself (the Continents and the Elements). On the whole, as an interior decorator Abildgaard avoided the neatness of the Empire style for the sake of a more grandiose vision of antiquity, preferring strong simplicity and striking colours. To complete the general effect he designed furniture that came to influence several generations of the Danish Golden Age era and fell within that peculiar field called 'artist's furniture' (i.e. that designed by painters to furnish their own homes). Abildgaard used and reinterpreted ancient Greek and Roman models. For his own home he designed, among other things, eight gilt chairs of the *klismos* type, with wickerwork seats and a palmetto frieze on the top rail, of exquisite taste and elegance, albeit hardly functional for the user. He tried his hand in almost every field within the applied arts. In 1779 he made costume designs for a production of Johannes Ewald's *Balder's Death* at the Kongelige Teater in Copenhagen. He designed various medals, and in his *Apis Clock* (Copenhagen, Kstindustmus.) a Renaissance-style bronze bull is integrated in the work, wearing a round clock on its back.

P. Kirkeby: *N. A. Abildgaard* (Hellerup, 1993)

Abramtsevo. Russian estate near Sergiyev Posad (57 km north of Moscow), the site of an artists' colony from the 1870s to the 1890s. A workshop established in 1884 produced caskets, dishes and furniture, decorated primarily with bas-relief carving (Abramtsevo-Kudrinskaya carving), which employs vegetable and geometrical ornament with representations of birds and animals. In 1890 a ceramics workshop was also set up at Abramtsevo, which instigated the production of maiolica; Mikhail Vrubel' (1856–1910) produced notable examples of maiolica at the Abramtsevo workshop.

The nearby town of Khot'kovo contains a factory producing carved artistic items, its craftsmen continuing the traditions of Abramtsevo-Kudrinskaya carving. The wood-carvers are taught in the Vasnetsov Abramtsevo Art College in the same town.

W. Salmond: 'The Russian Avant-Garde of the 1890s: The Abramtsevo Circle', *J. Walters A.G.*, lx–lxvi (2002–3), pp. 7–13

Abtsbessingen. German pottery factory in Thuringia founded *c.* 1739. In the second half of the 18th century the factory produced beer tankards, floral table decorations, tureens and vases, some decorated with the arms of the Schwarzburg family. The factory mark is a fork.

Acajou moucheté. French term for the spotted mahogany (*acajou*); the usual English term is fiddle-back mahogany.

Acanthus. Ornamental motif based on the leaves of the acanthus plant, an evergreen shrub native to the Mediterranean area. In various forms, it was one of the most widely used types of foliage motif from antiquity until the late 19th century. From classical antiquity throughout the Middle Ages, the acanthus motif was primarily architectural. In the Renaissance it retained its architectural importance, but was also applied to decorative arts, such as furniture, woodwork and ceramics, frequently in a hybrid acanthus/palmette form (e.g. Faienza maiolica dish, showing the *Arrival of Aeneas at Delos*, 1497; Sèvres, Mus. N.

Cér.). Alessandro Vittoria (1525–1608) used the acanthus in the stucco fireplace (1552–3) in the Palazzo Thiene, Vicenza, and Wendel Dietterlin (1550/51–99) in his book *Architectura* (Stuttgart, 1593, rev. ed. 1598) used the motif in a purely decorative way, with only brief consideration for its Classical architectural function.

In furniture and metalwork the motif was used in an upright rather than a curved form, in keeping with the restraint of the Neo-classical style (e.g. console table designed by William Kent, 1727–32; London, V&A). In late Regency England the acanthus motif had become commonplace and unrestrained and was used indiscriminately, without regard for its classical associations (e.g. porcelain teapot, Spode, *c.* 1830; London, V&A). In the USA it was applied to furniture both as a decorative motif, for example as freehand painted scrolling leaves (e.g. couch, 1810–25), and with an acknowledgement of its classical origins, for example on the capitals of columns used as supports for a pier table (1820–35; both Winterthur, DE, Du Pont Winterthur Mus.). William Morris revitalized the motif by studying early examples and the behaviour of real plants (e.g. 'Acanthus' wallpaper, 1875; London, V&A; see colour pl. I, fig. 2), and Christopher Dresser, a botanist and designer, not only studied the growth patterns of the acanthus but also formalized it into a design called 'Power', which was applied to a number of Wedgwood cane-ware vases and wine-coolers (e.g. pair, *c.* 1880; Barlaston, Wedgwood Mus.). With the advent of modernism and the consequent reduction in ornament and decoration, the acanthus motif was little used in the mid- and late 20th century.

M. Sherer: *The Acanthus Motive in Decoration* (New York, 1934)

Acier, Michel-Victor. *See under* MEISSEN.

Acorn cup. Covered silver cup shaped like the cupulate involucre in which the acorn grows, usually mounted on a botanical stem. Acorn cups were popular in Elizabethan and Jacobean England.

Adam, Robert (*b* Kirkcaldy, Fife, 3 July 1728; *d* London, 3 March 1792). Architect and designer, second son of the Scottish architect William Adam (1689–1748). He left an indelible stamp on British architecture and interior decoration and on international Neo-classicism. Adam designed a multitude of decorative objects for his domestic interiors, from furniture, carpets, door-knobs and escutcheons to stove-grates, candelabra, silverware, ink wells and (even) sedan chairs. This is not to say he designed everything that was included in any one commission or that Neo-classical furniture made for an Adam house was necessarily made to his designs. For many clients he designed only wall furniture—pier-tables, mirrors, bookcases—or a decorative object or two, but in some cases he designed a great deal. For Robert Child (*d* 1782) at Osterley Park, London, NT, for example, this included chairs for the dining-room, a commode and carpet for the drawing-room, a bed for the State Bedroom and chairs and a chimney-board for the Etruscan Dressing-room (all *in situ*); other pieces at Osterley were executed by such professional cabinetmakers as John Linnell; this was also true of Adam's other commissions. Those pieces that he did design are characterized by delicate and refined structures ornamented with elegantly flattened Classical motifs in relief (see colour pl. I, fig. 3).

ODNB
E. Harris: *The Furniture of Robert Adam* (London, 1963)
R. Rowe: *Adam Silver* (London, 1965)
D. Stillman: *The Decorative Work of Robert Adam* (London, 1966)
M. Tomlin: *Catalogue of Adam Period Furniture* (London, 1972)
G. Beard: *The Work of Robert Adam* (New York, 1978)
Robert Adam and Kedleston (exh. cat by G. Jackson-Stops and L. Harris; London, 1987)
S. Parissien: *Adam Style* (London, 1996)
E. Harris: *The Genius of Robert Adam: His Interiors* (New Haven, 2001)

Adam & Co. *See under* TYNESIDE.

Adams, **William.** Name of at least four potters in Staffordshire in the late 18th century and early 19th. The most distinguished William Adams (1746–1805) was the founder of Greengates Pottery, where the design and high quality of his jasper ware has led to the mistaken inference that he had been trained by Josiah Wedgwood; in fact he trained with John Brindley, brother of the canal builder James Brindley. His wares, of which some 300 examples are known to survive, are stamped Adams and Co. Apart from jasper ware, he also made underglaze blue-printed ware. He was succeeded by his son Benjamin, who ran the business until its closure in 1820.

The works of Adams of Greengates are sometimes confused with those of his three namesakes: William Adams (1748–1831) of Brick House, Burslem and Cobridge; William Adams of Stoke-on-Trent (1772–1829), who exported many blue-painted wares to the USA; and William Adams (1798–1865) the son of the Stoke-on-Trent potter, who succeeded his father.

ODNB (on Adams 1746–1805)

Robert Adam: chimney board from the State Bedchamber at Osterley Park House (London, Victoria and Albert Museum)

Adams & Company. Pittsburgh glasshouse founded in 1851 and active throughout the second half of the 19th century. The factory produced tableware and lamps; its glass included flint glass, lime glass and cut glass and, in the 1870s and 1880s, opal ware.

J. Shadel Spillman: 'Adams & Company', *Glass Club Bull.*, clxiii (1990–91)

Adlerglas and adlerhumpen. *See under* HUMPEN.

Admiral carpet. Type of 15th-century Spanish carpet, possibly woven in the Mercian villages of Letur or Liétor. Like Alcaraz carpets, they are tied with the Spanish knot. The name derives from the fact that many carpets of this type bear arms of the Enríquez family, hereditary admirals of Castile; others embody the arms of Maria of Castile (queen of Alfonso V of Aragon).

R. Pinner and W. B. Denny: *Carpets of the Mediterranean Countries, 1400–1600* (London, 1986)

Aegeri, Carl. *See* EGERI, CARL VON.

Aegricanes. Technical term, borrowed from Greek, for the ram's head or goat's head used to decorate altars in classical antiquity and revived in the Renaissance as an ornamental device, and used up to the 19th century on furniture and pottery.

Aelst, Pieter van (*b* ?Alost; *fl* 1509–55). Flemish tapestry-maker who trained in his father's workshop in Brussels. His mark, PVA, has been found on four tapestry series, all made in collaboration with others: on five of eight *History of Noah* tapestries (Kraków, N.A. Cols), part of a series made by six Brussels workshops for the King of Poland; on seven of ten *History of Abraham* tapestries, after Bernard van Orley (Vienna, Ksthist. Mus.); on two of eight *History of Odysseus* tapestries (Hardwick Hall, Derbys, NT); and on three of six *History of Moses* tapestries (San Francisco, CA Pal. Legion of Honor).

Pieter van Aelst is sometimes confused with Pieter Coecke van Aelst (1502–50), the South Netherlandish painter, sculptor, architect and designer of woodcuts, stained glass and tapestries.

M. Roethlisberger: 'The Ulysses Tapestries at Hardwick Hall', *Gaz. B.-A.*, lxxix (1972), pp. 111–25.
J. Szablowski, ed.: *The Flemish Tapestries at Wawel Castle in Cracow* (Antwerp, 1972)
A. Bennett: *Five Centuries of Tapestry from the Fine Arts Museum of San Francisco* (San Francisco, 1976)
G. Delmarcel: *Los Honores: Flemish Tapestries for the Emperor Charles V* (Antwerp, 2000)

Aemilia Ars [Società Cooperativa Aemilia Ars]. Workshop founded in Bologna in 1898 by the architect Alfonso Rubbiani (1848–1913), modelled on the English ARTS AND CRAFTS MOVEMENT; its formal name was Società Cooperativa Aemilia Ars. At first the workshop produced a wide range of products, including glass and pottery, but from 1902 to 1914 its principal products were textiles, especially lace.

Aesthetic Movement. Movement of the 1870s and 1880s that manifested itself in the fine and decorative arts and architecture in Britain and subsequently in the USA; it had no discernible influence on continental Europe. Reacting to what was seen as evidence of philistinism in art and design, it was characterized by the cult of the beautiful and an emphasis on the sheer pleasure to be derived from it.

The Aesthetic Movement was championed by the writers and critics Walter Pater (1839–94), Algernon Charles Swinburne (1837–1909) and Oscar Wilde (1854–1900). In the decorative arts, the most important product of the Movement was the 'Anglo-Japanese' furniture of E. W. Godwin, constructed in simple and elegant designs—solid balanced by void—occasionally with painted decoration. His preferred material was ebonized mahogany, which he used for the buffet that he designed originally for himself in 1867 (e.g. London, V&A), inset with panels of embossed Japanese leather paper. In the house in London that he decorated for himself there were Japanese fans on the ceiling and skirting, and Japanese vases. Such items were imported and sold at Liberty & Co. in London and could be found in fashionable 'Aesthetic' interiors of the 1870s and 1880s.

In 1876 F. R. Leyland (1831–92) commissioned Thomas Jeckyll to design the dining-room (now in Washington, DC, Freer) of 49 Princes Gate, London, which was to be the setting for his collection of porcelain and Whistler's painting *La Princesse du pays de la porcelaine* (1863–4). The walls behind Jeckyll's elaborate shelving were covered with Spanish leather, which Whistler overpainted in 1877 in gold on a blue ground with motifs based on the eye and tail-feathers of the peacock; opposite his picture, which hung over the fireplace, he painted two peacocks in full plumage. In the fireplace stands a pair of wrought-iron fire-dogs designed by Jeckyll in the form of sunflowers. With the peacock, the sunflower was a characteristic motif of the Aesthetic Movement, appearing in tiles painted by William De Morgan, embroidery designed by C. R. Ashbee, chintz and wallpaper designed by Bruce J. Talbert and in the painted face of a clock (1880; London, V&A) that was probably designed by Lewis Foreman Day.

The artists and craftsmen of the Aesthetic Movement sought to elevate the form of furniture, ceramics, metalwork and textiles to the status of fine art. William Morris, although at odds with much of the philosophy of the Aesthetic Movement, helped to extend its influence to the USA. By 1870 Morris's wallpapers were on sale in Boston, and two years later *Hints on Household Taste* (1868) by Charles Locke Eastlake was produced in an American edition. This was important to the dissemination of the notion that art should be applied to all types of decoration.

In 1876 the Centennial Exposition in Philadelphia did much to familiarize Americans with reformed taste in England, and in 1882–3 Wilde made a lecture tour of the USA. Though satirized for his effeteness and posturing, he increased awareness of the Aesthetic Movement.

In the USA Herter Brothers produced its own version of Godwin's 'Anglo-Japanese' style (e.g. wardrobe, 1880–85; New York, Met.), and Ott & Brewer of Trenton, NJ, made ceramics in the Japanese taste. Louis Comfort Tiffany designed jewellery and silver (e.g. vase, 1873–5; New York, Met.), as well as glass and interiors, and must be regarded as one of the principal American exponents of the Aesthetic Movement, as he was to be of Art Nouveau. John La Farge contributed decorations to the Japanese Parlor (1883–4) of the house (destr.) of William Henry Vanderbilt (1821–85) in New York, which was the epitome of fashionable taste.

D. Bolger Burke: *In Pursuit of Beauty: Americans and the Aesthetic Movement* (exh. cat., New York, Met., 1986)
L. Lambourne: *The Aesthetic Movement* (London, 1996)

Affenkapelle [Ger.: 'monkey band']. Term for a type of porcelain *singerie* manufactured in Meissen from the mid-18th century and thereafter imitated at other potteries. The sets typically consisted of some twenty simian musicians and a conductor (e.g. set at Clandon Park, Surrey, NT).

Affleck, Thomas (*b* Aberdeen, 1740; *d* Philadelphia, PA, 5 March 1795). American cabinetmaker of Scottish birth. He trained as a cabinetmaker in London. In 1763 John Penn, Governor of Pennsylvania, invited Affleck to Philadelphia, where the latter opened a shop on Second Street in the Society Hill area. He made stylish mahogany furniture for the governor's mansion at Lansdowne, PA, and for many of the most prominent families in the city, including the Mifflins, the Whartons and the Chew family at Cliveden.

The large body of surviving furniture attributed to Affleck, which includes wall-brackets, chairs (New York, Met.), grand chest-on-chests and elaborately carved tallboys or high chests-of-drawers, confirms his reputation as the leading cabinetmaker in Philadelphia in the 18th century. Much of his furniture was derived from designs in his personal copy of *Gentleman and Cabinet-maker's Director* by Thomas Chippendale. He also made furniture in the Neoclassical style. After his death, his son Lewis G. Affleck carried on the business for a short time until he went bankrupt.

D. M. Price: 'Cabinetmaker to the Colonial Stars', *A. & Ant.*, xxii/1 (Jan 1999), pp. 54–60

Agano. Japanese region in Buzen Province (now part of Fukuoka Prefect.), northern Kyushu, where stonewares were manufactured at various sites from *c.* 1600. The first potter to make Agano ware was the Korean master Chon'gye (Jap. Sonkai; 1576–1654). Deported to Kyushu during one of the Japanese invasions of Korea in 1592 and 1597, he entered the service of Hosokawa Tadaoki (1563–1645), the newly appointed governor of Buzen. On the completion of Tadaoki's fortress at Kokura (now Kitakyushu), Chon'gye built the Saienba kiln, probably within the castle precincts. A site thought to be Saienba was found beneath Myōkōji, the temple that replaced the castle in 1679, and excavations took place between 1979 and 1983. Sherds of both tea ceremony and everyday wares have been found there; they have transparent glazes made with a wood-ash flux, opaque glazes made with a straw-ash flux or brown-black glazes pigmented with iron oxide. Inscriptions on surviving pieces and entries in contemporary diaries indicate that these early products were also called Buzen or Kokura ware. After a few years the Saienba kiln closed, and Chon'gye, apparently still in Tadaoki's service, moved to the much larger Kamanokuchi kiln in the town of Akaike. Excavations there in 1955 uncovered thin-walled, finely finished wares mainly with transparent glazes; similar characteristics are found in early examples of Karatsu, Takatori and Hagi wares. Roughly coeval with the Kamanokuchi kiln was the Iwaya Kōrai kiln, a private enterprise that operated in nearby Hōjō. It made thick-walled vessels coated with an opaque glaze that is suggestive of north Korean origins. Both kilns produced wares for the tea ceremony and for utilitarian purposes.

A new phase began *c.* 1624, when the Saruyama Hongama kiln was opened, also in Akaike. It is believed to have been founded by Chon'gye and his assistants, who abandoned the Kamanokuchi kiln to a group of potters from the recently closed Takatori-ware kiln at Uchigaiso in the next valley. Initially the Saruyama Hongama kiln maintained the elegant standards of Kamanokuchi, but it ceased to make fine tea wares after 1632, when Hosokawa Tadaoki was made governor of the adjacent province of Higo (now part of Kumamoto Prefecture), and Chon'gye followed him there. Production of Agano wares continued for 250 years under the Ogasawara family, who succeeded the Hosokawa as lords of Buzen. In response to intense competition from the porcelain kilns at Arita, the Agano potters sought greater diversity and technical finesse. In the late 18th century Totoki Hoshō, a descendant of Chon'gye who worked at the Saruyama kiln, was sent to Kyoto and Edo to study the latest techniques, and the use of polychrome glazes and virtuoso textural effects dates from that time. Agano declined after the dissolution of the feudal domains in 1868, but production of wares in the Old Agano style was revived in the 20th century.

Agate glass [Ger. *Schmelzglas*; It. *calcedonio*]. Striped-pattern glass in which the coloured bands resemble those of natural agate. The bands are created by mixing molten glass of two or more colours. The technique was known in classical antiquity and was revived in 15th-century Venice and Germany.

Agate ware. Pottery made of clays of different colours; as the clays spin on the potter's wheel, striations similar to those in natural agate are formed. A similar effect is sometimes achieved with surface slips. Agate ware was made in classical Rome, and was revived in 18th-century Staffordshire, notably in the Wedgwood and Whieldon factories. In the late 20th century the American potter Michelle Erickson (*b* 1960) revived the tradition of agate ware.

P. Philip: 'Achieving Agate', *Cer. Rev.*, cxvi (March–April 1989), pp. 8–11

R. Hunter: 'The Stylistic Works of Michelle Erickson', *Ceramics*, xlvi (2001), pp. 46–51

Agitprop. Russian acronym derived from *agitatsion-naya propaganda* ('agitational propaganda'), in use shortly after the Bolshevik Revolution of 1917 for art applied to political and agitational ends. The prefix *agit-* was also applied to objects decorated or designed for this purpose, hence *agitpoyezd* ('agit-train') and *agitparokhod* ('agit-boat'), decorated transport carrying propaganda to the war-front.

The characteristics of the new art forms were defined as public, political and communal in purpose and execution. Trams were decorated with geometric designs, as were banners and posters, and, in response to Lenin's call in 1918 for monumental propaganda, temporary monuments to the Revolution and its heroes appeared in city streets. Printed works too played a role in agitprop, from the hand-stencilled posters known as 'ROSTA-windows' (posters published by ROSTA, the Russian Telegraphy Agency, and displayed in shop windows) by Vladimir Mayakovsky (1893–1930) to advertisements for state produce by Aleksandr Rodchenko (1891–1956). Even sweet wrappers and tableware reflected the aims of agitprop. The state porcelain factory produced a dish elegantly bearing the word *Golod* ('Famine'), Sergey Chekhonin decorated a plate with the slogan *Kto ne s nami, tot protiv nas* ('Who is not with us is against us'), while another by Maria Lebedeva (1895–1942) declared *Kto ne rabotayet, tot ne yest* ('Who does not work does not eat'). Agitational vehicles included the trains *V. I. Lenin No. 1* (1918), *Oktyabr'skaya Revolyutsiya* ('October Revolution', 1919), *Krasnyy Vostok* ('Red East', 1920) and the boat *Krasnaya Zvezda* ('Red Star', 1920).

Agostino Veneziano [Musi, Agostino dei] (*b* Venice, *c.* 1490; *d* ?Rome, after 1536). Italian engraver and draughtsman. His monogram ('A.V.') and in five instances his full name appear on 141 prints. Of these 85 are dated from 1514 to 1536. He began his career in Venice. His earliest dated prints (1514) are copies after Giulio Campagnola (*c.* 1482–after 1515; *The Astrologer*) and Albrecht Dürer (1471–1528; *Last Supper*). A print dated 1515 after Baccio Bandinelli (1493–1560; *Cleopatra*) and another dated 1516 after Andrea

del Sarto (1486–1530; *Dead Christ Supported by Three Angels*; B. 40) indicate his presence in Florence in these years.

In 1516 Agostino went to Rome, where over the next ten years he produced numerous prints after Raphael (e.g. *Blinding of Elymas*, 1516), Michelangelo (1475–1564), Giulio Romano (?1499–1546) and Rosso Fiorentino. He left Rome at the time of the Sack in 1527 and went to Venice; he also visited Mantua, where he engraved prints after Giulio Romano (e.g. *Lo Stregozzo* [the Witches' Procession], early 1520s, *Hercules and the Nemean Lion*, 1528), and Florence. Between 1531 and 1536 he worked in Rome, where he produced numerous prints, including a set of 12 *Antique Vases* (1531) and several contemporary portraits (e.g. *Francis I, King of France*, 1536).

P. Emison: 'Truth and Bizzaria in an Engraving of *Lo stregozzo*', *A. Bull.*, lxxxi (1999), pp. 623–36

Air-twist. Spiral of air bubbles used for decorative effect in the stem of a wine-glass, popular in English glasses from the 18th century.

Ajouré. French term for openwork, used in the decorative arts principally with reference to metalwork, bookbinding and heraldry. In metalwork, it denotes the piercing or perforation of sheet metal, a practice found as early as the ancient Egyptian period. In bookbinding, the term *ajouré* binding refers to a style that emerged in late 15th-century Venice in which bindings were embellished with pierced or translucent patterns, typically open designs of foliage. In heraldry, an *ajouré* is a field pierced by a square charge in a contrasting colour.

Alabaster. Term used to denote two types of stone, one of gypsum and one of limestone. 'True' alabaster is hydrated calcium sulphate, a finely fibrous form of gypsum. Alabaster is slightly soluble in water and therefore not suitable for outdoor works; it is very soft and readily cut and polished with the simplest tools. It provides an excellent surface for painting and gilding, without priming being necessary. Geologically ancient deposits provided material for sculptors, although gypsum continues to form in suitable environments in the Middle East, the USA and elsewhere. European sources exploited for decoration since the Middle Ages are present in England (S. Derbys and Staffs), France (Paris), Spain (e.g. nr Mérida) and Italy (nr Volterra and Castellina), while German deposits have given material since the 18th century. More recently alabaster from the USA and the former USSR has been used.

The second type is the stone that was referred to as alabaster by Theophrastus and Herodotus and that is now known as calcite alabaster, onyx-marble, Egyptian alabaster or Oriental alabaster (although alabaster is still used as a synonym in the eastern Mediterranean area). Onyx-marble is a stalagmitic lime-

Apulian Red-figure alabastron depicting Eros (Genoa, Museo Archeologico di Pegli)

translucent form of gypsum, became famous as a material for finely carved tomb figures and altar furnishings. It was revived as a medium for decorative objects in late 18th-century Italy, and since then has been used for objects such as clock cases and vases. The type of alabaster known as 'satin spar' (a vein-like form with the fibres in regular parallel arrangement, giving the mass a silk-like lustre) was mined at East Bridgeford, Notts, and shaped into beads and other ornaments for the American market.

A. Gardner: *Alabaster Tombs of the Pre-Reformation Period in England* (Cambridge, 1940)
F. W. Cheetham: *English Medieval Alabasters with a Catalogue of the Collection in the Victoria and Albert Museum* (Oxford, 1984)

Alabastra [Lat.: pl. of 'alabaster']. Bottles made of alabaster in which the ancient Egyptians and Greeks sealed up unguents. The singular Greek form, alabastron, is often used to denote these small cylindrical bottles, and the term is also used to denote later bottles of similar shape made of other materials, such as glass or pottery.

Albany slip. Slip clay that can produce a dark brown glaze. Albany slip was mined near Albany, NY, from the early 19th century, and was used on American stoneware. It is no longer mined commercially, but is imitated by colouring similar clays.

'Slip Sliding Away', *Cer. Mthly*, xxxvi (Jan 1988), pp. 57–8
G. Rowan and others: 'Living without Albany [slip]', *Cer. Mthly*, xxxvi (Oct 1988) p. 49–50

Albarello [It. *alberello*]. Maiolica jar, without handles, used especially as a container for dry drugs. The neck and foot are often slightly narrower than the body of the jar. The form originates in the Islamic world. An albarello with a procession of peacocks (Ann Arbor, U. MI, Kelsey Mus.) was excavated at Fustat (Egypt) in an undisturbed find-spot datable *c.* 1075, and there are many Persian examples. The albarello first appeared in Europe in early 14th-century Spain, and by mid-century was being manufactured in Italy. They were later made in potteries all over Europe, but the principal centre of production up to the 19th century was Italy. The form of the albarello has been imitated by modern potters such as Patrick Collins of Tasmania.

H. Wallis: *Italian Ceramic Art: The Albarello, a Study in Early Renaissance Maiolica* (London, 1904)
D. Klaosen: 'The Ceramics of Patrick Collins', *Cer. Tech.*, xii (2001), pp. 34–9

Albertolli, (Giuseppe) Giocondo (*b* Bedano, 24 July 1742; *d* Milan, 15 Nov 1839). Italian interior decorator and architect. He worked first in Parma, executing decorations in S Brigida (1765), decorations from a design by Ennemond-Alexandre Petitot (1727–1801) for a triumphal arch (1768, destr. 1859) for the wedding celebrations of Ferdinand, Duke of Parma, and Maria Amalia of Austria and ceiling decorations in the palace of the Duca di Grillo (begun 1769). From 1770 to 1775 Giocondo carried out the

stone marked with patterns of swirling bands of cream and brown. It was an admired decorative stone in the Ancient Near East and the Mediterranean region. During the Middle Ages in Western Europe, where useful deposits of stalagmitic limestone are rare, other material of similar appearance was named as, and used in place of, the rare stone, then available only as salvage from Roman ruins. At this time, English alabaster, a massive, fine-grained, stuccowork in the Gran Salone of the villa of Poggio Imperiale, outside Florence, for Leopold, Grand Duke of Tuscany. French designs were sent from Vienna, and the resulting room, later painted white, recalls the Petit Trianon, Versailles, though the scale is very large, with a Corinthian order of pilasters along the walls. These serve to mark off the garlands, trophies and low reliefs in frames that are applied in decoration. During his time in Florence he became familiar with Tuscan stuccowork of the 15th and 16th centuries, which was fundamental for his future career. In 1774 Giuseppe Piermarini (1734–1808), imperial and royal architect in Milan, invited Albertolli to decorate the Palazzo Reale. In 1774 and 1775 he divided his time between Milan and Florence, having been summoned again to Florence by the architect Gaspero Maria Paoletti (1727–1813) to decorate the ceilings of the Sala degli Stucchi and the Palazzina della Meridiana in the Palazzo Pitti. He also began the decoration of the Sala delle Niobi in the Uffizi Gallery. All his Tuscan projects were completed by his brother Grato (d 1812). In Milan he took two years to complete the room of the caryatids in the Palazzo Reale.

In addition to decorating many rooms in the Palazzo Reale to designs by Piermarini, Giocondo undertook commissions for the Teatro alla Scala (1778), for the Galleria Vecchia in the Palazzo Ducale in Mantua (to his own design, 1779) and for various rooms in the Villa Reale, Monza (to his own design, 1780–83). Piermarini supplied him with designs for the decoration of the Palazzo Casnedi (c. 1775), Milan, the Palazzo Greppi (c. 1776), Milan, and the Palazzo Belgiojoso (late 1770s), Milan, while he himself devised decorative schemes for the Palazzo Serbelloni (c. 1793), Milan, and the Palazzo Busca Arconati, Milan.

G. Albertolli: *The Architecture, Decoration and Furniture of the Royal Palaces in Milan* (Boston and New York, 1903)

Albini, Franco (*b* Robbiate, Como, 17 Oct 1905; *d* Milan, 1 Nov 1977). Italian architect, urban planner and furniture designer. One of the group of Rationalist architects who formed around the magazine *Casabella*, his work in the 1930s ranged from workers' housing in Milan to an ideal flat and furniture, exhibited at the Triennale in Milan in 1936. Albini's international reputation as an architect was also based on his exhibition and museum design, including the conversion of the Palazzo Bianco (1950–51), Genoa, into a museum. His reputation as a designer of furniture was established in his exhibition (with Gino Colombini (*b* 1915)) at the Low Cost Furniture Exhibition held in New York in 1950. His furniture was minimalist in design, and was built from inexpensive materials. The furniture with which he is now associated was produced in the 1950s, notably his woven cane Margherita and Gala chairs (1950), his Fiorenza armchair for Arflex (1950), his austere Luisa chair (1955) and his Rocking Chaise (1956), which combined features of a rocking chair and a hammock.

F. Helg, C. De Seta and M. Fagiolo: *Franco Albini, 1930–1970* (London, 1981)
S. Leet: *Franco Albini: Architecture and Design, 1934–1977* (New York, 1990)
M. Mulazzani: 'L'Iripetibilita della tradizione', *Casabella*, lxv/695–6 (Dec 2001–Jan 2002), pp. 156–67
A. Bassi: 'Franco Albini e la poltroncina Luisa: La definizione di un tipo per l'arredo', *Casabella*, lxvii (April 2003), pp. 106–9

Albisola. Italian town near Savona, in Liguria, which became a flourishing centre of maiolica production during the Renaissance, and continued to produce increasingly distinctive pottery in the 17th and 18th centuries. Important families in the pottery business included the Grosso, Chiodo, Corrado, Salomone, Pescio, Seitone, Seirullo, Levantino and Siccardi, all of whom produced large quantities of polychrome plates, albarelli and vases, which were sometimes inspired by silverware and contemporary Delftware; in the late 18th century the principal potter at Albisola was Giacomo Boselli. In some cases, yellow and an olive green were used on a turquoise ground. Wares were decorated in a calligraphic style with an emphasis on naturalistic motifs including such animals as leverets; this style later evolved into Baroque forms painted with soft, loose brushstrokes.

In the 1920s the Futurist potter Tullio Mazzotti (1899–1971), who took the name Tullio d'Albisola, revived Albisola's reputation as a pottery centre. The town is still a centre for pottery, especially the white and blue pottery known as Antico Savona. The Museo della Ceramica Manlio Trucco houses a collection of Albisola pottery from every period.

V. Conti: *Presenza di artisti degli anni ottanta nelle fornaci Albisolesi* (Albisola, 1986)
S. Grant: 'Ceramics Biennial in Italy', *Cer. Mthly*, 1/3 (March 2002), p. 16

Alcaraz. Spanish centre of carpet production in Murcia. Alcaraz was one of the two principal centres (together with Cuenca) of carpet production in 15th- and 16th-century Spain. The hand-knotted carpets are tied with a single-warp symmetrical knot (known as the Spanish knot) on an undyed woollen foundation. Several surviving 15th-century examples imitate Turkish carpets of the 'Holbein' variety, but the colouring is often different (Turkish red being replaced by blue and gold) and in the borders the Kufic inscriptions are replaced by geometrical or floral patterns. In the 16th century the red colouring became less vivid, possibly because of problems with the cochineal dye imported from Mexico. There was considerable variety of design, but in the 15th century the most common pattern consisted of wheels in rectangular compartments; in the 16th century the wheels softened into wreaths and the compartments assumed a variety of shapes or disappeared altogether.

A. Bartolomé Ariza, C. Partearroyo and A. Schoebel: *Alfombras españolas de Alcaraz y Cuenca*, vols XV–XVI (Madrid, 2002)

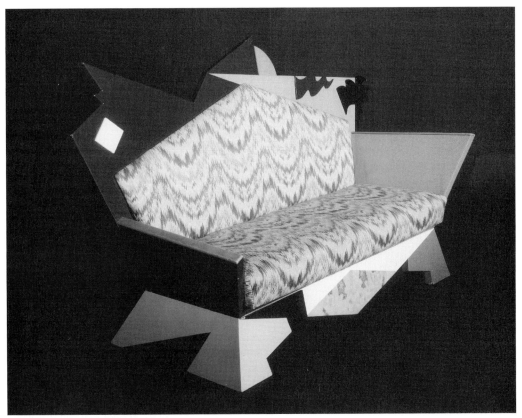

Alchimia Kandissi Sofa, designed by Alessandro Mendini, wood, leather and textile, 990 × 2050 × 870 mm, 1979 (Paris, Musée National d'Art Moderne)

Alcarraza [Sp.: 'the pitcher', from Arab. *al-kurraz*]. Porous earthenware vessel used for cooling water by evaporation.

Alchimia [Alchymia; Studio Alchimia]. Radical Italian design group known as Studio Alchimia founded in Milan in 1976 by the architect Alessandro Guerriero (*b* 1943) and his sister Adriana; they were later joined by the designer Alessandro Mendini (*b* 1931), who became the principal spokesman of group. The Studio was a manifestation of the anti-design movement, which sought to subvert austere Bauhaus design and mock conventional notions of good taste by championing experimental designs that caricatured the products of earlier schools of design. In 1980 a breakaway group formed MEMPHIS, a more commercial version of the Alchimia.

P. C. Bontempi and G. Gregori: *Alchimia* (The Hague and Milan, 1985)
C. Besemer: 'Studios: Alchimia', *Novum*, lviii (Feb 1987), pp. 16–21

Alcora Pottery. Spanish pottery manufactory. In 1727 a pottery factory was established in Alcora, in the Catalan province of Castellón. The most important products of the factory in its early years were plaques and glazed floor titles; the plaques were typ-

Alcora plate decorated with grotesques, faience, 18th century (Paris, Musée des Arts Décoratifs)

ically decorated with biblical or mythological scenes set within moulded frames, and the floor tiles used religious motifs (for churches and convents) and secular subjects such as maps and theatrical scenes. Later in the century the factory began to produce tableware, notably fruit bowls, sugar bowls, and pyramidical centrepieces. At the end of the 18th century Italian models were displaced by French design, and the factory began to produce tableware of soft porcelain in the Sèvres style. In this period the factory also started to manufacture the polychrome earthenware terrines known as *Fauna d'Alcora* because they were the shape of animals. The factory closed in 1895. A good selection of Alcora pottery is displayed in the local Museo de Cerámica.

M. C. McQuade: *Splendor of Alcora: Spanish Ceramics of the Eighteenth Century* (New York, 2000)

Aldegrever [Trippenmeker], **Heinrich** (*b* Paderborn, 1502; *d* Soest, Westphalia, 1555–61). German engraver, painter, medallist, glass painter and designer. He was the most important graphic artist in Westphalia in the 16th century. His reputation rests largely on his ornamental designs, which make up about one third of his *c.* 300 engravings. They were principally intended as models for metalworkers but were also adapted by other craftsmen for such decorative arts as enamel, intarsia and book illustration. Aldegrever followed Albrecht Dürer (1471–1528) and the Nuremberg Little Masters, deriving models for his paintings and subject prints as well as a full repertory of Renaissance ornamental motifs: fig and acanthus foliage, vases and cornucopia, combined with putti and satyrs, tritons, mermaids and dolphins, sphinxes, masks and medallions.

The Prints of Altdorfer and Aldegrever (exh. cat., Cambridge, Fitzwilliam, 1983)
F. W. H. Hollstein and others: *Heinrich Aldegrever* (Rotterdam, 1998)

Aldine binding. Style of late 15th- and early 16th-century North Italian bookbinding associated with ALDUS MANUTIUS but not restricted to the publications of the Aldine Press. The design of the bindings, which were usually in brown or red morocco, was relatively simple, consisting of geometrical strapwork or rectangular panels of gold fillets. The arabesques in the corners of the panels are called 'Aldine fleurons' or 'Aldine knot leaves'.

Aldus Manutius (*b* Bassiano, ?1450; *d* Venice, 6 Feb 1515). Italian printer, publisher, teacher and translator. In 1489–90 he moved to Venice, where soon afterwards he published the *Musarum panegyris* (1491). His Greek publications formed the core of his activities: he issued *c.* 30 first editions of literary and philosophical Greek texts including a five-volume Aristotle (1495–8). The first book printed with his own newly cut Greek type was the *Erotemata* (1495) by Constantinos Lascaris (1434–?1501). Three further Aldine Greek types were developed, the last in 1502.

Typographically his major achievement was the type cut by Francesco Bologna, il Griffo, for Pietro Bembo's *De Aetna* (February 1495), a truly modern type still used in modified form.

M. Lowry: *The World of Aldus Manutius: Business and Scholarship in Renaissance Venice* (Oxford, 1979)
N. Barker: *Aldus Manutius and the Development of Greek Script and Type in the Fifteenth Century* (Sandy Hook, 1985)
In Praise of Aldus Manutius: A Quincentenary Exhibition (exh. cat. by H. G. Fletcher, New York, Pierpont Morgan Lib.; Los Angeles, UCLA, Res. Lib.; 1995)
M. Davies: *Aldus Manutius: Printer and Publisher of Renaissance Venice* (Tempe, AZ, 1999)

Ale glass. *See* YARD-OF-ALE GLASS.

Alençon lace [Fr. *point d'Alençon*]. Type of lace produced in France. In 1675 a group of 30 Venetian lacemakers was settled in the Norman town of Alençon by Jean-Baptiste Colbert (1619–83; Louis XIV's minister of finance). The Venetians instructed local needlewomen in *point de Venise*, but by the 1690s the distinctive local style known as *point d'Alençon* had emerged. Needlewomen adopted the net ground technique, and invented a series of new stitches.

Lace production was halted at the Revolution because of its association with the *ancien régime*, but revived under Napoleon (*reg* 1804–1814) and again under the Second Empire. Lace is still produced in Alençon, supported by the Atelier National du Point d'Alençon founded in 1976, and there are good collections of Alençon lace in the Musée de la Dentelle au Point d'Alençon and the Musée des Beaux-Arts et de la Dentelle.

The term *point d'Alençon* now denotes a style as well as a place of origin. The style is characterized by a uniform mesh (called the *fond* or the *réseau*), numerous and elaborate fillings (*modes*) and bold motifs outlined by prominent whipped cords (the *cordonnet*).

E.-A.-M. Despierres and R. Morgan: *Alençon Lace* (Aberdeen, 1987)
Dentelles de haute vol: Robes du soir et haute couture. (exh. cat., Alençon, Mus. B.-A. & Dentelle, 1993)

Alentours. *See under* TAPESTRY, §II, 4.

Algardi, Alessandro (*b* Bologna, 31 July 1598; *d* Rome, 10 June 1654). Italian sculptor, architect and draughtsman. He was, with Gianlorenzo Bernini, the most important sculptor active in Rome in the middle years of the 17th century. Though primarily a sculptor, Algardi was also active in the decorative arts. In about 1622 he left his native Bologna for Mantua, where he made small ivory *objets d'art* and produced small models to be cast in bronze and silver for the Gonzaga court; none of these is known to survive.

In 1625, after a period spent in Venice, Algardi moved to Rome, where he was to remain for the rest of his life. In 1634 Algardi began his connection with Marcantonio Borghese, Prince of Sulmona (1730–1800), who commissioned models for the six bronze herms that bear the jasper slab forming what is known as the Borghese Table (Rome, priv. col.). Algardi was later commissioned by the same patron to design or make models for a whole range of smaller objects, such as silver room fountains and bronze braziers. The only surviving objects that can be associated with these commissions are a black marble urn, resting on the Borghese dragons, executed by Silvio Calci, and two black marble vases with serpent and eagle handles (all Rome, Gal. Borghese).

J. Montagu: *Alessandro Algardi*, 2 vols (New Haven, 1985)
G. Bozzo: *Alessandro Algardi: I bronzi della Chiesa di San Carlo a Genova* (exh. cat., Bologna, Mus. Civ. Med., 1998)

Alicatados. *See under* TILE, §I, 3.

Alkaline glaze. *See under* GLAZE.

Allis. American family of joiners and cabinetmakers, active in Hadfield, MA. The brothers John Allis (1642–91) and Samuel Allis (1647–91), whose maternal great-uncle was NICHOLAS DISBROWE, were both joiners, as was John's son Icabod (1675–1747). The firm was managed by John Allis the elder, and employed his brother and sons; John the elder's partner was SAMUEL BELDEN, and so the firm was called Belden & Allis. Many HADLEY CHESTS are attributed to members of the interconnected Allis and Belden families.

Allison, Michael (*b* 1773; *d* 1855). American cabinetmaker, active in New York throughout the first half of the 19th century; the principal competitor of his neighbour DUNCAN PHYFE. Allison's furniture is characterized by the use of high-quality mahogany and a principled austerity in the use of decoration. His early work is in the Hepplewhite style, and his later work is modelled on Sheraton.

Allwine, Lawrence (*b* 1756; *d* 1833). American chair-maker, active in Philadelphia, specializing in Windsor chairs, which were painted or gilded. His relatives (possibly sons) John and Peter Allwine were apprenticed to him. The first family workshop opened on South Front Street in 1791, and the last, on Sassafras Street (now Race Street), closed in 1809, when Lawrence and John migrated to Zanesville, in Muskingum County, OH; they continued to make chairs, and also ran a tavern. Lawrence Allwine is the eponym of the varnish known as 'Allwine Gloss'.

Almeida, Sebastião Inácio de (*d* Lisbon, 1779). Portuguese potter and painter. He became director and painting master of the REAL FÁBRICA DO RATO in Lisbon after the expulsion in 1771 of the first director TOMÁS BRUNETTO. With his predecessor, Almeida is associated with the factory's most successful and distinctive period. Initially he collaborated with the potter and painter Severino José da Silva (*d* 1797)

who was also vice-director and head of the potters' workshop. There was a marked change in style in the wares produced at the factory under Almeida's direction. In particular, the large pieces enamelled with polychrome decoration were abandoned in favour of smaller and more delicately executed items of blue-and-white tableware that were influenced by wares from the Rouen faience factories.

Almeida, Valentim de (*fl* Lisbon, *c.* 1720–60). Portuguese decorative artist. His apprenticeship was probably undertaken with Master PMP, the painter of glazed tiles. His most important commission between 1729 and 1731 was for the panels of blue and white tiles, made in Lisbon, that cover the lower storey of the cloister of Oporto Cathedral, which represent scenes from the Song of Solomon. Almeida's panels in the church of S Pedro, Sintra, contain scenes from the life of St Peter (*c.* 1740), in which the Miracle of the Fishes is based on Raphael's tapestry cartoon of the same subject (London, V&A). The attractive blue and white panels (*c.* 1735–45) in the cloister of the monastery of S Vicente de Fora, Lisbon, are attributable to Almeida.

Almorratxa [Almorrata]. Blown glass rose-water sprinkler with four spouts, made in Catalonia since the 17th century and subsequently produced in Venetian glasshouses. The Catalan dance known as the morratxa is so called because the dancers carry almorratxes.

Alpujarra rug. Type of Spanish rug made in the Alpujarra mountains south of Granada. The carpets are coarsely woven, usually in two colours, and have a separately-woven fringe, often in other colours. In some examples, exposed parts of the linen base constitute part of the design, which is often floral.

Altare. Italian town near Savona, in Liguria, where glass has been made since the 11th century. At first utilitarian objects were produced, but during the Renaissance pieces became more artistic, undoubtedly due to the contribution of craftsmen from Murano who had initiated the local craftsmen into the secrets of the art. While the activity in Altare is documented by early sources, it has not been possible to identify with certainty any piece produced there, as the typological and aesthetic characteristics were indistinguishable from those of Venetian glass. As they gained experience the Ligurian craftsmen refined their taste and techniques and contributed to the development of technical processes, especially for mirrors. They played an important role in creating the market for glass *à la façon de Venise* throughout Europe as they migrated in great numbers to Provence, Normandy and Belgium. The glassmakers of Altare were organized in a guild, the Università dell'Arte Vitrea, which adopted a statute in 1495 and worked to facilitate contacts and exchanges and establish new glassmaking centres in other countries.

G. Malandro: *I vetrai di Altare* (Savona, 1983)
M. B. Brondi: *Storia del vetro: Il vetro preindustriale dalla Liguria a Newcastle* (Genoa, 1999)

Altenburg. German town in Saxony and centre for stoneware pottery since the 1620s. Excavated fragments of the earliest pottery made in Altenburg are very similar to pottery from WALDENBURG, but by the end of the century Altenburg pottery had developed a distinctive style. Its principal products were stocky beer steins and (from 1690) the cylindrical jugs known as pearl jugs. The 'pearls', which were made from white fired material, decorated Altenburg ware throughout the 18th century. Altenburg potteries also made a spherical medallioned jug which was decorated with pewter medals.

Aluminium [Amer. aluminum; It. *alluminio*]. Silvery white metal produced by smelting after the extraction of alumina from bauxite. Following the discovery of processes for separating the metal from the oxide, at first experimentally in 1825, then commercially in 1854 and industrially in 1886–8, aluminium rapidly came to be valued as an adaptable material with both functional and decorative properties. At the time of its discovery it was thought to be a rare and precious metal, and so was used in fine jewellery.

From the 1920s and 1930s aluminium was widely used for industrial design, household products and interior features, due to its lightness and durability. At the Bauhaus in the 1920s aluminium was used experimentally in fabrics, and Marianne Brandt and others incorporated it into lighting fixtures. Alumin-

Frederick Kiesler: nesting coffee table, cast aluminium, 837×241×635 mm and 559×241×413 mm, 1935–8 (New York, Museum of Modern Art)

ium staircase railings and light fixtures were used in the De La Warr Pavilion, Bexhill-on-Sea, Sussex (1936), by Serge Chermayeff (1900–96) and Erich Mendelsohn (1887–1953). During this period it was particularly favoured by American designers, for example DONALD DESKEY (e.g. furniture and lamps in the Radio City Music Hall, New York, 1932) and RUSSEL WRIGHT. It was cast and wrought for ornamental gates, lift and radiator grilles and has been used for jewellery making, notably by the English designer Jane Adam (*b* 1954), who uses anodized aluminium. The stacking chair (1938) by Hans Coray (1906–91) was mass-produced for parks and gardens, the seat and back being formed of a single piece of aluminium. After World War II such designers as ERNEST RACE used aluminium for furniture, due to timber shortages. Eero Saarinen used aluminium as the base of his fibre-glass tulip chair (1956–7) produced by Knoll. In the early 1970s powder colour coatings were introduced and proved to be highly resistant to impact and corrosion. In the late 20th century a 'superplastic aluminium' was developed, which, when heated, acts like plastic and can be blown into a mould with compressed air to produce intricate shapes.

M. L. Bierman: 'Aluminum Styling', *Interior Des.*, lxvii (Oct 1996), pp. 144–5
S. Nichols: *Aluminum by Design* (Pittsburgh, 2000)
J. Ruyak: 'Rich Alchemy: Jane Adam', *Ornament*, xxvi/4 (Summer 2003), pp. 54–7

Alzata. Type of Italian plate, mounted on a high thin stem, often for use as a centrepiece or fruit bowl; sometimes a series of plates and stems is mounted on top of each other. The plates are usually made of glass or pottery.

Amastini [Mastini]. Italian family of gem-engravers. Angelo Antonio Amastini (*b* Fossombrone, the Marches, 1754; *d* after 1816) and his son Niccolò Amastini (*b* Rome, 1780; *d* Rome, 1851) worked in Rome; they may also have been active in Florence. A gem-engraver known as Angelo Tesei Mastini could possibly be the same person as Angelo Antonio Amastini. Carlo de Giovanni Amastini (*d* 1824) from Fossombrone was also a gem-engraver, but his relationship to Angelo Antonio Amastini and Niccolò Amastini is unknown. He was active in Berlin, where he taught gem-cutting and was a member of the Akademie der Künste. Surviving examples of work by the Amastini family include onyx cameos of *Cupid and Psyche* and of *Psyche*, signed A. MASTINI (both London, BM), of a woman's head, signed AMASTINI (Vienna, Ksthist. Mus.) and the *Education of Bacchus*, signed N. AMASTINY in Greek letters (New York, Met.). Their workshop in Rome also made series of casts of their own and others' stones, including the work of the Pichler family and Nathaniel Marchant.

Amber. Fossilized, water-insoluble resin, 20–120 million years old, which exuded from giant coniferous trees and became buried below them. Amber is amorphous, of resinous lustre and usually found in small pieces: irregular lumps, grains, drops and stalactites. It feels warm, is lightweight and porous and may fluoresce naturally under daylight, especially when freshly extracted. Inclusions of organic matter—insects, crustacea (some now extinct), flora, bark etc—resulted from these being trapped in the liquid resin as it flowed downwards. When in contact with atmospheric air, its surface becomes oxidized and forms a crust. Transparent, opaque (due to an abundance of tiny bubbles) or osseous, it is commonly yellow to honey-coloured, but approximately 250 different colour varieties including white and black are known, the rarest being red, blue and green. On lengthy exposure to air, golden-yellow amber slowly darkens to red. Green amber is thought to have formed in marshy areas through inclusions of decaying organic material. When burnt or rubbed vigorously amber emits a resinous pine aroma, and friction causes it to produce static sufficient to pick up small particles of paper. It is soft and carves easily but can be brittle, and skill is required to prevent fracturing. It tends to craze when subjected to sustained and extreme heat. Imitations include Chinese dyed sheep's horn and such plastic substitutes as phenolic resin. Amber has been confused with the fossil resins copal, dammar and kauri gum, of more recent date.

Amber was for centuries worked by hand. In the 18th century a spinning wheel was adapted into a crude lathe for turning objects, which were shaped with the aid of a piece of broken glass held against the amber. Industrialization reintroduced lathes and drills (which had been used by the Romans), but hand methods persisted with various saws, files, graving tools, sandpapers and such polishing compounds as tripoli, aluminium oxide and rouge; power-driven lapidary equipment used at slow speeds prevents shattering or melting.

For 200 years Baltic amber supplies were controlled by the Teutonic Order of Knights, who imposed strict discipline over the valuable raw material. The conversion to Lutheranism in 1525 of the Grand Master of the Teutonic Order, Albert of Hohenzollern-Ansbach, Duke of Prussia (reg 1525–68), a patron of amber-carving, encouraged the manufacture of such secular objects as tankards, goblets, caskets, game-boards and candlesticks, some with metalwork mounts. Devotional objects in amber (e.g. Florence, Pitti) continued to be produced in Catholic countries in the 16th century. The Duke of Prussia also lowered the cost of raw amber and expanded the market in Europe. As the craft flourished, guilds were established along the Baltic coast, and amber was distributed from Danzig (now Gdańsk) throughout northern Europe. The market extended to Turkey and India, and Armenians travelled to Königsberg (now Kaliningrad), a leading centre for amber-carving, in order to barter silk carpets for raw amber. One of the most outstanding carvers from Königsberg was Georg Schreiber (fl 1616–43). An example of Königsberg

work is a set of 18 amber and silver-gilt plates (1585; Copenhagen, Rosenborg Slot).

By the mid-17th century Danzig was patronized by the Polish court and flourished as the prime centre for amber working. The technique of 'incrustation' practised in Danzig was a major development: a wooden core was introduced for the construction of larger amber pieces, and slabs of amber were cemented to a wooden carcass to make such large objects as house altars and cabinets. An amber throne commissioned in 1677 for the Habsburg Emperor Leopold I of Austria, of which only fragments (Vienna, Ksthist. Mus.) and drawings (Berlin, Altes Mus.) survive, may have been partly worked by the ivory- and amber-carver Christoph Maucher, who also made two fine groups of the *Judgement of Paris* (late 17th century; London, V&A). Amber veneers in geometric and pictorial designs were used for cabinets and game-boards (e.g. of 1594; Kassel, Hess. Landesmus.). A mosaic effect was achieved with different coloured ambers—as on an altar (c. 1650–1700; V&A from Danzig—with contrasting opaque and clear amber panels, or with a combination of ivory and amber. The last spectacular court commission was an amber room designed for Schloss Charlottenburg near Berlin in 1709; it was presented to Peter the Great in 1717 and reconstructed at Tsarskoye Selo (now Pushkin) in Russia (untraced).

By the mid-18th century the use of amber was waning as fashions changed, patronage was withdrawn and the Baltic guilds declined. In the 19th century it was used chiefly in the Middle East and India for the decoration of horses' saddles and bridles. Ambroid (or Spiller) was made from small chips and offcuts of amber that were pressed hydraulically in a steel mould to form a cake, which was then cut to the required shape. Marketed in Vienna from 1881, Ambroid formed mouthpieces for pipes and cigarette holders. Amber jewellery became fashionable in late Victorian and Edwardian England, with plain round beads and cabochons occasionally set in gold. Georg Jensen and others combined it with silver (e.g. necklace, 1908; Copenhagen, Kstindustmus.), a trend followed on a silver bowl with an amber finial (c. 1934; London, V&A). In the 1920s, when amber vied with diamonds as the top gem import to the USA, bead necklaces with insect inclusions and faceted beads of clear amber were eagerly sought (e.g. in Chicago, IL, Field Mus. Nat. Hist.). Imitation and synthetic ambers enjoyed a peak of popularity from 1930 to 1935 for wireless casings, writing sets, table lamps, jewellery and decorative objects.

J. Grabowska: *Amber in Polish History* (Edinburgh, 1978)
M. Trusted: *Catalogue of European Ambers in the Victoria and Albert Museum* (London, 1985)
H. Fraquet: *Amber* (London, 1987)
C. Scott-Clark and A. Levy: *The Amber Room: The Fate of the World's Greatest Lost Treasure* (New York, 2004)

Amberg, Adolf (*b* Hanau, July 1874; *d* Berlin, 3 July 1913). German silversmith, sculptor and painter.

From 1894 to 1903 he worked at the renowned silverware factory of Bruckmann & Söhne in Heilbronn, modelling goblets, cutlery, sports prizes and medals etc. In collaboration with Otto Rieth (1858–1911), professor at the Kunstgewerbeschule in Berlin, Amberg made a silver fountain (h. 3.2 m) for the Exposition Universelle, Paris, in 1900. After designing the silver for the Town Hall of Aachen (1903) and spending a year in Rome (1903–4), Amberg completed his most important work, the design of the *Hochzeitszug* (Berlin, Tiergarten, Kstgewmus.), a table centre for the wedding of Wilhelm (1882–1951), Crown Prince of Germany and Prussia, and Herzogin Cecilie von Mecklenburg-Schwerin (1886–1954) in 1905. The designs were, however, rejected by the royal household and sold to the Königliche Porzellan-Manufaktur (KPM) in Berlin, which finally produced them in porcelain (1908–10): an ensemble of twenty figures, two candelabras, one jardinière and several fruit-bowls. Their theme is the homage and presentation of gifts to the bridal couple by representatives of foreign peoples and cultures. The figures were put on sale both unpainted and painted (under- and overglaze).

Amberg Pottery. German porcelain manufactory in the Bavarian town of Amberg that was founded in 1759 and produced household wares and occasional display pieces until it closed in 1910.

Amberina glass. Type of American glass patented in 1883 by Joseph Locke (1846–1936; head designer of the New England Glass Co.) and Edward Libby (1827–83; owner of the glassworks). Amberina glass is usually amber at the bottom, shading to red at the top, but there is also glass in which the colours are reversed (known as 'reverse amberina'). The effect is created by reheating the top (or, in 'reverse amberina', the bottom) of the glass before it has fully cooled.

Amberina glass was soon made at other factories, with or without a licence from the New England Glass Co. Amberina produced by Hobbs, Brockunier & Co. in Wheeling, WV, was made under licence, but the amberina made without a licence by Mt Washington Glass Works of New Bedford, MA, was the subject of litigation that first caused the company to change the name of its glass (to 'Rose Amber') and then, in 1886, to discontinue production. In Europe the manufacturers included Baccarat. Amberina glass is still made, notably by Boyd's Crystal Art Glass in Cambridge, OH.

Amberina (Toledo, OH, 1970) [includes Locke's Amberina sketchbook]

Amboyna wood. Mottled and curled wood of the *Pterocarpus indicus* tree found in Ambon, in the Moluccan Islands (Indonesia); has been used in marquetry since the 16th century.

Ambry [aumbry]. Cupboard, either in the recess of a wall or as a separate article of furniture), variously used as a pantry or a meat-safe. In ecclesiastical use, it denotes a cupboard, locker, or closed recess in the wall, for the storage of books, sacramental vessels and vestments

Amelung, **John Frederick** [Johann Friedrich] (*b* Hettlingen, nr Hannover, Germany, 26 June 1741; *d* Baltimore, MD, 1 Nov 1798). American glass manufacturer of German birth. He was associated with his brother's mirror-glass factory in the town of Grünenplan before his venture to make table wares and utility glass in America began in 1784. With backing from investors in Bremen, Germany, Amelung brought 68 glass craftsmen and furnace equipment to the USA. He purchased an existing glasshouse near Frederick, MD, close to the fast-growing Baltimore market. The factory, which he named the New Bremen Glassmanufactory, had been founded by glassmakers from Henry William Stiegel's defunct operation in Manheim, PA. During the following decade Amelung built housing for his 400–500 workers, many of whom were of German origin. It is believed that he built four glasshouses.

Although Amelung's craftsmen made window glass, bottles and table glass, the most important group of objects associated with the factory are the high-quality, wheel-engraved presentation pieces (e.g. sugar bowl, 1785–95; Winterthur, DE, Du Pont Winterthur Mus.) made as gifts for friends and for such politicians as President George Washington, whom Amelung hoped to impress. These wares shared some of the *Waldglas* lily-pad decoration associated with Caspar Wistar's earlier glassworks, but Amelung's products are more spectacular in conception and execution. They are unique among American glasswork products of the time in often being signed and dated. In 1787 Amelung published a pamphlet entitled *Remarks on Manufactures, Principally on the New Established Glass-house, near Frederick-Town in the State of Maryland*, in which he related the founding of his enterprise and speculated on its future.

Amelung's operations virtually ceased following his stroke in 1794, and he went bankrupt in 1795. His son, John Frederick Magnus Amelung, continued to make glass in the glasshouse given to him in 1795 by his father (the site was not included in his father's bankruptcy), but in 1799 he transferred the property to his partners Adam Kohlenberg and George Christian Gabler.

J. F. Amelung: *Remarks on Manufactures, Principally on the New Established Glass-house, near Frederick-Town in the State of Maryland* (Frederick-Town, 1787)

E. S. Delaplaine: *John Frederick Amelung, Maryland Glassmaker* (Frederick, MD, 1971)

D. P. Lanmon and others: *John Frederick Amelung: Early American Glassmaker* (London, 1990)

Amen glass. *See* JACOBITE GLASS.

American China Manufactory. *See* TUCKER CHINA FACTORY.

American Flint Glass Manufactory. *See under* STIE-GEL, HENRY WILLIAM.

American Pottery Manufacturing Co. American pottery manufacturer. Beginning in 1828 D. & J. Henderson made award-winning Rockingham ware in a factory previously occupied by the Jersey Porcelain and Earthenware Co. in Jersey City, NJ, but in 1833 David Henderson (*c.* 1793–1845) took control of the company and changed the name to the American Pottery Manufacturing Co. In addition to the fine Rockingham modelled by the Englishman Daniel Greatbach (*fl* after 1839; *d* after 1866), the company was the first to make transfer-printed pearlware in the USA and *c.* 1833 reproduced Ridgway's 'Canova' pattern. Many English potters who settled in the USA during the second quarter of the 19th century started their American careers in Henderson's pottery. After Henderson's death in 1845, the firm continued until 1852, when John Owen Rouse (*d* 1896) and Nathaniel Turner (*d* 1884) took over the works for the production of whiteware, which was made there until 1892.

Amethyst. Precious stone of a clear purple or bluish violet colour, of different degrees of intensity, consisting of quartz or rock-crystal coloured by manganese; it is valued as the only purple gemstone. From the 7th century AD it was used as the gemstone of bishops' rings.

Amol. City in northern Iran, close to the Caspian Sea, and from the 11th century to the 13th, centre for the production of a distinctive white slip pottery with incised designs.

Ampel [Ger.: 'hanging lamp']. Ceramic term used to denote a medieval oil lamp.

Amphora. In classical antiquity, a two-handled vessel, variously shaped, used for holding oil and wine.

Ampulla [ampul]. Small vessel, usually made of glass, used in ancient Rome and later in the Western church, for holding consecrated oil, or for other sacred uses.

Amstel Porcelain. Dutch porcelain factory near Amsterdam, originally founded at Weesp (1764; *see* WEESP PORCELAIN FACTORY), then moved to Oude Loosdrecht (1771), Oude Amstel (1784) and Nieuwe Amstel (1799); it closed in 1810. The term 'Amstel porcelain' is sometimes used to denote the products of the period 1784–1810, when the factory was in Oude Amstel and Nieuwe Amstel, but is also used to denote all the products of the factory from 1764 to 1810. The original workmen were from Dresden, and the early pottery resembles white Dresden pottery with landscape and figure decorations; the late

Black-figure Panathenaic amphora, late 6th century BC (Rome, Vatican, Museo Gregoriano Etrusco)

pottery tends to follow French models, especially Sèvres. Amstel tableware and utilitarian containers suited bourgeois tastes, and apart from a few busts in biscuit there was no attempt to mimic the refined technical mastery of Delft pottery. Decoration and shape were eclectic, so the pottery never developed a strong visual identity. Some pottery is entirely white, with ornament in low relief; piercings are sometimes outlined in blue; cartouches contained a wide variety of pictures, often portraying flowers or landscapes; Sèvres cornflowers are a common adornment.

The wares of the four stages of the factory are not easily distinguished, but the marks are distinctive. The Weesp mark is the crossed swords of Dresden with dots on either side; the Oude Loosdrecht mark was MOL; the Oude Amstel mark was sometimes 'Oude 14 Amstel', but sometimes a simple 'A'.

W. M. Zappey: 'Amstelporselein', *Vrienden Ned. Cer.: Medebl.*, lxxxvi–lxxxvii/2–3 (1977)

Andersen, David (*b* 1843; *d* 1901). Norwegian silversmith. Founder of the Oslo company of silversmiths now known as David-Andersen. In 1876 Andersen established a workshop and retail shop in Christiania (Oslo). His early work, mostly in 830 silver, uses traditional Nordic motifs. David's son Arthur (1875–1970), who became the principal designer for the firm and inherited it in 1901, introduced enamel (*cloisonné* and *plique-à-jour*) and up-graded to sterling silver. Arthur changed his surname to David-Andersen, and the company is now run by members the same family. David-Andersen is now regarded as the finest manufacturer of enamelled jewellery.

I. David-Andersen and A. David-Andersen: *David-Andersen, 1876–1951* (Oslo, 1951)

Andiron. *See under* FIREPLACE FURNISHINGS.

Andreoli, Giorgio [Giorgio da Gubbio; Mastro Giorgio] (*b* Intra or Pavia, *c.* 1465–70; *d* Gubbio, 1555). Italian potter. He seems to have moved to GUBBIO *c.* 1490, together with his brothers Giovanni Andreoli (*d c.* 1535) and Salimbene Andreoli (*d c.* 1522). He became a citizen of Gubbio in 1498. He is particularly well known for his lustrewares (e.g. vase and cover, 1500–10; V&A), and other potters, especially from the Metauro Valley, sent their work to be lustred in his workshop. His wares made in 1518–19 were frequently signed and dated. His *istoriato* (narrative) wares (e.g. plate decorated with *Hercules and the Hydra*, *c.* 1520; Oxford, Ashmolean) can be dated until at least 1537. In 1536 the workshop seems to have been taken over by his sons Vincenzo Andreoli (Mastro Cencio) and Ubaldo Andreoli.

P. Mattei and T. Cecchetti, eds: *Mastro Giorgio: L'uomo, l'artista, l'imprenditore* (Perugia, 1995)

Andries [di Savino], **Guido** (*b* ?Castel Durante, *fl* 1512; *d* Antwerp, 1541). South Netherlandish potter of Italian birth. He probably worked in Venice before

settling in Antwerp at the beginning of the 16th century. In 1512 he purchased a house called De Groote Aren in the Oude Veemerct and in 1520 established the Den Salm workshop in the Kammenstraat, which became the most important in Antwerp. His five sons also worked as potters in Antwerp and abroad: Guido Andries the younger (1535/41–*c.* 1587) in Antwerp; Frans Andries (*b* before 1535; *d* after 1565) in Seville; Joris Andries (*c.* 1535–*c.* 1579) in Middelburg; Jaspar Andries (1535/41–*c.* 1580) in Norwich and London (LAMBETH); while Lucas Andries (*b* before 1535; *d c.* 1573), the eldest son, eventually inherited his father's workshop in Antwerp. Guido Andries the elder produced faience pots and paving-tiles, the most remarkable of which are those from the abbey of Herkenrode, which are influenced by Venetian maiolica (1532–3; Brussels, Musées Royaux A. & Hist.), and the paving-tiles in The Vyne (*c.* 1525; The Vyne, Hants). After Andries's death, his widow married Franchois Frans, who managed the workshop from 1543 to 1561–2.

C. Dumortier: 'Pots de pharmacie en majolique anversoise conserves aux Musées royaux d'Art et d'Histoire', *Rev. Belge Archéol. & Hist. A.*, lxix (2000), pp. 113–32

Angarano. Italian town near Bassano and centre of ceramics production during the 18th century. The best-known pottery family in the town was the Marinoni. In 1778 Baldassare Marinoni was granted permission to manufacture porcelain at Angarano; he presumably employed workers from nearby Nove; a figure group from this factory dated 1779 was recorded in 1876. The factory seems to have closed in 1781.

Angell, Joseph (*b c.* 1816; *d c.* 1891). English silversmith and goldsmith who produced highly decorated tableware in London from 1849; his family remained prominent throughout the 19th century.

J. Angell: *Descriptive Particulars of a Collection of Silver, Silver Gilt, & Enamel'd Plate* (London, 1851)

Angermair, Christoph (*b* Weilheim, Bavaria, *c.* 1580; *d* Munich, 6 June 1633). German ivory-carver and sculptor. In 1611 Angermair was working in Augsburg with Philipp Hainhofer (1578–1647) on an ivory chess set (Berlin, Tiergarten, Kstgewmus.) for the *Kunstschrank* (collector's cabinet) Hainhofer was making for Duke Philip of Pomerania (*reg* 1606–18). This is one of a number of chess sets dating from Angermair's early years (e.g. St Petersburg, Hermitage; Brunswick, Herzog Anton Ulrich-Mus.) in which the rank of the figures is differentiated not only by their attributes but also by their bearing and gestures. In this period he also made portrait medallions of *Duke William V of Bavaria* (*c.* 1610; Vienna, Ksthist. Mus.) and *Prince Sigismund Bathory* (1613; Munich, Bayer. Nmus.), notable for their detailed depiction of physiognomy and dress; and reliefs of *St Sebastian* (boxwood, 160×124 mm; Frankfurt am

Giorgio Andreoli: vase and cover, tin-glazed earthenware with lustre decoration, h. 260 mm, 1500–10 (London, Victoria and Albert Museum)

Main, Liebieghaus) and the *Temptation of Christ* (ivory, 162 × 121 mm, London, BM). The latter were carved between 1610 and 1620. Angermair achieved the maximum effect of depth by the different treatment of foreground and background—the figures nearest to the viewer are sculpted almost in the round, whereas the other parts of the relief become flatter as they recede.

Angermair's most important and ambitious work is the coin cabinet made in 1618–24 for Duke Maximilian (Munich, Bayer. Nmus). Its exterior is decorated with ivory reliefs and statuettes. Their complex programme was designed to emphasize that the Duke's interest in numismatics was primarily related to the history of ancient empires. Thus, the exterior panels have, in addition to reliefs of the Colosseum, Trajan's Column and a woman personifying Collecting, representations of Nimrod, the founder of Babylon, and Romulus, the founder of Rome. Constantine, the model for the Christian monarch, is shown in the equestrian statuette (inspired by Giambologna) that surmounts the cabinet. His presence underlines the necessity of God's blessing on earthly empires. When opened, the cabinet displays the colours of Bavaria, blue and white, in lapis lazuli and ivory. The reliefs inside the doors are of music-making; their intimate tone contrasts with the exterior, and they may have held private allusions for Angermair's patron. Angermair also carved ivory decorative mounts for pieces of furniture and made ivory candelabra. Several late reliefs in ivory survive. Among them are a *Crucifixion* (Munich, Residenz), a *Holy Family* (Munich, Bayer. Nmus), and a *St Jerome* (Munich, Bayer. Nmus.). The ivory figure of *Christ at the Column* (h. 299 mm; Munich, Residenz) dates from the master's final years, as does a second *Tödlein* (Dresden, Grünes Gewölbe).

M. D. Grünwald: *Christoph Angermair: Studien zu Leben und Werk des Elfenbeinschnitzers und Bildhauers* (Munich, 1975)
K. A. Möller: *Elfenbein: Kunstwerke des Barock,* Schwerin, Staatl. Mus. cat. (Schwerin, 2000)

Angers, 'Apocalypse' tapestries. Set of Medieval French tapestries that form the largest surviving ensemble of historiated tapestries and the largest cycle of monumental images from 14th-century Europe in any medium. They were woven in six pieces (not seven, as earlier scholars maintained), each piece over 23 m long and over 4.5 m high, consisting of two rows of seven scenes prefaced by a large canopy rising the full height of the tapestry and sheltering a seated figure reading from a lectern. Originally, each scene also had a panel below it with an inscription, but so little evidence of these survives that their content cannot be ascertained. In addition, a ground strip along the bottom edge depicted a flower-strewn lawn, while at the top was a strip containing musician angels among heavenly clouds; these have survived only in part. Altogether, the set would have been over 130 m long, illustrating the Apocalypse in 84 scenes. Four of the reading figures and about sixty-nine scenes have survived. Since the tapestries have been cut into segments comprising at most two, and more usually one scene, and since some of the scenes have been lost, the reconstitution of the original sequence of scenes is problematic, particularly for the second piece. The difficulty is compounded by the fact that in two instances the scenes were woven in reverse sequence (scenes 6–5 and 55–54).

The tapestries rank among the highest accomplishments of contemporary French pictorial arts (see colour pl. II, fig. 1). The scenes display a limited but well-defined interest in pictorial space, with a shallow ground plane and consistent modelling of figures and objects in light and shade, from a generally centralized light source. The architectural structures represented, particularly the large canopies of the reading figures, display a surprisingly accomplished perspective. The designs are far more vivacious and exciting than any known Apocalypse manuscript. The virtuosity of weaving, particularly in hands and faces, is remarkable, and pictorial effects are achieved through a variety of weaving techniques, notably the gimping, which emphasizes contours by means of rows of small holes in the fabric surface.

The tapestries were bequeathed to Louis II, Duke of Anjou (*reg* 1384–1417), and his widow, Yolande, bequeathed them to their son, René I, who in turn bequeathed them to Angers Cathedral, in which they were hung on important feast days until 1767. In 1782 the cathedral canons unsuccessfully tried to sell the tapestries as a set, and it was probably shortly after that date that they were disastrously dismembered. It was only in 1848 that a concerned custodian, Canon Joubert, made an effort to gather together all the remaining pieces, which were restored and sewn back together between 1849 and 1863. In 1902 the tapestries were classed among the Monuments Historiques, and they became the property of the state; since 1954 they have been displayed in their own gallery in the castle at Angers.

R. Planchenault: *The Angers Tapestries* (Paris, 1980)
G. Henderson: 'The Manuscript Model of the Angers *Apocalypse* Tapestries', *Burl. Mag.*, cxxvii (1985), pp. 208–19

Angoulême. French city that was a centre of faience production from 1748 until 1914. The pottery, which resembles the wares of Mostiers and Rouen, includes large figures of animals, possibly intended for outdoor display.

M. Latier: *Faïences et faïenciers d'Angoulême de 1748 à 1914* (Mansle, 1971)

Angster. *See* KUTTROLF.

An hua decoration [Chin.: 'hidden']. Term applied to Chinese porcelain where the decoration can only be seen under a clear glaze or through transmitted light. Such decoration is sometimes found in Song dynasty (960–1279) Ding and Xing wares, and becomes very common in the white porcelain of the

Yongle period (1403–24) of the Ming dynasty. By the mid-16th century *an hua* decoration is regularly found in blue-and-white porcelain.

Anichini [Annichini; Nichini; Nichino]. Italian family of gem-engravers. Francesco Anichini (*b* Bagnacavallo, *fl* 1449–1526; *d* ?1545), active in Ferrara, supplied Isabella d'Este, Marchioness of Mantua, in 1492 with a turquoise *Head of a Child* (1492), gems for rings (1494) and two turquoises with figures of *Orpheus* and *Victory* (1496) after a design by the Marchioness, and a gem with a symbolic emblem (all untraced). For a physician from Ferrara, Francesco carved a glow-worm in lapis lazuli (untraced) in such a way that the natural gold veins of the stone appeared as the luminous parts of the insect's body. In 1500 Francesco moved his atelier to Venice.

Francesco had five sons: Luigi Anichini (*b* Venice, ?1500–10; *d* Ferrara, after 1559); Andrea Anichini (*fl* 1526–53); Callisto Anichini (*b* Ferrara, before 1527; *d* Venice, ?1553); Alvise Anichini and Pietro Anichini, who were also gem-engravers and worked in Ferrara and Venice. Luigi has often been confused with his father and, like him, received lavish contemporary praise from Vasari and others. In 1540 a *Ganymede* in lapis lazuli is recorded, in 1544 a carnelian with *Apollo* and a cameo portrait of *Giovanni delle Bande Nere* and in 1547 a seal with a head of *Medusa* for Pietro Aretino (all untraced). Of the other brothers, it is known that Callisto was also a jeweller and was probably active in Venice, where it is thought that he worked with his father.

Animal carpet. Type of carpet made in Persia, Turkey and Mughal India and decorated with animals; the term sometimes includes and sometimes excludes the related type known as 'hunting carpets'. The three earliest animal carpets (all of which have been dated to the 14th or 15th centuries by reference to paintings that depict similar carpets) are knotted in wool with symmetrical knots of fairly low density in a limited colour range, including various tones of red, yellow and blue. One acquired by the Metropolitan Museum of Art in New York in 1990 shows a rectangular field with four stylized quadrupeds, themselves decorated with stylized quadrupeds; the one in Berlin (Pergamonmus.) shows stylized dragons and phoenixes within octagons. The Marby Carpet (Stockholm, Stat. Hist. Mus.), found in the Swedish village of Marby in 1925, displays confronted birds separated by a Tree of Life within squares.

C. J. Lamm: 'The Marby Rug and Some Fragments of Carpets Found in Egypt', *Svensk. Orientsällskapets Åb.*, (1937), pp. 51–130

R. Ettinghausen: 'New Light on Early Animal Carpets', *Aus der Welt der islamischen Kunst: Festschrift für Ernst Kühnel*, ed. R. Ettinghausen (Berlin, 1959), pp. 93–116

L. W. Mackie: 'An Early Animal Rug at the Metropolitan Museum', *Hali*, liii (1990), pp. 154–5

Ankh [*crux ansata;* key of life]. Figure resembling a cross, with a loop or ring forming a handle instead of the upper arm. The ankh was used in ancient Egyptian decorative art as a symbol of life.

Annaberg. German pottery centre in the Erz mountains of Saxony. Annaberg pottery is loosely known as stoneware, but the term is inaccurate, because the clay did not vitrify. This obstacle was surmounted by covering the pottery with 'brownstone', a brown vitrifying engobe (slip) that opened the way for salt-glazing. Production of engobe ware began *c.* 1630 and continued till the third quarter of the 18th century. In the 1630s the tankards and jugs produced in Annaberg were decorated with scalloped patterns and cartouches. In about 1640 wares began to be painted with enamel colours and then given a second firing. The most distinctive products of the pottery are the beer steins and pear-shaped jugs introduced in the 1680s, often decorated with portrait heads.

Annealing. Tempering or toughening of glass after fusion; in this sense, the term is also used of cast iron, pottery and silver. In historic usage, annealing could also denote the burning of metallic colours into glass.

Anreiter von Zirnfeld. Austrian family of porcelain painters active also in Italy. Johann Karl Wendelin Anreiter von Zirnfeld (1702–57) moved to Vienna where he worked as a *Hausmaler* until 1737, when he moved to the newly established DOCCIA PORCELAIN FACTORY as its principal painter. His son Anton (*c.* 1725–1801) trained under his father in Doccia, and then moved in 1754 to Vienna, where he was the principal porcelain painter at the VIENNA porcelain factory until his death in 1801. Both father and son specialized in the painting of landscapes, some of which include closely observed architectural details and solitary figures.

Ansbach. Bavarian centre of ceramics production, *c.* 40 km south-east of Nuremberg. A faience factory was established by Matthias Baur and J. C. Ripp in Ansbach *c.* 1710–12. Wares included jugs and tankards at first decorated in blue and later in the *famille verte* (green, yellow, iron-red, blue and purple) palette; painters included J. H. WACKENFELD (1717–19). In 1757 a porcelain factory was established beside the faience factory at the behest of Margrave Karl Alexander (*d* 1806), who in 1763 transferred it to Schloss Bruckberg. The secret formula for porcelain was brought to Ansbach by Johann Friedrich Kändler (1734–91), a nephew of the Meissen Modellmeister JOHANN JOACHIM KÄNDLER, who had worked at the factory of Wilhelm Caspar Wegely (1714–64) in Berlin, as had the superb miniaturist and colour specialist Johann Carl Gerlach (1723–86) and the modeller Carl Gottlob Laut (*d* 1802). The shapes produced at Ansbach are therefore reminiscent of Berlin wares. Meissen was the inspiration for the relief decoration developed by Kändler, which was retained throughout the 18th century. The 'Ansbach' pattern consisted of four symmetrically arranged landscapes within Rococo cartouches on a basket-ware border (e.g. plate, 1765–70; Hamburg, Mus. Kst. & Gew.). Rococo motifs with applied acanthus leaves were used as three-dimensional decoration on handles, and small ladies' heads were used to decorate handles and spouts (e.g. teapot, *c.* 1760; Hamburg, Mus. Kst. & Gew.). On teapots or chocolate-pots the spouts end in a dog or dragon's head. Painted motifs included flowers by Johann Wolfgang Mayerhöffer (1699–1771) and Johann Jakob Schreitmüller (*fl* 1779–1807), fruit and garlands by Alexander Telorac (1749–92), animals and birds by Gottlob Büttner (*fl* 1785–93) and Albrecht Hutter (*c.* 1754–1804), scenes after Antoine Watteau (1684–1721), and genre scenes and landscapes by Johann Melchior Schöllhammer (1745–1816) and Johann Eberhard Stenglein (*fl* 1765–95). In addition to utilitarian wares, services and ornaments, one of the main production lines was figures for the Margrave's court; the inspiration for these came from the work of such artists as Johannes Esaias Nilson (1721–88), Claude Gillot (1673–1722), Jacques Callot (1592–1635) and Johann Balthasar Probst (1673–1750). The faience factory closed in 1839 and the porcelain factory in 1860.

A. Bayer: *Ansbacher Porzellan* (Brunswick, 1959)

Anse de panier [Fr.: 'basket handle']. The term is used to denote a decorative motif shaped like a basket handle, and is applied to metalwork (from the 16th century) and chairbacks (from the 18th century); in architecture the term denotes a three-centred arch.

Antefix. Ornamental tile used on the eaves and cornices of ancient buildings, to conceal the ends of the tiles; the term also used to denote the ornamental heads of animals making the spouts from the gutters.

Anthemion [honeysuckle; palmette]. Floral ornament, typically with alternating PALMETTE and lotus motifs.

Anthing, Johann Friedrich (*b c.* 1753; *d* 1805). German silhouettist and military historian. Anthing entered Russian military service, rising to the rank of colonel. While at the imperial court and travelling around Russia, he made silhouette portraits of notable persons; he visited London in 1789, and there made silhouettes of the Prince of Wales, the Duke of York and the Duchess of Devonshire. In 1791 he published a book of 100 silhouettes, the *Collection de cent Silhouettes des personnages illustres et celebres.*

C. Schüddekopf: *Johann Friedrich Anthing: Eine Skizze* (Weimar, 1913)

Antimacassar. Covering placed on the backs or arms of upholstered sofas and chairs to protect them from grease in the hair, or other soiling, or merely as an ornament. The term, which became popular in the last half of the 19th century, derives from Macassar, the proprietary name of a kind of hair-oil. In American English of the same period, an antimacassar is called a 'tidy'.

Antler. *See* HORN AND ANTLER.

Antonio di Neri. *See* BARILI, ANTONIO.

Antunes, Bartolomeu. (*b* Lisbon, 1688; *d* Lisbon, 1753). Portuguese tile painter and decorative artist. His output was enormous, and his work was distributed throughout Portugal and Brazil. He worked in partnership with his son-in-law, the painter Nicolau de Freitas (*c.* 1703–65). Under the influence of Joanine wood-carving and silver, the decorative borders of their tiles became richer and more elegant, dominated by grimacing masks and cascading palm and acanthus foliage. The tile makers adapted the convention of using arched frames, which end in garlanded volutes often accompanied by cherubs, for their high dado panels.

Two chapels in the church of Vilarde Frades, Barcelos, dated 1736 and 1742 are decorated with scenes, signed by Antunes and Freitas, from the *Life of the Virgin.* In S Francisco, Salvador, Brazil, two large panels of *St Francis* are dated 1737 and signed by Antunes. Antunes and Nicolau de Freitas collaborated on the panels in four rooms of the Mitra Palace, Lisbon, in which they incorporated decorative subjects, landscapes and *fêtes galantes*; on the staircase, which has painted balustrades, shells and figures representing the elements (*c.* 1735–45); and in the Quinta dos Arcebispos in S Antão do Tojal, Loures, where three of the rooms contain tiles of the four seasons and an allegory of the arts (*c.* 1730–40). Some of Antunes's figurative panels, painted in perspective and framed by dramatically exuberant borders, are monumental and have great decorative impact: these include those with sculptural motifs, medallions, landscapes and religious figures (*c.* 1730–40) in the nave of the Albertas church, Lisbon, and some of the panels of scenes from the *Life of St Augustine* (*c.* 1740) in the Pópulo church, Braga, where more care and imagination appear to have been spent on the decoration than on the figures. Antunes carried out ornamental compositions with lovely Baroque motifs, such as the *Symbols of the Virgin*, with floral swags and Baroque ornament, in the sanctuary of the hermitage of Porto Salvo, Oeiras, in 1734.

R. C. Smith: 'French Models for Portuguese Tiles', *Apollo*, xcvii (1973), pp. 396–407
J. Meco: 'A azulejaria do palácio da Independência, em Lisboa', *Bol. Cult. Assembl. Distr. Lisboa*, i (1981), pp. 5–76
J. Meco: 'O palácio da Mitra em Lisboa e os seus azulejos', *Lisboa-Rev. Mun.*, xii (1985), pp. 13–31; xiii (1985), pp. 25–40; xiv (1985), pp. 7–17

Antwerp [Flem. Antwerpen; Fr. Anvers]. Belgian city and port on the River Scheldt, *c.* 90 km from the sea. In the 16th and 17th centuries it was one of the leading centres of art in northern Europe.

1. Ceramics. 2. Gemstones and pearls. 3. Lace. 4. Tapestry.

1. CERAMICS. Major centre for faience production during the 16th century. About 1512 three Italian maiolica potters, Janne Maria de Capua, Jan Frans de Brescia and GUIDO ANDRIES, settled in Antwerp. In 1520 Andries bought the Den Salm workshop in Kammenstraat. From 1545, at the height of Antwerp's faience production, Henric van Grevenbroeck of the Dmoelenyser workshop and Jan Bogaerts (*fl* 1552–71) of De Maeght van Gent had workshops in the same street. Andries's five sons also directed workshops in Antwerp and abroad. Jan Floris (Juan Flores; *d* 1567) was made a master craftsman of the Guild of St Luke in 1550 and was famous for his work as a faience painter; in 1563 Philip II of Spain summoned him and bestowed on him the title Maestro de Azulejos. From 1550 to 1626–7 some 30 faience potters were admitted to the Guild of St Luke as master craftsmen. During the Wars of Religion (1562–98) many potters emigrated and spread their craft to Spain, the northern Netherlands, England and Germany. During the 17th century the Antwerp factories went into a slow but inexorable decline because of the competition from Holland. Antwerp's faience production comprised floor- and wall-tiles, *albarelli*, tablewares and plaques. Forms and decoration were influenced by Italian maiolica and by Hispano–Moresque wares. Antwerp's finest wares are those decorated with biblical subjects, strapwork and grotesques inspired particularly by engravings by such Netherlandish artists as Enea Vico (e.g. tile-picture of the *Conversion of St Paul*, 1547; Antwerp, Mus. Vleeshuis).

C. Dumortier: 'Pots de pharmacie en majolique anversoise conserves aux Musées royaux d'Art et d'Histoire', *Rev. Belge Archéol. & Hist. A.*, lxix (2000), pp. 113–32
J. Veeckman and S. Jennings: *Majolica and Glass: From Italy to Antwerp and Beyond: The Transfer of Technology in the 16th–Early 17th Century* (Antwerp, 2002)

2. GEMSTONES AND PEARLS. Antwerp has been a trading centre for gemstones and pearls since the Middle Ages. A decree of 1447, the first of its kind, ordered the prosecution of merchants trading in fake stones. In the 15th century a number of Jews, including diamond-cutters who had been expelled from Spain and Portugal, migrated to Antwerp. In 1483 diamond-cutters are recorded as working in the city, and by 1577 the guild of diamond-cutters, which at this time included cutters of all gemstones, numbered between 30 and 40 members. The extent of the gemstone-cutting industry was such that from 1584 to 1642 the ruby-cutters (who cut all coloured gemstones) formed their own guild. During the 16th century Antwerp became the main centre of jewellery production in the southern Netherlands. Hans Collaert, for example, designed pendants that departed from the Renaissance style.

Exotic shells and pearls continued to be traded through Antwerp harbour (e.g. ewer, 1544; Moscow,

Serpentine ewer by Siger van Steynemeulen, green porphyry with silver-gilt mounts, Antwerp, *c*. 1485 (London, Victoria and Albert Museum)

Kremlin); in the last decades of the 16th century nautilus cups were popular (e.g. double nautilus cup, *c*. 1550; Florence, Pitti; others in Brussels, Mus. Royaux A. & Hist.; Kassel, Staatl. Museen; London, BM), and from 1600 to 1610 there was a guild of pearl-drillers. Cameo-carving was also practised in the 16th century and the early 17th, although little is known about this trade. A large cup (gold, enamel, diamonds, emeralds, rubies and pearls, 1530–40; Vienna, Ksthist. Mus.) and a smaller cup (silver gilt, *c*. 24 cameos, 1625; Amsterdam, Rijksmus.) are thought to have been made in Antwerp. Intaglios in the style of Giovanni Bilivert were also produced, as were, probably, porphyry objects, for example a ewer (mounted *c*. 1485; London, V&A) by Siger van Steynemeulen (1443–1508).

During the 17th century the trade in diamonds expanded, and by 1618 Antwerp had 164 workshops with an average of three employees per workshop. Towards the second half of the 17th century a lower demand for coloured gemstones led to a decline in the number of ruby-cutters, and by 1642 the ruby-cutters' and the diamond-cutters' guilds were amalgamated. The diamond trade also declined after the mid-17th century, and by 1670 only about 100 workshops were still operating. Many cutters emigrated to Amsterdam or to Paris, where Cardinal Jules Mazarin (1602–61) promoted the brilliant cut, which was introduced to Antwerp only from the end of the 17th century. During the 18th century the industry lost its creative energy, although a large amount of diamonds were still cut in Antwerp: in 1788, for example, the French crown jewels (destr.) were recut there.

During the 1820s, in the depression following the Napoleonic Wars, there were only about 20 or 30 gem-cutters in Antwerp, who were largely dependent on Amsterdam for their supplies of rough stones and for providing a market for the cut stones. From 1840 mechanization, introduced to Antwerp by the merchant J.-J. Bovie, made cutting on a large scale possible and led to the growth of the diamond-cutting industry during the second half of the 19th century. During the 20th century demand decreased, although craftsmanship of the stones continues to develop, and Antwerp remains the most important centre for the trading and processing of cut diamonds.

A.-M. Adriaensens: *Diamond Museum Antwerp* (Antwerp, 1988)

I. Kockelbergh, E. Vleeschdrager and J. Walgrave: *The Brilliant Story of Antwerp Diamonds* (Antwerp, 1992)

J. Walgrave, P. Nolens-Verhamme and V. van Grotenhuis van Onstein: *Living Diamonds: Fauna and Flora in Diamond Jewellery* (Antwerp, 2002)

3. LACE. Antwerp has been a centre for lacemaking since the 17th century; much of its production was exported to Spanish America. Various kinds of lace were made in Antwerp, but the one known as Antwerp lace is a pillow lace decorated with pots or vases, and so is sometimes known as Antwerp pot lace.

M. Coppens: 'Reglementation de l'apprentissage du metier de dentelliere sous l'Ancien Régime: Quelques exemples', *Rev. Belge Archéol. & Hist. A.*, lxvii (1998), pp. 93–112

4. TAPESTRY. Until 1415 the tapestry-weavers of Antwerp were part of the guild of linen-weavers, but in July of that year they formed their own guild with their own statutes, which included regulations concerning the duration of an apprenticeship, the fee for becoming a master and salary. No work of this period has survived, but it would be wrong to suggest that only *verdures* were woven in Antwerp in the 15th century.

The tapestry-worker and painter Pieter van Uden settled in Antwerp in 1553 and brought 400 weavers with him from Brussels. His workshop contained 126 looms and employed 33 master weavers, all of whom were granted the freedom of the city. In order to aid the expansion of the trade in Antwerp the collegial act of 20 July 1559 extended this grant to all Brussels tapestry-workers who wished to settle in Antwerp. The imperial edict of 1544 was an attempt by the government to combat certain types of fraud and ensure the high quality of wall hangings. Weavers were required to work the mark of the city and a weaver's monogram into their tapestries; this regulation was not imposed in Antwerp until 1562. The influx of workers from Brussels included Michel de Bos (*fl* 1560–67) and the Brussels cartoon painter Jan Collaert, who arrived in 1563. They were followed by Joos van Herzeele (*fl* 1576–89), to whom the city granted a house near the castle to be used as a workshop for at least 40 workers.

The art of tapestry-weaving was encouraged in Antwerp not only by the municipal government but also by the new school of painting. Numerous expert cartoon painters also settled in Antwerp. The earliest of these was Pieter Coecke van Aelst (1502–50). In 1544 the Brussels cartoon painter Leonard Knoest gained the freedom of the city and enrolled himself in the Guild of St Luke. In the same year Karel de Riddere of Mechelen and Hans de Duytscher (pseud. Singher; *fl* 1544–58) from Hesse were also enrolled as cartoon painters in the guild. Other cartoon painters included Joris van Liecke (*fl* 1564), Maarten van Tiegem (*fl* 1580), Lucas Floquet (*fl* 1589), Artus Vermylen (*fl* 1589) and Otto van Veen (1556–1629). By the mid-16th century Antwerp had become the main centre of the international tapestry trade. The construction of the Pant, a tapestry hall, took place in 1550–54, and this became the main centre for the sale and display of tapestries, cartoons and sketches in Flanders.

Makers' marks added to the borders of several wall hangings enable works to be definitely attributed to Antwerp. The city mark (a stylized image of the city castle flanked on either side by a hand) is clearly derived from the blazon of the Margrave of Antwerp. Sometimes the mark is highly simplified, as in a *Hunting Tapestry* (*c*. 1600; Stuttgart, Württemberg. Landesmus.), which has only a single hand and the letter A. In other cases, the city mark of Brussels was woven in an altered form into the underside of the Antwerp tapestries—instead of the initials B-B (Brabant-Brussels), with the traditional miniature red shield in the middle, the initials B-A (Brabant-Antwerp) were woven into the borders of the work; this can be seen on two tapestries now in the château of Azay-le-Rideau, as well as on a *Grotesque Tapestry with Nebuchadnezzar and the Children in the Fiery Furnace* (*c*. 1585; Amsterdam, Rijksmus.). A weaver's monogram is sometimes woven into the border, which enables an accurate attribution. A few of the monograms have not yet been identified, such as that on the above-mentioned *Hunting Tapestry* and that on a scene from the *Life of Moses* and from the *Story of Esther* (*c*. 1560; Oxford, St John's Coll.). The borders of these tapestries are filled with flowers and fruit, as well as fantastic figures and personifications of Faith, Hope and Love.

Among the most characteristic Renaissance tapestries is a series depicting the *Deeds of Hercules*, with its typical blue ground and fine grotesque borders. The series comprises 13 (originally 14?) wall hangings and 10 window hangings depicting the *Arms of Bavaria and Austria* (1567; Munich, Bayer. Nmus.). It was woven for Albert IV, Duke of Bavaria (*reg* 1463–1508), in the workshop of Michel de Bos, whose name appears repeatedly in the borders of the *Hercules* tapestries. The mythological illustrations were derived from a fresco cycle by Frans Floris, which was published in part as engravings by Cornelis Cort (1533–78) in 1563. A monogram, IVH, appears on three of the four above-mentioned grotesque tapestries; this could be the monogram of the Brussels weaver Jan van den Hecke (*fl c*. 1575–1600), but is more likely that of the Antwerp weaver Joos van Herzeele. The same monogram appears in three of the series of eight tapestries with scenes from the *Life of Alexander the Great* (last quarter of 16th century; Vienna, Ksthist. Mus.). Another series consisting of eight tapestries on *The Six Ages of the World* (1566) woven for Archduke Ferdinand of Tyrol (*reg* 1564–95) is now in the Kunsthistorisches Museum in Vienna.

In 1576, during the war with Spain, the Pant was closed after heavy looting of the tapestries, trade materials and designs. Economic activity revived in 1578, and the building was re-opened, but the emigration of weavers to other European centres soon became a problem. By 1586 Joos van Herzeele seems to have moved to Hamburg, and in December 1594 Frans Spierincx (*c.* 1550–1630) arrived in Delft; around 1607 Maarten Steurbout (*fl* 1591–1607) travelled to Moscow, although it is not certain whether or not he planned to work there as a tapestry-weaver. Emigration continued throughout the 17th century. In April 1693 Balthazar Bosmans (*fl* 1687–1717) left for Paris; many weavers from Antwerp went to work at the Mortlake factory in England; and Jacques van der Goten (1659–1724) went to Madrid on 30 July 1720 and set up an important tapestry workshop, which continued to produce tapestries in the late 20th century.

In many of the workshops, wall hangings were produced, which were frequently sold through dealers or brokers. The latter made sure that monograms or weavers' signatures were excluded from the pieces sold, so that the buyers would not be able to trace the origin of the tapestry. The tapestry merchants also occasionally took the liberty of weaving their own names into the borders of the tapestries that they sold, to publicize their own businesses. In the wall hanging of a *Bacchanale* (*c.* 1650; Deurne, Prov. Mus. Sterckshof) the city mark of Antwerp and the subtitle *Anvers* are in the lower left-hand corner, and on the right there is a cartouche enclosing the words *Cura Simonis Bouwens*. Simon Bouwens was probably concerned only with the sale of tapestries; this is confirmed by the Latin tag in the cartouche, which is translated as 'under the supervision of Simon Bouwens'. Pieter Wouters (*fl* 1664–82), an important tapestry dealer and tapestry printer in the second half of the 17th century, signed his merchandise in this same way.

In many cases it is still difficult to determine who the weaver (or dealer) was. It often happened that an important tapestry-weaver, at the head of a busy workshop, was also an important dealer. The most significant dealers include the Vrancx, van Welden and de Bie families, as well as Jacob Tsantels (*fl* 1635–83), Hans Bos (*fl* 1626–46), Bernard Gerstelinck (*fl* 1629–53), Peter van Camp (*fl* 1679–89), Jan Frans Cornelissen (1640–78) and Joris Rombout (*fl* 1649–79). Another was Joost van Butsel (*b c.* 1609) of Enghien, who was active in Antwerp in the late 1640s. His son, Andries van Butsel, owned a series of cartoons depicting the *History of Tamburlaine and Bajazet* (1675–). After his death, these were probably passed to Maria Anna Wauters (1654–*c.* 1696), who had them made into tapestries. The wall hangings on this theme (Kremsmünster, Stiftsgal., and Vienna,

Dom- & Diözmus.) may well have come from the workshop of van Butsel. The separate pieces in the Hermitage, St Petersburg, and the Kunsthistorisches Museum, Vienna, which were probably once part of the same series, may have been woven in the workshop of Wauters. The latter works rank both technically and artistically among the most beautiful products of the Antwerp workshops of this period.

Jan van der Goten (1642–1700) must also be considered one of the most important tapestry-workers in the second half of the 17th century. From 1677 he produced different series for the Antwerp dealer Nicolaas Nauwelaerts (*fl* 1677–1709), including the *History of Rinaldo and Armida, Perseus and Andromeda, Bacchic Feasts*, the *Four Continents* and *verdures* with small figures in conversation. The series of the *Story of Jephtha* carries the signatures of van der Goten and his brother-in-law Peter Kolvenaar. Balthazar Bosmans was also the head of an important workshop, the productions of which included the *Story of St Kilian* (1687–8; destr. 1945) made for the Chapter of the Dom in Würzburg.

The tapestry workshop of the brothers Michiel Wauters (*d* 1679) and Philip Wauters (1617–79) enjoyed an international reputation. The intervention of numerous dealers meant that their wall hangings were offered for sale in most of the principal cities abroad. They produced simple series, mentioned in the documents as 'rough' work, and also the 'royal' series, which could be used by their owners for purposes of display. In many cases production was adapted to local taste. They repeatedly produced low-pile tapestries, which they called the 'English' style. They also requested the aid of well-known painters for the production of cartoons: Giovanni Francesco Romanelli (*c.* 1610–62), for example, supplied the designs for the *Story of Dido and Aeneas* (*c.* 1675–1700; examples in Piacenza, Coll. Alberoni; Milan, Castello Sforzesco; Cleveland, OH, Mus. A.), and ABRAHAM VAN DIEPENBEECK made cartoons for the nine-piece *Story of Moses* and the *Story of Semiramis*. Others were active in the same way, either directly or indirectly, as cartoon painters for the firm, including Thomas Willeboirts Bosschaert (1614–54), Peter de Witte (1586–1651), Pieter Boel (1622–74), Daniël Janssens (1636–82) and the French artist Philippe de La Hyre (1640–1718). In 1678 Michiel Wauters purchased no fewer than 29 cartoons from Jacob Jordaens (1593–1678).

At the beginning of the 18th century Cornelis de Wael (*d* 1723), Jacobus de Bock (*fl* 1693–1705) and Jan van der Goten were still active as producers and dealers in tapestries. The industry, however, was encountering increasing difficulties, including rising production costs, the closing of many foreign markets, growing competition from abroad and, above all, changes in taste and cheaper, alternative wall coverings, all of which contributed to the collapse of the industry. The death of de Wael marked the virtual end of the tapestry industry in Antwerp.

E. Duverger: 'Antwerp Tapestries of the Seventeenth Century', *Connoisseur* (April 1977), pp. 274–87

K. Nelson and J. Jordaens: *Jacob Jordaens: Design for Tapestry* (Turnhout, 1998)

I. Buchanan: 'Michiel de Bos and the Tapestries of the *Labours of Hercules* after Frans Floris (*c.* 1565): New Documentation on the Tapestry Maker and the Commission' [with appendix], *Rev. Belge Archéol. & Hist. A.*, lxiii (1994), pp. 37–61

R. Bauer: 'Die Sechs Weltzeitalter: Eine Tapisserienserie aus dem Besitz Erzherzog Ferdinands von Tirol', *Jb. Ksthist. Mus. Wien*, iv–v (2002–3), pp. 342–9

Antwerp–Louvre school. Modern name for a group of unidentified workshops that produced embossed parade armours and shields for the court of Henry II in the third quarter of the 16th century. Some of these armours were produced by Etienne Delaune (1518/19–1583) in a hypothetical French royal workshop assumed to be in Paris and long known as the Louvre School of Armourers. It was discovered that some of these armours had been decorated in the early 1560s in Antwerp by a goldsmith called Elisius Libaerts (*fl* 1557–64), who made armours for the court of Eric XIV of Sweden. It is possible that Elisius Libaerts worked for a time in Paris and that some of his armours were designed for the French court.

Aogai. *See under* LACQUER, §1(III).

Aoki Mokubei [Hyakurokusanjin; Kokukan; Kukurin; Rōbei; Ryūbei; Sahei; Seirai; Teiunrō; Yasohachi] (*b* Kyoto, 1767; *d* Kyoto, 1833). Japanese potter, painter and scholar. He was born into the Kiya family of restaurateurs and adopted the surname Aoki only after becoming a painter. Mokubei, one of his many artist's names, was created by combining the Chinese characters for 'tree' and 'rice' (a character anagram of his given name Yasohachi). His most familiar studio name (*gō*), Rōbei ('deaf [Moku]bei'), dates from the time when he had become deaf from the clangour of his ceramic kilns.

Although now best known as a painter, Mokubei was most famous in his day as a potter. In 1805 he opened a kiln at Awataguchi, one of the old pottery centres in the hills to the east of Kyoto, sponsored by Prince Shōren'in no Miya, to whom he was called into service as imperial ceramic master. From 1806 to 1808 he was invited to make ceramics at Utatsu and Kasugayama in Kanazawa, the latter at the behest of the daimyo of Kaga Province (now Ishikawa Prefect). He also gave instruction in ceramics. His association with the literati artists of the period resulted in his producing numerous implements for the *sencha* (green tea) tea ceremony, such as teapots, freely potted stoneware teabowls and cooling hearths. He also made Korean- and Japanese-style pieces popular among *matcha* (whipped tea) devotees. He was the first potter in Japan in the late Edo period (1600–1868) to make celadon ware (*aoki*).

Mokubei mastered both Chinese and Japanese ceramic traditions, including *kōchi* (type of polychrome ware), *sometsuke* (underglaze cobalt blue, or blue-and-

white porcelain), *iroe* (polychrome [overglaze] enamels), *hakuji* (porcelain), *kinrande* ('gold and enamel') and *Nanban* ('Southern barbarian') wares. Even the motifs and shapes based on clay types carry the distinctive stamp of Mokubei's technique. The relief decorations that appeared on his works such as braziers were also highly valued. The sheer range of Mokubei's work attracted many clients and influential patrons. Clients paid a thousand *ryō* (gold pieces) for his works, for which they had to wait years.

Apengeter, Hans [von Sassenlant] (*fl* 1332–42/4). German worker in bronze and brass. He was born in Halberstadt, and worked throughout northern Germany. He made and signed the brass font in the Marienkirche, Lübeck, in 1337, that in the Nikolaikirche, Kiel, in 1344, and a seven-armed bronze candelabrum in Kolberg Cathedral in 1327.

Apostle spoon. Small silver spoon, the handle of which ends with an apostle figure. Such spoons were manufactured in England and Germany from the late 15th century to the late 17th and were the usual present of sponsors at baptisms. When manufactured in sets of 13, the handle of the 'master spoon' was a figure of Jesus.

C. G. Rupert: *Apostle Spoons* (Oxford, 1929)

Two apostle spoons from a set of thirteen, St Matthew (left), Virgin Mary (right), silver, l. 195 mm, London, 1536–7 (London, British Museum)

Apparel. Middle English term, revived in mid-19th century, for ornamental embroidery on certain ecclesiastical vestments.

Applique. French term for a fitting (e.g. a sconce) designed to be attached to a wall or a piece of furniture; it is distinguished from *appliqué* by the lack of an acute accent.

Appliqué. Technique of decorating textiles with motifs cut from one material, which are attached or 'applied' to another with embroidery stitches.

Aprey Pottery. French pottery manufactory. In 1744 Jacques Lallemant, Baron d' Aprey, established a pottery on his estate at Aprey (near Dijon). In 1760 his brother Joseph joined the factory, and the brothers engaged the Swiss pottery painter Protaix Pidoux (who had been working in MENNECY PORCELAIN FACTORY); in the course of the next three years Pidoux produced many fine examples of elegant floral decoration for Aprey pottery. In 1769 Jacques withdrew from the partnership, and Joseph invited the potter François Ollivier to join the factory; Ollivier became the director of the factory in 1774, and managed it until his death in 1792. Under Ollivier's directorship the factory produced its finest pottery, which was decorated with birds, flowers and landscapes by Antoine Ergot, Antoine Mège and Jacques Jarry, and sold at the factory's shop in Paris and its outlets in Lyon and Angoulême. After the Revolution the factory continued to make pottery of a modest quality until it closed in 1885.

Apron piece. In architecture, a small piece of timber supporting the joists under the landing-place in a stair; in the transferred sense applied to furniture, it is an ornamental wooden support under the seat rail of a chair or under a cabinet.

Apt Pottery. French pottery manufactory in Le Castellet, near Apt (about 65 km north of Marseille) established in 1723 by César Moulin, who produced a distinctive marbled yellow-glazed pottery; the designs are modelled on English pottery (perhaps Wedgwood's), and look more English than French. The success of this pottery encouraged others to open in and around Apt, which is still an important pottery centre.

Aqua Fresca. Italian family of gunsmiths, active in the village of Bargi (near Bologna) from the mid-17th century, when Sebastiano Aqua Fresca was making guns, until 1809, when Pietro Antonio Aqua Fresca died. The most prominent member of the family was Matteo Aqua Fresca (1651–1738), a superb steel-chiseller and engraver who specialized in gun locks but also made steel snuff-boxes.

Aquamanile. Type of ewer, usually of metal, used for the washing of hands in a liturgical or secular context. It is often zoomorphic in form and usually has two openings, one for filling with water and the other for pouring. The earliest production of aquamanilia is associated with Mosan art of the Meuse Valley in northern France, and with Lower Saxony in north-east Germany. Most surviving examples are made of a variety of bronze that resembles gold when polished, while nearly all those made of precious metals are known only from church inventories.

Church documents refer to aquamanilia as early as the 5th century, when canon regulations stipulated that on ordination the subdeacon should receive such a vessel. Various documents from the 5th century to the beginning of the 11th sometimes use the term to denote both the ewer and its basin. Sometime after the beginning of the 11th century the term became transferred to a type of vessel, usually in the shape of an animal (e.g. lion, stag, horse), bird (cock, peacock, dove) or fantastic beast (dragon, griffin, unicorn), but sometimes also shaped as a human figure, bust or head. Some aquamanilia have clear iconographic meaning, for example those in the shape of a dove symbolize spiritual cleansing (Psalm 26:6), those in the shape of a hart signify the celebrant's spiritual devotion (Psalm 42:1), while aquamanilia in the form of demonic creatures served as exhortative warnings to the clergy to remain obedient to their vows and to live virtuous lives.

Non-liturgical aquamanilia were increasingly widespread from the 12th century until the late 16th and were used in banquets, monastic refectories, inns and private homes, for hand ablutions after meals. Mo-

Peacock-shaped aquamanile, copper alloy with engraved decoration, Spain or Sicily, 10th century–12th (Paris, Musée du Louvre)

nastic refectory aquamanilia were cast in the form of creatures such as those carved on the capitals in the cloisters from which the water was drawn. The earliest examples of secular aquamanilia were cast in the form of mounted knights. Later, some aquamanilia evolved into sculptural table decorations, while others took on humanistic subjects such as the humiliation of Aristotle by Phyllis (New York, Met.). In the 14th century they began to influence dinanderie ewers, which, although usually referred to as ewers rather than aquamanilia, often had figured spouts, lids, handles and feet. German bellarmines imitated the secular aquamanilia, as did English pottery. In the 19th-century Gothic Revival, German workshops began to reproduce aquamanilia, many of which have been confused with authentic pieces and have found their way into both private and public collections.

G. Swarzenski: 'Romanesque Aquamanile of the Guennol Collection', *Brooklyn Mus. Bull.*, x (1949), pp. 1–10
E. Meyer: 'Romanesque Aquamanile in the Form of a Dragon', *Burl. Mag.*, xcii (1950), pp. 102–5

Aquamarine. Bluish-green variety of beryl; it is related to emerald (also a beryl), but paler and capable of brilliance if facet-cut.

Arabesque. Distinctive kind of vegetal ornament that flourished in Islamic art from the 10th to the 15th century. The term 'arabesque' (and the obsolete form *rebesk*, It. *rebesco*) is a European, not an Arabic, word dating perhaps to the 15th or 16th century, when Renaissance artists used Islamic designs for book ornament and decorative bookbindings. Over the centuries the word has been applied to a wide variety of winding and twining vegetal decoration in art, but it properly applies only to Islamic art.

The vegetal elements of the arabesque were drawn from Sasanian and Late Antique art. They include, and for many centuries were limited to, acanthus and grape leaves, grape clusters and the derived, abstracted form usually known as the PALMETTE. These elements became standard, and only in the 14th century were other vegetal forms such as flowers introduced into the arabesque, particularly in Persian and Turkish art.

The fully geometrized arabesque appeared no earlier than the mid-10th century, when foliate motifs such as the vine or acanthus scroll were made to interlace with geometric frames. At roughly the same time the stem pattern of the vegetal scroll was assimilated to the geometric framework: the stems of the scroll were given the shape of what had formerly been a non-vegetal pattern, or conversely, the geometric framework came to life and leaves sprouted directly from it. The arabesque was probably invented in Baghdad, the cultural capital of the Islamic world in the 10th century, as the arabesque was disseminated quickly to all Islamic lands. The earliest datable example of this distinctive and original development may be found in carved marble panels

Carved teak door panel decorated with arabesques terminating in horses' heads, 330 × 215 mm, Egypt, 11th century (Cairo, Museum of Islamic Art)

flanking the mihrab of the Great Mosque of Córdoba.

The arabesque was displaced from the 14th century, both by freer designs employing chrysanthemum, peony and lotus motifs from Chinese art and by the new fantastic foliage of the Saz style, which became popular under the Ottomans in the 16th century. Both kinds of foliage can be made into arabesques but generally were not treated in that fashion. By the late 17th century the arabesque fell out of use as Baroque vegetal forms were imported into Islamic art and became extremely popular. In the 19th century, with the rise of Western interest in Islamic arts and crafts, traditional techniques and motifs, including the arabesque, were revived in the Islamic world. In some cases these revivals proceeded openly, and objects were made in historical styles; in other cases historical styles were revived for the purpose of producing forgeries.

The arabesque was introduced into Western art in the 15th and 16th centuries by Venetian craftsmen imitating Islamic metalwork and bookbinding, which in turn was connected with the influence of Islamic techniques and sources of materials (e.g. 'morocco' leather). Although the famous intertwining illumination of the Book of Kells and related manuscripts was in some ways a development parallel to the arabesque, such illumination remained without a strict geometric basis and employed animate rather than vegetal motifs.

E. Kühnel: *The Arabesque: Meaning and Transformation of an Ornament* (Graz, 1976)

M. Khazāie: *The Arabesque Motif (islimi) in Early Islamic Persian Art: Origin, Form and Meaning* (London, 1999)

M. Brüderlin and E. Beyeler: *Ornament and Abstraction: The Dialogue between Non-Western, Modern and Contemporary Art* (Basle and Cologne, 2001)

Arabesque style. Term used, mainly in France, to describe painted ornament in the late 18th century incorporating grotesques and foliate scrollwork enriched with grotesque figures. Contemporaries referred to the style, which was in evidence from 1775 and developed until the collapse of the *ancien régime*, as 'goût étrusque' or 'genre arabesque', or sometimes used the double appellation 'goût arabesque et étrusque'. It derives in part from surviving examples of the grotesque in Rome and is characterized by naturalistically shaped ornamental motifs, which pivot on a central axis to form a mirror image. The principle of composition of the style lies in the curvilinear ACANTHUS scroll, symmetrically aligned on an axis and rolling up to form a spiral. Spirals are also found in the scroll friezes, in scroll motifs turning in on themselves to become spirals and in flutings. This naturalistic imagery is diametrically opposed to the heavy forms, sober abstract friezes and the severe and solemn pictorial inventions of early Classicism and the *goût grec*.

The earliest example of the style in France was the decoration by Charles-Louis Clérisseau (1721–1820) for the salon of the Hôtel Grimod de la Reynière, Paris (1774). Clérisseau also used arabesque decoration for the salon of another mansion (1779–81; now London, V&A) on the Rue Boissy d'Anglas. The court did not begin to adopt the arabesque style until after 1785. In 1787 Rousseau de La Rottière decorated a games-room and a boudoir with a 'cabinet turc' at Fontainebleau for Marie-Antoinette. These rooms represent the apogée of the French 'style arabesque', and some of the motifs employed in them formed a transition to Pompeian decoration. In its late phase the 'arabesque style' corresponds closely to the DIRECTOIRE STYLE.

Arabia Porcelain Factory. Finnish ceramics manufactory established in 1873 in Helsinki (Swed. Helsingfors) as a subsidiary of the Swedish Rörstrand Factory; it became the leading Finnish ceramics factory for the domestic and Russian markets. In the early period, it followed Rörstrand's styles and decoration. Porcelain was manufactured there from 1877. Arabia's first independent designs date from 1893, when the manufacture of maiolica also began. The most important artist was the Swedish-born potter Thure Öberg (1871–1935), who was the factory's artistic director and who produced some distinguished Art Nouveau vases. In the post-war period the factory's most innovative lines were 'Kilta' (designed by KAJ FRANCK in 1948, sold from 1953 and relaunched in 1981 as 'Teema'), 'Ruska' (designed by Ulla Procopé (1921–68) in 1960), 'Paratiisi' (designed by Birger Kaipiainen (1915–88) and sold from 1970) and 'Arctica' (designed by Inkeri Leivo, and sold from 1979); 'Arctica' was the first series to be made of vitreous china. The company now trades as Arabia Finland; its products are displayed in the company's museum.

A. Kolehmainen and others: 'The Obligation of Tradition: 130 years of the Arabia Porcelain Factory', *Form Function Finland*, xvii (2003), p. 60

Arad, Ron (*b* Tel Aviv, 1951). Israeli designer, active in Britain. In 1981 Arad founded, with Caroline Thorman, One Off Ltd, a design studio, workshops and showroom in Covent Garden, London. In 1989, again with Caroline Thorman, he founded Ron Arad Associates, an architecture and design practice in Chalk Farm. In 1994 he established the Ron Arad Studio in Como (Italy). His most famous design is the Rover Chair, which recycled used Rover car seats. He has long had an interest in the use of steel, and the Bookwork bookshelves (1996), which are made from plastic by the Italian Kartell firm, were originally produced in a limited edition in steel.

D. Sudjic: *Ron Arad* (London, 1999)

Arazzeria Barberini. *See* BARBERINI TAPESTRY WORKSHOP.

Arazzeria Medicea. *See under* FLORENCE, §3.

Arbalète [Fr.: 'cross-bow'; Eng. arbalest]. Term used in descriptions of furniture to denote a similar shape.

Arcanist. Person who has knowledge of a secret process of manufacture, especially of the manufacture of porcelain. The secret formula is known as the arcanum.

Archambo, Peter (*b* Parish of St Martin's in the Field, Middx; *fl* 1710–*c*. 1750; *d* 1759). English goldsmith. He was the son of a Peter Archambo, a Huguenot refugee who worked in London as a stay-maker. In 1710 he was apprenticed to the goldsmith Jacob Margas (*c*. 1685–after 1730) and, like Margas, became a freeman of the Butchers' Company (rather than the Goldsmiths' Company) on 7 December 1720. He first registered his mark at Goldsmiths' Hall, London, in 1721, when he gave his address as the Golden Cup in Green Street. One of his apprentices was THOMAS HEMING. He produced fine quality domestic silver, and a wide range of objects, including cups, candlesticks, cream jugs and cake baskets, bearing his mark survives. His work is French in influence, and he is often credited with helping to introduce the Rococo style into England. His work also often incorporates marine motifs. His most important patron was George Booth, 2nd Earl of Warrington (1675–1758), who commissioned such pieces as a wine-urn (1728; London, Gold-smiths' Co.), chased with masks, shells and strap-work, a wine-cistern (1729; Dunham Massey, Ches, NT) and six sconces (1730). Other surviving works are a hot-water urn and a set of three caddies (Los Angeles, CA, Gilbert priv. col., on loan to Co. Mus. A.) and a plain ewer (New York, Met.).

J. Lomax: 'Parsimony by Candlelight: Lord Warrington's Silver Lighting Equipment', *Apollo*, cxxxvii (April 1993), pp. 244–7

Architrave [epistyle]. The lowest division of the entablature, consisting of the main beam that rests immediately upon the abacus on the capital of a column. The term is also used as the collective term for the various parts (lintel, jambs, and their mouldings) that surround a doorway or window and for the ornamental moulding round the exterior of an arch.

Archizoom (Associati). Italian architectural and design partnership formed in Florence in 1966 by Andrea Branzi (*b* 1939), Gilberto Corretti (*b* 1941), Paolo Deganello (*b* 1940) and Massimo Morozzi (*b* 1941). These were joined by Dario Bartolini (*b* 1943) and Lucia Bartolini (*b* 1944) in 1968. Numerous projects and essays reflected the group's search for a new, highly flexible and technology-based approach to urban design, and in the late 1960s exhibition and product design began to form a significant part of their work. The 'Superonda' and 'Safari' sofas, designed for the Poltronova company, combine modular flexibility with kitsch-inspired shiny plastic and leopard-skin finishes. The group was disbanded in 1974.

A. George: 'Archizoom Hydra', *Archit. Des.*, xliii (1972), pp. 2–16
M. Pidgeon: 'Archizoom', *Space Des.*, cxxi (1974), pp. 124–36
A. Branzi: *The Hot House: Italian New Wave Design* (London, 1984)
M. T. Stauffer: 'Utopian Reflections, Reflected Utopias: Urban Designs by Archizoom and Superstudio', *AA Files*, xlvii (Summer 2002), pp. 23–36

Ardabil carpets. Pair of carpets woven in Ardabil, a city in Azerbaijan in north-west Iran. Two of the most spectacular carpets of the Safavid period of Iranian history were purportedly made for the shrine of Shaykh Safi al-Din Ishaq (*d* 1334). Known as the Ardabil carpets, they were woven in 1539–40 as a matched pair (London, V&A, Los Angeles, CA, Co. Mus. A. and a border fragment in Textile Museum, Washington). Both were damaged, and part of the carpet of which the central portion survives in Los Angeles was used to repair the London carpet.

R. Stead: *The Ardabil Carpets* (Malibu, CA, 1974)
D. King: 'The Ardabil Puzzle Unravelled', *Hali*, lxxxviii (Sept 1996), pp. 88–92
P. Scott: 'Carpets in the Victoria and Albert Museum', *Apollo*, clviii (Nov 2003), pp. 32–4

Ardus Pottery. French pottery manufactory. In 1737 Baron François Duval established a pottery on his estate of Lamothe; it became a Manufacture Royale in 1749. In 1774 Duval's son Joseph de Varaire as-

Ardabil carpet, wool knotted pile, 10.5 × 5.3 m, Iran, 1539–40 (London, Victoria and Albert Museum)

sumed responsibility for the pottery; his death in 1789, together with the advent of the Revolution, marked the end of high quality production, and thereafter only utilitarian white wares were made. The early pottery of Ardus included tableware in the style of Berain. Enamel decoration was introduced in the 1770s, when the pottery's production included fine pharmacy jars.

E. Forestié: *Les anciennes faïenceries de Montauban* (Montauban, 1929)

Arfe [Arphe]. Spanish family of artists, of German origin. They were the most important dynasty of gold- and silversmiths active in Spain in the 16th century.

1. Enrique de Arfe [Heinrich von Harff] (*b* Julich or Harff, nr Cologne, *c*. 1475; *d* León, 1545). Goldsmith who established himself in León *c*. 1505. He introduced new types of ecclesiastical silver into Spain, for example the so-called 'seated' monstrances, transforming tower-shaped structures into free-standing objects. He executed monstrances for

León Cathedral (begun 1506; destr.), the monastery of S Benito, Sahagún (Sahagún, Ayuntamiento, Mus.), Córdoba Cathedral (1518; *in situ*) and possibly also that in Cádiz Cathedral (1528; *in situ*). Cardinal Francisco Jiménez de Cisneros, Archbishop of Toledo, commissioned from de Arfe a magnificent processional cross (1515–24; Toledo Cathedral) decorated with silver-gilt statuettes. De Arfe also executed a number of silver pieces for the diocese of León, for example the processional cross of Villamuñio, the shrine of S Froilán (1519–20; *in situ*) in León Cathedral and the processional cross and the Reliquary of the Holy Cross of the Colegiata de S Isidoro, León. He also made the four sceptres (1527) in Oviedo Cathedral. His style is idiosyncratic, as he used a complex Gothic style found in contemporary German silver. Despite producing the same types of object throughout his career, he developed variations of form and style, although the architectonic conception of all his pieces is outstanding. He gradually adopted Renaissance ornamental elements in his work without abandoning the Flemish style of northern Europe. His son Antonio de Arfe (*c.* 1510–75) was also a notable silversmith and was active in Valladolid from 1547. Antonio's work is in the Plateresque style, for example large silver tabernacles in Santiago de Compostela Cathedral (1539–45).

2. Juan de Arfe (y Villafañe) (*b* León, 1535; *d* Madrid, 1 April, 1603). Goldsmith, sculptor and writer, son of Antonio de Arfe. Juan carried out works in both Valladolid (where he spent his early years) and Ávila. His book on assaying, *Quilatador* (1572), was intended for the use of artists engaged in similar work. He moved to Seville in 1580, when he was commissioned to make the *custodia* (portable tabernacle) for Seville Cathedral (sacristy; *in situ*). Signed and dated, it was completed in 1587. It was altered in the 17th century, but its original form is known from de Arfe's description of it in *Descripción de la traça y ornato de la custodia de plata de la Sancta Iglesia de Sevilla* (1587), accompanied by engravings. *De varia commensuración* (Seville, 1585), an influential work that was widely circulated, reflected de Arfe's aesthetic ideas as well as his theoretical and practical knowledge.

In 1587 Juan de Arfe returned to Valladolid, where he made the magnificent funerary statues of the *Duque and Duquesa de Lerma* (Valladolid, Mus. N. Escul.). During this period he also made a series of tiered *custodias*, notably those for Ávila Cathedral (1564–71; *in situ*) and Valladolid Cathedral (1587–90; *in situ*; signed and dated); his *custodias* for Segovia Cathedral 1588–92) and Burgos Cathedral (commissioned 1588) are now lost, but the small one that he made for the church of Carmen in Valladolid survives (commissioned 1592; Toledo, Mus. S Cruz).

In 1596 de Arfe was summoned to court to restore damage to the bronze sepulchres in El Escorial that had been made by Leone Leoni and Pompeo Leoni, and from 1596 he was commissioned to execute other works there, such as a series of 64 coloured reliquary busts in bronze plate (1597–1605), including a bust of *St Martha* (1599–1603; Madrid, Escorial). His last works were for the Lerma family, who commissioned him in 1602 to complete and cast in bronze the funerary statues of the *Duque and Duquesa de Lerma* (Valladolid, Mus. N. Escul.), the plaster models for which had been made in 1601 by Pompeo Leoni, and to make the funerary statues in bronze of the Duque's uncle *Cardinal Bernardo de Sandoval y Rojas, Archbishop of Toledo* (may have been unfinished; untraced) and of *Don Cristóbal de Rojas, Archbishop of Seville* (Lerma, Colegio S Pedro), which was finished after the artist's death by his son-in-law, the silversmith Lesmes Fernández del Moral (*fl* 1590–1608).

De Arfe's work as a goldsmith established the high quality of this art at the end of the 16th century, and his use of architectural forms was highly influential. His ability as a sculptor is apparent in his decoration, including reliefs and free-standing figures depicted with skilled Mannerist foreshortening. The valuable theoretical works of this important figure also express his humanist views.

M. J. Sanz Serrano: *La custodia procesional: Enrique de Arfe y su escuela* (Córdoba, 2000)
M. d. C. Heredia Moreno: 'Juan de Arfe Villafane y Sebastiano Serlio', *Archv Esp. A.*, lxxvi (Oct–Dec 2003), pp. 371–88

Argand lamp [Fr. q*uinquet*]. Type of oil lamp invented in Geneva by Aimé Argand in about 1782. The lamp has a cylindrical wick (or concentric wicks) that allows a current of air to pass to both inner and outer surfaces of the flame, thus securing improved combustion and brighter light; after 1810 there was a mechanism for adjusting the flame. The term also denotes a ring-shaped gas burner constructed on the same principle. Argand lamps were made in England by MATTHEW BOULTON, in France by Quinquet and in the USA by CORNELIUS & CO..

R. C. Chinnici: 'The Manufacture of Argand Lamps in Philadelphia', *Mag. Ant.*, clxi/2 (Feb 2002), pp. 62–7
G. T. Gowitt: *19th Century Elegant Lighting: Argand, Sinumbra and Solar Lamps* (Atglen, PA, 2002)

Argentan. Alloy of nickel, copper and zinc, also known as NICKEL SILVER (from which it is sometimes distinguished by its lower proportion of copper) and German silver and Argentine.

Argentan lace. Needlepoint lace made in the French town of Argentan; the lace, like that of Alençon, has floral motifs on a hexagonal network ground.

Argyll [Argyle]. Vessel of silver or other metal or pottery, shaped like a small coffee-pot, in which to serve gravy; the gravy was kept warm by a surround filled with hot water.

Arita. Region in Japan, now part of Saga Prefecture, and the name of a type of porcelain first produced there during the early Edo period (1600–1868). The ware was originally known as *Imari yaki* ('Imari ware') because it was shipped from the port of Imari (Saga Prefect.). During the Meiji period (1868–1912) porcelain was produced throughout the country. The need to distinguish it from other porcelain wares led to the use of the name Arita (*Arita yaki*). As a result, the names Imari and Arita wares were used interchangeably. In the West, Arita porcelain was known by several names, including Imari, Amari, Old Japan and Kakiemon.

Porcelain production is said to have begun in Japan in 1616, when the Korean ceramicist Ri Sanpei [Jap. Kanagae Sanbei] (1579–1655) discovered porcelain clay near Arita in Izumiyama. The earliest wares, which were *sometsuke* ('blue-and-white'; cobalt underglaze decorated porcelain) imitations of late Ming period (1368–1644) wares, are called *Shoki Imari* ('Early-period Imari'). From *c.* 1660 Arita ware was extensively exported, and *Kakiemonde* ('Kakiemon style' *see* KAKIEMON WARE) and *somenishikide* ('polychrome style') overglaze enamels (*iroe*) wares were popular. They were exported for about 80 years. In addition to blue-and-white wares, overglaze enamels, which were called *Koimari keibutsu* ('Old Imari-patterned objects'), and which imitated the technique of *kinrande* ('gold-brocade style') wares of the Ming period, were highly appreciated in foreign markets. At the end of the Edo period, kilns principally producing overglaze enamels became more active, with the production of large plates.

I. Finch: 'The Lost Century: Japanese Arita Porcelain 1720–1820 in Britain', *A. Asia*, xxvii (July–Aug 1997), pp. 64–75
L. Smith: 'Some Aspects of Tradition in Arita since 1945', *Orient. A*, xliv/2 (Summer 1998), pp. 55–8

Armada chest. Heavy iron or iron-bound coffer made in Germany and Flanders from the 16th century to the 18th, when they were supplanted by the safe. The chests had a dummy keyhole in the front and were fastened by a lock on the underside of the lid. The word 'Armada' may allude to the Spanish Armada, but there is no historical connection with the chests of the Armada.

Armadio. Italian cupboard, used in the 15th century to denote a CASSONE with doors instead of a lid, and thereafter a large two-storied cupboard. An example from the 1730s in the oratory of S Giuseppe in Urbino is decorated with a thickly impastoed imaginary landscape by Alessio de Marchis (1684–1752).

Armoire [Fr.: 'cupboard']. Cupboard or ambry. In medieval usage the term denotes any large cupboard for storage, and in the 16th and 17th centuries it often denotes a large cupboard decorated with architectural motifs such as pilasters. In the 1740s the same term was used to denote a type of secrétaire (now known as a *secrétaire à abattant*) that resembled an armoire when closed, and so was known as a *secrétaire en armoire*. An *armoire à deux corps* is the modern term for a two-storey cupboard in which the front and sides of the upper tier are recessed (see colour pl. II, fig. 2).

Armorial porcelain. Porcelain bearing heraldic arms, often used to denote porcelain with coats of arms imported into Europe and the USA from China from the late 18th century to the early 20th.

D. S. Howard: *Chinese Armorial Porcelain* (London, 2003)

Armour. Military equipment designed to protect the wearer against weapons.

1. Europe. 2. Japan.

1. EUROPE. The most important type of metallic armour in early medieval Europe was mail, worn over

Arita ware dishes, porcelain decorated in overglaze enamels in Kakiemon style, diam. 143 mm, late 17th century–early 18th (Newark, NJ, Newark Museum)

a padded or quilted garment. Garments of mail were constructed from thousands of interlocking rings or links. Although expensive and time-consuming to produce, mail provided an effective, completely flexible defence, which weighed between about 10 and 16 kg.

The mail shirt (hauberk) in use in 11th-century Europe usually had elbow-length sleeves, an opening at the front of the neck and knee-length skirts split at the front and rear to permit the wearer to move about on foot or sit astride a horse. The shirt was extended upwards in the form of a mail hood (coif), which was later made as a separate item. Over this coif was worn a conical iron helm made either of one piece of metal or of four triangular plates either riveted directly together or to narrow iron bands at the front, rear and either side. It was fitted with a defence for the nose (nasal). This type of helmet, now described as a *Spangenhelm*, was derived directly from those used in the late Roman period. The legs were usually unprotected, other than by fabric defences, though occasionally mail leggings (chausses) were worn. The man-at-arms was protected additionally by a long, kite-shaped, wooden shield, supported by straps (enarmes) for the left arm and suspended round the neck by a longer strap (guige).

In the mid-12th century, probably under the influence of the dress of the Islamic troops encountered on the Crusades, a long, sleeveless, fabric coat (surcoat or coat-armour) began to be worn over ar-

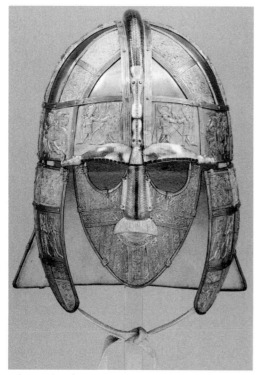

Helmet (replica) from the ship-burial at Sutton Hoo, early 7th century AD (London, British Museum)

mour. A round-topped version of the helm, without a nasal, also became popular, and from about 1180 a flat-topped helm appeared, together with a defence for the face pierced with slits for vision (sights) and ventilation holes (breaths). These face defences were augmented in the early 13th century by defences for the rear of the neck, so that by about 1240 the 'great helm', a cylindrical defence protecting the whole head, had become the standard type of head defence for the knightly classes. The mail coif, supplemented by a padded arming cap worn over or under it, continued to be worn with the great helm. From about 1200 the brimmed kettle-hat became one of the characteristic head defences for the infantry, though it was also used extensively by the knightly classes. The other important development in helmet types was the evolution of the basinet, a simple, hemispherical headpiece worn either in conjunction with or as the upper part of the mail coif. The basinet was also used by infantry, on its own, and by men-at-arms, under their helms.

The earliest reference to an iron-plate defence for the body appears *c.* 1225, and by the end of the 13th century 'pairs of plates' or 'coats of plate' seem to have become common; these were fabric garments, inside which iron plates were riveted, worn over mail but under surcoats. Such defences survive in quantity only in the grave finds from the site of the Battle of Wisby (1356) in Sweden (Stockholm, Nmus.). The widespread introduction in the period *c.* 1320–50 of complete defences of iron plate worn over mail was rapid. Limb defences of iron plate became popular; initially these were made in individual elements and tied by points and straps to the body. The arm defences (vambraces) were made in upper and lower sections (cannons), with an additional elbow defence (couter), and leg defences were of similar arrangement, the thigh defence (cuisse) being joined to the knee defence (poleyn), which was strapped over the top of the defence for the lower leg (greave). Gauntlets and sabatons of plate were produced for the hands and feet respectively.

Although the great helm continued to be used in the tournament, from about 1370 it ceased to be important on the battlefield, perhaps because of the increasing tactical use of men-at-arms in a dismounted role and the need for enhanced vision. It was replaced by the basinet, which had been worn under it; this headpiece was fitted with a visor with sights and breaths and attached to the skull by pivots at either temple or at the centre of the brow (the *Klappvisier* type). By the end of the 14th century the 'pig-faced' basinet was the most widely used helmet of the knightly classes throughout Europe.

About 1410 it became fashionable for the various coverings of armour to be discarded, thus revealing the complete 'white' armour of plate. The coat of plate was replaced by a back and breastplate, each composed of an upper and lower plate, attached together at the centre by a strap and buckle. When the solid breastplate appeared, it was fitted with a bracket on the right of the chest on which to rest the lance, so that when the lance struck something the impact did not shoot it backwards. The basinet was replaced in popularity by the great basinet, in which the mail aventail of the former was replaced by a solid defence of plate.

Before the 15th century the forms of armour had been remarkably homogeneous throughout Europe, but at this time differences appeared between armour made in Italy (predominantly Milan) and Germany. The advent of complete armour of plate made the use of the shield unnecessary on the battlefield, though it continued to be used in the joust. Instead, Italian arm defences were reinforced on the left arm, making the armour asymmetrical. Otherwise defences were of smooth, rounded forms. Large defences, known as pauldrons, were worn at the shoulders, overlapping the cuirass at the front and rear; the left pauldron was large and fitted with a reinforce, while the right pauldron was smaller and cut out at the armpit to accommodate the lance. Two new, characteristically Italian helmets were introduced: one, described by modern scholars as an armet, fitted with large, hinged cheekpieces fastening at the front and with a pivoted visor; and the open-faced barbuta, which closely resembles the ancient Greek Corinthian helmet. Italian armour of this period is quite well represented by surviving examples, primarily in the Trapp family armoury at Schloss Churburg (Castello Coira) in the Italian Tyrol, which contains by far the greatest quantity of early medieval European armour in the world, but also from a number of archaeological finds.

Unlike Italian armour, German armour in the first half of the 15th century remained symmetrical in form. The breastplate was fitted with a deep fauld (skirt) extending almost to the knees. Very few examples of German armour of this period survive, so knowledge of it comes mainly from artistic representations. In northern Europe a new open-faced helmet, the sallet, also appeared and became by far the most commonly used headpiece in this region.

By the mid-15th century plate armour was used in one form or another by the great majority of troops on the battlefield. It was, in its finest form, an extremely expensive commodity, the manufacture of which was at the forefront of technological advance and on which the finest artists and craftsmen were engaged. By the mid-17th century, however, technical developments in fire-arms had led to a decline in the use of armour, and complete plate armour at least had disappeared from the battlefield.

In the second half of the 15th century German armour was made in the Gothic style, with all the elements embossed with fluting that imitated the pleating of fashionable garments, and with an overall tendency to slender, elongated forms. On the finest examples internal edges were cusped and fretted, and external edges were often decorated with applied brass borders, similarly cusped. The most important examples of this type are the armours (c. 1480; Vienna, Ksthist. Mus.) of Archduke Maximilian of Austria (later Holy Roman Emperor Maximilian I) and

Archduke Sigismund, Count of Tyrol (1427–96), both made by Lorenz Helmschmied (d 1517) of Augsburg. As early as 1485 such armourers at Innsbruck as Kaspar Rieder (fl 1482–99), Hans Prunner (fl 1482–99) and various members of the Treytz family were producing armour that, though following German methods of construction, incorporated Italian forms and was probably the precursor of the synthesis of the German and Italian styles in the early 16th century. Milan remained the most important centre of armour production in Italy, and the dominant armourers there were members of the Missaglia family, identification of whom remains difficult despite a proliferation of makers' marks. The style of Italian armour remained constant throughout the second half of the 15th century.

Maximilian I was probably the greatest patron of armourers in the late 15th century and the early 16th, and his influence on the stylistic development of armour was profound, particularly on that of tournament armour. With the codification of the rules for the types of joust, foot combat and tourney within the tournament, different types of armour were needed for the various events. Jousts were divided into jousts of war (Rennen), in which sharp lances were used and for which armours of great weight, fitted with sallets and closely fitting shoulder-shields of wood and leather, were made, and jousts of peace (Gestechen), in which rebated (coronel-tipped) lances were employed and for which armours with frogmouthed helms were produced. Within these basic divisions there were numerous different forms of joust, for each of which a particular form of armour was made, and the same applied to the foot combat and tourney.

As well as patronizing armourers at Augsburg, those such as Matthias Deutsch (fl 1479–97) at Landshut and others at Nuremberg, Maximilian set up in 1504 an imperial workshop at Innsbruck. In the early 16th century the so-called 'Maximilian' style of armour, consisting of overall fluted decoration, usually found on every element of an armour except the greaves, started to be produced in the German centres. This style dominated central European production from about 1505 to 1530 and was also evident in Italian armour. A small number of armours exhibit a transitional style, with rounded breastplates and symmetrical limb defences, but with no fluting.

An important development during this period was the use of etching for the decoration of armour. In this method the plates were firstly either covered in a resist and the required design scratched through the coating, or the basic design was painted in reverse in wax and the details filled in by scraping; the plates were then placed in weak acid until a satisfactory etching of the uncovered surface had taken place. The first surviving example of etching on armour is the decoration of the horse armour (1477; Vienna, Ksthist. Mus.) of the Emperor Frederick III, though the technique was in use earlier for swords. By about 1510 the technique had become the most common method for decorating armour. Italian etchers tended

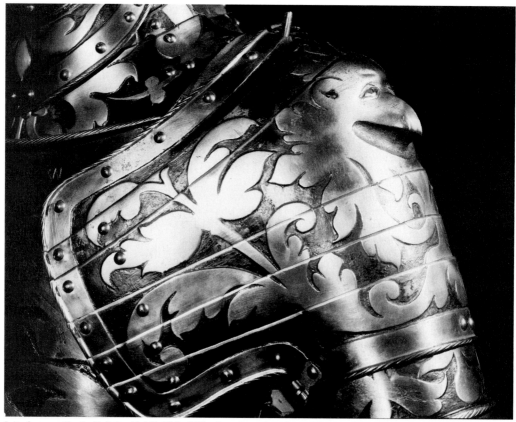

Suit of armour (detail of left shoulder) by Michael Witz the younger, iron decorated with embossed scrollwork and niello, Innsbruck, *c.* 1550 (Graz, Landeszeughas)

to use either a plain, hatched or cross-hatched background, while German artists tended to use a stippled ground. Etched decoration is usually confined to the borders of plates or to bands running vertically or diagonally; it is also usually combined with fire-gilding of either the back or the foreground, and sometimes with niello or occasionally enamelling.

As early as 1510 extra pieces began to be provided for an armour in order to render it suitable for the tourney, and from about 1530 this practice was extended, so that an armour could be used for the joust and foot combat, as well as for the field and tourney, thus obviating the need for owning a number of these exceedingly expensive different forms of armour. These extended armours are now known as garnitures, a term devised by modern German scholars. Many of the important surviving 16th-century armours were originally made as garnitures. A derivation of the coat of plates was the brigandine, produced by a similar technique, by riveting columns of small, overlapping plates inside a fabric doublet. Manufacture of these defences continued until the mid-16th century, mainly in Italy. Brigandines were primarily worn by infantry, but also, together with complete defences of plate for the rest of the body, by men-at-arms. Another defence, produced mainly in England and Scotland, was the jack of plate, consisting of small, square plates sewn with twine inside

a quilted doublet (jack). These were worn almost exclusively by infantry, including longbowmen, and were most popular during the mid- to late 16th century.

After 1450 the use of plate armour for the infantry became more common, and from the late 15th century a number of light, half armours with long, laminated tassets and no lance rest survive. German examples of the first half of the century, made mostly in north Germany and described in England as 'Almain rivets', had simple arm defences, protecting only the outside of the arm and back of the hand. These infantry armours were worn with open-faced helmets: during the 15th century and the early 16th sallets, and from the mid-16th century burgonets or morions. The burgonet is an open-faced helmet with a peak, neckguard (sometimes articulated) and hinged cheekpieces. It was often fitted with a buffe: a face and throat defence composed of articulated lames. The morion, the descendant of the kettle-hat, was an open-faced helmet with a broad brim, usually dipping down at the sides, and fitted with cheekpieces on internal leathers. By the mid-16th century half armours with open-faced helmets had become the normal equipment for the heavy infantry pikeman or halbardier. In England the great majority of these half armours (corslets) were imported from Flanders or Germany, although many were produced in Italy; the latter were often decorated with so-called 'Pisan' etching of very poor quality. The development of the form of 16th-century armours is particularly evident in that of the breastplate, the shape of which followed that of the civilian doublet: it remained globose until *c.* 1535, then took on a deep, bellied form from *c.* 1540 to *c.* 1560, then a peascod shape that was at its most extreme *c.* 1585, and then attenuating into the vestigial peascod form of the 17th century.

In Italy the Missaglia family was superseded in importance in the mid- and late 16th century by the Negroli family, also of Milan. They specialized in embossed decoration and damascening. German centres continued to produce fine armour in the 16th century. At Innsbruck Konrad Seusenhofer (*d* 1517) was followed by his brother Hans Seusenhofer (*d* 1555), the latter's son Hans Seusenhofer (*d* 1580) and Jakob Topf (*d* 1597). At Augsburg Lorenz Helmschmied was followed by his son Koloman Helmschmied (1471–1532) and Koloman's son Desiderius Helmschmied (1513–*c.* 1578). Other important armourers in Augsburg were Matthias Frauenpreiss (*d* 1549) and Anton Peffenhauser (1525–1603). In Nuremberg the most important master was Kunz Lochner the younger (*c.* 1510–67), though much of the production in that city was restricted to black and white munition armours. At Landshut a large amount of armour of the highest quality was made by Wolfgang Grosschedel (before 1515–63), who had also worked in the royal workshop at Greenwich, and Franz Grosschedel (*d* 1580). In Flanders, armour of high quality with embossed decoration by Elisius Libaerts (*fl* 1557–64) was made in Antwerp *c.* 1560 for royal patrons, and a small group of decorated pieces was produced in the 1580s by a member of the Collaert family, probably Hans Collaert (1566–1628), in the same city.

In the mid-16th century technical advances in firearms ignition systems brought about major changes in the tactics of warfare, and these had a significant impact on the development of armour. The availability of wheel-lock pistols led to the introduction of a new type of cavalry, known in Germany as *Reiters*, who were equipped with three-quarter armour, similar to that of the infantry, and open-faced burgonets. This type of cavalry largely replaced the completely armoured lancers in battle, though the need for some shock cavalry led to the retention of some lancers in three-quarter armour, known in England as demi-lances. The increasing importance of firearms and a type of warfare in which greater mobility was necessary led to the heavy infantry discarding, quite literally, their arm defences.

By the early 17th century the pikeman's armour comprised only headpiece, gorget, backplate and breastplate. The breastplate had tassets, each made in one piece and embossed to simulate the articulated lames of which they would have been made a generation earlier. About 1620 the fastening of shoulder-straps was improved, straps and buckles being replaced by straps with terminal plates pierced with

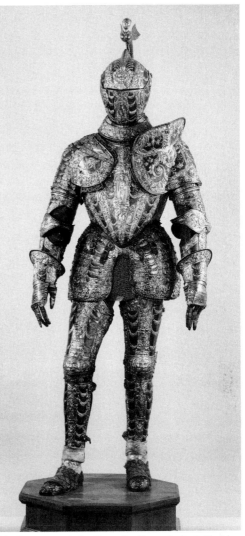

Suit of armour made for Alessandro Farnese by Lucio Piccinino, damascened iron, 1578 (Vienna, Kunsthistorisches Museum)

holes, which fitted over pierced studs with swivel hooks. From about 1630 the headpieces used by infantry were known in England as potts, though they were merely versions of the comb morions that survived in northern Europe.

The heavy cavalry or cuirassiers were similar to the demilances of the late 16th century but were armed with pairs of pistols. These troops were the most heavily armoured of this period, having three-quarter armour usually fitted with a close helmet. Far more numerous were the light cavalry harquebusiers, armed with sword and carbine, and protected with an open-faced pott, and a cuirass or buff coat or both. English harquebusiers' potts had characteristic triple-bar face-guards, while their continental counterparts, known as *Zischägge* after the Turkish *çiçak* ('chichak') from which they had evolved, had single nasal defences.

While armour of high quality continued to be produced at Greenwich until 1635 and at Innsbruck, the finest armours in western Europe were produced in France, where enamelled decoration was sometimes employed, and in the Netherlands under the patronage of Maurice, Prince of Orange. Dutch armours, only recently identified, are characterized by punched and incised decoration combined with gilding, sometimes with sheets of gold leaf. Complete armours were still made for the tournament, which survived in a vestigial form beyond 1650 in Germany and until the end of the 17th century in Scandinavia, but which lost popularity in France in the mid-16th century and in England in the early 17th. Most armours, however, were intended primarily for ceremonial purposes.

In western Europe infantry armour had become redundant by 1650, although light cavalry armour for the harquebusier, comprising a cuirass (breastplate and backplate), pott and sometimes a long elbow gauntlet, continued to be made until the end of the 17th century. The finest example of this type is probably the armour (London, Tower) of James II, King of England (*reg* 1685–8), made by Richard Holden of London (*fl* 1658–1709). In general, however, the buff coat became the only common form of body armour, and the pott was replaced by the secret, a skull defence worn under a hat. After the 17th century body armour continued to be worn by a small number of continental cuirassiers and forms part of ceremonial uniforms even in the 21st century; it was reintroduced in the uniform of the British Household Cavalry for the coronation of William IV in 1830. Although helmets were worn by many units of both infantry and cavalry during the 19th century, these were largely fashionable pieces of headgear and lacked any serious defensive properties.

With the changes in the character of warfare in the late 19th century a number of different types of thoracic defences, for example the Dayfield body shield, were used experimentally. During World War I the prevalence of shrapnel injuries led to the reintroduction on a large scale of protective helmets, and some quite heavy body armour was developed by the German forces. By World War II the need for body defence for key, immobile personnel, particularly aircrew, led to the development of the flak jacket, which was consciously based on the 16th-century jack of plate. In the second half of the 20th century the invention and application of polyaramid fibres (kevlar) and light ceramic trauma pads considerably expanded the effectiveness of defences for the body and led to their more extensive use on the battlefield than at any time since the 17th century. Kevlar remains the principal material for body armour in the early 21st century.

G. F. Laking: *A Record of European Armour and Arms through Seven Centuries*, 5 vols (London, 1920–22)

R. E. Oakeshott: *European Weapons and Armour: From the Renaissance to the Industrial Revolution* (Rochester, NY, 2000)

E. Wagner: *Medieval Costume, Armour and Weapons* (New York and Newton Abbot, 2000)

D. Nicolle: *A Companion to Medieval Arms and Armour* (Woodbridge and Rochester, NY, 2002)

A. Williams: *The Knight and the Blast Furnace: A History of the Metallurgy of Armour in the Middle Ages & the Early Modern Period* (Leiden and Boston, 2003)

2. JAPAN. The warriors of Japan have been protected by armour since at least the 5th century, when they wore heavy, flexible cuirasses made of small plates of iron tied together and extending over the hips or shorter, inflexible torso coverings constructed of large, riveted iron plates. There were also matching helmets with flat, crescent-shaped visors and cup-shaped ornaments or prominent front crowns and short visors. In the 8th century the new steel weapons and more powerful bows required a new type of armour, the Great Harness, derived from the cuirass. The Great Harness cuirass was a large box with front, back and left panels of leather, with the right side protected by a separate rib protector to increase freedom of movement. The panels bear stencilled images of esoteric Buddhist deities, patrons of warriors. Four panels, each composed of tiers of leather plates tightly bound with bright silk lacing or leather thongs, formed the skirt. A small upper chest plate on the right and another on the left provided mobility while protecting. Over-sized shoulder-guards of tightly laced leather were tied on to the back of the cuirass with cords formed into a firefly-shaped bow. Matched helmets had crowns of multiple overlapping plates secured with large exposed rivets and steeply pitched visors. Matching neck guards extended on either side of the face, forming blowbacks. These helmets had large, two-pronged ornaments called hoe shapes (*kuwagata*), which actually represented antlers. Warriors wore these unlined helmets over a soft cap tied on with a white headband. Fabric sleeves, later highly decorated with chainmail and metalwork, brocade undershirts and skirts, hammered and hinged iron greaves with raised knee caps and bear-fur or straw footwear worn over split-toed socks of leather completed the ensemble. Lower ranks wore a simple, one-piece suit with tassels or a breastplate without tassels.

In the late 12th century the victory of the Minamoto clan over the Mongol invaders transformed armour from battle gear into ceremonial objects. Examples of armour of this time include the elaborate 'red suit', the Great Harness and helmet in the Kushibiki Hachimangū Shrine (Aomori Prefect.) and other National Treasures in the Hachimangū (Kamakura, Kanagawa Prefect.) and Kasuga Taisha (Nara). In the 14th century arms and armour reverted from ceremonial objects to implements of war, and so were simplified. Mounted archers now wore *dōmaru*-type armour, but kept their Great Harness shoulder-guards. Helmets were made of a maximum of 32 ridged plates without exposed rivets, the ridges encased in gilt copper and the crown decorated with long, flat, gilt arrows. The size of frontal horns, their brackets and the crown opening were reduced. A new horsehoof-shaped visor accommodated a rudimentary iron cheek and forehead protector.

Eventually, halberd-wielding foot-soldiers dominated the battlefield. Armour was made with half the previous number of plates by using a new double-plate, and it fitted better at the waist. More complex lacing composed of eight strands appeared. Examples of such armour can be found in the Ichinomiya Oyama Shrine (Ehime Prefect.). The tassets of the Great Harness began to be detached and suspended by cords from the lower edge of the cuirass. The incessant warfare of the 15th and 16th centuries led daimyo to increase the size of their armies, necessitating more equipment, which in turn required faster production. Furthermore, the introduction of European technology after the arrival of the Portuguese in 1542 provoked dramatic changes in Japanese military hardware. Helmets changed to a new pumpkin shape made of 12 to 32 plates, with fewer crown ornaments and smaller blowbacks. Only the neck guard remained large and round. The chest plate on the cuirass changed in shape to the form of a ginkgo leaf. Leather decorated with floral prints in browns and reds stencilled on a pale ground replaced metalwork and lacquering on the visor, blowbacks and upper plate of the shoulder-guards. A thin, indigo-dyed deer hide stencilled with white iris designs also appeared. A lower jaw cover with movable nose and a separate tiered and laced throat guard replaced the earlier forehead and cheek cover.

The second stage in the development of arms in this period began with the arrival of the Portuguese and the introduction of the matchlock musket. Armour had to be strong enough to ward off musket balls yet remain light enough for long-distance travel. Daimyo began to adopt the highly individualized *kawari kabuto* ('spectacular helmet') with its fantastic shapes. Although spectacular in appearance, the helmet itself consisted of a simple, round, close-fitting bowl with an integral curved visor. This helmet could be worn alone or as the basis for the more elaborate designs executed in leather, iron, fur or lacquered papier mâché.

One traditional form of helmet also survived but made with an average of 62 plates. This helmet had a horsehoof-shaped visor, smaller blowbacks and, in place of the horns, various ornaments in forms taken from nature and legend. The neck guard shrank in closer to the head as the oversized shoulder-guards were replaced by smaller versions or omitted. The most popular type of neck guard was one that sloped off the shoulders.

Tōsei gusoku ('modern armour') developed from a combination of European and Japanese components and consisted of a helmet, face mask, a two- to five-plate cuirass that opened on the left side, sleeves and a new apron-like thigh guard of chainmail and/or small plates and greaves. *Tōsei gusoku* was mostly of

Suit of armour with tassets (*dōmaru*) (detail), iron, silk and leather, *c.* 1750 (L. J. Anderson Collection)

metal or leather with very little lacing (this, when present, was usually in pairs). Many cuirasses incorporated an interior cushion attached to a reinforced collar and epaulettes to reduce the discomfort caused by wearing a small flag on a pole thrust into a bracketing system attached to the back. Some early *tōsei gusoku*, for example that of Tokugawa Ieyasu (1543–1616), used pigeon-breasted cuirasses with Japanese additions (Nikkō, Tōshōgū Col.).

In the late 16th century Daimyo began to commission European-style arms and armour from native craftsmen and to use European motifs in their family crests (*mon*), horse trappings and armour. The Japanese made their own versions of the European cuirass (*wasei nanbandō*) and by turning around the peach-shaped helmet (*momo kabuto*) made it resemble the Iberian morion. Daimyo also began to wear surcoats (*jinbaori*) based on European clothing.

In the 17th century the ceremonial function of arms and armour revived. Although the country was at peace, the ruling military élite required arms and armour as outward symbols of rank (*omote dōgu*) and patronized nine major schools of armourers (Myōchin, Saotome, Haruta, Iwai, Yukinoshita, Bamen, Nio, Ichiguchi and Nakasone), in addition to many independent artisans. Some of these hereditary lines of armourers had been patronized earlier by the Ashikaga shoguns. There were 11 configurations of *tōsei gusoku* and several forms of the Great Harness. Some armourers continued to make spectacular helmets, but others made older forms, now sometimes worn with a full face mask. Low-ranking warriors wore foot-soldiers' helmets (*jingasa*) of iron or lacquered papier mâché. In the 1870s the government abolished the samurai class. Traditional arms and armour gave way to European uniforms.

H. Robinson: *Japanese Arms and Armour* (New York, 1969)
Nippontō: Art Swords of Japan, the Walter A. Compton Collection (exh. cat., ed. W. Compton and others; New York, Japan House Gal., 1976)
K. Kaneda-Chapplear: *Japanese Armour Makers for the Samurai* (Tokyo, 1987)
W. M. Hawley: *Japanese Armour Terms* (Hollywood, 1998)
An Introduction to Japanese Armour, Royal Armouries (Leeds, 2002)

Arms (European edged weapons). All swords and daggers consist basically of a blade with a handle (grip), which may be an entirely separate feature attached to the blade but which is usually either formed as an extension of its upper end or, more commonly, built round such an extension. In addition, a guard for the hand may be formed or fitted at the point where the grip and top of the blade proper meet; the pommel is a shaped counterweight for the blade at the top of the handle. The whole assembly of guard, grip and pommel is now called the hilt. Until the end of the 15th century the guard was never more—and, in earlier periods, usually much less—than a simple cross-bar, either straight or arched, while the most popular blade form was straight and double-edged, though single-edged and curved swords were also used, the latter especially in Eastern Europe.

The simple cruciform hilted sword remained in general use until the end of the Middle Ages, and its typological development during this period consisted merely of variations on this shape. Pommels and grips of hardstone or crystal are sometimes found, but decoration was mainly applied, and most of the techniques of the goldsmith—casting, chasing and enamelling—were used for this purpose. Surviving works from among the many rich examples mentioned in documents are rare but include an 11th-century sword, the two imperial coronation swords (early 13th century; Vienna, Schatzkam.) and the swords of Sancho IV, King of Castile and León (*c.* 1284; Toledo Cathedral), Henry, Earl of Derby, later Henry IV, King of England (*c.* 1390–99; Dublin, City Hall; used since 1403 as the civic sword of Dublin), the Holy Roman Emperor Frederick III (1440–52; Vienna, Ksthist. Mus.) and Charles the Bold, 4th Duke of Burgundy (*c.* 1470; Vienna, Schatzkam.), of which the last has a hilt and scabbard of narwhal's horn mounted in enamelled gold. The sword of Sancho IV has an inscription on the blade that appears to be the earliest-known example of the use of etching, while the silver-gilt decoration on the sword of Henry IV is unique in England for its period in being attributable to a known goldsmith, Herman van Cleve. A magnificent example is the sword of Duke Christopher of Bavaria (*d* 1493), of which the hilt and the scabbard-mounts are of silver-gilt, cast and chased with running Gothic foliage and with small figures in niches in the grip. Of equal magnificence are the highly distinctive, and now extremely rare, Hispano-Moresque swords, known as *espadas jinetas*, of which the best-known example (Madrid, Mus. Ejército) is that of Abu Abdallah Muhammad XI ('Boabdil'; *reg* 1482–3), the last Nasrid king of Granada, on which the pommel- and scabbard-mounts are of silver-gilt with partly enamelled filigree ornament. Originally from the same source but also widely used in Christian Spain and, to a lesser extent, elsewhere, was the so-called 'ear-dagger', of which the distinguishing feature is a pommel formed of two ear-like lobes set at an angle to each other. An example (Madrid, Real Armería) formerly owned by Boabdil has a scabbard with mounts decorated in a similar manner to that of his sword.

The cruciform sword survived in regular use until the 17th century, and, for ceremonial purposes, until modern times. In the mid-15th century in Italy the first swords showing the influence of the Renaissance in their design were produced. An example is the hilt of the sword (Madrid, Real Armería) given to John II, King of Castile and León (*reg* 1406–54), by Pope Eugenius IV in 1446–7, the earliest surviving example of the papal swords that were presented annually to Christian rulers. By the beginning of the 16th century these swords had succumbed completely to Renaissance styles and were being fitted with silver-gilt hilts that were splendid, but quite impractical, pieces of goldsmiths' work, for example the hilt by the papal goldsmith Domenico da Sutri on the sword (Edinburgh Castle) presented in 1507 to

James IV, King of Scotland (*reg* 1488–1513), by Pope Alexander VI and subsequently used as the Scottish Sword of State. By this date some Italian sculptors were working with the decoration of swords: a number of hilts survive with pommels involving or set with gilt-bronze plaquettes, while the gilt-bronze cruciform hilt of a sword (Turin, Arm. Reale) bearing a spurious Donatello signature is attributed to Andrea Riccio.

During the second half of the 15th century, again in Italy, blades decorated with fire-gilt etching appeared and became common by *c.* 1500. On the most elaborate specimens the etching consisted of Classical motifs and scenes, executed in fine lines, of the same general type as those found on other contemporary Italian works of art and often derived from the same graphic sources. It is probable that a number of artists were involved in decorating blades in this way. The style is, however, particularly associated with the artist whose signature, OPVS HERC(VLIS), appears in the decoration on the blade of a sword (Rome, Fond. Camillo Caetani) made for Cesare Borgia between 1493 and 1498 and also on a finely tooled leather sword sheath (Paris, Mus. Armée). The 19th-century identification of this Hercules with a goldsmith of Ferrara named Ercole dei Fedeli is no longer accepted, and he remains anonymous.

Another decorative technique used on blades (and armour) and introduced at the same period, probably in Germany, was *Goldschmelz*, whereby designs with broad gold surfaces were set against a blued background. The bluing was a natural—though controlled—result of the heating of the steel blade; the gold surface was produced by filling the shallowly etched designs with fire gilding. The technique is particularly associated with Hans Summersperger of Hall, Tyrol, who was supplying swords (Vienna, Schatzkam. and Ksthist. Mus.) to the Holy Roman Emperor Maximilian I in the 1490s. The major development during this period was the introduction of the rapier, the civilian sword. During most of the Middle Ages a dagger was commonly worn with civilian dress, but a sword was not, except when travelling or on ceremonial occasions. From *c.* 1500, however, it was increasingly the practice, for some reason that has yet to be explained, for men to wear a sword as part of their everyday dress. By the 1520s this had become normal all over Europe, and, until the second half of the 18th century, the wearing of a sword came to be regarded as a badge of gentility. There is some evidence to suggest that the fashion for wearing a sword regularly with civilian dress had started in the Iberian Peninsula, probably as early as the 1430s, and it is reasonable to assume that the Spanish term *espada ropera* ('robe sword'), first recorded in 1468, refers to a sword used for this purpose. The term rapier, first recorded in a Scottish document of 1505, almost certainly derives from this, via the late 15th-century French *épée rapière*. The rapier was, therefore, essentially a civilian sword, though for reasons mentioned below, it has come to be regarded as specifically a sword designed for fenc-

ing. The general adoption of the rapier produced three important results. Firstly, it and the sword designed for use in warfare or the tournament began to follow separate, though mutually influential, lines of development. Secondly, the fact that gentlemen carried swords regularly meant that they might have to use them at short notice and also encouraged the practice of duelling; this stimulated the development of systems of fencing, which, in turn, affected the design of the rapier. Thirdly, for the same reason, the rapier became a dress accessory as well as a weapon, and in consequence many gentlemen demanded that it should be decorative as well as functional.

So long as the sword was chiefly used in battle in conjunction with armour, the simple cross-guard was adequate. In the late 14th century, however, as a result of the practice of hooking the forefinger over one arm (quillon) of the cross, a small semicircular guard was sometimes added at the base of one side of the blade. During the second half of the 15th century two such guards were introduced, to which, from the end of the 15th century, a curved knuckle-bar was sometimes added. The developments in fencing already mentioned, with the need to provide better protection for the unarmoured hand, led from about 1520 to the addition of further bars, both above and below the cross, so producing by about 1550 the complex guard, involving diagonal curved bars, to which the modern term 'swept hilt' is applied.

The early rapier was a rather cumbersome weapon, with a long, double-edged blade designed for slashing as well as thrusting. The fencing systems of the 16th century and the early 17th led to its employment mainly for attack, parrying being carried out with the left hand, which was either protected by a gauntlet or by a cloak wrapped round it, or which held a parrying-dagger (poignard). Such daggers normally had a simple cross-guard, often arched so that it could be used to trap an opponent's blade and also often fitted with a small, central side-ring.

Rapiers and daggers were normally made *en suite* as sets, while it is known from written records that the richer examples, which were, in effect, masculine jewellery, were often accompanied by alternative scabbards, girdles and hangers made to match different suits of clothing. Every technique and virtually every material known to the goldsmith and jeweller was used in the decoration of their hilts and mounts, some of which, under Mannerist influence, were highly impractical in shape, though the weapons remained functional in design. Decoration of this kind was not confined to rapiers and their accompanying daggers but was also applied to other forms of dagger, hunting-swords and what can only be described as 'parade' swords, worn on semi-theatrical occasions by rulers and their nobility and which by this period included a moderate number of curved sabres, a type derived from eastern Europe. Staff-weapons, notably those carried by princely bodyguards, also became more decorative, although, apart from trimmings on the staff, the decoration was normally confined to etched designs, often gilt, on the blade. Very few examples of the richest of these swords survive outside the remaining armouries of European princely houses, among which the Austrian imperial armoury (Vienna, Ksthist. Mus.) and that of the Electors and Kings of Saxony (Dresden, Hist. Mus.) are outstanding. The most splendid example is the Spanish or Italian rapier with an enamelled gold hilt, presented to the future Emperor Maximilian II about 1550, but equal in quality, if perhaps not in design, are the rapier and dagger (Dresden, Hist. Mus.), with enamelled gold hilts by the Spanish goldsmith Pery Juan Pock, presented by the same Emperor to Augustus, Elector of Saxony, in 1575. Both collections contain many comparable rapiers and swords, which, though functional in design, are rendered unsuitable for serious practical use by the fragility of the material or the decoration of their hilts (some hilts are even made of rock crystal). Examples of such decoration on weapons other than rapiers are a series of hunting sets (Dresden, Hist. Mus.) with silver-gilt mounts by the goldsmith Gabriel Gipfel (*fl* 1591–*c.* 1615/20) decorated with applied, cast scenes of the chase and set with precious and semi-precious stones. It should be emphasized that weapons of this kind are, and always were, enormously outnumbered by entirely functional swords and daggers, modestly decorated or not decorated at all.

Two decorative techniques that became popular during the 16th century were damascening with gold or silver, and chiselling, probably because they were not only particularly appropriate for decorating iron (and steel) but also could be used without weakening it. Neither technique was new, and damascening especially has a very long history, though it does not appear to have been much employed in the West during the late Middle Ages. It survived, however, in Islamic lands and was used, for example, on the blades of some of the Hispano-Moresque swords and daggers mentioned above. There are two forms: the first—often referred to as true damascening—involves engraving designs, with lines of dove-tail section, into the metal and then filling these with thick gold or silver wire. The second form, known as counterfeit or false damascening, involves hatching all over the surface of the iron, which can be heat-blued first, with a special tool that roughens it sufficiently to retain designs formed of fine gold or silver wire or, for simple plating, thin sheets of gold or silver, applied with a burnisher. Counterfeit damascening was the form used almost entirely throughout the West, and its production in the form of tourist souvenirs has been one of the main industries of Toledo, Spain, since the beginning of the 20th century. Counterfeit damascening is less durable than true damascening, but it permits greater flexibility in the treatment of designs. A technique related to damascening, and often used with it, is what is now known as encrustation, in which small pieces of gold or silver are keyed into recesses punched into the surface of the metal in such a way as to leave them standing proud and are then chiselled into decorative shapes.

Damascened decoration seems to have become popular again in Europe from the 1530s and was thereafter widely used for the decoration of arms of all kinds, but especially swords and daggers, and also, to a more limited extent, of armour. It is possible that the technique was reintroduced into the rest of Europe from Moorish Spain. One of the earliest-known references to it is in a letter of 1524 from Federico II Gonzaga, Marchese of Mantua, about obtaining the services of a Spaniard who 'works in damascening [*azamino*] extremely well'. This may refer to Diego de Çaias, the earliest-known damascener whose work can be identified and who is recorded as working for Francis I, King of France, from 1538 to 1542 and for Henry VIII and Edward VI, Kings of England, from 1543 to after 1549. He is described as a Spaniard in English records, and his damascened ornament includes minute figures, many of Spanish type, and sometimes Kufic lettering and the coat of arms of the Nasrid kingdom of Granada. Pieces signed by or attributed to him include a hunting-sword (Windsor Castle, Berks, Royal Col.) made for Henry VIII, two maces made for the future Henry II, King of France (signed, New York, Met.; unsigned, Paris, Mus. Armée), an ear-dagger of Spanish type (New York, Met.) and a signed cross-hilted dagger (Dresden, Hist. Mus.). The hilt of a rapier (Vienna, Ksthist. Mus.) of the same period, decorated in an identical style, is signed DAMIANUS DE NERVE[N?], an otherwise unrecorded artist.

Chiselling involved, in effect, sculpting the iron or steel, either into a three-dimensional shape or relief decoration or both. Very simple chiselled linear ornament occurs on some medieval and early 16th-century hilts. After 1540, however, more elaborate motifs, such as foliage, strapwork, masks and small human figures, were increasingly employed and had become the norm by *c.* 1560. They were often gilded or silvered and picked out with, or accompanied by, damascening or encrustation in gold or silver, for example on the two swords, a mace and a boar-spear accompanying the Milanese Armour (Vienna, Ksthist. Mus.) bought by the Archduke Ferdinand of Austria in 1559 from Giovanni Battista Serabaglio and Marc Antonio Fava of Milan. Unadorned chiselled ornament was, however, equally popular. Among the finest surviving examples of the technique are the hilts of two rapiers chiselled with minute scenes, those on one taken from the Old Testament and on the other from the New, which are merely blued: the former (New York, Met.) is signed M.I.F., which, it has been suggested, rather doubtfully, is for Mathieu Jacquet (Fecit), sculptor to Henry IV, King of France, while the other (Paris, Mus. Armée) bears chiselled portraits of the same king and the date 1599. Similarly, the work of the steel-chisellers of Dresden and neighbouring Torgau during the second half of the 16th century is often simply blued (examples, Dresden, Hist. Mus.).

The most distinguished steel-chisellers of the late 16th century and the early 17th in the field of arms (though they also decorated other objects) were craftsmen who worked for the Dukes and Electors of Bavaria in Munich and who were known collectively as the Munich school: Ottmar Wetter (*d* 1598), Emanuel Sadeler (*d* 1610), his brother Daniel Sadeler (*d* 1632) and Casper Spät (*d* 1691). With the work of the two Sadelers in particular, the art of the steel-chiseller probably reached its apogee in Europe. Their work is characterized by minute figures—often after designs by the French engraver and medal die-cutter Etienne Delaune—chiselled in high relief and brilliantly blued against a gold background (examples, Munich, Bayer. Nmus.; Vienna, Ksthist. Mus.; New York, Met.; London, V&A).

No surviving graphic designs specifically for arms and their decoration dating from before the second quarter of the 16th century are known. Thereafter, however, they become available for study in increasing numbers. Some are manuscript, but the majority are engraved, forming part of the stream of such designs for all the decorative arts from the mid-16th century onwards. Most of the artists responsible were of comparatively minor stature, but among the important artists was Hans Holbein the younger, who produced a number of designs for swords and daggers, including some for a distinctive type of early 16th-century Swiss civilian dagger with a hilt shaped like a letter I and a scabbard covered in gilt brass, cast, chased and pierced with scenes (examples, Zurich, Schweiz. Landesmus.; London, Wallace). For this reason these daggers are sometimes now called 'Holbein daggers', though there is no evidence to suggest that he originated the type. A unique collection of mid-16th-century goldsmiths' lead patterns (Basle, Hist. Mus.) includes patterns for such scabbards as well as other sword- and dagger-mounts. The earliest recorded artist specializing in designs for arms and armour appears to have been Filippo Orso or Urso of Mantua, who produced a volume of such designs, including many for sword-hilts, of which two slightly differing manuscripts dated respectively 1554 and 1558–9 exist (London, V&A; Wolfenbüttel, Herzog-August Bib.). Nothing is known about him apart from his own description of himself as *Pictor Mantuanus*. An exact contemporary was Pierre Woeiriot, an artist from Lorraine working during the mid-16th century in Lyon, where he produced eight sheets of designs (six in 1552) for hilts and scabbard-mounts. In addition to Etienne Delaune, already mentioned, other artists—some well known, others obscure—who either produced designs for swords and their decoration, or actually decorated them, were the painter, engraver and goldsmith Heinrich Aldegrever of Soest, Westphalia, the engraver Hans Collaert the elder of Antwerp, the engraver Ambrosius Gemlich (*fl* 1527–42) of Munich, the engraver, embosser and damascener Giorgio Ghisi (1520–82) of Mantua, the printmaker and designer Daniel Hopfer (*c.* 1470–1536) of Augsburg, the goldsmith and engraver Erasmus Hornick of Prague, the goldsmith Wenzel Jamnitzer of Nuremberg, the goldsmith Jakob Mores (*d* before 1612) of Hamburg, the painter Hans Mielich (1516–73) of Munich and the engraver and painter Virgil Solis of Nuremberg. Mention must also be made of the designs (Barcelona, Inst. Mun. Hist.) for masterpieces submitted to the goldsmiths' guild of Barcelona, which include a number for sword-hilts and daggers, dating from 1537 onwards.

In the early 17th century in France new and much faster fencing techniques were developed—the direct precursors of modern ones—in which the rapier blade was used for parrying as well as for attack. This led to the abandonment of the left-hand dagger and the development, by about 1630, of a much shorter, lighter rapier with a much simpler guard, though the older forms lingered until the 1640s. In Spain and in Naples, where Spanish influence was strong, a long rapier with a cup-hilt, often chiselled and pierced, and a matching left-hand dagger with a solid triangular guard for the back of the hand, remained in use until the early 18th century. Elsewhere, the light form of rapier with a slender blade and simple hilt, known as the small-sword, came increasingly into use from the 1640s and within a decade or so had been universally adopted for wear with civilian dress. The development of the military sword followed similar lines during the same period, though its blade remained much heavier and its guard normally more complex. From the mid-18th century, however, the light cavalry of a number of countries adopted the curved sabre, which had a simple cross-guard, of the Hungarian and Polish hussars. From the second quarter of the 17th century there was a fashion for

Coronation sword of the kings of France, from the treasury of St Denis, gold, lapis lazuli, steel and glass, 10th–14th centuries (Paris, Musée du Louvre)

more restrained decoration, which also influenced arms. Long-established decorative techniques continued to be used, however, and the small-sword continued the role of its predecessor as masculine jewellery, many hilts and mounts being made by the same craftsmen who produced snuff-boxes and similar objects. The most remarkable surviving examples of this are the swords in the sets (*c.* 1720; Dresden, Hist. Mus.) made by Johann Melchior Dinglinger, the prominent Saxon goldsmith, for Frederick-Augustus I, Elector of Saxony, which are decorated with gemstones and enamelled and accompanied by costume jewellery and such accessories as snuff-boxes, watches and stick handles, all *en suite*. At a more modest level, steel chiselling became especially popular, and numerous exponents of it, mostly anonymous, appeared in various parts of Europe. The steel-chisellers of Brescia—among whom Carlo Botarelli (*fl c.* 1660–65) was outstanding—had a particularly high reputation, but there were many artist–craftsmen elsewhere whose work was superior, for example Pietro Ancino (*fl c.* 1660–70) of Reggio Emilia, Matteo Acqua Fresca (*d* 1738), of Bargi, Bologna, the medallist and sculptor Gottfried Christian Leygebe of Berlin, and the medallist Franz Matzenkopf (*d* 1776) of Prague and Salzburg. A distinctive form of steel chiselling is cut-steel work, which, in effect, involves the use of faceted, highly polished steel studs in the same manner as brilliants. Possibly first used in Russia in the late 17th century, the technique is particularly associated with the factory at Soho, Birmingham, of Matthew Boulton in partnership with John Fothergill (*d* 1782) and, later, James Watt (1736–1819), during the period 1762–1800. Some of the cut-steel small-sword hilts and jewellery produced there incorporate Wedgwood jasperware cameos (examples, London, V&A). One new material occasionally used for mid-18th-century sword-grips was porcelain. These were produced by a number of factories, including Meissen.

In the second half of the 18th century, probably in the 1760s, gentlemen began to give up wearing swords with civilian dress, and by the 1780s the small-sword had gone generally out of use, except for special purposes, such as accompanying ceremonial dress. A few such occasions survive: new members of the Académie Française, for example, are presented with a sword, often designed by a distinguished artist. Because of these and the practice of presenting swords of honour for meritorious naval and military service, finely decorated weapons continued to be made regularly until the end of the Napoleonic Wars, in France notably by Nicolas Noël Boutet (*d* 1833), of the Manufacture de Versailles, and occasionally since. The great industrial exhibitions of the 19th century also led to the production of a crop of 'exhibition pieces' that were commonly in a pseudo-Renaissance style, often technically the equal of the originals but rarely so in design. In this connection special mention must be made of the work of Eusebio Zuloaga (*d* 1898) and his son Plácido Zuloaga (*d* 1910), both of Eibar and Madrid.

H. L. Peterson: *The American Sword, 1775–1945* (Philadelphia, 1954, rev. 1965) [incl. 1965 exh. cat.]
American Silver Mounted Swords, 1700–1800 (exh. cat., Washington, DC, Corcoran Gal. A., 1965)
C. Burns: *Golden Rose & Blessed Sword* (Glasgow, 1970)
A. V. B. Norman: *The Rapier and Small-sword, 1460–1820* (London, 1980)
V. Harris, ed.: *Sword and Hilt Weapons* (London, 1989)
H. L. Peterson: *Daggers and Fighting Knives of the Western World: From the Stone Age till 1900* (Mineola, NY, 2001)
G. Weland: *A Collector's Guide to Swords, Daggers & Cutlasses* (Edison, NJ, 2001)
H. Kreutz: *Edged Weapon Accouterments of Germany, 1800–1945* (Pottsboro, TX, and Fredericksburg, VA 2002)
M. O. Ortner: *With Drawn Sword: Austro-Hungarian Edged Weapons from 1848 to 1918* (Vienna, 2003)
E. Wagner: *Swords and Daggers: An Illustrated Handbook* (Mineola, NY and Newton Abbot, 2004)
S. C. Wolfe: *Naval Edged Weapons: In the Age of Fighting Sail, 1775–1865* (London, 2005)

Arnhem Pottery. Dutch pottery manufactory. In 1759 Johan van Kerckhoff started a faience factory in Arnhem staffed partly with German workers. The best Arnhem pieces in blue, purple and polychrome (using both high-fired colours and enamels) were decorated with fairly large-scale flowers, figures and landscapes with ornamental borders. The scale of the decoration in relation to the size of the object attracted attention, as Delft faience painters were accustomed to filling completely the surface with small figures surrounded by overlapping motifs. The pottery closed on van Kerckhoff's death in 1773.

H. Havard: *La céramique hollandaise: Histoire des faïences de Delft, Haarlem, Rotterdam, Arnhem, Utrecht, etc* (Amsterdam, 1909)

Arnold, John (*b* 1735–6; *d* 1799). English watch and chronometer maker. He was the son of John Arnold (1702–76), a clockmaker who worked in Bodmin, Cornwall. He opened a watch shop at Devereux Court, Strand, in May 1762, moving in 1769 to St James's Street, and in 1771 to 2 Adam Street, Adelphi. In addition to domestic clocks and watches he made marine timekeepers (two of which were carried on Cook's second voyage) and regulator clocks for use in observatories. In 1783 he opened a new shop at 102 Cornhill, in the City of London.

Arnold was the inventor of the helical spring (1775) and of terminal curves (1782). His celebrated watch no. 36, for which he coined the term 'chronometer', was his first to incorporate a compensation balance, and was welcomed enthusiastically by the astronomical community. Arnold's son John Roger Arnold (*b* 13 February 1769) entered into partnership with his father in about 1783; thereafter the company traded as John Arnold & Son.

ODNB
John Arnold & Son, Chronometer Makers, 1762–1843 (London, 1972)

Arnoult de Nimègue [Aert de Glaesmakere; Aert Ortkens; Arnold of Nijmegen; Arnoult de la Pointe; Arnoult van der Spits; Arnt Nijmegen; Artus van Ort de Nieumegue] (*fl c.* 1490; *d c.* 1536). South Netherlandish glass painter. He began his career in Tournai, where his most famous works are the transept windows of the cathedral (*c.* 1500), over-restored by Jean-Baptiste Capronnier *c.* 1845. Shortly after 1500 Arnoult was called to Rouen, where he influenced a generation of Norman glass painters. His work is exemplified in windows in Rouen Cathedral; the *Crucifixion* now in York Minster, England, originally from St Jean, Rouen; and windows in St Vincent or St Godard, Rouen.

Arnoult's figures have small heads and long bodies swathed in layers of richly worked materials, seen, for example, in a magnificent *Tree of Jesse* (*c.* 1506) in St Godard, Rouen, and in the window of *SS Romanus and Adrian* (*c.* 1510) donated by Guillaume Toustain de Frontebosc in Ste Foy, Conche-en-Ouche (Eure). Arnoult then returned to the southern Netherlands, where he was admitted as a member of the Guild of St Luke in Antwerp (1513). The window of the *Three Marys* (*c.* 1520) in Notre-Dame, Louviers (Indre-et-Loire), which was shipped from Antwerp, continues to display his exquisitely delicate draughtsmanship in the elaborate clothing and intricate architectural settings, and the brilliant contrast of deeply saturated colours and silver-stain yellows. The influence of Albrecht Dürer's graphic work is apparent but subsumed into grandiose compositions exploiting both the graphic surface and unique colour impact of stained glass.

J. Helbig: 'Arnold de Nimègue et le problème de son identité', *A. & Vie*, iv/9 (1937), pp. 279–90

A. Van der Boom: 'Een Nederlands glasschilder in den vreemde: Aert Ortken van Nijmegen', *Ned. Ksthist. Jb.*, ii (1948–9), pp. 75–103

J. Lafond: 'Le Peintre-verrier Arnoult de Nimègue et les débuts de la Renaissance à Rouen et à Anvers', *Actes du XVIIe Congrès international d'histoire de l'art: Amsterdam, 1952* (The Hague, 1955), pp. 333–44

Arraiolos. Portuguese centre of carpet production; also the name applied to carpets made elsewhere in the same tradition. Arraiolos carpets are embroidered with strands of thick wool, or more rarely silk, on linen, jute or hemp canvas, using a large-eyed needle and a long-armed cross stitch, which gives the effect of braiding. The reverse side of the carpet shows no trace of finishing off and appears to be hatched. The pattern is drawn on squared paper, and then the main points of reference are marked on the canvas by counting the threads. The border and all the motifs are first outlined and then filled; the background is embroidered last. The carpet is finished with a continuous plain or polychrome edging of looped or cut fringe. In the days when natural dyes were used, the colours were predominantly red, blue and yellow, obtained from brazil-wood, indigo, dyer's weed or spurge respectively. Originally the carpets were used to cover the floor of the hall or bedroom in noble houses and were surrounded by a strip of polished wooden floor.

These carpets have been made in the Alentejo region since the early 17th century, particularly around Arraiolos, where their production became a cottage industry. The oldest examples date from the early 17th century and were perhaps produced in monastic houses. They are executed on linen and show clearly the influence of Persian carpets (common in noble and monastic houses from the 15th century) in their use of colour, symmetry of design (with floral and animal motifs) and Oriental symbols (e.g. lotus flowers, pomegranates, birds of paradise and clouds). During the 18th century the carpets became larger, and Persian motifs gradually gave way to European ones: carnations, palms, tulips, narcissi and sometimes stylized human figures. They were embroidered in a medium-sized stitch using thinner wool, and the choice and variety of colours became greater, sometimes as many as 18 shades being used. During the 19th century the Persian theme almost totally disappeared, and the quality of the carpets gradually declined.

Carpet manufacture was revived in the middle of the 20th century, and examples are now made almost everywhere in Portugal, retaining the generic name Arraiolos. Similar carpets are made in centres of Portuguese emigration such as Brazil and Canada. The largest collections of Arraiolos carpets are in the Museu Nacional de Arte Antiga, Lisbon, the Museu Nacional de Machado de Castro, Coimbra, and the Palacio Nacional de Queluz, Queluz.

C. Overby: 'Stitching across Centuries: The Carpets of Arraiolos, Portugal', *Piecework*, vii/5 (Sept–Oct 1999), pp. 38–41

Arras. French centre of ceramic and tapestry production. The city of Arras, which was once part of the Netherlands but has been French since 1659, has been an important centre of tapestry production since the early 14th century. The reputation of Arras tapestries spread to the extent that the name Arras came to mean tapestry in several languages (It.: *arrazzi*). The story of *SS Piat and Eleuthère* (1402; Tournai, Cathedral) made by Pierrot Feré (*fl* 1395–1429) is the only remaining piece that can definitely be attributed to Arras, although the scroll, which bore the date and an inscription, no longer exists. Stylistically, however, the tapestries of the *Romance of Jourdain de Blaye* (early 15th century; Padua, Mus. Civ.) and the *scènes galantes* linked to the *Roman de la rose* (Paris, Mus. A. Déc.) and the *Annunciation* (*c.* 1400; New York, Met.) can be tentatively attributed to the same place of production. The workshop patronised by the Walois family specialized in hunting scenes, famously those of the *Devonshire Hunting Tapestries* (1430; London, V&A). During the second half of the 15th century the production of high-warp tapestries spread to the north. It is therefore difficult to establish attributions, particularly as the cartoons were used in more than one centre. The *Story of St Peter* (1460; examples in Beauvais, Cathedral; Boston, MA, Mus. F.A.; Paris, Mus. Cluny; Washington, DC, N.G.A.) has been attributed to Arras. The town declined as a centre of tapestry production after the mid-15th century: in 1477 it was besieged by Louis XI and the repression that followed discouraged tapestry production (see colour pl. II, fig. 3).

Arras is primarily known for its tapestries, but it was also the location of a porcelain factory that produced tableware from 1770 to 1790; most of its pottery was unexceptional, but from 1782 to 1786 it produced tableware of the highest quality. From the 17th century to the 19th Arras was also an important centre of lace-making.

Arrasene. Embroidery material of wool and silk which is stitched into a fabric in the same way as crewels; the term derives from 'Arras'.

Arrost, **Jan.** *See* ROST, JAN.

Art à la Rue. Radical movement among radical artists and architects in the 1890s and early 1900s, mainly in Brussels and Paris. Proponents of Art à la Rue sought to bring art to the working class. The main arena for this art was the street, where ordinary people spent most of their leisure time. Streets were enlivened with bright colours by means of lithographic posters (e.g. those of Jules Chéret (1836–1932) and Théophile-Alexandre Steinlen (1859–1923)) and by artistically designed signs, lights and drinking fountains. Such art was to be deliberately popular in appeal, accessible and intelligible to people of all ages and educational backgrounds. Decorated building façades and shop fronts, too, were singled out as an especially good means of transforming sombre streets into free outdoor museums.

E. Dapporto and D. Sagot-Duvauroux: *Les arts de la rue: Portrait économique d'un secteur en pleine effervescence* (Paris, 2000)

Art Deco. Style of decorative arts that was widely disseminated in Europe and the USA during the 1920s and 1930s. Derived from the style made popular by the Exposition Internationale des Arts Décoratifs et Industriels Modernes held in Paris in 1925, the term has been used only since the late 1960s, when there was a revival of interest in the decorative arts of the early 20th century. Since then the term 'Art Deco' has been applied to a wide variety of works produced during the inter-war years, and even to those of the German Bauhaus.

1. France. 2. USA.

1. FRANCE. Louis Süe founded the Atelier Français in Paris in 1912 and tried to create a modern style that made explicit references to the French tradition. Many of the characteristics of what was to become the Art Deco style were presented in a manifesto written by one of Süe's associates, the landscape artist and garden theorist André Vera (1881–1971). Entitled 'Le Nouveau Style', this was published in *L'Art décoratif* in January 1912: in it Vera contended that a modern style of decorative arts should reject internationalism and also pastiche but nevertheless continue French traditions, especially the rationalism of the Louis XVI (*reg* 1774–92) pe-

riod and the more comfortable and bourgeois Louis-Philippe style. For decoration, contrasts of rich, bold colours should supplant the pale tones typical of Art Nouveau, and baskets and garlands of flowers should replace the 18th-century repertory of torches, bows and arrows. The decorator Paul Follot created one of the earliest designs with these characteristics, which is deemed one of the first Art Deco works: a dining-room ensemble in sycamore, ebony and amaranth, which was exhibited at the Salon d'Automne of 1912 (Paris, Mus. A. Déc.). The chair backs were sculpted in an openwork design representing a basket of fruit and flowers.

This decorative and rather traditional current continued after 1918, reinforced by notions of a *retour à l'ordre*, which was the leitmotif of much post-war art in France. References to French classical art could be seen especially in decorative painting, sculpture and ceramics. The Art Deco movement was then led by Süe and the decorator André Mare (1885–1932), through their Compagnie des Arts Français (founded in 1919), together with André Groult (1884–1967), Clément Mère (*b* 1870), Paul Follot and the master cabinetmaker Jacques-Emile Ruhlmann. Their work continued the traditions of French *ébénisterie* and featured unusual combinations of luxurious and exotic materials, especially those from French colonies in Africa and Asia, such as ebony, palm-wood, rosewood and shagreen. They based their aesthetic on contrasts of textures, colours and materials and on complicated techniques such as lacquerwork, marquetry and inlaid work using such materials as ivory and mother-of-pearl. Other references to the *ébénistes* of the Louis XVI (*reg* 1774–92) period can be seen in the ingenious devices incorporated into furnishings, such as swivelling or inclinable desktops, drawers and flaps (e.g. the desk by Mère, *c.* 1923; Paris, Mus. A. Déc.). Influenced by Japanese art, these decorators tended to give a pictorial treatment to such large pieces of furniture as armoires and buffets, applying the decoration all over the surface rather than restricting it to joints or mouldings (e.g. Ruhlmann, cabinet, 1925; Paris, Mus. A. Déc.; and Süe and Mare, cabinet, 1927; Richmond, VA Mus. F.A.).

The Art Deco movement encompassed a wide variety of decorative arts that were characterized by a certain sensuousness of curving forms, a lavish employment of luxurious materials and bold combinations of colours and floral patterns. The lacquered screens and furniture by Jean Dunand (1877–1942), who was also a master of *dinanderie*, were often engraved or sculpted and decorated with incrustations of mother-of-pearl or eggshell. In the work of the most important silversmith of the period, Jean Puiforcat, the clean lines and smooth surfaces, occasionally decorated with semi-precious stones, testify to a new architectural approach that departs from the exaltation of surface decoration typical of traditional silverwork. The painter Charles Dufresne brought the Art Deco style to tapestry; many of his designs were produced by the Beauvais factory. Georges Fouquet (1862–1957), Jean Fouquet (1899–

1984), Louis Cartier (1875–1942), Raymond Templier (1891–1968) and Gérard Sandoz (*b* 1902) were the master jewellers of Art Deco. They replaced traditional precious stones and naturalistic floral settings with hardstones such as onyx, coral and jade in compositions of stylized motifs with strong colour contrasts (e.g. the pendant by Georges Fouquet). Decorative forged ironwork, with lively motifs of stylized roses and arabesques, was popular in domestic and public interiors of the period. Raymond Henri Subes (1893–1970) and Edgar Brandt (1880–1960) were two of the major exponents of this medium. The most important Art Deco bookbinders were Pierre Legrain (1881–1955) and Rose Adler (1890–1959).

The Art Deco style reached its apogee at the Exposition Internationale des Arts Décoratifs et Industriels Modernes of 1925. In the climate of a post-war return to normality the exhibition lost much of its original emphasis on a union between art and industry and became instead a showcase for the finest products of the French luxury-goods industries. The most popular French pavilions were those devoted to a specific theme that demanded the collaborative effort of a group of artists. Among them was the sumptuous Hôtel d'un Collectionneur presented by Ruhlmann, its architecture by Pierre Patout. It featured furniture by Ruhlmann, lacquerwork by Dunand, forged ironwork by Brandt, sculpture by Joseph-Antoine Bernard (1866–1931), François Pompon (1855–1933) and Emile-Antoine Bourdelle (1861–1929), and the large decorative painting *The Parrots* (New York, priv. col.) by Jean Dupas (1882–1964), one of the few painters to whom the appellation Art Deco can justly be applied. The Société des Artistes Décorateurs presented decorative ensembles destined for a French embassy. Paul Poiret (1879–1944) presented his collections in three *péniches* (barges) entitled *Amours*, *Délices* and *Orgues* decorated by Raoul Dufy (1877–1953). In the pavilion entitled Musée d'Art Contemporain, Süe and Mare presented a grandiose music-room furnished with a desk in ebony and bronze and a grand piano with curved legs in a modernized Louis XV style. The interior decoration studios of the major department stores in Paris—Au Printemps (Primavera), Galeries Lafayette (La Maîtrise), Au Bon Marché (La Pomone) and the Grands Magasins du Louvre (Studium)—each had their own pavilions and were important in diffusing the Art Deco style.

Art Deco began to decline in France after the exhibition of 1925, as a more functionalist and internationalist group of designers emerged who were opposed to the decorative extravagance, nationalism and traditionalism of Art Deco. They formed the Union des Artistes Modernes in 1929. It could be argued that the influence of Art Deco continued in France during the 1930s in such ensembles as the liner *Normandie* (1935), but by 1930 proportions were becoming more monumental and forms heavier and fuller, without the ornamental exuberance so characteristic of Art Deco.

2. USA. Because of the popularity of the 1925 exhibition, and through the diffusion of luxurious government-sponsored publications featuring the works displayed in the French section, the Art Deco style had a widespread international influence, especially in the USA. The Metropolitan Museum of Art in New York made numerous purchases from the exhibition and a display of 400 objects travelled to major American cities in 1926. The New York department store Lord & Taylor held yet another exhibition of the *Style moderne* in 1928. In spite of this, little that was produced in the USA during the late 1920s and early 1930s truly corresponds to the French works dating from 1920 to 1925, so the term 'Art Deco' should be used with caution. The USA simply did not have the luxury craft tradition that lay at the heart of Art Deco. Most of the best designers working in the USA from 1926 to 1930, and whose work has been labelled 'Art Deco' in popular publications, were industrial designers born and trained in Europe. Joseph Urban (1872–1933), Paul Frankl and Kem Weber (1889–1963), for example, were from Vienna, and the rationalism and geometry of the furnishings produced by the Wiener Werkstätte, rather than the French *Style moderne*, are clearly the source of their design. Frankl integrated the Viennese style with a specifically American skyscraper aesthetic (e.g. the 'Skyscraper' bookcase, *c.* 1928; Cincinnati, OH, A. Mus.). Other designers in America incorporated the rich colours and decorative geometries of the French *Style moderne* with a machine aesthetic. The interiors designed by DONALD DESKEY for Radio City Music Hall (1931) testify to the pervasive influence of French Art Deco, especially in their refinement and polychrome decoration, but they were infused with a rationalism, urban sophistication and modern use of materials that were not prevalent in France until the 1930s. Art Deco, in addition, should not be used to describe a style of architecture, but rather its surface ornament. If the Chrysler Building (William Van Alen (1888–1954), 1929) in New York displays certain Art Deco influences in the decorative stainless-steel sunburst of the upper floors, its mechanistic iconography referring to automobiles was not part of the Art Deco repertory. The lobby, however, with its expensive marbles and richly decorated elevator doors with an intarsia design in the form of a papyrus flower, is a masterpiece of the Art Deco style. One can find the decorative motifs of the French *Style moderne* applied to the entrance of the Goelet Building (E. H. Faile, 1930) at 608 Fifth Avenue, New York, and to the top floors of the Kansas City Power and Light Company Building (Hoit, Price & Barnes, 1932).

A highly exaggerated and commercialized version of Art Deco was popular in cinemas and theatres during the late 1920s, notably in the Pantages Theatre (Marcus B. Priteca, 1929–30) in Los Angeles. By the mid-1930s the Art Deco influence on American design gave way to the horizontal, flowing, streamlined style that was evocative of speed and a technological Utopia.

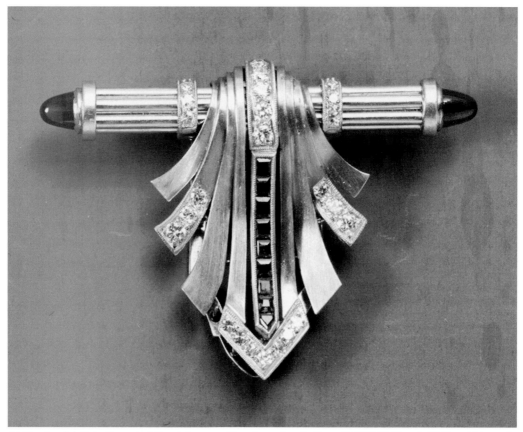

Art Deco jewelled clip by Krementz & Co., platinum, sapphires, diamonds and yellow gold, 1920–30 (Newark, NJ, Newark Museum)

B. Hillier: *Art Deco of the 20s and 30s* (London, 1968)

V. Arwas: *Art Deco* (London, 1980, rev. 1992)

A. Duncan: *Art Deco Furniture: The French Designers* (London, 1984)

A. Duncan: *American Art Deco* (London, 1986)

P. Frantz Kery: *Art Deco Graphics* (London, 1986)

Y. Brunhammer and S. Tise: *French Decorative Art, 1900–1942* (Paris, 1990)

M. Dufrene, ed: *Authentic Art Deco Interiors* (Woodbridge, 1990)

C. Benton, T. Benton and G Wood: *Art Deco 1910–1939* (Boston, 2003)

A.-R. Hardy: *Art Deco Textiles: The French Designers* (London and New York, 2003)

Y. Peyré and H. G. Fletcher: *Art Deco Bokbindings: The Work of Pierre Legrain and Rose Adler* (New York, 2004)

Artesonado. Spanish term for a type of intricately joined wooden ceiling in which supplementary laths are interlaced into the rafters supporting the roof to form decorative geometric patterns. *Artesonado* ceilings were popular in the Islamic architecture of North Africa and Spain from the 13th to the 15th century and were also used widely in Jewish and Christian architecture. They continued to be popular into the 16th century when they were effectively integrated with Renaissance motifs.

Wooden ceilings of proverbial richness are preserved in the Alhambra and other palaces of Granada. Particularly fine examples are the ceiling of the throne-room of the Palacio de Comares (*c.* 1333–54), in which thousands of individual wooden elements are joined together to represent the seven heavens of Islam, and the rounded ceiling of the Sala de la Barca (destr. 1890; rest.), named for its boatlike shape. *Muqarnas* elements could be placed in various parts of the ceiling, such as squinches, pendentives and lanterns, to create an even more spectacular effect.

Magnificent ceilings of the same type adorned many palaces, monasteries and chapels of the 15th and 16th centuries. At Alcalá de Henares, near Madrid, splendid ceilings were erected in the great hall of the Archbishop's Palace, the chapel of S Ildefonso and the Paraninfo (assembly hall) of the university. In the 16th century, when Renaissance styles of architecture were imported from Italy, they were incorporated into traditional *artesonado* ceilings. Islamic strapwork and Renaissance floral themes are blended in the coffered ceilings of the chapter house of the cathedral of Toledo and in the throne-room of the Aljafería at Saragossa.

Artifort. *See* WAGEMANS.

Artigas. Spanish Catalan family of ceramicists. Josep Llorens Artigas (*b* Barcelona, 16 June 1892; *d* Barcelona, 11 Dec 1980) studied art in Barcelona at the Escuela de Artes y Oficios de la Lonja, at the

Cercle Artístic de Sant Lluc and in 1915 at the Escola Superior de Bells Oficis. In 1923 he went for a lengthy stay to Paris, where he carried out a profound reconsideration of his pottery, divesting it of all decoration. In 1941, once more in Barcelona, he joined the Escuela Massana as a teacher, giving new impetus to Spanish pottery. His vessels, made of monochrome earthenware on the wheel, were not particularly unusual in their shape, but they were distinguished by the extraordinary quality of their glazes.

Llorens Artigas collaborated with several major painters, beginning in 1923 with Raoul Dufy (1877–1953) in Paris and later with Georges Braque (1882–1963) during 1948–9, and above all with Joan Miró (1893–1983), whom he met as early as 1912 and with whom he developed a close friendship. With Miró he produced pots, sculptures and large ceramic murals, such as those for the UNESCO building in Paris (1955–6, installed 1958), which won the Guggenheim Foundation's first prize; for Harvard University (1960); and for Barcelona Airport (1971). Six of his vases (all 1969) are in the collection of the Fondation Maeght at Saint-Paul-de-Vence.

His son Joan Gardy Artigas (*b* Boulogne-Billancourt, Seine-et-Oise, 1938) studied at the Ecole du Louvre in Paris in 1958. In 1959 he started a ceramics studio in Paris, where he worked with Georges Braque and Marc Chagall. In 1960, the year in which he met Alberto Giacometti, he made his first sculptures, but he also continued working as a ceramicist, notably in collaborations with Miró in 1961, 1967 and 1969.

J. Llorens Artigas and J. Corredor Matheos: *Spanish Folk Ceramics of Today* (New York, 1974)

R. Griffith: 'Jose Llorens Artigas and Joan Miro', *Studio Potter,* xiv (Dec 1985), pp. 20–28

G. McElroy and G. Miro: 'Playing with Fire', *Ceramics* (Australia), *xlviii* (2002), pp. 59–61

Art Nouveau [Fr.: 'new art']. Decorative style of the late 19th century and the early 20th that flourished principally in Europe and the USA.

1. Introduction. 2. Britain. 3. Belgium. 4. France. 5. Germany. 6. Austria. 7. USA. 8. Other countries. 9. Conclusion.

1. INTRODUCTION. The term Art Nouveau was first used in 1895, when Siegfried Bing (1838–1905) opened a gallery in Paris that he called L'Art Nouveau. Although it influenced painting and sculpture, the chief manifestations of the style were in architecture and the decorative and graphic arts. It is characterized by sinuous, asymmetrical lines based on organic forms; in a broader sense it encompasses the geometrical and more abstract patterns and rhythms that were evolved as part of the general reaction to 19th-century historicism. There are wide variations in the style according to where it appeared and the materials that were employed. Art Nouveau is also known as Glasgow style (Scotland); *Modern style, Style nouille, Style coup de fouet* (Belgium); *Style Jules Verne, Style Métro, Style 1900, Art fin de siècle, Art belle époque* (France); *Jugendstil* (Germany and Austria); *Sezessionstil* (Austria); *Arte joven* (Spain); *Modernisme* (Catalonia); *Arte nuova, Stile floreale, Stile Liberty* (Italy); *Nieuwe kunst* (the Netherlands); *Stil' modern* (Russia); Tiffany style (USA).

The decorative repertory of Art Nouveau was derived principally from the observation and imitation of nature, in particular of exotic flowers and plants. This is epitomized in the work of Victor Horta in Belgium and Emile Gallé and Hector Guimard in France. From EUGÈNE-EMMANUEL VIOLLET-LE-DUC in France and John Ruskin (1819–1900) and William Morris in Britain came the idea of the alliance of form with need: that all the arts should have their roots in utility. The more angular manner of the later phase of Art Nouveau, after about 1904, apparent in the work of the Belgian, Henry Van de Velde, active in Germany, and the Austrian, Josef Hoffmann, looks forward to modernism.

The forms and designs of Art Nouveau were disseminated through the numerous periodicals that existed and were founded at the time; the best-known of these were *The Yellow Book, The Studio, The Savoy, La Plume, Jugend* and *Dekorative Kunst.* Such international events as the Exposition Universelle of 1900 in Paris and the Esposizione Internazionale d'Arte Decorativa Moderna of 1902 in Turin brought the style, in its various guises, to the notice of the public as well as architects, artists and designers.

2. BRITAIN. Among the earliest examples of the flowing asymmetry associated with Art Nouveau are the book illustrations of A. H. MACKMURDO, Aubrey Beardsley (1872–98) and WALTER CRANE, in particular Mackmurdo's title page for his *Wren's City Churches* (1883). Mackmurdo, together with C. R. ASHBEE, C. F. A. VOYSEY and M. H. BAILLIE SCOTT, all of whom practised as designers as well as architects, provide the link between the Arts and Crafts Movement and Art Nouveau in Britain; Voysey, however, later despised the continental version of the style that he so strongly influenced. In Scotland, the Glasgow style was a manifestation of Art Nouveau. CHARLES RENNIE MACKINTOSH, HERBERT MACNAIR and the sisters Margaret and Frances MACDONALD were all students of the Glasgow School of Art, the director of which, Francis Newbery (1855–1946), was much influenced in his ideas by the Arts and Crafts Movement. They came together as the Four. Their cool, attenuated designs for interiors, furniture, bookbindings and needlework were much admired on the Continent and particularly in Vienna, where they were an important influence on the development of a geometrical version of Art Nouveau.

3. BELGIUM. The architect VICTOR HORTA is regarded as the 'father' of Belgian Art Nouveau. A disciple of Morris, he took charge of the interior decoration as well as the furnishings of his buildings. He made designs for woodwork, glass, textiles and, most notably, ironwork, in which the ideas put forward by Viollet-le-Duc are discernible. The inspiration for his style was nature itself (the only source of imitation

he considered permissible), on which he based the interlacing *coup de fouet* (whiplash) that characterizes his work.

PAUL HANKAR, another of the creators of Belgian Art Nouveau, was influenced both by Japanese art and the Arts and Crafts Movement. His early work was in a traditional neo-Renaissance manner; the most important Art Nouveau characteristic of his later work was his treatment of façades as decorative ensembles, as in the façade (1897) of Niguet's Shirt Shop in Brussels.

The other leading figure in Belgian Art Nouveau was HENRY VAN DE VELDE, who in 1892 gave up painting for design and, much influenced by Ruskin and Morris, was one of the most important forces in Europe for the reform of design from the late 19th century. Conscious of the disparity between his social and political convictions and his love of craftsmanship (by means of which only unique and expensive pieces could be produced), he set up a company in Brussels in 1898 in an attempt to coordinate the production and distribution of his work. He is remarkable for the multiplicity of his talents, being as successful as a designer of furniture as of lamps, wallpaper, textiles, fashion, silverware, porcelain and jewellery. He moved to Germany in 1899, and his style grew more sober and less ornamental after about 1902.

4. FRANCE. French Art Nouveau flourished most fully in the field of the applied arts rather than in architecture. Providing encouragement in the development of the style was the well-established tradition of craftsmanship in France and the support that the well-to-do gave to it. Another factor that contributed to its development was the existence of the Union Centrale des Beaux Arts Appliqués à l'Industrie (later the Union Centrale des Arts Décoratifs), founded in 1864, which from the outset professed the aim of 'supporting in France the cultivation of those arts that pursue the creation of beauty in utility'. The two centres where French Art Nouveau was created and from which the style was disseminated were Nancy and Paris and they witnessed the development of two rather different tendencies: while the former leaned towards the floral, the latter favoured the more symbolic aspects of Art Nouveau.

The Union Centrale exhibition of 1884 marked the birth of the floral style and proved to be a showcase for the ceramics and glassware of EMILE GALLÉ. A glassmaker, potter and cabinetmaker, Gallé combined a poetic spirit with determined industrial enterprise. At the same time as he developed techniques for creating his unique and expensive pieces, he set up a business for the commercial production of his glassware, using one activity to finance the other.

From the beginning of the 19th century architecture in Paris had been dominated by Neo-classicism. HECTOR GUIMARD, who studied at the Ecole des Beaux-Arts, instead of undertaking the traditional pilgrimage to Greece and Rome, went to Britain to study architecture and in 1895 visited Brussels, where he met Horta. On his return he re-worked a project begun in 1894, which he completed in 1897—the Castel Béranger, an apartment block in Paris. Here Guimard broke with the character of the surrounding buildings to give pride of place to sculpture and to colour, both on the exterior and in the interior. He designed every detail—the stained glass, ceramic panels, doors, locks, wallpaper and the furniture. In 1896 Guimard won the commission to design the Métro stations in Paris. The entrances are remarkable for the integration of decorative elements into the structure. Their appearance was halfway between that of a pavilion and a pagoda constructed of glass and iron. They were to make Guimard a household name and gave rise to the term *Style Métro*.

At the end of 1895, S. Bing opened his new gallery in Paris, *L'Art Nouveau*, for which Van de Velde designed three rooms and Louis Comfort Tiffany executed the stained glass. It became a rallying-point for the creators and devotees of Art Nouveau. Bing, one of the principal promoters of the style, brought together a number of artists and designers, among them GEORGES DE FEURE, EDOUARD COLONNA and EUGÈNE GAILLARD. All three designed rooms for Bing's pavilion (destr.) at the Exposition Universelle in Paris in 1900: de Feure's furniture for the model sitting room of a modern house included a gilt-wood sofa, its undulating lines abstracted from plant shapes.

After 1900 the Art Nouveau style in France was expressed mainly in interior decoration, notably in the shop (1900–01; destr.) in Paris designed by Alphonse Mucha (1860–1939) for the jeweller Georges Fouquet (1862–1957). Art Nouveau restaurants, such as Maxim's (remodelled 1899; architect Louis Marnez, painter Léon Sounier), and boutiques proliferated until about 1910. Originality in French Art Nouveau culminated in objects of vertu, such as those designed by Félix Bracquemond, and the sublime jewellery and accessories designed by René Lalique.

See also ECOLE DE NANCY.

5. GERMANY. Art Nouveau in Germany came into being as a reaction to the historic eclecticism epitomized by the castles built for Ludwig II, King of Bavaria. In January 1896 *Jugend: Illustrierte Wochenschrift für Kunst und Leben* was launched; this was to give its name to the Art Nouveau movement in Germany, *Jugendstil*. Most of the important figures associated with *Jugendstil* followed Morris and Van de Velde in abandoning painting to devote themselves to decorative art. OTTO ECKMANN was, with PETER BEHRENS, AUGUST ENDELL, HERMANN OBRIST, BRUNO PAUL and RICHARD RIEMERSCHMID, one of the founders of *Jugendstil* in Munich. He stopped painting in 1894 and began to study nature; some of his imaginative floral compositions were published in *Pan* and *Jugend*. He became interested in printer's type and made his name by developing the typeface known as the Eckmann type. The newly established periodicals promoted the move into graphic art, *Ju-*

gend, for example, employing 75 illustrators during its first year of publication. *Jugendstil* manifested itself in the designs that appeared not only in magazines but also in programmes and posters, revolutionizing the country's graphic art to such effect that it soon acquired an international reputation.

In glass, jewellery and ceramics German craftsmen generally did not compare favourably with the French, although there were a few exceptions, among them the glassmaker Karl Kaepping (1848–1914) and the potters Max Laeuger (1864–1952) and Julius Scharvogel (1854–1938). They excelled in furniture-making, however: Riemerschmid, Endell and Obrist were all part of the tendency that strove for overall unity in interior decoration, one of the principal aims of Art Nouveau internationally. All three made interesting sets of furniture, like Van de Velde eventually abandoning a floral style for simpler forms.

6. AUSTRIA. Art Nouveau made its appearance in Austria later and more abruptly than elsewhere in Europe in the form of the *Sezessionstil*. It was dominated by two figures: Gustav Klimt (1862–1918), in his decorative paintings, and Otto Wagner (1841–

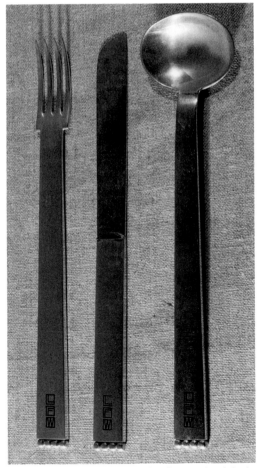

Art Nouveau cutlery designed by Josef Hoffmann and made by the Wiener Werkstätte for Lilly and Fritz Wärndorfer, silver, 1904–8 (Vienna, Österreichisches Museum für Angewandte Kunst)

1918), in his architecture. On 25 May 1897 Klimt and 18 other artists left the Künstlerhaus in Vienna to found the Vereinigung Bildender Künstler Österreichs, the Viennese Secession; Klimt was its first President. From the first this new association, which gave its name to the *Sezessionstil*, took note of artistic currents abroad and was receptive to new ideas in every branch of art.

The magazine *Ver Sacrum* was founded by the Secession in January 1898, with one of the artists responsible for designing the cover for each issue. They also produced the illustrations inside, which are of exceptionally high quality. Although publication of *Ver Sacrum* ceased in 1903, its impact on the spread of Art Nouveau in Austria was considerable; here as in Germany, the style began as a revolution in the graphic arts and in surface decoration.

In 1892 JOSEF HOFFMANN entered the Academie der Bildenden Künste in Vienna, where Wagner was his teacher. In 1898 he was employed on the Stadtbahn project and joined the Secession. He taught architecture and interior decoration at the Kunstgewerbeschule, and in 1900 he designed the Secession display at the Exposition Universelle of 1900 in Paris. He discovered the work of Mackintosh on a visit to Scotland, and Mackintosh was to be an important influence on the WIENER WERKSTÄTTE, founded by Hoffmann and KOLO MOSER in 1903. The principal aim of the Wiener Werkstätte was to re-introduce art into objects of everyday use, revitalize the workers' love of their craft and give them a role in the design and distribution of the objects they made, all of which was close to the theories of Morris.

7. USA. In the USA, Louis Comfort Tiffany was the leading designer and interior decorator in the Art Nouveau style, which was often known as the Tiffany style. Many of his designs for electric lamps, made of bronze, his own 'Favrile' glass or mosaics of opalescent glass are based on natural forms. He was an influential designer of furniture, textiles, wallpaper, silver and jewellery as well as glass. In the 1890s GORHAM became the most important manufacturer of Art Nouveau wares.

8. OTHER COUNTRIES. In Italy, Art Nouveau was known as *Arte nuova*, *Stile floreale* or *Stile Liberty* (after Liberty & Co., the shop in London). In Russia, the workshops of TALASHKINO produced Art Nouveau crafts. In Spain there emerged the isolated phenomenon of Catalan *Modernisme*, closely associated with the city of Barcelona. The last years of the 19th century were dominated there by the figure of ANTON GAUDí, whose buildings, sculptures and mosaics exemplify his fantastical style incorporating encrusted organic forms.

9. CONCLUSION. Art Nouveau was born of the desire by a section of society to reject historicism and to abolish the distinction between the major and minor arts. It was to lead on the one hand to ART DECO and on the other to Modernism in architecture. The end of Art Nouveau came with World War

I, but there had been some strong opposition to it much earlier. In 1901 Guimard had been criticized for the 'extravagance' of his designs for the Métro, for example; in 1903 Art Nouveau was described by Crane in the *Magazine of Art* as 'this strange decorative disease'; and the editors of *Art et décoration* were of the opinion that the Glasgow style, as represented at the Esposizione Internazionale of 1902 in Turin, 'does not appear to be in harmony with our artistic aspirations or our everyday needs'. Gaudí, like Mackintosh, thought little of Art Nouveau, although both had played a part in its development. In the 1920s and 1930s in France it was referred to dismissively as the *Style branche de persil* (stick of parsley style) or the *Style guimauve* (marshmallow style). It was not until the 1960s, through a series of exhibitions, that the reputation of Art Nouveau was re-established and that it was seen as more than a transitory phase linking 19th-century historicism and 20th-century Functionalism.

S. Tschudi Madsen: *Sources of Art Nouveau* (Oslo and New York, 1956, rev. New York, 1976)
P. Greenhalgh: *Art Nouveau: 1890–1914* (London and Washington, 2000)
J. Miller and others: *Art Nouveau* (London and New York, 2004)

Arts and Crafts Movement. A movement in architecture and the decorative arts that championed the unity of the arts, the experience of the individual craftsman and the qualities of materials and construction in the work itself.

1. Introduction. 2. British Isles. 3. Europe. 4. USA. 5. Conclusion.

1. INTRODUCTION. The Arts and Crafts Movement developed in the second half of the 19th century and lasted well into the 20th, drawing its support from progressive artists, architects and designers, philanthropists, amateurs and middle-class women seeking work in the home. They set up small workshops apart from the world of industry, revived old techniques and revered the humble household objects of pre-industrial times. The movement was strongest in the industrializing countries of northern Europe and in the USA, and it can best be understood as an unfocused reaction against industrialization. Although quixotic in its anti-industrialism, it was not unique; indeed it was only one among several late 19th-century reform movements, such as the Garden City movement, vegetarianism and folksong revivals, that set the Romantic values of nature and folk culture against the artificiality of modern life.

The movement was not held together by a statement of ideas or by collective goals and had no manifesto; its members simply shared, more or less, certain attitudes. The scalding critique of industrial art by John Ruskin (1819–1900) in *The Stones of Venice* (1851–3) taught them to see factory work as soulless and degrading; the pleasure in working in the traditional crafts was the secret of the object's beauty. They condemned the decorative arts of their own day as revivalist in style, machine-made and heavy

with meaningless ornament, and looked instead for fresh, unpretentious design, honest construction and appropriate ornament. They wanted to break down the hierarchy of the arts, challenging the supremacy of painting and sculpture and rejoicing in the freedom to work in wood, metal, enamel and glass. The philanthropists among them saw the crafts as therapy for the poor, educationalists saw them as a way of learning about materials. It was in some ways a serious movement, in others merely playful and self-indulgent, and its professed ideals did not always accord with its practices.

2. BRITISH ISLES. The earliest, and perhaps the fullest, development of the movement was in the British Isles, where its history falls into four phases. Its beginnings, in the 1850s, 1860s and 1870s, can be seen in the encouragement of church craftsmanship by GOTHIC REVIVAL architects, in the growth of a public taste for progressive decorative arts during the aesthetic movement, in such art potteries as that of the Martin brothers and above all in the work of WILLIAM MORRIS, who was an inspiration to the whole movement, less for his pattern designs than for his exploration of old or abandoned craft techniques and his lecturing on the decorative arts (see colour pl. III, fig. 1). In 1883 Morris became an active Socialist. He was, arguably, taking Ruskin's critique of industrial society to its proper conclusion, but only a few Arts and Crafts people followed him.

In the 1880s the pace quickened; the movement acquired its name—the phrase 'Arts and Crafts' was coined by T. J. Cobden-Sanderson in 1887. In addition, some of its principal organizations were founded: the Art Workers' Guild (1884), a club that served as the social focus of the movement in London; the Arts and Crafts Exhibition Society (1888), which brought members' work before the public in its annual and later roughly triennial exhibitions; and the Home Arts and Industries Association (1884), which encouraged craft classes for the urban poor and the revival of such rural industries as lacemaking. Alongside the named designers there were many anonymous workers, including amateurs and middle-class women excluded from the world of work by the code of gentility.

In its third phase, during the 1890s and 1900s, the movement grew in extent, but it did not change its character greatly. Important workshops were started, such as that of ERNEST GIMSON and Ernest and Sidney BARNSLEY. The movement influenced teaching in art schools, particularly at the Central School of Arts and Crafts in London under W. R. Lethaby, and it flourished outside London, for example in Haslemere, Surrey, and in Birmingham. In Scotland there was an extraordinary flowering of Arts and Crafts talent at the Glasgow School of Art, marked by the separate character of the Glasgow style, while the Arts and Crafts in Ireland, though dependent on the movement in England for guidance and expertise, was a vehicle for Irish nationalism.

The work produced while the movement was at

its height did not all look alike. Unlike Art Nouveau, the Arts and Crafts cannot be identified with a single style. There were debts of style in Arts and Crafts work to India, Japan, the Middle East, Scandinavia, Celtic Ireland, Byzantium, medieval Europe, Renaissance Italy and most of all to 16th- and 17th-century England. Many styles were used, but there were also common qualities, and there is a consistent, if not very precise, meaning in the phrase 'Arts and Crafts' when it is applied to objects.

Arts and Crafts people usually liked their designs to show how they worked and what the objects were made of: they thought of this as honesty. In Arts and Crafts houses the loose massing of the parts, irregular fenestration and ad hoc arrangement of gables, bays and other features are meant to suggest a house designed from the inside out, a relaxed assembly of different and comfortable spaces. In furniture and metalwork the jointing is often made obvious, in contrast to the long craft tradition of concealing it. In stained glass designers preferred a coarse and gritty glass that draws attention away from the pictorial and translucent qualities to the material of the window itself. Similarly ornament in metalwork is often confined in such a way as to direct the eye to the plain surfaces of silver, copper and brass.

The Arts and Crafts Movement looked both to the past and to the future, and the objects reflect this. The 'old work' that Arts and Crafts people sketched in the countryside and studied in museums provided them with models and meanings for their designs: the tradition and aura of the small English manor house stands behind many Arts and Crafts houses. They revived and adapted archaic decorative techniques, such as lustre painting and so-called Limoges enamelling. Yet they also looked forward. The mature furniture designs of M. H. Baillie Scott, C. R. Ashbee and C. F. A. Voysey were usually deliberately fresh in style and anxious to underline their modernity. Taking old work as a point of departure, these designers used such novel forms as simple squared-off timbers and, in the case of Voysey, delicately tapered verticals. In the Arts and Crafts, tradition and modernity were not necessarily at odds. While most Arts and Crafts books, printed on handmade paper with dense typography, seem archaic, almost medievalizing, the Renaissance-inspired typography of the books printed at the Doves Press, though no less traditional, was so clear and fresh that it exercised a wide influence on English typography in the early 20th century.

There was much talk of the need for simplicity in design in Arts and Crafts circles and a streak of puritanism in Arts and Crafts taste. But not all Arts and Crafts designs were simple and austere. Most Arts and Crafts interiors were light and reserved, decorated with panelling and perhaps some plasterwork, but Baillie Scott and the architects Joseph Crouch (1859–1936) and Edmund Butler designed interiors hung with tapestries, gleaming with beaten metalwork and glowing with stained glass. The early metalwork of the Arts and Crafts was generally simple

in character: W. A. S. Benson, in particular, produced tableware and lamps in brass and copper assembled from simple machine-made parts, while the silver tableware designed by Ashbee in the 1890s was sparingly decorated with coloured stones or enamel plaques. In the late 1890s and early 1900s, however, Henry Wilson, John Paul Cooper (d 1933), Alexander Fisher (1864–1936) and others began designing ceremonial silver encrusted with exotic materials and heavy with ornament. In pottery, conversely, the early work by William De Morgan and the Martin brothers was decorative, pots and tiles covered with naturalistic and figurative ornament; but then in the early 1900s W. Howson Taylor (1876–1935) and Bernard Moore (1850–1935) produced pots decorated with random, abstract glaze patterns in austere emulation of Oriental pottery.

Arts and Crafts objects are often rich in associations, carrying suggestions in their structure and decoration of things beyond themselves. Most ornament consisted of natural forms conventionalized, but in the work of Morris and many others it is a nature somehow so fresh and real that it carries the mind out to the country. Gimson and Sidney Barnsley incorporated details from hay rakes and farm wagons in their sophisticated furniture with something of the same effect. Narrative ornament was also used, the stories being drawn from myth and legend, particularly the *Morte d'Arthur*. It is not surprising that the imagery of the movement should refer to the twin Romantic dream-worlds of the countryside and the past, for the Arts and Crafts was, in many ways, a late expression of Romanticism.

The Arts and Crafts was also an avant-garde movement and, as such, a movement of reaction against prevailing middle-class taste. Arts and Crafts designers looked at what was in the shops, condemned it as 'commercial' and went away and designed the opposite. Late 19th-century jewellery, for instance, was dominated by the diamonds mined in great quantities in South Africa, usually set in small gold mounts and surrounded by other pale stones. Arts and Crafts designers despised diamonds as a vulgar display of wealth. Their designs had large silver mounts set with enamel or cheap and colourful stones, the difference proclaiming them as art. The sturdy and often uncomfortable-looking furniture of the Arts and Crafts can also be seen as a gesture of protest against the spindly upholstered furniture of late Victorian drawing-rooms.

These qualities can be found, overlapping one another, in most Arts and Crafts objects. The decanter designed by Ashbee, for example, is simple in its construction, the silver wires being soldered into place without disguise or even refinement. Ornament is concentrated around the finial, and otherwise the metal is left plain, the hammermarks on its surface witness to the fact that it was handmade. It belongs to the type of late Victorian handled decanter sold in the shops as a claret jug, all but the cheapest of which were decorated by faceting or cutting of the glass; Ashbee's design makes a point of being plainer. The design is both old and new, for it was based on some glass bottles, probably of the late 17th century, that Ashbee found on the site of a house he was building in London. Yet with its linear elegance and hint of Art Nouveau, it is unmistakably *c.* 1900. Ashbee was able to add a further dimension to the design, for he thought the bottles he had found were Elizabethan, bringing with them connotations of bluff English hospitality—a clumsy and romantic view of history that was a characteristic feature of the Arts and Crafts.

The fourth and last phase of the movement in the British Isles ran from *c.* 1910 into the 1920s and 1930s. These were years of transition, for the Arts and Crafts movement was going out of fashion around 1910. Little radically new work was seen at Arts and Crafts Exhibitions, and in 1912 the Exhibition lost a good deal of money. The Arts and Crafts was edged out of the public mind by new developments, Post-Impressionism in art, the admiration for French classicism in architecture and in design by those associated with the Design and Industries Association, who wanted to apply the standards of the craft movement to the productive power of industry. The essence of the Arts and Crafts, however, was not to be fashionable, and after World War I it carried on in an altered mood. Some major figures, such as Eric Gill, went on working, and a second generation continued the decorative traditions. There were also important new figures, particularly among weavers, such as Ethel Mairet (1872–1952), and studio potters, such as Bernard Leach and Michael Cardew. They were more exclusively concerned with materials and technique, and there was no longer any hint of the anti-industrialism of Ruskin. Their work was essentially revived hand-craftsmanship, done for the sake of creative satisfaction.

3. EUROPE. The earliest continental Arts and Crafts activity was around 1890 in Belgium, where such artists and architects as Gustave Serrurier-Bovy

Bernard Howell Leach: earthenware dish with slip decoration, St Ives, 1923 (London, Victoria and Albert Museum)

and Henry Van de Velde were inspired by the freshness of English Arts and Crafts work and the example of artists taking up the crafts: this seemed to be a less precious, more democratic art than easel painting. In 1894 the group of avant-garde artists known as Les XX reformed themselves as La Libre Esthétique with a new commitment to the decorative arts, and their first exhibition included work by Morris, Walter Crane, T. J. Cobden-Sanderson and Ashbee. Stylistically their work was influential in France, but it is not clear how large a part specifically Arts and Crafts ideas and practices played in the decorative arts in France, or indeed Spain or Italy. The main developments were in northern and central Europe.

The Arts and Crafts Movement in Germany was coloured by the strong spirit of nationalism following unification in 1871. The Arts and Crafts cult of the primitive and the vernacular was attractive to Germans, whose sense of national identity was rooted in a vigorous German culture of the past; local crafts, for example, were fostered by the Bund für Heimatschutz, founded in 1903 to preserve the traditional life and fabric of Germany. A progressive Arts and Crafts Movement could also contribute to Germany's struggle for industrial supremacy. Arts and Crafts workshops were set up in many parts of Germany; the two most important were the Vereinigte Werkstätten für Kunst im Handwerk, founded in Munich in 1897 by a group of artist–designers of whom Richard Riemerschmid and Bruno Paul were the most prolific, and the Dresdener Werkstätten für Handwerkskunst, started at Hellerau in 1898 by Karl Schmidt (1873–1954); both produced furniture, lighting, textiles and ceramics. Although modelled on English workshops, they had none of the scorn for trade that inspired and confined English Arts and Crafts, and they quickly developed into large commercial undertakings. In 1905 they both began producing standardized machine-made furniture with the idealistic purpose of reaching a larger public. Their business realism and experiments in standardization gave support to the reforming programme of Hermann Muthesius, who believed that if German industry could perfect pure, standardized Germanic designs, supremacy in world trade would follow, though in fact the Werkstätten themselves remained attached to the values of craft rather than industry, with machine production firmly under the control of the artist–designers.

The principal centre of Arts and Crafts in Austria was Vienna, a city whose cultural life, though long and distinguished, had become parochial in the late 19th century. Its younger artists looked eagerly to France, Belgium and the Netherlands and to English Arts and Crafts; they wanted to enlarge the scope of painters to include the decorative arts, and they made Viennese Arts and Crafts to some extent a painters' movement. In 1900, at the eighth exhibition of the Vienna Secession, the work of Charles Rennie Mackintosh and Ashbee was greeted with enthusiasm. In 1903 two leading Secessionists, Josef Hoffmann and Kolo Moser, set up craft workshops known as the

Wiener Werkstätte. They were organized along the lines of the English and German Arts and Crafts, and their manifesto spoke of the dignity of everyday objects, pleasure in work and the value of fine workmanship. Their work, which consists of furniture, metalwork, jewellery and bookbinding, is in a distinctive manner, a stylish rectilinear version of Art Nouveau that contrasts with the deliberate naivety of English Arts and Crafts and with German experiments in cheap furniture; the Wiener Werkstätte catered to the luxury trade. There were also Arts and Crafts workshops in Prague, notably Artěl, founded in 1907, in whose work the influences of folk art and Cubism were mixed.

Folk art influenced Arts and Crafts design in other parts of central Europe and also in Scandinavia, partly because the movement in these countries was inspired by nationalism: where political independence was at stake, folk art became an emblem of national identity. This was the case in Hungary, dominated by Austria and the Habsburg emperors during the last quarter of the 19th century, and in Finland, which was an unwilling part of the Russian Empire. The nationalist impulse fostered both the practice of folk crafts in their traditional form and the incorporation of folk-art motifs in original designs. At Hvittrask, for example, in the idyllic colony of artists' houses near Helsinki, designed by Gesellius, Lindgren & Saarinen, peasant motifs decorate the interiors.

4. USA. In the USA there was the same mixture of social concern and dilettantism and the rejection of historical styles in favour of a traditional simplicity. Many of the same groups of people, too, were involved: social reformers, teachers and women's organizations, as well as architects and designers. Ruskin and Morris were the prophets of craftsmanship for Americans as for Britons, though Thoreau, Ralph Waldo Emerson and Walt Whitman provided a sympathetic intellectual climate. Morris was also influential in book design and Voysey and Baillie Scott in architecture and furniture, and French artist–potters influenced their American counterparts. The Americans, however, were bolder than the British in making and selling large quantities. 'The World of Commerce', wrote Elbert Hubbard, 'is just as honorable as the World of Art and a trifle more necessary'. Compared with Europe, the American Arts and Crafts movement was much less influenced by Art Nouveau. There was a sturdy, four-square quality about much American Arts and Crafts that appealed, as Theodore Roosevelt appealed, to an American ideal of strong, simple manliness.

The movement in craftsmanship started in the 1870s and 1880s, in response to a demand from such architects as H. H. Richardson (1838–86). The art pottery movement began in Cincinnati, OH, in the 1880s; in quantity and quality the work of, among others, the Rookwood Pottery, the Van Briggle Pottery and the Grueby Faience Co. claims pride of place alongside furniture in American Arts and Crafts. The East Coast was always more aware of British and European developments, and the first Arts and Crafts exhibition in America was held at Copley Hall in Boston in 1897. This was followed by the foundation of the Society of Arts and Crafts, Boston, which sponsored local exhibitions, salerooms and workshops with great success; the Society's Handicraft Shop produced fine silverware. In 1901 the Arts and Crafts silversmith ARTHUR STONE opened a workshop in Gardner, MA. In Philadelphia the architects of the T-Square Club looked particularly to England and exhibited Arts and Crafts work in the 1890s, and in 1901 the architect William L. Price founded an idealistic and short-lived craft colony at Rose Valley, outside Philadelphia, devoted to furniture, pottery and amateur theatricals.

Upper New York State was another important centre of the Arts and Crafts, partly perhaps because of the attractions of the Catskill Mountains. At the Byrdcliffe Colony in Woodstock, for example, pottery, textiles, metalwork and furniture were produced in a romantic backwoods setting; the Arts and Crafts shared some of the pioneering mystique of the log cabin for Americans. The most important figure in the area, and arguably in American Arts and Crafts as a whole, was GUSTAV STICKLEY, a furniture manufacturer in Eastwood, Syracuse, NY, who began producing simple so-called Mission furniture about 1900. The design of Stickley's furniture was not as important as the scale of his operations and his power of communication. From 1901 he published *The Craftsman* magazine, which became the mouthpiece of the movement in America, and in 1904 he started the Craftsman Home-Builders Club, which issued plans for self-build bungalows; by 1915 it was estimated that ten million dollars' worth of Craftsman homes had been built. The furniture, houseplans and magazine together presented the Arts and Crafts as a way of life instead of a specialist movement. Simple, middlebrow, traditional, slightly masculine and slightly rural, it appealed to a large American market. The most flamboyant figure in New York State was ELBERT HUBBARD. At his Roycroft works in East Aurora, he produced metalwork, printed books and furniture very like Stickley's and published *The Philistine* magazine. Hubbard, too, created a powerful image for his craft enterprise, a slightly ersatz blend of bonhomie and culture, which made him seem almost a parody of Stickley or, more subtly, of himself.

In Chicago the focus of the movement was at first at Hull-House, the settlement house run by the social reformer Jane Addams (1860–1935), where the Chicago Society of Arts and Crafts was founded in 1897. Here immigrants were encouraged to practise their native crafts, such as spinning and weaving, less to perfect the craft than to soften the shock of the new city. There were more Arts and Crafts societies and workshops in Chicago than in any other American city, a witness to its aspiring culture. Perhaps the most distinguished of the workshops were those of the metalworkers and silversmiths, such as the Kalo Shop, which was founded in 1900 by Clara Welles

(1868–1965) and continued production until 1970. It was in Chicago, also, that the Arts and Crafts made one of its most important contributions to American architecture, for Arts and Crafts influence can be seen in the work of the Prairie school architects Walter Burley Griffin (1876–1937), George Washington Maher (1864–1926), Purcell & Elmslie and most notably Frank Lloyd Wright. In their sense of materials, their creation of a regional style echoing the horizontals of the prairies and their interest in designing furniture, metalwork and decorative details in their interiors, they continued the Arts and Crafts tradition.

Arts and Crafts workshops and activities in California began only in the early 1900s and were often stimulated by architects and designers from the East settling in California. Although Californian Arts and Crafts showed a debt to the beauty of the landscape and to the building traditions of the Spanish Mission, it had no single stylistic character. It ranged from the richly carved and painted furniture made by Arthur F. Mathews and his wife Lucia in San Francisco, through the simple, almost monumental, copper table-lamps of Dirk Van Erp (1859–1933), to the outstanding work of the architects Charles Sumner Greene and Henry Mather Greene. Between c. 1905 and 1911 GREENE & GREENE designed a number of large, expensive, wooden bungalows in and around Pasadena and equipped them with fine handmade furniture. These houses lie along the contours of their sites, inside and outside merging in the kindness of the climate. Their timber construction, panelling and fitted and movable furniture all show the gentle and authoritative ways in which the Greene brothers could make one piece of wood meet another, with Japanese and Chinese jointing techniques transformed into a decorative Californian *tour de force*. Although most products of the American Arts and Crafts are strong and simple in character, the Greenes' finest houses, the masterpieces of American Arts and Crafts architecture, are delicate and exquisite.

R. J. Clark: *The Arts and Crafts Movement in America, 1876–1916* (Princeton, 1972)
A. Callen: *Angel in the Studio: Women in the Arts and Crafts Movement, 1870–1914* (London, 1979)
The Arts and Crafts Movement in New York State, 1890s–1920s (exh. cat., ed. C. L. Ludwig; Oswego, SUNY, Tyler A.G., 1983)
A. Crawford, ed: *By Hammer and Hand: The Arts and Crafts Movement in Birmingham* (Birmingham, 1984)
'The Art that Is Life': The Arts and Crafts Movement in America, 1875–1920 (exh. cat., ed. W. Kaplan; Boston, Mus. F.A., 1987)
E. Cumming and W. Kaplin: *The Arts and Crafts Movement* (London, 1991)
K. Trapp, ed.: *The Arts and Crafts Movement in California: Living the Good Life* (Oakland, CA, and New York, 1993)
B. Denker, ed.: *The Substance of Style: Perspectives on the American Arts and Crafts Movement* (Winterthur, DE, 1996)
M. Boyd Meyer, ed.: *Inspiring Reform: Boston's Arts and Crafts Movement* (Wellesley, MA, 1997)
W. Kaplan and P. Bayer: *The Encyclopedia of Arts and Crafts* (London, 1998)
P. Todd: *The Arts & Crafts Companion* (New York, 2004)

Arzberg Porcelain Factory. German porcelain factory founded in 1887 in the Bavarian city of Arzberg.

The factory's most famous design is a set of tableware known as 'Form 1382', which was designed by Hermann Gretsch (1895–1950) and has been sold since 1931. In August 2000 the company merged with three smaller manufacturers to become SKV-ARZBERG-Porzellan GmbH, which since June 2004 has been trading as ARZBERG-Porzellan GmbH.

Asam, Egid Quirin [Aegidius Quirinus] (*b* Tegernsee, *bapt* 1 Sept 1692; *d* Mannheim, 29 April 1750). German stuccoist, sculptor, painter and architect, descended from a family of artists. In 1724 he became a valet and court stuccoist to the Prince-Bishop of Freising and in 1730 a valet to the Elector of Bavaria. He collaborated with his brother Cosmas Damian Asam (1686–1739) on the the decoration of Mariae Himmelfahrt (1720) at Aldersbach, where rich stuccowork adorns the pillars and vaulting, not merely providing a framework for the frescoes, but forming a connection with the paintings. Egid Quirin's stuccowork is often markedly three-dimensional, with clouds and figures seeming to spring out from the architecture. The finest examples of his stuccowork are the abbey church in Rohr (1717–23) and the church of St Margaretha in the former Premonstratensian abbey of Osterhofen (1731).

E. Hanfstaengel: *Die Brüder Cosmas Damian und Egid Quirin Asam* (Munich, 1955)
G. Hojer: *Die frühe Figuralplastik E. Q. Asams* (Witterschlick, 1967)

Ash, Gilbert (*b* 1717; *d* 1785). American furniture-maker whose New York workshop specialized in chairs in the Chippendale style. His reputation is largely based on attributed pieces, such as the sets of chairs made for Sir William Johnson (now divided, examples in Winterthur, DE, Dupont Winterthur Mus. and New Haven, CT, Yale U. A.G.) and for the Van Rensselaer family (New York, Met.).

Ashbee, C(harles) R(obert) (*b* Isleworth, Middx, 17 May 1863; *d* Godden Green, Kent, 23 May 1942). English designer, writer, architect and social reformer. As a young man he was deeply influenced by the teachings of John Ruskin and William Morris, and particularly by their vision of creative workmanship in the Middle Ages; such a vision made work in modern times seem like mechanical drudgery.

In 1888, while training to be an architect, Ashbee established the Guild and School of Handicraft in the East End of London. The School lasted only until 1895, but the Guild, a craft workshop that combined the ideals of the Arts and Crafts Movement with a romantic, apolitical socialism, was to be the focus of Ashbee's work for the next 20 years. There were five guildsmen at first, making furniture and base metalwork. In 1891 they moved to Essex House, an 18th-century mansion in the Mile End Road, and work was expanded to include jewellery, silverwork and enamelling. The last workshop to be added, in 1898, was the Essex House Press, which took over staff and equipment from William Morris's Kelmscott Press.

The products of the Guild were designed mostly by Ashbee, whose talents reached maturity *c.* 1900. His early work was uncertain in design, and the details often incorporated 16th- or 17th-century motifs in a prominent, ill-digested way. But in the early 1890s he began to design jewellery that was simple in form and radical in taste; made out of silver wire and cheap coloured stones, and without obvious historical precedents, it was the first distinctly Arts and Crafts jewellery. In the later 1890s he designed some marvellously assured silver table ware, including dishes and decanters; he chose to work with a few simple elements, such as plain hammered silver, coloured stones set sparingly and fluent wirework. He produced a remarkable variety of designs, which had a wide and enduring appeal (examples in London, V&A).

In 1902 Ashbee moved the workshops of the Guild of Handicraft to Chipping Campden, Glos, a small town with a wealth of fine stone buildings and almost no experience of the Industrial Revolution. It was a bold move, inspired by current concerns over degeneracy in cities and by the rural nostalgia of the Arts and Crafts Movement. At first it was a success and an enlargement of Ashbee's ideals; he repaired local buildings and started a craft school. The limited company went into liquidation at the end of 1907, though the Guild of Handicraft continued in a reduced form until 1919.

ODNB

C. R. Ashbee: *A Few Chapters in Workshop Re-construction and Citizenship* (London, 1894)

C. R. Ashbee: *An Endeavour towards the Teaching of John Ruskin and William Morris* (London, 1901)

C. R. Ashbee: *Craftsmanship in Competitive Industry* (London, 1908)

C. R. Ashbee: *Modern English Silverwork* (London, 1909, rev. 1974)

C. R. Ashbee: *Should We Stop Teaching Art* (London, 1911)

C. R. Ashbee: *Where the Great City Stands: A Study in the New Civics* (London, 1917)

F. MacCarthy: *The Simple Life: C. R. Ashbee in the Cotswolds* (London, 1981)

A. Crawford: *C. R. Ashbee: Architect, Designer and Romantic Socialist* (London, 1985; rev. 2005)

F. Ashbee: *Janet Ashbee: Love, Marriage, and the Arts and Crafts Movement* (New York, 2002)

C. R. Ashbee: loop-handled dish, silver and lapis lazuli, h. 198 mm, 1901 (New York, Museum of Modern Art)

Ashbury metal [Ashberry metal]. Type of pewter used mainly for cutlery; the metal is an alloy of tin, antimony and zinc.

Askew, Richard (*fl* 1772–95). English porcelain painter who specialized in figures. He is first recorded in the CHELSEA PORCELAIN FACTORY, and in 1772 moved to the DERBY factory. Several attributed works survive, but no known work is signed or otherwise documented.

Asplund, (Erik) Gunnar (*b* Stockholm, 22 Sept 1885; *d* Stockholm, 20 Oct 1940). Swedish architect and designer. Asplund is rightly known as an architect, but the design of interiors and furniture always formed an essential part of his work. His design for a kitchen and living-room for the *Home Exhibition of the Swedish Society of Arts and Crafts* (1917) in Stockholm was widely praised. He subsequently designed neo-classical furniture of which simplified versions were presented at the Exposition Internationale des Arts Décoratifs et Industriels Modernes, Paris (1925). His detailing often used symbolic elements, but its very elaboration lent an air of fragility in striking contrast to the massive shapes it adorned. His most important work as a designer of interiors was the Skandia Cinema (1923–4), Stockholm. Here his use of classical motifs was partly symbolic, partly in a more light-hearted spirit of pastiche. A miniature Pantheon adjoined the vestibule, with a false night sky above its oculus for pictures of film stars. In the auditorium he similarly created the illusion of night in a piazza surrounded by decorated 'buildings': the cinema's boxes and balconies. The vaulted ceiling, painted bluish-black, arched like a dark sky over dim pendant lamps (later removed). Gilt mouldings and pilasters reinforced the opulent classical effect, in part indebted to the neo-classical tradition of Gustavian theatre and garden architecture.

P. Blundell Jones: *Gunar Asplund* (London, 2005)

Assay groove. Small gouge under a piece of silver, made when a sample was removed for assaying.

Assisi work. Modern term for a type of embroidery made in Italy and elsewhere; there is no ascertainable connection with the Italian city of Assisi. The pattern, outlined in black or red with a double running or Holbein stitch, is left blank, and the ground is worked in cross stitch. The stitch is identical on both sides, so the fabric is reversible.

Assyrian Revival. Style of the second half of the 19th century and the early 20th, inspired the excavation and display of Assyrian artefacts of the 9th to 7th centuries BC. Assyrian revivalism first appeared in England in the decorative arts, such as the 'Assyrian style' jewellery that was produced as early as 1851 and flourished until at least the late 1870s. In tomb architecture, the most famous example of the Assyrian style is Jacob Epstein's tomb of Oscar Wilde (1909–12; Paris, Père-Lachaise Cemetery), which was modelled after an Assyrian winged bull.

F. N. Bohrer: 'Assyria as Art: A Perspective on the Early Reception of Ancient Near East Artifacts', *Cult. & Hist.*, iv (1989), pp. 7–33

C. Gilbert and V. Kurshan: *130 West 30th Street Building, 130 West 30th Street, aka 128–132 West 30th Street Manhattan: Built 1927–28: Cass Gilbert, Architect* (New York, 2001)

Astbury, John (*b* Shelton, Staffs, 1688; *d* Shelton, Staffs, 3 March 1743). English potter. He worked mainly in earthenware and furthered the development of white, salt-glazed wares, which replaced the earlier, drab, salt-glazed stoneware and the brittle, yellow-brown slipwares. He was interested in the nature of clays and carried out experiments with combinations of different types; he is often credited (along with Thomas Heath) with the introduction of calcined flint into the clay body to enable the production of finer, crisper work. His output included teapots and other red earthenwares—some with applied, white relief decoration—including cow creamers and a variety of animal figures. He is perhaps best known, however, for his charming figures of soldiers (e.g. *Grenadier*; London, BM), musicians and horsemen modelled in brown-and-white clay with transparent lead glazes. Although these figures were cheaply produced from moulds they required a great deal of hand finishing. Similar but later figures, stained with underglaze metallic oxides, are referred to as 'Astbury Whieldon'. Astbury's rolled, pipeclay figures possess a cheerful, enthusiastic quality and he is also sometimes credited with modelling the naive and humorous 'Pew Groups' of seated men and women in finely detailed contemporary dress. From *c.* 1735 he is also reputed to have made figure jugs, precursors of the popular 'Toby' jugs. His work was not signed; where the name does appear it belongs to a later member of his family, after *c.* 1760. His name is used to classify the work of many other potters by type and of the period 1730 to 1740.

ODNB

R. K. Price: *Astbury, Whieldon and Ralph Wood Figures and Toby Jugs* (London, 1928)

D. Barker: 'An Important Discovery of Eighteenth-century Ceramics in Stoke-on-Trent', *W. Midlands Archaeol.*, xxxv (1992), pp. 11–5

D. Barker and W. D. Klemperer: 'An Important New Discovery of Staffordshire Ceramics', *Ars Ceramica*, ix (1992), pp. 28–32

Asterism [*asterismus*]. In jewellery and mineralogy, the appearance of light in the shape of a six-rayed star seen in some crystals, as in star sapphire and star ruby.

Astragal. In architectural decoration and in furniture, a small moulding, of semicircular section, sometimes plain, sometimes carved with leaves or cut into beads; in gunnery, a ring or moulding encircling a cannon near its mouth.

Astrarium. *See* DONDI.

Athénienne. Lidded urn on a carved tripod stand in the style of the metal tripod on the choregic monument of Lysikrates. JAMES STUART reconstructed the tripod, and invented the motif, which he used at Kedleston Hall (Derbys, NT) as painted wall decoration, as incense burners on chimneypieces, as candelabra in front of mirrors, and in friezes above doors. The name derives from the use of the depiction of the tripod in Joseph-Marie Vien's painting *La Vertueuse Athénienne* (1763; Strasbourg, Mus. B.-A.). It soon became a type of French furniture, and was used as a wash-stand (e.g. 1804–14; New York, Met.) or plant-holder.

Atlantid [atlantes; atlas; telamon]. Figure of a man used as a column to support an entablature in the architecture of classical antiquity (i.e. a male CARYATID), and for decorative effect in European metalwork and furniture from the 16th century.

D. Hourde: 'Atlantes & Caryatides: Le fonctionnel et le sacre', *A. Afrique Noire*, cxxxi (Autumn 2004), pp. 14–17

Atterbury Glass Company. American glass manufactory. In 1860 James and Thomas Atterbury (the grandsons of Sarah Bakewell, whose brother founded the glass company Bakewell & Co.) joined their brother-in-law James Hale to form the Pittsburgh glass company of Hale, Atterbury and Company. In 1862 Hale was replaced by James Reddick as the company's glassblower, and the firm became known as Atterbury, Reddick, and Company. On Reddick's departure in 1864 it became Atterbury & Company (the name by which it is generally known) and in 1893 it became the Atterbury Glass Company, under which name it traded until 1903.

The Atterbury glassworks made milk glass tableware. Its most famous designs are its covered dishes, in which the covers were shaped like animals. 'Rabbit' appeared in 1886, 'Duck' in 1887 and the 'Boar's Head' in 1888. The glass menagerie also included dish covers called 'Chick and Eggs', 'Entwined Fish' and 'Hand holding a Bird'.

Aubusson. Town situated on the River Creuse in the Creuse département (formerly La Marche) in central-southern France. Tapestries have been produced at Aubusson and the nearby town of Felletin since the 16th century, and carpet manufacture was established in Aubusson in 1743.

1. Carpets. 2. Tapestry.

1. CARPETS. The production of carpets began at Aubusson in 1743. As the products of the SAVONNERIE in Paris were reserved for the exclusive use of the king, and as the best imported Turkish carpets were both expensive and difficult to obtain, Jean-Henri-Louis Orry de Fulvy (*d* 1751), Louis XV's Intendant des Finances, decided that Aubusson should

Atlantid from the Odeon, Pompeii, 1st century AD

also produce carpets to meet the growing demand. Early carpets were imitations of Turkish designs, but in 1753 the painter Louis-Joseph Le Lorrain created a new style of carpet design called *à grande mosaïque*, which referred to a central medallion of flowers of a completely French style (e.g. carpet, *c.* 1770; Paris, Mus. Nissim de Camondo). The new carpet designs were completely French in character, although they were much simpler than the complex arrangements of those of the Savonnerie. Two types of carpet were made at Aubusson: knotted-pile carpets woven on vertical looms, and from *c.* 1767 tapestry-woven carpets produced on horizontal looms. Aubusson carpets were cheaper than those of the Savonnerie and were not exclusive, which enabled the workshops to flourish; inventories show that several carpets were used in the smaller rooms at the château of Versailles.

During the French Revolution the factory had only four workshops in operation. The advent of the First Empire in 1804 revived the insustry, but by 1843 the number of orders for hand-woven carpets had decreased significantly, and many weavers were made redundant. After 1880 the crisis became more acute: orders for carpets were few, sales were poor, and the workshops were sustained only by the weaving of tapestry wall hangings. In the 20th century well-designed carpets once again began to play an important role in interior design. By the mid-1920s contemporary artists gave a new impetus to the production of hand-knotted carpets, with Aubusson workshops leading the way. In the 1990s craftsmen at Aubusson made carpets for the refurbishment of the Grand Trianon at Versailles based on the original designs.

M. Jarry: *Carpets of Aubusson* (Leigh-on-Sea, 1969)

2. TAPESTRY. It seems likely that the first looms in Aubusson were set up in the 14th century by Flemish refugees, although tapestry production did not begin until the 16th century. Local buyers who were unable to afford expensive, high-quality tapestries, so the Aubusson weavers specialized in the cheaper, low-warp weaving technique. The cartoons from which the weavers worked were also of rather poor quality; they were often taken from contemporary engravings, which were simplified when copied.

With the end of the Wars of Religion (1559–93) Henry IV was keen to restore France's economic health, and in 1601 he promulgated an edict forbidding the import of Flemish tapestries in an attempt to reduce foreign competition. The industry revived, and by 1637, 2000 weavers were recorded as working there. In 1625 a set of tapestries was commissioned from the weaver Lambert for the chapter house of the cathedral of Notre-Dame, Reims, and in 1649 a three-piece set was woven for the collegiate church of St Mainboeuf d'Angers. Subjects were taken from contemporary works: the painter Claude Vignon (1593–1670) made copies of engravings by Abraham Bosse (1602–76), which were used at Aubusson, and subjects from other workshops were copied with equal lack of respect. The *Loves of Gombault and Macée* (Guéret, Mus. Guéret), a tapestry modernized some time after 1650 by Laurent Goyot for the Paris workshops, was woven at Aubusson. As in the 16th century, the cartoons were mainly of inferior quality, and the wools and dyes were unrefined.

The low standard of the tapestry production at Aubusson was highlighted in 1664. Jean-Baptiste

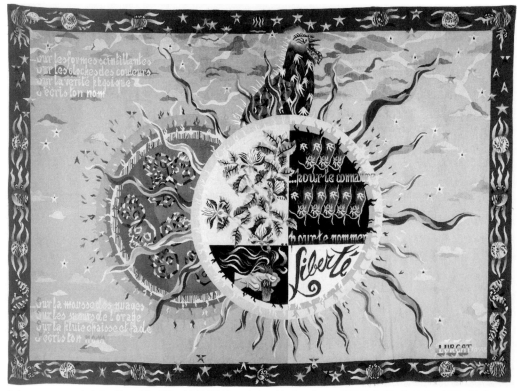

Aubusson tapestry depicting *Poem of Paul Eluard,* 2.35 × 3.31 m, designed by Jean Lurçat, 1943 Paris, Musée National d'Art Moderne

Colbert (1619–83), Louis XIV's Surintendant des Bâtiments, Arts et Manufactures, was eager to encourage the tapestry industry and bring all the concerns in France under his power. As part of this consolidation he ordered an inquiry into the weavers in La Marche and their needs. The main request from the weavers was for a painter and a dyer to be sent to Aubusson. Colbert responded in 1665 by issuing letters patent organizing the industry and giving it an official royal charter and the title of Manufacture Royale; the corporative nature and freedom of administration of the workshops were, however, maintained. Each tapestry was to have MRD or MRDB (Manufacture Royale Daubisson/Da Bission) woven into the fabric, and all tapestries were to have blue selvages. Felletin received its royal charter in 1689 and to differentiate its work from that of Aubusson it had to produce tapestries with brown borders. Despite the new charter, Aubusson was not very prosperous during the second half of the 17th century. The important request for a painter and a dyer had been ignored, and the revocation of the Edict of Nantes (1685) hit the industry badly: at least 200 Huguenot weavers fled and settled in more tolerant countries, especially Germany.

The 1730s and 1740s marked the beginning of a successful period for the workshops in La Marche. Many small workshops expanded, and several merchants bought shops in Paris as well as Aubusson as production increased. The tapestries of this period mainly depict pastoral landscapes or chinoiseries, re-flecting the change in taste from the heavy *verdures* of the Baroque to lighter Rococo subjects and designs. The work of Jean-Baptiste Atria was frequently copied, especially his *Fables of La Fontaine*. In 1761 Aubusson was given cartoons by Atria of the *Metamorphoses* by the Beauvais factory. These were very popular, and the weaver François Picqueaux wove a total of seven sets. The paintings of François Boucher were popular, and many chinoiserie tapestries woven at Aubusson were inspired by his designs; the designs of Jean Pillement (1728–1808) were also influential. The weavers, however, also continued to copy engravings (e.g. after Nicolas Lancret (1690–1743)). Large quantities of furnishing fabrics for upholstery, often with oval vignettes of a pastoral scene framed by wreaths of flowers, were also produced at Aubusson during this period.

The French Revolution forced some of the workshops in La Marche to close, as the weavers lost many of their richest clients. Napoleon (*reg* 1804–14), however, took great interest in the textile industry and by commissioning several carpets from Aubusson helped revive it. During this period very few wall hangings were woven; carpets and furnishing textiles were almost exclusively produced. The fashion for patterned wallpapers had made wall hangings less popular for interiors. The factories at Aubusson, however, continued to prosper throughout the 19th century, mostly reproducing old designs. In 1869 a school of industrial art was founded at Aubusson, which became the Ecole Nationale des Arts Décoratifs in 1884.

During the 1920s and 1930s tapestries were produced at Aubusson after designs by such famous contemporary painters as Pablo Picasso, Henri Matisse (1869–1954), Fernand Léger (1881–1955) and Georges Braque (1882–1963). In 1938 JEAN LURÇAT designed for Aubusson a set of upholstery covers to accompany his series of hangings the *Illusions of Icarus* (The Hague, Kon. Huisarchf), which had been made at the Gobelins. In 1939 Lurçat was appointed permanent designer at Aubusson. His ten-panel series called *Song of the World* (1957–64; Angers, Mus. Lurçat), made at the workshop of François Tabard (1902–69) in Aubusson, was directly inspired by the 14th-century ANGERS 'Apocalypse' tapestry series. His work is full of natural forms, animals and fish, and his palette limited to a series of strong colours. Lurçat's involvement in the art and promotion of tapestry helped ensure its revival in France in the late 20th century.

Audenarde. *See* OUDENAARDE.

Auffenwerth. German family of HAUSMALERs, active in Augsburg. Johann Auffenwerth (*d* 1728) was the first recorded Augsburg *Hausmaler*; he decorated porcelain from Meissen in polychrome and gold (e.g. cup and saucer, *c.* 1725; London, BM). His daughters Anna Elisabeth Wald (*b* 1696) and Sabina Auffenwerth (*b* 1706) were also accomplished porcelain *Hausmalers*. A tea bowl and a milk jug decorated by Sabina are in the Gardiner Museum in Toronto.

Augusta, Cristóbal (de) (*fl* 1569–84). Spanish potter born in Navarre and settled in Seville, where he became a prominent maker of *azulejos*. His tiles for the Alcázar include two remarkable sets installed in the Palacio Gótico between 1577 and 1583, one depicting the Conquest of Tunis. His panel of the *Virgin of the Rosary* is in the Museo de Bellas Artes in Seville.

Auguste. French family of gold- and silversmiths. Robert-Joseph Auguste (*b* 1723; *d* ?1805) became a master in 1757 after an apprenticeship that included work for Louis XV (*reg* 1715–74). His repertoire was unusual in that it embraced both silver tableware and gold objects of vertu; the latter includes four gold boxes made between 1762 and 1763, and 1769 and 1771 (Paris, Louvre; New York, Met.; London, V&A; Althorp House, Northants). In 1775 he received payment for the royal crown and other regalia (destr.) made for the coronation of Louis XVI in 1774. The majority of his work in silver is tableware and includes partial or complete services for the courts of Denmark (Copenhagen, Kon. Saml.) and Russia (St Petersburg, Hermitage) and for Gustav Filip Creutz of Sweden (1775–6; Stockholm, Kun. Slottet). He also made a service for George III of England

(1776–85; Paris, Louvre). Auguste's style is characterized by a light and graceful Neo-classicism, in which festoons and figures of children as handles or finials are prominent.

Robert-Joseph's son Henri Auguste (*b* 1759; *d* 1816) became a master in 1785. He was *Orfèvre du Roi*, like his father, and produced plate for the French royal family between 1784 and 1786. William Beckford was among his clients during the French Revolution (e.g. teapot stand, 1788; Brodick Castle). Henri Auguste subsequently executed commissions for Napoleon (*reg* 1804–14) and for the City of Paris, which commissioned a large table service (1804; Malmaison, Château N.) on the occasion of Napoleon's coronation. Henri Auguste was awarded a gold medal in the third Exposition de l'Industrie in Paris of 1802, but by 1809 he was bankrupt and had fled the country. A large collection of designs for his work, some by Jean-Guillaume Moitte (1746–1810), who worked for Robert-Joseph in the 1770s, was purchased by JEAN-BAPTISTE-CLAUDE ODIOT (examples in New York, Met.). The streamlined profiles of Henri Auguste's pieces, which are sparingly decorated with relief ornament, defined the transition from the late Neo-classical to the Empire style.

P. Glanville: 'A George III Silver Service at Waddesdon Manor', *Apollo*, clvii (April 2003), p. 29

E. Lambert: 'His Majesty's Silver Service', *Archit. Dig.*, lx/7 (July 2003), pp. 62, 64

Auliczek, Dominikus. *See under* NYMPHENBURG PORCELAIN FACTORY.

Ault pottery. *See* BRETBY ART POTTERY.

Aumbry. *See* AMBRY.

Aumonier, Frederic. *See under* WOOLLAMS & CO.

Aurene glass. *See under* STEUBEN GLASS WORKS.

Auricular style [Dut. *Kwabornament*; Ger. *Knorpelwerk, Ohrmuschelstil*]. Term used to describe a type of ornament popular in the 17th century, characterized by smooth, curved and rippling forms resembling the human ear. This highly plastic style evolved during the first two decades of the 17th century in Utrecht, and in its fully developed form is found only in metalwork. The style in this medium is characterized by the use of amorphous, lobate scrolls and embossed, relief ornament that emphasize the malleable nature of the metal. At its most extreme, it exaggerates this quality by suggesting that objects were modelled in a semi-molten state. The goldsmiths Adam van Vianen and Paulus van Vianen of Utrecht are credited with the invention of the style, although its origins seem to lie in the graphic designs of such 16th-century Italian Mannerist artists as Giulio Romano

(?1499–1546) (e.g. drawing for a fish-shaped ewer; Oxford, Christ Church) and Enea Vico (1523–67).

W. K. Zülch: *Enstehung des Ohrmuschelstils* (Heidelberg, 1932)

Aust, Gottfried (*b* Heidersdorf, 5 April 1722; *d* Lititz, PA, 28 Oct 1788). American potter of German birth. Although originally trained as a weaver, he was apprenticed to a potter in Herrnhut, Germany, where the Moravian Brethren were centred. In 1754 he arrived in Bethlehem, PA, the Brethren's first colonial outpost. After ten months' work at the pottery there under master Michael Odenwald, Aust went to the new settlement in Bethabara, NC, where he established its first pottery. In 1768 the pottery was moved to another new settlement at Salem, NC. All the wares necessary for daily life were made in Aust's potteries, including large stoves. Aust's most distinctive work is found on decorative plates embellished with floral or geometric ornament delineated in green, red, brown, white and dark brown slips (e.g. earthenware dish used by Aust as a trade sign, diam. 555 mm, 1773; Winston-Salem, NC, Old Salem). He trained a number of apprentices who worked in the Piedmont region, thereby creating a 'school' of his style that is associated with the area.

S. A. South: *The Ceramic Types and Forms of the Potter, Gottfried Aust of Bethabara, North Carolina, 1755–1771* (1966) [MS in North Carolina Department of Archives and History, Raleigh, NC]
J. Bivins jr: *The Moravian Potters in North Carolina* (Chapel Hill, 1972)
M. Hewitt: 'Stuck in the Mud: The Folk Pottery of North Carolina', *Cer. Rev.*, cli (Jan–Feb 1995), pp. 30–33

Austria. Ceramics *see* GMUNDEN; VIENNA.
Glass *see* BAKALOWITS; INNSBRUCK GLASSHOUSE; LOBMEYR, J. & L; SWAROVSKI AUSTRIAN GLASS COMPANY.

Autio, Rudy (*b* 1926, Butte, MT). American potter and sculptor of Finnish descent who is best known as a figurative ceramicist but has also worked in bronze, concrete, glass and metal. He normally works in stoneware with incised decorations, but began to work in porcelain while working at the ARABIA PORCELAIN FACTORY in Helsinki in the 1980s.

L. M. Lakey and R. Autio: *Rudy Autio* (Westerville, OH, 2002)

Avelli, Francesco Xanto (*b* Rovigo, ?1486–7; *d* ?1542). Italian maiolica painter. More is known about Avelli than any other maiolica painter because of his many signed works and the autobiographical details included in his sonnets in honour of Francesco Maria I della Rovere, Duke of Urbino. He seems never to have directed his own workshop, but he is known to have worked in Urbino from 1530, the year of his first unequivocally signed and dated plate; some pieces from the 1520s signed F.R. and F.L.R. may also be ascribed to him. His familiarity with Classical and contemporary literature is evident in his choice of secular and religious subjects, taken from such authors as Virgil and Ovid, Ariosto and Petrarch (e.g. plate, 1531; London, BM). He also depicted contemporary events, sometimes in allegorical form, for example the Sack of Rome (1527). His style is characterized by a strong sense of line, an interest in anatomy and architecture and the use of a broad and usually harmonious palette that sometimes included iridescent lustres (see colour pl. III, fig. 2). His imaginative compositions frequently relied on a montage technique in which he juxtaposed figures drawn from prints, occasionally borrowing an entire scene from one graphic source. Several of his commissions were for important services, among them one for a member of the Pucci family of Florence.

F. Cioci: *Xanto e il Duca di Urbino* (Milan, 1987)
A. Holcroft: 'Francesco Xanto Avelli and Petrarch' *J. Warb. & Court. Inst.*, li (1988), pp. 225–34
J. Lessmann: 'Xanto's Panels', *Burl. Mag.*, cxxxii (May 1990), pp. 346–9
T. Wilson: 'Xanto and Ariosto', *Burl. Mag.*, cxxxii (May 1990), pp. 321–7
J. C. Triolo: *The Armorial Maiolica of Francesco Xanto Avelli* (University Park, PA, 1996)

Aventurine. Brown glass with golden specks, manufactured in antiquity and rediscovered in the 16th century by the glassmakers of the Venetian island of Murano; the name (It.: *avventurina;* Venetian: *aventurina*) implies that its rediscovery was accidental, Aventurine was made by the admixture of copper crystals to molten glass, and was used both for glassware and as a porcelain glaze. A similar effect was subsequently achieved with lacquer. Since the 19th century the term 'aventurine' has also been used in a transferred sense to denote a variety of quartz in which the golden specks are pieces of mica.

L'Avventurina: L'Oro di Murano (exh. cat. by A. Bova and others, Venice, Gal. Rossella Junck, 2004)

Avisseau, Charles-Jean. (*b* Tours, 25 Dec 1796; *d* Tours, 6 Feb 1861). French potter. He was apprenticed in a faience factory at Saint Pierre-des-Corps. In 1825 he entered the ceramic factory of Baron de Bezeval at Beaumont-les-Autels where he saw a dish made by the Renaissance potter Bernard Palissy, which was to inspire his work. In 1843 Avisseau established an independent factory on the Rue Saint-Maurice in Tours, where individual ceramics inspired by and in the style of Palissy's 'rustic' wares were produced (e.g. lead-glazed dish, 1857; Bagnères-de-Bigorre, Mus. A.). Although critics complained that his works merely imitated the Renaissance master, he never directly copied Palissy's pieces.

L. N. Amico: 'Beastly Feasts', *F.M.R. Mag.*, lxxxix (Dec 1997–Jan 1998), pp. 105–28
C. -J. Aviseau: *Un bestiaire fantastique: Avisseau et la faïence de Tours (1840–1910)* (Paris, 2002)

Axminster. English centre of carpet production. In 1755 Thomas Whitty (*d* 1792), a weaver from Axminster (Devon), built a large vertical loom, taught his daughters to tie the symmetrical or Ghiordes knot and began to produce hand-knotted carpets. After his death his son Thomas Whitty (1740–99) and later his grandsons Thomas Whitty (1775–1810) and Samuel Rampson Whitty (1784–1855) took over the factory and continued production until a disastrous fire in 1828 destroyed most of the workshops. The company was declared bankrupt in 1835 and was purchased in 1836 by a Mr Blackmore, who moved the workshops and weavers to Wilton, where fine hand-knotted carpets in the Axminster tradition were woven until the 1950s.

In modern usage the term 'Axminster carpet' rarely denotes hand-knotted carpets from Axminster, but is rather used to denote three types of mechanically woven carpet, none of which has ever been woven at Axminster; the Chenille Axminster (1839), the Spool Axminster (1876) and the Gripper Axminster (1890).

See also under CARPET, §I. 8.

B. Jacobs: *Axminster Carpets* (Leigh-on-Sea, 1969)
B. Jacobs: *Axminster Carpets (Hand-made), 1755–1957* (Leigh-on-Sea, 1970)
B. Rose: 'Early Axminster Carpets', *Hali*, cxx (Jan–Feb 2002), pp. 92–100

Azulejos. Spanish and Portuguese name (from Arabic *al-zulayj*, 'the tile') for the glazed polychrome tile used in Moorish architecture for exterior and interior walls and for floors.

See also TILE, §§1(ii) and (iii).

Da Pena Palace with azulejos, Sintra, 17th century

B

Baccarat. French glassworks near Lunéville founded in 1764. At first the factory produced soda glass for household and industrial purposes. In 1816 it was purchased by the Belgian manufacturer Aimé-Gabriel D'Artigues (1778–1848), who transferred his Vôneche glassworks near Namur to Baccarat, built a new factory and began the production of lead glass. In 1823 the factory changed its name to the Compagnie des Cristalleries de Baccarat and made plain crystal, opaline and some alabaster and agate glass. In 1846 Baccarat began producing millefiori glassware and paperweights, followed by paperweights with flowers, fruits or reptiles. From 1848 the factory produced sulphides (opaque portrait medallions or cameos) to be inserted in clear glass and in the 1850s introduced coloured glass to its range. Its main output, however, was tableware, and services for Louis XVIII (1823), Charles X (1828) and Louis-Philippe (1839–40) were made at Baccarat. The factory exhibited at the Exposition des Arts Décoratifs et Industriels Modernes of 1925 in Paris and now produces fine tableware based on traditional patterns, as well as new lines by contemporary designers.

A. E. MacSwiggan: 'Baccarat', *Ant. J.*, xxviii (1973), pp. 16–18

G. Manners: 'Galleries: Baccarat', *Connoisseur*, cxxxix (1975), p. 89

A. Noakes: 'Baccarat at Asprey's', *Ant. Dealer & Colr's Guide*, vii (1975), pp. 88–91

P. Fitzpatrick: 'Baccarat: Crystal of Kings', *Ant. J.*, xxxi (1976), pp. 12–14

Museum of Compagnie des Cristalleries de Baccarat: Visitors' Guide (Paris, 1986)

M. Boyer: 'A Cut Above', *World Int.*, xxiii/9 (Sept 2003), pp. 120–25

Bacchus, **George**, & Sons. English glasshouse founded in Birmingham in 1818 as Bacchus, Green & Green; it became Bacchus & Green in 1834 and Bacchus & Sons in the 1840s. In the 1830s the company became the first to produce pressed glass in England. Its products included cased glass, tablewares and paperweights.

Baccio d'Agnolo [Bartolommeo d'Agnolo di Donato Baglione] (*b* Florence, 19 May 1462; *d* Florence, 6 May 1543). Italian wood-carver and architect. He was the son of a hosier turned woodworker, and he trained as a wood-carver, becoming the foremost Florentine craftsman of his day for picture frames, intarsia inlay, ceilings and all manner of wooden ornament.

Baccio's first important work in wood was the panelling (*c.* 1485–90) for the high altar chapel of S Maria Novella, and between 1490 and 1530 he produced frames for many painted altarpieces in Florence, collaborating with such artists as Filippino Lippi (*c.* 1457–1504), Perugino (*c.* 1450–1523), Domenico Puligo (1492–1527), Andrea del Sarto (1486–1530) and Jacopo da Pontormo (1494–1556). He seems subsequently to have acted as an entrepreneur, negotiating commissions for painters and designing elaborate settings for their work, including the celebrated bedroom (from 1515) of Pierfrancesco Borgherini in the Palazzo Borgherini (now Roselli del Turco), Florence, with its paintings by del Sarto, Pontormo, Francesco Granacci (1469–1543) and Bacchiacca (1494–1557), and the antechamber (from 1523) of Giovan Maria Benintendi, with panels by del Sarto, Franciabigio (1484–1525), Bacchiacca and Pontormo.

In 1496 Baccio began a long association with the fabric and decoration of the Palazzo della Signoria (now Palazzo Vecchio), Florence, when he collaborated on the ceiling of the great hall of council (later Salone del Cinquecento). He gradually assumed a dominant role, becoming head of the office of works in 1499, a position he occupied with only a few interruptions until the end of his life. There, as well as furnishing woodwork of all kinds, the frame for Filippino Lippi's altarpiece (1501–2) and the apartment (from 1502) of Piero Soderini (1452–1522), he designed (according to Vasari) the door in the Sala de' Dugento (*c.* 1506–12) with trophies and republican inscription, as well as the chapel of the Priors and the rearranged great hall (1512–13) for the newly returned Medici regime. His last works in the Palazzo della Signoria were carved and painted coats of arms (1531 and 1534) for the first Medici duke, Alessandro. Baccio's last important work in wood was the choir (1532–3) of S Agostino in Perugia.

A. Cecchi: 'Percorso di Baccio d'Agnolo legnaiuolo e architetto fiorentino dagli esordi al Palazzo Borgherini: 1', *Ant. Viva*, xxix/1 (1990), pp. 31–46

A. Cecchi: 'Percorso di Baccio d'Agnolo legnaiuolo e architetto fiorentino dal Ballatoio di Santa Maria del Fiore alle ultime opere', *Ant. Viva*, xxix/2–3 (1990), pp. 40–55

J. Nelson: 'The High Altarpiece of SS Annunziata in Florence: History, Form and Function', *Burl. Mag.*, cxxxiv (Feb 1997), pp. 84–91

Bachelier, Jean-Jacques (*b* Paris, 1724; *d* Paris, 13 April 1806). French painter, writer and administrator. In 1752 he was made artistic director of the Manufacture de Vincennes, and he was Directeur of the Manufacture de Sèvres from the factory's move there in 1756 until 1793. He exercised considerable influence on the porcelain industry: under his direction chinoiseries were abandoned and replaced by birds and bouquets of flowers. In addition to his responsibility for painting, he twice assumed responsibility for modelling (1751–7 and 1766–74), and seems to have been the first person to use BISCUIT for statuettes and busts.

D. Posner: 'Mme de Pompadour as a Patron of the Visual Arts', *A. Bull.*, lxxii (March 1990), pp. 74–105

Bacini. Round, hollow maiolica dishes that from the 11th century were set into the walls of churches and public buildings. Examples in the Palazzo Mansi, Lucca, and S Piero a Grado, Pisa, have bold, geometric patterns in green and manganese in-glaze colours. *Bacini* are Islamic in origin; the earliest examples were long thought to have come from Tunisia, but analysis of the clay has demonstrated that they were made in Mallorca.

M. Iozzi: 'Bacini corinzi su alto piede', *Annu. Scu. Archeol. Atene & Miss. It. Oriente*, lxiii (1985), pp. 7–61

Back stool. Four-legged stool to which a back has been added; in historic usage the term is sometimes used loosely to denote a chair without arms.

Badier, Florimond (*fl* 1630–45). French bookbinder who is primarily associated with the *pointillé* style. He used a distinctive finishing stamp, the profile of a man's head in dotted outline. Only three surviving bindings are authenticated with a signature; some of the unsigned bindings attributed to Badier may be his work, but many are the work of imitators, some of whom used his finishing stamp.

Badlam, Stephen (*b* Milton, MA, 1751; *d* Dorchester Lower Mills, MA, 25 Aug 1815). American cabinetmaker. His father, also Stephen Badlam (1721–58), was a part-time cabinetmaker and tavern keeper. Orphaned at a young age, Badlam was trained both as a surveyor and as a cabinetmaker. Soon after the outbreak of the American Revolution he was commissioned as a major in the artillery. He resigned within a year because of illness but after the war was made a general in the Massachusetts militia. On his return to Dorchester Lower Mills, he opened a cabinetmaking shop in his house and became active in civic affairs. He built up a substantial business, which included participation in the thriving coast trade, and even sold furniture through the warehouse of Thomas SEYMOUR in Boston. He also provided turning for other cabinetmakers in the neighbourhood and sold picture-frame materials and window glass. Several chairs in the Federal style with characteristic carved and stopped fluted legs are stamped with his mark, but his fame rests on the monumental mahogany chest-on-chest (1791; New Haven, CT, Yale U. A.G.) that he made for Elias Hasket Derby (1739–99), a Salem merchant and one of the wealthiest men in the country, who ordered it as a wedding present for his daughter Anstis Derby. Ionic columns flank the upper case, and carved chamfered corners resting on ogee bracket feet border the lower, serpentine section. John Skillin and Simeon Skillin executed the extraordinary figures that surmount the pitched pediment thought to represent *Virtue* flanked by the reclining goddesses of *Peace* and *Plenty*.

M. Swan: 'General Stephen Badlam: Cabinet and Looking-glass Maker', *Antiques*, lxv (1954), pp. 380–83

G. W. R. Ward: *American Case Furniture in the Mabel Brady Garvan and other collections at Yale University* (New Haven, 1988), pp. 171–7

D. Levison and others: 'Identifying Regionalism in Sideboards: A Study of Documented Tapered-leg Examples', *Mag. Ant.*, cxli (May 1992), pp. 820–33

Badorf ware [Badorfer ware]. Carolingian pottery (8th–10th cent.) associated with the German town of Badorf, between Bonn and Cologne. Vessels are characteristically decorated with girth grooves. The pottery was widely traded (e.g. examples excavated in 1990 at Flixborough Anglo-Saxon Settlement in Lincolnshire).

Baerdt [Baardt], **Claes Fransen** (*b* Bolsward, Friesland, 1628; *d* Bolsward, 1691). Dutch silversmith. His use of embossed botanical decoration on silverware was part of the Dutch late 17th-century expression of floral naturalism in the decorative arts. He appears to have remained in Bolsward throughout his life, producing domestic and church silver. The small number of objects attributed to him includes presentation and alms dishes, salts and such smaller objects as hinges, plaquettes and brush backs. Three objects dating from 1680–81 (Leeuwarden, Fries Mus., 8023, 1949–260, 1955-521) demonstrate his different approaches to the floral theme: the rim of one large dish is divided into sections, each containing an individual embossed flower, whereas another has a swirling pattern of flowers tumbling out of cornucopias and fruits, vegetables and insects; a pair of hinges is decorated with a tight symmetrical design of flower heads and leaves. In other examples fish and crustacea are included in the decorative scheme, and putti playing musical instruments appear on dish rims and centres.

Fries Zilver (exh. cat., Leeuwarden, Fries Mus., 1968)

Baggs, Arthur Eugene (*b* New York, 27 Oct 1886; *d* Columbus, OH, 15 Feb 1947). American potter. As a young man he helped to establish a pottery for occupational therapy at a sanatorium in Marblehead, MA. In 1908 the Marblehead Pottery was reorganized on a commercial basis. Baggs designed the wares, which were mostly simply shaped vases covered with muted matt glazes and contrasting stylized decorations. In 1915 he purchased the pottery and continued to be associated with it until its closure in 1936. Between 1925 and 1928 he developed brilliant blue and green glazes while working as a glaze chemist at R. Guy Cowan's Pottery Studio in Cleveland, OH. During the 1930s he revived interest in salt-glazing stoneware, and his 'Cookie Jar' (1938) is considered a key work in the use of this method for studio ceramics.

R. S. Persick and A. E. Baggs: *Arthur Eugene Baggs, American Potter* (1964)
H. Hawley: 'Cowan Pottery', *Studio Potter*, xix (June 1991), pp. 70–80

Baglione, Bartolommeo d'Agnolo di Donato. *See* BACCIO D'AGNOLO.

Bagnall, Benjamin (*b* 1689; *d* 1740). American clockmaker. He was was born in England and emigrated *c.* 1710 to Boston, where he became the city's first clockmaker; his products included eight-day clocks in pine and walnut cases. His business was carried on by his son Samuel till *c.* 1760. The most distinctive feature of Bagnall clocks is the relatively small size of the dial.

Three New England Clockmakers Claggett, Bagnall, Brown, National Association of Watch and Clock Collectors (New York, 1966)

Bahut. In furniture, the term denotes an ornamented chest (especially one with a rounded top) or cabinet; in earlier French usage it denoted a small box attached to a large chest, used for the storage of items for which ready access was required when travelling. In clothing, a bahut is a dress for masquerading.

Baier, Melchior, the elder (*b c.* 1495; *d* Nuremberg, 3 Aug 1577). German gold- and silversmith based in Nuremberg. Baier collaborated closely with PETER FLÖTNER, who produced the models for almost all Baier's gold figures (Kohlhausen). Symmetrically arranged foliage with flowers, leaves and berries evenly covering the surface is a typical feature of Baier's work, as is his skilled use of enamel. A large number of his drawings, probably preliminary studies for his gold pieces, have been preserved (Basle, Kstmus.; Erlangen, Ubib.), although few of his works have survived.

King Sigismund I of Poland (*reg* 1506–48) was probably Baier's main patron, for whom he made, in collaboration with Flötner and others, a parcel-gilt, silver winged altar (1531–8; Kraków Cathedral). During the work on this magnificent altar, which depicts the Passion of Christ on its painted panels and the life of the Virgin on 12 silver reliefs, Baier also produced a reliquary for Sigismund in 1533, which the King donated to Kraków Cathedral (*in situ*); this is in the Gothic style but also incorporates the figural parts typical of Baier's work. A small embossed silver

box (St Petersburg, Hermitage), with four diagonally placed griffins holding escutcheons as feet, was made by Baier in 1533 for Sigismund's daughter Hedwig (1513–73). Two further works for Sigismund, including the silver mounts for a sword and two silver candlesticks (both in Kraków Cathedral), date from between 1536 and 1540. Baier also produced a lidded box with a silver-gilt surround and sides formed of mother-of-pearl (1534; Kraków, St Stephen).

Baier worked for several wealthy patrician families, particularly those in Nuremberg. For Melchior Pfinzing (1481–1535) of the Pfinzing von Henfenfeld family he created the gold Pfinzing Bowl (1534; Nuremberg, Ger. Nmus.), with enamelled leafwork on parts of the foot and the convex surface of the lid. The models for the three reliefs of the heads of the donor's brothers (Sigmund Pfinzing, 1479–1554, Martin Pfinzing, 1490–1552, and Seifried Pfinzing, 1485–1545) on the lid were produced by the carver and medallist Matthes Gebel (*c.* 1500–74). For the marriage in 1536 of Erasmus von Starhemberg (1503–60) with Anna von Schaunberg (*b* 1513) Baier created a goblet with lid (Eferding, Schloss Eferding), the form of which is reminiscent of Venetian glassware; its sides are decorated with short, fine, stamped striations. Before 1540 Baier produced, in collaboration with Flötner, what is probably his most important work, a silver-mounted coconut goblet commissioned by the Holzschuher von Asbach family of Nuremberg (Nuremberg, Ger. Nmus.). The models for the gold figures were made by Flötner, who also carved the coconut shell. Baier cast the superbly chased figural and ornamental parts. Further works, mainly ceremonial drinking vessels, for the Tucher von Simmelsdorf family and the Scheurl von Defersdorf family and for the council of Nuremberg are mentioned in documents.

Several other miscellaneous important pieces are preserved. On a coin-decorated goblet dating from 1534 (Padua, Mus. Civ.) Baier used 45 ancient Roman silver *denarii*. The structure of the goblet is in the Renaissance style, and the surface is embellished with stamped grooves. For an agate bowl (1536; Munich, Residenz) Baier produced the richly ornamented circular foot and emphasized the bizarre shape of the gemstone with delicate gold clasps and a lid ornamented with designs in relief. Around 1538 he produced the mounts for another coconut goblet (Vienna, Ksthist. Mus.), also carved by Peter Flötner. A shallow bowl on a round foot, with escutcheons at the centre and large bulges at its edges (Munich, Residenz), probably dates from after 1541. Baier was undoubtedly one of the most important German goldsmiths before the Renaissance period.

Nürnberg 1300–1550, Kunst der Gotik und Renaissance (exh. cat., Nuremberg, Ger. Nmus., 1986), pp. 451–4

Bail. Hoop or half-hoop or ring, often used to denote a handle on a cradle or basketwork, or the hoop-handle of a kettle, or the handles on furniture brasses.

Baillie Scott, M(ackay) H(ugh) (*b* Ramsgate, 23 Oct 1865; *d* Brighton, 10 Feb 1945). English architect, interior designer, garden designer and writer. He was a leading member of the ARTS AND CRAFTS MOVEMENT in Britain. Baillie Scott's most important contribution to the movement was a new kind of open planning in domestic architecture that led to the elimination of Victorian parlours. These he replaced with a living-room, a space he often called the 'houseplace'. The space is closely interrelated to adjacent dining, study and sleeping areas, which were made subordinate. The focal point of these spaces is invariably an immense fireplace surrounded by built-in furniture and often covered by a projecting copper repoussé overmantel emblazoned with a heart, meant to symbolize the very 'heart' of the house. In his planning in terms of areas and levels rather than rooms and floors, he was a pioneer of Modernism. This originality was complemented by furniture and interior design. His simplified, usually box-like furniture eliminated any hint of classical or medieval ornament and usually features, as do his wallpaper designs and bas-relief friezes, brilliant pure colour similar to that used by van Gogh and Gauguin with the dominant floral and faunal symbolism characteristic of the period. For a number of years his furniture was mass produced by J. P. White in Bedford and a number of designs were executed by Ashbee's Guild and School of Handicraft or by German Werkstätten.

ODNB

J. D. Kornwolf: *M. H. Baillie Scott and the Arts and Crafts Movement: Pioneers of Modern Design* (Baltimore and London, 1972)

G. Zelleke: 'Harmonizing Form and Function: Mackay Hugh Baillie Scott and the Transformation of the Upright Piano', *A. Inst. Chicago Mus. Stud.*, 19 (1993), 161–73

M. H. Scott Baillie: ladies' drawing-room, Waldbühl, Uzwil, 1908–14

D. Haigh: *Baillie Scott: The Artistic House* (1995)

G. Breuer: *Haus eines Kunstfreundes: Mackay Hugh Baillie Scott, Charles Rennie Mackintosh, Leopold Bauer* (2002)

Bakalowits. Austrian glass retailer E[lias] Bakalowits & Söhne was established in Vienna in 1845. Inspired by LOUIS COMFORT TIFFANY, Bakalowits designed iridescent glass, which was manufactured by Lötz. The company's designers included KOLO MOSER, Joseph Maria Olbrich (1867–1908) and the architect Emil Hoppe (1876–1957). The company is now best known for its crystal chandeliers. In 1955 it began to manufacture architectural lighting for Viennese buildings that had been damaged during World War II. The company is now known in English as Bakalowits Light Design and in German as Bakalowits Licht Design.

D. Micucci: 'Antiques: Modern Austrian Glass', *Archit. Dig.*, lii (May 1995), pp. 142–7

Bakelite. *See under* PLASTIC.

Bakewell, Robert (*b* Uttoxeter, 1682; *bur* ?Derby, 31 Oct 1752). English metalworker. The son of a blacksmith, in 1700 Bakewell made railings for a house in St James's Place, London (*in situ*), belonging to Thomas Coke, Vice-Chamberlain to Queen Anne and King George I. He subsequently received a second commission from Coke for a garden arbour at Melbourne Hall, Coke's country house in Derbyshire (*in situ*); Bakewell opened his forge in a house opposite the hall in 1707. The arbour, which is Bakewell's best-known work, was completed in 1711; the panels of the cupola are filled with delicate scrollwork, with oak and laurel leaves at the front. The decorative elements are quite restrained and representative of the trend towards simplification of design in early 18th-century English ironwork. In 1711 Bakewell was employed by the Earl of Cholmondeley to make staircase rails and banisters for Cholmondeley Castle, Cheshire (*in situ*). In the 1720s and 1730s Bakewell completed numerous commissions for screens, gates and balustrades for buildings in Derbyshire; such works as the church furnishings (1725) of All Saints' Cathedral (*in situ*), Derby, include decoration of swirling acanthus and delicate scrolls and foliage characteristic of his work. From 1744 to 1746 he produced seven iron gates for the Radcliffe Camera, Oxford (*in situ*). Although little of Bakewell's work is signed, it is much better documented than that of his contemporaries, partly due to his distinctive style and use of motifs.

S. Dunkerley: *Robert Bakewell: Artist, Blacksmith* (Cromford, 1988)

Bakewell & Co. American glass factory founded in Pittsburgh, PA, by Edward Ensell and purchased by Benjamin Bakewell (1767–1844) and Benjamin Page in 1808. Its prominent role in the development of the American tableware industry in the 19th century made it the most famous glasshouse in Pittsburgh.

Bakewell's glasshouse produced the first successful lead crystal in America; it made the first American table glass ordered for the White House by Presidents James Monroe (1817, untraced) and Andrew Jackson (1829, White House Collection, Washington DC), and it held the first recorded American patent for pressed glass (1825). The firm established Pittsburgh's reputation for high-quality engraved glass. In addition to table glass, the factory produced tubes for table lamps, globes, lanterns and apothecary's equipment. Its glassware was free-blown, mould-blown, pressed lacy, pattern-moulded or cut and engraved. The factory closed in 1882.

L. Innes: *Pittsburgh Glass, 1797–1891* (Boston, 1976)
A. M. Palmer: *Artistry and Innovation in Pittsburgh Glass, 1808–1882: From Bakewell & Ensell to Bakewell, Pears & Co.* (Pittsburgh, 2004)

Baldachin [baldquin]. *See* BAUDEKIN.

Balin, Paul (*b* Paris; *fl* 1861; *d* Paris, 1898). French wallpaper manufacturer. He was an apprentice at the Desfossé factory from 1861 to 1863 when he took over the Genoux & Cie factory at 236 Faubourg Saint-Antoine, Paris, and ran it with his brother until 1868, and then on his own until 1898. Between 1866 and 1869 he began and completed proceedings to take out a patent on stamped wallpapers. He used powerful *balanciers*, a special type of press that enabled him to produce wallpaper in relief, imitating with unrivalled perfection the very stuff of the materials he copied, such as Cordovan leather or historic textiles from his own collection. Some of his luxury printed and stamped wallpapers were shown in 1873 at the Weltausstellung ('Universal exhibition') in Vienna where they attracted a great deal of attention. His career was dogged by financial difficulties. From 1877 he launched a series of court cases against various competitors for unauthorized imitation before committing suicide in 1898. His business was taken over by the Alfred Hans factory. Examples of Balin's production have been preserved in the Musée des Arts Décoratifs, Paris, in the Victoria and Albert Museum and the Sanderson collection, London, and in the Musée du Papier Peint, Rixheim, which also has an extensive dossier on Balin's court cases.

Ball, Tompkins & Black. American silversmiths, active in New York. The company was founded by the silversmith Isaac Marquand in 1810, and traded as Marquand & Co. In 1839 the company was bought by Henry Ball, Erasus Tompkins and William Black, and was known as Ball, Tompkins & Black until 1851, when it became Ball, Black & Company. In 1876 new partners entered the company, which became Black, Starr & Frost, the name under which it now trades; from 1940 to 1962 there was a partnership between Black, Starr & Frost and The Gorham Manufacturing Company, and the retailer's mark changed to Black Starr Frost Gorham Inc. The company has been a retailer rather than a manufacturer for most of its history; some of its finest products were made in the workshop of JOHN CHANDLER MOORE.

Balla, Giacomo (*b* Turin, 18 Aug 1871; *d* Rome, 1 March 1958). Italian Futurist painter, sculptor, stage designer, decorative artist and actor. He supplied an effervescent stage set and designed the lighting for Stravinsky's *Feu d'artifice* (1917; Milan, Mus. Teat. alla Scala) and the furniture and décor for the *Bal Tik-Tak* (1921; Rome, priv. col.). He also invented a particularly functional stage design with revolving panels and mobile floors that allowed for continuous and simultaneous action without intervals. In such interdisciplinary and collaborative works Balla unified all the visual arts. In the same way he designed luminous ties and brightly coloured suits and furniture (e.g. designs for a Children's Room, 1920; Rome, priv. Col.) whose cheerfulness and playfulness contrasted with the boring solemnity of traditional furnishings. Balla also worked on graphics for advertising and, following the example of Luigi Russolo, on musical instruments; he also made ceramics at ALBISOLA.

S. B. Robinson and G. Balla: *Giacomo Balla, Divisionism and Futurism, 1871–1912* (1981)
M. Fagiolo dell'Arco and G. Balla: *Balla: The Futurist* (New York, 1988)
Giacomo Balla: Abstract Futurism: June 8 to July 14, 1995 (exh. cat. by P. Baldacci, G. Balla and M. Fagiolo dell'Arco; New York, Paolo Baldacci Gal., 1995)

Ball clay. Fine-textured clay, found mainly in southwestern England (Devon and Dorset), which is used in the manufacture of earthenware. It was so called because it was transported to the potteries of Staffordshire in balls.

Ball foot. Round furniture foot, more spherical than a BUN FOOT, common in late 17th-century and 18th-century furniture.

Ballin. French family of goldsmiths and bronze-founders. Members of the Ballin family were active in Paris from the 16th century to the 18th. Claude Ballin I (*b* Paris, 3 May 1615; *d* Paris, 22 May 1678) became a master goldsmith in 1637. He was granted lodgings in the Louvre, Paris, before 1671 and became Orfèvre Ordinaire du Roi. Nicknamed 'the Great Ballin', he was one of the most prominent French goldsmiths of the 17th century. He worked extensively for Louis XIV (*reg* 1643–1715), providing an enormous quantity of silver and silver-gilt objects, including vases, bowls, display stands and incense-burners that formed part of the silver furnishings (destr. 1690) of the château of Versailles. Ballin's work in the classical style also included ecclesiastical pieces (untraced) for the cathedrals of Paris and Reims that are known from numerous drawings (Berlin, Kstbib. & Mus.; Stockholm, Nmus.; Beauvais, Archvs Dépt.), and which also feature in some wall-hangings, for example the *History of the King* and the *Royal Houses*. Some of his works influenced the bronzework of André-Charles Boulle. Ballin was succeeded in his appointment as Orfèvre Ordinaire du Roi by Nicolas de Launay, his nephew by marriage.

Claude Ballin II (*b* Paris, 1661; *d* Paris, 18 March 1754) was the nephew of Claude Ballin I, son of the painter Michel Ballin and brother-in-law of Nicolas de Launay, with whom he worked at the Louvre, Paris. He became a master goldsmith on 26 August 1688 and also became Premier Orfèvre Ordinaire du Roi. He had an exceptionally long career, although few of his works survive. His earliest work is a silver-gilt monstrance (1707; destr.) for the cathedral of Notre-Dame, Paris. Pieces (Munich, Residenzmus.) made by him between 1712 and 1713 bearing the coat of arms of Maximilian II Emanuel, Elector of Bavaria, are typical examples of the Louis XIV classical style, while the centrepieces for Peter I, Tsar and Emperor of Russia (1725–7; St Petersburg, Hermitage) signify the development of the Louis XV style in Ballin's work.

Claude Ballin II also worked for Louis XV (*reg* 1715–74): he worked on several important dinner services, notably the 'Gold Plate' (1727), the Choisy Service (1740–41) and the Versailles Officers Service (1750), and in 1733 he also supplied a travelling set. Among his clients were the most important French and foreign patrons, including Prince Eugène of Savoy, as well as members of the Spanish, Portuguese, Austrian, Russian, Danish, Saxon and Bavarian courts. Claude Ballin II also made several bronze pieces and modified designs for bronzework by the sculptor Corneille van Clève (1646–1732) for execution by Nicolas de Launay, including a pair of candlesticks (London, Wallace) depicting a man and a woman each supporting an infant. Jacques Ballin (*b* Paris, 1700; *d* Paris, 8 March 1764) was the son, pupil and collaborator of Claude Ballin II. He became a master goldsmith on 12 December 1750, was granted lodgings in the Louvre, Paris, and became Orfèvre Ordinaire du Roi. At the end of the 1750s he worked with François-Thomas Germain (1726–91) on plate for Joseph, King of Portugal (*reg* 1750–77).

C. Hernmarck: 'Claude Ballin et quelques dessins de pièces d'argenterie du Musée national de Stockholm', *Gaz. B.-A.*, xli/5 (1953), pp. 103–18

Ballin, (Francesco) Mogens (Hendrik) (*b* Copenhagen, 9 March 1871; *d* Copenhagen, 28 Jan 1941). Danish painter and metalworker. In his early career he worked as a painter, but in 1893 he converted from Judaism to Catholicism. He became interested in religious artefacts and abandoned painting for metalwork. In 1899 he opened a metal workshop with the sculptor Siegfried Wagner (1874–1952), which later became important to such Danish silversmiths as Georg Jensen and Just Andersen (1884–1943). Ballin specialized in works in pewter and silver, and his metal pieces are among the Danish works closest to international Art Nouveau: he combined its arabesque forms with simple, taut linear ornament. His importance lies in his encouragement of good design in less expensive materials (e.g. his simple pewter dish, *c.* 1899–1907; Stockholm Nmus.). He wanted to create a people's art which, following the principles of William Morris, would be a real handicraft and not machine work. Pewter was his favourite material, and he chased and beat it to highly textural effect, sometimes combining it with other metals, as in the pewter and brass christening font he made with Siegfried Wagner in 1899 for Hellerup church. In 1907 Ballin sold his workshop in order to work as an instructor at Copenhagen's Catholic high school.

Baltimore. American centre of furniture production. In the early 19th century Baltimore, MD, emerged as an important centre for the design and production of furniture. From 1800 until 1812, when the war with England cut off imports, Baltimore cabinetmakers satisfied new patronage with elegant Federal style interpretations of Hepplewhite and Sheraton designs. They specialized in marquetry and inlay using colourful contrasts of flame grains with lustrous satin-wood in swags, bellflowers, cross-banding, urns and eagles. Painters applied fancy designs in black-and-gold on red and yellow grounds. The most elaborate examples also used *verre eglomisé* panels set into the frame of a table or the prospect door of a secretary desk. The foremost practitioners of these techniques included John Finlay (1777–1851) and Hugh Finlay (1781–1831), who advertised 'Elegant Fancy Japanned Furniture'. Another was William Camp (1773–1822), who was trained in Philadelphia, moved to Baltimore in 1801 and by 1809 ran the largest shop in the city. Furniture attributed to Camp and his workshop represents the range of design and technical competence achieved by Baltimore furniture-makers during the period 1790 to 1812.

W. V. Elder: *Baltimore Painted Furniture, 1800–1840* (Baltimore, 1972)

F. J. Puig and M. Conforti: *The American Craftsman and the European Tradition, 1620–1820* (Minneapolis, 1989)

L. Humphries: 'Provenance, Patronage, and Perception: The Morris Suite of Baltimore Painted Furniture', *Amer. Furn.*, (2003), pp. 138–212

Baltic chest. Type of 16th-century chest carved with religious scenes that reflect Protestant sensibilities. Most surviving examples are in England, but the chests may have been manufactured in Baltic Hanse cities for the English market. Baltic chests are sometimes distinguished from NONESUCH CHESTS, but the term is sometimes used to denote both types of chest.

Baluster. Short pillar or column, of circular section and curving outline (properly, double-curved), slender above and swelling below into an elliptical or pear-shaped bulge; usually applied in a series called a 'balustrade'. In older usage, the plural can denote the upright posts or rails that support the handrail of a staircase, and could be applied to the whole structure of uprights and handrail; in this sense the term has been supplanted by 'banister'. The term is often used in the transferred sense of 'having the shape of a baluster', as in baluster handle, jug, pitcher, stem or vase.

Balustrade. *See* BALUSTER.

Balzac, **Edmé Pierre** (*fl* 1739–*c*. 1781). French silversmith in the service of the crown, active in Paris. His works include tureens (e.g. of 1757–8; New York, Met.) with covers modelled with figures of hounds attacking a stag. His younger brother Jean-François Balzac was also a silversmith in royal service.

Bamboo. Common name given to members of the variety *Bambuseae* of the grass family (*Gramineae*), found mainly in tropical and sub-tropical regions; some 76 genera and over 1000 species have been described.

Bamboo is an extremely versatile material that has a wide variety of uses in Africa, Asia and South America, including arms and armour, basketry, furniture making and paper making. Bamboo has long been associated with the arts in East Asia, where it is both the raw material for the implements of calligraphers and painters and a popular theme in literati ink-painting. As a decorative motif, it is ubiquitous, being found on lacquerware, metalwork and ceramics.

One of the most common and widespread uses of bamboo is for making containers. These come in two forms: those made from a segment or segments of a cane, retaining the internodal septum to form a bottom, as in the brushpots of East Asia, and baskets made from woven canes. Bamboo is carved into decorative and functional objects, ranging from pipes in Vietnam to *netsuke* in Japan. The Toba Batak of northern Sumatra use bamboo containers decorated with incised texts of divination, spells and magic formulae in Batak language and script, and with geometric designs. The Toraja and other South-east Asian groups decorate containers similarly with incised geometric patterns accentuated with pigment. These containers are sometimes fitted with carved hardwood stoppers bound with intricately woven rattan bands and mounted with carved horn or wood hangers.

The flexibility of bamboo makes it an ideal material for bows, which can be made from simple, split and shaped poles, such as those used in New Guinea, or complex laminates, such as Japanese *kyūdō* ('way of the bow', traditional Japanese archery) bows. Arrows and quivers are also made of bamboo. Bamboo clappers, rattles, slit gongs and Jews' harps are made in several parts of Asia. The *angklung* is a rattle found only in West Java, Indonesia. It is composed of two bamboo tubes in a bamboo frame, which emit a single note when shaken. The most common instrument made from bamboo is the pipe or flute, an example of which is the multi-piped mouth organ. The double clarinet is found in countries as far apart as Brazil, among the Dayak people of Borneo and India. Bamboo flutes, end blown (known in Japan as *shakuhachi*) and side blown (Chin. *dizi*; Jap. *fuye*) are found in many regions. Before the invention of paper, books were made of bamboo tablets and silk; bamboo is also used as a raw material for making paper. Other common uses include equipment for

Coffer with bamboo design, gold, silver and lacquer, Japan, Edo period, late 17th century–early 18th (London, Victoria and Albert Museum)

sports and games (e.g. polo sticks, mahjong sets) and shipbuilding (e.g. masts, spars and other fittings, as well as whole rafts) and even for clothing. Bamboo furniture is common virtually throughout the world.

In southern and western China, where some 250 varieties exist, bamboo is widely used for furniture and domestic articles. Tiny low stools, low chairs with high backs, slatted reclining chairs, beds and children's chairs and perambulators, or walking frames, are made, often out of the decorative black-spotted bamboo. Mats of all sorts (often woven in attractive patterns from coloured strips), baskets, fish-traps, woven frames for carrying small children on the back, and cooking steamers, strainers and scoops of all sizes are made from bamboo. These are rarely carved, but the bamboo bases of birdcages often had small sections carved with floral motifs; wrist-rests and brushpots for calligraphers were often made of bamboo carved with floral motifs or inscribed.

G. Walking: *Antique Bamboo Furniture* (London, 1979)
K. Ueda, R. Austin and D. Levy: *Bamboo* (Tokyo, 1981)
D. Farrelly: *The Book of Bamboo* (San Francisco, 1984)
N. Berliner and S. Handler: *Friends of the House: Furniture from China's Towns and Villages* (Salem, 1995)
Design and Manufacture of Bamboo and Rattan Furniture (Vienna, 1996)
C. Clunas and I. Thomas: *Chinese Furniture* (London, 1997)

Bampi, Richard (*b* 1896; *d* 1965). German potter who after an early career as a sculptor established a pottery workshop in Kandern. Initially he made pottery statuettes, and then cubist vases. In the 1940s he became interested in East Asian (especially Japanese) glazes, and *c.* 1950 became the first German potter to produce asymmetrical work with experimental viscous glazes and broken, irregular surface textures.

M. Schüly and R. Bampi: *Richard Bampi: Keramiker der Moderne* (Stuttgart, 1993)

Band. In woven textiles a distinction is drawn between stripes (in the direction of the warp) and bands (in the direction of the weft)

Bandelwerk. Ornamental motif (derived from STRAPWORK) of interlaced bands, used in early 18th-century Germany on furniture, metalwork and pottery.

Banderol [banderole; bandrol; bannerol]. Small flag or streamer with a cleft end, variously flown on the mast-heads of ships, hung from trumpets, and carried in battle attached to the lance of a knight; the term also denotes a ribbon-like scroll bearing a device or inscription, and the banners placed over coffins at funerals.

Bandhana. Hindi term for 'tie and dye', a mode of dyeing in which knots are tied in the fabric to prevent knotted parts from absorbing the dye. The term was imported into Europe (with the spelling bandana or bandanna) to denote a richly coloured silk handkerchief, with spots left white or yellow by the process described above; the term is now applied to cotton handkerchiefs and headscarves.

Banding. In furniture, a decorative effect achieved by using thin bands or strips of contrasting woods to finish off the edges. Straight banding is cut along the length of the grain and cross-banding across the grain. Feather-banding or herringbone banding may be cut diagonally across the grain, but may also be constructed by using two bands of veneer with grains in opposing directions.

Bang, Hieronymus (*b* 1553; *d* 1630). German goldsmith from Osnabrück who worked from 1588 in Nuremberg. His prints of ornamental designs include GROTESQUES for cups and beakers.

F. Lipperheide: *Hieronymus Bang* (Nuremberg, 1999)

Banko. Japanese centre of pottery and porcelain production. Kilns were established in the mid-18th century in Ise Province (Mie Prefecture); production eventually spread as far as Edo (now Tokyo); '*banko*', which was imprinted on the seals, means 'eternal'. In the 18th century the area produced raku ware and Satsuma types and decorative patterns taken from Ming Dynasty red and green porcelain. The rise in the use of steeped tea (*sencha*) in the 19th century opened the way for the introduction to Japan of a new type of unglazed ceramic, *zisha* (Chin. 'purple sand') ware from China. Teapots of this fine, hard stoneware were first imported through Nagasaki, but soon domestic production took over the bulk of demand, and the finest examples were produced at the Banko kilns.

B. Till: *The Whimsical World of Japanese Banko Ceramics* (Victoria, BC, 2000)

Banquette. In furniture, an upholstered bench-like seat, originally French, usually on six or more legs; a *banquette de croisée* is a banquette designed as a window seat. In military usage, a banquette is a raised platform running along the inside of a rampart or parapet, or bottom of a trench, on which soldiers stand to fire at the enemy.

Bantam work. Carved and painted work that imitates COROMANDEL LACQUER; the name derives from Bantam, the Dutch trading settlement in Java through which Japanese lacquer was imported. In early usage the term sometimes denoted genuine imports, but now is used to denote English imitations made in the late 17th century.

Baranówka Porcelain Factory. Porcelain manufactory in Volhynia founded by Michael Mezer in 1801;

Baranówka was then in Poland, which had been annexed by Russia, so it was an imperial factory; Baranówka is now in the Ukraine. The products of the factory, particularly its porcelain Easter eggs, resemble those of the St Petersburg Porcelain Factory, with which it competed. Its factory mark, spelt 'Baranovka', is often adjacent to the double eagle of the Russian empire.

U. Jastrzembska: *Porcelana polska: Korzec i Baranówka: katalog* (Malbork, 1973)

Barbedienne, Ferdinand (*b* Saint-Martin-de-Fresnay, Calvados, 10 Jan 1810; *d* Paris, 21 March 1892). French metalworker and manufacturer. After an early career as a manufacturer of wallpaper, he changed professions in 1838 and became a founder. He went into partnership with Achille Collas (1795–1859), who had invented a method for making reductions of sculpture. The firm, called Collas & Barbedienne, specialized in reproductions of antique and modern sculpture. By 1850 the firm was also producing a wide range of decorative objects—chandeliers, vases and furniture—in a variety of revival styles (e.g. Néo-Grec, Gothic and Louis XVI). Between 1850 and 1854 the firm, by then known as Barbedienne, provided furnishings in the Renaissance Revival style for the Hôtel de Ville, Paris. Some of Barbedienne's finest work is in enamel (e.g. gilt metal vase with champlevé enamel, *c.* 1862; London, V&A). The business was carried on by his nephew after his death.

F. Barbedienne: *Catalogue des bronzes d'art* (Chicago, 2002)
F. Rionnet: 'Barbedienne et la naissance de l'art industriel', *Conn. A.*, dcxiii (Feb 2004), pp. 84–9

Barberini Tapestry Workshop [Arazzeria Barberini]. In 1625 Cardinal Francesco Barberini (1597–1679) visited France, where King Louis XIII gave him seven tapestries, designed by Peter Paul Rubens (1577–1640), of scenes from the *History of Constantine* (1623–5; Philadelphia, PA, Mus. A.). After his return to Italy he founded a tapestry factory, the Arazzeria Barberini, at the Palazzo Barberini in Rome. The factory, which operated from 1627 to 1683, produced the *History of Constantine* cycle (1630–41; Philadelphia, PA, Mus. A.) by Pietro da Cortona (1596–1669), its six designs complementing the series by Rubens. The factory also produced series on the *Life of Christ* (1643–56; Cathedral of St John the Divine, New York; two were damaged in the fire of 2002) and on the *Life of Pope Urban VIII* (1663–83, now divided between the Musées Royaux d'Art et d'Histoire, Brussels, and Museum for Fine Arts, Boston, MA).

E. S. Garfinkle: *The Barberini and the New Christian Empire: A Study of the History of Constantine Tapestries by Pietro da Cortona* (MA thesis, Montreal, McGill U., 2002)

Barber's basin. Round metal dish with a broad edge having a semicircular opening for the neck, so as to allow the chin to reach into the bowl while being

Ferdinand Barbedienne: mirror, gilt bronze, *c.* 1878 (Paris, Musée d'Orsay)

shaved. The basins were usually made of pottery or pewter; sometimes they were hung outside as a barber's sign.

Barbizet, Maison. *See* MAISON BARBIZET.

Barbotine. Thin creamy mixture of kaolin clay used to ornament pottery; the term also denotes pottery ornamented with barbotine. Barbotine was used in late antiquity in Rhenish potteries. In the 1870s the use of barbotine was revived by ERNEST CHAPLET, who developed an underglaze technique called *procès barbotine*. In the USA its greatest exponent was MARY LOUISE MCLAUGHLIN.

Barco y Minusca, Gabriel del (*b* Sigüenza, Spain, 1649; *d* ?Lisbon, *c.* 1703). Portuguese tile painter of Spanish origin. He arrived in Lisbon in 1669 and began his career as a decorative painter in the workshop milieu of the city. From 1690 he confined himself to the painting of *azulejos* (glazed tiles). He contributed to the development of a monumental conception of figured panels and to the use of cobalt blue as the characteristic colour for Portuguese tiles. He developed the use of *azulejos* to form a unified pictorial design and created a repertory of decorative elements such as friezes of vases, flowers, single motif tiles and patterns. His important works include panels with scenes from the *Life of St John the Baptist* (1691) in a chapel at Barcarena, near Deiras. The magnificent wall coverings in the nave of S Vitor, Braga, depict saints from the Minho and Galiza and saints who were bishops of Braga. In the sanctuary are scenes from the *Life of St Vitor* (1692), all of which are surrounded with borders of Baroque foliage.

Barco decorated the nave walls of the church of Santiago, Évora, with panels showing scenes from the Old Testament and New Testament (1699–1700), which are also framed with bands of Baroque foliage. The frames and decorative elements were inspired by the designs and borders of 17th-century Flemish tapestries. He provided panels for the church of the Lóios, Arraiolos, which completely cover the interior of the building; those in the nave show scenes, arranged on three levels, from the *Lives of the Canons of the Order of St John the Evangelist* (1700). His best-known secular work is the vast panoramic *View of Lisbon* (Lisbon, Mus. Azulejo). Among his most important decorative works are the *azulejos* from the Palácio Tancos, Lisbon, where two rooms are decorated with Baroque compositions, of which the ornament of volutes and swags of flowers and foliage derive from painted ceiling decoration.

J. Meco: 'Azulejos de Gabriel del Barco na região de Lisboa', *Bol. Cult. Assembl. Distr. Lisboa*, lxxxv (1979), pp. 69–124

J. Meco: 'O pintor de azulejos Gabriel del Barco', *Hist. & Soc.*, vi (1979), pp. 58–67; vii (1981), pp. 41–9

Bargello work. Type of embroidery worked in flame stitch patterns in a single graduated colour, several examples of which (worked on silk) could formerly be seen at the Bargello in Florence; it is also known as Hungarian point or Hungarian stitch. In England crewel was customarily used instead of silk.

Barili, Antonio [Antonio di Neri] (*b* 1453; *d* 1516). Italian intarsia designer, civil engineer, architect and engraver, was a native of Siena. From 1483 to 1502 he worked in Siena Cathedral, providing carving and intarsia for the choir-stalls in the chapel of San Giovanni (1483–1502; seven panels survive in La Collegiata in San Quirico d'Orcia and one in the Kunstgewerbemuseum in Vienna) and building the benches for the Piccolomini library (1496) and the cathedral's organ case, organ loft and cantoria (1510). He also built the choir-stalls in S Maria Nuova in Fano (1484–9; 19 survive in the church).

Antonio's nephew Giovanni Barili (*d c.* 1529) worked as his assistant until 1514 and then settled in Rome, where his work included the implementation of Raphael's designs for doors and door-cases in the Vatican *Stanze*.

Bark cloth. Unwoven cloth made from the bast (inner bark) of a tree. It is also known as '*tapa*', with reference to the Polynesian bark cloth made from the bark of the paper mulberry and used for clothing. There is a huge collection of Polynesian bark cloth in the Bernice Pauahi Bishop Museum in Honolulu.

In sub-Saharan Africa bark cloth was traditionally decorated with free-hand painting applied with grass brushes, and was used for room-dividers and screens as well as clothing. Its widest application was in Japan, where bark cloth was used for windows, screens, kites, flags and umbrellas.

L. Terrell and J. Terrell: *Patterns of Paradise: The Styles of Bark Cloth around the World* (Chicago, 1980)

M. J. Pritchard: *Siapo: Bark Cloth Art of Samoa* (Samoa, 1984)

D. R. Severson: *Specimens of Polynesian Tapa Assembled from Various Institutions and Private Collections* (Honolulu, 1984)

J. Frederick: 'Lacandon Maya Bark Cloth: Hu'un', *Hand Papermaking*, xix/2 (Winter 2004), pp. 23–30

Barker, Benjamin. (*b* Pontypool, 1776; *d* Totnes, 28 Feb 1838). Painter and printmaker born into an English family of artists who worked in Bath. He painted (along with his sons) landscape scenes for the trays produced by the Pontypool japanning factory.

Barnsley. English family of furniture designers and artist-craftsmen. Ernest (1863–1926) and his brother

Kavat mask made by the Baining people of New Britain, Papua New Guinea, wood and bark cloth, h. 1.14 m, 1988 (Newark, NJ, Newark Museum)

Sidney (1865–1926) worked with ERNEST GIMSON in the design and construction of furniture in the tradition of the Arts and Crafts Movement. Sidney's son Edward (1900–87) carried on the business at a shop established in Froxfield (Petersfield, Hants) in 1923 and still manufacturing hand-made furniture.

A. Carruthers and E. Barnsley: *Edward Barnsley and His Workshop: Arts and Crafts in the Twentieth Century* (Wendlebury, 1992)

Barovier. Italian family of glassmakers. The family are recorded as working in Murano, Venice, as early as 1324, when Iacobello Barovier and his sons Antonio Barovier and Bartolomeo Barovier (*b* Murano, ?1315; *d* Murano, 1380) were working there as glassmakers. The line of descent through Viviano Barovier (*b* Murano, 1345; *d* Murano, 1399) to Iacobo Barovier (*b* Murano, ?1380; *d* Murano, 1457) led to the more noteworthy Barovier family members of the Renaissance. Iacobo was responsible for public commissions in Murano from 1425 to 1450. From as early as 1420 he was a kiln overseer, with a determining influence on the fortunes of the Barovier family.

During the 15th century Iacobo's sons, notably Angelo Barovier (*b* Murano, ?1400; *d* Murano, 1460), and his sons Giovanni Barovier, Maria Barovier and Marino Barovier (*b* Murano, before 1431; *d* Murano, 1485) were important glassmakers. From as early as 1441 Angelo owned a glass furnace. As a pupil of the philosopher Paolo da Pergola, he gained a scientific education, which, together with the empirical nature of his trade, enabled him to invent *cristallo* (*c.* 1450) and probably *lattimo* (milk) and chalcedony glass. In 1455 he was a guest at the court of the Sforza family in Milan, and in 1459 he was invited, without success, to work for the Medici family in Florence. His son Marino worked with him in 1455 at the Sforza court, where he met Antonio Filarete, who referred to both father and son in his *Trattato di architettura* (1461–4). After his father's death, Marino inherited the furnaces in Murano. As a steward of the glassworkers' craft (1468, 1482), he was active in the promotion and defence of Muranese glassworking. During the 16th century one of Marino's sons, Angelo Barovier or Anzoleto Barovier, owned a famous glass furnace, the emblem of which was an angel. Between the 16th and 17th centuries various members of the Barovier family moved to other European countries where they continued making glass.

The family regained its former prestige during the second half of the 19th century when, in 1884, Giovanni Barovier (*b* Murano, 1839; *d* Murano, 1908) and his nephews Giuseppe Barovier (*b* Murano, 1853; *d* Murano, 1942) and Benvenuto Barovier (*b* Murano, 1855; *d* Murano, 1931) became proprietors of the glassworks of Antonio Salviati (1816–90). During the 20th century Giuseppe created Art Nouveau wares. Ercole Barovier (*b* Murano, 1889; *d* Venice, 1974) was a noteworthy designer during the 1920s, and, together with the brothers Artemio Toso and Decio Toso, he established Barovier

& Toso, which is the present name of the company. Both families are still involved: the president is now Giovanni Toso, and the chief executive Jacopo Barovier. In the post-war years a variety of new glass techniques has been developed, including wares in *vetro diafono* (e.g. bowl and vase, *c.* 1975; Venice, Barovier & Toso, col.).

In 1995 the Company opened a museum which is primarily a collection of glass since 1880, but also contains the late 15th-century 'Barovier Wedding Cup', a blue enamelled cup that is one of the finest surviving glass pieces of the Renaissance.

D. R. McFadden and others: *Venetian Glass* (New York, 2000)
R. Barovier Mentasti: *Glass throughout Time: History and Technique of Glassmaking from the Ancient World to the Present* (Milan and New York, 2003)

Barr, Martin. *See under* WORCESTER.

Barry, Joseph (*b* 1760; *d* 1838). Irish-American cabinetmaker. He was a native of Dublin who trained in London before emigrating in late 1794 to Philadelphia, which was then the capital of America. In 1812 he entered into partnership with his son and advertised his 'fashionable Cabinet Furniture, superbly finished in the rich Egyptian and Gothic style'. Surviving examples of his furniture are in Neo-classical style, such as the sideboard in the Utah Museum of Fine Arts in Salt Lake City.

D. L. Fennimore and others: 'Joseph B. Barry, Philadelphia Cabinetmaker', *Mag. Ant.,* cxxxv (May 1989), pp. 1212–25
D. L. Fennimore: 'Egyptian influence in Early Nineteenth-century American Furniture', *Mag. Ant.,* cxxxvii (May 1990), pp. 1190–201
D. Ducoff-Barone: 'Philadelphia Furniture Makers, 1800–1815', *Mag. Ant.,* cxxix (May 1991), pp. 982–95

Basaltes, Black. *See under* WEDGWOOD.

Basile, Ernesto (*b* Palermo, 31 Jan 1857; *d* Palermo, 26 Aug 1932). Italian architect, teacher and designer, originator of a peculiarly Sicilian version of Art Nouveau. He was primarily an architect, but also worked in the decorative arts. His Hotel Villa Igiea (1899–1904) in Palermo is particularly important, as its main dining-room is almost the only surviving Basile interior. All the details here, including doors, mirrors and screens, are part of the overall architectural design in a manner typical of Art Nouveau, where ornament seems to be about to devour the room and its contents. Much derives from Belgian, French and English Art Nouveau; the apparently fluid, but oddly frozen forms, like cloth soaked in plaster, derive from Henry Van de Velde, and the medieval references come from William Morris and Viollet-le-Duc. Nevertheless, the mural depicting women and swans is more realistic than it would have been elsewhere, and the poppy, ubiquitous in northern versions of Art Nouveau, appears only in the capitals of columns and the doorframes. The interiors of other villas, such as the luxurious Villino Florio, owed much to

William Morris and Victor Horta. Another notable interior by Basile was for the Caffé Ferraglia (1901), Rome. By 1903, when he designed the Villino Basile, his work was marked by a new rigour: planning was stressed with clear-cut volumes and deliberate asymmetry, while decoration concentrated on wrought iron and mosaic work.

The blurring of distinctions between interior and exterior, natural and artificial are important themes in Ernesto Basile's work. They are epitomized by his designs for street furniture, which included kiosks in an Arab style seething with vegetal forms (and in which horizontal and vertical forms receive similar treatment) and garden sculpture. Much of Basile's work in Sicily has been destroyed.

G. Pirrone: 'Ernesto Basile and the Liberty Style in Palermo', *Connoisseur*, clxxxviii/757 (Mar 1975), pp. 194–201

G. Pirrone: *Villino Basile, Palermo* (Rome, 1981)

F. Amendolagine: *Villa Igiea* (Palermo, 2002)

Basketwork. Artefacts of more or less rigid construction produced by the interlacing of linear materials. Basketwork is of considerable antiquity (dating from at least 8000 BC in Egypt and Peru) and in one form or other has been practised almost everywhere in the world. Baskets are still woven in developing countries, but there have been no developments in technique since the Neolithic period. Decoration may be added to baskets in the form of painting (e.g. in Australia), feathers and beads (e.g. in California), cowrie shells (Nigeria) or strips of leather (East Africa). In South Sumatra ceremonial food baskets are sometimes coated inside and out with layers of black or red lacquer with an underlayer of gold leaf. Recent developments include baskets made of coloured plastic-coated telephone wire (southern Africa) and metal wire (the Tohono O'Odham people of southern Arizona). Although basketwork is ubiquitous, it is of particularly important in the cultures of sub-Saharan Africa and Native North America, each of which is the subject of a separate entry.

Stake and strand baskets are woven in much the same way as textiles, but without the aid of a loom. The warp and weft, which may be of different materials and widths, are interlaced at right angles to produce a fabric. The warp elements remain passive, while the weft passes actively over and under them, one row at a time. Many European willow baskets are of stake and strand construction, and the technique is found in many other parts of the world, particularly in Asia and the Americas.

Twined baskets are woven using two or more wefts at once, crossing over each other at intervals between the warps. In the simplest form of twining, two wefts cross between each warp; in wrapped twining, one weft remains passive, while the other binds it to the warps. There are particularly fine twined basketry traditions in California, on the north-west coast of North America and in Australia. Twining is found on openwork fish-traps in many parts of the world.

Plaited baskets are made with two or more sets of elements, usually all of the same material and width; there is no distinction between warp and weft, all elements being equally active. The use of three sets of elements results in a hexagonal lattice. Plaiting with palm fronds can produce a variety of interesting shapes, as seen in the baskets of the Amazon rain forest and Polynesia.

Twill effects can be produced on woven, twined and plaited baskets by passing elements over and under particular combinations of the opposing set (e.g. over two, under two) and shifting each successive row to the left or right to produce a diagonal pattern. The twilled baskets of Sarawak, Malaysia and the Amazon are particularly fine.

Rib baskets, which tend to be oval in shape, are woven over a rigid framework. They seem to be of European origin and are also made in south-eastern North America and in the West Indies.

Coiled baskets are made by a sewing process, built up spirally from the centre of the base. The two elements involved are the foundation—one or more rods or a bundle—and the sewing material, which simultaneously binds the foundation and stitches the coils together. The related technique of looping, more widely used for bags and nets, does not involve a foundation; a row of loops is first created around a holding thread, and subsequent rows link into the previous row. Coiled baskets were made in ancient Egypt and have a long history in the rest of Africa, the Middle East and the Americas; they are also made in India and the Pacific. The early tradition of coiled basketry in northern Europe (e.g. in Iceland, Scandinavia and the Orkney, Shetland and Faroe islands) has few exponents in the 21st century.

Basketwork is used primarily for making baskets, but also serves other purposes. Basketwork clothing takes the form of shoes, hats and rain-shields. Basketwork used for defence includes the body armour of Kiribati in Micronesia and the shields used by the ancient Romans, by many African tribes and by the Nagas of Nagaland in north-eastern India. Basketry is used to make blowpipe dart quivers and spear grips in tropical South America; it was also used for gun emplacements in Europe until the early 19th century and for shell-cases until World War I. Baskets have often been used ceremonially to hold shamanic equipment and medicines; they also form the basis of many masks (e.g. the female crest masks of the Jukun of Nigeria) and are used in dances. They may be given to people on special occasions, such as weddings, or buried or burnt with their owners after death.

E. Rossbach: *Baskets as Textile Art* (London, 1973)

D. Wright: *The Complete Book of Baskets and Basketry* (London, 1977/R 1983)

K. Kudo: *Japanese Bamboo Baskets* (Tokyo, New York and San Francisco, 1980)

W. Arbeit: *Baskets in Polynesia* (Honolulu, 1990)

L. Mowat, H. Morphy and P. Dransart, eds: *Basketmakers: Meaning and Form in Native American Baskets*, Oxford U., Pitt Rivers Mus., v (Oxford, 1992)

B. Sentence: *The Art of the Basket: Traditional Basketry from around the World* (New York, 2001)

I. Africa. II. Native North America.

I. Africa.

A great variety of baskets for storing food, spoons and trinkets and for serving food is made almost everywhere in Africa. In some areas, for example among the Shilluk of Sudan and the Somali, baskets are so tightly sewn that they become waterproof as the fibres swell. In these areas, therefore, baskets can be used for storing milk, water and other liquids. Winnowing baskets are often made from square mats, their corners trimmed off before they are pressed and stitched into a circular hoop. Another specialist basket is bottle-shaped, for sifting cassava flour. In Southern Africa traditional beer-making involves the use of long strainer baskets and openwork basketry spoons. Around Lake Victoria basketry drinking straws with fine sieves at the ends are used. Some large gourds and earthenware pots are reinforced with a twined basketry casing; other vessels may be encased in a basketry sling; and some have a basketry rim added for strength and decoration. Pottery and gourd vessels often have a decorative basketry lid.

Basketry techniques are used in some traditional house-building where the roof framework is of wattles, trimmed branches or stems twined with bast ties and the walls are of wattle-and-daub. Basketry is also used in making various forms of granaries, pigeon houses and chicken coops. Some houses in the Zaïre basin area and around Lake Victoria may be walled with large, screenlike mats, often patterned in black. Elsewhere others are roofed with decoratively plaited mats. In many parts of Africa, house doors are made of reeds twined together. Basketry mats are used as tent roofs among nomadic peoples in Somalia. Almost everywhere in Africa mats are used for sleeping or sitting on. In north-eastern Zaïre beds traditionally were made of mats tied on to a wooden frame. The headrests of the Turkana of Kenya have twined thongs between the legs to prevent splitting.

In some areas basketry is used to make conical fish traps, sometimes of great size; where fish poison is employed oval floating baskets are used to gather the catch. Finger-stall-shaped traps that contract and grip cane rats and other small animals have a wide distribution. In the Sahel, a special basket is used to harvest grain knocked off the plant. Large, open-mesh baskets of various forms are made for carrying tubers and other crops. Crudely made baskets are used for carrying chickens to market, while twined nets are used for stacks of pottery. Among the Lozi of Zambia and the Ndebele of Zimbabwe, basketry sleds made of wattlework on wooden runners are used for transporting bulk. In north-eastern Zaïre strong basketry shields made of split cane of palm leaf patterned in black on natural straw colour were used.

Basketry hats come in a great variety of forms, often embellished with fur, feathers, beads and tufts of raffia. In Zaïre basketry visors were used to protect the wearer's face from being cut by long, sharp grass. In Uganda basketry hoods protect a baby on its mother's back from the sun, and baby-carriers of wickerwork and wood were used in Liberia. Long ear-plugs covered with finely plaited, colourful grass were made in Uganda and Rwanda; in Mali fine straw is plaited in imitation of filigree gold; plaited bracelets of split palm leaves are made in Southern Africa. Basketry masks, though uncommon, do exist. The Chewa of Zambia make vast basketry masks, while in north-western Zambia and eastern Angola masks are made of painted barkcloth on a basketry frame.

Nearly all the materials used in African basketry are vegetable, but animal materials such as rawhide, leather and sinew are also used. In the 20th century plastic fibres from grain sacks and telephone wire were added to the range of African basketry materials.

African Furniture and Household Objects (exh. cat., ed. R. Sieber; Indianapolis, IN, Mus. A., 1980)
R. Levinsohn: *Art and Craft of Southern Africa* (Craighall, 1984)
M. Shaw: 'The Basketwork of Southern Africa: Part I. Technology', *An. S. Afr. Mus.*, c/2 (1992), pp. 53–248
T. Katzenellenbogen: 'Imbenge', *J. Mus. Ethnog.*, iv (1993), pp. 49–72
M. E. Terry and A. Cunningham: 'The Impact of Commercial Marketing on the Basketry of Southern Africa', *J. Mus. Ethnog.*, iv (1993), pp. 25–48
N. Tobert: 'Rizekat Wedding Baskets', *J. Mus. Ethnog.*, iv (1993), pp. 73–82
P. Gerdes: 'Titja Coiled Baskets', *Women, Art and Geometry in Southern Africa* (Trenton, NJ, 1998), pp. 11–19

II. Native North America.

The native American peoples of North America have made basketwork since at least *c*. 9000 BC. By *c*. 8000 BC they had invented the three basic basket-making techniques: twining, the oldest, comprises single or double wefts twisted around a group of warps; plaiting is done by weaving splints or stems over and under each other; and coiling is done with bundles of fibres or sticks bent into a spiral, then wrapped and sewn together with finer splints.

1. Arctic. 2. Subarctic. 3. Northwest Coast. 4. California and the far west. 5. Southwest. 6. Woodlands.

1. ARCTIC. Two basket techniques were used in the Arctic: hand twining and sewn coil. All Aleut basketwork is twined, using the two-strand weave technique, in which a double weft is wound around the warp strands. The baskets are suspended by a string or placed on a stake and worked upside down. The weaver weaves from bottom to top with the fine fringe of the top edge hanging down. Ornamentation is usually sewn on afterwards, using embroidery floss or coloured grasses. Inuit basketry is almost exclusively coiled. Collections of Arctic basketwork are held in Anchorage, AK (Hist. & F.A. Mus.), Vienna (Mus. Vlkerknd), Juneau, AK (State Mus.), Washington, DC (N. Mus. Amer. A.), and New York (Mus. Amer. Ind.).

(i) *Aleut*. The exact provenance of Aleut baskets is difficult to determine but is judged according to the fineness of the weave, the shape of the basket and

Basket made from split spruce roots, Tlingit culture (Chicago, IL, Field Museum of Natural History)

the style of the corners and knobs. Aleut women created baskets from wild rye grass, finely split with the fingernail. These were the most delicate baskets made in North America, and their surface texture is often compared to linen; one square inch of the basket fabric could have up to 1300 stitches. Numerous techniques were used to vary the texture of the weave: plain, open and three-element twining, crossed and divided warps, different coloured weft strands and false embroidery. The Attu women made the finest baskets of all: an example in the Alaska State Museum in Juneau has 1980 meshes to the square inch.

As early as 1805 most Aleut basketwork was created for the souvenir trade and included such basketwork products as mats, miniature baskets, pocketbooks, cigar cases and belts. Decoration most often comprised geometric designs, until the 19th century, when floral patterns became popular on items made for the tourist trade. Also in the 19th century imported raffia (fibre made from a type of palm-tree) replaced beach grass as the basic weaving material, and silk replaced reindeer hair as thread. After reaching its peak in the 1880s, Aleut basketwork became more coarse in the 20th century, and only a few skilled weavers remained.

(ii) Inuit.

(a) South Alaskan. Coiled grass basketwork, typically of cylindrical or globular shape, is a traditional Inuit craft. Most of it is made of grass or other materials with contrasting colours woven as part of the weft into the basket itself. Only in the later 20th century were baskets further embellished with imbricated or overlaid decoration in embroidery floss or raffia. Inuit twined and coiled basketry is far coarser than its Aleut counterpart. Yet, as Aleut basketwork declined, South Alaskan Inuit basketwork increased in quantity and improved in quality.

Two Alaskan archaeological sites—Bristol Bay and Cape Denbigh—yielded examples of prehistoric coiled basketwork. After European contact only a few coiled baskets were collected, even though Inuit women made hundreds of them for the souvenir trade, which developed during the gold rush of the Seward Peninsula. Traditional Inuit twined basketwork designs consisted of simple horizontal or vertical patterns, rendered in subtle contrasting colours. Coiled basket designs were also simple originally: tufts of yarn, tiny beads and natural objects, such as bird's feet, were employed in repeat patterns. The type of grass used for the weft was also changed frequently for a mottled effect. In the 1930s basketmaking became a chief source of income for South Alaskan Inuit women. Accompanying this expansion was a shift to bolder geometric designs and the use of representational motifs, especially fish, flies, crabs, dogs, birds and sleds.

Coiled basketry among the South Alaskan Inuit reached its height of sophistication during the 1960s and 1970s. Almost any subject-matter was considered suitable: yo-yos, dolls, kerosene lamps and dance fans all served as inspiration for basket shapes. Snowmobiles were used as design motifs, and basket lids were made to represent faces. Still more recently, Southwest Native American motifs were incorporated. By the 1980s most Inuit baskets produced for sale were coiled; Mary Black was well known for her grass and sealgut baskets.

(b) North Alaskan. Traditional North Alaskan baskets were made of birch-bark. Their envelope form dates back to *c.* AD 1–500. There is evidence that the western Thule people made twined baskets, but little is known about basketwork in North Alaska after European contact, except that, at some point before the 19th century, twining was abandoned for coiled basketwork techniques, learnt from the South Alaskans.

Like their South Alaskan counterparts, North Alaskan Inuit women made baskets in response to the demands of the souvenir trade. Decorated with tufts of fur, beads, small ivory carvings and imbrication, their grass coiled baskets were made in miniature and large sizes to the exclusion of any twined basketwork. However, an influenza epidemic in 1918 marked the almost complete abandonment of basketwork by North Alaskan Inuit women and a shift to the sewing of furs.

Baskets of baleen, a flexible, hornlike material found in the mouth of the baleen whale, were made for the tourist trade from 1905. Working baleen baskets takes great strength, and it is therefore men who most often make them. Using a single-rod coiling technique, in which adjacent weft strands alternate over warp strands, a six-inch diameter basket takes approximately fifty hours to finish. Two of the best-known weavers of baleen baskets are Kingoktuk and Marvine Sakvan Peter.

J. D. Ray: *Eskimo Art: Tradition and Innovation in North Alaska* (Vancouver, 1977)
J. D. Ray: *Aleut and Eskimo Art: Tradition and Innovation in South Alaska* (Seattle and London, 1981)

Interwoven Expressions: Works by Contemporary Alaska Native Basket-makers (Fairbanks, 1989)

(c) *Labradoran and Québécois.* Basketwork of the Inuit in Arctic Canada appears to have been restricted to the sewn-coil technique. At the time of early contact with Europeans, small baskets were used to store women's sewing equipment or tinder for starting fires. In the manufacture of these early baskets a foundation of dried grass, willow twigs or spruce roots was arranged in a spiral and held together by over-and-over sewing with dried grass, spruce root, willow bark or sinew. In the early 19th century Moravian missionaries in Labrador began to encourage the Inuit in their congregations to produce coiled-grass baskets and mats for sale in Europe through the mission trading operation. From that time the development of basketwork as a saleable craft spread throughout northern Labrador and neighbouring Arctic Quebec, where it has since provided a source of cash income to Inuit, mostly women.

The coiled grass plaques and baskets produced for sale display a wide variety of shapes and decorative features. Typical of the Labrador area is the frequent incorporation of zigzag openwork, a form of ornamentation probably introduced from Europe via missionaries or settlers. In Arctic Quebec, basket lids are often provided with handles that have been carved from soapstone, ivory or antler in the shape of birds or animals. Geometric patterns are commonly added to basketwork by using grasses that have natural colour variation, or else have been dyed, and also by incorporating wool, raffia, strips of black sealskin, whale sinew or black vinyl.

Grass Work of Labrador (exh. cat., ed. E. Goodridge; St John's, Mem. U. Nfld, A.G., 1979)

2. SUBARCTIC. Basketwork was important in the Subarctic before European contact. Late prehistoric sites have yielded bark basket fragments. Ethnographic evidence reveals that girls perfected basketwork skills during puberty confinement. Throughout the Subarctic, birch-bark was the primary material for containers for berry picking, storage, stone boiling, serving and eating. Bark was cut and folded, usually into rectangular-based, round-rimmed containers. The wrapped spruce-root rim was sometimes coloured in sections. Western Athapaskan bark containers were often ornamented with horizontal bands of lines or triangles scraped away to reveal the lighter inner bark (e.g. Chilcotin containers, New York, Mus. Amer. Ind.). On Algonquian containers foliate and figural motifs were created by scraping away background rather than the motifs themselves. The Naskapi made bark trays. Across the Subarctic basketwork traps were widely used with fish weirs.

Coiled basketwork was more rare. In the mid-19th century some Mackenzie and Cordillera Athapaskans coiled grass baskets (e.g. Slavey baskets, Edinburgh, Royal Scot. Mus.), as occasionally did Southern Shield Algonquians. Chilcotin and Carrier women created coiled imbricated spruce-root baskets similar to those made by the Salish.

By the late 20th century, baskets were made primarily for sale. Lower Yukon Athapaskan women coiled willow trays and baskets (e.g. Fairbanks, U. AK Mus.); and Slavey women ornamented large cylindrical birch-bark containers with porcupine quill insertion or incising (e.g. Providence, RI, Haffenraffer Mus. Anthropol.).

F. G. Speck: *Montagnais Art in Birchbark: A Circumpolar Trait* (New York, 1937)

J. Steinbright, ed.: *From Skins, Trees, Quills and Beads: The Work of Nine Athapaskans*, Institute of Alaska Native Arts (Fairbanks, 1983)

3. NORTHWEST COAST. Native American women of the Northwest Coast developed different approaches to basketwork design within three major traditions: plaited basketry, twined basketry and coiled basketry. The continuity of traditions between 18th-century and 19th-century baskets indicates that basketwork was highly conservative. Nonetheless, the late 19th century and the early 20th century were times of considerable innovation and experimentation with new materials, techniques and forms. In several regions contemporary basket-makers continue to work innovatively in long-established traditions.

Geometric design, executed within an essentially rectangular format, is characteristic of all regions of the coast and developed particularly on plaited bark baskets and mats. The definition of the field ranges from the simple placement of a single motif at the mid-point of a container wall, through stripes executed in a single colour, to a composition in two colours occupying the entire surface of a container or mat. The principal colours are black, appearing alone in contrast to the natural colour of the bark, or black and red in combination. In all regions designs sometimes incorporate optical illusion, achieved through variations in the weave. The basketwork of the Haida and Kwakiutl features design based on optical illusion without added colour, although Haida women also made mats with geometric designs in black and red. The repertory of geometric motifs is substantial, with some variation from one region to another.

Approaches to design on twined basketwork vary across the region. In the north, Tlingit twined basketwork is distinguished by bands of geometric motifs executed in false embroidery around the walls, the motifs of the upper and lower bands often identical and contrasting with motifs in a central band. Haida basketwork is similar in approach, with the decorative bands composed in solid colours or short vertical or diagonal lines created through the substitution of coloured wefts for plain. The use of false embroidery on Haida basketry is limited and appears to represent innovations by certain basket-makers in the early 20th century. In the late 19th century and early 20th twined basketwork made of cedar bark and decorated in false embroidery was produced in certain Coast Tsimshian communities, particularly Metlakatla, but this had a limited distribution. On these baskets motifs appear individually, rather than in bands. An older tradition of twined spruce-root basketwork was practised among the Gitksan; the few examples that exist show an approach to design different from that of the Tlingit and Haida; geometric motifs are applied with an overlay technique in diagonal bands (Quebec, Mus. Civilis.; Chicago, IL, Field Mus. Nat. Hist.).

The small, wrapped-twine baskets and mats that became common on the west coast of Vancouver Island and the Olympic Peninsula during the 19th century exhibit a distinctive approach to design based on concentric circles (Washington, DC, N. Mus. Nat. Hist.; Chicago, IL, Field Mus. Nat. Hist.; Quebec, Mus. Civilis.; Victoria, Royal BC Mus.). The essential technique is substitution. Motifs in strong colours—green, purple, orange and red—achieved with commerical dyes, are placed against a light background of bleached grass.

Motifs are arranged in bands encircling the basket. Baskets and mats from the early periods often have bands consisting only of coloured lines, with the colours arranged symmetrically within the band. On later baskets geometric or representative motifs appear in bands encircling the basket at the mid-point of the wall, framed above and below with bands of colour. Baskets in this tradition often have lids that are fully incorporated into the composition, with the centre of the lid a focal point of the design. Looking down at a basket, the viewer sees the design in concentric bands with the centre of the lid as the central point. The overall composition of wrapped-twine basketwork design may be derived from the composition of design on the traditional whaler's hat. In the approach to design, particularly of small containers, there are also strong correspondences with Aleut twined grass basketwork of the 19th century.

In the later 19th century and early 20th wrapped-twine baskets had bands of colour and geometric motifs. In the early 20th century the repertory of design expanded to include such representative motifs as ducks and other birds, and whaling scenes reminiscent of those on whalers' hats, and these became prominent. There was also considerable experimentation with stylized representative designs and floral patterns. From the 1890s basket-makers working in this tradition brought an innovative approach to the use of technique and the development of design.

Although there are substantial regional differences between the basketwork from Puget Sound and from the Columbia River area, the twined basketwork of these regions of the southern Northwest Coast is distinguished by an approach to design, in which motifs are arranged in vertical bands beneath a horizontal band following the line of the rim.

Contemporary Coast Salish people recognize the geometric motifs of cedar-root coiled basketwork as part of their heritage. Originally an Interior Salish tradition, coiled baskets have been found in Coast Salish homes for generations. Interior Salish basketwork design is complex, with a large repertory of geometric motifs, the composition of motifs and designs governed by rules concerning the alternation

of colour and spacing, and regionally distinct approaches to the definition of the design field. A Coast Salish style, developed in the 19th century, has, as a distinctive decorative feature, representative motifs in black or red, each built from several narrow decorative strips placed against a single coil.

G. T. Emmons: 'The Basketry of the Tlingit', *Mem. Amer. Mus. Nat. Hist.*, iii (1903), pp. 229–77

F. Boas: 'The Kwakiutl of Vancouver Island', *Mem. Amer. Mus. Nat. Hist.*, v/2 (1909), pp. 389–90

H. K. Haeberlin, J. Teit and H. Roberts: 'Coiled Basketry in British Columbia and Surrounding Regions', *Annu. Rep. Bureau Amer. Ethnol. Secretary Smithsonian Inst.* (Washington, DC, 1928), pp. 119–484

From the Tree Where the Bark Grows: North American Basket Treasures from the Peabody Museum, Harvard University (exh. cat. by J. S. Brandford, Cambridge, MA, Harvard U., Peabody Mus., 1987)

R. L. Hudson: 'Designs in Aleut Basketry', *Faces, Voices and Dreams: A Celebration of the Centennial of the Sheldon Jackson Museum, Sitka Alaska, 1888–1988*, ed. P. L. Corey (Anchorage, 1988), pp. 63–92

F. W. Porter III, ed.: *The Art of Native American Basketry: A Living Legacy* (New York, 1990)

J. Daly: *Woven History: Native American Basketry* (Vancouver, 2004)

4. CALIFORNIA AND THE FAR WEST. Like pottery and other forms of weaving, basketwork in western North America is an art traditionally practised exclusively by women. Two basket-weaving techniques dominate in the Far West: twining, in which the rigid foundation rods radiate from the basket centre like the spokes of a wheel, bound together by two or more flexible wefts passed simultaneously over and under them; and coiling, in which the foundation material spirals outward from the centre like a clockspring, bound together by sewing with a single weft element. In coiling, an awl is used to make the hole through the previous round, through which the flexible material is then passed. In western North America, coiled basketwork predominates in southern California and the Southwestern states, while twining predominates in northern California and the Northwest Coast, with a pocket of coiled basketweaving in northern Washington and southern British Columbia.

Designs in California and Far West basketwork are created primarily by variation in colour, using naturally contrasting plant fibres, dyed materials or both. Because the basket is woven in an inexorable spiral from centre to rim, it is not possible to complete a colour area at one time, as in tapestry weaving. The weaver must break off one material and shift to material of contrasting colour according to the dictates of the pattern. The design may be created either by the weft material or by an overlay that is carried simultaneously with it. In coiling, the delineation of design with overlay materials is usually called imbrication and is characteristic of the coiled basketweaving groups spanning the US–Canadian border. The use of overlay for design in twining, often called false embroidery, is prominent in northern California and the Northwest Coast.

The importance placed on basketwork decoration differs with each group. Where many types of baskets are developed to suit a variety of functions, designs are usually more elaborate on those baskets that receive lighter wear. The most highly ornamented basketwork is that involving social interaction outside the immediate family, such as dress caps, gambling trays and gift or offering baskets. In the latter types, aesthetic appreciation outweighs practical considerations of form or design.

Historically, the most elaborate schemes of ornamentation developed in the valleys and coastal regions of California, where a beneficent environment fostered larger and less nomadic populations with more leisure time and opportunity for social interaction. The contrasting simplicity of ornamentation among Great Basin tribes before the development of the curio trade correlates with the region's harsher environment, which limited population and required much more mobility in the seasonal round.

Mission macrostyle is associated with the mission peoples of southern California. Although the spheroid shape and the preference for black and brown design on light ground is distinctive to the region, the use of the curved tray and radiating or starlike patterns, which grow naturally from the coiling technique, are shared by the basketwork styles of Arizona.

Southern macrostyle is associated with the several Yokut groups, as well as Tubatulabal, Kawaiisu, Koso (Panamint) and Monache (Western Mono). The preferred coiled basket shapes include a flat tray, truncated cooking basket and collared gift basket with distinctive sharp shoulder and short cylindrical neck. Designs are usually formed by contrasting stepped rectangles, diamonds or triangles of red and black, or by outlining a red motif with black line. In both cases the black and red are separated by an intervening row of the light ground. These elements are kept small to allow multiple repetitions, arranged in horizontal, diagonal or vertical bands or band segments. Vertical and diagonal bands are often further ornamented by repeating a flaglike motif known as the 'quail plume'. Bands of simple human figures are sometimes ascribed to Euro-American influence. Most baskets combine bands of several different motifs, separated by bands of plain ground, which allows for increase of stitches as the basket expands. Often the scale of the design elements actually decreases as the basket diameter increases. This discontinuity between scale of design and form, like the multiplicity of design elements and the sharply segmented profile of the fanciest gift baskets, arises from a controlling aesthetic of variety and contrast.

Northern macrostyle is associated with groups from San Francisco north to the Canadian border and includes both twined and coiled decorated wares. Best illustrated in the literature are baskets of the Pomo, Maidu and Washoe groups, the lower Klamath River peoples, the Achomawi and Atsugewi, the Modoc of the upper Klamath and Salish imbricated coiled wares of the North-west. Preferred basket shapes include conical gathering or burden baskets, truncated conical cooking vessels and spheroid gift baskets, as well as flat gambling trays, sphe-

roid or conical hats and baby carriers. Designs are usually executed in one dark colour on a light ground—the polychrome style of the Lower Klamath River groups (Hupa, Yurok, Karok etc) representing a spectacular exception. The basic design elements employed are serrated diagonals, variously ornamented and arranged in discontinuous parallel bands or in a continuous zigzag band. Usually a single design element is repeated throughout the basket, with an interlocking and sometimes reciprocal relationship between dark pattern and light ground, and allowed to expand and contract with a basket's diameter. This approach promotes homogeneity and organic unity between shape and design, so that it is not the individual element or band that the eye perceives but the continuous web of pattern.

Some of the most innovative and complicated basketwork traditions developed at the interfaces of the three macrostyles described above. For example, the twined basketwork of the Twana on the west side of Puget Sound and the coiled basketwork of the Klickitat and other groups on the east side combine the serrated diagonal web of the Northern macrostyle with the rectilinear outlines and intricate light–dark contrasts of the Northwest Coast. To the south, Chumash basketwork combines preferences of the Mission macrostyle, such as the spheroid shape, the brown-black-light colour scheme and complete coverage of the basket with design, with other traits characteristic of the Southern macrostyle, such as the banded, cylindrical-necked gift basket, the flatter tray and the banded arrangements of diverse designs.

Even richer contrasts appear at the interface between the Southern and Northern macrostyles, since many peoples in these regions (Maidu, Washoe, Mono Lake Paiute and the Pomoan groups) make both twined and coiled baskets for different functions. For example, among these groups the conical gathering basket is always twined, while baskets used for cooking acorn mush may be twined or coiled. Among the Washoe and Paiute, Southern banded designs are conventionally applied to twined baskets, while Northern zigzag designs appear in coiling. The greatest diversity appears in basketwork of Pomoan groups, for which three different design schemes have been noted. On twined burden and cooking baskets, the Northern preference for a single dark colour and serrated zigzags is used but arranged according to the Southern scheme in contrasting and separated horizontal bands. Coiled gift baskets are frequently decorated with triangular designs in vertical bands, the overall discontinuity and heterogeneity of which are also characteristic of styles to the south. A third scheme, which appears identically on both twined and coiled Pomoan wares, is the serrated diagonal or zigzag in an expansive, organically unified pattern, with carefully controlled negative spaces that are completely within the aesthetic of the Northern macrostyle.

B. Sennett-Graham: *Basketry: A Clue to Panamint Shoshone Culture in the Early 20th Century* (Ann Arbor, 1991)

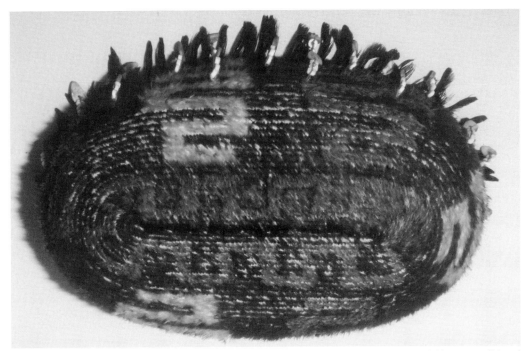

Pomo Indian basket, decorated with hummingbird, woodpecker and quail feathers, California (Chicago, IL, Field Museum of Natural History)

C. S. Fowler and others: 'Bound by Tradition: Contemporary Northern Paiute/Washoe Beaded Baskets', *Amer. Ind. A. Mag.*, xxix/ 2 (Spring 2004), pp. 32–9

T. Ames: 'The Jump Dance Basket of Northwestern California', *Amer. Ind. A. Mag.*, xxix/3 (Summer 2004), pp. 46–53

5. SOUTHWEST. Peoples of the Palaeo-Indian and Archaic (*c.* 9000–*c.* 200 BC) Southwest have made basketwork since *c.* 9000 BC (Berkeley, U. CA, Hearst Mus. Anthropol.; Salt Lake City, U. UT, Mus. Nat. Hist.; Carson City, NV, State Mus.). By 8000 BC they had invented the various basket-making techniques used in later centuries, including twining and plaiting. These techniques are still used in the Southwest to create many kinds of baskets, using almost every kind of vegetal material: stems, roots, wood, leaves, grass and other materials. Basketmakers had to be knowledgeable botanists to identify and to understand the gathering and preparation of these materials. The earliest baskets were twined. They were used to gather seeds, nuts and roots, to carry them to camps, to process them by parching and perhaps to cook them with hot stones. Coiled baskets appeared *c.* 5000 BC and quickly became popular because they were better than twined baskets for parching seeds and nuts.

The ancestors of the Pueblo peoples, the Basketmakers (*c.* 200 BC–*c.* AD 700) continued to practise the basket-making traditions of the Archaic period, as did later Pueblo peoples, but the only modern Pueblo people to have preserved the ancient tradition is the Hopi. Most early decoration comprised highly structured geometrical designs. The Hopi make baskets for ceremonial use, to use as gifts among themselves and for sale to collectors and tourists. The villages on Second Mesa produce fine baskets with coils of galleta grass sewn with yucca splints. On Third Mesa brightly coloured wicker baskets are plaited with rabbit-brush wefts over sumac warps. Both kinds of basket are decorated with *kachina* figures, rain symbols and other traditional designs. They also make plaited yucca ring baskets, similar to those made *c.* AD 1000. In the other Pueblo villages few baskets were still made by the end of the 20th century: yucca ring-baskets and a few coiled baskets at Jemez; openwork plaited wicker bowls at Jemez and several other Rio Grande towns.

The peoples of the circum-Pueblo region also make many kinds of basket. Most of them are coiled on slender sticks or rods—usually three—and sewn with strands of willow or sumac. The Havasupais, Walapais, Yavapais and Chemehuevis decorated their bowls and vase-forms with geometric designs of black 'devil's claws', a technique used also by the Western Apaches. The beautiful baskets the Apaches made until the mid-20th century were covered with geometric patterns and figures of people and animals. All these people also made twined baskets: squat jars with flat rims by the Walapais; fine conical carriers and water jars by all groups; and bucket-shaped burden baskets by the Apaches. Although coiling almost disappeared among the Apaches, twining survived because the twined burden baskets were used ceremonially. By the 1990s their chief products were conical twined baskets from *c.* 1 m in height to miniature baskets used on earrings. The Cibecue Apaches in particular still twine water jars and cover them with melted pine gum.

The Eastern Apaches of New Mexico formerly made distinctive baskets. The northern Jicarilla Apaches produce stout baskets coiled with three or five rods and sewn with sumac splints. They are brightly coloured with aniline and vegetal dyes and are important in the economic life of many families. Large shallow bowls are the commonest shapes, and they also make unique water bottles, coated white and sealed only on the inside surface. The Mescalero Apaches of southern New Mexico once made a unique type, coiled with two stacked rods and a bundle of fibre, and sewn with tan yucca splints. Their broad bowls and covered 'boxes' are no longer produced.

The Apaches' linguistic relatives, the Navajos, learnt from the early Pueblo peoples to make baskets with two-rod and bundle coils, but they stopped making them before the start of the 20th century to concentrate on weaving rugs. Nevertheless, because baskets were important in many Navajo rituals, they turned their basketwork needs over to the Great Basin San Juan Paiutes, who, from that time on, produced most of the famous 'Navajo wedding baskets', the shallow bowls, with encircling red bands with black terraced triangles along each edge, that are used in ceremonies to hold corn meal and/or pollen. In the 1970s these Paiutes and the Navajos produced a notable renaissance of basket-making. Both groups began to produce coiled baskets of varied sizes, decorated with an eclectic assortment of coloured designs: crosses, butterflies, yei figures (the highly stylized human figures representing supernatural spirits that are used in sand paintings) and other attractive patterns that have made their creations an economic success.

A different tradition of coiling is found among the Pimas and Papagos of southern Arizona. In Pima baskets the narrow coils have a foundation of rush fibres, while the Papagos use bear-grass. Both tribes traditionally sewed their baskets with willow splints and used 'devil's claw' for geometric designs. Pima basketwork became almost extinct in the late 20th century, but the Papagos invented a new type of basket with thick coils of bear-grass sewn with splints of yucca leaves. Such baskets could be produced quickly and easily, and sold cheaply. They also created complex new stitches that both enhanced the appearance of the baskets and facilitated their production. In the 1970s and 1980s some Papago women produced beautifully made baskets coiled with black and white horsehair and decorated with many tiny figures of snakes and/or people. The Yuman-speaking desert tribes of the lower Rio Grande never made such basketwork, except for fish traps and large coiled granaries. In the rest of the Southwest basket-making continues, and the number of basketmakers may be increasing.

B. Robinson: *The Basket Weavers of Arizona* (Albuquerque, 1954)
J. M. Adavasio: *Basketry Technology: A Guide to Identification and Analysis* (Chicago, 1977)
C. L. Tanner: *Apache Indian Baskets* (Tucson, 1982)
C. L. Tanner: *Indian Baskets of the Southwest* (Tucson, 1983)
H. Whiteford: *Southwestern Indian Baskets: Their History and Their Makers* (Santa Fe, 1988)
Woven Wonders: Southwest American Indian Basketry, Logan, UT State U., Nora Eccles Harrison Mus. A. (Logan, 1995)
B. B. Potter: *Reflections of Culture: Basketry from the Southwest Museum* (Los Angeles, 2000)

6. WOODLANDS. Basketwork is of considerable antiquity in the Woodlands. The earliest evidence for plaiting probably dates to before 8000 BC; coiling (limited to the southern Plains, where it was introduced from the Southwest) and twining were practised by the 1st millennium BC at the latest. Plaiting is the most widespread type of basketwork in the Woodlands. In the Southeast, river-cane splints of equal width were generally twilled to produce a wide range of shapes, from shallow winnowing trays to voluminous pack baskets. Besides simple single weaves, there were double-woven baskets consisting of two layers of warps and wefts showing different patterns on the inside and outside. Geometric designs were produced by using black, red (rarely orange and yellow) and natural-coloured splints. While most of these patterns were rectilinear, the complex curvilinear patterns used by the Chitimacha and their neighbours transcended the limitations of the technique.

On technical, stylistic and distributional grounds, a Euro-American origin has been postulated for the woodsplint basketwork of the north-eastern Woodlands. A tradition of plaited bags, mats and perhaps even baskets made of strips of bark before European contact must have favoured the adoption of woodsplint basketwork. However, the manufacture of thin and regular splints of white ash, white oak and other hardwoods was at least greatly simplified by specialized iron implements (splint splitters, gauges and planes). Some constructive features—such as the use of carved wooden handles—and the use of block-stamp decoration also betray European influence. Historically, there is evidence for the presence of Native American woodsplint basketwork in the north-eastern Woodlands since at least the early 18th century, whence the basic technique had spread to the western Great Lakes region by the early 19th century. Among the Cherokee, where it exists side by side with river-cane basketwork, it may have been introduced in the 18th century either from indigenous or European sources.

As in other adopted crafts, there was considerable indigenous innovation, which gave rise to some local peculiarities. Patterns are formed by splints of different width and colour, but since twilling is less common than in cane basketwork, chequerwork and banded designs predominate. Other features that distinguish woodsplint basketwork are the use of overlay and false embroidery, hexagonal weaves and the twisting of wefts to produce curls. Painted and stamped decoration—produced by means of potato, cork or wooden stamps—is especially characteristic of New England Algonquian basketwork.

The plaited wickerwork practised by the Cherokee and Virginia Algonquians using honeysuckle or buckbrush vines as wefts over rigid warps is of late 19th-century origin. Although inspired by their Euro-American neighbours, the craft was independently developed by Native American makers, for example in the double-woven root-runner baskets of the Oklahoma Cherokee. Sweetgrass and sweetgrass braids are used with woodsplint warps by the Iroquois and some of their neighbours for plaited wickerwork. Twilled burden baskets of strips of willow and box-elder bark (sometimes also leather) were plaited by the sedentary peoples of the Upper Missouri, exhibiting a limited number of simple geometric, two-colour patterns of diamonds, zigzags and other motifs.

The oldest historically collected baskets (Providence, RI Hist. Soc.; Paris, Mus. Homme; Wörlitz, Schloss) from the north-eastern Woodlands (New England and the Great Lakes), dating from the 17th and 18th centuries, were twined in a variety of techniques, including compact and spaced weft twining. Designs consisted of horizontal bands of geometric patterns, often in false embroidery with dyed porcupine quills or moose hair as decorative material. The same techniques and designs were also used in the area for two-dimensional textiles, which survived into the 19th and 20th centuries in the manufacture of soft bags. In three-dimensional basketwork, twining was almost completely replaced by plaited woodsplint basketwork, with the exception of the undecorated, bottle-shaped salt and tobacco containers and some cornhusk masks of the Iroquois, both of which are now more commonly made of sewn coiled husk braids.

Whereas two types of coiled gambling trays were traditionally made on the Plains, coiling seems to be a relatively recent basketwork technique in much of the Woodlands. As products for the tourist trade, coiled sweetgrass baskets appeared in the Great Lakes region in the 19th century and among the Florida Seminole in the 1930s. The latter produced simple designs of parallel rows created by the coloured thread used for stitching to hold the coils; these were modified into stepped geometric patterns by the 1990s. Elsewhere in the south-eastern Woodlands, coiled pine-needle baskets are similarly of 20th-century origin and may have as much Afro-American as Euro-American background. Effigy baskets made in this technique are an even more recent innovation. Yet another post-European contact style in the south-eastern Woodlands is represented by the baskets of braided bands of split palmetto leaves, made by the Houma.

F. G. Speck: *Decorative Art and Basketry of the Cherokee*, Milwaukee Public Museum Bulletin, ii/2 (Milwaukee, 1920)

M. Lismer: *Seneca Splint Basketry* (Washington, DC, 1941)

T. J. Brasser: *A Basketful of Indian Culture Change*, N. Mus. Man Mercury Series, Canadian Ethnology Service Paper, xxii (Ottawa, 1975)

C. Medford jr: 'Chitimacha Split Cane Basketry Weaves and Designs', *Amer. Ind. A.*, iii/1 (1977), pp. 56–61, 101

G. Pelletier: *Abenaki Basketry*, Canadian Ethnology Service Paper, National Museum of Man Mercury Series, lxxxv (Ottawa, 1982)

J. E. McGuire: *Old New England Splint Baskets and How to Make Them* (West Chester, 1985)

K. Bardwell: 'The Case for an Aboriginal Origin of Northeastern Indian Woodsplint Basketry', *Man NE*, xxxi (1986), pp. 49–67

A. McMullen and R. G. Handsman: *A Key into the Language of Woodsplint Baskets* (Washington, CT, 1987)

Downs: 'Contemporary Florida Indian Patchwork and Baskets', *Amer. Ind. A.*, xic/4 (1990), pp. 56–63

Bataille, Nicolas [Colin] (*fl* ?1363; *d* Paris, 1398–9). French tapestry-weaver and dealer. He was one of the most successful of several French luxury textile merchants based mainly in Paris and Arras during the late 14th century and the only one whose work is known to have survived. He was a citizen of Paris and is referred to variously as a weaver of high-warp tapestries, a merchant of *tapis sarrazinois* and, more generally, a merchant. His second wife, Marguerite de Verdun, who came from a family of weavers in Troyes, continued his business after his death with his son Jean (*b c.* 1371).

Batavian ware. Western name for Chinese porcelain of the Kangxi period (1662–1722) imported by Dutch merchants through the Dutch trading station at Batavia (now Jakarta). This porcelain, which was brown-glazed, decorated with panels and usually painted in blue, was imitated by European manufacturers, notably at Meissen and Leeds, and these imitations are known as Batavia ware.

Bateman, Hester [*née* Neden or Needham] (*b* London, *bapt* 7 Oct 1708; *d* London, 16 Sept 1794). English goldsmith. She married John Bateman (*c.* 1704–60), a gold chainmaker, in 1732. She entered the first of her nine marks in 1761, after her husband's death, revealing the paucity of her formal education by an inability to sign her name on the goldsmiths' register. From 1760 to 1790 she presided over a flourishing business at 107 Bunhill Row, London. From *c.* 1761 to 1774 the majority of silver produced in the Bateman workshop was commissioned by other silversmiths and consequently was often over-stamped. A large and varied output of Bateman-marked domestic silver dating from the late 1770s and the 1780s survives, including flatware (e.g. pierced and engraved fish slice, 1783–4; Colonial Williamsburg, VA), salvers, cruet frames, jugs, salts, tankards and tea and coffee equipage, as well as civic and church plate, for example a communion cup (1786; London, St Paul's, Covent Garden). Simplicity of design and extensive use of thin-gauge silver (e.g. bread basket, 1788; Washington, DC, N. Mus. Women A.), factory-made silver components and such machine processes as punching and piercing ensured a large and rapid turnover of low-priced silverware and helped meet the competition from Sheffield plate. Bateman silver is characterized by its graceful forms and by the use of bright cutting and piercing in foliage, festoon, medallion, and diaper patterns, edges of minute beading and urn finials.

Hester Bateman retired in 1790 and was succeeded by her sons Peter Bateman (1740–1825) and

Jonathan Bateman (1747–91). In 1791 the first steam-driven silver flatting mill (for rolling silver into sheets) in London was installed in the Bateman workshop. After Jonathan's death Peter entered a mark with his brother's widow, Ann Bateman (1748–c. 1812). They were joined by Ann's son William Bateman (1774–1850) in 1800, who, on Ann's retirement in 1805, registered a joint mark with Peter. William became sole head of the firm on Peter's retirement in 1815. Control of the firm was taken over by his own son William Bateman (c. 1800–c. 1876) in 1839. The Bateman workshop closed c. 1843.

ODNB

D. S. Shure: *Hester Bateman: Queen of English Silversmiths* (London, 1959)

G. B. Hughes: 'An 18th Century Woman Silversmith', *Country Life*, cxxviii (8 Sept 1960), pp. 508–10

English Silver by Hester Bateman and Other Makers from the Mrs. E. Claiborne Robins Collection, Richmond, VA Mus. F. A. (Richmond, VA, 2001)

Batik. Resist dyeing technique. Patterns are created on cloth (usually undyed cotton or silk) by painting, printing or stencilling designs in wax, rice or cassava paste, mud or some other dye-resistant substance on to those areas intended to retain their original colour after dyeing. Further patterns and colours can be introduced by altering or adding to the resist areas before redyeing. Finally, the resist media are removed by rubbing or washing. Delicate lines within the patterns, where the resist substance has cracked and allowed the dye to seep in, are characteristic of the technique.

The term 'batik' is thought to derive from the Malay *tik*, to drip or drop, but exactly where and when the technique was first practised is uncertain; it seems likely that the principle was discovered independently in several different areas. The earliest known batiks (London, V&A, nos 1552–1899 and 1103–1900; Basel, Mus. Vlkerknd.), dated to the 5th–6th century AD, were excavated in Egypt and included a linen cloth with white patterns showing biblical scenes on a blue background. Indigo blue was the commonest early dye: it is especially suitable for batik as the indigo dye process does not involve heat, which might destroy the resist. Cotton fragments dated to the 12th–16th centuries excavated at Fustat, Cairo, may have been imported from India, where batik is believed to have flourished from the 5th century AD. Although no Indian examples have survived from that time, 6th–7th-century AD frescoes at Ajanta, Maharashtra, show garments decorated with batik-type patterns, suggesting contemporary knowledge of the technique. Indian batik (New Delhi, N. Mus.) export has been documented since the 17th century, and painted, stamped and woodblock-printed cotton and silk resist textiles continue to be produced in the subcontinent (Udaipur, Batik A. Res. & Training Cent.).

Excavations in Central Asia at Loulan and Kucha in Xinjiang have yielded many examples of batik textiles (Beijing, Hist. Mus.; Guizhou, Batik A. Acad.),

mainly dated to the 7th–11th centuries. Some silk batiks may have been imported to China, but local production is suggested by the patterned garments shown in wall paintings at Kucha Oasis. The oldest examples of Japanese wax resist textiles (*rōkechi*) are in the Shōsō-in repository of imperial treasures, Nara, and belong to the Nara period (AD 710–94). They include silk screens representing trees, mountains and animals on glowing yellow, green, red or dark-blue backgrounds. These designs appear to have been painted free-hand, but other textiles (Tokyo, N. Mus.; Osaka, N. Mus. Ethnol.) suggest resist application by stamping, block-printing or stencilling. Some wax and rice paste resist textiles are still produced in Japan (Kyoto, Juraku Int. Textile Cent.). There is also a long and continuous tradition of batik production among the Miao (Hmong) hill peoples of southern China and northern Thailand, who draw geometric patterns with wax on to hemp and cotton using a pen. This practice probably predates the flourishing silk batik trade of the Tang period (AD 618–907), through which batik textiles and techniques could have spread to other parts of the world.

However, the best-known batiks are produced in South-east Asia, chiefly in Indonesia. Batik-like patterns are represented on the walls of the Loro Longgrang Temple at Prambanan (c. AD 800) and also in sculpture. There is an ancient tradition of rice paste resist batik cotton cloth (*kain simbut*) in West Java (Yogyakarta, Batik Res. Cent.) and the Toraja region of Sulawesi. Wax batik, especially in Java, was perfected by the Indonesian invention of the wax applicator (*chanting*): this consists of a bamboo handle attached to a small brass container for hot wax, which is applied to the cloth through a curved spout. The batik artist, usually a woman, uses a number of *chantings* with spouts of different diameters, which allow her to draw, free-hand, an immense variety of patterns: mythical or geometric, or derived from plants, animals or clouds. The design is usually drawn on both sides of the cloth to ensure complete exclusion of the dye. Natural dyes used include the different shades of indigo blue, yellow (rare), red and brown. As the demand for Indonesian batik increased in the 19th century, metal stamps (*cap*s) came into use for applying the hot wax to the cloth more speedily. The *cap*, which is usually operated by men, consists of thin, shaped copper strips shaped together with pins soldered on to a metal base with a handle on the reverse side. The repetitive *cap* batik print is less valued than batik *tulis* (writing) drawn with a *chanting*. Both techniques are also practised in Malaysia, especially Kelantan. In the mid-19th century a number of Dutch factories developed a mechanical process for reproducing Indonesian batiks.

In Africa, resist dyeing (e.g. London, BM, Dept. of Ethnog.; Lagos, N. Mus.) is an ancient tradition that is still practised, with the main centres of production in West Africa, in Nigeria, Senegal, Sierra Leone and the Gambia. Cassava and rice paste, applied with palm fronds, brushes, sticks, woodblocks or stencils, were originally used, but in the late 20th

Batik with *wayang* (shadow-puppet) design, Indonesia (Prague, private collection)

century hand-painted wax batiks depicting African scenes and motifs have become popular. In Senegal, the Soninke people cover the whole cloth with rice paste, which is then combed to form line patterns into which the dye can penetrate. In Mali the Bamana people practise a discharge-dye method called *bogolanfini*: the cloth is initially coloured with a yellow dye before passing through several processes, involving the application of designs using mud and caustic soap, to produce eventually a light-coloured design on a dark background. Batik methods have spread to many parts of the world. The best-known centres that continue to flourish are found in Indonesia, Malaysia, India and Africa. While traditional designs are still made, the 20th-century trend is to follow contemporary fashion in design and home decoration, often using synthetic rather than natural dyes, to achieve a wide colour range. Individual artists and designers in the older established centres and elsewhere, including Europe, have discovered in batik methods a new creative medium of expression.

J. L. Larsen and others: *The Dyer's Art* (New York, 1976)
S. Fraser-Lu: *Indonesian Batik* (Singapore, 1986)
N. Dyrendorth: *The Techniques of Batik* (London, 1988)
N. Dyrendorth: *Batik: Modern Concepts and Techniques* (London, 2003)
D. J. Harper: *Batik from the Courts of Java and Sumatra: Rudolf G. Smend Collection* (Singapore, 2004)
F. Kerlogue: *Batik: Design, Style & History* (London and New York, 2004)

Battam, Thomas (*b c.* 1810; *d* 1864). English painter of pottery and porcelain and the proprietor of a China decorating firm. In 1834 he began to work for Copeland, and during this period he may have developed the formula for PARIAN WARE. He is given credit for its invention in the catalogue of the Great Exhibition of 1851; this may be so, but several potteries subsequently claimed credit for its invention. His firm made imitation Greek vases that are known as Battam ware.

Battersea Enamel Factory. English enamel factory. In 1763 Stephen Theodore Janssen (*c.* 1705–77) founded an enamelling factory at York House, Battersea. The renowned engravers who worked with Janssen included Simon François Ravenet (1706/21–74), ROBERT HANCOCK and JOHN BROOKS, who claimed to have invented the TRANSFER PRINTING process while working at the factory. Enamel snuffboxes, framed plaques and wine labels (examples by Ravenet, *c.* 1754; London, V&A) produced at Battersea were transfer-printed in soft monochrome shades or gold, and some were over-painted in delicate translucent colours. The factory closed in 1756.

Baudekin [baldachin, baldaquin, cloth of baudkin]. Rich embroidered stuff, originally made with warp of gold thread and woof of silk; in later usage the term broadened to include any rich brocade or rich shot silk. The term derives from Baldacco, the Italian word for Baghdad. The forms 'baldachin' and 'baldaquin' are sometimes used to render Italian *baldacchino*, an architectural canopy made of wood, stone or metal but originally made from baudekin.

Baudisch, Gudrun (*b* Pöls, 17 March 1907; *d* Salzburg, 16 Oct 1982). Austrian potter and stuccoist. She studied at the Österreichische Bundeslehranstalt für das Baufach und Kunstgewerbe in Graz and in 1926 became an assistant in the ceramic design section of the Wiener Werkstätte under Josef Hoffmann; from 1930 to 1936 she worked for several ceramic workshops in Vienna. During this period she created the stucco ceiling in the Ataturk Palace (1931) in Ankara, Turkey. From 1936 to 1944 Baudisch stayed in Berlin where she made the stucco decoration for the Italian Embassy and also large figural sculptures. In 1946 she founded the Keramik Hallstatt, which was her base until 1977. While creating her own work in this studio she also (from 1968) made numerous designs for the Vereinigte Wiener und Gmundener Keramik and founded, in connection with them, the Gruppe *H*. From 1959 to 1966 she created the stucco decoration for the main Festspielhaus (1955–60) in Salzburg. In 1977 she left the Keramik Hallstatt and moved permanently to Salzburg.

G. Baudisch and others: *Keramik: von der Wiener Werkstätte zur Keramik Hallstatt* (Linz, 1980)

Baudouine, Charles A. (*b* New York, 1808; *d* New York, 1895). American cabinetmaker. He opened his first cabinetmaking shop in Pearl Street, New York, about 1830. Ten years later he moved to Broadway, near his competitor John Henry Belter, whose work, in particular the laminated rosewood chairs, Baudouine is claimed, perhaps unjustly, to have imitated. Baudouine's production was huge; he employed up to 200 workers, including 70 cabinetmakers. He favoured the Rococo Revival style based on simplified versions of Louis XV designs and frequently travelled to France to purchase upholstery material, hardware and trim. He also brought back furniture made in France, which he sold in his shop along with his own stock. Anthony Kimbel (*d* 1895) was Baudouine's designer in the years before the shop closed about 1856.

The documented pair of card-tables (Utica, NY, Munson–Williams–Proctor Inst.), two parlour settees and six chairs (Utica, NY, Munson–Williams–Proctor Inst.) that James Watson Williams purchased from Baudouine in 1852 for his home at Fountain Elms in Utica, NY, are in rosewood. Baudouine used little mahogany, no cheap walnut and only a limited amount of oak, mainly for dining-room furniture.

E. Ingerman: 'Personal Experiences of an Old New York Cabinetmaker', *Antiques*, lxxxiv (1963), pp. 576–80
B. Franco: 'New York City Furniture Bought for Fountain Elms by James Watson Williams', *Antiques*, civ (1973), pp. 462–7

T. D'Ambrosio: *Masterpieces of American Furniture from the Munson-Williams-Proctor Institute* (Utica, NY, 1999)
C. H. Voorsanger and J. K. Howat: *Art and the Empire City: New York, 1825–1861* (exh. cat, New York, Met., 2000)

Baudry, François (*b* 1791; *d* 1859). French cabinetmaker from Nantes who was working in Paris by 1822. He was appointed cabinetmaker to the king (*ébéniste du roi*) by Louis Philippe, and made many splendid pieces (e.g. a bed exhibited in 1827 and now in the Musée des Arts Decoratifs in Paris), but under the July Monarchy (1830–48) his work for the royal family consisted entirely of unadorned mahogany dining tables.

Bauer, Adam. *See under* LUDWIGSBURG PORCELAIN FACTORY.

Bauernmöbel [Ger.: 'folk art furniture']. The name given in German-speaking countries to furniture made in village workshops from the late 18th century to the early 20th, characteristically painted with folk-art motifs. In America, the tradition is embodied in Pennsylvania Dutch furniture.

A. Kugler: *Bauernmöbel* (Munich, 1988)
S. Seidl: *Bauernmöbel der Oberpfalz: Alte bemalte Möbel zwischen Donau und Fichtelgebirge* (Grafenau, 1991)

Bauhaus. German school of art, design and architecture, founded by Walter Gropius (1883–1969). It was active in Weimar from 1919 to 1925, in Dessau from 1925 to 1932 and in Berlin from 1932 to 1933, when it was closed down by the Nazi authorities. After the closure of the Bauhaus, its members were dispersed across Europe and the USA. Some became highly influential teachers: Gropius took up a professorship at the Graduate School of Design at Harvard University in 1937 and, perhaps more importantly, Josef Albers (1888–1976) accepted a post at Black Mountain College in North Carolina. Through the workshops and courses, they disseminated Bauhaus design and teaching methods in the USA. Elsewhere numerous establishments came to model themselves on the Bauhaus, for example the New Bauhaus or the School of Design in Chicago, both founded by László Moholy-Nagy (1895–1946), and after World War II the Hochschule für Gestaltung in Ulm. As well as setting standards for the development of modern design and the International Style, the Bauhaus established concepts for the teaching of art and design that are still influential.

The Bauhaus's name referred to the medieval Bauhütten or masons' lodges. The school re-established workshop training, as opposed to impractical academic studio education. It exemplified the contemporary desire to form unified academies incorporating art colleges, colleges of arts and crafts and schools of architecture, thus promoting a closer co-operation between the practice of 'fine' and 'applied' art and architecture. The origins of the school lay in attempts in the 19th and early 20th centuries to re-establish the bond between artistic creativity and manufacturing that had been broken by the Industrial Revolution. According to Walter Gropius in 1923, the main influences included John Ruskin (1819–1900) and William Morris, and various individuals and groups with whom he had been directly involved: for example Henry Van de Velde; such members of the Darmstadt artists' colony as Peter Behrens; the Deutscher Werkbund; and the Arbeitsrat für Kunst.

In the decorative arts the most important stage of Bauhaus design was the period in Dessau, where the metal workshop and the furniture workshop were among the most successful departments. In the furniture workshop Marcel Breuer, who had been at the Bauhaus as a student since 1920, succeeded in developing armchairs and chairs made of tubular steel, a breakthrough in designing furniture appropriate to its function and adapted to the potential of industrial mass production. The most outstanding characteristics of this metal furniture were its small mass, its transparency, lightness and ease of movement (the base of the frame acting as a skid). Under Moholy-Nagy the metal workshop continued to set the standards for the gradual transformation of the Bauhaus into a modern laboratory of prototypes for industrial mass production. This applies particularly to the classic, innovative designs of light fittings by such designers as Marianne Brandt, Karl J. Jucker (1902–97), Wilhelm Wagenfeld and Gyula Pap (1899–1983).

G. Naylor: *The Bauhaus* (London, 1968)
A. Rowland: *The Bauhaus Source Book* (Oxford, 1990)
E. S. Hochman: *Bauhaus: Crucible of Modernism* (New York, 1997)
M. Kentgens-Craig: *The Bauhaus and America: First Contacts, 1919–1936* (Cambridge, MA, 1999)
A. Bartram: *Bauhaus, Modernism, and the Illustrated Book* (New Haven, 2004)

Baumgarten, William (*b* 1845; *d* 1908). American interior decorator and founder of the first tapestry factory in the USA. He worked for Herter Brothers (*see* CHRISTIAN HERTER) on the decoration of a series of grand houses, notably William H. Vanderbilt's house on Fifth Avenue, New York, and William Welsh Harrison's Grey Towers Castle (now part of Arcadia University) in Philadelphia. When the Vanderbilt house was completed in 1882, Christian Herter returned to Germany and Baumgarten took over the company. In 1891 he started his own company, William Baumgarten and Company, Inc., and in 1893 complemented his interior decoration business with a tapestry factory in his Fifth Avenue premises. He recruited weavers and dyers from the Royal Windsor Tapestry Manufactory (which had closed in 1890), including five weavers from the Foussadier family. The factory's tapestries include one at Grey Towers (1898).

W. Baumgarten: *A Short Résumé of the History of Tapestry Making in the Past and Present* (New York, 1897)
Old Panellings in the Collection of Wm. Baumgarten & Co., Inc. (New York, n.d. [1930s])

Baumgartner, Bernát (*b c.* 1704; *d* after 1767). Hungarian wood-carver and Jesuit. He was a novice in the Society of Jesus at Trencsén (now Trenčín, Slovakia) and worked as a wood-carver in the Jesuit workshop until 1735; following this he worked in Esztergom and Vienna. From 1749 to 1760 he was the head of the Jesuit workshop at Székesfehérvár. The furnishings and fittings of the former Jesuit church there, St John of Nepomuk, and the rich, ornamental carvings of the priory and pharmacy (all *in situ*) were made under his direction. From 1764 to 1767 he worked in the Jesuit workshop in Kolozsvár, Transylvania (now Cluj-Napoca, Romania).

Baumgartner, Ulrich (*b c.* 1580; *d* 1652). German cabinetmaker, active in Augsburg, where he was employed by Philipp Hainhofer (1578–1647). Baumgartner's finest work, the carving of the ebony cabinet known as the Pommeranian Cabinet, is largely destroyed (1611–15; fragments in Berlin, Tiergarten, Kstgewmus.). His surviving work includes the carving of an ebony cabinet (1625–31; Uppsala, U. Kstsaml.) presented to Duke Ferdinando II of Tuscany (1619–26, Pitti Palace, Florence) and the carving of the ebony cabinet designed by Hainhofer for presentation by the town of Augsburg to Gustav II Adolf of Sweden (*reg* 1611–32).

Baumhauer, Joseph (*d* Paris, 22 March 1772). French cabinetmaker of German birth. About 1749 he became Marchand Ebéniste Privilégié du Roy Suivant la Cour et Conseils de Sa Majesté. He was active during the reign of Louis XV (*reg* 1715–74) and was the only French cabinetmaker who was equally competent in both the Louis XV and Neo-classical styles. His pieces were few but of an extremely high standard; he employed fine wood marquetry, Japanese lacquer and Boulle marquetry, as well as producing rigorous bronzes. His extant works in the Louis XV style include desks fitted with porcelain plaques, a series of sumptuous marquetry commodes (e.g. *c.* 1755; Toledo, OH, Mus. A.) and an astonishing upright writing-table (1758; Philadelphia, PA, Mus. A.) made for the Comte de Coblenz. About 1756 he made the famous *bureau plat* (Chantilly, Mus. Condé) in an early Neo-classical style for Ange-Laurent de La Live de Jully (1725–70), which was based on architectural designs by Louis-Joseph Le Lorrain (1715–59). Baumhauer's son Gaspard Baumhauer used his father's stamp until 1777 on works in his father's style.

J.-D. Augarde: '1749. Joseph Baumhauer: Ebéniste privilégié du roi', *Estampille*, cciv (1987), pp. 14–45

Baxter, Thomas. *See under* SWANSEA *and* WORCESTER.

Bayeux Porcelain Factory. French porcelain factory established in Bayeux (Normandy) in the early 1820s. It produced porcelain for both industrial and domestic purposes until its eventual closure in 1951. Examples of the factory's wares are displayed in the Musée Baron Gérard in Bayeux.

M. Vasseur: *La porcelaine de Bayeux et des autres manufactures bas-normandes* (Caen, 1985)

Bayeux Tapestry. Needlework depiction of the events that led to the Battle of Hastings and the Norman Conquest of England in 1066; despite its name, it is an embroidery, not a tapestry. It is made up of eight conjoined sections of different lengths. The scenes at the end of the tapestry are damaged and some are lost, but its surviving length is 68.38 m and its depth varies between 457 and 536 mm. The linen is relatively fine and the embroidery is in wool, in laid-and-couched work, defined by stem or outline stitch. The latter is also used for all the linear detail and the lettering. No trace of any construction lines or of tracing from a cartoon remains on the tapestry. The earliest possible mention of the tapestry is in 1463 in the accounts of Bayeux Cathedral. In 1476 it was listed in the cathedral inventory, at which time it was 'hung round the church on the day of the Relics and throughout the octave'. First published in 1729, it was put on permanent display as a whole in 1842. It is now shown in a purpose-built gallery (Bayeux, Mus. Tap.).

The inscription and the style of the Bayeux Tapestry suggest that it was embroidered in England. It could have been made at Canterbury or Winchester between 1066 and the death in 1097 of Odo, bishop of Bayeux, or more probably before his fall from power in 1082; these dates would fit the stylistic evidence. The Bayeux Tapestry depicts a total of 1515 different objects, animals and persons. Dress, arms, ships, towers, cities, halls, churches, horse trappings, regal insignia, ploughs, harrows, tableware, possible armorial changes, banners, hunting horns, axes, adzes, barrels, carts, wagons, reliquaries, biers, spits and spades are among the many items depicted. If used critically, they provide a useful source for the appearance of 11th-century material culture in England and Normandy.

F. M. Stenton, ed.: *The Bayeux Tapestry* (London, 1957)
D. M. Wilson: *The Bayeux Tapestry* (London, 1985)
S.-A. Brown: *The Bayeux Tapestry: History and Bibliography* (Woodbridge, 1989)
D. M. Wilson: *The Bayeux Tapestry* (London, 2004)
G. Beech: *Was the Bayeux Tapestry Made in France?: The Case for Saint-Florent of Saumur* (New York, 2005)
A. Bridgeford: *1066: The Hidden History of the Bayeux Tapestry* (New York, 2005)

Bayreuth. German centre of ceramics production. In 1719, at the behest of Markgraf Georg Wilhelm, a faience factory was founded in St Georgen am See, Bayreuth. Ten years later it was leased to the merchant Johann Georg Knöller (*fl* 1729–44). Dishes and tankards accounted for much of the production, although trays, inkstands and candlesticks were also made. Favourite decorations were still-lifes with flowers and fruit painted in pale blue surrounded by

Bayeux Tapestry (detail of a knight), linen with wool embroidery, probably before 1082 (Bayeux, Musée de la Tapisserie de la Reine Mathilde)

borders of *Laub und Bandelwerk*. Tankards were decorated with cartouches containing coats of arms and monograms, and the *famille verte* palette (green, iron-red, yellow, blue and purple) was also sometimes used. The most important painter was Joseph Philipp Dannhöffer (1712–90), who came to Bayreuth from Vienna in 1737 and stayed until 1744. Adam Friedrich von Löwenfinck, who had fled from the porcelain factory in Meissen, also spent a brief period in Bayreuth in 1736. The best known of the firm's own painters were Johann Friedrich Metsch (*d* 1766) and Johann Christoph Jucht (1721–*c*. 1782). In 1745 the firm was taken over by the burgomasters Adolf Fränkel and Johann Veit Schreck (*d* 1747). After Schreck's death Johann Georg Pfeiffer (*d* 1767) took over his share of the business. After Pfeiffer's death the standard of production declined with an increasing quantity of cheap stoneware being produced; in 1835 production ceased and the factory was sold. The Braune Porcelain Fabrique (est. 1714) was a subsidiary of the faience factory and there production continued until 1800. Red stonewares covered in a dark-brown, black or yellow glaze, decorated with delicate chinoiseries and coats of arms in gold and silver, were manufactured, in imitation of JOHANN FRIEDRICH BÖTTGER's stoneware at Meissen (e.g. *Walzenkrug*, 1731; Hamburg, Mus. Kst. & Gew.).

Bay State Glass Company. American glass company founded in 1849, incorporated in 1857 and closed in 1879. The glass works was in Bridge Street, Cambridge, MA, and the sales outlet was in State Street, Boston. The Company's flint glass wares were variously blown, cut, engraved, moulded and pressed.

Bead and reel. Carved enrichment consisting of a pattern of round or elliptical beads alternating with disks. It is the characteristic decoration for the small bead or astragal moulding in Classical architecture, and is widely used in the decorative arts, especially furniture and silverware. In the 16th and 17th centuries it was commonly used as a decorative border on furniture such as NONESUCH CHESTS.

Beadwork. Decorative assembly of beads, usually incorporated into a piece of weaving, netting or knitting or sewn on to a ground. At its simplest, beadwork is just a string of beads, but the term is generally applied to more elaborate constructions.

Primitive beads are known from the advent of *Homo sapiens* 40,000 years ago. Few examples exist from this early date, but they appear in numbers from the Upper Palaeolithic period (38,000–8000 BC). The first beads were simply grooved pebbles, bones, teeth etc, but by 16,000 BC abrasives and bow-drills were being used to form and drill beads from other materials. From the beginning beads had talismanic and symbolic connotations, which have continued to this day. These, and the desirability and rarity of particular materials, meant that beads were highly valued, and there is clear archaeological evidence that they have been traded since the earliest times. It is probable, for example, that etched cornelian beads were being exported from the Indus Valley to Sumer as early as 2500 BC.

From the mid-15th century AD beads were used as currency, either singly or in strings, by explorers, traders and missionaries. In pre-industrial societies beads were painstakingly handmade from such materials as stone, shell, wood and metal, so glass and other imported beads constituted an exchange medium that was highly valued for its rarity and novelty; at the same time it cost the foreign supplier little and was a means of getting trade goods cheaply. Venice, the chief source of glass trade beads in the Western world, supplied them strung on cotton threads, bunched according to number, or, in the case of the small 'seed' beads, by weight, hence the alternative name of 'pound' beads. These beads went by the shipload to Africa and the Americas to be traded for ivory, slaves, furs and other commodities.

Wampum is a form of currency beadwork. It was made and used in eastern North America as an exchange medium between Native American groups of the coastal and interior regions, as well as Europeans. Traditional wampum beads are 7 mm long by 3–4 mm in diameter and are made of the hard quahog seashell (*Venus mercenaria*), which has a purple interior. These beads seem to have been produced after the arrival of the Europeans, when iron awls became available; before that, wampum beads were made of wood. Purple beads were more valued than white, which might also have been made from conch shells.

Wampum came in currency strings, in jewellery or threaded into belts. Beadwork was sometimes used as a form of communication. The design on a wampum belt, for example, could encode a message or ratify a treaty, and the beadwork 'love-letters' of the Zulu used colour symbolism and bead-stringing order to convey messages from a girl to her betrothed. Generally, however, beadwork has been used for personal adornment, ceremonial and talismanic purposes and, in Europe, for craftwork and various objects.

1. Personal adornment. 2. Ceremonial and talismanic uses. 3. Craftwork and other uses.

1. PERSONAL ADORNMENT. In this context beadwork may be found in jewellery or in clothing. Almost any part of the body can be ornamented, and there is hardly any part of the world where such ornamentation has not occurred. The first-known examples date from *c.* 28,000 BC and include shell, stone and ivory. Later jet, amber, cornelian, lapis lazuli and gold were utilized. Beadwork often reflects the status of the wearer, distinguishing him or her as of royal or noble blood, of the priesthood, or as a headman. Elaborate bead ornaments worn by deceased royalty have been found, for example, in ancient sites in the Middle East, Egypt and Mesoamerica (e.g. the bead cloak of Queen Pu-abi from the Royal Cemetery at Ur, 2500 BC; Philadelphia, U. PA, Mus.; and the pectoral from the grave of Tutankhamun, *c.* 1323 BC; Cairo, Egyp. Mus.). Beadwork may also indicate the age and personal circumstances of the wearer. Among women, unmarried girls, brides, young mothers, senior wives and widows may all wear different bead ornaments to show their position, especially at weddings and special occasions. In the Americas, Africa and much of Asia, beadwork is also a sign of tribal identity.

Beadwork for personal adornment is seen most notably among the Plains Indians of North America, who wore beaded leather garments and moccasins (see colour pl. III, fig. 3), and in eastern and southern Africa, where the pastoral tribes in particular use beaded leather aprons, cloaks and blankets to indicate a woman's age and identity. Further examples include the Native Americans of Guyana, who also wear beaded pubic aprons; the Greenland Eskimos, who wear bead-mesh shoulder capes over their fur clothing; and the tribeswomen of Mongolia and Thailand, whose headdresses include rich assemblies of coral, amber and turquoise beads.

In Europe jet and imitation jet beads were lavishly applied to mourning and other day clothes during the later 19th century; a wider range of beads was used for evening dresses, particularly *c.* 1900. After the more severe styles of the 1910s, beads and sequins again dominated evening dresses in the 1920s, and solidly beaded handbags and garments retained their popularity into the 1930s.

2. CEREMONIAL AND TALISMANIC USES. The bead cloak from Ur is one of many instances in which beadwork is used to identify and set apart those in

high position, often royalty and court officials. Royal burials in Mesoamerica have been similarly identified by the presence of fine jade necklaces, and in Egypt the bead ornaments in royal burials included protective gold amulets. Beaded child's garments found in the tomb of Tutankhamun confirm that beadwork was not restricted to a funerary context. Although evidence is scant, it is likely that beadwork collars were worn by both sexes on such ceremonial occasions as banquets; high-ranking ladies also wore elaborate beaded overdresses on top of their simple, everyday linen shifts. A king, his family and court might wear elaborate beadwork; late 20th-century examples include the *oba* of Benin, Nigeria, with his coral bead headdress, collars and tunic, and the king of the Kuba of Zaïre, whose state costume, covered with beads and cowrie shells, weighs 84 kg, comprises almost 50 elements and takes hours to put on. The priesthood in a tribal society is often marked out by its beaded regalia; examples include the Ifa diviners among the Yoruba of Nigeria and the Xhosa diviners of South Africa, who wear white bead ornaments signifying purity. In Tibet the tantric priests wore aprons made of beads fashioned from human bones as a reminder of the transience of earthly life.

Through the ages grave goods have included beadwork: for instance, the shell and stone beads used by the Indus Valley civilization of the Indian subcontinent; the jet necklaces in Neolithic European burials; and the ancient Egyptian mummy shrouds, made of a network of blue faience beads or of amulets (gods' faces and scarabs) in white, black, blue and terracotta disk beads. Anglo-Saxon graves contained strings of beads with amber from the Baltic and mosaic beads from the eastern Mediterranean, showing how beads were traded over great distances. From the Chimú culture (*c.* AD 1200–*c.* 1470) of Peru come pectoral collars made of small disk beads strung on cotton with a mosaic-like design in pink and red *Spondylus* shells, other white shells and greenstone. In France and Germany, during the 19th and 20th centuries up to *c.* 1950, funeral wreaths were made of beads strung on wire and shaped into flowers and crosses (e.g. white beads from Paris, Père-Lachaise Cemetery; Santa Fe, NM, Mus. Int. Flk A.)

Weddings are an occasion of celebration and display. In Saurashtra, western India, a woman's dowry may include friezes to hang above the doorway and square hangings made of mesh-sewn seed beads. The bridegroom might wear a beaded bridal sash and pouch and receive a beadwork *parchese* gaming board. Among the Straits Chinese of Malaysia during the 19th century, women of good family spent much of their time threading or embroidering ornaments with minuscule glass beads for use as decorations for the wedding bed or as room-hangings or table-covers. Elsewhere, the dowry necklace may include beadwork: of coral, as in Italy, Romania and Poland, where the red colour is thought to bring good luck and fertility; of heirloom or amber beads, as in parts of Africa; or of silver, turquoise and lapis lazuli, along with silver coins, as in Asia. Brides among the Iraqw of Tanzania, the Maasi of Kenya and the Ndebele of South Africa may wear beautiful beaded wedding skirts and other finery. Ornaments in the form of long, beaded, conical hanging baskets decorate the wedding house in Ethiopia, and a Kamba bride from Kenya serves her husband his first meal in a specially beaded gourd, which later becomes a house ornament.

Beadwork may single out individuals who are important to the community, especially babies. The Plains Indians of North America and some Dayak peoples of Sarawak make elaborately beaded baby-carriers to protect the infant during its first vulnerable months of life; in Africa a pregnant Zulu woman may wear as a 'maternity apron' a beaded skin, which later becomes the baby's carrying-skin; a string of beads on a baby's neck may include a charm against infant sicknesses. Also, among many African peoples, a beaded doll is a charm to ensure pregnancy or cure sterility.

3. CRAFTWORK AND OTHER USES. Beadwork in Europe dates back at least to the medieval period, when glass beads, coral and pearls were used for embroidery. In the 17th century it flourished in England, where young ladies were expected to complete a series of needlework projects that often included beadwork. These could take the form of pictures, gloves, purses and, occasionally, jewellery boxes, with the beads embroidered in spot stitch on to a satin ground. Elaborate baskets were made entirely of beads threaded on to wire. In the 18th century the finest beadwork, *sablé* work, was made in Paris in professional workshops, using tiny, densely worked glass beads. It was made into such small, luxurious items as parasol handles, purses, needlecases, perfume bottles and boxes, using designs taken from contemporary engravings. One particular collection of this beadwork, in the Museum of Fine Arts, Boston, MA, includes a design reflecting the craze for ballooning that took place in the 1780s and 1790s.

Professional beadwork continued into the 19th century, particularly in Germany where there was a home-based industry in beaded bags and purses dating back to the 17th century. Professional patterns were used, and the beads (larger than those used for *sablé* work) were obtained from Bohemia. There was also a fashion for beaded caps, knitted or crocheted with very fine yarn and tiny beads. In the middle of the century, however, there was a surge in craftwork, and beading became a favourite pastime; in England this was encouraged by the abolition in 1845 of the excise duty on glass, which had included beads. A number of magazines published patterns for beadwork, the most popular items being purses to be knitted, netted or crocheted. Beads were often used to highlight Berlin woolwork (*see* BERLIN, §4). In the early 20th century, from *c.* 1913 to the 1920s, 'Indian' beadwork strips, made on table looms from printed patterns, were popular for decorative wristbands and belts.

L. S. Dubin: *The History of Beads from 30,000 BC to the Present* (London, 1987)

Wing Meng Ho: *Straits Chinese Beadwork and Embroidery* (Singapore, 1987)

J. D. Horse Capture and G. P. Horse Capture: *Beauty, Honor and Tradition: The Legacy of Plains Indian Shirts* (Washington, 2001)

C. Crabtree and P. Stallebrass: *Beadwork: A World Guide* (New York, 2002)

B. Dean: *Beading in the Native American Tradition* (Loveland, 2002)

M. S. Dubin: *North American Indian Jewelry and Adornment: From Prehistory to the Present* (New York, 2003)

L. Gillow: *African Textiles* (San Francisco, 2003)

C. K. Moore: *Navajo Beadwork: Architectures of Light* (Tucson, 2003)

A. K. Kanungo: *Glass Beads in Ancient India: An Ethnoarchaeological Approach* (Oxford, 2004)

D. K. Washburn and D. W. Crowe: *Symmetry Comes of Age: The Role of Pattern in Culture* (Seattle, 2004)

Beaker. In current scientific usage, an open-mouthed glass vessel, with a lip for pouring, used in experiments; in historic usage, a large drinking vessel with a wide mouth; in archaeological usage, a type of tall wide-mouthed vessel found in the graves of a people of Iberian origin who spread throughout Europe in the early Bronze Age.

Bear jug. Pottery jug shaped like a bear, which in some examples holds a dog in a posture meant to suggest bear-baiting. Bear jugs were made in the 18th century in Nottingham potteries (in brown stoneware) and in Staffordshire potteries (white salt-glazed stoneware); modern forgeries appeared in the art market in the 1980s.

Beatty & Sons. American glass factory founded in Steubenville, OH, *c.* 1850 by Alexander J. Beatty and relocated in Tiffin, OH, in 1888. Its blown and pressed tableware included goblets, of which it was able to make 500,000 per week. The company merged with the United States Glass Company in 1892, and became one of its 19 factories.

Beau Brummell. Type of dressing table (for men) or gaming table; many examples are 18th century, and so were built before the dandy and socialite Beau Brummell (1778–1840) became an arbiter of taste.

Beauvais Tapestry Factory. French tapestry manufactory. Although there was a strong weaving tradition in Beauvais, especially from the 11th century, the town became an important centre for tapestry production only in the late 17th century. On the instigation of Jean-Baptiste Colbert (1619–83), Louis XIV's Surintendant et Ordonnateur Général des Bâtiments, Arts et Manufactures, a tapestry factory was founded by the Parisian tapestry dealer Louis Hinart (*d* 1697) on 5 August 1664.

Colbert's intention was to discourage the purchase of Flemish verdure tapestries, which, despite prohibitions, continued to be bought. Contrary to his wishes, production was guaranteed when the Garde Meuble purchased 254 tapestries, mostly verdures, between 1667 and 1683. From this period tapestries from Beauvais were given by the King as diplomatic gifts, for example the series depicting the Story of Polyphemus, which was delivered to the King of Guinea in 1671.

Hinart was, however, unable to run a financially self-sufficient establishment and the King became sole owner of the factory. On 1 March 1684 Philippe Béhagle, a tapestry merchant from Oudenaarde who had been working in Tournai since 1678, was put in charge of production. From this time the first great tapestries were woven at Beauvais, including the *Conquests of Louis the Great* (Florence, Candido Casini priv. col.), the *Battle of Cassel* (Château Lafitte, nr Pouillac) in the style of Martin des Batailles and the *Acts of the Apostles* (Beauvais, Cathedral; version Paris, Mobilier N.) after Raphael. Several of these bear witness to the stylistic innovations introduced at Beauvais before the Gobelins. In the famous series known as the *Grotesques* (Paris, Louvre; Paris, Mus. A. Dec.; Aix-en-Provence, Mus. Tap.; Aix-en-Provence, Bishop's Pal.; Stockholm, Town Hall; Baden, Schloss Bruck-sal), which were on a yellow ground, the painter Jean-Baptiste Monnoyer was clearly inspired by the engravings of Jean Berain. These tapestries were precursors of the Rococo style, as were the chinoiserie tapestries known as the *Chinese Hangings* in the style of Monnoyer, Jean-Baptiste Belin and Vernansal.

In 1726 Jean-Baptiste Oudry was employed as a painter in the tapestry works, where he subsequently played a considerable role in the revival of Beauvais, which became, according to Voltaire, 'the kingdom of Oudry'. Between 1734 and 1756 the administration was in the hands of Nicolas Besnier, a goldsmith famous during the reign of Louis XIV (*reg* 1643–1715). During this time the design studio was organized, new cartoons were designed and an administration similar to that of Charles Le Brun at the Gobelins was introduced. Oudry closely supervised factory production to ensure both technical and artistic quality, and he demanded a faithful transfer of design and colour for his works, which included the COMEDIES OF MOLIÉRE (woven after 1732) and the FABLES OF LA FONTAINE (woven after 1736; New York, Met.). He also called on such famous painters as Charles-Joseph Natoire (1700–77), who designed a wall-hanging of the *Story of Don Quixote* (1735; Aix-en-Provence, Bishop's Pal.; cartoons, Compiégne, Château). In 1734 Oudry became director of the factory and shortly afterwards employed François Boucher as factory painter. The lengthy collaboration with Boucher was one of the reasons for the success of Beauvais in the 18th century. Between 1736 and 1755 Boucher produced no fewer than 45 compositions for 6 wall-hangings, which included the *Story of Psyche*, *Fêtes Italiennes* (c. 1762) and *Loves of the Gods* (Rome, Pal. Quirinale). The use of chinoiseries, mythological themes and pastoral scenes assured the success of the factory for several years, and from 1737 it was annually funded by Louis XV (*reg* 1715–74).

In the second half of the 18th century the rise of Neo-classicism led to the gradual abandonment of the designs of Boucher and Oudry in favour of those of such artists as Jean-Baptiste Deshays (1729–65; e.g. *L'Astrée*), Jean-Baptiste Le Prince (1734–81; *Russian Games/Russian Sports*; Paris, Petit Pal.; Paris, Mus. Jacquemart-André; Paris, Mobilier N.; Aix-en-Provence, Mus. Tap.) and Francesco Casanova (1727–1803; *Amusements de la Campagne* and *The Bohemians*; e.g. ex-Thiérard priv. col.). The production of furnishing tapestries, in particular those by Oudry, also contributed to the factory's growing success. From 1760 a set of furnishing tapestries was woven to complement each new wall-hanging. From the last years of the *ancien régime* date such important hangings as the *Four Corners of the World* (Hôtel de M Gaston Ménier), after Barbiers, and the *Alexander* series (1792) after Etienne de Lavallée-Poussin (1735–1802).

During the French Revolution the factory was administered by De Menou, a contractor who was granted a concession for 20 years starting in 1780. Now a private enterprise operating in premises belonging to the king, production at Beauvais slowed down and by 1793, when annual orders for official gifts were eliminated, sales were almost completely at a standstill. The proposed transfer of the factory to the Gobelins, demands for the abolition of the factory by the revolutionary politican Jean-Paul Marat and the rebelliousness of the poorly and irregularly paid workers all contributed to the difficulties of the revolutionary period. De Menou resigned; the factory was nationalized in November 1793. Conditions, however, did not immediately improve: there was a lack of raw materials and a limited number of weavers because many had been conscripted. The factory's prospects improved when the Bonaparte family became involved in the running of the concern. As Ministre de l'Intérieur et des Arts, Lucien Bonaparte devoted a great deal of attention to the old royal factories. In 1800 he put one of his protégés, Jean-Baptiste Huet I, in charge of Beauvais. In 1802 the factory was visited by Napoleon Bonaparte (*reg* 1804–14) and in October 1804 the Emperor decided to include Beauvais in the Civil List. Activity was immediately revived in the workshops. From this time production was reserved for furnishing the imperial palaces, with the main focus on the manufacture of seat coverings, which were often based on such old designs as those of *Military Convoys*, after Casanova. These tapestries were destined for such châteaux as Saint-Cloud, Fontainebleau, Compiègne, and the Tuileries. From the Restoration (1815) new models were created for the factory by such designers as Louis Saint-Ange Desmaisons and JEAN-DÉMOSTHÈNE DUGOURC, and their decorative inventiveness was reflected in the overall production. Important and imposing collections of furniture tapestries were made, sometimes accompanied by allegorical *portières*.

The direction of production remained the same under the other 19th-century administrations. New designs for royal residences were produced by such artists as Chenavard, Starke, Adam, and Couderc during the July monarchy (1830–48), and by Pierre-Adrien Chabal-Dussurgey or Diéterle during the Second Empire (1852–70). The same high standards were maintained throughout this period, an example of which are the unusually exquisite tapestries created after designs by Viollet-le-Duc for ecclesiastical vestments. Despite these successes, the lack of large orders and of resources led to the use during the last quarter of the 19th century of 18th-century cartoons in the style of Desportes, Oudry and Le Prince for screens or folding partitions. A few decorative panels, such as the *Garden of Luxembourg* by Ernest Quost (*b* 1844), continued to be made, especially at the beginning of the 20th century.

A clearly marked evolution followed the appointment of Jean Ajalbert as director in 1917. He realized that the causes of the decline were the lack of funds and the absence of new designs; he decided therefore to call on the services of such contemporary artists as Paul Poiret (1879–1944), Leonetto Capiello (1875–1942), Gaudissart and Paul Véra. Raoul Dufy (1877–1953) was commissioned to create the famous ensemble *Paris* (1924–9). From 1 January 1936, the factory was annexed to the Mobilier National under the management of the same general administration, which the following year also ran the Gobelins and Savonnerie factories. The aim of this reorganization was to unify the creative effort. In 1936, just prior to the revival of tapestry weaving for wall-hangings Jean Lurçat was commissioned to design a series of covers for the 'Icarus' range of furniture and Charles Dufresne was commissioned to make cartoons for tapestry covers for chairs for a series known as the *Beach and the Pleasures of Summer* (exh. Salon d'Automne 1941).

In November 1939 the workshops were moved near to Aubusson. In June 1940 the buildings of the old factory built by Colbert were destroyed. A few months later the factory was moved to the Gobelins enclosure in Paris. In 1946 Beauvais commissioned Matisse to design two wall-hangings called *Polynesia, the Sea* and *Polynesia, the Sky* (both 1946; Paris, Pompidou) from cut-paper cartoons, thus renewing the Beauvais wall-hanging tradition.

In the late 20th century works produced at Beauvais were used for the decoration of official buildings. In January 1989 President Mitterrand opened the new premises in Beauvais, created from 19th-century buildings that used to house the abattoirs.

B. Jestaz: *The Beauvais Manufactory in 1690* (San Francisco, 1979)

C. Bremer-David: *French Tapestries & Textiles in the J. Paul Getty Museum* (Los Angeles, 1997)

La Manufacture de Beauvais, du Consulat à la IIe République: Tapisseries, cartons, maquettes (exh. cat. by C. Gastinel-Coural, Beauvais, Gal. N. Tapisserie, 1998)

Becerril, Francisco (*b* Cuenca, 1506–7; *d* Cuenca, 1573). Spanish silversmith. His principal work was the monumental standing monstrance (destr. 1808) for Cuenca Cathedral, begun in 1528 and unveiled in 1546, although unfinished until 1573; only five statuettes (*c.* 1550; London, V&A) are preserved out of the hundreds that adorned it. Between 1527–8 and 1537 Becerril made the standing monstrance of Villaescusa de Haro (Cuenca, Mus. Dioc.-Catedralicio), with the collaboration of Juan Ruiz and Luis del Castillo. He later created three other tower-shaped monstrances: those in Iniesta (1556) and Buendía—both with three layers: the lower two square, the upper one circular—and the monstrance of S Pedro de Huete (untraced). Becerril was silversmith for Cuenca Cathedral and made a set of *coronas* (1543) and a set of paxes (1550–51) for use there. He executed several crosses: those made in the mid-16th century (e.g. the cross of La Puerta, *c.* 1540; parish church of Guadalajara) reveal the influence of Michelangelo in their wealth of reliefs and statues; the later crosses, made between 1555 and 1570, in El Salvador de Cuenca, Villar del Saz, Villar de Domingo García, Requena and Gaudix Cathedral, display abstract Mannerist decoration. His chalice at Mucientes (Valladolid), which is relatively plain and was executed late in his career, was the prototype for the 'Cuenca' type of chalice, popular in central Spain at the end of the 16th century. His secular pieces include a magnificent ewer set (Madrid, Inst. Valencia Don Juan). His son Cristobál Becerril (*fl* 1575; *d* 1584), also a silversmith, made the standing monstrance of Alarcón (New York, Hisp. Soc. America).

E. A. Lopez-Yarto: 'Relaciones de Francisco Becerril con otros centros de platería nacionales', *Archv Esp. A.* lxi (July–Sept 1988), pp. 323–5

E. A. Lopez-Yarto: 'El platero conquense Cristobal Becerril', *Archv Esp. A.,* lxviii/271 (July–Sept 1995), pp. 255–69

Bed. Type of furniture for sleeping or resting. Fragments of beds have survived from the 1st Dynasty of Pharaonic Egypt (*c.* 2925–*c.* 2775 BC). They had rectangular frames, typically spanned by hide or skin, and were usually set at an incline with a footboard at the lower end and a detachable headrest at the top. They were supported on short feet often shaped like bulls' hooves and, later, lions' paws. By the New Kingdom (*c.* 1540–*c.* 1075 BC) the slope had disappeared, although the frame now often had a concave profile. Simple linen bedding was supported on woven cord. Beds were very much luxury items—most people slept on mats or simple mattresses either laid directly on the floor, or on raised benches of mudbrick—and consequently were often given such rich finishes as sheet foil gold or silver or gilded gesso. Such precious timbers as ebony were also used in combination with simple ivory inlay.

The beds of the Greeks derived their basic form from those of Egypt, although footboards and separate headrests were not used. Beds were now used for banqueting as well as sleeping and were therefore the most important furniture type. Although early examples have legs in the form of animal monopodiae, they soon acquired rectangular supports decorated with scrolls and palmettes. These supports were relatively wide and flat, an effect offset by shaped profiles. One end of the bed was usually raised into an elegant scroll to provide a headboard. Although bronze frames seem to have been used, beds were normally of timber, which could be treated with a wide range of decorative finishes including painting and silver inlay. The most elaborate examples were fitted with delicately moulded bronze mounts.

The Romans inherited the Greek form of couch; however, the rectangular supports had now largely disappeared to be replaced by turned legs, often of elegant baluster form. During the 2nd century AD the raised headboard (fulcrum) was replaced by scrolling rests at each end. A further rest sometimes ran along the back. Byzantine beds were often formed from elaborately turned members set within a framework of wooden planks. Alternatively, the frames could be of simple chestlike construction, placed on two trestles or on four legs. Such beds were often surrounded by hangings. These boxlike beds, fitted with head- and footboards, continued to be used well into the Middle Ages. In southern Europe they were often painted (e.g. Italian painted bed, 1337; Pistoia, Osp. Ceppo), while in northern Europe they were often decorated with carved ornament and in the Late Gothic period usually panelled.

Hangings were an increasingly important feature of the grandest beds, particularly in colder climates. The itinerant nature of many medieval households meant that such movable furnishings as hangings were often lavish, while fixed furniture was relatively plain. Bed frames were therefore comparatively simple, and the value of any state bed lay in the richness of its hangings. Grand state beds with full testers (canopies) appeared towards the end of the Middle Ages. At the head of the bed a celure stretched to the ceiling. Above the bed, suspended from the ceiling, was a tester. Hangings at the front of the bed were gathered into loops. Alternatively a pavilion, fitted with curtains, was erected as a canopy at the bedhead (*see also* UPHOLSTERY, §2(i)).

From the later Middle Ages the wooden framework of Italian and Spanish beds became more elaborate. The mattress was raised on a panelled platform that was fitted with lidded lockers around its edge. In northern Europe the great medieval state beds began to be superseded at the end of the 15th century. Beds were now given a permanent timber framework, with a post at each corner, often elaborately carved. Increasingly, and particularly in northern Europe, these posts were extended upwards to support a wooden tester. The tester was often given a heavy cornice and the canopy was sometimes domed. Although rich hangings remained important they were now confined within the decorative carving of the framework. A valance was suspended from the tester, and curtains were tied back at the corner posts when not in use. Fabrics varied according to taste and wealth, but the richest examples were hung with damask and velvet, trimmed with gold or silver fringes. In southern Europe beds assumed an increasingly architectural form, but testers were not as widely used.

During the 16th century beds were among the most important of all furniture types, and designs for them appear among the engravings of the most influential architects. Although some examples survive in the Late Gothic style, such beds were essentially products of the Renaissance. Such designers as Jacques Androuet Du Cerceau the Elder and Hans Vredeman de Vries applied the full Mannerist vocabulary of strapwork, caryatids and grotesques to four-poster bed designs. Posts often took the form of columns and were carried on lion-paw feet or griffin monopodiae. In England elaborate headboards carved with arcading or fielded panels reached to the tester and replaced the back posts. Front posts were often very sturdy, turned like massive balusters. A fine example of an English bed of this period is the Great Bed of Ware (c. 1590; London, V&A). In northern Germany and the Netherlands boxlike beds were incorporated into the wainscoting of the room.

In the first half of the 17th century beds with massive carved frames began to be replaced by a much simpler type that had originated in France. The frame was a simple cubelike form, broken only by plumed finials at the corners of the tester, and covered entirely in fabric. In France beds of this type were known as *lits à housse* ('loose-cover beds') because they resembled a grand state bed swathed in its protective covers. The *lit à housse* had a deep valance, normally embroidered and trimmed with braid and fringe, and four similarly worked curtains. Two wide curtains went from the centre of the foot of the bed round the outside of the footposts and to the centre of the sides; two narrow curtains went from the bedhead to the centre of the sides. The panels that hung round the footposts outside the curtains were known as cantoons or *cantonnières*; those that hung outside the curtains at the head of the bed were known as *bonnegrâces*. The main fabric was lined with a contrasting material, which was also used for the counterpoint and headcloth. The bedhead was often worked with strapwork appliqué. The fabrics used ranged from coarse woollen cloth to 'Genoa' velvets. Integrated colour schemes were a popular feature of interior decoration during this period, and the fabric of seat covers, wall hangings and bed-hangings in a bedchamber were often *en suite*. Towards the end of the century the *lit à housse* became more elaborate and much taller, although the frame continued to be covered entirely by fabric. In England and in the Netherlands the testers of the finest beds were given elaborate broken cornices with pierced crestings, and the strapwork patterns that

Wooden bed, 16th century (Kreuzenstein, Schloss-Museum)

The Great Bed of Ware, oak with carved and inlaid decoration, 2.67 × 3.35 × 3.35 m, c. 1590 (London, Victoria and Albert Museum)

decorated the valance and bedhead became ever more exuberant. In France new types of grand bed that reflected the spirit of the Baroque began to appear, chief among which was the *lit d'ange* with its swagged flying tester. The engravings of Daniel Marot I give an impression of what such a bed might have looked like in an integrated decorative setting. In German-speaking countries carved bed-frames continued to be important (e.g. The Prince Eugene Bed, 1711; Markt St Florian, St Florian Abbey). In Italy beds with posts but without testers continued to be made. Frames were of walnut and were given broadly classical ornament; luxurious beds were gilded and richly carved with vigorous Baroque ornament, the posts taking the form of caryatids or solomonic columns. Portuguese beds of the 17th century divide into the *cama de bilros* type, which had four elaborately turned posts with footboards and headboards formed from conforming turned members (e.g. Évora, D. Celesta Cabral priv. col.), while the 'Herera' type, which was also popular in Spain, featured an elaborate architectural headboard.

For much of northern Europe elaborate or modest variations of the *lit à housse* remained the norm well into the 18th century. However, changing social customs led to the introduction of new types of bed

from the late 1600s. In France in less formal rooms beds were often placed sideways in alcoves, lying parallel to the room. Hangings were suspended from the alcove itself, and consequently beds were given padded head- and footrests known as chevets. The exposed frames of such beds were carved with the sinuous curves of the emergent Rococo style. By the 1760s these beds had emerged from their alcoves, and their hangings were now suspended from dome-like testers, which in turn could be suspended from the wall or ceiling. A popular variant known as the *lit à la polonaise* featured a dome supported on iron struts issuing from each corner of the frame. Chevets were now of more geometric form and carved with leaves and guilloche as their decoration took on a more architectural character. In England carved bed-frames had reappeared in the 1750s. Thomas Chippendale's *Gentleman and Cabinet-maker's Director* (1754) included many designs for fourposter beds in the Rococo style, with testers of scrolling contour supported on slender colonnettes. Given a straighter profile and applied with antique ornament, this lighter type of bed was easily adapted to the Neoclassical style in the 1770s.

Although *lits à la polonaise* were common throughout Europe well into the 1790s, a new type of bed, pioneered by Charles Percier (1764–1838) and Pierre-François-Léonard Fontaine, became increasingly important *c*.1800. In contrast to the elegant *menuiserie* of 18th-century beds, the monumental form of the Empire bed, veneered with mahogany and applied with gilt-bronze mounts, owed more to the art of the *ébéniste*. Their characteristic boxlike form was scooped at the front to ease access, and their ends were often over-scrolled in imitation of antique couches. This prowlike form earned them the name *lit-en-bateau* (e.g. *c*. 1825; Azay-le-Ferron, Château). Hangings, which could be extremely elaborate, were normally suspended from the ceiling or the wall but were separate from the bed. The popularity of this type of bed spread throughout Europe with the victories of Napoleon Bonaparte (*reg* 1804–14) and the engravings published in such pattern-books as Pierre La Mésangère's *Meubles et objets de goût*, which began to appear in 1802. Designers as diverse as Karl Friedrich Schinkel and Agostino Fantastici were all to create widely differing versions of the *lit-en-bateau* (e.g. bed designed by Schinkel for Queen Louise, 1811; Berlin, Schloss Charlottenburg). In German-speaking countries and Scandinavia the form was adapted to native timbers and the clean lines of the Biedermeier style. The Empire-style bed, essentially antique in its inspiration, remained important into the middle of the 19th century, when it was displaced by other forms that drew on the plethora of competing historicist revivals. From the 1840s beds with carved half, and occasionally full, testers enjoyed renewed popularity, although the testers were rarely supported on four posts. Such beds were usually decorated in a Renaissance Revival or Gothic Revival style. Rigid testers with boxlike wooden frames replaced the swagged drapery of the Empire style. Despite these changes, however, beds with testers fell from favour in the second half of the 19th century, and beds with metal frames—usually iron and brass—appeared in large numbers. Towards the end of the century designers turned again to the 18th century, and such furniture-makers as Julius Zwiener (*b* 1849) produced beds that fused the veneers and gilt-bronze mounts of the Louis XV style with the sinuous contours of Art Nouveau, while in England such firms as Heal & Son produced 'Sheraton' style bedroom suites. Paradoxically such progressive designers as Charles Rennie Mackintosh, Josef Hoffmann and Richard Riemerschmid were to design some of the last fourposter beds, using the characteristic rectangular shape to enhance the abstract geometry of their styles.

E. Harris: *Going to Bed* (London, 1981)
P. Thornton: *Authentic Décor: The Domestic Interior, 1620–1920* (London, 1984)
N. de Reyniès: *Le Mobilier domestique*, I (Paris, 1987)

Bedeschini, Francesco (*d c*. 1688). Italian engraver, designer, painter and architect, worked in Aquila. He worked as a designer of maiolica for Carlantonio Grue, and published sets of engraved ornaments.

H. Coutts: 'Francesco Bedeschini Designer of Maiolica' *Apollo*, vi (1987), pp 401–3

Bedfordshire. English county noted for its lace production. Commercial bobbin lacemaking was introduced in the 17th century to the English county of Bedfordshire by Flemish migrants. Documentary evidence indicates that English lace followed Flemish modes, but no examples from this early period survive. In the second half of the 19th century coarse laces such as Maltese, Cluny and Yak were made in Bedfordshire. Bedfordshire laces were revived by amateur enthusiasts in the late 20th century.

C. Freeman: *Pillow Lace in the East Midlands* (Luton, 1958)
J. Fisher: *The Bedfordshire Family of Laces* (Kenthurst, 1991)

Beefeater. Pewter flagon produced in the late 17th century with a lid that is similar in shape to the hat worn by the Yeomen of the Guard who serve as Warders of the Tower of London, popularly known as Beefeaters.

Beek, Jan Bontjes van (*b* 18 Jan 1899, Vejle, Netherlands; *d* 5 September 1969, Berlin). Dutch ceramicist who pursued his career in Germany. He opened a workshop near Bremen in 1922, manufacturing simple vessels to which (from 1929) he added lustre glazes. He moved to Berlin in 1933, and for the next ten years produced stoneware with feldspar glazes. He was uncompromised by the Nazi government (his daughter Cato Bontjes van Beek was executed for resisting Nazi rule), and survived to become one of the most important ceramicists of post-war Germany. There is an important collection of his work in the Museum für Kunst und Gewerbe in Hamburg.

R. Scherpe and F. G. Winter: *Jan Bontjes van Beek* (Krefeld, 1971)

Beetham [née Robinson], **Isabella** (*b* 1744, Sedgefield, Lancs; *d* after 1809). English silhouettist. In 1764 she eloped with her lover, the actor and inventor Edward Beetham. They worked as actors in London, and Isabella began to cut profiles at Clerkenwell. She initially painted on card, and then on glass. Her portraits were backed with plaster or, when painted on the back of convex glass, with wax. Edward Beetham, by now her husband, had invented the Beetham's Patent Washing Mill, an early form of washing machine. They bought a building at 27 The Strand where Edward ran a shop and warehouse and Isabella a silhouette studio.

Beham [Behem; Beheim; Böhm; Peham], **Sebald** [Hans Sebald] (*b* Nuremberg, 1500; *d* Frankfurt am Main, 1550). Engraver, etcher, designer of woodcuts and stained glass, painter and illustrator. In contemporary documents and prints he was nearly always identified as Sebald Beham although since the 17th century and into the early years of the 20th he has mistakenly been called Hans Sebald Beham on the basis of his monogram: HSP or HSB. Sebald is best known for his prints, of which he produced a prodigious quantity: approximately 252 engravings, 18 etchings and 1500 woodcuts, including woodcut book illustrations. These included utilitarian prints designed to serve as ornament and decoration of various kinds: on playing cards, title-pages, wallpaper, coats of arms, and as patterns for use by architects, metalworkers and other craftsmen. Sebald's brother, Barthel Beham (1502–40) was also a painter, engraver, etcher and, possibly, designer of woodcuts.

R. A. Koch and A. von Bartsch: *Early German Masters: Barthel Beham, Hans Sebald Beham* (New York, 1978)

A. Stewart: 'Paper Festivals and Popular Culture: The Kermis Woodcuts of Sebald Beham in Reformation Nuremberg', *16th C. J.*, iiiv (July 1993), pp. 301–50

Behrens, Peter (*b* Hamburg, 14 April 1868; *d* Berlin, 27 Feb 1940). German architect, designer and painter. Progressing from painting and graphics to product design and architecture, Behrens achieved his greatest successes with his work for the Allgemeine Elektrizitäts-Gesellschaft (AEG), in which he reconciled the Prussian Classicist tradition with the demands of industrial fabrication.

Behrens regularly exhibited paintings and woodcuts in the 1890s. His colour woodcut *The Kiss* (1899; Philadelphia, PA, Mus. A.) depicts a kissing couple, their faces framed and joined by voluptuous *Jugendstil* curves formed by their own tresses. At the end of the decade Behrens decided to abandon painting in favour of the applied arts. His first graphic works and designs for glass, porcelain, jewellery and furniture appeared in 1898 and 1899, and his monogram for the Insel Verlag (1899) is still in use in a modified form. In July 1900 work began in Darmstadt on his own house, which he had designed, together with all its furnishings and tableware.

In 1907 Behrens was called to Berlin as artistic adviser to AEG, for which he produced an incomparable series of product, graphic and architectural designs, with which Behrens created the world's first corporate image. In the sphere of product design this was achieved by offering a number of models based on various permutations of standardized parts, colours and finishes. This technique was applied to arc lamps, electric fans, electric clocks and, most successfully, to a range of electric kettles introduced in 1909. Behrens was also responsible for the firm's graphic design and in 1907–8 produced the Behrens Antiqua script used in the firm's initials. It drew on previous Behrens designs (Behrens-Schrift, 1902; Behrens Kursiv und Schmuck, 1907) and has been described as the 'maturest product' of the calligraphy course developed by Behrens, Anna Simons (1871–1951) and Fritz Hellmut Ehmcke (1878–1965) on behalf of the Prussian Ministry of Commerce for use in colleges of art and technology. In 1909 Behrens and Simons also designed the lettering of the inscription on the pediment of the Reichstag building in Berlin: 'Dem deutschen Volke'.

A. Windsor: *Peter Behrens: Architect and Designer* (London, 1981)

Peter Behrens: electric kettle, nickel-plated brass and rattan, 222 × 229 × 159 mm, 1909 (New York, Museum of Modern Art)

T. Buddensieg and others: *Industriekultur: Peter Behrens and the AEG* (Cambridge, MA, 1984)

S. Anderson: *Peter Behrens and a New Architecture for the Twentieth Century* (Cambridge, MA, 2000)

Beilby. English family of glassware enamellers. In 1760 William Beilby (1705–65), a goldsmith, moved his family from Durham to Newcastle upon Tyne, where his son Ralph Beilby (1743–1817) worked as an heraldic engraver. In 1755 William Beilby jr (1740–1819) was apprenticed to the Birmingham enameller John Haseldine. He was then employed with his sister Mary Beilby (1749–97) at the Dagnia-Williams glasshouse in Newcastle upon Tyne, where they decorated drinking glasses called 'light balusters' or 'Newcastle' glasses and decanters. Their early work is thought to have been influenced by the heraldic work of their brother Ralph: the decoration includes the royal coat of arms of George III and the Prince of Wales's feathers, painted in full heraldic colours on enamel-twist goblets. Their work then became more Rococo in style, displaying rustic scenes, such architectural fantasies as classical buildings and ruins, baskets of fruit, floral subjects, fruiting vines, exotic birds, gardens and landscapes, using only white enamelling. Designs often incorporated standard vine scroll and hop-and-barley motifs. They used white, monochrome or a combination of enamel colours, and some glasses have gilded rims. Their glasses are often signed with only the surname. Before 1765, when their father died, William signed his pieces *W. Beilby junr*. Although Mary was involved in the firm, her precise role is unclear as no work has been specifically attributed to her. In 1774 she had a paralytic stroke and moved with William to Fife in Scotland.

ODNB
J. Rush: *The Ingenious Beilbys* (London, 1973)
S. Cottle: 'The Other Beilbys: British Enamelled Glass of the 18th Century', *Apollo*, cxxiv (1986), pp. 315–27
S. Cottle: 'Enamelled Glass: The Beilbys Recollected', *Apollo*, cxxix (June 1989), pp. 393–8
R. J. Charleston: 'A Group of Enamelled Opaque-white Glasses', *Burl. Mag.,* cxxxii (May 1990), pp. 328–35
I. J. D. Murray: *Eighteenth Century English Glass* (Paddington, NSW, 2003)

Beinglas. Type of semi-opaque glass similar to lattimo. The milky colour was achieved by adding the ash of calcinated bone powder to the glaze mix. It was produced in the late 18th century and early 19th in the glasshouses of Bohemia and Thuringia, often with enamel decoration.

Bélanger, François-Joseph (*b* Paris, 12 April 1744; *d* Paris, 1 May 1818). French architect, interior designer and landscape designer. Although his fame rests on his accomplishments as a landscape architect, his mercurial talents are perhaps best characterized in his drawings for interior decoration and court festivals.

In 1767 Bélanger became a Dessinateur du Roi at the Hôtel des Menus Plaisirs under Charles Michel-Ange Challe. Since the Menus Plaisirs were responsible for the temporary decorations and stage scenery for court festivities, Bélanger was involved with preparations for the marriage celebrations in 1770 of the Dauphin, the future Louis XVI (*reg* 1774–92). One of his first commissions (1769) was for a jewel cabinet (destr.) made by Maurice-Bernard Evalde, with mounts by Pierre Gouthière, for the Dauphine Marie-Antoinette.

From 1769 Bélanger began to receive independent commissions, largely gained through his amorous liaison with the celebrated singer and actress Sophie Arnould. In 1770 he designed a pavilion after the Antique at the Hôtel de Brancas, Paris, for one of Arnould's wealthy admirers, the Comte de Lauragais. Its interior represented a completely innovative form of Neo-classical decoration: the walls were no longer divided into panels but instead were articulated by columns, niches and statues. Coupled Ionic columns carried the ceiling architrave, which was illusionistically painted in heavy garlands and grotesques. This type of decoration, inspired by Charles-Louis Clérisseau (1721–1820) and Nicolas Lhuillier (*d* 1793), a young sculptor who had trained in Rome, rapidly spread throughout Paris and influenced the Etruscan style during the 1770s and 1780s.

In 1770 Bélanger constructed and furnished the small Château de Bagatelle in the Bois de Boulogne. For the interior he introduced grotesques in coloured plaster to articulate the walls. The Comte d'Artois's bedroom was designed to represent a military tent, complete with a chimney supported by cannon-balls

and grenades, alluding to his office of Grand Maître de l'Artillerie. Bélanger's other projects for him included remodelling two dining-rooms and a billiards room for the 17th-century château of Maison (1777–9), where delicate illusionistic paintings were suspended between slender columns and pilasters in a manner influenced by engravings in *The Works in Architecture of Robert and James Adam* (1773).

J. Stern: *A l'ombre de Sophie Arnould : François-Joseph Bélanger* (Paris, 1930)

Belden [Belding], **Samuel** (*b* Norwalk, Staffs, 16 Sept 1632; *d* Hatfield, MA, 3 Jan 1713). American joiner. He was brought to America by his parents *c.* 1640. In 1661 he moved to Hadley (now Massachusetts) in the Connecticut River valley, and entered into partnership with John ALLIS. Belden's son Samuel (1665–1738) and Allis's son Ichabod (1675–1747) ran Belden & Allis after the deaths of their fathers.

Belfast Glasshouse. Northern Irish glass manufactory. In 1771 Benjamin Edwards (*d* 1812) was brought from Bristol by the Tyrone Colleries, and by 1776 he had opened a glass factory in the port of Belfast. From there he advertised enamelled, clear and coloured glass, cut and plain wine-glasses, decanters and all kinds of chemical wares. By 1783 he was selling glass-making machinery and moulds to glasshouses elsewhere in Ireland. The glasshouse closed *c.* 1829.

Bel Geddes, Norman (*b* Adrian, MI, 27 April 1893; *d* New York, 9 May 1958). American designer. He initially worked as an illustrator, making portraits of operatic luminaries for the *New York Times*. After producing plays in Los Angeles (1917), he joined the Metropolitan Opera in New York (1918) and became a leading stage designer; he invented the high wattage spotlight and developed modern theatrical productions that blended the play, its lighting, its performers, and their costumes into a cohesive whole. He gained international attention for his stage set (1921; unexecuted) for Dante's *Divine Comedy*, which revolutionized theatrical and operatic productions; it was conceived as a single, massive set with lighting coming first from below, signifying Hades, then, as the play progressed, from high above, signifying Paradise. This led Max Reinhardt, the distinguished German producer, to commission him to design the settings for a production of *The Miracle* in New York (1923), and for this Bel Geddes transformed the entire interior of the Century Theater into the nave of a Gothic cathedral, with pews replacing seats to make the audience part of the cast.

In 1925 Bel Geddes went to Paris to design a production of the play *Jeanne d'Arc*. There he was attracted by the new forms of art shown at the Exposition Internationale des Arts Décoratifs et Industriels Modernes (1925), and he determined to leave the world of the theatre for industrial design. In 1929 he collaborated with Otto Koller on the design (unexecuted) of an airliner as a massive 'flying wing' that would provide accommodation for 400 passengers in the style of ocean liners. He became one of the main exponents of streamlining, the 'moderne' style inspired by speed and dynamism, and he produced designs and patents for a streamlined train (1931), ocean liner (1932) and buses and automobiles (1932) whose forms foreshadowed the Volkswagen Beetle. His influential book *Horizons* (1932) predicted that design in the environment and for machines and objects of daily use would dominate the modern era.

Bel Geddes was as well known for his unrealized projects as for his completed works. His vision ranged from the practical design of typewriters, radios, refrigerators and stoves to the redesign of the Ringling Brothers Barnum and Bailey circus and a project for a floating airport in New York Harbor that would rotate to keep its single runway facing into the wind. He also carried out interior design commissions.

N. Bel Geddes: *A Project for a Theatrical Presentation of the Divine Comedy of Dante Alighieri* (New York, 1924)
N. Bel Geddes: *Horizons* (Boston, 1932)
F. J. Hunter: *Catalog of the Norman Bel Geddes Theater Collection* (Boston, 1973)
D. H. Dyal: *Norman Bel Geddes: Designer of the Future* (Monticello, 1983)
F. Engler and C. Lichtenstein: *Norman Bel Geddes, 1893–1958* (Bologna, 1994)
A. Morshed: 'The Aesthetics of Ascension in Norman Bel Geddes's Futurama', *J. Soc. Archit. Hist.,* lxiii/1 (March 2004), pp. 74–99

Belgium. Ceramics *see* ANTWERP, §1; BOUFFIOULX; BRUSSELS, §1; RAEREN; TOURNAI, §1.

Glass *see* LIÈGE; NIZET GLASSWORKS; VAL-SAINT-LAMBERT GLASSHOUSE.

Textiles *see* ANTWERP, §§3 and 4; BINCHE LACE; BRUGES; BRUSSELS, §§2 and 3; ENGHIEN; GRAMMONT; MECHLIN LACE; OUDENAARDE; TOURNAI, §2.

Belkein [Belkin, Bellekin, Belkyn, Bellequin]. Dutch family of shell-carvers, based in Amsterdam and active in the 16th, 17th and early 18th centuries. Their work included MOTHER-OF-PEARL relief carvings with additional black line-engravings of mythological or genre scenes (e.g. shell depicting *Perseus and Andromeda*; Stuttgart, Württemberg. Landesmus.) and NAUTILUS SHELLS.

Bell, **Vanessa**. *See under* OMEGA WORKSHOPS.

Bell and baluster turning. In furniture legs, a baluster or vase shape is surmounted by an inverted cup (the 'bell'). This type of turning is common in English furniture, especially in the 17th century, and also appears on American furniture *c.* 1690–1720.

Bellangé. French family of furniture-makers. Pierre-Antoine Bellangé (1758–1827) made furniture for the courts of Napoleon (*reg* 1804–14), Louis XVIII (*reg* 1814–24) and Charles X (*reg* 1824–30). His furniture is characteristically made from mahogany and other dark woods. As part of the reconstruction of the White House in 1817, President James Munroe ordered 53 pieces of furniture from Bellangé: a pier table, two sofas, two *bergères*, two screens, four upholstered stools, six footstools, 18 armchairs and 18 side chairs. Many of these pieces were dispersed in the auction of 1860. The process of reassembling this collection in the White House was initiated in 1961 by Jacqueline Kennedy; the White House now has the pier table, a *bergère,* a sofa and four armchairs.

Pierre Antoine's brother, Louis François Bellangé (1759–1827) was also a furniture-maker; furniture that he designed himself is usually decorated with porcelain plaques, but his workshop also used Boulle designs. When the brothers died in 1827, Pierre Antoine's son Alexandre-Louis (1799–1863) inherited both workshops, but ran them separately and maintained the distinctive styles of the workshops. He became one of the most prominent furniture-makers in France, and in 1842 was appointed *ébéniste du roi* to Louis-Philippe.

D. Ledoux-Lebard: *Le mobilier français du XIXe siècle, 1795–1889: Dictionnaire des ébénistes et des menuisiers* (Paris, 1989)

Bellarmine [Ger.: *Bartmannskrug*; 'bearded-man jug']. Type of German glazed stoneware jug produced from the 15th century through to the 19th, and known in English from the 17th century as the bellarmine, the eponym of which was Cardinal Roberto Bellarmino (1542–1621), who was detested in England because of his anti-Protestant polemics. The jugs, which are decorated with the moulded face of a bearded man (sometimes with a coat-of-arms below it) are also known as 'Greybeards' and as 'd'Alva bottles'; the latter name alludes to the third Duke of Alba (1507–82), who persecuted Protestants in the Netherlands.

Belleek Porcelain Factory. Irish ceramics factory built in the village of Belleek, Co. Fermanagh (now Northern Ireland) between 1857 and 1863, when production began. The factory was close to sources of such essential materials as feldspar, kaolin, flint, shale and water. During the early years potters from Staffordshire, England, were employed to assist in the technical developments at the factory. The pottery was funded by the Dublin entrepreneur David McBirney (*d* 1884), who also owned shares in the Sligo and Bundoran Railway; a branch line was built to the factory, which aided distribution. The architect Robert Williams Armstrong (*d* 1884) probably designed the factory building and was the factory's first artistic director. He was particularly interested in developing high-fired ceramic bodies, especially stoneware and porcelain. Three types of wares were produced at the factory: utilitarian, transfer-printed earthenwares, which continued to be made until 1947; stonewares, including telegraphic insulators and vases, and porcelain. Belleek is most famous for its very thin porcelain, the glaze of which has a nacreous lustre; wares included vases, centrepieces, sweetmeat dishes (e.g. of *c.* 1865–70; London, V&A) and openwork baskets. Between 1865 and 1870 the factory concentrated production on its porcelain and developed its export markets to Britain, Europe, Canada, the USA, South Africa and Australia. In 1884 the factory was sold to local businessmen, who traded as the Belleek Pottery Works Co. Ltd until 1918, producing individual wares or limited editions. In 1919 the company began trading as Belleek Pottery Ltd; it has changed hands several times, and is now owned by the Irish-American Dr George Moore.

J. B. Cunningham: *The Story of Belleek* (Belleek, 1992)

R. K. Degenhardt: *Belleek: The Complete Collector's Guide and Illustrated Reference* (Radnor, 1993)

M. Langham: *Belleek Irish Porcelain: An Illustrated Guide to over Two Thousand Pieces* (London, 1993)

J. W. Keefe: *Belleek: Innovation, Form and Technique: The Geraldine Colby Zeiler Collection*, New Orleans, LA. Mus. A. (New Orleans, 2002)

H. M. Mann: *Ireland's Belleek: A Collector's Reference Guide* (Victoria, BC, 2005)

Bellevue (France). French centre of ceramics production. A pottery was founded in the village of Bellvue (near Toul, in Meurthe-et-Moselle) in 1758. In 1771 it passed into the hands of Charles Bayard (former director of the Lunéville pottery) and François Boyer, who in 1773 were given the right to style the pottery 'Manufacture Royale de Bellevue'. Bayard left in 1788, and Boyer ran the factory until 1806. In the 19th century it was managed by successive generations of the Aubry family. Bayard and Boyer made biscuit figures from models supplied by PAUL-LOUIS CYFFLÉ (who also worked for Toul and Lunéville). The company also made tableware (both earthenware and faience) and terracotta garden figures.

Bellevue (UK). English centre of ceramics production. A pottery was founded in the town of Hull (near what is now the Albert Dock) in 1802; the proprietors included Job RIDGWAY. It soon closed, but in 1826 it was bought by William Bell, who called it Bellevue; it closed in 1841. The factory produced large quantities of earthenware, much of which was exported to Germany through the Company's depot in Hamburg. Very few examples of its wares survive; some are marked Belle Vue.

Belli. Italian family of gold- and silversmiths. Vincenzo Belli I (*b* Turin, 1710; *d* Rome, 1787) settled in Rome in 1740, where he worked with Roman masters on the altar for the chapel of St John the Baptist in S Roque in Lisbon. The works produced for this altar were the most important set of liturgical furnishings made in Rome during the 18th century (e.g. ewer and basin, 1745–50; Lisbon, Mus. S Roque). He created prototypes that influenced the taste of the period, especially in the field of secular silverware, for example a ewer and basin (Rome, Pal. Venezia),

a pair of soup tureens, trays and other tableware (priv. col.). These are richly decorated in a Baroque style, though the forms are classical. Under Vincenzo's leadership the family shop employed *c.* 20 people, which made it possible to maintain a steady rate of production to satisfy the constant commissions from nobles and churchmen.

On Vincenzo's death the shop was taken over by his son Giovacchino Belli (1756–1822), who had worked with his father on various pieces of elaborate tableware. Later Giovacchino favoured a more rigorous style, with precise references to the Antique in his decorative repertory, for example a reliquary (Rome, S Carlo al Corso); statues in silver and gilt bronze of *SS Peter and Paul* (priv. col.); a ewer (Rome, Vatican, Mus. Stor. A. Tesoro S Pietro); desk furnishings, lamps and tableware (priv. col.). Giovacchino was succeeded by his son Pietro Belli (1780–1828) and his grandson Vincenzo Belli II, who developed the style of their predecessors into a production of great formal and technical mastery.

Belli [Vicentino], **Valerio** (*b* Vicenza, *c.* 1468; *d* Vicenza, 1546). Italian gem-engraver, goldsmith and medallist. The most important part of his career was spent in Rome, where he worked for Clement VII and his successor Paul III. He also spent a short period in Venice, returning from there to Vicenza in 1530 and remaining in the latter city for most of the time until his death. No specimens of his work as a goldsmith survive, but he is called 'aurifex' in contemporary documents and may have made the settings for his carved gems.

Belli specialized in cutting gems and crystal and in carving dies for coins and medals. His style was governed by his study of ancient coins and gems. His best-known works are those made for his papal patrons, many consisting of or incorporating carvings in rock crystal or semiprecious stones. The most splendid of these is a silver-gilt casket adorned with 24 carvings in crystal showing scenes from the *Passion* (1532; Florence, Pitti); it was made for Clement VII as a wedding gift for the French Dauphin (later Henry II) and Catherine de' Medici.

Belli is also known to have been connected with the papal mint, although no specific issues of coins can be attributed to him, and the remains of his work as an official medallist are scanty. The best known of his works in this field is a private rather than an official work, a medal bearing a portrait of *Pietro Bembo* (e.g. Washington, DC, N.G.A.), with a reverse representing him reclining in a pastoral setting. Specimens also survive of a portrait medal that is almost certainly a self-portrait from dies engraved by Belli. This is known in several versions (e.g. Washington, DC, N.G.A.), each bearing a classicizing mythological scene on its reverse. Vasari attributed to Belli a series of portraits of the *Twelve Caesars*. No complete set is known to survive, although there are many copies (e.g. Berlin, Bodemus.). More interesting and unusual is a group of some 50 medals representing mythological and historical figures of the ancient world. These combine portraits, imaginary or based on ancient coins, with a variety of reverses inspired more or less directly by ancient models. Struck specimens are rare (e.g. *Helen of Troy*, Washington, DC, N.G.A.), but many reproductions of them in the form of metal casts survive (e.g. Washington, DC, N.G.A.; London, BM).

B. Barsali: *Medieval Goldsmith's Work* (London and New York, 1969)
D. Thornton: 'Valerio Belli and after: Renaissance Gems in the British Museum', *Jewel Stud.*, viii (1998), pp. 11–20

Bellini carpets. *See under* CARPET, §II. 3(III)(A).

The Gloucester Candlestick, gilt, bell metal, h. 510 mm, early 12th century (London, Victoria and Albert Museum)

Bell metal. Alloy of copper and tin of which bells are made, the tin being in larger proportion than in ordinary bronze. The proportions of the constituents vary within the limits of 3¼ and 4 of copper to 1 of tin: the former is suited for large bells, the latter for small house-bells. Bell metal has on occasion been used for other objects that would ordinarily have been made with bronze (e.g. Gloucester Candlestick, *c.* 1110; London, V&A). Usage is not consistent, in that bell metal is sometimes understood to be a type of bronze; the Gloucester Candlestick is described by the Victoria and Albert Museum as bronze.

Bellosio, Eugenio (*b* Milan, 1847; *d* Magreglio, 1927). Italian silversmith. He was known for his complex designs of flatware, chalices and inkwells. His flatware designed *c.* 1885 was Renaissance Revival in style, while that designed *c.* 1887 (Milan, Castello Sforzesco) is more reminiscent of the Mannerism, the handles being adorned with the forms of nymphs and satyrs. Bellosio is also well known for his silver altar for the church of S Marta at Magreglio.

Belper Pottery. English pottery factory established in the Derbyshire village of Belper in the mid-18th century. It made light brown stoneware, and became well-known for its grotesque portraits of reform leaders. In 1834 the pottery was closed and moved to Derby.

Belter, John Henry (*b* Hilter, nr Osnabrück, 1804; *d* New York, 15 Oct 1863). American cabinetmaker of German birth. He arrived in New York in 1833 and was established as a cabinetmaker by 1844. In 1854 he opened a five-storey factory on 76th Street near Third Avenue. In 1856 Belter's brother-in-law John H. Springmeyer joined the firm. William Springmeyer and Frederic Springmeyer joined in 1861, and in 1865 the firm's name was changed to Springmeyer Bros; it went bankrupt in 1867.

Belter's fame is for technical innovation, reflected in four patents: the first, in 1847, for a device to saw openwork patterns into curved chair backs; the second, in 1856, for a two-piece bedstead of laminated construction; the third, in 1858, for a refinement to his process for achieving laminated construction with three-dimensional curves; and the fourth, in 1860, concerned with laminated construction and central locking. Belter's furniture—curvaceous rosewood chairs, sofas, tables, *étagères*, beds etc—is in a coarse and exuberant Rococo Revival manner, characterized by elaborate open crestings and aprons, decorated with C and S scrolls, leaves, flowers and grapes, partly in high relief, where extra sections were glued to the laminated base.

M. D. Schwartz, E. J. Stanek and D. K. True: *The Furniture of John Henry Belter and the Rococo Revival: An Inquiry into the Nineteenth-Century Furniture Design through a Study of the Gloria and Richard Manney Collection* (Edina, MN, 2000)

Beltrami, Giovanni (*b* Cremona, 26 Oct 1770; *d* Cremona, 1854). Italian gem-engraver and medallist. His work, executed with meticulous attention to detail, consists primarily of cameo reproductions of paintings on large size stones. His masterpiece is considered to be the *Tent of Darius* (1828; Cremona, Mus. Civ.), carved in white Brazilian topaz and based on the painting by Charles Le Brun (Versailles, Château). The former work was commissioned by Bartolomeo Turina of Cremona, as were *Angelica and Medoro*, *Wealth Conquered by Cupid*, the head of *Niobe* and *Rinaldo and Armida* (all Cremona, Mus. Civ.). Beltrami also received sizeable commissions from the Bonaparte family; these include portraits of *Napoleon and Josephine* and the *Myth of Psyche*, portrayed on 16 white cornelians (untraced) supplied to him for that purpose by the Empress Josephine. Other commissions were from the Austrian imperial family, among them an onyx cameo of a wreathed bust of *Francis I* (Vienna, Schatzkam.). Many works were also executed on behalf of Bartolomeo Soresina Vidoni and Conte Giovanni Battista Sommariva, for whom Beltrami produced numerous gem-engravings of the paintings in Sommariva's collection in Paris and at Tremezzo on Lake Como. Of these the following are extant: the agate *Communion of Attala* (priv. col.), after a painting by Anne-Louis Girodet (1767–1824; Paris, Louvre), the rock-crystal engraving of *The Kiss* from a painting by Francesco Hayez (1791–1882; untraced) and an engraving of *Curtius* (London, BM). Beltrami also carried out at least 90 medallions of pewter and copper (Cremona, Mus. Civ.), comprising a series of portraits of famous personalities. His work is signed, and many pieces carry the date of execution and a reference to the iconographic source.

G. Tassinari: 'Glyptic Portraits of Eugène de Beauharnais: The Intaglios by Giovanni Beltrami and the Cameo by Antonio Berini', *J. Walters A.G.*, lx–lxi (2002–3), pp. 43–64

Belvedere Factory. *See under* WARSAW.

Bencharong ware. Type of decorated ceramics made in China for the Thai market. During the 18th century, and possibly earlier, the Thai court at Ayutthaya started ordering enamel-decorated table-ware from China, made to their own designs. When the new dynasty established the capital at Bangkok in 1782 after the destruction of Ayutthaya by the Burmese, the use of these Bencharong ('five-coloured') wares (e.g. Bangkok, N. Mus.) grew and ceased to be a royal monopoly. It is known that on occasions the king sent artists to supervise the work of decoration, which was probably carried out at Canton using undecorated wares (Zhen-te-Zhen blanks).

Decoration of Bencharong wares is usually in the *famille verte* or, in the later wares, *famille rose* palette. By the middle of the 19th century gold was sometimes added: the Thai name for this group is *lai nam thong*. The enamel tends to cover the whole body in bright, regular and repetitive patterns. The commonest motif is the angel (Thai *thephanom*) but other mythical creatures such as the *garuda* or the royal lion (Skt *rājasimha*) are also depicted. A whole range of tableware and household utensils was produced: covered rice-bowls, spittoons, stemmed bowls and trays, cups and spoons. In the second half of the 19th century attempts were made to decorate Chinese wares in the blank in Thailand but these could not compete in quality, scale or price with the imported goods. In the first years of the 20th century the collapse of the Qing dynasty in China and the taste in Thailand for all things European ended both the production of, and demand for, Bencharong wares.

The Artistic Heritage of Thailand: A Collection of Essays, National Museum Volunteers (Bangkok, 1979)
T. B. Arapova and others: 'Sino-Thai Ceramics in the Hermitage: Contacts between Thailand and Russia at the end of the Nineteenth Century', *Apollo*, cl/ 453 (Nov 1999), pp. 19–24

Bendigo Pottery. Australian pottery founded in 1858 by a Scot, George Guthrie (1808–1909), in the Victoria town of Bendigo. The factory made household wares, including acid bottles, bricks, clay pipes, roof tiles, and tableware. During World War I it also made portrait jugs of military commanders, and in the 1930s it made agate-ware vases that were marketed as Waverly ware. The pottery is still active, but since 1971 has also been a tourist destination with an excellent museum built around the largest surviving collection of wood-fired kilns (5 bottle kilns, 3 circular kilns and 2 rectangular kilns). The walls are glazed from a century of salt-glaze firing.

R. Trower: *Bendigo Pottery* (Mulgrave, 1983)
K. Terpstra: 'Australia's Bendigo Pottery', *Cer. Mthly*, li/1 (Jan 2003), pp. 66–8

Beneman [Bennemann], **Guillaume** (*d* after 1804). French cabinetmaker, possibly of German birth. In 1785 he became a *maître-ébéniste* and was appointed Ebéniste du Roi. The next year he became the main supplier to the Garde Meuble under the direction of the sculptor Jean Hauré, who was in charge of furniture production. Beneman understood how to create a unified style in furnishings for royal residences, which is shown by his copying of old pieces: the writing-desk (Waddesdon Manor, Bucks, NT) for Louis XVI (*reg* 1774–92), for example, was based on the Bureau du Roi Louis XV (1769; Versailles, Château) made by Jean-Henri Riesener and Jean-François Oeben. There are few identifiable works by Beneman, so his contribution to the period is difficult to ascertain. The few pieces of furniture created during the Directoire (1795–9) indicate that he could adapt his forms to the new, fashionable styles.

F. de Salverte: *Les Ebénistes du XVIIIème siècle: Leurs Oeuvres et leurs marques* (Paris, 1923, rev. 5/1962)
P. Verlet: *Le Mobilier royal français*, 4 vols (Paris, 1945–90)
P. Verlet: *French Royal Furniture* (London, 1963)

Bénitier. Metal or faience vessel, normally mounted on a wall, used to hold holy water.

Bennett, John (*b* 1840; *d* 1907). Anglo-American potter. He was born in Staffordshire and as a young man worked for Doulton, where he developed a distinctive method of underglaze painting. In 1877 he emigrated to New York, where he established a studio; at first he imported English biscuit clay, but then developed his own compound. His pottery, in which he favoured Arts and Crafts styles or Islamic styles, was distributed through Tiffany & Co. Examples of his work at the Metropolitan Museum of Art, New York, include a vase of 1882.

Bennett Pottery. American pottery manufactory in Baltimore, MD, founded in 1846 by Edwin Bennett, a Staffordshire potter, and his brother William. The company was known as Bennett & Brothers and in 1890 was incorporated as the Edwin Bennett Pottery Company. It closed in 1936. The early products were household wares with a brown glaze (known in America as Rockingham ware) and jugs of biscuit porcelain resembling Parian ware, but with a blue or sage-green ground and white decorations. In 1853 the company became the first in America to make industrial porcelain. The best-known product of the factory was the Rebekah at the Well teapot, modelled by Charles Coxon and usually known as the Rebekah teapot.

E. C. Holland: *Edwin Bennett and the Products of His Baltimore Pottery* (Baltimore, 1973)
J. G. Stradling: 'Puzzling Aspects of the Most Popular Piece of American Pottery Ever Made', *Mag. Ant.*, cli (Feb 1997), pp. 332–7

Bennington. American centre of ceramics production and generic name for the pottery produced in and around Bennington, VT, since the late 18th century. The principal companies were Norton Stoneware and the United States Pottery Company. The first pottery was established in 1785 by Captain John Norton, who initially made earthenware and by 1815 had begun to make stoneware; thereafter the company was called the Norton Stoneware Company. On John Norton's retirement in 1823 the company was taken over by his sons (Luman and John), and remained a family business until 1894, when pottery production was ended; the company continued to operate as a wholesaler until 1911. Norton stoneware was brightly decorated, usually with flowers, birds and animals. Some of its finest pottery was painted by John Hilfinger (*fl* 1852–88), a native of Württemberg who migrated to America, where he worked for five potteries, including Bennington (1855–64); his birds and animals are characteristically painted in cobalt blue.

In the early 1840s Julius Norton (1809–61), Luman's son, entered into partnership with Christopher Webber Fenton (1806–65) to produce high quality wares; in 1846 they employed an English potter (and former employee of Spode) called John Harrison, who inaugurated the production of biscuit porcelain, which was used both for figures and for jugs. The company also made agate wares, granite wares, and yellowware with Rockingham and flint enamel glazes. In 1848 this company became Lyman and Fenton, and the following year it became the United States Pottery Company. Daniel Greatbach, a noted English potter who had worked from 1839 to 1850 for the American Pottery Company in Jersey City, joined the company in 1852 and modelled some of their best pieces. Greatbach used the 'flint enamel' glaze developed by Christopher Fenton, as in the 'Apostle' pattern water cooler (1849; New York, Brooklyn Mus. A.) attributed to him. The United States Pottery Company closed in 1858, but the factory survives. The most prominent pottery now is Bennington Potters, which was founded in 1948 by David Gil, whose designers have included Yusuke Aida (1961–4).

The Bennington Pottery Gallery and Study Center contains a good collection of pottery and an archive of the pottery companies in Bennington.

R. C. Barrett: *Bennington Pottery and Porcelain* (New York, 1958)
R. C. Barrett: *A Color Guide to Bennington Pottery* (Manchester, VT, 1967)
C. Osgood: *The Jug and Related Stoneware of Bennington* (Rutland, VT, 1971)
C. Zusy: *Norton Stoneware and American Redware: The Bennington Museum Collection* (Bennington, 1991/R 2003)

Benson, W(illiam) A(rthur) S(mith) (*b* London, 17 Oct 1854; *d* Manorbier, Dyfed, 5 July 1924). English designer. He was educated at Winchester and Oxford, and in 1877 he was articled to the architect Basil Champneys. In 1880, encouraged by William Morris, Benson established a workshop in Hammersmith specializing in metalwork. Two years later he established a foundry at Chiswick, a showroom in Kensington and a new factory at Hammersmith (all in London), equipped with machinery to mass-produce a wide range of forms, such as kettles, vases, tables, dishes and firescreens. Benson's elegant and spare designs were admired for their modernity and minimal use of ornament. He is best known for his lamps and lighting fixtures, mostly in copper and bronze, which are fitted with flat reflective surfaces (e.g. *c.* 1890; London, V&A). Many of Benson's designs were patented, including those for jacketed vessels, which keep hot or cold liquids at a constant temperature, and for a 'Colander' teapot with a button mechanism for raising the tea leaves after the tea has infused. Benson sold his designs, labelled 'Art Metal', through his showroom on Bond Street, which opened in 1887, and at the showroom of Morris & Co., both in London.

Benson designed furniture for J. S. Henry & Co., and fireplaces and grates for the Coalbrookdale and Falkirk foundries. He designed furniture and wallpaper for Morris & Co., of which he became managing director after Morris's death in 1896. He retired in 1920.

ODNB
I. Hamerton: *W. A. S. Benson: Arts and Crafts Luminary and Pioneer of Modern Design* (Woodbridge, 2005)

Bentley, **Thomas**. *See under* WEDGWOOD.

Bentwood. Wood curved by machinery, used for making furniture. In the 18th century wood was softened by heating in water or steam and then shaped and clamped onto a mould. In America the principal innovator in bentwood furniture was Samuel Gragg (1772–1855), a Boston furniture-maker who in 1808 patented a bentwood 'elastic' chair. At about the same time German furniture-makers working in the Biedermeier idiom began to use plywood for shaped chairbacks. The greatest exponent of bentwork in Germany was MICHAEL THONET. In Poland, the Bentwood Furniture Company in Jasienica was founded in 1881 by Joseph Hofman, a cabinetmaker from Vienna; the company is still making bentwood furniture. In America bentwood furniture was developed by JOHN HENRY BELTER. In the 20th century bentwood was an important element in the furniture of designers such as ALVAR AALTO, MARCEL BREUER, Charles EAMES and EERO SAARINEN.

D. E. Ostergard, ed: *Bent Wood and Metal Furniture 1850–1946* (New York, 1987)
M. Friedman: 'All the Right Moves', *ID*, li/3 (May 2004), pp. 42–5

Berain, **Jean** (*b* Saint-Mihiel, Lorraine, *bapt* 4 June 1640; *d* Paris, 24 Jan 1711). French designer, ornamentalist and engraver. The Berain family moved to Paris *c.* 1644. Berain's father, also called Jean Berain, and his uncle Claude Berain were master gunsmiths. In 1659 Berain published a series of designs for the decoration of arms, *Diverses pièces très utiles pour les arquebuziers*, reissued in 1667. In 1662 he engraved for the guild of locksmiths a series of designs by Hugues Brisville (*b* 1633), *Diverses inventions nouvelles pour des armoiries avec leurs ornements*. Around 1667 he decorated and signed a hunting gun (Stockholm, Livrustkam) for Louis XIV (*reg* 1643–1715), which probably served as his introduction to the court. Through the influence and support of Charles Le Brun, in 1670 Berain was employed by the crown as an engraver. In January 1671 he received 400 livres in payment for two engravings (Paris, Bib. N., Cab. Est.) recording the ceiling decoration by Charles Le Brun of the Galerie d'Apollon in the Louvre, Paris, for which he also designed the painted stucco grotesques.

In 1674 Berain was appointed as Dessinateur de la Chambre et du Cabinet du Roi and began to design stage scenery; in 1680 he became chief designer of scenery and stage machinery for the Paris Opéra, and in this capacity provided designs for costumes and decorations for all manner of royal festivities and ceremonies. His costume designs included those for *Le Triomphe de l'amour* (1681; Paris, Louvre); he also produced costume designs for court masques and carrousels, fireworks, funeral decorations and mausoleums.

Jean Berain: *Pluto*, costume design for a masquerade (Paris, Musée du Louvre)

Although Berain was fully employed by the crown he had a number of other influential patrons. His designs for aristocratic and royal clients represent the decoration usually associated with his name: grotesques, SINGERIES, elements of the exotic, perfume burners, lambrequins, dais with draperies, masks, foliage and STRAPWORK. In 1685 the Marquis de Seignelay asked Berain for designs (*c.* 1685; Stockholm, Nmus.) for the decoration of the dining-room at his château at Sceaux, executed in the style of Jean-Baptiste Monnoyer, and designs (Paris, Ecole B.-A.) for ceilings at the Hôtel de Seignelay, Paris, the composition of which was spacious and airy and comprised such motifs as jets of water. In 1686–7 Berain designed the ceiling decoration (Stockholm, Nmus.) for several rooms in the Hôtel de Mailly-Nesles, Paris, carried out by André Camot (*d* 1689), which feature in the *Nouveau livre d'ornements de plafonds* (1690). These designs show a dense arrangement of exotic animals and fantastic creatures, caryatids, herms and female masks. The ceiling designed for Marie-Anne de Bourbon dowager Princesse de Conti (1666–1739), for the *pavillon des bains* in her hôtel in Versailles in 1691 shows by contrast a more delicate and refined composition.

Berain's ornamental style can also be seen in the tapestries woven from his designs. Two *portières* and four panels survive (Paris, priv. col.) from the series *Attributes of the Navy* (1689–92), woven by Jean-Baptiste Hinard. Designs by Berain (1696; Stockholm, Nmus.) for tapestry borders for the series *Conquests of Karl XI* (Stockholm, Kun. Slottet) were woven by G. Behayle (*d* 1710) for Drottningholm Slott, Stockholm, with one section woven in 1699 at the Manufacture de Beauvais. Berain also designed another suite of tapestries, the *Naval Triumphs*, for the Comte de Toulouse (design, *c.* 1696, Marseilles, Mus. Borély; tapestries, 1697–8, Paris, Banque de

France). In 1695 Daniel Cronström requested tapestry designs for upholstery, which were woven at the Gobelins in 1697 (Stockholm, Nmus.; New York, Met.).

Few objects designed by Berain survive. They include a silver candelabrum (1702; Stockholm, Nmus.) and the state coach of Karl XI (Stockholm, Livrustkam.), which survives in modified form.

Berain's work symbolized the later stages of the Louis XIV style and was a precursor of the more fanciful Rococo style. His important work undoubtedly had significance on such later designers as Claude Audran III and the Slodtz family. For many years after his death, Berain's work continued to inspire such artists as the cabinetmaker André Charles Boulle (his designs often appear of the tabletops of Boulle furniture), and decoration after Berain was frequently to be found on ceramics produced at Moustiers and Rouen. Berain's work was widely disseminated through series of prints, among which was the *Oeuvre de Jean Berain, recueillies par les soins du sieur Thuret* (Paris, 1711). Jean Berain II, also employed by the crown, succeeded his father as Dessinateur de la Chambre et du Cabinet du Roi in 1711.

F. P. Tollini: *Scene Design at the Court of Louis XIV: The Work of the Vigarani Family and Jean Berain* (Lewiston, NY, 2003)

E. Coquery: 'Les Attributs de la Marine, d'après Jean Berain et Jean Lemoine: Une tenture d'exception entre dans les collections du Louvre', *Rev. Louvre*, liii/ 5 (Dec 2003), pp. 56–67

Berettino [berrettino; bertino]. Blue tin glaze on which decorations were painted in white or polychrome. It was used in the 16th and 17th centuries in Faenza (especially at Casa Pirota) and the Veneto (especially Venice). A variation on this technique was a deep-blue ground decorated with light-blue or gold decoration; in Venice work of this kind was known as *smaltino*.

Bergère. Large armchair, fashionable in the 18th century, typically with canework sides, back and seat, fitted with an upholstered seat or, in later chairs, a loose cushion; it differs from other armchairs in that the area between the arms and seat is upholstered. A *bergère* hat is a large straw hat.

Berlage, **H(endrik) P(etrus)** (*b* Amsterdam, 21 Feb 1856; *d* The Hague, 12 Aug 1934). Dutch architect, urban planner and writer. Berlage is primarily known as an architect, but his desire to cast off historicist forms from his buildings and to encourage an integrity of workmanship consistent with his socialist ideals can also be seen in his ventures into the decorative arts, which include an oak buffet (*c.* 1900) and a canary-yellow glass breakfast service (1924, with Piet Zwart), an oak buffet (both Gemeentemuseum, The Hague, Berlage's finest building) and glass designs for the Pantin glasshouse (see colour pl. IV, fig. 1).

S. Polano: *Hendrik Petrus Berlage* (Milan, 2002) [Eng. Trans.]

Berlin. German capital city.

1. Iron jewellery. 2. Porcelain. 3. Tapestry. 4. Woolwork.

1. Iron jewellery. The Königliche Eisengiesserei bei Berlin (founded 1804) began *c.* 1806 to produce jewellery, including long chains of cast links and, later, necklaces formed of medallions joined by wirework mesh (*fer de Berlin*). The royal foundry's association with such artists as Schinkel (who designed the Iron Cross) and Leonhard Posch, the creator of a number of important portrait medallions that were incorporated into jewellery, was a decisive factor in its success. A number of private jewellery-making foundries were also established in Berlin. The most prominent designers were the two goldsmiths Johann Conrad Geiss (1771–1846), who began to design jewellery ornaments for the royal foundries of Berlin and Gleiwitz in Silesia in 1806, and Siméon Pierre Devaranne (1789–1859), both of whom developed new jewellery forms. Alfred Richard Seebass (1805–84) and August Ferdinand Lehmann (*b* 1806; e.g. belt ornament, *c.* 1820; London, V&A) had their own foundries and mostly copied the designs of others. Iron jewellery production was at its peak in 1813, when the Prussian royal family exhorted all women to donate their gold jewellery towards funding the uprising against the Napoleonic occupation. In return they were presented with iron brooches and rings bearing the inscription *Gold gab ich für Eisen* (e.g. iron ring, 1813) or *Für das Wohl des Vaterlands*. Iron jewellery, which had previously been worn only for mourning, became a symbol of patriotism. Combs, necklaces, bracelets, brooches, rings and buckles in the finest openwork casting survive from this period. Ornaments were initially made in the Neo-classical style; from 1810 miniature tracery in the Gothic Revival style was also used, as were such naturalistic motifs as vine leaves and butterflies from *c.* 1815 (e.g. pair of earrings, *c.* 1815–20; London, V&A). Most iron jewellery made in Berlin is lacquered black and is occasionally combined with fine gold (e.g. three iron and gold necklaces, *c.* 1820; London, V&A; London, BM) or silver settings or with polished steel (e.g. parure, iron with polished steel, 1820–30; Stockholm, Nordiska Mus.). In 1916 another attempt was made to promote the manufacture of iron jewellery, and a medallion inscribed *Gold gab ich zur Wehr, Eisen nahm ich zur Ehr* was given in exchange for gold jewellery, but this attempt was unsuccessful.

A. Clifford: *Cut-steel and Berlin Iron Jewellery* (Bath, 1971)

2. Porcelain. The first attempt to produce porcelain in Berlin was made between 1740 and 1746, when the chemist Dr Heinrich Pott was commissioned by Frederick the Great to manufacture porcelain (e.g. of 1744; Berlin, Märk. Mus.). In 1751 the Swiss wool manufacturer Wilhelm Caspar Wegely was given a concession to manufacture hard-paste porcelain, but his factory closed in 1757. Production was renewed in 1761 when Johann Ernst Gotzkowsky, a Berlin merchant and financier, began to

manufacture porcelain. Two years later the King purchased the factory, which was then in debt, transformed it into the Königliche Porzellan-Manufaktur (KPM) and directed it until his death in 1786. In 1918 the factory was nationalised, and became the Staatliche Porzellanmanufaktur.

Although there are few extant pieces from Pott's period of manufacture, products dating from the Wegely period can be recognized by the use of underglaze blue or coloured enamels. Similarities between the wares of Berlin and those of Höchst are evident, as many of the workers were employed at both establishments. The range of wares included coffee- and tea-services as well as vases and squat groups of figures. As a result of the siege of Meissen during the Seven Years' War and the influx of workers from there, Gotzkowsky porcelain was clearly influenced by this factory. Wares were decorated with such new patterns as the 'willow', 'broken rod', and 'Brandenstein', low-relief decoration, scale borders, trelliswork, flowers and subjects based on paintings by Watteau. These forms of decoration, in conjunction with often highly contrasting colours, resulted in the production of exceptionally fine pieces of Rococo porcelain. The most outstanding examples were the services commissioned by the King for his palaces: for example the Potsdam Neues Palais service (1765–6; Hamburg, Mus. Kst. & Gew.), which was decorated with relief trelliswork and with pierced and 'Mosaik' (diaper and imbricated pattern) borders.

The main stylistic influence on figure production during this period was the chief-modeller Friedrich Elias Meyer (1723–85), who had previously worked at Meissen. Such restrained colours as grey and a soft purple-pink perfectly complemented the simple, practical shapes of the Neo-classical services. The busts in biscuit porcelain, however, based on models by Johann Gottfried Schadow (1764–1850), were particularly unusual. Schadow was probably responsible for the creation of the figures in the centrepiece of the 'Prussian' service (1817–19; London, Apsley House), which was a gift from Frederick William III to Arthur Wellesley, 1st Duke of Wellington.

During the 19th century fine, ornamental decoration (drawing on such new technical innovations as transfer-printing) were typified by portraits and views of Berlin and its environs. The modelling department created new shapes on which a wide range of decoration was applied, reflecting the diverse artistic trends of the 19th century (see colour pl. III, fig. 4). The porcelain works maintained its position as one of the leading avant-garde factories during the 20th century, creating new and innovative porcelain (e.g. 'Urbino' service, 1930–31; Munich, Bayer. NMus. Neue Samml.).

W. Baer: *Berlin Porcelain* (Washington, DC, 1980)
E. Köllmann and M. Jarchow: *Berliner Porzellan*, 2 vols (Munich, 1987)
D. E. Ostergard and I. Baer: *Along the Royal Road: Berlin and Potsdam in KPM Porcelain and Painting, 1815–1848* (New York, 1993)
A Century of Berlin: Wednesday 1 May 2002 (sale cat., London, Christie's, 2002)

3. TAPESTRY. In October 1685, in the wake of the revocation of the Edict of Nantes (which had afforded toleration to Huguenots), Huguenot weavers left Aubusson, and some, including the tapestry-weaver Pierre Mercier (*d* 1729), settled in Berlin. In the following years he produced an extensive series of tapestries from sketches by various Berlin painters, featuring the exploits of Frederick William of Brandenburg, the Great Elector. In 1714, Mercier went to Dresden. His place in Berlin was taken by his nephew, Jean Barraband II (1687–1725) and (from 1720) by Charles Vigne (*d* 1751); their tapestries were variously modelled on *commedia dell'arte* figures, chinoiseries, the fables of La Fontaine and hunting and genre scenes.

Medieval, Renaissance and Later Works of Art, Rugs, Textiles, Tapestries, Pewter and Furniture (sale cat., New York, Sotheby Parke Bernet, 1975)
C. Keisch and S. Netzer: *Herrliche Künste und Manufacturen: Fayence, Glas und Tapisserien aus der Frühzeit Brandenburg-Preussens 1680–1720* (Berlin, 2001)

4. WOOLWORK. Type of *gros-point* embroidery, so called because in the early 19th century the wools, patterns and canvases were exported to Britain and the USA from Berlin. By mid-century the term 'Berlin woolwork' had ceased to reflect the origin of the materials and had become the name of a style of embroidery, characterized by biblical scenes and phrases such as 'Home Sweet Home'. Initially patterns were printed on paper and then coloured by hand, but soon counting patterns were introduced. In the kits now sold as Berlin work coloured patterns are printed directly onto the canvas. Modern Berlin work is less intricate than its 19th-century predecessor, but is much more imaginative, in that copying patterns is merely a preparation for independent creative work.

M. G. Proctor: *Victorian Canvas Work: Berlin Wool Work* (London, 1986)
U. Bergemann: 'Berliner Stickereien des Biedermeier. Entwicklung und gesellschaftliche Bedeutung', Jb Berlin. Mus., xliv (2002), pp. 93–128

Bernabé, Felix [Felice Antonio Maria] (*b* Florence, 27 July 1720). Italian gem-engraver. While still young he attracted commissions from eminent Florentines. His surviving works include a portrait of *Alexander the Great* on a cornelian, *Cupid and Psyche* (Rome, Mus. Capitolino) in chalcedony and the Farnese *Hercules* (Naples, Mus. N.). He also engraved armorial seals. He signed his name in Greek characters, sometimes using his first name only, a fact that has on occasion caused his work to be confused with Felix, a Roman engraver of the Augustan period. Some of his gems are reproduced in the collections of James Tassie (examples in Edinburgh, N.P.G.) and Tommaso Cades (examples in Rome, Dt. Archäol. Inst.).

Bernardes. Portuguese family of tile painters.

1. António de Oliveira Bernardes (*bapt* Beja, *c.* 1660; *d* Lisbon, 4 Oct 1732). He was the leading artist in a group of tile painters who worked during the first third of the 18th century. António's first works (*c*. 1699) were tiled panels depicting the *Life of the Virgin* and the *Infancy of Christ* for the Ramada Chapel near Loures (Cascais, Casa de S Maria); they are reminiscent of Dutch tiles in the use of colour, the depth and translucence of the painting and in the strength of draughtsmanship. In works from the early years of the 18th century his painting developed a very personal and expressive *sfumato*, achieved by means of subtle gradations of cobalt blue. This is seen in the signed panels (*c*. 1705–10) showing scenes from the *Life of St Pedro de Rates* and the *Life of St Geraldo* in the chapels of the same name, Braga Cathedral. These qualities are also seen in the mythological scenes decorating two rooms in the Palácio Tancos, Lisbon, and in the monumental panels of the *Life of St Dominic* in the transept and chancel of S Domingos, Benfica, near Lisbon; some of the latter were executed with António Pereira (ii). The impact of these outstanding compositions lies in Bernardes's use of contrasting intensities of light.

António's tile paintings from the second decade of the 18th century contain complex borders of elaborate Baroque acanthus foliage, volutes and putti enriched with finely modelled sculptural and architectural motifs. These elements can be seen in the large panels of tiles (1713; executed with the monogrammist painter PMP (*fl c*. 1700–25)) completely covering the nave of Nossa Senhora do Terço, Barcelos, which have tapestry-like scenes depicting the *Life of St Benedict*. The fine acanthus borders resemble the acanthus foliage on the carved and gilded woodwork in the church. Other works from this period that show António's fine draughtsmanship are large-scale scenes from the *Life of St Laurence Giustiniani* (1711) in S João Evangelista, Évora; those of the *Nativity* and *Passion* (*c*. 1712) in the choir of the convent of Esperança, Ponto Delgada, Azores; those from the *Life of Christ* (1716) in the Misericórdia, Évora; and scenes from the *Passion* and landscapes (*c*. 1721) in the Capela da Piedade, Colares, near Sintra.

Towards the end of his life António worked with his son and pupil Policarpo. Among their collaborative works are the scenes of the *Life of the Virgin* in the Santuario dos Remedios, Peniche, and scenes from the Old Testament in the chancel of S Lourenço, Azeitão, near Setúbal (all *c*. 1725–30), which are all surrounded by elaborate and decorative Baroque borders. António continued to help in the family workshop until 1730.

2. Policarpo de Oliveira Bernardes (*b* Lisbon, 1695; *d* 1778). Policarpo's first important works were the signed panels representing scenes from the *Life of the Virgin* and the *Infancy of Christ* (1720) in the chancel of the church of the Misericórdia, Viana do Castelo. The scenes showing the *Acts of Mercy*, in the nave, are probably a result of collaboration with António, to whom they have often been attributed. All these scenes have an expressive force created by Policarpo's painstaking technique of shading with

hatched brushstrokes, and they are monumental in conception, especially in the perspectival architectural setting. These characteristics mark all his work.

Policarpo's independent work includes a *Gloria* (1730), surrounded by a complex perspectival composition that covers the nave and chancel of the church of S. Lourenço, Almansil, near Faro; and scenes from the *Life of the Virgin* (1736) decorating the chapel of the Castelo de S Filipe, Setúbal. The scene of the *Assumption of the Virgin* was taken from an engraving by Rubens that António had also used at the Santuário, Nazaré, in 1714. Other signed or attributed works of this period include the panels framed with complex Baroque ornament showing scenes from the *Life of the Virgin* and the *Birth of Christ* in the chancel of the Penha Church, Braga; the decorative panels containing atlantids and seraphims in a lateral chapel of the church of Nossa Senhora da Conceição, Vila Viçosa; and the Marian symbols and moralizing scenes set in painted architectural frames of tiles that decorate the sacristy of the convent at Varatojo, near Torres Vedras. In 1738 Policarpo moved to Loures, near Lisbon. His last documented works are the signed and dated panels of 1740 showing the *Flight into Egypt* and the *Return from Egypt*, which cover the facde and nave of the hermitage chapel of Porto Salvo, near Oeiras.

Bernardi, Giovanni (Desiderio) [Giovanni da Castel Bolognese] (*b* Castel Bolognese, 1494; *d* Faenza, 22 May 1553).

Italian gem-engraver and medallist. He was first instructed as a gem-engraver by his father, the goldsmith Bernardo Bernardi (1463–1553). His earliest works, which dated from the three years he spent in Ferrara at the court of Alfonso I d'Este, were an engraving on crystal of the *Battle of La Bastia* and steel dies for struck medals representing *Alfonso d'Este* and *Christ Taken by the Multitude* (untraced). By 1530 Giovanni Bernardi was in Rome, where he worked for the cardinals Giovanni Salviati and Ippolito de' Medici. He was commissioned to produce a portrait of

Giovanni Bernardi: *The Punishment of Tityus,* rock crystal intaglio, Italian, *c*. 1530 (London, British Museum)

Pope Clement VII for the obverse of a medal struck with two different reverses: *Joseph Appearing to His Brothers* (e.g. Modena, Gal. & Mus. Estense; London, V&A) and the *Apostles Peter and Paul* (e.g. Milan, Castello Sforzesco; Paris, Bib. N.). For Clement VII he engraved on rock crystal the *Four Evangelists* (Naples, Capodimonte), a work that was praised by Benvenuto Cellini. For the coronation of Charles V as Holy Roman Emperor in Bologna (24 Feb 1530), Bernardi presented him with a splendid gold medal bearing his portrait (silver version, Vienna, Ksthist. Mus.).

From 1534 until 1538 Bernardi held a post at the Papal Mint. During these first years in Rome, Bernardi made other engravings on crystal for Cardinal Ippolito; surviving examples, skilfully adapted from drawings by Michelangelo (Windsor Castle, Berks, Royal Col.; London, BM), include various versions of *Tityus* (e.g. London, BM) and the *Fall of Phaëthon* (e.g. *c.* 1533–5; Baltimore, MD, Walters A.G.), which is inscribed IOVANES. Two further engraved gems may be attributed to Bernardi at this time, one on chalcedony with the portrait of *Cardinal Ippolito* and the other on jasper, the *Damned Soul* (both Florence, Pitti); the latter is elaborated from a drawing by Michelangelo (1475–1564; Florence, Uffizi).

In 1535, on the death of Cardinal Ippolito, Bernardi entered the service of Cardinal Alessandro Farnese, for whom he executed many works, including a medal with a portrait of *Pope Paul III* (Milan, Castello Sforzesco). He also made two exceptionally fine cameos, one a portrait of *Giovanni Baglioni* and the other that of *Margaret of Austria* (both Brit. Royal Col).

In 1539 Bernardi settled in Faenza, remaining there for the rest of his life except for the years 1541–5, when he was again in Rome, working at the Papal Mint as a master engraver. His most important works include two series of rock crystals depicting episodes from the *Life of Christ*: the first series (1539) engraved after drawings by Perino del Vaga (1501–47; e.g. New York, Pierpont Morgan Lib.; Paris, Louvre); the second, representing the *Passion*, was completed in 1546–7. Of the rock crystals, 13 survive, mounted on a cross and on two silver-gilt candlesticks (all 1582; Rome, St Peter's, Treasury) commissioned for St Peter's, Rome, by Cardinal Farnese and made in 1570–80 by the goldsmith Gentile da Faenza. Four other engraved rock crystals are mounted on a 17th-century casket (Copenhagen, Nmus.); there are also a *Crucifixion* (Paris, Bib. N.), a *Christ before Pilate* (Baltimore, MD, Walters A.G.), an *Adoration of the Shepherds* (London, V&A) and *Christ Driving the Moneychangers from the Temple* (Washington, DC, N.G.A.).

Six of Bernardi's most important rock crystals depicting mythological and historical themes are mounted on the Farnese Casket (Naples, Capodimonte), which was made between 1548 and 1561 by the Florentine goldsmith Manno di Bastiano Sbarri (1536–76), a pupil of Cellini. Working from drawings by Perino del Vaga (Paris, Louvre; Chatsworth, Derbys), Bernardi engraved four of these crystals with scenes representing the *Battle of the Amazons*, the *Battle* of the *Centaurs and the Lapiths*, the *Triumph of Bacchus* and the *Kalydonian Boar Hunt*. The other two, of which the designer is unknown, show a *Naval Battle* and a *Chariot Race in the Circus*. A seventh engraved crystal, of the *Battle of Tunis* (New York, Met.), had been intended for the Farnese Casket but was not used.

V. Sloman: 'Rock-crystals by Giovanni Bernardi', *Burl. Mag.*, xlviii (1926), pp. 9–23
V. Donati and G. D. Bernardi: *Pietre dure e medaglie del Rinascimento: Giovanni da Castel Bolognese* (Ferrara, 1989)

Bernburg. German centre of ceramics production. The term 'Bernburg Pottery' is used to describe both Prehistoric pottery made in Thuringia *c.* 3000 BC, and the product of two faience factories that flourished in the 18th century. The first operated from *c.* 1725 to *c.* 1775, and produced blue-and-white wares (e.g. chinoiserie vase, 1725; Halle, Kstgewmus.); the second operated from 1794 to 1885, and made glazed earthenware and stoneware.

U. Dirks: *Die Bernburger Kultur in Niedersachsen* (Rahden, 2000)

Bernini, Gianlorenzo [Gian Lorenzo; Giovanni Lorenzo] (*b* Naples, 7 Dec 1598; *d* Rome, 28 Nov 1680). Italian sculptor, architect, draughtsman and painter. He is rightly known as the most outstanding and the most influential sculptor of the 17th century. He was not often active in the decorative arts, but was nonetheless influential on furniture design. The wooden plinth shaped like a burning log that he designed for his marble statue *St Lawrence on the Grill* (*c.* 1618; Florence, Pitti) proved to be a seminal influence on the design of plinths for tables. He is also known to have designed silver (a reliquary and candlesticks), but none survives, nor does the coach that he designed for Queen Christina of Sweden (*reg* 1632–54).

A. Gonzáles-Palacios: 'Bernini as a Furniture Designer', *Burl. Mag.*, cxii (1970), pp. 719.–24
C. Scribner: *Gianlorenzo Bernini* (New York, 1991)
I. Lavin: *Essays on Style and Meaning in the Art of Gianlorenzo Bernini* (London, 2003)

Bernward, Bishop of Hildesheim (*b c.* AD 960; *bur* Hildesheim, 22 Nov 1022; *can* 1192). German saint, bishop and goldsmith. The finest art produced in the Hildesheim workshops is traditionally attributed to Bernward, but his precise role in design and fashioning of these objects is uncertain, so some are described as 'Bernwardine' to associate them with his workshop. Surviving works attributed to Bernward include the two silver candlesticks from his tomb (*c.* 1000; Hildesheim, Magdalenenkirche), the huge 'bronze' (actually brass) doors (1007/8–1015) and the Column of Christ (*c.* 1020; both Hildesheim Cathedral).

J. Tschan: *Saint Bernward of Hildesheim*, 3 vols (Notre Dame, IN, 1942–52)
S. D. Walther: *Bernward's Column at Hildesheim and the Rise of Monumental Art in the Middle Ages* (Providence, 1977)

Bishop Bernward: Brass west doors (detail), Hildesheim Cathedral, 1015; originally in the church of St Michael, Hildesheim

Berretino [bertino]. *See* BERETTINO.

Bertoia, Harry (*b* San Lorenzo, nr Reggio di Calabria, 10 March 1915; *d* Barto, PA, 6 Nov 1978). Italian-American sculptor and designer. He moved to the USA in 1930, working initially at the Cranbrook Academy of Art in Bloomfield Hills, MI (1937–9), where he taught metalworking and produced abstract silver jewellery and colour monoprints. In 1943 he moved to California to assist in the development of the first of a series of chairs designed by Charles EAMES. In 1950 he established himself in Bally, PA, where he designed the Bertoia chair (1952), several forms of which were marketed by Knoll Associates Inc. His furniture is characterized by the use of moulded and welded wire; in the case of the Bertoia chair, the chromium-plated steel wire is reshaped by the weight of the sitter.

F. Bertoia: *Chairs by Harry Bertoia* (New York, 1969)
N. Schiffer and V. O. Bertoia: *The World of Bertoia* (Atglen, PA, 2003)

Beryl. In mineralogical usage, a mineral species that includes emerald and aquamarine; it is a silicate of aluminium and glucinum, and crystallises in hexagonal prisms. In lapidary usage, beryl is distinguished from emerald (a rich green colour) and aquamarine (a pale bluish green) by its pale green colour; if there is a pronounced yellow colour, it is called chrysoberyl; the greenish-yellow variety is called helidore, the pink variety morganite and the colourless variety

goshenite. The term beryl is sometimes used loosely to describe crystal or glass.

Bettisi, Leonardo (*fl* 1566–89). Italian potter. He was born in Ascanio and worked in Faenza, initially with CALAMELLI, from whose widow he bought the workshop in 1570. Bettisi made huge maiolica services, including one of several hundred pieces made for Albert V of Bavaria in 1576; there is a broad-rimmed bowl from this service in Fitzwilliam Museum, Cambridge. His wares and those of his workshop are marked 'Don Pino'.

Betts, Thomas (*d* 1767). English glasscutter. He sold cut glass and mirrors from his London shop from *c.* 1740. In about 1756 he became the first Englishman to use a water-powered cutting wheel, using the Ravensbourne river at Lewisham to drive iron lapidary and glass-cutting wheels.

A. Werner: 'Thomas Betts: An 18th Century Glasscutter', *J. Glass Assoc.*, i (1985), pp. 1–16

Beurdeley. French family of cabinetmakers, antique dealers and collectors. The dynasty was founded by Jean Beurdeley (1772–1853), who in 1830 bought the Pavillon de Hanovre, 28 Boulevard des Italiens, Paris, which was the Beurdeley firm's principal gallery until 1894. His son (Louis-Auguste-)Alfred Beurdeley (1808–82) dealt in antiques and works of art and was also a cabinetmaker specializing in reproductions of 17th- and 18th-century furniture. Alfred Beurdeley's illegitimate son (Emmanuel-)Alfred Beurdeley (*b* Paris, 11 Aug 1847; *d* Paris, 20 Nov 1919) took over the gallery and workshops in 1875 and until 1894 concentrated on making luxury furniture, continuing the models sold by his father.

D. Ledoux-Lebard: *Le mobilier français du XIXe siècle, 1795–1889: Dictionnaires des ébénistes et des menuisiers* (Paris, 1989)

Bevan, Charles (*fl* London, 1865–82). English furniture designer and manufacturer. In 1865 Bevan advertised a 'New Registered Reclining Chair', made by MARSH & JONES of Leeds, whose London showrooms were near his own premises off Cavendish Square. In 1865 Marsh & Jones supplied the Yorkshire mill-owner Sir Titus Salt with a large group of furniture, including a bedroom suite, and in 1867 with the case of an Erard grand piano (all Leeds, Temple Newsam House) designed by Bevan; described at the time as 'medieval', the pieces are decorated with geometric marquetry ornament. Bevan designed a bookcase for the Manchester firm James Lamb, which was shown in the Paris Exposition Universelle of 1867, and by the following year was also designing for Gillows. At the International Exhibition of 1872 in London, Gillows exhibited two ebonized cabinets (London, V&A) by Bevan decorated with Doulton stoneware plaques. In 1872 Bevan and his son, George Alfred Bevan went into partnership as C. Bevan & Son at 100 High Holborn,

London, remaining at this address for the next ten years.

S. Jervis: 'Charles Bevan and Talbert', *The Decorative Arts in the Victorian Period*, ed. S. Wright (London, 1989), pp. 15–29

Gothic-revival Furniture by Charles Bevan (sale cat., London, H. Blairman & Sons Ltd., 2003)

Beyer, **Christian Friedrich Wilhelm** (*b* Gotha, 27 Dec 1725; *d* Vienna, 23 March 1806). German sculptor, painter and architect. After a long period of training in Paris and Rome as a painter and sculptor, Beyer returned in 1759 to Germany, to take part in the decoration of Charles-Eugene's Neues Schloss in Stuttgart. In Stuttgart Beyer's activities included work at the Ludwigsburg porcelain manufactory, for which he modelled porcelain figures, eschewing the customary gallant Rococo pastoral scenes in favour of themes and figures from Classical mythology. Examples of his work may be seen in Stuttgart (e.g. the bust of a *Young Faun*, Stuttgart, Württemberg. Landesmus.) and Hamburg (Mus. Kst & Gew.). In 1767 Beyer moved to Vienna, where he again worked at the porcelain manufactory.

Bezel. In lapidary usage, the oblique sides or faces of a cut gem. A bezel setting is a metal rim that holds the gem in a finger ring. The term is used in a transferred sense by horologists to denote the ring that secures the glass in a watch or clock, and by metal specialists to describe the ring inside the lid of silver and pewter objects.

Bianchetto. Type of Italian earthenware made waterproof by dipping the clay into a white slip before firing. *Bianchetto* was used for ceramics that were to be painted; in modern examples it is often decorated with graffiti.

Bianchi [Bianciho] **di Faenza.** Type of maiolica covered with a thick white glaze. Bianchi ware was often extravagantly shaped and pierced but tended to be lightly decorated, usually in blue and orange. The decorative technique was known as *compendiario* (It.: 'perfunctory') and characteristically consisted of boldly drawn figures which left most of the glazed surface untouched. It was introduced in the Faenza potteries in the 1540s but was eventually produced all over Europe. The most prominent Faenza manufacturers of *bianchi* were LEONARDO BETTISI, Virgiliotto CALAMELLI and FRANCESCO DI ANTONIO MEZZARISA.

Bianco sopra bianco [It.: 'white on white']. Italian earthenware decorated with an opaque white pigment on a tin glaze of slightly contrasted colour, normally white tinted with blue. The phrase is sometimes written *blanco sopra blanco* or *bianco sopra blanco*.

Biarelle. German family of decorative designers. Brothers Paul Amadeus (*fl* 1737–52) and Johann

Adolf (*fl c.* 1743) both worked with the Bavarian court architect François de Cuvilliés on Schloss Brühl, a German Electoral castle halfway between Bonn and Cologne; they worked on the interiors of the Falkenlust (1729–34), an intimate pavilion in the garden. They subsequently worked for the architect Leopoldo Mattia Retti (1705–51), decorating the interiors of the ducal Residenz at Ansbach in a style that became known as Ansbach Rococo.

Bibelot. Small curio or object of vertu (e.g. a snuff-box).

Biccherna. Small painted panel, initially created as a cover for official documents of the civic government of Siena between the 13th and 17th centuries. The Italian word derives from the chief financial office of Siena, the Biccherna. The term has also been extended to designate painted covers and small panels connected with other Sienese civic offices and institutions, such as the tax office (Gabella), the hospital of S Maria della Scala, the Opera del Duomo and various lay confraternities.

Each volume of accounts prepared for official presentation to the council received a painted wooden cover. In the mid-15th century the subjects of the paintings begin to extend beyond official details in covers such as *Allegory of the Plague* (1437; Berlin, Schloss Köpenick; see colour pl. V, fig. 1), attributed to Giovanni di Paolo (*c.* 1399–1482), and the *Coronation of Pope Pius II* (1460; Siena, Pal. Piccolomini, Archv Stato) with a view of Siena, attributed to Vecchietta (1410–80). At the same time, as a result of damage done to the covers, the practice of attaching panels to the financial registers was replaced by the creation of small panels to hang on the walls of the Biccherna. Because dimensions no longer had to accord with the size of the registers, the *biccherne* grew in size. The last surviving example is dated 1682.

R. W. Lightbown: *The Tavolette di Biccherna of Siena* (London, 1963)

D. T. Baker: *The Artistic and Sociological Imagery of the Merchant-banker on the Book Covers of the Biccherna in Siena in the Early Renaissance* (PhD, Seattle, U. Washington, 1998)

G. Mace: 'Biccherne, les registres du bon gouvernement', *L'Oeil*, dxiii (Feb 2000), pp. 82–7

Bidet. Small washing basin formerly used solely for feminine hygiene. The bidet originated in France, *c.* 1710, and was initially a metal basin on a walnut stand; later basins were often porcelain, and stands sometimes took the form of chairs. In 1750 the first bidet with an upward water spray (*bidet à seringue*) appeared, powered by a hand pump. Until the 20th century, when bidets began to be plumbed into a space beside the toilet, bidets were an item of bedroom furniture. The original purpose of bidets was to fend off sexually transmitted diseases; later they were regarded as a mechanism for birth control.

Bidri ware. Form of Indian metalwork characterized by inlaid and overlaid decoration and even, in

Bidri ware hookah base, inlaid silver, h. 165 mm, Bidar, Deccan, late 17th century–early 18th (London, Victoria and Albert Museum)

some Lucknow wares, encrusted decoration. The name of the technique is derived from the Deccan city of Bidar, and although it has been claimed that it was introduced by 'Ala' al-Din Bahmani (*reg* 1436–58) from Iran, there is no evidence for this; the earliest surviving pieces dating from the late 16th century.

To produce bidri ware, objects are first cast from an alloy in which zinc predominates but which may include small amounts of lead as well as copper and tin. The surface of the object is smoothed and a solution of copper sulphate applied to darken it temporarily for the next stage, engraving. The engraved design is lighter in colour than the darkened surface, enabling the pattern to be seen more clearly. The piece is passed on to the inlayer, who uses silver or brass, the brass often having a goldlike appearance owing to its high zinc content. The inlay may be of wire or sheet metal, and some of the finest pieces have a design cut out of sheet silver so that it appears silhouetted against the body of the object. In pieces of later date the decoration may be hammered on to a crosshatched surface. The final stage of the process is to blacken the dull grey of the zinc alloy so that the inlay is seen in dramatic contrast. This is done by applying a paste of ammonium chloride, potassium nitrate, sodium chloride, copper sulphate and mud, which darkens the body while having no effect on the inlay. The paste is removed, and the piece is rubbed with oil to deepen the matte black ground.

Bidri decoration consists of floral, arabesque and non-figurative motifs, with the inclusion of small animals, birds and fish in Lucknow wares. Rare exceptions include a hookah base (New Delhi, N. Mus.) that depicts narrative scenes from the *Padmāvat*, a 16th-century Hindi poem by Muhammad Jayasi of Avadh. In the 20th century, bidri production became limited to the Deccan region. Modern production is largely confined to Hyderabad, with a small industry remaining at Bidar. As well as such items as buttons, jewellery, cigarette- and pill-boxes and decorative ornaments, 20th-century craftsmen are turning back to traditional forms, making, for example, hookah bases in 18th-century style.

S. Stronge: *Bidri Ware: Inlaid Metalwork from India* (London, 1985)

S. La Niece and others: 'The Technical Examination of Bidri ware', *Stud. Conserv.*, xxxii (Aug 1987), pp. 97–101

K. Lal: *National Museum Collection Bidri ware* (New Delhi, 1990)

S. Markel: 'Bidri ware: Lyric Patterns', *Marg*, xliv/1 (1992), pp. 45–56

Biedermeier. Term applied to bourgeois life and art in Germanic Europe (including Copenhagen and Prague) from 1815 (the Congress of Vienna) to the revolutions of 1848. It originated in 1854 as a pseudonym, Gottlieb Biedermeier, created by the poets Ludwig Eichrodt (1827–92) and Adolf Kussmaul (1822–1902). There is a Biedermeier style in painting, but the term is generally used with reference to the decorative arts, especially furniture but also interior design and household goods such as carpets, glass and porcelain. In the years from 1815 through the 1820s, design was characterized by a cool and restrained style in which severity of line was valued; in the 1830s and 1840s, design became more complex, catholic and sentimental, and was characterized by historicism and eclecticism and an increase in pattern and upholstery in interiors.

The design of Biedermeier furniture was determined by concern for comfort and practicality and reduced economic circumstances. It was influenced by both English Sheraton furniture and the early classicism of Louis XVI. The strongest influence, however, was the French Empire style, from which it took Neo-classical symmetry, a preference for simple geometric shapes and flat surfaces and an architectural vocabulary of columns, mouldings and pediments. It rejected ornate decoration, costly materials and aristocratic references. The aesthetic dimension came from the skills of fine craftsmanship: proportion, simplicity, formal clarity and the natural beauty of the materials. Favourite materials included fruitwoods, walnut and ash, with ebonized wood for accent. Comfort dictated the introduction of upholstery and new curved shapes for chair legs and backs. The most popular furniture types were those used for daily life: the sofa, chair, desk (especially secrétaire), cabinet, *étagère*—used to display collections of Biedermeier porcelain and glass—and such smaller pieces as plant-stand, night-table, wine cooler, wastebasket and needlework holder. Regional variations ranged from the elegant, delicate and imaginative Viennese designs typified by the work of Joseph Ulrich Danhauser (e.g. sofa, *c.* 1820; Vienna, Bundesmobiliensamml.) to the massive architectural forms of Berlin furniture under the influence of Karl Friedrich Schinkel. Furniture produced after 1830 had more historicizing ornamentation and more opulent materials, reflecting the increased prosperity of the middle classes (see colour pl. IV, fig. 2).

The concern for comfort and convenience also dominated the design of the Biedermeier interior. Furniture was no longer aligned against the wall but was used to create groupings known as *Wohninsel*. These arrangements, usually composed of sofa-table-chair combinations, established small informal areas sympathetic to family life and abandoned the formality of Empire room design. From 1815 to 1830 furnishings were sparse; subsequently wallpaper, textile hangings, parquet floors and carpets became the norm. Floral arrangements and floral motifs in fabrics were especially popular, just as the garden itself became an extension of the interior living-space.

G. Himmelheber: *Biedermeier Furniture* (London, 1974)

Vienna in the Age of Schubert: The Biedermeier Interior 1815–1848 (exh. cat., London, V&A, 1979)

R. Waissenberger, ed.: *Vienna in the Biedermeier Era, 1815–1848* (New York, 1986)

A. Wilkie: *Biedermeier* (New York, 1987)

S. Sangl, B. Stoeltie and R. Stoeltie: *Biedermeier to Bauhaus* (New York, 2000)

R. Pressler, S. Döbner and W. L. Eller: *Antique Biedermeier Furniture* (Atglen, PA, 2002)

L. Winters: 'An Introduction to the Biedermeier Period', *Mag. Ant.*, clxv/1 (Jan 2004), pp. 178–83

Biemann [Bimann], **Dominik** (*b* Harrachsdorf, 1 April 1800; *d* Eger, 29 Sept 1857). Bohemian glass-engraver. He was the son of a carpenter and pattern-maker at the Harrachsdorf glassworks and received his training as a glass-engraver at the Nový Svět glassworks on the estate of the counts of Harrach. He worked for the wholesale glass dealers Muttoni and Steigerwald, but spent his summers in the spa town of Franzenzbad (now Františkovy Lázně) in western Bohemia, where he depicted landscapes, hunting scenes and mythological and religious scenes on glasses and cups for affluent guests. In 1826 he tried for the first time a *tiefschnitt* (deep-cut) portrait and soon became an outstanding master of this technique. Biemann travelled for portrait commissions to Gotha and Coburg (1830–31), Berlin (1834) and Vienna (1839–40), where he executed profile portraits of members of the different ruling houses and the court entourage, an example of which is a beaker with a portrait of *Duke Ernst I von Saxe-Coburg-Gotha* (Coburg, Veste Coburg). Most of the several hundred glasses and plaques on which Biemann is known to have worked are unsigned, so very little of his work can be identified with confidence. One of his brothers, Vincenz Biemann (1811–48), was also a glass-engraver, and a cup with a lid decorated with a representation of *Apollo and the Muses* (Berlin, Tiergarten, Kstgewmus.) has been attributed to him.

S. Pesatová: 'Dominik Biemann', *J. Glass Stud.*, vii (1965), pp. 83–106

K. Pittrof and D. Biemann: *Dominik Biemann: Böhmischer Glasgraveur des Biedermeier* (Stuttgart, 1993)

Biennais, **Martin-Guillaume** (*b* Lacochère, Orne, 29 April 1764; *d* Paris, 26 March 1843). French cab-

Martin-Guillaume Biennais: *nécessaire* of Napoleon I, silver, enmamel and crystal, 540 × 140 × 350 mm, 1806 (Paris, Musée du Louvre)

inetmaker and silversmith. By 1789 Biennais had established himself at 283, Rue Saint-Honoré, Paris, as a cabinetmaker and *tabletier* (a dealer in and maker of small objects). After 1797 he expanded his business to include the manufacture of silver. During the Consulate, Biennais became Napoleon's personal silversmith, although he may have provided Napoleon with silver as early as 1798, when it is said that he supplied him with a *nécessaire de voyage* prior to his Egyptian campaign (1798–1801) and trusted him to pay for it on his return.

Biennais produced large amounts of silver for Napoleon and his family, including, in 1804, the crown and sceptre for his coronation and a number of *nécessaires* of different types, remarkable for the combination of forms of varying shapes and sizes that are ingeniously accommodated in a restricted space. One (*c*. 1800; Edinburgh, Royal Mus. Scotland) supplied to Napoleon's sister, Pauline Bonaparte, Princess Borghese, contains 97 items in a case 570 × 400 × 185 mm. Much of the silver in these cases was made by independent goldsmiths working to Biennais's specifications, including Jean-Charles Cahier (*b* 1772; *d* after 1849), Marie Joseph Gabriel Genu (*fl* after 1788) and Pierre-Benoit Lorillon

Martin-Guillaume Biennais: washstand of Napoleon I, gilt wood, silver basin and pitcher, 1800–04 (Paris, Musée du Louvre)

(*fl* after 1788). Biennais also provided silver for a number of other European monarchs including those of Russia, Austria and Bavaria. Increased demand for his work led him to expand his workshop, where he employed possibly as many as 600 workers. Many of Biennais's best designs for both silver and furniture were supplied by Percier and Fontaine.

Biennais's furniture, generally small in scale and often based on antique models (e.g. Egyptian Revival coin cabinet, *c*. 1800–14; New York, Met.), is of great sophistication and elegance. An *athénienne* (*c*. 1804–10; New York, Met.) is after a design by Charles Percier (1764–1838; Paris, Mus. A. Déc.).

A. Dion-Tenenbaum: *L'Orfèvre de Napoléon: Martin-Guillaume Biennais* (Paris, 2003)

Bierfreund, Sigmund (*b* 1620; *d* 1702). Prussian goldsmith who worked in Nuremburg. He is best known for his cups (sometimes lidded) in the shape of tulips.

K. Tebbe: 'Tulpenmanie', *Weltkunst*, lxxiv/1–2 (Feb 2004), pp. 46–8

Biggin. In clothing, a child's cap or a night-cap; in metalwork, a coffee-pot (originally silver but later in other metals) containing a strainer for the infusion of the coffee.

Bigot, Alexandre (*b* Mer, nr Blois, 5 Nov 1862; *d* Paris, 1927). French ceramics manufacturer. He was initially a physics and chemistry teacher and in 1889 visited the Exposition Universelle in Paris, where he saw Chinese porcelain with opaque glazes that enhanced the ground colours and emphasized the forms of the body. He transferred this technique to stoneware, a less expensive material that has the advantage of being able to withstand great variations of temperature when fired. In this way, with one type of ceramic body, it is possible to vary the degree to which enamels are fused in order to obtain dull, oily or crystalline finishes in the greatest possible variation of colours.

The catalogue produced by Bigot's firm in 1902, *Les Grès de Bigot*, placed the greatest value on one-off, made-to-order objects, which were fired directly from clay models without passing through a casting stage. This was the procedure he followed for the windows, door, doorframes and balcony of 29, Avenue Rapp, Paris, designed by Jules Lavirotte (1864–1924). Bigot concluded that it was no more expensive to decorate a façade with high-fired stoneware than it was to do so with sculpted stone; furthermore, by this method one obtained everlasting colours. He embellished numerous buildings both inside and out, with ornaments in fired stoneware, including the Villa Majorelle (1898) in Nancy by Henri Sauvage (1873–1932), and, in Paris, Castel Béranger (1894–5) by Hector Guimard (1867–1942), the church of St Jean (1897–1904) in Montmartre by Anatola de Baudot (1834–1915) and the block of flats (1903) at 25, Rue Franklin by Auguste Perret (1874–1954). He also mass-produced objets d'art, vases and statues, from bathtubs to teapots, and such architectural ornaments as friezes, tiles, decorative bosses and balusters, based on the designs of the greatest architects associated with the Art Nouveau style. Bigot's firm in Rue des Petites Ecuries, Paris, closed in 1914.

Bijlivert, Jacques [Jacopo [Giacomo] Biliverti] (*b* Delft, 17 Nov 1550; *d* ?Florence, between Jan and April 1603). Dutch goldsmith, active in Italy. He served his apprenticeship in Delft or Augsburg and travelled to Florence in 1573 to head the workshops of Grand Duke Francesco I de' Medici, supervising small groups of goldsmiths from various countries. In 1577 Bijlivert began work on the new Medici ducal crown (destr.), completed in 1583: a gold circlet with 17 gem-set rays and the red fleur-de-lis of Florence at its centre. It is depicted in several Medici portraits, including Scipione Pulzone's portrait of *Cristina di Lorena* (1590; Florence, Pal. Medici-Riccardi), and an 18th-century drawing, perhaps by Giovanni Cassini, inscribed *Corona di Casa Medici* (London, V&A). The Rospigliosi Cup (New York, Met.), previously attributed not only to Bijlivert but to Benvenuto Cellini, is now known to be a 19th-century fake by the German restorer Reinhold Vasters (1827–1909). Bijlivert is known to have created the gold mounts for the sculpted lapis lazuli urn (*c.* 1583; Florence, Pitti), which was designed by Bernardo Buontalenti (*c.* 1531–1608). The neck of the urn is flanked by two attenuated human necks of enamelled gold, terminating in female grotesque heads. The foot, neck and lid are also ornamented with enamelled gold bands (see colour pl. VI, fig. 1).

Y. Hackenbroch: 'Jacopo Bilivert and the Rospigliosi Cup', *Connoisseur*, clxxii (1969), pp. 174–81

Bill, Max (*b* Winterthur, 22 Dec 1908; *d* Zurich, 9 Dec 1994). Swiss architect, sculptor, painter, industrial designer, graphic designer and writer. He attended silversmithing classes at the Kunstgewerbeschule in Zurich from 1924 to 1927, but then decided to become an architect and enrolled in the Bauhaus, Dessau, in 1927. He practised as an architect, but after World War II Bill worked increasingly in the field of applied art. His designs were based on the idea (articulated in his book *Form*, 1952) that the aesthetic component of an object was defined not only as arising from a function but as being the actual function of form. This concept of 'good form' was implemented in the products that he designed for Braun and for his independent designs, which centred on furniture but also included the Patria typewriter.

Max Bill (exh. cat. by L. Alloway and J. N. Wood, Buffalo, NY, Albright–Knox A.G., 1974)
E. Hüttlinger: *Max Bill* (New York, 1978)
G. Fleischmann: 'A Poster by Max Bill, or the Love of Geometry', *Des. Issues*, xvii/2 (Spring 2001), pp. 53–63

E. Heathcote: 'Max Bill: Simplicity and Ordinariness', *Archit. Des.*, lxxii/4 (July 2002), pp. 17–21
J. Sergison: 'Moments of Brilliance', *Archit. J.*, cc/15 (Oct 2004), p. 51

Biller [Bühler]. German family of goldsmiths furniture-makers and engravers. Lorenz Biller I (*fl c.* 1664–85) achieved prominence with works for Emperor Leopold I, for whom he made a centrepiece with a knight on a horse (1680–84; Moscow, Kremlin, Armoury) that was sent to Moscow as an ambassadorial gift. Lorenz Biller I's sons, Johann Ludwig Biller I (1656–1732), Albrecht Biller (1663–1720) and Lorenz Biller II (*fl c.* 1678–1726), supplied silverware of the highest quality to several German courts, especially that of Prussia, for which Albrecht made large wine-coolers and 'pilgrim' bottles (1698; Berlin, Schloss Köpenick). Albrecht Biller's abilities as a sculptor are also evident in his reliefs and in seven splendid silver vases he supplied to the court of Hesse-Kassel (*c.* 1700; Kassel, Hess. Landesmus.). The silver vases ordered by the court usually followed French fashions, yet the form and lavish decoration of these pieces are quite different. A pair of vases by Lorenz Biller II (Florence, Pitti) with views of Hungarian forts are similarly overdecorated. In 1716 Albrecht also published designs for embossed silver and furniture in the style of Jean Berain. Johann Jacob Biller (*d* 1723), descended from Lorenz II, was a goldsmith and engraver of ornament.

Johann Ludwig I's sons, Johann Ludwig Biller II (1692–1746) and Johannes Biller (1696–1745), also achieved renown as goldsmiths. Johann Ludwig II's French-influenced style is clear in the four *pots à oille* and a number of platters that are strictly classical in style (1721; priv. col.). He received commissions from several courts: he supplemented the 17th-century gold service of the court of Bavaria, for example, with two large *pots à oille*, and in 1731 he supplied George II, King of England and Elector of Hanover (*reg* 1727–60), with a silver table decorated with a relief of *Hercules Supporting the Vault of Heaven* (Nordstemmen, Schloss Marienburg). For King Frederick William I of Prussia, Johann Ludwig II made a pair of tureens and a pair of enormous pâté tins (1731–3; Berlin, Schloss Köpenick). The three-dimensional eagles and lions on this piece may have been designed by a sculptor. About the same time Johann Ludwig II produced part of the Riga Service, commissioned by the Russian court for William Augustus, Duke of Cumberland (St Petersburg, Hermitage). One of Johann Ludwig II's outstanding works is the gold service that he made for Anna, Empress of Russia (1736–40; St Petersburg, Hermitage). It comprises a toilet mirror, a ewer and basin, a covered bowl, various boxes, candlesticks, covered beakers and tea and coffee utensils. The forms show French influence; the decoration—*Bandelwerk* (ornament in the style of Jean Berain) with interwoven cartouches and monograms—is more elaborate than that of most German plate of this period.

The surviving work of Johannes Biller is less extensive. He also supplied several courts with silverware and worked as a silver trader. In 1738 he was appointed court gold- and silversmith to the Prussian royal family. Four pedestal tables (Nordstemmen, Schloss Marienburg) with the coat of arms of the Braunschweig-Wolfenbüttel family were supplied with the table by Johann Ludwig II to King George II. A mounted chalcedony bowl by Johannes was kept in the *Kunstkammer* of the Dukes of Württemberg (Stuttgart, Württemberg. Landesmus.). Johannes's son Johann Martin Biller appears to have worked only as a dealer of silver.

D. Alcouffe: 'Le Louvre présente un mobilier d'argent qu'il partage avec le musée d'Augsbourg', *Rev. Louvre*, xxxvii/1 (1987), pp. 1–4

Billet. Architectural ornament used extensively in the Romanesque period, particularly in the 12th century. It is formed of small blocks, either flat and square or cylindrical, spaced out in horizontal bands. The term 'billet' is also used to denote the thumbpiece of a flask, and in heraldry, a bearing of the shape of a rectangle placed on end.

Billingsley, William (*b* Derby, *bapt* 12 Oct 1758; *d* Coalport, 16 Jan 1828). English ceramic artist and porcelain manufacturer. In 1774 he was apprenticed to William Duesbury at the DERBY porcelain factory, where his father, William Billingsley (*d* 1770), was a flower painter. He became one of their chief flower painters and some ten years later developed a new, soft, naturalistic style of painting flower petals on ceramics that came to be widely, though poorly, imitated at other English factories. His innovative technique involved painting with a heavily loaded brush, and then wiping away much of the paint with a virtually dry brush to produce more delicate colours and highlights (e.g. two-handled tray, *c.* 1790; Derby, Mus. & A.G.). Though particularly famous for his 'Billingsley roses', he also painted landscapes, buildings and other botanical subjects. In 1795 he helped John Coke (1776–1841) to set up a porcelain factory at Pinxton, Derbys. By 1799 he was working as a decorator of blanks, first in Mansfield, then moving in 1802 to Brampton-in-Torksey, Lincs, and in 1808 to Worcester. In 1813 he and his son-in-law, Samuel Walker (*fl* 1813–35), established a porcelain factory at Nantgarw, near Cardiff. Production difficulties caused financial problems and in 1814 they joined L. W. Dillwyn (1778–1855) at his larger and better equipped factory in SWANSEA. In 1817 they returned to Nantgarw where they succeeded in producing a popular soft-paste porcelain ware with deep green, turquoise and claret grounds and lavishly decorated with highly burnished gilding. Production continued until 1819 when the moulds were bought by the COALPORT PORCELAIN FACTORY, with which Billingsley remained associated until his death.

W. D. John: *William Billingsley, 1758–1828: His Outstanding Achievements as an Artist and Porcelain Maker* (Newport, 1968)

J. Norie: 'A Billingsley-decorated Service', *Apollo*, cxxiii (April 1986), pp. 242–5

J. Robinson and R. Thomas: *William Billingsley (1758–1828)* (Lincoln, 1996)

Bilston. English centre of production for objects of vertu. A Staffordshire village, and town from 1824, in and around which japanning factories produced small japanned objects (mostly snuffboxes) from the 1690s to the early 20th century. Bilston was also an important centre for enamels (especially enamel boxes) from 1749 to 1831. In 1970 the modern successor to these factories, Bilston & Battersea Enamels PLC, entered into a collaboration with Halcyon Days Ltd, a London antique shop, to revive enamelling-on-copper in the 18th-century manner. In the 21st century these enamelling techniques have continued to be employed to embellish jewellery and objects of vertu.

R. J. Charleston: 'Battersea, Bilston or Birmingham', *V&A Mus. Bull.*, iii (1967), pp. 1–12

E. Benton: 'John Brooks in Birmingham: The Bilston Enamellers', *Trans. Eng. Cer. Circ.*, vii/3 (1970), pp. 162–6

T. Cope: *Bilston Enamels of the 18th Century* (Tipton, 1980)

Bimann, Dominik. *See* BIEMANN, DOMINIK.

Binche lace. Type of lace made since the 17th century at Binche, near Brussels and Valenciennes, both of whose laces it resembles. It is a heavy lace with decorative grounds, and was used for bedspreads and as a costume trimming. The name has since become the generic term for the type of lace once made at Binche.

M. Giusiana and L. Dunn: *Binche Lace* (London, 1989)

Bindesbøll, Thorvald (*b* Copenhagen, 21 July 1846; *d* Copenhagen, 27 Aug 1908). Danish architect and designer. Bindesbøll's chief achievement was the rejuvenation of the Danish applied and decorative arts. The fine vigorous lines of his decorative work were applied with inexhaustible variety to every sphere of design and all types of interior. The best of his Art Nouveau designs were pioneer works, forerunners of much 20th-century abstract art. Most noteworthy were his ceramics (e.g. enamelled earthenware plate, 1901; Paris, Mus. A. Déc.), inspired by Italian *sgraffito* techniques and produced between 1883 and 1906. His style developed from classical neatness through the vogue for Japanese motifs towards liberated, asymmetrical and forceful abstraction, often characterized by tautly rounded and hard-edged contrasting forms. He produced book designs and other graphic work from the 1880s, and the clean lines of his labels for Carlsberg Pilsner (1897–1904) became world-famous. At the Exposition Universelle in Paris in 1900 his silverware received international recognition. From about 1890 he designed furniture in three distinct styles: he continued to work in the style of his father; he revived traditional Danish designs; and he created Art Nouveau pieces covered with metal inlay or upholstery based on the embroidery designs of his childhood (e.g. white lacquered pine chair, exh. Exposition Universelle, Paris, 1900; Copenhagen, Kstindustmus.).

S. Hammershøi: *Thorvald Bindesbøll in Memoriam, 1846–1946* (Copenhagen, 1946)
P. Brandes and others: *Thorvald Bindesbøll: Ceramic Works* (Copenhagen, 1997)

Bing & Grøndahl. Danish porcelain factory founded in Copenhagen in 1853 by Frederik Vilhelm Grøndahl, a former employee of Bing & Grøndahl's only predecessor, the Kongelige Porcelainsfabrik (Royal Copenhagen Porcelain Factory, established 1775); Grøndahl's partners were the art dealers Jacob Herman and Meyer Herman Bing, whose chain of retail outlets sold the products of the factory. Grøndahl's two sons later became managers in the company. The company made (and still makes) table and display wares in porcelain and stoneware. Its designers have included the painter Pietro Krohn (1840–1905), who made the 'Heron' dinner service (1888); Jean René Gauguin (1881–1961; son of the painter Paul Gauguin), who made figures; Ingeborg Plockross-Irminger (1872–1962), who made statuettes of women and children; Jens Peter Dahl-Jensen (1874–1960), who later started his own factory; and the silversmith Henning Koppel (1918–81), who famously designed for GEORG JENSEN. The Company has issued Christmas plates annually since 1895. Bing & Grøndahl was bought by Kongelige Porcelainsfabrik in 1987.

E. Lassen: *En københavnsk porcelænsfabriks historie: Bing & Grøndahl, 1853–1978* (Copenhagen, 1978)
P. Owen: *Bing & Grøndahl Christmas Plates, The First 100 Years* (Dayton, OH, 1995)
C. Pope and N. Pope: *Bing & Grøndahl Figurines* (Atglen, PA, 2002)
L. Christoffersen: *Christmas Plates & Other Commemoratives from Royal Copenhagen and Bing & Grøndahl* (Atglen, PA, 2004)

Binns, Charles Fergus (*b* Worcester, UK, 4 Oct 1857; *d* Alfred, NY, 4 Dec 1934). American potter and teacher. He was born in England, where his father was director of the Worcester Royal Porcelain Co. Ltd. After holding various positions in the Worcester firm, he moved in 1897 to Trenton, NJ, where he was appointed director of the Technical School of Arts and Sciences and superintendent of the Ceramic Art Co. In 1900 he became the first director of the New York College of Clayworking and Ceramics at Alfred University, NY, and subsequently became a founder-member of the American Ceramic Society, through which he greatly influenced the development of American ceramics. His own technically exquisite stoneware, produced at Alfred, was inspired by early Chinese ceramics and emphasized the interrelationship of classical shape and finely textured glazes.

M. C. Xie: 'Charles Fergus Binns: The Father of American Studio Ceramics', *Studio Potter,* xxi (Dec 1992), pp. 67–72
M. Carney and others: *Charles Fergus Binns: The Father of American Studio Ceramics* (New York, 1998) [including a catalogue raisonné]

M. B. A. Rasmussen: *A Crusade for Porcelain in America: The Mission of English Ceramist Charles Fergus Binns, 1897 to 1922* (1999)

Bird-beaked jug [sparrow-beaked jug]. Milk or cream jug with a pouring lip shaped like a beak. These porcelain jugs were made at several English factories, notably Bow, Lowestoft and Worcester.

Birdcage clock. Iron or brass weight-driven wall clock of a type manufactured in the 17th century.

Birdcage support. Type of hinge under a table that enables the top to be tilted or revolved.

Bird's-eye maple. Wood of the sugar maple when full of little knotty spots, used in cabinet-making. A bird's eye veneer was originally one made from this maple, but the term is now used for veneer made from any light wood of similar appearance.

B. Keenan: 'Bird's eye Maple', *Fine Woodworking,* lxxiv (Jan–Feb 1989), pp. 78–80
T. Masaschi: 'Three Finishes for Bird's-Eye Maple', *Fine Woodworking,* clxiii (May–June 2003), pp. 44–7

Birmingham. English centre of metalwork production. Birmingham has been a major producer of domestic metal wares since the 16th century. Originally it was known for ironwork, followed in the 17th century by the expansion of brass and copper manufacture and in the 18th century by small silverware. The growth of Birmingham's brass industry in the second half of the 17th century was largely a result of the ban on imported buttons in 1662 and the prohibition of trade with France in 1688. By the 18th century it was established as the main centre of production of small metalwork or 'toys', and Edmund Burke described it as the 'toy shop of Europe'.

The 'toy' manufacturers made increasing use of silver during the 18th century, although the history of large-scale silver production begins with MATTHEW BOULTON. The output of silver in Birmingham expanded steadily in the 19th century, although the industry was still largely based on small workshops. The manufacture of Sheffield plate also grew, and the leading makers were Waterhouse & Ryland and Edward Thomason (1769–1849). The latter in particular competed with some success with the London retailers Rundell, Bridge & Rundell. The brass industry also expanded, as new developments in the smelting of zinc led to a reduction in manufacturing costs. Small objects—chimney ornaments, boxes and inkstands—were made by casting or die-stamping.

The mid- and late 19th century was dominated by the huge firm of G. R. ELKINGTON & Co. Other important firms in the second half of the 19th century were Hardman & Co. (*see* JOHN HARDMAN) and Hukin & Heath; the latter's products, in contrast to Hardman's, promoted the severe minimalist electroplate designed by CHRISTOPHER DRESSER.

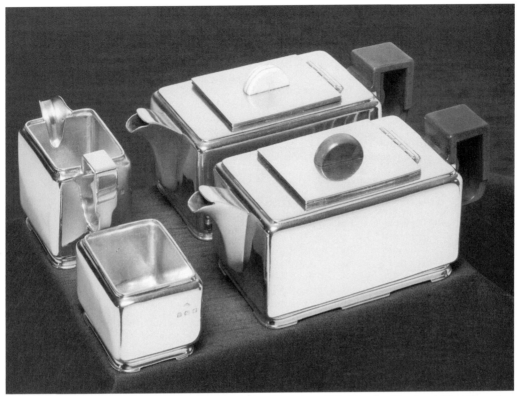

Silver tea service, designed by Harold Stabler and made by Adie Bros, Birmingham, 1935–6 (London, Victoria and Albert Museum)

Although remaining the leading centre of manufactured silverware in England, the industry never fully recovered from the reversal of trade caused by World War I. The War was followed by the merging of many firms and most production concentrated on relatively cheap reproductions of antique forms. The role of designers in most firms was reduced, with a few exceptions such as W. H. Haseler, who produced silver for Liberty's, and A. Edward Jones.

Birmingham Gold and Silver, 1773–1973 (exh. cat., Birmingham, Mus. & A.G., 1973)

K. Crisp Jones, ed.: *The Silversmiths of Birmingham and Their Marks, 1750–1980* (London, 1981)

H. J. Allen: *Notes on the Armorial Engraving on Silver in the Collection of the Birmingham Assay Office* (Birmingham, 1982)

B. Tilson: 'Finely Taught, Finely Wrought', *Crafts*, cviii (Jan–Feb 1991), pp. 54–5

K. Quickenden and N. A. Quickenden: *Silver & Jewellery: Production & Consumption Since 1750* (Birmingham, UK, 1995)

Biscuit. Name given to porcelain and other pottery after having undergone the first firing, and before being glazed, painted, or otherwise embellished. The term is also used to denote the unglazed white porcelain that resembles marble and has been used since the mid-18th century (initially by JEAN-JACQUES BACHELIER) for statuettes and busts.

Bishop's bowl. Type of bowl shaped like a mitre from which 'Bishop', the name of a sweet drink made from wine, citrus fruit and sugar, was traditionally

drunk. Other shapes appeared later, including one- and two-handled cups. Faience bishop's bowls were made at Danish factories in the late 18th century.

Bizarre silk. Style of silk fashionable in late 17th- and early 18th-century Europe, especially in Italy, England and France. The bizarre style first appeared in the late 1680s, when chinoiseries and vegetable forms derived from Indian textiles began to be mixed with European floral sprigs. By the mid-1690s, the plant forms, although still small, were becoming more angular and elongated, with an increasingly vigorous left-right movement. The patterns, typically asymmetrical, were brocaded with metal threads on damask grounds, which were already patterned with even stranger motifs.

From *c.* 1700 to 1705 the designs were at their most bizarre, incorporating strange gourds, serpentine vegetable stems, intertwined plants and unidentifiable shapes, some angular and others reminiscent of sea creatures or rock formations. They were brocaded with gold and silver threads and coloured silks on damask grounds and had repeats measuring as much as one metre. This exaggerated length suited the elongated lines of womens' dress in the early 18th century, and the silks were also used for covering furniture and wall panels.

The earliest English silk designs made by James Leman (1688–1745) in Spitalfields, London, from 1706 are in the bizarre style. They are the first of an unbroken line of designs that make it possible to follow the development of the style through a less bizarre phase, when clearer, but still strange, chinoiserie and japonaiserie motifs were combined with images derived from architecture and others taken from Indian floral filling patterns (e.g. of *c.* 1709; London, V&A). The repeats became shorter and, by *c.* 1712, vertical bands and more naturalistic flowers began to be introduced. Abundant foliage became the dominant feature; it was controlled by various forms of band or serpentine line, arranged symmetrically, in place of the asymmetrical plan of most bizarre silks. By *c.* 1720, the bizarre elements had virtually vanished.

V. Slomann: *Bizarre Designs in Silks: Trade and Tradition* (Copenhagen, 1953)
L. Teisseyre-Sallmann: *L'Industrie de la soie en Bas-Languedoc: XVIIe-XVIIIe siècles* (Paris, 1995)
H. C. Ackermann and V. Otavská: *Seidengewebe des 18. Jahrhunderts* (Riggisberg, 2000)

Bizen. Japanese centre of ceramics production. High-fired ceramic wares were manufactured from the end of the 12th century in and around the village of Inbe, Bizen Province (now Okayama Prefect.). This region had been a centre for manufacturing Sue-style stonewares and Haji-style earthenwares from the 6th century AD. At the end of the Heian period (794–1185) the potters moved from the old Sue-ware sites around Osafune village to Inbe, just to the north. In response to increased agricultural development, the new kilns manufactured kitchen mortars (*suribachi*), narrow-necked jars (*tsubo*) and wide-necked jars (*kame*). During the thirteenth century the wares show less of the grey-black surfaces typical of the old Sue tradition and more of the purple-reddish colour characteristic of Bizen. In the 14th century Bizen-ware production sites shifted from the higher slopes to the foot of the mountains. Kilns expanded in capacity, ranging up to 40 m in length. Vast quantities of Bizen wares, particularly kitchen mortars, were exported via the Inland Sea to Kyushu, Shikoku and numerous points in western Honshu, establishing Bizen as the pre-eminent ceramics centre in western Japan. By the fifteenth century the Bizen repertory had expanded to include agricultural wares in graded sizes; wares then featured combed decoration and such functional additions as lugs and pouring spouts. Plastic–forming was assisted by the introduction of a fusible clay found 2–4 m under paddy-fields. This clay, which fires to an almost metallic hardness, is still in use today.

That Bizen adjusted quickly to demands from cultural centres is seen in its early manufacture of tea ceremony wares, particularly water jars (*mizusashi*) and flower vases. Bizen teaware is first mentioned in the diary of the tea master Tsuda Sōtatsu in 1549. Tea practitioners were particularly fond of the decorative accents that occurred in the long, high-temperature firing: *hidasuki*, red scorch marks left by the straw cords in which the pots were wrapped for kiln packing; *hibotan*, blush marks created by the irregular play of the fire on the pots; *botamochi*, resist patterns created when wares are stacked one on top another; *goma*, a speckled pattern created by a shower of ashes on the pots.

In the 17th century, in response to competition from the nascent porcelain industries, the Bizen potters manufactured a crisply formed product called *Inbede*. A line of decorative earthenware and stoneware figurines, variously known as *Ao Bizen* ('blue Bizen'), *Shiro Bizen* ('white Bizen') and *Saishiki Bizen* ('coloured Bizen'), began to be produced a century later. Some of these were exported to the West. The Bizen kilns declined in the Meiji period (1868–1912) but revived in the tourism and ceramic boom that began after World War II. The most distinguished of the 20th-century Bizen potters was Toyo Kanashige (1896–1967), who was descended from a long line of Bizen potters; he specialized in rough and irregular red clay vessels intended for use as TEA CEREMONY WARE. The Bizen area now has about 300 potteries.

B. Chang and others: 'Bizen: A Living Tradition', *Ceramics* (Australia), xxxviii (1999), pp. 90–92

Black jack. Large leather beer jug, coated externally with tar to make it watertight, and sometimes fitted with a metal rim. Black jacks were used widely throughout late medieval and early modern Europe; 'bombard' is an alternative name, derived from a resemblance to the early cannons known as bombards.

O. Baker: *Black Jacks and Leather Bottles* (London, 1921)

Black metal. Term used in mining to denote black bituminous shale and in metalwork to denote a pewter in which the proportion of lead is doubled to 40%; black metal (or 'black pewter') was used for centuries for household wares and for soldering, but the awareness of lead poisoning reduced its popularity.

Blackwork. Type of embroidery done in black silk on linen, was popular in the 16th and 17th centuries, especially in England, Spain and northern Holland; in Friesland and the island of Marken, blackwork was much in favour among peasant women for caps and shifts; upper-class women in the towns also often wore blackwork caps, and handkerchiefs with fine black embroidery formed part of Friesian betrothal rituals.

R. Drysdale: *The Art of Blackwork Embroidery* (New York, 1975)
M. Gostelow: *Blackwork* (Mineola, NY, 1998)

Blanc de chine. European name for white glazed porcelain made since the Ming period (and still made) at DEHUA, in Fujian Province

P. J. Donnelly: *Blanc de Chine* (London, 1969)

Blaze. *See* FLOSS SILK.

Bleeding bowl [cupping dish]. Shallow bowl with a flat handle, used by surgeons when bleeding their patients; the bowls were made of pewter or pottery, and occasionally of silver. In the USA bleeding bowls are sometimes called PORRINGERS.

Blind Earl. Pattern used on Worcester dishes from *c.* 1760, later named in honour of George William Coventry, 6th Earl of Coventry (1722–1809), who lost his sight in 1780. The pattern consists of emerald green rose leaves some of which are slightly raised on the surface of the plate.

Blind tooling. In bookbinding, the technique of impressing an ornamental design without gilding; if gold is applied the technique is called 'gilt tooling' or 'gold tooling'.

Block front furniture. Design common in some of the finest American furniture of the 18th century, first developed in Boston in the 1730s and then built elsewhere in New England, including Rhode Island. The contours on the front of the cases were formed of three blocks, two convex blocks flanking a concave block. In the finest examples the drawer front is carved from a single piece of wood, which had originally to be very thick in order to accommodate the curves. The finest exponents of block front furniture were the Newport families of GODDARD and TOWNSEND.

M. A. Norton: 'More Light on the Block Front', *Antiques*, iii/2 (Feb 1923), pp. 63–6

Blanc de chine porcelain figurine, Dehua, Fujian province, China, Qing period (1644–1911) (Rome, Museo Nazionale d'Arte Orientale)

M. M. Lovell: 'Boston Blockfront Furniture', *Boston Furniture of the Eighteenth Century*, eds W. M. Whitehill, B. Jobe and J. L. Fairbanks (Boston, 1974), pp. 77–136
P. D. Zimmerman and others: 'An Important Block-front Desk by Richard Walker of Boston', *Mag. Ant.*, cxlvii (March 1995), pp. 436–41

Blonde lace. Type of lace produced in northern France. *Blonde* lace is a floss silk lace of two threads, twisted and formed in hexagonal meshes; early examples are the colour of raw silk, but later ones are sometimes black or white. *Blonde* laces were first made *c.* 1745, principally in Bayeaux, Caen, Chantilly and Dieppe. The laces are sometimes known as 'blondes' (not 'blonds') or 'nankins'; the latter term, a corruption of Nanjing, reflects the Chinese origin of silk.

C. Bouvot and M. Bouvot: *Dentelles normandes: La blonde de Caen* (Condé-sur-Noireau, 1997)

Blue-and-white ceramic. Category of ceramics defined by the use, on a white surface, of blue derived from cobalt oxide, the most powerful of the colouring oxides in tinting strength. Depending on its concentration, colours range from a pale blue to a near blue-black. Cobalt produces good colours on all ceramic bodies, from low-fired earthenwares to high-fired porcelains. It was used as a colourant on figures found in Egyptian tombs of the 5th Dynasty (*c.* 2465–*c.* 2325 BC), and glass beads coloured with cobalt and dating to *c.* 2250 BC have been discovered in north-west Iran. Its use in ceramic glazes is datable to 1200 BC from tomb objects found in Ethiopia, Mycenae and Tiryns, which probably originated in Egypt or Phoenicia. Persian and Syrian potters used cobalt on earthenwares for several centuries before they introduced it to China, where it was first used as an underglaze colour on earthenware during the Tang period (AD 618–907) and then later on porcelain. The opaque white, tin-glazed earthenware that originated in Mesopotamia during the 9th century AD or early 10th should be considered the first blue and white. The technique was later introduced into Europe during the Arab conquests of North Africa and Spain. Merchants from Persia (now Iran) established communities on the coast and in the large cities of China, where they influenced the production of ceramics and constituted one of the earliest and largest markets for Chinese blue-and-white decorated porcelains; blue-and-white porcelain was first really appreciated in the Middle East, which was unable to produce its own high-fired ceramic due to the lack of appropriate materials and techniques.

The Portuguese were the first Europeans to arrive in China by sea (1517) and to begin direct trade with China. They were the major exporters of Chinese blue-and-white wares throughout the 16th century and were therefore the first Europeans to be directly influenced by these porcelains. By the 1520s shipments of mostly blue-and-white porcelain to Portugal amounted to between 40,000 and 60,000 pieces, many of which were re-exported to the Netherlands.

One outstanding example of the mania for Chinese blue and white is the Santos Palacio (now the French Embassy) in Lisbon: in what an inventory of 1704 calls the 'Casa das Porçolanas', a pyramidal ceiling was covered with 261 Chinese blue-and-white dishes and plates dating from the 16th century to the early 17th.

Because of Venice's early efforts in maritime trade, the importation of silk and other luxuries from Asia made Italy a viable location for the introduction of Chinese porcelain to the European Continent. In 1461 the Sultan of Egypt presented 20 pieces of Chinese blue-and-white porcelain to Doge Pasquale Malipiero of Venice and later even more to Lorenzo the Magnificent in Florence. Francesco I, Grand Duke of Tuscany, was the first to develop a close replica of Chinese porcelain; a soft-paste porcelain was made in his court workshops (est. *c.* 1565) in Florence *c.* 1575 using clay from Vicenza, which contained some kaolin. Only 57 pieces are recorded and all are decorated with blue winding stems and coiled foliage resembling similar decoration on Chinese porcelain of the 15th and 16th centuries. Similar Chinese motifs had already been used on Italian maiolica in a style known as *alla porcellana*. At the end of the 16th century Italian potters dispersed the technique of maiolica production, including the blue-and-white palette, throughout Europe.

In 1609 the Dutch were granted permission to establish a trading post at Hirado in Japan, and in July 1610 the first ship arrived in the Netherlands

Covered jar, porcelain with underglaze blue decoration, China, Ming period, 1522–66 (Paris, Musée Guimet)

from Japan carrying Chinese blue-and-white porcelains, which had previously been brought by Portuguese ships. In 1636, 259,000 pieces of 'kraak' were shipped from Batavia, and the passion for blue and white in the Netherlands was thus established. From the second quarter of the 17th century the declining Delft breweries became the site for a pottery industry where tin-glazed earthenware was produced in such profusion that the name of the town has become synonymous with its product, Delftware. The enormous quantities of Chinese blue and white imported by the Dutch East India Company affected the local ceramics industry to the extent that at first they directly copied the imported blue-and-white porcelain and only later introduced Dutch motifs and designs. In the Netherlands wares were covered with a clear lead glaze to resemble more closely the finish of the Chinese porcelains. Plates, chargers, ewers and tiles were decorated with designs in cobalt in the Chinese style. The Dutch East India Company records show requests for Delftwares by Japanese warlords and wealthy merchants from 1634 until 1668, when Japanese sumptuary laws prohibited the importation of foreign pottery. These wares were thought to be especially suitable for the tea ceremony, and a set of small, irregularly shaped dishes (*mukozuke*) for this ceremony, made in Delft and decorated by Frederik van Frytom (1632–1702), have been found in Japan.

Centres for the production of tin-glazed wares were established at Hamburg, Frankfurt am Main and Jannau in the late 17th century in order to compete with Dutch imports. The first fine earthenware factory established in Frankfurt am Main in 1666 was influenced by Chinese blue and white, either directly or through the Dutch wares. As with the Dutch tin-glazed wares, these were covered with a clear lead glaze.

Early examples of Chinese blue and white in Britain suggest that blue and white was rare in the 16th century, but after the accession of William III to the English throne in 1688, the stylistic influences from the Dutch court were strong and included the extensive use of blue and white, especially in interior design. The display of blue-and-white wares became one of the primary styles of interior decoration, mainly through the work of the Huguenot Daniel Marot, who had worked for Queen Mary II in the Netherlands.

This passion for blue and white naturally led to its being imitated by English potters producing tin-glazed earthenwares, especially at the London potteries of Southwark and Lambeth. In the 18th century the production of tin-glazed wares—mostly tablewares—was particularly centred in Bristol and Liverpool. Soft-paste porcelain was first produced at the CHELSEA PORCELAIN FACTORY in London *c.* 1745. Other porcelain factories were established in England, including the BOW PORCELAIN FACTORY in London's East End, which, after 1749, specialized in the production of blue-and-white decorated with chinoiseries. Not until the New Hall Factory in New Hall, Staffs, was established in 1781 were blue-and-white, hard-paste porcelains produced in quantity. By 1800 Josiah Spode had perfected bone china at Stoke-on-Trent, Staffs, making blue-and-white ware less expensive and thus available to a wider public.

In the 1750s transfer-printing was introduced at such factories as Worcester; the designs from an engraved copper plate were transferred with tissue paper on to the ceramic object. One of the most ubiquitous patterns in this category of ceramic ware is the WILLOW PATTERN. 'Flow blue', a category of transfer-printed blue and white, was an early 19th-century development that, by firing in an atmosphere containing volatile chlorides, created a soft appearance resulting from the diffusion of the pigment into the glaze.

The production of blue and white first began in France when Chinese-style faience was produced at Nevers. Made between 1650 and 1680, typical pottery of this type is decorated with a deep-blue ground and yellow and orange motifs; it was erroneously known as *bleu persan*. It was imitated at Rouen as well as in the Netherlands and England. The French East India Company was established in 1664, after which many French ceramics reflected an increased interest in Chinese wares. From *c.* 1700 factories in Normandy began to produce blue-and-white faience in the *style rayonnant*, identified by blue lacy borders sometimes accented by red, yellow and green. A similar style was developed at the factory of Pierre CLÉRISSY in MOUSTIERS in southern France.

D. Macintosh: *Chinese Blue and White Porcelain* (Newton Abbot, 1977, rev. Woodbridge, 3/1994)
M. Lerner: *Blue and White: Early Japanese Export Ware* (New York, 1978)
Blue and White: Chinese Porcelain and Its Impact on the Western World (exh. cat. by J. Carswell, U. Chicago, IL, Smart Gal., 1985)
W. H. Van Buskirk: *Late Victorian Flow Blue, Other Ceramic Wares: A Selected History of Potteries & Shapes* (Atglen, PA, 2002)
P. F. Ferguson: *Cobalt Treasures: The Robert Murray Bell and Ann Walker Bell Collection of Chinese Blue and White Porcelain* (Toronto, 2003)

Blue-dash charger. Large circular earthenware dish made in England (especially Bristol and Lambeth) in the late 17th century and early 18th; the name derives from the dashes of blue around the rims. The dishes are usually decorated with portraits of Stuart monarchs or pretenders, but some portray an Adam and Eve in which the fruit is an orange, an allusion to William and Mary of Orange. There are no makers' marks on the dishes.

Blue John. Local name of a blue fluorite (formerly known as fluor-spar) mined near Castleton, Derbys, since the mid-18th century. The name Blue John derives from the French *Bleu Jaune* ('blue yellow'). It is a form of fluorite and was discovered as miners were exploring the cave systems of Castleton for lead. Banded Blue John fluorite has long been carved into ornaments in both England and France; its modern industrial uses include toothpaste. MATTHEW BOULTON used Blue John for candelabra.

T. Ford: *Derbyshire Blue John* (Ashbourne, 2000)

Blue Mountain Pottery. Canadian pottery founded in Collingwood, Ontario, in 1947. Its earthenware figures were moulded from a rich red clay and used two glazes, one dark and one light; during firing the lighter glaze ran as it passed through the darker glaze. The pottery is associated with its characteristic green figures and vases, but in the 1960s produced earthenware in other colours and also made tea and coffee sets. The pottery closed in 2004.

Blue Willow. *See* WILLOW PATTERN.

Board chest [boarded chest]. Medieval or early modern chest constructed from planks nailed to end pieces, often reinforced with iron at the corners. This method of construction is distinguished from joined construction that uses mortise and tendon joints. Board chests that use a single plank on each of the six surfaces are known as 'six-board chests'.

E. K. Gronning: 'New Haven's Six-Board Chests', *Mag. Ant.*, clxiii/5 (May 2003), pp. 116–21

Bobbin lace. *See under* LACE, §1(ii).

Bobbin-net [bobbinet]. Type of machine-made cotton net, originally imitating the lace made with bobbins on a pillow; the Bobbinet machine patented by John Heathcoat (1793–1861) in 1808 produced a perfect imitation of the simple twist net of Lille lace.

Bocage. Representation of shrubs or sylvan scenery in ceramics, often used as background to a figure.

Boccaro [bucaro; buccaro]. Scented red earthenware brought originally by the Portuguese from Mexico; the word derives from Portuguese *búcaro* (clay cup). The term also denotes similar earthenware made in Portugal and Spain (especially Talavera) from the 16th to the 18th centuries, and the imitation made by JOHANN FRIEDRICH BÖTTGER at Meissen; the name is also applied to the red Chinese stoneware made in YIXING.

Boehm, Edward Marshall (*b* 1913; *d* 1969). American potter famed for his hand-painted porcelain figures of American birds. He maintained an aviary on the Delaware River, and the captured life specimens were the models for the work of his studio in Trenton, NJ. The largest collection of his porcelain birds is housed in the Stark Museum in Orange, TX.

C. Marren: *The New and Complete Porcelain Art of Edward Marshall Boehm: America's Fine Porcelain Art Studio* (Loxahatchee, FL, 2003)

Boelen, Jacob (*b c.* 1657; *d* 1729–30). American goldsmith and silversmith of Dutch origin, based in New York. His most characteristic products are spoons, teapots, beakers and tankards (with coins set in the lids); his pieces are marked with the letters IB in a shield. The Metropolitan Museum of Art in New York has a fine silver teapot and a silver seal made for civic use in Marbletown (Ulster County, NY). Jacob's son Henricus was also a silversmith.

H. S. F. Randolph and Mrs R. Hastings: 'Jacob Boelen, Goldsmith, of New York and His Family Circle', *New York Gen. & Biog. Rec.*, lxxii/ 4 (Oct 1941), pp. 265–94

Bog oak. Oak preserved in a black state in peat-bogs; used from the 16th century for inlays and sculptures.

R. Barnes: 'As the Crow Flies', *Crafts*, cxi (July–Aug 1991), pp. 40–41

Böhm, August (*b* 1812; *d* 1890). Bohemian glass-engraver who worked in London and Hamburg before moving to America. His goblets and plaques, which are engraved with portraits and scenes (battle, landscape and religious), are unusual in that they are normally signed.

Böhm, Sebald. *See* BEHAM, SEBALD.

Bois durci ['hardened wood']. Hard, highly polish-able material patented in France and England in 1855 by François Charles Lepage. His composition was made of fine hardwood sawdust mixed with alumen (blood from the Paris slaughterhouses, or eggs) and coloured to simulate wood; the mixture was steam-heated and then pressed into a heated steel mould. The invention was bought by A. Latry, who pro-duced it at his factory in Grenelle. La Société du Bois Durci specialized in desk ware (especially ink stands) and plaques, but also made household items such as combs and decorative elements (e.g. medallions) for furniture. In about 1898 the company was bought by MIOM (La Manufacture d'Isolants et Objets Moulés), which manufactured Bois Durci until about 1920.

E. H. Pinto and E. R. Pinto: *Tunbridge and Scottish Souvenir Woodware, with Chapters on Bois Durci and Pyrography* (London, 1970)

Boiserie. French term for wood panelling, often used with reference to 18th-century French panel-ling, designed by an architect or a sculptor–orna-mentalist. Generally of oak, but also of walnut or pine, the panels might be carved with such decora-tive motifs as garlands of fruit and flowers, trophies, the architectural orders or symbols specific to the owner. The panels were rarely left natural and were generally painted white or pastel, highlighted with gilding. *Boiserie* was sometimes lacquered in VERNIS MARTIN.

N. Powell: 'Precious Paneling', *A. & Auction*, xxiii/8 (Sept–Oct 2001), pp. 76–87

Boizot, Louis-Simon (*b* Paris, 9 Oct 1743; *d* Paris, 10 March 1809). French sculptor. Although he even-

tually became known for his portrait sculpure, the first years of Boizot's career were dedicated primarily to decorative sculpture, such as the model for the elaborate allegorical gilt-bronze clock known as the 'Avignon' clock (*c.* 1770; London, Wallace), some caryatids for one of the chimney-pieces at the châ-teau of Fontainebleau (marble and bronze, 1772; now Versailles, Château) and various works for the château of Louveciennes, Yvelines. In 1773 he was appointed artistic director of the sculpture studio at the Sèvres porcelain manufactory, and during his time there he made more than 150 models that were reproduced in biscuit porcelain. In addition to mod-els for official portrait busts such as those of *Louis XVI* and *Marie-Antoinette* (both 1774–5) and numer-ous allegorical groups, he executed some unusual and prestigious pieces, for example the *surtout de table*, the 'Russian Parnassus' (1778; Sèvres, Mus. N. Cér.), a toilet set (1782; Pavlovsk Pal.) for the Comtesse du Nord (later the Tsarina) and the so-called large 'Me-dici' vases (1783; Paris, Louvre).

V. Marchi: 'Le Parnasse selon Boizot', *L' Oeil*, dxxxi (Nov 2001), p. 78
Louis-Simon Boizot (1743–1809): *Sculpteur du roi et directeur de l'atelier de sculpture à la Manufacture de Sèvres* (Paris, 2001)

Bokhara carpets. *See under* BUKHARA.

Bolection. Term applied to mouldings, usually ogee in section, which project before the face of the work which they decorate, as a raised moulding round a panel. The purpose of bolection mouldings is to

Louis-Simon Boizot: centrepiece with the Apotheosis of Catherine II ('Russian Parnassus'), porcelain, made by Sèvres, 1778 (Sèvres, Musée National de Ceramique)

cover the join between two members with differing surface levels. The term is used both in architecture and in the decorative arts, such as cabinet-making and silverwork.

Bologna. Italian centre of ceramics production. Pottery has been made in the Italian city of Bologna since the early 14th century. By the late 15th century Bologna had become a major centre for the production of lead-glazed, incised slipwares, the finest of which competed with the colourful tin-glazed earthenwares of Faenza and other maiolica centres for the luxury market. Signed and dated *sgraffito* pieces are extremely rare, and attribution is often difficult. Patrons include such prominent local families as the Bentivoglio, whose arms appear on certain pieces (e.g. inkstand, *c.* 1500; London, V&A). Among the best works are elaborate, large plates, tazze and modelled inkstands decorated with putti, figures of youths, portrait busts, animals and occasional genre, allegorical or religious scenes, bordered by patterns of stylized, Gothic-influenced leaves. The typical restrained palette is comprised of a whitish slip, through which a design was scratched to reveal the red earthenware beneath; the designs were then heightened with yellow, green, brown, purple and blue pigments and finally covered with a transparent glaze. Unlike the decoration of maiolica, which is characterized by a painterly quality and complex colour range, incised slipwares rely on the linear directness of the artist's draughtsmanship for their effect.

Maiolica was frequently imported into Bologna from Florence, Venice and Faenza. By 1595, however, maiolica workshops had been established in Bologna and production of both types of wares continued. During the late 19th century the factory of Angelo Minghetti (1822–92) was known for its excellent reproductions of Renaissance maiolica, some of which were bought as genuine Renaissance pieces. AEMILIA ARTS (founded in Bologna in 1898) also produced some fine ceramics.

W. B. Honey: 'Bologna Pottery of the Renaissance Period', *Burl. Mag.*, xlviii (1926), pp. 224–35

Bombard. *See* BLACK JACK.

Bombé [Fr.: 'swollen']. Having an outward swelling curve. The term is used with particular reference to French Rococo chests of drawers, which first appear in the *bombé* shape in the 1740s. The swollen section is normally in the upper half; when it is in the lower half, it is sometimes known as 'kettle shape'. In colonial America *bombé* furniture was mostly made in Massachusetts, primarily in Boston but also in centres such as Salem. In American *bombé* the swollen part is in the lower section in forms such as chests of drawers, desk and bookcases, chest-on-chests, and dressing tables.

G. T. Vincent: 'The Bombe Furniture of Boston', *Boston Furniture of the Eighteenth Century*, eds W. M. Whitehill, B. Jobe and J. L. Fairbanks (Boston, 1974), pp. 137–96.

M. S. Podmaniczky and others: 'Two Massachusetts Bombe Desk-and-bookcases', *Mag. Ant.*, cxlv (May 1994), pp. 724–31
M. K. Brown: 'Topping off Thomas Dawes's Desk-and-bookcase', *Mag. Ant.*, clvii/ 5 (May 2000), pp. 788–95

Bonbonnière. Small decorated box for holding sweets.

Bone china. Type of porcelain invented in England during the 1740s at the BOW PORCELAIN FACTORY and which was improved throughout the 19th century. Refinement of the paste increased its translucency and visual similarity to hard-paste porcelain; these improvements were achieved by the addition of kaolin and china stone to the bone ash (calcium phosphate). THOMAS FRYE of Bow patented bone china in 1748, but within a few years it was being manufactured elsewhere in England (especially Lowestoft, Chelsea and Derby) and in France (notably at Sèvres).

G. B. Hughes and T. Hughes: *English Porcelain and Bone China, 1743–1850* (New York, 1968)
S. Wardell: *Porcelain and Bone China* (Ramsbury, Crowood, 2004)

Bonheur du jour. Small lady's writing-table or desk, usually fitted with shelves or pigeonholes for writing materials or toiletries, and often closed with a fitted tambour shutter. The earliest examples were made in France in the mid-18th century.

Bonhomme. *See under* LIÈGE.

Bonnet top. Collectors' term for a broken pediment running from front to back on the top of a case piece of 18th-century American furniture; it may be a solid piece of wood, or may be a pair of pediments (at front and rear) joined by side pieces.

Bonnin & Morris. American soft-paste porcelain manufacturer. Gousse Bonnin (*b* ?Antigua, *c.* 1741; *d c.* 1779) moved in 1768 from England to Philadelphia, where he established the first porcelain factory in America. The factory produced its first blue-decorated bone china wares in late in 1770. Newspaper advertisements listed such wares as pickle stands, fruit baskets, sauce boats, pint bowls, plates, plain and handled cups, quilted cups, sugar dishes in two sizes, cream jugs, teapots in two sizes and breakfast sets. The enterprise proved unviable in the face of foreign competition, and production had ceased by November 1772.

G. Hood: *Bonnin and Morris of Philadelphia: The First American Porcelain Factory, 1770–1772* (Chapel Hill, NC, 1972)
E. H. Gustafson: 'A Rare Pair', *Mag. Ant.*, clxi/4 (April 2002), pp. 40–42

Bontemps, George (*b* 1801; *d* 1882). French glassmaker. He was a director of the glassworks of Choisy-le-Roi from 1823 to 1848, when he went into political exile in England, where he joined Robert Lucas Chance's glassworks in Smethwick (near Birmingham). In Choisy-le-Roi he initiated the production of opaline (1827) and of filigree glass in the Venetian style (1839). In Smethwick he initiated the manufacture of specialized optical glass.

G. Bontemps: *Report on Glass* (London, 1857)

Bony, Jean-François (*b* 1754; *d* 1825). French painter and designer of textiles and embroideries. He trained with Philippe de Lasalle and went on to become one of the most celebrated designers of textiles and embroidery for Lyons silk manufacturers. His clients included the Empress Josephine, for whom he designed the furniture fabics at Malmaison (near Paris), and the Empress Marie Louise, for whom he designed a coronation robe. His work in every medium is chiefly remarkable for its flowers. It is sometimes difficult to attribute work with confidence to Bony or de Lasalle; the silk wallpaper for Marie-Antoinette's bedroom in Versailles (of which some is now in the Musée Historiques des Tissus in Lyon), for example, could be by either artist.

Bonzanigo, Giuseppe Maria (*b* Asti, 6 Sept 1745; *d* Turin, 18 Dec 1820). Italian furniture-maker, sculptor and ornamentalist. He belonged to a family who owned a workshop of wood-carvers and organcase-makers in Asti. He started working for the Savoy family in 1883, and thereafter the royal accounts record him as supplying numerous stools, chairs, armchairs, benches, sofas, screens, prie-dieux, beds and mirrors, as well as many ornamental panels and chests-of-drawers, for the Palazzo Reale in Turin and for royal residences at Moncalieri, Rivoli, Stupinigi, Venaria and Govone. His work is characterized by its departure from the traditional school of Franco-Piedmontese inlay and marquetry cabinetmaking in favour of a more predominant use of carving. He adhered to Neo-classical forms in their most plastic, solid and vigorous, yet elegant, expression, in which the profusion of carvings always had a symbolic, allegorical and commemorative significance, with great use of garlands, emblems and trophies.

P. Cannon-Brookes: 'A Frame by Giuseppe Maria Bonzanigo', *Mus. Management & Curatorship*, ix (Sept 1990), pp. 322–3
G. Ferraris and G. M. Bonzanigo: *Giuseppe Maria Bonzanigo e la scultura decorativa in legno a Torino nel periodo neoclassico, 1770–1830* (Turin, 1991)

Booge. *See* BOUGE.

Bookbinding. Cover of a book and process of creating and attaching it by hand. Mechanization of the various binding processes started in the 1820s, radically changing the traditional processes and turning the craft into an industry; handbinding continued in the early 21st century, but only as a small part of the luxury and collectors market.

1. Europe. 2. Islamic world. 3. Jewish.

1. EUROPE. The mechanization of the various binding processes started in the 1820s, radically changing the traditional processes and turning the craft into an industry; handbinding continued in the late 20th century, but only as a small part of the luxury and collectors market. This article is principally concerned with the gentile tradition of decorative bookbinding in Western Europe; the distinctive Islamic and Jewish traditions are the subjects of separate entries.

Decorated bindings form only a small proportion of all books bound. They are collectors' items, presentation copies produced by top craftsmen, rather than the protective covers of books for daily and constant use. Bindings may be decorated in numerous ways, with metalwork, jewels, enamel, ivory, carved or painted wood, embroidery, painting, staining, stencilling, onlaying or inlaying with pieces of material in contrasting texture and/or colour, moulding or sculpting. The most widespread method of decorating leather bindings is by impressing them with engraved brass tools, either cold (obtaining a 'blind' impression) or heated through gold leaf.

(i) Covers before *c.* 1400. (ii) Covers *c.* 1400–*c.* 1700. (iii) Covers after *c.* 1700. (iv) Fasteners and leaf edges.

(i) Covers before c. 1400. The most extravagant medieval bindings are of precious metals or ivory and are usually found on liturgical books. Silver or silver gilt covers were engraved or show relief or filigree work, with or without precious stones or hardstones. Repoussé or separately cast figures often represent Christ, the Virgin, the four Evangelists or saints. Carved ivory book covers were modelled on Late Antique diptychs. They too show saints or scenes from the Old and New Testaments. Book covers were sometimes enamelled, particularly from Limoges between *c.* 1180 and *c.* 1230. In Siena painted wooden covers were used to protect and adorn the local tax accounts from the 13th century to the 18th (*see* BICCHERNA). The earliest surviving embroidered binding, made in England, covers the early 14th-century Felbrigge Psalter. The upper cover shows the *Annunciation* and the lower cover the *Crucifixion*. Textile and embroidered bindings continued to be popular in England during the following centuries, especially for religious books. They were less common in Holland, France, Spain and Italy.

Very few medieval European decorated leather bindings are known. The earliest surviving European decorated binding, that on the Stonyhurst Gospel, was produced in England. It probably dates from the end of the 7th century and is covered in red–brown goatskin, decorated with a different design on each cover. The upper cover has an embossed floral design, surrounded by incised lines filled with coloured paint; the lower cover has a much simpler incised step design, also showing traces of colour. During the 12th and early 13th centuries blind-tooled Romanesque bindings were produced in France, England, Germany and Austria. Several show stamps or tools depicting biblical subjects side by side with

Book cover of the Dagulf Psalter showing scenes of *David* and *St Jerome*, ivory, h. 168 mm, Carolingian, Aachen, AD 783–95 (Paris, Musée du Louvre)

figures from Classical antiquity and mythology, monsters, dragons, birds and other animals. The tools are fairly large and their motifs bear strong resemblance to those found on Romanesque stone-carvings. They are usually arranged in circles, rows or concentric panels.

(ii) Covers c. 1400–c. 1700. The monastic reforms on the Continent early in the 15th century contributed to a revival in book production, and the invention of printing gave a substantial boost to the book trade. An increase in the output of decorated leather bindings followed. In Germany, France and Italy and a little later in Spain, a large number of leather bindings decorated with small hand tools used in blind were produced, mainly in monasteries. Interlacing strapwork, effected with very few small rope or knot tools, were popular in Italy and Spain in the second half of the 15th century and persisted well into the 16th. In France small animal, bird, insect and floral tools were used in vertical strips.

The earliest 15th-century English blind-tooled bindings were made in London. Other early centres were Oxford, Canterbury, possibly Salisbury, Winchester and, a little later, Cambridge. Small engraved tools showing animals, birds, stylized flowers, roundels, squares, triangles, monsters and fleurs-de-lis abound. Two designs, widely used on both sides of the Channel, show a frame of intersecting lines around a diamond and a saltire, or lines dividing the centre into smaller diamond-shaped and triangular compartments. Designs formed by arranging the tools in rows are frequently found in Oxford and sometimes in London, as well as in France. The influences of continental binding and tool design on English bookbinding of the last quarter of the 15th century and the first half of the 16th is marked. Rolls (engraved brass wheels) were introduced at the very end of the 15th century, while panels (engraved or, more probably, cast blocks) had been used in the Netherlands as early as the second half of the 13th

Upper cover of the Lindau Gospels, repoussé gold studded with gemstones, 350 × 275 mm, from the Abbey of St Gall, Switzerland, *c.* AD 880 (New York, Pierpont Morgan Library, MS. M. 1)

century. They came into frequent use during the late 15th century and the early 16th, and are most commonly found in the Netherlands and England, but also in France and Germany. A technique that used a knife or other sharp instrument to draw a design into the leather or to cut or carve the leather away, leaving the decoration to stand out against the cutaway, sometimes punched, background, was popular in German-speaking countries between the end of the 14th and the beginning of the 16th centuries. Many of these cut-leather ('Lederschnitt') bindings have pictorial designs.

The technique of impressing heated brass tools through gold leaf into the leather is of Islamic origin. Gold-tooled bindings were made in Morocco from the 13th century and the practice was well established by the second half of the 14th century in the Mamluk empire and Iran. Gold-tooling reached Italy early in the 15th century, where by the third quarter of the century it was widely known. The technique came to Spain by the end of the 15th century and was used in Hungary, on bindings for Matthias Corvinus (*reg* 1458–90). Early in the 16th century gold-tooled bindings were produced in France. The best-known French binding collector of the 16th century, Jean Grolier, acquired his earliest bindings in Milan, but the pride of his collection was bound in Paris between 1520 and 1565. In France the binding trade was divided into forwarders (binders) and finishers (decorators) and it is frequently difficult to attribute French bindings purely on the basis of their finishing tools, the more so as the person who was paid for the bindings may well have been a bookseller or stationer who ordered rather than made them. The

most stunning gold-tooled bindings were produced in Paris during the reign of Henry II (*reg* 1547–59), using a wide variety of designs showing linear frames, arabesques, or interlacing strapwork combined with solid, open and hatched tools. In the 1540s, 1550s and 1560s many famous collectors had their books bound in Paris, for example Thomas Mahieu (*fl* 1536–72) and the Englishman Thomas Wotton (1521–86). Thin pieces of onlaid leather in contrasting colour were combined with gold-tooling to produce the finest bindings of the period. Those commissioned by Mahieu are known as Maioli bindings, because they are stamped 'Thos Maioli'.

The technique of gold tooling came to England from France, the earliest example dating from 1519 (Oxford, Bodleian Lib., MS. Bodley 523). For the next ten years it was still largely an experimental technique, but from *c.* 1530 many fine gold-tooled bindings were produced, most of which show French or Italian influence. Gold-tooling was also practised in the Netherlands and in Poland. German binders continued tooling in blind, often on white-tawed pigskin, well beyond the mid-16th century. They also used rolls and panels longer than their colleagues in other countries and employed them either in blind or with low quality gold during the second half of the century. Italy continued to produce fine bindings. The bibliophiles Apollonio Filareto (*fl* 1537–50) and Giovanni Battista Grimaldi (*c.* 1524–*c.* 1612) used their own medallion-shaped devices. Bindings with plaquettes modelled on antique coins or Classical inta-

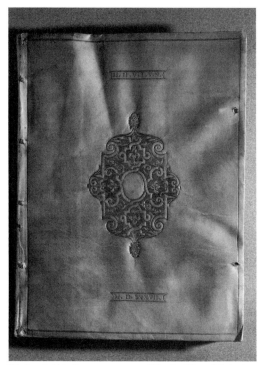

Blind-tooled binding, upper cover of *Travels of Marco Polo*, leather, 1577 (Vienna, Österreichische Nationalbibliothek)

glios and cameos were a typical Italian phenomenon, but they are also found in France, and to a lesser degree in England and Germany. During the reign of Elizabeth I (*reg* 1558–1603) fine gold-tooled bindings were made in England, the designs of many of which show French influence. Interlacing ribbons, combined with solid and hatched tools, as well as designs showing large corner and centre pieces prevailed. The latter continued to flourish during the reign of James I (*reg* 1603–25). The Dudley Binder (*fl* 1558), the Morocco Binder *fl* 1571), the Initial Binder (*fl* 1562–3), Jean de Planche (*fl* 1567–80), the McDurnan Gospels Binder (*fl* 1566) and Matthew Parker's private bindery, among others, all produced first-rate work in London.

In France during the second half of the 16th century interlace developed into the fanfare style. Echoes of this style are found in Holland and England in the 17th and 18th centuries and in Italy and Germany in the 18th. In France, later in the 17th century, this style developed into mosaic designs, when the compartments were frequently made of inlays or onlays of contrasting colours and filled with small dotted tools. At the end of the 16th century and during the 17th other designs that covered the whole of the boards in a regular way were also popular in France and a little later in Holland; they were effected by a sprinkling of small tools, sometimes as the background of a central arms block, or with drawer-handle tools and fleurons. The habit of sprinkling the covers with small tools was still current in England during the reign of Charles I (*reg* 1625–49). In the 1630s and 1640s dotted or *pointillé* tools became fashionable in France; they were much used in Holland later in the 17th century and continued in the 18th; they occur in Italy in the later part of the 17th century; and they first appeared in Cambridge in the 1640s and 1650s, soon to become one of the typical features of English Restoration binding. Characteristic designs, either circular or formed of concentric panels, and made with small tools, were prevalent in Cambridge in the first half of the 17th century.

Corner and centre designs, formed by whole or quarter fan shapes, were fashionable in Italy in the 1640s; they also occurred in Spain in the 17th century. The movement towards the use of smaller *pointillé* tools and polychrome leather onlays in England started early in the 1650s and developed into the splendours of the golden age of English bookbinding, the period following the restoration to the throne of Charles II. The cottage roof design, typical of the Restoration binding, remained in use until the early 18th century. The best-known binders of this period are John Houlden (*fl* 1631–*c.* 1670) in Cambridge, Stephen Lewis and Thomas Lewis (*fl* 1653–61), Charles Mearne (*fl* 1675–86) and Samuel Mearne (*fl* 1653–83), Robert Steel (*fl* 1677–1710), the Queen's Binders, the Naval Binder (*fl* 1670–90), the Centre Rectangle Binder (*fl* 1674–96), Richard Balley (*fl* 1680–*c.* 1711) and Alexander Cleeve (*fl* 1678–91), all in London, and Roger Bartlett

(*fl c.*1666–1711) and Richard Sedgley (*fl c.* 1680–1719) in Oxford.

(iii) Covers after c. 1700. During the first decade of the 18th century, the Geometrical Compartment Binder introduced some new designs to replace the cottage-roof style or 'all-over' designs of his predecessors and contemporaries; a number of his bindings recall the French fanfare style. The library founded by Robert Harley, Earl of Oxford, gave its name to a design formed by roll-tooled borders and a diamond-shaped centrepiece, built up of small tools. Developed by Thomas Elliott and Christopher Chapman (both *fl* 1719–25) for the Harleian Library, it persisted well into the 1760s in London and Cambridge. Bindings decorated with emblematic tools were made for Thomas Hollis and Jonas Hanway (1712–86) from the 1750s till the 1780s and are also found on Masonic bindings of the second half of the 18th century. Neo-classical bindings were designed by James Stuart and Robert Adam in the early 1760s.

In the second half of the 18th century numerous German binders immigrated to England and ran the fine binding trade in London, including Andreas Linde (*fl* 1751–63), John Ernst Baumgarten (*fl* 1771–82), Christian Samuel Kalthoeber (*fl* 1780–1814), Henry Walther, L. Staggemeier (*fl* 1791–1804) and Samuel Welcher (*fl* 1791–1817), and Charles Hering. Native English binders working during the latter part of the 18th century include Roger Payne (1738–97), who was an outstanding finisher and employed finely cut tools to comparatively simple designs, and the firm of Edwards of Halifax, best known for parchment bindings with scenes painted on the transparent under-surface and for so-called Etruscan bindings. Parchment bindings painted on the top surface were made in Italy in the 18th century and also in Hungary and Germany.

Very fine bindings were produced in Dublin in the 18th century with characteristic white onlays (made of paper, parchment or thin leather) and floral or fan tooling. During the 18th century in France two binding styles prevailed. One achieved a lace effect with the help of small tools (dentelle); the other used onlays and inlays to form colourful, often floral or pictorial, mosaics. The best known Paris binders of this period were Derome, Monnier and Padeloup. Pictorial designs are also found in Germany, Austria and Italy, often tooled or blocked but sometimes painted or made of onlaid straw. Decorated paper bindings, already produced in Italy and Germany in the 16th century, became more popular during the 18th, especially on pamphlets, and survived well into the 19th century when they gradually lost their artistic merit. Printed woodblocks, marbling, coloured paste and embossed metal plates were all employed. Printed and painted silk bindings are found in France, Italy and the Netherlands in the 19th century, especially on almanacs.

During the first half of the 19th century a number of different styles were current: Neo-classical designs, simple panel designs, sometimes combined with elaborately tooled *doublures*, more complex designs effected with small tools, and designs making use of thick (sometimes double) boards with sunk panels, tooled and blocked in blind and gold. In the late 1820s, the process of embossing bindings was introduced in France and Germany, but it was soon practised in England where embossed designs often depicted cathedrals, although floral and chinoiserie designs were not uncommon. Painted parchment persisted, but black moulded papier mâché on a metal frame, often in elaborate Gothic designs, was also used. During the second half of the century pastiches of earlier periods were in vogue, both in France and in England. Breaking away from these traditional designs, Marius Michel produced bindings in Art Nouveau designs, while Thomas James Cobden-Sanderson designed his own (frequently floral) tools and used them in a variety of ways, always with great taste and restraint. He gave rise to the amateur school of English bookbinding which has dominated binding design in the 20th century both in the UK and in the USA.

During the 20th century, especially after World War II, binding design reached remarkable standards in France and in England. Interesting work is also produced in Germany, Holland, the USA, and Japan. Styles have become more individual and designs tend to be determined by the book they embellish rather than by tradition. A wide variety of materials such as metal, stone, perspex and plastics have taken the place of or been combined with the more traditional leathers, parchment, paper or cloth. In some cases it is hard to draw the line between bookbindings and sculpture.

(iv) Fasteners and leaf edges. Straps, clasps or ties, necessary to keep books shut, also offer scope for decoration. Medieval luxury bindings tend to have elaborate, often jewelled clasps. Finely chased, engraved, or otherwise decorated clasps occurred from the 12th century onwards and elaborately ornamented clasps are frequently found on textile bindings of the 15th and 16th centuries, as well as on leather work, or—in the 17th and 18th centuries—on tortoiseshell or as part of chased or repoussé metal covers, especially in Holland and Germany. Clasps were often combined with metal bosses or with metal corner and centre pieces and these are a typical feature of German bindings of the 15th century and later.

Decorated leaf edges may be stained, painted, marbled, sprinkled, gilt, or gilt and gauffered. Coloured edges seem to be as old as the codex itself and purple edges have been found on a 4th-century book. Edges painted with decorative designs are found at least as early as the 10th century. Marbled edges are most frequently found on 17th and 18th century books. Edge gilding started in Italy in the second half of the 15th century and gilt edges, sometimes also gauffered (decorated with heated finishing tools), were widespread from the 1530s in Italy, France, Spain, Holland and a little later in England, Germany and Scandinavia. The peak of elaboration, when paint was combined with gilding and gauffering, was reached during the second half of the 16th century, and continued in Holland, Germany and Scandinavia in the 17th and 18th centuries.

Stained edges are more common on retail bindings but are also found on finer work, especially in Germany and Holland, while sprinkled edges occur on English books of the 18th century and continued to be popular. The painting of designs underneath the gold of the edges dates back in England to the 1650s and was quite common during the Restoration Period. This practice continued in England during the first half of the 18th century and was much employed by Edwards of Halifax in the 1780s; it was still carried on in the first three decades of the 19th century and was revived early in the 20th century.

2. ISLAMIC WORLD. Bookbinding was one of the most esteemed arts in the Muslim world because of its close association with the written word. Islamic bindings are distinguished from Western ones by a right-hand hinge, a fore-edge flap on the left and boards that do not project beyond the body. After paper replaced parchment in the 10th and 11th centuries as the usual body material, bindings were made in a standard two-step process: preparation of the body and preparation of the cover. The two were only loosely joined in the areas most subject to flexing, and the cover often became detached from its intended body. The two could be rejoined or a new cover could be made, but usually elaborate covers were preserved separately or reused with other bodies, explaining why the earliest Islamic bindings known are detached from their bodies.

Most of the earliest Islamic bindings preserved come from North Africa. The most important are the 179 fragments that were found in the library of the Great Mosque of Kairouan in Tunisia and date from the 9th to the 13th century. These, along with other fragments preserved in Cairo (N. Lib.), show that binders continued many of the techniques and motifs used in Coptic bindings, such as blind-tooling, coloured inpainting, incising, cutting and geometric diaper patterns. As the typical vertical format for manuscripts was replaced by the horizontal format preferred for early parchment Korans, the typical layout of the cover evolved from a square central panel with narrow friezes above and below to a single oblong panel filled with twisted band ornament and surrounded by a wider border. The earliest designs were small in scale, with motifs used in a frieze or repeat to form frames and borders or to fill a larger decorative form. Complex decorative areas were built up with fillets, bars, arcs and dots. Different designs were also used for the front and back covers. For example, the upper and lower covers of a 9th-century binding from Kairouan are decorated with a blind-tooled torsade circumscribing a rectangular field containing a kufic inscription. The three-word inscription begins on the front cover and ends on the back, a common arrangement. In other cases, the two covers show variations on the same design. The front cover of a square binding from Egypt (10th–11th cent.; Baltimore, MD, Walters A.G.) is decorated with openwork tracery of spiral *rinceaux* ending in palmettes or leaves over a gilded ground; the back cover is a simplified version of the front.

The widespread production of paper manuscripts was accompanied by a return to the vertical format. The group of bindings in Kairouan attributed to the 12th and 13th centuries typically has a central geometric figure in a plain field with tooled borders of fillets and twists and triangular corner elements. These bindings are similar to a group preserved in the Ben Yusuf Madrasa in Marrakesh, Morocco, attributed to the period of Almohad rule (*reg* 1130–1269). The binding on a magnificent copy of the Koran (1256; London, BL, Or. MS. 13192), written in Marrakesh by the penultimate Almohad sultan Abu Hafs 'Umar al-Murtada (*reg* 1248–66), is an early example of gold-tooling and strapwork in reserve against a tooled ground, although two centuries earlier Ibn Badis mentioned a more primitive form of stamping with gold. Gold-tooling did not appear on European bindings for another two centuries.

Regional variations can be detected in bindings produced after the 14th century. 'Arab' bindings, comprising those ascribed to Egypt and Syria, Spain and North Africa, and the Yemen, are generally simpler, with less elaborate tooling than those ascribed to Iran, Turkey or the Indian subcontinent. Two types of geometric layouts predominate in Arab bindings: central medallions and strapwork patterns emanating from a central star. Colour is used sparingly, and the main effect is achieved by contrasting gold against untooled strapwork bands. Typical doublures are made of light-brown or cream leather that is block-pressed with arabesque and floral designs. Bindings from North Africa and Spain are done in dark, coarse-grained leather and have somewhat simple patterns; a cover in London (180 × 130 mm; V&A, 366/22–1888) attributed to North Africa in the 14th or 15th century has a central roundel filled with strapwork and plain, triangular corner-pieces. Examples from Egypt and Syria are often particularly fine, with tooling and cut-outs adding a sense of vitality, and gold, silver and blue paint enhancing the pattern. The bindings on a 30-volume copy of the Koran (371 × 275 mm; Baltimore, MD, Walters A.G.; Dublin, Chester Beatty Lib.; London, BL, and V&A; Washington, DC, Freer, and Lib. Congr.) made for Aytmish al-Bajasi (*d* 1400), an amir of the Mamluk sultan Barquq, all have central medallions composed of geometric interlaces radiating from an eight-pointed star worked in blind- and gold-tooling and stamping. The medallions are set in plain fields, the corners of which are filled with quarter medallions. A binding in Dublin made of brown goatskin over pasteboard is decorated with blind- and gold-tooling in strapwork patterns. The upper and lower covers have the same frames, but the fields have different patterns. Bindings produced for the Zaydi rulers of Yemen in the 15th century form another coherent group. Most are of light-brown leather, quarto size with polished surfaces decorated with flat blind-tooling and calligraphic stamps with religious mottoes or binders' signatures (e.g. U. Chicago, IL, Orient. Inst. Mus., A12125, signed by al-Rabi').

Iranian bindings are laid out with central medallions and corner-pieces or overall patterns in the field. Borders are often filled with elaborate cartouches. In contrast to the angular geometry of Arab bindings, Iranian bindings are more curvilinear. Colour is more prominent and motifs are more elaborate and naturalistic. The same techniques of stamping and tooling were used to more elaborate effect. A binding in Dublin (1435; Chester Beatty Lib., MS. 5282) has 550,000 blind stamps and 43,000 gold stamps; it must have taken about two years to complete. Gilding was often applied with a fine brush. Poetic texts often had quatrains stamped on the fore-edge flap or spine so that the contents could be identified when the books were stacked. One of the earliest surviving Iranian bookbindings encloses a copy of Ibn Bakhtishu's bestiary, *Manāfi' al-hayawān* ('Usefulness of animals'; 1297 or 1299; New York, Pierpont Morgan Lib., MS M.500), copied at Maragha in north-west Iran. Measuring 339 × 254 mm, the covers are made of dark reddish-brown leather decorated with blind-tooling applied with a small number of punches. There are no traces of gilding. The front and back covers have almond-shaped medallions with three different radiating elements. All the patterns are symmetrical, except two graceful arabesques on the flap. The total effect is of austere dignity.

In the early 15th century the arts of the book in Iran were transformed under the patronage of the Timurid prince Baysunghur (1397–1433) at Herat. The typical layout of a central medallion with quarter medallions in the corners was elaborated by relief and lobing. New techniques—such as leather filigree, often on a blue ground, and varnish—were introduced, colour was increased through the use of silk inlays and paint, and naturalistic vegetal and figural motifs were added. These innovations suggest that manuscript painters were closely involved in the design and execution of bindings. The decoration of inner covers was often as elaborate as that on the outer covers, and the protected location often ensured better preservation. The binding on a copy of *Kalila and Dimna* made for Baysunghur (1429; Istanbul, Topkapı Pal. Lib., R. 1022) has a landscape in relief filled with birds, animals and flowers. Two confronted dragons fill the triangular flap. Even more spectacular is the binding for a copy of the *Sitta* ('Six poems') of 'Attar made for Baysunghur's father, Shahrukh, in 1438 (Istanbul, Topkapı Pal. Lib., A. 3059). The upper cover, depicting a fantastic landscape inhabited by deer, monkeys, dragons and ducks, was stamped with a single large block; the flap depicts Chinese-style lions amid dragons, ribbons and foliage in the same technique. The fore-edge bears a stamped dedication to Shahrukh. The inner covers, worked in filigree against a deep-blue ground, are equally splendid. The upper cover has a central medallion containing a tree flanked by dragons; the quarter medallions, borders and flap are inhabited by ducks, rabbits, monkeys, deer and lions in a foliate ground. Leather covers could also be decorated with gold and varnish, as on the binding of a copy of Jalal al-Din Rumi's mystical poem, the *Masavī*, made for Sultan Husayn Bayqara at Herat. The outer covers have been stamped with central medallions and lobed quarter-panels, varnished in black and painted with peonies and other flowers in gold. The similarly executed fore-edge flap bears a quatrain admonishing the reader to read the book. The inner covers bear a spectacular example of leather filigree set against a blue ground, depicting wild animals cavorting in a landscape.

In the 16th century a layout of the central panel surrounded by block-stamped border panels and cartouches became increasingly popular for Iranian bindings. They were often gilded to create an impression of great sumptuousness; decoration included arabesques, cloud-scrolls, medallions, inscriptions and landscapes. To save money, paper filigree often replaced leather, and large metal blocks allowed half the cover to be stamped at once. An early 16th-century binding enclosing an album of calligraphy attributed to the royal scribe Mir 'Ali (232 × 137 mm; London, V&A, 685–1876) depicts a landscape showing three birds perched in a tree. Cranes and ducks fly between clouds, and rabbits cavort on the ground. The inner covers, with the traditional layout of a central medallion and quarter panels, are inlaid with gold paper filigree set against a red, blue, green and black paper ground. Painted and varnished covers often depict princely pastimes, such as hunting and feasting and scenes from literature. The outer covers of a varnished set in London (304 × 185 mm; V&A, 353–1885) have single fields with figural scenes. The upper cover depicts a prince in a garden surrounded by servants roasting food and playing musical instruments; the lower shows the prince hunting. The inner covers, done in the same technique but with a medallion format, show *Majnun among the Animals* from the *Khamsa* ('Five poems') of Nizami and a tiger attacking a deer. The iconography suggests that the covers may have belonged to a manuscript of the *Khamsa* made for a royal patron.

From the 17th to the 19th century book covers continued to use the same formats and techniques but were simpler in execution. A complete leather cover in London (378 × 265 mm; V&A, 1948–1981), for example, is done with gold block-stamping and traces of gold paint. The field has an almond-shaped medallion with two pendants at either end and scalloped corner panels; the narrow border is stamped with cartouches and quatrefoils. The single-field format became increasingly popular; leather was replaced by pasteboard when varnished covers became standard, and the flap tended to disappear. The single field often contains arabesques, floral or figural scenes; the art of the bookbinder was subsumed by the art of the painter.

Bindings produced in Turkey under the Ottomans (*reg* 1281–1924) generally followed the Iranian layout of a central medallion and quarter medallions in the corners, but they used a greater combination of coloured leathers and distinctive Ottoman motifs, such as the sawtoothed leaf (Turk. *saz*), carnation, arabesque (Turk. *rumi*) and Chinese cloud band. The quarter medallions were often joined to form ogee arches, and medallion contours are often scalloped (e.g. Washington, DC, Sackler Gal., S86.0478). Medallions on the inside covers show a wide range of colours (blue, orange, turquoise, black and red) and material (paper, silk and cotton), as on a complete cover in London (V&A, 123–1897). Production was centralized in Istanbul, where 700 binders are said to have worked in the 17th century. The impact of European books in the 18th and 19th centuries led binders to drop the characteristic Islamic flap in favour of slipcases and to adopt Europeanizing decorative motifs. The European-format covers to a book of prayers (182 × 106 mm; March 1825; London, V&A, 801–1942) are made of papier mâché painted and varnished with an overall design of trees, leaves and acorns on a green ground within a narrow cable border.

Islamic bindings from the Indian subcontinent continue the styles and techniques of their Iranian models, as for example in the stamped leather covers to a *Būstān* ('Orchard') of Sa'di made for Nasir al-Din Khalji (*reg* 1500–10; New Delhi, N. Mus., 48.6/4). In the 19th century a distinct local school of book production flourished in Kashmir. Typical bindings are of varnished pasteboard painted with floral scenes: a Koran in London (382 × 232 mm; V&A, 1392–1922) has an elaborate all-over floral pattern of pink and yellow blossoms against a black ground.

3. JEWISH. The Iberian peninsula is the source of the largest number of documents mentioning medieval Jewish bookbinders. Four are known in Portugal in the 14th and 15th centuries. In Spain, 11 are known in the 14th century. The fact that a papal bull was issued in 1415 expressly forbidding Jews to bind Christian religious books confirms that they were still practising their craft at that time. Moreover, archives show that many bookbinders, forcibly converted at the end of the 14th century, and their descendants continued to practise the craft during the 15th century, and for the same clientele. With a single exception, all the notarized deeds refer to bindings executed for Christians, mainly for ecclesiastical or royal customers but also occasionally for the bourgeoisie. One surviving contract for a Jewish customer, however, indicates that Jewish bookbinders also undertook commissions for their fellow Jews. A few deeds referring to bindings commissioned for devotional works at a very high price are clear proof that Jewish bookbinders had achieved a high level of skill.

These bindings were not of cloth but of *guadameci*, leather worked after the manner of the Arabs in Spain (known as Mudéjars until the taking of Granada in 1492, then as Moriscos), as is known from extant bindings on more than 20 Hebrew books executed for Jewish clients and from the imprints left by leather bindings with openwork geometrical decorations on half-a-dozen others. Most of these bindings date no earlier than the last decades of the 15th century, although some were used for manuscripts written in the 13th and 14th centuries, replacing older bindings. Most were executed in Castile. They were all MUDÉJAR in technique and style, decorated with interlaced bands against a background stamped with small blind tools and punches, and overall they are among the finest Iberian bindings of this kind. Nine of them are box-bindings of a unique type, with sides that protected the edges of the book attached to three sides of the lower cover, which acted as the bottom of the box, and an upper cover that closed over this like a lid, both covers being joined to a spine of the usual European type with raised bands.

Documents show that in the comtat Venaissin (the papal state) the popes and Petrarch retained the services of Jewish binders. Three Hebrew manuscripts (early 15th century) copied for Jewish clients have been preserved with their original bindings. Their decoration of fillets and blind tooling is closer to Italian bindings influenced by the western Islamic style than to any Mudéjar work.

Although Jews certainly bound Hebrew books for Jewish use in medieval and renaissance Italy, some such books displaying stamps and decorative schemes widely used on non-Jewish bindings were doubtless the work of gentiles. The work of Jewish binders can be identified only in the case of a few bindings almost certainly made by refugees from the Iberian peninsula.

In the Germanic countries, written sources on Jewish binders and bindings are even rarer. They were mentioned at the beginning of the 13th century in the *Sefer ha-hasidim* ('Book of the pious', a major work of Ashkenazi teachings on ethics) and in other documents of the late 14th century and the 15th. Twelve bindings dating from the 14th and 15th centuries have been preserved on Hebrew manuscripts. Of five others, at least four are thought to have been used originally to cover Hebrew manuscripts, on the basis of their structure and decoration. All were richly decorated with incised motifs showing plants and animal, human and hybrid figures. Stamps were rarely and sparingly used. Only one of these bindings (Munich, Bayer. Staatsbib., Cod. hebr. 212) is signed—with the name Meïr Jaffé in Hebrew—but there is no reason why some or all of the others should not prove to be Jewish handiwork too, as may also be true of some of the bindings made for gentile books. The Munich binding is the only one of all the cuir-ciselé (cut leather) bindings, either Jewish or gentile, to bear the artist's signature and has consequently attracted much scholarly attention and controversy.

L. Avrin: 'The Sephardi Box Binding', *Scripta Hierosolymitana*, xxix (1989), pp. 27–43, pls 1–24

A. R. A. Hobson: *Humanists and Bookbinders* (Cambridge, 1989)

H. M. Nixon and M. M. Foot: *The History of Decorated Bookbinding in England* (Oxford, 1992)

Silver repoussé book cover with clasps, 117 × 174 × 54 mm, Venice, 1772 (Paris, Musée d'Art et d'Histoire du Judaïsme)

M. Foot: *Studies in the History of Bookbinding* (Aldershot, 1994)

M. Foot: *The History of Bookbinding as a Mirror of Society* (London, 1998)

P. J. M. Marks: *The British Library Guide to Bookbinding: History and Techniques* (Toronto, 1998)

A. R. A. Hobson: *Renaissance Book Collecting: Jean Grolier and Diego Hurtado de Mendoza, Their Books and Bindings* (Cambridge, 1999)

M. Foot and D. Pearson: *For the Love of the Binding: Studies in Bookbinding History Presented to Mirjam Foot* (London, 2000)

H. Petroski: *The Book on the Bookshelf* (New York, 2000)

J. Greenfield: *Notable Bindings* (New Haven, Conn., 2002)

G. Fernández Lapeña: *Arte del libro: La encuadernación Española en Nueva York/Book Art: Spanish Bookbinding in New York* (Madrid and New York, 2004)

S. Bennett: *Trade Bookbinding in the British Isles, 1660–1800* (London, 2004)

M. M. Foot, ed.: *Eloquent Witnesses: Bookbindings and Their History* (London, 2004)

Bookplate [Ex-libris]. Engraved or printed mark of ownership affixed to a book. The earliest, woodcuts from *c.* 1470, were for Hans Igler, called Knabensberg, with a hedgehog as a pun on his name, and two that recorded gifts to the Carthusian monastery of Buxheim by Wilhelm von Zell and Hildebrand Brandenburg. Usage spread quickly in Germany, encouraged by the participation of Albrecht Dürer, Lucas Cranach the elder, the Little Masters of copperengraving and others. Their works inspired some fine bookplates of later centuries; but though many distinguished artists have subsequently lent their talents to bookplate-making, until the latter part of the nineteenth century most bookplates were the work of trade engravers. Many early British and 17th-century American bookplates were printed labels, often with ornamental borders. Labels have continued as a minority option, and engraved versions, common since the 18th century, have latterly been cut on wood with distinction. An armorial was, however, until recent times the most familiar bookplate form, engraved on copper or often in the 1800s on steel.

Among 17th-century British bookplates the terms Tudoresque and Carolean embrace the stylistic vagaries of some early examples. The few bookplates by William Faithorne are superb, and other armorials of the period echo their robust mantling, except where mantles are of cloth. William Jackson (*fl* 1698–1714), working near the Inns of Court in London, popularized bookplate usage. Concurrently using the Early Armorial and Jacobean styles, he made bookplates for the nobility and for most English university colleges. Many others worked in these styles before Chippendale or Rococo became the vogue, *c.* 1745–80. Spade shield compositions with wreaths and festoons superseded them, giving way to plain armorials ('die-sinkers') for most of the 19th century. After 1860 an armorial renaissance was effected by Charles William Sherborn (1831–1912) and George W. Eve (1855–1914), and engravers including John Augustus Charles Harrison (1872–1955) and Robert Osmond maintained similar quality and prolific output from *c.* 1900 to *c.* 1950.

Pictorials or pictorial-armorials have, however, as old a history, their stereotyped styles overlapping and longer lived. The stolidly tiered bookpile devised in 1698 by Samuel Pepys, long remained modestly pop-

ular. Allegories (showing gods, goddesses, cherubs and the like) appeared *c.* 1700, continental artists aiding their popularity. Their finest exponent was Francesco Bartolozzi, but many trade engravers used allegory, sometimes combined with 18th-century library interior subjects. Urn pictorials appeared from *c.* 1750, but though isolated landscape bookplates were used decades earlier, it was the wood engravings of Thomas Bewick and his followers that brought that style to its apogee.

After 1860 fresh impetus was afforded bookplate art in Europe and North America by the wide participation of book illustrators, engravers and artists. Diverse reproductive processes were exploited, bookplates were recognized as artistically significant, and the bibliographical and genealogical importance of their usage was recognized. Societies of collectors in many countries assisted their documentation, and bookplate production proliferated among Europe's printmakers and illustrators. In the twentieth century bookplates were made by the inheritors of a tradition inspired notably by Eric Gill (1882–1940) and Reynolds Stone (1909–79).

B. N. Lee: *Early Printed Book Labels* (London, 1976)

B. N. Lee: *British Bookplates* (Newton Abbot, 1979)

J. P. Keenan and G. Plimpton: *The Art of the Bookplate* (New York, 2003)

B. N. Lee: *Some Bookplates of Heralds and Related Ex-libris* (London, 2003)

D. Roberts: *Rockwell Kent: The Art of the Bookplate* (San Francisco, 2003)

Boote, T. and R. English ceramics manufactory founded in 1842 by Thomas Latham Boote and Richard Boote at the Central Pottery, Burslem, Stadffs; in 1850 the company bought the Waterloo Potteries, Burslem from Thomas Edwards. The Company produced unglazed pavement tiles, Parian ware (notably a group consisting of Repentance, Faith and Resignation) and earthenware with inlay decoration (which they called 'Royal Patent Ironstone'). In 1888 the Company discontinued most of its decorative lines, and thereafter concentrated on the manufacture of plain white granite ware for the American market and on the production of glazed and unglazed pavement tiles; the company supplied the tiles for the Blackwall Tunnel (Greenwich, London), which opened in 1897. Decorative tiles included a set of 'The Four Seasons' (1891) designed by the children's book illustrator Kate Greenaway (1846–1901). After 1906, production was restricted to tiles. In 1963 T and R Boote was bought by T & R Boote Richards Tiles, and it now trades as H & R Johnson Tiles Ltd. Boote wares were variously marked as T & R B , T & R BOOTE and T B & S; Victorian marks often included the royal arms.

Boote, T. & R. (Burslem, England) (sale cat., Geo. Harrison & Son, 1876)

Bordeaux. French centre of faience production. Production of faience began in Bordeaux *c.* 1710 when a potter from Nevers, Jacques Fautier, settled

Bookplate for John Lumsden by Aubrey Beardsley, photogravure, 1893 (London, Victoria and Albert Museum)

there and continued in several workshops until the 1840s. However, the only really important factory, which operated from 1715 to 1780, was that of Jacques Hustin (1664–1749) and his son Ferdinand Hustin (1696–1778), then of his wife Victoire. Hustin's factory was protected by a royal privilege, which entitled him to exclusive production rights until 1762. Utilitarian items included table-services, apothecary-style pots and tobacco jars, which were produced in large quantities and served a local and transatlantic market until other such factories were established. Most Bordeaux wares are thick and robust, decorated with high-fired colours including blue, azure, orange, almond-green and a pale or brownish mauve. Decoration was influenced by wares from other French centres of production including Nevers, which inspired the use of blue grounds with stylized flowers and palmettes; Rouen, from which came the idea of blue or multicoloured lambrequins, occasionally picked out in iron-red; Moustiers, which inspired the use of grotesques and arabesques by Jean Berain in blue monochrome, and later chinoiseries in green monochrome; and also Montpellier, whence came a more naturalistic, mainly floral, polychrome decoration, using a pinkish-mauve obtained from manganese. During the last years of production, designs and colours became stereotyped and schematized. The finest Bordeaux pieces date from c. 1740 and include such items as water jugs, basins and tableware.

J. Du Pasquier, V. de Raignac and G. Devaux: *La faïence de Bordeaux au service de la santé* (Bordeaux, 1996)
J. Du Pasquier: *J. Vieillard & Cie: Histoire de la faïence fine à Bordeaux de l'anglomanie au rêve orientaliste* (Bordeaux, 2002)

Boreman, Zachariah (b 1738; d 1810). English porcelain painter who specialized in monochrome landscape scenes. He originally worked at the Chelsea factory, but from 1783 to 1794 he worked in Derby, and his landscapes from that period depict Derbyshire scenes. There is a collection of Boreman's work in the Derby Museum and Art Gallery.

Borne, La. *See* LA BORNE.

Boselli, Giacomo (b Savona, 1744; d ?1808). Italian ceramics painter who worked in Savona (Liguria) and Marseille. The production of his Savona workshop included maiolica, porcelain and cream-coloured earthenware decorated with both enamels and high-temperature colours. His wife Clara [Chiarina] Boselli was a skilled painter of flowers and small figures; after Boselli's death she continued to run the factory.

P. Torriti: *Giacomo Boselli e la ceramica savonese del suo tempo* (Genoa, 1965)
L. Pessa and G. Boselli: *Giacomo Boselli: Cultura e genio di un ceramista del Settecento* (Genoa, 1994)

Bossi work. Style of inlaid marble in the manner of Robert Adam, usually found in chimney pieces (and

sometimes in table tops) made in Dublin in the late 18th century. The eponymous Bossi is an obscure figure, but is assumed to be an Italian who worked in Dublin in the 1780s and 1790s.

Boston. American city, capital and financial and commercial centre of Massachusetts on the northeast coast of the USA.

1. Ceramics. 2. Furniture. 3. Silverwork.

1. CERAMICS. In 17th-century New England a large supply of red clay along the Mystic River fostered the brickmaking and pottery industries in Boston's nearby towns of Charlestown and Medford. By the late 1630s Philip Drinker and his sons Edward and John were established as earthenware potters in Charlestown and more than 40 potters are known to have worked in Charlestown before the end of the century; in 1750, approximately eight or nine shops were in simultaneous operation. The proliferation of potters in Charlestown explains why so few potters worked in Boston and why references are often found to what was called 'Charlestown ware'.

Although attempts were made from the mid-18th century to make stoneware in Boston, beginning with Isaac Parker, domestic production was not stimulated until after the American Revolution, when charges levied on the weight of imported goods made stoneware an economically attractive commodity. After 1793 a Boston stoneware factory was established by Frederick Carpenter (1771–1827) and Jonathan Fenton (1766–1848). Their goods were made of clay shipped from Perth Amboy, NJ; they made redware and stoneware, and some fine ceramics as tortoiseshellware.

By the mid-19th century one of the major potteries was the East Boston Crockery Manufactory. It was first established in Weston in 1765 by Abraham Hews (1741–1818); by the Civil War it had moved to North Cambridge, where porcelain, yellowware, Rockingham and Parian wares were produced in addition to an expanded line in ornamental ceramics.

HUGH CORNWALL ROBERTSON, who had worked as a manager of the East Boston Crockery Manufactory, established the Chelsea Keramic Art Works in Chelsea, MA (1872–89), and later the Dedham Pottery, Dedham, MA (1896–1943), which were prominent art potteries in the region. Other Arts and Crafts potteries included the Grueby Faience Co. (*see* WILLIAM HENRY GRUEBY), the Marblehead Pottery, Marblehead, MA (1904–36; *see* ARTHUR EUGENE BAGGS), and the Low Tiles, Chelsea, MA (1878–1907). The Paul Revere Pottery (1911–42) of Boston and Brighton was a reform-minded, subsidized pottery that employed young immigrant Italian and Jewish women. One of the few art potteries to flourish until the mid-20th century was the Dorchester Pottery, Dorchester, MA (1895–1979), which was best-known for its salt-glazed wares.

In the late 20th century many university programmes devoted to ceramics were established. The subsequent proliferation of studio potters in the Boston area in the late 20th century was partly due to such professors as William Wyman (1922–80) at Massachusetts College of Art. Norman Arseneault (1912–84), who was particularly interested in glazes, taught in the ceramics department at the School of the Museum of Fine Arts, Boston, for many years, and devoted his career to perfecting a tourmaline glaze. During the 1970s Richard Hirsch (*b* 1944) taught at Boston University's short-lived but prestigious Program in Artisanry (1975–85).

2. FURNITURE. In the 17th century the dominant furniture workshops in Boston were those of Ralph Mason (1599–1678/9) and Henry Messinger (*fl*1641–81), both London-trained joiners who worked in the Anglo-Dutch Mannerist style using split turnings, bosses, triglyphs and dentils of exotic hardwoods reminiscent of Dutch furniture; a panelled chest-of-drawers with doors (New Haven, CT, Yale U. A.G) is apparently their collaborative work, and its drawers are the earliest in America known to have been constructed using dovetail joints. The turner Thomas Edsall (1588–1676) arrived in Boston from London *c.* 1635; he made turnings and bosses for joined furniture and chairs with London-style ball-turned stretchers and stiles. By the late 17th century Mannerism in Colonial furniture had been superseded by the Baroque style with its sculptural forms and rich, unornamented surfaces (e.g. high chest-of-drawers, prob. Massachusetts, pine, walnut and maple, 1700–25; Boston, MA, Mus. F. A.). In Boston, this fashion manifested itself primarily in such pieces as the high chest-of-drawers with figured walnut veneer on a pine carcass that rests on a frame with turned legs; the use of walnut and maple burls created a visual richness without recourse to ornament. Such styles suited the tastes of the newly arrived royal officials who from the 1680s displaced the Puritan oligarchy. The shift in taste was accompanied by a technological shift from joinery to cabinetwork.

In the early 18th century Boston craftsmen provided furnishings for a growing anglophile élite. This first generation of artisans was tightly interconnected through loyalty and an unofficial barter system that prevented many immigrants from establishing their own shops. Nevertheless, many new arrivals trained in London were employed by local cabinetmakers, who utilized their skills and knowledge of up-to-date fashions to produce furniture in the latest styles. Such journeymen were probably responsible for veneered chest-on-chests (e.g. chest-on-chest, Boston, MA, black walnut, burl walnut veneer and eastern white pine, 1715–25; Boston, MA, Mus. F. A.) in the Georgian style with canted corner pilasters and pull-out folding boards that were originally attributed to English makers.

The typical forms of 18th-century case furniture were high chests, dressing-tables, chest-on-chests and bureau-bookcases. The pad foot was employed in New England, particularly Massachusetts, during the first half of the 18th century on chairs, small tables, case pieces and high chests. It extends from a slender cabriole leg and flares outward in a circular fashion before canting inwards to a smaller round base. Japanning was a Boston speciality, a result of the thriving trade with China and the corresponding popularity of chinoiserie decoration; an example is the high chest (*c.* 1736; Baltimore, U. MD Mus. A.) by the japanner Robert Davis *fl* 1733–9). However, until the mid-18th century most examples were veneered, such as those produced by the Charlestown cabinetmaker Ebenezer Hartsherne or Hartshorn (1690–1781), while others were decorated with a block front, a contouring of the façade with three vertical panels of which the outer two were raised and the central one recessed—an innovation of Boston cabinetmakers that was popular from the 1730s until the 1780s. Other shaped case pieces were *bombé* in form, with the sides of the lower section swelling outwards in serpentine curves that are sometimes echoed by shaped drawers (e.g. desk, Salem, MA, mahogany and white pine, 1760–90; Boston, MA, Mus. F. A.). Although the form was derived from imported English bureau-bookcases, the complicated construction techniques were mastered only by such Boston craftsmen as Benjamin Frothingham sr of Charlestown, George Bright (1726–1805), John Cogswell (1738–1818) and a few others in nearby towns. In mid-century the most skilled and prolific carver in Boston was John Welch (1711–89). In the 1770s many case pieces were modified with serpentine or oxbow fronts; some of the finest examples were embellished with carvings and figural sculpture by John SKILLIN. The demand for Neo-classical furniture was met by John SEYMOUR, who arrived from England *c.* 1784; he and his son Thomas produced elegant tambour desks and semicircular commodes with mahogany and satinwood veneers.

Boston continued to be an important centre for furniture-making in the 19th century. In the early decades furniture in the bolder Empire style was produced by George Archibald and Thomas Emmons (*fl*1813–24) as well as Isaac Vose and Joshua Coates (*fl* 1805–19). Closely related to French forms, their work incorporated broad expanses of figured mahogany veneer punctuated by cut brass inlay and ormolu. By 1850, the furniture industry produced Rococo and Renaissance Revival furniture for a burgeoning middle-class market. Among the well-known makers were Augustus Eliaers (*fl* 1853–65), George Croome (*fl* 1845–*c.* 1880) and George Ware (*fl c.* 1860). New forms ranged from pier tables and étagères to large sideboards and included a variety of specialized furniture, some with folding or mechanical parts for invalids, libraries or travel.

Despite the Great Fire of 1872 and the financial panic of the following year, Boston's furniture industry flourished until the end of the century. The leading furniture carver of the Arts and Crafts period was Johannes Kirchmayer (1860–1930), who emigrated to Boston from his native Oberammergau in 1880. High productivity was due partly to the influx of unskilled Irish immigrants to man such new steam-powered factories as the A. H. Davenport Co. (1880–1906), which executed commissions for architects H. H. Richardson and McKim, Mead & White among others. In 1916 A. H. Davenport merged with Charles R. Irving & Robert Casson Co. (1893–c. 1970) and manufactured furniture in various styles (notably Gothic Revival) for Boston's commercial and ecclesiastical clients. In 1917 Wallace Nutting (1861–1941), one of the best-known exponents of the Colonial Revival, began manufacturing furniture nearby Framingham, MA.

After World War II the studio crafts movement flourished in Boston. The Program in Artisanry at Boston University, instituted in 1975, became a dynamic centre for furniture-making under its founder, Dan Jackson (b 1938), and subsequently under Jere Osgood (b 1936) and Alphonse Mattia (b 1947). Although it ceased in 1985, it inspired many careers in furniture-making, some of which were featured in the exhibition *New American Furniture* in 1989 (Boston, MA, Mus. F.A.).

3. SILVERWORK. The craft of silversmithing began in Boston in 1652, when John Hull (1624–83) and Robert Sanderson (1608–93) became the first Masters of the Mint for the Massachusetts Bay Colony. Sanderson (who had trained in London) and Hull fashioned the first coins of the colony and much of its earliest plate and were well-respected members of the Puritan oligarchy. Their hollowware followed the latest fashions in silver imported from London and is characterized by a Mannerist style that features strong contrasts in shapes and textures (e.g. caudle cup, 1660–70; Boston, MA, Mus. F.A.).

After 1692, in the wake of the change in the Massachusetts Bay Colony Charter, the authority of the Puritan founders yielded to the power of a new group of merchants whose religious, political and commercial interests were orientated towards England. These new arrivals, some of whom were officials of the provincial government, patronized Jeremiah Dummer (1645–1718), JOHN CONEY and Edward Winslow (1669–1753), the first Boston-born silversmiths. During this second period, vessel forms included monteiths, chocolate pots and sugar-boxes in the Baroque style with elaborate repoussé chasing and cast ornament. The need for church plate also grew along with burgeoning congregations. Craftsmen derived their designs primarily from imported English wares, but they also utilized the skills of immigrant craftsmen who brought with them specialized skills, new techniques and the latest fashions. Their lack of family and religious connections prevented most immigrant craftsmen from establishing their own workshops; instead they performed specialized tasks or worked as anonymous journeymen in some of the larger Boston establishments.

Despite the talents of Boston's native-born and immigrant silversmith population, the economic slump of the 1730s resulted in the production of silver that was conservative in style, as seen in the work of Thomas Edwards (1701–55), Jacob HURD

and Samuel Edwards (1705–62). The craft as a whole concentrated less on evolving new forms than on creating finely raised and chased vessels, some engraved with coats of arms. Porringers, mugs and domed tankards changed little, while the apple-shaped teapot of the 1730s and 1740s gradually gave way to the more fashionable inverted pear form in the Rococo style by the 1760s (e.g. teapot by PAUL REVERE, 1760–65; Boston, MA, Mus. F.A.). The greatest piece of Boston silver is Revere's Sons of Liberty Punch Bowl (1768, Boston, MA, Mus. F.A.), which is one of the icons of colonial America.

With some exceptions, Boston silver from the 1760s to the end of the 18th century is conservative in contrast to the more elaborate decoration found on the silver made in such rapidly growing cities as New York and Philadelphia. Boston patrons generally preferred heraldic engravings to the ciphers chosen by stylish New Yorkers, and they did not embrace the fashionable Rococo style as enthusiastically as did Philadelphians. The careers of Paul Revere and Benjamin Burt (1729–1805) spanned the latter half of the 18th century and the early decades of the 19th. Both produced a large quantity of silver for Boston patrons in the Rococo style, and towards the end of the 18th century both also made elliptical fluted vessels in the newly popular Neo-classical vein (e.g. teapot and stand by Benjamin Burt, 1790–1800; Boston, MA, Mus. F.A.). The following generation of silversmiths, which included Lewis Cary (1798–1834) and Obadiah Rich (fl 1830–50), produced more robust forms in the Empire style with mechanically produced naturalistic decoration.

During the second half of the 19th century such Boston firms as Shreve, Stanwood & Co. (1860–69), Crosby & Morse (1848–76) and Goodnow & Jenks (1893–c. 1905) created tea services and coffee services in the newly fashionable Renaissance Revival and Greek Revival styles. But by 1900 few workshops remained in Boston, for such larger concerns as Reed, Barton & Co. (founded 1886) of Taunton, MA, and the silverware firm of GORHAM (founded 1831) of Providence, RI, could produce their wares more competitively. One of the last apprentices to Goodnow & Jenks was George Christian Gebelein (1878–1945), a skilled practitioner of the Colonial Revival style, a dealer in antique American silver and a member of the Society of Arts and Crafts, Boston. Founded in Boston in 1897, the Society was the first such group to be established in America. The metals department of the Society's Handicraft Shop offered classes in silversmithing in the Arts and Crafts and Colonial Revival styles, and fostered the development of silversmiths Mary Knight (b 1876) and Katherine Pratt (1891–1978). The most prominent and prolific silversmith in the Boston area was Arthur J. Stone (1847–1938). Born and trained in Sheffield, England, Stone moved to Gardner, MA, in 1896 and produced work on commission for many of Boston's prominent families.

By the late 1920s, few silversmiths were working in Boston. Gebelein, Pratt and Karl Leinonen (1866–

Paul Revere: *Sons of Liberty Bowl*, silver, h. 140 mm, diam. 279 mm, 1768 (Boston, MA, Museum of Fine Arts)

1957) continued to make some Colonial Revival pieces, but demand for locally made silver declined. Although metalworking classes were offered at the Museum School of the Museum of Fine Arts and at the Massachusetts College of Art, it was not until the establishment in 1975 of the Program in Artisanry at Boston University that a new group of metalsmiths developed. In 1989 the Program in Artisanry was relocated to the University of Massachusetts at Dartmouth, MA; all three schools maintain active metalsmithing programs. One of the most important 20th-century metalsmiths in Boston is Kansas-born Margret Craver (*b* 1907), who trained under Arthur Nevill Kirk in Detroit and *c.* 1930 with Baron Erik Fleming (1894–1954), silversmith to King Gustav VI Adolf of Sweden. Following her move to Boston in 1967, she revived the 16th-century enamelling technique of *en résille sur verre*, which she used in the production of jewellery (e.g. necklace in gold, enamel and African black glass beads, *c.* 1981; Boston, MA, Mus. F.A.). After its closure in 1989 Craver's workshop was acquired by the Smithsonian Institution.

L. W. Watkins: *Early New England Potters and Their Wares* (Cambridge, MA, 1950)

N. Carlisle: 'Revolutionary Acts: Selections from the SPNEA Collection', *Mag. Ant.*, clxiv/2 (Aug 2003), pp. 60–69

R. H. Randall jr: *American Furniture in the Museum of Fine Arts, Boston* (Boston, 1965/R 1985)

W. M. Whitehill, B. Jobe and J. L. Fairbanks, eds: *Boston Furniture of the Eighteenth Century* (Boston, 1974)

J. L. Fairbanks: *New England Begins: The Seventeenth Century*, 3 vols (exh. cat., Boston, MA, Mus. F. A., 1982)

J. Seidler: 'A Century in Transition: The Boston Furniture Industry, 1840–80', *Victorian Furniture*, K. Ames (Philadelphia, 1983), pp. 65–83

New American Furniture: The Second Generation of Studio Furnituremakers (exh. cat. by E. S. Cooke jr, Boston, MA, Mus. F.A., 1989)

P. Talbott: 'The Furniture Trade in Boston, 1810–1835', *Antiques*, cxli (May 1992), pp. 842–55

L. Keno, J. B. Barzilay and A. Miller: 'The Very Pink of the Mode: Boston Georgian Chairs, Their Export, and Their Influence', *American Furniture 1996*, L. Beckerdite (Hanover, NH, 1996), pp. 267–306.

M. B. Meyer and D. Acton: *Inspiring Reform: Boston's Arts and Crafts Movement* (Wellesley, MA, and New York, 1997)

S. P. Feld and P. Talbott: *Boston in the Age of Neo-classicism, 1810–1840* (New York, 1999)

T. J. Hardiman and others: 'Maine Cabinetmakers of the Federal Period and the Influence of Coastal Massachusetts Design', *Mag. Ant.*, clxv/5 (May 2004), pp. 128–35

K. C. Buhler: *American Silver, 1665–1825, in the Museum of Fine Arts, Boston*, 2 vols (Boston, 1972)

B. M. Ward: 'Boston Goldsmiths, 1690–1730', *The Craftsman in Early America*, I.M.G. Quimby (New York, 1984)

B. M. Ward: '"In a feasting posture": Communion Vessels and Community Values in Seventeenth- and Eighteenth-century New England', *Winterthur Port.*, xxiii/1 (Spring 1988), pp. 1–24.

B. M. Ward: 'The Edwards Family and the Silversmithing Trade in Boston, 1692–1762', *The American Craftsman and the European Tradition, 1620–1820*, F. J. Puig and M. Conforti (Minneapolis, 1989), pp. 136–51

E. C. Chickering and S. M. Ross: *Arthur J. Stone, 1847–1938, Designer and Silversmith* (Boston, MA, 1994)

M. B. Meyer and D. Acton: *Inspiring Reform: Boston's Arts and Crafts Movement* (Wellesley, MA, and New York, 1997)

P. E. Kane and others: *Colonial Massachusetts Silversmiths and Jewelers: A Biographical Dictionary* (New Haven, 1998).

D. R. Friary: 'Silver from the First Church of Deerfield, Massachusetts', *Mag. Ant.*, clxiv/3 (Sept 2003), pp. 82–91

Boston & Sandwich Glass Co. American glass factory formed by Deming Jarves (1790–1869), who left the New England Glass Co. in 1825 and built a glasshouse in Sandwich, MA. The factory produced table glass, lighting devices and ornamental wares, including free-blown, mould-blown, cut, engraved, colourless and cased products, and various art wares, especially opaline, 'Peachblow' and satin glass. The company is best known for its lacy pressed glass, which gave rise to the generic term 'Sandwich Glass' for American examples of this type. The firm's products were of very good quality but, as with many other New England glasshouses, its fortunes declined after the Civil War (1861–5), and the works closed during the strike of 1888.

R. E. Barlow, J. Kaiser and L. Nickerson: *A Guide to Sandwich Glass*, 4 vols (Windham, NH, and Atglen, PA, 1985–99) [originally published as *The Glass Industry in Sandwich*]

Bott, Thomas (*bapt* Bromsgrove, Worcester, 25 Jan. 1828; *d* St Martin's, Worcester, 12 Dec 1870). English porcelain painter and designer, was born near Kidderminster, Worcestershire, the son of a maker of spade handles. He was trained from 1846 as a glass painter at Richardson's glassworks at Wordsley near Stourbridge. In 1853 he moved to Worcester to work as a painter for the Worcester Porcelain Factory, where he developed 'Worcester enamel', a tinted white enamel on a dark ground (often blue); the resemblance to 16th-century Limoges enamels led to his work being sold as 'Limoges ware'.

Bott's son, Thomas John Bott (1854–1932), continued to work in the Limoges style for the Worcester Porcelain Factory and subsequently became art director of the Coalport China Company (1890–1932).

ODNB

Bottengruber, Ignaz. *See under* HAUSMALER.

Böttger, Johann Friedrich (*b* Schleiz, 4 Feb 1682; *d* Dresden, 13 March 1719). German inventor of European hard-paste porcelain. After an early career as an alchemist, Böttger first developed a red stoneware called *Jaspis-porzellan* and then on 28 March 1709 discovered 'true' or hard-paste porcelain, which had until then only been produced in China and Japan. A factory was established in the Albrechtsburg in Meissen on 6 June 1710. There Böttger refined the new material and created the colours to decorate it. Initially the shapes were designed by the court goldsmith Johann Jacob Irminger (1635–1724), who in 1712 assumed the role of artistic director at the factory. Böttger's porcelain was creamy white and could be potted very thinly. His discovery was to create a fashion for porcelain all over Germany for the next 60 years.

Böttger was also the inventor (*c.* 1715) of the lustre known as Böttger lustre or *Perlmutterglasur*, a pale purple lustre based partly on gold; it was used at Meissen until the late 1730s.

Johann Friedrich Böttger: *Die Erfindung des europäischen Porzellans* (Leipzig, 1982)
Johann Friedrich Böttger zum 300. Geburtstag (exh. cat. by W. Goder and others; Dresden, Staatl. Kstsammlungen, 1982)
K. Hoffmann: *Johann Friedrich Böttger: Vom Alchemistengold zum weissen Porzellan: Biografie* (Berlin, 1985)
J. Gleeson: *The Arcanum: The Extraordinary True Story* (New York, 1999)

Bottle vase. Type of Chinese vase, made since the 9th century AD, shaped like a narrow-necked pear with a flared lip.

Boucher, François (*b* Paris, 29 Sept 1703; *d* Paris, 30 May 1770). French painter, draughtsman, etcher, tapestry designer and stage designer. Arguably it was he, more than any other artist, who set his stamp on both the fine arts and the decorative arts of the 18th century. He reinvented the genre of the pastoral, creating an imagery of shepherds and shepherdesses as sentimental lovers that was taken up in every medium, from porcelain to *toile de Jouy*, and that still survives in a debased form.

In about 1734 Boucher was invited to design tapestries for the Beauvais factory. Boucher's first three designs for the *Fêtes de village à l'italienne* were ready by 1736. The *Fêtes italiennes* (as they are commonly known) eventually consisted of eight pieces, apparently designed in two sets of four: the first set, which had been woven by 1739, was more rustic in character but with the Italianate settings that gave the series the second part of its name; the second, woven from 1742 onwards, showed more refined figures celebrating and playing at pastoral love in the open air, justifying the first part of the title. Tapestries from the two sets were equally popular, but it was those from the second set that contributed most to the diffusion of Boucher's pastoral imagery throughout Europe. They were succeeded at Beauvais by the five tapestries in the *Story of Psyche* series (1741–2) and by *La Tenture chinois*, for which Boucher made ten coloured oil sketches (Besançon, Mus. B.-A.). From these, Jean-Joseph Dumons de Tulle (1687–1779) worked up the cartoons. Boucher painted the first two cartoons of the next series, the *Loves of the Gods*, in 1747, but the first weaving did not come off the looms until 1749. The first two tapestries of the *Fragments of Opera* were woven in 1752; finally, in the same vein as the *Fêtes italiennes* but with a much greater element of artificiality, the first tapestries of the set known as *La Noble Pastorale* were woven in 1755.

Also in 1755, however, Boucher was appointed Inspecteur sur les Ouvrages at the Gobelins tapestry factory, replacing Oudry, who had recently died. The Gobelins, which had long been worried by the commercial success of Boucher's designs for the rival factory at Beauvais, insisted that he should cease to supply Beauvais with models. He had already worked for the Gobelins, but only by supplying paintings to be used as designs for unique weavings for the Marquise de Pompadour, the most notable examples being the *Rising of the Sun* and the *Setting of the Sun* (both 1753; London, Wallace). After his appointment at the Gobelins, however, Boucher supplied as models small paintings rather than full-scale cartoons; none was as successful as his Beauvais designs. He did produce the full-scale design (1757; Paris, Louvre) for the tapestry of *Venus in the Forge of Vulcan* (London, Osterley Park House) as one of a set of four in the series the *Loves of the Gods* commissioned by the king. Ironically, the only successful series, the so-called 'Tentures de Boucher', was designed by Maurice Jacques (*c.* 1712–84), and Boucher's part in it was confined to providing models for the figures. By this date, however, the use of tapestry to make up the complete décor of a room was no longer fashionable in France, and almost every set of the Tentures de Boucher was exported, mostly to England; the first (1764–71; New York, Met.) was sold to Croome Court, Hereford & Worcs.

Boucher worked as a stage designer for the Académie Royale de Musique (the Opéra) from 1737 to 1739 and again (or possibly without interruption) from 1744 to 1748. The oil sketch *Le Hameau d'Issé* (1741; Munich, Alte Pin.) may have been a stage design for the pastoral opera *Issé*, performed in 1742. He also provided costumes and stage designs for such productions of the Théâtre de la Foire as Favart's *L'Ambigu de la Folie* (1743) (see colour pl. V, fig. 2).

E. A. Standen: 'Fêtes Italiennes: Beauvais Tapestries after Boucher in the Metropolitan Museum of Art', *Met. Mus. J.*, xii (1977), pp. 107–30

R. Savill: 'François Boucher and the Porcelains of Vincennes and Sèvres', *Apollo*, cxv (1982), pp. 162–70

G. Brunel: *François Boucher* (Paris, 1986; Eng. trans., 1986)

A. Laing with P. Rosenberg and F. Boucher: *The Drawings of François Boucher* (New York, 2003)

François Boucher. Seductive Visions (exh. cat. by J. Hedley; London, Wallace, 2005)

Boucheron. Italian family of gold- and silversmiths. Andrea Boucheron (*b* Turin, *c.* 1692; *d* Turin, 1761) was apprenticed in Paris to Thomas Germain. He was called back to Turin by Victor-Amadeus II of Savoy (*reg* 1720–30), where he opened two workshops and became goldsmith to the court of Charles Emanuel III (*reg* 1730–73) in 1737. Almost all of his works have been lost; all that remains is the bronze and silver tabernacle of the Sacro Pilone in the church at Vicoforte near Mondovì, produced between 1750 and 1752 in collaboration with François Ladatte. Andrea's son Giovan Battista Boucheron (*b* Turin, 1742; *d* Turin, 1815), after being taught by his father, went to Rome in 1760. There he completed his training by studying sculpture in the Collini brothers' workshop. He was active in Paris and Rome and from 1763 succeeded his father as court goldsmith. In 1776 he became director of the royal goldsmiths' workshop. His drawings (Turin, Mus. Civ. A. Ant.) and his theoretical writings on his craft as well as his various pieces in gold and silver confirm his role as one of the main figures in the field of secular silverwork in the second half of the 18th century and the early 19th. His style was primarily classicist but with French and English elements (e.g. a silver-gilt pair of candlesticks, 1783; London, V&A).

C. LeCorbeiller: 'Andrea Boucheron: Inkstand', *Met. Mus. A. Bull.*, lvi/2 (Fall 1998), pp. 34–5

Boudin, Léonard (*b c.* 1735; *d* Paris, 20 Nov 1807). French cabinetmaker and dealer. In 1761 he became a *maître-ébéniste* in Paris. He was a particularly talented marquetry craftsman, as seen on his secrétaires (e.g. Cleveland, OH, Mus. A.), including one (Paris, Petit Pal.) stamped R.V.L.C. While managing his workshop, he dealt in both new and antique furniture. After 1770 he made this his main business and he added his own stamp to those of his subcontracted colleagues.

Bouffioulx. Belgian centre of ceramics production, near Charleroi. Potters were working in Bouffioulx from the 13th to the 15th century. The first mention of a master potter at Bouffioulx was in 1528, brown and grey salt-glazed stoneware being made from *c.* 1530. During the first half of the 16th century wares produced included tankards with ovoid bodies (often decorated with a figure) and ovoid pitchers, sometimes with three handles and decorated with three faces. During the second half of the 16th century production also included *schnellen* (tall, tapering tankards). The influence of the Raeren workshops is evident especially in the decoration, which included armorial bearings, medallions, figures, flowers and foliage.

A. Matthys: *Les grès communs de Bouffioulx et Châtelet XVIe-XVIIe s. Catalogue des pièces conservées dans les collections du Musée archéologique de Charleroi* (Brussels, 1971)

Bouge [booge]. Hollow running inside the rim of a plate made from silver, pewter or ceramic.

Bough-pot. Pot or other vessel, usually pottery or porcelain, for holding boughs for ornament; it normally has a cover with holes through which the boughs or branches are inserted. In the 19th century the term was used in a general sense to denote a flower-pot, and also to refer to a bouquet of flowers.

Bouillotte lamp. French table-lamp, named after the card game called *bouillotte*. Bouillotte lamps are normally made of metal (brass or gilt-bronze) and are fitted with a metal shade (usually green) through which the shaft (often ending in a finial) protrudes. Two or three candle brackets are mounted under the shade. The base is dish-shaped, and there is sometimes a smaller dish mounted on the shaft.

Boulard, Jean-Baptiste (*b* 1725; *d* 1789). French furniture-maker. He was received as a master menuisier 17 April 1755. Several of the chairs that he made for the French royal family are now in the Musée du Louvre; they are characterized by strong moulding and by restraint in sculpted elements. His son Michel-Jacques Boulard continued the business after his father's death; his patrons included Napoleon (*reg* 1804–14).

C. Baulez: 'Paire de chaises a carreau', *Rev. Louvre*, xlii (July 1992), pp. 14–15

Boulle, André-Charles (*b* Paris, 11 Nov 1642; *d* Paris, 28 Feb 1732). French cabinetmaker. His family were originally from Guelderland in the Netherlands and went to Paris, where his father worked as a 'menuisier en ébène'. Boulle became a master before 1666, and by 1685 employed at least 15 workmen; by 1720 his workshop had 20 work-benches and equipment for 6 bronzeworkers. His work for the Crown was principally carried out for the Bâtiments du Roi, the state department in charge of the royal buildings. It consists mostly of marquetry and

André-Charles Boulle: marquetry panel from a cabinet depicting a bird and a butterfly, ebony and bronze (Paris, Musée du Louvre)

parquet floors and gilt-bronze decorative details, his masterpiece being the marquetry floors and wainscoting (destr.) in the Dauphin's apartments (completed 1683) at the château of Versailles. Pieces from the Boulle workshops were not stamped, and documentation exists for only a few pieces, so attributions remain tentative.

Boulle's work is characterized by the use of fine, gilt-bronze mounts and magnificent marquetry of two main types: extraordinarily naturalistic floral marquetry in wood and that composed of metal (usually brass, pewter or copper) and tortoise-shell or ebony, which became known in the 18th century as boullework or buhl work, whether produced by the Boulle workshops or not. The form of his furniture ranges from the late 17th-century cabinets supported by a pair of three-dimensional figures and veneered with floral marquetry (examples in London, Wallace; Malibu, CA, Getty Mus.; Duke of Buccleuch priv. col.) to the new forms, current in the 18th century, of the commode, bookcase, low armoire and *bureau plat*; the workshops also produced a substantial number of clockcases (see colour pl. VI, fig. 4).

Although the production of Boulle's workshops was aimed at the top end of the market, it was not composed of one-off pieces; rather, specific models were made repeatedly, often with minor variations. The pair of commodes (1708–09; Versailles, Château) made by the Boulle workshops for Louis XIV's bedchamber in the Grand Trianon at Versailles were later reproduced by his workshops: there are at least five surviving examples (New York, Met.; Petworth House, W. Sussex, NT; a pair at Vaux-le-Vicomte; and one ex-Jean Lombard col.). In the 1720s the *marchand-mercier* Thomas Joachim Hebert (*d* 1773) commissioned from the Boulle workshops replicas of successful models. Variations in the same model were produced through the use of marquetry panels and mounts of different designs. Among surviving examples of the six-legged side-table depicted in *Nouveaux Deisseins* are those with the top veneered with a boulle-marquetry triumphal carriage drawn by oxen (ex-Duchess de Talleyrand col.; ex-Dennery col.; London, Wallace) and, alternatively, with a birdcage drawn by monkeys (London, Wallace). Boulle-marquetry furniture, particularly the productions of the Boulle workshops, remained in demand throughout most of the 18th century. Models were still being copied in the 19th century: a pair of commodes (New York, Frick) made originally for the Grand Trianon are marked BLAKE OF LONDON, and three commodes (two Rouen, Mus. B.-A.; one Madrid, Pal. Real) were made by the Fordinois firm in Paris. Boulle's posthumous influence continued and his reputation was international. See fig. on p. 136.

G. Wilson: 'Boulle', *Furn. Hist.*, viii (1972), pp. 47–69

J.-P. Samoyault: *André-Charles Boulle et sa famille* (Geneva, 1979)

P. Fuhring: 'Designs for and after Boulle', *Burl. Mag.*, cxxxiv (1992), pp. 350–62

P. Fuhring: *L'Armoire "au char d'Apollon" par André-Charles Boulle provenant de la collection de M. Hubert de Givenchy* (Paris, 1994)

A Pradere: 'Les armoires a medailles de l'histoire de Louis XIV par Boulle et ses suiveurs', *Rev. A.*, cxvi (1997), pp. 42–53

J. Ronfort: *Boulle* (Dijon, 2005)

Boullework [Boulle marquetry]. *See under* MARQUETRY.

Boulsover, Thomas. *See under* SHEFFIELD PLATE.

Boulton, Matthew (*b* Birmingham, 14 Sept 1728; *d* Birmingham, 17 Aug 1809). English manufacturer and engineer. At the age of 17 he entered his father's silver stamping and piercing business at Snow Hill, Birmingham, which he inherited in 1759. Three years later he established a factory in Soho, Birmingham, in partnership with John Fothergill (*d* 1782). Boulton progressed from the production of 'toys' in tortoiseshell, stone, glass, enamel and cut steel to that of tableware in Sheffield plate, on which he obtained a monopoly, and later ormolu (e.g. two pairs of candelabra, *c.* 1770; Brit. Royal Col.; London, V&A) and silver, and enjoyed a reputation for fine craftsmanship.

Boulton & Fothergill produced some of the best-designed plate and silver in the last quarter of the 18th century and fully exploited the technical ad-

André-Charles Boulle: commode with two drawers, gilt wood, h. 860 mm (Paris, Musée du Louvre)

vances of Joseph Hancock and R. A. F. de Réaumur (1683–1757). The thinner gauges of Sheffield plate available from the 1770s, and the precision of machine-produced, fly-punched parts that were cut, stamped and pierced in repeated patterns were suitable for regular, uniform Neo-classical designs, in which a clear distinction can be discerned between structure and decoration. As the items produced in silver, for example dinner services, tureens, coffee- and teapots and candelabra, were made increasingly for stock rather than to order, Boulton also adopted the manufacturing techniques of items in Sheffield plate for those in solid silver, especially for objects with simple forms requiring little chasing or hand-finishing. Notable among Boulton's products are a silver helmet-shaped ewer (1774; Birmingham, Mus. & A.G.), a similar silver-gilt ewer (1776; Boston, MA, Mus. F.A.), a pair of silver sauce tureens (1776; Birmingham, Assay Office), and a pair of Sheffield plate candelabra (1797; Birmingham, Mus. & A.G.). Many of his pattern books are in the Reference Library, Birmingham.

For his silverware products Boulton commissioned designs both from silversmiths (notably Thomas Heming and Michelangelo Pergolesi) and from architects, including Robert Adam, who designed a set of eight sauceboats (1776–7; one London, V&A), James Adam (1732–94), William Chambers, Robert Mylne (1733–1811), James Stuart and James Wyatt (1746–1813). Boulton also collaborated with his friend Josiah Wedgwood, who used similar design sources, production methods and marketing techniques and produced cut-steel frames for jasper cameos.

Boulton was less a craftsman and designer than an industrial entrepreneur, organizing factory production of metalwork and managing designers both within and outside his extended workshop system, thereby revolutionizing the silver manufacturing trade and challenging the monopoly of silversmiths in London. He produced silver and Sheffield plate to the highest technical standard in the most fashionable styles and made such small wares as buckles and fittings available to a wider market. A large part of the production of silver, however, continued to consist of ornamental pieces that were expensive to produce. His production of ormolu, which ceased in the 1780s, was only partially successful, as he tried to compete with French manufacturers. As the processes involved in the manufacture of ormolu were not suited to mass-production, this part of his business failed to be profitable.

Boulton's factory was known from 1781 as the Matthew Boulton Plate Co., continued after his death, producing such pieces as J. Widdowson's silver copy (1827; Birmingham, Assay Office) of the Warwick Vase (2nd to 4th century AD; Glasgow, Burrell Col.); it remained in operation until the 1840s and was sold in 1850.

ODNB

H. W. Dickinson: *Matthew Boulton* (Cambridge, 1937)
N. Goodison: *Matthew Boulton: Ormolu* (2/2002)
J. Uglow: *The Lunar Men: The Friends Who Made the Future* (London, 2003)

Bouquetier. Small glass holder for a bunch of flowers, especially one carried in the hand; the design, which derives from late 18th-century France, is a trumpet-shaped mouth and a deep handle to hold the stems of the flowers. Sometimes the mouth is perforated to allow pins to hold the flowers in place. The spelling *bouquetière* is erroneous, but has become common in English-language publications.

Bourdalou. Oval chamber pot for ladies, designed for use when travelling, and so in England sometimes sold as 'coach pots'. The eponym of the *bourdalou* is popularly believed to be the Jesuit preacher Louis Bourdaloue (1632–1704), whose sermons were said to be so long that ladies began to bring to church these chamber pots concealed in their muffs with a view to using them hidden under their capacious dresses. The earliest surviving examples, however, were made at Delft *c.* 1710. Thereafter they were made (in porcelain, pottery and silver) by European factories and (for export) by Chinese and Japanese factories. Wedgwood sold cream-coloured earthenware 'coach pots', and European manufacturers of porcelain *bourdalous* included Chantilly, Höchst, Meissen and Sèvres; these delicately decorated products are sometimes mistaken for gravy boats. There is a *bourdalou* museum in the Zentrum für Aussergewöhnliche Museen (ZAM, the Centre for Unusual Museums) in Munich. In modern French this sense of *bourdalou* has fallen out of all but specialized usage, and the term now denotes (as it does in Greek) a leather hatband.

Bourgeoys, **Marin Le.** *See* LE BOURGEOYS, MARIN.

Bourne, **Joseph** & Son. English manufacturer of stoneware and earthenware in Derbyshire from 1809 to the present. In 1806 a Derbyshire potter called William Bourne leased the rights to a seam of clay in Denby, and in 1809 established a pottery to make bottles; he installed his son Joseph Bourne as manager of the Denby Bottle Works, which became known as Joseph Bourne and later as Joseph Bourne & Son. Joseph Bourne opened a second pottery in Belper in 1812, and in 1833 acquired the Codnor Park Pottery, which had been making stoneware bottles since 1821. The company's bottles were mostly utilitarian containers for ink, medicines and ginger beer. Jopseh Bourne & Son became DENBY POTTERY, under which name the modern company operates.

Joseph Bourne & Son: Background to Denby (Derby, 1959)

Boutet, **Nicolas-Noël** (*b* 1761; *b* 1833). French gunsmith. He worked in the service of Louis XVI (*reg* 1774–92) as Directeur-artiste of the Manufacture d'Armes de Versailles and at the Revolution became technical director of the state arms factory. While working as a manager he also made decorated swords and luxury firearms, some for Napoleon (*reg* 1804–14). In the historiography of the gun, Boutet is regarded as the last of the great artist-gunsmiths.

D. G. Taylor: 'Nicolas-Noël Boutet and the Manufacture of Arms at Versailles' in *Arms Collect.*, xx (1982), pp. 107–26.
La Manufacture d'armes de Versailles et Nicolas-Noël Boutet: Manufacture nationale, impériale et royale, 1793–1818 (Versailles, 1993)

Bow-front. Having a convex curved front; the term is used with reference to case furniture and to buildings

Bow Porcelain Factory. English ceramic manufactory in the east end of London. The first Bow patent for 'a certain material whereby a ware might be made . . . equal to . . . China or Porcelain ware imported from abroad' was taken out in east London in December 1744 by the Irish artist Thomas Frye (*c.* 1710–62) and by Edward Heylyn (1695–1765). The early undertaking, significantly named 'New Canton', was founded to undercut Chinese imports and was probably financed by Alderman George Arnold (1691–1751). John Weatherby (*d* 1762) and John Crowther (*d* 1790), who had been partners in pottery and glassmaking ventures since 1725, completed the board of proprietors. An important ingredient in the original paste and mentioned in the 1744 patent was 'Unaker', possibly a china clay imported from Carolina. The soft paste used at Bow was unique in being the first to incorporate calcined bone-ash (mentioned as 'Virgin earth' in the second Bow patent of 1749–50) to increase strength and whiteness. Bow had a seminal influence on the course of English porcelain-making through its pioneer use of bone-ash, which continued to be an important ingredient in later bone china.

Bow's early wares were simply shaped, utilitarian pieces decorated in Chinese style in underglaze blue, the earliest shade being a distinctive royal blue. White wares decorated in relief with applied sprigs of prunus blossom, imitating Chinese Dehua wares made in Fujian Province were also produced. From about 1750 both Chinese and Japanese overglaze enamelled designs were used, especially those in 'Kakiemon style', and the forms of wares derived from both Europe and East Asia. Figures made during the early period were often inspired by French prints and by engravings of contemporary stage characters, such as Kitty Clive as the 'Fine Lady' in Garrick's *Lethe* (1750; London, BM), engraved by Charles Mosley (*d* ?1770) and copied from Thomas Worlidge's watercolour (untraced). Few names of individual workers or modellers have survived, but the anonymous 'Muses' Modeller', whose subjects included Classical gods and the Muses, produced an unmistakable personal style through the use of disproportionately small heads, with heavy-lidded eyes, wide brows and receding chins, on long-armed bodies dressed in heavily folded draperies.

Bow's trading was widespread at home and overseas, especially in the American colonies, and it was during the 1750s that the factory was most prosperous. About 1756 overglaze transfer-printing in brickred, purple, lilac or black was introduced at Bow, with many of the prints originating from French engravings. After 1756 the oriental influence gradually lessened. Underglaze blue was much less bright than at first, and, though some wares continued to be decorated in Chinese style, and a powder-blue ground was popular, European styles became dominant by 1760. Figures were often straight copies of Meissen originals. There was no regular factory mark.

By 1762, after the death or bankruptcy of most of the original partners, John Crowther remained the sole proprietor of the company. His firm made great efforts to produce the more florid Rococo wares typified by the Chelsea factory's 'Gold Anchor' pieces (1758–70) but was hindered by underfiring of the heavy bone-ash paste and sometimes by inexpert workmanship. Although some of the later figures are noteworthy, standards generally declined. Bow had first opened a retail City Warehouse on Cornhill in 1753. This moved to the Poultry and then to St Paul's Churchyard, where it closed finally in 1773. The factory itself was closed by March 1774, and then let to a china maker, William Brown, in 1774–6. By 1780 it had become a tar and turpentine factory. The equipment and stock were reputedly sold to William Duesbury (1725–86) and moved to his Derby porcelain factory.

E. Adams and D. Redstone: *Bow Porcelain* (London, 1981, rev. 1991)
P. Begg and others: *A Survey of the Bow Factory from First Patent until Closure: 1744–1774* (Hawksburn, Australia, 2000)

Boxwood. Hard, close-grained wood of the box-tree (or box), much used by turners and wood-engravers, and in the manufacture of mathematical and musical instruments. This boxwood is the genus (*Buxus*) of evergreen shrubs native to Europe and Asia; the species normally used in carving and furniture is *Buxus sempervirens*, the common or evergreen box-tree. It is not the same tree as American boxwood (*Cornus florida*) or Jamaica boxwood (*Tecoma pentaphylla*) or the various Australian species of eucalyptus known as boxwood.

Boyvin, René (*b* Angers, *c.* 1525; *d* ?Angers, *c.* 1625). French engraver, etcher and designer. Vasari, in his *Vita* of Marcantonio Raimondi, mentions that 'after the death of Rosso [Fiorentino], we saw the arrival from France of all the engravings of his works'. He attributed this upsurge of engraved reproductions 'to the copperplate engraver René', that is René Boyvin. He came to Paris *c.* 1545 from Angers. In 1553 he completed two plates that the engraver Paul Milan had failed to finish for the music publisher Guillaume Morlaye (*c.* 1510–after 1558); one of these was the *Nymph of Fontainebleau* (Levron, 169). He later opened his own workshop, but his production was intermittent, because he was persecuted and for a time imprisoned for his Calvinist beliefs. The canon of his work is problematical, in part because of confusion between his work and that of Milan. In his most famous work, *Le Livre de la conqueste de la toison d'or par le Prince Iason de Tessalie* (1563), which reproduced the drawings of Léonard Thiry (*fl* 1536; *d*

1550) in 26 plates, Boyvin displayed a particular aptitude for chiaroscuro effects. Although he was primarily a reproductive engraver, Boyvin also designed and executed numerous refined decorative prints that served as models for goldsmiths and jewellers (e.g. the *Panneaux d'ornements* and the *Livre de bijouterie*).

J. Levron: *René Boyvin, graveur angevin du XVIe siècle* (Angers, 1941)

Bracket clock. Wood-cased, spring-driven clock designed to stand on a shelf or wall-bracket; the term is misleading, in that these clocks were portable, and many early examples from the late 17th century and early 18th were fitted with a handle or pair of handles to enable them to be carried from one room to another, typically back and forth from living room to bedroom.

The bracket clock may have been invented by Jost Bürgi (1552–1632), the Swiss clockmaker at the court of Rudolf II in Prague, but production of these clocks began in Restoration England and spread thereafter to the Netherlands, Germany and Austria. Those by Edward East were made of dark oak in architectural designs, complete with pillars and pediments. Later makers, such as Thomas Tompion (1639–1713) and JOSEPH KNIBB, toned down the architectural elements in the design. From *c.* 1710 square dials were superseded by arched dials. Many examples have a silvered hour-ring and pierced hour-hands; both front and rear doors are usually glazed, and the vertical backplate of the clock movement is often engraved.

R. C. R. Barder: *The Georgian Bracket Clock, 1714–1830* (Woodbridge, 1993)
D. Roberts: *The Bracket Clock* (Newton Abbot, 2003)

Bracket clock, wooden case with panels of mirror glass, from England, 1710 (London, Victoria and Albert Museum)

Bracket foot. In furniture, a right-angled foot, with each inner end curved. Bracket feet may be straight or ogee (a double curve, also known as a cyma curve, common in Chippendale designs) or French (a flared foot common in the furniture of Hepplewhite and his successors).

Bracquemond, Félix(-Auguste-Joseph) (*b* Paris, ?28 May 1833; *d* Sèvres, nr Paris, 27 Oct 1914). French printmaker, designer, painter and writer. Bracquemond produced almost 900 plates, divided about equally between original and reproductive prints. In the 1860s he began to design ceramics. He worked for a while in the studio of JOSEPH-THÉODORE DECK, where he learnt the technique of enamel painting. In 1866 he was commissioned by Eugène Rousseau (1827–91) to design a large faience service. The 'Rousseau service' incorporates motifs from his animal etchings: for example, *The Duck*, published in *L'Artiste* (1856), was reused on one of the plates (Nevers, Mus. Mun.), as were some motifs from the etching *Teal* (1853; dinner plate, Paris, priv. col.), which shows his interest in Japanese aesthetics combined with a more delicate and sophisticated sense of composition and colour. The more abstract style of his 'Flower and ribbon service' of 1879 anticipates the designs of the Art Nouveau movement. From 1873 to 1880 he was head of the Auteuil studio (near Paris) of the Haviland Limoges factory, where he personally designed individual pieces and several important porcelain services including the 'Parisian service' of 1876.

Bracquemond also designed furniture, gold and silver jewellery and tableware, bookbindings and tapestry in collaboration chiefly with Auguste Rodin (1840–1917) and Jules Chéret (1836–1932). His furniture designs for Baron Joseph Vitta's Villa La Sapinière at Evian were shown at the Salon of 1902. At the end of his life he produced designs for decorative art for his friend and devoted admirer, the writer and critic Gustave Geffroy, who was then director of the Gobelins.

Bracquemond's wife Marie Bracquemond (née Quivoron-Pasquiou; *b* Argenton, nr Quimper, 1 Dec 1840; *d* Sèvres, 17 Jan 1916) was a painter, draughtswoman, printmaker and designer. She was involved in her husband's work for the Haviland Limoges factory and produced in particular several dishes and a wide panel of ceramic tiles entitled the *Muses*, shown at the Exposition Universelle in Paris in 1878. Félix and Marie's son Pierre Bracquemond (*b* Paris, 26 June 1870; *d* Paris, 29 Jan 1926) was a pupil of his father and as such was involved in works for the Gobelins. He pursued a career as an interior decorator (carpets, tapestries) and painter.

Félix et Marie Bracquemond (exh. cat., ed. J.-P. Bouillon; Mortagne-au-Perche, Maison Comtes du Perche, 1972)

J.-P. Bouillon and E. Kane: 'Marie Bracquemond', *Woman's A. J.*, v/2 (1984), pp. 21–7

T. Garb: *Women Impressionists* (Oxford, 1986)

Le Service 'Rousseau' (exh. cat. by J.-P. Bouillon, C. Shimizu and P. Thiébaut, Paris, Mus. Orsay, 1988)

Félix Bracquemond (exh. cat. by C. van Rappard-Boon, Amsterdam, Rijksmus. van Gogh, 1993)

F. Bracquemond, C. Méryon and R. Porter: *Meryon, Bracquemond & the 19th Century Etching Renaissance* (Sydney, 1998)

J. P. Bouillon and F. Bracquemond: *Félix Bracquemond, 1833–1914: Graveur et céramiste* (Paris, 2003)

Bradley, Will(iam Henry) (*b* Boston, MA, 10 July 1868; *d* La Mesa, CA, 25 Jan 1962). American book-illustrator and designer of posters, typefaces and furniture. In 1893 Bradley began designing for *Vogue* magazine. He subsequently worked for *Ladies' Home Journal*, and in 1901–2 published an influential series of eight articles on 'The Bradley House'; the designs in these articles (and another three in 1905) seem not to have been implemented, but they nonetheless exerted a seminal influence on public taste and on subsequent furniture design; his designs for pianos were used by Chickering & Sons of Boston. Bradley also designed two series of plates for Royal Doulton: 'Golfers' (1905) and 'Proverbs' (1911). He is the eponym of the Bradley blackletter typeface (1894).

R. Koch: 'Will Bradley and the Art Nouveau Poster', *Mag. Ant.*, cxxxiv (Oct 1988), pp. 812–21

R. Koch: *Will H. Bradley: American Artist in Print: A Collector's Guide* (New York, 2002)

Bradshaw, George Smith (*b* 1717; *d* 1812). English tapestry-weaver, upholsterer and cabinetmaker. In 1755 he assumed control of the Soho tapestry works owned by his relative WILLIAM BRADSHAW. In 1757 he worked with the tapestry-weaver Paul Saunders (1722–71) to make tapestry and furniture for Holkham Hall, the Norfolk seat of the earls of Leicester; their work (designed to match a set of Brussels tapestry panels) can still be seen in the Green State Bedroom. Bradshaw subsequently supplied furniture to Admiralty House in London (1764–74).

Bradshaw, William (*b* Cockerham, 1700; *d* after 1762). English furniture-maker and tapestry-weaver. He founded a London workshop in 1728, and in 1755 passed control of the workshop to GEORGE SMITH BRADSHAW. He was unusual in his ability to undertake both the joinery and the tapestry upholstery for furniture (e.g. four armchairs. New York, Met).

G. Beard: 'William Bradshaw: Furniture Maker and Tapestry Weaver', *Met. Mus. J.*, xxxvii (2002), pp. 167–9

Bradwell Wood Pottery. *See under* ELERS.

Braid. Woven fabric in the form of a band, typically made of silk, wool, cotton, gold or silver thread; it is used primarily for trimming or binding articles of dress. In the vocabulary of lace, a braid is a narrow flat band woven of linen thread, with an open-work border on each side, used to form the outline of the pattern in point-lace work. In embroidery, braids were often couched to the foundation, sometimes in place of the embroidery stitch.

Bramah [Bramma], **Joseph** (*b* 2 April 1749, Stainborough Lane Farm, nr Barnsley, Yorkshire; *d* 9 Dec 1814, Pimlico). English locksmith and inventor of the flush toilet. He trained as a cabinetmaker and in the early 1780s opened a workshop in Eaton Street, Pimlico. In 1778 he patented a design for a watercloset in which the traditional side valve was replaced by a hinged flap valve, which largely solved the problem of the system freezing in winter; in the next 20 years he manufactured some 6000 toilets at a Denmark Street workshop, and production continued throughout much of the 19th century.

In 1784 Bramah patented the Bramah Cylindrical Lock, which achieved an unprecedented level of security through the use of a series of notched sliders which made the lock difficult to pick. He offered a prize of 200 guineas to anyone who could open his lock without a key; the prize was eventually claimed in 1851, but the American locksmith who succeeded (Alfred Charles Hobbs) took 51 hours to open it.

ODNB
J. Bramah: *A Dissertation on the Construction of Locks* (London, *c.* 1785)
I. McNeil: *Joseph Bramah: A Century of Invention, 1749–1851* (1968)

Brameld. *See under* ROCKINGHAM CERAMIC FACTORY.

Brampton. English centre of ceramics production. Town in Derbyshire where a group of manufacturers of household wares in brown stoneware were active from the 18th century to the early 20th. The most prominent factories were Oldfield & Co. and S. & H. Briddon. The Brampton potter Thomas Davenport (1815–88) emigrated to Utah, where he and his descendants worked as potters.

Below the Salt (exh. cat., Derby, U. Derby; Portsmouth, City Mus. & A.G.; Nottingham Castle Mus.; 2000)

Brancas, Louis-Léon-Félicité, Duc de (*b* 1733; *d* 1824). French inventor of hard-paste porcelain, using kaolin from Alençon; he made a small number of pieces from 1763–8, most of which are in the museum at Sèvres. He secured an English patent in 1766, but it specified neither materials nor method, and so did not inhibit William Cookworthy from developing English porcelain.

Brandenburg. German centre of glass production. The first Brandenburg glassworks was established in 1602 by Joachim Frederick, Elector of Brandenburg, and was run by Bohemian glassmakers. The earliest products included coloured and marbled glass. In 1607 the factory was transferred to Marienwalde, near Küstrin (now Kostrzyn, Poland), and another factory was built in Grimnitz in 1653. Both factories produced window glass and simple drinking vessels based on Bohemian models and painted with enamels or, from the mid-17th century, engraved. In 1674 Frederick William, Elector of Brandenburg, built another factory at Drewitz (near Potsdam) for the production of glass crystal. The glass-engraver Georg Gondelach came from Dessau to work there from 1677, accompanied by the engraver Christoph Tille and the enamel-painter Ruel. After the arrival of the glassmaker Johann Kunckel (1630–1703), the great period of Brandenburg glass began. Kunckel operated the glassworks in Drewitz from 1679 to 1682, while the Elector built a new glassworks in Potsdam. In 1679 Kunckel published his *Ars vitraria experimentalis*, which was the most important account of glassmaking during this period. In a secret laboratory that the Elector had given him on the Pfaueninsel in the Wannsee, Kunckel carried out various experiments, reducing crizzling by adding chalk to the batch and creating the process for making gold-ruby glass. In 1680 the Elector hired Martin Winter (*d* 1702) and in 1683 his nephew Gottfried Spiller (1663–1728) as glass-engravers. In 1688 Winter introduced relief-cutting and built a water-powered engraving workshop. Spiller produced the most outstanding figurative engravings on Brandenburg glass; in addition to his work in *tiefschnitt* (intaglio) and *hochschnitt* (relief; e.g. covered goblet, *c.* 1700; London, V&A), he also worked in gold-ruby glass. Spiller was succeeded by the engraver Elias Rosbach (1700–65), who had worked in Berlin from 1727. Around 1742 Rosbach went to Zechlin, to which the glassworks at Potsdam had been relocated (1736). In addition to the engraving and cutting, high-quality gilding is a mark of Potsdam and Zechlin glass. During the first half of the 19th century Zechlin produced cut glass in the Empire and Biedermeier styles, including pieces with cameo incrustations. From *c.* 1840 primarily simple, utilitarian wares were produced.

R. Schmidt: *Brandenburgische Gläser* (Berlin, 1914)
C. Keisch and S. Netzer: *'Herrliche Künste und Manufacturen': Fayence, Glas und Tapisserien aus der Frühzeit Brandenburg-Preussens 1680–1720* (Berlin, 2001)
A. Klauke and F. Martin: *Glasmalereien des 19. Jahrhunderts: Berlin, Brandenburg Die Kirchen* (Leipzig, 2003)

Brandewijnskom. Brandy bowls made in Holland and Friesland in the 17th and 18th centuries. The bowls were associated with ceremonies of childbirth and are usually octagonal or oval with two flat, cast handles. They are decorated either with engraved or embossed ornament (e.g. of 1651; Leeuwarden, Fries Mus.).

Brandon. English centre of flint-knapping in Suffolk during the 19th century and early 20th. Brandon was the principal source of gun-flints, and of flints for building and ornamental purposes.

Brandt [née Liebe], **Marianne** (*b* Chemnitz, 1 Oct 1893; *d* Kirchberg, 18 June 1983). German metalworker and designer in the BAUHAUS tradition. Around 1923 she went to study at the Bauhaus in Weimar and joined the metal workshop there. Her early designs, for example the hand-crafted nickel-silver teapot (1924; New York, MOMA) and brass

Marianne Brandt: teapot, nickel silver and ebony, h. 178 mm, 1924 (New York, Museum of Modern Art)

and ebony tea-essence pot (1924; Berlin, Bauhaus-Archv), are based on pure geometrical forms—cylinders, spheres and hemispheres. Functional considerations are secondary to aesthetic concerns. Her later designs, particularly those for lighting fixtures, reflect the influence of László Moholy-Nagy. Under his direction the metal workshop concentrated on producing prototypes for mass production. Notable among Brandt's lamp designs are a ceiling fixture (1925), equipped with chains so the globe could be lowered to change the bulb, an adjustable ceiling light (with Hans Przyrembel; 1926; e.g. at Berlin, Bauhaus-Archv) and the 'Kandem' bedside table lamp on a flexible stem (1927). The last was one of several lamps by Brandt that were commercially manufactured by Körting & Mathiesson, Leipzig, from 1928.

D. Norton: 'The Bauhaus Metal Workshop: 1919–1927', *Metalsmith*, vii (Winter 1987), pp. 40–45
R. Price and others: *New Worlds: German and Austrian Art, 1890–1940* (New York, 2001)

Brandt, **Reynier** [Reinier; Reijnier] (*b* Wesel, Gelderland, 1702; *d* Amsterdam, 1788). Dutch silversmith. In his youth he moved to Amsterdam, where he was active from *c.* 1734. He specialized in delicate bread- and cake-baskets in the Rococo style, all of which have the same basic form: a graceful ogee-shape with an openwork body and curving sides tapering into handles at either end. They are decorated with openwork patterns of trellis or foliage. The rims and bases are trimmed with linked volutes or fillets and groups of flowers and fruits, and Rococo scrolls form the feet (e.g. basket, 1770; Amsterdam, Rijksmus.). In the later 18th century, with increasing

mechanization, some components of his baskets were machine-made. Though chiefly known for these elaborately decorated objects Brandt also produced relatively plain ones, for example an inkstand of 1735 (Amsterdam, Rijksmus.), which is undecorated except for a small pierced lid, and a large tureen and salver (1765; Amsterdam, Hist. Mus.), whose only decoration is the figure of a cow that forms the handle of the tureen cover, and rocaille motifs on the feet and handles of the tureen itself.

Brangwyn, Sir **Frank** (*b* Bruges, 13 May 1867; *d* Ditchling, Sussex, 11 June 1956). English painter, graphic artist and designer of furniture, textiles and carpets. Through his father, the decorative artist William Curtis Brangwyn (1839–1907), he was introduced as a boy to A. H. MACKMURDO, who in turn commended Brangwyn to WILLIAM MORRIS, who in the early 1880s employed him as a glazier and subsequently in work on inlay, embroidery, and wallpaper.

In 1895 Brangwyn received his first decorative commission, for the façade of Siegfried Bing's Maison de l'Art Nouveau in Paris. At about the same time he designed the 'La Vigne' carpet (Bruges, Stedel. Musea), which draws on the design of Morris's 'Trellis' wallpaper. For the rest of his career he combined painting (including a huge number of murals) with designs for ceramics, furniture, glass, metalwork and textiles; he also made many etchings, lithographs, and woodcuts

ODNB
H. E. A. Furst: *The Decorative Art of Frank Brangwyn, RA* (London, 1924)

Bras de Lumière [Fr.: 'sconce']. The term is used in English to denote a 17th-century French wall-light in which the bracket is modelled in the shape of a human arm and hand.

Brass. The alloy of copper and zinc. The alloy of copper and tin is bronze, while alloys with both zinc and tin are known as gunmetals. Many of the alloys that are described as bronze are in fact brass.

1. China. 2. Europe. 3. Indian subcontinent. 4. Islamic world.

1. CHINA. Brass sprang to prominence very quickly *c.* 1500, when coins, which had long been made from bronze, began to be made from copper and a 'new' tin, almost certainly metallic zinc. In art metalwork, brass replaced bronze almost completely from the 16th century. The technology and indeed the basic design of the ritual vessels and statuettes remained much the same, and the difference between the colour of the earlier, heavily leaded bronzes and the golden, high-zinc brass would have been nullified by the dark varnish or patination that almost invariably covers the later metalwork.

2. EUROPE. In the West the watershed between the general use of bronze and that of brass seems to

have come with the fall of the Western Empire in the 5th century AD. Virtually all the sources of tin on which the Middle East and the Mediterranean relied were in the north-west of the Empire, so the loss of the tin-producing provinces of Britannia, Hispania and Pannonia must have severely curtailed production and supply. Analyses of Coptic metalwork, for example, show that by the 6th and 7th centuries AD brass had already largely replaced bronze. By the time of Charlemagne (*reg* 742–814) the brass industry was capable of producing major items of considerable artistic and technical sophistication, for example the doors of the Palatine Chapel, Aachen, and of the cathedrals of Hildesheim and Mainz, together with crosses, fonts and other major ecclesiastical fittings. In the medieval period the industry was centred in such small towns as Dinant (hence the term dinanderie to describe medieval decorative brasswares) and Huy on the river Meuse, and in other centres throughout the Meuse Valley. The workshops in these towns produced a wide range of cast and hammered domestic vessels but are especially renowned for the church fittings, for example memorial brasses and lecterns, which once adorned the churches of all Christendom but, after centuries of strife and neglect, survive chiefly in England. Another centre developed in the late medieval period at Nuremberg, utilizing the metal deposits at Rammelsberg and other mines in the Harz Mountains. This seems to have produced smaller, more domestic wares but on a very large scale. Documents from the early 16th century list enormous quantities of brassware shipped out to West Africa, with thousands of brass vessels being sent to individual trading stations. This trade demonstrates that brass production was now a major and increasingly international industry. The rise of the British brass industry dates from the end of the 17th century. Bristol was the first substantial centre and always specialized in sheet metalwork, including all manner of pots and pans. Much of the trade was for export.

Brass has been the predominant copper alloy for centuries' owing to its attractive appearance, relative cheapness and ease of working. Although for utilitarian purposes it has been largely replaced by enamelled iron or aluminium, it has continued to be used for sculpture and decorative items.

3. INDIAN SUBCONTINENT. Brasses have been found among the metalwork excavated at Taxila, in Pakistan, a city that rose to prominence as a trading centre in the last centuries of the 1st millennium BC, after Alexander's campaigns had opened up contact and commerce between the Mediterranean and the East. Many of the metal vessels found at Taxila are local brass copies of Greek types, whereas the originals would have been of bronze. From the Gupta period (4th–5th century AD) copper-alloy statuettes of deities etc. were produced in quantity in north India, and analysis has shown that these are almost all of brass. This tradition of image-making in brass continued all over north India and Tibet until the

mid-20th century; it still flourished in Nepal in the late 20th century. Brass is an important element in BIDRI WARE.

4. ISLAMIC WORLD. Tin is not available in the Islamic world, so copper alloys usually take the form of brass (though they are often described as bronze). Islamic metalwork is of two types: the cast metalwork that tends to be of brass, with *c.* 10% zinc and similar amounts of lead and a little tin, and the thinner pieces made from sheet brass that tend to have *c.* 20% zinc and only traces of other metals. The sheet metalwork was generally shaped by hammering, but by the 13th century some vessels were formed by spinning. Islamic brassware was often richly decorated by chasing, emphasized by bitumen, and inlaid with silver or, more rarely, with gold. From the 16th century brass became less popular for everyday use and was replaced by tinned copper.

P. T. Craddock, ed.: '2000 Years of Zinc and Brass', *BM Occasional Papers*, 1 (1990)

Brasses, monumental. Term used to denote any inscription, figure, shield of arms or other device engraved for a commemorative purpose in flat sheet brass. Such memorials became established in 13th-century Europe as a very satisfactory form of inlay for grave slabs in churches.

Brasses were manufactured almost exclusively in north-western and central Europe, although they were exported as far south as Madeira. This form of monument was initially patronized by the higher clergy, although very occasionally royalty chose to be so represented, as in the brass of *King Eric VI of Denmark and Queen Ingeborg* (1319) at Ringsted Cathedral. By the 14th century production was prolific, catering for all persons of high status and extending to merchants, minor officials, tradesmen and ultimately any person of means, leading in England and Flanders to the laying of numerous small memorials. Production fell on the Continent in the 16th century, but remained high in England until the 1630s.

The main centres of production were evidently Paris, Tournai, Ghent and London, with Cologne, Nuremberg and Breslau (now Wrocław, Poland) important for short periods. There was, moreover, much provincial work, evidence in Britain indicating the importance of Bury St Edmunds, Coventry, Norwich, York and probably Boston (Lincs). Immediate access to all raw materials was not necessary, most if not all the plate used in England being imported. Access to stone and to waterways facilitating transport was more important than access to metal.

The design of most brasses followed workshop patterns, and most can be studied as examples of series rather than individual works of art. The basis of the design was a representation of the deceased, but in its simplest form a brass consisted of an inscription, which was frequently complemented by a shield of arms or merchant mark or occasionally a rebus. Representations of full- or half-length figures were common, and in more elaborate examples the figures were framed by a canopy of honour, the whole bordered by an inscription. Evangelist symbols were commonly placed at the corners of the inscription, having a protective symbolism. In many large Flemish compositions and a few English ones, angels supported cushions behind the heads. Footrests took many forms, mainly lions and dogs, but heraldic or canting devices were frequently preferred. Flemish 14th-century canopies derived inspiration from the miniature architecture of metalworkers, with massed tabernacles and representations of saints, prophets and angels, while in Germany in the late 15th century and early 16th canopies took the form of entwined branches. Following the designs of incised and relief slabs, in 14th-century England cross compositions were adopted, showing a half- or full-length figure of the deceased in the expanded centre of a cross, latterly of octofoil form, the stem decorated with leaves and resting on a stepped base.

While the oldest surviving brasses are in Germany, at Augsburg (SS Ulrich und Afra; 1187), Verden (St Andreas; 1231) and Hildesheim Cathedral (1279), in the 13th century the French workshops seem to have been the most productive, although the brasses are recorded only in drawings. During the 14th century the most internationally sought-after brasses were the rectangular plate and separate inlay compositions of the Franco-Flemish school, of which Tournai was the main centre. The very stylized treatment and elaboration of canopy and background design are well illustrated on the brass of *Bishops Serken and Mul* in Lübeck Cathedral (1350). Yet the best London work was of very good quality, as shown by the *Camoys* and *Seymour* series, named after brasses of these families at St George, Trotton, W. Sussex (*c.* 1310) and St Mary, Higham Ferrers, Northants (1337), and standards remained high until the mid-15th century.

Widespread destruction in the mid-16th century had a marked effect on production in the European mainland and on the English provincial workshops; an interesting consequence was the common reuse of brasses by engraving on the reverse. The revival in Britain owed much to émigrés such as the Cure and Janssen families, and brass design complied with the new demands for realism and classical settings, the memorials becoming essentially secular in purpose. With such notable exceptions as the works of Edward Marshall at SS Peter and Paul, East Sutton, Kent (1629), and St Mary, Chigwell, Essex (1631), the quality of English brasses was deteriorating significantly at the time when renewed iconoclasm discouraged all but the very occasional production of memorial effigies. In continental Europe the decline was even more marked, and there are very few 17th-century brasses, some of which, as that of *Pedro de Valencia* at St Jacobskerk, Bruges, are engraved on the reverse of earlier memorials. The revival of brasses in Britain in the 19th century was inspired by the return to favour of Gothic art.

M. Stephenson: *A List of Monumental Brasses in the British Isles* (London, 1926, rev. 1938/*R* Ashford, 1964)

H. K. Cameron: *A List of Monumental Brasses on the Continent of Europe* (London, 1970, rev. 1973)
M. W. Norris: *Monumental Brasses: The Craft* (London, 1978)
M. W. Norris: *Monumental Brasses: The Memorials* (2 vols, London, 1978)
J. Bertram, ed.: *Monumental Brasses as Art and History* (Phoenix Mill, 1996)
W. Lack and P. Whittemore: *A Series of Monumental Brasses, Indents and Incised Slabs from the 13th to the 20th Century* (London, 2000)

Bratina. Type of Russian loving cup, typically a large rounded drinking bowl, often with two handles, used to pass a drink from person to person. Surviving medieval examples are ceramic or wood, but from the 16th century they were also made in silver and occasionally in gold. The main centre of production was Moscow.

Brattishing. Cresting of open-carved work on the top of a medieval screen or shrine

Break-front [broken front]. Piece of furniture, typically a cabinet or bookcase, in which the line of the front is broken by a curve or angle with the effect that the centre or central section protrudes slightly.

Brechtel, Hans Conraet (*b* 1608; *d* 1675). German silversmith, active in the Netherlands. Conraet trained as a silversmith in his native Nuremberg, and in 1640 moved to The Hague, where he become one of Holland's greatest exponents of embossed display silver. His surviving works include a silver layette basket designed to hold the linen of babies (1652; Dutch Royal Col.) and the so-called Coronation Cup of Frederik III of Denmark (1653, Copenhagen, Rosenborg Slot); this elaborately decorated gold cup may have been made for the planned (but unrealised) swearing of the oath of allegiance to Frederik III in Hamburg in 1654.

Breguet, Abraham-Louis (*b* 1747; *d* 1823). Swiss watch-maker. In 1762 Breguet left his native Neuchâtel for Paris, where he remained for the rest of

Bratina by Carl Fabergé, silver and enamel, 1905 (Moscow, Kremlin Museums)

his life except for a period in the early 1790s when he fled the Revolution to live in Switzerland and England. Breguet was the greatest innovator in the history of horology, and a long series of technical advancements made him the greatest exponent of the precision watch. His company, Breguet et Fils, continued to make watches and other precision instruments throughout the 19th and 20th centuries. In 1870 the company was taken over and split up, and the watch-making element was bought by the English watchmaker Edward Brown. In 1970 Brown's family sold the company, and after a series of changes in ownership it was bought in 1999 by the Swatch Group, which now manufactures mechanical Breguet watches (the brand has never been used for quartz watches) and maintains a Breguet museum.

Bréguet: Watchmakers Since 1775: The Life and Legacy of Abraham-Louis Breguet (1747–1823) (Paris, 1997)

Bretby Art Pottery. English pottery established in 1883 by Henry Tooth and William Ault; its formal name was H.Tooth & Co. Ltd. Tooth had recently left LINTHORPE ART POTTERY, where he had worked with CHRISTOPHER DRESSER, who continued to contribute designs to the Bretby pottery. The pottery was initially housed in Church Gresley, Derbys, but with a year it had moved to Woodville, Derbys, where it was to remain until it closed in 1996. In 1887 Ault moved to nearby Swadlincote and established the Ault Pottery. When Linthorpe closed in 1889, he acquired some of the moulds, and produced Dresser's designs until 1904, when Dresser died. The Ault pottery operated until 1919, when when it merged with the Ashby Potters' Guild.

M. D. Ash: *Bretby Art Pottery: A Collector's Guide* (Swadlincote, 2001)

Breuer, **Marcel (Lajos)** (*b* Pécs, 21 May 1902; *d* New York, 1 July 1981). American furniture designer and architect of Hungarian birth. He studied at the Bauhaus at Weimar, where he led the carpentry workshop in its endeavours to find radically innovative forms for modern furniture. In practice, this meant rejecting traditional forms, which were considered symbolic of bourgeois life. The results of these experiments were initially as idiosyncratic as those of other workshops at Weimar, including the adoption of non-Western forms (e.g. an African chair of 1921) and an aggressively castellated style inspired by Constructivism.

Breuer was impressed by De Stijl, whose founder Theo van Doesburg (1883–1931) made his presence felt in Weimar in 1921–2. Breuer interpreted the De Stijl aesthetic in his designs, which were characterized by asymmetry, discrete elements and a tendency to view the design of a chair, for example, as an architectural experiment. Gerrit Rietveld's Red–Blue chair (1917; New York, MOMA) taught Breuer to distinguish between the frame of a chair and the supports for the sitter. Encouraged by Walter Gropius to think in terms of standardization, he used ele-

Marcel Breuer: B32 side chair, chrome-plated tubular steel, wood and cane, 800×445×476 mm, 1931 (London, Victoria and Albert Museum)

ments of the same width to facilitate manufacture. From 1923 he also turned to less expensive woods such as plywood, particularly in his children's furniture. After a brief period working as an architect in Paris (1924), Breuer rejoined the Bauhaus in Dessau as leader of the carpentry workshop. By 1925 he insisted on the complete rejection of formalism: if an object was designed in such a way that it fulfilled its function clearly, it was finished. Suitability for a particular function was not, however, enough in itself; there was also the quality factor. Ornamentation was not necessary to form a coherent set of furniture: a good chair would go with a good table.

In spring 1925 Breuer began to experiment with tubular steel, beginning with his Wassily chair; next he developed a side chair with sled-like runners instead of legs. The following crucial stage was the cantilevered side chair; his best-known side chair is the B32 (1928; New York, MOMA) in chrome-plated steel, wood and cane, which is still mass-produced. He also produced tables in materials such as steel tube and wood. Breuer's chairs and the glass-topped tables that accompanied them were intended to be light, transparent and non-specific in function. Thus, for example, his small stacking stools could also be used as occasional tables. He also developed a range of modular furniture (cabinets, desktops, shelving) that could be assembled according to need (examples in New York, MOMA).

In 1933 Breuer won the International Aluminium Competition in Paris for aluminium furniture by exploiting the material's lightness and flexibility. In October 1935 he followed Gropius to England and on his suggestion designed a plywood version of his aluminium lounge chair for Jack Pritchard's Isokon Company. The Isokon long chair (1935; New York, MOMA), an early example of biomorphic design, was followed by plywood nesting tables and stacking chairs.

C. Wilk: *Marcel Breuer: Furniture and Interiors* (London, 1981)
M. Breuer and others: *Marcel Breuer: Design and Architecture* (Weil am Rhein, 2003)

Briati, **Giuseppe Lorenzo** (*b* 1686; *d* 1772). Italian glassmaker, active in Venice. In 1724 he became director of the school for glassmakers in Murano, and in 1739 he moved to Venice, where he established a glasshouse at the Carmine that continued to produce glass till 1808. He played an important role not only in the propagation but also often the actual invention of some types of glass products that enabled the Venetian factories to meet foreign competition. Briati was famous for his table centrepieces called *deseri* or *trionfi*, which were perfectly suited to the late 18th-century taste for rich and magnificent furnishings. These centrepieces adorned the banquets of doges and aristocrats on important ceremonial occasions. They were composed of numerous small pieces and represented miniature architectural complexes, gardens and fountains and were worked and decorated with *lattimo*, enamelling and coloured vitreous pastes. Briati was also famous for his chandeliers, called *ciocche*, in which the very slender metal armature was completely covered with glass branches set one within the other. These in turn were enriched with multicoloured floral bouquets, droplets and swags. The chinoiserie 'pagoda' type followed; one by Briati with dolphin-shaped arms from the mid-18th century is in the Museo Vetrario, Murano. His chandeliers provided a perfect complement to the luxurious furnishings of the aristocratic dwellings of the time (e.g. of *c.* 1740–50, Venice, Ca' Rezzonico).

Briati was also probably responsible for an innovation in the design of mirrors, which enabled Venice to overcome the fierce French competition: the frames were no longer made of wood but entirely of glass, composed of many small pieces in varied forms and colours (e.g. of mid-18th century; Murano, Mus. Vetrario). The competition, however, particularly from Bohemia and England, increased, and Murano was forced to adopt new 'imported' techniques and typologies. Briati experimented with a type of glass based on potassium, similar to Bohemian crystal.

R. Gallo: *Giuseppe Briati e l'arte del vetro a Murano nel XVIII secolo* (Venice, 1953)

Brickard [Brick], **Servatius** (*b* 1676; *d* 1742). German cabinetmaker. In 1705 he moved from his native Brabant to Bamberg, where he entered the service of the Prince-bishop Lothar Franz von Schönborn. In 1724 he became chief cabinetmaker in succession to Ferdinand Plitzner, and 1735 he was appointed 'court-cabinetmaker' (*Hofschreiner*). His surviving work includes the crucifixion altar (1720–30) and the choir stalls (completed 1730) in St Michael's Church in Bamberg. Several examples of his furniture are preserved at Schloss Weissenstein (Pommersfelden), notably a baroque writing desk (1727) richly decorated with marquetry.

Bride-lace. Piece of lace, sometimes of gold or silk, used to bind the sprigs of rosemary carried or worn at weddings in the 19th century.

Briggle, **Artus Van.** *See* VAN BRIGGLE, ARTUS.

Bright-cut. Form of engraving of precious metal, usually silver, popular in the late 18th century. The metal is cut away with a bevel to create glittering geometrical designs.

Brilliant. Lapidary term indicating a diamond that has been cut to achieve the highest degree of fire and brilliancy. The brilliant cut has 57 facets (or 58 if the base is cut with a culet): the crown has 33 facets consisting of a table (the large octagonal facet at the top), 8 triangular star facets, 8 quadrilateral facets (4 templets and 4 quoins), and 16 other triangular facets; the base (apart from the culet) has 24 facets consisting of 8 pentagonal facets (4 pavilion facets and 4 quoins) and 16 triangular facets. The American brilliant has a smaller table but more facets around it, giving 66 facets in all, including table and culet. The French brilliant consists of two truncated pyramids placed base to base.

In the vocabulary of glass, a brilliant cut is a design produced on flat glass with abrasive and polishing wheels.

Brin. Single filament of raw silk fibre as spun by the silk-worm; two brins bonded together by sericin form the bave.

Briosco, **Andrea**. *See* RICCIO, ANDREA.

Briot, **François** (*b* Damblain, Lorraine, *c.* 1550; *d* ?Montbéliard, *c.* 1612). French metalworker and medallist. He was born of Huguenot parents and moved in 1579 to Montbéliard (Mömpelgard), then in Germany, to escape religious persecution. In 1585 he was appointed Graveur de son Excellence to Duke Frederick I of Württemburg-Mömpelgard (*d* 1608) and specialized in cutting dies for coins and medals. Briot is best known for his fine pewter vessels decorated in relief with densely packed Mannerist ornament (e.g. ewer, *c.* 1600; Paris, Louvre). Because of the softness of the metal these would not have been suitable for practical use and were intended as a cheap, decorative substitute for fine plate. The Temperantia dish (so-called from its ornament, *c.* 1585; Dresden, Mus. Ksthandwerk) and accompanying ewer are in the same style as gold-smiths' work of the Fontainebleau school. His vessels were widely imitated, especially by the Nuremberg pewterer Caspar Enderlein and in ceramics by Bernard Palissy.

H. Demiani: *François Briot, Caspar Enderlein* (Leipzig, 1897)

Briot, **Nicolas** (*b* Damblein in Bassigny, duchy of Bar, France, 1579; *d* London, Dec 1646). French medallist, also active in England and Scotland. Between 1606 and 1625 he was engraver-general at the Paris mint, whereupon his mechanized system of coin production failed, forcing him to flee to London. He was appointed engraver at the Royal Mint in 1634, and the following year became Master of the Scottish Mint.

Briot was responsible for the coronation medal of *Louis XIII* (1610; e.g. London, BM), whose portrait is probably from a wax by Guillaume Dupré (*c.* 1574–1642), and a series of small, jetton-like struck medals made to commemorate events in England during the reign of Charles I. His other medals include a large cast medal of the King's physician *Theodore de Mayerne* (1625; e.g. London, BM), the well-known *Dominion of the Seas* (*c.* 1630; e.g. London, BM), a highly detailed view of London on his struck medal celebrating Charles I's return to London in 1633 (e.g. London, BM), the Prince of Wales (1638) and Peace or War (1643).

ODNB
M. Jones: *A Catalogue of French Medals in the British Museum*, 2 (London, 1988), pp. 143–76

Bristol. English city and seaport, the county town of Avon.

1. Ceramics. 2. Glass. 3. Metalwork.

1. CERAMICS. A number of potteries were producing tin-glazed earthenware in the English seaport of Bristol from *c.* 1650 until the late 18th century. The principal potters were Richard Frank and Joseph Flower. Tableware dominated production, in particular blue-dash chargers, which were decorated in maiolica colours with portraits of notables, including Charles II and William III. Chinoiserie decoration dominated from *c.* 1720, and wares included punch-bowls and posset-pots. From 1755 wares were often decorated with *bianco-sopra-bianco*. By 1770 the production of tin-glazed earthenware had virtually ceased; it was superseded by cream-coloured earthenware. Towards the mid-18th century a tin-glazed earthenware factory was started at Wincanton (Somerset), south of Bristol; its products are difficult to distinguish from those made in Bristol.

Soft-paste porcelain was made in Bristol (1749–52) by Benjamin Lund, who used soapstone (steatite) from the Lizard, Cornwall, and employed a formula he developed with William Cookworthy. Wares produced included cream jugs and sauceboats decorated with chinoiseries in underglaze blue or polychrome enamels. Dr Wall's Worcester Porcelain Factory ac-quired Lund's establishment in 1752. Cookworthy was a chemist who worked in Plymouth and introduced hard-paste porcelain to Bristol. About 1768 he obtained a patent to exploit the kaolin (china clay) deposits in Cornwall. In the same year he founded the porcelain factory at Plymouth, which in 1770 he transferred to Bristol. The production concentrated on everyday utilitarian wares, and the decoration shows influences from the porcelain factories of Sèvres and Derby. In 1774 Cookworthy's patent was taken over by Richard Champion (1743–91). Fine, elaborately decorated, armorial dinner services, vases and figure groups were produced under Champion's direction, and later he became the proprietor. Pierre Stephan was a modeller at Derby (1770–73) and then became an independent modeller at Bristol. In 1780, after financial difficulties, the factory was forced to close, and the patent was sold to the New Hall Factory in Shelton, Staffs.

R. K. Henrywood: *Bristol Potters, 1775–1906* (Bristol, 1992)

2. GLASS. The first recorded glasshouse in Bristol was established *c.* 1651 by a branch of the Dagnia family from Italy, who were brought to England *c.* 1630 by Robert Mansell (1573–1656). Some members later moved to Newcastle upon Tyne to establish a glasshouse. The earliest production was dominated by window glass and bottles. However, during the 1760s Bristol became a centre for high-quality, enamelled wine-glasses with opaque-twist stems. These glasses, with waisted bucket-bowls, often recorded the privateers based at Bristol during the Seven Years War and are decorated with diamond- and wheel-engraved ships.

Bristol is especially noted for its opaque white glass, said to have been first made *c.* 1757 at the Redcliff Backs Glasshouse. It was made to emulate porcelain and was often decorated with chinoiseries by Michael Edkins (1734–1811). In 1785 Edkins was employed by Lazarus Jacobs (*d* 1796) at the Temple Street Glasshouse as a gilder and enameller. In 1788 the Nailsea Glasshouse was established about seven miles outside Bristol by John Robert Lucas (1754–1828) with William Chance. At first it made crown glass for windows and then sheet glass and bottles; later it made cheap domestic wares such as jugs, vases, friggers (objects such as rolling-pins and tobacco pipes) and bowls in various shades of green, flecked with red and white glass. In 1805 Lazarus Jacobs's son, Isaac Jacobs (*fl* 1790–1835), set up the Non-Such Flint Glassworks, where he decorated blue-glass wine coolers, decanters and finger bowls with gilt, key-fret borders.

K. Vincent: *Nailsea Glass* (Newton Abbot, 1974)
C. Witt, C. Weedon and A. Palmer Schwind: *Bristol Glass*, Bristol, Mus. & A.G. (Bristol, 1984)

3. METALWORK. The manufacture of pewter in Bristol began in the 15th century and reached its peak in the late 17th century and early 18th, with pewterers such as Richard Going (*fl* 1715; *d* 1764). His shop is portrayed in an oil painting in the City of Bristol Museum and Art Gallery. The success of

pewter was based on local demand as well as on exports and depended on the supply of tin from Cornwall. In the 17th century there were between 30 and 60 pewterers in Bristol, more than in any other English city except London. Most Bristol pewterers concentrated on flat or sadware. A good collection of plates, including some by the Edgar family who traded *c.* 1776–1852, are housed at Blaise Castle House Museum, Bristol. Large quantities of pewter were exported to the USA in the late 18th century and early 19th, but as elsewhere, the industry was in decline after 1830.

The availability of copper from Cornwall, calamine (zinc carbonate) from the Mendip Hills, Somerset, and the abundance of coal from the Forest of Dean, Glos, and Radstock, Avon, led to the establishment of the first brass manufacturing works in the area of Bristol *c.* 1700. The Bristol Brass Wire Co. was also established in 1702. Until 1770 there was large-scale development of brassmaking, and the manufacture of finished brass goods increased in the valley of the Avon and those of its tributaries. The first brass mills were in Keynsham, Avon, and these were followed by others along the valleys. In 1729, for example, there were 36 furnaces operating in the area. The works in Warmley, Avon, were opened in 1741, and soon after 17 copper furnaces, 12 brass-making furnaces and 4 calamine zinc furnaces were operating, employing over 800 men at the peak of production. The gradual development of Birmingham as a centre of brassworking, however, led to a decline in the importance of Bristol, and after 1800 the industry there was of relatively little importance.

J. Day: *Brass in Bristol: A History of the Industry* (London, 1973)

Britannia metal. *See under* PEWTER, §1.

Britton, Alison (*b* Harrow, Middx, 4 May 1948). English potter, teacher and writer. She began her career decorating tiles. Her first solo exhibition was at the Amalgam Gallery, London, in 1976. In 1979 the Crafts Council, London, held an important show of her colourfully glazed and painted jugs, decorated with naive, figural motifs. The jugs gained her fast recognition and with hindsight were regarded as a breakthrough for British ceramics. Her pots were not thrown on a wheel, but rather hand-built from slabs of earthenware that were rolled flat, painted and then cut and used to construct asymmetrical vessels. The early naive motifs of 1976 to 1979 (jugs, 1978; London, V&A) gave way in the 1980s to abstract patterns, and her forms became tougher and more complex (green vessels set, 1983; London, V&A). The surfaces of her pots seem not so much to be glazed as painted in a modernist idiom. The angular planes of her pottery are sometimes architectural, consisting of overhanging upper and lower storeys; she has also made large, headless, ceramic torsos.

The Work of Alison Britton (exh. cat. by J. Houston and others, London, Crafts Council Gal., 1979)

P. Dormer and D. Cripps: *Alison Britton in the Studio* (London, 1985)

P. Dormer, A. Britton and D. Cripps: *Alison Britton: A View* (London, 1985)

T. Harrod: *Alison Britton: Ceramics in Studio* (London and Aberystwyth, 1990)

L. Sandino and A. Britton: *Complexity and Ambiguity: The Ceramics of Alison Britton* (London, 2000)

Broadcloth [broad cloth]. Plain, dressed, double-width, black woollen cloth, used chiefly for hangings and men's clothing; in early modern usage the term implied width, but subsequently it has been used loosely to denote a densely woven woollen cloth.

Broad glass. Window glass, or flat glass made by the 'broad' method whereby glass is blown into a cylinder and then reheated so that it can be flattened.

Brocade. Woven fabric with a pattern of raised figures; in early modern English, the Spanish form '*brocado*' is sometimes used. In appearance brocade resembles embroidery, but the techniques are wholly distinct: embroidery is added to the cloth ground, whereas brocade is made during the weaving process. A brocaded weft is one that is introduced only for the width of its motif; for example, if a daisy has a yellow centre, a yellow thread is carried on a small brocading shuttle from side to side of this centre and no farther. Before the use of the Jacquard loom a brocade was a draw-loom-woven textile, the entire pattern of which depended on brocaded wefts. These might float on the surface or be bound by a binding warp to give the designer greater freedom to use larger areas of colour. Because the weft travels only the width of its motif, the textile is very light. The favourite English dress-silk of the mid-18th century was a brocaded lutestring, which had a ground of lightweight taffeta specially treated to produce an extra gloss, with a brocaded pattern of naturalistic flowers on the front and very little wasted silk on the back. As the weaver had to insert the appropriate shuttle individually for each motif in every line, weaving a brocade was very slow work. The term became meaningless after the introduction of the Jacquard loom, when brocading became not impossible but uneconomic as the speed of the Jacquard would have been lost had the weaver stopped to brocade instead of passing the shuttle from selvage to selvage.

Brocard, Philippe-Joseph (*d* 1896). French glassmaker. In the 1850s Brocard began to study the Islamic tradition of glass-making and to experiment with Islamic decorative techniques, such as staining and enamelling. He made reproduction 14th- and 15th-century Syrian glass which he first exhibited at the 1867 *Exposition Universelle*. Brocard could not read Arabic, but nonetheless used Arabic calligraphy to decorate his glassware; he sold to Europeans to whom the numerous errors in the Arabic were not apparent. Some of his best-known designs were based on mosque lamps in the Musée de Cluny, Paris.

'Butterfly' brocatelle furnishing fabric, silk, designed by E. W. Godwin and made by Warner, Sillett & Ramm, *c.* 1874 (London, Victoria and Albert Museum)

Brocatelle. Lampas-woven imitation of brocade, usually made of silk or wool, used for tapestry, upholstery and women's clothing.

Brocatello. Type of variegated marble, clouded and veined white, grey, yellow and red. Brocatello has long been quarried near Siena, and in the 18th century was often used for table tops.

Broché [Fr. b*rocher*: 'to stitch']. In needlework, *broché* work is a type of embroidery which follows patterns woven into the ground, as in damasks and fabrics for furnishing. In bookbinding a broché book is one that is stitched but not bound.

Broderie anglaise. Type of whitework embroidery characterized by patterns of small holes edged with buttonhole stitches, used from the 18th century for making dresses.

J. Kliot and K. Kliot: *Cutwork, Hebedo & Broderie Anglaise* (Berkeley, CA, 1992)

Broncit. In glassware, a type of black geometrical decoration first used by Josef Hoffmann in 1914 for a glass service and later manufactured by the glass decorators J. & L. Lobmeyr of Vienna.

Brongniart, Alexandre-Théodore (*b* Paris, 15 Feb 1739; *d* Paris, 6 June 1813). French architect. His distinguished career as an architect was arrested by the Revolution. In 1800 he turned to designing porcelain and furniture. He was employed by the Sèvres

porcelain factory and designed the 'Table des Maréchaux' (1808; London, Buckingham Pal., Royal Col.), made for Napoleon (*reg* 1804–14).

J. Silvestre de Sacy: *Alexandre-Théodore Brongniart, 1739–181: Sa vie, son oeuvre* (Paris, 1940)
D. E. Ostergard, ed.: *The Sèvres Porcelain Manufactory: Alexandre Brongniart and the Triumph of Art and Industry, 1800–1847* (New Haven and London, 1997)

Bronze. Alloy of copper and tin. In the West bronze was largely superseded by BRASS, the alloy of copper and zinc, by the 5th century AD; many brass artworks, however, are commonly described as 'bronze'. In early times most languages had just one term for copper and copper alloys, thus for example the Chinese had the word *tang*, the Tibetans *li*, the Greeks *khalkos* and the Romans *aes*. The equivalent Anglo-Saxon general term was 'brass', and up to the 17th century this simply meant copper or one of its alloys. In late medieval Italy the term *bronzo* came into use to denote the copper alloys used in the ancient world. In particular, it was applied to the corroded, copper-base metals of the antiquities that were being dug up in Italy. These had an attractive patina, which was held to be due to some lost alloy. Much of this Classical metalwork was of copper alloyed with tin, whereas in Renaissance Italy copper alloyed with zinc was prevalent. Thus, the quite accidental association of bronze with patinated metal and of brass with a bright, clean finish was established.

By the time the word 'bronze' entered the English language, sometime in the late 17th century or the early 18th, it was associated with decorative or art metalwork, especially ancient metalwork and thus, by implication, with copper–tin alloys, while the term 'brass' continued to be used for everyday metalwork, which tended to be of copper and zinc. However, as late as the mid-18th century Samuel Johnson still regarded the two words as synonymous when he compiled his *Dictionary*. Only in the 19th century did engineers and metallurgists (and the *Oxford English Dictionary*) specify that bronze was an alloy of copper and tin, and brass an alloy of copper and zinc. Popular usage, however, continued to apply the terms quite loosely.

Brooks, Hervey (*b c.*1779; *d c.*1864). American potter who made red earthenware domestic wares in Goshen, CT, for 72 years. There is little documentary evidence of the activities of most American potters of the period, but Brooks is an exception. The extensive records, together with the archaeological excavation of the site of his pottery, has meant that he is the best understood American potter of the 19th century. His workshop is now a working exhibition in Old Sturbridge Village, where a replica of his kiln was built in 1979.

Brooks, John (*b* Dublin, *c.* 1710; *d* Chester, after 1756). Irish mezzotint engraver, active also in En-

Alexandre-Théodore Brongniart: salon in the Hôtel de Bourbon-Condé, Paris, late 18th century

gland. He learnt the technique of mezzotint engraving in London and on his return to Dublin opened a workshop with Andrew Miller (*d* 1763). Their workshop became the training ground for a group of Irish engravers who moved to London, where they influenced the development of mezzotints of Old Master and contemporary paintings. On returning to London in 1746 Brooks became a partner of the enamelling factory at York House, Battersea, where he worked until it closed in 1756; he claimed (possibly justly) to have invented the transfer-printing process, and attempted (unsuccessfully) to patent it for enamels and ceramics in Birmingham (1751), where he had a workshop, and London (1754 and 1755).

ODNB

E. Benton: 'John Brooks in Birmingham: The Bilston Enamellers', *Trans. Eng. Cer. Circ.*, vii/3 (1970), pp. 162–6

Brooks, Thomas (*b* 1811; *d* 1887). American furniture-maker based in New York. He was active from 1841, when he entered into a partnership, and was based in Brooklyn from the 1850s. The best-known examples of his furniture are a Gothic Revival armchair (*c.* 1847; New York, Met.) and an elaborately decorated cabinet (built to accommodate a set of Audubon's *Birds of America*) presented by the firemen of New York to the singer Jenny Lind on the occasion of her visit to the city (1850; New York, Mus. City NY).

Broome, Isaac (*b* 1836; *d* 1922). American sculptor, ceramic modeller and teacher of Canadian birth. He

trained at the Pennsylvania Academy of Fine Arts in Philadelphia. In 1854 he assisted Thomas Crawford with the statues on the pediment of the Senate wing of the US Capitol in Washington, DC, and tried unsuccessfully to establish a firm for architectural terracotta and garden ornaments in Pittsburgh and New York. From 1875 Broome was employed as a modeller by the firm of OTT & BREWER in Trenton, NJ. The Parian porcelain sculpture he created for their display at the Centennial International Exhibition of 1876 in Philadelphia won him medals for ceramic arts. Thereafter he worked as a modeller for potters in Ohio and Trenton, including the Trent Tile Co. and the Providential Tile Co., producing major work as late as 1917, when he modelled a parian portrait bust of Walter Scott Lenox (Lawrenceville, NJ, Lenox Inc.).

Brosamer, Hans (*b* ?Fulda, *c.* 1500; *d* ?Erfurt, 1554 or after). German painter, draughtsman, engraver and woodcut designer. He worked in Fulda from *c.* 1520 to the mid-1540s, and thereafter in Erfurt, where he concentrated on making copper engravings and woodcuts, either as single prints or as book illustrations. He produced more than 30 copper engravings, in which he achieved a characteristic dense texture by using very closely hatched lines. He engraved Christian, mythological and Classical themes as well as a few genre scenes. Three plates that must have formed part of a larger set devoted to Old Testament subjects (then currently popular) are particularly successful: *Samson and Delilah*, *Samson Worshipping*

Idols and *Bathsheba Bathing* (all 1545); they are all the same size and have ambitious architectural backgrounds incorporating groups of figures, following Netherlandish models.

In contrast to the engravings, which have a certain unity of style, Brosamer's woodcuts present a more confused picture. Single prints are notably outnumbered by book illustrations, but of the many illustrations with the initials HB that appeared in Protestant works published in Frankfurt am Main, Wittenberg and Magdeburg, many must be the work of other artists, such as Hans Baldung. However, illustrations in Martin Luther's Bible, printed in Wittenberg (1550) by Hans Lufft (1495–1584), were the work of Hans Brosamer, some dated 1549 and 1550 (particularly those for the Old Testament, the epistles of St Paul and Revelation), as well as those for Luther's *Catechism* (1550), published by Weygand in Frankfurt am Main.

Brouwer, **Willem C(oenraad)** (*b* Leiden, 19 Oct 1877) *d* Zoeterwoude, 23 Oct 1933). Dutch potter and sculptor. He trained as a drawing teacher but took a particular interest in bookbinding, decorative woodcuts and household pottery. From the example of the Arts and Crafts Movement he learnt the value of traditional techniques and craftsmanship. In 1898 he settled in Gouda in order to perfect his technical knowledge of pottery-making. Three years later he started his own ceramics firm in Leiderdorp. His ceramics are characterized by their intentionally plain shapes, combined with mostly geometric linear ornament and frequently with sculptural decoration applied in low relief. Around 1907 Brouwer began to experiment with large-scale ceramic decoration. His terracotta ornaments and façade sculptures were greatly admired by contemporary architects, who secured him important commissions in this field, for example the Vredespaleis in The Hague, the Scheepvaarthuis in Rotterdam, and the railway stations at Maastricht and Zandvoort. His architectural sculptures survive in large numbers on buildings throughout the Netherlands.

Brown. English family of gem-engravers active in the export market to Russia. Nothing is known of the early training and apprenticeships of the brothers William Brown (1748–1825) and Charles Brown (1749–95), although their address in 1769 was that of the seal- and gem-engraver John Frewin. William exhibited at the Society of Arts from 1766 until 1770, when both brothers began to show annually at the Royal Academy, London (until 1785). William offered a large number of subjects from the Antique (e.g. *Head of Hygeia*, cornelian intaglio, before 1705; St Petersburg, Hermitage) and portraits of contemporaries, which were his forte; Charles rarely showed more than one gem at a time, among them the animal subjects for which he became famous (e.g. *Horse Frightened by Lion*, before 1782, after George Stubbs's painting; St Petersburg, Hermitage).

In 1786 the Brown brothers ceased to exhibit, having received the first of many lavish orders from the Russian court, which they supplied from London with almost 200 gems during the lifetime of Catherine II, Empress of Russia. Although their total output was large, amounting to perhaps twice that number, their work for other patrons has been dispersed, while their work sent to Russia has been preserved in the collections of the Hermitage Museum, St Petersburg. Among these gems, the many-figured intaglio scenes from Classical mythology, some depicting figures in violent movement (e.g. *Rape of Proserpina*, before 1794), others in Classical repose, show a remarkable mastery in composition and the recession of planes, while the most delicate engraving is shown in such jugate busts as *Mars and Bellona* (before 1785, signed C. BROWN, INVT) or William's *Muse of Tragedy* (before 1772). Their Russian commissions were only briefly interrupted by a successful excursion to the court of Louis XVI (*reg* 1774–92) in 1788, from which they returned to London the following year. In subsequent years they worked in the new genre of historical allegory, perhaps inspired by the intaglios of Jacques Guay (1711–97) in France: such commissions as the large cameo medallions *Catherine II Crowning Potemkin* (1789) and the *Allegory of the Victory of Russia over Turkey* (before 1794) are allegories of contemporary Russian history. Many of their gems are signed BROWN and may have been worked in collaboration. Their last joint production for Catherine before Charles's early death in 1795 was a comprehensive cameo series of the *Kings of England*, followed by the early numbers of the *Kings of France*, which show a considerable decline in quality. Thereafter William occasionally exhibited at the Royal Academy, showing portraits of such contemporaries as *Sir Walter Scott* and *George Gordon, 6th Baron Byron* (both untraced) and especially of 'political characters', which he advertised in the *Monthly Magazine* (no. 185, 1809). A cameo portrait of *George III* is in the British Museum, London.

Bruges. Belgian centre of tapestry production. Tapestries have been woven in the town of Bruges since at least 1302, but there are no extant examples of 14th- or 15th-century Bruges tapestries. By the beginning of the 16th century a series depicting the *Life of St Anatolius* (1502–6; Paris, Louvre) had been woven for the church in Salins in the Franche-Comté. At about the same time pieces depicting coats of arms with intertwining branches filled with flowers and leaves and a distinctive border were also being produced. The principal motif was a blazon surrounded by a laurel wreath. In Bruges grotesque tapestries, large-leaved *verdures* and pieces with historical and religious scenes were all produced. The *Story of Gombaut and Macée*, a series that was produced several times *c.* 1600, showed links with the past. In a landscape filled with flowers, shrubbery and birds, scenes from pastoral life were portrayed. The exceptional success of this series was due to more than the ribald verses written on the tapestry.

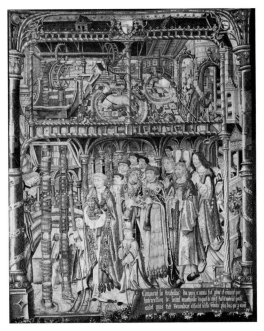

Jean Sauvage: *Tapestry de St Anatoile de Salins*, detail of the miracle of the water, linen and silk, atelier de Jean Sauvage, Bruges, 1501–6 (Paris, Musée du Louvre)

During the 17th century, and possibly as late as the early 18th, many tapestries were produced, some in local monastic workshops, others in private workshops. Some of the best work was of a quality equal to that of Brussels, but it could not compete with the enormous output of Oudenaarde. The range of subjects displayed in Bruges tapestries at this time is almost equal to that of the major tapestry centres, although the cartoons that were used did not always reflect contemporary artistic developments and would have been considered outdated in other cities. The charmingly coloured borders are noticeably less crowded than tapestries from other towns; in this way they could be completed more rapidly. Although very little is known of the cartoon painters who were active during this period, some can be identified: for example, Cornelis Schut I (1597–1655) painted the cartoons *c.* 1640 for a repeatedly utilized series of the *Seven Liberal Arts*, and Pauwels Ricx (*c.* 1610–68) may have contributed the designs for the *Story of Astrée*. Nevertheless, it is certain that the primary source for Bruges tapestry designs was—with a few alterations—drawings and engravings after masters from Antwerp and elsewhere. The Bruges workshops also made use of cartoons from the preceding century, including the Renaissance cartoons by Lukas van Nevele (*fl* 1548–65) of the *Months of Luke*; these were altered only slightly, betraying the advent of the Baroque style.

J. Versyp: *De geschiedenis van de tapijkunst te Brugge* (Brussels, 1954)
G. Delmarcel and E. Duverger: *Bruges et la tapisserie* (Bruges, 1987)

Brûle parfum. French term, sometimes used in English, for a CASSOLETTE.

Brunetto, Tomás (*b* ?Turin; *d* Rato, 1771). Portuguese potter of Italian birth. In 1767 he left his native Turin (where he probably had some experience of maiolica manufacture) for Lisbon, where he became the first director of the REAL FÁBRICA DO RATO. Under his direction shapes and patterns were based on Italian prototypes, especially those from the factories in Turin and SAVONA. Production included polychrome table services, tureens in the form of animals, birds, vases, figures and fish tanks supported by dolphins (e.g. of 1767–71; Barnard Castle, Bowes Mus.).

Brunswick [Ger. Braunschweig]. German centre of faience production. The first faience factory in Brunswick was founded in 1707 by Anton Ulrich, Duke of Brunswick-Wolfenbüttel, and directed by Johann Philipp Frantz. Output was extensive and varied, and at first mainly blue-and-white faience, imitative of Delftware, was produced. The large, rather clumsy figures and ewers bearing the ducal monogram are particularly striking. In 1749 the factory was taken over by Johann Erich Behling and Ernst Heinrich Reichard (*d* 1764). The famous vases and jugs with moulded Rococo decoration painted with bright, high-temperature colours date from this period. In 1776 the factory was bought by Johann Benjamin Heinrich Rabe (*d* 1803) who directed it until his death; the factory closed four years later. The second faience factory was founded in 1747 by Rudolf Anton Chely (*d* 1770) and his sons. Large items such as vases, tureens and figures, which were based on designs by Christoph Rudolf Chely, were a speciality. The factory closed in 1757.

G. Spies: *Braunschweiger Fayencen* (Brunswick, 1971)

Brussel, Jan van. *See* ROOME, JAN VAN.

Brussels [Flem. Brussel; Fr. Bruxelles]. Capital city and administrative region of Belgium. It is situated in the centre of the country, in the former duchy of Brabant.

1. Ceramics. 2. Lace. 3. Tapestry.

1. CERAMICS. In 1705 Corneille Mombaers (*d* 1729) obtained a monopoly for the manufacture of faience and with Thierry Witsenburg (*fl* 1705) established a faience factory in Brussels, which manufactured wares for daily use. In 1724 the business was taken over by Mombaers's son, Philippe Mombaers (1693–1754), who made the concern very successful. In 1754 Philippe Mombaers's son-in-law, Jacques Artoisenet (1719/20–65), also established a factory despite Mombaers's monopoly. The two factories produced similar wares, including such decorative items as tureens in the shape of ducks, fish or vegetables. The factories that most influenced Brussels were Strasbourg and Saint-Amand-les-Eaux, although other centres of production were also inspirational: for example the blue *style rayonnant* was

derived from wares from Rouen, while chinoiserie decoration was taken from wares from Sinceny, near Laon. Decoration unique to Brussels consists of dominant green lines, bright-yellow butterflies and snails. This decorative faience, however, did not resist competition from *faience fine* (lead-glazed pottery) and porcelain. By the end of the 18th century production concentrated solely on everyday wares.

Porcelain was produced in Brussels at the end of the 18th century. The factory of Montplaisir (1786–90) in the Schaerbeek district of Brussels produced wares decorated with sprays of small flowers or landscapes in green. The factory in the Etterbeek district (1787–1803) was established by Chrétien Kühne (*c.* 1744–*c.* 1815). Wares included tablewares decorated with polychrome flowers and chinoiseries.

At the beginning of the 19th century many workshops for decoration were established. Painters such as Louis Cretté (*c.* 1758–1813) ordered pieces of plain white porcelain from Paris, which were then painted with scattered flowers, exotic birds, landscapes and chinoiseries. In 1824 Frédéric Théodore Faber (1782–1844) set up a factory with the sculptor Charles-Christophe Windisch (*d* 1842) in Ixelles, which from 1830 was run by Faber's son Henri Faber (*b* 1808); it was purchased by Jean-Baptiste Cappellemans the elder (1766–1841) in 1849, but closed down in 1870. The factory's most successful wares were those decorated with views of Brussels and genre scenes embellished with gold. In 1833 Windisch set up another factory in Ixelles. He produced white porcelain, which was sometimes gilded, and wares included openwork baskets carried by figures of winged women. Subsequently, a decorative workshop was added. From 1852 to 1901 the factory was managed by the Vermeren-Coché family and until 1959 by their descendants, the Demeuldre-Coché family. Traditional wares were produced but adapted to the various styles in vogue. Decoration included flowers, landscapes, birds and sometimes mythological scenes.

G. Dansaert: *Les Anciennes Faïences de Bruxelles* (Brussels, 1922/*R* 1979)
M. Pinckaers: *La Porcelaine de Bruxelles, 1767–1953* (Brussels, 1984)

2. LACE. By the second half of the 16th century cutwork, needle lace and bobbin laces were being produced in Brussels, and there were already such competent lace merchants as Jacqueline Masqueliers (*fl c.* 1563–87), who supplied the firm of Plantin in Antwerp between 1563 and 1587. At this time Brussels-made laces were being exported to Paris and elsewhere, and in the 17th century exports grew so phenomenally that many countries tried to prohibit them for economic reasons; when France banned Flemish lace in 1662, Brussels lace was sold as point d'Angleterre. Brussels dominated this rapid expansion, early demonstrating its ability to adapt to changing fashions by innovation with the introduction of the flexible part-lace technique, first mentioned in 1646. Bobbin lace now became all-important, although needle lace continued to be made. In

the 17th century Brussels largely followed the practice of the workshops in Venice and then France in design. Leading manufacturers and designers were the Gandussis, father and son, but in the 18th century Brussels had plenty of good designers. Its numerous rich lace merchants now enjoyed considerable standing. The firm of Godefroy-Durondeau supplied the imperial court in Vienna and agents in such cities as Paris, Hamburg and London with all the classic bobbin laces, all made in Brussels, and exquisite, expensive needle lace. The Brussels industry was rescued from the collapse following the French Revolution by Napoleon Bonaparte (*reg* 1804–14), who made several visits there, placing large orders.

Much of the handmade lace now sold in Brussels is made in China, but the city plays a leading role in the development of lace as an art form, with its Atelier du XXe Siècle and the International Lace Biennials staged since 1983.

A. I. Blanco and A. M. Isasi-Díaz: *Brussels Lacemaking* (Jacksonville, 1985)

3. TAPESTRY. The tapestry industry in Brussels may well have begun in the 13th century, and the names of many weavers are known from the 14th and 15th centuries, but the earliest surviving tapestries date from the late 15th century. The *Story of Herkinbald* tapestry (Berne, Hist. Mus.) was produced between 1450 and 1460; this was based on the four *Scenes of Justice* panels (*c.* 1439–50; destr. 1695) by Rogier van der Weyden (*c.* 1399–1464) and was originally in the Hôtel de Ville in Brussels. The composition of the *Adoration of the Magi* (Berne, Hist. Mus.) also recalls the work of van der Weyden. The large *Passion* tapestry (Brussels, Musées Royaux A. & Hist.) was probably made in the workshop of Gillis van de Putte (*fl* 1477). The *millefleur* tapestries showing the arms of Philip the Good and Charles the Bold (*c.* 1466; Berne, Hist. Mus.) were woven by Jan de Haze (*fl* 1465–72), the head of a fairly large Brussels workshop and also a well-known dealer.

After 1480 Brussels became the principal centre of the tapestry industry in Brabant. It maintained its position until the end of the 18th century, largely due to its favourable situation, an abundance of skilled workers and the activity in the area of painting and other branches of the arts. Production between 1480 and 1490 is stylistically close to that of the sculpted retables of the period. The tapestries are neatly and regularly woven, and progress is evident in the attempts to reproduce certain details and to portray people realistically. Typical examples of this work include the *Allegory of the Blessed Virgin as a Fount of Living Water* and the *Angel's Annunciation to Mary* (both Paris, Louvre). The cartoons for these tapestries are attributed respectively to the Master of the Embroidered Foliage (*fl c.* 1495–1500) and the Master of the Redemption of the Prado. The arrangement of the figures within the frame of a retable makes a somewhat illogical impression. Flowers fill the foreground of the compositions. Towards the end of the 15th century there was a reaction against the pictorial trend in tapestry, which was replaced by a monumental style that prevailed until the introduction of Romanism in Brussels. The first group in this new style includes many woven patterns. In a *Mass of St Gregory* (1495; Nuremberg, Ger. Nmus.), which carries the arms of Franz Holzschuher of Nuremberg, a pattern appears on the floor, on the altar and in the clothing of the figures. Around the tapestry there is also a narrow border with representations of precious gemstones. The second group comprises the so-called 'golden' tapestries, in which considerable amounts of gold and silver thread were used (e.g. *Coronation of the Virgin*, *c.* 1502; Madrid, Pal. Real). The third group includes a series of wall hangings that are associated with JAN VAN ROOME. Among this group is a piece with the *Story of Herkinbald* (early 16th century; Brussels, Musées Royaux A. & Hist.), which was designed after work by this master. It was ordered in 1513 by the Brotherhood of the Blessed Sacrament and woven in the workshop of Léon de Smet, recorded as a citizen of Brussels in 1490. The border is decorated with flowers, bunches of grapes and the symbols of the Blessed Sacrament. The composition is relatively shallow and is more decorative than earlier works. The figures are unusually stately in their long and luxurious drapes, with deeply sculpted folds. The various scenes in the tapestry are separated by pillars. Another tapestry that belongs to this group portrays the *Finding of the Cross* (Brussels, Musées Royaux A. & Hist.): the threshold of one of the buildings bears the word *Knoest*, the name of the cartoonist who designed the tapestry, Leonard Knoest, who came to Brussels from Cologne in 1501. All of these tapestries still have a distinctive style and are not so-called 'paintings' in wool and silk, as is the fourth tapestry from the series, the *Legend of Our Lady of Zavel* (Brussels, Musées Royaux A. & Hist.). The composition of this piece is conceived as a triptych and is close to the style of contemporary panel painting. The design is ascribed to Bernard van Orley and appears to date from *c.* 1517.

At the beginning of the 16th century, however, there were some instances of serious negligence in tapestry production. The first to react was the City Board of Magistrates, which executed an ordinance in 1528 requiring the addition of the city mark to all tapestries of six square ells (685.8 sq. mm) or more. The mark consisted of two BS (one for Brussels and one for Brabant), surrounding a small red shield. After this, the central government published the imperial ordinance of 1544, which among other things required that all large and expensive tapestries must be signed with the city and the weaver's marks.

Orders for tapestries after cartoons by Italian painters helped to establish a new tapestry style. Between 1513 and 1515 Pope Leo X commissioned Raphael to paint a series of cartoons of the *Acts of the Apostles* (London, V&A). These cartoons, which broke completely with the Flemish tradition, give a good idea of the new trend in painting. Artists now tried to achieve more depth and perspective in their compositions by exploiting large empty spaces and expansive skies. The clothing of the figures was no longer patterned, and the borders featured a series of allegorical figures or scenes related to the life of the patron instead of the earlier decoration of flowers and foliage. It would, however, have been impossible to copy these cartoons exactly; they were conceived as frescoes and went completely against the Flemish style, making them somewhat unsuitable for tapestry work. The tapestry-maker Pieter van Aelst, who received the commission to weave the tapestries (Rome, Pin. Vaticana) from these cartoons, was an experienced craftsman and managed to circumvent all the difficulties he encountered. He tried to make the entire composition richer, filling the foreground and background with foliage and decorating the cloak of Christ with golden suns. The series was immensely successful and was copied by various workshops throughout Europe until the late 18th century. The best copy (1562–70; Madrid, Pal. Real) was made in the workshop of Jan van Tieghen in Brussels.

Brussels cartoon painters also produced valuable work at this time. Bernard van Orley was the leading figure of Netherlandish Romanism in tapestry production. He broke new ground as a cartoon painter, and his inventive and good-quality designs were very influential. His broadly constructed compositions and sense of monumentality and his familiarity with the work of Raphael enabled him to usher in a new period of tapestry manufacture. He produced cartoons for the two *Passion* series (1520–28; Madrid, Pal. Real; Washington, DC, N.G.A.; Paris, Mus. Jacquemart-André; New York, Met.), the *Hunts of Maximilian* (1528–33; Paris, Louvre) and the *Story of Jacob* (Brussels, Musées Royaux A. & Hist.). The decorative borders are sensitively and successfully adapted for tapestry. Van Orley had several students, and such other artists as Lucas van Nevele, to whom the cartoons for the *Months of Lucas* are attributed, followed his example.

Another important cartoon painter was Pieter Coecke van Aelst (1502–50), who was active in Antwerp, but lived in Brussels towards the end of his life. Only three series can be definitely traced to his cartoons, the *Story of Joshua* (Vienna, Ksthist. Mus.), the *Life of St Paul* (e.g. Vienna, Ksthist. Mus.) and the suite portraying the *Seven Deadly Sins* (1560–75; examples in Vienna, Ksthist. Mus.; New York, Met.), although cartoons for the *Tobias* tapestries (Gaasbeek, Kasteel) are also ascribed to him. Coecke's work is more decorative, lively and brilliant than that of van Orley. His crowded scenes are filled with particularly tall, elegant figures with small feet. He also devoted considerable attention to the decoration of the borders, which included grotesques and strapwork.

The importance of Michiel Coxcie (1499–1592) as a cartoon painter is indisputable. He studied the Renaissance style in Rome, concentrating particularly on the work of Raphael. For some years Coxcie was the official cartoon painter for the city of Brussels.

Among the works credited to him are cartoons for the *Story of the First Human Beings* and the *Life of Noah* (Kraków, N. A. Cols). Although his compositions are very well balanced and he was a skilled master, he had little independence of style. The wonderful borders, filled with all sorts of animals, were very successful and were copied until the early 17th century.

The cartoons for the series the *Conquest of Tunis* (1545–54; Madrid, Patrm. N.) were commissioned from Jan Cornelisz Vermeyen (*c.* 1500–*c.* 1559) by Emperor Charles V. The tapestries are remarkable for their soft, yellow palette and borders filled with moresques. The cartoons for a series of the *Fables from Ovid* (Madrid, Pal. Real) and another depicting the *Story of Vertumnus and Pomona* (*c.* 1560; Madrid, Pal. Real) are also attributed to Vermeyen, partly because in both series the borders are decorated with moresques.

The painter Peeter de Kempeneer (*c.* 1503–*c.* 1580) was also an important tapestry designer. At first he lived and worked away from the tapestry industry, but was associated with a few tapestry-workers. He spent some time in Italy and settled in Spain in 1537. He returned in 1564 to Brussels, where he was appointed the official city cartoon painter. The ten cartoons for *SS Peter and Paul* (1556–67; five France, priv. col.; three Ghent, Oudhdknd. Mus. Bijloke), with the arms of the abbey of St Peter, Ghent, and of Abbot François d'Avroult, are attributed to him.

Little is known of the activities of the other cartoon painters of the second half of the 16th century. Nevertheless, there was a noticeable reaction during the last decade against earlier stylistic conceptions: the work became more involved, flatter and more monotonous, with a relatively high horizon. Artists appear to have wanted to return to concepts current *c.* 1500: there was a deliberate retreat from movement and depth in composition and little realism in the depiction of flora. A restricted and monotonous palette, very deep borders and indistinct decoration marked the low level of this work compared to that of the mid-16th century. These Brussels hangings were imitated in other centres, but the colouring was usually less rich and the weave frequently coarser and more cheaply executed.

The Brussels weavers were particularly important in the development of tapestries. Among the most important masters of the first half of the 16th century, in addition to Pieter van Aelst, were Pieter and Willem de Pannemaker, Gabriël van der Tommen (*fl* 1500–25), Frans Geubels (after 1520–before 1585) and Hendrik Tsas (*fl* 1550–1600). The second half of the century was dominated by Jan van Tieghen, Jacob Tseraerts (*c.* 1535–after 1592), Leo van den Hecke (*fl* 1575–1600), Maarten Reynbouts (*fl* 1576–1618) and Jacob Geubels (*d c.* 1605), the son of Frans, as well as the Leyniers family. Those who established tapestry-maker dynasties passed on their technical knowledge and artistic abilities from generation to generation. Their tapestries, however, were not sold from the factory but in the Antwerp Pant. The export of wall hangings abroad was an important part of the industry.

The designs of Peter Paul Rubens (1577–1640) resulted in a revolution in the art of tapestry-weaving, comparable to the one caused by Raphael's *Acts of the Apostles*. His cartoons for the *Story of Decius Mus* (1617–18), which had never been portrayed in tapestry, resulted in numerous orders. The first set of tapestries from these cartoons was made in Brussels for Francisco Cattaneo (*fl* 1600–50) of Genoa. The tapestries were surrounded by a border that was completely independent of the main tapestry. The assignment was a difficult one for weavers to realize: compositions on such a large scale, bursting with energy and blazing with colour. Subsidiary details were reduced to a minimum, and attention was focused on the enormous figures and their muscular bodies. In Rubens's cartoons for the *Story of Achilles* (1630–35; examples Brussels, Musées Royaux A. & Hist.; Boston, MA, Mus. F.A.) the border has lost its independent character and is closely related to the subject. There are herms to the left and right of the central scene, at the bottom, where they appear to stand not on but in front of a plinth, and at the top, where they are connected by a superstructure of putti and garlands, with a richly worked cartouche in the centre.

Rubens's style was spread by his students and followers, including Cornelis Schut (1597–1655), Theodoor van Thulden (1606–69), Justus van Egmont (1601–74) and Jan Boeckhorst (*c.* 1604–68), but a certain relaxation could already be seen in their work. They adapted more completely to the flatness of the tapestry, designing clear, easy compositions, dominated by concern for detail. Gradually the larger figures disappeared from the designs, resulting in a more harmonious composition. The heavy borders, inspired by architecture and sculpture, disappeared and were replaced by frames filled with flowers and plants. In the designs of Jan van den Hoecke (1611–51) for the *Months*, the *Seasons*, the *Four Elements* and the *Story of Zenobia* (1660; Madrid, Pal. Real), Rubens's pathos has been completely eliminated. The loving treatment of the abundant details and the sparkling depictions of flowers, fruits and putti prompt the classification of these designs as some of the most successful compositions for tapestry at this time.

A similar evolution can be seen in the tapestry designs of Jacob Jordaens (1593–1678). He was a highly gifted master with an interest in the decorative character of his art. Throughout his life, however, he was so overwhelmed with commissions that he freely used figure and groups from one series in another. Jordaens is thought to have started painting cartoons as early as 1620. The best and most familiar examples include the *Story of Odysseus* (*c.* 1630–35), the *Story of Alexander the Great* (*c.* 1630–35), *Scenes from Country Life* (*c.* 1635), the *Proverbs* (1644) and the *Riding School* (1645; Vienna, Ksthist. Mus.). His other designs include the series *Famous Women of Antiquity* and the *Story of Charlemagne* (1660s). The compositions are usually well balanced and well adapted to the typical style of tapestry work.

The painter David Teniers the elder (1582–1649) was also highly influential in the art of tapestry. Many thousands of tapestries were woven in Brussels, Oudenaarde, Lille, Beauvais and Aubusson, all of which were called *fins Teniers* or *Tenières*, featuring kermesses with rural people returning from the fields or market. It is not clear whether the cartoons for these pieces were painted by David Teniers or whether the scenes were merely inspired by his paintings. It is in any case certain that both he and his son, David Teniers the younger (1610–90), designed cartoons for allegorical scenes and armorial tapestries.

At the end of the 17th century the increasing influence of the Gobelins factory in Paris is noticeable, particularly in tapestries with mythological and historical scenes and, occasionally, religious scenes. An outstanding example is the beautiful series *Worship of the Gods* (1717; Ghent, Mus. S. Kst.), which came from the Brussels workshops of Urbaan Leyniers (1674–1747), Daniël Leyniers II (1669–1728) and Hendrik Reydams II (1650–1719). The cartoons were painted by the gifted Brussels master Jan van Orley (1665–1735), who took his inspiration not only from the work of Charles Le Brun but also from the designs of Antoine Coypel (1661–1722) and Charles-Antoine Coypel (1694–1752). The French influence is clear in the elegant, idealized figures, charmingly set in the composition, the rich foreground colouring and the delicate pastels of the background, as well as the virtuosic treatment of the light. The border is filled with foliage in the Louis XIV style and is actually an imitation of the frame of a painted picture. Similarly charming and fashionable figures, lively colours and landscapes constructed like theatrical sets can be seen in a *Story of Psyche* and a series on *Alexander* from the workshop of Jan-Frans van den Hecke (*fl c.* 1660–95), in the *Story of Achilles* signed by Jodocus de Vos and in a suite on the *Life of Christ* (Bruges, St Saviour's Church) from the workshop of Jaspar van der Borght (*fl* 1700–50). All of these works date from the late 17th century or the first half of the 18th and indicate how the Gobelins exercised a growing influence on Brussels tapestry work.

After 1750 decline was rapid, although Jacob van der Borght, son of Jaspar, was still active in Brussels. In 1785 he produced four rather unsuccessful tapestries on the *Legend of the Blessed Sacrament of Miracles* for St Michael's Church, Brussels. He was the last tapestry-maker of Brussels; when he died on 13 March 1794, his workshop was closed down and the contents offered for sale. This meant the end of a once-famous craft in the southern Netherlands. For more than three centuries the Brussels tapestry-weavers had produced work of high artistic quality and had played a leading role in other European countries. Not until the second half of the 19th century was there renewed interest in tapestry work, when workshops like those of Arthur Lambrecht in the Schaerbeek district of Brussels helped to revive an age-old branch of the arts.

A. Wauters: *Les Tapisseries bruxelloises* (Brussels, 1878)
E. A. Standen: *European Post-medieval Tapestries and Related Hangings in the Metropolitan Museum of Art*, 2 vols (New York, 1985)
P. Junquera de Vega and C. Herrero Carretero: *Cátalogo de tapices del Patrimonio nacional*, 2 vols (Madrid, 1986)
S. Cavallo: *Medieval Tapestries in the Metropolitan Museum of Art* (New York, 1993)
G. Delmarcel: *Flemish Tapestry* (New York, 1999)
T. P. Campbell: *Tapestry in the Renaissance: Art and Magnificence*, Metropolitan Museum of Art (New York and New Haven, 2000)

Brussels carpet. Type of carpet; *see under* CARPET, §I. 5.

Brustolon, Andrea (*b* Belluno, 20 July 1662; *d* Belluno, 25 Oct 1732). Italian sculptor and draughtsman. He worked almost exclusively in wood. In 1675 he may have executed a group of angels for the parish church of S Fermo, near Belluno; for the same church he sculpted the group of the *Four Evangelists* and the tabernacle of the high altar. In 1695 or 1696 he sculpted the *Custody of St Theodora* in Swiss pine for the Augustinian nuns of Feltre (Feltre, S Giacomo Maggiore), and ecclesiastical commissions in and around Belluno occupied him throughout the late 1690s.

In addition to these local commissions, Brustolon made elaborate furniture for Venetian patrician families, including the Pisani, the Correr and the Venier families. For the Pisani he made 12 large chairs in boxwood, incorporating symbols of the *Months* (Rome, Pal. Quirinale). The naturalistic plant forms that decorate these chairs are of a Baroque magnificence. Natural motifs also predominate in the Correr chairs and in the items of furniture, mainly pedestals, for the Venier family, which feature figures—grouped and single—representing the seasons or the elements, warriors and Ethiopian slaves, horses and marine creatures, and Hercules triumphing over the Hydra or Cerberus. The sprightly figures often showed a tendency to elongation that recalls the art of the Hellenistic era. These works (all Venice, Ca' Rezzonica) were made during a time of great creativity and imagination in Brustolon's career.

In 1715 Brustolon's reliquary of *St Innocent* (Hamburg, Mus. Kst & Gew.), carved in boxwood and ebony, was delivered to Polcenigo, Bishop of Feltre. In 1722 the artist was working on the altar of *Our Lady of Sorrows* for the church of Dosoledo di Comelico. In about 1724 he executed the tabernacle with caryatids and putti for the parish church of Cortina d'Ampezzo. Meanwhile, in 1723, he had signed the contract for the great wooden altarpiece of the *Death of St Francis Xavier* (Belluno, Mus. Civ.) for S Ignazio at Fasola di Belluno. This was commissioned from him by the noble Miari family and completed in 1728. It was the first of the magnificent wooden altarpieces executed during the last period of Brustolon's activity. For the same church he executed an altarpiece of the *Crucifixion* (1729; Belluno, Mus.

Andrea Brustolon: guéridon, boxwood and ebony, late 17th century (Venice, Ca' Rezzonico)

Civ.). During this period Brustolon continued to carve objects and furniture for private patrons. In 1727 he carved a series of mythological divinities with their accompanying pedestals (priv. col.) for the Piloni, an aristocratic Bellunese family. He continued to produce suites of furniture and had such a productive workshop that for many years dealers attributed to him any piece of furniture of 18th-century origin that happened to include carved figures.

G. Biasuz and M. G. Buttignon: *Andrea Brustolon* (Padua, 1969)
S. S. Jervis: 'From Abbotsford to Australia: A Set of "Brustolon" Chairs', *Burl. Mag.*, cxlvi (June 2004), pp. 400–04

Bruxelles, Jean de. *See* ROOME, JAN VAN.

Bruyn van Berendrecht, Michiel de (*b* Utrecht, *c.* 1608; *d* ?London, *c.* 1664). Dutch silversmith. In 1622 he was apprenticed to Adam van Vianen of Utrecht, and after his marriage in 1636, he set up house in the Mariaplaats, Utrecht. His work was strongly influenced by that of Adam van Vianen and, after the latter's death in 1627, by his son Christiaen van Vianen. Bruyn van Berendrecht became known as a producer of Catholic church silver: candelabra, chalices, ewers and salvers, decorated with a mixture of swag ornament and Baroque floral designs. His best-known works include a pair of silver kneeling

angels (1648) and a pair of Baroque wall sconces (1653) with wax-catchers in the shape of tulips (Amsterdam, Rijksmus.). In 1660 he formed a partnership with Christiaen van Vianen and accompanied him to England, where he seems to have stayed until his death.

Bucaro [buccaro]. *See* BOCCARO.

Buch, Iver Winfeldt [Windfeldt; Bukh, Ivar Venfel'd] (*b* 1749; *d* 1811). Norwegian goldsmith, active in Russia. His best-known work is a gold chalice of 1791 (Washington, DC, Hillwood Mus.), which was part of a liturgical set commissioned by Catherine the Great and presented by her to the Aleksandr Nevsky Monastery in St Petersburg on 29 August 1791. Catherine provided Buch with the materials for the chalice: gold and diamonds from the State Treasury, and carved gems (chalcedony, bloodstone, nephrite, carnelian) from her private collection. The Hermitage Museum in St Petersburg has an extensive collection of Buch's works, notably a silver vase on a pedestal with the monograms of Emperor Paul I and his family (1796).

A. B. Polak: *Iver Winfeldt Buch, Imperial Russian Goldsmith* (London, 1968)

Buchan Pottery. *See under* PORTOBELLO.

Buckinghamshire. English county noted for its lace production. The Buckinghamshire towns of Aylesbury, Great Marlow, Hanslope, Newport Pagnell, Olney and Stony Stratford were important centres of a domestic lace industry. Bobbin lace had been made in the county since the 16th century. By the 19th century it had established a county style (similar to the laces of Lille) consisting of a ground mesh of two threads twisted into either a hexagon or a six-pointed star, with simple floral patterns in thicker thread.

L. Bartlett: *Lace Villages* (London, 1991)
British College of Lace: *Fine Buckinghamshire Point Lace Patterns Belonging to the Misses Sivewright and Pope* (Rugby, 1994)

Bucrane [bucranium]. Sculptured ornament representing an ox-skull, a classical motif revived in the late 18th century for the decoration of furniture and porcelain.

Buczacz. Town in Podolia, Ukraine, formerly in Polish territory, known as a centre for weaving in the 18th and 19th centuries. In the 18th century the town belonged to the magnate family Potocki, and the art of weaving kilims with floral designs flourished. About 1870 Oskar Potocki founded a large factory to produce wall hangings made of silk interwoven with gold and silver thread. These hangings carried on the Polish tradition of brocade weaving but were made on mechanical looms. They are distinguished by subtle shades of pink, orange and red, with tiny motifs, or are predominantly gold with a beautiful sheen. They were expensive and much prized by connoisseurs. The workshop labels, which give the size of each piece (usually about 1.5 × 2.5 m), show the Pilawa coat of arms of the Potocki family (a cross with two-and-a-half arms), the name *Buczacz* and sometimes the initials *AP* for Artur Potocki, the manager. These were woven in or stitched on a separate piece of fabric. The Potocki factory closed in 1939.

Budapest. Hungarian centre of ceramics production. In the Middle Ages the potters of Buda and Pest produced simple earthenwares: jugs, pots, dishes and plates, as well as fireplace tiles, of which many richly decorated examples remain. The first unglazed decorative wall tiles and ornate dishes in Hungary were made in Buda. From 1470 until 1480 faience was produced in a workshop in the Royal Palace of Buda, probably established by Petrus Andrea da Faenza of the bottega Bettini in Faenza. The coloured roof tiles of the Stephansdom in Vienna were made in Buda. In 1785 Domokos Kuny (1754–1822) opened a faience and stoneware factory, and wares were influenced by those of Holics and Tata. The factory closed in 1813. In 1864 Ignác Fisher established a stoneware factory in Pest, which produced high-quality, richly decorated dishes, imitative of wares from the Zsolnay Ceramic Factory, in Pécs; the two factories merged in 1895. The son of Ignác Fisher, Emil Fisher, also owned a stoneware factory. The Drasche Brickworks produced fine porcelain dinner-services and ornamental wares from 1909. The earthenware works in Kispest (est. 1922) produced dinner, tea and coffee services and decorative ornaments; after 1930, under the new title of Granit, the factory also produced porcelain. The Hüttl Porcelain Factory (est. 1854) developed from a small workshop for painting ceramics, and their fine porcelain dinner-services were much sought after. The factory was nationalized in 1948 and continued to operate throughout the 20th century under the name Aquicum. In the 20th century several studio potters including Géza Gorka (1894–1971), Margit Kovács (1902–77) and Hajnalka Zilzer (1893–1957) worked in Budapest.

T. Artner: *Modern Hungarian Ceramics* (Budapest, 1974)

Buen Retiro Pietre Dure and Mosaic Workshop [Laboratorio de Piedras y Mosaico]. Spanish hardstone workshop next to the BUEN RETIRO PORCELAIN FACTORY, Madrid, founded by Charles III (*reg* 1759–88) in 1759. As he had done at the Real Laboratorio delle Pietre Dure in Naples, he imported craftsmen from Florence; in October 1761 Domenico Stecchi (Domingo Stequi), active in the Opificio delle Pietre Dure in Florence, and Francesco Poggetti and his son Luigi Poggetti arrived in Madrid to practise their craft. In 1764 five artisans were em-

ployed under Stecchi and Francesco Poggetti, and by 1784 nineteen people were working under their direction. In 1786 Luigi Poggetti became the new director after Stecchi's death, while the administration—as distinct from its artistic supervision—was conducted until the end of the 18th century by two other Italians, the Bonicelli, who also superintended the Real Fábrica del Buen Retiro. Artists approved by the court were engaged to create designs that were then realized in pietre dure.

There are eight documented pietre dure mosaic table-tops (all Madrid, Prado) created by craftsmen at the Laboratorio, all finished before the death of Charles III in 1788. A ninth table (Lisbon, Pal. N. Ajuda), though not documented, undoubtedly belongs to the same series. The first of these to be made, decorated with a port scene surrounded by musical instruments, bears an inscription with the dates 1779–80 and the names of Domenico Stecchi, Francesco Poggetti and *Josh. Flipart Pintor de Cámara dei S. M. C.* Although the name of Charles-Joseph Flipart (*fl* from 1753) appears only on this table, it seems likely that he designed the whole series. The two tables constructed last, with scenes of the games of *pelota* and shuttlecocks bordered by garlands, shells, flowers and fruits, show similarities with the figurative and ornamental designs of the painter Giuseppe Zocchi (1711/17–67), whom Flipart may have known from the studio of the printmaker Joseph Wagner (1706–80) in Venice. Giovanni Battista Ferroni (*d* 1804), a bronze specialist, designed bronze mounts for the eight tables; these commissions are documented by a series of payments made to Ferroni from 1768 to 1796. In 1789 he is recorded as having designed and selected the stones for a cabinet to be made for Charles IV.

Other products of the Buen Retiro workshop include mosaic pictures, for example those of a *View of Bermeo*, based on a drawing by Luis Paret (1746–99), and *Virgil's Tomb* (both Madrid, Prado) after Gaspar van Wittel (1652/3–1736). A sumptuous marble table centrepiece depicting a small temple (Malmaison, Mus. N. Château Bois-Préau), with polychrome stones and bronze ornaments chased by Ferroni, was begun in the 1790s. It was presented by Charles IV (*reg* 1788–1808) to Napoleon (*reg* 1804–14) in 1808; in the same year the Laboratorio was destroyed in the Napoleonic Wars.

A. González-Palacios: 'Il Laboratorio delle Pietre Dure del "Buen Retiro" a Madrid (1762–1808)', *Splendori di pietre dure: L'Arte di corte nella Firenze dei granduchi* (exh. cat., ed. A. M. Giusti; Florence, Pitti, 1988–9), pp. 260–67

Buen Retiro Porcelain Factory [Real Fábrica del Buen Retiro]. Spanish porcelain manufactory. The Real Fábrica del Buen Retiro was named after the garden and palace on the outskirts of Madrid, where the factory was established in 1759 by Charles III, after he ascended to the Spanish throne. He was married to Maria Amalia of Saxony (1724–60), a member of the family of Saxon sovereigns who founded the porcelain factory at Meissen. Under her influence the porcelain factory of Capodimonte in Naples was created; when she moved to Spain she was accompanied by 53 artists from Capodimonte, with all the necessary material for the art to be continued in Madrid. In 1760 the Real Fábrica del Buen Retiro began to function with the Italian craftsmen and ten Spaniards under the direction of Gaetano Schepers. Giuseppe Gricci executed the Gabinete de la Porcelana (1760–65; *in situ*) at the Aranjuez Palace, near Madrid, which is totally covered with white porcelain plaques enhanced with coloured relief chinoiserie motifs, animals and plants. From 1770 to 1775 another Gabinete de la Porcelana, decorated in a similar style, was installed in the Palacio Real, Madrid. Sculptures, dinner-services and imitation flower bouquets were also produced by the factory. Before 1789 soft-paste porcelain was manufactured, and the pieces executed in a Baroque style derived from that of Capodimonte. At the end of the 18th century, however, the Neoclassical style was introduced, and English Wedgwood Jasperwares were imitated. After the death of the King, a warehouse was opened for sales to the public. Until 1803 all the directors were Italian; between 1803 and 1808, however, the factory was directed by the Spaniard Bartolomé Sureda, who had visited France to study Sèvres porcelain. On his return hard-paste porcelain was introduced to Buen Retiro, and the forms and decoration of Sèvres wares were copied. Despite these influences, and although some pieces are similar to those made at Sèvres, Buen Retiro porcelain is generally unmistakable. The building, on a strategic site, was occupied by the French in 1808 and was completely destroyed on 10 August 1812.

M. C. Santos: '18th-Century Buen Retiro Porcelain', *Cer. Mthly,* li/10 (Dec 2003), pp. 57–9

Buffet. In early modern English, a low three-legged stool. From the early 18th century the French sense of an ornamental sideboard or side-table for the display of plate became the dominant meaning in British English. In colonial America the term was sometimes used to denote an architectural cupboard for the display of plate, glass, ceramics and other small objects.

Bugatti, Carlo (*b* Milan, 16 Feb 1856; *d* Molsheim, Alsace, April 1940). Italian furniture and silver designer. His furniture is self-consciously original in design, though sources for its style can be found in the Islamic and Japanese decorative traditions and in Romanesque architecture. He often covered his pieces with vellum or parchment, with inlays of brass and pewter in the wooden supporting members. In his earlier work the vellum is sometimes painted in brown monochrome with Japanese-inspired motifs, but after about 1900 he favoured painted, polychrome geometric designs. Elaborate fringes and tassels often decorate his pieces. Circles, round arches and, later, curving planes are usually encountered in his furniture designs. Once his formal vocabulary was established, Bugatti produced a varied series of works using a limited number of motifs. A stylistic progression is observable in his designs towards unified, plastic forms, which culminated in the organic shapes of the tables and chairs (e.g. mahogany and parchment chair, 1902; Paris, Mus. Orsay) of the Snail Room, shown at the Esposizione Internazionale d'Arte Decorativa of 1902 in Turin. The precise chronology of this development is not clear, and it seems that early designs continued to be manufactured over a long period of time.

About 1904 Bugatti and his family moved to Paris. He sold his Milanese furniture-making shop to the De Vecchi firm, and this and other Italian firms made furniture after his designs or in his style for some years after his departure. In France he turned his attention primarily to designing silver, often incorporating fantastic human and animal forms, which was exhibited and sold by the Parisian firm of Adrien Hébrard. Some furniture designed by Bugatti was produced in France but probably not in large quantity. He also made plaster models for interior architectural schemes, but they seem not to have been realized. Many of his plaster models for silver and architecture are in the Musée d'Orsay, Paris.

P. Dejean: *Bugatti* (Paris, 1981; Eng. trans., New York, 1982)
H. Hawley: 'Carlo Bugatti's French Furniture', *Mag. Ant.*, clvi/1 (July 1999), pp. 82–9
L. Salmon: 'Le salon escargot de Carlo Bugatti', *Beaux-A.*, cciii (April 2001), pp. 98–9

Bühler. *See* BILLER.

Bukhara. Centre of carpet production in Uzbekihstan. The oasis that eventually grew into the city of Bukhara has been a centre of textile production since the 6th century AD. Bukhara was also the main centre for the sale of carpets knotted by Turkoman nomads, and the name Bukhara (Bokara) has come to identify a distinctive red-ground carpet with geometric designs, produced after 1700 by the tribes who migrated seasonally in search of pasture for their flocks and herds. Unlike their counterparts elsewhere in the Islamic lands, these carpets are almost exclusively the products of tribal weavers. These Turkoman carpets can be distinguished from Anatolian, Caucasian and Iranian examples by the presence of the characteristic *gul* (*göl*), an octagonal medallion of variable shape, often decorated with geometric patterns or stylized animals and birds. The medallions are arranged in regular rows of dominant and subordinate elements.

In all types of Turkoman carpets, warp, weft (usually two) and pile yarns are Z-spun and S-plied. Red predominates as the ground colour, because of the ubiquitous use of madder root and insect dyes. Different dyeing techniques, however, and the use of mordants, most commonly alum, produced many shades of red, ranging from dark walnut brown through mahogany to purple-crimson and brilliant scarlet. The red ground is complemented by blue, green, yellow, ivory (undyed), brown and orange. Natural dyes were used until the late 19th century, when the introduction of aniline dyes resulted in harsher tones. Pile and foundation are usually sheep's wool, although goat or other animal hair is sometimes used. Silk and occasionally cotton, purchased from merchants, are sometimes employed for small accents in the pile. Various knots are used among the different tribal groups: Salor pieces have asymmetrical knots open to the left and sometimes right, and closely packed warps on two levels; Tekke carpets have symmetrical or asymmetrical knots open to the right, often with a single weft; Saryk carpets have symmetrical knots; Yomut and Ersari carpets may have any of the three types of knots; while Arabatchi and Chodor carpets have both types of symmetrical knots.

Turkoman tribal weavings include knotted pile and tapestry weavings for use as tent furnishings and animal trappings. The extreme popularity of these pieces among 20th-century collectors and the wide range of uses to which they were put have led to a bewildering variety of terms in the literature. In general, large pile carpets (*khali, chaly*) and flatweaves were laid on the floor. Felts were used on the floor and as tent walls. Tents were decorated with doorhangings (*ensi, engsi*), door surrounds (*kapunuk, deslik*) and horizontal bands. Storage bags (*torba*) ranged in size from the larger *chuval* (*juval, tschowal*) to the

Turkoman rug, Jekke (London, Victoria and Albert Museum)

smaller *mafrash*. Pentagonal animal trappings (*asmalyk*), sometimes embroidered, and rectangular ones (*kejebe, kedshebe*) were woven for special occasions, as were trappings for the bridal litter (*khalyk*).

S. Azadi: *Turkoman Carpets and the Ethnographic Significance of Their Ornaments* (Fishguard, 1975); Eng. Trans R. Pinner
Turkmen Tribal Carpets and Traditions (exh. cat., ed. L. Mackie and J. Thompson; Washington, DC, Textile Mus., 1980)
I. Bennett and others: *Oriental Rugs* (Woodbridge, 1989)

Bullet teapot. Spherical teapot mounted on a footring. The earliest silver teapots were pear-shaped, but *c*. 1730 this design was superseded by the bullet teapot, which was in turn superseded by the drum-shaped teapot of the 1770s.

Bullion. Metal knob or boss used for decoration on a book or harness. The term can also denote a bull's eye in glass and (in early modern English) trunk-hose that is puffed out at the top. It is also used to describe a heavy textile fringe in curtains, pelmets and the top covers of seat furniture.

Bullock, George (*b* 1782–3; *d* London, 1 May 1818). English cabinetmaker and sculptor. In 1804 he entered into partnership with a looking-glass maker, William Stoakes of Church Street, Liverpool. They advertised themselves as 'Cabinet Makers, General Furnishers and Marble Workers' and in 1805 supplied Gothic furniture designed by Bullock to Cholmondeley Castle, Ches (*in situ*). The following year Bullock set up on his own in Bold Street, Liverpool, selling furniture and bronze ornaments. By 1806 he had acquired the Mona Marble quarries in Anglesey and sold 'fashionable and elegant Sculptured and Plain Chimney Pieces' at a separate showroom in Church Street. Around 1809 or 1810 Bullock was briefly in partnership with the architect Joseph Michael Gandy, as 'architects, modellers, sculptors, marble masons, cabinetmakers and upholsterers', probably working together at Storrs Hall, on Lake Windermere, Cumbria, and Bolton Hall, N. Yorks, both for Colonel John Bolton (1756–1837). Gandy may have been involved in Bullock's antiquarian refurbishment of Speke Hall, Liverpool, for Richard Watt (*d* 1812) in 1811.

In 1813 Bullock transferred his business to London, where he set up his own Grecian Rooms in the Egyptian Hall (a museum managed by his brother) in Piccadilly; he moved the following year to a large house in Tenterden Street, with manufacturing premises in Oxford Street adjoining his back garden. These included polishing rooms for marble and a Calico Room for printing upholstery fabrics in addition to furniture workshops. Bullock's major furnishing commissions during the remainder of his life were at Blair Castle, Tayside, for John Murray, 4th Duke of Atholl (begun 1814); Longwood, St Helena, for the use of Napoleon Bonaparte (1815); Tew Park, Oxon, for Matthew Robinson Boulton; Abbotsford (nr Melrose, Borders) for Sir Walter Scott; and Battle

Abbey, E. Sussex, for Sir Godfrey Webster (all from 1816). The designer Richard Bridgens, who had known Bullock in Liverpool, was involved in the antiquarian schemes at both Abbotsford and Battle Abbey.

Most of Bullock's furniture is in a massive Regency Neo-classical style, although he also designed in the Gothic, Elizabethan and Jacobean manners. He pioneered the use of native British materials, using such woods as larch for cabinets at Blair Castle, and Mona and Scottish marbles. His Neo-classical furniture is often finely decorated with stylized marquetry of various woods and metals, and splendid brass or ormolu mounts.

ODNB

George Bullock: *Cabinet Maker* (exh. cat., London, Blairman & Sons; Liverpool, Sudley A.G.; 1988)
M. Levy: 'Napoleon in Exile: The Houses and Furniture Supplied by the British Government for the Emperor and his Entourage on St Helena', *Furn. Hist.,* xxxiv (1998), pp. 2–211

Bun foot. Foot shaped like a flattened sphere, first used on furniture in the late 17th century

Bunzlau. The Silesian town of Bunzlau (now Polish Bolesławiec) has been an important pottery centre for centuries. Its principal wares were hard earthenware vessels, which have since the 19th century been decorated with blue and brown dots forming the so-called 'peacock's-eye pattern' (e.g. coffeepot from Bunzlau, *c.* 1900; Berlin, Mus. Dt. Vlksknd.); until the end of the 19th century this type of ware was produced in large quantities. Bunzlau potters also produced utilitarian and display stoneware from the 16th century, and in the 18th and 19th centuries specialized in coffee pots and tankards.

In the 20th century pottery production in Bunzlau was industrialised, and with the encouragement of the Keramische Fachschule Bunzlau (Bunzlau Ceramic Technical School, founded 1898), new lines of pottery were introduced under the influence of the Arts and Crafts Movement; traditional storage vessels for agricultural and industrial use were displaced by dinner services, decorative bowls and vases. From the late 1920s to the 1950s air-brushed Art Nouveau designs were the main product of the factories, though during the Nazi years a taste for 19th-century Prussian designs led to the formation of the Aktion Bunzlauer Braunzeug (Bunzlau Brown Wares Consortium) to make pottery that suited Nazi aesthetics. After the war many Bunzlau potters settled in Germany and continued to make pottery in the Bunzlau style; Polish potters now produce high-quality wares in Bolesławiec.

C. R. Mack and I. S. Mack: 'The Bunzlau Pottery of Germany and Silesia', *Mag. Ant.,* clii (July 1997), pp. 88–95

Bureau. Writing-table incorporating drawers or a type of case furniture with a hinged writing surface. The first furniture types to bear the name bureau evolved in France in the middle of the 17th century.

Their antecedents, however, existed in the early medieval period, and the word 'bureau' is a corruption of the medieval French for a kind of coarse linen used as a surface for writing. In Sweden a simple desk has been preserved (*c.* 1200; Gotland, Vallstena Church), which has a sloping writing surface supported on the turned uprights typical of Romanesque furniture. Most medieval desks, however, were not free-standing and took the form of a writing-box with a hinged, sloping writing surface. Cabinets with a drop-leaf writing surface appeared in Italy during the Renaissance, and in Spain the *vargueño*—a cabinet, often carved and gilded, with a drop-leaf concealing an elaborate arrangement of drawers—began to appear at around the same time (e.g. walnut and gilt *vargueño*, early 16th century; London V&A).

An early type of bureau developed in France in the mid-17th century, sometimes known as a *bureau Mazarin*, took the form of a writing-table, initially pushed against the wall like a pier table. Below the writing surface were two banks of drawers flanking a central kneehole. The drawers were carried on an arrangement of eight tapering legs joined by stretchers. Many examples survive, typically decorated with boulle inlay or floral marquetry. A variation of this type was the *bureau brisé*, which had a hinged horizontal top that concealed a writing surface and an arrangement of small drawers. During the early 18th century the bureau Mazarin gradually evolved into the more elegant form known as the *bureau plat* (e.g. *bureau plat*, attributed to André-Charles Boulle, 1710–15; Paris, Louvre). The banks of drawers were replaced by single drawers flanking a shallow drawer in the kneehole, while the complex arrangement of eight legs was replaced by four sinuous cabriole supports. The *bureau plat* was one of the most successful French furniture types of the 18th century. Although its elegant curving contours were straightened with the advent of Neo-classicism, its overall configuration remained almost unchanged into the 1820s.

In England the bureau had, typically, a hinged sloping flap that enclosed a fitted interior and opened out into a writing surface. Some early models were raised on legs, but by 1700 most bureaux were carried on an arrangement of drawers reaching almost to the floor. A particularly successful variation on this type was the bureau-cabinet, where the bureau supported a tall cabinet with one or two doors often faced with mirrored panels. Although such pieces were usually given the restrained boxlike form of 18th-century English case furniture, the grander examples were enlivened by architectural outlines with scroll pediments or arched crestings, while the doors could be flanked by pilasters. Until the 1730s most examples were veneered with walnut, although some of the most decorative examples were japanned in bright colours (e.g. bureau-cabinet japanned in blue and gold, *c.* 1745–9; London, V&A). After *c.* 1730 mahogany succeeded walnut as the timber most commonly used.

The English type of bureau and bureau-cabinet was adopted widely throughout northern Europe, although its form was often altered beyond recognition. Initially Dutch bureaux and bureau-cabinets were almost indistinguishable from their English counterparts, but during the second quarter of the 18th century they acquired complex *bombé* profiles and broad, canted corners. The cabinets that surmounted them were usually given domed outlines. From 1750 to 1775 the form of the Dutch bureau-cabinet became more restrained, and a cylinder replaced the simple sloping flap. Mahogany again replaced walnut as the favoured timber. In German-speaking countries bureaux assumed complex serpentine forms contained within broad canted corners. The cabinets or banks of drawers that surmounted them were usually slightly narrower than the bureau and were often divided into three parts with a slightly higher central section. These *Schreib-schränke* were normally veneered with walnut inlaid with strapwork or panels of burr-wood or marquetry. In Mainz the development of the *Schreibschrank* reached a peak in the 1760s when its elaborate form was framed by detached scrolling volutes (e.g. *Schreibschrank*, 1764; Karlsruhe, Bad. Landesmus.). Although such bureaux were to lose their popularity towards the end of the century, the form persisted in Neo-classical guise in northern Germany. In Denmark, the bureau-cabinet with a roll-top and tripartite superstructures known as a *chatol* was still one of the more important household pieces around 1800.

The bureau-cabinet was also widely popular in Italy, where it was adapted to regional characteristics. In Genoa the gently swelling forms were decorated with finely figured veneers laid in contrasting directions; in Venice lacquering and japanning were a common form of decoration, although walnut was widely favoured. Some of the most extraordinary bureaux were made in Piedmont. In the Rococo era Pietro Piffetti created a series of fantastic pieces of elaborate *bombé* and serpentine form inlaid with rare woods and ivory (e.g. bureau-cabinet, 1738; Rome, Pal. Quirinale). In the Neo-classical period Giuseppe Maria Bonzanigo produced a fabulous bureau-cabinet (*c.* 1780; Stupinigi, Mus. A. & Ammobil.) decorated with delicately carved white-painted grotesques set against a turquoise background.

The bureau-cabinets and bureaux closest to English prototypes were made in the USA. Although inspired by English pattern books, they were given regional inflections. Those in Newport, RI, for example, had blocked fronts with convex and concave panels headed by shell lunettes. Cabinetmakers such as John Cogswell (*fl* 1769–1818) from Boston gave their bureaux a pronounced *bombé* profile.

Towards the middle of the 18th century in France such *ébénistes* as Bernard van Risamburgh the younger produced small writing-tables known as *secrétaires en pente* for the luxury end of the market. The *secrétaire en pente* was rather smaller than the *bureau plat*, and its writing surface and fitted interior were concealed beneath a sloping fall-front. It was carried on cabriole legs rather than banks of drawers (e.g. *secrétaire en pente*, 18th century; Paris, Mus. Jacquemart-

André). The luxurious *bureau à cylindre*, pioneered by Jean-François Oeben, reached its apogee with the bureau of King Louis XV (*reg* 1715–74) commissioned from Oeben in 1760 and finished and delivered to Louis XV by Jean-Henri Riesener in 1769 (Paris, Louvre). Other famous *bureaux à cylindre* were made by David Roentgen (e.g. 1785; Paris, Louvre). The *secrétaire à abattant*, also known as the *secrétaire en armoire*, was a shoulder-height piece of case furniture that stood against the wall, with a vertical fall-front enclosing a fitted interior above a cupboard. Although Rococo secrétaires of this type exist, its box-like form suited the rectangular shapes of Neo-classicism, and it achieved pre-eminence in the later part of the 18th century, often being made *en suite* with a commode. Its rectangular form was ideal for trellis parquetry and floral and pictorial marquetry. Riesener made several examples distinguished by the extraordinary quality of their gilt-bronze mounts, including a lacquered commode and secrétaire (1784; New York, Met.) for Marie-Antoinette's appartements at Saint Cloud. During the late 1780s and 1790s finely figured veneers framed with simple gilt-bronze or brass mounts were increasingly favoured as an alternative to complex marquetry (e.g. *secrétaire à abattant* by Riesener, *c.* 1783; London, Wallace).

By the 1790s the *secrétaire à abattant* had replaced the bureau throughout most of Europe. In the Netherlands such secrétaires were often of satin-wood decorated with marquetry or set with panels of lacquer or *verre églomisé*. In German-speaking and Scandinavian countries the *secrétaire à abattant* was particularly suited to the simple geometric forms of the Biedermeier style.

In England the bureau-cabinet had become outmoded by the 1780s, although bureaux continued to be produced until the turn of the century. It was replaced by the secrétaire-bookcase, which substituted a fitted secrétaire drawer for the sloping fall-front of the bureau. The doors of the cabinet were usually glazed and divided by thin astragals arranged in elegant patterns. Although mahogany remained the primary timber, rosewood and satinwood were also used. Such designers as Thomas Sheraton, however, drew inspiration from such French types as the *bonheur-du-jour*, the most successful of which was the D-shaped Carlton House writing-table, with a bank of drawers surrounding a writing surface (the original was supposed to have been supplied to the Prince Regent, later George IV, at Carlton House, London). The importance of the library grew during the Regency period, and there was a concomitant development of a variety of small writing-tables carried on legs or end standards. The Davenport—a small desk with a sloping writing-surface above a single bank of drawers—was particularly popular from 1800 to 1875. For much of the 19th century, however, the writing-tables and pedestal desks developed during the 18th century replaced bureaux and secrétaires, although the Sheraton revival at the end of the century caused a return to favour of the Carlton House desk.

During the same period such French luxury manufacturers as François Linke (1855–1945) continued to produce a wide range of bureaux and secrétaires that drew their inspiration freely from 18th-century types. Other *ébénistes*, notably Henri Dasson (1825–96), produced high-quality replicas of 18th-century originals. During the Art Nouveau period such designers as Henry Van de Velde and Louis Majorelle successfully reinterpreted the bureau form through the sinuous abstractions of the Art Nouveau style.

Burgau [burgaudine; Burgos mother-of-pearl]. Decorative material used for inlays derived from a group of tropical shells of which the most common is *Turbo marmoratus*. It was long used in Europe for the decoration of weapons, cutlery and small boxes. In China and Japan the technique known in Europe as *laque burgauté* or *lac burgauté* used the shell of the sea-ear (*Haliotis*) to create inlays for lacquer ware. The term 'Burgos shells' is often used for modern reproduction shells cast in precious medals (especially silver) for use as pendants.

Burgau Porcelain Factory. German porcelain factory near Jena, Thuringia, which produced fine domestic wares from 1901 to 1929. The company was owned by Ferdinand Selle, and its designers included HENRY VAN DE VELDE and Albin Müller (1871–1941), both of whom designed well-known breakfast services (1907 and 1910).

B. Fritz and B. Hellmann: *Porzellan-Manufaktur Burgau a.d. Saale Ferdinand Selle 1901–1929* (Jena, 1997)

Burges, William (*b* London, 2 Dec 1827; *d* London, 20 April 1881). English architect and designer. As an architect he is best known for his work at Cardiff Castle and Castell Coch for his patron, the Marquess of Bute. His designs for the decorative arts, particularly furniture and metalwork, are equally inventive and elaborate. He was friendly with the leaders of the Pre-Raphaelite movement, employing a number of Pre-Raphaelite artists and craftsmen in his decorative work.

Burges tightly controlled details of interior design, and numerous detailed drawings in his hand survive for woodwork, stonework, sculpture and wall decoration. He also designed his furniture and metalwork in detail before his craftsmen set to work. His furniture is heavy and massively sculptural, with elaborate carving. It is richly painted and highly architectural. Cabinets have pitched roofs, dormers, chimneys and gables. Shelves are supported by Gothic columns, beds have Gothic arcades and many pieces are capped with crenellations. There are figurative panels with painted medieval scenes and there is a lavish use of geometric and stylized stencilled work. His furniture is witty, inventive and erudite. Among his earliest pieces of painted furniture was the first Yatman Cabinet (1858; London, V&A), which was decorated by Edward John Poynter

William Burges: washstand, carved, painted and gilded wood, marble top and bowl inset with silver, and bronze tap and fittings, h. 1.6 m, 1880 (London, Victoria and Albert Museum)

(1836–1919). Other examples of his furniture are the Vita Nuova washstand and Golden Bed (both London, V&A) from the Guest Bedroom, Tower House. His metalwork shows a similar witty invention, evident in his church plate as well as his elephant inkstand (untraced). Good examples are his two decanters of 1865 (Bedford, Cecil Higgins A.G. and Cambridge, Fitzwilliam).

J. M. Crook: *William Burges and the High Victorian Dream* (London, 1981)
Cooper: *Victorian and Edwardian Furniture and Interiors* (London, 1987)
G. Davies: 'Gothic Desserts: William Burges and the Story of Sneyd's Wedding Present', *Apollo*, cli/456 (Feb 2000), pp. 28–32

Burmantoft. English ceramics manufactory (also known as Wilcox and Co.) founded in Leeds in 1858, originally for the manufacture of bricks and building materials. In 1879 the firm began to produce tiles, display pottery and architectural faience; tiles from this period survive in the sumptuous bathroom of Gledhow Hall in Leeds (decorated for the visit of the Prince of Wales, *c.* 1885) and in the Centurion Café (originally the first-class lounge) in Newcastle Central Station. Burmantoft wares were decorated with glazes (typically green, yellow, brown and dark blue) with relief decorations, often in oriental motifs. The principal products were clock cases, jardinières, pedestals, umbrella stands and vases.

Burmantofts Pottery (exh. cat., Bradford. A. Gals & Museums and Leeds, City Mus., 1984)
Ceramic Design 1860–1945, Including a Private Collection of Burmantofts and Linthorpe Art Pottery (sale cat., London, Bonhams, 26 Feb 2004)

Burmese glass. Type of glass first manufactured in the USA *c.* 1885 by the MT WASHINGTON GLASS COMPANY in New Bedford, MA, and subsequently made in England by THOMAS WEBB & Sons of Stourbridge (who called it 'Queen's Burmese') and in America by the Fenton Art Glass Company in Williamstown, WV, and other manufacturers. American Burmese glass shades from rose pink at the top to golden yellow at the bottom; the English variety is salmon pink at the top and shades to lemon yellow at the bottom. The glass has nothing to do with Burma apart from a whimsical association with Burmese sunsets.

D. Coe and R. Coe: *Fenton Burmese Glass* (Atglen, PA, 2004)

Burnap, Daniel (*b* 1759; *d* 1838). American clockmaker and silversmith. After an apprenticeship in Norwich, CT, he established a business in East Windsor, CT. He made fine long-case clocks with brass works and faces of engraved silver. His daybooks and ledgers survive, and show that he made and sold only 49 clocks in the course of 20 years.

P. R. Hoopes: *Shop Records of Daniel Burnap, Clockmaker* (Hartford, 1958)
R. C. Cheney: 'Roxbury Eight-Day Movements and the English Connection, 1785–1825', *Mag. Ant.,* clvii/4 (April, 2000), pp. 606–15

Burne-Jones, Sir **Edward (Coley)** (*b* Birmingham, 28 Aug 1833; *d* London, 17 June 1898). English painter and decorative artist, a leading figure in the Pre-Raphaelite movement. His designs for stained glass, tapestry and many other media played an important part in the Aesthetic Movement and the history of international Symbolism. In the decorative arts, stained glass was his particular forte; in 1857 he designed the first of a number of windows for James Powell & Sons, and he also worked for the rival firm of Lavers & Barraud. In April 1861 he helped to found the firm of Morris, Marshall, Faulkner & Co., 'Fine Art Workmen', soon becoming their chief designer of figure subjects for stained glass and tiles; the firm was dissolved in 1875.

Burne-Jones's talents as a decorative artist reached their fullest development in his last years. Although Morris, Marshall, Faulkner & Co. had been wound up in 1875, he continued to provide William Morris with a seemingly endless flow of stained-glass cartoons; their work in this field culminated in the four enormous windows made for St Philip's Cathedral, Birmingham (1885–97). During the 1880s Morris turned his attention to tapestry; again Burne-Jones supplied the designs, their greatest achievement being the Holy Grail series completed in 1894 for Stanmore Hall, Uxbridge, near London. In 1879–80, collaborating with Broadwood, he designed and painted the 'Orpheus' piano (priv. col.) for Graham's daughter Frances, a close friend of later years. In 1881 he was commissioned to design mosaics for the American Episcopal church of St Paul in Rome by G. E. Street (1824–81), adopting a Byzantine idiom that

permeated much of his work in the ensuing period. Nor did his invention stop here, embracing needlework, gesso panels, jewellery, tombstones, ceremonial seals, stage design, book covers, even shoes and garden seats. Many of his later designs were shown at the exhibitions of the Arts and Crafts Exhibition Society, founded in 1888.

In 1890 Morris launched his last great venture, the Kelmscott Press. Once more Burne-Jones was closely involved, illustrating 12 books. By far the most important was the celebrated edition of Chaucer's works (May 1896), for which he made 87 designs.

A. Vallance: 'The Decorative Art of Sir Edward Burne-Jones, Bt.', *A. Annu.* (1900) [special Easter no. of the *Art Journal*]
A. C. Sewter: *The Stained Glass of William Morris and his Circle,* 2 vols (New Haven, 1974–5) [cat., incl. all Burne-Jones's windows]
Poulson: 'Costume Designs by Burne-Jones for Irving's Production of *King Arthur*', *Burl. Mag.,* cxxviii (1986), pp. 18–24
R. Ash: *Sir Edward Burne-Jones* (New York, 1993)
S. Wildman and others: *Edward Burne-Jones, Victorian Artist-dreamer* (New York, 1998)
D. Peters Corbett: *Edward Burne-Jones* (London, 2004)

Burslem. *See under* STAFFORDSHIRE.

Burt, John (*b* Boston, 5 Jan 1692; *d* Boston, 23 Jan 1745). American silversmith, active in Boston. The most important collection of his silverware is held by Harvard University (notably a pair of candlesticks dated 1724); the Historical Society of York, PA, holds a thimble (*c.* 1740), and Yale University has a fine tankard (*c.* 1745). John Burt's sons William (*b* 1723; apprenticed to his father but died young), Samuel (1724–54), and Benjamin (1729–1804) succeeded him in the family business. Benjamin's surviving works include a caster (*c.* 1750) and a sauceboat (*c.* 1760; both Boston, MA, Mus. F.A.).

Bustelli, Franz Anton (*b* Locarno, ?1723; *d* Munich, April 1763). German porcelain modeller of Swiss birth. Although little is known about his early life, he is recorded as joining the Neudeck factory near Munich in November 1754 as Modellmeister; the factory was later moved to the Nymphenburg Palace, from which it then took its name (*see* NYMPHENBURG PORCELAIN FACTORY). From that time until his death he produced one of the most remarkable series of porcelain figures ever modelled. Beginning with small Ovidian gods (e.g. *Flora*, 1755–8; Frankfurt am Main, Mus. Ksthandwk), nude putti with various classical attributes on fairly simple bases, he then made a series of figures of street vendors including an egg seller (e.g. *c.* 1755; Hamburg, Mus. Kst & Gew.) and a mushroom seller. These early figures do not reflect the full Rococo movement of Bustelli's later work. They do, however, display one essential characteristic of his entire oeuvre: a tendency to conceive his figures with faceted planiform surfaces, more reminiscent of wood-carving than clay-modelling, which may suggest that he was trained as a wood-carver. His figures seem to carry on in porcelain the rich traditions of the south German Rococo, and his first major compositions, including a Crucifix, a Virgin and a St John, are all in the direct tradition of south German ecclesiastical sculpture; at one time they were even ascribed to the sculptor Ignaz Günther (1725–75).

Bustelli's greatest period, however, began with his Chinese and Turkish figures, whose rich and vigorously scrolled bases surrounding and supporting them were to assume an important part of the whole creation. This phenomenon is also a vital feature of Bustelli's groups the *Sleeper Disturbed* and *Lovers among Ruins* (e.g. 1756; Hamburg, Mus. Kst & Gew.), in which the figures play an almost subsidiary role to their Rococo surroundings. His reputation as one of the greatest porcelain modellers was secured by his characters from the *commedia dell'arte*; the series (1759–60), consisting of 16 figures, is the most extensive and is considered the most daring and beautiful of its kind. The figures are arranged in eight pairs, each of a male and a female character. The two people in each couple appear to react physically as they gaze at one another across the space framed by each integral composition. Bustelli departed from the canon of the *commedia dell'arte* in porcelain by the inclusion of the characters Ottavio, Corine, Anselmo, Julia, Leda (e.g. 1759–60; Hamburg, Mus. Kst &

Gew.), Lalage, Lucinda and Donna Martina. Corine and Anselmo are paired together, while the others are matched with the more usual members of the cast of the Comedy. Unusually, too, these figures bear the Wittelsbach shield, impressed into the scrolls on which they stand.

R. Ruckert: *Bustelli* (Munich, 1963)
K. Hantschmann and others: 'Neue Bustelli-Figuren', *Weltkunst*, lxxiv/11 (Oct 2004), pp. 72–5

Butler's tray. Tray mounted on a folding stand, popularly in England in the 18th and 19th centuries

Buttenmann. *See* TANZEMANN.

Buzaglo, Abraham (*b* 1716; *d* 1788). Moroccan ironfounder who settled in England in 1762. He invented an innovative three-tier cast-iron stove decorated with extravagant reliefs. His name was so strongly associated with his stove that Richard Tickell, in his poem *The Project* (1778), could refer to a 'Buzaglo', which Tickell maintained could raise the standard of debate in the House of Commons by warming members who become irritable because of the coldness of the chamber. Only two examples are known to survive: the one

Franz Anton Bustelli: *Capitano* porcelain figure (detail) from the *commedia dell'arte* series, made at Nymphenburg, 1759–60 (Hamburg, Museum für Kunst und Gewerbe)

in the DeWitt Wallace Decorative Arts Gallery in Williamsburg, VA(1770), has flamboyant rococo decoration and the one in Knole, Kent (1774), which is decorated with classical reliefs. The Williamsburg stove, which was originally in the Virginia House of Burgesses, was extravagantly praised in an accompanying letter by Buzaglo, who assured the recipients that 'the elegance of workmanship and impression of every particular joint, does honour to Great Britain; it excels in grandeur any thing ever seen of the kind, and is a Masterpiece not to be equalled in all Europe, and could not be sufficiently admired'.

E. Pitzer Gusler: 'Buzaglo's "Masterpiece" in Iron—London Iron Founder Abraham Buzaglo', *Mag. Ant.*, (Jan 1997)

Byzantine Revival. Revivalist style that affected all the arts (including visual and literary), but primarily architecture and the decorative arts, especially mosaic. The style was prevalent in Europe and North America during the second half of the 19th century and into the early 20th. The initial impetus for the Revival came from 18th- and 19th-century accounts of travels to Italy, Greece and Turkey, containing descriptions of Early Christian and Byzantine buildings, and from early specialist books on Byzantine and Early Christian architecture. In mosaic decoration the Byzantine Revival was promoted by the Venetian firm of Salviati (founded 1859), who led an international revival of mosaic mural decoration, combining Byzantine pictorial imagery with industrialized methods of production.

J. B. Bullen: *Byzantium Rediscovered* (London, 2003)

C

Cabaret. Porcelain tea or coffee service consisting of a small table or tray and matching cups, pots and bowls. If designed for one person it is called a *solitaire*, and if for two (as most are) a *tête-à-tête*; if intended for use at breakfast it is called a *déjeuner*.

Cabinet. Piece of furniture which contains drawers and pigeon-holes for the storage of small precious objects. The name is derived from the French *cabinet*, which came into use *c.* 1500, and can also mean a small private room. The form of the cabinet seems to have originated in Spain, where a Moorish tradition of piecing together small refined wooden objects survived, in contrast to the more structural carpentry tradition of northern Europe. About 1500 a new form appeared, the *cofre de Valencia*, outwardly resembling a chest, but with on one side a door concealing a nest of small drawers. The next development seems to have been the *escritorio*, a box filled with drawers whose fall-front, when let down and resting on a table, or on lopers incorporated in a stand, served as a writing surface. Such a practical portable combination of document case and writing-desk circulated rapidly through the Habsburg Empire, and the form now known as a *Schreibtisch* was produced in quantity in the great mercantile cities of Augsburg and Nuremberg. The form was also copied in Japan. By this date the fall-front had usually given way to doors, and the cabinet was associated with the princely cult of the precious microcosm, which was so important an aspect of Mannerism. Thus in 1568 Bernardo Buontalenti (*c.* 1531–1608) designed an octagonal cabinet (untraced) for the Tribuna of the Uffizi, Florence (Italian terms were *studiolo*, *stipo*, or in Naples, reflecting the trade with Spain, *scritorio*), and in the early 17th century Philip Hainhofer (1578–1647), an Augsburg merchant, orchestrated the production of a series of monumental cabinets packed with works of art and nature.

'Solitaire' cabaret breakfast service, made at Nymphenburg, 1770–75 (Hamburg, Museum für Kunst und Gewerbe)

From the 1570s ebony was the preferred material for cabinets, whether they were made in Augsburg, Naples or Florence. In Paris ebony cabinets began to be made in the 1630s: hence the French word for cabinetmaker is *ébéniste* (It. *ebanista*). At this date cabinets were much larger, and their stands were a more integral part of their composition. In many cases the doors were dispensed with, and the cabinet, once a miniature and secretive form, became increasingly monumental and splendid, decorated with paintings, gilt and silver mounts, tortoiseshell, marquetry, lacquer and pietre dure, a process that culminated in the magnificent cabinet (priv. col.), 3.8 m high, delivered from the Grand Ducal workshops in Florence to Henry Somerset, 3rd Duke of Beaufort (1707–45), in 1732. Cabinets of this form continued to be made: one was presented by the City of Paris to Marie-Antoinette in 1787 (Versailles, Château), and Henri Fourdinois (1830–1907) showed an elaborate Fontainebleau-style cabinet (London, V&A) at the Exposition Universelle of 1867 in Paris. New cabinet types also emerged, however: at Gripsholm Castle in Sweden, for instance, there is an amber cabinet dated 1712, which looks back to the 16th century, shown in a possibly contemporary glazed cabinet. Secrétaires, however various in outward form, often preserved an interior arrangement, including secret drawers, ultimately inherited from the 16th-century cabinet.

Jewellery cabinet, ebony, inlaid with pietre dure, made by Gobelin, *c.* 1685

G. Himmelheber: *Kabinettschränke* (Munich, 1977)
D. Alfter: *Die Geschichte des Augsburger Kabinettschranks* (Augsburg, 1986)
M. Riccardi-Cubitt: *The Art of the Cabinet: Including a Chronological Guide to Styles* (New York, 1992)

Cable moulding. *See* ROPEWORK.

Cable stitch [rope stitch]. Embroidery stitch used for outlining stems and flowers; it is technically a buttonhole stitch worked backwards.

Cabochon. In lapidary use, a precious stone when domed and polished, without being cut into facets. The double cabochon has a curved or domed surface on both top and bottom; stones in which the curve above and below the plane was formed by the edge of the girdle were long used as pendants or charms. A hollow cabochon is one in which the back or underside is concave. Cabochon cutting was largely superseded by brilliant cut, and is still in use for amethyst, garnet (carbuncle), ruby, and sapphire.

In cabinetmaking, a cabochon is a carved ornament in the form of a convex polished oval, typically on the knees of chair legs, where it is surrounded by decorative carving.

P. D. Kraus: *Introduction to Lapidary: Rock Tumbling, Cabochon Cutting, Faceting, Gem Carving, and Other Special Techniques* (Radnor, PA, 1987)
W. Peck, D. Duffy and S. Cote: *The Art of Making a Cabochon* (Phoenix, 1997)

Cabriole [Fr.: 'caper'; Lat. *capreolus*: 'goat']. In late 18th-century usage, a cabriole is a small stuffed armchair or sofa. In late 19th-century usage, it denotes a curved furniture leg, common in Queen Anne and Chippendale furniture, that resembles the foreleg of a capering animal and curves and narrows downward, ending in a club, hoof or paw; the term derives from the movement of the leg of a quadruped performing a caper or capriole (standing leap). The distinction between the two senses is sometimes observed by expanding the word to 'cabriole chair' or 'cabriole leg'.

H. A. Tipping: *English Furniture of the Cabriole Period* (London, 1922)

Cachemire (ceramics). Ribbed octagonal covered vase, originally made in Delft in the early 18th century and subsequently imitated elsewhere; the name refers to the Himalayan kingdom of Kashmir, the source of the design.

Cachemire (textiles). *See* CASHMERE.

Cache-pot. Ornamental container for a flower-pot, typically made of pottery or porcelain; some were used as wine coolers.

Cachet, A. C. Lion. *See* LION CACHET, A. C.

Caddinet. Small, flat, rectangular stand, of gold, silver or silver gilt, with a box standing proud at its end to hold personal cutlery, napkins and condiments. It probably originated in the 16th-century French court as a *cadenas* (Fr.: 'padlock', 'clasp') and was used by royal families and high nobility. English caddinets are recorded from *c.* 1660 although the trencher-of-state recorded in the 16th century may be a precursor. There are two extant English examples that are engraved with the royal arms of William and Mary (e.g. of silver gilt by Anthony Nelme, 1689; London, Tower). The caddinet appears to have become obsolete by the early 18th century.

Caddy spoon. Short-handled silver spoon, often of a whimsical shape, used for measuring tea out of the TEA-CADDY.

The Society of Caddy Spoon Collectors Present a Loan Exhibition of Teacaddy Spoons at Goldsmiths' Hall, London, June 16th–30th, 1965, (exh. cat., London, Goldsmiths' Co., 1956)
J. Norie: *Caddy Spoons* (London, 1988)

Cadinen Pottery. Germany pottery manufactory. In 1904 Emperor Willliam II founded an imperial pottery on his private estate near the East Prussian town of Cadinen (now the Polish town of Kadyny). The factory made imitations of classical and Renaissance pottery, and also produced original works by artists such as ADOLF AMBERG, Ludwig Manzel (1858–1936) and the painter and etcher Emil Pottner (1872–1942); the factory also made architectural ceramics (notably the Kaiser-Friedrich-Bad, a public spa in Wiesbaden) and domestic stoneware. The factory closed in 1945; there is a collection of its products in the Ostpreussische Landesmuseum in Lüneburg.

Cadogan teapot. One-piece teapot with no lid, filled through a hole in the bottom; the tea runs through a tube from the bottom to the top, and when the teapot is turned to an upright position the tea can be poured through the spout. The design was based on a Chinese wine-pot, of which an example must have been brought to England in the late 18th century, possibly by a member of the family of the Earl of Cadogan. Cadogan teapots were first manufactured in the early 19th century at the Rockingham Porcelain Factory and thereafter by other English manufacturers.

Cafaggiolo Ceramic Factory. Italian maiolica factory established in 1498 in the Medici villa of Cafaggiolo (near Florence), by the brothers Piero and Stefano SCHIAVON from Montelupo. The factory was in production throughout the 16th century, and the products made for the grand dukes of Tuscany and other noble Florentine families reveal a remarkable pictorial zeal, which developed from decorative schemes influenced by the style of wares from Faenza, including *alla porcellana* (blue-and-white deco-

Cafaggiolo maiolica plate decorated with Tornabuoni coat of arms, mid-16th century (Florence, Museo Nazionale del Bargello)

ration inspired by Chinese porcelain) and grotesques and the rather showy and heraldic *istoriato* (narrative) scenes. Many of these works are stamped or marked underneath with the words *in Chafagiollo* or *Chafaguotto* or sometimes stamped with the famous SP monogram, by tradition ascribed to the Fattorini family (e.g. jug with a portrait of Pope Leo X, *c.* 1515; Faenza, Mus. Int. Cer.). The strong incentive of an important, rich clientele lasted for several decades, but thereafter quality declined, and by 1599 all the surviving potters who had trained at Cafaggiolo seem to have transferred to other centres of production.

G. Cora and A. Fanfani: *La maiolica di Cafaggiolo* (Florence, 1982)
Maioliche marcate di Cafaggiolo (exh. cat. by G. Cora and A. Fanfani, Florence, Bargello, 1987)

Caffiéri [Caffieri; Caffier]. French family of artists of Italian descent. Philippe Caffiéri the elder and three generations of his family were sculptors in the French naval yards at Le Havre and Brest. One of his sons, Jacques Caffiéri, was one of the most celebrated bronzeworkers in the reign of Louis XV (*reg* 1715–74). Jacques's eldest son, Philippe Caffiéri the younger, was also a bronze-caster and chaser; Jacques's younger son, Jean-Jacques Caffiéri, became one of the most eminent sculptors of the second half of the 18th century. In the decorative arts, the three most important members of the family were Philippe the elder, Jacques, and Philippe the younger.

1. PHILIPPE [Filippo] CAFFIÉRI the elder (*b* Rome, 1634; *d* Paris, 7 Sept 1716). Sculptor, wood-carver and bronze-founder. In 1660 he was summoned by Cardinal Mazarin to Paris, where he worked for the Gobelins manufactory (with DOMENICO CUCCI) and for the Bâtiments du Roi (under CHARLES LE BRUN). He was principally a wood-carver, contributing decorative carving to the Tuileries (1666) and the Louvre (1668)—sometimes working in collaboration with

Mathieu Lespagnandelle (1617–89)—and also to the Château de St-Germain-en-Laye, Yvelines, where in 1669 he provided carvings for the chapel; none of this work survives. At Versailles he executed many carvings, most notably for the sumptuous Appartement des Bains of Louis XIV and for the queen's oratory (both destr.), as well as providing carved doors and furniture for the king's apartments. The carved and gilded frames on the series of the *Labours of Hercules* by Guido Reni (1575–1642) (Paris, Louvre) have been attributed to him. In 1680 he provided bronze architectural ornaments after models by Le Brun in the Galerie des Glaces (*in situ*), Versailles, and bronze Ionic capitals for pilasters on the Escalier des Ambassadeurs (destr. 1750).

2. JACQUES CAFFIÉRI (*b* Paris, 25 Aug 1678; *d* Paris, 23 Nov 1755). Bronze-caster, sculptor and designer, son of Philippe Caffiéri. Of his bronzework only small, decorative pieces are extant. He is known to have made gilt-bronze mantelpieces (destr.) for four chimney-pieces commissioned for the château of Versailles in 1747, but only those from the Dauphin's Bedchamber survive. Similarly, the numerous bronze ornaments for coaches, including those commissioned by the court, are lost. Of his work for cabinetmakers, only the bronzes for the commode (1739; London, Wallace) by Antoine-Robert Gaudreaus for Louis XV (*reg* 1715–74) are extant, although those for the desk (Baron Edmond de Rothschild, priv. col.) of the Duc de Choiseul (1719–85) have also been attributed to him. He specialized in the Louis XV style. Animals and fantastic beasts, figures of gods and heroes inspired by Ovid's *Metamorphoses* and genre subjects, all combined with elaborate curves that are emphasized by leafy, flowered branches, typical of the asymmetrical Louis XV style, feature prominently in his earlier works. Examples with this type of decoration include the *Diana* and *Apollo* clocks (Pushkin, Pal.-Mus.; Duke of Buccleuch, priv. col.); the *Diana and Endymion* cartel-clock (Amsterdam, Rijksmus.); Queen Marie Leczinska's candelabra (Paris, Louvre); wall-lights (Malibu, CA, Getty Mus.) made for the Infanta Elizabeth, Louis XV's daughter (1727–59); fire-dogs decorated with hunters (Rome, Pal. Quirinale); and the chandeliers (Paris, Bib. Mazarine) of the Marquise de Pompadour, which include putti playing among bouquets of roses, as well as representations of castles similar to those that feature on the Marquise's coat of arms. Caffiéri's later works are in the symmetrical version of the Louis XV style, for example the chandelier (1751; London, Wallace) from the collection of the dukes of Parma and the Passament astronomical clock (1753; Versailles, Château) for Louis XV (*reg* 1715–74).

3. PHILIPPE CAFFIÉRI the younger (*b* Paris, 19 Feb 1714; *d* Paris, 8 Oct 1774). Bronze-caster, collector and designer, son of Jacques Caffiéri. He inherited the family workshop, but rejected the Louis XV style in which his father had worked, favouring instead the richly decorative technique of black patination with gilding, which he used particularly for Neo-classical works. After 1756 he modelled bronzes based on the designs of Louis-Joseph Le Lorrain for the desk (Chantilly, Mus. Condé) of Ange-Laurent de La Live de Jully (1725–70), which is one of the finest examples of French Neo-classical furniture. Caffiéri later produced the mantelpiece, designed by Ange-Jacques Gabriel (1698–1782), for the chimney-piece of the Salle des Maréchaux in the Ecole Militaire, Paris, which, with its lions' heads, draperies and frieze with a repeating scroll motif, incorporates most of the decorative themes of the Neo-classical style. The lamp brackets (1759; Rome, Pal. Quirinale) with trophies of the Arts and the Sciences also illustrate his modernism. Like his father, Philippe produced many different types of bronzework. He made the bronzes for a medal-cabinet by Jean-François Oeben for François Boucher and decorated pendulum clocks (New York, Frick; Versailles, Château) made by Berthoud and Lieutaud with bronze bas-reliefs, including one of the *Chariots of Apollo*. He also modelled vase and pedestal decorations for the Duc d'Aumont (Paris, Louvre), Paul Randon de Boisset, La Live de Jully and Stanisław II Poniatowski, King of Poland. He also designed a toilet-table for the Princess of the Asturias in 1765, altar bronzes for the cathedral of Notre-Dame and the church of St Nicolas du Chardonnet, Paris, and for Bayeux Cathedral, as well as numerous works at Versailles. Some of his most notable bronzes are those commissioned for the Palais-Bourbon, Paris, for which only the designs (Chantilly, Mus. Condé) are extant, and the candelabra mounted around statues by Martin Desjardins (1637–94) (London, Buckingham Pal., Royal Col.) illustrating the *Four Seasons*, for the Comte d'Orsay. From 1766 to 1768 he took part in the redecoration of the Łazienki Palace, Warsaw, for Stanislav II, together with Jean-Louis Prieur and Victor Louis (1731–1800), providing ornaments for four chimney-pieces, six tripod candelabra with cornucopias and a set of wall-lights with illusionistic drapery (all Warsaw, Royal Castle).

J. Guiffrey: *Les Caffiéri: Sculpteurs et fondeurs-ciseleurs* (Paris, 1877)

B. Metman: *Documents sur la sculpture française; et, Répertoire des fondeurs du XIXe siècle* (Paris, 1989)

J. Guiffrey: *Les Caffiéri, sculpteurs et fondeurs-ciseleurs: Etude sur la statuaire et sur l'art du bronze en France au XVIIe et au XVIIIe siècle* (Paris, 1993)

Cahier, Jean-Charles (*b* 1772; *d* after 1849). French silversmith. He was apprenticed to MARTIN-GUILLAUME BIENNAIS and established as an independent silversmith by 1806. He made both secular and ecclesiastical plate, and his work shows the transition between the Empire and Renaissance Revival styles.

Cailloué [Fr.: 'pebbled']. Porcelain decoration consisting of ovals and irregular circles in gold set against a coloured background, often dark blue. The motif was first used at Sèvres in the mid-18th century and subsequently used on English porcelain, including that of Derby, Swansea and Worcester.

Cake basket. Openwork silver container used since the mid-18th century for holding cakes and fruit, memorably described by Keats in 'The Eve of St Agnes', in which fruits are heaped 'in baskets bright of wreathed silver'. The openwork can either be woven like a basket (as in the Keats poem) or pierced.

Calamander. *See* COROMANDEL.

Calamelli, Virgiliotto [Virgilio] (*fl* Faenza, 1531; *d* Faenza, *c.* 1570). Italian potter. His pottery was in the San Vitale quarter of Faenza, and he sold his wares in Bologna. His workshop produced huge table-services, including water jugs, salt-cellars, dishes and vases (e.g. vase with lion handles, *c.* 1550–60; Brunswick, Herzog Anton Ulrich-Mus.). In 1566, for health reasons, he handed his shop over to Leonardo Bettisi. Calamelli is recognized as an important exponent of the *Compendiario* (sketchy) style, which was typical of the so-called *bianchi di Faenza* wares. His most important works were stamped with the monogram VR FA.

G. Gennari: 'Virgiliotto Calamelli e la sua bottega', *Faenza*, xlii (1956), pp. 57–60

Calcedonio. *See* AGATE GLASS.

Caldas da Rainha. Portuguese centre of ceramic production. Pottery has been made in Caldas da Rainha since the 15th century, but the modern ceramics tradition with which the town is associated dates to the time of a certain D. Maria 'dos Cacos', who is recorded as having attempted to sell his wares in fairs all over Portugal between 1820 and 1853. Pieces attributed to him are rare. He was succeeded by Manuel Cipriano Gomes (*fl* 1853–7) from Mafra. In addition to producing faience that resembled wares made in the Oporto factories, Gomes also produced a body of wares that were strongly influenced by the work of BERNARD PALISSY.

In 1884 the Fábrica de Faianças das Caldas da Rainha was established in Lisbon, under the artistic direction of the painter Rafael Bordalo Pinheiro, who transferred the concern to Caldas da Rainha. Bordalo Pinheiro also worked in the Palissy tradition, so his jars, pots and plates feature vegetation, crustacea, fish and reptiles. In the 1890s he produced the large Beethoven Vase (1895; Rio de Janeiro, Mus. N.) and figures of such popular Portuguese characters as Zé Povinho in various postures. Bordalo Pinheiro's son Manuel Gustavo Bordalo Pinheiro succeeded his father; the factory closed in 1908.

M. P. Katz: *Portuguese Palissy Ware: A Survey of Ceramics from Caldas da Rainha, 1853–1920* (New York, 1999)
A terra e a chama: António Dias Ribeiro: cerâmica, vitral, vidro arquitectónico (exh. cat., Caldas da Rainha, Osíris-Gal. Mun., 2001)

Caldwell, J. E., & Co. American jewellers and silversmiths founded in Philadelphia in 1839, when James Emott Caldwell, a watchmaker from Poughkeepsie, opened a workshop and retail outlet on Chestnut Street. The company's fourth Chestnut Street shop was the Widener Building, which it occupied for 87 years until it closed in 2003; it now operates in six suburban locations. In the 19th century the company made silver plate, but in the 20th century it became primarily a retail outlet.

J. E. Caldwell & Company: Jewels, Goldware, Silverware Stationery (Philadelphia, 1926)
L. Meyer: *The J. E. Caldwell Story: When Once Bought, Worth Keeping* (New York, 1989)

Calico. In early use, a generic name for cotton cloth from India, which was imported from Calicut (now Kozhikode), on the Malabar Coast of Kerala. The term subsequently came to denote similar European cloths. In late 19th-century England it was applied to any white unprinted cotton cloth, though in the USA and Scotland such cloths were called 'cotton'. In modern American English it now denotes a coarse printed cotton cloth (see colour pl. VI, fig. 2).

P. E. Rivard: *A New Order of Things: How the Textile Industry Transformed New England* (Hanover, NH, 2002)
D. A. Farnie and D. J. Jeremy: *The Fibre That Changed the World: The Cotton Industry in International Perspective, 1600–1990s* (Oxford and New York, 2004)

Camaiue [Fr. *en camaieu*: 'like a cameo']. Painting with a single colour (monochrome) in two or three tones only; the technique is often employed to give the spectator the illusion that the image is carved (*see also* GRISAILLE).

M. Krieger: *Grisaille als Metapher: Zum Entstehen der Peinture en Camaieu im frühen 14. Jahrhundert* (Vienna, 1995)

Cambrian Pottery. *See under* SWANSEA.

Cambric. Type of fine white linen, originally made at Cambrai in French Flanders and widely used for handkerchiefs; the term is also applied to an imitation made of hard-spun cotton yarn.

Cameo. Design engraved, carved or moulded in relief on gemstones, glass, ceramics etc; it uses layers of different colours, which can be transparent or opaque, so that the background and raised ground contrast. There are often just two colours: one dark colour, the other lighter, often white. The most common form is a medallion with a profile portrait. The cameo technique is the opposite of INTAGLIO. Cameos were made in classical Greece and Rome and revived during the Renaissance.

See also SHELL CAMEO.

Cameo binding. Bookbinding with a central medallion in low relief, produced by the pressure of an

Cameo cup with portrait of Empress Josephine, made by Sèvres (Rueil-Malmaison, Châteaux de Malmaison et Bois-Préau)

intaglio stamp directly into the leather; it is also known as a 'plaquette binding'. The form is popular in Italian Renaissance bindings.

Cameo glass. Product of a technique first used in ancient Egypt and later developed in ancient Rome. The outer of two superimposed layers of glass was ground away to leave a pattern consisting of a pattern standing in relief on a contrasting ground, usually white on dark blue. The finest surviving example is the Portland Vase (early 1st cent. AD; London, BM).

R. Grover and L. Grover: *English Cameo Glass* (New York, 1980)
Cameo Glass: Masterpieces from 2000 years of Glassmaking (exh. cat. by S. M. Goldstein, L. S. Rakow and J. K. Rakow; Corning, NY, Mus. Glass, 1982)
Cameo Glass and Related Art Glass (sale, cat., London, Christie's, 1998)

Camlet. Mixed cloth combining wool, silk and, sometimes, Angora goat- or camel-hair. The camlet of Cyprus was for centuries deemed to be of the highest quality. From the 17th century European manufacturers produced imitations; in the 18th century it became the favoured cloth for bed hangings, though the grandest beds continued to be hung with silk.

Canabas [Gegenbach, Joseph] (*b* 1712; *d* 1797). French furniture-maker of German origin. In 1745 he settled in Paris, where he became a prominent *ébéniste*. He worked in mahogany, and specialized in individual sideboards, called *tables servantes* or *rafraîchissoirs*, which could be used for intimate meals without service; rounded corners and legs were inspired by English models. Some of his furniture was designed for travellers or soldiers on campaign, and so could easily be taken apart. There are examples of

his furniture in the Musée des Arts Décoratifs in Paris.

Canada. Ceramics *see* BLUE MOUNTAIN POTTERY; STAFFORD POTTERY.
Furniture *see* MONTREAL.

Canadella. Ewer, usually of glass, made in Catalonia since the Middle Ages. The body is pear-shaped and the neck long and cylindrical.

Candelabrum. Support for one or more lights, consisting of a base, usually three-footed, a shaft and a receptacle or tray, which became a highly developed decorative art form in the ancient world.

Candlestick. Portable stand for a candle. One of the earliest extant candlesticks is of silver and was made in the reign of the Emperor Justinian I (AD 527–65; London, BM). Medieval candlesticks, however, were made from iron, brass or wood and had a pricket—a thin spike of metal—on which the candle was impaled. Few pricket candlesticks dating before 1400 survive. Some 12th-century candlesticks

Candlestick by Egide Rombaux and Frans Hoosemans, silver, ivory and onyx, h. 360 mm, Brussels, 1900 (Berlin, Schloss Köpenick)

include representations of beasts and human figures, for example the Gloucester Candlestick (1104–13; London, V&A) and the surviving fragments of a candlestick made near Reims (late 12th century; Reims, Mus. St Rémi), with a foot in the form of a winged dragon. In the 12th and 13th centuries copper candlesticks with champlevé enamel decoration were made at Limoges (e.g. London, V&A).

Candle holders or sockets, in which the candle was set, appeared in Europe in the late 13th century, in particular on domestic candlesticks. Until about 1500 the pricket form of candlestick and the type with a socket were used concurrently. A cup was also incorporated at the top of the stem below the pricket or socket to hold the accumulation of wax. In the 16th century a drip tray, often half-way up the stem, was added, while many candlesticks were made with a concave depression in the base.

During the late Middle Ages most pricket candlesticks had three feet, but c. 1450–1500 a new style with a round base appeared. This form is probably derived from earlier Near Eastern brass candlesticks that have drum-shaped bases (e.g. base of a candlestick probably from Iran, first half of the 14th century; Edinburgh, Royal Mus. Scotland). In the late 15th century socketed candlesticks were made with

notches to facilitate the removal of the stub; the notches were often crudely cut, rectangular and usually carrying file marks that show they were cut after casting. Notches were replaced in the late 16th century by a round, drilled hole, in which a lever could be inserted to eject the spent candle. Mouldings or knops also appear on 16th-century brass candlesticks.

Pewter candlesticks were particularly popular in the 17th century. Few silver candlesticks made before 1600 survive: extant examples from the 17th century follow the form of those in base metals (e.g. pair of silver trumpet-shaped candlesticks, 1649; Boston, MA, Mus. F.A.). Candlesticks in wood, bone or ceramic from this period are also similar to base metal examples. During the 17th century baluster stems were introduced, the drip tray having become unfashionable. At this time candle holders or sockets were made without apertures, and in the 18th century mechanical grips and other devices (often patented) that ejected the stubs were developed.

In the late 17th century and early 18th candlesticks were produced in a wide variety of fashionable styles. While certain features that were common to all areas of production appeared, each region developed its own variations of the main forms. Silver and brass

Pair of candlesticks in the form of jesters, Germany, 16th century (Florence, Museo Nazionale del Bargello)

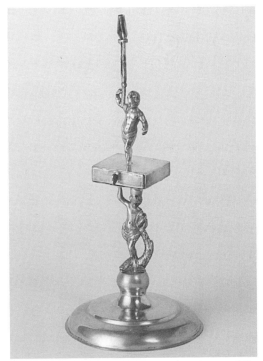

Candlestick for havdala, silver, h. 250 mm, from Germany, 16th–17th centuries (Paris, Musée d'Art et d'Histoire du Judaïsme)

candlesticks were cast in two halves (including stem, base and socket) and then soldered together. During the 1730s and 1740s elaborate Rococo candlesticks in silver, porcelain and earthenware were made. George Michael Moser produced designs for candlesticks that incorporate twisted human figures supporting the socket (e.g. of 1740; London, V&A). Paktong, an artificial silver alloy of 20% nickel with brass, began to be used for candlesticks during the first half of the 18th century, but the cost of production and a shortage of the zinc-based alloy meant that it was not widely popular. By the 1760s developments in core-casting (i.e. casting in one piece using a removable core) enabled candlesticks to be produced more inexpensively by using less metal. Simpler Neo-classical forms appeared with reeded or fluted stems on a square base and sockets in the form of Corinthian capitals. This type of hollow candlestick often has a loaded base to provide stability. Candlesticks in the Neo-classical style were designed by such architects as Robert Adam in order to harmonize with other interior furnishings (e.g. pair of 1767; Leeds, Temple Newsam House).

During the 19th century ornamental candlesticks continued to be made in the prevailing styles (e.g. pair of Gothic Revival candlesticks designed by A. W. N. Pugin, 1844–5; London, V&A), although a number of more practical forms were introduced. Telescopic candlesticks were patented in 1795: they are in the form of a cylindrical stem with a number of telescopic slides and are adjustable from about 5 cm to 50 cm. SHEFFIELD PLATE was also a popular material for candlesticks during the early 19th century. By the mid-19th century, however, candle lighting had been superseded by oil lamps.

It is often difficult to date candlesticks by style, as many forms, for example chamber candlesticks, continued to be manufactured over a long period. Ecclesiastical candlesticks with triangular stems and

were the most commonly used materials. Small silver candlesticks on square bases, often with elaborate embossed decoration, formed part of the large toilet services of the Baroque period (e.g. pair in French toilet service from Paris, 1658–76; Copenhagen, Rosenborg Slot).

Octagonal faceted brass candlesticks were also popular, as improvements in casting ensured that a greater variety of forms could be produced: most

Pair of candlesticks for travelling, c. 1820 (Vienna, Judaica Collection Max Berger)

bases were made in southern Europe from the 16th to the 19th century. The use of special silver candlesticks for the *havdalah* ceremony remains traditional in Jewish communities. Candlesticks continued to be made in modern styles after 1900 (e.g. pair of modernist pewter candlesticks by Reed & Barton, 1928; New Haven, CT, Yale U. A.G.), although antique styles remained popular.

See also CHAMBER CANDLESTICK.

J. Burke: *Birmingham Brass Candlesticks* (Charlottesville, VA, 1986)

J. Bourne and V. Brett: *The Art of Lighting in the Domestic Interior* (London, 1991)

E. F. Koldeweij: *The English Candlestick: 500 Years in the Development of Base-metal Candlesticks, 1425–1925* (London, 2001)

T. Felt, E. Stoer and R. Stoer: *The Glass Candlestick Book: Identification and Value Guide*, 3 vols (Paducah, KY, 2003–5)

J. Gadd: *Pewter Candlesticks : English Candlesticks of the Second Half of the 17th Century* (London, 2004)

Cane. Stem of the rattan palm. The technique of interweaving split cane to form an open mesh originated in East Asia; it was first used in England during the Restoration period in the second half of the 17th century for the bottoms and backs of seat furniture, supplies of the palm being shipped to Europe from the Malay Peninsula by the East India Co. Caning was also widely used by Dutch Colonial furniture-makers. After declining in favour, caning again became popular in the late 18th century for chairs, cradles, bedheads and, as Thomas Sheraton observed, 'anything where lightness, elasticity, cleanness, and durability, ought to be combined'. In the late 19th century and the early 20th there was a worldwide demand for furniture constructed entirely of the tough, fibrous core of the rattan palm; a wide range of articles, often described as 'art cane furniture', was available for gardens, conservatories, steamers, cafés, drawing-rooms and hotels. The cane is sometimes combined with fixed upholstery, and some makers used brightly coloured stains. A large collection of Edwardian trade catalogues issued by leading cane manufacturers, including W. T. Ellmore & Son (Leicester), E. A. Day and Morris Wilkinson & Co. (both Nottingham), is owned by the City Art Gallery, Leeds.

See also WICKER.

P. Kirkham: 'Willow and Cane Furniture in Austria, Germany and England *c.* 1900–14', *Furn. Hist.*, xxi (1985), pp. 128–33

R. Conniff: 'Antiques: Wicker Furniture: Versatile Charm of an American Classic', *Archit. Dig.*, li (June 1994), pp. 150–55

M. Connors: 'Raising Cane: Collectors are Clamoring for Colonial Danish West Indian Furniture', *A. & Ant.*, xxi/8 (Sept 1998), p. 114ff

Canephorus. In ancient Greek art, a sculpture of a young woman carrying a basket on her head. The motif was subsequently adopted in architectural decoration (sometimes with a young man instead of a woman) and in furniture from the Renaissance and later periods.

Caneware. Buff-coloured stoneware pioneered by Wedgwood in the 1770s and subsequently made by other manufacturers.

Cannelé silk. *See* SILK CANNELÉ.

Canopic jars. In ancient Egyptian art, a set of four vases into which a mummy's internal organs were deposited. In the Middle Kingdom, all four lids were made in the shape of human heads. This design was later to be imitated by Wedgwood in his *rosso antico* ware. It was also a feature of Neo-classical reconstructions of the Roman columbarium (a tomb with small niches intended to hold cremation urns) in settings such as THOMAS HOPE's house in Duchess Street, London.

A. Dodson: *The Canopic Equipment of the Kings of Egypt* (London and New York, 1994)

P. Dorman: *Faces in Clay: Technique, Imagery, and Allusion in a Corpus of Ceramic Sculpture from Ancient Egypt* (Mainz am Rhein, 2002)

Cantagalli, Ulisse (*b* 1839; *d* 1901). Italian pottery manufacturer. In 1878 he founded (together with his brother Giuseppe) the Manifattura Cantagalli in Florence. The factory made Islamic style tin-glazed earthenwares, and also produced imitations and copies of earlier Italian maiolica. In 1892 William De Morgan began spending winters in Florence, where he employed decorators at the Cantagalli pottery to paint his new designs and fired some of his pottery in the Cantagalli kilns; some pieces bear their joint signatures.

D. Thornton: 'Lustred Pottery from the Cantagalli Workshop', *Apollo*, cli/456 (Feb 2000), pp. 33–40

Canterbury. In furniture usage, a partitioned tray on legs. It was used both as a music stand and as a plate and cutlery stand (sometimes called a 'supper canterbury').

Càntir [Sp. *cántaro*]. Catalan drinking vessel with two spouts: a short one for filling and a long one through which the liquid is poured into the mouth without the spout touching the lips of the drinker. There is a Museo del Càntir in Argentona, near Barcelona.

M. A. Arnabat and O. Calvo: *Imatges del Càntir: Les representacions pictòriques d'un atuell de la Mediterrània en la història de l'art* (Argentina, 2003)

R. Violant i Simorra, R. Noé and S. Palomar: *El càntir per aigua* (Reus, Tarragona, 2003)

Canton enamel. Chinese enamelware, particularly that made in Guangzhou (Canton). In the early 18th century, Guangzhou became a centre of painted enamels. Three distinct types of painted enamel made in Guangzhou in the Qianlong reign period have been identified: copies of European painted enamels, items such as snuff bottles produced according to court designs, and typical Guangzhou products such as bowls, probably designed to hold goldfish and often decorated with fish and boxes with fit-in trays. Some enamels were painted in imitation of cloisonné, with outlines painted in gold to represent metal *cloisons*, though this style declined after the Jiaqing reign period (1796–1820). Painted enamels were made elsewhere in China, and in English the term 'Canton enamel' was used loosely to denote any Chinese painted enamels, not just those made in Guangzhou.

Caparra. *See* GROSSO, NICCOLÒ.

Cape Cod Glass Company. American glass factory. In 1858 Deming Jarves (1790–1869) was forced out of the Boston & Sandwich Glass Co. by its directors, and together with his son established his own glass works a mile away; the company produced coloured and opaque glass until its closure in 1869.

B. Burgess and C. M. Stow: *History of Sandwich Glass* (Yarmouthport, 1925)
Glass-making in Sandwich (Yarmouthport, 1931)

Capitonné. In upholstery, the French term for stuffing that is buttoned; the term reflects the fact that this technique had formerly involved the use of a tuft (or *capiton*) of material.

Capodimonte Porcelain Factory. Italian porcelain factory. It was founded in 1743 in the grounds of the Palazzo Reale di Capodimonte by Charles VII, King of Naples (later Charles III, King of Spain). The clear, white, soft-paste porcelain was developed by Livio Schepers (*d* 1757) and Gaetano Schepers (*d* after 1764). The chief modeller was GIUSEPPE GRICCI and the principal painters were Giovanni Caselli (1698–1752), Giuseppe della Torre (*fl* 1744–*c*. 1764) and Johann Sigismund Fischer (*fl* 1750–58). The factory produced useful wares, sculpture and snuff-boxes. Some early decorative schemes were based on prototypes from the Saxon factory of Meissen. Painted subjects included battle scenes, allegorical figures and still-lifes stippled or painted in a subdued palette of browns, blues and greens and chinoiseries in brilliant colours. Religious figures were also produced, but most were of peasants or characters from the *commedia dell'arte*, composed as narrative couples or groups. Modelling was simple and effective more through mood and gesture than detail. Figures were sparsely decorated and costumes were simply trimmed with coloured or gilded borders. One of the factory's most extraordinary achievements was the *Salottino di Porcellana* of painted and relief chinoiserie tiles created for the Palazzo Reale in Pórtici between 1757 and 1759 (now Naples, Capodimonte). When Charles succeeded to the Spanish throne in 1759, the factory closed and was transferred to the new building in the Buen Retiro, Madrid.

A. Caròla-Perrotti: *Le porcellane dei Borbone di Napoli* (Naples, 1986)
Porcellana di Capodimonte: La Real Fabbrica di Carlo di Borbone, 1743–1759 (Naples, 1993)
R. Palmer: 'Capodimonte Porcelain [Villa Floridiana, Naples]', *Apollo*, cxxxix (March 1994), p. 89
S. M. Guida: 'Chinoiserie in the Boudoir', *F.M.R. Mag.*, lxxviii (Feb 1996), pp.105–23 [the porcelain Salottino at Capodimonte, Naples]

Capparoni [Caparroni; Capparone; Capperoni], **Gaspare** (*b* Rome, 20 June 1761; *d* Rome, 13 Dec 1808). Italian gem-engraver. His works, signed КАП, КАППА, КАППАРОΝΙ and CAPPARONI, include engravings in both intaglio and cameo, although he seems to have preferred the latter technique. Among his documented signed works are: *Maecenas* (Rome, priv. col.); *Hebe Giving Water to the Eagle* (Vienna, Ksthist. Mus.); a *Veiled Head of a Woman* (St Petersburg, Hermitage); and a bust of *Napoleon*, copied from a statue by Antonio Canova (1757–1822) (London, Apsley House).

L. Pirzio Biroli Stefanelli: 'Gaspare Capparoni, scultore in gemme', *Xenia*, ii (1981), pp. 85–98

Caqueteuse [caquetoire]. 'Conversation' chair (from Fr.: *caqueter*, 'to chatter') introduced into Britain from France in the late 16th century. It was a type of light open-backed chair with a flared seat narrowing to a typically elongated back with angled or outcurved arms that enclosed the sitter, and proved to be an important influence on Scottish furniture. An important group of 16 Scottish caqueteuse chairs survives at Trinity Hall, Aberdeen, where they were used and documented by successive Deacons of the Incorporated Trades. Seven of the chairs, including one in mahogany, dated 1661, have crestings comprising inward-scrolling volutes put down on capitals, a form echoed in the furniture of other provincial centres on the east coast. Examples from St Monans and Balmerino in Fife have a distinctive combination of lobed rosettes and diagonal palmette motifs.

In the 20th century the Scottish furniture designer GEORGE WALTON produced a modern interpretation of the caqueteuse chair which inspired German designers such as RICHARD RIEMERSCHMID.

Carabin, (François-)Rupert (*b* Saverne, Lower Rhine, 17 March 1862; *d* Strasbourg, 1932). French sculptor, decorative artist and draughtsman. He is best known for a small number of pieces of furniture which have more in common with sculpture than with the work of traditional cabinetmakers. He often made use of female nudes in his furniture, not as decoration but literally as construction; in a writing table of 1890 a table-top like a book is supported by four carved figures of women supporting the table-top with their uplifted arms (Strasbourg, Mus. B.-A.). See fig. on p. 176.

L'Oeuvre de Rupert Carabin, 1862–1932 (exh. cat. by Y. Brunhammer and C. Merklen; Paris, Pal. Luxembourg, 1974)
M. Frechuret: 'Charles Maurin et Francois Rupert Carabin: Les échanges de deux artistes à la fin du XIXe siècle', *Rev. Louvre*, xliii (April 1993), pp. 64–70

François-Rupert Carabin (see p. 175): bookcase, chestnut-wood, wrought iron and glass, 2.9×2.15×0.83 m, 1890 (Paris, Musée d'Orsay)

N. Lehni and others: *F. R. Carabin, 1842–1932* (Strasbourg, 1993)

Caradosso [Foppa, Cristoforo] (*b* Mondonico, nr Pavia, *c.* 1452; *d* between 6 Dec 1526 and 1 April 1527). Italian goldsmith, coin- and gem-engraver, jeweller, medallist and dealer. Son of the goldsmith Gian Maffeo Foppa, from 1480 he served at the Milanese court with his father, eventually becoming personal goldsmith and jeweller to Ludovico Sforza (il Moro), Duke of Milan. In the late 1480s he twice worked in Hungary in the service of King Matthias Corvinus. Caradosso moved to Rome in 1505 and received a constant stream of commissions, from the popes from Julius II to Clement VII and from members of the papal court.

To his contemporaries, Caradosso was most famous as a jeweller, but none of his jewellery works can now be identified. His most famous work was a papal tiara made for Julius II in 1509–10 and recorded in a drawing (*c.* 1725; London, BM) by Francesco Bartoli (*c.* 1675–*c.* 1730). Caradosso also made a matching clasp for the Pope's cope; this was of sheet-gold and silver, with the Four Doctors of the Church grouped around a magnificent diamond. He made an inkwell for which John of Aragon was reputed to have offered 1500 gold pieces; Ambrogio Leone's description (*Dialogus de nobilitate rerum*, 1525) of this piece has led to the identification of numerous replicas of two of the reliefs that originally decorated it: the *Rape of Ganymede*

and *Battle of the Lapiths and Centaurs* (specimens of both in Washington, DC, N.G.A.); other plaques have, consequently, also been attributed to Caradosso. He carved gemstones with such skill that they were mistaken for antique works. Lomazzo and Vasari reported that he made portrait medals of Gian Giacomo Trivulzio, Julius II and Donato Bramante, and this has provided the basis for all the additional attributions made by modern writers, although none of his coins or medals is documented. The attribution of the base of the *Calvary* of Matthias Corvinus (Esztergom, Mus. Christ.) to Caradosso would seem to be correct on both historical and technical grounds, but other attributions, such as Pius IV's pax (Milan, Tesoro Duomo), are much more problematical.

J. Pope-Hennessy: 'The Study of Italian Plaquettes', *Stud. Hist. A.,* xxii (1989), pp. 19–32
C. M. Brown and others: 'Caradosso Foppa and the Roman Mint', *Artibus & Hist.*, xxii/43 (2001), pp. 41–4

Carbuncle. Name variously applied to precious stones of a red or fiery colour; the carbuncles of the ancients were probably sapphires, spinels or rubies, and garnets; in medieval and early modern usage, it denotes the ruby and a mythical gem said to emit a light in the dark; in modern lapidary usage it denotes the garnet when cut *en cabochon*.

Carder, Frederick (*b* Brockmoor, Staffs, 18 Sept 1863; *d* 10 Dec 1963). American glass designer and technician of English birth. He trained as an assistant in his father's salt-glazed stoneware factory in Stourbridge, Staffs, and in 1880 joined the Stourbridge firm of Stevens & Williams. During this period Carder developed his *Mat-su-no-ke* glass (which uses the application of clear or frosted glass in high relief outside the vessel). He also collaborated with JOHN NORTHWOOD to make coloured art glass and cut and cased glass.

In 1902 Carder established a factory at Corning, NY, to produce blanks for T. G. HAWKES & Co. In 1903 Carder, who was inspired by the Art Nouveau style, joined with Thomas G. Hawkes (1846–1913) to found the STEUBEN GLASS WORKS, Corning, for the production of ornamental art glass. During his 30 years as Art Director, Carder developed new techniques of enamelling and etching. Some of the types of art glass produced include 'Aurene', 'Calcite' and 'Tyrian' glass. In 1918 Steuben became a subsidiary of the Corning Glassworks, and Carder continued as Art Director. The huge range of ornamental glasswares developed by Carder has resulted in him being generally regarded as the founder of the modern tradition in American art glass. He retired from Corning in 1933.

Steuben Glass: The Carder Years (exh. cat., St Petersburg, FL, Mus. F.A., 1984)
P. V. Gardner and F. Carder: *Frederick Carder: Portrait of a Glassmaker* (Corning, NY, 1985)
Play of Light: The Glass Lamps of Frederick Carder, Rockwell Museum (Corning, NY, 1991)

T. P. Dimitroff, C. R. Hajdamach and J. S. Spillman: *Frederick Carder and Steuben Glass: American Classics* (Atglen, PA, 1998)

P. V. Gardner and P. N. Perrot: *The Glass of Frederick Carder* (Atglen, PA, 2000)

M. Ketchum and others: *Frederick Carder's Steuben Glass: Guide to Shapes, Numbers, Colors, Finishes and Values* (Atglen, PA, 2002)

Cardew, Michael (*b* Wimbledon, London, 26 May 1901; *d* Truro, Cornwall, 11 Feb 1983). English potter. In 1923 he joined Bernard Leach as a student in the Leach Pottery at St Ives, Cornwall. They shared an interest in English slipware, and in 1926 Cardew left St Ives to set up his own workshop where he planned to revive the tradition. He leased the pottery at Greet, near Winchcombe, Glos, where, from 1926 until 1939, he worked with earthenware clay (e.g. earthenware pie dish, *c.* 1938; Bristol, Mus. & A.G.). In 1939 Cardew moved to St Tudy on the edge of Bodmin Moor, Cornwall, where he founded Wenford Bridge pottery, which was to be his base for the remainder of his life.

In 1942 Cardew began his long association with Africa when he went as Pottery Instructor to Achimota College on the Gold Coast (now Ghana). Here he built and ran Alajo Pottery, making domestic ware and tiles and training West African potters. When the project closed in 1945 Cardew moved to Vumé Dugamé, on the Volta River, where he built a pottery and made stoneware pots glazed a dark bronze-green (e.g. stoneware jar, 1947–8; Brit. Council Col.). His

Michael Cardew: cider jar, earthenware, *c.* 1938 (London, Victoria and Albert Museum)

health broke down in Africa, and he returned to Wenford Bridge, where he made stoneware pots from 1949 to 1951, when he returned to West Africa as Pottery Officer for the Nigerian Government. His job was to protect native women potters from exploitation and to teach pottery skills. He built the pottery and training centre at Abuja, where he again made stoneware pots with dark-toned glazes. Cardew 'retired' to Wenford Bridge in 1965, and for the next 18 years continued to make stoneware pots.

ODNB

M. Cardew: *Pottery in Nigeria: Incorporating "A preliminary survey of pottery in West Africa"* (Washington, 1950/*R* 1993)

M. Cardew: *Pioneer Pottery* (London, 1969/*R* 2002)

G. Clark: *Michael Cardew* (London, 1978)

Michael Cardew and Pupils (exh. cat. by T. Sidey, York, C.A.G., 1983)

M. Cardew: *A Pioneer Potter: An Autobiography* (London, 1988)

International Contemporary Ceramics: Tuesday 10 May 2005 (sale cat., London, Bonhams, 2005)

Carlin, Martin (*b* nr Freiburg im Breisgau; *d* Paris, 6 March 1785). French cabinetmaker of German birth. He became a *maître-ébéniste* on 30 July 1766 and established a workshop in the Rue du Faubourg Saint-Antoine, Paris, and produced luxurious furniture for a distinguished clientele which included the daughters of Louis XV, who decorated the Château Bellevue in Paris with some of Carlin's most beautiful, lacquered furniture (see fig. on p 178). Some of his furniture was inset with porcelain plaques from the factory of Sèvres. His masterpieces include two commodes and a *guéridon* table (Paris, Louvre) and a writing-table with porcelain plaques (Lisbon, Mus. Gulbenkian) for the Comtesse Du Barry, a commode (London, Buckingham Pal., Royal Col.) with panels of pietra dura for Mademoiselle Laguerre, a lacquered commode (Paris, Louvre) for Madame Victoire and a writing-desk with porcelain plaques (Malibu, CA, Getty Mus.) for Empress Maria Fyodorovna. Among Carlin's most sophisticated pieces are his *bonheurs du jour* (e.g. Paris, Mus. Nissim de Camondo), which combined a writing-table and toilet accessories decorated with porcelain plaques and similarly decorated secrétaires (e.g. of 1776–7; Malibu, CA, Getty Mus.).

P. Lemonnier: 'Les Commodes de Martin Carlin', *Estampille*, clxxi–ii (1984), pp. 6–19

W. Rieder: 'A Meuble à Corbeil in the Metropolitan Museum', *Met. Mus. J.*, xxxvii (2002), pp. 257–8

M.-L. de Rochebrune: *Le guéridon de Madame du Barry* (Paris, 2002)

Carouge. Swiss centre of ceramics production. There were three potteries producing creamware in 19th-century Carouge, which was part of Savoy from 1786–1816 and thereafter joined the Swiss canton of Geneva, of which it is now a suburb. The first ran from 1779–1829, the second from 1803–*c.* 1820 and the third (founded by Abraham Baylon) from 1813 till the early 20th century. Some of the finest pottery was made between 1813 and 1820 at the second of the three potteries; during this period JOHANN JACOB DORTU owned the pottery, and the manager was Jacques-François Richard. In the 20th century the

Martin Carlin (see p.177): commode, ebony, lacquer and gilt bronze with a white marble top, made for the Château de Bellevue, 1785 (Paris, Musée du Louvre)

most important potter was Marcel Noverraz (1899–1972), who settled in Carouge in 1922. The Musée de Carouge has a collection of earthenware produced by the Carouge factory between 1810 and 1930 and of Noverraz art deco ceramics made between 1930 and 1960. Carouge is still an important pottery centre, and since 1987 has hosted a biennial international ceramics competition.

Carpet. Originally a thick cover for a bed or table. From the 16th century the term included knotted carpets from the Middle East; it gradually became exclusively associated with knotted carpets placed on the floor. By the early 18th century other forms of fabric floor covering had assumed the same name.

I. Types and techniques. II. History.

I. Types and techniques.

1. Hand-knotted. 2. Tapestry-woven. 3. Flat-woven. 4. Embroidered and needle-worked. 5. Pile-woven. 6. Power-loom woven. 7. Warp-printed. 8. Machine-tufted.

1. HAND-KNOTTED. This is considered the quintessential carpet. Woven originally in Asia, such carpets were highly prized and later copied in many parts of Europe. The knots, tied in cut lengths of yarn, the ends of which formed the pile, were inserted during the process of construction, or weaving; they were tied in rows across the warps, each row of knots being separated by one, two or three picks of weft, laid in as alternate rows of plain weave. Hand-knotted carpets can be divided into several categories, according to the knot used; this is, consequently, a means of establishing a carpet's provenance. There are four types of knot, each type known by several names. The first is the Turkish, Ghiordes or symmetrical knot and the second the Persian, Senna or asymmetrical knot. A third type, based on the first two but worked over four warps instead of two, is known as the jufti knot; depending on the style, this may be the Turkish jufti or the Persian jufti. The fourth type of knot is the Spanish or single-warp symmetrical knot.

The warp of Middle Eastern carpets was almost exclusively tightly spun wool, often a dark natural colour; in some very fine Persian carpets, tightly spun silk was used for the warps, as it was stronger and less bulky than wool, and a loosely spun silk for the wefts. In Persian and Indian carpets the silk warps were later replaced by factory-spun cotton. In Turkish carpets wefts were usually of a softer wool, often dyed red; cotton was sometimes used, especially in Caucasian rugs. In 19th- to 21st-century rugs a combination of materials has sometimes been used for the weft, and some late Indian carpets have employed jute. The knots of Middle Eastern carpets were almost invariably of wool, although of widely differing qualities. Silk was used in particularly rich carpets, and occasionally small amounts of cotton were used. The density of the knots varied enormously according to the quality of the carpet, and could range from 5 knots to 2000 knots per 25 sq. mm, a broad average lying between 10 and 40 knots per 25 sq. mm.

See also RYIJY AND RYER RUGS.

2. TAPESTRY-WOVEN. Such carpets and rugs, which have been woven in many parts of the world, have a plain woven weft-faced structure in which the weft is beaten down very hard to cover the warp entirely. Their distinctive feature is the use of discontinuous coloured weft threads, which travel only a short distance along the pick in creating the pattern. Differently coloured areas of the pattern are not necessarily joined in the weaving process, and slits running in the direction of the warps may form between two colours. In the type produced in West Asia, known as kelims, kilims, khelims or ghilleems (*see* KILIM), such slits are common, but they are not invariable, and various joining methods are employed. Interlocking techniques are found in early Peruvian tapestry, in Navajo rugs and blankets and in Swedish and Norwegian *rølakan* rugs.

With single interlocked joins, like those found in Norwegian *rølakan*s and in some kilims from central to south-west Persia, the finish is the same on both sides of the weaving. With double interlock joins, as used on Swedish *rølakan*s and some Persian kilims, particularly those woven by the Baktari tribes, although the front looks the same as single interlock, on the back the join is more obvious, and a ridge is visible. Another method of making vertical joins is dovetailing, which gives a jagged saw-tooth line; it is used in kilims from Thrace and north-west Persia. Hatching is a steep zigzag joining technique that gives a softer edge. In intricate or curved areas of the design, wefts sometimes travel around a contrasting pattern area, instead of remaining strictly perpendicular to the warp; known as eccentric or curved-weft tapestry, this is also found mainly in Thracian kilims. In large areas of a single colour, 'lazy lines' can sometimes be seen; these were created when the weaver, having taken the weft over a limited number of warps, moved it along to work on the next area, forming a diagonal line in the weave. Such lines have sometimes been used as a pattern feature, progressing across one or two warps at a time to produce a smooth line, while a stepped diagonal line was a distinctive feature of patterns in kilims. Soumak and small areas of brocading were occasionally used in kilims.

3. FLAT-WOVEN. Rugs and carpets woven without a pile or raised surface texture have been made in all parts of the world and vary from the highly prized and richly adorned to the simplest and most basic of matting. Carpets can be woven using basic plain weave, with simple or complex patterns ranging from warp- or weft-faced stripes to intricate designs. Looms with three, four, six and eight shafts give vast scope for pattern and surface texture on the warp or weft face; these range from simple twills, with all their variations of diaper and broken twills, to shadow weave, spot weave, honeycomb, block patterns and brocades.

Warp-faced carpets and rugs, in which only the warp yarns are visible, are considered to be more hard-wearing, because warp yarns have generally tended to be stronger and more tightly spun. Examples include Bedouin saha or tent curtains made of goat hair, and Venetian carpets, first recorded in 1803, which had a striped worsted warp and a wool weft (by the end of the 19th century this was often replaced by jute). References to Venetian carpeting show that it was used for halls and stairs; it is known to have been made in KIDDERMINSTER, Yorkshire and Scotland and had no known connection with Venice. List carpets, first recorded in 1747 and noted to be like an inferior version of the Venetian, were wiry, plain-weave coarse carpets in which the weft was made of selvages, then called lists, cut from other fabrics. Such carpets were made of cotton, with narrow, coloured stripes.

Soumak is a weft-faced technique, used in Caucasian rug-making, that involved repeatedly wrapping the weft yarn around the warps to create a distinctive surface texture. The yarn may travel from selvage to selvage, using a continuous weft, but its path is not direct; it can be wrapped around each individual warp or around two or more, while the progress of the weft moves one warp along with each wrap (rather like backstitch in needlework), giving a diagonal appearance to the surface. This diagonal can be alternated with the ground weave, in which case it is called soumak brocading, or it can be worked without any ground weaving in between, called soumak wrapping. The diagonal can also be reversed, giving a zigzag effect. There are many different variations: the soumak wefts are sometimes used for patterning across part of the warp, employing discontinuous wefts, to produce blocks of different colours or textures.

Hard-wearing double and triple cloths used as floor coverings are known as Kidderminster, Scotch, Ingrain, Union or two- or three-ply carpets. A double cloth has two independent sets of warps and wefts of plain weave, one on top of the other. They can be crossed, so that the top set intersects the lower one and changes places with it. If different colours are used for each set of warps and wefts, a pattern can be formed by moving the sets back and forth at chosen intervals. This method gives a reversible product with a choice of two sets of colours. Triple cloth works in a similar fashion, but with three sets of warps and wefts, giving a choice of three sets of colours. The first mention of carpets of Kidderminster cloth is found in 1634 in an inventory of the Countess of Leicester, but it is not known whether that cloth corresponded to KIDDERMINSTER double cloth, first made there in 1735. Double-cloth carpets were introduced in 1778 to Kilmarnock, Scotland, where in 1824 the triple-cloth technique was perfected. These types of carpet were mainly all-wool products and tended to have worsted yarn in the warp and wool in the weft. Early carpets using double and triple cloths were made by sewing together strips 910 mm wide, with approximately 15 ends and picks per 25 mm. By the early 20th century improved technology had made possible the weaving of wide seamless carpets.

4. EMBROIDERED AND NEEDLE-WORKED. Embroidered carpets could be worked in a variety of stitches on a canvas ground. Early embroidered carpets, dating from the 16th century, were on single-thread canvas; those of the 19th century and after seem to have favoured double-thread canvas. As early as the 17th century patterns already drawn on the canvas were sold with a set of wools or silks, ready to be executed. The stitches, although sometimes coarser, were the same as those used for other canvaswork, using primarily wool and occasionally small amounts of silk. The most common stitches found in early examples are tent stitch and cross stitch; from the 19th century embroiderers made use of variations of cross stitch, half-cross stitch and herringbone stitch, as well as knotted stitch, chain stitch and rice stitch.

Two types of hand-knotted pile rug that were popular in the late 19th century and the 20th were the long-pile rug and the short-pile rug. Both used a canvas ground and almost exclusively used wool for the pile. The long-pile method used pre-cut lengths of wool (an instrument known as a 'turkey gauge' was sometimes used to ensure evenness of length) that were drawn through the canvas and knotted one at a time using a latched hook. In the short-pile method, a needle threaded with a long piece of yarn was used to make a knot or double stitch on the canvas; the thread was taken around a gauge, and a second knot or double stitch was made one space further along. Repeating this process created a row of the pattern; the loops were cut before the gauge was moved on to a new area.

5. PILE-WOVEN. The techniques employed for these carpets contributed towards the eventual mass production of carpets; the looms used to produce them were subsequently fitted with jacquard montures (a mechanism for controlling the selection of heddles to be lifted in weaving) and were later adapted to become power looms.

In Chenille carpets, originally called Patent Axminsters, the pile was created by means of a specially prepared form of chenille yarn, made by weaving a flat cloth with a wool weft, and a warp, usually of linen, arranged in groups with spaces between. The cloth was then cut along the length of the warp between the groups. The resulting long strips were used as pile warps in the carpets; the cut wool wefts formed the tufts. In the weaving of the chenille cloth, the colour of the weft could be changed, so that the cut strips used as pile warps formed the pattern. Colour changes along the strip could range from 12 to 20 per 25 mm. The density of chenille in construction is 3.5–5 per 25 mm, corresponding roughly to 42–100 knots per 25 sq. mm. In weaving chenille carpets, it was difficult to maintain accurate registering of the pattern; also, the chenille was apt to break away from the surface of the carpet, as it did not have a very strong anchor, while a binding warp that was too strong sometimes crushed the pile.

The looped-pile or Brussels carpet was first patented in England at Wilton in 1741 and the first loom for weaving it was built at Kidderminster in 1749. The construction was like that of terry-towelling but woven with multi-coloured supplementary warps, from which groups of threads were looped proud of the ground warp when required to form the pattern. Up to six colours could be used, but often only two were required, and self-coloured Brussels carpets were also made. Brussels carpet was considered durable and clean and could render a wide variety of patterns, although the complicated shedding motion made it unsuitable for long pattern repeats. It was uneconomic in patterning, as much expensive worsted yarn lay below the surface. The weaving of wide carpets was impractical, and even with a jacquard monture, the heavy machinery could not be worked at great speed. The carpets were usually 700 mm wide and up to 46 m long; several widths could be joined, the borders being woven separately. There were 40 to 100 loops per 25 sq. mm. The surface quality was considered to be lacking in richness, and on poorer versions the foundation weave showed through.

WILTON carpets were originally made around Wilton, near Salisbury, in large quantities. The technique was almost the same as that of Brussels, but the pile was cut. The number of colours, or pattern warps, varied from two to six, although again, self-coloured carpets of this type were also made. The carpets were woven in widths ranging from 690 mm to 910 mm, with 50–150 loops per 25 mm. Carpets up to 2.7 m wide were known, but they were rare, being technically difficult and therefore expensive. Wilton had the same disadvantages as Brussels, but the cut pile gave it a richer surface texture and more covering power. It was considered the best kind of machine-made carpet; the close-piled quality was sometimes called velvet carpeting.

6. POWER-LOOM WOVEN. Up to the 1830s and 1840s the looms used in factories to produce Kidderminster, Ingrain, Brussels and Wilton carpets did not differ greatly from those used domestically. In 1825 a jacquard monture was first used in Kidderminster for Ingrain carpets and soon after for Brussels and Wilton. This simplified the weaving process and made possible looms operated by only one person. In 1842 Wood of Pontefract patented the first steam loom to be used for Brussels carpets. In 1847 John Crossley of Halifax purchased Wood's patent and tried it for tapestry, or warp-tinted carpets. In 1839 Erastus Brigham Bigelow (1814–79), an American engineer, had begun to work on perfecting a power loom for Ingrain carpets. The early results were technically excellent, producing a superior article, but the loom did not at first increase speed or productivity. In 1846, when his Ingrain loom was being launched, Bigelow took out a British patent for a new power loom for Brussels carpet. The final version was said to combine the driving motions of Bigelow's Ingrain loom, the power of the Jacquard loom and, for the pile, a terry wire mechanism that Bigelow had previously devised for a coach-lace

loom. It was only after he had displayed his looms in London at the Great Exhibition of 1851 that carpet manufacturers began to show enthusiasm for power-loom weaving. Crossleys of Halifax bought Bigelow's patent for £10,000 and proceeded to sell licences to build the looms to various British manufacturers.

7. WARP-PRINTED. These are sometimes misleadingly known as tapestry carpets, although they are not tapestry-woven but have a ground warp and a pattern warp and are woven in a similar way to velvet. The pattern warp is six times longer than the ground warp and is woven in over rods to create a looped pile, which can, as in velvet, be cut or can be left in loops. Before weaving, the pattern warp is dyed or printed in different colours so as to form a pattern in weaving. Because the quality of dyefastness is poorer in partially dyed or printed textiles, these carpets were not considered to have the durability of other carpets, where the whole yarn was immersed in the dye vats. Another disadvantage was that the pattern did not always register perfectly in the weaving. This kind of carpet could be woven up to 2.7 m or 3.65 m wide, with 7–9 tufts per 25 mm, 64 per 25 sq. mm.

8. MACHINE-TUFTED. Although AXMINSTER was known as a weaving centre for carpets, the carpet known as machine-tufted, and also as Axminster, has apparently no connection with the town. It was Tomkinson & Adam who introduced machine-tufted carpets, which were woven on a loom developed from a patent bought from Halcyon Skinner, an American. They were known as Royal Axminster carpets and were closer in general appearance to hand-knotted carpets than anything so far achieved. Unlike Brussels and Wilton carpets, they entailed no waste of valuable worsted. A separate row of warp rollers, sometimes known as spools, was made up for each line or pick of pattern in the carpet; these rotated in sequence above the loom, and at the appropriate time the correct roller was presented to the loom. The necessary amount of yarn was then taken for each tuft and cut. The row of rollers then moved on, and the next one in the sequence was presented. The texture was not very fine; the first Royal Axminsters had about 30 tufts per 25 sq. mm, and the Imperial Axminsters marketed by Tomkinson & Adam in 1893 had 48 tufts per 25 sq. mm. By the 1930s this had improved to 63 tufts per 25 sq. mm. The number of colours that could be used was virtually unlimited, and carpets up to 2.7 m wide could be woven. In 1910 Tomkinson & Adam acquired machines from the French company of Renard, which made knotted carpets resembling hand-made ones. In 1927 Jacquard or Gripper Axminsters were introduced, dispensing with the need to pre-arrange colours on a series of rollers or spools. The colours required for the whole pattern were set up; the jacquard device selected those that were needed for each row and, by means of a gripper, pulled off the required lengths of yarn, cut them and took them to the correct place on the loom. Up to 16 colours were practicable, which was ample for most designs. These carpets wasted less wool than Imperial Axminsters, and the method could be used for making both small and large quantities. The spool and gripper methods were later combined in the Spool Gripper Axminster to maximize the advantages of both types.

Since World War II many changes in carpet-making have taken place. In the 1950s looms that weave face-to-face carpets were introduced. Two separate backings were woven, with a single set of loops between them, which, when cut, produced two identical carpets. New synthetic fibres, such as nylon, acrylic, rayon, polyester and polypropylene, were introduced. Perhaps the most radical change was mechanical tufting, introduced by an American carpet manufacturer. Instead of weaving the pile in, cut tufts were attached to a ready-made backing; this was at first a woven backing and later a sheet backing. This method was found to be 10 to 20 times faster than any other method of carpet weaving. In the 1960s and 1970s methods of introducing patterns to tufted carpets were explored. First, the tufts could be made high or low, giving a self-coloured, raised pattern. Then printing of colours on to an uncoloured tufted base was developed, using machinery that resembled sets of hypodermic needles. A third way was to move the backing back and forth during tufting to produce simple geometric patterns. Since the 1970s hand-held tufting guns have been used by designer-craftsmen to make one-off gallery pieces or individual commissions.

C. E. C. Tattersall: *Notes on Carpet Knotting and Weaving* (London, 1920/*R* 1927)

C. E. C. Tattersall: *A History of British Carpets* (London, 1934)

A. H. Cole and H. F. Williamson: *The American Carpet Manufacture* (Cambridge, MA, 1941)

A. F. Stoddard: *The Carpet Makers* (Elderslie, 1962)

I. Bennett, ed.: *The 'Country Life' Book of Rugs and Carpets of the World* (London, 1978)

Y. Petsopoulis: *Kilims: The Art of Tapestry Weaving in Anatolia, the Caucasus and Persia* (London, 1979/*R* 1982)

The Eastern Carpet in the Western World (exh. cat., ed. D. Sylvester and D. King; London, Hayward Gal., 1983)

I. Bennett: *Rugs & Carpets of the World* (London, 1997)

E. Milanesi: *The Carpet: Origins, Art and History* (Buffalo, NY, 1999)

II. History.

1. Europe. 2. Indian subcontinent. 3. Islamic world.

1. EUROPE.

(i) Before 1500. (ii) 1500–1680. (iii) 1681–1800. (iv) 1801–1914. (v) After 1914.

(i) Before 1500. It is not known how or when the art of carpet-knotting was introduced into Europe. It is apparent that carpet-weaving was well established in the southern provinces of Spain by the 12th century and that the products of these looms were of high quality: carpets from Andalusia were used at the court of the Fatimid caliphs in Cairo, and in 1154 the Arab geographer El Idrisi mentioned that it would be difficult to surpass the quality of the wool-

len carpets from Chinchilla de Monte Aragón and Cuenca. Two other 12th-century Arab authors, Ibn Sa'id and El Saqundi, confirmed that Spanish carpets were being exported to the Middle East. From the 13th century there is increasing evidence that Spanish carpets were also being traded northwards into Europe: when Eleanor of Castile arrived in London in 1254 to marry Prince Edward (later Edward I), she brought carpets and textiles from Spain that aroused the admiration and envy of many. So well organized was the industry that Pope John XXII (*reg* 1316–34) was able to order carpets to be woven in Spain for the episcopal palace in Avignon, and Spanish carpets are listed in several other European inventories of the period. There is, however, nothing to indicate that carpet-weaving ever became established in medieval Europe, except in Spain.

The oldest, almost complete Spanish carpet to have survived is probably that in the Islamisches Museum, Berlin: it appears to date from the 14th century. Sometimes called the Synagogue carpet because the main motif is thought by some to resemble or represent the Ark of the Covenant, it is a unique piece and one that illustrates the characteristic feature of Spanish carpet-weaving: the knot is always tied around a single warp thread, unlike the symmetrical or asymmetrical knots of the Middle East, which encircle two warp threads. The single-warp knot has been found in early carpet fragments from Central Asia (3rd–6th century AD; some on loan to London, V&A), and it was used by Coptic weavers in Egypt to produce a looped pile; it is, however, not possible to establish what connection, if any, existed between these three areas, although it is known that Coptic weavers were employed in Spain in the 10th century. From the 11th century the carpet-weaving towns referred to in medieval texts gradually came under Christian rule, but it is thought that the weavers continued to be Muslims, or *mudéjar*s, who had chosen to remain.

In the 15th century the main centres of production that can be identified from texts include Liétor, Letur (*see* ADMIRAL CARPET) and Alcaraz, in Murcia, but surviving carpets cannot be attributed to specific towns with any degree of certainty. It is known that quantities of Turkish carpets were imported to Spain, some of which were faithfully copied by local weavers while others were adapted to include elements of native art. Large-pattern Holbein carpets, which were very popular in Europe, were copied in Spain

and appear in inventories as 'wheel' carpets. They combine the large octagons of the Turkish originals with the detailed interlacing of Hispano-Moresque art. Frequently an additional border at the top and bottom was decorated with human figures, birds and animals, probably derived from Iberian folk art.

The end of the 15th century was a turning-point in carpet design: until then the Spanish had coloured their wool with rich vegetable dyes—predominantly red, dark blue, green and yellow—used for centuries throughout the Mediterranean, but after the discovery of the Americas cochineal became available, enabling the weavers to experiment with new shades.

(ii) 1500–1680. Although by the early 16th century artistic patronage in Spain lay entirely in the hands of Christian nobles, Turkish carpets were still being imported and copied. In the Turkish models the strong geometric patterns of the previous century were gradually being replaced by a curvilinear court style based on floral motifs, but when copied by Spanish weavers the proportions of these new designs were frequently distorted, probably unintentionally, and the predominant reds of the originals were often replaced with blues and yellows to make them more acceptable to European taste. Other European elements were introduced, including the double-headed eagle of the Habsburg dynasty and religious symbols. The latter indicate that particular carpets were commissioned for church use; the practice seems to have become more common as the Counter-Reformation progressed. Contemporary silk patterns and fashionable Renaissance motifs continued to influence carpet design, and by the end of the 16th century Spanish carpets had become entirely European in style. The single-warp knot, which was difficult to tie but had enabled the weavers to produce fine, curving lines and detailed patterns, was replaced in the mid-17th century by the Ghiordes (symmetrical) knot, and the main areas of production moved north to be centred on Cuenca and Madrid.

Outside Spain, knotted pile carpets were almost unknown in Europe until the beginning of the 16th century: even in grand houses rushes were still scattered on the floors. Turkish carpets were imported into England at the beginning of the 16th century; Cardinal Thomas Wolsey imported 60 carpets in 1520 as part of a diplomatic agreement. The oldest surviving carpet made in England, in East Anglia, is dated 1570 (Earl of Verulam priv. col.). Three sur-

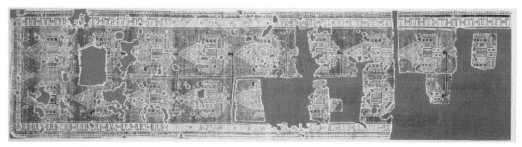

Synagogue carpet, 4.2×0.94 m, southern Spain, 14th century (Berlin, Museum für Islamische Kunst, Staatliche Museen zu Berlin)

viving Star Ushak carpets (Duke of Buccleuch priv. col.) are thought to have been made in Norwich; two are dated, one 1584 and the other 1585.

By the end of the 16th century the English had adapted Turkish weaving techniques to local artistic traditions and were weaving carpets with designs based on the common flowers and shrubs found in many English gardens—roses, honeysuckle, pansies, strawberries and oak leaves. From the late 16th century inventories in England began to differentiate between 'turkie carpetts', which were imported from the Middle East, and carpets of 'turkie work', meaning the knotted carpets made in England. As large carpets were expensive, small panels suitable for cushion-covers and upholstery became popular; they were often made domestically as well as commercially. These remained in demand throughout most of the 17th century, and production did not decline until the 1680s, when the importation of Turkish and Persian carpets increased. Then, with the greater use of Eastern carpets and the popularity of inlaid floors, almost all production of knotted carpets in England seems to have ceased. It was not revived until the middle of the 18th century, and then only with help from France.

In France, Pierre Dupont (d 1640) obtained a licence in 1608 to use a workshop under the Palais du Louvre in Paris in which to manufacture carpets in the *façon du Levant* and the *façon de Turquie*. In 1627 he took one of his former pupils, Simon Lourdet (d 1666), into partnership and installed him in a former soap factory near Colline de Chaillot, Paris. Lourdet began to weave carpets, screens, seat-covers and wall hangings at the SAVONNERIE.

(iii) 1681–1800. In 1712 orders were placed for the furnishing of rooms in the châteaux at Versailles and Fontainebleau, and the Savonnerie was given the title Manufacture des Meubles de la Couronne de Tapis Façon de Perse et du Levant. The architect Robert de Cotte (1656/7–1735), also director of the Gobelins, was put in charge. There was a noticeable collaboration between the tapestry workshops at the Gobelins and the carpet workshops at the Savonnerie: not only did they have the same director, but they frequently shared the same designers, including Jean-Baptiste Belin, Pierre Josse Perrot (*fl* 1724–35) and François Boucher. Under their influence the designs were changed to mirror contemporary taste; although the carpets continued to be enormous, graceful curvilinear lines and Rococo motifs began to replace the landscapes and allegorical tableaux of the previous century. It was not uncommon for two or three carpets to be woven from the same cartoon. In one case three identical carpets were required to cover the dais of the king's throne at Versailles, and in another, three identical ones were sent to three châteaux, at La Muette, Choisy-le-Roi and Fontainebleau (all these carpets now Paris, Mobilier N.).

Since the Savonnerie worked exclusively for the monarch and as imported carpets were not always easy to obtain, nor in keeping with French taste, there was considerable incentive for enterprising manufacturers to produce reasonably priced alternatives. In 1743 it was agreed that the tapestry workshops at AUBUSSON should weave carpets to meet this demand. The Crown continued to finance the venture until the workshops were taken over as a private enterprise in 1746.

The art of carpet-knotting was reintroduced into England in 1750 by two craftsmen from the Savonnerie, Pierre Poiré and Louis Théau. They made a carpet for the Duke of Cumberland to present to his sister-in-law, Augusta, the Dowager Princess of Wales. In 1753 they moved to Fulham to share a tapestry-weaving studio, but the venture failed, and the premises were sold at public auction in July 1755. The carpet looms and designs were bought by a Swiss Huguenot, Claude Passavant of Exeter, who took some of the workmen back to Exeter. The workshop seems to have lasted only six years. Three signed carpets have survived: one dated 1757, the other two 1758 (Petworth House, W. Sussex, NT; priv. col.). All three exhibit marked French qualities in both composition and palette, with Rococo designs in strong reds and blues on a black ground.

After the sale of the Fulham workshop, some of the weavers stayed in London and were employed by Thomas Moore (c. 1700–88) of Chiswell Street, Moorfields. This workshop quickly gained a reputation for fine carpets that were said by many to be superior to imported ones. Moore acted as a wholesaler for upholsterers and seems, from an early date, to have supplied clients with Brussels, Wilton and Ingrain carpets. In 1763 he received a royal warrant, and after his death the workshop continued to be run by his family until 1793, when it seems to have ceased production.

A third important English workshop also owed its existence to the Fulham enterprise. Thomas Whitty (d 1792), a weaver from Devon, had been inspired by the sight of a Turkish carpet but had found the English horizontal loom unsuited to its manufacture. It was not until he persuaded an apprentice to show him the Fulham workshop that he realized that vertical looms were needed. He began work on his first carpet in AXMINSTER in 1755.

All hand-knotted carpets, imported or locally made, were expensive and beyond the means of all but the most prosperous. There were, however, cheaper alternatives. From at least the 16th century strong woollen cloth had been used as a relatively inexpensive floor covering. From the mid-17th century a patterned worsted double cloth known as an Ingrain, Kidderminster, Scotch or Union carpet was very popular in Britain and North America. It remained in use until c. 1914 and in the 19th century was also woven as a triple cloth. It was made on horizontal looms in long strips 915 mm wide, which could be stitched together to form wide carpets, often with contrasting borders. It was woven by outworkers in Scotland and northern England, and the first factory devoted to its production was established by a Mr Pearsall in KIDDERMINSTER in 1735.

Despite its popularity, it was not as durable as pile carpet, and the number of colours that could be used was limited.

A looped-pile carpet called Brussels, woven in the manner of an uncut velvet, was very hard-wearing. It too was produced in long lengths, but usually only in widths of 69 mm. Although woven before then in Tournai, the first patent to weave such carpeting was taken out in 1741 by a London merchant and two Wilton men, John Barford, an upholsterer, and William Moody, a clothier. It was possible to weave a great variety of designs, but the foundation was apt to show through in poor-quality pieces, and the looped pile did not produce a rich, luxurious texture. This, however, could be achieved by cutting the pile to give a type of carpet called Wilton.

Both types proved popular, and by the 1750s they were being supplied to the royal family. They represent a technological breakthrough necessitated by the growing demand for good-quality floor coverings—weavers were now able to produce a sturdy pile carpet without having to tie each knot by hand. Not only were the carpets quicker to make and therefore cheaper than hand-knotted ones, but the purchaser could have the strips cut and sewn to cover the entire floor, fitting into alcoves and around hearths, and he could order the design and colours of his choice, advantages seldom available with imported Eastern carpets. Brussels carpets were also widely used in France, where they were known as *moquette*. There, as in England, they helped fill the increasing market for carpets.

(iv) 1801–1914. In France the establishment of the First Empire in 1804 marked the beginning of a period of prosperity. This gave a new lease of life to both the Savonnerie and Aubusson workshops, with orders from the imperial household for magnificent carpets to replace those damaged or lost in the Revolution. The designs of most of these were inspired by the work of Charles Percier (1764–1838) and Pierre-François-Léonard Fontaine, the creators of the Empire style, but although many of the carpets woven for the imperial palaces were decorated with such classical war motifs as shields, helmets, spears and trophies, the floral tradition continued, often with the addition of classical muses, graceful swans and peacocks. Work slowed after the fall of Napoleon, but large carpets continued to be woven at the Savonnerie. In 1825 the Savonnerie was finally amalgamated with the Gobelins workshops, and after this its carpet designs were influenced increasingly by those of the tapestry-weavers. By the end of the 19th century it was common for the same cartoons to be used in both techniques. The privately owned Aubusson workshops found themselves competing with industrial manufacturers in the 19th century, and demand for their hand-knotted products declined rapidly in the 1830s, when even the royal household was ordering machine-woven carpets for the Grande Galerie of the Palais des Tuileries. In order to survive, Aubusson employed English work-

men to set up looms for weaving Brussels and Wilton carpets, and by the 1850s their products were rivalling English ones in their quality and beauty. Although a few hand-knotted carpets were commissioned, from the 1840s the workshops produced mainly machine- and tapestry-woven ones.

In the 19th century there were similar changes in England. After the demise of the Moorfields workshop, Thomas Witty of Axminster was the sole producer of hand-knotted carpets. He followed the French fashion for enriched classical designs so closely that some of his carpets are almost replicas of contemporary Savonnerie products. In 1828 his factory, by then run by his sons, was nearly destroyed by fire. It never recovered: the stocks and surviving looms were bought by a Mr Blackmore in 1836 and transferred to Wilton, where production continued side by side with the increased use of mechanical and power looms. Technological advances followed in quick succession as manufacturers sought to provide cheap floor coverings to satisfy a growing market. In 1832 Richard Whytock of Edinburgh adapted a method of pre-printing the required colours on to the warp before weaving. With this he produced 'Tapestry Brussels' and 'Tapestry Velvet' carpets with up to 150 colours in the pattern. In 1839 James Templeton, a shawl manufacturer in Glasgow, developed a way of weaving carpets with chenille thread. These were known as CHENILLE AXMINSTER.

In the USA, Erastus Brigham Bigelow (1814–79) of Massachusetts invented a power loom *c.* 1839 that could weave both double and triple cloth, and in 1848 he invented one that could weave Brussels and Wilton carpets; these machines were eventually capable of weaving up to 50 m per day, compared with a hand-loom weaver's daily 6.5 m. In 1878 Tomkinson & Adam of Kidderminster purchased from New York a loom for making machine-tufted carpets, and in 1910 they introduced one that could make knotted pile. These, and many other inventions, made it possible to weave carpets in a fraction of the time that it would have taken to knot the pile by hand. Production costs dropped dramatically, and by the end of the 19th century reasonably good-quality, durable floor coverings were available to most people.

As the mechanized production of carpets increased in Europe, the number of Eastern carpets being imported also increased. Both had their critics, of whom the most prominent was William Morris. He decried in British carpets the prevalent taste for extravagant and full-blown floral patterns, with such disparate elements as scrolls, landscapes and urns, and in imported carpets the indiscriminate use of aniline colours and Westernized designs. Morris had designed carpets for several machine techniques since 1875, but in 1878 he began to weave small carpets in his studio in Hammersmith, developing the designs from classical Persian models. Larger hand-knotted carpets were subsequently commissioned, but the venture was never commercially viable, and in 1912 the carpet looms were transferred to the Wilton Royal Carpet Co. Another attempt to re-establish the production of hand-knotted carpets took place in western Ireland. In 1896 the government asked Alexander Morton (1844–1921) to provide work in the Donegal area to alleviate economic distress. Initially, Morton started a workshop to make lace, but he then established a factory to make hand-knotted carpets in Killybegs. It proved to be very successful and quickly gained a reputation for quality in both material and design, but the social and economic face of Europe was changing, and the market for exclusive, expensive carpets was growing smaller.

(v) After 1914. In France several exhibitions of Algerian and Moroccan art (1917, 1919 and 1923) included thick-pile Berber carpets, which caught the imagination of such designers as Da Silva Bruhns and Stéphany. The effect of these ethnic influences, combined with contemporary artistic trends, especially with Cubism, was to change attitudes towards carpet design to such an extent that even well-established, traditional workshops began to commission modern designs from artists. Designs by Robert Bonfils (1886–1971) and Gaudissart were used at the Savonnerie, and the small-scale patterns of Edouard Bénédictus (1878–1930) were used by the Beauvais carpet factory to produce machine-made *moquettes.* The Exposition des Arts Décoratifs in Paris in 1925 confirmed that there was a revival in the craft of the hand-knotted carpet. Amid the modern, stark interiors of the exhibition brilliantly coloured carpets, especially those designed by Jean Lurçat and by Mlle Max Vibert, were used to add texture and warmth.

British designers in the 1930s responded well to France's challenge. Firms as the Wilton Royal Carpet Co. and the Edinburgh Weavers moved away from tried and tested patterns to experiment with designs based on the work of Pablo Picasso and Georges Braque (1882–1963) and interpreted by such artists as E. McKnight Kauffer (1890–1954), Marion Dorn (1899–1964), Betty Joel (1896–1985) and Ronald Grierson (1901–92). These carpets were usually machine-woven, either for individual clients or for hotels, cinemas or luxury liners. Such large workshops and factories as Donegal Carpets Ltd in Ireland and the Wilton Royal Carpet Co. continued to weave hand-knotted carpets, but less for private houses and increasingly for government property, embassies and international companies. The designs tended to be copies or pastiches of late 18th-century and early 19th-century carpets, which gave a sense of classical grace to well-proportioned state rooms and boardrooms. By the late 20th century commissions for large hand-made carpets had diminished dramatically, and at one time even these large workshops were facing the serious threat of extinction. Ironically, many commissions came from the royal houses of the Middle East.

The interior designers of the 1950s and 1960s exploited the texture and colour of carpets to contrast with the white walls and light woods that were typical of the popular Scandinavian style. Such flatweaves as kilims and durries were imported into Europe from as far afield as Mexico and India and were used with machine-woven shag-pile carpeting. In the 1970s, perhaps in reaction, there was a revival of interest in the even-textured, machine-woven Axminsters and Wiltons, which were produced in an eclectic repertory of designs incorporating both traditional and modern elements. Imported Eastern rugs continued to be popular, and some European artists and craftsmen, for example Helen Yardley (*b* 1954) and Grace Erickson (*b* 1950), made rugs and small carpets, sometimes hand-knotted and sometimes machine-tufted, with designs similar to those of the 1930s.

C. E. C. Tattersall and S. Reed: *British Carpets* (London, 1966)

M. Jarry: 'Designs and Models for Savonnerie Carpets in the 18th Century', *Burl. Mag.,* cx (1968), pp. 258–62

C. Gilbert, J. Lomax and A. Wells-Cole: *Country House Floors,* Temple Newsam Country House Studies, no. 3 (Leeds, 1987)

B. Faraday: *European and American Carpets and Rugs: A History of the Hand-woven Decorative Floor Coverings of Spain, France, Great Britain* (Woodbridge, 1990)

S. B. Sherril: *Carpets and Rugs of Europe and America* (New York, 1996)

S. Day: *Art Deco and Modernist Carpets* (London and San Francisco, 2002)

M. Thompson: *Woven in Kidderminster: An Illustrated History of the Carpet Industry in the Kidderminster Area Including Stourport, Bridgnorth and Bewdley: 1735–2000* (Kidderminster, 2002)

2. INDIAN SUBCONTINENT. Woollen knotted-pile carpets have probably been manufactured in India for at least two millennia, but they have never been the subcontinent's predominant floor covering. Traditionally, the majority of the population has relied more on cotton floorspreads, cotton and woollen flatweaves, thick cushions, grass mats and even felts. Written records document carpets and carpet-making in India since the 2nd century AD, but the earliest surviving carpets are Mughal carpets from the late 16th Akbar period. One well-known example is the Ames Carpet (Boston, MA, Mus. F.A), which portrays domestic and mythological scenes. A second example (Vienna, Österreich. Mus. Angewandte Kst) with birds, trees and flowers is drawn in the style of the late Akbar period or early Jahangir period (*reg* 1605–28). A third example, the Widener Carpet (Washington, DC, N.G.A.), combines elements of the painterly style with a more conventional format of animal combats and individual vignettes within floral scrolls. The borders of all three carpets contain monstrous faces within palmettes (imagery borrowed from carpets of Safavid Iran), while their fields display features that are considered characteristic of Indian carpets, including *ton-sur-ton* (unoutlined floral elements in light shades of one colour superimposed on darker shades of the same colour) and the display of sinuous, wisteria-like racemes. Other probable Akbari-period carpets include at least 16 fragments of a red-ground 'grotesque' animal carpet or carpets, possibly woven in Lahore for the wealthy Rajput rulers of Amer/Jaipur in the late 16th century or early 17th (e.g. Detroit, MI, Inst. A., and Glasgow, Burrell Col.).

The best documented of all Mughal examples, the somewhat later Girdlers Carpet (*c.* 1631; London,

Girdlers' Co.) and the Fremlin Carpet (*c.* 1640; London, V&A), borrow minor details from 'picture-format' carpets to create what are essentially standard 'Indo-Persian' carpets modified for the European market. Both were woven in Lahore as commissions for resident Europeans. The Girdlers Carpet superimposes five European heraldic motifs on a considerably narrowed red central ground. The borders are conventional in-and-out palmette meanders, and the field is decorated with standard scrolling vines, buds, blossoms, elaborate palmettes and wisteria-like racemes. *Ton-sur-ton* colouring is much in evidence. The Fremlin Carpet has European heraldic devices superimposed on both the in-and-out palmette borders and the field. The basic vine scroll and palmette pattern of the field is largely obscured by disjointed vignettes of animal combats amid blossoming trees. The simple drafting of the floral elements of these two carpets conforms to the earlier Akbar-period style and demonstrates the difficulty of assigning dates to Mughal carpets solely on the basis of comparable styles in other media.

Similar carpets without heraldic devices include the large Morgan Carpet (New York, Met.), in which the field is composed of symmetrically repeated animal combats under trees. It is better drawn and coloured than the Fremlin Carpet, and its finely composed border of interpenetrating stars and cartouches suggests the existence of workshop production capable of modifying both the level of quality and the design elements of a basic repertory. A fourth carpet, known as the Illchester (England, priv. col), reflects the drafting and colour saturation of the Girdlers Carpet, while its blue ground exhibits even more skilfully drawn animals than the Fremlin Carpet. All four carpets were probably woven in Lahore between 1630 and 1650.

Carpets with floral elements within niches represent another original Mughal format, one that can be more precisely associated with stylistic developments within painting. Mughal artists began depicting flowers in a new manner in the 1620s as a result of encouragement from the emperor, Jahangir. The Mannerist naturalism of newly introduced European herbals was copied and then modified to produce sensitive studies of Kashmiri flora. This unique Mughal floral style was not pure naturalism; relative proportions were ignored, and elements of one genus were often combined with those of another. One result of this decorative innovation was a small number of Mughal carpets featuring a single, large flowering plant arising from a mound, enclosed within a cusped arch. Often known as 'prayer rugs' but more probably wall or tent hangings, these carpets range in quality from the relatively coarse construction of the McMullan Carpet to the superb silk foundation and fine goat-hair pile of the Altman fragment (both New York, Met.). Production was gradually expanded to include carpets with several horizontal registers of large, alternating flowering plants or trees. The finest example is the Frick 'Tree' Carpet

(New York, Frick). All of these examples were probably produced between the late 1620s and *c.* 1650.

By the middle of the 17th century the standard 'Indo-Persian' carpet was still popular and was produced in vast numbers, but more elaborate variations were also woven. In its most sophisticated form, the standard in-and-out palmette border was replaced by bands of elaborate strapwork, stars and cartouches or graceful double guillouches supporting twisting leaves, bracts and colourful rosettes. The spiralling vines of the ground were similarly enhanced by a detailed elaboration and increased variety of buds, blossoms, palmettes and racemes. This is best observed in the Gulbenkian fragment (Lisbon, Mus. Gulbenkian). Other carpets emphasized the centre of the field by producing single or multiple central medallions (e.g. Detroit, MI, Inst. A. and Lisbon, Mus. Gulbenkian). As more complex borders and a greater variety of larger floral elements were added to carpets with animal combat motifs, the animals came to play a less important role (e.g. New York, Met.) and eventually disappeared.

The large, well-drafted flowers and trees of the earlier examples became more regimented during the second half of the 17th century. Unconventionally shaped and rectangular carpets woven in Lahore and purchased for use in the Rajput palace of Amer (Jaipur, Maharaja Sawai Man Singh II Mus.) bear acquisition labels ranging from 1664 to 1673. Graceful but static rows of small flowering plants cover their fields, and their borders usually consist of a single column of similar plants. The field of an exceptional pair of floral carpets purchased for the Jaipur palace in 1656 also displays those same flowers on a rich red ground, while its borders consist of more conventional leaf and blossom meanders. Another common treatment of flowers in the carpets of this period is their enclosure within lattices. Single blossoms, groupings of two or more floral varieties or bouquets rising from vases were used to fill uniform diamond or ogival lattices formed by serrated lancet leaves or European strapwork (e.g. Paris, Mus. A. Déc.; Los Angeles, CA, Co. Mus. A.; New York, Met.). Floral lattice carpets of the late Shah Jahan period are the most finely constructed of all classical knotted-pile carpets. They are characterized by striped, coloured silk warps, silk wefts and fine goat-hair pile. The knot density of one example (Washington, DC, Textile Mus.), 2070 knots per square inch (3105 knots per square decimetre), is unequalled by any other contemporary carpet.

During the third quarter of the 17th century simple lattices were replaced by more complex arrangements of alternating shapes and sizes. Individual recognizable blossoms evolved into composite floral fantasies combining elements from different plants. The abandonment of robust draughtsmanship in favour of precise, small-scale detailing eventually produced the *millefleurs* carpets of the early 18th century to the early 19th. Every surface (borders and field) of these superbly constructed carpets was filled with tiny, repetitive floral patterns. When this aesthetic was applied to lattice carpets, the floral elements were miniaturized and the framework eventually eliminated (e.g. Oxford, Ashmolean). When the model was the single plant within a cusped arch, the result was the *millefleurs* 'prayer carpet' (e.g. Vienna, Österreich. Mus. Angewandte Kst).

With the decline of Mughal political power during the 18th century, patronage was withdrawn from many carpet-weavers. Artisans of all crafts migrated to emerging provincial centres in Rajasthan, the Punjab, Avadh (Lucknow), Bengal (Murshidabad) and the Deccan (Hyderabad), where many 18th-century carpets were woven. In the first two decades of the 19th century bold 'tile pattern' carpets with fields of interlocked stars and crosses appear in miniature paintings. Similar carpets with unconventional blue cotton wefts are known and must represent an early 19th-century development.

Knotted-pile carpets had been woven at Eluru, Godovari District, in the Deccan since the 17th century, and the establishment in the early 18th century of the nizam's court at Hyderabad encouraged new production in old centres such as Warangal and Machhilipatanam (Masulipatam). Simply drawn silk pile lattice carpets in the north Indian style of the second half of the 17th century were probably woven in the Deccan or at Ayyampet in Thanjavur District during the 18th century and early 19th (e.g. Kuwait City, N. Mus., and Lyon, Mus. Hist. Tissus). A series of woollen knotted-pile *saf*s (Arab.: 'multiple-niche prayer rugs') as well as a number of distinctive *dari* (Urdu and Hindi: 'cotton flatweave carpet') *saf*s may also be attributed on the basis of colouring and construction to Deccani centres in the late 18th century or early 19th (e.g. Washington, DC, Textile Mus., and Ahmadabad, Calico Mus. Textiles).

By the second half of the 19th century the knotted-pile carpet industry was virtually extinct in north India. *Dari*s were still produced in vast numbers, and fine *millefleurs* carpets were still being made in the Deccan for the Hyderabad court, but elsewhere the demand for traditional carpets was insufficient to support large-scale, high-quality weaving. After the 1870s an entirely new knotted-pile carpet industry using modern materials and techniques was established by Europeans to produce inexpensive copies of Persian, Chinese, French and simplified Indian carpets for the European and North American markets. A small number of high-quality, knotted-pile carpets were produced in Indian prisons, where the most technically superior pictorial *dari*s ever woven were made from *c.* 1900 to 1920. In the 20th century India became one of the world's largest exporters of woollen knotted-pile carpets and cotton flatweaves.

E. Gans-Ruedin: *Indian Carpets* (London, 1984)
D. S. Walker: *Flowers Underfoot: Indian Carpets of the Mughal Era* (New York, 1997)
S.Venkatesan and A. Herle: *Crafting Culture: Pattamadai Mats from South India* (Cambridge, 2002)
N. Chaldecott: *Dhurries: History, Pattern, Technique, Identification* (New York, 2003)

3. Islamic world.

(i) Introduction. (ii) Before *c.* 1450. (iii). *c.* 1450–*c.* 1700. (iv) *c.* 1700 and after.

(i) Introduction. In the Islamic lands, carpets occupy a place of prominence not found in other artistic traditions, as these textiles provided comfortable and attractive surfaces for seating and sleeping in a region where hard furniture was largely unknown. They have been woven in a wide geographical area known as the 'Rug Belt', distinguished by a temperate climate, terrain suitable for sheep grazing, and historical and cultural links to a nomadic or tribal past. The major areas of traditional carpet production in the central Islamic lands are Anatolia (including northern Syria and the south-eastern Balkans), Iran, the Caucasus and western Central Asia (including western China, parts of Afghanistan, Uzbekistan, Tajikistan and Turkmenistan). There is also a historic tradition of carpet production in Spain and North Africa, in northern India and for a brief period in Egypt, the only carpet-producing land that fulfils none of the normal environmental conditions for carpet production. The concept of the 'Oriental' carpet has become so all-pervasive that carpets with Oriental designs are produced by machine in France, Belgium, the United States, Britain and even the Middle East, and carpets with traditional hand-knotting in Romania, China, India and other areas that have cheap labour and a need for hard currency.

The vast majority of traditional carpets in the Islamic world are made exclusively or primarily of sheep's wool and similar animal fibres by a variety of processes. The simplest carpets are felted, largely from undyed, carded and unspun wool. This is usually white, but can often be light or dark brown; it is fulled with hot water and an alkaline solution. Felt carpets may be plain or patterned, with designs added either in the felting process or afterwards using appliqué or mosaic techniques. Woven carpets fall into two main categories: pile carpets, where knots of yarn are tied on the warp foundation, with varying numbers of wefts between the rows of knots, to produce a fur-like surface; and flat-woven carpets, produced by a variety of techniques. Among the best-known types of flat-woven carpets are tapestry-woven pieces, which usually have slits where two colours meet along a warp line; and brocaded carpets, which have extra decorative wefts creating patterns on a warp and weft ground (*see* Kilim). Embroidery is rarely encountered in carpets of the Islamic lands.

Pile-woven carpets are categorized according to the material used and the technique of construction. Most examples use wool for the pile, but the warp and weft may be wool, goat or camel hair, cotton or silk, among other fibres. Although the thickness, disposition and relative numbers of warps and wefts in the foundation may vary extensively, from relatively coarsely knotted pieces in wool with 1000 knots per sq. decimetre to the finest silk carpets with over 12,000 knots per sq. decimetre, the technical cate-

Lotto carpet, wool knotted pile, from Ushak, Anatolia (Florence, Museo Nazionale del Bargello)

gories of pile carpets are usually defined by the type of knot used: the symmetrical (Turkish or Gördes) knot, the asymmetrical (Persian or Sehna) knot and the single-warp (Spanish) knot. These techniques of construction are to some extent geographically or ethnically specific; with the exception of the extreme western part of the Islamic world, where the single-warp knot predominates, and the Caucasus, where the symmetrical knot predominates, both symmetrical and asymmetrical knots are found in carpets produced in Iran, Anatolia and western Central Asia.

Most carpets are rectangular and have a field framed by borders and guard bands. The field is often filled with a symmetrical pattern which is cut off at the edges but could continue into infinity. Many carpets have a central medallion; in Iranian examples this is often framed by quarter medallions in the corners of the field. Some carpets have a design that is intended to be viewed from only one direction, as in the case of prayer-rugs and *sff* (row) carpets used to indicate the direction of prayer. Given the techniques of production, the simplest motifs to weave are geo-

metric; but with increased fineness, curvilinear designs are also possible. These include not only scrolling arabesques and floral motifs, but also animals and figures. Garden carpets have a grid design showing a bird's-eye view of a garden, in which the rectangular field is divided into compartments filled with trees and flowers by water channels which are themselves filled with fish and which intersect to form pools. Borders are filled with repeating geometric motifs such as cartouches, palmettes or pseudo-kufic or kufesque inscriptions, often joined by an arabesque scroll. A small number of carpets have other woven inscriptions giving the name of the weaver, place of production or date.

M. Dimand and J. Mailey: *Oriental Rugs in the Metropolitan Museum* (New York, 1973)
Prayer Rugs (exh cat. by R. Ettinghausen and L. Mackie, Washington, DC, Textile Mus., 1974)
K. Erdmann: *History of the Early Turkish Carpet* (London, 1977)
F. Spuhler: *Islamic Carpets and Textiles in the Keir Collection* (London, 1978)
W. B. Denny: *Oriental Rugs* (Washington, DC, 1979)
Ş. Yetkin: *Historical Turkish Carpets* (Istanbul, 1981)
The Eastern Carpet in the Western World (exh. cat. by D. King and D. Sylvester, London, Hayward Gal., 1983)
D. Black, ed.: *The Macmillan Atlas of Rugs and Carpets* (New York, 1985)
F. Spuhler: *Die Orientteppiche im Museum für Islamische Kunst Berlin* (Berlin, 1987)
C. G. Ellis: *Oriental Carpets in the Philadelphia Museum of Art* (Philadelphia, 1988)
J. Thompson: *Oriental Carpets from the Tents, Cottages and Workshops of Asia* (New York, 1988)
P. R. J. Ford: *The Oriental Carpet: A History and Guide to Traditional Motifs, Patterns, and Symbols* (New York, 1989)
V. Gantzhorn: *The Christian Oriental Carpet: A Presentation of its Development, Iconologically and Iconographically, from its Beginnings to the 18th Century* (Cologne, 1991)
N. Ma'ruf: *Traditional Carpets and Kilims in the Muslim World: Past, Present and Future Prospects* (Istanbul, 2002)

(ii) Before c. 1450. The evidence for the production of floor coverings made of woven, knotted and felted wool in western Central Asia and the Near East in the period before *c.* 1450 is very patchy. A nearly intact knotted carpet (1.8 × 2.0 m; St Petersburg, Hermitage) discovered in a tomb at Pazyryk in southern Siberia has been dated to the end of the 4th century BC. The rectangular field shows 24 framed squares containing stylized flowers; the broad borders show either friezes of fallow deer and horses, or medallions with stylized lions. Fragments found in Sasanian levels (6th century AD) at Shahr-i Qumis in northern Iran (New York, Met.) include a looped pile carpet and a flat-woven floor covering of wool and cotton.

Evidence for the production of carpets from the advent of Islam in the 7th century to the Mongol conquests in the mid-13th combines a rich literary tradition with scant and fragmentary remains. Three fragments of pile carpets, believed to date from the 11th century, were excavated in 1980 at Fustat (Old Cairo) in Egypt. All are made of Z-spun wool, which is found everywhere in the Islamic world but Egypt, suggesting that these carpets were imported. One has a single-warp knot typical of later Spanish carpets, while two have symmetrical knots with multiple weft shoots and may well have come from carpet-weaving centres in northern Iran and Armenia. In 1986 the Asian Art Museum in San Francisco acquired a small (1.68 × 0.89 m), symmetrically knotted carpet with a large stylized lion in the field. This carpet is also said to have been found at Fustat. Radiocarbon analysis produced results consistent with an 8th- or 9th-century date, and the carpet is commonly attributed to the Iranian world.

The techniques for the production of knotted carpets were apparently introduced to Anatolia with the arrival of Islam in the region in the 12th century. The group known as the Konya Carpets comprises 18 large pieces discovered in central Anatolia at the congregational mosques of Konya in 1903 and Beyşehir in 1925, and smaller fragments subsequently discovered in Cairo. The carpets (of which 8 are in the Istanbul, Mus. Turk. & Islam. A.) are rather coarsely knotted, with less than 1000 symmetrical knots per sq. decimetre, and show a limited range of strong colours (medium and dark red, medium and dark blue, yellow, brown, and ivory). The typical layout consists of a central field with small, angular motifs arranged in staggered rows and a contrasting border with large pseudo-kufic designs or stars. The date of the carpets is uncertain, but they were made no later than the first half of the 14th century, and so constitute some of the earliest evidence for the production of knotted carpets in Anatolia

The known ANIMAL CARPETs date from the 14th century and early 15th.

L. W. Mackie: 'Covered with Flowers: Medieval Floorcoverings Excavated at Fustat in 1980', *Orient. Carpet & Textile Stud.*, i (1985), pp. 23–5
T. Kawami: 'Ancient Textiles from Shahr-i Qumis', *Hali*, lix (1991), pp. 95–9

(iii) c. 1450–c. 1700.

(a) Anatolia. (b) Mediterranean lands. (c) Iran. (d) Indian subcontinent.

(a) Anatolia. The types of carpets attributed to commercial production in Anatolia between the mid-15th century and the 17th are numerous and interrelated, and large numbers of them were exported to Europe where they were depicted by contemporary artists and preserved as valuable items. Many are classified by similarities in technique and design; but the names commonly used for groups of related carpets are taken either from the painters in whose works they are shown, among them Carlo Crivelli, Gentile Bellini, Hans Holbein, Hans Memling and Lorenzo Lotto, or from the towns in which it is thought the carpets were made, the most notable being USHAK (now Uşak) in western Anatolia. All these carpets are knotted entirely in wool, with a symmetrical knot of fairly low density. In the 15th and 16th centuries the colour range was limited to varying tones of red, yellow and blue; in the 17th century the range was expanded, although tones of red still predominated. Designs are almost entirely geometric; even animal and floral motifs are reduced to angular forms.

The Crivelli type, depicted in paintings that Carlo Crivelli executed in the 1480s, is related to earlier so-called animal carpets, but the composition is more elaborate, consisting of large stars in various colours that enclose confronted animal motifs; a fragmentary example is preserved in Budapest (Mus. Applied A.). A carpet of the Bellini type first appears in Gentile Bellini's *Virgin and Child Enthroned* (London, N.G.), attributed to the last two decades of the 15th century. This type has a meandering inner border that forms a geometric niche terminating in a cusp at the top; at the bottom the border projects into the field in a keyhole shape, whence the alternative names Keyhole or Re-entrant carpet. Bellini carpets may also contain a pendant (lamp) at the top or a medallion in the middle of the niche and pseudo-kufic inscriptions in the outer border. Sub-groups of this type continued to be produced into the early 17th century.

There are two types of Holbein carpet. Those with large patterns, sometimes called Wheel carpets (e.g. Berlin, Mus. Islam. Kst), usually have two or three broad octagons separated by connecting bands that link them to the borders. Both the number of octagons (sometimes depicted as a single medallion surrounded by four smaller ones) and the colour arrangement can vary. Small-pattern Holbeins (e.g. Istanbul, Mus. Turk. & Islam. A.) have two types of geometric motif—octagons and cross-shaped lozenges—arranged in a diaper pattern. The design is executed with great freedom of colour and is arranged without a fixed scheme. The borders are often decorated with elegant pseudo-kufic inscriptions with intertwined stems. Both Large- and Small-pattern Holbein carpets date from the 15th and 16th centuries, and both seem to have been knotted in Spain (e.g. Boston, MA, Mus. F.A.) as well as in Anatolia. The relatively rare Memling carpets have an all-over pattern of octagonal medallions, arranged in parallel or staggered rows (e.g. a fragment in Budapest, Mus. Applied A.). The medallions contain stepped lozenges with small hooks at the corners.

The large group of Lotto carpets is characterized by an elaborate all-over design of an arabesque invariably executed in yellow on a red ground with small fields of blue, green or black. The design is inspired by the stylized floral repertory and represents a variation of the octagon and cross-shaped lozenge design of Small-pattern Holbeins. Borders vary considerably, from alternating medallions and cartouches to pseudo-kufic inscriptions and floral motifs of different complexity and geometric design. One example (New York, Met.) was presumably commissioned by a Western patron for a wedding, as it bears the coat of arms of the Doria and Centurione family. These carpets vary considerably in quality and in size, ranging from large examples measuring 5.0 × 2.5 m (Florence, Bargello) to small pieces in Transylvanian churches, which measure 1.7 × 1.0 m; this range indicates a long period of production.

Commercial production in Anatolia continued in local centres during the 17th century. Commercial commissions were influential in spreading certain types, such as the Lottos and white-ground Ushaks, to Europe. Both Lotto carpets and star Ushaks were copied in England during the late 16th century and the 17th and perhaps in south-eastern Europe as well. Some carpets of Anatolian manufacture take the name Transylvanian from the region in Romania where large numbers, taken there by merchants, were found in the 19th century; small and distinctive, they have a centralized design with flowers within four corner spandrels (e.g. Ham, Surrey, Keir priv. col.). It seems likely that other western Anatolian centres known for the manufacture of carpets in later times, such as Lâdik (or Konya-Lâdik), Gördes, Kula, Milâs and Mucur, produced carpets as early as the 17th century, although surviving examples are not securely dated. Many of these carpets are small carpets of the so-called prayer-rug type (Turk. *seccade*), the design of which includes a niche-like element recalling the mihrab in a mosque. A tradition of flatweaving must have co-existed alongside the knotting of pile carpets, but the earliest surviving flatweaves date from the 18th century.

The Splendor of Turkish Weaving (exh. cat. by L. W. Mackie, Washington, DC, Textile Mus., 1973)
K. Erdmann: *The History of the Early Turkish Carpet* (London, 1977)
The Eastern Carpet in the Western World (exh. cat. by D. King and D. Sylvester, London, Hayward Gal., 1983)
W. B. Denny and S. B. Krody: *The Classical Tradition in Anatolian Carpets* (Washington, DC, 2002)

(b) Mediterranean lands. In contrast to contemporary production in Anatolia, where the symmetrical knot was used, another group of carpets was knotted with an asymmetrical knot open to the left. These have been attributed to several centres on the eastern and southern shores of the Mediterranean in the period from the 15th to the 17th century, and most have been identified conventionally with the Mamluk sultans (*reg* 1250–1517) in Egypt and Syria and the Ottoman dynasty (*reg* 1281–1924) in Anatolia and the eastern Mediterranean. On technical and stylistic grounds, four sub-groups (Mamluk, Para-Mamluk, Ottoman Court and Compartment carpets) have been distinguished, but their traditional names should not be seen as accepted indications of places of production or patronage. Indeed, the provenance of these carpets remains a matter of lively debate.

Mamluk carpets are one of the most readily recognizable types, characterized by intricate centralized designs, executed in red, green, blue and yellow, revolving around one or more large octagonal medallions. There may be a single octagon, as in the many surviving small examples; three medallions, as in the large carpets belonging to the Scuola di S Rocco in Venice (1541) and the Medici family in Florence (1557–71; Florence, Pitti); or five medallions, as in the splendid Simonetti carpet (New York, Met.). Generally, the entire field is densely decorated with geometric motifs composed of more-or-less regular octagons, hexagons and triangles that produce an almost kaleidoscopic effect. Warp, weft and pile are S-spun, a technique normally associated with Egypt,

and Z-twined. Mamluk carpets are made of wool except for one three-medallion silk example (Vienna, Österreich. Mus. Angewandte Kst). The provenance of these carpets, which were particularly popular in Italy, has long been debated. Mamluk carpets were long attributed to Damascus, recent scholarship suggests that Cairo was the principal centre of production, beginning in the second half of the 15th century and continuing to the mid-16th, despite the Ottoman conquest of the region in 1516–17.

Three types of carpets manufactured in the eastern Mediterranean lands during the 16th century are technically and iconographically analogous to the Mamluk type, but they are knotted with Z-twist wool and use madder instead of lac to dye the wool red. One grouping, the Para-Mamluk carpets (e.g. Philadelphia, PA, Mus. A.), has distinct octagonal designs in which a central large octagon is flanked by smaller ones at either end. Cypress trees are characteristic filler motifs, and borders have bands of elegant pseudo-kufic designs. Para-Mamluk carpets are thus related to both Mamluk carpets and Large-pattern Holbeins. The provenance of Para-Mamluk carpets is controversial. Despite some claims for Anatolia, they should arguably be attributed to Cairo or North Africa.

Octagonal designs recur in Compartment carpets, also known as Chequerboard or Chessboard carpets, of which some 30 examples are known (e.g. Washington, DC, Textile Mus.). The field of the typical carpet is subdivided into squares, within which are hexagons, octagonal stars and other small connecting motifs including cypress trees. The palette, although limited, is more varied than in Mamluk carpets. As with Para-Mamluk carpets, the provenance of Compartment carpets is controversial: they have been attributed to Damascus, Cairo, Adana in Anatolia, and even the island of Rhodes. Although Rhodes was an important entrepôt, it was never a centre of production; Damascus is plausible, but in the absence of positive evidence the most likely attribution is Cairo or North Africa.

Ottoman Court carpets share with Para-Mamluk and Compartment carpets the use of an asymmetrical knot, but in this case warp and weft are often silk, and the pile is knotted in cotton as well as wool. Their floral patterns differ markedly from the geometric ones of the other two groups. The repertory includes such motifs as large buds, tulips and long leaves with jagged edges, all of which are identical to those used to decorate ceramic tiles, textiles and the margins of manuscripts associated with the Ottoman court in the mid-16th century. The shared vocabulary implies a common design source in the court workshop (Ott. *nakkaşhane*), which produced cartoons used in a variety of media; hence the name Ottoman Court to distinguish them from those contemporary carpets thought to have been manufactured in Anatolia without imperial patronage. The characteristic floral ground of Ottoman Court carpets supports central round and oval medallions, lateral half medallions and angular quarter segments, which are all probably derived from Persian designs. Although Persian designs had already been influential in the Ottoman design studios, a more markedly Persian character appears following the Ottoman victory over the Safavids at Chaldiran in 1514 and the sack of the Safavid capital at Tabriz, after which artists and art objects were brought to the Ottoman capital.

Ottoman Court carpets vary considerably in size. Unusual cruciform examples (e.g. San Gimignano, Mus. Civ. and London, V&A) were special orders from Europe intended as table covers. One subgroup of Ottoman Court carpets depicts either a niche filled with ornate floral motifs (e.g. Vienna, Österreich. Mus. Angewandte Kst) or two columns supporting an arch with floral elements on a monochrome field (e.g. the Ballard Rug; New York, Met.). The borders of these carpets were done with particular care. Three possible centres of manufacture have been proposed: Cairo, Istanbul and Bursa. Production probably took place in all three at different but overlapping times.

E. Kühnel and L. Bellinger: *Cairene Rugs and Others Technically Related* (Washington, DC, 1957)

J. Thompson: *The Sarre Mamluk and 12 Other Classical Rugs* (London, 1980)

Hali, iv/1 (1981) [special issue devoted to Mamluk carpets]

R. Pinner and W. B. Denny: *Carpets of the Mediterranean Countries, 1400–1600* (London, 1986)

(c) Iran. The tradition of carpet-making in Iran can be documented with examples beginning only in the late 15th century or early 16th, but the high technical quality of the early pieces indicates that carpets had been made there for some considerable time. This is confirmed by the few fragments from the earlier period that may be attributed to Iran, representations of carpets in manuscripts and references to them in texts. Those illustrated in Persian manuscripts of the 14th century and early 15th have geometric patterns, some of which are related to the Small-pattern Holbein carpets of Anatolia. Carpets with floral patterns began to be depicted in the mid-15th century. Although they do not show an abrupt departure from earlier types in terms of the underlying principles of composition, they introduce a new decorative vocabulary typical of the arts produced under the patronage of the Timurid dynasty (*reg* 1370–1506).

Only one small fragment of a 15th-century carpet in the geometric style is known to have survived (Athens, Benaki Mus., 16147), but there exist a few floral carpets, similar in spirit to those depicted in manuscript paintings of the Timurid period, that may date from the second half of the 15th century. A spectacular example (Lisbon, Mus. Gulbenkian) has a central lobed medallion framed by four medallion segments in the corners of the field, a composition typical of contemporary bookbinding and manuscript illumination. The carpet has cotton warps and wefts and asymmetrical wool knots in a wide range of colours, including red, light and dark blue, green, white, yellow and salmon pink. The turbulent field of double split-leaf motifs, stylized lotus blossoms, flowers and palmettes is held in check by a trellis of stems.

The refined and sophisticated aesthetic of Timurid court workshops continued under the patronage of the Safavid dynasty (*reg* 1501–1732). Approximately 1500 carpets and fragments survive from this period. Compositions with a central medallion and quarter medallions repeated in the corners continued to be favoured. Field patterns became increasingly complex: some are entirely floral, while others show birds and animals in idealized natural settings. Carpet weavers were able to achieve such detail thanks to the introduction of silk for warps, wefts and even pile.

Early 16th-century carpets are thought to have been made in Safavid capitals at Tabriz and subsequently Qazvin. Later Safavid rulers established royal factories in such other cities as Kashan, Kirman and Isfahan, but records do not link specific carpets or types of carpet to particular centres. Only three signed and dated carpets survive from this period. One (Milan, Mus. Poldi Pezzoli) has silk warps and three shoots of cotton weft after each row of asymmetrical knots, with approximately 4100 knots per sq. decimetre. The lobed central medallion, depicting 40 flying cranes, is surrounded by a lively hunting scene. The huntsmen—some mounted, others on foot—fight ferocious lions, cavorting deer and other animals. The figures wear the distinctive Safavid turban, a white cloth wrapped around an upright red baton, which can be seen in contemporary book illustration. The medallion is red, the field is dark blue and the pattern is worked in a wide range of colours. The inscription gives the name Ghiyath al-Din Jami, perhaps to be identified with the weaver, and a date that can be read as either AH 929 (1522–3) or, more probably, AH 949 (1542–3). The other two signed and dated carpets of the period are a matched pair known as the ARDABIL CARPETS.

In the mid-16th century one of the most important weaving centres was Kashan. In addition to the Ardabil carpets, which may have been woven there, a small group of carpets is generally attributed to its workshops in the mid-16th century. Characterized by brilliant colour and technical perfection (sometimes over 12,000 knots per sq. decimetre), they are woven entirely in silk and usually measure less than 3 × 2 m. In colour, design and texture, they recall velvets attributed to Kashan. Ten of these carpets have centralized compositions of medallions in a field of floral ornament and double split-leaves; four others contain directional scenes with animals. One example in 14 colours (New York, Met.) depicts a woodland scene in which a range of animals play and fight while others, including two ferocious winged lions of decidedly Chinese character, look on. Pairs of pheasants flanking lotus blossoms create an elegant border.

In the second half of the 16th century the best carpets seem to have been produced in provincial centres. A large group of carpets with varied designs, but all woven with the same structure, is usually attributed to Kirman in southern Iran and dated to the late 16th century and early 17th. They have de-

Detail of Persian tapestry of hunting scenes illustrating the tales of the poet Nizami, Kashan or Kirman, 16th century (Paris, Musée des Arts Decoratifs)

pressed warps and three weft shoots, the first and third of which are wool and the second silk or cotton, a structure characteristic of 19th- and 20th-century carpets from Kirman. Some 15 carpets and fragments are known as Sanguszko carpets after the finest example (Paris, Prince Roman Sanguszko priv. col.), said to have been captured from the Ottomans at the battle of Khotim in Ukraine in 1621. Sanguszko carpets maintain the classical composition of a centralized medallion on a field of animals and birds, but both the rendering of motifs and the use of muted colours differ from those in earlier Safavid carpets. The medallions in the borders are similar to tiles on buildings commissioned by Ganj 'Ali Khan, governor of Kirman from 1596 to 1621. Another sub-group known as Vase carpets have directional rather than centralized compositions (e.g. Berlin, Mus. Islam. Kst; Vienna, Österreich. Mus. Angewandte Kst; London, V&A and New York, Met.). The field appears as a random assortment of flowers (peonies, lotuses and lilies) as well as palmettes, floral sprays, pomegranates and rosettes, among which vases sometimes appear, but the composition is highly regular, often laterally symmetrical, and usually structured on an intricate lattice composed of three planes of stems from which blossoms issue at regular intervals. The blossoms, once the back-

ground motif, have expanded to dominate the composition. Several examples of Garden carpets (e.g. Glasgow, Burrell Col.; the Wagner Garden Carpet) are related in technique and style to the group with depressed warps. The field schematically shows a bird's-eye view of a Persian garden, the parterres of which are bisected by watercourses emanating from a central pond. Each parterre is filled with a variety of flowers, shrubs, trees and birds; the streams may contain fish. In such an arid land as Iran, garden iconography remained popular. Garden carpets of a more stylized character were made in the 17th and 18th centuries and are often ascribed to Kurdistan.

Another group of carpets, characterized by a deep pink field and a blue-green border, is assumed to have been made in Herat (now in Afghanistan). The best-known examples are the Emperor's Carpets (New York, Met.; Vienna, Österreich. Mus. Angewandte Kst), which Peter the Great of Russia gave to Leopold I of Austria in 1698. Knotted in wool on silk warps with some 5500 asymmetrical knots per sq. decimetre, the carpets are worked in 18 colours. Fantastic large blossoms facing in all directions run a stately dance over the field, while animals and birds sport amid a tracery of twirling stems, rosettes and cloud bands. Cartouches in the inner guard band contain Persian poetry celebrating nature and lauding the shah, presumably Tahmasp. In other Herat carpets, parts of the ground were brocaded in gold and silver thread.

Carpets with gold and silver thread were also among the gifts that 'Abbas I (*reg* 1588–1629) bestowed on those he wished to please or impress. He presented the English entrepreneur Sir Anthony Shirley with six mules, each carrying four carpets, of which four were of silk and gold and twenty of 'crewel'. Those in silk and gold were probably examples of a type later known as Polish or Polonaise carpets. Much sought after in the great houses of 17th-century Europe, some 300 of them survive. Some must have been special commissions, for they bear European coats of arms, including one example (Kraków, N. Mus.) with arms once thought to be those of the Czartoryski family. They acquired the misnomer Polonaise when several were exhibited at the International Exhibition at Paris in 1878, but they are known to have been woven in Safavid court factories established by ?Abbas and his successors. Knotted in silk on silk or cotton warps and wefts, these carpets are now faded but were once bright green, blue, yellow and pink, enriched with silver and gold. Their designs vary considerably but are composed of fleshy overblown blossoms or palmettes and swirling leaves arranged in compartments or around a central medallion. Similar designs of a central medallion framed by quarter medallions appear on flatweaves (*see* KILIM), including several (Munich, Residenzmus.) bearing the arms of Sigismund III, King of Poland. In contrast to the pile carpets, the flatweaves often include representations of animals, birds and human figures. With their meticulously rendered designs and restrained colours, these carpets are strikingly different from those of the early 16th century and mark the heyday of the Iranian carpet. In later years, classical motifs and designs became increasingly stiff and stylized.

Carpets of Central Persia (exh. cat., ed. M. H. Beattie; Sheffield, Mappin A.G.; Birmingham, Mus. & A.G.; 1976)

F. Spuhler: 'Carpets and Textiles', *The Timurid and Safavid Periods* (1986), vi of *The Cambridge History of Iran* (Cambridge, 1968–91), pp. 698–727

L. M. Helfgott: *Ties that Bind: A Social History of the Iranian Carpet* (Washington, 1994)

(d) *Indian subcontinent.* Knotted woollen floor coverings may have been made in India for centuries, but the earliest surviving examples (e.g. Boston, MA, Mus. F.A.) are dated to the end of the 16th century. The evident similarities to the carpets of Safavid Iran suggest that designs or weavers were brought from Iran. Characteristic Indian features include lively asymmetrical designs in the field which depict foliage and figures, and wisteria-like clusters of flowers. The finest carpets were produced during the reign of Shah Jahan (*reg* 1628–57), when some examples had silk warps and wefts and a pile of fine goat hair with 39,500 knots per sq. decimetre (e.g. the Altman fragment, New York, Met.). Typical Indo-Persian carpets, in which Indian single-flower motifs were combined with Iranian-style palmettes, were modified for the European market by the addition of heraldic motifs (e.g. *c.* 1631; London, Girdlers' Co.). Indian carpets of the period are epitomized by red-ground pieces with rows of flowering plants (e.g. New York, Frick). In the middle of the 17th century the typical palmette borders were replaced by strapwork and guilloche bands (e.g. Lisbon, Mus. Gulbenkian, T. 72), and in the second half of the century the typical tree and flower motifs became more rigid (e.g. Jaipur, Maharaja Sawai Man Singh II Mus.) or enclosed within lattices. Compositions became increasingly elaborate, eventually culminating in the *millefleurs* carpets (e.g. Oxford, Ashmolean) produced at the end of the Mughal period.

(iv) c. 1700 and after.

(a) Anatolia and the Balkans. (b) Caucasus. (c) Iran. (d) North Africa.

(a) *Anatolia and the Balkans.* The three traditions of carpet-weaving embedded in Turkish Anatolian culture—commercial, village and nomadic—continued to flourish *c.* 1700, long after the court-controlled weaving establishments that provided a major part of their historical and artistic heritage had ceased to operate. Commercial carpet-producing establishments were located in such centres as Uşak (Ushak) and Gördes (Ghiordes) in west Anatolia and Konya in western central Anatolia, where access to the Mediterranean markets had made carpets important for export as well as the domestic economy. The declining interest of Europeans in Oriental carpets after 1700 coincided with Louis XIV's *grand goût* in France and the heyday of such manufactories as GOBELINS and SAVONNERIE, where carpets were produced in a style consistent with other contemporary French decorative arts, although some copies of Turkish models were produced. When carpet-weaving re-emerged as an important commercial undertaking in the Middle East in the later 19th century, it was often under the aegis of European economic and political control, which influenced not only the means of production but also style. Carpet-weaving in Anatolia and the Balkans in the 18th and 19th centuries therefore combines local and foreign artistic sources, old and new economic systems, social conservatism and change, and Western and Turkish tastes.

By the end of the 19th century the distinctive products of several Anatolian weaving centres had become important items of commerce in the Ottoman empire, and dealers and subsequently some scholars assigned various names to carpets in an attempt to identify their geographic origins. Among large format carpets, the traditional Turkey carpet, coarsely woven with a preponderance of red and blue, was produced in Uşak, Isparta and surrounding areas. Nevertheless, most Anatolian carpets entering the market were small, for the small prayer-rug (Turk. *seccade*) with the design of an arch at one end had predominated in traditional village weaving, and small rugs filled a new Western taste for decorating with scatter rugs. A wide variety of small carpets using traditional Anatolian techniques and dyestuffs combined with designs recalling local village and nomadic traditions as well as the great age of Ottoman court art was produced at Lâdik, Mucur (Mudjur, Mujur) and Kırşehir (Kirshehir) in central Anatolia. The designs of many of these pieces can be traced to prayer-rugs and small medallion carpets of the Transylvanian type. The production of more finely woven carpets using non-traditional techniques, materials and designs was developed by entrepreneurs in Kayseri during the 19th century for urban markets at home and abroad.

In western Anatolia the market-town of Bergama (ancient Pergamon) gave its name to the long-piled and coarsely woven products of nomadic and village weavers in north-west Anatolia, often bearing designs of great antiquity. For example, a 19th-century fragment (Berlin, Mus. Islam. Kst) bears a design derived from that of a Large-pattern Holbein carpet. The towns of Gördes, Milâs and Kula also gave their names to distinctive carpet types. The products of Gördes became the best known and commanded the highest prices, being highly prized in the West. Gördes carpets, which sometimes use cotton rather than wool in both foundation and pile, often employ muted colours. The non-traditional and intricate designs reflect both domestic embroideries and European styles. Cottage industries throughout Turkey—from Thrace and Bandirma in the north-west to Kayseri in the east—used traditional Gördes designs, eventually prompting large numbers of copies from the Iranian looms of Tabriz as well. Gördes carpets, in common with those of Kayseri, Istanbul and Kula, were often altered for the market by the addition of elaborate false fringes and the application of bleach to mute the colours. Thus the commercial magic of the Gördes name led to its attachment to carpets of entirely different provenance, design and technique.

Carpets attributed to Lâdik in Konya province stand at the opposite pole from the traditional Gördes type: woven in brilliant colours using traditional materials, Lâdik carpets reflect a distinctively Anatolian blend of nomadic designs and the classical Ottoman style. The triple arch in the field and the border motifs all derive from 16th-century prototypes, but are strongly geometricized. Together with the carpets traditionally attributed to Mucur and Milâs, Lâdik carpets represent a weaving tradition that long resisted Western designs and coloration and only succumbed to cheap aniline dyes with the economic and social upheavals of the late 19th century and early 20th. By contrast, the traditional type of Kırşehir carpet was produced well into the 20th century alongside examples using a totally Europeanized design vocabulary.

Traditional modes of carpet-weaving and design persisted in many places in Anatolia even after the growth of commercially oriented cottage industries serving domestic and foreign markets. Because the market virtually ignored slit tapestry-woven kilims until the last third of the 20th century, they continued to be woven in traditional formats and designs throughout Anatolia and the Balkans long after ani-line dyes had blighted their glorious tradition of colours. Traditional techniques persisted in east and south-east Anatolia, in the Taurus Mountains along the south coast, in certain Anatolian towns and above all in the north-west, where many kinds of tribal weaving persisted into the later 20th century. That of the Yüncü nomads, for example, had a distinctive palette dominated by red and blue and a preponderance of powerful interlocking geometric shapes, while nomadic weaving of the north-west traces its designs directly back to early Holbein and Lotto carpets and often shows striking parallels with the weaving of nomadic Turkic peoples of Transcaucasia, Turkmenistan and Kazakhstan.

Other areas of Anatolia also preserved traditional techniques and styles of carpet-weaving together with a thriving production through much of the 19th century. These include the districts of Karapinar in Konya province and the 'Yörük Triangle' to the east, which extends from the Taurus mountains in the south to the market town of Şarkişla in the north. Certain groups of carpets can be localized on the basis of evidence gathered by anthropologists and historians and from the collection of carpets preserved as religious endowments (Turk. *vakf*) in local mosques.

As Ottoman political and military fortunes declined after 1700, a shifting of economic power and the establishment of independent Western commercial ventures on a large scale within the Ottoman empire meant that the production of Turkish carpets began to be affected by European markets. Although Western entrepreneurship and markets had some impact on Gördes and Kayseri carpets, Western tastes became even more dominant in the realm of large carpets. As the fashion for the brightly coloured red Turkey carpet waned in the second half of the 19th century, manufactories at Uşak and other centres turned to making large carpets of coarse weave in pale colours, often depending on aniline dyestuffs and on the process of 'washing' carpets with chemicals after weaving to make their palette more acceptable in Western markets. Eventually, Turkish manufactories responded to the popularity of Iranian styles by producing cheaper Iranian-style carpets in Kayseri and more expensive ones in Sivas and in the state-controlled manufactories established at Hereke near Istanbul in 1844.

In the 20th century Turkish production was further affected by the development of carpet collecting in the West. Imitations of Gördes carpets were made in a variety of centres; finely knotted reproductions of classical Persian and Ottoman carpets were produced at Hereke and in ateliers in the Armenian quarter of Kukapı in Istanbul. In the late 20th century a renaissance in the use of traditional dyestuffs in Anatolia, together with the spectacular performance of older Turkish village and nomadic carpets on the art market, led to the weaving of reproduction carpets that were new and faithful versions of older village and nomadic types. Some of these have been subjected to clipping and bleaching to make them more acceptable to buyers with a preference for old carpets, while others reach the market as they left the loom, honest modern re-creations of traditional carpet types.

A. N. Landreau, ed.: *Yörük: The Nomadic Weaving Tradition of the Middle East* (Pittsburg, 1978)

B. Balpinar and U. Hirsch: *Flatweaves of the Vakiflar Museum ıstanbul* (Wesel, 1982)

W. Brüggemann and H. Böhmer: *Rugs of the Peasants and Nomads of Anatolia* (Munich, 1983)

B. Balpinar and U. Hirsch: *Vakiflar Museum ıstanbul: Carpets* (Wesel, 1988)

U. Ayyildiz: *Contemporary handmade Turkish carpets* (Istanbul, 1996, 3rd edn)

(b) Caucasus. Carpets and flatweaves were probably produced in the Caucasus, the rugged isthmus bordered by the Black and Caspian seas and crossed by the Greater and Lesser Caucasus mountains, long before the 17th century, when the region was nominally under the control of the Safavid dynasty (*reg* 1501–1732) of Persia. 'Abbas I (*reg* 1588–1629) is reported to have established carpet manufactories in Shirvan and Karabagh provinces, but no example of their products has yet been identified, and the earliest examples are datable *c.* 1700.

Early Caucasian carpets are typically long (often over 5 m) and relatively narrow with narrow borders. They feature symmetrically knotted wool pile on undyed warps, and their wool wefts are almost always dyed red. The knot count is usually well under 15.5 per sq. cm. These carpets once bore the trade name Quba carpets after the town in eastern Dagestan, but they were probably not manufactured there, as the town only developed late in the 18th century. It is more likely that they were manufactured to the south and west in the urban centres of Shusha in Karabagh province and Shemakhy in Shirvan, since 19th-century carpets produced in Karabagh have the same heavy coarse texture and bold motifs.

Dragon carpets are the oldest, largest and most discussed group of early-Caucasian carpets. The field of a typical Dragon carpet—red, or less often blue or brown—is covered with a large-scale trellis of jagged leaves, overlapped at their intersections by large palmettes. Within irregular compartments formed by the trellis appear the dragons after which the carpets are named: upright and S-shaped with vestigal crests and flaming shoulders and haunches. Older examples include such other fauna as lions battling dragon-headed stags (*chi'lin*) in the compartments not occupied by the dragons, and ducks and pheasants in the leafy latticework. Even in the oldest carpets of the group, the animals are so stylized as to be barely recognizable. Despite the Chinese ancestry of the animal motifs, Dragon carpets probably derived from Safavid carpets. Many Dragon carpets and other early Caucasian pieces share with the Vase carpets of 17th-century Kirman a directional trellis pattern and the structural peculiarity of the periodic addition of a heavy single weft.

Despite the important role played by Armenian weavers and clients in the carpet production of the Caucasus, theories proposing an Armenian origin for

Dragon carpet, Asia Minor, 16th–17th century (London, Victoria and Albert Museum)

Dragon carpets must be discounted. No Dragon carpet is inscribed in Armenian; the only signed piece (Washington, DC, Textile Mus.) bears the name of Husayn Beg written in Arabic script and a date readable as either 1001 or 1101 (AD 1592 or 1689). As this carpet is anomalous in so many ways, however, including the unusual colours and drawing and the central medallion imposed on the latticework, it is thought to be a freely adapted 19th-century Kurdish recreation of a Dragon carpet. Only later do designs taken from Dragon carpets appear on many carpets inscribed in Armenian. The Gohar carpet (USA, priv. col.), for example, is inscribed 'I, the sinful Gohar, made this with my newly learned hands, may the reader pray for me', and has a date in the form of a chronogram, which can be read as 1679–80, 1699 or 1732. In the field, vestiges of dragons in addorsed pairs surround palmettes that have become pendants to a large central medallion. The design is clearly transitional between the directional, overall latticework of Dragon carpets and the centralized format of some 19th-century carpets from the Karabagh region.

Other pieces with technical similarities to Dragon carpets display different designs. The leafy trellis of Dragon carpets may be maintained, although the dragons and other fauna are omitted in favour of long-stemmed flowering plants (e.g. Philadelphia, PA, Mus. A.). Cypress trees may alternate with medallions that sprout curving, serrated leaves in X-shaped groups of four (e.g. Washington, DC, Textile Mus.). Sunburst carpets are named for the arresting, white-rayed floral motif that appears singly or in multiples among large palmettes and leaves (e.g. Washington, DC, Textile Mus.). Towards the end of the 18th century patterns that were dramatically reduced in scale and probably borrowed from brocaded silks became fashionable. The semé design (Pers. *afshān*: 'scattering'), featuring an endless repeat of vines, palmettes, roundels and forked lilies (e.g. a fragment, Washington, DC, Textile Mus.), proved so successful that it continued to be reproduced virtually unchanged in 19th-century carpets from several districts of the Caucasus.

In the last quarter of the 19th century the making of carpets in the Caucasus was transformed from a local craft supplying the home and bazaar into a major industry producing exports for Europe and America. Marketing considerations led to the choice of some Western designs, the most common being the European rose. The weaving economy was destroyed by World War I, but revived early in the Soviet period (*c.* 1926) when motifs from traditional patterns of Caucasian carpets were reused separately. The result was a distinctive type of scatter rug (less than 3 × 2 m) with a central field of one colour surrounded by borders of another; both contrast with the colours used in the superimposed pattern. This creates a geometric art with strong centres and repeated and alternating motifs. Although animals are present, floral motifs predominate and the main border pattern is a stylized vine with blossoms and tendrils.

Current nomenclature includes 35 to 40 terms referring to sites, areas or ethnic groups; nonetheless, two main types of pile carpets can be distinguished. One group comes from the western Transcaucasus and is called Kazakh/Borchaly (Bordjalou) after the small districts in north-west Azerbaijan and southeast Georgia settled centuries earlier by Kazakhs from western Siberia. This type has thick yarn and a high pile. Several wefts pass between rows of knots and are visible on the back, and cotton wrapping is occasionally used for side finishes. The designs are spacious because of the wide separation between motifs (which are relatively abstract), the abrupt jumps in motif size, and the use of contrasting colours, mainly bright reds and violets made from cochineal. By 1910 the quality of the Kazakh group had declined considerably.

The second group comes from the eastern lowlands along the Caspian Sea and is called Quba or Shemakhy after the towns in the heartland of Baku province, although the type was produced northward into coastal Dagestan (Kiurin district) up to Derbent and southward to the Djevat and Lenkoran districts. The typical carpet has fine-spun yarn and short pile. The two wefts between each row of knots are barely visible on the back of the carpet. Many, often complementary, colours are used; blue is the most common. Motifs are quasi-representational and of graduated sizes, and patterns are intricate. The highest quality and the most numerous pieces came from Quba itself: in 1913 its 40,000 weavers comprised 80% of the district's craft-industry labour force. Quba carpets also show the greatest fidelity to traditional designs and dyes. Products from Shemakhy are similar, but less fine; those of Lenkoran are poorly dyed. A sub-set of the Quba/Shemakhy type

is comprised of pictorial carpets, bearing representations of stories, scenes and people. They were rarely exported.

Other carpets show some characteristic features of the two main types. One intermediate group originated in Elizabetpol province and can be called Gandja/Karabagh after its northern and southern cities. This group is technically similar to the Kazakh/Borchaly type, but resembles the Quba/Shemakhy type in design. Other intermediate carpets resemble the Quba/Shemakhy type, but with coarser materials, motifs and patterns. They probably came from several still unidentified sites. Shusha was the capital of Karabagh (Kariega) where the surge of commercial weaving began in the 1880s. Some of the ten principal Shusha patterns are curvilinear and resemble Persian ones rather than the indigenous Gandja/Karabagh type.

The Transcaucasus was also the source of many handsome flatweaves (*see* KILIM). A large group from the Quba district are woven with a floating weft, which gives them a thick, matted back, a technique known as sumak after the town of Shemakhy. Many bear the same patterns as pile carpets, with a main field enclosed by borders composed of a continuous meander-and-bar pattern or a repeated single motif. Other flatweaves from the western Transcaucasus, known as verneh, are made of narrow strips sewn together and brocaded with depictions of stylized camels, dragons or snakes. Reversible types of flatweaves include covers woven in narrow bands of different colours, covers with a unitary or repeat pattern, and all-purpose fabrics made from a composite of narrow strips, which bore supplemental designs.

U. Schürmann: *Teppiche aus dem Kaukasus* (Brunswick, 1964; Eng. trans., London, 1965/*R* Accokeek and Basingstoke, 1974)

S. Yetkin: *Early Caucasian Carpets in Turkey*, 2 vols, trans. A. and A. Mellaarts (London and Atlantic Highlands, 1978)

Early Caucasian Rugs (exh. cat., ed. C. G. Ellis; Washington, DC, Textile Mus., 1978)

R. E. Wright: *Rugs and Flatweaves of the Transcaucasus* (Pittsburgh, 1980)

L. Kerimov and others: *Rugs and Carpets of the Caucasus: The Russian Collections* (Harmondsworth and Leningrad, 1984)

Weavers, Merchants and Kings: The Inscribed Rugs of Armenia (exh. cat., ed. L. der Manuelian and M. Eiland; Fort Worth, TX, Kimbell A. Mus., 1984)

R. E. Wright and J. T. Wertime: *Caucasian Carpets & Covers: The Weaving Culture* (London, 1995)

(c) *Iran*. Production in 18th-century Iran is exemplified by a carpet woven (and signed) by Muhammad Sharif Kirmani (1758; Tehran, Archaeol. Mus.) bearing a traditional design of a lattice with flowering plants in its compartments. Knotted with the same technique of depressed warps used in Vase carpets and associated with the city of Kirman, from which the weaver (or his ancestors) evidently came, it serves as the basis for identifying a group of related carpets and fragments. Other examples with non-traditional motifs, including fields strewn with small flowers (often called *millefleurs* or *millefiori*; e.g. London, V&A) and the repeated pear or teardrop shapes familiar from paisley patterns (Pers. *buta*, *boteh*), are attributed to Shiraz because carpets bearing these designs are depicted in contemporary paintings of Zand notables.

By the second quarter of the 19th century sizeable numbers of carpets were being produced in both traditional and new centres, including Herat, Kirman, Yazd, Borujerd, the Turkoman areas of Khurasan, Isfahan and Azerbaijan. A popular design of the period combined different types of floral motifs, such as the graceful symmetrical schemes of floral palmettes on a background of close-textured leaves (e.g. a carpet made in Faraghan in 1817; London, V&A). Popularized through international expositions, museum exhibitions, the Arts and Crafts Movement in Britain and changes in styles of interior decorating, Iranian carpets were produced and exported in increasing numbers from the 1870s. Villages weavers adapted to Western demands for carpets to fit rooms, areas, hallways and stairs. Furthermore, long-wearing knotted carpets were produced for export, in anticipation of use in Western interiors where street shoes are worn indoors, bringing dirt onto the carpet and grinding it into the pile. Colours were adapted to Western taste; typical schemes balance deep red, dark blue and orange with lighter tones of green, turquoise and beige. Synthetic dyes were introduced by the 1870s, but the harsh colours were unsuited to Western taste, so to subdue them the carpets were washed in chemical baths.

By the late 19th century flamboyant floral designs similar to those on architecture and tilework had become popular. Large-scale pictorial carpets were introduced in the mid-19th century. Often inscribed with graceful calligraphy in the border, they present scenes from such literary works as Firdawsi's *Shāhnāma* ('Book of kings') and Nizami's *Khamsa* ('Five poems'). From the 1870s pictorial carpets also bore images from Western sources, including scenes from Classical mythology and portraits of European figures. The images were derived from newspapers, books, postcards, paintings and photographs, and the carpets were very fine in technique, particularly when imitating stippling and hatching in the original image.

Carpets have been made in Azerbaijan, the Turkish-speaking region in north-west Iran, since Safavid times, and are known by various names. The oldest known carpets of the Heriz type date from the 19th century and are woven on an all-wool foundation. Often called Serabi/Serapi, Heriz carpets combine the dignity of large Persian formats with the appeal of geometric designs typical of carpets produced in nearby Anatolia and the Caucasus. In the late 19th century extremely fine silk carpets (up to 2500 knots per sq. decimetre) were woven at Tabriz; their designs were based on Anatolian and European prototypes (e.g. Springfield, MA, Smith A. Mus.).

In Kurdistan to the south of Azerbaijan such types as Hamadan, Senna (Sanandaj) and Bijar (Bidjar) were made. These carpets are distinguished by their technical variety, ranging from the sturdy, hard-wearing quality of many Hamadan carpets (e.g. London, V&A) to the astonishing fineness and suppleness associated with the relatively small, asymmetrically knotted carpets of Senna (e.g. Berlin, Mus. Islam. Kst, with 2030 knots per sq. decimetre). The single weft between each row of knots gives the back of Senna carpets a distinctive granular texture. Senna also produced flat-woven carpets of extraordinary fineness (e.g. London, V&A), and production there was apparently less affected by the Western market than elsewhere. The extremely thick and stiff carpets associated with Bijar were woven on a wool foundation with closely set warps and tightly beaten knots (e.g. Amherst Coll., MA, Mead A. Mus.).

The district to the south-east of Hamadan around Arak became a major centre of commercial production in the 19th century, particularly after Ziegler & Co. established its enterprise there. It was largely a home-based industry, employing weavers in towns and surrounding villages; only gradually were factories established in the cities. The 19th-century carpets of Sarouk are finely woven small carpets with traditional floral medallion designs in a limited range of muted colours, including pink. Other names applied to carpets of the district include Sultanabad and Ziegler (carpets primarily made for Europeans), and Faraghan (Ferahan) and Lilihan, villages in the surrounding district. Faraghan carpets (e.g. Berlin, Mus. Islam. Kst, with 1400 knots per sq. decimetre) are finely woven with designs based on the traditional *herati* pattern, derived from the International Timurid style of the 15th and 16th centuries.

The city of Kashan in central Iran had been a centre of carpet production in Safavid times, and in the late 19th century workshops in the surrounding villages began to produce velvety wool and occasionally silk carpets based on traditional designs for both local and Western markets (e.g. Berlin, Mus. Islam. Kst, with 5000 knots per sq. decimetre). Kirman had also been a centre of carpet production since the 16th century, but in the 19th century large carpets were produced there for the Western market. They are distinguished by subdued colours, fine weave (up to 5500 knots per sq. decimetre) and hard-wearing qualities. Designs (e.g. Washington, DC, Textile Mus, with 7500 knots per sq. decimetre) were often transferred from the famous goat-hair shawls of Kirman, although other patterns were based on floral medallions, flowering trees, interpretations of classical Iranian and European carpets, and pictorial themes.

The supple and thin carpets of the province of Khurasan in north-east Iran are often known after Mashhad, its principal city. They have a common structure of asymmetrical knots around two pairs (Pers. *jufti*) of cotton warps, three shoots of cotton weft between each row of knots, and side finishes of a single bundle of warps, usually overcast in red. The distinctive and intense palette of pinky red, pale blue and ivory is often set against a dark blue ground, with a typical *herati* design (e.g. London, V&A). Other typical designs include zigzag floral scrolls (e.g. a carpet made in Mashhad in 1876; London, V&A).

Carpets produced by nomads throughout Iran are generally smaller and more geometric in design than their urban counterparts. The carpets are generally loosely woven and knotted in brilliantly coloured soft wool, showing an astonishing variety of designs and techniques. Such nomad groups as the Qashqa'i and the Bakhtiari in south-west Iran continued to weave traditional pieces into the 20th century. Qashqa'i carpets, generally identified with Shiraz, the main marketing centre, often bear geometricized figural motifs; the ends are often extra weft-brocaded with herringbone or chequered stripes. Bakhtiari carpets are distinguished by bright colours and compartmentalized patterns; the loosely strung warps and tightly pulled single wefts give them a granular texture similar to but much coarser than that of Hamadan carpets. Nomadic carpets were relatively unaffected by the commercialization of production in the 19th century and were not discovered by collectors until the 20th century. In south-east Iran the Afshar produced large carpets with European-style floral designs in the 19th century; Baluch carpets show a limited palette of varying shades of red and blue, and sometimes beige. Nomads also produced many flatweaves in a variety of techniques, from interlocking tapestry to sumak brocading (see KILIM).

B. W. MacDonald: *Tribal Rugs: Treasures of the Black Tent* (Woodbridge and Wappingers Falls, NY, 1997)
L. Harrow: *The Ballantyne Collection: Rugs and Carpets from Persia* (London, 1998)
P. Willborg: *Chahar Mahal va Bakhtiari Including the Feridan Area: Village, Workshop & Nomadic Rugs of Western Persia* (Stockholm, 2002)

(d) North Africa. Carpet-weavers may have been among the emigrés from southern Spain to north-west Africa after the fall of the Kingdom of Granada in 1492, bringing with them the distinctive techniques of Spanish carpet-weaving, and the Ottoman domination of most of the region from the mid-16th century introduced Anatolian carpets to North Africa. Nevertheless, the earliest surviving carpets from the region can only be attributed to the 19th century.

The long tradition of carpet production in North Africa is confirmed by the weavings of the Berber tribes, generally very conservative, who produced pile carpets using diverse and sometimes original procedures. The white woollen *tanchra*, a thick, loop-knotted carpet, which could be used as a mattress, of the Mzab region in central Algeria, has long, barely twisted tufts coiled into loops which stand out from the warp and are held in place by the weft; these carpets have no decoration and are thought to imitate sheepskins. The knotted carpets used in tents known as *qtif* or *qatifa*, made by nomads throughout the region, are more refined in technique and design, but are based on the same principles. Specialized male weavers (*reggam*) tie the knots, while women behind the loom cut the loops, shear the surface, and beat the weft tight with a special heavy comb. These very long carpets (*c.* 2×6 m) have red grounds and geometric patterns in many colours. They are made in Tunisia by the Hamama and Mahadba tribes and in Algeria by the Nemencha and Harakta tribes in the region south of Constantine. Those made in the Djebel Amour to the south of Oran have geometric decoration in blue or black pectinate lines and woven bands of various colours at both ends; they remained true to local tradition into the 20th century.

The Berber pile carpets of the High and Middle Atlas mountains in Morocco are similar to the *qtif* and show an extraordinary variety. The carpets produced in the Haouz, the plains surrounding Marrakesh, are also known as Chichaoua carpets after the town some 70 km south-west of the city. These large (2.2×5.5 m maximum) carpets with overlapping rows of coarse symmetrical knots have red grounds with sombre decoration of triangles, squares or even figures in green, browns or orange. The fine carpets of the Aït Ouaouzguit, made by the Glaoua tribes of the High Atlas Mountains to the south of Marrakesh, have more elaborate compositions: narrow borders enclose a field filled with a single lozenge or a lattice forming lozenges in various colours on a red or brown ground. The carpets range in size from small rectangular or square pieces meant to be used as prayer- and saddle-rugs to large examples used as floor coverings and mattresses. The knotted carpets of the tribes inhabiting the Middle Atlas Mountains have a high pile (80 mm maximum). Various kinds of knots are used, including distinctive Berber or overlapping knots, tied around four warps. The designs also vary widely. Zemmour carpets have a red ground and very regular patterns, while others have designs of diamond patterns with pectinate lines. Zaïane carpets have multicoloured diamond patterns on a red ground, those of the Beni M'tir have parallel vertical bands, those of the Beni Mguild have a red ground with decoration often reduced to sparse elements on a white ground, and those of the Marmoucha have decoration of pectinate lines.

The best known of the urban pile carpets (Arab. *zerbiya, sajjada*) are those of Kairouan in Tunisia, which began to be produced in the 18th or 19th century. Their designs, with borders of stylized kufic script enclosing a central elongated hexagon, are modelled on those of Anatolian carpets, but Kairouan carpets are not as finely woven (4 knots per sq. cm). The introduction of aniline dyes in the late 19th century led to a decline in quality; in the 20th century fine undyed carpets (*alloucha*) began to be woven in shades of white, beige, brown and grey wool. Algerian Guergour carpets are similarly dependent on Anatolian prototypes, particularly Gördes carpets. These large carpets have red grounds with motifs woven in shades of green, blue, yellow, pink and white. The *qtif* of the Bedouin also became dependent on Anatolian models, featuring large central lozenges with corner-pieces decorated with such floral motifs as carnations and tulips. Carpets were also produced at Rabat and Mediouna (near Casablanca) in Morocco, beginning in the late 18th century. The finest may have 19 knots per sq. cm and, like most North African carpets, are long and narrow (e.g. Rabat, Mus. A. Maroc; 19th century). They generally have red grounds and show a wide variety of colours, including yellow, orange, green, blue and brown. Their designs recall those of Gördes carpets, but compositions are stiffer. Mediouna carpets have a longer pile and brighter colours; the field design of three large medallions overwhelms the borders. The carpets from Qal'at Bani Rashid to the south-east of Oran have designs of multiple compartments and a finely nuanced colour range. They are presumably related to the carpets of Andalusia, as Andalusians emigrated to this region in the 16th century, but they also share similarities with the carpets of the Djebel Amour. Carpets have been made in factories at Tlemcen since the beginning of the 20th century and are a great commercial success, although they retain no element of traditional production. The commercial production of pile carpets was established throughout North Africa in the 20th century.

Flat-woven carpets (*klim, mergoum*) have remained faithful to the tradition of purely geometrical decoration and are some of the most distinctive weavings from North Africa. The heavy *mergoum*s of Kairouan often have a pale green ground and a design of parallel zigzag bands or a more complicated pattern of chevrons and diamonds in the field. They also use the pectinate lines so typical of Berber art. Similar weavings are also produced in the Tunisian Sahel (e.g. the *ksaya* or wall-covering and *mouchtiya* or shawl of El Djem) and in the south where they share similarities with the flatweavings of Tripolitania (*klim trabelsi*). At Gafsa in central Tunisia, the distinctive bright weavings have bold geometric designs, often including lines of camels and even people. In the region south of Constantine, very long, magnificently decorated hangings (*draga*) served to separate men from women in the tent. Similar pieces were known in the Djebel Amour as *tag*. The variety and splendour of Moroccan flat-woven carpets exceed those produced elsewhere in the Maghrib. Woven in both the High and Middle Atlas mountains, they are the glory of museums in Marrakesh, Fez, Meknès and Rabat, and are vibrant proof of the high quality of Berber art. Other flat-woven textiles of the Bedouin include the *flij*, a long band of wool mixed with goat or camel hair. Undecorated or striped examples were sewn together to form the roof of the tent; more elaborately decorated pieces were sewn together as floor coverings. Among the most beautiful are the hangings of Oulad Naïl (in the region of Laghouat, Algeria), which have red grounds and geometric patterns in orange, green and yellow.

P. Ricard: *Corpus des tapis marocains*, 4 vols (Paris, 1923–34)

R. P. Giacobetti: *Les Tapis et tissages du Djebel-Amour* (Paris, 1932)

L. Poinssot and J. Revault: *Tapis tunisiens*, 4 vols (Paris, 1937–57)

From the Far West: Carpets and Textiles of Morocco (exh. cat., ed. P. L. Fiske, W. R. Pickering and R. S. Yohe; Washington, DC, Textile Mus., 1980)

I. Reswick: *Traditional Textiles of Tunisia and Related North African Weavings* (Los Angeles, 1985)

D. W. Fraser: *Weft-twined Rugs and Related Textiles of North Africa and the Middle East* (Philadelphia, 1991)

Carr, **Alwyn Charles Ellison**. *See* RAMSDEN, OMAR.

Carrickmacross work. Type of appliqué work in lace or muslin made in and near Carrickmacross (Co. Monaghan, Ireland); the process consists of the application of cambric to a net ground. In 1808 John Heathcoat (1793–1861) invented a machine to make cotton net, and the embroidered net laces of Carrickmacross were based on this technology. This form of appliqué led in turn to a type of lace scissors with a protruding tip to one blade for use in 'Carrickmacross' work, where the top layer of fabric has to be removed without damaging the net base.

D. C. Preston: *Needle-made Laces and Net Embroideries: Reticella Work, Carrickmacross Lace, Princess Lace, and Other Traditional Techniques* (New York, 1984)

Carrier-Belleuse [Carrier], **Albert-Ernest** (*b* Anizy-le-Château, Aisne, 12 June 1824; *d* Sèvres, 3 June 1887). French sculptor and designer. He signed his works A. Carrier until *c.* 1868, thereafter adopting the name Carrier-Belleuse. As a young man he made small models for commercial manufacturers of porcelain and bronze, but no work from this period can now be identified. By 1850 he was in England, employed as a designer at the Minton ceramic factory. In addition to the many decorative objects and statuettes that he modelled for Minton, such as *Seahorse with Shell* (1855; London, V&A), he supplied models for ceramics and metalwork to other English companies, including such Staffordshire-based firms as Wedgwood and William Brownfield & Sons. In 1855 he returned to France but continued to collaborate with English firms until his death.

Carrier-Belleuse was one of many sculptors to benefit from Baron Haussmann's rebuilding of Paris, begun during the Second Empire (1851–70). He contributed to the embellishment of the Louvre, the Tribune du Commerce, the Théâtre de la Renaissance, the Banque de France and Charles Garnier's Opéra. His magnificent electrotyped *torchères* (1873; *in situ*) for the grand staircase of the Opéra, each with its three over-life-size figures derived from the work of such 16th-century sculptors as Jean Goujon and Germain Pilon, perfectly illustrate Carrier-Belleuse's talent for combining historicist styling with the most recent technical innovations.

Supported by his reputation as a serious sculptor, Carrier-Belleuse executed lavish one-off pieces, for instance a silvered bronze chimney-piece (1866) for the mansion of the courtesan and patron Païva, on the Champs-Elysées, Paris. He also continued to collaborate with commercial manufacturers to exploit the opportunities inherent in mass production, devoting as much care to the design of such a mass-produced object as his zinc clockcase (e.g. 1867; London, V&A) as to a unique de luxe one.

In 1876 Carrier-Belleuse was made artistic director of the Sèvres porcelain manufactory to reform what were seen at the time as the aesthetic excesses of the previous decades. He devoted himself to revitalizing Sèvres with dozens of new designs, such as the 'Vase Carrier-Belleuse' (e.g. 1883; Paris, Hôtel du Sénat). In 1884 he published *L'Application de la figure humaine à la decoration et à l'ornementation industrielles*, a collection of 200 designs of anthropomorphic objects, which underlined his belief that since the human figure was traditionally the focus of art, its application to everyday objects would elevate their status.

J. Hargrove: *The Life and Work of Albert Carrier-Belleuse* (New York, 1977)
C. Espinosa Martin: 'La Faiencerie de Choisy-le-Roi a traves de los modelos de Albert Ernest y Louis Robert Carrier de Belleuse en el Museo Lazaro Galdiano', *Goya,* cclxxiv (Jan–Feb 2000), pp. 35–43

Carriès [Cariès], **Jean(-Joseph-Marie)** (*b* Lyon, 15 Feb 1855; *d* Paris, 1 July 1894). French sculptor and ceramist. After an early career as a sculptor began in 1888 to experiment with ceramics. He revived and established a fashion for sturdy hand-made vases plainly decorated with mottled or flambé matt glazes. His most ambitious ceramic work, a monumental Symbolist doorway (destr.) commissioned in 1889 by Winaretta Singer (1865–1943), Princesse de Scey-Montbéliard, was intended to adorn the room in which she kept the manuscript of Wagner's opera *Parsifal*. He died before it was completed, but the plaster maquette, together with a collection of pottery by Carriès donated by his friend GEORGIES HOENTSCHEL, is at the Musée du Petit Palais, Paris. He signed his works *Joseph Carriès* until 1890–91 and *Jean Carriès* thereafter.

G. P. Bellanger: *Jean-Joseph Carriès, 1855–1894* (Paris, 1997)
M. Ducret and P. Monjaret: *L'Ecole de Carriès: L'Art céramique à Saint-Amand-en-Puisaye, 1888–1940* (Paris, 1997)
Jean Carriès, imagier et potier, Nevers, Mus. Mun. (Nevers, 2001)

Carron Iron Co. Scottish ironworks established in 1759 near Falkirk; by 1800 it was the largest smelting works in Europe, with 1000 employees. Its revolutionary iron-smelting techniques enabled the company to mass-produce fire-grates and stoves; its designers included Robert Adam, who designed a number of elegant fire surrounds, stoves and grates. In the late 18th century the company made some items of cast-iron furniture; it later supplied architectural ironwork for the Edinburgh New Town. James Watt made his first steam engine at Carron, and Henry Shrapnel made his exploding shell in the ironworks. Carron is also the eponym of the carronade, a small naval cannon used by the British at Trafalgar.

The company closed in 1982. Its complete archive, which documents its relationship with Adam and other designers, was deposited in the Scottish Record Office in Edinburgh. Falkirk Museum houses the entire collection of the ironworks museum, including many castings and trade catalogues. A new company called Carron Phoenix operates beside the original foundry, manufacturing kitchen sinks and hardware.

Cartlidge, Charles, & Co. American soft-paste porcelain factory in Greenpoint, NY. The factory opened in 1848 and closed in 1856; it made porcelain doorknobs and buttons, but is best known for the Parian portrait busts and porcelain pitchers displayed in the New York Crystal Palace Exhibition of 1853.

E. A. Barber: *Historical Sketch of the Green Point (N.Y.) Porcelain Works of Charles Cartlidge & Co* (Indianapolis, 1895)

Cartonnier [serre papier(s)]. Piece of furniture for holding papers, and so fitted with pigeon-holes or compartments; it was an early form of filing cabinet–usually with drawers faced with leather–which stood on a desk or was free standing at the end of a desk; many had a matching desk. A rococo desk with matching *cartonnier* (Château de Pregny, Edmond de Rothschild priv. col.) is one of the most famous pieces of 18th-century French furniture. One of the finest surviving works of JEAN-FRANÇOIS LELEU is the desk (London, Wallace) and cartonnier (New York, Met.) decorated with porcelain plaques produced for J. B. Vandenyver.

Cartoon. Drawing, sometimes coloured, made specifically as a pattern for a painting, textile or stained-glass panel. It is produced on the same scale as the final work and is usually fairly detailed. In textile design cartoons have always been necessary. Silk-weavers used to work from full-colour cartoons that reproduced one section of the repeat, and embroiderers still pounce designs through to the ground fabric. In tapestry-weaving the cartoons were coloured (e.g. the series by Raphael depicting the *Missions of SS Peter and Paul, c.* 1514–17; British Royal Col., on loan to London, V&A).

See also STAINED GLASS.

Cartouche. Ornamental tablet or shield bearing an inscription, monogram or heraldic arms framed in elaborate scrolls, shell-shaped volutes or similar devices. The term has been extended to include the lozenge-shaped frames inscribed with the names of pharaohs in Egyptian hieroglyphs. The cartouche was a minor ornament in the vocabulary of European Renaissance and Mannerist design. Used in both ecclesiastical and secular contexts, it adorned exterior and interior walls and furniture (e.g. *cassone* with shield cartouche flanked by putti, carved wood and gilt, Roman, mid-16th century; London, V&A).

The use of the cartouche developed more fully in the Baroque era, however, and in its more opulent 17th-century form it spread rapidly as a decorative device throughout Europe and eventually to the New World. It became the dramatic focus of pedimental designs above façades, doorframes and windows, as well as in chimney-pieces, keystones and balconies. Deeply carved in stone, marble and wood or in cast plaster or stucco, its commonly shared characteristics were lavish back or forward scrolls resembling parchment or a profusion of scrolling

Cartoon for the tapestry of *Paul Preaching at Athens* by Raphael, bodycolour on paper mounted onto canvas, 3.4 × 4.4 m, 1515–16 (British Royal Collection: on loan to London, Victoria and Albert Museum)

plant forms. Shields were frequently surmounted by crowns or mantled helmets and flanked by figures, animals or birds and heavy floral swags (e.g. shield cartouche flanked by ostriches, carved and painted wood, façade, Uppark, W. Sussex, *c.* 1686); variations included trophies, flags and sunburst surrounds. In the first half of the 18th century cabinetmakers used cartouches in the open pediments of armoires, cabinets and tallboys. During the Neo-classical period following the 1750s, the cartouche was largely replaced by evenly dispersed roundels, urns and vases executed in shallow relief. It was reintroduced with the revival of interest in Baroque forms at the end of the 19th century.

Carver. Term used to denote two quite different chairs: one is an armchair among a set of dining-chairs, usually set at the head of the table for the host, who is expected to carve the meat; the other is an American chair with a rush seat, arms, and a back usually consisting of three horizontal and three vertical spindles. The eponym of the latter is John Carver (*d* 1621), the first governor of Plymouth Colony in America, who owned a chair of this type (now Plymouth, MA, Pilgrim Hall Mus.). The term is also used as a shortened form of 'woodcarver'.

L. R. Pizer and others: 'Furniture and Other Decorative Arts in Pilgrim Hall Museum in Plymouth, Massachusetts', *Mag. Ant.,* cxxvii (May 1985), pp. 112–20

Caryatid. Sculpted female figure (equivalent to the male ATLANTID or telamon) used in place of a column in Greek and Roman architecture. Non-architectural, caryatid figures occur as decorative elements in the minor arts of Greece, Etruria and Imperial Rome. The most notable are the stands supporting mirror-discs, usually dating from the 6th and 5th centuries BC. Caryatids were revived in 18th- and 19th-century architecture, and during this period were also used in furniture (see fig. on p. 202), often as bronze mounts.

E. Shanes: 'Brancusi and the Caryatid: Raising Ideals on to a Pedestal', *Apollo,* cxxxvi (Aug 1992), pp. 106–11
D. Hourde: 'Atlantes & Caryatides: Le fonctionnel et le sacre', *A. Afrique Noire,* cxxxi (Autumn 2004), pp. 14–17

Cased glass. Glass covered with one or more layers of coloured glass. In medieval stained glass, the red and yellow panels were made of cased glass. It is also the glass from which cameo glass is made. It is sometimes known in English by its French name, *verre doublé.*

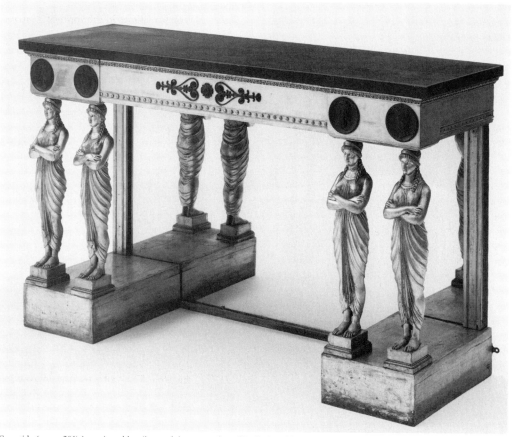

Caryatids (see p. 201) in a pier-table, gilt wood, bronze and marble, designed by Thomas Hope, 1800–07 (London, Victoria and Albert Museum)

Caserta Maiolica Factory [Real Fabbrica di Caserta]. Italian maiolica factory. In 1753 the Bourbon king Charles VII of Naples (from 1759 King Charles III of Spain) established a royal maiolica factory in Caserta (20 miles from Naples). The factory, which was known as the Real Fabbrica di Faenza San Carlo di Caserta, was managed by Lorenzo Neroni, who assembled potters from Faenza (Gennaro Chiaiese), Cerreto (Lorenzo Festa, Gennaro Del Vecchio) and Castelli (FRANCESCO ANTONIO XAVIERO GRUE). The factory closed in 1756, but in the three years that it was open it made plaques and tableware in a Rococo style. The mark on the factory's wares was a Bourbon lily in relief.

G. Donatone, *La Real Fabbrica di Maioliche di Carlo Borbone a Caserta* (Caserta, 1973)

Cashmere [cachemire]. Term that originally referred to a shawl made from the fine soft wool of the Kashmir goat, and later applied to the fabric from which the shawls were made and the woollen European imitations of that fabric.

See also under TEXTILE, §I. 1(i)(c).

Casket. Small case or lidded box for storing various objects. Among the early types are nuptial caskets, which functioned as courtship gifts or marriage chests, miniature precursors of the Italian CASSON. They were popular from the 4th century AD and were usually made of ivory or wood. An outstanding Early Christian example in silver is Projecta's Casket (4th century; London, BM), which combines a Christian inscription and secular scenes. In the Byzantine period ivory caskets were produced with rosettes, scrollwork and delicately carved figural reliefs. About 50 complete examples survive, including the 10th- or 11th-century Veroli Casket (London, V&A). Some of the Byzantine caskets (e.g. Troyes, Trésor Cathédrale) appear to have had an ecclesiastical use, as storage boxes for pyxides, incense boats and other small liturgical utensils (see colour pl. VI, fig. 5). Secular ivory caskets were produced in France in the 14th century. They were usually decorated with low reliefs illustrating romances (e.g. London, V&A) or allegorical scenes, but their function is unclear.

Caskets were also used for storing important books and papers. For example, Bible boxes were used by both ecclesiastic and lay owners for storing Bibles. They were particularly common in the Renaissance and made of wood, usually walnut or oak, with either a flat or a slanting hinged lid. They were decorated with foliate strapwork or similar designs

Medici casket by Gasparo Mola, chiselled steel, 254 × 184 × 254 mm, 1609–21 (London, Victoria and Albert Museum)

and were sometimes inscribed and dated. Epistolary cases are another type of wood casket, used especially from the 11th century to the 16th for storing important letters or documents. They were frequently covered with cuir-bouilli (boiled leather), which was applied when soft to take its required form. They were made with hinged lids, sometimes with iron locks, and various ornamentation, usually incised or punched. Small bronze epistolary caskets were also produced, for example *c.* 1500 in Padua, with reliefs of classical figures and foliate ornamentation.

In France during the Baroque period porcelain and faience caskets were produced, the latter, for example, at Marseille. Some of these were in the form of miniature armoires, with *fête champêtre* representations or heraldic coats of arms on the doors. The shelved interiors were painted with floral sprays, with gilt fleurs-de-lys. A distinctive type of English casket developed in the early 17th century. These boxes were used for storing jewellery or toilet articles and were usually made of wicker or embroidered, with glass beadwork, stumpwork and petit point decoration and such ornaments as glass-bead flowers attached to the lid. Other types of English casket were metal, or of wood veneered with oyster marquetry and with elaborate gilt-bronze hinges and a fall front, or with two doors opening at the front to reveal small drawers. They were commonly owned by the aristocracy and royalty (e.g. jewel casket of Mary II, *c.* 1690; London, V&A) and were frequently depicted in European painting of the period. In the 19th century English caskets were also produced in agate ware and contained animal figures on the lid in a manner typical of Romantic art.

See also CABINET and RELIQUARY.

Cassapanca. High-backed bench with storage space beneath the seat, sometimes in the form of a *cassone* with an upright back. The *cassapanca* originated in Italy during the Renaissance, and was subsequently imitated elsewhere, e.g. the 17th-century box-seat chair from Hungary.

U. Raffaelli and D. Scarpa: *Arte e tradizione in Trentino. La cassapanca* (Trento, 1989)

Cassel. *See* KASSEL.

Cassolette. Either a vessel in which aromatic pastilles are burned (or liquid perfumes vaporised) or, in 19th-century usage, a box for perfumes with a perforated cover that allows the odours to diffuse. In the 17th century heated cassolettes were vase-shaped, but in the late 18th century they often took the form of an ATHÉNIENNE. The brazier was often made of silver, but sometimes porcelain with a metal lining was used. The English version, which was known as a pastille burner or a perfume burner, was sometimes created in a pastoral idiom (e.g. as a shepherd's cottage).

Cassone [It.: pl. *cassoni*: 'chest']. Large, lavishly decorated chest made in Italy from the 14th century to the end of the 16th. The word is an anachronism (taken from Vasari), the 15th-century term being *forziero*. Wealthy households needed many chests, but the ornate *cassoni*, painted and often combined with pastiglia decoration, were usually commissioned in pairs when a house was renovated for a newly married couple and were ordered, together with other

Covered cassolette with ram's head handles by Pierre Gouthière, green porphyry and gilt bronze, h. 380 mm, *c.* 1770 (Paris, Musée du Louvre)

furnishings, by the groom. Florence was the main centre of production, though *cassoni* were also produced in Siena and occasionally in the Veneto and elsewhere.

1. Painted. 2. Pastiglia. 3. Carved.

1. PAINTED.

(i) Florence. (ii) Siena. (iii) The Veneto.

(i) Florence. The earliest *cassoni* were simple structures with rounded lids, probably painted in solid colours, such as the red *cassone* in the *Annunciation to St Anne* (*c.* 1305; Padua, Arena Chapel) by Giotto (1267/75–1337). The earliest known chests with painted designs are all from the same shop (e.g. Florence, Mus. Pal. Davanzati). Like the much more numerous contemporary chests with gilded low-relief in pastiglia, they have an all-over repeat pattern derived from textiles. They have been dated from the early 14th century to the early 15th, but the patterns of the decorative edges suggest they were made in Florence between 1360 and 1380.

Narrative, too, made a tentative appearance in *cassoni* at this time with allusions to the Garden of Love (London, V&A; Venice, Col. Cini). By the last quarter of the 14th century small painted scenes were routinely set into the chests, but at first pastiglia decoration and story were given almost equal prominence (e.g. *Messer Torello and Saladin*; Florence, Bargello). Both the pastiglia relief and the painting were probably done in the same workshop, because the same gesso served as the base for the gilded framework as well as for the painted portion.

One anonymous Florentine artist active in the last quarter of the 14th century ran a large workshop that can be distinguished by its pastiglia decoration, its painting style and its subject matter. In some of his *cassoni* the story (usually taken from Boccaccio) was spread over both chests, as in that of *Messer Torello and Saladin* taken from the *Decameron*; several examples of the first part of the story survive (e.g. Florence, Bargello) but only one of the second part (Venice, Col. Cini). In other cases a chest displays stories that are complete, so that the pendant must have had a different cautionary tale illustrating the same theme.

The Late Gothic courtly style, introduced into Florence during the first decade of the 15th century, quickly made itself felt in the sphere of *cassoni* and continued to dominate the *cassone* market through the 1430s because its romanticism was ideally suited to marriage celebrations. The most common subjects were the Garden of Love and illustrations of novellas, such as Boccaccio's *Caccia di Diana* (Florentine, late 14th century; Florence, Mus. Stibbert) and *Ninfale fiesolano* (Brunswick, ME, Bowdoin Coll. Mus. A.); others are tales of Classical heroines, such as Lucretia.

Leading artists of the Late Gothic style painted *cassoni*, including Rossello di Jacopo Franchi (1377–1456), Lorenzo di Niccolò (*fl* 1392–1412) and the Master of the Bambino Vispo (believed by some to be Gherardo Starnina; *c.* 1360–1413), who painted the *Battle of Saracens* (Altenburg, Staatl. Lindenau-Mus.). In the 1420s Francesco d'Antonio (before 1393–after 1433), Giovanni Toscani (1370/80–1430) and Giovanni dal Ponte (1385–1437/8) all produced *cassoni*; the *cassoni* that can be attributed to Giovanni dal Ponte all date from the 1430s, when, despite a preference for gold backgrounds, he had largely abandoned the Late Gothic style. A favourite subject of his was that of allegorical figures of the Seven Virtues with, on the pendant chest, the Seven Arts, each accompanied by one of its most famous exponents—Hercules with Fortitude, Tubalcain with Music etc (e.g. Madrid, Prado).

In the 1440s the *cassone* assumed a new painting style (Renaissance instead of Gothic), a new structural form and new subject matter. The simple rectangular body of the chest was masked by elements taken from contemporary architecture—heavy, classical cornices, mouldings, volutes or pilasters at the ends and all the vocabulary of Classical architectural ornament. Lids were flat, with the central section raised, as in the *cassone* with the *Conquest of Trebizond* (1461–5; New York, Met.) from the workshop of Apollonio di Giovanni (*c.* 1416–65). The chests also became much more massive in order to be in scale with the larger rooms of the new palaces. As it was easy to salvage the front panel, few complete cassoni from this period have survived, and most chests now in museums were made in the 19th century with 15th-century painted panels incorporated into them.

Although the older subjects were not completely discarded (e.g. ?Domenico di Michelino, *Susanna and the Elders*; Avignon, Mus. Petit Pal.), from the 1450s the majority of panels depicted Classical subjects, most taken from Greek and Roman mythology or Roman history. Some subjects, such as the *Continence of Scipio* (e.g. attributed to the workshop of Apollonio di Giovanni; London, V&A; U. London, Courtauld Inst. Gals.), in which the hero returns his beautiful prisoner untouched to her parents and betrothed, not only exemplify ancient heroism but also allude indirectly to the stresses of marriage and advocate generosity on the part of the husband.

All flat surfaces of a chest were painted, although the less prominent parts were usually left to assistants. Occasionally the *testate* (panels on the short ends of the chest) were decorated with narrative scenes, for example the *Judgement of Paris* (Glasgow, Burrell Col.) attributed to the Paris Master (*fl c.* 1440–60), but more usually there were only a few figures—mounted knights or putti—or coats of arms. The painting on the back of the chest, seen only when it was carried to the bride's new home, was cursory and often omitted several steps in the normal method of panel painting. The designs consisted mainly of large-scale textile patterns or imitation marble revetments (e.g. New York, Met.; Cincinnati, OH, A. Mus.). Textile patterns also adorned the tops of lids.

The insides of lids were more elaborately decorated. There are three types: a large-scale textile pattern that echoed the practice of lining the chests with cloth (Vasari); putti with coats of arms and/or flowers (e.g. Apollonio di Giovanni, *Two Heraldic Putti*; Bloomington, IN, U. A. Mus.); and a pair of reclining figures, a nude female in one lid and a youth, fully or partially clothed, in the other (e.g. Copenhagen, Stat. Mus. Kst). The putti holding garlands of red and white roses and/or arms refer to love and marriage, as do the pairs of reclining figures, though they are more difficult to interpret (e.g. ?Paolo Schiavo, *Reclining Venus with Cupid*; Los Angeles, CA, Getty Mus.). One youth is identified by inscription as Paris (Florence, Mus. Horne), and they may all depict ancient figures.

Cassoni were occasionally produced in the workshops of major artists. Pesellino (*c.* 1422–57) favoured calm themes such as Petrarchian triumphs (e.g. a pair in Boston, MA, Isabella Stewart Gardner Mus.). Apollonio di Giovanni and his prolific workshop specialized in secular work for private houses. Masaccio's brother, Scheggia (1406–86), also painted cassoni, *deschi da porto*, *spalliere* and other domestic works. The vast majority of *cassoni* defy attribution. Most shops can, however, be characterized by their palette—particular colours and overall tonality—and by a body of specific motifs recurrently used. By the last third of the 15th century, painted *cassoni* had been gradually replaced by chests decorated with reliefs or intarsia.

Throughout the 14th and 15th centuries more modest travel chests were also produced, variously called 'nuns' coffers' or 'travel chests' because they occur in paintings of the Journey of the Magi or the Queen of Sheba, strapped one on each side of a horse. They are low, flat-topped coffers with a deeply curved front and flat backs that are painted with several large, alternating sections of coats of arms, devices and mottoes.

(ii) Siena. In Siena painted *cassoni* appeared in the second quarter of the 15th century. The earlier of the two distinct types of *cassone*, generally dating from the mid-15th century, had two or three painted compartments, each wider than it was high, enclosed in broad, low-relief frames. Such panels are associated with Giovanni di Paolo (*c.* 1399–1482), Domenico di Bartolo (*c.* 1400–before 1445), Sano di Pietro (1405–81), Pellegrino di Mariano (*fl* 1448) and their circle. Attributions fluctuate widely because the pieces are not major works, and their execution was left largely to assistants who may have moved from shop to shop.

Although the choice of subjects and the dependence on antiquity are as great as with Florentine *cassoni*, the tone of Sienese examples is generally less fiercely didactic and more romantic. In the most archaic the figures are set into a complex architectural setting seen from a bird's-eye view. This revival of early 14th-century views is felicitous for pictures seen from above, as in Pellegrino di Mariano's *Story of Lucretia* (Avignon, Mus. Petit Pal.) and the *Journey of the Queen of Sheba* (New York, Met.). In his late

works Pellegrino adopted the single scene of the *cassone* front then in vogue (e.g. the *Story of Hippo*; Baltimore, MD, Walters, A.G.). In other panels the architecture achieves a unified space that frames and encloses the composition, particularly when interiors are shown (e.g. pair illustrating the *Story of Joseph*; Sienese, *c.* 1450–75; Cambridge, Fitzwilliam).

The artists active from the 1460s to 1500 introduced a single, spatially unified picture, often flanked by shield bearers, either in pastiglia or painted, set between pairs of pilasters (e.g. *Tobias and the Angel*, attributed to Liberale da Verona (*c.* 1445–1527/9; Florence, priv. col.). The figures are much larger in scale, and the architecture is a heavy, rather visionary display of Renaissance forms and motifs. In continuous narratives, large rocks and trees or architectural elements separate the scenes. Most of these works are attributed to Francesco di Giorgio Martini (1439–1501) or Neroccio de' Landi (1447–1500), who shared a workshop from 1468–9 to 1475, when Francesco left Siena (e.g. the *Caccia di Diana*, Florence, Mus. Stibbert).

(iii) The Veneto. In North Italy painted *cassoni* were rarely produced, except briefly in the Veneto *c.* 1490–1520. At that date the usual *cassone* decoration consisted of either three historiated rectangular compartments (e.g. North Italian school, *cassone* with scenes of *Lucretia and Mucius Scaevola*, U. London, Courtauld Inst., Gals; *cassone* with *Stories of Aeneas*, Chicago, IL, A. Inst.) or two tondi set into pastiglia work (e.g. *Tuccia and the Sieve* and *Duilius and his Wife*; Milan, Mus. Poldi Pezzoli). Most of these are poorly preserved, some completely effaced, and only a few were salvaged when damaged chests were discarded, such as the pair of tondi of the *Marriage of Antiochus and Stratonice* and the *Story of the Vestal Claudia* attributed to Bartolomeo Montagna (*c.* 1450–1523) (Oxford, Ashmolean). Verona was the main centre of production (e.g. *Perseus and Andromeda*; Venice, Col. Cini). Narrative subjects concerning heroines from ancient history or mythology abound, and the story of Atalanta was a favourite.

G. Hughes: *Renaissance Cassoni, Masterpieces of Early Italian Art: Painted Marriage Chests 1400–1550* (London, 1997)

C. L. Baskins: *Cassone Painting, Humanism, and Gender in Early Modern Italy* (Cambridge and New York, 1998)

J. Miziolek: 'Cassoni Istoriati with "Torello and Saladin": Observations on the Origins of a New Genre of Trecento Art in Florence', *Stud. Hist. A.*, lxi (2002), pp. 442–69

S. Ferino-Pagden: 'The Gonzaga Dowry: Andrea Mantegna and Paola Gonzaga's Wedding Chests', *F.M.R. Mag.*, cxiii (Dec 2001–Jan 2002), pp. 17–64

2. PASTIGLIA. These wooden *cassoni*, decorated with reliefs in a very fine plaster, were made in Italy from the 14th century until well into the 16th. The wood was covered with several layers of plaster, first *gesso grosso* then *gesso sottile*, which could be modelled while still soft or carved, or high-relief elements could be moulded separately and then attached. The whole surface was then gilded, and on later examples details were also painted. Pastiglia is so brittle that extant *cassoni* are often heavily restored.

Cassone, wood and gilt gesso, with a panel of *Solomon and the Queen of Sheba*, tempera, 990 × 1905 × 660 mm, from the workshop of Francesco di Giorgio Martini, Siena, 1469–75 (London, Victoria and Albert Museum)

Most of the earliest works (*c.* 1330 to 1425, possibly Tuscan) have overall patterns that cover the front and ends of the chest and consist of such single, repeated emblems as a lion, eagle or rosette, often set into a cordlike network, a design derived from textiles. Another early type, traditionally associated with Siena, has two or three large subdivisions with arms, devices and inscriptions. In Tuscany during the last quarter of the 14th century *cassoni* with three small painted scenes set into foliate pastiglia work came into use. Here pastiglia decoration and painting were given almost equal prominence and were both probably made in the same workshop. About the same time allegorical figures in quatrefoils were introduced, and this type of decoration continued throughout the first half of the 15th century, as seen in the *Four Cardinal Virtues* (*c.* 1400–25; Glens Falls, NY, Hyde Col.). Not much later, *cassoni* were decorated with simple, large-scale chivalric scenes or wedding processions (e.g. of mid-15th century; New York, Met.) and show a strong dependence on contemporary sculpture. In Umbria and North Italy by the mid-15th century more complex narratives came into vogue, as in the *cassone* decorated with the *Story of Lucretia* (Perugia, G.N. Umbria). Figures are smaller, compositions crowded, and the continuous narrative is often separated by pilasters or arches. The relief is lower, and the images are closer to popular art and less influenced by monumental sculpture.

At the end of the 15th century a new type of pastiglia *cassone* was introduced in Florence: the form of the chest was similar to the earlier painted ones, but the pastiglia work was based on ancient sculpture. Many examples exist and show such figures as

the Four Cardinal Virtues in classical garb, flanked by candelabra, centaurs and nereids. Roman candelabra appeared in Florentine art by the last quarter of the century, and the centaurs are best known from North Italian bronze caskets of *c.* 1500. The various examples of friezelike pairs of *cassoni* depicting the *Rape of Persephone* (Philadelphia, PA, Mus. A.) and *Demeter's Descent into Hades* (New York, Met.) imitate Roman sarcophagi and are from the same workshop. Concomitantly, high-relief, free-flowing foliate *cassoni* emerged (e.g. of *c.* 1490–*c.* 1515; Milan, Castello Sforzesco). During the early 16th century in the Veneto and possibly Lombardy, a low, often curved type of *cassone* evolved, which in structure closely resembled carved *cassoni* but was decorated with delicate, low-relief, classical ornament.

3. CARVED. During the Late Gothic period in North Italy *cassoni* were carved with tracery decoration on the front and sides. However, during the early 16th century carving began to supplant other forms of ornament as the main decorative treatment, and several drawings of designs have survived. *Cassoni* were normally of walnut and were given a simple polished finish (e.g. mid-16th century; London, V&A). In Tuscany and Rome, where the influence of antiquity was strongest, the rectangular forms imposed by the use of painted and intarsia panels were frequently discarded, and *cassoni* began to assume a wholly sculptural character. Lids were raised on bands of carved mouldings, while the bases were often bulbous and deeply fluted. The *cassone* was usually raised on lion-paw feet between which ran a scroll-carved apron. The main bodies of the grandest *cassoni* are carved with scrolling foliage or elaborate contin-

uous scenes, broken sometimes by a cartouche painted with an armorial. Carvers were heavily influenced by the decoration of antique sarcophagi, and triumphal and mythological scenes were typical subjects. Carvers also responded to contemporary trends, and the influence of artists as diverse as Giulio Romano and Benvenuto Cellini is apparent in the attenuated figures and densely packed compositions. Gilding was sometimes used to highlight certain areas of carving and to form a background to the figures (e.g. walnut *cassone*, *c.* 1560; London, V&A).

Carved *cassoni* continued to evolve during the 16th century. Whereas those of the late 15th century and early 16th had been flared towards the base, *cassoni* of the mid-16th century were often adapted to the waisted form of Roman sarcophagi, and the whole of the front might be gadrooned or fluted to emphasize its swollen contours, while the angles were often marked by curved herm figures (e.g. Florence, Bargello). *Cassoni* of simpler, rectangular form continued to be made in such northern areas as Lombardy, Piedmont and Venice, where French and German influence was important. In Venice carved ornament was often shallow and dense, resembling pastiglia. Later in the 16th century the influence of Jacopo Sansovino (1486–1570) can be discerned in the use of elaborate strapwork designs. Large central panels were set between uprights, often carved with grotesques, and the *cassoni* were raised on feet carved as volutes. Even in Florence *cassoni* of severe architectural form, decorated only with panels outlined with crisp leaf mouldings, continued to be made. A particularly fine group of this type, carved with a distinctive volute motif at the angles, has been attributed to the workshop of Domenico del Tasso. In Bologna *cassoni* followed Florentine and Roman shapes, but continuous scenes were replaced by friezes carved with griffins, scrolling foliage and even bucrania. Later in the century Lombard chests resembled those of southern Germany and were given the dense architectural treatment familiar from the engravings of Jakob Guckeisen (*fl* 1590s).

Castel Bolognese, Giovanni da. *See* BERNARDI, GIOVANNI.

Castel Durante [now (since 1636) Urbania]. Italian centre of maiolica production near Urbino. Ceramics were manufactured in the town as early as the 14th century, and it was among the most prolific Italian centres of production for pottery during the first half of the 16th century. Its fine maiolica was remarked on by Vasari and by CIPRIANO DI MICHELE PICCOLPASSO, a native of Castel Durante and author of the treatise *I tre libri dell'arte del vasaio* (1557–9). Extensive interchange occurred between Durantine artists and those of Urbino, Gubbio, Pesaro and Faenza.

Among the most famous ceramics of Castel Durante were maiolica plates and jars decorated with candelabra, trophies, musical instruments, oak leaves and designs imitating Chinese porcelain (see colour pl. VI, fig. 3). One important example is a bowl decorated with candelabra (1508; New York, Met.), with the arms of Pope Julius II and inscribed with the name GIOVANNI MARIA VASARO, either the painter or workshop owner. Other notable Durantine wares include pharmacy jars with imaginative, colourful grotesque designs. *Bella donna* dishes with idealized portraits of women and men were a popular product of the 1520s; attribution of these lyrical works to particular artists, including NICOLA DA URBINO (formerly identified as Nicolò Pellipario), remains unclear. The tradition of *istoriato* (narrative) wares developed in Castel Durante and Urbino in the 1520s and 1530s and was transferred to other areas by painters trained there. Some *istoriato* pieces were sent to Gubbio for the addition of its famous metallic lustre glazes. Among the identifiable painters of Castel Durante are Cipriano di Michele Piccolpasso, Sebastiano di Marforio (*fl c.* 1509–41), the 'In Castel Durante Painter', an artist who created colourful narrative compositions in the mid-1520s, and Maestro Simone (*fl* 1550s–60s), whose name appears on pharmacy wares.

Castel Durante continued to be an active centre of ceramics production in the 17th and 18th centuries, and in recent years has been restablished as an important centre for ceramics.

G. Raffaelli: *Memorie istoriche delle maioliche lavorate in Castel Durante o sia Urbania* (Fermo, 1846)

Castellani. Italian family of jewellers. The firm founded in Rome by Fortunato Pio Castellani (*b* Rome, 6 May 1794; *d* 1 Jan 1865) shortly after 1820 and expanded by his sons Alessandro Castellani (*b* 1823; *d* 1883) and Augusto Castellani (*b* 10 Jan 1829; *d* 1914) was foremost in reviving period style in jewellery design. Their reputation was established in Rome by the mid-19th century, and in the 1860s they opened shops in Paris and Naples. Designs were closely inspired by, and in some cases reproduced, antique and medieval pieces, often from their own considerable study collection. Their jewellery is notable for its use of gold; the family perfected processes for simulating the techniques of filigree and granulation used in antique jewellery. A variety of chainwork and hinged pieces with repoussé decoration are characteristic of the firm. Among their most popular designs were pieces ornamented with fine glass mosaic inspired by Byzantine jewellery. Decoration in enamels, either applied or in the prevailing taste for cloisonné, was derived from medieval examples. Gemstones and hardstones were either set as cabochons or engraved in a similar way to the cameos that were frequently incorporated in their designs.

The firm offered a wide range, from complete parures to brooches and rings. The Castellani monogram of two Cs within a cartouche sometimes forms part of the decorative design. The success of the firm was sustained by two subsequent generations, until it closed after the death in 1930 of the last member

Fortunato Pio Castellani: sapphire and diamond brooch (Washington, DC, Smithsonian Institution)

of the family. Examples of their jewellery are in the Castellani Collection, bequeathed by Alfredo in 1919 to the Museo Nazionale di Villa Giulia, Rome, and in London in the Hull Grundy Collection at the British Museum and in the Victoria and Albert Museum.

A. Castellani: *Antique Jewellery and its Revival* (London, 1862) [privately pubd]
G. C. Munn: *Castellani and Giuliano: Revivalist Jewellers of the Nineteenth Century* (London, 1984)
S. W. Soros and S. Walker: *Castellani and Italian Archaeological Jewelry* (New Haven, 2004)

Castelli. Italian centre of ceramic production in the Abruzzo region. The oldest examples of Castelli pottery, the Orsini-Colonna pharmacy jars (*c.* 1520–40) such as those produced by the Pompeo family, display tasteful and popular variations of the *istoriato* (narrative) style. In the 17th century, the families of the Gentili, Cappelletti and particularly FRANCESCO ANTONIO XAVIERO GRUE made vessels and shields decorated with rural landscapes, allegorical and mythological themes, all of which were painted in naturalistic tones of olive-green, browns, yellows and sometimes gold. The decorative schemes were usually inspired by the Baroque style of painting and were frequently derived from contemporary prints. Towards the end of the 18th century (when there were 35 ceramic factories in Castelli) Gesualdo Fuina (1755–1822), a follower of the Castellian School, skilfully decorated Rococo style tablewares with refined, floral decoration or figures. The town is still an important centre for ceramics.

C. Hess: *Maiolica in the Making: The Gentili/Barnabei Archive* (Los Angeles, 1999)
L. Arbace: *I protagonisti della maiolica di Castelli* (Colledara, 2000)
A. A. Amadio: 'Under a Majolica Sky: The Ceramics of Castelli', *F.M.R. Mag.,* cviii (Feb–March 2001), pp.107–28

Castiglioni. Italian family of designers and architects. Livio Castiglioni (*b* Milan, 16 Jan 1911; *d* Milan, 30 April 1971) and his brother Pier Giacomo Castiglioni (*b* Milan, 22 April 1913; *d* Milan, 27 Nov 1968) designed the bakelite Phonola radio-set (1938) in collaboration with the architect Luigi Caccia Dominioni; it came to be considered the first significant example of Italian product design integrating technical, functional and figurative aspects. After World War II the most famous of the brothers, Achille Castiglioni (*b* Milan, 16 Feb 1918; d. Milan 2 December 2002), joined the studio, and after 1952, when Livio Castiglioni began independent work on lighting design, Achille and Pier Giacomo Castiglioni maintained a partnership until the latter's death. Although they produced architectural projects until *c.* 1960, their reputation is based on famous shop displays and their industrial design work, which was distinguished by attention to the inherent functionalism of objects and the use of basic technology. Their approach is best exemplified by the ironic humour of the Mezzadro stool (1955), with its metal tractor seat, and a series of innovative lamp designs.

The Arco and Toio standard lamps, both 1962, and the Parentesi suspended lamps of 1971, all three produced in the Flos factory in Milan, reveal the designers' intention to invent more liberated and diverting versions of conventional domestic objects while maintaining a formal quality that transcended any stylistic or ideological constraints.

Achille Castiglioni and Pier Giacomo Castiglioni: Mezzadro stool, tractor seat, steel and beech, h. 514 mm, Zanotta S.p.A., 1957 (New York, Museum of Modern Art)

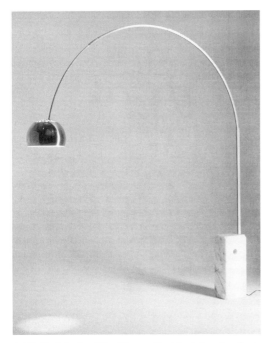

Achille Castiglioni and Pier Giacomo Castiglioni: Arco floor lamp, carrara marble and stainless steel, maximum h. 2.4 m, Flos S.p.A., 1962 (New York, Museum of Modern Art)

Changing Light: The Sixth Arango International Design Exhibition: 30 Years, the Lighting of Achille Castiglioni (exh. cat. by M. Kreitman; Miami, FL, Cent. F.A., 1987)
Achille Castiglioni: Design! (exh. cat. by P. Antonelli; New York, MOMA, 1997)
S. Polano and A. Castiglioni: *Achille Castiglioni: Complete Works* (Milan, 2002)

Castle, Wendell (*b* Emporia, KS, 6 Nov 1932). American furniture designer. He normally works in wood (sometimes exotic wood), but has also made furniture in plastic and fibreglass; his finest work reflects his mastery of laminated wood. Castle's decorative furniture is strongly sculptural; his designs are markedly individualistic, but nonetheless evince debts to the traditions of Art Nouveau and the Arts and Crafts Movement. His best-known designs are the Molar chair and loveseat designed for Stendig in 1969; these designs, which are shaped like back teeth, were inspired by the Italian Pop movement.

W. Castle and D. Edman: *The Wendell Castle Book of Wood Lamination* (New York, 1980)
D. S. Taragin and others: *Furniture by Wendell Castle* (New York, 1989)
E. S. Cooke, G. W. R. Ward and K. H. L'Ecuyer: *The Maker's Hand: American Studio Furniture, 1940–1900* (exh. cat., Boston, MA, Mus. F. A., 2003)

Castleford Pottery. English pottery factory established in the Yorkshire town of Castleford in 1790 by David Dunderdale, whose company (David Dunderdale & Co) produced fine cream-coloured earthenware and white stoneware decorated in blue and black; the best-known products of the factory are

teapots. The mark, which was impressed, was D D & CO CASTLEFORD POTTERY; the factory closed in 1821.

D. E. Roussel, *The Castleford Pottery, 1790–1821* (Wakefield, 1982)

Castle Hedingham. English ceramics factory. The factory was founded in 1837 by Edward Bingham (*d* 1872) in Castle Hedingham, Essex, where there were good-quality deposits of clay. The earliest output was earthenware for local use. During the 1850s Bingham's son Edward Bingham (1829–*c.* 1900) took over the factory, and more decorative wares were produced. The first pieces of ornamental ware were red terracotta baskets introduced in 1853 and trelliswork cache-pots in 1854. By 1860 over 60 different types of unglazed vases, baskets and bowls were being produced. In the 1870s more ambitious glazed wares were made. From 1875 lead-glazed wares with moulded reliefs and *sgraffito* decoration were manufactured in quantity. Included in the range were wares that reflect Bingham's interest in ceramic products of the 16th and 17th centuries. The range of wares include tygs (two-handed cups), mugs, candlesticks, miniature vessels and large vases. In 1899 Bingham's son Edward William Bingham (*b* 1862) took over the concern until 1901, when he sold it to the Essex Art Pottery Co., but he remained as manager until it closed in 1905. A good collection of Castle Hedingham wares is in the Colchester and Essex Museum, Colchester.

D. J. Bradley: 'The Story of Castle Hedingham', *Connoisseur*, clxvii (1968), pp. 77–83, 152–7, 210–16

Castor. *See* DREDGER.

Cat. Double tripod with six legs, formed by three bars joined in the middle and so placed that it always rests on three legs; it was used as a stand for dishes to be warmed by the fire.

Cathedral binding. Early 19th-century French bookbinding decorated with motifs from Gothic architecture.

Caudle cup. Lidded vessel, also known in British English as a porringer, from which caudle (a warm drink for invalids, consisting of thin spiced gruel, mixed with wine or ale) might be drunk. In American English a caudle cup is distinguished from a porringer by the fact that it is two-handled.

Caughley Porcelain Factory. English ceramic manufactory. Production at the Salopian China Manufactory on the Caughley estate, near Ironbridge, Salop, was started in 1775 by Thomas Turner (1749–1809) and Ambrose Gallimore (*fl c.* 1749–*c.* 1787); Robert Hancock, the former Worcester engraver, was briefly associated with the venture. Until *c.* 1794 a wide range of useful wares was produced in a soapstone soft-paste porcelain similar to that used at the Worcester factory. Simple shapes and underglaze blue, transfer-printed or painted decoration emulated the style of the wares produced at the Worcester, Chantilly and Tournai factories. A variety of engraved designs was based on Chinese handpainted patterns. Between 1789 and 1794 Humphrey Chamberlain and Robert Chamberlain of Worcester decorated much Caughley porcelain, often to order. About 1794 the body changed, eventually to a hard-paste porcelain, and overglaze decoration was undertaken at Caughley. In 1799 Turner sold the works to the Coalport partners John Rose (1772–1841) and Edward Blakeway (1720–1811), and the Caughley premises were operated as part of the Coalport factory until 1814, when Caughley was closed.

G. A. Godden: *Caughley and Worcester Porcelains, 1775–1800* (London, 1969, rev. Woodbridge, 1981)
R. S. Edmundson: 'Separating Caughley from Coalport', *J. N. Cer. Soc.*, vii (1989), pp. 71–117

Cauliflower ware. Earthenware made in the form of a cauliflower, notably mid-18th century Wedgwood teapots but also similar wares made in other Staffordshire potteries.

Causeuse. *See* SOFA.

Cauvet, Gilles-Paul (*b* Aix-en-Provence, 17 April 1731; *d* Paris 14 Nov 1788). French architect, sculptor, interior decorator and silversmith. His surviving metalwork includes a gilded bronze pair of candlesticks depicting Minerva and Victory (Louvre, Paris).

G. P. Cauvet: *Recueil d'ornemens à l'usage des jeunes artistes qui se destinent à la décoration des bâtiments* (Paris, 1777)

Cavetto. Concave moulding, at least a quarter of a circle in section.

Celadon. European term for a type of Chinese stoneware also known as greenware; the name derives from the colour of the dress worn by the shepherd Céladon in the stage version of Honoré d'Urfe's 17th-century pastoral romance, *L'Astrée*. The natural presence of small percentages of iron and titanium oxide in the glaze raw materials gave a wide range of celadon greens when fired in a reducing atmosphere. The glaze was later imitated in the stoneware of Japan and Korea, and still later in Cambodia, Thailand and Vietnam. China began to export celedons to Japan in the Song period (960–1279); the Japanese gave the name *kinuta* ('mallet') to the finest Longquan celadons, which have a cloudy, blue-green colour.

For information on northern celadons *see* YAOZHOU.

G. St G. M. Gompertz: *Chinese Celadon Wares* (London, 1958, rev. 1980)
Ice and Green Clouds: Traditions of Chinese Celadon (exh. cat. by Y. Mino and K. R. Tsiang; Indianapolis, IN, Mus. A., 1986)
R. Tichane: *Celadon Blues* (Iola, 1998)
Y. Pak and R. Whitfield: *Earthenware and Celadon* (London, 2003)
M. Bailey and others: 'Electric Kiln Celadons', *Cer. Rev.,* ccxii (March–April 2005), pp. 54–5

Pair of celadon-glazed, double-gourd vases (1736–95) and slip-decorated celadon brushpot (1662–1722), China, Qing dynasty (private collection)

Cellaret. Drinks cabinet, sometimes housed in a deep lead-lined drawer (partitioned for wine bottles) of a sideboard, but often designed as a separate unit standing beneath the sideboard. If made of silver and designed to hold ice, it was variously known as a wine-cooler and a wine-cistern.

A. Gale: 'Wholesome Simplicity', *A. & Ant.,* xxvii/4 (April 2004), pp. 36, 38–9

Cellini, Benvenuto (*b* Florence, 3 Nov 1500; *d* Florence, 13 Feb 1571). Italian goldsmith, medallist, sculptor and writer. He was one of the foremost Italian Mannerist artists of the 16th century, working in Rome for successive popes, in France for Francis I and in Florence for Cosimo I de' Medici. Between the autumn of 1540 and the spring of 1543 Cellini executed what is probably the most famous work by a Renaissance goldsmith: the salt of Francis I (Vienna, Kunsthistorisches Mus.; see colour pl. VII, fig. 1). The virtuosity of the composition in such a limited space (260 × 330 mm) is astonishing. The elegant figures of *Neptune* and *Earth* derive from Tusco-Roman Mannerism; by contrast, the opulence of the precious materials encrusted with tightly interwoven heraldic symbols, as well as the triumphal arch at the side of the figure of *Earth*, are clearly based on models from the Fontainebleau school. The personifications of *Morning, Day, Evening* and *Night* that decorate the base are, in turn, copies of the same sculptures by Michelangelo (1475–1564) in the New Sacristy, S Lorenzo, Florence, works that Cellini knew well, having seen them during his visits to Florence, but before their installation on the sarcophagi of the tombs of *Lorenzo de' Medici* and *Giuliano de' Medici.*

C. R. Ashbee, trans.: *The Treatises of Benvenuto Cellini on Goldsmithing and Sculpture* (London, 1888/*R* New York, 1967)
B. Cellini: *The Life of Benvenuto Cellini: Goldsmith to Popes and Kings* (Geneva, 1980)
M.A. Gallucci and P. L. Rossi: *Benvenuto Cellini: Sculptor, Goldsmith, Writer* (New York, 2004)

Celtic Revival. Style rooted in 19th-century antiquarian studies of ancient Celtic art in Britain and Ireland. It was a mainly decorative style and first appeared in the 1840s, remaining fashionable from the 1890s to *c.* 1914 and lingering on through the 1920s. Derived from the complex, intertwining, linear motifs of ancient Celtic ornament, it was employed in metalwork, jewellery, embroidery, wall decoration, wood inlay, stone-carving and textiles. The Celtic Revival was closely related to the English Arts and Crafts Movement's aim of social and artistic reform and was part of the general upsurge of Romantic interest in the Middle Ages. Its chief characteristics were raised bosses, tightly enmeshed roundels and

Benvenuto Cellini: figure of Day from the salt of Francis I, gold and enamel, 1540–43 (Vienna, Kunsthistorisches Museum)

bands of sinuous, criss-crossing lines, similar to but more abstract than Art Nouveau designs.

In Ireland the Celtic Revival coincided with a renewed interest in the country's visual and literary heritage and in traditional Irish arts and crafts. Celtic-style objects and 'archaeological' jewellery were popular from the 1840s. Scottish and Irish jewellers also excelled at creating reproductions of 8th-century Celtic body ornaments and utilized such indigenous materials as Irish gold, agates, cairngorms, amethysts, Connemara marble and river pearls (e.g. 'Arbutus Berry' torc shawl brooch made by G. & S. Waterhouse, c. 1851; London, V&A). In the 1850s G. & S. Waterhouse of Dublin made two copies of the Tara Brooch in parcel gilt (Belfast, Ulster Mus.) for Queen Victoria (reg 1837–1901), which led to a vogue for jewellery with such Irish motifs as harps, Celtic crosses and Tara brooches, carved from Irish bog oak with gold or silver mounts. Both the Belleek Porcelain Factory and W. H. Goss Ltd of Hanley, Stoke-on-Trent, manufactured souvenir Celtic crosses of Parian porcelain from the 1850s, and Irish stonecutters did a lively local and export business in carved gravestones copied from old Celtic wheel-head crosses (examples at Glasnevin and Mount Jerome cemeteries, Dublin; Maynooth, Co. Kildare). Ecclesiastical and domestic embroidery in Celtic and medieval designs was also produced (e.g. banners by Susan Mary Yeats (1866–1949) for Loughrea Cathedral, 1902–3).

The Celtic Revival reached the height of its popularity in the 1890s throughout Britain and Ireland. The silversmith Edmond Johnson (fl 1881–1927) adapted Celtic ornament in his metalwork and jewellery, shown at the Irish Arts and Crafts Society's first exhibition in Dublin in 1896 (e.g. Ardagh silver sugar sifter and bowl, c. 1896; priv. col). In Scotland, Tudor floral motifs and modified Celtic interlaced ornament appeared among the designs of Charles Rennie Mackintosh and the artists working in the Glasgow style. In England, Arthur Lasenby Liberty achieved great success with his distinctive Cymric range of Celtic-style silver objects and jewellery, launched at the Liberty & Co. store, London, in 1899, followed in 1903 by his Tudric line of pewter-ware. Silver and pewter objects were inset with blue or green enamel, hardstones or mother-of-pearl and decorated with interlaced strapwork (e.g. casket set with heart-shaped opal matrix by Archibald Knox, 1903; London, V&A); the inlays, exposed rivets and hammered surfaces gave the desired handmade look. Among Liberty's designers were ARCHIBALD KNOX, who had studied Celtic and Runic monuments on the Isle of Man and in Ireland, Rex Silver (1879–1965) and Bernard Cuzner (1877–1956). Some studio pottery sold by Liberty & Co. also bore Celtic motifs, for example the Compton Pottery's moulded terracotta garden wares. In 1903 the Grafton Galleries in London mounted an exhibition entitled *Modern Celtic Art*, and such was the style's popularity that Liberty continued to produce Cymric and Tudric designs into the 1920s.

J. Sheehy: *The Rediscovery of Ireland's Past: The Celtic Revival, 1830–1930* (London, 1980)

C. E. Karkov, M. Ryan and R. T. Farrell: *The Insular Tradition* (Albany, NY, 1997)

P. Harbison: 'Culture of Creation', *Irish A. Rev.*, xxi/2 (Summer 2004), pp. 96–9

Censer [thurible; Lat. *incensarium, thuribulum, thymia-materium*]. Footed brazier, chafing-dish or portable grate for burning incense or coals to produce aromatic fumes for liturgical and secular purposes. Censers commonly have two to four rings on the outside of the bowl, with chains or rods attached for holding and swinging. There is frequently a pierced lid or cover, attached by rings, through which the chains or rods pass. Typically the finial or knob of the lid has a separate chain attached.

Centrepiece. *See under* TABLE SERVICES AND ORNAMENT.

Century Guild of Artists. English group of painters, designers and craftsmen, active between c. 1883 and 1892. It was one of the earliest Arts and Crafts groups and initiated the practice of attributing designs to individual craftsmen, which became a firm principle of the ARTS AND CRAFTS MOVEMENT. Although output was limited and sporadic, the group had considerable influence by exhibiting its products and publishing a quarterly magazine, the *Century Guild Hobby Horse* (1884–92). Perhaps 20 craftsmen in all were associated with the Guild, but the only members were A. H. Mackmurdo, Herbert Horne (1864–1916) and Selwyn Image (1849–1930).

The Guild's work was mainly domestic. It offered textiles, wallpapers, furniture, stained glass, metalwork, decorative painting and architectural design, all of which were displayed at the *Inventions Exhibition* (London, 1885), the *Exhibition of Navigation and Manufacture* (Liverpool, 1886) and the *Royal Jubilee Exhibition* (Manchester, 1887). The style adopted was formal and based on 18th-century sources, although some patterns were of an Art Nouveau character. The Guild's work at Pownall Hall (1886–7; Cheshire) is regarded as its major commission, but only fragments of this scheme survive. Its work is represented in the collection of the William Morris Gallery, London.

S. E. Overal: *Catalogue of A. H. Mackmurdo and the Century Guild Collection*, London, William Morris Gal. cat. (London, 1967)

S. Evans: 'The Century Guild Connection', *Art and Architecture in Victorian Manchester*, ed. J. H. G. Archer (Manchester, 1985), pp. 250–68

A. N. Sprague: 'The British Tempera Revival: A Return to Craftsmanship', *Brit. A. J.*, iii/3 (Aug 2002), pp. 66–74

A. Powers: '1884 and the Arts and Crafts Movement', *Apollo*, clxi (April 2005), pp. 60–65

Ceramic Art Co. *See under* LENOX, WALTER SCOTT.

Ceramics. Items of clay fashioned using a variety of techniques and hardened by heat.

Ramsey Abbey Censer, silver gilt, h. 108 mm, diam. 53 mm and incense boat, silver parcel-gilt, from ?Ramsey Abbey, England, *c.* 1375 (London, Victoria and Albert Museum)

See also BONE CHINA; EARTHENWARE; GLAZE; KAOLIN; PORCELAIN; STONEWARE; TERRACOTTA.

Cerbara. Italian family of gem-engravers and medallists. Giuseppe Cerbara (*b* Rome, 15 July 1770; *d* Rome, 6 April 1856) was the son of Giovanni Battista Cerbara (*b* Rome, 1748; *d* Rome, 1811) and was one of the best-known gem-engravers and medallists working in Rome in the 18th century and the early 19th. From 1822 he held the post of Incisore Camerale to the papal mint with Giuseppe Girometti; the artists were responsible for producing a medal on alternate years. Appointed Incisore Particolare dei Sommi Pontefici by Leo XII (*reg* 1823–9), Giuseppe Cerbara also executed seals and coins and prepared dies for the *zecca* (mint) of Bologna. From 1823 he began the series of medals known as *Della Lavanda* (Rome, Mus. Cent. Ris.). Among his most significant medals are that commemorating the new Museo Chiaramonti (1822), that for Cardinal Ercole Consalvi (1824), those commemorating the visit of Leo XII to the Ospedale del S Spirito (1826), the visit of Gregory XVI to the Ospizio Apostolico (1831), the

monetary reform (1835), the new Museo di S Giovanni in Laterano (1853) and the restoration of the Porta Pia (1854). A catalogue (Balbi de Caro) of his more important works (15 medals and 44 engraved gems), all in the Neo-classical style, is in the Accademia di S Luca, Rome.

His numerous gem-engravings and cameos, signed G. C., G. CERBARA, CERBARA or KEPBAPA, are well documented by several sets of casts of his work, with their related catalogues (Rome, Accad. N. S Luca; Rome, Pal. Braschi). Extant works by Giuseppe Cerbara in museums and private collections are often attributed to one or other member of the family, as the initial G is frequently omitted. Examples of Giuseppe's work with subjects taken from mythology or antiquity are illustrated in *Memorie enciclopediche romane* by G. A. Guattani, and engraved gems with similar subjects are in the Kunsthistorisches Museum, Vienna. These are attributed to both Giovanni Battista and Giuseppe; likewise those in the British Museum, London, are attributed to Nicola Cerbara (see below) but are partly by Giuseppe. The cameo with the head of *Livia di Firenze* (Florence, Bargello) is also attributed to Giuseppe.

Nicola Cerbara (*b* Rome, 29 Feb 1796; *d* Montepulciano, 28 June 1869) was the younger brother of Giuseppe. His works in steel may be identified by his signature: N. CERBARA, NIC. CERBARA, NIC. C, N. C. As an engraver of dies for the papal mint, he produced medals for the popes from Leo XII (*reg* 1823–9) to Pius IX (*reg* 1846–78). Of particular interest are the medal for Cardinal Alessandro Albani (1830) and the iconographical series of famous Italian men, begun in collaboration with Pietro Girometti in 1841. Nicola Cerbara also produced coins for the mints of Rome and Bologna. On his medals he often reproduced paintings by Old Masters, as well as drawing on Classical subjects.

I. S. Weber: 'Fur Napoleon', *Weltkunst,* lxxiv/11 (Oct 2004), pp. 94–5

Cerreto Sannita. Italian pottery centre in Campania. The first potteries were founded in 1688 by Neapolitans. Flasks or vases in the form of the female figure and spire-shaped centrepieces, inspired by marble prototypes in the Neapolitan piazzas, were manufactured. In the 18th century members of the GIUSTINIANI family worked in Cerreto Sannita on projects as the panel (1727) set in the tympanum of the congregation of S Maria in San Lorenzello, which is signed and dated by Antonio Giustiniani. The town is still an important pottery centre.

G. Donatone: *La ceramica di Cerreto Sannita* (Rome, 1968)
Un museo a Cerreto Sannita: Inaugurazione del Museo civico e mostra di antiche maioliche cerretesi: Chiostro monumentale di Sant'Antonio, Cerreto Sannita, 1995 (Cerreto Sannita, 1995)
S. Cipolla and A. Maddonni: *L'Immaginario religioso: 2 Biennale della ceramica contemporanea, Cerreto Sannita* (exh. cat., Cerreto Sannita, 2000)
G. Donatone: *Maioliche meridionali da collezione: Ariano Irpino, Cerreto Sannita, Ischia, Napoli, Vietri sul Mare* (Naples, 2003)

Certosina. Type of intarsia MARQUETRY that was especially popular in Lombardy, Venice and the Veneto in the 15th century. It was made with polygonal tesserae of wood, bone, metal and mother-of-pearl arranged in geometrical patterns.

Chaffers, **Richard** (*b* 1731; *d* 1765). English potter. He was the son of a Liverpool shipwright and in 1752 he established a pottery factory which made blue-and-white earthenware, principally for export to the American colonies. In 1755 he discovered and secured the rights to a vein of soapstone (or soaprock) at Mullion in Cornwall, and thereafter his wares rivalled those of Wedgwood After his premature death in December 1765, his company was taken over by his partner, Philip Christian, who ran the pottery till 1776.

K. Boney: *Richard Chaffers, a Liverpool Potter* (Liverpool, 1960)
D. Goldstein: 'Rediscovering Liverpool Porcelain', *A. & Ant.,* xxiii/6 (June 2000), pp. 62–6

Chafing dish. Portable grate fuelled by charcoal, designed for use in a dining room to heat food.

P. Dunne and others: 'Some Like it Hot', *Hist. Preserv.,* xlvi (March–April 1994), p. 76ff

Chair. Type of seat furniture for use by one person.

1. *c.* AD 500–*c.* 1450. 2. AFTER *c.* 1450.

1. *c.* AD 500–*c.* 1450.

(i) China. During the 10th century in China it became common practice to sit on chairs, which subsequently became an important furniture type. During the Song dynasty (960–1279) chairs began to conform to the shape of the body and became more comfortable, with curved armrests and curved or S-shaped splats, which were adopted in England during the 17th century. There are many extant examples of chairs from the Ming dynasty (1368–1644). During this period two basic forms—waisted and waistless—were developed, and several different types were produced: side chairs, armchairs, folding chairs and thrones.

(ii) Europe. In the Middle Ages a chair was recognized as the seat of authority and was accorded to the person of highest social standing on any particular occasion. Seats of authority were frequently provided with footstools or incorporated a footrest. Although few chairs from this period survive, manuscript illuminations illustrate the different types and their uses. Inventories and accounts to tailors and saddlers show that the covering of a chair was at least as important as its basic carpentry. Chests or boxes could be used as chairs when covered with cushions, carpets or tapestries; one of the most commonly illustrated types of seat is simply a box with a large cushion on it. The box could be pierced with open-work or moulded, and the cushion might be plain, embroidered or tasselled.

In common with most medieval furniture, many chairs were designed to be portable and had leather carrying-cases. The folding X-seat, the *sella curulis* used by Roman officials, was known in the Middle Ages as a faldstool and retained its association with authority. In its Classical form it had animal-claw feet and animal-head finials. Generally the seat was made of leather straps or canvas webbing, with the X-frame at the front and back or occasionally on the sides; the frames were made of iron (e.g. ?6th century; London, BM), bronze or wood. The Coronation Gospels (795–810; Vienna, Schatzkam.) shows an example with a pair of wooden legs turned in a bobbin-reel pattern, while a relief in the choir of Amiens Cathedral shows six interlocking wooden Xs braced together to form a wooden seat. The upper terminals of the X could be lengthened and the two rear members joined by webbing with either a wooden brace or leather strap slung between the back and side members (e.g. 1372; The Hague, Rijksmus. Meermanno-Westreenianum. MS. 10 B. 23).

The term 'post seat' refers to any chair with a vertical post at each corner joined to the seat; the posts may also be joined to the back and arms by further posts and rails. The posts may be turned on a lathe or carved in free forms, possibly from wood or from wood covered with bronze sheets or ivory. The legs or arms of post chairs could be made of ivory; only the Throne of Maximian (6th century; Ravenna, Mus. Arcivescovile) survives intact, but there are a few fragments from northern Europe, for example a slender ivory arm from a chair carved with animal interlace (1150s; Florence, Bargello) and another chair arm or leg carved in Norway from a walrus tusk (*c.* 1150; London, BM).

Turned post seats were found throughout Europe in the Middle Ages, but few survive. Among the oldest examples are the Bishop's Chair (*c.* 1200) at Hereford Cathedral and a chair (12th–13th century) at the church in Husaby, Sweden, both of which have Romanesque arcading on the base. Other examples are found in the medieval churches at Urnes, Norway (12th century), and in Herrestad (Östergötland; 12th–13th century; now Stockholm, Stat. Hist. Mus.) and Källunge (Gotland; 12th–13th century; now Visby, Gotlands Fornsal) in Sweden.

Post chairs produced without a lathe took several forms. An iron-framed example decorated with iron leaves and rosettes, probably dating from the 13th century, is illustrated in the *Dictionnaire raisonné du mobilier français* (Viollet-le-Duc, 1858). The Essen Madonna (late 10th century; Essen, Münsterschatzmus.) sits on a post stool with four rectangular moulded legs and no back or armrest. The Bayeux Tapestry (1070s; Bayeux, Mus. Tap.) depicts many types of chair, often being used as thrones. In the scene with Halley's comet, for example, Harold is sitting on a post chair that has an openwork base, low arms and a high back. The finials of the back posts end in gaping dragon heads and are joined by a bowed rail. Chairs of this type dating from the 13th and 14th centuries survive in Norwegian churches, but their carving is entirely secular, and their style and iconography are clearly related to much earlier models. The pine Blaker chair (13th century; Oslo, U. Oldsaksaml.) has a boarded base and back but can be considered part of this group because of its secular carving of geometric and vegetal interlace, dragonhead terminals and knights fighting on horseback and on foot. Another example is the birch Tyldal chair (1150–1200 Oslo, U. Oldsaksaml.), which is carved with fighting beasts and geometric knot patterns.

In contrast to the post seat, the boarded seat has a more boxlike appearance, with the base and possibly back and sides solidly boarded over. Most examples of this type were designed as permanent fixtures, and many are specifically thrones. However, the chair (?12th century) in St James's, Stanford Bishop, Hereford & Worcs, was designed to be portable. It was made without nails, and the boards slot together with the uprights so that it can be dismantled. The chairs used by the Lewis chessmen (1150–1200; examples in London, BM; Edinburgh, N. Mus. Ant.) appear to be of board construction, with solid armless sides and back, carved with intricate animal and interlace designs; however, this type of chair,

with a somewhat more curved form, also corresponds to the traditional Norwegian *kubbstol*, hollowed out of a tree trunk. More elaborate 14th-century board chairs with openwork tracery are illustrated in the *Romance of Alexander* (Oxford, Bodleian Lib., 360) and the Psalter of Jean, Duc de Berry (*c.* 1386; Paris, Bib. N. MS. fr. 13091). In the latter the seat is spacious enough to accommodate a man wearing elaborate gowns, the front and back posts are like miniature towers with crocketted spires, and the back is decorated with a mosaic panel, but the arms are two narrow, uncomfortable bars. The chair is shown without cushions or upholstery, but it was probably designed to be softened with textiles. A surviving chair (*c.* 1450) of equal intricacy and beauty is in St Mary's Guildhall, Coventry. It was designed as part of a set of three for the guildmasters. From *c.* 1400 board seats in England, France and the Netherlands were decorated with Gothic tracery and the linenfold motif.

P. Eames: 'Medieval Furniture: Furniture in England, France and the Netherlands from the Twelfth to the Fifteenth Century', *Furn. Hist.*, xiii (1977) [whole issue]

2. AFTER *c.* 1450. In 1500 the chair in Europe was still predominantly Gothic in character, although from *c.* 1450 Classical motifs were being applied to Italian furniture. After his invasion of Italy (1494), Charles VIII returned to France with a number of Italian craftsmen; through their influence French craftsmen assimilated Renaissance ornaments and applied them to French furniture. A chair characteristic of the new style was the armchair or *fauteuil*; this had a narrow, carved backrest and semi-octagonal seat with supports in the form of columns and was popular in England and the Netherlands. Until recently it was referred to as the *caquetoire*; it has now been established that *caquetoires* were almost always upholstered. In England, Renaissance or 'romayne' motifs began to appear *c.* 1520; surviving chairs show a mingling of Italianate grotesques with Gothic ornament (e.g. London, V&A). From about 1550 French, Netherlandish and German pattern books by such designers as Jacques Androuet Du Cerceau and Hans Vredeman de Vries provided a wealth of ornament that was applied to chairs, in particular to the flat expanse offered by the chair back. The Italian *sgabello*, a chair or stool, the legs and back of which were made up of a series of elaborately carved slabs, spread throughout Europe and was introduced to England in the 1630s, largely through such designers as Francis Cleyn and Inigo Jones.

During the 17th century France, while still owing a great deal to Italian fashions, became the major centre for innovation in chair design. By the 1600s one of the dominant forms was the more elegant upholstered chair known as the *chaise au vertugadin* in France and the 'back stool' in England (e.g. *c.* 1625; Knole, Kent, NT). Rectangular upholstered seats and backrests were joined by supports in the form of turned Doric columns. Armchairs usually had straight, padded arms until the 1670s; thereafter the arms sloped down from the back to the armrests. Further comfort was achieved by hollowing the backs on what in England were called 'French chairs'. However, throughout the 17th century dignity took precedence over comfort, more care being lavished on fringes and tassels than on seat padding. An exception to this was the development in the late 16th century of chairs with adjustable backs, one of the earliest examples being an invalid chair (Brussels, Bib. Royale Albert 1er, MS.) for Philip II, King of Spain. Originally luxury items, these became widespread in Europe. They were known as *fauteuils de commodité* in France and first appeared in England in the 1660s (e.g. sleeping-chair, 1670s; London, V&A).

The furniture of the court of Louis XIV at Versailles remained highly formal. By the end of the 17th century, however, the lighter, less formal Régence style became fashionable. Rococo-style suites of chairs—*sièges meublants*—were placed against the wall to enhance the internal architecture of a room, while *sièges courants* were used for reading or writing. Chairs had curving, flowing lines and were often padded for comfort. The more generous use of upholstery resulted in the enlargement of chair backs and the concealment of more of the woodwork with textiles. The most lavishly upholstered versions were referred to as *bergères* in French and easy-chairs in English. Curved legs gave greater stability than straight or tapering ones, and by the 1730s stretchers uniting the legs were dispensed with. The Rococo style spread throughout Europe, with FRANÇOIS DE CUVILLIÉS working in Germany and Chippendale in England; the latter's *Gentleman and Cabinet-maker's Director* (London, 1754) includes many different designs for Rococo-style chairs. French fashions also led the way when Rococo designs were superseded by the Neoclassical style in the mid-1750s. An early example is the furniture made for Ange-Laurent de La Live de Jully (1725–70) by Louis-Joseph Le Lorrain. Such English designers as William Chambers and Robert Adam were swift to exploit the new taste, while the pattern books of George Hepplewhite (1788) and Thomas Sheraton (1793) helped to spread the English domestic version throughout Germany, Scandinavia, Russia, Spain and Portugal, where carved mahogany chairs in the English Neo-classical style became prevalent (particularly in the latter two countries). The English version was even popular in France from 1775. Chair legs that had previously been curved and embellished with rocaille ornament were now straight and were decorated with Classical motifs.

In the late 18th century and the early 19th there was a revival of Greek styles based on the examples depicted in ancient vases. Such designers as Charles Percier (1764–1838) and Pierre-François-Léonard Fontaine exploited the possibilities of the klismos chair (a Greek easy-chair that was light, elegant and comfortable; it had a curved receding back and legs that curved outwards both to the front and rear), as did such furniture-makers as Georges Jacob. The newly acquired palaces of Napoleon, gained through conquest, were decorated in the Empire style by Percier and Fontaine and furnished by Jacob; this did much to spread the style throughout Europe, and chairs freely based on the klismos became almost universal and retained their popularity, particularly in Italy, until well into the 1830s.

In the 19th century the emphasis in chair design was on comfort rather than dignity. Coiled upholstery springs were introduced in the 1830s, and shortly afterwards deep buttoned seats and backs became widespread. A variety of chairs developed, such as the *pouffe*, a cylindrical stool with no visible woodwork, the *confidant*, two seats joined to form an S curve, or the *indiscret*, formed of three seats. Chairmakers became increasingly eclectic in their choice of styles: some examples hark back to the Gothic (e.g. Gothic Revival armchair, possibly designed by Schinkel, c. 1840; London, V&A), while others took the Rococo Revival form, the extravagances of which went hand in hand with luxurious upholstery. Such designers as Henry Lawford (*fl* 1830s–1850) in England, Théodore Pasquier (*fl* 1840s) in France and John Henry Belter in the USA vied with each other to produce greater comfort. In contrast, simple bentwood chairs were mass-produced by MICHAEL THONET of Vienna.

From the mid-1860s in England the designs of William Morris (e.g. the 'Sussex' chair, 1865), Charles

Charles Eames and Eero Saarinen: high-back armchair, moulded wood shell, foam rubber upholstery, h. 1.07 m, 1940 (New York, Museum of Modern Art)

Locke Eastlake and Bruce J. Talbert resulted in a less extravagant type of chair. The Arts and Crafts Movement looked back to such vernacular designs as the simple, robust, ladder-back chair (e.g. by Ernest Gimson, *c.* 1890s; London, V&A). Such developments were influential in the USA, for example on chairs made by Gustav Stickley and Greene & Greene. The Deutscher Werkbund in Germany and the Wiener Werkstätte in Austria produced chairs that often drew inspiration from traditional designs and were stripped of unnecessary ornament. Such Viennese designers as Otto Wagner and Josef Hoffmann made use of the bentwood techniques pioneered by Thonet. In England, C. F. A. Voysey designed such austere pieces as the 'Swan' chair (1883–5; e.g. Cheltenham, A. G. & Mus.) and helped to develop the Art Nouveau style, although he disapproved of the more sinuous, asymmetrical version developed by such French designers as Emile Gallé or Louis Majorelle. The avant-garde designs of Charles Rennie Mackintosh ranged from sturdy chairs reinforced by intersecting verticals and horizontals to long, narrow chairs surmounted with elliptical panels, such as those made for the Argyle Street Tea-room of Glasgow. Among the most important American innovators was Frank Lloyd Wright, famous for his pioneering office furniture (e.g. desk chair, 1904, from the Larkin Building, Buffalo, NY; London, V&A).

Towards the end of and after World War I chair design reflected the modern style, which was severely geometrical and owed little to historical ornament. An early example is GERRIT RIETVELD's 'Red–Blue' chair (1918) made up of a series of machine-processed rectangles. At the Bauhaus in Weimar, MARCEL BREUER pioneered the use of tubular steel, which could be bent in different directions to give the appearance of a continuous curve (e.g. the 'Wassily' chair, 1925). In Finland Alvar Aalto created the same visual effect with laminated plywood, for example in 'Armchair Model 41' designed between 1930 and 1933 (e.g. London, V&A). He was also one of the pioneers in the design of stacking chairs, with his three-legged stools that neatly pile one on top of the other. This concept took on increasing importance, with the avant-garde British firm PEL producing the PEL stacking chair in the 1930s, Robin Day designing the 'Q-Stak' chair for S. Hille & Co. in the 1950s, and Ernest Race designing the 'Antelope' and 'Springbok' chairs for the Festival of Britain in London in 1951 and the 'Polyprop' stacking chair in 1963. Meanwhile, the Danish architect Kaare Klint was producing such innovative designs as the 'Safari' chair and the 'Deckchair' (both 1933). In the USA Charles Eames and Ray Eames exploited the possibilities of moulded wood surfaces.

In the second half of the 20th century designers worldwide exploited the opportunities provided by increased standardization in furniture production and by new synthetic materials that can be made into any shape. Peter Murdoch (*b* 1940) used three different papers and five different laminations to produce his child's chair; Eero Aarnio (*b* 1932) used fibreglass for his 'Pastille' chair (1968); the Zanotta Poltrone Co., Milan, used plastic for its blow-up chair; the 'Sacco' chair consists of a leather bag stuffed with polystyrene granules that adjust to the position of the sitter. From the late 1970s the science of ergonomics was increasingly important, especially in Scandinavian design, producing revolutionary chair forms. Chair designs in the early 21st century range from such Post-modernist pieces as Charles Jenks's 'Spring' chair, which looks back to Classical motifs, to the Craft Revival pieces of John Makepeace (*b* 1939) and David Colwell (*b* 1944) and to the minimalist pieces by Jan Dranger (*b* 1941) of Sweden and Jaspar Morrison (*b* 1959) of England.

J. Gloag: *The Englishman's Chair* (London, 1964)
Modern Chairs, 1918–1970 (exh. cat., London, Whitechapel A.G., 1970)
R. Bishop: *Centuries and Styles of the American Chair, 1640–1970* (New York, 1972)
P. E. Kane: *300 Years of American Seating Furniture: Chairs and Beds from the Mabel Brady Garvan and Other Collections at Yale University* (Boston, 1976)
F. Russell and J. Read: *A Century of Chair Design* (New York, 1980)
G. McClendon: *The Master Chair-maker's Art: France 1710–1800* (New York, 1984)
E. S. Cooke Jr, ed.: *Upholstery in America and Europe* (New York, 1987)
L. Knobel: *Office Furniture* (London, 1987)
G. Cranz: *The Chair: Rethinking Culture, Body, and Design* (New York, 1998)
Master Chair Makers of Continental Europe, 1725–1825 (New York, Cummings Antiques, 1999)
C. Fiell and others: *1000 Chairs* (Cologne, 2000)
C. Fiell and P. Fiell: *Chairs* (Cologne, 2001)
P. Bueno: *Just Chairs* (New York, 2003)

Chaise longue. Sofa with a rest for the back at one end only, also known as a 'couch', a 'lounge' or (elliptically) a 'chaise'; the DUCHESSE is a form of chaise longue. See fig. on. p. 218.

V. Fischer: *The LC4 Chaise Longue by Le Corbusier, Pierre Jeanneret and Charlotte Perriand* (Frankfurt am Main, 1997)
R. Schuldenfrei: *Design-recline: Modern Architecture and the Mid-century Chaise Longue* (exh. cat., Cambridge, MA, Busch-Reisinger Mus., 2004)

Chaise percée. *See* CLOSE STOOL.

Chalcedony. Fibrous variety of quartz which includes a wide range of stones, among which certain types are more widely used and valued for carving. The types that are light and generally uniform in colour are called 'common' chalcedony; these were used, for example, by the Grand Ducal Workshops in Florence for flesh tones in polychrome pietre dure sculpture. One of the best-known and most valued types is cornelian, a translucent stone that varies in colour from bright red to light yellow; it was widely used by the Romans, who obtained it in the Near East and India. Another type of chalcedony especially famous and valued in classical antiquity is bloodstone, which is dark green with small blood-red flecks or veins. It comes mainly from India and

Bubbles chaise longue (see p. 217) by Frank Gehry, corrugated cardboard with fire-retardant coating, 889 × 1854 × 724 mm, 1987 (New York, Museum of Modern Art)

was often used for goblets and vases in Roman times and in the Renaissance. Agates, known by different names according to the type of colouring and markings, are the semi-transparent or translucent varieties of chalcedony, of various colours, with a structure of parallel or concentric striations. Agate sardonyx, from India, Asia Minor and China, is a translucent type with zones of black or brown sard (a type of chalcedony). Onyx-chalcedony, with black zones alternating with bluish-grey or white ones, was often used for cameo work, using the light strata for the figure. Vast deposits of German agate, with regular zones of various colours, were widely exploited in the Middle Ages. In Renaissance Italy, Sienese agate was frequently used; this type has parallel striations in various shades from ochre to brown.

See also CORNELIAN; ONYX.

Chalice [Lat. *calix*: 'drinking vessel']. Liturgical implement in which the eucharistic wine is offered, consecrated and distributed to communicants. Other names for it are scyphus, crater, proculum and fons. In the Early Christian period the same materials were used for the eucharistic chalice as for secular drinking vessels: glass, rock crystal, hardstones and wood, horn and ivory, but especially precious and base metals. This diversity reflects the lack of restrictions governing the materials to be used for its manufacture until the Carolingian period. Thus most surviving chalices from pre-Carolingian and Carolingian times—even such a splendid example as the Tassilo Chalice (*c.* 769–88; Kremsmünster, Stiftskirche, Schatzkam.)—were still made from gilt-copper. From the late 8th century, however, synodal decrees repeatedly forbade the use of materials such as glass, wood, copper, bronze, ivory, horn and pewter. The chalice was instead to be made at least from silver, with the inside of the bowl gilded. This rule seems to have met with only qualified observance. Chalices were made not only from materials that were regarded as equivalent in value to gold and silver because of their rarity or their origin (e.g. chalices in the Tesoro di S Marco, Venice); many copper chalices were also still being used in the late Middle Ages. In these a distinction was nevertheless made between the base-metal foot and the bowl, which was made of precious metal. Pewter chalices were still in use in the 18th century (especially in poorer and Protestant churches), while gilt-copper ones were being used as late as the 19th century. Gold and silver were always considered to be the most suitable materials for making chalices, however. The Roman Missal prescribes that the bowl at least must be gold or silver, and it must in any case be gilded inside. In the 11th century (as again today) the knop was often made from a ball of rock crystal. Small funerary chalices, while often made from gold and silver, were even more frequently fashioned from simple materials such as lead, wood, pewter and leather.

The form of the chalice, unlike the materials used to make it, was not determined by ecclesiastical decree but simply developed over the centuries. The starting point was again the secular drinking vessel of the Early Christian period; this applies both to chalices with two handles and to those with none. The basic components of both are the goblet-like bowl of varying depth (*cuppa*, *vas*) and the base, which in turn consists of the foot (*pes*) and the knop (*nodus*) and intervening between them, from at least the second half of the 12th century, the stem (*stilus*) (e.g. the chalice from Fritzlar Cathedral; *c.* 1180). From ancient times it had been customary to use the two-handled cantharus-shaped chalice to offer to the faithful when they were receiving Communion under both kinds, especially in the Byzantine area. No doubt as a result of the decision to restrict the reception of the holy blood to the celebrant, the han-

Chalice, onyx, silver-gilt mounts, semi-precious stones and enamel, Byzantine, *c.* 10th century AD (Venice, Tesoro di San Marco)

dled chalice fell into disuse from the 13th century onwards. The Council of Constance (1414–18) determined that the chalice should not be given to the laity. Surviving examples such as the 'Heinrichskelch' (*c.* 1020; Munich, Residenz) were thenceforth happily put to other uses during services. After that time chalices were handleless, with a semi-spherical bowl, a round foot with a rimmed edge and a knop shaped like a slightly flattened sphere or ribbed to resemble a pomegranate.

The proportions were lengthened by the insertion of a cylindrical stem both above and below the knop. From the 13th century onwards the shape became more slender, with a longer stem and a more beaker-like bowl. At about the same time a new shape of foot began to become widespread, characterized by concave scalloping, usually six-lobed (more rarely four-lobed). This design was soon extended to the shaping of the whole base. The knop was also structured correspondingly, usually with six oval patellae, lozenge-shaped or four-lobed. In the 15th century these horizontally projecting 'cones', often richly decorated, might bear the letters IHESVS. The decoration on the Gothic chalice, which had an increasingly slender bowl on an ever more elongated stem section, was further enriched by architectural motifs.

While chalices with this typically Gothic shape were to some extent widespread outside Italy until the 17th century, a more clearcut and unified shape gradually won favour, first in Italy and then, from the mid-15th century, north of the Alps as well. Typically, these chalices had a bowl with an out-turned lip, a round foot and a knop that was generally oviform or pear-shaped. The alteration in shape was preceded by a change in ornamental decoration. The often very large Baroque chalices are generally covered with a luxuriant profusion of sculpted decoration. While the typical Rococo chalice with a weakly formed knop can often appear to lack clear structuring, Neo-classical chalices are marked by simple, severely structured shapes. Development from that period to the present is characterized by the adaptation of historical prototypes, their further development and new forms, which again place greater emphasis on the bowl.

Goldsmiths used a wide variety of techniques and materials to decorate the chalice. From the 8th century, inscriptions (sometimes relating to the donor) were often engraved on the rim of the foot, on the bowl or on both. Alongside simple, undecorated chalices and those decorated with ornamental motifs, from the early Middle Ages there were also chalices

Chalice by Skidmore & Sons, silver gilt and enamel, h. 204 mm, *c.* 1851 (London, Victoria and Albert Museum)

Chalice by Beatrice Wood, ceramic, h. 194 mm, 1986 (Newark, NJ, Newark Museum)

with a distinctive iconography, emphasizing the vessel's role as a symbol of the fount of life or indeed as the tomb of Christ. This could be expressed in representations of the sacrifice on the Cross and of the Lamb. This complex iconographic tradition was continued in the 12th century by important chalices sometimes bearing extensive pictorial representations and inscriptions, often in relief; these created a typological scheme based on the 'life-giving' chalice and the unbloody renewal of the sacrifice on the Cross through the celebration of the Eucharist (e.g. the chalice from Wilten Monastery, *c.* 1160–70; Vienna, Ksthist. Mus.). As well as having an overall filigree decoration, chalices from the 12th century were decorated, particularly on the foot, with enamels and nielli or relief medallions, the pictorial imagery of which generally indicates a trend away from typological schemes. The typical High Gothic chalice is characterized by the use of small-scale architectural motifs with decoration made up of ornamental struts and sometimes rich finials, tracery and crockets. In the Baroque period there was an increased tendency to make the chalice a vehicle for contemporary ornamental forms. Rococo taste largely confined the decoration of the chalice to secular rocaille ornamentation. Most 20th-century chalices are notable for an emphasis on simplicity.

W. W. Watts: *Catalogue of Chalices & Other Communion Vessels* (London, 1922)

J. R. Harris: *Glass Chalices of the First Century* (Manchester, 1927)

M. Ryan: *Early Irish Communion Vessels* (Dublin, 2000)

J. Y. Ulrich: 'Ratselhafter Silberkelch', *Ant. Welt,* xxxv/5 (2004), pp. 40–42

Chalkware. American term for figurines made from plaster of Paris, often imitating Staffordshire pottery; chalkware was not glazed, but rather painted in oils or watercolours. In the early 18th century chalkware moulds were imported from Italy, but thereafter moulds and figurines were made in America.

A. E. Lange and J. A. Reilly, *Chalkware* (New York, 1994)

A. E. Lange and others: 'Chalkware', *Mag. Ant.,* cxlvi (Oct 1994), pp. 496–505

Chamber candlestick. Portable candlestick mounted on a base with a handle, often fitted with a snuffer and wax drip holder; the form first emerged in the late 17th century, and by the 18th century fine examples in porcelain and silver were being manufactured. A folding version (known as a Brighton bun) for travellers in use from *c.* 1735 to 1925 unscrewed to make two chamber candlesticks.

N. A. Brawer: 'Brighton Buns: Ingenious Folding Candlesticks for Travelers', *Mag. Ant.,* clxiv/6 (Dec 2003), pp. 90–95

Chamberlain, Robert (*bapt ? 1736; d 1798*). English enameller and porcelain manufacturer. In 1751 he was apprenticed at the Worcester Porcelain Company 'to learn pot painting', and eventually became the head of the decorating department; his apprentices included his sons Robert (1755–1832) and

Humphrey (1762–1841). In 1783 the company was sold to Thomas Flight, whereupon Chamberlain left and established an independent decorating company with his son Humphrey. They began to decorate porcelain for Thomas Turner of CAUGHLEY PORCELAIN FACTORY, and by 1789 had opened a shop in Worcester High Street, where they sold high quality 'Chamberlain's Worcester' (*see* WORCESTER). In the early 1790s the Chamberlains began to manufacture hybrid hard-paste porcelain, and so became competitors to those whose wares they had formerly decorated.

In the 19th century the firm secured noble and royal patrons; Lord Nelson ordered a set of armorial tableware in 1802, and in 1807 the Prince of Wales conferred a royal warrant on the company; the prince became regent in 1811, whereupon Humphrey Chamberlain created a line of Regent China. Dinner services with the Regent body were manufactured for royalty and for organizations such as the East India Company. In 1814 the company opened a London shop at 63 Piccadilly, and in 1816 moved the shop to 155 New Bond Street. In 1840 the company merged with the Worcester Porcelain Company which traded as Chamberlain & Co. until 1852, when the name of Chamberlain was finally dropped from the name of the firm.

ODNB

G. A. Godden, *Chamberlain–Worcester Porcelain, 1788–1852* (London, 1982)

S. F. G. Parkinson, 'Chamberlains of Worcester: The Early Years of a Family Enterprise', *J. North. Cer. Soc.*, viii (1991), pp. 33–60

Chambers, Sir **William** (*b* Göteborg, Sweden, 23 Feb 1723; *d* London, 8 March 1796). English architect and writer, of Scottish descent. Chambers was primarily an architect (his best-known building is Somerset House), but on occasion he also designed interiors and furniture. For Melbourne House (1771), in Piccadilly, he designed everything from side tables and overmantel mirrors to silver urns and candelabra, and his success in these fields of design (Chambers confessed he was a 'very pritty connoisseur in furniture') can be compared to that of his rival Robert Adam. The interior of Melbourne House was destroyed when it was converted into Albany in 1803. Chambers also designed the furniture for the Great Room (painted by James Barry (1741–1806)) of the Society of Arts in London; only the President's chair is known to survive.

ODNB

W. Chambers: *A Treatise on the Decorative Part of Civil Architecture* (1759, rev. 1971/*R* New York, 2003)

M. Snodin and J. Harris, eds: *Sir William Chambers* (London, 1996)

S. Jenkins: 'The External Sculptural Decoration of Somerset House, and the Documentary Sources', *Brit. A. J.*, ii/2 (Winter 2000–01), pp. 22–8

Chambrette, Jacques. *See under* LUNÉVILLE.

Champion, Richard (*b* Bristol, 6 Nov 1743; *d* Camden, SC, 7 Oct 1791). English porcelain manufac-turer. In the mid-1760s Champion met WILLIAM COOKWORTHY, a fellow Quaker, who had long been developing the techniques requisite for the production of hard-paste porcelain. In 1768 Cookworthy patented his discoveries and opened a factory in his native Plymouth; Champion entered into a partnership with Cookworthy in the same year, probably in connection with the Plymouth factory but possibly in connection to an otherwise undocumented factory in Bristol. In 1770 the Plymouth factory was closed and its production transferred to Castle Green, Bristol; in 1773 Cookworthy sold his patent and his share in the Bristol factory to Champion.

Under Champion's management the factory specialized in high-quality figures and tea wares. The finest product of the factory was a tea-set given by Champion and his wife Judith to Jane Burke (wife of Edmund Burke); the teapot, milk jug, and sugar bowl are in the Royal Scottish Museum in Edinburgh. The factory failed in 1781, whereupon Champion sold his patent to a group of Staffordshire potters who established themselves as the New Hall Factory. The last surviving dated piece made by Champion's factory is a figure of Grief commemorating his daughter Eliza, who died on 13 October 1779 (Mint Museum of Art, Charlotte, North Carolina). In 1784 Champion emigrated to South Carolina, where instead of establishing a porcelain factory he ran a plantation.

ODNB

F. S. Mackenna, *Champion's Bristol Porcelain* (Leigh-on-Sea, 1947)

Champlevé *See* ENAMEL, §2(II).

Chandelier. Lighting fixture suspended from the ceiling, equipped with multiple lamps or candles. The massive, crown-shaped, Romanesque chandeliers, for example that made *c.* 1166 for Frederick I, King of Germany and Holy Roman Emperor, for the Palatine chapel in Aachen Cathedral, were gradually superseded by a form that emerged in the 15th century in the Low Countries. This type comprises a central moulded shaft, from which 6–36 upward-curving branches radiate, embellished with Gothic ornament and sometimes human, bird or animal figures. These bronze chandeliers were used in public buildings, churches and the houses of the wealthy, as depicted in Jan van Eyck's *Arnolfini and his Wife* (1434; London, N.G.). In the later 15th century the solid shaft was replaced by a traceried niche containing a figure, often a Virgin and child (e.g. Amsterdam, Rijksmus.).

The mid-16th-century type, with a shorter, spherical shaft surmounted by a figure (e.g. Amsterdam, Rijksmus.), evolved into the Baroque baluster-shaped design that became the standard form in the Low Countries, Germany and England. This design relied for its aesthetic effect on simplicity and the glow of the highly polished bronze or brass globes and balusters that constitute the shaft. In contrast, Italian Baroque examples have elaborate decorations of fruit, leaves, scrolls and figures.

Chandelier, glass, Venice, 1719 (Mira, Villa Widmann-Foscari)

Silver chandeliers are recorded in French and English royal inventories from the late 16th century. They were sometimes described as 'branches'. Surviving examples include one by Daniel Garnier (c. 1695; Colonial Williamsburg, VA). The development in the 17th century of rock-crystal (and later glass) chandeliers composed of beads threaded onto metal armatures to form chains and drops increased the intensity of lighting. Court reception rooms were lit by several glass chandeliers, known as *lustres* in France, hanging low on a chain or cord. The cord was later disguised by a silk or taffeta sleeve. In the early 18th century the Venetian glassmaker GIUSEPPE BRIATI responded to the competition from Bohemian gilded and coloured glass chandeliers with his crystal *ciocche*. These have many branches and consist of white crystal tubular elements on metal frames, ornamented with naturalistic polychrome flowers. They were used in theatres and the rooms of the nobility (e.g. of c. 1740–50; Venice, Ca' Rezzonico). The chinoiserie 'pagoda' type followed; one by Briati with dolphin-shaped arms from the mid-18th century is in the Museo Vetrario, Murano. At about the same time porcelain, gilded and painted metal or wood chandeliers resembling flower-laden arbours with colourful birds were developed in Piedmont and chinoiserie chandeliers in the factory of Capodimonte outside Naples.

English and Irish glass examples imitate the traditional Flemish Baroque form, with added brilliance achieved by faceting. From the mid-18th century they comprised cut-glass spires and festoons of faceted drops hanging from grease pans and pagoda-like canopies. Around 1790 the body lengthened,

Neo-classical vase and urn shapes appeared and prismatic drops were strung in lengths and festooned from arm to arm. The advent of the Regency 'tent' or 'bag' shape radically changed the design of chandeliers. The central shaft was concealed within a curtain of long strings of glass beads cascading from a canopy at ceiling height and fixed to a large horizontal ring below, from which shortened arms sprang. A chandelier of oriental character (previously thought to be a gasolier) made for the Prince Regent (later George IV) in 1817 (Brighton, Royal Pav.) is suspended from a large silver dragon beneath a group of lotus leaves. Another type of Regency chandelier has concentric rings of prisms named 'finger-fringes'. These chandeliers were hung in ranks to decorate large state rooms during the Empire period. The 'dish' light, consisting of a wide, shallow dish of glass or metal suspended by three chains, was also popular.

In the 19th century chandelier forms were adapted to gas and later electric light; hoop-shaped lights and the branches of the Baroque baluster form support lights encased in globular or mushroom-shaped shades. In the 20th and 21st centuries large, ornate glass chandeliers have continued to be made for reception rooms and auditoria (see colour pl. VII, fig. 3).

M. Mortimer: *The English Glass Chandelier* (Woodbridge, 2000)
Early 20th Century Lighting: Electric and Gas, Beardslee Chandelier Mfg Co. (Atglen, PA., 2002)
A. Voulangas: 'Suspended Animation', *Glass,* xliii (Winter 2003), pp. 38–43

Channon, John (*b* Exeter, 1711; *d* London, *c.* 1783). English cabinetmaker. It is likely that he was apprenticed to his older brother Otho Channon (*bapt* 1698; *d* 1756), a chairmaker, in 1726. By 1737 he had established a cabinetmaking business in St Martin's Lane, London. A spectacular pair of bookcases at Powdersham Castle, near Exeter, Devon, bear brass plates engraved 'J Channon Fecit 1740'. They are of architectural character featuring inlaid brass linear designs, arabesques and grotesques in a retardataire style associated with JEAN BERAIN and are further embellished with highly finished, Rococo gilt-brass mounts in a style reminiscent of German, especially Dresden, furniture. On the stylistic evidence of engraved brass inlay combined with a flamboyant repertoire of ornamental mounts representing dolphins, satyr and female masks, foliage and waterfalls etc, other pieces are attributed to the Channon workshop, including a library desk (*c.* 1740; London, V&A) and the Murray writing-cabinet (Leeds, Temple Newsam House). The latter masterwork embodies all the elements of the Powdersham bookcases plus a plethora of drawers and concealed compartments, the pediment surmounted by classical figures in gilt bronze; the mounts feature satyrs and petrified fountains.

C. Gilbert and T. Murdoch: *John Channon and Brass-inlaid Furniture, 1730–60* (New Haven, 1993)

John Channon: bookcase made for Powdersham Castle, oak and pine with padouk veneer and brass inlay, 3.83 × 2.50 × 1.04 m, 1740 (London, Victoria and Albert Museum)

C. Gilbert and others: 'Channon Revisited', *Furn. Hist.*, xxx (1994), pp. 65–85

L. Wood: 'John Channon and Brass-inlaid Furniture', Burl. Mag., cxxxvi (Feb 1994), pp. 131–3

Chantilly. French town in the Oise region, *c.* 40 km north of Paris, and the site of a famous château. It is also known as a centre of production of porcelain and lace.

1. Lace. 2. Porcelain.

1. LACE. Although the production of cheap linen-thread laces and large quantities of black-and-white silk lace had been established in the region north of Paris since the 1650s, the town of Chantilly emerged into prominence only during the revival of lace under Napoleon Bonaparte (*reg* 1804–14). In the early 19th century bands of white silk lace were chiefly made there, alongside black laces intended primarily for export. With the decline of *blonde* silk lace in the 1840s, Chantilly switched to making black silk lace in the matt thread called grenadine. For a time it was noted for the highest-quality lace of this type, but after the early 1850s it was superseded by Caen and Bayeux, and women began deserting lacemaking for more lucrative trades. Thus, as the lace called Chantilly came into its own, the industry in the town itself dwindled away.

Chantilly in der Mode, 2 vols (Ubach-Palenberg, 2000–02)

2. PORCELAIN. The manufacture of porcelain began at Chantilly after Louis-Henri de Bourbon, Prince de Condé (1692–1740), was exiled to his estate at Chantilly in 1726. By letters of 5 October 1735, Louis XV (*reg* 1715–74) authorized Ciquaire Cirou (1700–51) to make porcelain 'in imitation of Japanese porcelain' for 20 years, although the factory had already been established *c.* 1725 and had been installed by the Prince in Chantilly in 1730. Cirou is known to have been a painter at the porcelain factory of Saint-Cloud and was working at the Rue de la Ville l'Evêque, Paris, in 1728. The painters Gilles Dubois (*b* 1712) and Robert Dubois (1709–59) and the carpenter Claude-Humbert Gérin (1705–50) left Chantilly in 1738 to establish a new factory at Vincennes (*see* VINCENNES PORCELAIN FACTORY). In 1751 Cirou sold the factory to Jean-Baptiste Suzanne Buquet de Montvallier, Etienne Roussière and François Baudin. After 1760 a number of directors were in charge, including (1776–9) Louis-François Gravant, until the factory was sold in 1792 to CHRISTOPHER POTTER, an English porcelain-maker working in Paris, who retained control until 1800, when the factory closed.

Early Chantilly porcelain is quite unique in the history of European porcelain as the soft-paste body was covered in a milky-white tin glaze, probably to mask the yellowish-green ('citronée') Luzarches clay. By *c.* 1750 wares were covered with a lead glaze, but tin glaze continued to be employed until the late 18th century, as seen in the 'Villers-Cotterets' service (*c.* 1770; Paris, Louvre). The Prince de Condé inherited a large collection of Japanese and Chinese porcelain, and he and both his wives continued to collect porcelain from East Asia as well as from European factories. Forms at Chantilly were based on such Japanese shapes as the gourd and melon, and lobed, octagonal and fluted forms were also popular. Figures were rare (e.g. *Buddha* with lobed jar; Paris, Mus. Cluny), while knife handles and 'toys' were produced in great numbers. By the mid-18th century, forms were influenced by contemporary metalwork.

Chantilly successfully imitated the simple, asymmetrical designs and characteristic palette of Kakiemon porcelain made in the kilns in Arita, Hizen Province (now Saga and Nagasaki Prefecture) in Japan (e.g. pair of cups; Chantilly, Mus. Condé). At the same time the factory also produced copies of Meissen adaptations of Japanese ware; for example the Meissen 'red dragon' pattern was introduced at Chantilly *c.* 1730 and known as the 'Prince Henri' pattern. Also characteristic of the Kakiemon-inspired designs were the Chantilly versions of the flying squirrel, banded hedge, and quail and pomegranate patterns. *Indianische Blumen* were later used, as were chinoiseries based on designs by Jean-Antoine Fraisse, designer to the Prince de Condé from 1733 to 1740. Due to the edict of 1752 to protect Vincennes's monopoly, the factory was obliged, to some degree, to decorate wares in monochrome, as seen in the flower-pot (London, V&A) bearing the arms of the Condé and the Order of Saint-Esprit, in blue. From *c.* 1755 there was a large production of useful wares and tablewares, typical decoration being the 'Chantilly sprig', which was much imitated throughout Europe.

G. Le Duc: *Chantilly: Un certain regard vers l'Extrême-Orient, 1730–1750,* French Porcelain Society (London, 1993)

G. Le Duc: *Porcelaine tendre de Chantilly au XVIIIe siècle: Héritages des manufactures de Rouen, Saint-Cloud et Paris et influences sur les autres manufactures de XVIIIe siècle* (Paris, 1996)

S. Miller: 'Images of Asia in French Luxury Goods: Jean-Antoine Fraisse at Chantilly, *c.* 1729–36', *Apollo,* cliv/477 (Nov 2001), pp. 3–12

Chapin, Eliphalet (*b* Somers, then MA, now CT, 1741; *d* East Windsor, CT, 1807). American furniture-maker. He made cherrywood highboys and chairs in a style derived from the Philadelphia version of Chippendale, but is not known to have signed any of his furniture. Attributions are based on four documented chairs and a tripod table. From 1774 to 1783 his partner in East Windsor was Aaron Chapin (1753–1838), who was a second cousin. Aaron Chapin moved to Hartford in 1783, and there made furniture in a Federal style influenced by Hepplewhite. From about 1807 Aaron worked alongside his son Laertes (1813–47).

J. Lionetti and others: 'New information about Chapin chairs', *Mag. Ant.,* cxxix (May 1986), pp. 1082–95

M. G. Dowling: *The Enigmatic Eliphalet Chapin, Connecticut's Premier 18th-Century Cabinetmaker, and a Representative Catalogue of his Work* (MA Thesis, New York, Cooper-Hewitt Mus. & Parsons Sch. Des., 1990)

T. Kugelman and A. Kugelman: *Connecticut Valley Furniture by Eliphalet Chapin and His Contemporaries, 1750–1800,* Connecticut Historical Society Museum (Hartford, 2005)

Chaplet, Ernest (*b* Sèvres, Hauts-de-Seine, 1835; *d* Choisy-le-Roi, Val-de-Marne, 1909). French potter. He was apprenticed at the Sèvres porcelain factory, studying historic styles and techniques. From 1857 to 1874 he produced painted earthenware at the Laurin factory in Bourg-la-Reine, Hauts-de-Seine. In 1875 he joined an experimental workshop in Auteuil, Paris, where he worked with Félix Bracquemond. The studio was owned by Charles Haviland (1839–1921) and provided moulds and underglaze decoration for the Haviland factory at Limoges. In the early 1870s Chaplet pioneered BARBOTINE, a method of underglaze painting in coloured slips. With the help of in-house and freelance artists, skilled copies were made of works by Jean-Honoré Fragonard (1732–1806), Antoine Watteau (1684–1721) and the Italian masters, or landscapes and still-lifes of fruit and flowers. Barbotine vases, jugs and bottles quickly became fashionable, but the pieces were difficult to fire and after a few years the factory abandoned the technique. The Haviland company made a second studio available to Chaplet in Vaugirard, Paris, where he made painted, unglazed stoneware after the peasant pottery of Normandy. Chaplet took over the studio in 1885 and was succeeded in 1887 by Auguste Delaherche. In 1886 Bracquemond introduced Chaplet to Paul Gauguin who, stimulated by the new French art pottery, was experimenting with ceramics. During that winter (1886–7) Gauguin attended the Vaugirard studio and with Chaplet created some 55 stoneware pots with applied figures or ornamental fragments, multiple handles, painted and partially glazed. In 1887 Chaplet settled in Choisy-le-Roi where he perfected coloured glazes, especially a flambé glaze derived from the early Chinese *sang de boeuf* (e.g. vase, 1896; London, V&A). In 1904 he lost his sight and gave up the workshop to his son-in-law, Emile Lenoble (1876–1939).

J. d'Albis and others: *Ernest Chaplet, 1835–1909* (Paris, 1976)

Chareau, Pierre (*b* Bordeaux, 3 Aug 1883; *d* East Hampton, New York, 1950). French architect and designer. His work as an architect culminated in the Maison de Verre (1928–32) in Paris. His first important work as a designer was an impressive series of lamps (1923) in floating secant planes of alabaster, revealing an interest in Cubist explorations of space. After 1925 Chareau's highly sculptural furniture, which pivoted or expanded in fan-shaped configurations, became a feature of his designs. Also characteristic of Chareau's work were his unusual combinations of materials such as lightly hammered, unpolished metal and rich mahogany.

In 1940 Chareau emigrated to the USA, where he designed the studio (1948; destr.) in East Hampton, NY, for the painter Robert Motherwell (1915–91), constructed from American army surplus materials.

M. Vellay and K. Frampton: *Pierre Chareau: Architect and Craftsman, 1883–1950* (New York, 1985)

B. B. Taylor and P. Chareau: *Pierre Chareau: Designer and Architect* (Cologne, 1992)

B. Loyaute: 'Le design epure de Pierre Chareau', *Conn. A.,* dlix (Nov 2002), pp. 100–05

Charger. Large circular or oval dish or platter of metal, ceramic or wood, used since the Middle Ages for carrying food to the table and for carving meat. Some have a shallow well or deeply incised lines or troughs to catch the juices from the meat. Ornamental ceramic chargers with relief or painted decoration were intended for dresser or wall display. Metal examples are characterized by gadrooning, a

Charger decorated with four mirhabs, faience, from Morocco, 18th century (Paris, Musée du Quai Branly)

lobed or shaped rim or richly embossed ornament. Ceramic versions in tin-glazed earthenware include the BLUE-DASH CHARGERS of the 17th century and early 18th.

Charpentier, Alexandre(-Louis-Marie) (*b* Paris, 10 June 1856; *d* Neuilly, Hauts-de-Seine, 3 March 1909). French sculptor, medallist and designer. From the early 1890s Charpentier was a key figure in the movement to revive the arts related to interior decoration and design. His furniture and domestic ornaments, inspired more by naturalism than Symbolism, are typical examples of ART NOUVEAU. In both his collaborative interior design schemes, such as that for the Villa la Sapinière in Evian, Haute-Savoie (*c.* 1897–9), with Félix Bracquemond and Jules Chéret (1836–1932), and his individual work, such as the dining-room for Adrien Bénard (1846–1912) at Champrosay (*c.* 1901; Paris, Mus. Orsay), Charpentier acted more as a decorator than a sculptor, carefully creating a perfectly homogenous ensemble, down to the details of the locks and doorhandles. More than these spectacular but rare commissions, it was his innumerable decorative plaquettes in bronze, tin, ceramic, leather and embossed paper (e.g. Paris, Mus. Orsay) that brought him lasting success.

Alexandre Charpentier (Paris, 1902)
R. Froissart Pezone: *Le groupe de l'Art dans tout (1896–1901) un art nouveau au seuil du XXe siècle* (Lille, 2000)

Chasing. Embossing or engraving in relief of metal (often silver and gold); the term also denotes the figures or designs chased on the metal with the chasing-chisel or chasing-hammer.

Chatelaine. Decorative appendage worn by ladies at their waist and by gentlemen suspended on their thighs (to conceal the flap on the breeches). The name alludes to the bunch of keys carried by a medieval châtelaine. The chatelaine consisted of a number of short chains attached to the girdle or belt, bearing articles of household use and ornament, such as as keys, a watch, charms, scissors and thimble-cases. Elaborate chatelaines were fashionable in the second half of the 18th century; in the 1780s factories such as those of MATTHEW BOULTON produced cut-steel chatelaines for men.

J. Zapata: 'Watch Chatelaines in the Munson-Williams-Proctor Arts Institute', *Mag. Ant.,* clix/4 (April 2001), pp. 610–17
H. Meininghaus: 'Necessaires: Ein Modeaccessoire des 18. Jahrhunderts', *Weltkunst,* lxxiii/14 (Dec 2003), pp. 2096–8

Chatoyant. Lapidary term for the cat's-eye effect which can be found in some chrysoberyls and tourmalines. The floating lustre is a band of light that seems to emanate from the gemstone and to move across the surface as the position of the stone is adjusted.

Checker work. *See* CHEQUER-WORK.

Chekhonin, Sergey (Vasil'yevich) (*b* Valayka Station, Novgorod Province [now Lykoshino, Tver' region], 1878; *d* en route from Germany to Paris, 22 Feb 1936). Russian graphic artist, ceramicist, painter and designer. In 1904 he worked in the pottery studio at the ABRAMTSEVO colony. At this period he employed Art Nouveau elements in his work, as in the majolica decorations for the Hotel Metropole, St Petersburg (early 1900s) and the majolica panel *St George Triumphant* for the Municipal Primary School on Bol'shaya Tsaritsynskaya [now Bol'shaya Pirogovskaya] Street in Moscow (1909). In 1917 he joined the State Porcelain Factory in Petrograd, where from 1918 to 1923 and from 1925 to 1927 he was the artistic director. In an attempt to produce his work on a mass scale, Chekhonin worked from 1923 to 1925 at the Novo-Gubfartrest (the former Kuznetsov factory in Volkhov). Porcelain plates and bowls with revolutionary monograms and slogans, and cups and services with portraits of political leaders were produced there. Chekhonin was one of the pioneers of mass agitational porcelain (*see* AGITPROP). Dissatisfied with pre-existing methods and techniques, he combined the precise use of black and white characteristic of graphic art with colour and gilding, adapting gold engraving extensively. His style was labelled 'Soviet Empire' by his followers. Examples of porcelain designed by Chekhonin are preserved in Moscow (Tret'yakov Gal. and Kuskovo Mus.) and in St Petersburg (Rus. Mus. and Lomonosov Mus.).

A. Efros and N. Punin: *S. Chekhonin* (Moscow, 1924)
Art into Production: Soviet Textiles, Fashion and Ceramics (exh. cat., intro D. Elliot, essays L. Andreeva, V. V. Filatov, T. Strizhanova and others; Oxford, MOMA; London, Crafts Council Gal.; 1984)

Chelsea Keramic Art Works. *See under* ROBERTSON, HUGH CORNWALL.

Chelsea Porcelain Factory. English ceramic factory. The date of the foundation of the factory, situated in the London village of that name, is uncertain. It is likely that a French jeweller, Charles Gouyn (*d* 1785), founded the factory jointly with NICHOLAS SPRIMONT and that they obtained technical help from a German chemist, whose name is given, perhaps unreliably, as 'd'Ostermann'. Around 1749, following initial losses, Gouyn left the partnership but continued to make, at Bennet Street, St James's, or near Hyde Park Corner, 'very beautiful small porcelain figures' thought to include the scent bottles and seals of the so-called 'Girl-in-a-swing' class, which used formerly to be confused with Chelsea products. Sprimont's first known connection with the Chelsea factory site was on 12 September 1744, and the earliest datable products are the 'goat-and-bee' jugs inscribed 1745; this seems a probable date when commercial production began. The factory expanded in size and productivity until 1757, when

Sprimont's ill-health and the withdrawal and subsequent death of Sir Everard Fawkener (1694–1758), seemingly a principal financier of the factory since at least 1746, checked the firm and probably induced Sprimont to concentrate on a smaller production of luxury porcelains. Sprimont sold the business to James Cox (*fl* 1749–91), a London jeweller, in August 1769, and Cox resold it in February 1770 to WILLIAM DUESBURY, who ran it in tandem with his porcelain factory at DERBY, until he closed the Chelsea branch in 1784.

Chelsea porcelains are usually classified into five periods named after the marks then in use: during the first or 'Triangle' period (*c.* 1744–9) a triangle was often incised before the piece was fired; more rarely it was painted in underglaze blue. Probably *c.* 1749 an underglaze-blue crown and trident mark was occasionally substituted. Figures and some wares were slip-cast. The glassy paste is highly translucent, and its slightly yellow appearance was, from *c.* 1747 to 1755, counteracted by the application of a glaze opacified and whitened with tin oxide. Enamelling was technically successful but at first artistically uneven.

The 'Raised Anchor' period (*c.* 1750–52) and the 'Red Anchor' period (*c.* 1752–8) show a continuous development. A wide variety of shapes and enamelled patterns, including the fable subjects associated with the painter Jefferyes Hamett O'Neale (1734–1801), was introduced, and the paste became less prone to slump in the kiln, which made it possible to produce an increasingly sophisticated variety of figures and, from *c.* 1754 to 1756, tureens formed as animals and vegetables (e.g. life-size Swan tureens, *c.* 1755–6; London, V&A and Bedford, Cecil Higgins A.G.). From 1748 to 1766 the factory's figure modeller is thought to have been a Flemish sculptor, Joseph Willems (*c.* 1715–66). On the other hand Brolliet, an industrial spy who appears to have worked at Chelsea in 1758–9, reported that 'the modeller is one named Flanchet, a pupil of Mr. Duplessis', presumably Jean-Claude Chambellan DUPLESSIS, who was a leading modeller of wares and vases at Sèvres, so it is likely that Flanchet modelled similar things at Chelsea. Brolliet adds, 'the draughtsman is named Du Vivier: he is Flemish'. It is possible to recognize many models and styles of decoration from surviving auction catalogues of the factory's annual production in 1755 and 1756. Though Japanese Kakiemon patterns were still in production during these years, it is evident that floral decoration in the style of the Meissen Porcelain Factory was more popular, and many of the figures were also copied from the MEISSEN PORCELAIN FACTORY.

Wares made during the 'Gold Anchor' period (1758–70) contain bone-ash, and the glaze is thick and clear. Gilding, which had been increasingly used since the 'Raised Anchor' period, became more frequent and elaborate. A rich 'MAZARIN BLUE' and other ground colours inspired by porcelain made at Vincennes and Sèvres were much used, with such decoration as exotic birds filling reserved panels. Figures were also often elaborate, set on gilded Rococo scroll bases, or backed with tree-like bocages supporting candle-nozzles. Miniature scent bottles and other 'toys' (trifles), introduced in the late 'Red Anchor' period, were much in vogue, as were elaborately gilded and painted sets and pairs of vases.

Probably little was made under Cox's management, and under Duesbury after 1770 a fusion of Chelsea and Derby styles and techniques rapidly occurred, so that it is difficult to determine which pieces were made at which factory. The gold anchor mark of the preceding period seems to have remained in at least occasional use as late as 1779, though by then a crown and anchor mark and an interlaced anchor and D (for Duesbury) had both been used. The glaze on Chelsea-Derby porcelains is usually thinner and less inclined to 'pool' than that on Sprimont's 'Gold Anchor' porcelains. Neo-classical forms and decoration were introduced, but a diluted Rococo style was continued. Seals and other miniatures are known to have been made or at least enamelled at the Chelsea branch of the combined firm.

F. Severne Mackenna: *Chelsea Porcelain*, 3 vols (Leigh-on-Sea, 1948–52)

S. Spero: 'Chelsea Porcelain, 1744–1769', *Mag. Ant.,* cxxxv (Jan 1989), pp. 260–71

H. Young: 'Anti-gallicanism at Chelsea: Protestantism, Protectionism and Porcelain', *Apollo,* cxlvii/436 (June 1998), pp. 35–41

E. Adams: *Chelsea Porcelain* (London, 2001)

Chenille [Fr.: 'caterpillar']. Velvety cord, having short threads or fibres of silk and wool standing out at right angles from a central core of cotton thread or wire. Chenille is used in trimming and bordering dresses and furniture. The term also denotes a type of embroidery needle.

C. Anderson-Shea: 'Metamorphosis: From Yarn to Fabric', *Shuttle Spindle & Dyepot,* xxvi (Summer 1995), pp. 25–7

N. Holmberg: *New Directions in Chenille* (Bothell, WA, 2000)

D. Maglio: 'Function Plus Fashion: Victorian Smoking Caps', *Piecework,* xii/1 (Jan–Feb 2004), pp. 52–5

Chenille Axminster. Type of carpet invented in 1839 by James Templeton, a shawl manufacturer in Glasgow, who had developed a way of weaving carpets with chenille thread. The pile was woven separately, with tufts of the correct number and colour to form the pattern, then inserted as weft on the surface of a linen or jute base. This had the advantage of keeping all the expensive wool on the surface, and there was practically no limit to the number of colours that could be used, but the resulting fabric was intrinsically fragile and not really suited to its purpose. In 1841 his firm was asked to weave a chenille carpet for St George's Chapel, Windsor Castle, for the baptism of Prince Edward (later Edward VII), and among other royal commissions was a chenille carpet for the opening of the Great Exhibition of 1851 in London.

Chequer-work [checker work]. Designs of alternating squares imitating the pattern of a chess-board.

The motif is common in mosaics, basketwork and 16th- and 17th-century furniture inlays.

Chéret, Gustave-Joseph (*b* 1838; *d* 1894). French sculptor and ceramic artist, and the younger brother of Jules Chéret (1836–1932), the lithographer and poster designer. Gustave-Joseph was a pupil of ALBERT-ERNEST CARRIER-BELLEUSE, and initially worked for a porcelain factory in Boulogne. He produced designs for several manufacturers, including the Cologne furniture manufacturer Jacob Pallenberg (*c.* 1870). From 1877 he produced designs for BACCARAT. He subsequently made models for the Sèvres Porcelain Factory, of which he was artistic director from 1886 to 1887.

Chertsey tiles. Set of English Medieval tiles. In 1852 excavators at the ruined Benedictine Abbey of St Peter in Chertsey, Surrey, discovered fragments of a large 13th-century tiled pavement. The designs portray scenes from the mediaeval romances of 'Sir Tristrem' and 'Richard, Coeur de Lion'; these tiles, which are the finest example of medieval pavement art in England, are now in the British Museum. In July 1996 a further 11 tiles were found on the site, and are now in Chertsey Museum.

R. S. Loomis: *Illustrations of Medieval Romance on Tiles from Chertsey Abbey* (Urbana, IL, 1967)
M. Shurlock and D. Bryce: *Arthurian and Knightly Art from the Middle Ages* (Lampeter, 1989)

Chess set. Chess is a game in which players use pieces and a board divided into 64 squares, coloured light and dark. Chess is played by two players, with the opposing sides known as the 'black' and the 'white'. Each player's pieces, called chessmen, are shaped three-dimensionally to represent a king, a queen, two bishops, two knights, two rooks or castles and eight soldiers or pawns. Chess was first played exclusively in royal and noble circles. Many chess sets are, therefore, highly decorative and made from such fine materials as ivory and amber, although bone, wood, metal, marble, glass and ceramics were also employed.

1. India. 2. Islamic world. 3. East and South-east Asia. 4. Europe and Western Asia.

1. INDIA. Chess was first recorded in northern India during the 6th century AD and was derived from an ancient Hindu game of chance known as *caturanga* (Skt *catur*: 'four'; *anga*: 'component parts'), a four-handed game of war played across a board using 32 pieces and dice. The players were ranged two against two, each controlling carved ivory or teak chessmen, led by a maharaja (king), his counsellor, later his maharani (queen), two elephants (bishops), two chariots or boats (rooks), two horses or camels (knights) and eight foot-soldiers (pawns). These represented the four traditional units of an Indian army: elephants, cavalry, chariots and foot-soldiers.

The Indian game spread westward through the Islamic world to Europe and eastward to China and other parts of Asia, and by the 16th century the dice were discarded. Indian chess pieces were carved and etched in fine detail and were often gilded or lacquered with many colours. Human and animal forms were characterized by their realism, with kings, queens and courtiers depicted in splendid robes, enthroned beneath canopies or seated in howdahs on caparisoned elephants or horses. To represent the

Chertsey tiles, detail depicting *Richard and Saladin,* lead-glazed encaustic tiles, 171 × 104 mm, *c.* 1250–60 (London, British Museum)

opposing armies, the ivory was frequently left natural for the pieces of one side and stained red or green for those of the other (e.g. viridian-stained and natural ivory chessmen, 17th century; London, V&A).

By the Mogul period and during the 19th century, richly decorative sets with wooden chessboards were inlaid with designs in metal, ivory, horn and tortoiseshell, with ivory or mother-of-pearl and ebony squares. Wooden boxboards with hinged lids were introduced in the early 19th century. In some royal chess sets the pieces are of cast and chased gold, silver gilt or carved ivory, painted with coloured enamels and inlaid with rubies, emeralds and pearls. Under British colonial rule European-style figures appeared with pieces generally depicting British cavalry and troops in uniform, arrayed against a native ruler's army on elephants and horses (e.g. polychromed ivory chessmen from Rajasthan, late 18th–early 19th century; London, V&A). Later portrait-bust sets include king pieces as personifications of a local raja or British colonel.

Special lathes for turning ivory ornaments were imported in the 19th century, and workshops all over India produced sets for home consumption or for export, particularly to Britain. Craftsmen in Muslim India also made abstract chess pieces, often in plain, baluster or spool-like columnar designs.

2. ISLAMIC WORLD. Chess probably appeared in Iran in the 6th century AD, where it was known as *shatranj*. As a result of the Islamic conquests in the 7th century, the game (Arab. *shatranj*) was carried to Syria, North Africa and Spain, as well as to the Byzantine Empire. Islamic chess pieces follow the Indian model: king (*shāh*), counsellor (Pers. *dastūr*, *farzīn*; Arab. *wazīr*), elephant (Pers. *pīl*; Arab. *fīl*), horse (Pers. *asp*; Arab. *faras*), rook (Pers. *rukh*; Arab. *rukhkh*, often represented as a bird) and foot-soldiers (Pers. *piada*; Arab. *baydaq*). Chessmen in the Islamic world were generally non-figurative, abstract shapes, such as

cones or ringed cylinders, made of wood or clay. The earliest known examples (New York, Met. and London, BM), dating from *c.* 750–800, were excavated at Nishapur in north-east Iran; a few of the pieces are clay, but most are of natural and green-stained ivory. Chessmen were also made of luxurious materials. A set made of carved rock crystal, reportedly from the parish church of Ager, a village near Urgel in Catalonia, is attributed to 10th-century Egypt (Kuwait City, Mus. Islam. A.; al-Sabah priv. col.; ex-countess of Béhague priv. col.). Other popular materials were turned, carved or inlaid ivory, bone and wood, and cast, chased or enamelled gold and silver. Stylized figures and animals did appear, for example an ivory elephant from 10th-century Iraq (Florence, Bargello). In some examples the animal pieces have been generalized into vaguely conical shapes with two protrusions to represent ears or tusks. Blue, red and green were popular colours for Islamic chess pieces. Boards were made of inlaid wood, stone and other hard materials as well as dyed leather and embroidered cloth. They were normally monochrome, at least until the 15th century, and later examples were decorated with elaborately patterned or strapwork borders around alternating squares of inlaid ivory strapwork.

3. EAST AND SOUTH-EAST ASIA. A version of chess (*xiang qi*: 'elephant chess') was played in China by *c.* AD 800, and although it differed considerably from the Indian game, its roots lay in *caturanga*. Contemporary chroniclers described the game as confined solely within the circle of the Chinese court. In *xiang qi* the board was divided by a 'river', and the main characters shown as emperors or government officials, usually richly attired and seated on lotus thrones; the bishops represented ministers, and the rooks appeared as elephants mounted on concentric or 'puzzle' balls. By the 13th century the game, modified by the loss of the 'river' on the board, had

Set of chessmen, gilded and lacquered ivory, Jodhpur, India, 1800 (London, Victoria and Albert Museum)

spread to Korea and from there to Japan, where it was called *shōgi*. The Islamic game was played in other parts of Asia, notably in Burma, where it was known as *chit-tha-reen* and where carved ivory sets featuring bamboo foliage, huts, birds and insects were later made for export to the West. From the end of the 18th century a flourishing trade in Chinese carved ivory chess sets was conducted with Britain, France and other parts of Europe through the port of Guangzhou (Canton), Guangdong Province. In these sets the chessmen are invariably represented as warring Chinese and European armies, often led by English monarchs (e.g. 'Edward VII' puzzle-ball ivory chess set made in China, late 19th century; London, V&A) or Napoleon for France. Intricately carved chess sets for export were also made in the Portuguese colonies, chiefly in Macao, and from the 19th century in Malaysia, Sumatra and Burma. There are also sets where the pieces are simple ivory or wooden discs engraved with Chinese characters. Chinese craftsmen used Indian ivory painted with polychrome enamels or stained brown or green on one side. The pieces are often lavishly etched and carved with details picked out in black, and peculiar to Chinese.

4. EUROPE AND WESTERN ASIA. Chess is believed to have reached Europe by way of Moorish Spain, although in the Cathedral Treasury at Osnabrück, Germany, there is a group of carved rock crystal chessmen of Arab design, similar to the 11th-century Ager group, from a set traditionally supposed to have been a gift from an Eastern caliph to Charlemagne. The Islamic game is presumed to have passed to Russia from Byzantine countries in the 8th and 9th centuries; Islamic-style pieces (St Petersburg, Hermitage) dated to between the 12th and 15th centuries have been excavated at Novgorod.

Abstract pieces based on Islamic models were initially used in Europe, but with the flowering of Gothic naturalism chessmen in human and animal forms were common. The mid-12th-century Lewis chessmen (London, BM; Edinburgh, Royal Mus. Scotland) are the largest extant group of European

Lewis Chessmen, walrus ivory and whales' teeth, h. of tallest piece 102 mm, made in ?Norway, *c.* 1150–1200 (London, British Museum)

pieces and are thought to be of Scandinavian or British origin. Discovered in 1831 on the Isle of Lewis, Outer Hebrides, the hoard included 78 chessmen in carved walrus tusk. The figures are seated, standing or riding caparisoned horses. The king and queen pieces wear crowns, the knight pieces carry long, pointed shields, and the traditional elephant-bishop piece is replaced by a figure in a mitred hat.

By 1200 chess was the most popular board game in Europe among the aristocracy and clergy. European chess pieces were carved from ivory, walrus tusk, bone and wood or made from cast metal. By the 13th century sets displayed figurative pieces up to 120 mm high, accompanied by large chessboards. Medieval kings and queens were shown seated beneath elaborate, architectural canopies, often replete with entwined foliage and attendants (e.g. queen chess piece, walrus ivory, ?English, 13th–15th century; London, BM).

In the 13th century an Italian Dominican friar, Jacobus de Cessolis, composed a manual, *De Ludo Scaccorum*, on the theme of morality and the various occupations of men under the guise of a game of chess. William Caxton (*c*. 1422–91) printed this book under the English title of *The Game of Chesse* (*c*. 1483), and the woodcuts illustrate the standard shapes for chessmen: hemispherical bases topped by crowns, plumes, mitre and tulip-shaped hats, pinnacles and abbreviated horses' heads. The knight piece in the form of a realistic horse's head mounted on a long pedestal was popular in Renaissance sets of the late 15th century and was particularly favoured in France, Italy and Spain.

In the 16th century new chess rules were introduced that both modernized and Westernized the game. New subjects appeared, sometimes drawn from ancient Greek myth or Roman history or representations of contemporary kings, patrons and heroic figures. Semi-abstract chess pieces in a variety of schematic designs that combined columnar or baluster shafts with naturalistic symbols were also popular. The bishop piece as a figure in ceremonial robes was by now firmly entrenched, although in sets made in central Europe, mainly Austria, and in Russia the elephant shape with a tower on its back prevailed. In Russian sets the queen was usually replaced by a general and the rook depicted as a boat, as in many Bengali sets.

During the 16th and 17th centuries craftsmen in Nuremberg and Augsburg produced carved wooden chessmen mounted on silver bases, as well as all-silver and silver gilt sets. Elsewhere in Germany a few rare amber sets were made (e.g. of *c*. 1700; Dresden, Grünes Gewölbe), possibly in Königsberg (now Kaliningrad, Russia), which was one of the main centres of production of carved amber. Different European countries incorporated national symbols in sets, for example the Maltese cross finial in carved ivory sets from Malta; many Swiss chess sets feature the Bears of Berne. Sets similar to both French and German figurative examples, although of simpler design, were made in ivory and bone in Catalonia.

From the 17th century high-quality ivory chess sets were produced in Dieppe, supported by France's ivory trade with West Africa, and until the French Revolution large numbers of chess sets were exported to England.

In the 18th century many chess pieces were designed in the elaborate styles of the period. From 1700 to *c*. 1750 Spanish turners and carvers made ivory 'pulpit' sets with delicate balustrades of acanthus leaves surrounding figures and symbols (e.g. New York, Met.). In France, fanciful half-figure ivory and bone sets were developed, the knight piece often transformed into a sea horse (e.g. painted bone chessmen from Dieppe, early 18th century; New York, Met.).

Many chess designs were influenced by Islamic pieces, for example the porcelain and pottery sets made from the 18th century at Meissen (e.g. 'Turks versus Saracens' porcelain chess set, mid-18th century; Munich, Bayer. Nmus.) and other German ceramics factories. Some ceramic chess sets were made in England at the Wedgwood, Minton and Doulton factories (e.g. Wedgwood 'Jasper' ware chessmen, late 18th–early 19th century; Barlaston, Wedgwood Mus.). By the late 18th century and the early 19th a return to more formal design led to the production of chess sets in the Directoire style. Sets of the 'St George' type made in tin-glazed earthenware at Rouen in plain, compact, baluster shapes painted with floral designs in red-on-white or blue-on-white were also popular.

The successful Staunton pattern of chessmen was designed in 1835 in England by Nathaniel Cooke and patented in 1849; it continues to be the internationally accepted standard set. Staunton pieces are stable, well balanced and easy to handle, with columnar shafts rising from flared bases; the kings and queens bear stylized crowns, the knight is a horse's head and the bishop a pointed ball, sliced diagonally. In the 20th century innovative chess pieces were designed by such artists as Man Ray (e.g. abstract silver chess set, 1926; New York, MOMA) and Max Ernst (e.g. abstract boxwood chess set, 1944–5; Philadelphia, PA, Mus. A.).

R. Keene: *Chess: An Illustrated History* (Oxford, 1990)
I. M. Linder: *The Art of Chess Pieces* (Moscow, 1994)
M. Mark: *British Chess Sets* (n.p., 1996)
M. Mark and O. Dietze: *Antique Indian Chess Sets* (Kelkheim, 1997)
E. S. Munger and L. A Smith: *Cultures, Chess & Art: A Collector's Odyssey across Seven Continents* (San Anselmo, CA, 1996–2000)
G. Williams: *Master Pieces: The Architecture of Chess* (New York, 2000)
G. Williams: *Master Pieces: The Story of Chess: The Pieces, Players and Passion of 1,000 Years* (London, 2000)
Italfama: The Historical and Artistic Chess Collection (Florence, 2000)
G. LeC. Taylor: *For Show Not Play: Glass Chess Sets* (Millville, NJ, 2002)
The Kaspar Stock Collection of Chess Sets (sale cat., London, Christie's South Kensington, 2004)

Chest. Large box container with a hinged lid. When the lid is domed, or if the chest is reinforced, it can also be known as a coffer or *cassone*. During the Middle Ages chests were the most important single furniture type and, given the itinerant nature of medieval households, were also items of luggage. They can be divided into two main types: those with flat lids carried on feet and those with domed lids, resting directly on the ground. Chests were used to store almost everything, and their construction was as diverse as their functions. Basic chests were hollowed out of tree trunks and bound with iron bands. Simple plank construction was also common, with horizontal timbers framed at the corners between vertical timbers or stiles. In the hutch chest the stiles were extended to hold the chest above floor level. Alternatively, the sides of the chest could be lowered to form feet. Ecclesiastical chests had three locks for increased security. The simplest chests were decorated with rudimentary chip-carving, usually in the form of roundels filled with geometric patterns (e.g. oak chest, *c*.1300; London, V&A). Chests decorated with simple arcading survive from the Romanesque period (e.g. *c.* 1250; Sion, Mus. Cant. Valère). During the Gothic period more elaborate chests, probably originating in France, were decorated with architectural motifs, usually in the form of tracery. By the late 15th century the carving of such chests had reached impressive levels of sophistication in terms of design and execution and often approached the level of such contemporary church fittings as screens (e.g. oak chest, 15th century; Hamburg, Mus. Kst. & Gew.). Many chests were carved in low relief with continuous scenes taken from the Bible or the lives of the saints. Jousting was another popular theme (e.g. carved oak chest, 14th century; London, V&A); in England such pieces are known as 'tilting chests'. Many chests were reinforced with iron; however, during the late 13th century some chests had purely decorative wrought ironwork that reflected the elaborate decoration applied to contemporary cathedral doors (e.g. chest, ?St Denis, *c.* 1300; Paris, Mus. Carnavalet). Travelling chests, known in England as trunks, were often covered with leather protected by studs. Chests were sometimes given polychromed decoration and painted with scenes or armorials. Panelled construction became widespread in northern Europe during the late 14th century, and linenfold panelling seems to have been a particularly popular form of decoration throughout northern France, the Low Countries and England by the late 15th century.

The Renaissance had a considerable impact on the design of chests throughout Europe. In Italy the CASSONE was often adapted to the forms of the Classical sarcophagus. In France elaborate Gothic tracery was replaced by low-relief carving that drew heavily on Classical sources. Chest fronts were often faced with large panels carved with profile heads enclosed by wreaths, a motif derived from antique coins. The panels were divided by foliate balusters and the spandrels carved with delicate arabesques. Architectural treatments continued to be popular but now took their inspiration from the four orders of Classical architecture; joins were masked by such motifs as pilasters or caryatids. In Germany chests were often given a heavy, architectural treatment.

The fronts were normally emphatically divided by pilasters and applied with aedicular motifs. This vigorous three-dimensional decoration was combined with inlay of grotesques or complex architectural vistas. The design of this kind of chest was spread through pattern books such as Jakob Guckeisen's *Etlicher architectischer Portalen, Epitapien, Caminen und Schwefflen* (Cologne, 1596). In England the impact of the Renaissance was less immediate. The most advanced chests, which boasted elaborate architectural treatment (sometimes known as 'Nonsuch' chests), seem to have been the work of immigrant German craftsmen. A number of chests survive from the 16th century decorated in the 'Romayne' or Roman style, a less sophisticated adaptation of contemporary French and Flemish models, but linenfold panelling remained in use well into the later part of the century.

During the 17th century the evolution of other types of storage eroded the pre-eminence of chests as important decorative objects, although their practical nature ensured their continued use in more humble households and provincial areas. Less attention was paid to their decoration; in a period that saw enormous advances in cabinetmaking techniques, chests were rarely veneered or inlaid, and their construction remained relatively simple. Consequently, 17th-century chests are usually developments of earlier types, though there were some exceptions. During the later 17th century the fashion for all things lacquer meant that japanned chests, often supported on low gilt-wood stands, were relatively common in England. In France JEAN BERAIN designed elaborate coffers of sarcophagus form, and related groups of English chests, decorated entirely in gilt-gesso, are among the most splendid pieces of the early 18th century.

In America chests are chiefly remarkable for their regional variations, of which the best-known are the CONNECTICUT CHEST and the HADLEY CHEST. Construction took the form of either boards nailed together (the 'six-board chest') or boards joined with MORTISE AND TENON joints. Decoration normally consisted of shallow relief carving in regional styles, architectural mouldings, applied ornaments such as bosses, spindles and triglyphs, and paint.

M. H. Fabian: *The Pennsylvania-German Decorated Chest* (New York, 1978)

V. Chinnery: *Oak Furniture: The British Tradition* (Woodbridge, 1979)

J. L. Fairbanks: *New England Begins: The Seventeenth Century*, 3 vols (exh. cat., Boston, MA, Mus. F. A., 1982)

G. W. R. Ward: *American Case Furniture in the Mabel Brady Garvan and Other Collections at Yale University* (New Haven, 1988)

E. K. Gronning: 'New Haven's Six-Board Chests', *Mag. Ant.,* clxiii/5 (May 2003), pp. 116–21

Chesterfield. Stuffed couch or SOFA with a back and two ends, with no woodwork visible.

Chest-of-drawers. Large box or frame fitted with a set of drawers, formerly used for storing valuables, now used as an article of bedroom furniture in which clothes are kept. Some 16th-century CHESTS were

Heinrich Wilhelm Spindler: chest-of-drawers, 1765 (Potsdam, Neues Palais)

fitted with up to three drawers in the base, and by the 17th century the modern chest-of-drawers (sometimes with doors) had evolved. In America, chests-of-drawers (which were found in Boston by the 1640s) usually had turned feet, ball- or turnip-shaped, or feet formed by extending the sides or corner stiles below the bottom drawer. By 1700 they were often adorned with japanning, veneer or inlay. Single- or double-arched mouldings typically outlined each drawer. By 1700 drawers ran on the bottom edge of the drawer side instead of on grooves cut into the drawer sides. The earliest drawer handles were usually of wood, but by the end of the 17th century brass pear-shaped drops hung in front of rosette-shaped back plates, and matching cartouche-shaped brass escutcheons protected the wood around the keyholes. Such variations as brass knobs or ring pulls were also found.

See also BUREAU; CHIFFONIER; COMMODE; HIGHBOY; LOWBOY; SEMANIER; TALLBOY.

B. M. Forman: 'The Chest of Drawers in America, 1635–1730: The Origins of the Joined Chest of Drawers', *Winterthur Port.*, xx/1 (Spring 1985), pp. 1–30.
R. F. Trent, 'The Chest of Drawers in America: A Postscript', *Winterthur Port.*, xx/1 (Spring 1985), pp. 31–48

Cheval glass. Full-length mirror swung on a four-legged frame.

Cheveret [sheveret]. Small table or writing desk popular in England in the late 18th century. The cheveret typically has an oblong writing surface over a shallow drawer, and is supported by four thin legs joined with a shelf. Some examples have pigeonholes at the back of the top. Tall cheverets were designed to be used as standing desks.

Chichow. *See* JIZHOU.

Chiffonier. Term used to denote three distinct types of furniture. In 18th-century England, the term is an anglicised form of *chiffonière*, a small chest-of-drawers designed to hold fabric (Fr. *chiffon*); *chiffonières* were French in origin, but were also made by English cabinetmakers, notably Chippendale. In 19th-century England, the sense of 'chiffonier' shifted, and came to denote a piece of dining-room furniture consisting of a small cupboard with the top made so as to form a sideboard. In the same period it was also used to denote a type of folding bed in the shape of a chiffonier. In the early 20th century it was used to denote French-style chests in the Art Deco mode.

Our Latest Styles: Wardrobe and Chiffonier Folding Beds, Boyington Folding Bed Co. (Chicago, 1887)
P. Thiebaut and others: 'Paris, Musée d'Orsay', *Rev. Louvre*, I/4 (Oct 2000), pp. 100–01
T. Dann: 'Luxurios und Raffiniert', *Weltkunst*, lxxiv/7 (July 2004), pp. 23–6

Chimney furniture. *See* FIREPLACE FURNISHINGS.

Chimney-piece [mantelpiece]. Wooden, brick or stone frame surrounding a fireplace, which may include an overmantel above. As domestic wall fireplaces became common in medieval Europe, it became usual to make the fire on a hearth projecting from the wall into the room, surmounted by an incombustible hood made invariably of stone in grander houses but often of wattle covered in clay in lesser buildings. A particularly fine stone example of the 13th century is at Michelham Priory, E. Sussex, but English examples of hooded chimney-pieces later than the mid-14th century are rare, a result of the development of the modern, unhooded type of chimney-piece. In this form, the flue was entirely buried within the wall or chimney-breast, and the chimney-piece became simply the frame round the fireplace opening. Good examples of this new type, with Gothic panels and heraldry above, exist at Tattershall Castle, Lincs, built 1434–c. 1450 for Ralph Cromwell, Lord Treasurer of England; they are representative of court taste at this date.

During the Renaissance continental architects and builders continued to use the hood form, albeit in a modified fashion. Classical cornices and details were added, for example by Domenico Rosselli (*c.* 1439–97/8) in the chimney-piece (*c.* 1480) in the Sala degli Angeli of the Palazzo Ducale, Urbino. Throughout Europe, the unhooded chimney-piece eventually became more common in palatial interiors, such as the Rittersaal (*c.* 1580) of Schloss Heiligenberg, Baden-Württemberg; yet in the exactly contemporary and equally magnificent Cedernsaal of Schloss der Fugger, Kirchheim im Schwaben, the hooded form was still preferred. In England, the hood occasionally reappeared during the Renaissance, as in the Great Hall (*c.* 1565) at Burghley House, Cambs, or the Manor House (*c.* 1580), Swell, Glos, but in these circumstances it is likely that the patron was following continental fashion rather than a style largely defunct in England. As chimney-pieces were given more decorative importance in the 15th and 16th centuries by such influential figures as Sebastiano Serlio, impressively elaborate designs became common in great houses. One of the most splendid must have been the 'Belle Cheminée' in the Grande Salle of the château at Fontainebleau, commissioned by Henry IV in 1598 from Mathieu Jacquet (*c.* 1545–after 1611); this measured 7 × 6 m and included a life-size equestrian portrait of the King. Even far less grand houses could sport exuberantly carved, two-tier chimney-pieces combining heraldry (e.g. Loseley House, Surrey, *c.* 1570) and sculpted panels (such as the *Wise and Foolish Virgins* in the hall, *c.* 1610, of Burton Agnes Hall, Humberside). The materials used were predominantly marble, stone or wood and occasionally plaster, though this was more often employed in overmantels.

During the 17th century chimney-pieces tended to become simpler and smaller. In England the relatively plain designs of Inigo Jones (1573–1652), who adapted published French designs by Jean Barbet (1591–before 1654) and others, were in contrast to the elaborate, multi-tier confections of the previous generation, although Jones's influence on his immediate contemporaries was limited. By the late 17th century, chimney-pieces had been reduced to a simple frame of bolection moulding round the fireplace opening, usually, though not always, of stone or marble. In the grandest rooms, as at the château of Versailles or at Hampton Court Palace, additional carving, including putti or busts, might be added above. In the State Dining Room (*c.* 1695) at Chatsworth, Derbys, the simple marble moulding was surmounted by a virtuoso display of carved wood garlands surrounding a parquetry panel and an inset portrait, an increasingly common decorative feature of overmantels from the 1630s onwards. In small rooms such as closets, corner fireplaces allowed stepped display shelves to be built above them. These were sometimes called 'china steps', as they were used to display the blue-and-white ceramics so popular at this period.

In 18th-century England chimney-pieces based on classical principles were fashionable. The surround was thought of as a low, wide door, with jambs and an entablature above. Round the opening was an architrave, a narrow band that could be decorated or left plain. Above was the frieze, up to a foot wide, which could also be decorated. A plaque or tablet could ornament its centre, often decorated with a carved scene, Aesop's *Fables* being a popular source. At the top, the cornice was greatly widened to provide the mantelshelf. Elaborate designs could include free-standing figures (caryatids and atlantids) instead

of jambs. This fashion was also known on the Continent. A chimney-piece (*c.* 1685) in the Great Hall of the castle at Libochovice, Czech Republic, for example, has atlantids in the form of peasants, while Łazienki Palace, near Warsaw, has a chimney-piece that incorporates figures of Hercules and the Hydra. French chimney-pieces, on the other hand, were generally lower and smaller than English designs. In France, and wherever French fashions were followed in Europe, the chimney-piece was seen as a projecting box with the fire opening cut in its front. Sides and mantelshelf were of the same depth, and the entablature was omitted, leaving only the frieze.

The materials used in 18th-century England were usually stone and marble, carved or inlaid, and wood, always painted. Simple, repetitive, Neo-classical ornament of the type popularized by Robert Adam, such as roundels, swags, husks and urns, could be cheaply cast in metal or composition and nailed or glued on before painting. Josiah Wedgwood produced ceramic plaques for the same purpose, and even some complete chimney-pieces made up of plaques set into a marble framework: an example (*c.* 1786) from Longton Hall, Staffs, is now in the Lady Lever Art Gallery, Port Sunlight. Occasionally, more exotic materials could be incorporated, such as the Chinese painted marble panels reused in 1773 by Adam in the Upper Hall chimney-piece at Kenwood House, London. Scagliola was occasionally used: marble inlaid with scagliola is generally called Bossi work after an Italian chimney-piece-maker working in Dublin in the 1780s and 1790s, but he certainly did not invent the process, which was in use in London in the 1770s.

In the early 19th century chimney-piece designs became less imaginative. Most were utilitarian, and those of John Soane were particularly austere. For middle-class houses in Britain, the form throughout the 19th century generally remained a simple marble or painted wood surround with little ornament apart from pilasters or carved brackets, often with a large plate-glass overmantel mirror above. In the mid-19th century medieval themes were made popular by such artists as A. W. N. Pugin and William Burges, and Viollet-le-Duc was similarly influential in France. William Morris in England advocated a return to simple rustic craftsmanship, and the huge, open, cottage fireplace returned to fashion. In towns, the plain chimney-piece was enlivened by an overmantel loaded with shelves and brackets to display ornaments. In the 20th century the development of gas and later of electricity for heating greatly changed the design of the chimney-piece, which could now be much smaller or even be dispensed with completely. The continuing popularity of the fire as a focal point, however, led to some imaginative designs. Modern Movement architects sometimes omitted the chimney-piece as a surround entirely, leaving the fire in an unadorned hole in the wall, or used the chimney-breast as a room divider, with an open fire accessible on two sides. New materials such as stainless steel and fire-resistant glass were used, and the absence of soot allowed for a flowering of decorative tiles on the cheeks of the fire opening.

G. C. Rothery: *Chimneypieces and Ingle Nooks, Their Design and Ornamentation* (New York, 1911)

R. Adam and J. Adam: *A Book of Mantels: Thirty-seven Drawings in Color Reproduced from Recently Discovered Originals* (New York, 1915)

A. Kelly: *The Book of the English Fireplace* (London, 1968)

T. West: *The Fireplace in the Home* (Newton Abbot, 1976)

M. T. Gasser: *A Wood-carved Chimney-piece of the Early French Renaissance* (Hanover, NH, 1985)

M. Droth: *Ornament as Sculpture: The Sam Wilson Chimneypiece in Leeds City Art Gallery* (Leeds, 2000)

P. Fuhring: 'Jean Barbet's "Livre d'Architecture, d'Autels et de Cheminees": Drawing and Design in Seventeenth-century France', *Burl. Mag.,* cxlv (June 2003), pp. 421–30

A. J. Bicknell: *Victorian Architectural Details: Designs for over 700 Stairs, Mantels, Doors, Windows, Cornices, Porches, and Other Decorative Elements* (Mineola, NY, 2005)

China.

1. Ceramics. 2. Furniture

1. CERAMICS. Chinese potters developed the world's first porcelain in the 6th century AD and began exporting porcelain to West Asia and Japan as early as the 9th century AD. To meet domestic and foreign demand, production of porcelain in China expanded enormously between the 16th and 19th centuries, and a large part of the history of European ceramics represents various local responses to imported Chinese wares. This close identification of China with ceramics still survives in the English use of the word 'china' as a generic term for crockery.

Besides these influential export wares (mostly grey-green celadons, porcelains and unglazed red stonewares), Chinese ceramics include finely painted earthenwares from as early as the Neolithic period (*c.* 6500–*c.* 1600 BC), everyday stonewares, palace

Octagonal celadon porcelain bowl, h. 130 mm, diam. 180 mm, China, Yuan period (Paris, Musée Guimet)

wares, burial wares and figures, large temple vases, portrait sculptures, tomb guardians, elaborate architectural ceramics and even military ceramics in the form of bombs and grenades. In the aesthetic realm the court and country stonewares of the Song period (960–1279) are widely regarded as some of the finest ceramics ever produced.

Chinese ceramics may be divided into two main groups: those with low-fired (*tao*) and those with high-fired (*ci*) bodies, which are, respectively, permeable and impermeable. (Body refers to the clay and any added temper, as distinct from the glaze.) To the former group belong all the earthenwares, firing up to *c.* 1150° C, while to the latter belong all the stonewares, as well as porcelain, which fire at temperatures from *c.* 1200° C to *c.* 1500° C.

Earthenwares vary in both colour and grain size, ranging from white or pinkish-white wares of very fine grain through greys and buffs to wares that are almost black, some of which are very coarse-grained. High-fired wares first appeared as early as about the 13th century BC and were generally grey in colour. Whitewares were not fully developed until the 6th century AD. It was from these that the pure white vitrified wares known as porcelain evolved.

No other ceramic tradition in the world has achieved such a wealth of glaze qualities as that of China. At the peak of this tradition are the subtle monochrome stoneware glazes of the Song dynasties (960–1279), produced in many cases from suspended bubbles, micro-crystals and separated glasses that have developed in the thick glazes as they cooled. The main ingredients of Song high-fired glazes seem to have been the simple clays, rocks and woodashes of the Chinese countryside; their subtle colours came largely from iron and titanium oxide impurities, present naturally in the raw materials.

Besides these remarkable high-temperature compositions, Chinese potters also created an important low-fired glaze tradition. This includes the rich and colourful lead glazes of the Tang dynasty (AD 618–907) and the bright, polychrome porcelain enamels of the 15th–16th centuries as well as a number of low-firing monochrome glazes. Perhaps the most famous of these is the Chinese 'imperial yellow', a transparent lead glaze coloured with about 3.5% ferric oxide in solution and used as a monochrome overglaze on some early Ming porcelains.

Chinese ceramics have been produced in a tremendous variety of shapes, some inspired primarily by practical needs, others by considerations of aesthetics or ritual. As in other arts in China, clear differences between the aesthetics of northern and southern ceramics can be seen, especially before the Song period (AD 960–1279), when the economy of China remained essentially regional. Southern Chinese ceramics at this time were characteristically more inclined to fantasy and elaboration, while northern wares reflected a more severe aesthetic, a greater reliance on metal prototypes and greater access to foreign models.

Among the most familiar Chinese ceramic shapes is the *meiping* ('plum-blossom vase'), a shape singularly appropriate to the medium of clay in its sensuous, curvilinear profile. Many ceramic shapes were adapted from prototypes in other media, however: the cup-stand, for example, was originally a lacquerware shape. The pilgrim flask of the nomadic Liao dynasty (AD 907–1125) was inspired by leather saddle bags, and details specific to the original medium were retained in the ceramic version. The Ming-period (AD 1368–1644) pilgrim flask (178k) reflects a West Asian glassware shape. The archaistic bronzes of the Song period and after were also copied in ceramics, notably in the imperial Guan ware. A number of shapes of the Tang (AD 618–907) and Liao periods in particular reflect the Tang love of Asian silverwares. In the elevated form of the stem cup distant echoes may be detected of the ancient ritual bronze *dou* and *gu*.

Foreign models were especially inspirational during the Tang, an exuberant and self-confident period characterized by openness to foreign influences and to the richness of diversity. Ceramics reminiscent of Greek Hellenistic shapes were produced in China, for example the oinochoe and amphora. Other forms were particularly popular with specific foreign markets: in the Ming period very large blue-and-white bowls were produced for the Turkish and Persian markets, while the spouted water jar (Malay *kendi*) was exported to South-east Asia. In the Ming and Qing periods European merchants brought prototypes of shapes to be produced for their clients, resulting in the production of such vessels as beer mugs and cream jugs at Jingdezhen.

See also BATAVIAN WARE; BLANC DE CHINE; CELADON; CIZHOU WARE; DEHUA; DING WARE; GUAN WARE; HARE'S FUR; JINGDEZHEN; JIZHOU; JUN WARE; JU WARE; KRAAK WARE; LONGQUAN WARE; QINGBAI WARE; RU WARE; SANCAI; SANG DE BOEUF; SHIWAN; SWATOW WARE; TEA-DUST GLAZE; TEMMOKU; WUCAI; YAOZHOU WARE; YIXING; YUE WARE.

M. Medley: *The Chinese Potter: A Practical History of Chinese Ceramics* (Oxford, 1976, rev. 1980/*R* 1982)
M. Tregear: *Song Ceramics* (London, 1982)
B. Gray: *Song Porcelain and Stoneware* (London, 1984)
M. Medley: *T'ang Pottery and Porcelain* (London and Boston, 1981)
J. Rawson: *Chinese Ornament: The Lotus and the Dragon* (London, 1984/*R* 1990)
W. Watson: *Tang and Liao Ceramics* (London, 1984)
R. Kerr: *Chinese Ceramics: Porcelain of the Qing Dynasty, 1644–1911* (London, 1986)
S. Vainker: *Chinese Pottery and Porcelain, from Prehistory to the Present* (London, 1991)
A. Paludan: *Chinese Tomb Figurines* (Hong Kong, 1994)
R. Scott and R. Kerr: *Ceramic Evolution in the Middle Ming Period: Hongzhi to Wanli (1488–1620)* (London, 1994)
Cheng Xiaozhong and P. Lam: *Qing Imperial Porcelain of the Kangxi, Yongzheng and Qianlong Reigns* (Hong Kong, 1995)
Flawless Porcelains: Imperial Ceramics from the Reign of the Chenghua Emperor (exh. cat. by R. Scott and S. Pierson; London, U. London, SOAS, Percival David Found., 1995)
N. Wood: *Chinese Glazes: Their Origins, Chemistry and Recreation* (London, 1999)
Yang Houli, Fan Fengmei and Rita Tan: *Dated Qingbai Wares of the Song and Yuan Dynasties* (Hong Kong, 1999)
Song Ceramics, Museum of Oriental Ceramics (Osaka, 1999)
Heaven and Earth Seen Within: Song Ceramics from the Robert Barron Collection (exh. cat. by L. Rotando-McCord, New Orleans, Mus. A., 2000–01)

2. FURNITURE. Chinese furniture has a history going back as far as the 14th century BC, although few pieces are extant from periods earlier than the Ming (AD 1368–1644). The period often described as the Golden Age of Chinese furniture extends from the Ming to the early Qing (1368–1735).

Ming and early Qing furniture has two basic forms: waistless and waisted. Waistless furniture generally has legs set back from the edge; the legs are round, splayed slightly outward towards the base and have high stretchers. When tables were elevated to correspond to chair level, it was necessary to strengthen them without interfering with the legs of a seated person, and so waisted furniture, with an inset panel between the top and apron, developed, based on Buddhist pedestals and the box construction. Waisted furniture has legs at the corners, often square and terminating in an inward- or outward-facing upturned foot known as a horse-hoof foot (*mati*).

In Ming and early Qing furniture, function and form are inseparable. Functional details, such as the slight S-shape of the splat, were employed to create a beautiful interplay of curves. Wood was used in a supple manner to produce sculptural forms. The spaces around and between members were an integral part of the aesthetic effect: Chinese terminology names the voids rather than the solids. In hardwood furniture, the flatness of the surface was relieved by the use of different woods and other materials, beading, piercing and insetting. The cloud-head motif that had been applied to the feet of furniture in the Song period (AD 960–1279; lobed, open-scroll silhouettes ending in pointed feet) no longer occurred in the shaping of the legs and feet but rather as a surface decoration. Joinery was visible and part of the decorative scheme. Much attention was paid to grace, vigour and proportion.

It is difficult to date Chinese furniture exactly, because there are few dated pieces and because styles persisted for long periods of time. In general, Ming furniture gradually moved away from the rigidity, flatness and delicate grace of the Song and became flowing, fully three-dimensional and powerful in style. Subtle details and perfect proportions transformed simple pieces into works of art. In the late Ming a certain angularity was favoured. In the early Qing a softness and formalism were introduced, and there was a loss of vigour in detail. Craftsmen tried to produce interesting variations of Ming forms. By the mid-Qing the flowing grace of Ming ornamentation had become stiff and stylized.

In the Ming period, the cloud-head foot was transformed to make it stronger: the point became a moulded rectangular base surmounted by flanges retaining elements of the cloud-head motif. Similar cloud-head-derived flanges might be placed further up the leg. Legs were in general less flat than those of Song pieces and might have shaped, slightly convex front surfaces edged by beading and depressed in the centre by a double row of 'two-incense-stick' (*liangzhuxiang*) beading. Early pieces have inserted

Altar table, rosewood, Ming period, 16th–17th centuries (London, Victoria and Albert Museum)

shoulder joints and deeply cusped aprons with beaded edges continuing unbroken down the legs. Later, the moulding of the legs became more angular and the aprons straighter.

In houses, pieces of furniture were placed at right angles to each other, parallel to walls and away from the centre of room. In the public areas of a house they were arranged symmetrically, reflecting the Confucian social order. In the main halls, for instance, chairs, stools, tables and stands were made in multiples of two and placed in a hierarchical pattern radiating outward from the place of honour. In the private living quarters—women's rooms, pleasure pavilions and gardens—there were more asymmetrical arrangements, and pieces of different materials were combined. Tables, stools and chair seats had colourful brocade covers. For formal occasions the backs of chairs and one long side of tables were covered with silk, and for welcoming guests silk or woollen pile carpets were used.

G. Ecke: *Chinese Domestic Furniture* (Beijing, 1944)

G. Kates: *Chinese Household Furniture* (New York, 1948)

J. G. Lee: 'Chinese Furniture', *Philadelphia Mus. Bull.* (Winter 1963), pp. 41–80

L. Sickman: *Chinese Domestic Furniture: A New Gallery Opened 17 November 1966* (Kansas City, MO, 1966)

W. Drummond: *Chinese Furniture*, Sackler Collections, xiii, lecture 1 (New York, 1969)

R. H. Ellsworth: *Chinese Furniture: Hardwood Examples of the Ming and Early Ch'ing Dynasties* (New York, 1970)

L. Sickman: 'Chinese Classic Furniture', *Trans. Orient. Cer. Soc.*, xlii (1977–8), pp. 1–23

M. Beurdeley: *Chinese Furniture*, Eng. trans. by K. Watson (Tokyo and New York, 1979)

C. Clunas: *Chinese Furniture* (London, 1986)

Wang Shixiang: *Classic Chinese Furniture: Ming and Early Qing Dynasties* (Hong Kong, 1986)

Wang Shixiang: *Connoisseurship of Chinese Furniture: Ming and Early Qing Dynasties*, 2 vols (Hong Kong, 1990)

Folding chair, carved red lacquer on wood with a woven mat seat, h. 1.15 m, Ming period, 1500–60 (London, Victoria and Albert Museum)

G. Wu Bruce: *Dreams of Chu Tan Chamber and the Romance with Huanghuali Wood: The Dr S. Y. Yip Collection of Classic Chinese Furniture* (Hong Kong, 1991)

Lo Kai-Yin, ed.: *Classical and Vernacular Chinese Furniture in the Living Environment* (Hong Kong, 1998)

Pu Anguo: *Ming Qing Shushi jiaju* [Ming and Qing dynasty furniture in the Suzhou style] (Hangzhou, 1999)

Splendor of Style: Classical Furniture from the Ming and Qing Dynasties (Taipei, 1999)

S. Handler: *Austere Luminosity of Chinese Classical Furniture* (Berkeley, CA, 2001)

Ming: L'âge d'or du mobilier chinois/The Golden Age of Chinese Furniture: Collection

Lu Ming Shi (exh. cat by J. F. Jarrige, J.-P. Desroches and C. Pekovits; Paris, Mus. Guimet, 2003)

S. Handler: *Ming Furniture in the Light of Chinese Architecture* (Berkeley, CA, 2004)

See also CHAIR, §1(i).

OTHER ARTS *see* BRASS, §1; CANTON ENAMEL; CHESS SET, §3; COROMANDEL LACQUER; DOOR, §IV, 1; FAN, §1; ROCK CRYSTAL, §1; SNUFF BOXES AND SNUFF BOTTLES, §2; WALLPAPER, §II, 2.

China clay. *See* KAOLIN.

China stone. Talcose granite with partly-decomposed feldspar, used for producing a glaze in the manufacture of porcelain. China stone is a form of petuntse (*see under* PORCELAIN).

Chinese Chippendale. *See* CHINOISERIE.

Chini, Galileo (*b* Florence, 2 Dec 1873; *d* Florence, 24 Aug 1956). Italian painter and potter. He began his artistic activity at a very early age, as a decorator and fresco painter. In 1896 he began to make ceramics. His work as a potter was highly innovative and receptive to outside influences, especially from England and central Europe; he developed a brilliant and personal style, characterized above all by the results he obtained with lustre glaze on stoneware. In 1906 he opened the Fornaci di San Lorenzo (Florence) in partnership with his cousin Chino Chini (1889–1957); this pottery produced ceramics till 1944. The grandest of the pottery's tile decorations was for Le Nuove Terme in Salsomaggiore (1913–23).

F. Benzi and G. Citariello Grosso: *Galileo Chini* (Milan, 1988)

P. Pacini and G. Chini: *Galileo Chini: Pittore e decoratore* (Soncino, Cremona, 2002)

P. Pacini and G. Chini: *Galileo Chini, 1873–1956* (Florence, 2003)

M. Margozzi: *Galileo Chini: La primavera* (Milan, 2004)

Chinoiserie. Term derived from *chinois* (Fr.: 'Chinese') denoting a type of European art dominated by Chinese or pseudo-Chinese ornamental motifs. The term is most often applied to decorative arts produced from the second half of the 17th century to the early 19th, when trading contacts between Europe and East Asia were at their height.

1. Ceramics. 2. Interior decoration. 3. Lacquer. 4. Metalwork and objects of vertu. 5. Textiles.

1. CERAMICS. The first successful attempt to produce porcelain in Europe was made at the Medici court in Florence in 1575 by the architect Bernardo Buontalenti (*c.* 1531–1608). He produced basins, jugs and vases in blue-and-white soft-paste porcelain decorated with very early chinoiserie motifs; about 60 pieces have survived (e.g. London, V&A; New York, Met.). Nevertheless, until the 18th century it was Dutch tin-glazed earthenware that imitated most successfully the style and technique of Chinese export porcelain (*chine de commande*). The taste for Chinese blue-and-white ware prompted the development of Delftware, a tin-glazed earthenware with cobalt-blue decoration in the style of porcelain made in China during the Wanli period (1573–1620). Chinese motifs were used to decorate forms derived from Dutch silver or maiolica, or from imported East Asian wares. In China, export porcelain was produced specifically for the Western market at the same time. As design models were traded between East and West, individual motifs became increasingly fanciful; these included figures in Oriental dress with fans and parasols, exotic birds, bridges, pagodas and stylized landscapes, some of which can be seen on a wig stand (London, V&A) by Samuel van Eenhorn (*fl* 1674–86).

In England, factories in Southwark, Brislington, Bristol and Lambeth also produced blue-and-white Delftware decorated with chinoiserie motifs inspired by original Chinese or Dutch imitation prototypes. In France blue-and-white faience in the Dutch chinoiserie style was produced in Rouen, Moustiers and Nevers. Blue-and-white chinoiserie faience was fashionable throughout the 17th century and most of the 18th. Imported Chinese pieces were still avidly collected by the wealthy and were sometimes displayed in special rooms called Cabinets Chinois, in vitrines, on shelves or brackets, or massed on top of cabinets. Entire porcelain rooms were also created, including one designed *c.* 1690 by Daniel Marot I for Het Loo in the Netherlands, and later re-created (now destr.), by Queen Mary, at Hampton Court. After the formula for hard-paste porcelain was discovered in Meissen *c.* 1708–9, rooms were made wholly of European porcelain decorated with Chinese figures and scenes: the Salottino di Porcellana in the Palazzo Reale in Pórtici, near Naples, contained an entire room made of 3000 interlocking panels of porcelain made at the factory of Capodimonte and decorated with Chinese figures modelled in relief and painted in Rococo settings of rocaille and scrollwork (1757–9; Naples, Capodimonte). Until the mid-18th century chinoiserie porcelain combined Chinese forms and designs with motifs derived from the Imari and Kakiemon ceramics produced by the ARITA kilns in Japan. After 1752 porcelain produced at Sèvres and decorated with enamelled flowers, birds, or landscape paintings on richly coloured grounds became more fashionable.

2. INTERIOR DECORATION. In about 1650 Chinese wallpaper was imported into Europe, although it was often thought to be Indian; in 1753 the boudoir of the Duchesse de Mortemart was described as 'Un Cabinet de Papier des Indes'. Imitation Chinese wallpaper was produced in England by the 1680s and in America by 1700. Chintz and wallpaper were used primarily in private rooms, and reception

Chinoiserie fan painted with pastoral scene, gouache on paper, from France or the Netherlands, 1750–70 (London, Victoria and Albert Museum)

rooms were hung with japanned or painted panels in the Chinese manner.

During the 18th century the taste for chinoiserie reached its height in France, where the word was first used in conjunction with the Régence style of Jean Beain, Claude Audran III (1658–1734) and Antoine Watteau (1684–1721); it subsequently spread throughout Europe with the dissemination of the Rococo style. Rooms were decorated in a light-hearted, fanciful chinoiserie manner that reflected a new feeling for a more relaxed way of life. Watteau's graceful arabesques exemplified the gay and elegant spirit of the Régence, and in 1709 his panels (destr.) for the Cabinet du Roi at the château of La Muette were engraved by François Boucher as *Figures Chinoises et Tartares*, depicting an 'Empereur chinois' and a 'Divinité chinoise'. Christophe Huet followed the fashion at the château of Champs and the château of Chantilly, where his decorations, called SINGERIE, used monkeys in a chinoiserie type of grotesque first introduced by Berain. Watteau produced designs (Stockholm, N.Mus.) for singerie (destr.) at the château of Marly. The Rococo style developed in the early 1730s in the work of Nicolas Pineau and Juste-Aurèle Meissonnier, who assimilated chinoiserie elements into their designs for fanciful, assymetric ornament. Although chinoiserie survived the more rigorous Neo-classical style of the latter part of the 18th century, the Revival styles of the 19th century brought about its demise.

3. LACQUER. Lacquer was first imported from Japan in 1542 and soon became one of the most important export commodities of the East; it was imitated in Europe from the early 17th century. In the

Netherlands the first mention of japanning 'after the fashion of China' dates from 1609 with William Kick, a member of Lackwerken, the japanners' guild of Amsterdam (1610). Nuremberg, Augsburg and Hamburg also produced japanned wares. In France it was called 'Lachinage' and in 1661 PIERRE GOLE provided two japanned tables for the château of Vincennes. In England japanning became a fashionable pastime for ladies after the publication in 1688 of Stalker and Parker's *Treatise of Japanning and Varnishing*. The book provided technical hints and designs inspired by imported lacquer as well as by blue-and-white porcelain and the exotic 'Cathay' motifs of the engraver Matthias Beilter, whose designs were published in Holland in 1616. Many types of furniture and other objects were covered in naive chinoiserie figures. At the end of the 17th century the Netherlands, England and the town of Spa in Belgium were the most important centres for japanning, while in Boston, MA, there were several outstanding japanners, among them John Pimm (*fl* 1740–50), who created the japanned tallboy (1740–50) in the H. F. Du Pont Winterthur Museum, Winterthur, DE. Entire rooms were decorated with japanned panels; an example is the Japan Closet by Gerrit Jensen at Chatsworth, Derbys, completed in the 1680s.

In the 18th century, commodes, bureaux, encoignures and secrétaires were decorated with panels of lacquer set within japanned or *vernis Martin* surrounds and enriched with elaborate ormolu mounts. The nobility were carried around the streets of London in lacquered sedan chairs. The type of chinoiserie illustrated in Thomas Chippendale's *Gentleman and Cabinet-maker's Director* (1754) became known as 'Chinese

Chippendale'; the Chinese element consists largely of prominent latticework on seat furniture and small cabinets. In America, furniture with chinoiserie lattice work and fret work was one of the specialties of the Philadelphia workshops of the second half of the 18th century.

4. METALWORK AND OBJECTS OF VERTU. In metalwork, chinoiserie motifs for flat-chasing on toilet-sets and punch-bowls were designed by Daniel Marot I in the 17th century and by CHRISTOPHE HUET and Jean Pillement (1728–1808) in the 18th century. Such motifs are especially evident in English silver produced between 1680 and 1720. In the mid-18th century chinoiserie tea-caddies were especially popular, either lavishly embossed with oriental scenes or engraved with bands of ornament and pseudo-Chinese characters in imitation of tea bales shipped from China (e.g. silver tea-caddy by Louisa Courtauld and George Cowles, 1773; London, V&A). In France, exquisite snuff-boxes made during the first half of the 18th century featured enamelled chinoiserie decoration on a gold ground or Chinese or Japanese lacquer mounted in gold.

5. TEXTILES. Patterned silks were a major and early vehicle for the introduction of Chinese designs to the West. Dragons, dogs, lions and phoenixes feature in Italian silks of the 14th century, and the geometric fretwork in the background of German linen embroideries of the same date may also have a Chinese origin. A more conscious dependency followed the opening-up of trade with East Asia during the 16th century and its expansion in the 17th. The channelling of Chinese and Japanese goods through India blurred Western views of their individual traits and resulted, for example, in English embroideries of c. 1700 showing the Indian tree of life standing within a bamboo fence on Chinese rocks and alive with phoenixes and long-tailed cranes. Birds and blue-and-white china were the favoured Chinese motifs on amateur embroideries of the late 17th century and early 18th but, in professionally produced textiles, the dress and occupations of the Chinese were preferred; they feature, for example, in the masquerade costumes (c. 1700) designed by Jean Berain and in the wall panels of applied pieces of Indian painted cottons (1720s; Vienna, Mus. Angewandte Kst.) that were made for the summer palace of Prince Eugene of Savoy.

During the late 17th century and the first half of the 18th several tapestry series were woven in France, England and Germany on the theme of Chinese life. The Manufacture Royale des Tapisseries at Beauvais introduced the first set of 'Tentures chinoises' after cartoons by Guy-Louis Vernansal (1648–1729), Jean-Baptiste Belin (1654–1715) and Jean-Baptiste Monnoyer, also known as 'Baptiste'; a second set after designs by François Boucher was produced in 1742 and copied numerous times. Tapestries with chinoiserie motifs were also being produced at the Gobelins at this time. The silk designers were initially less obvious in their use of Chinese

motifs, although some figures, mixed with Indian images, appear in French and Italian silks of c. 1700, and Chinese-style buildings hide among the exotic foliage of the designs (c. 1705) of James Leman (1688–1745). In the mid-1730s the French designer Jean Revel (1684–1751) produced a number of chinoiserie silk designs in an early Rococo style, and from the mid-1750s Jean Pillement (1728–1808) engraved fanciful chinoiserie designs that were drawn upon by other textile designers in his *One Hundred and Thirty Figures and Ornaments and Some Flowers in the Chinese Style* (London, 1767). His designs were used by English cotton printers and, in the 1780s, by the Oberkampf factory at Jouy (e.g. Mulhouse, Mus. Impression Etoffes; London, V&A). Delicate floral designs showing varying degrees of Chinese influence appeared on embroideries, woven silks and printed cottons into the 1790s and there was a brief revival of printed cottons decorated with bamboo interlacing and Chinese flowers in the early 19th century.

H. Honour: *Chinoiserie* (London, 1961)
O. Impey: *Chinoiserie* (London, 1977)
M. Jarry: *Chinoiserie* (Fribourg, 1981)
D. Jacobson: *Chinoiserie* (London, 1999)

Chintz. Painted cotton cloth that was developed in India (where it was known as 'kalamkani') and susequently imitated in the West. The technique used mordants and resist-dyeing processes to produce a cotton fabric with brilliant fast colours that was washable because the colouring was produced by dyes. The colour palette encompassed black, reds, purples, browns, blue, green and yellow, although not all cloths have the full range, and in old examples the yellows have often faded. Limited colour ranges may be red and black, as for some Hindu temple cloths. The chintzes made for the Mughal courts and

Design for chintz, pen, ink and watercolour, 18th century (London, Victoria and Albert Museum)

the European market usually have large areas of white ground (e.g. chintz overdress, painted and dyed cotton; Toronto, Royal Ont. Mus.), and may be just in several tones of red on white. A large complex cloth could take months to decorate and would involve at least ten stages of production, the main reason being the difficulty, before the advent of suitable synthetic dyes, of dyeing cotton and other cellulose fibres. The best cloths also depend on finely spun cotton.

J. Irwin and K. B. Brett, *Origins of Chintz with a Catalogue of Indo-European Cotton-paintings in the Victoria and Albert Museum, London, and the Royal Ontario Museum, Toronto* (London, 1970)
The Chintz Collection, the Calico Museum of Textiles, India (Ahmadabad, 1983)
J. Burnard: *Chintz and Cotton: India's Textile Gift to the World* (Kenthurst, NSW, 1994)
S. Cohen: 'The Unusual Textile Trade between India and Sri Lanka: Chintz and Block Prints: 1550–1900', *Hali*, cxxxv (July–Aug 2004), pp. 16–27 [supp. special edition]

Chip-carving. Decorative carving in which the patterns are produced by chipping out the material with a chisel and gouge; chip-carved roundels are characteristic of medieval north European oak furniture.

Chipchase, Robert (*d* 1810). English furniture-maker who had established a workshop in London by 1767 and in 1790 entered into partnership with his son Henry, who described himself as an upholsterer. Robert's best-known commissions were for the dukes of Atholl, for whom he designed chairs and settees, some of which survive at Blair Castle in Perthshire.

Chippendale, Thomas (*bapt* Otley, W. Yorks, 5 June 1718; *bur* London, 13 Nov 1779). English furniture-maker. He probably received some early training from his father, who was a joiner. Chippendale moved to London in the late 1740s, and in December 1753 rented nos 60, 61 and 62 St Martin's Lane for his cabinetmaking business.

The term 'Chippendale' is regularly used to denote English Rococo furniture inspired by the designs in Chippendale's celebrated pattern book, the *Gentleman and Cabinet-maker's Director* (1754). The book contains 161 plates, the majority engraved by Matthias Darly. These include designs for a wide range of household furniture in the Gothic, Chinese and Rococo styles, as well as a repertory of plain domestic pieces. A virtually identical second edition of the *Director* was issued in 1755. The appearance in 1760 of William Ince and George Mayhew's rival publication, the *Universal System of Household Furniture*, with a parallel French text, prompted a third enlarged and revised edition of the *Director* in 1762, dedicated this time to Prince William Henry. The new plates include several featuring Neo-classical designs. The book sold well and helped the firm to attract fashionable clients, ranging from the nobility to David Garrick, the actor. The *Director* was influential abroad, particularly in North America, and the publication of the third edi-

tion in French gave a further boost to international sales: Catherine II, Empress of Russia, possessed a copy.

As well as furniture and room schemes, Chippendale designed wallpaper, chimney-pieces, carpets, ormolu and silverware, and his business ranged from the furnishing of state apartments to equipping servants' quarters and acting as an undertaker. On one occasion he made furniture to a design supplied by Robert Adam; this was a drawing-room suite (part at Aske Hall, N. Yorks) ordered in 1765 by Sir Lawrence Dundas for his London residence at 19 Arlington Street. Chippendale regularly conferred with architects when equipping the grand interiors they had designed, but at many houses he had sole control over the furnishing programme. It is unlikely that he personally made furniture after he had established himself in London; instead he seems to have concentrated on design, quality control and dealing with clients. Although his name is commonly associated with the Rococo designs of the *Director*, his finest furniture is in the Neo-classical style (e.g. the library table of inlaid satinwood supplied to Harewood House, 1771; Leeds, Temple Newsam House). The finest ensembles still in private houses include those at Dumfries House; Wilton House, Wilts; Nostell Priory, NT; Aske Hall; Petworth House, W. Sussex,

Thomas Chippendale cabinet bedstead, painted pine and glass with brass handles, 2.49 × 1.65 × 0.69 m, made for David Garrick, 1768–70 (London, Victoria and Albert Museum)

NT; Newby Hall, N. Yorks; Brocket Hall, Herts; Burton Constable and Harewood. A more light-hearted vein can be seen in the white-and-green painted furniture (some, *c.* 1768–78, at London, V&A) made for Garrick's villa. Large collections of Chippendale's manuscript designs are preserved in museums (New York, Met.; London, V&A), while others survive in country-house archives.

Chippendale's son, also called Thomas (*bapt* London, 23 April 1749; *d* ?Dec 1822), assisted in the family firm from an early age and became an accomplished draughtsman, publishing a suite of decorative designs, *Sketches of Ornament*, in 1779. After his father's death in the same year, he continued the business in partnership with Thomas Haig (*d* 1803). He operated on his own from 1796 to *c.* 1820. Some 30 commissions are recorded: the most important houses where documented furniture survives are Harewood House, W. Yorks, Paxton House, Borders, Luscombe Castle, Devon, and Stourhead, Wilts. The last contains a large and distinguished collection, including pieces in progressive Neo-classical and Egyptian Revival styles.

T. Chippendale: *Gentleman and Cabinet-maker's Director* (London, 1754, rev. 2/1755, rev. 3/1762/*R* New York, 1966)
C. Gilbert: 'Chippendale Senior and Junior at Paxton, 1774–91', *Connoisseur*, clxxx (1972), pp. 93–103
J. Kenworthy-Browne: 'Notes on the Furniture by Thomas Chippendale the Younger at Stourhead', *NT Yb.* (1975–6), pp. 93–103
C. Gilbert: *The Life and Work of Thomas Chippendale*, 2 vols (London, 1978)
N. Harris: *Chippendale* (Secaucus, NJ, 1989)
T. Chippendale and J. M. Bell: *The Chippendale Director: The Furniture Designs of Thomas Chippendale* (Ware, 1990)
J. Sellars and T. Chippendale: *The Art of Thomas Chippendale: Master Furniture Maker* (Leeds, 2000)
C. Gilbert and A. Firth: *The Chippendale Society: Catalogue of the Collections* (Leeds, 2000)
B. S. Mason: 'Furniture Virtuoso', *A. & Ant.*, xxvii/1 (Jan 2004), pp. 50–55
J. Goodison: 'Thomas Chippendale the Younger at Stourhead', *Furn. Hist.*, xli (2005), pp. 57–116

Choir-stalls. Places in the choir of a church set aside for the daily use of the clergy. They are usually made of wood and are found only in churches of the Western tradition. Choir-stalls were essentially places for standing, the clergy being required to do so during most of the services. Each stall consists of a folding seat, turning on hinges or pivots, with a MISERICORD under it, a standard on each side with elbow rest, a wainscot backing and, sometimes, a canopy above. Some form of book desk was provided in front.

Choir-stalls were usually made from oak, which has the required tensile strength for the production of substantial continuous lengths of foundation beams and tall standards for canopy-work. Pine was substituted in some parts of Europe where oak of suitable quality was hard to obtain. Walnut and lime-wood were also occasionally used; these woods are much easier to carve than oak but are less resistant to climate and disease. No limewood choir-stalls survive, and only some fragments in walnut. Stone, par-ticularly marble, was sometimes used, especially in Italy.

In Early Christian basilicas there were no individual stalls for the celebrants; the only seating consisted of a continuous stone bench behind the altar. By the 11th century, the choir was usually placed in front of, rather than behind, the altar. Choir-stalls from such churches have not survived, and their precise form is unknown, but the clergy may have sat on long wooden benches, such as the 12th-century example in the south transept of Winchester Cathedral. Canterbury Cathedral had wooden choir-stalls by the mid-12th century: their conflagration in the fire of 1174 is described by the monk Gervase. At that time the form of choir-stalls probably differed significantly between buildings and in different parts of Europe, but from the mid-13th century it seems to have been standardized. There was usually a single row of back stalls on each side of the choir, with return stalls at the west end. In secular institutions and in English monastic cathedrals, there were normally, in addition, substalls, with benches in front for the choir-boys. The capacity varied from *c.* 20–30 places in the smallest establishments to over 120. In eastern France and some parts of Germany it is common for there to be a single range of seats on one side only. The low 'desks' in the early 13th-century choir-stalls at Rochester Cathedral, Kent, may have been merely forms for leaning on when kneeling.

The earliest surviving choir stalls are of the 'single-screen' type, where the seats are backed by a low wooden structure instead of a wall (cf. the mid-13th-century stalls at Notre Dame de la Roche, Le Mesnil St Denis, near Paris). The 'double-screen' design, which appeared in England for the first time at Westminster Abbey, London, *c.* 1255, stands at the head of a distinguished succession of English canopied stalls. The extraordinary early 14th-century double-screen choir-stalls at Winchester Cathedral, with their arrangement of two seats per bay surmounted by an elaborate and intricately carved superstructure, surpass all surviving stalls of the time in Europe in size, ingenuity and architectural ambition.

The design of English choir-stalls became progressively more daring in the course of the 14th century, as at the cathedrals of Ely (*c.* 1342), Gloucester (*c.* 1350), Lincoln (*c.* 1370) and Chester (*c.* 1390). The aesthetic of Perpendicular architecture eventually enabled master carpenters to discard the traditional conventions and to create a style with tall, insubstantial structures that best exploited the fibrous nature of wood. The medium also enabled forms to be built up from a number of component parts, and this quality was exploited to produce highly wrought, complex canopies. These were light in weight since they were assembled from thin, carved members glued and nailed together. The combination of tenuous verticality and intricate detailing resembling metalwork in such choir-stalls as those at the cathedrals of Lincoln and Chester and St Mary's, Nantwich, Cheshire (*c.* 1390), produced a new, impressionistic effect quite different from Rayonnant. The

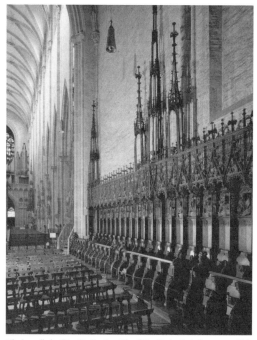

Choir-stalls by Jörg Syrlin the elder, Ulm Cathedral, Germany, 15th century

examples of Baroque and Rococo stalls in south Germany (e.g. the Klosterkirche, Ottobeuren, from *c.* 1754), France (e.g. Notre-Dame, Paris, 1715–17), Italy (e.g. Bergamo Cathedral) and the southern Netherlands (e.g. St Jacobskerk, Antwerp, 1658–70). Spanish wood-carvers produced fine Baroque stalls both in Spain (e.g. Malaga Cathedral) and in South America, as at Lima Cathedral in Peru (begun 1623, by Pedro de Noguera of Seville), where the decorative devices are strongly indebted to the work of the Antwerp Mannerists, in particular prints after Hans Vredeman de Vries. Most choir-stalls created in the 19th century were in the neo-Gothic style, but in the 20th century some novel forms were introduced: instead of traceried Gothic canopies, the choir-stalls of Coventry Cathedral (1962), by Sir Basil Spence, have clusters of three-point crosses that give the impression of birds in flight.

D. Kraus and H. Kraus: *Las sillerías góticas españoles* (Madrid, 1984; Eng. trans., London and New York, 1986)
U. Bergmann: *Das Chorgestühl des Kölner Domes*, 2 vols (Neuss, 1987)
C. Tracy: *English Gothic Choir-stalls, 1200–1400* (Woodbridge, 1987)
C. Tracy: *A Catalogue of English Gothic Furniture and Woodwork*, London, V&A (London, 1988)
C. Tracy: *English Gothic Choir-stalls, 1400–1500* (Woodbridge, 1990)
B. T. N. Bennett: *The Choir Stalls of Chester Cathedral* (Chester, 1994)
R. Hancock: *Notes on the 'Graffiti' Carved on the Panels Fronting the Side Stalls in Carlisle Cathedral* (Carlisle, 1995)
R. E. Roberts, G. Piper and T. Ruth: *Misericords and Other Carvings in the Great Quire, Christchurch Priory, Dorset* (Much Wenlock, 2000)
C. Tracy: *Continental Church Furniture in England: A Traffic in Piety* (Woodbridge, 2001)
E. C. Block: *Corpus of Medieval Misericords* (Turnhout, 2003)
C. Hourihane: *Objects, Images, and the Word: Art in the Service of the Liturgy* (Princeton, 2003)
C. Tracy and H. Harrison: *The Choir-stalls of Amiens Cathedral* (Reading, 2004)

choir-stalls at Lincoln (*c.* 1370) show an attention to detail that ensures that each crocket is individually treated and a different species of plant represented. At the same time, when seen from afar, the component motifs of the design start to merge into one another to produce an effect that would have been considerably enhanced by the overall application of colour and gilding. The English love of canopy-work continued for the rest of the Gothic period, as is demonstrated by the choir-stalls of York Minster (*c.* 1420; destr.), and those at Ripon Minster (*c.* 1488–94) and Manchester Cathedral (*c.* 1506). Finally, the furniture at St George's Chapel, Windsor (*c.* 1478–83), and the Henry VII Chapel, Westminster Abbey (*c.* 1512), show the influence of the latest trends in Netherlandish Gothic.

Choir-stalls have continued to be manufactured to the present day. In English reformed churches some fine examples were made in the 17th century at the cathedrals of Durham (1665; rest. 1870s) and St Paul's (1695–7), London. The stalls at Durham, installed by Bishop John Cosin (1660–72), combine Baroque and Gothic features, including swags, strapwork and traceried canopies. Those at St Paul's, executed by Grinling Gibbons to designs by Christopher Wren, have small rooms in the thickness of the structure, while decorative motifs include coupled Corinthian columns, openwork scrolls, cherubs' heads, swags and garlands of fruit and flowers. Some of the finest examples of the genre, however, were created in the Roman Catholic countries during the 17th and 18th centuries; at this time, the stalls ceased to form a barrier between nave and choir and often curved round the chancel wall at the east. There are notable

Choisy-le-Roi. French town and château some 8 km south-east of Paris, and the site of important pottery and glass. In 1788 Louis XVI (*reg* 1774–92) converted the 17th-century château into barracks, and it was sold during the French Revolution, becoming a pottery factory in 1804. In the 19th century the factory made architectural, industrial and ornamental wares on a large scale. The building was progressively dismantled, and after the factory closed (1939) the last remains were cleared away (1952). The glass factory (in operation 1821–51) was founded by M. Grimbolt; its technical director was GEORGES BONTEMPS, who produced some of French opaline glass from *c.* 1838. Bontemps's primary interest was sheet glass, and he rediscovered the manufacturing process for red sheet glass much used in the revival of stained glass in France.

C. Espinosa Martin: 'La Faiencerie de Choisy-le-Roi a traves de los modelos de Albert Ernest y Louis Robert Carrier de Belleuse en el Museo Lazaro Galdiano', *Goya*, cclxxiv (Jan–Feb 2000), pp. 35–43
F. Montes de Oca: *L'Age d'or du verre en France, 1800–1830: Verreries de l'Empire et de la Restauration* (Paris, 2001)

Chrétien, Gilles-Louis (*b* 1754; *d* 1811). French silhouettist and musician. In 1784 he invented a portrait cutting machine which he called a physionotrace; this apparatus, which consisted of a mechanical wooden instrument guided by a viewfinder, enabled Chrétien to draw quickly and to produce engraved drawings that could easily be reproduced.

W. Way and H. W. Chase: *The Story of Two Portraits* (Chapel Hill, NC, 1921)

R. Hennequin: *Avant les photographies; les portraits au physionotrace, gravés de 1788 à 1830. Catalogue nominatif, biographique et critique* (Troyes, 1932)

Chřibská [Ger. Kreibitz]. Czech centre of glass production. A glass factory was established in Chřibská in northern Bohemia on the Česká Kamenice estate in the Lužické Mountains at the beginning of the 15th century. Martin Friedrich (1582–1612) was a renowned glassmaker, and he and other glassmakers at the works were invited in 1601 by the Elector of Brandenburg, Joachim Frederick (*reg* 1598–1608), to establish a glass workshop at Grimnitz in north Brandenburg. From the list of products made at Grimnitz it is evident that the Chřibská glassworks produced cold-painted, enamelled, engraved and filigree glass. Dishes and goblets were decorated with the imperial eagle, the Electors, allegories of the Virtues, the Apostles and the Seven Ages of Man. During the 17th century the production of painted glass continued at Chřibská. In 1661 the first Bohemian guild of glassmakers, enamellers and glass engravers was established at Chřibská. From the 1660s local records indicate the names of the glass engravers, whose numbers increased after the 1670s. By the end of the 17th century the factory was producing a good-quality potash glass. Between 1696 and 1722 it was run as part of the estate, and among the tenants were the Kittels. In 1767 Johann Josef Kittel (*fl* 1748–86) bought the glassworks, and in 1785 his son Johann Anton Kittel took over. In the second half of the 18th century the works was producing ordinary clear, opaque white, dark blue, purple and opaque blue glass. After a crisis in the market during the Napoleonic blockade and a temporary cessation in production, the factory was revived at the end of the 1820s. At the Prague industrial exhibitions of 1828 and 1829 it exhibited agateware, glass decorated with biscuit-coloured enamel and wares decorated with black or multicoloured paintings of flowers or landscapes. During the 1830s high-quality crystal and coloured glass were produced. In the 1870s the works was owned by Anton Zahn, who decorated glass with a combination of techniques. Up to 1945 it was owned by the Mayer family. After World War II the factory became a project centre for coloured glass, specializing in decorative wares in delicate smoked colours. From the 1950s to the 1970s Josef Hospodka (1923–88) was employed as a designer, and other employees have included Vratislav Šotola (*b* 1931) and students from the Academy of Applied Art, Prague.

V. Lukáš: 'The North Bohemian Glassworks with the Oldest Tradition', *Glass Rev.*, xxiv (1974), no. 9, pp. 18–21; no. 11, pp. 17–21

Christiansen, **Hans** (*b* Flensburg, 6 March 1866; *d* Wiesbaden, 5 Jan 1945). German designer. After an early career as an interior designer he turned to the design of tapestries (subsequently woven at the Scherbeker Kunstge werbeschule), porcelain (table wares), drinking glasses (for the Theresienthaler Kristallglasfabrik) and silver cutlery. After 1914 he worked primarily as a painter and writer.

M. Zimmermann-Degen and H. Christiansen: *Hans Christiansen: Leben und Werk eines Jugendstilkünstlers* (Königstein im Taunus, 1985)

Christofle, **Charles** (*b* 1805; *d* 1863). French silversmith. In 1830 he founded the silver company Christofle et Compagnie of Paris, which produced silver in revival styles, made widely accessible by his introduction of electroplating (under licence from G. R. ELKINGTON) into France in 1842. By engaging a series of designers (e.g. Lino Sabattini, François Fauconnet) Christofle maintained its repertoire conservatively up to date and its position in the forefront of the manufacture and retailing of useful and decorative metalwork. The firm also produced large numbers of vessels in copper gilt using various enamelling techniques.

Christofle opened its first shop, the 'Pavillon de Hanovre', in Paris in 1856; it now has shops in 29 countries, and is France's largest producer of tableware, including silverware, porcelain, crystal and table linen.

M. de Ferrière Le Vayer: *Christofle, deux siècles d'aventure industrielle: 1793–1993* (Paris, 1995)

Chromium. Lustrous silvery metal obtained from lead chromates by smelting or aquaceous electrolysis. It was first produced *c.* 1797 in France and was named chrome (Gr.: 'colour') due to the pigments observed in its compounds. It is widely dispersed in natural deposits as dark brown to jet black chromite, the largest producer being Albania. Rarely used in its pure form, it is usually plated on to base metal above a coat of nickel, by a process that was first mentioned in 1854. As chromium is resistant to corrosion, it was used in World War I for projectile covers, although it was not until 1924 that it was commercially produced in the USA and Germany and later in Britain. The decorative potential of its colour and brilliance was quickly and enthusiastically recognized by the innovative designers of the 1920s and 1930s, for example Le Corbusier, Eileen Gray and MARCEL BREUER, who employed chromium-plated tubular steel in furniture (e.g. B32 side chair, 1928; New York, MOMA). Lighting fixtures, clocks and such decorative articles as figurines and car mascots were also chromium-plated. Chromium was utilized with superb effect in jewellery, both by French avant-garde designers and in cheaper mass-produced work where it was often combined with plastics. It continued to be used after World War II but has gradually declined in competition with stainless steel.

A. H. Sully and E. A. Brandes: *Chromium* (London, 1967)

J. K. Dennis and T. E. Such: *Nickel and Chromium Plating* (London, 1972; rev. 3/1993)

Chrysoberyl. In classical antiquity and for centuries thereafter, chrysoberyl was thought to be a variety of beryl, with a tinge of yellow; it is now known to be a quite distinct stone, an aluminate of glucinum. Two varieties are particularly prized: one with a bluish opalescence is chrysoberyl cat's-eye, which was formerly known as cymophane; one which in natural light is bluish-green is alexandrite, which was mined in the Urals in the early 19th century and named after Tsar Alexander I.

Chubb. English family of locksmiths. Charles Chubb (*b* ?Fordingbridge, Hants, 16 Jan 1772; *d* Islington, 16 May 1846), was trained as a blacksmith and then moved to Portsea, where he established a hardware business. There he invented a series of locks that incorporated the detector sign, whereby an attempt to pick the lock or use a false key causes the lever closest to the lock bolt functions to block the mechanism, so that when the correct key is inseted it must first be turned in the opposite direction to unblock the mechanism; the mechanism may have been invented with the needs of the Admiralty in mind, to create more security on the nearby docks and prison hulks. On 3 February 1818 Charles patented the lock together with his brother Jeremiah (*b* Fordingbridge, Hants, 10 June 1790; *d* Winchester, Hants, 10 Nov 1847). The brothers then moved to Wolverhampton, the principal centre of lockmaking in England. Jeremiah moved to France and then America, and Charles stayed to run the business. In 1820 he sold the lock to the Admiralty, and soon after opened offices in St Paul's Churchyard in London. From this base he sold locks to the Bank of England, the king and the Duke of Wellington (who called on a Chubb locksmith to pick the lock on the front door to Apsley House). Jeremiah returned to England in 1828, and thereafter worked as a travelling representative for Chubb locks.

John Chubb (*b* Portsea, Hants, 13 Nov 1815; *d* London, 30 Oct 1872) was the eleventh child of Charles Chubb. He was apprenticed in the family business and entered the partnership of Chubb & Sons in 1841. John Chubb expanded the business in England and abroad: by the 1840s Chubb locks and safes were being despatched to India and North America. The increase in turnover occasioned the relocation of the lock factory from Temple Street to the former workhouse in Horseley Fields, Wolverhampton, and the safe factory from Cow Cross Street to Glengall Road, Old Kent Road, in London. He had a gift for publicity, and impressed Queen Victoria (*reg* 1837–1901) with his locks when she visited his stand at the Great Exhibition of 1851. He also submitted his locks to a series of public lock-picking contests, and devised improvements to overcome any succeeses that his opponents may have enjoyed. He campaigned successfully to have Chubb locks fitted to the first pillar boxes (1856), and this contract was still in place in the 1990s. The company is now the Chubb Security Group, based in Leatherhead, Surrey.

ODNB

Churrigueresque. Term used from the late 18th century to denote the most exuberantly ornamental phase of Spanish and Spanish American architectural decoration, lasting from *c.* 1675 to *c.* 1750. The term derives from the Churriguera family, the principal exponents of the style, who worked mostly in Salamanca.

R. Ceballos: *Los Churriguera* (Madrid, 1971)

Ciacchi, Jacopo (*fl* 1820). Italian cabinetmaker, active in Florence. His surviving furniture includes two night-tables and a series of drum-shaped stools for Grand Duchess Elisa (Florence, Pitti) and, with Giuseppe Colzi, the furniture for Queen Mary Louise's bathroom in the Quartiere dei Volterrano in the Palazzo Pitti (e.g. commode; Florence, Pitti).

Ciborium. Covered, chalice-shaped liturgical vessel, used in churches of the Catholic (and some Orthodox) traditions to contain reserved, consecrated hosts. The basic type of ciborium consists of a broad-based foot, a stem with a knop, and a wide, rather shallow cup with a closely fitting cover. Examples are usually *c.* 400 mm high, although Late Gothic ciboria with tower-shaped covers, and some 19th-century ones from large churches, are over 600 mm in height. Before the Counter-Reformation of the 16th century, the term ciborium was also often applied to a monstrance; both could be placed on the altar for the veneration of the sacrament and carried in procession (the largest ciboria, weighing 2 kg and more, are suitable only for such purposes). A few Gothic pieces (e.g. Cologne, Schnütgen-Mus.) combine a footed ciborium with a monstrance in the tower-shaped upper portion.

Although ciboria of solid gold existed, most were made of silver or copper gilt with a silver cup. Pewter ciboria are rare; they were allowed in poorer parishes during times of political unrest, when country churches were threatened by looting armies, and after the confiscation of church silver by French republican occupying forces at the end of the 18th century.

The form of the receptacle for the reserved host has responded to changes in liturgical requirements; the size often depended on the frequency of communion. From the 10th century there are references to the eucharistic dove (symbol of the Holy Spirit); these were hanging, dove-shaped receptacles made from silver or bronze gilt, with a hole in the back for hosts. Many examples in Limoges enamel survive (e.g. Paris, Mus. Cluny). The boxes were of variable form and construction, usually round or polygonal and often with a convex cover. Sometimes they were

Ciborium, alabaster (Volterra, Museo Diocesano di Arte Sacra)

equipped with conical feet, which made them more convenient to handle. This type of footed pyx, often called a ciborium, is represented by two related English examples (*c.* 1160–70; New York, Pierpont Morgan Lib., and London, V&A) made of enamelled and gilded copper. They each bear 12 typological Old and New Testament scenes, with explanatory inscriptions, and medallions inside the bowl and lid depicting, respectively, the *Lamb of God* and *Christ Blessing.*

The oldest surviving ciboria of the chalice type date from the 13th century. They have a cylindrical cup with a hinged cover, a simple stem, often with a ribbed knop, and a lobed foot. The cover is usually crowned with an orb and crucifix, symbol of Christ's dominion over the world. Examples of this type include the ciboria of St Kunibert, Cologne, and two in Brussels (Musées Royaux A. & Hist.). A ciborium in Rome (Vatican) from the Meuse region, decorated with precious stones, filigree and niello, is related by its style and ornamentation to monumental reliquaries. At the same time a type evolved in which the cup and cover are mirror images of each other, forming an oblate spheroid. Examples include the great early 14th-century ciborium at Klosterneuburg, Mus. Chorherrenstiftes, which has enamelled *Passion* scenes on the bowl and, on the foot, repoussé prophets alternating with symbols of the Evangelists in medallions. Many smaller Limoges enamel ciboria follow this essential form. In the course of the 14th

and 15th centuries the foot of the ciborium followed the form of the chalice, with six or eight concave or convex sides. Cup, knop and cover are often polygonal as well (e.g. Anfang-Eltz, Burgkapelle). The cover is attached to the cup by a hinge, sometimes with a separate chain and pin. During this period, the cover developed a towering architectural superstructure, complete with miniature flying buttresses and spires and frequently with small images of the Ecce homo, the Virgin and angels (e.g. that of *c.* 1400 in St Johann, Cologne). The upper portion is closely related to that of contemporary monstrances. The gilt copper ciborium (1396) in St Mariä Himmelfahrt, Rees, which was made in Cologne, and that in Aachen (Aachen, Domschatzkam.) are fine examples of this type, which persisted in various forms until well into the 16th century. Like chalices, Gothic ciboria with lobed feet are often finely engraved with the figures of the saints or scenes from the Life of Christ. In Spain and Portugal, this basic type of ciborium acquired an exuberant decorative structure (e.g. *c.* 1530, London, V&A).

After the Counter-Reformation, the Roman Catholic Church emphasized eucharistic devotion; large exhibition ciboria were placed on altars for adoration or carried in processions. Particularly in the southern Netherlands, new brotherhoods that encouraged such devotions and brought the host in processions to the sick and dying used the confessional ciborium, which had a small vessel for Holy Oil, used for Extreme Unction, on its cover (e.g. that of 1654 in St Pauluskerk, Antwerp). The combined ciborium/ monstrance continued to be used in less affluent parishes (e.g. the Baroque example in Diest, Stedel. Mus.). Since many churches in northern Europe were looted during the Wars of Religion, and regulations for the quantity and construction of liturgical vessels became more severe, new receptacles were produced on a massive scale in the first half of the 17th century, often in a new flamboyant style.

The Renaissance ciborium has a hemispherical cup, a round or hexagonal foot, and an egg- or basket-shaped knop. The cover is attached to the cup by a bayonet mount and often carries a small figure of Christ in a niche crowned with a small cross. The relief work, which replaced engraving as the most common ornamental device, was initially nonrepresentational, with square bosses, egg-shaped borders and palmettes, but figures were included increasingly after 1610. The foot was usually provided with medallions, with scenes in relief often depicting the *Last Supper.* The knop was usually decorated with acanthus leaves and garlands of fruit and flowers (e.g. that of 1613 in the Holy Virgin Church, Rupelmonde, Belgium). Baroque features gradually appeared. The knop became pear-shaped, and a false, usually openwork cup covered the bowl. The foot remained polygonal and followed the stylistic evolution of the chalice foot. The cover, no longer attached to the cup, was frequently ornamented with a pelican on its nest, one of the symbols of the self-sacrificing Christ. Other motifs included large crowns or the figure of God the Father in a gesture of blessing. The whole was luxuriantly ornamented with relief work; winged angel heads and putti with bunches of grapes are common. Many examples of this type of ciborium survive in nearly all the churches of Belgium. In the early 18th century an angel, a figure of the Virgin or the personification of one of the three theological Virtues replaced the stem and knop. The foot was made up of between three and six accolades. Rococo ornamentation appears primarily in south German ciboria (e.g. 1751; Regensburg, St Emmeramkirche). Ciboria from central Europe (e.g. in Sabinov, Roman Catholic church) and those from Russian Orthodox churches often bore colourful enamel medallions on the cup and foot. Around the third quarter of the 18th century, when ornamentation generally became more sober, liturgical vessels also adopted a classicizing character. The foot became round, the stem took on the shape of an amphora, and the relief was lighter, dominated by acanthus. Neo-classical and Empire style ciboria are, however, rare, perhaps owing to the decline in religious observance after the Enlightenment. Like all other liturgical vessels in the 19th century, ciboria were made in a variety of historicizing styles. The few existing 20th-century ciboria are simpler and smaller in format and often resemble secular works, such as the Art Deco ciboria of the Sacred Heart Basilica of Koekelberg in Brussels. From c. 1950, and especially after the innovations of the Second Vatican Council, the ciborium was frequently replaced by a shallow silver basin.

Cimarre. Ceremonial wine tankard of tall, slender, baluster form, sometimes with a spout and usually made of pewter. It has a convex cover and two handles: one fixed at the side and the other hinged and pivoting over the top. The thumb-piece is often of linked acorns or berries. It was used to present wine to honoured persons to mark their entry into a town, and some bear town armorials. Cimarres are mentioned in documents from the 14th century, but most surviving examples date from the 17th and 18th centuries. Examples made in Switzerland often have a chain instead of the mobile handle.

Cire perdue [Fr.: 'lost wax']. Method of hollow bronze casting with wax. *Cire perdue* (also known as investment or precision casting) is used where very accurate reproduction of detail is required. The process was developed in the ancient Near East in the 4th millennium BC: initially it was used only for small objects, but by the 6th century BC it was employed in Greece for large-scale statuary. The shape to be cast is modelled in a material with a low melting-point, such as wax, and the sprue and risers are added in wax. In the 'direct' process the model is dipped in a fine clay slip, the consistency of batter mixture, and allowed to dry. This is repeated until a good coating has built up, and then a stronger, but coarser clay (the investment) is fitted around it for strength. The

mould is then heated, which bakes the investment and melts the wax, causing it to run out and leave the mould empty and ready to receive the metal. The mould is often rotated during casting, and the centrifugal force pushes the molten metal into the details of the mould. When the metal is set the mould is broken away to reveal the casting.

M. V. Krishnan: *Cire Perdue Casting in India* (New Delhi, 1976)
L. Jans, H. Scheerder and F. Villanueva: *A Cire Perdue* (Amersfoort, 1993)

Cirou, Ciquaire. *See under* CHANTILLY, §2.

Ciselure. Finishing process of chasing and tooling metals; a *ciseleur* is a chaser, one who carves metals.

Cistercian ware. Type of English pottery, so called because the first specimens were found in the ruins of Cistercian abbeys; it appears to have been manufactured by monks in the late 15th century or early 16th. The ware is very hard, and usually orange or red (but sometimes grey or purple), and has a chocolate-brown or black glaze and decorations in trailed yellow slip. The most common form is the drinking cup with two or more handles.

V. Eley: *A Monk at the Potter's Wheel: The Story of Charnwood-Cistercian ware* (Leicester, 1974)

Citrine. Glassy variety of wine-yellow quartz, also called false topaz.

Cizhou ware. Chinese stoneware made for popular use and named after the kilns at Cizhou (modern Ci xian), Hebei Province, though they were also produced at many other sites in Hebei, Henan and Shaanxi provinces. They are characterized by their robust forms and vivid black-and-white decoration, though other colours were also used. A wide range of decorative techniques was applied to Cizhou wares, some of them, such as the cut-glaze technique, not introduced until the Yuan period. In the Song period, among the most important techniques was SGRAFFITO, in which a layer of slip in one colour was applied on top of another in a different colour and then cut away to achieve a contrast. Cizhou wares were made in a wide range of practical shapes, reflecting everyday popular use.

Cizhou wares are especially noted for their great variety of decorative styles. The most effective and important decorative technique in the Yuan period, as in the Song, was painting in black on a white ground. The principal motifs are birds, flowers (peony and lotus in particular), butterflies, dragons, phoenixes and fish. Figures, animals, landscapes and the interesting composition of children in lotus ponds were not uncommon. Calligraphy was also used, either in the form of a single character such as *fu* ('good fortune') or *shou* ('longevity'), or in a poem or narrative passage. Decorations painted in brown on black or in black on brown are also found.

Cizhou wares were also often decorated with bands of pattern. The main band round the body of the vessel is sometimes divided into panels, usually ogival in form, which contain the main pictorial patterns. These pictorial bands are separated by bands of stylized repeats such as classic scroll, floral scroll, petal panel, diaper, angular meander lines, wavy lines, geometric motifs or a solid broad band.

Decorative techniques on Cizhou wares also included the cut-glaze technique, in which the basic design was cut out from the surface of a vessel covered with dark brown or black slip while still damp; then, after glazing, details were incised to reveal the buff or pale grey body.

Y. Mino: *Freedom of Clay and Brush through Seven Centuries in Northern China: Tz'u-chou Type Wares, 960–1600* AD (New York, 1981)

Clair de lune [Fr.: 'moonlight']. Term used to describe the a soft white or pale blue-grey glaze of Kangxi and Yong Zheng porcelain.

Clamp kiln ware. Pottery or bricks made by burning in the open air rather than firing in a kiln.

Claw-and-ball foot. Furniture foot, popular in the 18th century, characterized by the representation of an eagle's claw clasping a ball; in the Chinese bronzes from which the motif derives, the foot is a dragon's claw.

M. Headley: 'Carving a Ball-and-claw Foot: Tracing the Techniques of a Williamsburg Cabinetmaker', *Fine Woodworking*, lxxxiv (Sept–Oct 1990), pp. 83–7

Clayton & Bell. English firm of stained-glass manufacturers. John Richard Clayton (*b* London, 30 July 1827; *d* London, 5 July 1913) and Alfred Bell (*b* Silton, Dorset, 1832; *d* 1895) became partners in 1857 in order to improve stained-glass design, having worked as draughtsmen for the architect George Gilbert Scott (1811–78). Clayton was influenced by the Pre-Raphaelites, but Bell had a more medievalizing style. Their earliest designs were made up by HEATON & BUTLER, but from 1861 they manufactured their own windows, as well as producing murals and mosaics, in their workshop in Regent Street, London. Demand increased, and by the late 1860s the studio had expanded to 300 employees. Many of their pupils, including Henry Stacy Marks (1829–98), John Burlison (1843–91), Thomas John Grylls (1845–1913) and C. E. Kempe (1837–1907), later founded their own firms. Architects commissioning their work included Scott, G. E. Street (1824–81) and J. L. Pearson (1817–97). Their style was characterized by elegant figural drawing, inspired by—but not directly copying—medieval glass, combined with clear primary colours and such tones as umber and violet, which were new to glass. Good early examples are the windows in St Mary's, Hanley Castle, Hereford

& Worcs, executed in 1860, and All Saints, Denstone, Staffs, executed in 1861. Their colours became more muted, as in three windows (1860, 1870, 1890) in the south chancel of Ely Cathedral and those (1870) in St John's College Chapel, Cambridge, where the walls and ceiling were also painted by the firm. The massive west window (1878) for King's College Chapel, Cambridge, blends sensitively with the earlier glass. The firm was granted a royal warrant by Queen Victoria in 1883, and production continued into the 1980s.

P. Larkworthy: *Clayton and Bell: Stained Glass Artists and Decorators* (London, 1984)

Cleffius, Lambertius (*fl* 1671; *d* 1691). Dutch pottery manufactourer. He was the proprietor of a Delft pottery called De Metaale Pot, which produced blue-and-white wares and red earthenware teapots; the potter's mark was LC. The best-known product of the factory is a set of Delft Blue faience (*c.* 1685) which was made for Wenzel Ferdinand, Fürst von Lobkowicz; 125 pieces survive in the Lobkowicz collection in Nelahozeves Castle (north of Prague).

Clement, William (*b* Rotherhithe, 1633; *d* 1704). English clockmaker. After an early career as an anchorsmith and blacksmith, he turned in 1677 to clock-making, initially specializing in turret clocks (e.g. clock of 1671 for Chapel of King's College, Cambridge, now in the Science Museum, London). He subsequently became a maker of fine long-case clocks, which he fitted with the anchor escapement (of which he may have been the inventor) and a screw regulation of the pendulum; many have the long 1¼-second pendulum. This 'royal pendulum' length allowed a minute and second hand to be fitted to the clock face alongside the hour hand that had previously been the only hand on the face.

Clérissy. French family of potters. Antoine Clérissy I (*d* 1679) and his son Pierre Clérissy I (1651–1728) established the first pottery in MOUSTIERS (Provence) in the late 1670s; Antoine made earthenware, and Pierre initiated the production of faience. Pierre's son Antoine Clérissy II (*d* 1743) entered into partnership with his father in 1710 and ran the factory from 1728 (when his father died) until 1736 (when he retired); the business then passed to his son Pierre Clérissy II (1704–94), who sold the factory in 1783. The factory's wares were painted with armorial devices, historical scenes and hunting scenes (e.g. oval dish, *c.* 1700; Sèvres, Mus. N. Cér.) inspired by the engravings of Antonio Tempesta (1555–1660) and painted by François Gaspard Viry (1682–1750). Towards the end of the 17th century and the beginning of the 18th, wares were decorated in blue-and-white with lambrequin borders and strapwork in the style of Jean Berain (e.g. dish, *c.* 1710; London, BM).

Pierre's brother Joseph Clérissy (*c.* 1649–84) established a factory in Saint-Jean-du-Désert, a suburb of MARSEILLE.

Clews. English family of potters, active also in the USA. Ralph and James Clews (both *fl* 1818–36) owned a Staffordshire pottery at Cobridge, Stoke-on-Trent. Their pottery, which was largely made for export to America, is marked CLEWS or CLEWS WARRANTED STAFFORDSHIRE or CLEWS DRESDEN OPAQUE CHINA. In 1834 the factory closed, whereupon James Clews moved to Troy, IN, where he opened a pottery; when this venture failed he returned to England.

E. H. Gustafson: 'A Don Quixote Discovery', *Mag. Ant.,* cxxxii (Oct 1987), p. 740ff

Cleyn, Francis [Clein] [Frantz] (*b* Rostock, Mecklenburg-Schwerin, 1582; *d* London, 1658). German tapestry designer and decorative painter active in England. As a young man he lived in Italy and Denmark before settling in London in 1626. On his arrival in England Cleyn was granted denization and an annuity of £100. He was appointed chief designer of the Mortlake Tapestry Factory, near London, and, after King Charles I purchased the factory in 1637, he was retained at a salary of £250 a year and given an assistant. His work at Mortlake included the designs for the *Hero and Leander* tapestries completed in 1636 (Swedish Royal Col.), the *Horses* and the *Five Senses* series. He also produced distemper cartoons, together with border designs, for the *Acts of the Apostles*. His appointment continued under the Commonwealth (1649–60), and in 1657 he was consulted by the Council of State on the choice of fresh tapestry subjects. Cleyn was otherwise mainly employed in the internal and external decoration of country houses. His painted schemes and tapestry designs introduced to England an exuberant, if sometimes laboured, late Mannerist style whose language he had learnt in Italy from such artists as Polidoro da Caravaggio (*c.* 1499–*c.* 1543). His allegorical programmes can be cumbersome, and his work is perhaps at its best at its most unashamedly decorative (e.g. the painted scheme of ceiling decoration of 1637–9 in the Green Closet at Ham House, Richmond, Surrey, NT). Cleyn's other recorded decorations, including external frescoes at Carew House, London, are lost. His activities may also have extended to furniture design: a set of Italianate shell-backed chairs (London, V&A), supposedly from the Gilt Room at Holland House, London, are traditionally ascribed to him.

J. S. Grioni: 'Hero & Leander: The Morlake Tapestries of Bratislava', *Hali,* xlviii (May–June 1998), pp. 92–7

Clichy Glasshouse. French glass manufactory. In 1837 M. Rouyer and G. Maës founded a glasshouse at Billancourt in Paris. In 1844 it moved to Clichy-la-Garenne, and soon became the third of France's great glass companies (after Baccarat and Saint-Louis). The company concentrated on the production of cheap table glass for export, but also produced opaline, cased glassed and millefiore paperweights; one of its paperweights, a moss ground with a pink 'Clichy rose' at its centre, is the world's most prized paperweight. The factory was merged with the Cristallerie de Sèvres in 1885.

Antique French Glass Paperweights and Related Items: Baccarat, Clichy, St. Louis, Pinchbeck (sale cat., London, Spink & Son, 1982)

Cliff, Clarice (*b* Tunstall, Staffs, 20 Jan 1899; *d* Newcastle-under-Lyme, Staffs, 23 Oct 1972). English potter and designer. She left school in 1912 to work as a pottery apprentice at Lingard, Webster & Co. and in 1916 joined A. J. Wilkinson Ltd near Burslem. In the mid-1920s Wilkinson's had acquired thousands of pieces of old-fashioned earthenwares from the Newport Pottery, and Cliff led a small team which hand-painted them with brightly coloured, geometric patterns. She named the ware 'Bizarre' in January 1928, and it was a success by October of the same year. She then produced her most famous and popular design, 'Crocus', which features flowers between brown and yellow bands. From then, all Cliff's ware was stamped with: *Hand Painted Bizarre by Clarice Cliff, Newport Pottery, England.* Cliff then designed modern shapes; the 1929 'Conical' range consists of cone-shaped bowls, vases and teaware, with triangular handles or feet, decorated with sunbursts and lightning flashes; the 1930 'Stamford' teapot has flat sides and angular edges inspired by the French designer Jean Tetard.

By 1930 Newport Pottery was devoted to producing Cliff's range of wares. She no longer decorated the wares herself, but her designs were copied by 60 apprentices. Less popular than the various tablewares were Cliff's 'Age of Jazz' series of five figures, which were produced from 1930, and the face masks and wall medallions introduced in 1933. By 1932 there were 400 designs on as many shapes. 'Bon Jour' ware is round with flat sides, and 'Biarritz' tableware has oblong plates. Design ranges included 'Applique', 'Delecia', 'Latona' and 'Inspiration'. Cliff's most important range, 'Fantasque', is typified by stylized cottages in landscapes. The most popular ranges were those wares decorated with floral or fruit subjects.

In 1933 Cliff became involved in the 'Art in Industry' project, in which Duncan Grant (1885–1978), Vanessa Bell (1879–1961), Laura Knight (1877–1970), Frank Brangwyn and Graham Sutherland (1903–80) submitted designs for execution on Cliff's tableware, but these did not sell as well as 'Bizarre'. In 1936 the 'Bizarre' trademark was replaced with *Clarice Cliff*; the designs became more subtle, orders decreased and sales declined. After World War II hand-painting was not economical and Cliff concentrated on exporting traditional ware and managing affairs at Newport.

ODNB

L. R. Griffin, L. K. Meisel and S. P. Meisel: *Clarice Cliff: The Bizarre Affair* (London, 1988, rev. 1989)

H. Watson: *Collecting Clarice Cliff* (London, 1988)

L. Griffin: *Clarice Cliff: The Art of Bizarre: A Definitive Centenary Celebration* (London, 2001)

H. Watson and others: *The Complete Clarice Cliff: A Collector's Handbook* (London, 2003)

G. Slater: *Comprehensively Clarice Cliff: An Atlas of over 2,000 Patterns, Shapes and Backstamps* (London, 2005)

Clobbered ware. Porcelain with underglaze decoration that could be overpainted with lacquer or other paints that did not need to be fired. Initially the porcelain was made and underglazed in the East and overpainted in Europe, but eventually clobbered ware was made entirely in Europe.

Clocks and watches. Instruments, most commonly powered by mechanical or electrical means, for measuring the passage of time. The clock was the most sophisticated machine in the world until the 18th century. Clocks are either portable or a fixed architectural feature. A watch is commonly defined as a timepiece carried or worn on the person, although the earliest watches, made in the 16th century, are similar to clocks of the same date.

1. Before 1400. 2. 1400–1500. 3. 1501–*c.* 1590. 4. c. 1590–1700. 5. 1701–1830. 6. After 1830.

1. BEFORE 1400. Weight-driven mechanical clocks first appeared in Europe shortly before 1300. The use of an 'escapement', to enable the stored power of the falling weights to 'escape' in equal units commensurate with the passing of time, increased the accuracy of timekeeping. These clocks had no dials, were used only in religious establishments and merely sounded a bell at pre-arranged intervals to summon the fraternity to worship.

The first Strasbourg Cathedral clock, which took two years to build, was installed in 1354. It included a statuette of the Virgin, before which three figures representing the Magi bowed at noon. A large cock that surmounted the clock simultaneously crowed and flapped its wings. This clock was replaced in 1574 and 1842; of the original clock only the automaton cock survives (Strasbourg, Mus. A. Déc). In England Salisbury Cathedral probably had a clock as early as 1306, although the machine *in situ* was installed in 1386; the clock of Wells Cathedral (on loan to London, Sci. Mus.) dates from before 1392. There are also two 14th-century clocks in France: in the Rue du Gros Horloge at Rouen and on the church of Notre-Dame at Dijon, but only the former is reasonably complete.

2. 1400–1500. Large 15th-century automata clocks have been restored many times, and it is difficult to ascertain the amount of original machinery that survives. Examples include the automata clock (rest. 1948) on the Old Town Hall in Prague, previously thought to have dated from 1490, although now dated as early as 1410. It incorporates a lower dial with the signs of the zodiac, automata of the Twelve Apostles that appear every hour and a figure representing Death that tolls a bell and passes across two windows above the upper, astronomical dial. At the same time three other figures, described as the 'Miser', the 'Indulger' and the 'Turk', appear. A feature of many 15th-century tower clocks (also known as 'turret clocks') was the striking of a bell by two wooden automata known as 'jacks' or 'jaquemarts'. The first such figures were either angels or men-at-arms, but in the second half of the 15th century figures of blackamoors were introduced. This fashion can be seen on the clock (1499) on the Torre dell'Orologio in the Piazza S Marco, Venice.

Although large mechanical clocks originally performed no more than an alarm function in ecclesiastical establishments, one early example of a much smaller type of 'alarm' clock survives (priv. col.). Made in Italy probably in the 15th century, it is 250 mm high. The two pillars between which the mechanism is deployed have moulded capitals and bases, and one of the main wheels of the mechanism has crenellated 'teeth'. The 24-hour dial, which has holes to accommodate pins that trigger the alarm, rotates against a fixed hand. Small 'alarm' clocks, probably for religious use, were also made in Nuremberg; there are two examples in the Germanisches Nationalmuseum: the first, from the church of St Sebaldus, dates from *c.* 1400, while the second is probably from the very early 16th century. Both are completely plain and were designed to be mounted on the wall.

Surviving domestic clocks made before 1550 are rare and are usually scaled-down versions of tower clocks. In these smaller clocks the movement is contained within an open frame surmounted by one or more bells, which are supported by four metal straps springing from each corner and meeting over the top. These straps, together with the corner-posts of the open frame, are often decorated with crockets or similar Gothic ornament, hence their description as 'Gothic' clocks.

By the end of the 15th century the most elaborate clocks were produced in Italy, where smaller, portable clocks first appeared, leading eventually to the development of the watch. This was dependent on the use of a different type of mechanical power, since no clock that is weight-driven is easily portable. An Italian engineer, Comino da Pontevico, writing in 1482, referred to a clock driven by 'a ribbon of tempered steel fastened in a brass barrel': this is the mainspring.

3. 1501–*c.* 1590. Decoration on domestic clocks and watches, particularly those made in Germany and France, became more elaborate in the 16th century, reaching a peak in the 17th. Cases and dials were decorated, as well as movements, the back plates protecting the movement and the pillars that separate the back and front plates.

(i) Clocks. The earliest extant dated spring-driven clock (diam. 250 mm; London, Soc. Antiqua.) is drum-shaped, signed *Jacob Zech* (Jacob the Czech, *d* 1540) and bears on its spring-barrel the date 1525.

Figure-clock in form of a rooster, gilt bronze, copper, silver with painted cockscomb and feathers, from southern Germany, 1580 – 90 (New York, Private Collection)

Armorials included in the engraved decoration on the band (the central component of a drum-shaped clock- or watchcase, inside which the movement fits, between the dial and the back plate) indicate that it was made for Sigismund I, King of Poland (*reg* 1506–48), for presentation to his wife, Bona Sforza (1494–1557). The complicated horizontal dial incorporates various indications relating to astrology, including a band of signs of the zodiac enclosing a narrower band with the divisions BONUM, MEDIUM and MALUM, indicating the most propitious or unsuitable times to embark on enterprises. The figure 'II' on this dial is rendered as 'z', a feature adopted on later German watches. Spring-driven clocks with vertical dials from this period are similar to their weight-driven counterparts, with 'four-poster' movements in the manner of 'Gothic' clocks.

Drum-shaped, spring-driven table clocks from the second half of the 16th century are often square or hexagonal, usually mounted on feet and with a horizontal dial. Cases tend to be of gilt brass with the hour (or chapter) ring, which forms the main part of the dial, in silver. The feet—four for the square type but only three for the hexagonal—are often turned or carved grotesque feet or claws. Side panels are silver or silver gilt, with glass or rock crystal insets, and elements of the mechanism, even though normally hidden from view, are usually lavishly pierced and engraved with foliate and other motifs.

Two other clock styles appeared in the late 16th century. The tabernacle clock, derived partly from

the 'Gothic' type, is commonly 70–100 mm square and 150–250 mm high, with the movement made entirely of steel. This is enclosed within decorated gilt-brass plates, with the dial or chapter ring on the front. Pillar clocks, on the other hand, have a base housing the movement. The base is connected to the dial by a pillar, often taking the form of a figure holding the dial above its head. In later examples the pillar is surmounted by a rotating globe with an hour-band around its equator that indicates against a 'hand' fixed to the globe frame or carried by a figure mounted on the base.

The British Museum, London, has fine examples of table, tabernacle and pillar clocks, and its collection also includes a number of elaborate, late 16th-century clocks that fall into no clearly defined category. One example is the superb 'nef' or three-masted ship-clock, said to have been made *c.* 1580 by the clockmaker Hans Schlottheim (1547–1625) of Augsburg for the emperor Rudolf II. The dial is so small (diam. 60 mm) that it is obscured among the ornament; the striking of the hours and chiming of the quarters is performed by figures in the two crows' nests on the mainmast, in each of which there is an inverted bell. Originally mounted on a wheeled carriage, the ship was propelled by its clockwork while firing its cannon. Another example, made for Pope Pius V in 1589 by Isaac Habrecht (1544–1620), in imitation of the second clock for Strasbourg Cathedral (1574; also by Habrecht), is over 1.2 m high and operates on three levels. It includes two automata that move a scythe and an hour-glass every time the clock strikes, while the top level has four sections of automata and, at the apex, a cock that crows and flaps its wings when the quarters chime.

(ii) Watches. During the 16th century smaller versions of spring-driven clocks with horizontal dials for carrying on the person were made. In 1512 Johann Cochläus (1479–1552) of Nuremberg, in his *Cosmographia pomponii mele*, described Peter Henlein (*c.* 1479–1542) as making 'out of a small quantity of iron, horologia devised with very many wheels, and these horologia, in any position and without any weights, both indicate and strike for 40 hours, even when they are carried on the breast or in the purse'. The Nuremberg Staatsarchiv contains a record of a payment to Henlein of 15 florins for a gilt musk-ball with a watch in 1524. The only other recorded German watchmaker from this period is Caspar Werner (1528–57).

A number of watchmakers were also active in France during the 16th century. Florimond Robertet, Treasurer to three French kings, left 12 watches when he died in 1532, 'of which seven are striking and the other five silent, in cases of gold, silver and brass', according to the inventory prepared by his widow (*Mém. Soc. N. Antiqua. France*, 3rd ser., x (1868)). The inventory that describes these watches also includes the first use of the word *montre* as specifically applied to a timepiece carried on the person.

At Blois, the first centre of French clock- and watch-making, six craftsmen were active during the first half of the 16th century, two being Horlogers du Roi.

The earliest watches took one of two forms: spherical musk-balls (e.g. by Jacques de La Garde, 1552; London, N. Mar. Mus) or a drum-shaped form 50–80 mm in diameter with a horizontal dial. The spherical design was popular only for a short period, and by the mid-16th century the drum shape—described also as 'tambour'—became shallower and incorporated over the dial a hinged cover that was pierced so that the hand and hour numerals were visible. This type of watch remained fashionable from about 1540 to 1590. Watches from the last quarter of the 16th century in octagonal cases are also extant, though rare. The cases of all surviving 16th-century watches are of gilt metal. No English watch dating from before 1580 survives, and most extant early examples incorporate both French and German characteristics; English watchmakers of the late 16th century include Bartholomew Newsam (*fl* 1568–93), Randolf Bull (*fl c.* 1582–1617) and Francis Nawe (*fl* 1582–1613).

4. *c.* 1590–1700. British clock- and watchmaking was in the ascendant during the 17th century, during the second half of which the minute hand began to appear. Two great technical advances, both directed towards the more precise measurement of time, were the application of the pendulum to clocks from *c.* 1657, coupled with the addition of its counterpart, the balance spring, to watches in 1675, and the invention of the anchor escapement for clocks *c.* 1670.

(i) Clocks. (ii) Watches.

(i) Clocks. The spring-driven, gilt-brass table clock with a horizontal dial continued to be popular well into the 18th century. English table clocks from the 17th century are rare, most being German. In the second half of the 17th century, with the appearance of the wooden case, two new styles of clock were introduced, the so-called bracket clock and the longcase ('grandfather') clock. The first type is spring-driven and the second powered by weights, and both are controlled by a pendulum, which was introduced in the Netherlands. Despite its name, the bracket clock usually had no fixed position, although later French examples with matching brackets are extant. Until about 1675 both bracket and longcase clocks had many features in common. The longcase clock, however, never became popular in Europe, except in the Netherlands, where a style was developed incorporating a bulbous base and a hood surmounted by gilt figures instead of finials.

(a) Britain. In the first decade of the 17th century the lantern clock was introduced in Britain. Consisting of an enclosed 'four-poster' movement that can strike the hours and provide an alarm facility, this type of clock also has flat surfaces for engraved decoration on all four sides and often pierced cresting and finials. Longcase clocks appeared from 1659. The earliest examples are about 1.9 m high, with dials

203–215 mm square. The case is in three sections—plinth and trunk containing the weights and pendulum, and hood containing the mechanism and dial—and the trunk door, with three panels, is flush-fitting. At the top of the trunk is a convex moulding, on which the hood sits. The hood has no door and after releasing a locking catch must be lifted upwards on grooves in order to wind up the mechanism.

Most early bracket and longcase clocks have black wooden cases—usually oak veneered with ebony, but king-wood, olive-wood and lignum vitae were also used. The architectural design of both types incorporates a triangular pediment to the top or hood, often with a central gilt escutcheon and three gilt finials, while the base is supported on gilt feet. The square dial openings are often flanked by Corinthian columns with gilt capitals and bases.

A short-lived fashion between 1660 and 1675 was the 'hooded' wall clock: an eight-day clock (capable of going for 8 days after one winding) enclosed in a hood similar in design to those of longcase and bracket clocks but with the weights hanging exposed beneath. This type of clock was made by some of the best clockmakers in London. A transitional style of case for bracket and longcase clocks had a top or hood made of plain, chamfered panels supported on barley-twist columns, but from about 1670 the introduction of the so-called 'bell' top—dome-shaped and at first shallow but later deeper—made it possible to fit a carrying handle to bracket clocks. A plain, glazed door across the front of the clock was also used on bracket clocks. The frame of the door often bears gilt escutcheons: one for the keyhole and one on the other side to balance it aesthetically. The top part of the case generally incorporates a gilt-metal fret, backed with silk, to permit the sound of the bell to be heard.

Dials were also elaborately decorated in the 17th century. Narrow, silver or silvered chapter rings, either solid or 'skeletonized' (with the spaces between the hour numerals cut away), were mounted on plain, matted dial plates—the latter often engraved with the newly introduced tulip motif. The beautiful 'cherub' spandrel was used to fill the four triangular spaces outside the chapter ring. Although generally made of gilt metal, silver-winged cherubs' heads are also occasionally found. Other features on the dial include the maker's name, often in Latin, engraved on the dial plate below the chapter ring, a calendar aperture and, where appropriate, an alarm-setting dial in the form of a silver or silvered disc, about 50 mm in diameter, set centrally below the hands. The centre of the dial is also sometimes engraved with a spiral or floral pattern. Movements are generally plain, apart from a boldly engraved maker's name across the back plate and a Tudor rose or similar motif engraved on the striking mechanism count wheel (regulating how many times the hour bell was struck at each hour), which was mounted outside the back plate at this time. The movement plates are usually separated by baluster-shaped pillars.

Cases for bracket clocks with pedimented tops were not made after 1675; those with panelled tops and columns were popular until the 1680s. Flat-topped longcase clocks with an openwork cresting appeared *c.* 1675. The height of longcase clocks increased to 2.1 m from 1675, although miniature longcase clocks, only 1.5 m high but otherwise accurate in every detail, were used during this period. From about 1680, under the influence of Dutch cabinet-making, panels of inlaid decoration became common, usually with floral or star patterns and at first confined to trunk doors and plinths. Marquetry was introduced towards the end of the 17th century (*see under* MARQUETRY). Cases from the 1680s and 1690s are of olive-wood or walnut, sometimes veneered with laburnum in the 'oyster' pattern. From around 1680, to match an increase in the height of rooms in new houses, the domed tops and hoods of bracket and longcase clocks became larger. Pillars flanking the dial openings changed from barley-twist to plain slender columns by 1690. The lift-up hood remained in general use until 1700, but its pedimented top had disappeared by 1685.

From about 1675 dials were 255 mm square, and movement back plates were engraved with a variety of complex, decorative motifs, first the fashionable tulip variety but, after 1690, more abstract designs, sometimes incorporating the maker's name in a cartouche. From about 1690 it also became the general practice to inscribe the maker's name on the chapter ring rather than below it on the dial plate. The cock or bracket, screwed to the back plate and supporting the rear bearing of the pendulum, was also decorated.

During the last quarter of the 17th century the greatest English clockmaker, Thomas Tompion (1639–1713), was active in London. Admitted to the Clockmakers' Company in 1671, he developed the wider chapter ring, permitting larger, more legible hour and minute numerals, as well as a larger, more decorative hour-hand. Another dial feature, introduced by Tompion between 1690 and 1695, was the 'false pendulum', a slit in the dial behind which a gilt bob swung in unison with the pendulum. Tompion invented the break-arch dial (*see* §5(i)(a) below), a feature that appears on a clock that he made for William III in 1695 (London, BM). Tompion also replaced cherub spandrels with tiny corner dials for technical innovations concerning regulation, striking mechanisms and pendulum locking while the clock was in transit (e.g. of *c.* 1700; London, Clockmakers' Co.). At the end of the 17th century Tompion's partner, George Graham (1673–1751), was also active, initially only as Tompion's assistant, since he was not admitted to the Clockmakers' Company until 1695.

(b) Europe. Some notable clock styles were developed in Europe at this time. In the Netherlands, for example, Zaandam clocks were popular. These are beautiful, weight-driven, hooded wall clocks that rest on two brackets and have four corner pillars and a dial plate that is usually covered in velvet, on which a metal chapter ring and spandrel ornaments are displayed. Rare early pendulum clocks from the centres of Austrian clockmaking (Vienna, Prague and Innsbruck) have posted movements and stand either on a bracket or on a case with pillars. Some have complicated movements relating to astronomy that necessitate dials on all four sides; these display English influence by the inclusion of cherub spandrels. Clocks made almost entirely of wood were produced in the Black Forest area of Germany from the mid-17th century.

French clocks are totally different from those made in England, since clocks were viewed principally as furniture and, thus, as a part of interior decoration. In France the maker of the clockcase is considered just as important as the maker of the movement. The early French pendulum clock, known as the 'Religieuse', with a velvet-covered plate to set off the metal dial features, is rectangular, with a flat, arched or pedimented top. It either stands on feet or hangs on the wall.

(c) Japan. Clocks were manufactured in Japan from the early 17th century. These were initially weight-driven wall clocks, similar to lantern clocks, with side plates encasing the movement and surmounted by a bell. No other types were developed in Japan until the early 19th century. The dials of these clocks were adapted to the Japanese system of time measurement, used until 1873. Both day and night were considered to be six hours long throughout the year, and the counting of the hours was performed backwards from nine to four, as the numbers one, two and three were sacred and reserved for religious use.

(ii) Watches. At the end of the 16th century and the beginning of the 17th a type of watchcase recognizable as such in the 20th century emerged (e.g. by Hans Schniep, *c.* 1590; London, BM). It is circular, with its band bowed outwards and both lid and back slightly convex. Above 12 o'clock there is a loose ring for suspension, which is often balanced by an ornamental pendant at 6 o'clock, somewhat in the style of Renaissance jewellery. The appearance of this style probably overlapped the decline of the 'tambour' case; the late 16th-century type similarly disappeared *c.* 1640. During the early 17th century octagonal and then oval watches were made, the latter slowly developing by the middle of the century into the egg-shaped, British 'Puritan' watch, as it was later known. French and Swiss watchmakers also used oval and octagonal cases, while the German industry declined during the Thirty Years War. Watches were also disguised as skulls, books, dogs, birds, crosses and flower-buds; these novelties are known as 'form watches'. An enormous range of decoration was applied to watchcases in the 17th century. Casting, chiselling, piercing, engraving, chasing and embossing were widely used. Between 1600 and 1675 cases were made of rock crystal—usually clear but sometimes of the much rarer opaque type; amber, ivory and agate panels were also used. All the principal enamelling techniques can be found on 17th-century

watchcases and dials; these include champlevé, cloisonné and basse-taille.

The 'pair-case' style of watch, introduced at this time, consisted of the addition of a protective cover to an expensive watchcase. These outer cases were at first made of leather, sometimes tooled. By the mid-17th century it had become customary to use the outer case all the time, and consequently these cases were themselves elaborately decorated. By 1670 the inner case had become plain, and only the outer case was decorated; by about 1680 watches for daily use had two plain cases, the outer excluding dust and dirt from entering the movement through the keyhole in the back of the inner case. The 'pair-case' style was not adopted in France, where watches were wound through the dials. The style of watch known as an 'oignon', due to its rotund shape, is particularly French.

During the second half of the 17th century travelling or coach watches became fashionable. These are large watches, 75 mm to 125 mm in diameter, and are a form of 'clock-watch', striking the hours automatically; alarm and repeating facilities are also common (the latter involving an additional mechanism allowing the time to be sounded on demand on a bell or gong). This type was made until about 1800.

Throughout the century watch dials were made of silver, gilt metal or even gold, to match the material used for the cases. Multiple dials, incorporating calendar work to indicate the days of the month (and, later, the week), became fashionable. The chapter ring was initially simply engraved, but an applied silver ring or, occasionally, a silver disc gave a greater decorative contrast; the surrounding part of the dial was often further decorated with floral designs, a face or a reclining figure. Engraving at the centre of the dial usually depicted a pastoral scene. In the late 17th century high relief decoration became common;

deeply cut hour numerals filled with black engraver's wax are known as champlevé dials. Lavish enamelled watches were produced, for example by the Huaud family in Geneva.

From *c.* 1675 there was much experimentation directed towards indicating both hours and minutes on one dial; dial design did not become standardized until about 1700, even though concentric hour and minute hands and white enamel dials had been introduced by 1680. Four versions of dial design were established: the 'sun and moon' (which distinguished between daytime and nighttime hours), the 'wandering hour' (no hands; each hour numeral moved around a fixed semi-circular scale marked with the minutes), the six-hour dial and the rarer, differential dial (no hour hand; a small chapter ring, concentric with the minute hand, kept the appropriate hour numeral under the hand). Only the first type is relatively common, the last two being particularly rare. The 'wandering hour' version frequently incorporates the royal coat of arms displayed on the dial or the cock or a miniature painting of the monarch. The significance of such features has not yet been established.

Watch movements were also decorated. At first only the bracket on the back of the movement (the balance or watch cock) was pierced and engraved; this type of decoration gradually occupied more of the back plate, as well as the slide plate housing the regulatory mechanism, decorated *en suite* after 1675 (e.g. two movements by Daniel Quare, *c.* 1700; London, Clockmakers' Co.; priv. col.). The pillars between front and back plates were made in a great variety of styles in English watches, mainly the tulip, 'Egyptian' and baluster forms; French 'oignon' watches initially incorporated 'Egyptian' pillars (shaped like inverted and elongated pyramids) and then plain baluster versions.

5. 1701–1830. The use of elaborate decoration on clocks and watches declined in the 18th century, reflecting a greater interest in precision time measurement. In 1714 an Act of Parliament in Britain offered a substantial prize for a more precise means of calculating longitude and, by implication, a timekeeper with far greater accuracy. Marine chronometry was thus introduced; timepieces for use at sea are primarily scientific instruments and are largely devoid of decoration. Pocket chronometers, with smaller versions of the same mechanism, were made from the mid-1770s.

(i) Clocks. (ii) Watches.

(i) Clocks.

(a) Britain. In the first half of the 18th century English bracket clocks changed little in form and style. Ebony or ebonized fruit-wood continued to be popular, but walnut and lacquered cases became increasingly common. While cherub spandrels continued to be used in dial openings, a more common feature was a small head of a woman set into a formal design. By 1725 the break-arch dial was widespread, the arch projecting from the centre of its top edge

Watch by Edward East, silver, diam. 90 mm, London, *c.* 1645 (London, Victoria and Albert Museum)

providing added space above the chapter ring that was usually employed for a calendar or striking mechanism. The maker's name appeared either on the chapter ring or on the dial plate inside it, while spandrels became arabesque and of varying quality. Back plates were engraved, although designs became much simpler.

After 1750 a round glass held in a fixed brass bezel exactly matching the size and shape of the dial and inset into a solid door dispensed with the need for spandrels. The dial thus became a one-piece, engraved, silvered disc with the maker's name on the centre. This was followed *c.* 1770 by the break-arch case with a round dial. From 1780 to *c.* 1810 there was a short-lived fashion for the balloon clock, a type of bracket clock with a waisted case, often made in satin-wood with a gilt finial and feet and with an inlaid patera or similar decoration on its plinth. Around 1800 access to the dial of bracket clocks was achieved by hinging the brass bezel with its glass, obviating the need for a door to form the front of the case.

Longcase clocks made during the first half of the 18th century are also similar to those produced in the 17th century. Fashion dictated a slight increase in dimensions, with the height of the clock rising to 2.5 m with dials 300 mm square. The moulding supporting the hood became concave instead of convex, and hoods from this period have glazed access doors across the front, with the top consisting of a flat dome with three ball finials. The break-arch top was used from the mid-18th century, and lacquered and japanned cases remained popular, though walnut continued to be used for high-quality clocks. All-over marquetry deteriorated into the commonplace 'seaweed' pattern. The dial openings and features on mid-18th-century longcase clocks are similar to those on bracket clocks. The trunk door, originally rectangular, was now usually arched, while the angles of the case were chamfered. Broken pediments, evolving into curvilinear 'horns', often surmounted the hood.

From about 1750 mahogany became popular for longcase clockcases. The 'pagoda' top of the hood consisted of two concave curves joined by a convex one to produce a roughly bell-shaped pediment. The gilt-brass dial with applied chapter ring and spandrels was gradually superseded by a one-piece, silvered dial, as on bracket clocks, while, from about 1775, iron dials painted white with black numerals and coloured, painted spandrels, usually of flowers but sometimes representing the Four Seasons, became popular. Calendar work, moon phases or tidal indications or such simple automata as a windmill or a rocking ship were used in the break-arch. Towards the end of the 18th century longcase clocks with trunks that tapered towards their bases were made, following an original design by Chippendale.

During the 18th century a number of 'exhibition' clocks, inspired by the earlier, highly complex astronomical clocks, were produced in Britain. One example (Liverpool Mus.), made by Jacob Lovelace

(1695–1755) of Exeter, is said to have taken 30 years to build and weighs nearly half a tonne. It originally incorporated a variety of automata, for example a 'bird organ' and a belfry with six ringers, as well as an organ. Another example, known as 'The Microcosm' in the 18th century, was built by Henry Bridges (1697–1754) of Waltham Abbey, Essex, around 1734. Apart from its technical complexity—its mechanism was said to include 1200 wheels and pinions—its main feature was an organ that performed automatically or could be played from a keyboard. This clock, lacking its magnificent original case, is in the British Museum, London.

Charles Clay (*d* 1740) and the father and son John Pyke (*d* 1762) and George Pyke (*b* ?1715) were the most prominent makers of elaborate organ clocks. George Frideric Handel (1685–1759) composed melodies specially for their organs, while the dial paintings were executed by Jacopo Amigoni (*c.* 1685–1752) and the embossed silver dial mounts by Michael Rysbrack (1694–1770; examples in London, Kensington Pal., Royal Col.; London, Mus. London). From 1750 to 1830 a type of clock erroneously called an 'Act of Parliament' clock, but more properly described as a tavern clock, was popular: this is a wall clock with a wooden dial generally painted black with gold numerals and about 750 mm in diameter, with a small drop trunk case below it to house the weight and pendulum. The finest examples often have chinoiserie decoration. At the end of the 18th century the high-precision observatory clock, known as a regulator, was produced. It incorporates a case with severe lines and is usually in the architectural style of early bracket and longcase clocks.

(b) Europe and the USA. In the Netherlands a design from Friesland known as a *stoeltjesklok* (stool clock) appeared in the early 18th century. The clock sits on a 'stool' on a decorative wall bracket that incorporates a canopy. Both this feature and the dial are covered with gilded lead ornament; the iron dial plate is usually painted with floral and landscape designs. The *staartklok*, another type developed in Friesland that appeared in the second half of the 18th century, is similar in form to the hood of a longcase clock, but it hangs on the wall, with the pendulum contained beneath in a flat, glass-fronted case.

French bracket clocks (*horloges de cheminée*) usually had matching brackets in the 18th century, but they were also often placed on tall, tapering pedestals. These clocks, with curved cases decorated with boulle and ormolu, are totally unlike their English counterparts. The typical French clock dial, often called a '13-piece' dial, has a central enamel plaque surrounded by 12 small plaques inscribed with hour numerals. French clock cases made after 1750 are often signed and are usually supported on bronze animals or decorated with porcelain flowers. Wall-mounted cartel clocks set in a frame of cast and gilt bronze (e.g. of 1750–60; Paris, Mus. A. Déc) or carved gilt wood matched the contemporary French taste for carved and gilded wall panelling. Other pop-

Elephant clock, ebony, bronze and ormolu stand, from France, mid-18th century (London, Victoria and Albert Museum)

ular decorative techniques included painted horn panels set in ormolu, and a wide colour range could be obtained using *vernis Martin*. In the late 18th century symmetrical designs were revived, with smaller dials; marble with gilt-bronze decoration became fashionable for smaller clocks. The portico clock, with a portico top supported on columns or caryatids, the clock hung between them, and the lyre clock, in which the frame of the lyre surrounds the dial and the gridiron pendulum forms its 'strings', were both introduced at the end of the 18th century. The carriage clock was also invented at this time by Abraham-Louis Breguet (1747–1823) but was not widely popular until the mid-19th century.

In Austria, English influence was dominant in clock design, but there was a tendency for clockmakers to use the bulbous, provincial, French style of case. About 1780, however, the 'Vienna Regulator', a wall clock often with a pediment-shaped top and glass panels on all sides, first appeared, and versions were made until the end of the 19th century. Austrian bracket clocks, combining elements of both French and English styles, were replaced *c*. 1780 by a variety of styles generally known as *Stockuhr* or *Stutzuhr* (short clocks). Common features on these clocks include a colonnaded base supporting the dial and movement and flanking ormolu ornaments, often displaying a dolphin motif. In the early 19th century tiny 'zappler' clocks, so-called from the rapid motion of the pendulum, were developed.

American clocks dating before 1800 were made by immigrants and are indistinguishable from their English counterparts. Eli Terry (1772–1853) was the first craftsman in the USA to produce cheap clocks in large quantities, initially with wooden, later with brass movements. American wall clocks are found in three principal styles: the banjo, lyre and girandole. The first type, patented in 1802 by Simon Willard (1753–1848), has a square, boxlike base from which a tapering trunk rises, surmounted by a round dial with an eagle finial. The lyre design is similar to the banjo except that the trunk is lyre-shaped and heavily carved; the girandole is also like the banjo style but has a round base instead of a square one. Pendulum 'shelf' clocks, first marketed by Simon Willard and his brother Aaron Willard (1757–1814), reached a peak in the style known as 'pillar and scroll', introduced by Eli Terry in 1817.

(ii) Watches. During the 18th century white enamel dials on watches replaced the metal versions, and the use of concentric minute hands became common. The quality of decoration on movements, however, gradually degenerated. Dust caps to protect the movement, uncommon before 1725, are usually of gilt metal, although some are of silver. From about 1725 the 'foot' of the engraved balance cock—that part screwed to the plate—was solid rather than pierced, and by the last quarter of the century the 'table' protecting the balance became increasingly wedge-shaped (rather than round) and solid. Watchmakers in several European countries favoured the balance bridge—roughly oval in form and screwed to the plate in two places to give added rigidity—rather than the cock.

Repoussé work was increasingly used to decorate watchcases in the 18th century. Before 1715 this was generally confined to radial fluting. The best repoussé work was produced between 1725 and 1750; after 1770 it was rarely used. Deep relief could be obtained by working a second sheet of metal, which was then soldered to the main carcase. The best repoussé cases usually represent allegorical or mythological scenes and are signed by the artist. A third type of case, with a glazed back to display the repoussé work, was sometimes supplied for extra protection.

Outer cases could also be covered in black, green or white shagreen. Pinchbeck was used from 1720. Tortoiseshell and leather cases are often decorated with pinwork (*piqué*), and the tortoiseshell is often inlaid with fine patterns in silver or gold. Underpainted horn cases, first intended to simulate tortoiseshell but later depicting ferns, butterflies and other insects and figure scenes, also appeared. Enamel was less commonly used for watchcases in the 18th century and is often confined simply to a panel, sometimes heraldic, on the back of the case. Enginturning (guilloche) is rarely found on watchcases before about 1780; it is sometimes covered with translucent enamel with split-pearl bezels on the back and front. Watchcases made of idiosyncratic materials, for example Chelsea porcelain, are occasionally found.

In the second half of the 18th century in Europe, particularly in France, there was a dramatic change towards a slimmer, less ornamented and more elegant type of watch. One of the leading watchmakers in this movement was Abraham-Louis Breguet. In Britain, however, the so-called hunting and half-hunting watchcases—the first denoting a solid hinged cover over the dial, the second a cover with a small, round, glass 'window' in the centre, large enough to read the position of the hands without opening it—were popular from 1800 to 1810. 'Keyless winding', by means of a crown or button on the pendant, was invented by Thomas Prest (*c.* 1770–1855) in the 1820s; decoration on such watches is mostly restricted to engine-turning on the back, often with a buckled garter at the centre, within which a monogram may be engraved.

6. AFTER 1830. After 1830 the evolution of national styles in clocks and watches gradually declined; watches, in particular, became more utilitarian, with elegance inherent in their slim form rather than in applied decoration. In the USA, then in Germany and France and, by the 1870s, in Switzerland, mass production was adopted, although craft manufacture continued in Britain until the 1930s. In the 20th century modern technology and the use of electrically powered mechanisms enabled timepieces to be accurate to within one second in hundreds of years.

(i) Clocks. The opulence of French clocks continued well into the 19th century, with the elaborate, sculptural cases reflecting fashions in interior design. After about 1830, however, elements of Gothic Revival decoration appeared. The modern style of carriage

Henry Van de Velde: clock, 1916 (Otterlo, Hoge Veluwe National Park, St Hubertus Lodge)

clock was designed by Paul Garnier (1801–69) of Paris. France generated such a profitable export trade from carriage clocks that examples made after about 1850 often bear the name of the retailer rather than that of the maker. Dials on carriage clocks are of white enamel or have engine-turned decoration on gilt or silvered metal; both dials and side-panels are often decorative, with such materials as Limoges enamel, porcelain and marble replacing the original bevelled glass.

Two characteristic Japanese styles of clock appeared about 1830. The small, spring-driven, portable clock, similar to an English bracket clock but with elaborately decorated movement plates and glazed side panels, had a carrying handle on top, while the weight-driven pillar clock, so-called because it was intended to hang on the central pillar of a house, was the cheapest timepiece available. In both types, complex provisions were made to accommodate the peculiarities of the Japanese timekeeping system used until 1873.

An export business was developed in Germany in both cheap brass movements and the all-wood products that originated from the Black Forest region. The cuckoo clock, based on an earlier design, did not appear in its familiar 'chalet-style' case until about 1850. In Austria the 'Vienna Regulator' continued to be produced in the 19th century.

From about 1840 the average household clock in Britain was an American or German import. Some examples are in an over-elaborate Gothic style, with the metal dial and mounts similar to 15th-century 'Gothic' clocks. Yet fine clocks were also handmade in revival styles by a slowly declining number of firms. Small bracket clocks from this period, often resembling wooden-cased carriage clocks, are of high quality, as are the metal-cased carriage clocks that were produced by such firms as Dent, Frodsham & McCabe. Innovations in mechanisms also occurred: the use of electricity to drive a clock pendulum was pioneered by the Scotsman Alexander Bain (*c.* 1811–77) during a series of experiments conducted from 1840 to 1852. The most typically British type of clock made throughout the 19th century until the beginning of World War I was the skeleton clock, produced in London, Birmingham, Liverpool, Prescot on Merseyside and Derby. Skeleton clocks consist of an uncased movement, mounted on a base and covered with a glass dome, with its plates elaborately fretted to represent such Gothic churches as York Minster and Westminster Abbey or scrolled to depict hearts, lyres and similar motifs. The 19th century also saw the installation in 1859 of Britain's largest clock, the Great Clock of Westminster, more usually called 'Big Ben' after its hour bell (designed by Sir Benjamin Hall, Chief Commissioner of Works at the time).

No clearly identifiable style of clock emerged in the 20th century; clocks were normally based on earlier styles but were not usually of high quality. Printed paper dials, for example, largely replaced beautiful hand-painted white enamel dials. Two clock types are, however, notable. The electrically powered 'Eureka' clock, originating in the USA, was licensed for manufacture in 14 countries yet seems to have reached its greatest development in Britain. It was first marketed in 1909, but production ceased with the advent of World War I. This type of clock was beautifully made; an enormous variety of different case styles was available, and the movement is frequently ornamented with two splendid turned finials.

The so-called 400-day clock, although developed in the USA in the 19th century, was subsequently manufactured in Germany. It has an uncased movement covered by a glass dome, and its most notable feature is a torsion pendulum, with a 'bob' oscillating horizontally. In early clocks of this type, the 'bob' is a lead-loaded brass disc, but four brass balls were later used. The movement also incorporates such other small, decorative features as finials. Such clocks continue to be made. The 'Atmos' clock, first produced in 1926, represented a further development of the same basic mechanical principle, although it was wound by the movement of aneroid bellows in response to changes in atmospheric pressure. Another development was the domestic clock controlled by regular signals from a radio beacon. Indeed, the evolution of clocks throughout the 20th century was marked by the development of high-technology precision timekeepers for both home and scientific use, while the mechanical timekeepers that were still produced were derivatives of earlier styles.

(ii) *Watches*. During the 19th and 20th centuries national styles in watchmaking became less distinct; the decoration of watches diminished in direct proportion to the improvement in their timekeeping capability. Stylized decoration of the movement was confined to the wedge-shaped cock. The pair-cased watch, however, fashionable since the 17th century, was still popular in the mid-19th century in some rural areas of Britain, and, despite improvements in mechanisms, winding a watch with a key inserted through the back cover or through the dial remained the usual practice until around 1880.

In the USA, the companies of Elgin, Waltham and Hamilton produced factory-made precision watches with great success. By contrast, the firms of Auburndale, Waterbury and Ingersoll were known for their production of cheap and basic watches. A tiny number of craftsmen, however, for example Charles Fasoldt (1818–98) and Albert Potter (1836–1908), made custom-built, hand-finished watches of the highest quality.

The French industry was now in decline, with watchmakers becoming increasingly dependent on Switzerland for parts. In Germany high-precision watches and chronometers were produced by Adolph Lange at Glasshütte. In Switzerland, however, large-scale watch manufacture started to compete with that of the USA, which it was eventually to supersede. In 1867 Georges-Frédéric Roskopf (1813–89) produced a basic watch that sold for 20 francs; Switzerland's main success, however, was in the mass production of medium- to very high-grade watches.

By 1880 the Swiss firm of Girard-Perregaux was supplying German naval officers in Berlin with wristwatches about 250 mm in diameter in gold cases. In Britain the *Horological Journal* of December 1887 also reported that 'it has been the fashion for some time past for ladies, when riding or hunting, to wear their watches in leather bracelets strapped to the wrist'. These small watches, imported from Switzerland, could also be suspended from a brooch. Bracelets were also fitted with fixed or removable watches, and, consequently, the wristwatch was developed.

Wristwatches quickly became the most popular type of watch in the 20th century, with Switzerland the largest producer. Every feature that could be applied to a pocket watch—a self-winding facility, a calendar, hour-striking mechanisms, an alarm and a chronograph—could also be built into a wristwatch. The most prominent manufacturers include Rolex, Patek Phillipe, Universal and Longines, and the finest examples of their products from 1930 to 1960 are widely collected. Demand for pocket watches is mostly confined to the ultra-thin, so-called 'dress watch'.

In Britain craft methods of manufacture ceased during the Depression of the 1930s and World War II. There was no competition with the mass-produced watches made in Switzerland and Japan. Around 1957 the electric wristwatch was developed separately in France and the USA and later in Germany and Switzerland. By 1960 the Swiss Bulova 'Accutron' watch mechanism, which measured time by 'counting' the vibrations of a magnetically activated tuning fork, was developed in the USA for use as a time switch in space, as well as in the form of a wristwatch movement. Although the quartz crystal clock had been invented as early as 1929, its successful miniaturization was not accomplished until 1967; the Japanese firm of Seiko was the first to market a quartz watch. By the 1980s the 'Swatch', a quartz watch in a moulded plastic case from Switzerland, was produced in a vast variety of designs, often by important artists and often made in limited editions. Despite its amazing accuracy, the quartz watch had not wholly displaced the mechanical watch in the early 21st century.

C. Clutton and G. Daniels: *Watches: A Complete History of the Technical and Decorative Development of the Watch* (London, 1965, 3/1979)
C. Allix and P. Bonnert: *Carriage Clocks: Their History and Development* (Woodbridge, 1974)
B. Loomes: *The White Dial Clock* (Newton Abbot, 1974)
C. H. Bailey: *Two Hundred Years of American Clocks & Watches* (Englewood Cliffs, 1975)
C. F. C. Beeson: *English Church Clocks, 1280–1850* (Ashford, 1977)
R. E. Rose: *English Dial Clocks* (Woodbridge, 1978)
A. Nicholls: *English Bracket and Mantel Clocks* (Poole, 1981)
T. Robinson: *The Longcase Clock* (Woodbridge, 1981)
P. G. Dawson, C. B. Drover and D. W. Parkes: *Early English Clocks* (Woodbridge, 1982)
D. Roberts: *The Bracket Clock* (Newton Abbot, 1982)
L. Weiss: *Watch-making in England, 1760–1820* (London, 1982)
R. C. R. Barder: *English Country Grandfather Clocks: The Brass-dial Longcase* (Newton Abbot, 1983)
B. Loomes: *Grandfather Clocks and Their Cases* (Newton Abbot, 1985)
D. Roberts: *British Skeleton Clocks* (Woodbridge, 1987)
C. Jagger: *The Artistry of the English Watch* (Newton Abbot, 1988)

M. Cutmore: *Watches, 1850–1980* (Newton Abbot, 1989)

G. White: *English Lantern Clocks* (Woodbridge, 1989)

F. Leibe and J. Wachsmann: *Miller's Watches: A Collector's Guide* (London, 1999)

D. S. Landes: *Revolution in Time: Clocks and the Making of the Modern World* (Cambridge, MA, 2000)

M. Cutmore: *Collecting & Repairing Watches* (Newton Abbot, 2001)

D. Christianson: *Timepieces: Masterpieces of Chronometry* (Toronto, 2002)

M. Cutmore: *Watches: 1850–1980* (Cincinnati, 2002)

P. J. Foley: *Willard's Patent Time Pieces: A History of the Weight-Driven Banjo Clock 1800–1900* (Norwel, 2002)

C. M. Cipolla: *Clocks and Culture, 1300–1700* (New York, 2003)

R. J. Matthys: *Accurate Clock Pendulums* (Oxford, 2004)

R. W. Swedberg and H. Swedberg: *Encyclopedia of Antique American Clocks* (Iola, 2004)

H. Kahlert with R. Muhe and G. L. Brunner: *Wristwatches: History of a Century's Development* (Atglen, PA, 2005)

Cloisonné. *See* ENAMEL, §2(I).

Closegate Glasshouse. *See under* NEWCASTLE UPON TYNE.

Close stool. Chamberpot enclosed in a box, which was often upholstered; in the 18th century the close stool was sometimes built into a chair which was known in France as a *chaise percée*.

Cloth of baudkin. *See* BAUDEKIN.

Club foot. In furniture, a turned foot resembling a club, used with both cabriole and straight legs throughout the 18th century.

Cluny lace. Type of lace developed in France in the late 19th century in Mirecourt (Lorraine) and Le Puy; the name derives from the origins of the style in late medieval laces in the collection of the Musée de Cluny in Paris.

L. Paulis, *Technique and Design of Cluny Lace* (1921 / *R* Bedford, 1984)

Clutha glass. *See under* DRESSER, CHRISTOPHER.

Coaci, Vincenzo (*b* 1756; *d* 1794). Italian silversmith, active in Rome. He trained in the VALADIER workshop. His best-known piece is a bejewelled silver inkstand in the form of the Quirinal obelisk and Roman statutes of the *Dioscuri* and their rearing horses (1792, Minneapolis Institute of Arts); it was presented, together with a leather case in the form of a castle, to Pope Pius VI to mark Giovanni Antinori's rebuilding of the piazza outside the papal summer palace. Coaci also made a chalice (now in the Treasury of St Peter's) for presentation to Pius VI.

Coalbrookdale Iron Company. English iron foundry established in Shropshire in 1708 and still in business. From the late 18th century the Company supplemented its core business of domestic and industrial ironwork with a long succession of decorative designs. In the late 19th century CHRISTOPHER DRESSER designed hall and garden furniture for the company, W. A. S. BENSON designed fireplaces and grates, and the young Francis Wood, later to become a distinguished sculptor, worked as a modeller.

A. Raistrick, *Dynasty of Iron Founders: The Darbys and Coalbrookdale* (London, 1953)

J. Powell and others: 'Seating English Style', *F.M.R. Mag.*, lxxv (Aug 1995), pp. 104–21

E. Thomas: *Coalbrookdale and the Darby family: The Story of the World's First Industrial Dynasty* (York, 1999)

Coalport Porcelain Factory. English porcelain manufactory. The works, near Ironbridge, Salop, beside the River Severn and close to coal resources, were founded by John Rose (1772–1841), a former apprentice at the Caughley works, with backing from Edward Blakeway (1720–1811). After manufacturing from *c.* 1794 at the Calcut China Manufactory, Jackport, Salop, they moved to Coalport in 1796. In October 1799 they bought the Caughley works and used them until 1814, when all the production was consolidated at Coalport. In 1800 Rose's younger brother Thomas Rose (1780–1843) opened a smaller works in the former Coalport Pottery owned by William Reynolds (1758–1803), who was succeeded by Robert Anstice (1757–1845) and William Horton (1754–1833). Both works produced fine utilitarian and ornamental wares in hard-paste porcelain, emulating Chinese and French shapes and decoration. In 1814 John Rose & Co. took over Thomas Rose's works. Softer and more translucent bodies were produced by the 1820s, when Rose bought the moulds of the discontinued Nantgarw and Swansea factories. Between 1820 and 1840 designs evolved into the Rococo style; much of the large output was handpainted with flowers, fruit, landscapes and birds. Thereafter the wares were more simply designed and decorated, although elaborate pieces appeared in exhibitions from 1851 (e.g. Coalport vase and cover, handpainted by John Randall (1810–1910), of the type exhibited in 1871; Shrewsbury, Clive House Mus.). The factory was bought by the Bruff family in 1880, and the Coalport China Co. Ltd was revitalized under the art director Thomas John Bott (1854–1932). Between 1890 and 1920 it was renowned for its ornamental products. High quality decoration was executed by many artists from *c.* 1800, though their work was not signed until *c.* 1900. Manufacturing ceased at Coalport in 1926, after the business had been purchased by Cauldon Potteries Ltd of Stoke-on-Trent. In 1976 the surviving buildings were opened as one of the Ironbridge Gorge Museums.

G. A. Godden: *Coalport and Coalbrookdale Porcelains* (London, 1970, rev. Woodbridge, 1981)

Coal-scuttle. *See under* FIREPLACE FURNISHINGS.

Coaster. Low round tray or stand, usually of silver, for a decanter; it was so called because it was circulated around the 'coast' of the table after dinner. Usually the wooden base was fitted with baize on which it could slide, but some examples are wheeled.

Cobalt. Blue pigment derived from cobalt ore, used as a colourant for ceramics and glass since antiquity, and in medieval Europe used to colour stained glass.

Cobb, John (*b c.* 1715; *d* ?London, Aug 1778). English cabinetmaker and upholsterer. Little is known about him before 1751, when he formed a partnership with WILLIAM VILE, but it is assumed that he was the John Cobb apprenticed in 1729 to Tim Money (*fl* 1724–59), a Norwich upholsterer. When Vile retired in 1764, Cobb carried on in business with the assistance of his foreman, Samuel Reynolds (*fl* 1751–85). He made furniture to very high standards and earned a reputation for exquisite marquetry: Hester Thrale, the writer and friend of Dr. Johnson, compared the inlaid floors at Sceaux, France, to 'the most high prized Cabinet which Mr Cobb can produce to captivate the Eyes of his Customers'. Inlay in tropical woods, particularly satinwood, was an important element of Neo-classical furniture. In 1772–4 Cobb produced an 'Extra neat Inlaid Commode' and two stands *en suite* for Paul Methuen at Corsham Court, Wilts, which survive *in situ*. In 1772 he was implicated in the smuggling of furniture from France. His most extensive work was for the 6th Earl of Coventry at Croome Court, Worcs, between 1765

Clothes press, designed by Robert Adam and made by John Cobb for Croome Court, mahogany, *c.* 1764 (London, Victoria and Albert Museum)

and 1773. This included a large mahogany wardrobe and extensive seating in the new Neo-classical style.

ODNB
G. W. Beard: 'Vile and Cobb, Eighteenth-century London Furniture Makers', *Mag. Ant.,* cxxxvii (June 1990), pp. 1394–1405

Cobden-Sanderson, T(homas) J(ames) (*b* Alnwick, Northumb., 2 Dec 1840; *d* London, 7 Sept 1922). English bookbinder. He pursued an early career as a barrister, but in 1883 he responded to the suggestion of Jane Morris, William Morris's wife, that he pursue bookbinding in London. The Cobden-Sandersons' Doves bindery was established in 1893 at The Mall, Hammersmith, London. By April 1900 Cobden-Sanderson had obtained a printing press and in June of that year installed it in new premises at 1 Hammersmith Terrace and inaugurated the Doves Press. The unmistakable style of his books is derived from Cobden-Sanderson's early work, when he used tools he designed himself. Inspired by nature, he favoured such motifs as buttercups, roses, large and small tulips, poppy seed-pods and stylized leaves, supplementing them with interspersed dots and long, curved gouges. Leathers were primarily native-dyed Niger in reds and greens, but occasionally sealskin was used, as with his edition of the Bible (Hammersmith, 1903–4). If a project was particularly complicated, one pattern piece would be made for each of the covers, as well as for the lettering and tooling on the spine and for the turn-ins. Designs were not usually drawn out but if so, only roughly; most were tooled directly to thin handmade paper using smoke-blackened tools. Five or more free-leaves and plain end-papers were often used. Books were always sewn on to raised cords with silk thread, mostly on five slips. A standard Doves Press edition was bound in classic or figured vellum on tapes, with end-papers but no headbands; almost 11,000 of these were produced, and about 730 in Morocco leather.

In 1908, because of increasing ill-health, he announced the closure of Doves Press; in 1913, he destroyed his matrices by throwing them into the Thames; the type itself followed in 1916. Despite the fact that the Doves Press was (by comparison with other binderies of the day) very small, his work, particularly his original style, was extremely influential on subsequent generations of bookbinders.

ODNB
M. Tidcombe: *The Doves Bindery* (London, 1991)
M. Tidcombe: 'T. J. Cobden-Sanderson and the Doves Bindery', *Mag. Ant.,* cxliv (Aug 1993), pp. 202–11
A. Crawford: 'T. J. Cobden-Sanderson', *Crafts,* clxxi (July–Aug 2001), pp. 24–5
M. Tidcombe: *The Doves Press* (London, 2002)

Cockbead. Quirked or projecting beading applied to the edges of drawer fronts from about 1730 (when it began to replace lip moulding, which was altogether displaced by 1745) to about 1800.

Cockpit Hill Pottery. English ceramics manufactory, founded in Derby and officially known as the

Derby Pot Works. It made cream-coloured earthenwares from 1751 to *c.* 1780; its designers included Thomas Radford. One of the owners, John Heath, later became a founding partner in the DERBY Porcelain Company, some of whose early figures were probably made at Cockpit Hill.

F. Williamson: *The Derby Pot Manufactory Known as Cockpit Hill Pottery* (Derby, 1931)

Coconut cup. Decorative cup, popular in Renaissance Europe, where it appears in inventories as an 'Indian nut'. The body of the cup is a coconut shell carved in shallow relief, mounted on a silver stem and topped with a silver lid. There is a fine example (*c.* 1533–4) by Hans van Amsterdam in the Metropolitan Museum in New York.

R. Fritz, *Die Gefässe aus Kokosnuss in Mitteleuropa 1250–1800* (Mainz, 1983)

Codnor Park Pottery. *See* BOURNE, JOSEPH.

Coffee, William John (*b* 1774–*d c.* 1846). English painter and sculptor, active also in America. He worked in porcelain, plaster, and terracotta and after an early career in an artificial stone factory in London he moved *c.* 1792 to the DERBY Porcelain Factory, where he worked as a modeller. In 1816 he emigrated to America, where he contributed architectural decoration to the University of Virginia, including the plaster of paris friezes for the university buildings and internal plaster and lead ornaments for various buildings.

B. R. Bricknell: *William John Coffee: 1773–c.1846: Modeller, Sculptor, Painter and Ornamentalist: His Life and Work Reviewed* (Grantham, 1998)

Coffer. Chest or strong box for the secure storage of money or valuables; coffers were usually covered in leather and banded with metal.

Coggeshall lace. Type of English TAMBOUR lace made in the Essex village of Cotteswall in the late 19th century; it consisted of bobbin or machine net on which designs were worked in chain stitch.

J. Dudding: *Coggeshall Tambour Lace: A Short History* (2003)

Cogswell, John (*b* Ipswich, MA, 1738; *d* Boston, MA, 1819). American furniture-maker. From about 1760 he was working in Boston, where he was the most important exponent of BOMBÉ pieces carved in the American version of the Chippendale style. In the early 1780s, perhaps in response to Chippendale's *Gentleman and Cabinet-maker's Director*, Cogswell began to add double-serpentine shaping to the facades of his furniture. The number of secure attributions is small, but the existence of one signed piece has facilitated the identification of another 12 works by Cogswell.

R. Mussey and A. R. Haley: 'John Cogswell and Boston Bombé Furniture: Thirty-Five Years of Revolution in Politics and Design', *Amer. Furn.* (1994)

Coin glass. Type of drinking glass created in the 18th century with a coin embedded in a knop in the stem. In 1892 a new type of 'coin glass' was introduced by the Central Glass Company of Wheeling, WV: coins were used to make moulds that would leave impressions of the coin on glass. This glass, which took the form of drinking glasses, butter dishes, cake stands etc., was produced for five months, whereupon the Treasury declared that the process constituted counterfeiting, and the moulds were destroyed.

T. Timmerman: *U.S. Coin Glass: A Century of Mystery* (Beaverton, 1992)

Coins. Pieces of metal stamped with an inscription, device or other design and valid as units of currency. Coins have been studied in Europe as art objects since the Renaissance, when ancient Greek and Roman coins were highly regarded as examples of Classical art. They are also valued for the contemporary representations contained in their designs of many other art forms, such as architecture and calligraphy. Coins have two distinct characteristics that enhance their value as documents of art history. First, their function as money means that they are normally mass-produced and widely disseminated, so a large number of examples is usually available for the examination of any particular design or representation. Second, coins are issued for use as money by the authority of a ruler or state, and therefore the images on them usually have an official status and can be viewed as a public form of art.

Both design and manufacture of coins developed out of the use of seals. The first coins, made in the ancient kingdom of Lydia in Asia Minor during the late 7th century BC, were simply lumps of precious metal, the size of which was determined by weight, stamped with a mark by a seal-like metal die. The function of the impressed mark was to identify the authority responsible for guaranteeing the use of the coin as money.

The earliest coins were marked with designs closely resembling those on contemporary seals. These mostly featured animal designs—a recumbent lion or a lion forepart or head was used by the kings of Lydia. Other early designs include a horse head, a seal, a stag and a pair of cockerels. The close relationship between coin and seal designs is best illustrated by the inscription on a coin with a stag design, issued in the early 6th century BC, which states in Greek *I am the seal of Phanes*.

The force needed to stamp a seal-like design into one side of a lump of metal meant that the other side was also marked. At first the marks on the reverse of coins were made with the crude punches that served to push the metal into the seal-like die. It was soon realized that seal-like designs could also be en-

Coffer, wood decorated with mother-of-pearl and lacquer, from Japan, Momoyama period, late 16th century– early 17th (London, Victoria and Albert Museum)

graved into the rectangular faces of these punches. By the end of the 5th century BC the designs on the reverse of coins had become similar in appearance to those on the obverse, although the rectangular form of the original punches survived in some areas into the 4th century BC.

As the manufacture and use of coins spread from Asia Minor (as far as North Africa, Spain, the Crimea and India by the 4th century BC) many new coin designs were brought into use, although the techniques and artistic approaches of seal engraving continued to play an important part in their invention and execution. More varied elements, particularly of a religious and political nature, began to be used. Religious images, in the form of representations of both gods and divine symbols, were dominant, but, with the rise of the kingdoms following the death of Alexander the Great, King of Macedonia, royal portraits were also widely used. Inscriptions, normally naming the state, ruler or magistrate under whose authority the coin had been made, became a common feature of the design.

The first centuries of development in coin design in the Greek world established a formula that has been maintained in the Western tradition. Although style continues to evolve, the progress of coining technology has had little impact on the underlying principles governing the content, composition and function of coin designs. Although since the 15th century there has been a steady progression in the mechanization of coin production, only two significant advances have been made in the engraving of coin designs. First, from the medieval period punches began to be used to cut part of the designs on the dies, and, second, from the early 19th century die-cutting 'reducing machines', capable of translating larger modelled designs onto dies, also came into use. Both developments led to the standardization of coin design. Coins are now stamped on electrically powered presses using machine-cut dies.

Silver tetradrachm of Athens, showing the owl of Athena (reverse), 4th century BC (Vienna, Kunsthistorisches Museum)

Viking coin minted in England, 10th–11th century (London, British Museum)

Gold manen oban, 133×79 mm, from Japan, 1861 (Newark, NJ, Newark Museum)

The development of coinage design outside Europe and America has followed a slightly different path. Until largely replaced by the Western tradition during the 19th and 20th centuries, three other major traditions flourished. The Indian and Islamic coinages were influenced by early Western coins, but the Chinese tradition had an independent origin and evolution.

The Islamic tradition diverged from the Western one with the rejection by Islamic religious teaching during the Umayyad caliphate (661–750 AD) of the representation of living creatures. After the late 7th century AD pictorial designs were rarely used on Islamic coins, which are normally impressed with purely inscriptional designs, embellished with geometrical frames, symbols and ornamental calligraphy.

This type of coin has been used throughout the Islamic world from West Africa to Indonesia and from Spain to Central Asia.

Coinage was introduced to the Indian subcontinent from the Greek world during the 5th century BC, but the pictorial designs used on Greek coins were replaced by symbolic designs, probably of religious significance. Although further influence from the West later introduced pictorial designs, and the arrival of Islam brought those of an inscriptional type, religious symbolism continued to be the predominant feature of Indian coin design. The Indian coinage tradition also permeated into Central and South-east Asia.

The Chinese coinage tradition began during the 6th or 5th century BC. As they moved away from the use of cast-bronze tools as monetary units, the first coins were cast in bronze, shaped like the tools, and marked with inscriptions that resembled the 'factory marks' found on cast tools. These consisted either of the name of the place of casting or of a control or weight mark. The inscription was cut or stamped into the mould before casting. Although different information was later included in these inscriptions, they remained the dominant designs on Chinese coins until the 19th century, when machinery for producing Western-style coins was introduced in East Asia. As in the case of Islamic coins, however, ornamental calligraphy was also used as a means of embellishment. The Chinese coinage tradition was also adopted in Japan, Korea and Vietnam and mingled with the Indian and Islamic traditions in Central and South-east Asia.

R. G. Doty: *Encyclopedic Dictionary of Numismatics* (London, 1982)

P. Grierson and M. Blackburn: *Medieval European Coinage* (Cambridge, 1986)

Money: From Cowrie Shells to Credit Cards (exh. cat., ed. J. Cribb; London, BM, 1986)

J. Cribb, B. Cook and I. Carradice: *The Coin Atlas* (London, 1989)

P. Grierson: *Coins of Medieval Europe* (London, 1991)

L. Krause and C. Mishler: *Standard Catalogue of World Coins*, 2 vols (Iola, 1991)

M. E. Snodgrass: *Coins and Currency: An Historical Encyclopedia* (Jefferson, NC, 2003)

D. M. Schaps: *The Invention of Coinage and the Monetization of Ancient Greece* (Ann Arbor, 2004)

C. L. Krause, C. Mishler and C. R. Bruce: *2005 Standard Catalog of World Coins: 1901–Present* (Iola, 2004)

C. L. Krause, C. Mishler and C. R. Bruce: *Standard Catalog of World Gold Coins* (Iola, 2005)

Cold stamping. In medieval bookbinding, the technique whereby a design was stamped by hand on wet leather with metal dies; it was superseded in the 15th century by STAMPED BINDINGS that used a press.

Cold work. Metal worked in its natural state instead of when heated

Coleman, William Stephen (*b* Horsham, 1829; *d* St John's Wood, London, 22 March 1904). English book illustrator and painter. He trained as a surgeon, but never practised, instead working as a writer and illustrator of books on natural history and as a painter of watercolour landscapes. In 1869 Coleman embarked on a new career when he joined Copeland's (*see* SPODE CERAMIC WORKS) as a painter of china plaques. Later that year he moved to the MINTON CERAMIC FACTORY, attracted by the opportunity to work with their well-known turquoise colour. At Minton he designed table services, which were transfer-printed in colour with his scrupulously accurate depictions of flora (e.g. 'The Naturalist') and fauna (e.g. 'Game Place') and people (a series of dessert services with orientalised ladies). In 1871 he became head of the new Minton's Art Pottery Studio in Kensington Gore; there he designed porcelain plaques, many of which depict flora, fauna and lighly-clad girls and women. He resigned as director in 1873, but continued to paint porcelain at the studio till it was destroyed by fire in 1875.

ODNB

Colenbrander, T(heodoor) C(hristiaan) A(driaan) (*b* Doesburg, 31 Oct 1841; *d* Laag-Keppel, 28 May 1930). Dutch decorative artist. He trained as an architect but turned to pottery in the 1880s. From 1884 until 1889 he was the artistic director of the Rozenburg Delftware factory in The Hague, which was established by W. W. von Gudenberg in 1883. It was

not only Colenbrander's designs of ornamental china that were revolutionary but also the asymmetric, whimsical, but at the same time elegant, decorative patterns, which were applied in bright, transparent colours. His motifs seemed to indicate an awareness of oriental decorations, which he may have seen at Expositions Universelles, although for the most part they were original. After a disagreement with the management, he left Rozenburg in 1889 and spent several years working in different fields within the applied arts, including interior design and textiles.

In 1895 Colenbrander was asked to take over the artistic direction of the Amersfoortse Tapijtfabriek, a firm that had executed some of his carpet designs. The patterns of these colourful Smyrna carpets bear an obvious similarity to his ceramic decorations. Unlike his ceramic decorations his carpet designs are always symmetrical. When the factory was taken over by the Koninklijke Deventer Tapijtfabriek, he became aesthetic adviser at this large, reputable company, where his Smyrna carpets were hand-knotted until well into the 20th century. At a variety of national and international exhibitions the firm won considerable praise with its 'Colenbrander carpets'.

Although Colenbrander was involved with the Deventer Tapijtfabriek until *c.* 1920, he was also able to involve himself in other activities. For a short period in 1912–13, for example, he produced a series of ceramic designs for the Delftware factory Zuid-Holland in Gouda. In 1920 some of his wealthy friends founded a Delftware factory especially for him; at this firm, Ram, in Arnhem, the designs used were exclusively his until 1924. There were 75 different designs with *c.* 700 different decorations, each with its own name. A large number of the works from this period were executed in enamel so that the areas of colour could be filled in completely, and so that it was possible to make two areas meet precisely. The five-piece decorative vase set called 'Cathedraal' was made with this technique (1922), and there are examples at the Museum Boymans–van Beuningen in Rotterdam and one at the Gemeentemuseum in Arnhem. The excessive decoration on this set, which is made up of hundreds of areas of colour, is unusual in being symmetrical.

T. C. A. Colenbrander: *Plateelbakkerij 'Ram' te Arnhem* (exh. cat., Arnhem, Gemeentemus., 1986)

R. Mills: 'Kleurnuancen. T. C. A. Colenbrander als tapijtontwerper', *Jong Holland*, x (1994), pp. 26–31

R. Mills: 'Motif and Variations: A Study of Dutch Art Nouveau Ceramic and Carpet Designs by T. A. C. Colenbrander', *Stud. Dec. A.*, iv/1 (Fall–Winter 1996–7), pp. 85–117

R. Mills: 'Axes of Construction: An Analysis of Dutch Art Nouveau Carpet Designs by T. A. C. Colenbrander', *Stud. Dec. A.*, x/2 (Spring–Summer 2003), pp. 69–135

Collcutt, T(homas) E(dward) (*b* Oxford, 16 March 1840; *d* Southampton, 7 Oct 1924. English architect and furniture designer. He studied architecture under R. W. Armstrong (*d* 1884) and later G. E. Street (1824–81) in London, subsequently working for COLLINSON & LOCK, the fashionable furniture-makers. He designed their premises (1873–4; destr.) on Fleet Street, London, and a once-famous ebonized 'Art' cabinet (1871, London, V&A); he was also responsible for many of the designs in their 1872 catalogue. His Collinson & Lock dining chair set the pattern of chair design in late Victorian England.

Collinot, Eugène-Victor (*d* 1882). French potter and designer. He collaborated with Adalbert de Beaumont to publish a *Recueil de dessins pour l'art et l'industrie* [*A Collection of Designs for Art and Industry*], which contained 217 engravings, many of which portray Islamic ceramics and glass from their own collections or seen in their travels. This book was a seminal influence on the introduction of Islamic decorative art to French artists and craftsmen, notably JOSEPH-THÉODORE DECK. In 1863, Collinot and Beaumont founded their own faïence factory in the Bois de Boulogne, specializing in wares inspired by Persian and Iznik pottery.

Collinson & Lock. English firm of 'Art Furnishers' established in London in 1870 by Frank G. Collinson and George James Lock. The company sold high quality furniture, and became well known for furniture that combined rosewood and ivory and was decorated with scrolling foliage. The principal designer was T E. COLLCUTT, but the firm also employed E. W. GODWIN, who was responsible for the 'Lucretia' cabinet (1873, Detroit Institute of Arts). The firm of Collinson & Lock was established in London in the third quarter of the 19th century and quickly achieved both commercial success and a leading position in the field of design. In 1871 the firm issued an impressive illustrated catalogue of 'Artistic Furniture', with plates by J. Moyr Smith, assistant to Christopher Dresser, and in 1873 was trading from extensive newly built premises in St Bride Street. The firm went bankrupt in 1897 and was taken over by GILLOW.

Sketches of artistic furniture manufactured by Collinson & Lock: 109 Fleet St London (Collinson & Lock, 1871)
M. Donnelly: 'British Furniture at the Philadelphia Centennial Exhibition, 1876', *Furn. Hist.,* xxvii (2001), pp. 91–120

Cologne [Ger. Köln]. German centre of ceramic production. In Roman times Cologne was the centre of production of a variety of ceramic goods, some of high quality (examples in Bonn, Rhein. Landesmus.; Cologne, Röm.–Ger.-Mus.). The raw material was provided mainly by the clays present in large quantities near Frechen, which turn white when fired. The main manufacturing centre was to the west of the city on the road from Bavay (Rudolfplatz); a stretch of about 800 m was lined by numerous potteries. All types of ware were produced except *terra sigillata*, including some with green or yellow glaze and vessels with moulded decoration. Black-gloss cups with hunting or arena scenes using the barbotine technique were exported beyond Germany to Gaul and Britain. Terracotta figurines of native and

Collinson & Lock (attrib.): chair, mahogany, h. 972 mm, designed by A. H. Mackmurdo, c. 1883 (London, Victoria and Albert Museum)

Roman gods, statuettes (especially busts) of women and men, animals, toy figures and theatre masks were also widely exported: 13 signatures are known. Ceramic production died out in Cologne at the end of the 2nd century AD, although a revival in the first half of the 4th century included white clay mugs with reddish concentric circles.

The industry was again revived in the late 15th century, when Cologne became an important centre for the production of stoneware. Between 1520 and 1600 brown salt-glazed stonewares decorated in relief with tendrils of foliage and figures are characteristic of Cologne wares. Typical products included the globular *Bartmannkrüge* (bellarmines). During the last third of the 18th century several faience factories were established in Cologne. The best-known was LOUIS-VICTOR GERVEROT's Englische Porcelainsfabrik, which made dinner-services, coffee- and tea-services and such other utilitarian items as bowls and jugs.

Colombo, Joe [Cesare] (*b* Milan, 30 July 1930; *d* Milan, 30 July 1971). Italian designer. After an early career as a sculptor and painter he turned to design for what was to be the last decade of his short life. In 1962 he opened a design studio on Viale Pavia in Milan, and thereafter concentrated on interiors (in the first instance for alpine hotels) and furniture design. His furniture had neither straight lines nor corners, but consisted of curves and folds. His chairs include the fibreglass Elda Armchair (1963), the plywood Small Armchair with Curved Elements (1964) and the plastic Universale (1964, V&A, London), in which the legs and be detached and replaced with longer ones (see colour pl. VIII, fig. 1).

I. Favata: *Joe Colombo and Italian Design of the Sixties* (New Haven and London, 1988)
Joe Colombo (exh. cat., Bergamo, Accad. Carrara B.A., 1996)
G. D'Ambrosio: *Joe Colombo: Design antropologico* (Turin, 2004)

Colonna, Edouard [Klönne, Eduard; Colonna, Eugène] (*b* Mülheim, nr Cologne, 27 May 1862; *d* Nice, 14 Oct 1948). German designer and architect, active also in North America France. He studied architecture in Brussels and in 1882 went to New York where he worked briefly as a designer for Tiffany's Associated Artists. From 1885 onwards he produced railway wagons for Barney & Smith, Dayton, OH, and for a Canadian railway company, and he also worked in the field of interior decoration. In 1893 Colonna went to Europe, settling in Paris, where in 1898 he started work as a designer for S. Bing's Galerie Art Nouveau. His heyday came between 1898 and 1902, when he produced designs for jewellery, textiles and furniture, including exhibits in the famous Art Nouveau Bing pavilion (destr.) at the Exposition Universelle in Paris in 1900.

In 1902 Colonna returned to Canada, and for 20 years he worked as an interior decorator and designer there and in the USA. In 1923 he retired to the south of France, and in his last years he carved alabaster bowls after East Asian originals. He developed into an elegant exponent of *Jugendstil*. For his ornaments, he preferred abstract floral designs, and his favourite form in pieces of jewellery was the oval made from gold, enamel and pearls.

E. Colonna (exh. cat., essay M. Eidelberg; Dayton, OH, A. Inst., 1983)

Colt, Samuel (*b* Hartford, CT, 19 July 1814; *d* Hartford, 10 Jan 1862). American inventor and firearms manufacturer. He invented the first pistol to be successfully fitted with a revolving cylinder, so creating a multiple-shot firearm. He patented this revolver in England in 1835 and in America the following year. He opened a firearms factory, Patent Arms Manufacturing, but it closed in 1842; he returned to the industry five years later, when the army awarded him a contract to supply revolvers. In 1855 he opened a new arms factory in Hartford, the largest commercial arms factory in the world. The Colt 45 entered the popular imagination as the gun of the American West.

W. Hosley: *Colt: The Making of an American Legend* (1996)
D. K. Boorman: *The History of Colt Firearms* (London, 2000)
R. L. Wilson and R. Pershing: *The Paterson Colt Book: The Early Evolution of Samuel Colt's Repeating Arms* (Palo Alto, 2001)

Columbine cup. Silver goblet shaped like a columbine flower. They were manufactured in Nuremberg in the 16th century (they were first mentioned in 1513), often by candidates applying for admission to the guilds of goldsmiths. There are two fine examples in the Victoria and Albert Museum and another in the British Museum. GEORG WECHTER is sometimes said (in error) to have been the inventor of the Columbine cup, but his influential design was not published until 1579.

Comb, liturgical. Decorated comb, usually of ivory, used ceremonially by the celebrant before Mass in both Orthodox and Roman Catholic churches. From late antiquity the combs have been fashioned from a single rectangular piece with teeth along both long edges, and the quadrangle or lunette at the centre is often carved with Christian motifs; They have been found in 5th-century catacombs; a new one was placed in St Cuthbert's tomb early in the 11th century (Durham Cathedral, Treasury) and they were still being made in the 12th century. References to their use appear in ecclesiastical rituals until the 16th century. They are still used in the Greek rite. See fig. on p. 266.

Combed ware. The term is used in two distinct senses. In prehistoric archaeology (in which there is an eponymous 'combed ware culture'), the term denotes a pattern of pottery decoration in which the impressions of a comb-like stamp alternate with rows of small depressions. In medieval and modern pottery (especially of peasant origin), the term denotes pottery covered with slips of contrasting colours combed into feather patterns.

Cometti, Giacomo (*b* 1863; *d* 1938). Italian furniture designer, sculptor and cabinetmaker, based in Turin. The extravagantly curved lines of his early furniture (e.g. 'Scrittoio', 1898–1900) gradually yielded to the influence of north European designs, and by the 1920s he had become Italy's most distinguished exponent of ART DECO furniture.

Cominazzo. Italian family of gun-barrel makers, active in Brescia from the 16th century to the 19th. The most famous member of the family was Angelo Lazarino Cominazzo, from whom John Evelyn bought a carbine while visiting Brescia in 1646. Angelo signed his barrels 'Lazarino Cominazzo', and this signature was used on the family's gun barrels for generations; it also appears on the guns of many other makers.

Commesso di pietre dure. *See* FLORENCE, §1.

Commode. French term for a chest-of-drawers. In France it is the proper term for all chests-of-drawers, as the commode constituted the earliest occurrence in that country (shortly before 1700) of the form. In

Liturgical comb (see p. 265) showing scenes from the Life of Christ, ivory, 85 × 115 mm, ?St Albans, England, c. 1120 (London, Victoria and Albert Museum)

other parts of Europe, where chests-of-drawers had been in use for much of the 17th century, the novel features of the commode were its elaborate profile and virtuoso decoration; and some examples, notably in England, were not fitted with drawers at all but with shelves and cupboard doors.

The word 'commode' seems first to have come into currency to describe the sarcophagus-shaped chests-of-drawers manufactured by ANDRÉ-CHARLES BOULLE, among them the pair supplied by him to the Grand Trianon at Versailles in 1708. Contemporary with this type were various low-slung forms with three or four tiers of drawers, straight sides and curved or canted fore-corners, sometimes decorated with floral marquetry (e.g. c. 1700; London, V&A). Commodes of this date have wooden tops decorated to match the façade, but within a few years French commodes were invariably given marble tops.

During the Régence the serpentine form evolved in tandem with the fashion for parquetry decoration, and a two-drawer model on longer legs came into vogue. CHARLES CRESSENT and ANTOINE-ROBERT GAUDREAUS were responsible for some of the earliest Rococo versions of this form, in which marquetry is abandoned in favour of a proliferation of ormolu, completely overrunning the surface and obscuring the division between the two drawers: the

commode by Gaudreaus in the Wallace Collection, London, with mounts by JACQUER CAFFIÉRI, was supplied to Louis XV's bedchamber at Versailles in 1739. This is in fact a *commode à encoignures*, with drawers in the centre and cupboards in the ends, a type that seems to have evolved as an amalgamation of the commode and corner-cupboard. In the 1740s the *bombe* shape (serpentine in two planes) evolved, and floral marquetry was revived. A new fashion arose for veneers of Japanese lacquer, seen in commodes by Bernard VAN RISAMBURGH (e.g. c. 1745; Brit. Royal Col.; Paris, Louvre), ADRIEN FAIZELOT DELORME, Nicolas-Jean Marchand (b c. 1697; e.g. a piece dated c. 1755; London, Wallace) and others, a taste that was sustained in the Neo-classical period.

The growth of the *goût grec* brought about the development of the break-front form, of which JEAN-FRANÇOIS OEBEN produced some of the earliest examples. This type has a distinct frieze incorporating three short drawers (or occasionally one long one) and below two deep drawers veneered *sans traverse*, flanked by cupboard doors (on later examples this arrangement is replaced by full-length drawers). These transitional examples have vestigially Rococo cabriole legs and softened corners; but the Louis XVI version of the break-front form, in the hands of JOSEPH BAUMHAUER (e.g. c. 1770; Paris, Louvre;

Commode attributed to Augustin Gaudron, c. 1710–15 (Versailles, Château)

and c. 1770; Brit. Royal Col.), JEAN-HENRI RIESENER (e.g. c. 1785; Versailles, Petit Trianon) and GUILLAUME BENEMAN (e.g. pair with porcelain mounts from Sèvres, 1786; Fontainebleau, Château), became uncompromisingly rectilinear, and eventually even the shallow central projection was suppressed. Other Neo-classical forms include the D-shaped commode à encoignures, favoured by René Dubois (1737–99), CLAUDE-CHARLES SAUNIER, Riesener and others (when the end-doors were removed, exposing the internal shelves, this type was known as a commode à l'anglaise, although it undoubtedly originated in France); and the semicircular or semi-elliptical form, seen in the work of CHARLES TOPINO for example, which may owe a real debt to English developments under Robert Adam.

In the 1760s and 1770s a new fashion arose for commodes and other furniture mounted with Sèvres porcelain plaques; these were a speciality of both MARTIN CARLIN and ADAM WEISWEILER, working primarily for the marchands-merciers Simon-Philippe Poirier (c. 1720–85) and Dominique Daguerre (fl 1772; d 1796), who enjoyed, in succession, a virtual monopoly on the supply of Sèvres furniture mounts. In the same period a taste developed, perhaps under English influence, for plain mahogany veneers, the earliest examples of which were the remarkable series of mahogany commodes supplied by Oeben to the Marquise de Pompadour c. 1760. This fashion persisted, partly for economic reasons, up to and during the Empire period. Commodes assumed increasingly heavy four-square proportions, with three or even

four drawers, raised on short feet or a solid plinth; metal mounts, both ornamental and figurative, became central rather than peripheral to the decoration while at the same time growing increasingly coarse. Subsequent stylistic changes concern ornament more than form, the principal innovation being the fashion for bois clairs, introduced in the reign of Charles X, with contrasting marquetry of formal linear patterns and usually no mounts at all.

The stylistic developments of French commodes were broadly reflected all over Europe, although it took up to 40 years for the form to gain currency in other countries; and its evolution was of course modified by different national and regional predilections. The bombe form, in particular, was distorted in a variety of ways: the Germans were especially inventive, producing occasional monstrosities as well as more stylish models, such as one derived from Cressent with a vigorous in-turned C-scroll above the tall shoulder of the front angles; a peculiarly ungainly Germano-Danish model, on a coarse Rococo giltwood stand, has a dropped bulge and two vertical 'seams' down the front; Swedish examples are typically high-hipped with lozenge parquetry on the three drawers, attenuated mounts and gilt channels on the face of the dustboards; the north Italians favoured a disproportionately high bulge, and numerous Venetian examples were decorated in the characteristic lacca of that region. Neo-classical European commodes present less diversity of form—the rectangular type with canted corners and tapering legs, for instance, being almost universal—but their ornament is less reliant on French precedent and consequently more idiosyncratic: in Milan, GIUSEPPE MAGGIOLINI (e.g. Milan, Castello Sforzesco) developed a distinctive vocabulary of Pompeiian ornament and pictorial medallions; David ROENTGEN of Neuwied (and Paris) perfected an even more painterly marquetry style; and the Dutch adopted a quirky and rather arid geometric idiom, with distinctive chequer-board pattern borders.

English commodes were generally of simpler profile than French examples: the *bombe* form was little favoured, and even a short-cut serpentine form, with straight sides, was developed as a popular economy model. They were also less profusely mounted, and the majority were clad in plain veneers of mahogany or satin-wood, with minimal marquetry decoration or none. Of the more elaborately inlaid examples, a large proportion was produced by immigrant cabinetmakers of widely varying calibre; only a small number of English-born master craftsmen included such pieces in their repertory: among them were JOHN COBB (e.g. 1772; Corsham Court, Wilts), Thomas Chippendale (e.g. *c.* 1770 and 1770–73; Harewood House, W. Yorks, and Nostell Priory, W. Yorks, NT), John Linnell (attributed examples, *c.* 1768–70; Osterley Park, London, NT, and St Petersburg, Hermitage) and John Mayhew and William Ince (*see* INCE & MAYHEW; most notably the commode made in 1775 to Adam's design for Derby House, London). In the 1780s a fashion arose for painted decoration, either on satin-wood veneer, as produced by the firm of George SEDDON) among others, or on an all-over painted ground, the invariable practice of George Brookshaw (*fl* 1783–6), whose empanelled floral decoration was perhaps a response to French porcelain-mounted furniture (two commodes, *c.* 1785–90, attributed to his workshop are in the Lady Lever Art Gallery, Port Sunlight; others there are attributed to Chippendale, *c.* 1775–80; Cobb, *c.* 1770–75; Linnell, *c.* 1768–70; and Mayhew and Ince, *c.* 1773–*c.* 1780).

English commodes also differed from French ones in two more fundamental respects: in the predominant use of wooden tops rather than the marble slabs that almost always feature on French and other continental examples, and in the increasing preference for cupboard doors rather than exterior drawers. Sometimes the doors enclosed interior drawers (the occasional French occurrences of this type were known as *commodes à vanteaux*), but more often the interiors were fitted with plain shelves: a type that the French would class as an armoire, for a French commode was (at least in metropolitan terms) by definition formed with drawers. In England, however, commodes were so called by virtue of their profile, especially in so far as it approximated to French models: the serpentine shape thus came to be seen as the definitive commode form ('commode' was even used adjectivally in this sense), and the term was subsequently applied to examples of break-front, semi-circular and semi-elliptical profile. But with the fashion towards the end of the century for more aus-

tere rectilinear forms, commodes became indistinguishable from any other sort of low four-square cabinet, and in the early part of the 19th century the term gradually passed out of English usage. It was not until after 1900 that the word was resurrected, and then only as a historical term to describe 18th-century examples (or precise reproductions of 18th-century models, which were manufactured throughout Europe in large numbers in the second half of the 19th century). In France, by contrast, the term has remained in constant use as the word for a chest-of-drawers, regardless of style.

J. Yorke: 'A Signed and Dated Commode by Ignazio Ravello', *Furn. Hist.*, xl (2004), pp. 73–82

Compendiario. Restrained style of Italian pottery decoration that became fashionable in the second half of the 16th century, first in Faenza, where CAL-AMELLI and MEZZARISA were its most prominent exponents, and subsequently in other workshops in Central Italy. The decoration attempted to emphasize the items' form, and the potters took inspiration from contemporary silverwares. A decoration of blue and yellow was applied to the ground of thick, white enamel. The best-known examples were BIANCHI DI FAENZA that were usually sketchily decorated with coats of arms and floral motifs. This style lasted throughout the first half of the 17th century, when workshops in Naples and the Abruzzo produced inferior-quality imitations. There was also a Spanish version of compendiario used in the workshops of Talavera.

Compo [Composition]. Substance used in decorative arts from the 18th century. The usual formula combined animal glue, boiled oil and resin, which was then packed with powdered chalk to make a dough-like substance that could be pressed into moulds. Many gilded objects have sculptural or relief ornamentation that is made from 'gilder's compo': a composition of glue, resin, whiting and linseed oil. This is usually applied after the surface has been prepared with gesso and is attached with an adhesive. The use of compo in picture frames was initially regarded as fraudulent in 18th-century France (because they were sold as wooden frames), but eventually became common practice.

Comport. Glass dessert dish raised upon a stem or support; 18th-century examples are usually made from cut flint glass, and 19th-century examples from pressed glass.

Compound-twist stem. Glass stem, popular from 1760 to 1800, consisting of a pair of pair of intertwined AIR TWIST or enamel spirals (or one of each).

Coney, John (*b* Boston, MA, 5 Jan 1656; *d* Boston, 20 Aug 1722). American silversmith, goldsmith and engraver. The son of a cooper, he probably served his apprenticeship with JEREMIAH DUMMER of Boston. Coney may have engraved the plates for the first banknotes printed in the Massachusetts Bay Colony in 1690 and certainly engraved the plates for those issued in 1702. His patrons included important citizens of Boston, churches throughout New England, local societies and Harvard College. Active as a silversmith and goldsmith for 45 years, he produced objects in three distinct styles—that of the late 17th century (characterized by engraved and flat-chased ornament and scrollwork), the Baroque and the Queen Anne—and introduced specialized forms to New England, for example the monteith and chocolatepot. Although derived directly from the English silversmithing tradition and thus not innovative in design, Coney's work exhibits excellent craftsmanship in all technical aspects of gold- and silversmithing. Two lobed sugar-boxes (Boston, MA, Mus. F. A., and Manchester, NH, Currier Gal. A.), a large, gadrooned, two-handled cup (1701; Cambridge, MA, Fogg) made for William Stoughton (d 1701), the earliest New England chocolatepot (Boston, MA, Mus. F. A.) and a monteith made c. 1705–15 for John Colman (New Haven, CT, Yale U. A.G.) are among the objects he made in the Baroque style. His pear-shaped teapot of c. 1710 made for the Mascarene family (New York, Met.) and a two-handled covered cup (1718; Shreveport, LA, Norton A.G.) and a monteith (1719) made for the Livingston family (New York, Franklin D. Roosevelt Lib.) are superb examples of the curvilinear Queen Anne style that was never widely popular in Boston.

H. F. Clarke: *John Coney, Silversmith, 1655–1722* (Boston and New York, 1932/R New York, 1971)

P. E. Kane and others: *Colonial Massachusetts Silversmiths and Jewelers: A Biographical Dictionary* (New Haven, 1998)

B. L. Scherer: 'Silver', *A. & Auction*, xxiv/4 (April 2002), p. 108

Confessional. Closet-like piece of furniture used in the Roman Catholic Church and some other liturgically 'high' denominations for auricular confession. Confessionals are always made out of wood, since it was thought inappropriate to use more costly materials for non-liturgical church furnishings. For centuries there was no particular furinture or space associated with aural confession, though from the 14th century in Sweden, where men lived alongside women in double monasteries, grilles were inserted in special recesses in the choir walls to prevent the priest from coming into contact with the sisters. The first confessional rooms, with a grille opening into the church, appeared in Portugal in the early 15th century (e.g. at Guarda Cathedral); in the 16th century in northern Europe confessional grilles were inserted in the choir aisle windows so that confession could be made from outside the church.

The modern confessional emerged from these precedents in the late 16th century, after the Council of Milan (1565) specified that the confeesion box was to be clearly visible and to stand outside the choir; and it was to have a partition with a grille through which the priest could communicate with the penitent. The earliest confessionals of the Counter-Reformation consist of two parts and are closed off at the sides with a roof over the top. This, the alcove type, first gained popularity in Italy. Later a three-piece confessional of this form appeared in the southern Netherlands and south Germany. During the 17th century two further types consisting of three sections came into use: the cell type, which is similar to the alcove type but has no roof (e.g. the Klosterkirche, Stromberg, Germany), and the alcove-cell type, which has a roof over the priest's alcove but open cells for the penitents (e.g. Onze-Lieve-Vrouw, Aarschot, Belgium; 1647).

The confessional as it is known today is primarily a creation of the 17th century; it became popular in south Germany, and especially the southern Netherlands, where distinctive forms of decoration were developed, largely owing to losses of earlier models during periods of severe iconoclasm. The earliest examples dating from 1610 to 1640, however, have been mostly destroyed. The Onze-Lieve-Vrouwkerk in Nieuwmoer (Belgium, 1653) contains confessionals of the alcove type; decoration is limited to a pair of angel terms on either side of the priest's box and a continuous garland frieze on the two outer panels behind the penitents. Some confessionals were joined together with continuous panelling, with the imagery used as decoration continuing cyclically from one to the other. Most of these examples are of the alcove type with a cartouche in relief over the priest's box. Statues of angels on either side of the priest's alcove hold attributes that allude to confession and the Passion, while the outer panels are decorated with statues of saints depicted as penitents and priests. The finest example is the series of ten conjoined confessionals with related imagery in St Pauluskerk, Antwerp, made by Peeter Verbrugghen the elder and his workshop (1657–9). Gradually, however, the angels were replaced by symbolic figures and saints (e.g. the confessional in St Servaas, Grimbergen, by Guillielmus Ignatius Kerricx; 1718), and during the late Baroque period the use of statuary disappeared in favour of herms on the ends of each of the four partitions. Few, if any, changes were made during the Rococo period, but French influence, in the use of Louis XIV elements, is apparent in the introduction of elegant curves into the basic plan. Occasionally the confessional formed part of an extended sculptural ensemble. In the confessional by Theodor VERHAEGEN (1736) in the Onze Lieve Vrouwkerk, Ninove, for example, the box is flanked by figures holding symbols of Justice and Mercy (scales, a chalice and host), while saints above intercede for the penitent with the Risen Christ, beneath a representation of the Trinity. Figure sculpture, however, was gradually replaced by architectural elements, and, although the basic types of confessional continued in the 19th century, their decorative vocabulary depended on prevailing styles that included Neo-classical columns and cornices and Gothic Revival motifs. Earlier, in the late 17th century, a variant on the standard type of confessional had appeared in Italy and Westphalia (Germany), where confessionals and pulpits were combined in one structure (e.g. S Gaetano, Florence).

Confidante. *See under* SOFA.

Connecticut chest [Hartford chest; Sunflower chest]. American oak chest made in the Connecticut River valley in the late 17th century. The panels and drawer fronts carved with what have traditionally been called 'tulip and sunflower' motifs; they would be more accurately described as 'tulip and marigold'. The chests were sometimes decorated with split banisters applied to the verticals. The Connecticut chest has traditionally thought to have been developed by NICHOLAS DISBROWE or his successors in Hartford, CT, but the tulip and sunflower decoration is almost always associated with Peter Blin (*c.* 1640–1725), a joiner to whom of many Wethersfield sunflower chests are attributed, so it is possible that he is the originator of this type of chest.

H. W. Erving: *The Hartford Chest* (New Haven, 1934)
S. P. Schoelwer: 'Connecticut Sunflower Furniture: A Familiar Form Reconsidered', Yale *U. A.G. Bull.*, (Spring 1989), pp. 20–37

Conran, Sir **Terence** (*b* Esher, Surrey, 4 Oct 1931). English designer, retailer and entrepreneur. In 1956 he formed the Conran Design Group, and for the next 12 years he expanded the practice and the manufacture of his furniture and textile designs, which were sold into a mainly non-domestic market. He believed passionately that well-designed, reasonably priced products for the home should be available to the mass market, and in 1964 he opened the first Habitat shop in Fulham Road, London, which put his ideas into practice. He chose every article for its visual appeal and fitness for purpose, and his innovative settings of simple furniture and fabrics allied to massed displays of inexpensive glass, china, kitchenware and coloured enamel introduced aspiring homemakers to a new lifestyle. By 1983 some 50 Habitat shops were trading in Britain and abroad.

Conran was one of the most formative influences on the appearance of the average British domestic interior and on the changing perception of design. He shared William Morris's view of design as a social issue, and the Conran Foundation—a charitable trust that he established in 1979—sponsored the Design Museum, which opened in London's Docklands in 1989.

B. Phillips: *Conran and the Habitat Story* (London, 1984)

Console [modillion; mutule]. Carved ornamental bracket, derived from architectural use in classical antiquity, surmounted by a horizontal tablet and fixed upright against a wall.

Console table. Formal table that stands against the wall, supported by consoles, sculpture or one or more legs, commonly called a side, pier or sideboard table in the 17th and 18th centuries. The console table was an important design form for the Baroque,

Connecticut chest, 660×1270×597 mm, from Guilford, CT, 1650–80 (Newark, NJ, Newark Museum)

Rococo and Neo-classical styles. Most were made from carved and gilt wood and usually supported a stone or marble slab that was often more highly prized than the structure beneath. Italian carvers executed some of the most impressive Baroque tables for palazzi and churches, particularly in Rome. By the 1720s tables displayed cabriole legs and a lighter, more asymmetrical supporting structure in response to the emerging Rococo style. Important tables were often designed and/or executed by such wood-carvers as Pineau and François Roumier (*fl* 1701–48) in France, or Matthias Lock, Thomas Johnson and the cabinetmaking shops of Thomas Chippendale and of William Ince and his partner John Mayhew in England. In Germany the table designs of FRANÇOIS DE CUVILLIÉS and his son François II and of Johann Michael HOPPENHAUPT exemplify the Rococo and provide ample evidence of the creativity that the form inspired.

Neo-classicism resulted in more architectural console tables characterized by straighter vertical supports, reeding, classical mouldings and garlands. Urns often stood at the *noeud* or junction of cross-stretchers. Early examples tended to be heavy but progressed by 1770 to an elegant and refined lightness. Chronologically, the early phase is documented through the designs of Dominique Pineau (1718–86), François de Neufforge and Jean-Charles Delafosse.

Such leading Neo-classical designers as Robert Adam and James Adam exemplify the simpler, lighter British approach, which combined an oblong, semi-circular or semi-elliptical top with turned and carved legs. After 1775 the diminishing use of state-rooms and a growing emphasis on smaller, functional pieces of furniture (e.g. commodes and folding card- and tea-tables) all contributed to the decline of the console table as an important form in British furniture. In France it retained its importance and appeared among the published designs of Juste-François Boucher (1736–82), Pierre Ranson (1736–86), RICHARD DE LALONDE and Henri-Joseph Aubert Parent (1753–1835).

After 1800 the console table generally followed established or historic models. The widely made Regency/Empire form with a mirror below probably evolved from the furnishings found in German *Spiegelkabinette* (*see* CABINET) of the early 18th century. Wrought iron was an important material for console tables, particularly in the French Rococo and Art Deco periods.

Cookworthy, William (*b* Kingsbridge, Devon, 12 April 1705; *d* Plymouth, 17 Oct 1780). English chemist and ceramic manufacturer. His interest in china manufacture led him to experiment with kaolin (china clay) in Cornwall in the 1740s, although it was not until *c.* 1768 that he was able to take out a patent to protect his formula and to begin the manufacture of a fine, true porcelain at the Plymouth Porcelain Factory, which he established in the same year. The factory was transferred to Bristol in 1770; his principal partner in the new venture was RICHARD CHAMPION, who had also been at Plymouth. The white, true porcelain was closer to Chinese and German hard-paste porcelain than to any existing English porcelain, although it proved difficult to fire, and examples frequently exhibit imperfections and considerable 'smoking' of the glaze. Cookworthy's Plymouth porcelain was much influenced by the designs on Chinese wares, although after the move to Bristol it was Meissen porcelain from Germany that became the most important source of inspiration. Cookworthy's manufacture of figures, however, owed more to pieces from the Staffordshire potteries than the more sophisticated Meissen products. Plymouth wares occasionally bear the mark of the alchemists sign for tin. Cookworthy retired in 1774 and transferred his patent to Champion, who, after modest success, failed to compete with such Staffordshire manufacturers as Josiah Wedgwood; the factory was forced to close by 1780.

ODNB
F. S. Mackenna: *Cookworthy's Plymouth and Bristol Potteries* (Leigh-on-Sea, 1946)
J. Penderill-Church: *William Cookworthy, 1705–1780* (Truro, 1972)

Cooper, Susie [Susan] **(Vera)** (*b* Burslem, Staffs, 29 Oct 1902; *d* Douglas, Isle of Man, 28 July 1995). English ceramics designer and manufacturer. She joined A. E. Gray & Co. Ltd (Hanley) in 1922, initially on a work placement. At Gray's Pottery she had her own backstamp, designing surface patterns in lustre pigments and enamel colours for the white ware that Gray's bought in and decorated. Frustrated by the limitation of not being able to conceive the form and the pattern as a whole, Susie Cooper left Gray's in 1929 to start her own hand-painting ceramic decorating business in rented rooms at the George Street Pottery, Tunstall. By 1932 she was designing her own shapes, which were being made for her at Wood & Sons, Burslem, where she had her own production unit called Crown Works. The earthenware tableware body shapes of the 1930s were named after birds—'Kestrel', 'Curlew' (both *c.* 1932) and 'Falcon' (*c.* 1937). A few figures and some vases and plates with moulded surface designs were also made during this decade. By the mid-1930s she was exporting ware to Europe, Scandinavia and Australia and employed a workforce of 70–100 people.

Difficulty in buying white ware after the war led Cooper, in partnership with her husband, Cecil Barker (1908–1972), an architect, to buy Jason Works, a bone-china factory in Longton, Stoke-on-Trent. The white, light, translucent bone-china teaware made in Longton was sent to Burslem for decoration. The existing 'Fluted' body was revamped, and *c.* 1950 'Quail' was designed (coffeepot and cover, *c.* 1957; London, V&A), followed by the avant-garde geometric 'Can' shape designed in 1957. In 1958 Cooper joined R. H. & S. L. Plant, Longton, whose spare bottle-oven capacity gave her the chance to make dinnerware. Both companies were taken over by the

Wedgwood Group in March 1966. Following the closure of the Crown Works in 1980 Cooper continued to design for the Wedgwood Group, in particular for William Adams & Sons (Potters) Ltd, Tunstall, at a studio in the Adams's plant until her retirement in 1986 ('Florida' teapot and cover, 1986; London, V&A).

One of Cooper's major contributions to the pottery decoration industry was her detailed work on the development of transfer prints, which were indistinguishable from hand-painted designs. Working with Harry Taylor (1871–1956) of the Universal Transfer Co., she transformed the quality of lithographic prints, most of which were used in-glaze, trapped between two glaze layers for added protection.

ODNB

Elegance and Utility, 1924–1978: The Work of Susie Cooper RDI (exh. cat. by A. Woodhouse, London, Arthur Sanderson & Sons Ltd, 1978)
Susie Cooper Productions (exh. cat. by A. Eatwell, London, V&A, 1987)
A. Casey: *Susie Cooper Ceramics: A Collector's Guide* (1992)
B. Youds: *Susie Cooper: An Elegant Affair* (1996)
A. Eatwell and A. Casey: *Susie Cooper: A Pioneer of Modern Design* (Woodbridge, 2002)

Copeland Porcelain Factory. *See* SPODE CERAMICS WORKS.

Copenhagen Porcelain Factory [Kongelige Porcelainsfabrik]. Danish porcelain manufactory. In 1775 the chemist Frantz Heinrich Müller (1732–1820) founded a company to make hard-paste porcelain with kaolin (china clay) from Bornholm. The early wares were of a heavy, greyish body decorated with underglaze blue, which showed the influence of the Meissen porcelain factory. In 1779 Christian VII took control of the factory and styled it the Kongelige Porcelainsfabrik (Royal Porcelain Factory). The factory produced a wide range of dinner-services and figures, some of which were made by the German modeller Anton Carl Luplau (d 1795), who had worked at the porcelain factory of Fürstenberg. Production, however, concentrated on underglazed utilitarian wares decorated with such patterns as Meissen's 'Immortelle' and 'Blue Flower'.

Among the factory's most important early achievements was the 'Flora Danica' service (1790–1803; Copenhagen, Rosenborg Slot), which was originally intended for Catherine II, Empress of Russia. The service is decorated with polychrome plants executed by the German flower-painter Johann Cristoph Bayer (1738–1812) from illustrations in the botanical encyclopedia *Flora Danica* (Copenhagen, 1761–1883). The original service consisted of 1802 pieces decorated with 1260 different species of plants, identifiable by their Latin names on the underside of each piece.

In 1882 the Kongelige Porcelainsfabrik was bought by the Aluminia Faience Factory. In 1885 the architect and painter ARNOLD KROG was employed as artistic director. He raised the factory's reputation to an international level, introducing stylized Danish motifs that were inspired by the Danish landscape, flora and fauna, and Japanese woodblock prints in a series of underglaze muted blues and greys. He also renewed and revived the factory's 'Immortelle' service.

In 1906 Carl Martin-Hansen (1877–1941) made a series of figures in national costume. From 1909 the sculptor Gerhard Henning (1880–1967) made a series of figures inspired by erotic, Oriental and Rococo themes as well as by Danish folk traditions and characters from the fairy tales of Hans Christian Andersen. In 1924 a cooperative programme was established between the Kongelige Porcelainsfabrik and the Holmegaards Glasværker. Various glassware series were specifically designed to accompany the porcelain services. There was also a succession of fine tea- and dinner-services: Grethe Meyer (b 1918) designed the 'Blue Line' service (1962), Anne-Marie Trolle (b 1944) designed the restrained 'Domino' service (1970) and Gertrud Vasegaard (b 1913) designed the 'Capella' service (1975).

The principal competitor of Kongelige Porcelainsfabrik was BING & GRØNDAHL. In 1987 the two factories merged, and the new factory was styled Royal Copenhagen.

B. L. Grandjean: *The Flora Danica Service* (Copenhagen, 1950)
B. L. Grandjean: *Kongelig Dansk Porcelæn, 1775–1884* (Copenhagen, 1962)
B. L. Grandjean: *Kongelig Dansk Porcelæn, 1884–1980* (Odense, 1983)
H. V. F. Winstone: *Royal Copenhagen* (London, 1984)
D. R. McFadden: 'Porcelain in Denmark', *Mag. Ant.*, cxxxviii (July 1990), pp. 112–23
O. Willumsen Krog, ed.: *Flora Danica og det danske hof* (Copenhagen, 1990)
L. G. Dorenfeldt: 'Royal Danish Blue-decorated Porcelain', *Mag. Ant.*, clvi/2 (Aug 1999), pp. 166–75
R. J. Heritage: *Royal Copenhagen Porcelain: Animals and Gigurines* (Atglen, PA, 2002)

Coper, Hans (b Chemnitz, Lower Saxony, 8 April 1920; d Frome, Somerset, 16 June 1981). British potter of German birth. He arrived in England from Germany as a refugee in 1939 and in 1946 joined LUCIE RIE as a trainee assistant; together they produced sets of domestic ware (jug and beakers, 1950–55; London, V&A). Coper's first stoneware pots were small, incised or painted with lively designs. In 1959 he moved to Digswell, Herts, where he developed the flattened spade-, thistle- and tulip-shaped cup forms on cylindrical columns or bases for which he is known (1968, 1975; London, V&A). He produced wheel-thrown stoneware containers influenced by ancient Chinese, Egyptian and Mediterranean pottery. His work bridges the territory between vessel and art object, and he revived the old technique of hand-building. Among his early hand-built pieces are pilgrim-bottle vases on short columns with lightly textured or matt glazes in neutral colours or coated with manganese oxide and burnished. In 1983 the Hans Coper Memorial Collection was established at the Sainsbury Centre for the Visual Arts, Norwich.

ODNB
T. Birks: *Hans Coper* (London, 1983)
Hans Coper, 1920–1981 (exh. cat., ACGB, 1984)
C. Frankel: Modern pots: *Hans Coper, Lucie Rie & Their Contemporaries: The Lisa Sainsbury Collection* (Norwich and Wappingers Falls, 2000)
T. Birks: *Hans Coper* (Yeovil, 2005)

Copier, A(ndries) D(irk) (*b* Leerdam, 11 Jan 1901; *d* Wassenaar, 19 Dec 1991). Dutch glass designer. He worked at the royal glass factory in Leerdam (*see* LEERDAM GLASS), where his father was head of the etching and decoration department, and designed a large amount of consumer glass (1914–70). In addition to mass-produced items he also designed single pieces (sold as Unica) and limited editions (sold as Serica). In the late 1920s he began to design geometric abstract shapes, such as bulbs, cylinders and cubes; his bulb vases and cactus pots in red, yellow and blue graniver are particularly well known.

Nieuwe unica A. D. Copier (exh. cat., Arnhem, Gemeentemus., 1986)
R. Liefkes: *Copier, Glasontwerper/glaskunstenaar* (The Hague, 1989) [Dutch/ English text]
R. Liefkes: *A. D. Copier: Glass Designer, Glass Artist* (Zwolle, 2002)

Copland, Henry (*b c.* 1706; *d* 1753). English engraver, designer of trade cards and furniture designer. In 1746 he published *A New Book of Ornaments*, and subsequently collaborated with MATTHIAS LOCK on a second edition (1752). The *New Book* contains designs for side-tables, *torchères*, clocks, frames, pierglasses and fireplaces, very much in the Rococo idiom but also including such chinoiserie motifs as ho-ho birds and oriental figures. Copland also provided plates for the 1766 edition of ROBERT MANWARING's *The Chair-maker's Guide*. Copland and Lock also seem to have contributed to the designs in Chippendale's *Gentleman and Cabinet-maker's Director* (1754), but the nature of their collaboration with Chippendale is not clear.

Copper. Type of metal. As copper can be difficult to cast but is easy to shape by hammering, it has been used since very early times to make items of beaten sheet metal. Copper vessels have always been popular, although, as the unalloyed metal is rather soft, they are easily damaged and thus tend to form the more humble cooking utensils, with the golden-coloured bronze and brass used for more prestigious purposes. At the end of the 19th century beaten copper was favoured by the craftsmen of the ARTS AND CRAFTS MOVEMENT in Europe and North America.

Copper has been widely used in conjunction with a number of other materials. As it takes enamel very well, it has always been the favoured metal for this medium. Medieval Mosan and Limoges enamels, for example, are set in copper; where enamelwork was used on brasses in the medieval period, the actual enamelwork was often done on thin copper trays that were then let into the brass. The combination of enamelwork and copper was also popular among designers and craftsmen of the Arts and Crafts Movement. Copper also takes fire gilding better than its alloys, and many examples of the deliberate use of copper, rather than the more usual bronze or brass, for objects to be fire gilded are known. Copper has a pleasing and distinctive colour and has always been widely used for inlays into other metals, notably silver or the more golden bronze or brass. The black-patinated *shakudo* copper alloys inlaid with silver, gold and brass have been used extensively by the Japanese, particularly for sword guards and other sword fittings.

D. L. Fennimore and G. J. Fistrovich: *Metalwork in Early America: Copper and its Alloys from the Winterthur Collection* (Winterthur, DE, 1996)

Coquillage [Fr. *coque*: 'shell']. Decorative motif in the form of seashells.

Coral. Secretion of the coral polyp, largely consisting of calcium carbonate. Red or precious coral (*Corallium rubrum*) is the species most used by craftsmen and is most widely distributed in the Mediterranean; it is also found in the Fiji Islands and in the Japanese archipelago. Pacific coral may be distinguished from Mediterranean by its greater hardness, weight and size and by the diversity of its colour.

Throughout the Middle Ages coral continued was used for amulets and as a medical remedy, as well as for decorative beadwork in textiles. The earliest surviving works using coral carved into simple geometric forms are paternosters. Workshops in Genoa, TRAPANI, Paris, Lyon and Barcelona producing large numbers of these items were recorded in the 12th century. During the Middle Ages it was also believed that coral had the power to detect poison in food, and thus it was used in cutlery. In the 13th century silver-gilt spoons, forks and knives with coral handles were frequently recorded: some cutlery sets have survived that may be from 16th-century Genoa (examples in Dresden, Grünes Gewölbe; London, V&A). This magical property attributed to coral is highlighted in the case of credenzas, in which a coral branch, usually mounted in precious metal, is further set with fossilized sharks' teeth, also known for their power to detect poison (e.g. in Vienna, Schatzkam. Dt. Ordens). Coral is also recorded in connection with salts: the inventory (1401–16) of Jean, Duc de Berry, mentions a *saliera* of gold with a coral base.

Coral attained even greater significance in the Renaissance, when Trapani and Genoa were the principal centres of production. As a naturally occurring rare material that is soft enough to be worked by skilled carvers, it became one of the most sought-after items for collectors. William V, Duke of Bavaria, is said to have supported a coral-carving workshop in Landshut. The most important collections of 16th-century coral objects are in Schloss Ambras, Innsbruck, and the Galleria Doria-Pamphili, Rome. Goldsmiths' work was often decorated with coral during this period. Surviving examples include the *Crucifixion of St Sebastian* (Rome, Gal. Doria-Pamphili)

Coral amulet, from Palestine, 19th century (Jerusalem, Hechal Shalom Wolfson Museum)

and various other Crucifixions (e.g. Vienna, Ksthist. Mus.), the *Daphne* portraits by WENZEL JAMNITZER (Dresden, Grünes Gewölbe; Paris, Mus. Cluny), Archduke Ferdinand II's coral sabres (Vienna, Ksthist. Mus.; Innsbruck, Schloss Ambras), sabre-hilts (e.g. Florence, Pitti) and *Adam and Eve* figures (e.g. Munich, Bayer. Nmus.). The continued association of coral with blood, as well as its relative softness, made it the most suitable material for teething toys and rattles set in goldsmiths' work, which were popular from the late 16th century to the 19th.

A characteristic of coral work in the 17th century was the development of inlay: small pieces of coral were inset into gilded copper, bronze or silver. In addition to jewellery, textiles and figural statuary, there was at this time an increased use of coral for ecclesiastical objects, for example stoups, monstrances, devotional pictures and cribs, as well as secular household items. In the 17th century the most significant centre for coral work in Europe continued to be Trapani. The importance of Genoa, however, declined, partly because France held the monopoly on coral fishing off the North African coast until the French Revolution.

In the 18th century the art of coral-carving was revived in Naples, Livorno and Genoa, and work from these centres and Trapani was exported throughout Europe, as well as to India and China. The style of coral objects of this period reflected fashionable Baroque forms, with curving plant decoration as well as figurative ecclesiastical or secular subjects. Contemporary coral decoration was attached with pins rather than inlaid. It is often combined with such other colourful materials as enamel,

amber or tortoiseshell, for example in caskets (e.g. Pommersfelden, Schloss Weissenstein) and frames (e.g. Naples, Mus. N. Cer.). Northern artists, such as Peter Boy (1648–1727), continued to work in coral (e.g. a vessel, 1700; Pommersfelden, Schloss Weissenstein), although their style was quite different from that of the Italian workshops.

Coral was widely used for jewellery during the 19th century, a pale pink colour being particularly suitable for cameos (e.g. a pendant and pair of brooches carved with cameo portraits of *Bacchus*, *Apollo* and *Venus, c.* 1854; London, V&A). In the Art Deco period, coral continued to be used to introduce colour into jewellery and was often carved into abstract geometric shapes and contrasted with transparent gemstones, precious metals or lacquer.

Cordial glass. Type of drinking glass popular in 18th-century England, when it was used to drink gin and fruit liqueurs; the glasses have small bowls (either flute-shaped or cup-shaped) on proportionately tall stems.

Cordonnet. *See under* LACE.

Cori, Domenico dei. *See* DOMENICO DI NICCOLÒ.

Cork. Irish centre of glass production. In 1780 Ireland was granted permission to export glass and entrepreneurs were encouraged to establish glass houses in Cork because its location on the west coast of Ireland made it good for trade with the USA. In

1783 Atwell Hayes, Thomas Burnett and Francis Rowe founded the Cork Glass Co., which produced high-quality, richly cut lead glass, crown glass and black bottles until 1818. The most distinctive patterns of this glasshouse were engraved or cut band with vesical motifs, either joined point to point or separated by an eight-pointed star or bow-knot (e.g. jug, 1783–1818; London, V&A). Decanters attributed to this glasshouse are mallet-shaped with a medium-sized lip and three round or feathered rings. To celebrate the passing of the Act of Union (1800) engravers decorated some decanters with the national emblems of England (rose), Ireland (shamrock) and Scotland (thistle).

In 1815 the Waterloo Glass House Co. was established by a china retailer, Daniel Foley. Production concentrated on lighting and cut glass, but glass for medical purposes, phials and gallipots was also made. The management was sufficiently interested in technical development to introduce steam power to improve the process of annealing so as to warrant their glass hot-water proof. After the imposition of the Glass Excise Act (1825) the concern faced increasing financial difficulties and went bankrupt in 1835. After its closure there was an auction of wares, which included richly cut decanters, jugs, salad bowls, celery and pickle glasses, dessert plates and dishes, tumblers and wine glasses, hall and staircase globes and side-lights.

In 1818 the Terrace Glass Works was established by Edward Ronayne (d 1841) and Richard Ronayne. The factory produced lead-glass light fittings and cut and plain tableware. It employed first-rate artists to ensure high-quality designs and remained in production until 1841.

P. Warren: *Irish Glass: Waterford–Cork–Belfast in the Age of Exuberance* (London, 1981)

Cornelian. Variety of chalcedony, a semi-transparent quartz, of a deep dull red, flesh, or reddish white colour. It has been carved since the time of the ancient Egyptians, for whom supplies were available as pebbles that could be collected in the Eastern desert.

M. M. Bullard and others: 'Lorenzo de' Medici's acquisition of the Sigillo di Nerone', *J. Warb. & Court. Inst., lxii* (1999), pp. 283–6

Cornelius & Co. American metalwork company established in Philadelphia in 1810 by Christian Cornelius, a silversmith who had emigrated from the Netherlands in 1783. He soon turned to the casting of bronze, and by 1825 he had become a lamp manufacturer. The company passed to Cornelius's son Robert (1809–93), under whose management it became an important lighting business. The company made lamps and chandeliers, often finished in gold lacquer; it also made candlesticks, including the earliest documented American brass candlestick. The best known product of the company was the AR-GAND LAMP. The company's lamps were marked C Cornelius & Co or CCC. Production continued (for

a time as Cornelius & Baker) until the end of the 19th century.

D. L. Fennimore: *Metalwork in Early America: Copper and its Alloys from the Winterthur Collection* (Winterthur, DE, 1996)

Corning Glass Works. American glass manufactory in Corning, NY. In 1851 Amory Houghton (1813–82), a Boston businessman, became a director of a glass company in Cambridge, MA, and subsequently owner of his own glass factory. Later he sold his Massachusetts glass interests and bought the idle Brooklyn Flint Glass Works in New York. Transportation and labour difficulties caused him to move the equipment and some employees to Corning in 1868. The factory's chief product was blanks for glasscutting, and Houghton persuaded John Hoare (1822–96) to establish a branch of his successful Brooklyn cutting shop in Corning. This was the first of many cutting shops in the region, which became noted for the production of heavily cut glass. By about 1900 more than 500 glasscutters were employed in the Corning area.

In the 1870s Amory Houghtonjr (1837–1909) of the renamed Corning Glass Works developed an exceptionally visible and stable red glass for railway signal lanterns, which later became a railway standard, and in 1880 the firm blew the first light bulbs for Thomas Edison (1847–1931). After 1905 Corning phased out the manufacture of blanks for glasscutting, as this type of glass ceased to be fashionable, and developed the heat-resistant glass 'Pyrex' for use in laboratories and kitchens. The works expanded to become the largest speciality glass company in the USA, making all types of products except window glass and containers. In 1918 the STEUBEN GLASS WORKS became a subsidiary of Corning and now produces colourless, artistic glasswares with an ex-

Corning Glass Works frying pan, borosilicate glass and steel, diam. 177.8 mm, 1942 (New York, Museum of Modern Art)

ceptionally high proportion of lead, often decorated with copper-wheel engraving.

In 1951, to commemorate 100 years of involvement in the glass industry, the Houghton family opened the Corning Glass Center, which houses industrial displays, the Steuben glass factory and The Corning Museum of Glass, an educational institution devoted to the art and history of glassmaking. In 1990 the company changed its name to Corning Inc.

E. S. Farrar and J. S. Spillman: *The Complete Cut and Engraved Glass of Corning* (New York, 1979, rev. Syracuse, NY, 1997)
J. J. Matthews: *The Pursuit of Progress: Corning Glass Works, Alanson B. Houghton, and America as World Power* (Lexington, KY, 2000)

Coromandel [calamander]. Attractive and extremely hard cabinet wood from Sri Lanka and the Coromandel coast of south-east India; the wood is the product of *Diospyros quaesita* (family *Ebenaceae*), and so a type of ebony.

Coromandel lacquer. Chinese lacquer, which from the 17th century was exported to Europe; its name derives from the Coromandel coast of south-east India, where goods from China were often reloaded on their way to the West. Coromandel combined carving, lacquering, moulding in putty and polychrome painting. The design was built up on the surface, then lacquered, painted with oil pigments and carved to leave some areas free of lacquer. Scenes from famous dramas and stories of the Ming and Qing periods were represented. The best examples are large folding screens (e.g. a screen in 12 leaves of the Kangxi reign period (1662–1722), Copenhagen, Nmus.).

W. G. de Kesel and G. Dhont: *Coromandel: Lacquer Screens* (Ghent, 2002)

Corona. Circular chandelier consisting of one or more metal hoops on which lamps or candles were mounted. The corona (*corona lucis*: 'crown of light') was originally a form of lighting suspended from the roofs of church, but was later used in domestic interiors.

Cortelazzo, Antonio (*b* 1819; *d* 1903). Italian metalworker, active in Vicenza. Some of his early work imitated Renaissance metalwork so adeptly that it was sold by dealers as Renaissance metalwork. His virtuoso display pieces in gold, silver, enamel and steel attracted wealthy buyers in Europe and America. He designed for Lady Layard an elaborate metal belt, decorated with onyx cameos and miniature glass mosaics (1871; London, V&A), and for Sir William Drake a steel ewer and basin inlaid with gold and silver (*c.* 1870, since 2002 in the Indianapolis Museum of Art).

E. H. Gustafson: 'Museum Accessions', *Mag. Ant.*, clxiii/2 (Feb 2003), p. 30 [illustration; globes and ewers made by W. Bardin and A. Cortelazzo at Boscobel and the Indianapolis Museum of Art]

Cosmati. Traditional name for the marbleworkers of Rome (*marmorarii Romani*) active in the 12th and 13th centuries. Their characteristic use of polychrome marble and mosaic inlay is also known as cosmatesque art. The description of the marbleworkers as 'Cosmati' was based on the incorrect assumption that all Roman decorative marblework in the Middle Ages was produced by one family of artists of that name. The names of more than 50 'Cosmati' artists are so far known, most of them belonging to seven large family workshops, with documentary evidence of members from several generations in each family.

The art of the Cosmati was recognized throughout Europe as symbolizing the papal sphere of influence. If a patron wished to identify his interests with those of papal Rome, he employed Roman marbleworkers; one of the finest examples is the Cosmati floor (1268) by 'Odoricus' (probably Pietro di Oderisio) in front of the high altar in Westminster Abbey, London.

E. Hutton: *The Cosmati: The Roman Marble Workers of the 12th and 13th Centuries* (London, 1950)
D. F. Glass: *Studies on Cosmatesque Pavements*, Brit. Archaeol. Rep., Int. Ser. 82 (Oxford, 1980)
C. Napoleone: 'Marble Cosmesis', *F.M.R. Mag.*, lxxxix (Dec 1997–Jan 1998), pp. 34–58
L. Grant and R. Mortimer, eds: *Westminster Abbey: The Cosmati pavements*, Courtauld Research Papers, 3 (Aldershot, 2002)

Costanzi, Carlo (*b* Naples, 1705; *d* Rome, 1781). Italian gem-engraver. He was the son of the Roman gem-engraver Giovanni Costanzi (?1674–1754) and the younger brother of the painter Placido Costanzi (1702–59) and the gem-engraver Tommaso Costanzi (?1700–1747). Carlo secured commissions from courts all over Europe. His surviving gem-engraved portraits include *Benedict XIII* (sardonyx; Florence, Pitti); and *Baron Philipp von Stosch* (sapphire; Florence, Pitti). An emerald (untraced), engraved by Costanzi on one side with a portrait of *Benedict XIV* and on the other with *SS Peter and Paul*, was sent by the Pope to the Treasury of S Petronio in Bologna.

Costanzi's repertory also included portraits of figures from antiquity (e.g. Otto, Plato) and reproductions of ancient sculptures (e.g. *Antinous* from the marble at the Museo Capitolini, Rome), as well as reproductions of famous antique gems (*Aesculapius*, *Massinissa*; both untraced). A particularly noted work is the copy in chalcedony, for Cardinal Melchior de Polignac, of the famous antique intaglio of the *Head of Medusa*, then in the Strozzi collection; because of its perfect adherence to the model, it was long thought to be the original stone. Carlo's works, unlike those of his father and brother Tommaso, are often signed with *Cavalier Carlo Costanzi*, *Cavalier C. Costanzi f.* or *Eques Costanzi f.*

Costrel. Large bottle with an ear or ears through which a cord might be passed so it could be suspended from the waist; in later antiquarian use it is known as a pilgrim's bottle.

Maiolica costrel attributed to Flaminio Fontana, Urbino, mid-16th century (Florence, Museo Nazionale del Bargello)

Cotswold school. English school of furniture design. In 1892 ERNEST GIMSON and Ernest and Sidney BARNSLEY moved from London to the Cotswolds, where they made such Arts and Crafts furniture as rush-seated, ladder-backed chairs, plain oak pieces and more elaborate inlaid cabinets. They were joined in 1902 by C. R. ASHBEE, who moved the workshops of the Guild of Handicraft to Chipping Campden, Glos. In 1911 GORDON RUSSELL, who had spent much of his youth in Broadway (Hereford & Worcs) established his own workshop there, and in 1926 he founded his own furniture-making firm, Gordon Russell Ltd, in Chipping Campden.

Ceramics, Glass, Oriental Wares and Decorative Arts, Including Arts and Crafts, Jewellery, Gordon Russell and Cotswold School Furniture (sale cat., Bonhams, 2004)

Cottage-roof binding. *See under* BOOKBINDING, §1(III).

Cotterill, Edmund. *See under* GARRARD.

Cotton. Fibre made from the long, soft hairs (lint) surrounding the seeds of the cotton plant (*Gossypium*). Indigenous to India, the Sudan and Ethiopia, it was later grown in Egypt, China, western Central Asia, North America and elsewhere. Cotton is a very versatile fibre: used alone it can produce very fine,

light and quite strong textiles (lawn and muslin), and used alone or in combination with other fibres it can make extremely durable and heavy fabrics (e.g. for use in bedspreads, rugs and carpets). It takes dye-stuffs very well and can be painted or printed with designs.

1. Europe. 2. India. 3. Printed cotton.

1. EUROPE. Cotton was imported into the Middle East and North Africa in the 1st century AD and from there was traded throughout Spain and gradually through the rest of Europe. From its introduction into Europe, cotton was woven into cheap materials for underwear and stockings, and by the mid-18th century it was used for cotton velveteen and corduroy; an English corduroy waistcoat (London, V&A) is so decorative that it is comparable with contemporary silks. Also in the 18th century there was a steadily growing quilt-making industry in Bolton, Lancs: production was based on two types, one with a looped pile (caddy), and the other flat-woven in double cloth, imitating hand-quilted covers made in Marseille and hence called 'Marseille' or 'Marcella' quilts. The second technique was also used for men's summer waistcoats and for ladies' pockets, of which there are a few examples from the 18th century and many from the 19th, woven on power looms with jacquard control.

Lancashire cottons of all kinds dominated the European market for most of the 19th century. Cotton was also combined with worsted wool to make furnishings and men's waistcoats, thus meeting a new demand in the 19th century from a burgeoning middle class. Cotton was also used to make enormous SHAWLs in the 1850s and 1860s.

2. INDIA. Plain cotton cloth has for centuries been the basic ground for Indian decorative and folk arts. The spinning of cotton thread has been done on the spinning wheel (*carkhā*) for the past two or three centuries (or earlier), though in isolated areas hand-spinning on the spindle continued until towards the end of the 19th century. Until the 19th century, the winding of the warp was done on rows of sticks erected in the ground to the length of the cloth piece required, the warper crossing and re-crossing the threads as he walked, so that the threads were held in order for the simple handloom. The handlooms for cotton were of standard breadths and accommodated standard lengths, as most ordinary people wore a draped garment made from an uncut cloth length. The length for a *dhotī* (man's loin-cloth) or a *sārī* varied from region to region. In western India, the *sārī* was comparatively short; in Bengal and in parts of south India, it was long. For a shoulder wrap (*cādar*) or a woman's head cloth (*orhanī*), two breadths of cloth were stitched together; the term *dupattā*, sometimes used for a woman's head covering, literally means 'two cloths'. In areas with a large Muslim population, where cut-and-stitched garments were worn, a *thān* (length of cloth to make a garment) would also be woven.

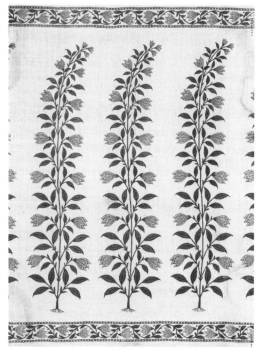

Cotton stencilled and hand-painted sash, from India, Mughal or Deccan, 18th century (London, Victoria and Albert Museum)

Indian cotton thread was comparatively loosely spun, giving the finished cloth a soft texture. It was the practice of the Indian cotton weavers to stretch the warp after tying the crossings of the threads and to brush in a starch of rice-paste (*koie*) before setting up the loom. The warp threads were thus strong and supple during weaving. The finished cloth was washed to remove all trace of starch; it was then bleached by drying in the sun.

Among India's most prized cotton textiles were its muslins, especially white cotton muslins from Dhaka (now in Bangladesh). Their fine quality has been attributed to a number of factors, including the variety of cotton plant grown in the region. Dhaka cotton grew especially well in the lands along the Brahmaputra River and its tributaries, where annual flooding brought alluvial and saline deposits. The cotton fibre produced was fine and soft and was spun on a small iron spindle, known locally as a *takwa*. Women spun the yarn and men did the weaving. As some moisture in the air was necessary to keep the thread supple, the spinners worked from soon after dawn until the sun dissipated the morning dew, and then for a short time in the late afternoon before sunset. The jawbone of the boalee fish (*Siluris boalis*) was used in carding the fibre before spinning. Its small, curved, closely-set teeth were ideal for combing out coarse fibres and extraneous matter and straightening the fine threads.

The starching of the warp thread with rice-paste, while the weft thread remained as spun, and the use of a small, smooth shuttle were also important factors. The soft, fine cloth produced was known by such names as *bāftāhavā* ('woven air') and *śabnam* ('evening dew'). Patterned muslins (*jamadānī*) were woven with floral sprigs (Hindi *būtī*) brocaded in thicker, softer white cotton on the delicate white ground. Fine hand-woven muslins were also produced in other parts of Bengal, in the Tapti Valley, around Madras. In Rajasthan, cotton from Gujarat was used to weave fine muslin *sārī*s with richly patterned coloured borders. The muslin *sārī*s of Rajastan were often printed.

3. PRINTED COTTON. The importing of painted cottons from India in the 17th century stimulated Europeans to create patterned cottons by printing instead of by weaving. By the late 17th century both the Dutch and the English were printing rather hesitantly in madder colours. The cottons produced have a naive charm but do not compare in quality with the cottons from India. By using different mordants, however, colours ranging from nearly black to pale pink could be achieved; it took another half century to achieve indigo printing. Despite the difficulties of using it, indigo yielded a crisp, fast blue that was particularly good for the large-scale, monochrome, copperplate-printed textiles made from the 1750s.

From the late 17th century a large number of snuff handkerchiefs were produced in Europe, the majority of which were copperplate-printed. Some printers concentrated specifically on the production of handkerchiefs, while others produced them as part of their range. Although many 18th-century handkerchiefs depicted such topical or political subjects as the *Trial of Dr Sacheverell* or the *Brentford By-election*, by the 19th century they were being produced for a much wider market. By the mid-18th century English block-printed textiles were printed in a full range of colours, which could copy both the patterns and the colouring of contemporary dress silks. Block-printing of cotton was used to great effect by William Morris in the 19th century. Even after American Independence (1776), English traders continued to export their cottons, thus discouraging the Americans from setting up their own cotton-printing industries. Only in the later 19th century were American cotton printers able to compete with the English.

In France it became legal to print cottons in 1759. A number of factories were set up in various regions, notably in Rouen, Nantes and Jouy-en-Josas. It is not always easy to identify a cotton printed in Mulhouse in France in the late 18th century from one printed in Lancashire, especially if it has a dark ground (very fashionable at the time), which would make it impossible to see the obligatory three blue threads of an English cotton dating from between 1774 and 1812.

Factories for printing cottons were also set up in other parts of Europe, especially in Germany, Switzerland and Bohemia. Most of their products were made to be sold locally or in nearby states. In Italy the factories produced printed cottons for local use, and the *mezzara* of Genoa, large shawls with patterns inspired by those of contemporary imported Indian painted bedspreads, became particularly well known throughout Europe. Another development, of the mid- and late 19th century, was the production of cottons printed for overseas markets. Turkey red printed cottons were produced in Scotland for the African market and in Moscow for the Central Asian and Swiss markets. Printed cottons were traded in both Europe and America through the use of pattern cards, which were sent by an agent to his counterpart abroad; the recipient then ordered the required fabric by number. Nathan Meyer Rothschild (1777–1836) from Frankfurt am Main was a particularly successful cotton printer: he traded Lancashire printed cottons all over Europe and established his family's fortune in Britain.

F. Montgomery: *Printed Textiles: English and American Cottons and Linens, 1700–1850* (London, 1970)
S. D. Chapman and S. Chassagne: *European Textile Printers of the Eighteenth Century* (London, 1981)
Colour and the Calico Printer (exh. cat., Farnham, W. Surrey Coll. A. & Des., 1982)
J. Brédif: *Toiles de Jouy: Classic Printed Textiles from France, 1760–1843* (London, 1989)
W. Hefford: *The Victoria and Albert Museum's Textile Collection: Design for Printed Textiles in England, 1750–1850* (London, 1992)
M. Riffel and S. Rouart: *Toile de Jouy: Printed Textiles in the Classic French Style* (London and New York, 2003)
D. A. Farnie and D. J. Jeremy: *The Fibre That Changed the World: The Cotton Industry in International Perspective, 1600–1990s* (Oxford and New York, 2004)

Couch. *See* SOFA.

Couched work. Embroidery with thread (often of gold) laid flat on the surface and secured by stitching.

Counter. In medieval and early-modern usage, a banker's or money-changer's table marked for counting money, sometimes fitted with a cupboard beneath; in more recent usage, the large surface in a shop on which the money paid by purchasers is counted out, and across which goods are delivered. In shoemaking, a counter is the piece of stiff leather forming the back part of a shoe or boot round the heel.

Counterchange. In design, a pattern consisting of juxtaposed materials of identical shape, contrasted in colour or texture.

Court, Suzanne de (*fl c.* 1600). French enameller, active in Limoges. She was the daughter of the enameller Jean de Court (*fl* 1541–64). Instead of using the *grisaille* technique, she developed a unique enamelling style noted for its vivid colours. An example of her work is *The Annunciation* (Limoges enamel plaques, *c.* 1600; Baltimore, MD, Walters A.G.).

B. A. L. Woytowicz: *Suzanne Court: A Study of Selected Enamels* (MA thesis, City College NY, 1981)

Courtauld. English family of silversmiths, industrialists, collectors and patrons, of Huguenot origin. Between 1708 and 1780 three generations of Courtauld silversmiths were registered at the Goldsmiths' Company. Augustine Courtauld (*c.* 1686–*c.* 1751) was apprenticed to SIMON PANTIN and in 1708 started a business as a plateworker in Church Court, off St Martin's Lane in London. Most of his work is of high quality, for example a silver tea-table (1742; St Petersburg, Hermitage) and the state salt of the Corporation of the City of London (1730; London, Mansion House). Augustine's brother Pierre Courtauld (1690–1729) registered a mark in 1721, but none of his works has been identified. Samuel Courtauld (1720–65), one of several Courtaulds to be called Samuel, was apprenticed to his father, Augustine, and entered his own mark in 1746. Like his father he produced many pieces in the fashionable Rococo style of the mid-18th century, for example a large two-handled soup tureen and cover (1751; Courtaulds plc, on loan to U. London, Courtauld Inst. Gals) and an oval shaving basin (1757; St Petersburg, Hermitage). In 1749 he married Louisa Perina Ogier (*c.* 1730–1807), and on Samuel's death she continued the business. In 1765 Louisa Courtauld registered her own mark, which appears on a silver table bell of 1766–7 (Oxford, Ashmolean). Three years later she took into partnership George Cowles (*d* 1811), and their joint mark appears on articles in the Neoclassical style made between 1768 and 1777. At the demise of this partnership Louisa entered a joint mark with her son Samuel Courtauld (1752–1821), but the partnership continued for only a further three years until he emigrated to the USA to pursue a career as a merchant. Louisa's other son, George Courtauld (1761–1823), became a silk-weaver, thus initiating the family's connection with the textile industry. George's son Samuel Courtauld (1793–1881) became an important silk manufacturer. The collector Samuel Courtauld (1876–1947), the eponym of the Courtauld Institute of Art, was the great-nephew of Samuel Courtauld the silk manufacturer.

ODNB [entries on Courtauld family and the two youngest Samuel Courtaulds]
J. F. Hayward: *The Courtauld Silver* (London and New York, 1975)
The Courtauld Family: Huguenot Silversmiths, Worshipful Company of Goldsmiths (London, 1985)
A Century of Silver: The Courtauld Family of Silversmiths, 1710–1780 (exh. cat by H. Braham; London, U. London, Courtauld Inst. Gals, 2003)

Court-cupboard. Low (the meaning of 'court') movable sideboard or cabinet used from the 16th century in England and the 17th century in America to display plate. Court-cupboards normally consisted of three shelves supported by legs of the cup and column type; the top shelf was used as a service table, the middle shelf sometimes accommodated a drawer and the bottom shelf was used for open storage. The stage between the upper and middle shelves was sometimes partly or wholly enclosed by doors, in which case it is sometimes known as a hall cupboard or a parlour cupboard or a press cupboard. By the 18th century court cupboards were usually called 'buffets'.

Southern Perspective: A Sampling from the Museum of Early Southern Decorative Arts (Winston-Salem, 2005)

Courteys [Courtois], **Pierre** (*b c.* 1520; *d c.* 1586). French enamel painter, active in Limoges. He executed large, decorative plaques and enamelled wares in the style of Pierre Raymond (whose pupil he may have been), but in a more vigorous and colourful manner. However, Courteys's two sons, Martial and Jean, left Limoges to become painters and goldsmiths at court; they both signed enamels in the style of Fontainebleau.

Courting mirror. Modern term for a type of 18th-century American mirror, sometimes given as a courting gift and often hung in hallways for last-minute grooming; early examples were imported (sometimes from the Netherlands), but thereafter most were made in New England. The frame typically consisted of painted glass strips, often in a metal moulding; some were surmounted with a crested area containing a picture.

Cousinet. French family of silversmiths. René Cousinet (*c.* 1626–92) was made a master in 1652 or 1654. An *Orfèvre du Roi*, he received payment between 1666 and 1684 for silver furniture (destr. 1689) made for Louis XIV (*reg* 1643–1715), including mirror-frames, large repoussé chargers, containers for orange trees and chandeliers. Two of René Cousinet's sons were associated with the Swedish court of Karl XII (*reg* 1697–1718). Jean-François Cousinet (*fl* 1686–*c.* 1711) became a master in Paris in 1686, but lived in Stockholm from 1694 to 1711. While there he executed a silver baptismal font (1696–1707; Stockholm, Kun. Slottet), designed as three caryatid putti emerging from a triangular pedestal and supporting a large shell-form basin. His brother, Nicolas-Ambroise Cousinet (*fl* 1696–*c.* 1715), became a master in Paris in 1696, but no silver by him is known. In 1703 he moved to Versailles, having been employed the previous year by Daniel Crönstrom, the Swedish envoy to the French court, to make drawings (Stockholm, Nmus.) of the French royal silver to be sent to Stockholm. These drawings are the single record of French royal domestic plate of the period. Henri-Nicolas Cousinet (*fl* 1724–68), son of Nicolas-Ambroise, made a travelling set (1729–30; Paris, Louvre) for Queen Maria Leczynska (1703–68). Ambroise-Nicolas Cousinet (*fl* 1745–*c.* 1765), brother of Henri-Nicolas, became a master in 1745. His only recorded work is a set of 16 large statuettes (Lisbon, Mus. N. A. Ant.) executed in 1757 for José Mascarenhas, Duke of Aveiro (1708–59). The figures, representing dancing couples of eight different nationalities, are the only such set of French silver sculpture for the dining-table from this period. The models for the figures may have been supplied by Henri-Nicolas Cousinet.

Cowan, **R(eginald) Guy** (*b* East Liverpool, OH, 1 Aug 1884; *d* Syracuse, NY, 1957). American potter and designer. Born into an Ohio pottery family, he studied ceramics under CHARLES FERGUS BINNS at Alfred University, Alfred, NY. In 1913 he opened his first pottery in Cleveland, OH. After World War I, he chose Rocky River, a suburb of Cleveland, as the site for a pottery where he produced limited edition vases and figurines. His Cowan Pottery Studio exclusively produced his designs until 1927, when he brought in the sculptor Paul Manship (1885–1966) to work with him, as well as other young potters and designers including Waylande Gregory (1905–71), Viktor Schreckengost (*b* 1906) and Edris Eckhardt (1910–98). The pottery closed in 1931, and Cowan went to Syracuse, NY, where he became art director for the Onondaga Pottery Co.

G. W. Scherma: 'R. Guy Cowan and his Associates', *Transactions of the Ceramics Symposium: Syracuse, 1979*, pp. 66–72
M. T. Bassett, R. G. Cowan and V. Naumann: *Cowan Pottery and the Cleveland School* (Atglen, PA, 1997)

Cow milk jug [cow-creamer]. Model of a cow in pottery, porcelain or (occasionally) silver, with the mouth and tail forming spout and handle; the jug is filled through a hole in the back. Early 18th-century examples are Dutch, but by the 1750s cow milk jugs were being manufactured in England.

Cox, **James** (*b c.* 1723; *d* 1800). English jeweller, clockmaker, toymaker and maker of automata. In 1745 he established himself in Fleet Street a goldsmith, jeweller, and toyman; 1756 he entered into partnership with Edward Grace and moved to 103 Shoe Lane. The business went bankrupt in 1758, but when Cox was discharged from bankruptcy in 1763, he started a new business, manufacturing mechanical clocks for export to the Far East. Few examples of his products survive, but they include the Swan automaton (Bowes Museum, Castle Barnard), and (probably) the *Peacock* clock (Hermitage, St Petersburg). In 1772 he opened Cox's Museum in Spring Gardens, Charing Cross, in which he housed 22 of his large automata, ranging in height from 3 to 5 metres.

In 1769 Cox bouught the CHELSEA PORCELAIN FACTORY from NICHOLAS SPRIMONT, but soon sold it on to DERBY Porcelain Factory. Cox & Son traded as jewellers in Shoe Lane until 1797.

ODNB
C. Pagani, 'The Clocks of James Cox', *Apollo*, cxli (Jan 1995), pp. 15–22
W. Meinz-Arnold: 'Lotterien: Goldschmiedearbeiten als Lotteriegewinne', *Weltkunst*, lxxiii/11 (Oct 2003), pp. 1592–4
R. Smith: 'James Cox (*c.* 1723–1800): A Revised Biography', *Burl. Mag.*, cxlii (2000), pp. 353–61

Coxe-DeWilde Pottery. American pottery in Burlington, NJ. It was founded in 1688 by Daniel Coxe (*b* ?Stoke Newington, England, 1640; *d* ?London, 19 Jan 1730) and John DeWilde (*b c.* 1665; *d* Doctor's Creek, NJ, 1708). A Cambridge-trained physician, Dr Coxe had extensive interests in the American colonies and was Governor of East and West Jersey from 1688 to 1692. His contract with DeWilde for a pottery 'for white and Chiney ware' was only one of the many ways in which he profited from his colonial holdings. From 1675 DeWilde had trained in London Delftware potteries and by the time of his association with Coxe was a master potter and maker of Delftware. Documents show that tin-glazed earthenwares were sold in the Delaware River Valley, Barbados and Jamaica, although no pieces from this pottery survive. The pottery was probably disbanded when Coxe sold his Jersey holdings to the West Jersey Society in 1692.

ODNB (on Daniel Coxe)

L. Springsted: 'A Delftware Center in Seventeenth-century New Jersey', *Amer. Cer. Circ. Bull.*, iv (1985), pp. 9–46

Cozzi Porcelain Factory. Italian porcelain factory. It was established in the Cannaregio area of Venice by the banker and ceramic technician Geminiano Cozzi (1728–97) in 1764. Cozzi had been trained at the Vezzi Porcelain Factory in Venice and later established a partnership with the Saxon potter Nathaniel Friedrich Hewelke, a porcelain expert (*see* HEWELKE PORCELAIN FACTORY). The factory produced mostly hard-paste porcelain but also some maiolica and cream-coloured earthenwares in the English style. Tablewares and vases were decorated with chinoiseries, carnival scenes and floral designs in bright colours and thick gilding. Painters and sculptors such as Domenico Bosello worked at the factory. Cozzi's brother Vincenzo Cozzi also worked with him, and the factory is known to have remained in production until 1812.

F. Stazzi: *Le porcellane veneziane di Geminiano e Vincenzo Cozzi* (Venice, 1982)

Crabeth, Dirck (Pietersz.) (*fl* Gouda, 1539; *d* Gouda, 1574). Dutch stained-glass artist, active in Gouda, sometimes with his younger brother (*fl* Gouda, 1559; *d* Gouda, 1589). His first important work is a group of stained-glass windows (1543; Paris, Mus. A. Déc.) for the cross-windows in the house of the Leiden bailiff Adriaen Dircksz. van Crimpen. The small scenes, framed by imaginary architecture, depict scenes from the *Lives of the Prophet Samuel and the Apostle Paul* and are stylistically so close to the work of Jan Swart that personal contact between the two artists can be assumed. The frames, unusual in the decorative arts of that time, demonstrate Crabeth's qualities as a designer of ornament.

The St Janskerk in Gouda was destroyed by fire in 1552, and the Crabeth family workshop (together with various Antwerp workshops) participated in the reconstruction. During the first five years, six designs by Dirck were executed, of which the three windows in the choir make a particularly beautiful group: the

Baptism (1555) with, on either side, *St John Recognizing Christ* (1556) and *St John Preaching* (1557). They combine an almost ascetic austerity with a love of landscape and a clever use of light effects. The royal window in the transept, nearly 20 m high, dates from 1557 and was donated by Philip II, then ruler of Holland. It shows the *Building of King Solomon's Temple* and the *Last Supper*. The majestic *Last Supper*, which features Mary Tudor, Philip II and his patron saint, is flanked by the building of the ideal church and a skilfully designed decorative cartouche. The *Baptism of the Eunuch* (1559) demonstrates Crabeth's distinctive manner of depicting compact rows of figures with individually characterized heads.

Although the Gouda windows survived the iconoclastic outbreak in 1566 and work on them continued afterwards, the glazing gradually came to a standstill. Dirck's design for *Christ Driving the Money-changers from the Temple*, probably commissioned as early as 1562, is dated 1567 but was not installed until 1569. Its donor, William the Silent of Orange Nassau, had by then instigated the resistance in the northern Netherlands to Philip II's rule. The donor's frame for the window was probably never installed, and William presumably never paid for the window. One more window, with *Judith and Holofernes* (1571), shows the full range of Dirck's skills. The artist used a relatively simple composition as an opportunity to provide eye-catching decoration and a brilliant landscape background, containing a view of the siege of the town of Bethulia. After the installation of this window the glazing work was suspended for 20 years. Full-size cartoons for most of the windows are kept at the church in Gouda, a unique but virtually inaccessible collection.

Apart from designing windows, Dirck drew maps and also made tapestry designs for Willem Andriesz. de Raedt (*fl* 1541–73/4), a Leiden weaver.

J. Q. van Regteren Altena and others: *De Goudse glazen, 1555–1603: Beschouwingen over Gouda, haar Sint Janskerk en de gebrandschilderde glazen* (The Hague, 1938)

Crabstock. In 18th-century stoneware (mostly English but sometimes French), handles and spouts (and occasionally lids) moulded to resemble the knotted branch of a crab-apple tree.

Crace. English family of interior decorators. During the 19th century members of the family headed the most important decorating firm in Britain. For 131 years the business was handed down from father to son, and commissions included interiors for a number of royal palaces, aristocratic seats and major public buildings. The family worked with leading architects and designed interiors in the most advanced styles of the day, their work informed by careful study of major European architectural monuments.

In 1718 Thomas Crace (*b c.* 1695) set up as a coachmaker in Rochester Row, London. His eldest son, Edward Crace (1725–99), was apprenticed in 1741 to the artist William Atkinson and in 1752 became a coach decorator in Long Acre, Covent Garden, London. Edward Crace made the natural transition to house decoration, establishing a decorating firm in 1768 in his Long Acre premises. In 1770 he provided gilt furniture, rich scagliola columns and arabesques in grisaille for the Pantheon (destr.), London, which was designed by James Wyatt and was the first major Neo-classical public building in Britain. Crace retired in the late 1780s.

Edward Crace was succeeded by his eldest son, John Crace (1754–1859), who traded as John Crace & Co. His three sons, Frederick Crace (1779–1859), Alfred Crace (1782–1849) and Henry Crace (*b* 1790), traded as John Crace & Sons from 1812 to 1826; their most important interior was the Royal Pavilion at Brighton, where John and Frederick created the first series of chinoiserie interiors (*c.* 1802–4) and where Frederick was recalled in 1815 to begin a new series of interiors in a spectacular Chinese style including the downstairs Corridor (*c.* 1815) and the Music Room (*c.* 1817–20; both altered). For the latter he designed curtains, a carpet (rewoven) and a large suite of furniture, made by the firm of Bailey & Saunders of London. In 1826 Frederick Crace became the sole head of the firm and between 1827 and 1834 carried out decorative painting and gilding at Windsor Castle, Berks.

Frederick's eldest son, John Gregory Crace (1809–89), became a full partner in Frederick Crace & Son in 1830 and continued to head the firm until his retirement *c.* 1880. After a visit to Paris in 1837 he decorated the firm's Wigmore Street showroom in a French Renaissance manner. Crace's first important patron was William Spencer Cavendish, 6th Duke of Devonshire, for whom he worked at Devonshire House (1840–45) in London and Chatsworth (1840–48), Derbys, providing carpets, upholstery, painted walls and ceilings, and some furniture. His most important work was for A. W. N. PUGIN, with whom he worked at Alton Towers, Staffs, in 1844. In the same year Frederick Crace & Son began to make furnishings in the Gothic style for Pugin's own house, The Grange, Ramsgate, Kent, and in 1846 they were awarded the contract for painting and gilding the New Palace of Westminster, designed by Sir Charles Barry (1795–1860) and Pugin. An important commission of the 1870s was the redecoration of the principal rooms of Grosvenor House, London, around the collection of Old Masters of Hugh Lupus, 3rd Marquess of Westminster.

Frederick's son John Dibblee Crace (1838–1919) designed Gothic- and Renaissance-style furniture for the International Exhibition of 1862 in London, and executed creditable work in the Gothic style at the Palace of Westminster (1869), London. His greatest patron was John Alexander Thynne, 4th Marquess of Bath (1831–1915), for whom he transformed the state rooms and east range (1874–82) of Longleat, Wilts, creating some of the most important Renaissance Revival interiors in Britain. Crace's travels to the Middle East in 1868–9 later inspired his interiors in the Islamic style, most notably his work at the

Royal Pavilion (1884–98). At the end of his career he worked for William Waldorf Astor, decorating Cliveden (*c.* 1895), Bucks, 18 Carlton House Terrace, London (1895–6), and the Astor Estate Office (*c.* 1892–5), London, in a sumptuous French Renaissance style, designing for Astor many items of furniture.

The Crace firm reached its largest extent in 1873, having 101 regular employees. This number declined towards the end of the 19th century, particularly after the death of John Gregory Crace. In 1899 John Dibblee Crace closed the firm.

ODNB (articles on Crace family, Frederick Crace, John Dibblee Crace and John Gregory Crace)

M. Aldrich, ed. *The Craces: Royal Decorators, 1768–1899* (London, 1990)

Crackle [craquelure]. Patterns of small cracks produced intentionally as a decorative effect in glazes, particulary on ceramics; the term 'crazing' is sometimes used to denote unintended crackle, but is also used to denote crackle that is deliberate. Crackle first emerged as a decorative feature in the Guan and Ru wares of the Song dynasty. Crackled glazes in Chinese pottery first became fashionable in Europe in 18th-century France, but were not used in European and American pottery and porcelain until the late 19th century; one of the pioneers was HUGH CORNWALL ROBERTSON, whose glazes in the late 1880s included a crackled apple-green turquoise. In 1895 a new pottery was established in Dedham, MA, using Robertson's distinctive crackled glaze for dinnerware, decorated in cobalt blue with stylized flowers and animals. In Demark, the Kongelige Porcelainsfabrik began experimenting with crackled glazes *c.* 1904.

Crackle has also been used to decorate glass. The techniques for producing crackle glass (also known as 'ice glass') were developed in Venice in the 16th century. In the late 19th century HOBBS, BROCKUNIER & CO.. inaugurated its lines of art wares with a cracked glass called 'Craquelle', and in the early 20th century Chris LEBEAU designed Art Deco glass with crackle decorations that look like snowflakes.

Crackle is also used as a decorative effect in batik. Before dyeing in indigo, the cloth is deliberately crushed in various ways to give 'crackle' effects where the dye penetrates the wax. In the past crackle was deliberately avoided in the East, but it now tends to be more popular, especially in Malaysia and the West.

S. L. Bucklow: *Formal Connoisseurship and the Characterisation of Craquelure* (Cambridge, 1996)

Cradle. Bed for an infant. In noble households during the Middle Ages cradles possessed much the same social significance as state beds. Aristocratic families generally had a splendid daytime cradle, in which the infant could be shown to visitors, and a simpler night cradle, in which the baby slept. State cradles were high, generally being suspended be-

Cradle given to King Vittorio Emanuele III on occasion of the birth of his daughter, early 20th century (Rome, Museo Boncompagni Ludovisi per le Arti Decorative)

tween wooden, inverted T-shaped standards, and were draped with textiles and furs. Ordinary cradles set on base rockers were low, permitting the nursemaids to attend the baby. The British Royal Collection includes a late 15th-century oak high cradle (Brit. Royal Col., on loan to London, Mus. London). The box, constructed of ribbed boards, swings between buttressed uprights surmounted by birds. An important state cradle (of the same design but now lacking its stand) of 1478–9 (Brussels, Musées Royaux A. & Hist.), made for either Philip the Fair or Margaret of Austria, is embellished with tracery, lavishly painted decoration and gold leaf.

Cradles of the 16th and 17th centuries were usually of box form, set on rockers, often with turned corner posts headed by ball finials so that the cradle could be easily rocked by hand. Many have a hood at one end (sometimes hinged or made to slide), and the exterior might have been covered with fringed and panelled velvet with gilt nails. The tomb of Princess Sophia (d 1607), daughter of James I, in Westminster Abbey, London, is carved in the form of a richly draped cradle. The commonest form of decoration at this time was bas-relief carving. A fine example dated 1670 at Townend, a manor house in Cumbria (NT), displays characteristic regional carvings.

Poor families made cradles of wicker or straw, known as bassinets, sometimes raised on simple stands. Although few survive, they are often depicted in paintings of cottage interiors. Many late 18th-cen-tury provincial cabinetmakers' books of prices include specifications for cradles. If these were made of pine the surface was normally grained. Thomas Sheraton published a design for a 'Swinging Crib Bed' in his *Cabinet Dictionary* (1803), which marked a return to the medieval system of suspending a cot between uprights. He recommended fitting a special clock spring, claimed to make the cradle swing for one and a half hours.

Royal cradles were still magnificent in the early 19th century. The cradle (Paris, Louvre) of Napoleon II, King of Rome, by François-Honoré-Georges Jacob-Desmalter and Pierre-Philippe Thomire, made of amboyna with gilt-bronze mounts, is of hooded design, fabric-lined, raised on an X-frame and surmounted by a figure of Fame. It is a simplified version of the silver gilt cradle given to him by the City of Paris (Vienna, Schatzkam.). During the late 19th century wicker cribs and cradles with canework sides were popular in wealthy households. See fig. on. p. 284.

Crailsheim Pottery. German pottery founded in 1720 by Georg Veit Weiss, run by his son Johann Georg Weiss from 1769 to 1800 and then by his grandson J. G. Weiss (and his widow) from 1800 to *c.* 1827. The factory's best-known products were tankards, typically decorated with hunting scenes.

H. Gretsch, *Die Fayencefabrik in Crailsheim* (Stuttgart, 1928)

Crane, Walter (*b* Liverpool, 15 Aug 1845; *d* Horsham, W. Sussex, 14 March 1915). English painter, illustrator, designer, writer and teacher. Crane's great skill was in the designing of decorative patterns and ornament. He is best known as a book illustrator, but his finest works also include the wallpapers printed by Jeffrey & Co., which he worked on from 1875; the designs for pottery for Maw & Co., Pilkington and Wedgwood; and the decorative schemes that he created (see colour pl. VII, fig. 2).

ODNB
W. Crane: *The Claims of Decorative Art* (London, 1892)
W. Crane: *Of the Decorative Illustration of Books* (London, 1896)
P. G. Konody: *The Art of Walter Crane* (London, 1902)
O. von Schleinitz: *Walter Crane* (Bielefeld, 1902)
I. Spencer: *Walter Crane* (London, 1975)
W. Crane, G. Smith and S. Hyde: *Walter Crane, 1845–1915: Artist, Designer, and Socialist* (London, 1989)
A. H. Lundin: *Victorian Horizons: The Reception of the Picture Books of Walter Crane, Randolph Caldecott, and Kate Greenaway* (Lanham, 2001)

Crapaud [Fr.: 'toad']. Usually heavily upholstered, deeply buttoned and richly embellished squat armchair, popular in the Netherlands and France in the mid-19th century.

Crape. *See* CRÊPE.

Craquelure. *See* CRACKLE.

Rocking cradle (see p. 282), from England, early 19th century (London, Victoria and Albert Museum)

Crayon manner. Type of copperplate-engraving process that reproduces a drawing in chalk or pencil in facsimile. It was invented in the 18th century, but it was superseded by the STIPPLE technique.

Crazing. *See* CRACKLE.

Creamware [cream-coloured earthenware; Fr. *faïence fine;* Ger. *Steingut;* It. *terraglia*]. Type of pottery made from clay enriched with calcined flint (silica) and Cornish soapstone (steatite) and finished with a liquid-lead glaze. The earliest extant example of the creamware body is dated 1743 and was potted by Enoch Booth (*fl* 1740–54) of Tunstall. Other potters associated with this improvement were JOHN AST-BURY of Shelton, THOMAS WHIELDON and Joseph Warburton (1694–1752) of Cobridge. A further refinement of creamware by WEDGWOOD established his 'Queen's ware' in honour of Queen Charlotte

(George III's consort), as the dominant useful pottery throughout Europe. From 1761 much creamware was decorated by the Liverpool-based partnership of John Sadler (1720–89) and Guy Green (1729–1803) with on-glaze transfer-printing.

Wedgwood's development of creamware radically changed the mechanics of the ceramics trade. It was hugely popular and was imitated all over Europe. It undercut Chinese porcelain and drastically reduced the ceramics trade with East Asia. Before the end of the century creamware was being produced in Sweden (Rörstrand and Marieberg from 1770, Gustavsberg-Vänge, near Uppsala from 1785), France (Pont-aux-Choux factory in Paris from 1772, Creil and Montereau from 1774, Douai, La-Charité-sur-Loire, Chantilly, Apt and Lunéville by 1776), America (in Salem, NC, by 1773), Slovakia (Holíč by 1786), and Ireland (in Downshire, Co. Wicklow, by 1787). Creamware is still made in many pottery centres, such as the Royal Creamware Company in Malton (North Yorks).

D. C. Towner: *Creamware* (London and Boston, 1978)
J. Kybalová: *European Creamware* (London, 1989)
P. Francis: *A Pottery by the Lagan: Irish Creamware from the Downshire Pottery, Belfast 1787– c. 1806* (Belfast, 2000)
'Weldon Creamware', *Cer. Rev.*, cxciv (March–April 2002), pp. 32–3
S. A. South, L. R. Hudgins and C. Steen: *John Bartlam: Staffordshire in Carolina* (Columbia, SC, 2004)

Credence [It. *credenza*]. Side table or sideboard on which vessels and dishes were placed ready for being served at table. In ecclesiastical use, a small side table or shelf on which the eucharistic elements are placed previous to consecration.

Creeper. *See under* FIREPLACE FURNISHINGS.

Creil Pottery. French pottery factory founded in 1795 at Creil (Oise) with a view to producing earthenware that would imitate and undercut English manufacturers of cheap tableware. The factory employed English craftsmen from the outset, and made pottery decorated with both English themes (e.g. hunting) and French themes (e.g. Napoleon). The factory merged with a creamware factory at Montereau from 1818–25 and from 1840–95. Creil closed in 1894, but Montereau continued to use the Creil name until 1955.

M. Ariès: *La Manufacture de Creil, 1795–1894* (Paris, 1974)
M. Ariès: *Creil: Faïence fine et porcelaine, 1797–1895* (Paris, 1994)
M. Boyer: 'House of Creil', *World Int.*, xix/4 (April 1999), pp. 158–65

Crêpe [crape]. Thin transparent gauze-like fabric, plain woven, without any twill, of highly twisted raw silk or other staple, and mechanically embossed, so as to have a crisped or minutely wrinkled surface. In France this material, formerly known in English as crape, is called *crêpe anglais*. *Crêpe de chine* is a white or other coloured crêpe made of raw silk; *crêpe lisse* is a smooth or glossy *crêpe*, which is not *crêpé* or wrinkled. The *crêpe* made in Norwich in the 18th and 19th centuries was a plain cloth of silk warp and worsted weft; it became associated with the dress of clergymen, and eventually with the black *crêpe* of Victorian mourning.

R. Reilly: *Crepe de Chine and Other Silky Woven Fabrics* (Ames, IA, 1980)

Crespin, Paul (*b* London, 1694; *d* Southampton, 25 Jan 1770). English goldsmith of Huguenot descent. He entered his first marks between July 1720 and December 1721 and established a workshop in Old Compton Street, Soho, London. An early example of his chasing skill can be seen on a cruet stand (1721; Colonial Williamsburg, VA), the rim of which is decorated with hunting scenes. He had a large number of aristocratic patrons to whom he supplied table services, ornate centrepieces, two-handled cups, tureens, candlesticks and such smaller items as spice-boxes. He drew on French designs in work such as the silver gilt ice buckets (1732; Blenheim Pal., Oxon), for example, which he made for Charles Spencer, 3rd Duke of Marlborough. Among the most remarkable examples of his work are the tureen and salver (1741; Toledo, OH, Mus. A.) made for Charles Seymour, 6th Duke of Somerset; the tureen is majestically supported on the backs of two goats amid a profusion of fruits. Crespin may have collaborated with NICHOLAS SPRIMONT (whose shop was nearby) on a silver gilt centrepiece made for Frederick, Prince of Wales (1741; London, Brit. Royal Col., Buckingham Palace).

E. A. Jones: *Paul Crespin, Huguenot Goldsmith* (London, 1940)
Queen Anne & Georgian Silver: Many Rare Examples by Paul Crespin, Orlando Jackson, Paul Storr and Other Well-Known Makers. Various Owners Including Property of Charles Percy Tyner, Estate of Mrs. Theodore Frelinghuysen, Estate of the Late Robert Goelet (sale. cat., New York, Parke-Bernet Galleries, 1966)
A. Delaforce: 'Paul Crespin's Silver-gilt Bath for the King of Portugal', *Burl. Mag.*, cxxxix (Jan.1997), pp. 38–40

Cressent, Charles (*b* Amiens, 16 Dec 1685; *d* Paris, 10 Jan 1768). French cabinetmaker and sculptor. He was taught by his father, François Cressent, a sculptor in Amiens, and became a *maître-ébéniste* on 9 January 1708. He obtained the title of Ebéniste du Régent in 1719, which allowed him to trade as a cabinetmaker free from guild restrictions. The richest French patrons, the Portuguese Court and many German princes bought furniture from him. His work is of exceptional quality and epitomizes the Régence and early Louis XV styles to which he remained faithful throughout his career. The forms of his pieces were perfectly curved and rendered sumptuous by abundant, virtuoso bronze mounts and emphatically serrated agraffe (hooked) ornaments and mouldings (see colour pl. VIII, fig. 4). His lavish mounts to some extent obscured the restrained veneering or geometric marquetry, for which he almost always used rosewood, purple-wood or satin-wood. Above all, however, he was a sculptor, and he contravened guild restrictions by modelling the bronzes that adorn his furniture himself; these included terminals depicting the *Four Continents* (e.g. book-cabinet; Lisbon, Mus. Gulbenkian), *Child Musicians* (e.g. commode) and *Seated Women Holding Cornucopias* (e.g. commode; both Munich, Residenzmus.), all *c.* 1740. These figures were combined with vegetation consisting of palms, vines and garlands of flowers, which emphasized the furniture's contours. He also mounted furniture with busts of *Mars* (e.g. desk, *c.* 1740; Paris, Louvre) and *espagnolette* heads (female head surrounded by a stiff ruff; e.g. commode, *c.* 1730; London, Wallace). He also made many, predominantly bronze, cartel-clocks, the most remarkable of which depicts the theme of *Love Conquering Time* (*c.* 1747; London, Wallace).

A. Pradère: *Charles Cressent: Sculpteur, ébéniste du Régent* (Dijon, 2003)

Cresson. French family of furniture-makers (*menuisiers*) in 18th-century Paris. At least ten members of the family were involved in the trade, and it is often difficult to attribute furniture to a particular member of the family, so pieces are described as 'Louis XV Cresson'. The most prominent members of the family were Louis Cresson (1706–61) and his brother Michel (1709–*c.* 1773), both of whom made sumptuous upholstered furniture, often for the royal court.

Cresting. Ornamental edging on a piece of furniture, mainly the decorated top of a mirror or frame; in medieval furniture it often consists of a repeated foliate motif.

Cretonne [Fr. *crétonne*] Strong fabric of hempen warp and linen weft; it was stronger than CHINTZ, which it displaced in the mid-19th century. In England the term denotes a strong unglazed cotton cloth printed on one or both sides with a pattern in colours, and used for chair covers and curtains; cretonne was first manufactured in England in the 1860s.

Cretonne and Its Uses for Every Room in the House, F. A. Foster & Co. (Boston, MA, 1922)
R. Norton: *Cretonne Solves the Problem: A Manual of Interior Decoration with Special Emphasis on the Selection, Use, and Care of Puritan Cretonnes,* F. A. Foster & Co. (Boston, MA, 1925)

Creussen [Kreussen]. German centre of ceramics production. Stoneware was produced at Creussen, near Bayreuth, as early as the end of the 15th century. Brown-glazed stoneware, however, was not manufactured until the end of the 16th century. The oldest-known dated piece was made in 1614. During the first quarter of the 17th century output was at its finest, and the most famous potteries belonged to the Vest and Speckner families. A number of special forms were developed, including the *Krause* (a low, wide tankard) and *Schraubflasche* (a globular-shaped flask with four or six flattened sides). Another speciality was vessels for chemists' shops, as Creussen wares were resistant to acids. The majority of the potteries' output consisted of wine jugs and tankards. Typical wares were decorated in relief and brightly coloured enamels. Favoured motifs included the Apostles (*Apostelkrüge*), biblical scenes, representations of the seven planets (*Planetenkrüge*), the Emperor with the seven Electors (*Kurfürstenkrüge*; e.g. of 1690; Hannover, Kestner-Mus.), hunting scenes and coats of arms. The manufacture of stoneware ceased in the 1730s. From 1618 to *c.* 1669 high-quality blue-and-white faience was also produced in Creussen at the workshop of Lorenz Speckner (1598–1669).

J. Kröll: *Creussener Steinzeug* (Brunswick, 1980)
C. Höreth:x *Creussen: Bilder aus vergangener Zeit* (Horb am Neckar, 1996)

Crewel. Thin worsted yarn used from the late 17th century for bedhangings, curtains, embroidery, fringes, hosiery, laces, tapestry and vestments. 'Crewel-work' is a type of embroidery (popular from the 1860s) in which a design is worked in crewel on a background of linen or cloth.

S. Amor: *Crewel Embroidery* (Bowral, 2002)
A-Z of Crewel Embroidery (Norwood, SA, 2005)

Criard, Mathieu (*b* ?Brussels, 1689; *d* Paris, 30 Jan 1776). French cabinetmaker of Flemish origin from the most prominent of a family of *ébénistes*. He worked independently before becoming a *maître-ébéniste* on 29 July 1738 His extant works, stamped with his mark M CRIAERD, include luxurious furniture, in general characterized by very turbulent forms and exuberant, fantastic decoration. Chequered marquetry or, more rarely, floral marquetry was used, as well as some varnished panels, either imitating Chinese lacquer or in *vernis Martin* with European decoration. In particular, he made beautiful commodes, including one (Versailles, Château) for the Dauphin's Cabinet de Retraite, which is typical of his work, as is the commode (Paris, Louvre) decorated with blue and silvered-bronze birds made for Madame de Mailly.

Criblé [Fr. *crible*: 'sieve'). Type of engraving on metal or wood or glass; such engravings depict shade or half-tones through the use of small dots. Dotted prints (Fr. *criblé*; Ger. *Schrotblatt*) made by relief-engraving on metal were produced by goldsmiths in the second half of the 15th century in the Natherlands, parts of the Rhine, Cologne, Basel and Lake Constance.

Crich. English centre of ceramics production. Brown stoneware pottery made in the Derbyshire town of Crich in the second half of the 18th century. The tradition was revived in 1973, when Diana and David Worthy established Crich Pottery, which exports all over the world.

Crieff. *See under* PORTOBELLO.

Crinoline. Stiff cloth made with a warp of cotton or linen thread and a woof of horse-hair (Fr. *crin*). It was originally used for shoes and half-boots (bottines), and in the early 19th century for dresses and bonnets; from the mid-19th century it was primarily used for hooped petticoats, which came to be known as crinolines.

W. B. Lord: *The Freaks of Fashion with Illustrations of the Changes in the Corset and Crinoline from Remote Periods to the Present Time* (London, 1959)
N. Waugh: *Corsets and Crinolines* (New York and London, 2004)

Crinoline group. Modern pottery term for a type of 18th-century German porcelain group consisting of a woman in a hooped skirt accompanied by a well-dressed man and one or two servants; the genre was designed by JOHANN JOACHIM KÄNDLER at Meissen in 1737 and was soon imitated by other German manufacturers.

Cripps, William (*fl* 1730–67). English silversmith based in London. He made domestic silver for the top end of the market, and is best known for his drinking vessels.

Criseby. *See* ECKERNFØRDE POTTERY.

Crisselling. *See* CRIZZELLING.

Cristallerie de Baccart. *See* BACCARAT.

Cristallerie de Clichy. *See* CLICHY GLASSHOUSE.

Cristallerie de Pantin. *See* PANTIN GLASSHOUSE.

Cristallerie de Saint-Louis. *See* SAINT-LOUIS GLASSHOUSE.

Cristallerie de Val-Saint-Lambert. *See* VAL-SAINT-LAMBERT GLASSHOUSE.

Cristallo. Transparent glass invented *c.* 1450 by Angelo BAROVIER and soon produced in large quantities by other Murano glassmakers. The finest examples of 16th-century Venetian glass are the thin *cristallo* chalices and goblets.

Cristóbal Augusta. *See* AUGUSTA, CRISTÓBAL.

Crivelli carpets. *See under* CARPET, §II. 3(III)(a).

Crizzelling [crizzling]. Roughened or crumpled surface feature on glass or stone or ice, characterized by a fine network of cracks

Crochet. Type of knitting or lacework done with a single hooked needle, usually with cotton or wool thread (see fig. on p. 288). The basic structure is the chain, on which stitches and patterns are built. Filet crochet consists of a groundwork of square mesh in which each square is made from two chain stitches with a triple stitch at each end; it is sometimes darned with a pattern.

The finest crochet work has traditionally come from Ireland, notably the early 19th-century examples made by children in the schools staffed by nuns from the Ursuline Convent at Blackrock (County Cork). In Irish crochet, double crochet is worked over a padding of linen thread to form the pattern; sometimes the motifs are worked separately and then attached by a network known as the filling. The two

Cristallo goblet, with enamel and gilt decoration, h. 160 mm, from Venice, *c.* 1475–1525 (London, Victoria and Albert Museum)

principal types of Irish crochet work are GUPIRE LACE (a heavy lace worked on a foundation that has a design stamped on it) and *bébé* lace (a light lace worked into geometrical patterns which are joined without a foundation).

A. L. Potter: *A Living Mystery: The International Art & History of Crochet* (n.p., 1990)
N. H. Scalessa: *Historic Reflections in Crochet* (Philadelphia, 2001)
M. Treanor: *Clones Lace: The Story and Patterns of an Irish Crochet* (Cork, 2002)
C. Bojczuk: *Crochet Unravelled: A Clear and Concise Guide to Learning Crochet* (South Ockendon, 2005)

Croft. Filing cabinet with drop leaves that enable it to be used as a writing table; it is named after its inventor, the writer and lexicographer Sir Herbert Croft (1751–1816).

ODNB (Sir Herbert Croft)

Crolius and **Remmey.** American pottery established by William Crolius [Johan Willem Crollius] (*b* Neuwied, near Koblenz, *c.* 1700; *d* New York, *c.* 1776) and John Remmey (*d* New York, Nov 1762). Crolius arrived in New York *c.* 1718 and established a stoneware pottery on Pot-Bakers Hill. Bound by intermarriage to the Corselius and families, who were also in the pottery business, the Crolius family figured prominently in Manhattan pottery history until about 1850. From *c.* 1735 William Crolius and John

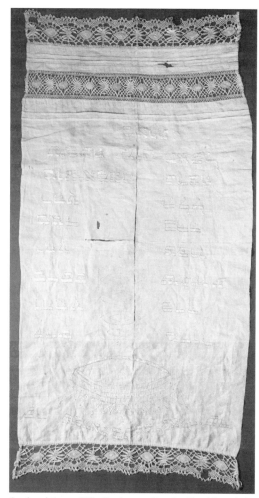

Crocheted (see p. 287) silk edge on silk-embroidered linen Seder towel, 610 × 559 mm, from Frankfurt, Germany, 1914 (New York, The Jewish Museum)

Remmey were in business together. Although salt-glazed stoneware was the principal product, lead-glazed earthenware was also made in the early years of the Crolius and Remmey potteries. Before the American Revolution, their stoneware closely resembled Rhenish stoneware with incised decoration filled in with a blue cobalt oxide glaze, but subsequent generations usually painted simple blue embellishments (e.g. pitcher, 1798; New York, NY Hist. Soc.). Remmey's grandson Henry Remmey Sr (*b c.* 1770; *d c.* 1865) and great-grandson Henry Remmey Jr left New York before 1817, when they were working in Baltimore. In 1827 the latter purchased a pottery in Philadelphia and established the Remmey name there.

W. C. Ketchum Jr : *Early Potters and Potteries of New York State* (New York, 1970); rev. as *Potters and Potteries of New York State, 1650–1900* (Syracuse, 1987)

Cros, (César-Isidore-)Henri [Henry] (*b* Narbonne, 16 Nov 1840; *d* Sèvres, 20 Jan 1907). French sculptor

and writer. Between 1869 and 1880 he researched techniques of making sculpture in polychromed wax, and produced 12 works in this medium (see colour pl. XV, fig. 5). His investigations into the way wax had been used in earlier art culminated in a study, undertaken in collaboration with the scientist Charles Henry, of the use of encaustic in the ancient world. From the mid-1880s Cros became interested in another ancient technique, that of making polychrome sculpture and decorative objects from fired glass-spaste imbued with metal oxides. He sought State sponsorship for his research and was rewarded in 1891 by being provided with a studio at the Sèvres Porcelain Factory, for the production of *pâte de verre* sculpture and decorative work, notably vases and imitations of antique carved gems

H. Cros and C. Henry: *L'Encaustique et les autres procédés de peinture chez les Anciens, histoire et technique* (Paris, 1884)
J.-L. Olivié: 'Un Atelier et des recherches subventionnés par l'état: Henry Cros à Sèvres', *La Sculpture du XIXe siècle, une mémoire retrouvée: Les Fonds de sculpture. Rencontres de l'école du Louvre: Paris, 1986*, pp. 193–9

Crosier [crozier]. Crook or pastoral staff of a bishop, abbot or abbess. It was originally a wooden staff used by itinerant monks, priests and bishops (and also teachers), possibly as an aid to walking and also as a badge of office. The use of such staves is first recorded during the 4th century AD. The crook-headed form had become common by the 9th century, and this form has remained dominant throughout the centuries, except for a period in the 11th and 12th centuries when some clerics carried tau-headed (T-shaped) crosiers. The occasional practice of popes carrying a crosier was abolished by Innocent III in the late 12th century, after which they were carried only by bishops, abbots and abbesses. Crosiers were abolished in the Anglican Church, along with many other appurtenances of the Roman Catholic Church, by King Henry VIII, and it was not until the revival of outward form stimulated by the Oxford and Liturgical movements that they again came into use; they are still in occasional use in the Roman Catholic church.

From an early period, the plain wooden crosiers of the saints were treated as relics and were encased in precious metal and encrusted with gems. The precious covering of the crosier of St Austreberthe of Montreuil-sur-Mer (Montreuil-sur-Mer, St Sauve) is supposed to date from the 7th century, and a Merovingian *Life of St Sylvanus* records the posthumous encasing of the saint's crosier in silver. This practice seems to have become common, and it may have had an influence on later crosiers, which, from about the 9th century, began to be made of semi-precious materials.

The earliest surviving crosiers that do not appear to have been thought relics are Frankish. They are made of various materials, such as jet (New York, Met.) and gilt bronze (Hildesheim Cathedral Treasury). Their heads are small and tightly curled into

Crosier head, enamel and gold-plated copper, from Limoges, France, *c.* 1220–35 (Paris, Musée du Louvre)

spiral form, unlike the encased relics, which have heads that are relatively large and just slightly bent. Crosiers survive in large quantities from the 11th century onwards. Throughout the medieval period ivory and enamel were the most common media, and the most common imagery was of serpents, fruit and foliage (a clear example is a 12th-century English crosier head in Florence, Bargello).

The traditional assumption that the crosier is based on a shepherd's crook did not affect their design until the 20th century; indeed there was no pastoral imagery until the 19th century, when the Good Shepherd appears on some of the more ornate examples. The serpents and foliage that appeared on most crosiers during their formative period between the 9th and 12th centuries probably refer to Aaron's rod, which became a serpent on several occasions. In later periods, the serpent ceased to appear on crosiers, although foliage remained widespread. Crosiers became increasingly precious and ornate until the later 20th century, when it became fashionable to bear an 'authentic' wooden shepherd's crook, except in the case of the Anglican Bishop of Lynn, who carried a boat-hook on the grounds that there were more boats than sheep at Lynn.

D. Gaborit Chopin: 'Bâtons pastoraux', *Trésors des abbayes normandes* (Rouen, 1979), pp. 233–4, 243

P. E. Michelli: *The Pre-Norman Crosiers and Metalwork of Ireland* (Norwich, 1987)

Cross. The central symbol of Christianity, widely represented in art in a great variety of types, contexts and materials. Although in its narrow sense the term denotes a cross without the *corpus* (figure of the crucified Christ), it is also commonly used to refer to a crucifix (a cross with a representation of the *corpus*); the cross was also adopted as the typical form for reliquaries of the True Cross (*see* RELIQUARY). The monumental cross is a large cross, usually sculpted in stone, often free-standing. The portable cross is a small cross that is not permanently fixed; the main types of portable cross are the altar, processional and pectoral cross.

1. Altar and processional. 2. Pectoral.

1. ALTAR AND PROCESSIONAL. The altar cross stands on the altar at all times or sometimes only during the celebration of mass. It marks the altar as the place where Christ's death on the cross is re-enacted through the celebration of the Eucharist; thus in a great many cases it includes the figure of Christ crucified on it. The processional cross is fixed onto a tall pole by means of a pin and carried at the front of processions. It is often difficult to distinguish between these two types of cross, particularly since the function and appearance of individual crosses mentioned in treasury inventories and other sources are not generally specified. In addition, most surviving crosses have or once had a pin, so that they could have been fixed either onto a pole or into a pedestal or a slot in the altar, a practice also corroborated by miniatures.

(i) Byzantine and medieval. (ii) Renaissance and after.

(i) Byzantine and medieval.

(a) Eastern Church. A number of silver crosses dating from the 6th and 7th centuries have been preserved (e.g. Washington, DC, Dumbarton Oaks); as well as serving as altar or processional crosses, they may also have been placed above the iconostasis or in the narthex, where people also prayed. The 6th-century Moses Cross (Mt Sinai, Monastery of St Catherine) is a superb example. It is a bronze cross with flaring arms, decorated on the front with a Greek inscription from Exodus and a dedication. At the ends of the cross arms are three engravings: one on the left depicts Moses ascending Mt Sinai, and one on the right shows him loosening his sandal. The reverse is blank.

From around the 6th or 7th century the preferred material for altar and processional crosses was silver with niello decoration or gilding, although bronze was more widely used from the 10th century. Most of these crosses have widened ends, although there are also examples with straight ends. They are often decorated with engraved or niello representations of the *Trisagion* [Gr.: 'thrice holy'], donors' monograms and dedicatory inscriptions (e.g. Washington, DC, Dumbarton Oaks), or occasionally with an engraved image of Christ crucified. Examples with a three-dimensional figure of the crucified Christ do not occur before the 10th century; such crucifixes often also include busts of the apostles or the evangelists as well as figures of the Virgin and St John the Baptist. The latter usually flank the central figure of Christ thus forming a Deësis arrangement. The Virgin or saints may be shown on the back of the cross, and other frequent depictions include the Virgin and Child, Christ Pantokrator and angels. Jewelled crosses were much less common. The earliest surviving *crux gemmata* is that of Emperor Justin II (*c.* AD 565–78, Rome, Tesoro di S Pietro); it has a relic container with a fragment of the True Cross as well as hardstones and inscriptions on the front, while on the reverse are medallion busts of *Justin* with his wife *Sophia, Christ,* and in the middle the *Agnus Dei* (see colour pl. VIII, fig. 2).

(b) *Western Church.* The earliest surviving example of an altar cross is probably the 11th century Bernward Cross (silver-gilt, *c.* 1007–8; Hildesheim, Diöz-mus. & Domschatzkam.). Later examples survive in the territory of the Holy Roman Empire, in Tuscany and Lombardy as well as in Denmark and Scania (Skåne, now Sweden). Surprisingly few Romanesque examples have been preserved in England, France and Spain. There were no regulations in the medieval period regarding the material to be used for altar and processional crosses. Most of those that survive are made of bronze, copper or brass, usually gilt. Records frequently mention crosses made of silver gilt or gold, although the latter may also have only been gilt as hardly any solid gold crosses survive. In poorer communities wooden crosses must also have been used. A few isolated examples survive of crosses or crucifixes made of walrus ivory; a splendid example is the Cloisters Cross (mid-12th century; New York, Cloisters), of English workmanship; other examples have originated in the Scandinavian countries (e.g. Gunhild Cross, before 1076; Copenhagen, Nmus.). Limoges enamel crosses became more widespread from the second half of the 12th century, and were exported all over Europe. Processional crosses were often decorated with gems and pearls; the intersection frequently containing relics, as in the Great Bernward Cross (*c.* 1130–40; Hildesheim, Diözmus. & Domschatzkam.), or emphasized by gems, as exemplified by the Lothair Cross (*c.* 1000; Aachen, Domschatzkam.).

The basic form for both altar and processional crosses is the Latin cross with straight ends, although variations are also found; the ends can, for example, be widened, trapeziform, crutch-headed or rounded. Widened ends are particularly frequent on early examples, for instance the jewelled crosses (9th–11th centuries) at the Camara Santa in Oviedo Cathedral and in the Münsterschatzkammer, Essen. The Imperial Cross (*c.* 1024; Vienna, Schatzkam.) is the earliest surviving cross with crutch-head ends. Lily or trefoil-shaped ends became more common from the 13th century and a few isolated crosses with branches appearing to grow from the sides have also been preserved (e.g. the Soltikoff Cross, 1150–60; London, V&A). The figure of the crucified Christ was not represented on altar and processional crosses before the end of the 10th century; the earliest examples are the cross of Abbess Mathilde and Duke Otto and the silver Bernward Cross at Hildesheim. The figure of the crucified Christ may be ac-

Pectoral cross, gold and cloisonné enamel, Byzantine, early 11th century (London, British Museum)

companied by renderings of the Virgin and St John the Baptist, the Hand of God, Adam resurrected or angels. Usually the back is either completely undecorated or shows such images as the *Agnus Dei* or the symbols of the Evangelists, often with inscriptions and vine tendrils or similar decorative motifs.

(ii) *Renaissance and after.* Altar and processional crosses continued to be predominantly made of gold, silver and silver gilt, and were occasionally decorated with hardstones, precious gemstones and enamels. As in the earlier period, the adjustable fittings that survive on a number of crosses show that in many cases the same object was used on the altar and in processions, although some crosses were apparently designed specifically for one purpose rather than both. Reliquary crosses were sometimes converted into altar crosses: for example the silver cross (Florence, Mus. Opera Duomo) from Florence Baptistery is thought to have been made in 1457 by Antonio Pollaiuolo as a reliquary cross and adapted by the same artist *c.* 1470 to serve as an altar cross.

The great demand for processional and altar crosses in the 15th century led a number of major sculptors and goldsmiths to specialize in their production. These artists developed new types that were then repeated by others, often for decades, with the result that numerous crosses from the period have the appearance of mass-produced objects. There are also, however, a great number of high-quality examples that are unique or unusual in design, for example the processional cross from Lislaughtin Abbey, Co. Kerry, with a long inscription on the arms stating that it was made by William, son of Cornelius. The cross has a finely modelled figure of the crucified Christ and is incised with a delicate vine motif with pierced leaves; the symbols of the Evangelists are represented in quatrefoils at the ends of the arms. The cross foot is shaped like a crown around which is repeated the figure of a priest blessing and holding a cross in his left hand. The crown rests on a twisted knop that has rhomboid silver panels decorated with floral motifs and a socket for fixing a wooden staff.

A great number of very ornate crosses survive from the 16th century, for example the processional cross (c. 1547; London, V&A) by Juan Francisco (c. 1500–1579/80). Important Italian examples include the gold cross (in situ) made by Manno di Bastiano Sbarri (fl 1548–61) and Antonio Gentili for the high altar of St Peter's, Rome; this cross was turned into a crucifix in the 17th century when a 16th-century corpus by Giacomo della Porta was affixed to it. Around 1657 Pope Alexander VII ordered two new altar crosses (in situ) for St Peter's, and they were produced to designs by Gianlorenzo Bernini and cast in bronze by Paolo Carnieri (fl 1658–61) from moulds by Ercole Ferrata (1610–86). One cross shows the living Christ while the other depicts Christ dead, showing signs of suffering.

Cross by Antonio Pollaiuolo, silver, 1478 (Florence, Museo Nazionale del Bargello)

In the 18th century such materials as porcelain were also used for making crosses. King Augustus III of Poland made at least two lavish gifts of porcelain altar sets designed by Johann Joachim Kändler. The smaller of the sets (1736; Urbino, Mus. Duomo) includes an altar cross, candlesticks and two statues of apostles and was given to Cardinal Annibale Albani. In the 19th century a tendency towards more simplified forms co-existed with a renewed interest in medieval designs, which was particularly strong in northern Europe where the GOTHIC REVIVAL flourished. In England the best examples of 'medieval' church furnishings, including crosses, were produced by A. W. N. Pugin. Many of his designs, including the silver plate processional cross (1850; London, V&A), were produced by John Hardman, director of a Birmingham metal workshop specializing in Gothic Revival plate. Designs in the 20th century were characterized by more simplified forms, well-exemplified by the parcel gilt altar cross (Godalming, Charterhouse School) by Gerald Benney (b 1930).

2. PECTORAL. Small cross worn on a chain or ribbon around the neck. It often comprises two hinged halves holding a relic, but it can also be solid.

(i) Byzantine and medieval. (ii) Renaissance and after.

(i) Byzantine and medieval. The earliest surviving examples of pectoral crosses, dating from the 5th and 6th centuries AD, are small and simple. They include a gold pectoral cross with a niello pattern (Rome, Vatican, Mus. Sacro) from a grave in S Lorenzo fuori le Mura, Rome. Most surviving pectoral crosses are made of metal, especially bronze, silver and gold, but it can be assumed that less expensive examples were made of wood or bone. Most have curved, straight or medallion-shaped ends, and in later examples these might also take the form of a crook or a lily. The crosses often have engraved or low-relief images, and less frequently are decorated with enamel (such as the 8th/9th-century Beresford Hope Cross; London, V&A) or niello (for example the 6th/7th-century bronze cross; Providence, RI Sch. Des., Mus. A.). Examples set with precious stones or pearls are less common. Although some simple pectoral crosses have only geometric patterning, most are decorated with figures, and frequently show Christ on the cross accompanied by the Virgin and St John the Evangelist or the Four Evangelists; the standing figure of the Virgin at prayer with apostles or saints is often shown on the reverse. Some 6th- or 7th-century examples survive with Christ the Judge flanked by the Virgin and St John the Baptist. Saints who were particularly venerated in a certain area may also be depicted; for example SS Boris and Gleb were often represented on Russian pectoral crosses from the 11th century and later.

(ii) Renaissance and after. The Western custom of wearing the pectoral cross as a sign of office followed the publication of Pius V's Missale Romanum (1570), which prescribed that bishops should wear a pectoral cross over the alb. Such crosses also came to be used as ornamental insignia by other high-ranking clergy, including the pope, cardinals, abbots and prelates and consequently are sometimes referred to as archiepiscopal crosses. In the Eastern Church in this period they were worn by archimandrites and archpriests, and in Russia by all priests. Renaissance and Baroque pectoral crosses were usually made of gold or silver and frequently decorated with hardstones and enamels. A fine gold example (Berlin, Schloss Köpenick) was made in the 16th century by the Netherlandish goldsmith Hieronymus Jacobs of Antwerp; it was purchased in 1562 by Abbot Mattheus Volders for the Premonstratensian Abbey of Averbode. A good example of a 17th-century archiepiscopal cross (Florence, Archv Opera Duomo) is the silver and gold cross made by Cosimo Merini (1580–1641). There were no great changes in the design and usage of pectoral crosses in the 18th, 19th and 20th centuries. They continued to be predominantly made of gold with hardstones, although such other materials as enamel and ivory were also used.

K. Weitzmann and I. Sevcenko: 'The Moses Cross at Sinai', *Dumbarton Oaks Pap.*, xvii (1963), pp. 385–9

P. Springer: *Kreuzfüsse: Ikonographie und Typologie eines hochmittelalterlichen Geräts*, Bronzegeräte des Mittelalters, iii (Berlin, 1981)

E. Cruikshank Dodd: 'Three Early Byzantine Silver Crosses', *Dumbarton Oaks Pap.*, xli (1987), pp. 165–79

R. Marth: *Untersuchungen zu romanischen Bronzekreuzen: Ikonographie—Funktion—Stil* (Frankfurt, 1988)

P. Bloch: *Romanische Bronzekruzifixe*, Bronzegeräte des Mittelalters, v (Berlin, 1992)

E. C. Parker and C. T. Little: *The Cloisters Cross: Its Art and Meaning* (New York, 1994)

C. Hourihane: *The Processional Cross in Late Medieval England: The Dallye Cross* (London, 2005)

C. E. Pocknee: *Cross and Crucifix* (London, 1962)

E. Dinkler: *Signum crucis* (Tübingen, 1967)

R. Schneider Berrenberg: *Kreuz, Kruzifix: Eine Bibliographie* (Munich, 1973)

G. F. Korzukhina and A. A. Peskova: *Drevnerusskie enkolpiony: nagrudnye kresty-relikvarii XI-XIII vv.* (St. Petersburg, 2003)

Cross-banding. Decoration on wooden furniture, balustrades or panelling by means of thin strips of veneer set across the grain; if set with the grain, the technique is called 'straight-banding'.

Cross-stitch. *See* GROS POINT.

Crouch ware. English brown Staffordshire stoneware made in the mid-18th century; it is sometimes called 'critch ware', which leads to confusion with Derbyshire CRICH ware.

Crown glass. Flat glass, used since late antiquity for windows, composed of silica, potash, and lime (without lead or iron), made in circular sheets by blowing and whirling. The place at the centre where the rod spins the glass leaves a point known as a bull's eye.

Crozier. *See* CROSIER.

Crucifix. *See* CROSS.

Cruet. Small bottle with a stopper, used for oil, vinegar and other condiments. Its earliest use was ecclesiastical, for wine, oil and water. Cruets were used domestically from the late 17th century, from which time they were made of glass imported from Italy, often with silver or silver-plated mounts. Cruets were grouped together on a stand in a frame or rack, sometimes with a central vertical handle and supporting feet. The number of bottles could vary from two to six or more, and they were often combined with casters. Their popularity was so great that by the late 18th century hundreds of different patterns were made by a single manufacturer. The term also refers to a condiment set for salt, pepper and mustard.

Crunden, John (*b c.* 1745; *d* 1835). English architect and designer. In 1765 he published 12 engravings of designs for ornamental ceilings, and the following year he published a set of drawings (by himself and some contemporaries) called *The chimney-piece-maker's daily assistant: or, a treasury of new designs for chimney-pieces*. In 1770 he collaborated with a joiner to produce *The Carpenter's Companion for Chinese Railing and Gates*, and in the same year published a collection of his own designs called *The Joyner and Cabinet-maker's Darling, or Pocket Director, containing sixty different designs, entirely new and useful*.

Crutched Friars Glasshouse. English glass manufactory established in London in 1570 by the Flemish glassmaker Jean Carré and his partner Peter Briet. The factory produced glass *à la façon de Venise*. The types of vessels produced were tapering conical or cylindrical medicine-bottles, stemmed goblets and ribbed beakers. At first predominantly Flemish workers were employed at Crutched Friars, but Italians from Antwerp were increasingly hired, including JACOPO VERZELINI, who managed Crutched Friars until Carré's death in 1572 and then took over the factory. In 1574 he obtained a licence granted by Elizabeth I for the production of Venetian-style glass for 21 years, which also prohibited the import of Venetian glass and the production of glass *à la façon de Venise* by other glasshouses. Anthony de Lysle (*fl* 1577–90) is thought to have done some diamond-point engraving for Verzelini's factory.

Crux ansata. *See* ANKH.

Crystal [crystal-glass; Ger. *Krystallglas*; It. *vetro di cristallo*]. Colourless glass with a high degree of transparency achieved by ther admixture of manganese to the FRIT. It is normally used for glass vessels, decanters and wine glasses, and is often cut. The technique was known in ancient Rome and rediscovered in 15th-century Venice, from where it was transmitted all over Europe.

For information on mineral crystals *see* ROCK CRYSTAL.

Crystalline glaze. Matt pottery (or porcelain) glaze marked by large crystals of zinc or calcium. The effect was long regarded as a fault caused by the kiln cooling too slowly, but in the 19th century it began to be used to decorative effect, notably by Hermann Seger (1839–93) at the Königliche Porzellan-Manufaktur (*see under* BERLIN, §2).

D. Creber: *Crystalline Glazes* (London and Philadelphia, 1997)

Crystallo-ceramie. Glass decorated with embedded ceramic cameos (typically portraits or figurines). The process was invented by the French glassmaker Barthélemy Desprez (*fl* 1773–1819) and brought to England by Apsley Pellatt (1791–1863), who owned the Falcon glassworks in Southwark, London; Pellatt called the technique 'crystallo-ceramie'. Production included goblets, paperweights and scent-flasks, which incorporated an embedded medallion made of a porcellanous material decorated with profile portraits, busts, coats of arms and landscapes.

A. Pellatt: *Memoir on the Origin, Progress, and Improvement of Glass Manufactures* (London, 1821)

Cucci, Domenico (*b* Todi, Italy, *c.* 1635; *d* ?Paris, 1704–5). French cabinetmaker, bronzeworker and carver of Italian birth. He was summoned to France *c.* 1660, probably by Cardinal Jules Mazarin (1602–61), to work at the GOBELINS, where he became head of the workshop that produced opulent, Italianate display cabinets of superb workmanship. Cucci can be seen presenting such a cabinet in the tapestry of *Louis XIV Visiting the Gobelins* (*c.* 1667; Versailles, Château). This cabinet is probably one of a pair of 'large ebony cabinets inlaid with pewter' with 'four large twisted columns in imitation of lapis and vine scrolls of copper gilt supported by lions' paws', made between 1667 and 1673, described in the royal records. The records provide detailed information on the cabinets produced by Cucci and his workshop, among them the War and Peace cabinets, and the Apollo and Diana cabinets with columns of aventurine marble and jasper. They were supported by columnar figures and surmounted by elaborate bronze figural or armorial groups illustrative of their iconographical programmes. These four cabinets were considered old-fashioned by 1748 and were placed in the Cabinet of Natural History, where they were probably dismantled and the mosaic panels and hardstones turned into mineralogical specimens. The two identifiable works by Cucci that survive are cabinets made between 1681 and 1683 (both Alnwick Castle, Northumb). These cabinets were at Versailles, possibly in the Galerie de Mignard, which Cucci had decorated with lapis lazuli, gilded tortoiseshell and bronze in the early 1680s, until 1751, when they were among items of royal furniture sold by auction.

Cucci also produced decoration in bronze and gilt copper, and produced ironwork for the windows and door furniture at Versailles. He was employed on the elaborate marquetry floor designed by Le Brun for the château of Saint-Germain and is known to have carved cases for an organ, a harpsichord and a spinet for the King at Versailles.

Cuerda seca and cuenca tiles [Sp.: 'dry cord'; 'hollow']. Spanish name for a technique for decorating tiles. If a number of differently coloured glazes are used close together on a flat tile, they tend to 'run' during firing. In Spain, where the tradition of Islamic pottery had been influential since the Moorish occupation, the *cuerda seca* technique provided an effective solution to this problem. The technique consists of drawing lines using a mixture of dark ceramic pigments and a greasy substance that keeps the water-based coloured glazes separate from each other. The grease burns away during firing and leaves a thin, sunken, unglazed line between the slightly raised glazed surfaces. This technique was much used in Spain during the 15th and 16th centuries (see colour pl. IX, fig. 1).

A modified form of the *cuerda seca* technique consists of imprinting a design in the soft clay with a mould. When the tile has been fired once, the incised lines of the design are filled with the greasy substance. This is a particularly labour-saving device as *cuerda seca* tiles have complex geometrical Moorish patterns that would be difficult to draw free-hand. A further simplification of this is known as the *cuenca* technique: moulds of individual parts of the design are sunk into the clay leaving a thin, raised line around each one. The hollows are then filled with coloured glazes. Both *cuerda seca* and *cuenca* tiles need to be stacked horizontally for firing to prevent the glazes from running out of their delineated areas.

See also TILE, §II, 3.

R. Puertas Tricas: *La cerámica islámica de cuerda seca en la Alcazaba de Málaga* (Málaga, 1989)

Cuir-bouilli. Moulded leather used for covering books, caskets and scabbards. Cuir-bouilli was also used for armour and shields as a cheap alternative to metal. Leather has a unique fibrous structure that allows it to be moulded. In the process known as cuir-bouilli, vegetable-tanned leather is soaked in cold water until it becomes saturated and highly pliable. It can then be moulded by hand over wooden forms or in a press. The surface may be decorated by punching or incising while it is still soft, after which it is dried in a moderate heat. The term has been used since the medieval period, and it has been suggested that the leather was boiled in order to harden it, but it seems more likely that 'bouilli' merely refers to the application of heat.

Cuir-ciselé [cut leather]. Bookbinding technique in which the design is cut into the surface and then widened with a tool.

Cul-de-lampe. In architecture and furniture, an ornamental support of inverted conical form; in printing, an ornament of similar shape used to fill up a blank space at the bottom of a page.

Culet. In lapidary usage, the horizontal face or plane forming the bottom of a diamond when cut as a brilliant. In the vocabulary of amour, a part of ancient armour, consisting of overlapping plates, protecting the buttocks.

Cumella, Antoni (*b* 1913; *d* 1985). Catalan potter. He was almost entirely self-taught, and his style, though influenced by Gaudí and the Bauhaus, was highly individualistic. His thrown wares and tile-pictures show an exuberant creativity. He also founded (1941) and directed a factory at Granollers for the production of architectural ceramics. In 1942 he married a chemist, Agnès Vendreil, and she helped him to develop the metallic glazes that distinguish his stoneware and porcelain.

E. Klinge: *Antoni Cumella* (Düsseldorf, 1982)

Cup and cover column. Bulbous baluster used in Tudor furniture; the bulge resembles a lidded communion cup.

Cupboard. Piece of case furniture enclosed by doors, generally used for storage. The word 'cupboard' derives from the term applied during Tudor and Jacobean periods to an open structure of shelves used to display plate, a type of furniture now known as a court cupboard (e.g. oak, *c.* 1620; London, V&A). Cupboards, in the modern sense, were widely used by the Romans. During the Byzantine period most cupboards were used for such specialized functions as the storing of books or vestments, as depicted in a mosaic of St Lawrence (early 5th century; Ravenna, S Vitale, mausoleum of Galla Placidia). Typically of plank construction, although sometimes panelled, they were often of architectural form and might be decorated with paintings. When used for storing books the interiors were fitted with shelves. Large cupboards continued to be used for ecclesiastical purposes in the Romanesque and Early Gothic period (e.g. sacristy cupboard, *c.* 1200; Halberstadt, Dom & Domschatz). The doors were generally symmetrical around a central axis and of plank construction bound by iron hinges. The sides could be panelled and carved with arcading. In northern Europe during the Middle Ages the ironwork covering the doors became increasingly elaborate and could be wrought into scrolls, and cast with such naturalistic details as fruit and foliage (e.g. cupboard doors, originally from the church of St Quentin, Somme, *c.* 1290–1320; Paris, Mus. A. Déc.). In Germany and Austria cupboards often assumed an architectural character, with two sets of doors one above the other, topped by a crenellated cornice and carved with Gothic motifs. In the Low Countries, France and England linenfold panelling was a common way of facing cupboards during the late 15th century and early 16th (see colour pl. X, fig. 1).

During the Renaissance shelves that had been open in court cupboards were frequently enclosed, creating cupboards in the modern sense. Livery cupboards, an adaptation of this form, were installed in bedrooms to hold 'livery'—food and drink left overnight for members of the household and guests (e.g. livery cupboard, late medieval; London, V&A). In France furniture of this type was known as a buffet or dressoir. In Italy large cupboards generally had a pair of panelled doors flanked by pilasters and topped by a cornice. The doors and sides could be decorated with applied panels of intarsia (e.g. cupboard with intarsia decoration, 1502; Monte Oliveto Maggiore, Abbey). In France various types of buffet and dressoir or *armoires à deux corps* were decorated with elaborate Mannerist carving of caryatids and grotesques, under the influence of Jacques Androuet Du Cerceau, but cupboards proper, or armoires, remained relatively plain. They usually had a single door flanked by thin columns. In southern Germany the Gothic two-tiered cupboard was quickly adapted to Renaissance motifs under the influence of the designer Peter Flötner of Nuremberg (e.g. 1541; Nuremberg, Ger. Nmus). Other impressive Gothic and early Renaissance cupboards have survived in Austria. In northern Germany cupboards became more complex in form. They were increasingly faced by a multitude of smaller doors, often arranged on different axes, while ornament became more sculptural, with small, densely packed scenes carved in relief.

In the Low Countries a distinctive type of oak cupboard emerged in the early 17th century, featuring a deep cornice and heavily panelled doors divided by half columns often of a darker wood such as ebony (e.g. Dutch cupboard, *c.* 1620–50; London, V&A). The form of German cupboards was simplified during the same period, and by 1660 they were usually faced by two long, panelled doors divided by three pilasters above a base containing a pair of drawers. Although oak was used earlier in the century it began to be replaced by walnut *c.* 1670. The shape of the cornice varied according to region. Cabinets made in Frankfurt had particularly distinctive door panels faced with heavily moulded concentric rectangles (e.g. 1700; Frankfurt am Main, Hist. Mus.). This type of cupboard was developed well into the 18th century, by which time it was decorated with fine walnut veneers inlaid with strapwork and marquetry panels. The grandest cupboards of this period were those associated with the workshops of André-Charles Boulle (e.g. *c.* 1700; Paris, Louvre). Initially their form was relatively simple, with a pair of doors faced by panels. The decoration of the panels, however, was particularly lavish, often combining brilliantly stained floral marquetry with panels of boullework. Later these armoires acquired elaborate crestings, and although floral marquetry fell from favour the boullework panels became more elaborate and were framed by gilt-bronze mounts.

During the 18th century grand cupboards were replaced as decorative pieces by such other types of case furniture as commodes and cabinets. In the Netherlands, however, cupboards remained relatively important; they were usually veneered with walnut and had a domed upper part and a *bombe* lower section fitted with drawers. In France armoires were usually of oak, walnut or fruit-wood and not veneered. They were given a domed cresting and carved with scroll ornament and set with shaped panels. In England the 'gentleman's press', or wardrobe, with its pair of doors above an arrangement of drawers, was the main form of storage cupboard.

In America, the splendid cupboards that graced the best rooms of many colonists' homes by the mid-17th century were used to display expensive silver, glass and tin-glazed earthenware, and so to impress visitors with the wealth of the household. The enclosed upper sections, on which a length of brightly coloured cloth was often laid, were framed by massive turned pillars; the panels were elaborately carved or, later, fielded, and further decoration was applied in the form of bosses and half-balusters. The lower sections often contained drawers (e.g. a cupboard from Massachusetts, *c.* 1675–90; New York, Met.). By the end of the 17th century these cupboards went out of fashion and were replaced by the HIGHBOY as the best piece of furniture in the house. This, along with the corner cupboard, assumed the role of the cupboard as a place to display finery (see colour pl. VIII, fig. 3).

Cupping dish. *See* BLEEDING BOWL.

Curfew. *See under* FIREPLACE FURNISHINGS.

Curstgen. *See* KNÜTGEN.

Curtains. *See under* UPHOLSTERY.

Custodia. Spanish term for a portable tabernacle. Some of the finest examples were made in the 16th century by members of the ARFE family.

Cut-card. Relief decoration on silverware in which a thin sheet of metal is cut ornamentally and soldered to the surface.

Cut glass. Thick glass decorated with geometrical or representational incisions made by grinding and polishing; the process had been used since classical antiquity for the decoration of rock crystal, and first used on glass by CASPAR LEHMANN in 16th-century Prague. Cut glass from the 18th and 19th centuries tends to be made from LEAD GLASS.

Cut-glass Passover goblet showing a family gathering, h. 215 mm, from the Netherlands, mid-18th century (Vienna, Judaica Collection Max Berger)

Cutlery. Domestic implements, predominantly of metal, used for a variety of purposes, particularly for eating. The term generally describes knives, forks and spoons for dining but also refers to scissors, edged tools and, formerly, edged weapons.

C. Pagé: *La Coutellerie depuis l'origine jusqu'à nos jours*, 6 vols (Châtellerault, 1896–1905)

J. F. Hayward: *English Cutlery, 16th to 18th Century* (London, 1957)

E. Lassen: *Knives, Forks and Spoons* (Copenhagen, 1960)

H. R. Singleton: *A Chronology of Cutlery* (Sheffield, 1973)

G. Benker: *Alte Bestecke* (Munich, 1978)

Masterpieces of Cutlery and the Art of Eating (exh. cat., London, V&A, 1979)

I. Pickford: *Silver Flatware* (Woodbridge, 1983)

S. J. Moore: *Table Knives and Forks* (Aylesbury, 1995)

K. Marquardt: *Eight Centuries of European Knives, Forks and Spoons* (Stuttgart, 1997)

S. J. Moore: *Cutlery for the Table* (Sheffield, 1999)

P. Brown: *British Cutlery: An Illustrated History of its Design, Evolution and Use* (London, 2001)

V. Beauchamp, J. Unwin and J. Symonds: *The Historical Archaeology of the Sheffield Cutlery and Tableware Industry, 1750–1900* (Oxford, 2002)

J. van Trigt: *Cutlery, from Gothic to Art Deco: The J. Hollander Collection* (Antwerp, 2003)

Collectors Encyclopedia of 19th Century Hardware: Cutlery Tools, Kitchen, Small Farm Equipment, and Miscellaneous Items: With a 2004 Price Guide (Gas City, IN, 2004)

1. Knives, forks and spoons. 2. Scissors.

1. KNIVES, FORKS AND SPOONS. Cutlery, in particular knives, probably has the longest history of any artefact. Edged implements made of stone (eoliths) for cutting or scraping animal carcasses were probably in existence about 2.5 million years ago or even earlier (see colour pl. X, fig. 3).

Surviving late medieval knives and spoons show that experiments in cutlery-making occurred at this time: new blade styles were introduced, although many evolved from Anglo-Saxon, Roman and even Bronze Age designs. Knife blades were normally strip-tanged, the haft, comprising two 'scales' of material, riveted on to the tang. From *c.* 1350 cutlers in London were obliged to strike a trademark on to knife blades. In the late 15th century brass knops were added to the ends of many knife hafts, a style that originated in the Netherlands or Flanders. Elaborate carving sets (examples in London, BM; Paris, Louvre) became popular at this time; noble households often included a pantler, who prepared diners' bread, and a carver, who set diners' places and carved their meat. Guests brought their own knives and spoons, the knife for cutting off pieces of meat, the spoon for eating broth or other liquid foods. Spoons were made from bone, wood and horn, although the majority were of base metal, frequently pewter and tinned brass. Those made from silver (and often also those in base metal) were often knopped in the Roman style. Medieval spoon shapes appear to have evolved from some late Roman designs with a slender handle (stele) joining on to a nearly circular to fig-shaped (ficulate) bowl. Ficulate spoon bowls reappeared during the early 14th century. Earlier spoon bowls were either round (French influence) or leaf-shaped (11th–12th centuries). During the medieval period Middle Eastern knives were characterized by long blades set into disproportionately short but heavy hafts. In East Asia knives only were used as preparatory tools for a meal; at table they were supplanted by chopsticks.

By the 16th century the uniformity of knife and spoon styles throughout Europe was declining; consequently, cutlery dating from this period onwards can be assigned to individual countries within (as well as outside) Europe. Netherlandish genre painters, particularly Pieter Bruegel the elder, depicted many items of cutlery in their work. In England, as dining halls were replaced by dining-rooms, knives and spoons became more refined and were fitted with such materials imported from newly explored lands as ivory, which became important for hafts. Knives with bolsters and whittle tangs largely replaced those with strip tangs. Slender knives tended to be made entirely from ferrous materials, with a steel blade forged on to a wrought-iron haft (see colour pl. IX, fig. 2).

Towards the end of the 16th century the fashion for pairs of knives, given from groom to bride at weddings, stimulated the production of knives of great artistry—blades and bolsters inlaid with precious metals and with ivory or amber hafts often carved into figures. The tradition of owning fine sets of knives started at about this time; a host of social standing was required to provide table cutlery, rather than the guests supplying their own. In England larger forks assisted in carving, while smaller ones were used to eat sticky sweetmeats. Spoons remained largely unchanged in style from their medieval forebears, although knops were more adventurous in form—seated lions, saints and other figures were popular.

In the early 17th century knives and spoons gradually became more austere in style; knife hafts made of ivory or bone were carved into simple club and cylinder shapes. After 500 years spoons with slender handles and fig-shaped bowls were phased out in favour of a type of spoon with an elliptical bowl and flattened plain handle, known as the 'Puritan' spoon. Its ancestry can also be traced back to the late Roman spoon period (5th–7th centuries AD); it was the prototype for modern table spoons.

With the Restoration in 1660 the English court, returning from exile on the continent, introduced the European trefid spoon, with Roman-style rat-tail bowl support down the centre of the bowl underside, which readily became popular. Soon after (1680–1700), the table-fork, another European refinement, began to find favour at English dining tables after many years of unpopularity. Matching sets of six or twelve spoons and a few sets of forks were made at this time. (The term 'flatware' is often applied to sets of matching spoons and forks made from metals other than steel.) At this time blades of eating knives became more varied, with triangular points or square or rounded ends; hafts tended to be cylindrical and, if made of metal, often engraved.

In the mid-17th century folding knives incorporated a backspring to hold the blade open or closed. The practicality of this invention encouraged a renaissance in the manufacture and use of the folding knife, which, for general purposes, gradually replaced the personal eating knife carried in a sheath. Folding knives generally resembled their table counterparts; many included more than one blade and were made in different sizes, mainly at Sheffield in England.

At the end of the 17th century a new style of knife blade, curving up at the end like a scimitar, was made. Although originally with a traditional cylindrical or cannon-shaped haft, the new type of blade was better balanced with a haft that turned down at the end like a pistol butt. 'Pistol-grip' hafts, as they became known, were made from bone, ivory (sometimes stained green or black), silver or ceramic; this style remained unchanged until about the 1770s. Spoon bowls, however, became more elongated, while the ends of handles of both spoons and forks were shaped like the top of a shield or a dog's nose. The latter type was soon phased out in favour of a spoon with the standard, round-ended handle that turns up at the end and is known as Hanoverian, since its introduction coincided with the accession in 1714 of George I; this type of spoon continues to be produced. During the 1740s spoons were also made with downturned handles; this form became known as the 'Old English' pattern. Forks to match 'Dognose' and 'Hanoverian' spoons were generally made with three tines, and although 'Old English' forks were made with four tines, the handles were still turned up at the end, ensuring that they were comfortable to hold. In the 18th century knives, forks and spoons were made in sizes according to their function at table:

spoons, especially, varied in size from the huge 'baster', 600 mm in length, stuffer and table (soup) spoons to the much smaller dessert, tea, snuff and toy spoons (the last two about 25 mm long).

The form of folding knives continued to evolve in the 18th century; some were effectively pocket tool kits, as cutlers skilfully crammed in more blades. Fine folding knives with silver or gold blades, as well as folding forks for eating fruit were also developed at this time. In France, particularly elegant examples with two blades (one steel, one silver or gold) and superbly enamelled and jewelled hafts were made as an offshoot of the manufacture of snuff-boxes. A few Swiss examples even contain a tiny musical box movement.

With the advent of machine production towards the end of the 18th century knife styles became more simple—straight-bladed and the hafts with slightly curved sides. Silver handles were cheaper and easier to make as silver sheets stamped out of moulds then filled with resin. In the 1780s the 'Fiddle' pattern spoon, similar to the 'Old English' but with a broader-ended handle and a pair of 'shoulders' on the handle just above the bowl, was introduced. At the same time a method for die-stamping spoons from sheet silver was devised by William Darby in Sheffield.

In the 19th century new methods of refining large quantities of steel were introduced by Henry Bessemer (1813–98) in Sheffield, reducing the amount of extra work in hand-processing blades, although such smaller items as knife and tool blades continued to be made from crucible steel well into the 20th century. Knives of a simpler form, with round-ended and parallel-sided blades, were made. Bolsters and tangs continued to be die-stamped as one unit and then forged on to the steel blade. Hafts were made from ivory, bone, horn and wood, although, with the invention of Bakelite and other plastics, ivory was soon substituted by cheaper ivorine, celluloid or xylo. In 1914 the first knife blades of stainless steel were made, and during the following years cutlery firms marked their blades in deference to the inventor, Harry Brearley (1871–1948), and the firm of Thomas Firth & Sons for whom he worked. Stainless steel was quickly adopted for the manufacture of cutlery throughout the world.

See also APOSTLE SPOON; CADDY SPOON; KNIFE BOX; LOVE SPOON; MARROW SPOON; RAT-TAIL SPOON; SEAL-TOP SPOON; SLIP-TOP SPOON; SPOON TRAY; SUCKET FORK; TREFID SPOON.

C. J. Jackson: *The Spoon and its History* (London, 1892)
N. Gask: *Old Silver Spoons of England* (London, 1926/R Feltham, 1973)
C. T. P. Bailey: *Knives and Forks* (London, 1927)
Knives and Forks in the Netherlands, 1500–1800, The Hague, Gemeentemus., (The Hague, 1972)
M. Snodin: *English Silver Spoons* (London, 1974)
R. F. Homer: *Five Centuries of Base Metal Spoons* (London, 1975)
G. Belden and M. Snodin: *Spoons* (London, 1976)
J. Emery: *European Spoons before 1700* (Edinburgh, 1976)
D. T. Rainwater and D. H. Felger: *A Collector's Guide to Spoons around the World* (Pennsylvania, 1976)
V. Houart: *Antique Spoons: A Collector's Guide* (London, 1982)

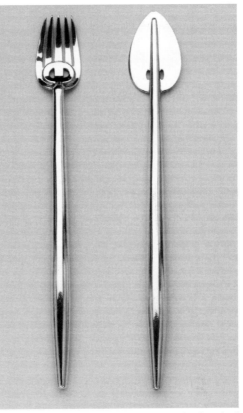

Fish knife and fork by Charles Rennie Mackintosh, silver-plated nickel, 235 × 35 mm (knife), 229 × 29 mm (fork), c. 1900 (New York, Museum of Modern Art)

S. J. Moore: 'The History of the Folding Knife', *N. Knife Mag.* (Dec 1983), pp. 5–7; (Feb 1984), pp. 8–13; (April 1984), pp. 8–10
S. J. Moore: 'The Evolution of Mediaeval English Knives', *N. Knife Mag.* (July 1985), pp. 15–17, 29–31
G. Boggiali: *La Posata* (Milan, 1987)
J. Cowgill, M. de Neergard and N. Griffiths: *Knives and Scabbards* (London, 1987)
S. J. Moore: *Spoons, 1650–1930* (Aylesbury, 1987)
S. J. Moore: *Penknives and Other Folding Knives* (Aylesbury, 1988)
J. Sargent: *American Premium Guide to Knives & Razors: Identification and Value Guide* (Iola, 2004)

2. SCISSORS. There are two types of scissors: those that work with a spring action (known as shears), which, although originally intended for general use, are employed for a limited number of purposes (e.g. carpet-making and weaving), and those with pivoted blades. Early scissors were relatively simple in design and construction: the bows or finger loops consisted of rings attached to the shanks of the blades; a rivet or screw held the two blades together. From the medieval period scissors were produced in a number of European centres, for example Solingen in Germany, and in 16th-century France cutlers in Moulins produced high-quality steel for scissors. According to an order dated 1560, the king's nails were trimmed with scissors made in the town. Large decorated scissors, often engraved with the owner's name and the date, were made in Spain in the 17th century. Some were damascened at Toledo, while others had pierced dec-

oration. The records of the Cutlers' Company of London (1624) refer to scissor-making in the city, although the quality of English-made scissors did not match that of continental scissors for another 100 years. A few English firms of scissor-makers, notably those of Beach, Macklin and Neesham, established a small but notable industry at Salisbury, Wilts, from the mid-17th century until the early 20th.

The 18th and 19th centuries represented the period of the greatest variety in construction and decoration of scissors throughout the world. Steel scissors inlaid with silver and resembling birds, the blades forming the beak while the bows formed part of the underbelly and the back, were produced in Iran. 'Dagger' scissors, the bows set one over the other, were also first produced in this region. Persian blades were ground hollow, it is said, for secreting notes. In Europe, scissors were often kept in attractive metal cases, so that they could be worn as part of the daily costume. Some of these cases also contained a small knife and spike, which were used to unpick gold and silver thread from fine material—a practice that, although popular in the 17th century, developed into near mania during the early 18th century and was known as 'drizzling' or *parfilage*. New methods of production were also developed: towards the end of the 18th century the bows and shanks of scissors began to be made in one piece, either in silver or steel.

The best quality English scissors were made in Sheffield from the end of the 18th century to the end of the 19th by such companies as Joseph Rodgers & Sons and Thomas Wilkinson & Sons. In 1837, to commemorate her coronation, Queen Victoria was presented with elaborately decorated scissors (which apparently took four months to make) by James Atherton, who was the chief scissor-maker for Wilkinson. The firm also had a fine display at the Great Exhibition of 1851 in London, including six pairs of scissors less than 50 mm long; the smallest were only *c*. 1.5 mm long and weighed 0.04 g, in contrast to a pair 600 mm long, weighing almost 4 kg.

The Victorians invented many gadget scissors, including lace scissors with a protruding tip to one blade for use in 'Carrickmacross' appliqué work, where the top layer of fabric has to be removed without damaging the net base, and 'stork' scissors in all sizes, which continue to be popular. Cases containing three scissors—nail, embroidery and paper—were a popular gift.

In the 18th and 19th centuries the most important French centres of steel production were Paris, Langres, Moulins and Thiers. In Paris, mother-of-pearl was also worked in the area around the Palais Royal, where ornate, fretted scissor shanks and bows in this material, depicting swans, dolphins, urns and other classical motifs, were made and fitted with steel blades. By the end of the 19th century in Germany, 3200 cutlers in Solingen specialized in the production of scissors; manufacture in Germany outstripped that of Britain, with cheaper products that were exported to the Americas, Italy and even to England.

The multi-bladed 'Universal', incorporating many sewing and personal tools, was also invented in Germany. Some included a 'Stanhope' or peep featuring a local view. In the early 20th century pinking 'shears', which do not have a spring action, were invented to cut a zigzag or scalloped edge to prevent fraying.

M. Andrere: *Old Needlework Boxes and Tools* (Newton Abbot, 1971)

S. Groves: *History of Needlework Tools and Accessories* (Newton Abbot, 1973)

G. A. Rogers: *An Illustrated History of Needlework Tools* (London, 1983)

Cutwork [It. *punto tagliato*]. Openwork linen fabric made by cutting away portions of the fabric and filling the gaps with ornamental designs made with needle and thread. The technique was evolved prior to that of LACE, of which it is an early form, and cutwork clothing became fashionable in 16th-century Italy. The most important designer of cutwork patterns was Matio Pagano.

Cuvilliés, (Jean) François (Vincent Joseph) de (*b* Soignies [Hainault], nr Brussels, 23 Oct 1695; *d* Munich, 14 April 1768). French architect of Flemish origin, active in Bavaria, to which he successfully imported the Parisian Rococo. In the 18th and 19th centuries de Cuvilliés's work was known chiefly from collections of his ornamental designs, which were made between 1738 and 1768.

In 1724 de Cuvilliés designed stucco ceilings at Schloss Schleissheim near Munich. He became court architect to the Elector, and worked on the Munich Residenz, where he built the Gelbes Appartement (1726; destr.) and parts of the Trierzimmer (1725–35; destr.) and designed the ceiling of the Ahnengalerie (1729). His first major task there was the modification of the state apartments known as the Reiche Zimmer (1730–37), following a fire in December 1729. In 1730 the Schatz-Gewölb had been built at the end of the Ahnengalerie: de Cuvilliés's playful décor in this room, from the free development of the cove into the ceiling, to the individual motifs—of springs, swinging putti and dragons—influenced his choice of décor in the Reiche Zimmer, for which he also created new types of rooms, not based on Parisian models. For example, he built the Grüne Galerie with an H-shaped ground-plan (1733), a vestibule on the ground-floor, which opened out on to an Italianate grand staircase with three flights of stairs (destr. 1764), and the Spiegelkabinett (1731–2). In the latter, the framed panels usually employed to articulate walls are replaced (except for the dados) by mirrors. The miniature cabinet known as the Rotes Kabinett is equally unusual (stucco completed 1733), for here the rectangular pictures are framed with a network of ROCAILLE, which completely covers the red lacquered walls. The décor in the Reiche Zimmer was very much in keeping with the *genre pittoresque*: the ornamentation consists of such a wealth of figures that, in addition to the masks, vases and trophies, allegories were realized in the stucco décor rather than in painted pictures.

De Cuvilliés' most significant work was the Amalienburg Pavilion (1734–9) in the gardens of Schloss Nymphenburg. The Amalienburg combines French ideas, taken from the Pavillon d'Aurore in Sceaux and the Trianon de Porcelaine in Versailles, with the new shape of the mirrored hall, which was round in the centre and flanked by connecting rooms which form two *appartements en enfilade*. The subdued exterior is marked by contrasts, particularly between convex and concave shapes. In the interior the corners of the rooms are rounded for the first time, and the rocaille is employed with an especial emphasis on its asymmetry. In the Spiegelsaal both the articulation of the wall bays and their border with the vaulting disappear.

From 1738 de Cuvilliés assembled three series of bound collections of engraved designs of Rococo decorative devices. *Series I* appeared from 1738 to 1742, *Series II* from 1742 to 1754 and *Series III* from 1755. A proportion of the engravings were assembled and after his death reproduced in the anthology *Architecture bavaroise* (unpublished) by de Cuvilliés's son François de Cuvilliés II (1731–77). The engravings were widely viewed and hugely influential. Essentially they deal with suggestions for the design of architectural features (e.g. frames, panelling, iron latticework), as well as furniture and caprices, which were fantasy landscapes in rocaille frames. The anthology, like the series, became dispersed (Munich, Staatsbib., Berlin, Kstbib.; Nuremburg, Ger. Nmus.; priv. cols).

W. Braunfels: *François de Cuvilliés* (Munich, 1986)
A. Schick: *Cuvilliés–Möbel* (Munich, 1993)

Cyfflé, Paul-Louis (*b* 1724; *d* 1806). Flemish sculptor and porcelain modeller. In 1746 he settled in Lunéville (France), where from 1752 he modelled figures for the Lunéville Porcelain Factory (*see under* Lunéville). He subsequently worked for the porcelain factories at Saint-Clément (1758), Ottweiler Factory (1765) and Niderviller (1772–80). In about 1765 he established a factory in Lunéville, which until 1780 made many biscuit figures in *terre de Lorraine*, a type of soft *terre de pipe*, whitened with lime phosphate; the figures were sentimental portrayals of rural figures.

Czech Republic. Ceramics see Gabel pottery; Klášterec nad Ohří porcelain factory; Pirkenhammer porcelain factory; Slavkov porcelain factory.

Glass *see* Chřibská; Falknov; Harrachov glassworks; Karlovy vary; Lötz witwe; Nové hrady; Nový bor; Nový svět.

D

Dagly, Gerhard (*b* Spa, French Flanders, 1657; *d* Bensberg, 1715). Walloon japanner, active in Berlin. He practised as a decorative artist in Spa before moving in the 1680s to Berlin, where he became famous for his painted furniture. By 1687 his proficiency in gilding and decorative painting, particularly japanning, which imitated lacquerwork from East Asia, gained him the post of Kammerkünstler to Frederick William, Elector of Brandenburg. On the accession in 1688 of Frederick III, Elector of Brandenburg (after 1701, Frederick I of Prussia) he retained responsibility for interior decoration and furnishings at the court and in 1696 was appointed Intendant des Ornements. His brother Jacques Dagly (1665–1729) joined him in the management of the firm, which provided gilded, polychromed and japanned cabinets as well as such other furnishings as treen painted to imitate porcelain for the royal palaces. Their clients included harpsichord manufacturers as well as the nobility, and such was their fame that in Paris their cabinets became known as 'Berlin' cabinets. They embellished snuff-boxes, cane knobs, sword guards and tin wares and invented methods of applying silver varnish in place of gold leaf on books and leather. Dagly's researches also included methods of reviving varnish on oil paintings, which resulted in his court appointment as Kunstkammer Meister and the publication of his *Recueil des mémoires des diverses expériences fait au sujet de la conservation des tableaux* (1706). In addition he promoted methods of embalming and taxidermy, as well as treatments for preserving stone, plaster, metal and timber. He closed his workshops in 1713.

Dahlin, Niels (*fl* 1761; *d* 1787). Swedish furniture-maker, based in Stockholm, who specialized in lacquerwork in the French style. His furniture for the Swedish court includes a desk of lacquered and gilded wood (*c.* 1765; Stockholm, Nordiska Mus.).

Dahlskog, Ewald (Albin Filip) (*b* 1894; *d* 1950). Swedish decorative artist who specialized in intarsia and in glass engraving. He designed and built fine intarsia furniture but is best known for his intarsia panels in public buildings, notably the Stockholm City Hall (1923), the Stockholm Concert Hall (1926) and the Göteborg (1935); he later decorated the Chi-cago Room in the American Swedish Historical Museum in Philadelphia (1937). In the late 1920s he revived the tradition of glass-engraving at the KOSTA GLASBRUK, of which he was director (1926–9)

Dalpayrat, Adrien (*b* 1844; *d* 1910). French potter. He left his native Limoges to work at the Jules Viellard pottery in Bordeaux, where he made tableware, and after a brief return to Limoges (1873–4), where he worked at the pottery of Léon Sazerat (1831–91), he moved in 1876 to Monaco, where he began to make stoneware. He left after the earthquake of 1887 and finally settled in Bourg la Reine, where in 1889 he founded a pottery with the sculptor Alphonse Voisin-Delacroix (1857–93); in 1894, after the latter's death, Dalpayrat's new partner was Jean Coulon (1853–1923). This change of partnership led to the introduction of more conventional china alongside

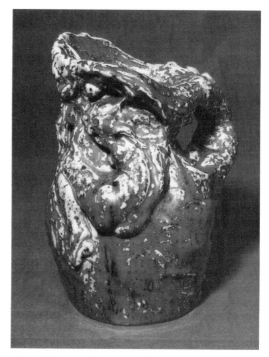

Adrien Dalpayrat: pitcher, enamelled stoneware (Paris, Musée d'Orsay)

PLATE I

1. Masséot Abaquesne: tile panel (detail), faience, l. 3.26 m, from the altar step of the chapel of the Château de La Bastie d'Urfe, 1557 (Paris, Musée du Louvre)

2. *Acanthus,* wallpaper by William Morris, 1875 (London, Victoria and Albert Museum)

3. Robert Adam: Kimbolton Cabinet, mahogany and oak, with marquetry in satinwood and rosewood, pietra dura plaques and ormolu mounts, 1.89×1.82×0.36 m, 1771−6 (London, Victoria and Albert Museum)

PLATE II

1. Apocalypse tapestry by Jan Boudoulf, Nicolas Bataille and Robert Poinçon: *The Woman Receives Wings to Flee from the Dragon*, scene 37, 1373–87 (Angers, Château et Galerie de l'Apocalypse, Collection des Tapisseries)

3. Arras tapestry depicting *Offering of the Heart*, wool and silk, 2.47×2.09 m, *c.* 1400–10 (Paris, Musée du Louvre)

2. Armoire by André-Charles Boulle, ebony inlaid with shell, pewter and copper, 1732 (Paris, Musée du Louvre)

PLATE III

1. Arts and Crafts 'Chrysanthemum' pattern fabric by William Morris, printed cotton, 939×958 mm (New York, Museum of Modern Art)

2. Francesco Xanto Avelli: maiolica plate depicting *Joseph and Potiphar's Wife*, Urbino, 1537 (Florence, Museo Nazionale del Bargello)

3. Sioux quilted mocassins decorated with beadwork and quillwork, *c.* 1895 (Cody, WY, Buffalo Bill Historical Center)

4. Berlin porcelain fruit vase, 19th century (Rueil-Malmaison, Châteaux de Malmaison et Bois-Préau)

PLATE IV

1. H. P. Berlage: tea-room at the St Hubertus Hunting Lodge, 1915 (Otterlo, Hoge Veluwe National Park)

2. Biedermeier wedding sofa, birch veneer over pine, lindenwood, paint, gilt and textile upholstered, 1600×970×710 mm, north Germany, 1838 (New York, Jewish Museum)

PLATE V

1. Biccherna cover depicting *Allegory of the Plague*, 1437 (Berlin, Schloss Köpenick)

2. François Boucher: study for a stage set, 520×670 mm (Amiens, Musée de Picardie)

PLATE VI

1. Jacques Bijlivert: lapis lazuli dish with gold and enamel handle, 16th century (Florence, Palazzo Pitti, Museo degli Argenti)

2. 'Surfers', printed cotton, Calico Printers' Association, 650×750 mm, 1937 (London, Victoria and Albert Museum)

4. André-Charles Boulle (attrib.): armoire, wood, copper and shell with bronze trimmings, 1.49×2.71×0.61 m, from Paris, *c.* 1680–90 (Paris, Musée des Arts Décoratifs)

3. Maiolica dish depicting the *Abduction of Ganymede*, from Castel Durante (Paris, Musée du Louvre)

5. Becket Casket, gilt copper and champlevé enamel on wooden core, Limoges, *c.* 1180 (London, Victoria and Albert Museum)

PLATE VII

1. Benvenuto Cellini: salt of Francis I, gold and enamel with ebony base, 260×330 mm, 1540–43 (Vienna, Kunsthistorisches Museum)

2. Walter Crane: six tiles depicting flower fairies, made by Pilkington's Tile & Pottery co., 1900–01 (London, Victoria and Albert Museum)

3. Rotunda Chandelier by Dale Chihuly, glass, 1999 (London, Victoria and Albert Museum)

PLATE VIII

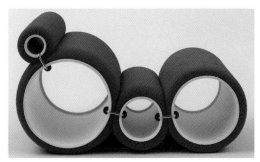

1. Joe Colombo: tube chair of nesting and combinable elements, PVC plastic tubes padded with polyurethane and covered in fabric, made by Flexform, 1955 (New York, Museum of Modern Art)

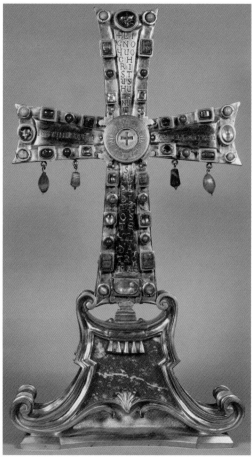

2. Cross of Justinian, silver and hardstones, Byzantine, 6th century (Rome, Vatican Museo Storico Aristico—Tesoro di San Pietro)

3. Child's cupboard, painted wood with nails and porcelain handles, 737×559×330 mm, USA, c. 1910 (Newark, NJ, Newark Museum)

4. Charles Cressent: commode mounted with gilt bronze cupids and monkeys, 900×1430×640 mm, c. 1745 (Paris, Musée du Louvre)

PLATE IX

1. *Cuerda seca* tile panel depicting a garden scene, from the Pavilion of Forty Columns, Isfahan, Iran, early 17th century (Paris, Musée du Louvre)

2. Travel cutlery and bag of Queen Elizabeth I, 1533–1603 (Alnwick Castle, Northumberland)

PLATE X

2. *Descho da parto* showing cherubs (reverse) by Domenico di Bartolo, 15th century (Venice, Ca' d'Oro)

1. Cupboard on supporting table by Edouard Lièvre, 1877 (Paris, Musée d'Orsay)

3. Handle of a sacrificial knife in the form of a kneeling deity, turquoise and shell mosaic, Aztec (Rome, Museo Nazionale Preistorico ed Etnografico 'Luigi Pigorini')

PLATE XI

1. Golden Throne of Maharaja Ranjit Singh by Hafiz Muhammad of Multan, wood and resin core covered with sheets of embossed gold, h. 940 mm, *c.* 1818 (London, Victoria and Albert Museum)

3. Bohemian glass tumbler showing Abraham and the Three Angels, *c.* 1850 (Vienna, Judaica Coll. Max Berger)

2. Johann Melchoir Dinglinger: *Court of Aurangzeb* (detail), gold and enamel, 1701–7 (Dresden, Grünes Gewölbe)

4. Bayeux Tapestry (detail of Harold and his falcon), linen with wool embroidery, probably before 1082 (Bayeux, Musée de la Tapisserie de la Reine Mathilde)

PLATE XII

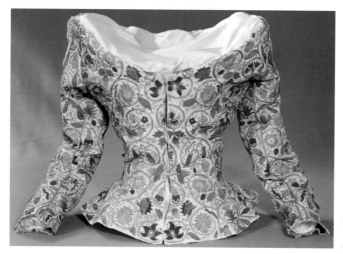

1. Woman's jacket, linen embroidered with silk and metal threads, h. 680 mm, England, early 16th century (London, Victoria and Albert Museum)

2. Teapot, enamel on copper, France, *c.* 1867 (London, Victoria and Albert Museum)

3. Goldenes Rössel (detail of page and horse), enamel *en ronde bosse* and silver gilt, Paris, France, 1403–4 (Altötting, SS Philipp und Jakob, Schatkammer)

PLATE XIII

1. Carl Fabergé: gold and enamel Easter eggs, executed by Fyodor Rückert, *c.* 1900 (private collection)

2. Tankard made of blue and white twisted glass canes *à la façon de Venise* and silver-gilt mounts, h. 128 mm, London, 1548–9 (London, British Museum)

3. Porcelain statuette of a European horseman decorated with *famille rose* enamels, h. 270 mm, 18th century (Paris, Musée Guimet)

PLATE XIV

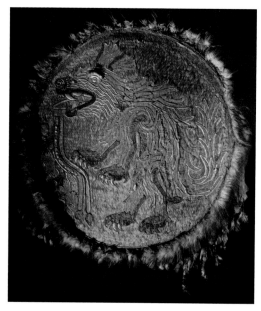

1. Featherwork shield (detail) showing a water beast holding a sacrificial knife in his jaws, Aztec (Vienna, Naturhistorisches Museum)

2. Alexandre-Georges Fourdinois: cabinet on stand, oak with ebony veneer and inlay, after designs by Hilaire and Pasti (figures) and Neville (arabesques), 2.49×1.55×0.52 m, 1861–7 (London, Victoria and Albert Museum)

3. Frankenthal porcelain Chinese pavilion and Chinese figurines, c. 1770 (Mannheim, Städtisches Reiss-Museum)

1. Wallpaper frieze, England, 1847–70 (London, Victoria and Albert Museum)

4. Ikat headcloth (*rūmāl*), cotton, Andhra Pradesh, India, 20th century (London, Victoria and Albert Museum)

2. Fra Giovanni da Verona: intarsia decoration depicting flutes and lutes, Monte Oliveto Maggiore

3. Owen Jones (attrib.): 'Alhambresque' furnishing fabric, jacquard-woven silk, 556×1270 mm, London, 1850s (London, Victoria and Albert Museum)

5. Henri Cros: *Prize of the Tournament*, polychrome wax relief, 600×510 mm (Paris, Musée d'Orsay)

PLATE XV

PLATE XVI

1. Hector Guimard: Porte Dauphine metro station entrance, Paris, c. 1905

3. Mahogany armchair with inlaid veneers, designed by Lawrence Alma-Tadema and made by Norman Johnstone, England, c. 1884 (London, Victoria and Albert Museum)

2. Emile Gallé: 'par une telle nuit' cup, glass with particles of metal and engraved ornaments, 1894 (Paris, Musée d'Orsay)

4. Inrō in the form of a top by Shibata Zeshin, coloured lacquer and shell, second half of the 19th century (London, Victoria and Albert Museum)

the flamed stoneware that had long been associated with the company; in the same decade Dalpayrat was joined by his four sons (Albert, Adolphe, Hyppolite and Paul). Dalpayrat continued to design display pieces, some of which were set in gilded bronze by Parisian jewellers such as Maison Cardeilhac. The pottery closed in 1906.

H. Makus: *Adrien Dalpayrat, 1844–1910* (Stuttgart, 1998)
Pierre-Adrien Dalpayrat, 1844–1910: Céramiste de l'art nouveau: Etude biographique (Sceaux, 1999)

D'Alva bottle. *See* BELLARMINE.

Damascene. Fabric with a moiré or water pattern.

Damascening. Technique of decorating metalwork with an inlay of precious metal. Damascened or pattern-welded iron relies on surface treatment or etching to bring out the pattern, but sometimes the whole surface can be uniformly patinated by careful heat treatment and quenching to produce an attractive blue-black surface that is usually inlaid with gold or silver.

Islamic blacksmiths produced a black-patinated steel inlaid with gold and silver. This is sometimes known as 'false damascening' or Toledo ware, after the city in Spain where the craft was and continues to be practised. The conquistadors introduced the craft to the Americas, and the small town of Amozoc, near Puebla, in Mexico is well known for the production of saddle and bridle fittings. The steel is inlaid with gold and silver, then oiled and plunged into hot nitre and quenched in water. Finally it is placed in boiling water, followed by a dip in oil to impart a peacock-blue colour to the metal.

A similar technique is used in the Indian subcontinent to make *kuftkäri* wares. A steel plate is first inlaid with fine silver or gold wire and then patinated by holding it over a charcoal fire until the desired purple-black colour is attained. It is then quenched and treated with vegetable oil to preserve the colour. Methods similar to these were widely used in Renaissance Europe to patinate or 'blue' armour and other steelwork.

S. N. Sen: *Catalogue on Damascene and Bidri Art in the Indian Museum,* Calcutta, Ind. Mus. (Calcutta, 1983)
J. D. Lavin and R. Larrañaga: *The Art and Tradition of the Zuloagas: Spanish Damascene from the Khalili Collection* (Oxford, 1997)
C. Rabinovitch: 'Matter into Metaphor: Transformation in Asian and Western Metals', *Metalsmith,* xxii/2 (Spring 2002), pp. 28–35

Damascus ware. *See under* IZNIK.

Damask. *See* LINEN DIAPER AND DAMASK.

Dammouse, Albert-Louis (*b* 1848; *d* 1926). French potter, glass-maker and sculptor. He was the son of a porcelain modeller at Sèvres, where Albert-Louis was eventually to have his own studio, where he be-

came an exponent of the PÀTE-SUR-PÀTE technique of ceramic decoration. His early work is maiolica designed under Italian influence, but from the early 1880s he turned to stoneware designed under Japanese influence. He designed for other manufacturers, notably the HAVILAND Auteuil workshop (1873–85), for which he designed stoneware with barbotine decoration, and from 1898 he made a type of cast glass called PÀTE DE VERRE.

P. Hollister: 'Pâte de Verre: The French Connection', *Amer. Craft,* xlviii (Aug–Sept 1988), pp. 40–47

Damm pottery. *See* HÖCHST CERAMICS FACTORY.

Danhauser, Josef Ulrich (*b* Vienna, 14 March 1780; *d* Vienna, 6 Jan 1829). Austrian furniture manufacturer. In 1804 Danhauser founded the Etablissement für alle Gegenstände des Ameublements, which manufactured all types of furniture, including gilded, silvered or bronzed ornaments made from woodpaste (a material composed of sawdust, glue and oil), which were used as a substitute for massive bronze mouldings. As well as furniture ornaments Danhauser also manufactured small pieces of decorative sculpture and lighting fixtures. In 1814 he eventually obtained the state manufacturing warrant 'to make all types of furniture', and to distinguish his wares from those made by his competitors he signed them: K.K. PRIVILEG. LANDESFABR:ALLER GATTUNGEN MEUBL:DES JOSEPH DANHAUSER IN WIEN.

Danhauser ran the first Viennese furniture and interior decoration shop, particularly promoting the BIEDERMEIER style. All items needed to equip a house—curtains, upholstered furniture, lighting fixtures and such decorative accessories as clocks and small pieces of sculpture—were manufactured and sold.

Dantesca chair. Nineteenth-century term for a type of late medieval Italian chair which had four legs with crossed scissor hinges connected by four bars

Darby, Abraham (*b* Old Farm Lodge, Wrens Nest, near Dudley, Worcs, 14 Apr 1678; *d* Madeley Court, Madeley, Salop, 5 May 1717). English iron founder, copper smelter, and brass manufacturer. In 1702 Darby entered into a partnership with three fellow Quakers and established a brass factory at Baptist Mills, in Bristol. In 1703 he established an iron pot foundry in Cheese Lane, Bristol, where he developed a new technique casting iron-bellied pots in sand; he patented the process in 1707.

Darby then established a series of businesses at Coalbrookdale, of which the most enduring was the CAOLBROOKDALE IRON COMPANY founded in 1708 and still in operation. The business was subsequently managed by his son Abraham (1711–63) and his grandson Abraham (1750–89).

ODNB

E. Thomas: *Coalbrookdale and the Darby Family: The Story of the World's First Industrial Dynasty* (York, 1999)

Dari. *See under* CARPET, §II., 2.

Darly, Matthias [Mathias; Matthew] (*fl c.* 1740–*d* early 1770s). English engraver, draughtsman and drawing-master. In 1751 he issued *A New-book of Chinese, Gothic & Modern Chairs*, a slight publication on eight leaves. Twelve examples with bizarre backs were described as 'Hall Chairs' in a reissue of 1766, but it is more likely they were intended for gardens and summer-houses. A shell-back chair (Stratford-on-Avon, Nash's House) corresponding to one of the designs was made for the Chinese temple erected at Stratford for the Shakespeare jubilee organized by David Garrick in 1769. Five plates from a second book of chairs (*c.* 1751), of which no copy survives, were apparently reprinted in Robert Manwaring's *The Chair-maker's Guide* (1766). Described as 'Parlour Chairs', they incorporate extravagant C-scroll motifs in the backs.

Darly shared a house in Northumberland Court, London, with Thomas Chippendale in 1753, and he engraved most of the plates in the first edition of Chippendale's *The Gentleman's and Cabinet-maker's Director* (1754). In collaboration with George Edwards (1694–1773), an ornithologist, he published *A New Book of Chinese Designs* (1754), which consisted of 120 sprightly chinoiserie compositions. The 21 plates feature furniture, including beds, pagoda-like girandoles, chairs and candle stands, all invested with an Oriental or whimsically Rustic character.

The success of the *Director* led William Ince and John Mayhew to employ Darly to engrave the plates for their *Universal System of Household Furniture* (1762). Another pattern book in which his engravings featured was Roger Sayer's *Houshold Furniture in Genteel Taste* (1760).

Darly's later publications on ornament featured Neo-classical elements: tripods, vases and frames occur in *The Ornamental Architect or Young Artist's Instructor* (1770) and *A New Book of Ornaments in the Present (Antique) Taste* (1772).

M. Darly: *A New-book of Chinese, Gothic & Modern Chairs* (London, 1751, 2/1766)

M. Darly and G. Edwards: *A New Book of Chinese Designs* (London, 1754)

M. Darly: *The Ornamental Architect or Young Artist's Instructor* (London, 1770)

M. Darly: *A New Book of Ornaments in the Present (Antique) Taste* (London, 1772)

C. Gilbert: 'The Early Furniture Designs of Mathias Darly', *Furn. Hist.*, xi (1975), pp. 33–9

Darmstadt Artists' Colony. German artists' Colony based in the city of Darmstadt in Hessen. For centuries Darmstadt was the seat of the grand dukes of Hesse-Darmstadt and in 1899 Grand Duke Ernst-Ludwig founded an artists' colony in the city's Mathildenhöhe park; the colony was eventually to become a leading centre for *Jugendstil* and the applied arts in Germany. The seven artists whom Ernst-

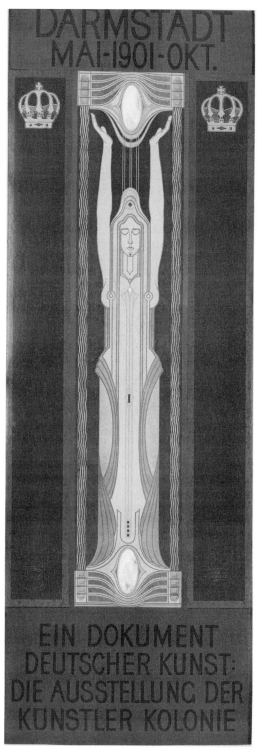

Peter Behrens: poster for the exhibition of the Artists' Colony at Darmstadt in 1901 (Berlin, Kunstbibliothek, Staatliche Museen zu Berlin)

Ludwig summoned to the colony included PETER BEHRENS, JOSEF MARIA OLBRICH, the medallist and sculptor Rudolf Bosselt (1871–1938), the painter and printmaker Paul Bürck (1878–1947), the painter and designer Hans Christiansen (1866–1945), the sculptor Ludwig Habich (1872–1949) and the interior decorator Patriz Huber (1878–1902). Olbrich, who led the colony until his death in 1908, designed most of the buildings and workshops; by designing the furniture and fittings as well, the colony was able to put into practice Olbrich's ideas of GESAMTKUNST-WERK, visible both in his panelled interior (1908; Darmstadt, Mus. Kstlerkolon.) from the Gluckert House and in Behrens's design for his own house.

The second generation of artists in the colony included designers of furniture, glass, ceramics and metalwork, such as Albin Müller (1871–1941), Ernst Riegel (1871–1939), Jacob Julius Scharvogel (1854–1938) and Josef Emil Schneckendorf (1865–1949). All aspects of the decorative arts were covered: examples of the colony's work include Huber's sinuous cherry-wood chair (1900–01), Müller's *Jugendstil* coffeepot (*c.* 1905; all Darmstadt, Hess. Landesmus.) and Schneckendorf's translucent lustreware glass vase (*c.* 1904; Zurich, Mus. Bellerive). The colony was closed in August 1914 at the outbreak of World War I, but Mathildenhöhe continues to be used as a venue for exhibitions.

Darned netting [It. *punto maglia*]. Loose network of knotted threads on which a pattern is darned

Dassier. Swiss family of medallists. Jean [John] Dassier (*b* Geneva, 17 Aug 1676; *d* Geneva, 15 Nov 1763) trained under his father Domaine Dassier (1641–1719), chief engraver at the Geneva Mint, and studied in Paris under Jean Mauger and Joseph Roettier. From 1711 he was assistant engraver at the Geneva Mint and in 1720 succeeded his father as chief engraver, a post he held until his death. Around 1720 he designed and executed his first series of medals: those of French monarchs (72 medals) and religious reformers (around 24). In 1728 he visited England, where he refused the offer of a position at the Royal Mint. In 1731 he issued a series of medals dedicated to George II, depicting British sovereigns from William I to George II. This consisted of 35 medals available in gold, silver and bronze, some of which were damascened. He was joined in this project by his second son, and the medals are described in his *A Sett of Medals of all the Kings of England* (London, 1731) and *An Explanation of the Medals of the English Monarchs Engraved by John Dassier and Son* (Birmingham, 1731). The Birmingham manufacturer Edward Thomason obtained the dies and continued to issue the series. Dassier also produced series depicting subjects from ancient Rome (silver and bronze) and remarkable men from the time of Louis XIV (*reg* 1643–1715; silver and bronze). Many of his portraits are not authentic, but the technical skill of his die-engraving placed him among the leading European medallists and ensured for him many commissions for commemorative medals.

Of Dassier's three sons, the eldest, Jacques-Antoine Dassier (*b* Geneva, 15 Nov 1715; *d* Copenhagen, 2 Nov 1759), studied in Paris and Rome before working as assistant engraver at the Royal Mint in London from 1741 to 1745. He later worked at Geneva and from 1756 at the St Petersburg Mint. Besides many individually commissioned medals, in the 1740s he produced a series of famous Englishmen, including *Sir Hans Sloane* (bronze, 1744), and contributed to his father's Roman series. Antoine Dassier (1718–80) and Paul Dassier (1719–55) were both goldsmiths; like his elder brother, Antoine worked with his father on his medallic series and at the Geneva Mint, as chief engraver, from 1777 until his death.

R. B. Waddington: 'The Iconography of Jean Dassier's Milton Medal', *Milton Q.*, xix/4 (1985), pp. 93–6

W. L. Eisler: *The Dassiers of Geneva: 18th-century European Medallists* (Lausanne, 2002)

Dasson, Henri (*b* 1825; *d* 1896). French *ébéniste* whose company specialized in producing high-quality replicas of 18th-century originals.

Daubenkrug. Beer stein mounted on pewter and fitted with an inlaid wooden handle and foot.

Daum. French family of glassmakers. In 1878 Jean Daum (*b* Bischwiller, 1825; *d* Nancy, 1885), from Alsace, acquired a glass factory, which he renamed Verrerie de Nancy, and there began to produce traditional tableware. His eldest son, Auguste Daum (1853–1909), joined the factory in 1879 and was followed by Antonin Daum (1864–1930), who managed the business from 1887. In the 1890s the brothers enlarged the range of coloured glassware, producing etched, moulded and cameo glass with naturalistic motifs in the Art Nouveau style inspired by the work of their fellow townsman EMILE GALLÉ. Painters and decorators, chief among them being Henri Bergé, provided designs executed by numerous skilled craftsmen under the supervision of Auguste. The originality of Daum glass lies in the diversity of such decorative techniques as enamelling, etching and casing developed for large-scale production, rather than in the quality of decoration. All pieces made after 1890 bore signatures.

During the 1890s the Daum brothers collaborated with LOUIS MAJORELLE in the design and production of lamps and vases. In 1906 a *pâte de verre* workshop was opened and directed by Almaric Walter (1859–1942). After World War I Auguste's sons, Paul (*b* 1890, deported 1944) and Henri (1894–1966), began producing clear glass in free forms with deep, acid-etched decoration. After temporary closure during World War II, the firm was reopened by Antonin's son, Michel (*b* ?Nancy, 1900), who aimed at a more exclusive market with sparkling crystal glass of a high lead content. Production of *pâte de verre* was resumed after 1966, with limited editions of glass sculptures from a variety of artists, including Salvador Dalí (1904–89). As president of the firm, Antonin's nephew Jacques (b ?Nancy, 1919; d 5 March 1987) was the last member of the family to have an official connection with the Compagnie Française de Cristal Daum.

N. Daum: *Daum: Maîtres verriers* (Lausanne, 1980)
C. Bacri, N. Daum and C. Pétry-Parisot: *Daum: Masters of French Decorative Glass* (New York, 1993)
C. Bardin: 'Le Reve d'Elsa, l'affirmation de l'entreprise Daume comme verrerie d'art', *Rev. Louvre*, lii/1 (Feb 2002), pp. 67–73, 117
C. Bardin: 'Au musée des Beaux-arts de Nancy, le Vase aux raisins roses de Daum, 1925: D'un passe prestigieux a une nouvelle esthetique', *Rev. Louvre*, liii /3 (June 2003), pp. 67–73
V. Bougault: 'Les Daum de Daum' *Conn. A.*, dcxxii (Dec 2004), pp. 72–7
X. Narbaits: 'Verrerie Daum: Un Style Incassable', *Beaux-A.*, ccxlvii (Dec 2004–Jan 2005), p. 140

Davenport (ceramics). English family of pottery and porcelain manufacturers. In 1794 John Davenport (b 1765) founded a pottery at Longport (Staffordshire) to manufacture earthenware. He was succeeded in 1830 by his sons Henry and William, and when Henry died in 1835, the firm became known as William Davenport and Company; it remained in the Davenport family till 1887. Initially the company only made underglaze blue printed earthenware, but from about 1815 it also manufactured porcelain. The company had a huge range of domestic wares (which included many willow patterns) and manufactured in large quantities for both domestic and export markets. The pottery is marked 'Davenport' (or occasionally 'Longport'), initially in lower case letters and later in upper case; after 1805 the mark sometimes includes an anchor.

T. A. Lockett: *Davenport Pottery and Porcelain, 1794–1887* (Newton Abbot, 1972)
T. A. Locket and G. A. Godden: *Davenport: China, Earthenware, Glass* (London, 1989)

Davenport (furniture). Small ornamental writing-table or escritoire with a sloping top above a set of drawers, made in England in the 19th century; in American English the term denotes a type of sofa-bed.

G. Walkling: 'Davenport Desks', *Connoisseur*, ccv (Sept 1980), pp. 2–7

David, Jacques-Louis (b Paris, 30 Aug 1748; d Brussels, 29 Dec 1825). French painter. David's reputation rightly rests on his painting, but he was also a furniture designer, and in the 1780s inaugurated a new fashion by designing replicas of ancient Roman furniture (especially chairs), which were made for him by the *menuisier* Georges JACOB.

Davis, Alexander Jackson (b New York, 24 July 1803; d Orange, NJ, 14 Jan 1892). American architect. Davis was the most influential American archi-

tect of the second quarter of the 19th century. His most respected works are his large Gothic Revival country houses, for which he sometimes designed furniture as well as interiors. The best-preserved of his large Gothic villas is Lyndhurst (originally 'Knoll'; 1838), at Tarrytown, NY, built for General William Paulding and for which Davis made 50 furniture designs in the Gothic style.

C. M. McClinton: 'Furniture and Interiors Designed by A. J. Davis', *Connoisseur*, clxx (1969), pp. 54–61
J. B. Davies: 'Gothic Revival Furniture Designs of Alexander J. Davis', *Antiques*, cxi (1977), pp. 1014–27
A. Peck: *Alexander Jackson Davis, American Architect, 1803–1892* (New York, 1992)

Davis, William. *See under* WORCESTER.

Day, Lewis Foreman (b Peckham Rye, London, 29 Jan 1845; d London, 18 April 1910). English designer and writer. In 1865 he entered the office of Lavers & Barraud, glass painters and designers. Some time later he became keeper of cartoons at Clayton & Bell and by 1870 had joined Heaton, Butler & Bayne, for whom he worked on the decoration of Eaton Hall, Ches. In late 1880 Day started his own business designing textiles, wallpapers, stained glass, embroidery, carpets, tiles, pottery, furniture, silver, jewellery and book covers. He designed tiles for Maw & Co. and Pilkington's Tile and Pottery Co., stained glass and wallpaper for W. B. Simpson & Co., wallpapers for Jeffrey & Co. and textiles for Turnbull & Stockdale where he was made Art Director in 1881.

Day was a founder-member and Secretary of the Fifteen, a group of artists interested in design who came together in 1882 to discuss the role of art and design in daily life. Day helped form the Art Worker's Guild in 1884. In 1888 he led several members of this group to form the Arts and Crafts Exhibition Society.

ODNB
L. F. Day: *The Anatomy of Pattern* (London, 1887)
L. F. Day: *The Planning of Ornament* (London, 1887)
L. F. Day: *The Application of Ornament* (London, 1888)
L. F. Day: *Nature in Ornament* (London, 1892)
L. F. Day: *Pattern Design* (London, 1903)
D. M. Ross: *Lewis Foreman Day: Designer and Writer on Stained Glass* (Cambridge, 1929)

Day, Robin (b High Wycombe, Bucks, 25 May 1915). English furniture designer. In 1948 he and his wife Lucienne Day (b 1917), a textile and wallpaper designer, opened a London office where he practised as a graphic, exhibition and industrial designer. That year he and Clive Latimer (b c. 1916) won first prize in the International Low-cost Furniture Competition, held at MOMA in New York, for their storage furniture design. Such storage units became standard elements in 1950s British homes, contributing to contemporary ideas of flexibility in interiors. The prize brought him to the attention of Hille International, a British manufacturer looking to produce modern, contract furniture in a post-war market and to whom he became a design consultant with the opportunity to explore new materials and techniques in the production of low-cost furniture. In 1950 he designed the 'Hillestak' stacking chair, made of plywood, using newly available plastic glues and with inverted V-shaped splayed legs, characteristic of the period. His most successful chair for Hille, the 'Polyprop', of injection-moulded polypropylene on a slim metal tube base, developed the principle of different materials for base and seat established in the mid-1950s by the American designer Charles Eames. Day designed seating for the Festival Hall (1951), for the Barbican Arts Centre (from 1968), both in London, and furniture for Gatwick Airport, W. Sussex (1958). His minimalist 675 chair has recently been revived by Habitat.

L. Jackson: *Robin and Lucienne Day: Pioneers of Modern Design* (New York, 2001)

Deal. Term denoting both a type and a size of wood. It loosely refers to fir or pine, specifically the wood of the Norway Spruce (*Abies excelsa*, known as white deal), the Scotch Pine (*Pinus sylvestris*, known as red deal) and American species such as the Yellow Pine (*Pinus mitis*, known as yellow deal), or kindred American species. These are the woods that from the 17th century began to displace oak for panelling and for the carcases of furniture that was to be veneered. As a measure of the size of a sawn plank, in British usage a deal is 9 inches (228 mm) wide, no more than 3 inches (76 mm) thick and at least 6 feet (1.8 m) long; in American usage it is 11 inches wide, 2½ inches thick and 12 feet long.

Debschitz, Wilhelm von (*b* Görlitz, 21 Feb 1871; *d* Lüneburg, 10 March 1948). German designer, painter, teacher and theorist. His designs, which were influenced by the English ARTS AND CRAFTS MOVEMENT, were exhibited in 1899 at the exhibition of the Bayerische Kunstgewerbeverein (Munich, Glaspal.) and in 1901 at the first Ausstellung für Kunst im Handwerk in Munich. In 1902 he founded the Lehr-und Versuch-Atelier für Angewandte und Freie Kunst with the Swiss artist HERMANN OBRIST; the school's practical training in arts and crafts anticipated the work of the BAUHAUS. When Obrist resigned from the school in 1904, Debschitz founded the Ateliers und Werkstätten für Angewandte Kunst and the Keramischen Werkstätten production centres attached to the school. He published essays on art theory in a number of periodicals, including *Dekorative Kunst*. In later years he lived at Bernau in the Black Forest, mainly producing textile designs.

Decalcomania. Decoration made by using cut up sheets of paper printed with lithographic designs stuck down and varnished on to a surface. In the late 18th century the process was used to decorate furniture with prints; in England in the early 1860s there was a fashion for decorating glass and porcelain through this process. In ceramics the decal has been revived by potters such as the American Howard Kottler (1930–89) and the Lithuanian-American Rimas VisGirda.

V. Halper and H. Kottler: *Look Alikes: The Decal Plates of Howard Kottler* (Seattle, 2004)

Decanter. Bottle of cut glass or (historically) clear flint, with a stopper, used for serving decanted wine at the table. This process ensures the removal of sediment from the wine and improves the taste by aeration.

A. McConnell: *The Decanter: An Illustrated History of Glass from 1650* (Woodbridge, 2004)

Deck, Joseph-Théodore (*b* Guebwiller, Alsace, 1823; *d* ?Paris, 1891). French potter. In 1856 he established a workshop in Paris, where he experimented with glazes, eventually creating his much-admired *bleu de Deck* (1861). He produced lustre and polychrome painted, tin-enamelled wares based on Isnik and Persian ceramics and Italian maiolica. He also made 'inlaid' pottery in the style of 16th-century wares from Saint-Porchaire. His reputation as the first 'modern' studio potter rests on the range and quality of his technical innovations and his successful use of historical methods. Many early pieces from his workshop (e.g. dish painted by Eléonore Escallier, *c*. 1867; Paris, Mus. A. Déc.) were painted by such other artists as Albert Anker (1831–1910), Félix

Joseph-Théodore Deck and Jean-Charles Davillier: Alhambra Vase, painted earthenware inlaid with coloured clays, h. 1.07 m, 1862 (London, Victoria and Albert Museum)

Bracquemond and Eléonore Escallier (1827–88). During the 1870s he became a pioneer of Japonisme and began experimenting with reduced copper glazes on porcelain, developing flambé glazes similar to Chinese glazes used during the period of the Qianlong emperor (*reg* 1736–96). Deck was appointed administrator (1887–91) at the porcelain factory of Sèvres, where he introduced a new type of glassy, soft-paste porcelain suitable for making reproductions of the factory's 18th-century styles. Under his direction Sèvres extended its production to include porcelain with rich, monochrome glazes (e.g. faceted urn vase, 1883; Paris, Mus. A. Déc.).

J.-T. Deck: *La Faïence* (Paris, 1887)

Deckel [Ger.: 'lid']. Term used to indicate presence of a lid, hence *Deckelkrug* (a jug with a lid), *Deckeldose* (a box with a lid), *Deckelkanne* (a jug with a lid), *Deckelpokal* (a goblet with a lid), *Deckelschüssel* (a dish with a lid), *Deckelterrine* (a tureen with a lid) and *Deckelvasen* (a vase with a lid). These terms are all in occasional use in English.

Decker, Paulus (*b* Nuremberg, 27 Dec 1677; *d* Bayreuth, 3 Oct 1713). German architect and designer. He published ornamental designs (including grotesques) for artists working in gold, silver, glass and lacquer.

Decorative paper. *See* PAPER, DECORATIVE.

Décor bois [Fr.: 'wood decoration']. *Trompe l'oeil* decoration resembling wood-grain and used on earthenware and porcelain in 18th century France, notably at NIDERVILLER.

Décorchemont, François-Emile (*b* 1880; *d* 1971). French glassmaker who established a studio at Conches, where he was an early exponent of PÂTE DE VERRE, which he used from *c.* 1900 to produce small glass sculptures and figures, initially in an ART NOUVEAU style and later in a more austere idiom. By 1904 Décorchemont had developed a method of colouring glass to make it resemble translucent stones.

Découpage. Term introduced into English in the early 1960s to denote the decoration of a surface with an applied paper cut-out or an object produced by this technique. In the fine arts, the greatest exponent of découpage was Henri Matisse (1869–1954), whose late work includes paper cut-out compositions such as *Memory of Oceania* (1953; New York, MOMA), *The Snail* (1952–3; London, Tate) and *Ivy in Flower* (1953; Dallas, TX, Mus. F.A.). Découpage has been popular as a domestic art since the 18th century. Paper cut-outs are assembled into a design and then fixed to a surface, usually under layers of varnish but sometimes under glass. There are national guilds of decoupeurs in Australia, Italy, Japan, South Africa, the USA and the United Kingdom.

Degoullons, Jules (*b c.* 1671; *d* 1737). Sculptor and wood-carver who from 1698 was employed as a sculpteur de roi. He collaborated with JACQUES VERBERCKT on decorations at Versailles (e.g. the Chambre de la Reine, 1730; *in situ*), and for the apartments of the Dauphin and for the Petite Galerie of the king's apartments (both 1736; *in situ*), and was a principal carver of the choir-stalls at the cathedral of Notre-Dame (Paris) designed (*c.* 1790) by Robert de Cotte (1656/7–1753).

Dehua. Chinese centre of ceramics production. The pure white porcelain commonly known in Europe since the middle of the 19th century as *blanc de Chine* was, and still is, made in the vicinity of Dehua in the Fujian Province of China. The kilns came into operation in the late part of the Southern Song period (1127–1279) but only achieved fame for high-quality wares in the 16th century. The finest material comprised the freely modelled figures for which the kilns are now best known. Among the key figures is the seated Guan Yu, god of war (1610; London, BM); Guanyin (goddess of mercy; Chinese form of the *bodhisattva* Avalokiteshvara), Bodhidharma, the Buddha and the Heavenly Twins of Harmony and Mirth, seated or standing, were also popular. Other wares include conical bowls, small cups (some of which resemble rhinoceros-horn cups) and incense burners with lion-head bosses. All of these forms are extremely simple, their beauty deriving from the warm ivory or slightly bluish, skimmed-milk colour of the glaze. For both vessels and figures the construction is always thick and heavy, with a perfect marriage of body and glaze. Because of the thickness of the body, figures tend to have drying or firing cracks extending up the inside from the hollow base.

J. Ayers and Y. Bingling: *Blanc de Chine: Divine Images in Porcelain* (New York, 2000)

R. H. Blumenfield: *Blanc de Chin: The Great Porcelain of Dehua* (Berkeley, 2000)

J. Ayers: 'Blanc de Chine and Europe' *Orient A.*, xlviii/5 (2002–3), pp. 2–9

E. J. Frankel: 'Early White Wares and Blanc de Chine', *A. Asia*, xxxii/5 (Sept–Oct 2002), pp. 140–42

H. Tan: 'The Hickley Collection of Blanc de Chine', *A. Asia*, xxxii/6 (Nov–Dec 2002), pp. 112–22

Déjeuner. *See* CABARET.

Delafosse, Jean-Charles (*b* Paris, 1734; *d* Paris, 11 Oct 1789). French decorative designer, engraver and architect. By 1767 he styled himself 'architecte et professeur pour le dessin'. In 1768 he published the first volume of his most important work, the *Nouvelle iconologie historique*. It contains 110 plates, nearly all engraved by Delafosse himself, with designs for furniture, decorative objects and architectural ornament in the heavy, classicizing, Louis XVI style. In addition, each design bears a particular, usually complex, symbolic or iconological meaning, pertaining to an almost encyclopedic range of subject-matter. In some of his designs he manipulated abstract shapes in new ways, using such forms as truncated columns, cones, pyramids, spheres, discs and rectangles, sometimes carefully shaded to appear simultaneously three-dimensional and flat.

J.-C. Delafosse: *Nouvelle iconologie historique*, 2 vols (Paris, 1768, 2/1771)

G. Levallet: 'L'Ornemaniste Jean-Charles Delafosse', *Gaz. B.-A.*, i (1929), pp. 158–69

J.-C. Delafosse: *Fragments énigmatiques: Allégories de J.-C. Delafosse* (Paris, 1994)

Delaherche, Auguste (*b* 1857; *d* 1940). French potter. As a young man he made architectural ornaments (principally tiles) in a ceramics factory near Beauvais. In 1887 he moved to Paris to assume responsibility for the Haviland studio of Ernest Chaplet; he specialized in stoneware vases with high-temperature flambé glazes, often decorated with Persian motifs. In 1894 he moved to Armentières, where he began to make porcelain as well as stoneware. In 1904 he stopped designing pottery that could be reproduced, and thereafter only made unique pieces. His glazes were an important influence on the work of the American potter WILLIAM HENRY GRUEBY.

A. Delaherche: *Auguste Delaherche: Rêves d'argile, secrets d'émail* (Paris, 2001)

F. Claustrat: 'Delaherche, recettes de ceramiste', *L'Oeil*, dxxviii (July–Aug 2001), p. 86

Delamain. Irish family of potters. In 1752 Captain Henry Delamain (*d* 1757) took over an existing pottery business in Dublin and employed foreign technicians. In 1755 the Dublin Society, which had offered a premium for improving the quality of earthenware, certified the quality of Delamain's tin-glazed wares. After Delamain's death the factory first passed to his wife, Mary Delamain (*d* 1760), and in 1760 to his brother, William Delamain, and Samuel Wilkinson. In 1770 the factory competed for the Dublin Society's prize for earthenware 'in imitation of flint or Paris ware', which was probably a lead-glazed creamware (cream-coloured earthenware), indicating the influence and increasing popularity of Josiah Wedgwood's invention. However, the Delamain factory ceased production *c.* 1770.

Delanois, Louis (*b* 1731; *d* 1792). French chair-maker who became a *maître* in Paris in 1761. He built furniture for many royal and aristocratic clients, including King Stanisław II Augustus Poniatowski of Poland and the Prince de Condé. In 1768 Pierre-Marie-Gaspard Grimod (soon to become Comte d'Orsay) bought the Hôtel de Chaulnes, otherwise known as Clermont (now 69 Rue de Varenne), in Paris, which he redecorated and furnished in the Neo-classical style; Delanois supplied the first Neo-classical seat furniture (untraced) to come from his workshop. In 1770 Delanois was commissioned to build the furniture for what is now known as the Pavillon du Barry in the grounds of the Château of Louveciennes. In 1777 sold his business and became a speculator in real estate; he became bankrupt in 1790.

S. Ericksen: *Louis Delanois, menusier en sièges (1731–1792)* (Paris, 1968)

Delaune, Etienne (*b* ?Paris, *c.* 1519; *d* Paris, 1583). French goldsmith, medallist, draughtsman and engraver. He was recorded as a journeyman goldsmith in Paris in 1546. A number of medals, including one of *Henry II* (Paris, Bib. N., Cab. Médailles), are attributed to him. He did not become an engraver until about 1557; his first dated prints, a series of 12 plates illustrating the Old Testament and two designs for hand mirrors, were made in 1561. His work was influenced by the Fontainebleau school, especially Luca Penni. As a Calvinist he left Paris at the time of the St Bartholomew's Eve massacre on 24 August 1572 and thereafter worked in Augsburg and Strasbourg. In Augsburg he made two engravings depicting a goldsmith's workshop (1576) and in Strasbourg he made a suite of 20 engravings of moral allegories (1580) based on drawings by his son Jean Delaune (*fl c.* 1580). His last dated engraving, a portrait of *Ambroise Paré*, dates from 1582.

Delaune was a skilled practitioner of the Italianate style favoured at the Valois court. His engravings of mythological and allegorical subjects, and especially his ornamental designs for jewellery and goldsmiths' work, of great precision despite their small dimensions, contributed to the spread of the Fontainebleau

Louis Delanois: *marquise*, carved white-painted and gilt beechwood, *c.* 1765 (Paris, Musée du Louvre)

style among a wide variety of artists and craftsmen in France and abroad. There are collections of his drawings in Paris (Louvre and Ecole N. Sup. B.-A.) and the British Royal Collection (Windsor Castle, Berks).

Y. Hackenbroch: 'New Knowledge on Jewels and Designs after Etienne Delaune', *Connoisseur*, clxii (1966), pp. 83–9

J. Jacquiot: 'Hommage à Etienne Delaune, célèbre graveur etmédailleur français, 1519–1583', *Bull. Club Fr. Médaille*, lxxx (1983), pp. 56–73, 77

C. Pollet: *Les gravures d'Etienne Delaune (1518–1583)* (Villeneuve d'Asq, 2001)

Delft. Dutch town in the province of Zuid-Holland and centre of ceramics production. Maiolica wares (those with a tin-glazed front and lead-glazed back) and tiles were made in Delft from *c*. 1580 following the trend set by such other Dutch towns as Haarlem, Amsterdam and Rotterdam. In reaction to the importation of Chinese porcelain by the Dutch East India Company, two potteries—the Porceleyne Schotel (est. 1616) and the Porceleyne Lampetkan (est. 1627)—were established in Delft for the production of faience (Delftware), which at that time was known as *Hollands Porceleyn*. From *c*. 1645 the importation of Chinese porcelain virtually ceased due to a series of domestic wars; this gave rise to an increasing number of new factories in Delft producing blue-and-white faience in the style of porcelain made in China during the Wan li period (1573–1620) and in the Transitional style (1620–44). Delft became the most famous centre for the production of faience in the Netherlands. About 1670 production was complemented by the manufacture of blue-and-manganese wares decorated with chinoiseries. About 1680 experiments were carried out with colours influenced by imported Japanese Kakiemon porcelain made in the kilns of Arita, Hizen Province (now Saga and Nagasaki Prefectures): blue, yellow, green, red, purple and sometimes gilding. A new direction in production was introduced by the Hoppesteyn family, owners of the faience factory Het Jonge Moriaenshoofd, who manufactured redwares decorated with gilding; red stoneware teapots, imitative of Chinese Yixing wares, were a particular speciality of the potter Ary de Milde. The influence of Delft is apparent in the number of factories that were either set up by or run by Dutch workers for the manufacture of blue-and-white faience and/or porcelain: Hanau (1661), Frankfurt am Main (1666), Saint-Cloud (1667/8), Lambeth, London (1671), and Berlin (1678). Between *c*. 1690 and 1695 decoration in white and yellow on a coloured (blue, brown, olive-green) ground was introduced. After 1700 a greater range of high-fired colours was used on a black ground. About 1705 wares decorated with both high-fired and enamel decoration were introduced, first imitating Japanese Imari porcelain and later Kakiemon porcelain, Chinese porcelain decorated with both the *famille verte* and *famille rose* palettes and Meissen porcelain.

In the early 1720s the factories entered a period of decline due to the economic depression in Europe, the increased competition from other faience and porcelain factories and the subsequent deterioration in standard and quality. In order to minimize the effects, a number of factory owners took action in 1724 by drawing up price agreements and limiting production. In the 1740s, however, some factories were forced to close. After the Seven Years War (1756–63) there was a short period of revival; production included figures and objects modelled as animals and fruit after Meissen porcelain and Strasbourg faience. The period of revival was, however, brief and the increased production of the hugely popular English creamware (cream-coloured earthenware) in the mid-1760s effectively marked the end of the Delftware industry. By 1800 there were only about eight factories left in Delft and from 1850 only one factory, the Porceleyne Fles, continued production.

J. D. van Dam: *Gedateerd Delfts aardwerk* [Dated Dutch earthenware] (Amsterdam and Zwolle, 1991)

J. D. van Dam: *Delffse porceleyne: Dutch Delftware, 1620–1850* (Rijksmuseum, 2004)

Delft, Thomas, & Co. *See under* TYNESIDE.

Delftfield Pottery. Scottish pottery established in 1748 in Glasgow; the potters, who were brought from England, used local clays to produce tin-glazed earthenwares for both home and colonial markets. When the Delftware market declined, such new products as creamwares, pearlwares, basaltes and later porcelain and brown glazed 'china' were produced. The factory closed in 1823 and merged with the Caledonian Pottery (1801–1925).

J. Kinghorn and G. Quail: *Delftfield: A Glasgow Pottery 1748–1823*, Glasgow Museums and Art Galleries (Glasgow, 1986)

Delftware. Modern term for tin-glazed earthenware manufactured in England or Ireland; the term (which replaced the earlier 'galleyware') is anachronistic, because such earthenware was introduced into England from Antwerp in 1567, when Jasper Andries (1535/41–*c*. 1580) and his brother Joris (*c*. 1535–*c*. 1579) established a pottery in Norwich, but Delft did not emerge as an important pottery centre until the 1650s; Jacob Jansen (*d* 1593), who had accompanied the Andries brothers to Norwich, established a pottery in Aldgate (London), and soon 'English Delftware' factories were established in Lambeth, Southwark (both on the south bank of the Thames opposite London) and Bristol.

By 1700 Delftware potteries at Southwark and Lambeth in London and at Bristol and nearby Brislington were making large quantities of plates, bowls, mugs and drug jars, mostly with cobalt-blue or manganese-purple decoration, generally inspired by Dutch and Chinese motifs. Towards the mid-18th century a Delftware pottery was started at Wincan-

Delftware plate depicting Taurus *by James Thornhill, one of a set of twelve signs of the zodiac, diam. 220 mm, 1711 (London, British Museum)*

ton, Somerset, while earlier in the 18th century an important industry had been founded at Liverpool; there was also a Delftware industry in Ireland. However, London was perhaps the biggest centre of production and made vast numbers of plates with lively painting and bold patterns until the early 19th century. Although many attempts had been made to improve the appearance of Delftware—powdered blue and manganese ground colours, polychrome patterns and even, at Liverpool, the rare use of *petit feu* enamels and transfer-printing—by the mid-18th century the material was clearly unsuitable for further development. The advent of creamware, the waning popularity of blue-and-white chinoiserie patterns in the 1780s and the labour-intensive manufacturing process, as well as the tendency of the glaze and body to chip and crack, all combined to cause the demise of a type of ware that, at its best, was highly decorative, cheap and popular both in England and as an export to North America.

L. L. Lipski and M. Archer: *Dated English Delftware* (London, 1984)
F. Britten: *London Delftware* (London,1987)
P. Francis: *Irish Delftware: An Illustrated History* (London, 2000)
A. Ray: *English Delftware in the Ashmolean Museum* (Oxford, 2000)
H. van Lemmen: *Delftware Tiles* (Princes Risborough, 2005)

Della Robbia. *See* ROBBIA, DELLA.

Delorme, Adrien Faizelot (*b* Paris, *c.* 1715–20; *d* after 1783). French cabinetmaker and dealer. He was the most famous member of a family of cabinetmakers; his father, François Faizelot Delorme (1691–1768), and his brothers Jean-Louis Faizelot Delorme and Alexis Faizelot Delorme were all *maîtres-ébénistes*. Adrien stamped his work delorme. He made and sold luxury furniture in the Louis XV style, decorated with japanning either in imitation of Chinese lacquer (e.g. Amsterdam, Rijksmus.) or with Eu-

ropean decoration (e.g. Waddesdon Manor, Bucks, NT). He also carried out sumptuous floral marquetry (e.g. Paris, Petit Pal.). His most distinguished work consisted of small pieces of furniture (e.g. Paris, Louvre; London, V&A; Washington, DC, Hillwood Mus.) embellished with floral marquetry or inlays of scrolls and foliation executed in end-grain wood on a dark-veined, light-wood ground forming a chevron pattern (e.g. Lyon, Mus. B.-A.).

Del Tasso, Giovan Battista di Marco. *See* TASSO, GIOVAN BATTISTA DI MARCO DEL.

Demay, Jean-Baptiste-Bernard (*b* 1759; *d* 1798). French furniture-maker (*menuisier*) who worked primarily for the court. His best-known chairs, typically in inlaid mahogany, had Marie-Antoinette's monogram on their pierced backs. He is the likely designer of the Montgolfier chair, which has a wooden splat shaped like a hot air balloon (Fr. *Montgolfière*); the chair was designed to mark the inaugural flight in 1784 of the balloon designed by the Montgolfier brothers.

De Morgan, William (Frend) (*b* London, 16 Nov 1839; *d* London, 15 Jan 1917). English designer, potter and novelist. One of the most original artist–craftsmen associated with the ARTS AND CRAFTS MOVEMENT. As a young man De Morgan worked for the firm of Morris, Marshall, Faulkner & Co. as a designer of stained glass and a painter of panels for furniture. His interest in the iridescence caused by the firing of the silver paint used to outline designs on stained glass led him to experiment with reproducing the effect on tiles. In 1873 he opened a studio and showroom (known as Orange House) in Chelsea, London; the principal product of the studio was a range of tiles with floral and foliate patterns in the style of William Morris and animal and bird designs, often grotesque or whimsical, painted in lustre glazes (examples in London, William Morris Gal.). In the early years of the Chelsea studio tile blanks were used, but by the late 1870s the factory was making its own tiles; in 1879 De Morgan produced tiles after Frederic Leighton's collection of Islamic tiles to complete the scheme (*in situ*) for the Arab Hall at Leighton House, London. Large ready-made dishes in the form of Chinese rice dishes were also decorated.

In 1882 De Morgan moved to a larger workshop at Merton Abbey, Surrey, close to William Morris's textile workshop. Orange House was kept as a showroom until 1886 when a new shop was opened at 45 Great Marlborough Street, London. At Merton Abbey De Morgan concentrated on producing hollowware and had pots thrown to his specifications. In addition to experimenting further with lustre glazes De Morgan developed his 'Persian' style of decoration, based on Middle Eastern ornament and executed in turquoise, blues and greens.

In 1888 De Morgan moved back to London, where he formed a partnership with the architect

Halsey Ricardo (1854–1928) in a new pottery at Sands End, Fulham, London. Here De Morgan developed his 'Moonlight' and 'Sunlight' series, which consist of wares with double and triple lustre effects (e.g. vase, *c.* 1890; London, V&A). Also in 1888, De Morgan was a founder-member of the Arts and Crafts Exhibition Society. In 1892 De Morgan began spending winters in Florence, where he employed decorators at the Cantagalli pottery to paint his new designs, which were then sent to Sands End. The partnership with Ricardo was dissolved in 1898 due to financial difficulties and another was formed with his long-time employees, kilnmaster Frank Iles (*fl* 1872–1911) and tile painters Charles Passenger and Fred Passenger. Leaving his partners to carry on the pottery, De Morgan retired in 1907 and pursued a successful career as a novelist.

ODNB

W. King: *Catalogue of Works by William De Morgan* (London, 1921)
R. Pinkham: *Catalogue of Pottery by William De Morgan* (London, 1973)
J. Catleugh: *William De Morgan Tiles* (London and New York, 1983)
M. Greenwood: *The Designs of William De Morgan* (Shepton Beauchamp, 1989)
C. Jordan: 'Tile panels by William De Morgan for the Peninsular and Oriental Steam Navigational Company' *Burl. Mag.*, cxliii/1179 (June 2001), pp. 371–4

Denby Pottery. English ceramics factory in Denby, Derbys; the successor of JOSEPH BOURNE & Son. In the 19th century the company was a manufacturer of stoneware bottles, but in the late 19th century the competition from cheaper glass bottles forced the company to diversify. It chose in the first instance to concentrate on decorative and kitchen wares with richly coloured glazes. Its decorative and giftware products (vases, bowls, tobacco jars) were stamped 'Danesby Ware'. In the 1930s the company introduced the bright 'Electric Blue' and the matt blue-brown 'Orient ware' giftware lines, and in the same period introduced kitchenware in 'Cottage Blue', 'Manor Green' and 'Homestead Brown', all of which continued in production till the early 1980s.

In the 1950s giftware production was reduced and Denby introduced new lines of tableware, especially dinner services. 'Echo' and 'Ode' were introduced in the early 1950s, followed by 'Greenwheat' (1956), 'Studio' (1961) and 'Arabesque' (1964; sold in the USA as 'Samarkand'). In the 1970s Denby became a major presence in the new fashion for 'oven-to-tableware' products that combined cooking and serving dishes; its most successful lines were 'Romany' (*c.* 1970), 'Gypsy' (1971), 'Troubadour' (1971) and 'Cotswold' (1973). In the 1980s, designs became simpler (e.g. 'Imperial Blue' and 'Regency Green') as the company attempted to accommodate its wares to less formal settings, and its products are now robust and informal.

I. Hopwood and G. Hopwood: *Denby Pottery 1809–1997: Dynasties and Designers* (Shepton Beauchamp, 1997)
G. Key and A. Key: *Denby Stonewares: A Collector's Guide* (Torrington, 1995)

Denière, Guillaume (*fl* 1797). French bronze-caster who established a factory in Paris *c.* 1797. He produced sculptures, candelabra, furniture (both bronze furniture and wooden furniture with gilt-bronze mounts), but increasingly came to specialize in clocks, sometimes in collaboration with a bronze caster called Matelin, with whom he made various objects for President Monroe, including the Hannibal clock (1817), which remains in the Blue Room of the White House. The clockcases and candelabra that Denière made for Louis-Philippe are in the Petit Trianon, Versailles. The company closed in 1903.

Denmark. Ceramics *see* COPENHAGEN PORCELAIN FACTORY; ECKERNFØRDE POTTERY; KASTRUP; KELLINGHUSEN; KIEL POTTERY; SAXBO; SCHLESWIG POTTERY FACTORY.

Textiles *see* ELSINOR TAPESTRY WORKSHOP; HEDEBO; TØNDER LACE.

Dennis, Thomas (*b* Portsmouth, NH, *c.* 1638; *d* Ipswich, MA, 1706). American furniture-maker. In the late 1660s Dennis moved from Portsmouth to Ipswich, where he entered into a partnership with William Searle (whose widow he was later to marry). Furniture by Dennis and Searle is represented in the collections of the Winterthur Museum in Delaware and the Museum of Fine Arts in Boston.

J. L. Fairbanks: *New England Begins: The Seventeenth Century*, 3 vols (exh. cat., Boston, MA, Mus. F. A., 1982)
R. Tarule: *The Artist of Ipswich: Craftsmanship and Community in Colonial New England* (Baltimore, 2004)

Dentelle binding. Type of 18th-century French bookbinding decorated with an ornamental tooling resembling lace (Fr. *dentelle*).

Dentil. Each of the small rectangular blocks, resembling a row of teeth, under a cornice.

Derby. English centre of ceramics production. A factory producing soft-paste porcelain was in operation in Derby, Derbys, by *c.* 1750, possibly started by Thomas Briand of the Chelsea Porcelain Factory. Early output included white cream jugs and some figures that have biscuit visible at the base and are therefore known as dry-edge figures. The main Derby factory was established *c.* 1756 by William Duesbury, who joined with John Heath, a banker who also had an interest in the Cockpit Hill Pottery, Derby, and the Frenchman André Planché. Early wares included tea and coffee services. About 1764 Richard Holdship of the Worcester factory had an agreement with Duesbury to improve the paste and to introduce transfer printing to the factory. Blue-and-white wares were also produced until 1770 but thereafter only for special commissions. Figures produced during the early years show the influences of the Chelsea and Meissen porcelain factories, and specifically the modelling of Johann Joachim Kändler. This was later intensified by the modeller Nicolas-François Gauron (*fl* 1753–88), who had previously worked at Mennecy, Vincennes and Tournai before moving to Derby in 1773.

In 1769, with financial assistance from John Heath, Duesbury bought the Chelsea factory and in 1775 acquired the Bow factory. The years 1769–84 are known as the Chelsea–Derby period; the Sèvres porcelain factory provided the main source of inspiration for the wares, and the production of biscuit figures also began. The best painters of the period were specialists, for example Zachariah Boreman (1736–1810) for landscapes, William Pegg (1775–1851) for flowers, Richard Dodson for exotic birds and William Billingsley for cabbage roses. In 1784 Duesbury closed the Chelsea factory and moved the men and equipment to Derby.

In 1786 Duesbury was succeeded by his son William Duesbury II (*d* 1797); he took Michael Kean as his partner from 1795 to 1797, when Kean took over until 1811. Many of the original wares continued to be made, as well as Neo-classical wares and figures. One of the best modellers during the 1790s was Johann Jakob Wilhelm Spengler, who had previously worked in Zurich. In 1811 William Duesbury III took over, but in 1815 he leased the factory to Robert Bloor, and there was a deterioration in the quality of the wares. Bloor's brother Joseph Bloor managed the factory until it closed in 1848.

During the 19th century several porcelain factories were set up in Derby, often making imitations of 18th-century products. The most significant was the Derby Crown Porcelain Co., which was founded in 1876 to make high-quality porcelain. The name was changed to the Royal Crown Derby Porcelain Co. following a visit by Queen Victoria in 1890. The factory continues to produce tablewares decorated with rich gilding and Japanese patterns.

F. B. Gillhespy: *Derby Porcelain* (London, 1961)
A. L. Thorpe and F. A. Barrett: *Derby Porcelain, 1750–1848* (London, 1971)
J. Twitchett: *Derby Porcelain* (London, 1980)
G. Bradley and others: *Derby Porcelain, 1750–1798* (London, 1990)
G. Daniel: *Recent Research on Ceramics of Derbyshire* (Derby, 1991)

Derby Pot Works. *See* COCKPIT HILL POTTERY.

Derome. French family of bookbinders, active for three generations. The most prominent members of the family were Jacques-Anthoine Derome (1696–1760) and his third son, Nicolas-Denis Derome (1731–88). Both made mosaic bindings, but Nicolas-Denis also made fine DENTELLE BINDINGS, often with a small bird in the borders; in his late bindings Nicolas-Denis eschewed the French tradition of dentelles in crimson morocco in favour of narrow, straight borders in the (English) medium of cross-grained blue morocco.

Deruta. Italian centre of maiolica production. It was the main centre of pottery production in Umbria during the Renaissance. By the early 16th century 30 to 40 kilns were in operation, of which only three or four used the metallic gold and red lustres for which Deruta and Gubbio are renowned. As in Gubbio, lustres were applied to local wares and to those brought from such other centres of production as Urbino for this specialized finish. In addition to lustred ceramics, quantities of polychrome maiolica were produced, the predominant colours of which are yellow, orange and blue. In the 17th and 18th centuries the quality of ceramic production declined and was characterized by the manufacture of votive plaques that were placed in churches and homes.

The tin-glazed earthenware produced at Deruta in the 16th century was noted for a conservatism and consistency, both in style and shape, which was probably engendered by its geographical isolation. The large, deep dishes, known as *piatti da pompa*, painted with idealized portraits of women or men set within formalized floral and geometric borders (e.g. of *c.* 1500–40; London, BM), were particularly popular. Other common subjects for these dishes were images of SS Francis, Jerome and Rocco, the Virgin, angels, equestrian figures or scenes based on local fables, allegories or proverbs. Products from Deruta of this period also include polychrome drug jars decorated with complex floral and grotesque designs, moulded plates with relief patterns and *istoriato* wares with religious, historical, literary or mythological subjects.

Giacomo Mancini (*fl c.* 1540–60; known as 'El Frate') was the most notable Deruta *istoriato* painter and one of the few who signed his works. His dated pieces were made between 1541, when he came to Deruta from Urbino, and 1545, although it is likely that he was responsible for some important tile pavements of the 1560s. His work, typified by a signed plate with the subject of *Alexander and Roxanne* (*c.* 1540–50; Paris, Petit Pal.), is characterized by a styl-

Maiolica plate showing two soldiers fighting, Deruta, *c.* 1520. (Florence, Museo Nazionale del Bargello)

ized linearity and somewhat awkward spatial conception.

L. De-Mauri: *Le maioliche di Deruta* (Milan, 1924)
C. Fiocco and G. Gherardi: 'Contributo allo studio della ceramica derutese', *Faenza*, lxix (1983), pp. 90–3
E. Helman-Minchilli, S. Cushner and D. Hamilton: *Deruta: A Tradition of Italian Ceramics* (San Francisco, 1998.)
Fatto in Deruta: Ceramiche Tradizionali di Deruta (exh. cat by G. Busti and F. Cocchi Deruta, Mus. Reg. Cer., 2004)

Descho da parto [It.: pl. *deschi da parto*]. Italian wooden birth tray designed for bringing food to women in labour. The tray was usually painted with mythological or domestic scenes, and sometimes had heraldic decoration (see colour pl. X, fig. 2). The finest surviving *descho da parto* is *The Triumph of Fame* (New York, Met.), which was commissioned by Piero de' Medici and Lucrezia Tornabuoni to commemorate the birth of Lorenzo, their first son, and painted by Scheggia (1406–86), the younger brother of Masaccio.

J. M. Musacchio: *The Art and Ritual of Childbirth in Renaissance Italy* (New Haven, 1999)
A. W. B. Randolph: 'Gendering the Period Eye: *Deschi da parto* and Renaissance Visual Culture', *A. Hist.*, xxvii (2004), pp. 538–62.

Desfossé & Karth. French wallpaper manufacturing company. It was founded in Paris in 1864 by Jules Desfossé (*d* 1889), who had been trained in the wallpaper business in Paris and in 1851 took over the Mader Frères factory in the Faubourg Saint-Antoine. In 1864 he took on his brother-in-law, Hippolyte Karth, as a partner and bought out the Clerc & Margeridon factory about 1866. The business continued to operate until it became part of the Isidore Leroy factory in 1947.

The Desfossé factory was known for high-quality work using both plates and machine-printing (examples in Paris, Mus. A. Déc). Its considerable reputation rested on its 'panoramic' wallpapers, based on images of nature, presented at the Exposition Universelle in Paris in 1855 and the International Exhibition in 1862 in London, for which the company had taken the innovative step of commissioning designs from such well-known artists as Thomas Couture (1815–79) and Auguste Clésinger (1814–83) on the theme of the Vices and the Virtues. The factory also printed a great number of other, highly elaborate designs. The Desfossé collection is part of the Leroy collection in the Musée des Arts Décoratifs, Paris.

Desk. *See* BUREAU.

Deskey, Donald (*b* Blue Earth, MN, 23 Nov 1894; *d* 29 April 1989). American interior and industrial designer. In 1926–7 he created New York's first modern window displays for the Franklin Simon and Saks Fifth Avenue department stores. In 1927 he was joined by the designer Philip Vollmer, and the partnership became Deskey–Vollmer, Inc. (to *c.* 1929). Deskey expanded into designing interiors, furniture, lamps and textiles, becoming a pioneer of the *Style moderne*. His earliest model for the interior of an apartment was shown at the American Designers' Gallery, New York, in 1929. With its cork-lined walls, copper ceiling, movable walls, pigskin-covered furniture and linoleum floor, it demonstrated his novel approach. He was one of the first American designers to use Bakelite, Formica, Fabrikoid, brushed aluminium and chromium-plated brass, which he would combine with more exotic materials (e.g. desk, macassar ebony, mixed woods and brass, 1929; New Haven, CT, Yale U. A.G.). In 1931, for the showman Samuel L. Rothafel and the Rockefeller family, he created the interiors of Radio City Music Hall, Rockefeller Center, New York, introducing aluminium foil wallpaper in the men's smoking lounge. His Radio City interiors, together with a luxury apartment he designed for Rothafel in the same building (*c.* 1931–2), survive as his masterpieces. At a more popular level, he designed the gooosenecked streetlights of New York City and was responsible for many popular package designs, including Tide laundry detergent and Crest toothpaste.

D. A. Hanks and J. Toher: *Donald Deskey: Decorative Designs and Interiors* (New York, 1987)
D. A. Hanks and others: 'Donald Deskey's Decorative Designs', *Mag. Ant.*, cxxxi (April 1987), pp. 838–45
M. Komanecky: 'The Screens and Screen Designs of Donald Deskey', *Mag. Ant.*, cxxxi (May 1987), pp. 1064–77
S. Gray: *Designers on Designers: The Inspiration behind Great Interiors* (New York, 2004)

Deutsche Blumen [Ger.: 'German flowers']. Painted naturalistic flowers, single or in bunches and often derived from prints, used as porcelain decoration at Vienna and Meissen (notably by JOHANN GREGORIUS HÖROLDT in the mid-18th century, and thereafter in French and English factories. If the flowers cast shadows, the decoration was known as *ombrierte teutsche blumen* or *Saxe ombré*.

Deutscher Werkbund. German association of architects, designers and industrialists. It was active from 1907 to 1934 and then from 1950. It was founded in Munich, prompted by the artistic success of the third Deutsche Kunstgewerbeausstellung, held in Dresden in 1906, and by the then current, very acrimonious debate about the goals of applied art in Germany. Its founder-members included Hermann Muthesius (1861–1927), Peter Behrens, Heinrich Tessenow (1876–1950), Fritz Schumacher (1869–1947) and Theodor Fischer (1862–1938), who served as its first president.

In 1907 Muthesius gave a lecture in Berlin, in which he condemned eclecticism and applauded the new directness and simplicity of design that had dominated at the Dresden exhibition. This was against current trends, for, as Muthesius noted, 'domestic furnishing and decoration in present-day Germany are based on social pretensions, and an industry working with imitations and surrogates provides the material for this'. The Dresden exhibition and

Muthesius's lecture were to lead to the establishment of the Werkbund.

Between 1908 and 1915 the Werkbund published the deliberations of its annual conference, originally in pamphlet form, later in handsomely illustrated and highly influential yearbooks. Among the important contributions published in these volumes were essays by Muthesius (1912; an account of the particularly German ability to achieve universally valid design solutions); Walter Gropius (1913; illustrated with the American grain silos that were to become canonical images of architectural Modernism in the 1920s); and Behrens (1914; on time, space and modern form).

The highpoint of the Werkbund's fortunes was from 1924 to 1929. For the only time in its history it was strongly linked to one style—to Functionalism and Neue Sachlichkeit—and concerned pre-eminently with architecture and urban design. This focus gradually occluded the interest in furniture and interior decoration that dominated the early years of the Werkbund.

J. Campbell: *The German Werkbund: The Politics of Reform in the Applied Arts* (Princeton, 1978)

M. Jarzombek: 'Joseph August Lux: Werkbund Promoter, Historian of a Lost Modernity', *J. Soc. Archit. Hist.*, lxiii/2 (June 2004), pp. 202–19

P. Overy: 'Visions of the Future and the Immediate Past: The Werkbund Exhibition, Paris 1930', *J. Des. Hist.*, xvii/4 (2004), pp. 337–57

Deutsche Werkstätten [Vereinigte Werkstätten für Kunst und Handwerk]. German manufacturing firm that was set up in Munich in 1898 with the idea of returning to high-quality craftsmanship. It formed the nucleus of the German *Jugendstil*, which unlike the Art Nouveau movement in England, aimed to work not against, but in cooperation with industry and machines. The Munich workshop produced both luxury furniture and routine cabinetwork working to designs by BERNHARD PANKOK and RICHARD RIEMERSCHMID, among others. Many of Pankok's designs are sculptural in character and combine a variety of materials. His sideboards are close to traditional types with relief carving in which animals combine with naturalistic plants or abstract organic forms. Riemerschmid, on the other hand, turned to folk art for his inspiration: his furniture is neat, practical, functional and well suited for mass production (e.g. walnut chair, 1899; London, V&A).

Dhurrie [dari]. Cotton flatweave carpet made in India; *see also under* CARPET, §II, 2.

N. Chaldecott: *Dhurries: History, Pattern, Technique, Identification* (New York, 2003)

Diamond-point engraving. Decorative technique used on glass and (occasionally) porcelain, effected with a stylus tipped with a fragment of diamond. The process of scratching or stippling glass with such a stylus began in 16th-century Venice but eventually became associated with North European glasshouses, notably HALL-IN-TIROL GLASSWORKS.

Diaper. All-over decoration of repeated geometric patterns such as squares or lozenges, which sometimes contain foliate ornament. Diaper can be found on architecture, metalwork, sculpture, painting and textiles. Linen diaper is the self-patterned, fine white linen that has been used in western Europe since the 15th century for tablecloths, napkins and handtowels. By the mid-16th century they were described as either 'diaper' or 'damask': small repeat patterns, often of a geometrical form, were described as 'diaper' and figurative patterns with longer repeats as 'damasks'.

For information on diaper as a kind of linen *see* LINEN DIAPER AND DAMASK.

Diasprum. Medieval term for a patterned silk weave in which the pattern and ground are distinguished by texture rather than colour.

D. King: 'Sur la signification de "diasprum"', *Collected Textile Studies*, ed. A. Muthesius and M. King (London, 2002), pp. 71–6

Dichroic glass. Type of glass created in the 1990s using the space-age technology known as 'thin film physics'. The term 'dichroic' (literally 'two-coloured') has traditionally referred to doubly refracting gems that exhibit different colours when viewed from different angles. The effect is achieved in glass by the application of extremely thin layers of silicon and titanium that cause the glass to become partially reflective, like tiny mirrors. The effect is intense colour without glare. In the past decade dichroic glass has become very popular with jewellery makers.

Diepenbeeck, Abraham (Jansz.) van (*b* 's Hertogenbosch, *bapt* 9 May 1596; *d* Antwerp, 31 Dec 1675). Flemish glass-painter, draughtsman, painter and tapestry designer. Van Diepenbeeck trained in the 's Hertogenbosch workshop of his father, the glass painter Jan (Roelofsz.) van Diepenbeeck (*d* 1619). In 1622–3 he became a master glass painter in the Guild of St Luke in Antwerp.

Abraham van Diepenbeeck's earliest activity apparently consisted mostly of designing and glazing stained-glass windows for various churches and monasteries in Antwerp. The design for the *Presentation in the Temple* (1622–5; ex-J. S. Held priv. col.; now Washington, DC, N.G.A.) is probably van Diepenbeeck's earliest datable work. It is a preliminary study for one of the 12 stained-glass windows depicting episodes from the *Life of the Virgin*. The figures' somewhat elongated body type and their long, sharply pointed fingers indicate a preference for Mannerist forms. The whole of van Diepenbeeck's oeuvre from this period onwards is remarkable for its vigorous articulation of musculature, pictorially suggested by a studied use of chiaroscuro. This pronounced sense of volume can also be found in the few surviving modelli (*c.* 1630–36) for the stained-glass windows depicting episodes from the *Life of St Paul* (commissioned by the Dominicans) for example an oil sketch of the *Conversion of St Paul* (*c.* 1633–6; Munich, Alte Pin.). Van Diepenbeeck's style is also characterized by a heavy, broad outline, which clearly sets off his figures.

In his later years van Diepenbeeck also made many designs for tapestry cartoons; his known works include a number of cycles from the Bible and ancient history, notably scenes from the lives of Moses, Marcus Aurelius and Semiramis, and the Acts of the Apostles.

D. Steadman: *Abraham van Diepenbeeck: Seventeenth-century Flemish Painter* (Ann Arbor, 1982)

Dietrich, Wendel (*b* Augsburg, *c.* 1535; *d* Augsburg, Nov 1621–April 1622). German cabinetmaker and architect. He was employed by Hans Fugger in 1569 to work on the new state apartments in the Fugger-haus on the Weinmarkt in Augsburg. By 1573 he had provided tables, chairs, wood panelling and vaults for Fugger's house. Other commissions from the Fugger family included the burial chapel (the Andreaska-pelle) in the abbey of SS Ulrich and Afra at Augsburg. Its decoration and furnishings included a large carved altar (1580) and choir-stalls (1581), which are generally attributed to Dietrich. The design for the marble screen enclosing the Fugger chapel may also have been by Dietrich. In 1582 he was commissioned to make the wooden ceiling and doorways of the Banqueting Hall and the adjoining rooms at Hans Fugger's country house at Kirchheim an der Mindel. The coffered ceiling covers an area of 375 sq. m, using different woods to produce a subtle range of colours. With its rich ornamentation of mouldings, cartouches, garlands of flowers and masks, it is a remarkable example of the German late Renaissance style.

Dietrich's later work, possibly in collaboration with his son, Jakob Dietrich (*b* 1559–60; *d* after 1636) includes the high altar (1586–9) and choir-stalls for the Jesuit church of St Michael (Munich)

Dimity. Stout cotton fabric, woven with raised stripes or fancy figures. Early examples are Italian, but dimity was manufactured in England from the 17th century, usually to be used undyed for beds and bedroom hangings, and sometimes for clothing.

Dinanderie. Decorative brassware, specifically kitchen ware. The term derives from the town of Dinant (on the Meuse near Liège), where brass kitchen utensils were made for centuries.

J. T. Perry: *Dinanderie: A History and Description of Mediæval Art Work in Copper, Brass and Bronze* (London, 1910)
D. Forest and M.-C. Forest: *La dinanderie française: 1900–1950* (Paris, 1995)

Dinglinger, Johann Melchior (*b* Biberbach, 26 Dec 1664; *d* Dresden, 6 March 1731). German goldsmith and jeweller. He was one of the most famous goldsmiths of his time, and almost all his works are in

the Grünes Gewölbe, Dresden. He is first recorded in Dresden in 1692. His two brothers, the enameller Georg Friedrich Dinglinger (1666–1720) and the jeweller Georg Christoph Dinglinger (1668–1728), are documented as active there in 1693; they remained his closest collaborators, particularly Georg Friedrich.

Dinglinger's principal patron was the Elector Frederick-Augustus I of Saxony. The jewellery produced for Frederick-Augustus's coronation as King Augustus II of Poland in 1697 was Dinglinger's first important commission. In 1698 he was appointed Court Jeweller, and thereafter seems to have produced most of the jewellery for the court: almost all the orders of chivalry and military decorations came from his workshop, including those in emeralds and diamonds for the revived Polish Order of the Knights of the White Eagle. Various designs for banquets for the King are also kept in the Grünes Gewölbe.

The large number of treasury pieces that Dinglinger supplied to the King, usually at his own expense, includes a gilt coffee-set of 1701. The fashion of coffee drinking gave rise to coffee-sets on trays, but Dinglinger's work was an exaggeration of this type. He arranged a coffeepot, cups, rinsing bowls, scent bottles, figurines and garlands of gold, silver, enamel, gems, ivory and wood, one on top of the other, in the manner of a Baroque display buffet but in the form of a free-standing pyramid. The painted enamels by Georg Friedrich Dinglinger simulate porcelain (see colour pl. XI, fig. 2).

This was followed in 1704 by *Diana Bathing*, an agate bowl on a foot. Diana, an ivory figure carved by Balthasar Permoser, sits on the rim of the bowl with her weapons and garments of gold and enamel scattered about her. In 1707, after six years' work, Dinglinger, his brothers and other collaborators completed the *Court of Aurangzeb*. It depicts the homage paid to the Mughal emperor on his birthday, with 165 enamelled gold figures on a silver-gilt stage.

The *Obeliscus Augusteus*, conceived for the Grünes Gewölbe and erected there in 1722, is a type of monument to the King: portraits of ancient rulers are set in a symbolic relationship to the enamel profile portrait of *Augustus II the Strong, King of Poland*, which imitates a cameo. In the centrepieces depicting the *Three Ages of Man* (1727–8) Dinglinger's growing interest in allegorical themes is evident. The structure, similar to that of a monstrance, rises from a stone pedestal with two figures to an immense sardonyx cameo framed by goldwork and gems. His last important work is the *Apis Altar* (1731), of which the overall form derives from the Baroque high altar. An immense cameo also forms the centre. Dinglinger's work gave rise to a school of goldsmithing in Dresden that remained active until the end of the 18th century and even influenced Fabergé in the 19th.

E. von Watzdorf: *Johann Melchior Dinglinger: Der Goldschmied des deutschen Barock* (Berlin, 1962)
J. Menzhausen and K.G. Beyer: *At the Court of the Great Mogul: The Court at Delhi on the Birthday of the Great Mogul Aureng-Zeb: Museum*

Piece by Johann Melchior Dinglinger, Court Jeweller of the Elector of Saxony and King of Poland, August II, Called August the Strong (Leipzig, 1966)

D. Syndram and J. M. Dinglinger: *Der Thron des Grossmoguls: Johann Melchior Dinglingers goldener Traum vom Fernen Osten* (Leipzig, 1996)

D. Syndram: *Die Ägyptenrezeption unter August dem Starken: Der 'Apis-Altar' Johann Melchior Dinglingers* (Mainz am Rhein, 1999)

Ding ware. Chinese pottery made in Ding Xian (Ding County) in Hebei Province. The pottery has a thin, white porcelain body and an ivory-coloured transparent glaze, fired at a temperature of 1300–1340° C in an oxidizing atmosphere. Ding wares were produced over a period of 600 years, beginning in the 8th century AD. Before the use of coal-fired kilns in the 10th century, glazes had a bluish tint, the result of firing in a reducing atmosphere. In the 11th century a new firing technique using stepped saggars was introduced: the bowls were placed rim-downwards on the steps of the saggars to prevent the thin walls from warping. The rim had to be wiped clean of glaze to stop it from sticking to the saggar, thus creating a rough mouth (*mangkou*), which was characteristically bound with copper, silver or gold after firing. Many shapes imitated such fine metalwork as the lobed silver bowls of the Tang and Song periods. Initially the decoration was carved; in the 11th century the technique of using hump moulds was introduced, in which the wet clay was moulded over a pre-carved mould, resulting in a denser style of ornament.

Z. Bing: 'Les imitations de porcelaines de Ding du Xe au XIVe siècle: :Le cas des officines de potiers de Jizhou and Jiangxi', *A. Asiatiques*, lvi (2001), pp. 61–80

Diptych. Two wood, ivory or metal panels of equal size, usually hinged together so that they can be folded, and closed with some form of clasp. There are usually images on the inside surfaces of the panels and sometimes also on the outer sides.

The diptych as a work of art seems to have originated in Late Antique ivory-carving as a luxury form of writing tablet. These ivories have carved images on the exterior faces, while a sunken field inside could be filled with wax for writing on with a stylus. Such objects commonly functioned as gifts from the imperial consuls at the beginning of their term of office. Similar ivory diptych writing tablets also served as marriage gifts and were decorated with mythological or cult subjects. A good example of such a diptych is the late 4th-century AD pair of plaques which has representations of pagan priestesses making offerings at altars (London, V&A; Paris, Mus. Cluny).

The diptych was revived by French Gothic ivory-carvers in the late 13th century and the 14th. Many examples survive, almost all produced in Paris. The most popular type seems to have incorporated numerous narrative scenes from the *Life of Christ*. Occasionally goldsmiths and enamellers also used the diptych format. The painted diptych remained popular until the 16th century, after which the form became rare though not obsolete.

W. Kermer: *Studien zum Diptychon in der sakralen Malerei* (Neunkirchen-Saar, 1967)

J. B. Friedman: *An Iconological Examination of the Half-length Devotional Portrait Diptych in the Netherlands, 1460–1530* (Los Angeles, 1977)

Directoire style. Style fashionable in France, especially in Paris, named after the short-lived Directoire period (Oct 1795–Nov 1799). The Directoire style is exhibited mainly in interior decoration and in the applied arts. Distinguishing characteristics are the use of colour that is light in tone and of grotesque motifs shown in outline. The classical forms of the lightly built furniture, by such cabinetmakers as Georges JACOB the younger, show restrained use of materials (e.g. chair, ebony, 1796–7; Paris, Mus. A. Dec.). Decorative motifs also included such Revolutionary symbols as the Phrysian bonnet or cap of Liberty, clasped hands as an emblem of Fraternity, fasces and oak leaves, applied to furniture, ceramics and textiles. In Germany the style was promoted in F. Bertuch's journal *Journal des Luxus und der Moden*, which published interior decorative schemes and fashion designs (Weimar, 1793–1810). See fig. on p. 316.

F. Contet: *Intérieurs Directoire et Empire* (Paris, 1932)

G. Janneau: *Le Style Directoire* (Paris, 1938)

M.-N. de Grandry: *Le mobilier français: Directoire, Consulat, Empire* (Paris, 1996)

T. Wilson-Smith: *Napoleon and His Artists* (London, 1996)

Disbrowe, Nicholas (*bapt* Saffron Walden, Essex, 16 June 1613; *d* Wethersfield, CT, 1683). American cabinetmaker. He emigrated from England to Hartford, CT in the mid-1630s. Some CONNECTICUT CHESTS have been attributed to his workshop, but he is no longer believed to have been the originator of the form. The signature of Disbrowe on the Hadley chest in the Bayou Bend collection in Houston is now considered to be fraudulent.

Dishcross stand [spider stand]. Stand, typically of Sheffield plate or silver, which served to prevent a hot container (or a spiritlamp that was heating a dish) from marking a table. In 18th-century Ireland the dish ring (or potato ring), which was often made of silver, served a similar purpose, but could support a bowl with a rounded bottom.

Divan. In 18th-century usage, a long seat furnished with cushions and consisting of a continued step, bench, or raised part of the floor, against the wall of a room. In later usage, the term denoted a low bed or couch with no back or ends.

Dixon, James, & Sons. English firm of silversmiths established in Sheffield *c.* 1806. The company was one of the pioneers of the new electroplating process (silver-plating on base metal) and was an important manufacturer of Britannia metal (*see under* PEWTER). Its designers included CHRISTOPHER DRESSER, who between 1879 and 1882 sold some 37 designs to

Directoire-style (see p. 315) interior at La Vallée aux Loups, Chatenay-Malabry, France, 19th century

Dixon's, many of which (notably his Japanese-inspired teapots) were put into production.

James Dixon & Sons, Cornish Place, Sheffield, Sheffield Industrial Museums (Sheffield, 1991)

Doat, Taxile (*b* 1851; *d* 1938). French potter. From 1877 to 1905 he was employed as a designer by SÈVRES PORCELAIN FACTORY, for which he created sophisticated floral and figural designs in the Art Nouveau style that he introduced to the factory. From 1892 he also had his own studio in Paris. Doat's display pieces were often decorated with fine enamels; his individualistic medallions were made with the pâte-sur-pâte technique. His vases often took the form of gourds. From 1909 to 1914 Doat taught ceramics at the University City Pottery (St Louis, MO), where his pupils included ADELAIDE ALSOP ROBINEAU, who translated Doat's treatise *Grand Feu Ceramics*.

Doccia Porcelain Factory. Italian porcelain manufactory. In 1737 a factory producing hard-paste porcelain works was founded at Doccia by the Marchese Carlo Ginori (1702–57), assisted by the painter Karl Wendelin Anreiter von Zirnfeld (1702–57) and the technician Giorgio delle Torri (*fl* 1737–43), both from Vienna. The early paste was rather grey, with a dull glaze. Between *c*. 1770 and 1790, however, a tin glaze was used to whiten the body, and after 1803 clays from Limoges were used for this purpose. Several formulae were in use throughout the 19th century. Until 1757 factory production was highly experimental; some early pieces are similar to wares from the factory of Claudius Innocentius Du Paquier (*d* 1751) in Vienna, where Anreiter is thought to have worked. Underglaze-blue, stencilled decoration was common between *c*. 1737 and 1745 (e.g. teapot, *c*. 1742–5; London, V&A). Useful wares were modelled with an emphasis on sculptural, relief and pierced decoration. Painted decoration included armorials, genre scenes and East Asian flowers in intense tones of puce, iron-red, acid yellow and green. Large-scale figures and groups were copied from bronze casts, moulds and wax models in the Marchese's collection by such sculptors as Massimiliano Soldani (e.g. *Deposition*, *c*. 1770; London, BM) and Giuseppe Piamontini (1664–1742; e.g. *Massacre of the Innocents*, *c*. 1700; Boston, MA, Mus. F.A.). The factory's chief modeller during this period was Gasparo Bruschi (*c*. 1701–80). After 1757 sculpture was smaller in scale, the figures were painted with pronounced stippled flesh tones and features picked out in brown-black and iron-red. Production during the 19th century was influenced by French wares. After *c*. 1850 the factory was modernized, but due to economic difficulties it was merged in 1896 with the Società Ceramica of Milan.

L. Ginori Lisci: *La porcellana di Doccia* (Milan, 1963)
G. Liverani: *Il museo delle porcellane di Doccia* (Florence, 1967)
18th century Doccia Porcelains of Ginori from New York Collections: A Loan Exhibition (exh. cat., New York, Parke-Bernet Galleries, 1969)
K. Lankheit: *Die Modellsammlung der Porzellanmanufaktur Doccia* (Munich, 1982)

Dōhachi. *See* TAKAHASHI DŌHACHI.

Dolls and dolls' houses. *See* TOYS AND GAMES, §§II AND III.

Domenico di Niccolò [dei Cori; Spinelli] (*b* Siena, *c.* 1363; *d* Siena, *c.* 1453). Italian sculptor, designer and architect. He is known primarily for the large number of carved and polychromed wood statuettes of the Virgin, Virgin and Child, Christ and saints that he produced throughout his career for churches in and around Siena but was also an important intarsiatore. Domenico executed intarsia choir-stalls for the new chapel in the Palazzo Pubblico, Siena (1415–*c.* 1428). His exceptional skill in this intricate and complex art form brought him high praise and the appellation 'dei cori'. The intarsie consist chiefly of decorative geometric designs and small scenes illustrating verses from the Credo.

Don Pottery. English pottery established in 1801 in Swinton, on the bank of the Don canal in Yorkshire. The proprietor was John Green, who had previously been a partner in both the LEEDS POTTERY and ROCKINGHAM CERAMIC FACTORY. The factory made earthenware and (*c.* 1810) also experimented with porcelain. John Green became bankrupt in 1834, by which time Don Pottery employed 600 people and exported its wares worldwide. The factory was bought in 1839 by Samuel Barker, who owned the nearby Mexborough Pottery; in 1848 he moved the production of both factories to the Don Pottery. The pottery closed in 1893.

J. Griffin: *The Don Pottery, 1801–1893* (Doncaster, 2001)

Door. Movable closure of an entranceway to a building or room

I. Western world. II. Islamic world. III. Indian subcontinent. IV. East Asia. V South-east Asia. VI. Africa.

I. Western world.

1. Early Christian and medieval, before *c.* 1400. 2. Renaissance, *c.* 1400–*c.* 1550. 3. Mannerist and Baroque. 4. After *c.* 1750.

1. EARLY CHRISTIAN AND MEDIEVAL, BEFORE *c.* 1400.

(i) Wood. (ii) Bronze. (iii) Iron.

(i) Wood. There are relatively few surviving historiated wooden doors. The earliest surviving example from

Christian times is at S Sabina, Rome, dated by inscription to *c.* 432. These cypress-wood doors originally contained 28 panels crowded with Old and New Testament scenes. Ten panels are lost, and the remainder have been rearranged at least twice. Of the 5th-century doors from S Ambrogio, Milan (Milan, Mus. Sacro S Ambrogio), only three original panels survive, showing scenes from the *Life of David* and some ornamental peacocks. The frames, mostly copies of the original, are carved with beautifully arranged foliage. The doors have been altered several times and were virtually rebuilt in 1750. These Italian wooden doors were clearly an important influence on Bishop Bernward of Hildesheim's bronze doors, but their direct descendants in wood are the 11th-century doors of St Maria im Kapitol, Cologne. These depict the *Life of Christ*, with traces of red, blue and green colour still surviving in the figures. Their construction, with the panels held by ornamental frames and rotating on a har post (a sturdy beam, projecting from the top and bottom of the door, which fitted into sockets on the lintel and threshold, allowing the door to rotate), relates them to both wooden and bronze Late Antique doors. In Italy the 12th-century doors at S Pietro, Alba Fucense, and S Maria in Cellis, Carsoli, both in the Abruzzi, also continue this tradition, although in a somewhat rustic fashion. These doors are carved with the Tree of Life motif and scenes from the *Life of Christ*.

The group of doors in the Auvergne (France), at Le Puy Cathedral (larch-wood; by 1189), St Gilles, Chamalières-sur-Loire (pine-wood; 1130s), St Pierre at Blesle (pine-wood; *c.* 1200) and Ste-Croix, Lavoute-Chilhac (after 1137), are an independent development. They are carved with flat, low relief in contrast to all the previous examples, which employ rounded forms. Furthermore, they are not made with the standard classical panel-and-frame construction. Those at Le Puy are made from vertical planks hinged to open in concertina fashion. In the other three examples a veneer technique is employed with decorative components applied to the backing planks by nails and interlocking joints. Scenes from the *Infancy* and *Passion of Christ* are carved on the two pairs of doors at Le Puy. Each scene is explained by an inscription, and around the edge of the doors is pseudo-Kufic ornament as well as the name of the carver, GAUZFREDUS. Each door has a foliate or interlace border and an inlaid Greek cross at the top. Their decoration is mainly geometric with several apotropaic knots and a few single human or animal figures.

At Gurk Cathedral, Austria, an original and attractive design was used to frame the scenes on the 13th-century west doors. Attached to the flat surface of the door are openwork lime-wood roundels linked to each other in a 'Tree of Jesse' design. Within the roundels are scenes from the *Life of Christ*, prophets and Christ with the Apocalyptic Beasts.

Quite outside the Mediterranean Christian tradition is the door of Urnes Church, Norway (*c.* 1060). The doorway is carved in high relief with the figure of a great beast fighting a serpent, and the door itself continues in low relief the theme of sinuous fighting animals. Although used for a Christian church, both the style and subject derive from pagan sources, close parallels being found on the low-relief carvings of the 11th-century Scandinavian grave stones. The Urnes door is presumably the last remnant of an earlier pagan Nordic tradition.

During the later Middle Ages the decoration of wooden doors became limited to abstract tracery designs. They frequently followed patterns used in window tracery. One of the earliest traceried doors was made in 1241–8 for the Ste Chapelle, Paris, but the fashion did not develop widely for another 50 years. Particularly splendid examples can be seen at York Minster (south transept), St Nicholas, King's Lynn, and Norwich Cathedral (north gateway). A few tracery doors have carved figures, sometimes under canopies. A crucifix, pelican and dove are carved at St John's, Finchingfield, Essex, while Evangelists and saints are found at St Lawrence, Harpley, Norfolk.

W. Cahn: *The Romanesque Wooden Doors of the Auvergne* (New York, 1974)
D. Bierens de Haan: *Het houtsnijwerk in Nederland tijdens de Gothiek en de Renaissance* ('s-Gravenhage, 1977)

(ii) Bronze. The panels and frames of bronze doors in classical antiquity were cast in separate pieces, but Carolingian doors were cast in one piece. The most spectacular examples are those now at Hildesheim Cathedral, where each leaf, covered in three-dimensional relief figures and including the lion-head ring bosses, is cast in one piece. In Italy the native medieval technique involved casting separate relief panels and frames and attaching them to a wooden core. Many doors in Italy were made by Byzantine craftsmen or in the Byzantine fashion: they consist either of small, flat bronze panels, incised and inlaid (damascened) with silver, enamel or niello, or of cut-out bronze motifs applied to the surface of the bronze.

The three pairs of doors at Charlemagne's palatine chapel (now the cathedral) at Aachen (*c.* 800) and those of Mainz Cathedral (*c.* 1000) are models of classic restraint, with between four and sixteen plain panels surrounded by frames of low-relief egg-and-dart, acanthus or simple mouldings. Each has a pair of lion-head door rings. Bishop Bernward of Hildesheim had clearly seen both these and the wooden doors of Milan and Rome, carved with biblical scenes, when he commissioned his bronze doors for St Michael's, Hildesheim (dated by inscription 1015; moved to the cathedral by Bishop Godehard, 1022–38). The panels bear eight pairs of Old and New Testament scenes, illustrating with poignant, expressive figures Man's Fall and Redemption. The doors at Augsburg Cathedral, also made in the 11th century, are more closely related to the Byzantine technique and style. They are made of panels and frames cast singly and attached to the wooden core of the door, and they illustrate single subjects such as *Samson and the Lion*, *King David* and centaurs. Some of the scenes are repeated from the same model. The iconography, including the secular subjects, seems to relate to the struggle between good and evil. The doors now at Novgorod Cathedral were originally (1152–4) made for Płock Cathedral (Poland) but were removed to Russia before the 15th century. The panels, fixed to a wooden core, include scenes from the *Life of Christ* and from the Old Testament and figures of bishops and of the bronze-founders and their tools.

In Italy, the two doors at Tróia Cathedral (Apulia), though roughly contemporary, are very different in style and technique. The west doors combine the animal exuberance of northern work with the flat severity of Byzantine doors. Divided into 28 panels by frames with lush foliage bosses, they have eight openwork, lion-head door rings and two free-standing scaly, winged dragons biting the knockers. Four panels of incised figures include the bronze-founder ODERISIUS OF BENEVENTO, while the inscription dates them to 1119 (eight panels were replaced in the 16th or 17th century). The south doors, made in 1127, also by Oderisius, are subdued by comparison: they have only four lion-head door rings with twenty further panels of incised, damascened figures of saints and bishops of Tróia. Oderisius also made bronze doors with winged dragons (now lost) for S Giovanni in Capua.

The doors of the Cappella Palatina, Palermo (ded. 1140), must have had an antique prototype. They consist of eight plain panels with two lush acanthus bosses and lion-head masks surrounded by broad acanthus borders, echoing the stone acanthus frame of the doorway. Severely classicizing doors are also found in the chapel of the Lateran Baptistery, Rome. Made in 1195–6, their four panels bear incised architectural designs and one relief figure of *Ecclesia*. At S Zeno Maggiore, Verona, both the figure style and the composition of the metal indicate that the bronze panels were made at two different dates, one before the rebuilding of the church in 1138 and the other slightly later. Each of the 48 panels and their frames is cast separately, with the earlier style found mainly on the left valve. They depict Old and New Testament scenes, the *Life of St Zeno* and allegorical figures.

The cathedral doors of Ravello, Trani and Monreale (north aisle) are all signed by Barisanus of Trani (*fl* 1179). The Ravello doors, dated 1179, are the earliest and the most important because the subjects of their 54 low-relief panels form a coherent iconographic programme. The other two doors are smaller and simply reuse the same moulds in a less coherent arrangement. At Ravello the panels bear a hierarchical programme starting with *Christ in Majesty* at the top, ranging down through scenes of *Redemption* and *Judgement*, the donor with his hopes of salvation and equestrian saints protecting the church.

Bonanus of Pisa (*fl c.* 1179–86) made the doors at both Pisa Cathedral (*c.* 1180, east door, south transept) and Monreale Cathedral (*c.* 1185, west door). The inscriptions on these doors contain the earliest surviving written examples of the Tuscan vernacular, mixed with Latin. The Pisan panels, surrounded by orderly rosettes applied to the frames, illustrate the *Life of Christ*, starting at the bottom with two panels of prophets and ending at the top with *Christ and the Virgin Enthroned*. At Monreale the scenes start with the Old Testament at the bottom and end with Christ and the Virgin, as at Pisa. The west doors of Benevento Cathedral with their 72 figural panels represented the most ambitious iconographic programme of all the Italian doors. They were almost totally destroyed in World War II, but earlier photographs and a few fragments survive (Benevento, Bib. Capitolare). The panels illustrated the *Life of Christ*, the Archbishop of Benevento and his 24 suffragans. The iconography is derived from Byzantine sources, while the style is related to local early 13th-century sculpture in Campania. Although many Italian churches enjoyed the prestige of bronze doors, Florence Cathedral had none until the guild responsible for the Baptistery decided in 1322 to commission a pair. Representatives were sent to Pisa to study and draw those in the cathedral, and founders were brought in from Venice. The gilt-bronze work produced by Andrea Pisano was in place by 1336. The lattice pattern of the crossbars of the framework enclose 28 square panels. Of these, 20 depict scenes from the *Life of St John the Baptist*, in Gothic quadri-lobed shapes and with great elegance and economy; the two bottom rows of panels, which would be hidden whenever there were crowds pressing round the doors at baptisms, were dedicated to the theme of the *Virtues*.

The Byzantine group of doors in Italy was either made in Constantinople or cast in Italy by Byzantine craftsmen. Most can be dated quite closely by inscriptions, which often identify the donor and his desire for salvation. Their iconography concerns the intercession of the Virgin and saints while their foliate crosses represent the Tree of Life.

Pantaleone of Amalfi gave the doors to S Paolo fuori le mura, Rome, in 1070 and to Amalfi Cathedral around the same time. The inscription at S Paolo asks the patron saint to open the doors of eternal life. Doors similar to those at Amalfi were given by Pantaleone Viarecta in 1087 to S Sebastiano, Atrani (later moved to S Salvatore). They depict on incised panels the Virgin of Intercession and Christ. Two original panels, inscribed with the dedication inscription of Maurus of Amalfi and the date 1066, are incorporated with nine later panels of silver-inlaid figures on the basilica doors at S Benedetto, Montecassino. A *domino* Pantaleone had doors made in Constantinople for S Michele Arcangelo, Monte Sant'Angelo (Puglia), in 1076. The door was dedicated to St Michael and illustrates the Archangel's intervention in the Old and New Testaments. At S Marco, Venice, there are four bronze doors in the narthex. Two on the exterior are of Classical style with panels of fish-scale designs, one made in the 6th century and the other in 1300 by Bertuccio. The door in the south portal of the nave was made in 1080 in Constantinople and depicts inlaid figures of Christ, the Virgin and saints. The central nave door,

Detail of St Andrew from the door at the Cathedral of Amalfi, bronze, from Constantinople, 1065 (Amalfi, Duomo)

commissioned by Leo da Molino in 1112, was made locally, influenced by the south door. It shows a heavenly hierarchy starting with Christ and proceeding through the prophets, saints and martyrs, with Molino himself prostrate before St Mark.

G. Matthiae: *La Porte bronzée byzantine in Italia* (Rome, 1971)
K. Clark and D. Finn: *The Florence Baptistery Doors* (London, 1980)
U. Mende: *Die Bronzetüren des Mittelalters, 800–1200* (Munich, 1983)
G. P. Carratelli, ed.: *Le porte di bronzo dall'antichità al secolo XIII* (Rome, 1990)
J. I. Daniec: *The Message of Faith and Symbol in European Medieval Bronze Church Doors* (Danbury, CT, 1999)
J. Gardner: 'Magister Bertucius Aurifex": et les portes en bronze de Saint-Marc, un programme pour l'annee jubilaire'. *Rev. A.,* cxxxiv (2001), pp. 9–26

(iii) Iron. In Britain, Scandinavia, Germany, Spain and France well over 1000 medieval doors have survived decorated with applied scrolls and figures of iron. The techniques for making cast iron were not widespread in Europe before the 14th century, so the metal used was always hammered or wrought iron. The doors of northern Europe generally hung from iron strap hinges, which naturally lend themselves to embellishment. The earliest surviving examples are from the 11th century at Urnes in Norway and Hadstock (Essex), but the heyday for this type of decoration was from the 12th century to the early 14th.

Because the iron was produced primarily by village blacksmiths, there are distinct regional varieties in design. In England, a few doors such as those at

All Saints, Staplehurst (Kent), and St Helen's, Stillingfleet (N. Yorks), are covered with enigmatic figurative designs, but the most common form of Romanesque hinge was the C shape. This was nonfunctional and attached to the front of the door, often with a load-bearing strap through its centre. The C and strap could be embellished with various terminals: fleurs-de-lis, barbs and lobes with tendrils. Typical examples are found at St John the Baptist, Kingston Lisle (Oxon), the Nativity of the Virgin, Madley (Hereford & Worcs), and St Nicholas, Castle Hedingham (Essex). Later in the 12th century greater interest was shown in surface decoration, foliage and geometric ornament. The hinges from the slype of St Albans Abbey, now St Albans Cathedral (1160s; London, V&A), have chiselled zigzag patterns, leaves and lively raised animal-head terminals. Also from this phase are the high-quality hinges at All Saints, Faringdon, and St Mary, Uffington (Oxon), and Durham Cathedral (nave, south-west door). In the 13th century the new technique of stamping the iron scrolls with dies enabled smiths to produce accurate repetitive motifs of leaves and flowers. This elegant technique was most widespread in the Ile-de-France and England. The smith Gilebertus stamped his name on the doors of St George's Chapel, Windsor (1247–9). They are covered in flowing spiral designs of leaves and flowers, as are the doors of York Minster chapter house (1280–85). The master blacksmith Thomas de Leghtune made the stamped iron grille around the tomb of Queen Eleanor in Westminster Abbey (1293–4), and he used stamps of the same design on doors at All Saints, Leighton Buzzard, and All Saints, Turvey (Beds). A simpler way of making the delicate foliage terminals was to cut out tiny sheets of iron, like biscuits. Although technically less sophisticated, many attractive designs were made using the cut-out method. Fine examples are found at Lichfield Cathedral (1290s), St Lawrence and All Saints, Eastwood (Essex), and Worksop Priory (Notts). After 1350 woodwork tracery eventually replaced iron decoration on doors, and the smiths responded to the change of fashion by making iron tracery. Much of this is crude punched and filed work, but iron tracery of the highest quality is found on the gates in front of the tomb of *Edward IV* in St George's Chapel, Windsor (1483).

In Sweden an exceptional number of iron-clad church doors survive from the late 12th century and the 13th. Bold figurative scenes are found, for instance, at Rogslösa and Väversunda (Östergötland), where the struggle between good and evil, the Fall and Redemption through the Crucifixion are illustrated. Many doors are covered with horizontal bands of geometric designs: interlocking circles, crosses and scrolls, as at Bjälbo (Östergötland). On Gotland a distinctive form of design was used between the 12th and 14th centuries, consisting of back-to-back C shapes, separated by a horizontal strap. Delicate cut-out foliage was also used from the 13th century onwards (e.g. Högby, Östergötland; Stockholm, Stat. Hist. Mus. 4779). A large collection of Swedish medieval doors is now preserved in the Statens Historisk Museum, Stockholm. The more modest survivals in Norway include a fine series of dragon-headed lock plates from Arnafjord (U. Bergen, Hist. Mus.), Hurum and Hedal (both *in situ*). The most outstanding group of doors in Denmark is found on the island of Funen. Their entire surface is decorated with horizontal rows of iron black-letter inscriptions, which generally cite their date and patron. Fine examples from the 15th and 16th centuries are at Sondersø, Hastrup and Indslev.

Clearly a great deal of iron has been lost from the wealthy churches of the former Holy Roman Empire, where the survivals are somewhat scattered. The Romanesque C shape is found at Maulbronn Abbey and St Ägidius, Mittelheim; horizontal rows of 'trees' are seen at the Liebfrauenkirche, Wiener Neustadt (Austria), and Heiligenleiten, near Pettenbach (Austria); and figurative scenes occur at the Dorfkirche, Wahren (now in Leipzig, Mus. Gesch.), and the Dorfkirche, Eisdorf, Germany. The finest cut-out work, of delicate leaves and branches, is at St Elizabeth, Marburg (1270s), while later, more rigid cut-out designs are in the Germanisches Nationalmuseum, Nuremberg, at St Vincenz, Hattenheim, and St Trinitatis, Kaub.

French ironwork can be divided into distinct regions. In the Massif Central the designs are distinguished by the extensive use of palmette leaves, raised human and animal heads and patterns based on a lozenge shape. Examples from the 12th and 13th centuries are at Auzelles, St Léger Abbey, Ebreuil, St Etienne, Gannat (London, V&A, M396–1924), St Barthélemy, Liginiac, St Etienne, Neuvy-Saint-Sépulchre, and Saint-Leonard de Noblat (New York, Cloisters). In both the French and Spanish Pyrenees, one style predominates for most of the Middle Ages and even recurs in the 17th century. It consists of pairs of tightly curled spirals arranged in rows along hinge straps, often covering the whole door. Vigorous examples of this type are found at Ste Marie, Corneilla de Conflent, La Trinité, Prunet et Belpuig, and the Assomption de la Vierge, Serralongue, France; others are at the Museu d'Art de Catalunya, Barcelona, and carved on a cloister capital at Girona Cathedral. In Burgundy the style is less homogeneous, but it can be characterized by elegant attenuated C shapes with scrolled terminals found at Notre-Dame, Montréal, St Martin, Chablis, from the 12th century and at Pontigny Abbey (if genuinely medieval). Possibly the finest hinges made in the Middle Ages were those decorating the west doors of Notre-Dame, Paris, from the 1240s. They were made with a profusion of stamped designs, sprays and bouquets of flowers and leaves. A few fragments of the original survive in the Musée de Cluny, Paris, but the present hinges are 19th-century replicas. Stamped ironwork achieved its greatest flowering in the Ile-de-France in the 13th century, being used for doors, candlesticks, grilles and chests. The largest collection of medieval ironwork is preserved in Rouen (Mus. Le Secq des Tournelles). It is quite likely that stamped ironwork originated in the Sambre-Meuse region, inspired by similar techniques in goldsmithing. Early 13th-century examples are found at St Jacques, Liège, and Liège Cathedral sacristy, and there is a sumptuous 15th-century door with cut-out terminals at Notre-Dame, Halle.

M. Mackeprang: 'Fyenske jaernbundne kirkedøre fra middelalderen' [Iron-bound church doors from the Middle Ages], *Aab. Nord. Oldknd. Hist.* (1943), pp. 1–30

L. Karlsson: *Medieval Ironwork in Sweden*, 2 vols (Stockholm, 1988) [excellent pls, covers most of Europe]

2. RENAISSANCE, *c.* 1400–*c.* 1550. The medieval tradition of covering doors with bronze reliefs was continued in the Renaissance only in Italy. In 1401, when Lorenzo Ghiberti (1378–1455) won the competition to make the second set of doors for the Baptistery in Florence, he exactly followed the pattern used by Andrea Pisano (*c.* 1295–1348/9) 70 years earlier. When Ghiberti was commissioned to make the third and last pair of doors (1425–52), he was able to persuade his patrons to abandon the cramped Gothic design in favour of ten large, square panels, which would permit a freer rendering of settings and backgrounds and a more modern and painterly approach. The doors were completely gilded, conspicuously advertising the affluence of the patron guild; Michelangelo famously called them the 'Gates of Paradise'. The original panels (Florence, Mus. Opera Duomo) have been cleaned and replaced by modern casts.

Probably in the 1430s, Donatello (1386/7–1486) contributed two pairs of bronze doors in the Old Sacristy of S Lorenzo, Florence, with hyperactive pairs of Apostles or martyrs in square fields against neutral backgrounds. These were followed by a commission (1437) to produce two larger pairs for the two sacristies of Florence Cathedral, but Donatello failed to deliver these, and in 1446 a new contract was drawn up with his associates Michelozzo di Bartolomeo (1396–1472) and Maso di Bartolommeo (1406–*c.* 1456), as well as Luca della Robbia, for one pair for the north sacristy. These were not completed until 1469. Luca played the major role and predictably created a series of ten panels that were blander than anything that Donatello would have designed: the four *Evangelists* and four *Fathers of the Church* were shown calmly writing or teaching, with the *Virgin and Child* next to *St John the Baptist* completing the sequence at the top. Heads project from the intersections of the frame, following the example of Ghiberti, and three are thought to be portraits of the sculptors involved.

In Rome, meanwhile, the architect–sculptor Filarete (*c.* 1400–*c.* 1469), aided by Simone Ghini (1407–91), had been furnishing an enormous pair of bronze doors, with some gilding and enamelling, for the main portal of Old St Peter's (*c.* 1433–45). Installed in the new basilica, they are impressive for sheer size and exuberance of ornament, which includes, for example, inhabited scrolls of acanthus with medallion portraits on the frame. The four rectangular panels depict *Christ* and the *Virgin Enthroned*, *St Paul* and *St Peter* with Eugene IV, the papal donor, at his feet; two square panels at eye-level show the *Decapitation of St Paul* and the *Crucifixion of St Peter*.

In the next generation (*c.* 1475) the example of Filarete's narratives, packed with anecdote, was followed by Guglielmo Monaco, an artillery founder, in his doors for the gateway of the Castel Nuovo in Naples (now in the Palazzo Reale). He depicted the recent victories of Ferrante I of Aragon over Jean d'Anjou in minute detail in four large, square fields, with an upper pair forming a lunette when closed. The junctions of the frame are marked with medallions with heraldic devices and the artist's self-portrait and signature.

During the High Renaissance in Italy only one bronze door was made, the concave one by Jacopo Sansovino (1486–1570) for the sacristy in S Marco, Venice. With only two large, square narrative panels (*Entombment* and *Resurrection*), a frame broad enough to contain niches with statuettes of Evangelists, and portrait busts projecting from the junctions, Sansovino's reliance on the *Gates of Paradise* is manifest.

In northern Europe and in Spain no significant doors were cast in bronze during the whole of the Renaissance (or indeed the Baroque). Oak was in common use because of its durability for external doors, while internally walnut might be preferred, as it takes a high polish. As in the Late Gothic epoch, the panels of such doors were carved in low relief, but a new, classicizing, repertory of ornament was introduced. Aediculae, round niches with figures and portrait medallions of heroes or heroines of antiquity or of contemporary grandees were particularly popular. They were interspersed with geometric patterns of raised mouldings, pertinent coats of arms and heraldic devices, mottoes or initials/monograms, with the proper coronets where applicable. In France, such doors are to be seen in the Palais du Louvre, Paris, and the châteaux of Chenonceaux and Ecouen and elsewhere. Trophies of armour, musical instruments or agricultural implements and Michelangelesque chained prisoners were popular. The principal subject-matter was often drawn from engravings after the work of great painters, such as Rosso Fiorentino or Francesco Primaticcio (1504/5–70). Series of allegories that lent themselves to symmetrical disposition, such as the *Four Elements* or the *Four Seasons*, were much favoured. Good examples from France and other countries are to be found in the Victoria and Albert Museum, London, the Metropolitan Museum, New York, the Musée des Arts Décoratifs, Paris, and the Musée de la Renaissance in the château of Ecouen.

3. MANNERIST AND BAROQUE. The next three noteworthy commissions for bronze doors span the Mannerist and early Baroque periods, around the turn of the 16th century. The earliest were cast for the four relatively modest doorways of the Santa Casa, within the basilica of S Maria di Loreto, by Girolamo Lombardo (*c.* 1505/10–84/9) and Ludovico Lombardo (1507/8–75) between 1568 and

1576. Their design was uniform, a simplified variant of Sansovino's sacristy door in Venice. More important by virtue of their size and location were the three pairs of bronze doors for the basilica itself commissioned a decade later (1590), the central pair from Guglielmo Lombardo and Antonio Lombardo the younger (*c.* 1564–1608/10), the northern pair from Tiburzio Bergelli (1555–1610) and Giovanni Battista Vitali (*d* 1640) and the southern one from Antonio Calcagni (1536–93), Sebastiano Sebastiani (*d c.* 1626) and Tarquinio Jacometti (1570–1638). Their general design was deliberately homogenous, although the larger central pair varies slightly. On the central doors the story of Genesis from the Creation to the Punishment of Cain is recounted in large, bold figures, reminiscent of those carved round the portal of S Petronio, Bologna, by Jacopo della Quercia (?1374–1438). Each door has three large, squarish narrative fields recalling Ghiberti's, with scope for much background detail, and a varying number of subsidiary panels with smaller figures. The central door has the traditional heads projecting from cartouches in its framework, while the other doors have statuettes or subsidiary scenes framed in ovals by strapwork ornaments. Finished at various dates between 1596 and 1610, they are a brilliant artistic and technical achievement, all too rarely acknowledged because of the seclusion of the town of Loreto.

When a fire (1595) in Pisa Cathedral destroyed the west doors by Bonanus of Pisa, replacements were commissioned (in 1600) from a team composed of Giambologna's followers, to work under his aegis: many younger sculptors or goldsmiths cut their artistic teeth on modelling individual panels. The higher central pair of doors, dedicated to the *Life of the Virgin*, has four horizontal rectangular panels of narrative on either leaf, while the lower doors on either side have only three panels, more upright in proportions, dedicated to the *Life of Christ*. Giambologna's methods of creating the effect of perspective were adhered to by all the participants, and the effect is uniform and satisfactory. The framework is richly encrusted with foliage inhabited by charming little creatures such as squirrels, owls, birds and lizards (as in the doorjambs by Vittorio Ghiberti (1418/19–96) for the south doors of the Baptistery in Florence, while other, more exotic animals, with symbolic meanings particular to the Medici, occupy some of the subsidiary panels. There are no projecting heads, let alone portraits of the artists, but the coats of arms of the Grand Dukes and of the cities of Florence and Pisa feature prominently. There are statuettes of apostles in niches at the corners of every door-leaf, with others inserted at the middle of those in the central doorway; these are cast from the same moulds as some of Giambologna's and Susini's own earlier independent statuettes.

4. AFTER *c* 1750. The tradition of making great doors in bronze re-emerged after almost two centuries of quiescence towards the close of the 19th century, as part of the general revival of interest in past historic styles. As in earlier days such doors represented confident statements of religious devotion and civic or national pride. Almost every city in Italy whose cathedral was not endowed with older sculpted doors sought to rectify this by commissioning some in an appropriate—usually neo-Gothic—style from the most renowned sculptors of the day. In Florence, where the cathedral was dedicated to the Virgin Mary, a Marian theme was mandatory. Six of her 'Joys' were spread over the main panels of the three pairs of doors, with her *Assumption* and *Coronation* reserved for the central ones. These Ghibertesque reliefs are framed by ogival canopies and surrounded by appropriate statuettes and busts in niches. The central and north (left-hand) pairs of doors (1897; 1903) are by Augusto Passaglia (1838–1918), while the south (right-hand) pair, which interestingly vary in design from the corresponding pair despite being set within a symmetrical frame, were by Giuseppe Cassioli (1865–1942). At Padua in 1895, for the basilica of S Antonio, Camillo Boito (1836–1914) designed and Guglielmo Michieli modelled a pair with a more restrained sculptural component, showing only the four *Fathers of the Church*, standing beneath transitional, Late Gothic canopies. These are set off by a foil of square panels above and below with holy monograms and symbols in low relief, all framed with a running frieze of Madonna lilies recalling Ghiberti and Luca della Robbia.

In Milan Ludovico Pogliaghi (1857–1950) modelled an amazing and masterly pair of bronze doors (1894–1906) for the restored façade of the cathedral. His swaying, graceful figures in the International Gothic style filtered through Ghiberti are infected with the added sinuosity of line and fluidity of surface characteristic of Art Nouveau. Nevertheless, all was held rigidly in control by a firm cruciform frame, with a great central quadrilobe on each leaf (containing the *Pietà* and the *Assumption of the Virgin*), a shape that was derived visually from the cope clasps of Gothic precious metalwork. The *Life of Christ* is disposed in rows of canopied rectangles that recall Flemish oak retables of the 15th century as well as Italian Gothic altar frontals in silver (for example at Pistoia). Above the hinged leaves is an openwork panel, set amid complex ogival tracery, which has at its centre (seemingly rising from a vertical shaft like a Tree of Jesse running up the central division) a deep relief of the *Coronation of the Virgin*. The Art Nouveau style of fluid modelling is also represented by a pair of bronze doors made by Pier Enrico Astorri (1882–1926) for the monument to Pope Pius X in St Peter's, Rome, which are centred with large female figures, allegorical of painting and music, with four subsidiary scenes on squarish panels above and below. After World War II, Giacomo Manzù made the *Door of Death* at St Peter's, a series of visual meditations on aspects of death

The most effective and celebrated bronze portal of the modern period in northern Europe is the monumental *Gates of Hell* by Auguste Rodin (1840–1917; Paris, Mus. Rodin), which was commissioned in 1880 and finally cast (posthumously) in 1925. Virtually every figure in Rodin's early repertory was pressed into service in the mêlée of distraught human beings that is the subject of the doors: colossal statues in bronze of *Adam* and *Eve* were to flank the door, and they are clearly indebted to Michelangelo, especially to the *Slaves* from the tomb of *Julius II*, which Rodin had seen in the Louvre. On top three casts of an identical figure, derived from Adam, stand in rotated positions to form a group of the *Three Shades*, while below them sat his best-known statue, *The Thinker*, a representation of man himself, sunk in contemplation of his destiny. A plethora of smaller figures, crouching, writhing, curled up in terror or flying in mid-air, most of them known also in separate casts, and to be seen individually, was employed to populate Rodin's deeply personal, psychological and encyclopedic vision of Hell. The huge low-relief sculpture that resulted was a phenomenal achievement by any standards and is a monument to Rodin's creative genius, technical facility and control of his chosen medium of modelling wax.

E. Rumler: *Portes modernes: Architecture, ferronnerie, sculpture* (Paris, *c.* 1910)

New Forms in Door Ornamentation: Executed in Metal, Crystal, Glass, Ebony, Enamel, Marble and Ceramics (exh. cat., New York, 1956)

A. Elsen: *Rodin's Gates of Hell* (Minneapolis, 1980)

L. Blumin: *Victorian Decorative Art: A Photographic Study of Ornamental Design in Antique Doorknobs* (Mill Valley, CA, 1983)

II. Islamic world.

Doors in the Islamic world were usually made of joined wood, as large planks were scarce throughout the region. Decoration, often elaborate, was applied to the interior and exterior doors of public and private buildings and to city gates. By far the largest number of doors survive from interiors. The standard arrangement consists of a pair of valves, each with two vertical stiles connected by four or more rails and enclosing three or more panels. The middle panel was often larger than the upper or lower ones. In earlier times, particularly under the Abbasid dynasty (*reg* 750–1258), the panels of interior doors were carved in the BEVELLED STYLE, and in Egypt under the Tulunid (*reg* 868–905) and Fatimid (*reg* 979–1171) dynasties, the abstract designs were sometimes transformed into representations of animals or accompanied by inscriptions. In later times the panels were also inlaid or painted, or replaced by turned spoolwork. In Anatolia, where wood was commonly available, large planks were sometimes carved with patterns to imitate joinery. Marquetry of ivory, bone, ebony and other woods provided colour, and under the Ottoman dynasty (*reg* 1281–1924) mother-of-pearl was added to wooden doors for the finest royal foundations. A pair of doors from a pavilion in the harem at Topkapı Palace (1578–9) in Istanbul, for example, has panels of minute marquetry in mahogany, lead, tin, ebony and ivory and veneer in ivory, ebony, mother-of-pearl and tortoiseshell, this last set over gold foil to add glitter. In Iran, interior doors were often painted and sometimes heavily varnished

in a technique known as 'Islamic lacquer'. In Egypt spoolwork (Arab. *mashrabiyya*) was occasionally used, as in the doors within the mausoleum (1284–5) of the Mamluk sultan Qala'un in Cairo.

Exterior doors often had fittings of metal. Several important fittings of iron or brass survive from the central Arab lands in the 12th and 13th centuries. For example, the striking door handles that once adorned the Great Mosque at Cizre (early 13th century) in eastern Turkey are of cast and incised bronze in the form of confronted dragons (e.g. Berlin, Mus. Islam. Kst; Copenhagen, Davids Saml.; Istanbul, Mus. Turk. & Islam. A.). Many buildings erected under the Mamluk sultans of Egypt (*reg* 1250–1517) had heavy wooden doors elaborately plated with metal in complex geometric designs, often further embellished with silver and gold inlay. Some of the most famous are those made for the complex of Hasan (1356–62) in Cairo, which were so magnificent that they were illegally removed and installed by al-Mu'ayyad Shaykh (*reg* 1412–21) in his nearby funerary complex. City gates, normally of huge, sturdy planks, were also adorned with metal fittings, which are often the only part to have survived. The Khatir Gate (1040–41) at Yazd in central Iran had iron plates decorated with figures, elephants and a foundation inscription naming the amirs who funded the work; the city gate (1063) from Gandja in Azerbaijan removed to the Gelati Monastery in Georgia was inscribed with the names of the ruler and the qadi who supervised the work.

Doors were often the focus of elaborate surrounds of carved stucco or stone. A rich tradition of figural sculpture developed in parts of Turkey, Syria,

Wooden doors, Islamic (Istanbul, Archaeological Museum)

Iraq and Iran in the 12th and 13th centuries, and door surrounds and the spandrels of gateways were decorated with real and imaginary creatures. The Talisman Gate (1221; destr. 1917) at Baghdad, for example, was decorated with a seated monarch, presumably the Abbasid caliph al-Nasir (*reg* 1180–1225), holding two dragons by their tongues. The portal to the funerary madrasa of al-Nasir Muhammad (*reg* 1294–1340 with interruptions) in Cairo is a Gothic portal made of white marble that had been removed by Khalil (*reg* 1290–94) from a crusader church in Acre. Door posts, a lintel with joggled voussoirs in two colours of marble and a panel with an Arabic inscription were added for the new setting. Many doorways were crowned by *muqarnas* semi-domes and framed by a flat masonry or brick structure known as a pishtaq.

III. Indian subcontinent.

In ancient India the entrance to a sacred space, for example a tree-shrine or stupa complex, was marked by a free-standing gate known as a torana. In early stone temples, built from the first half of the 5th century AD, doors generally had a frame of two or three jambs carved with rosettes and scroll motifs. The lintel often extended beyond the jambs to create a T-shape. Small figures of the river goddesses Ganga and Yamuna standing on mythic crocodiles, or tortoises, were set in the upper corners or flanking the bottom of the door. By the 9th century, doors had become more elaborate, typically comprising four main parts: the lintel, side jambs, threshold and projecting stepping-stone. The lintel often bore a depiction of the nine planets or flying divinities holding garlands and an image of a divinity in the keystone. The jambs, made of three, five, seven or nine parallel vertical sections, were ornamented with scrolls, entwined serpents, amorous couples, divinities, lions or pilasters. Door-guardians were positioned at the base of the jambs adjacent to the figures of Ganga and Yamuna and their attendants. The threshold could have scrolls, pots of plenty, lions, elephants and celestial beings. The semicircular stepping-stone known as a half-moon or moonstone was often carved with lotus petals and flanked by conches.

Entrances were usually closed by door panels. These could be wooden, brass or gilded and were often carved or painted with scenes from the lives of Krishna and Rama or with celestial beings. They could also be embossed and inlaid with brass and ivory, often in geometric or floral patterns. Hinges fixed the doors at top and bottom, and bolts closed and fastened the panels. Chains served as handles. Strips of copper, brass or iron cut in the form of creepers were added for additional strength. The intimate relationship between the temple door and the divinity is seen in the fact that the idol in a sanctum is always placed exactly opposite the door so that the ornate doorframe serves as a surround for the image.

J. Jain-Neubauer: *Dvāra: The Entrance to the Temple in North India* (New Delhi, 1995)

IV. East Asia.

1. China. 2. Korea and Japan.

1. CHINA. According to Chinese tradition, doors were invented in imitation of mussels and oysters. In the earliest Chinese dictionary, the *Showen jie zi* ('Dictionary of words and phrases', AD 121), the pictogram *men* denotes a door with two leaves and *hu* a door with one leaf. Modern scholarship dates the first appearance of both types of door to the Western Han period (206 BC–AD 9), but from the Han (206 BC–AD 220) to the Tang (AD 618–907) period the inward-opening double-leaf plank door (*ban men*) was the main type in use. The earliest extant example of this can be found in the east hall of Foguang Temple (Foguang si) in Shanxi Province (AD 857). Depending on the method of construction, plank doors can be divided into three kinds. The chequer-board door (*qipan men*) consists of a frame with vertical timber boarding fitted into it. The boarding is flush with the frame on the front of the door, while three to five ledges are fixed to the frame at the back with mortise-and-tenon joints. If the front was made smooth with no seams visible, the door would be called *jing-mian men*, or mirror-surfaced door. The pierced plank door (*shita men*) consists of three to five timber vertical planks of the same thickness fastened at the back with ledges. In the *Yingzao fashi* ('Building standards', 1103) the outermost planks on the left and right for this type of door are thicker than the other planks. Sometimes two-pointed nails were also used between adjoining planks. The ledges are fixed to the planks either by iron nails or by fitting the ledges on to rebates 10–12 mm deep on the boarding; occasionally both means are employed to make a door more durable.

From the Five Dynasties period (AD 907–60), plank doors continued to be used in the gateways of palaces, temples and residences, but lattice doors—which opened inwards, admitted light into the interior and were dismountable—also became common. Generally, four door-leaves were fitted between each pair of columns on a façade, but the number varied from two to eight depending on the distance between the columns. In the Song period (960–1279), the width-to-height ratio of a door-leaf was 1:2 or a little less than 1:3; under later dynasties it was 1:3 or 1:4, with ratios of 1:5 and 1:6 in the domestic dwellings of Jiangsu and Zhejiang provinces. The major components of the lattice door are the latticework, a lower panel (*qun ban*, sometimes called a skirtboard), a number of ledges and, sometimes, one to three small panels (*taohuan ban*). In the Qing period (1644–1911) it was common to make two layers of latticework, with the inner layer dismountable and gauze or thin paper pasted on it. The latticework, constructed with small timber pieces, commonly carried geometric designs, sometimes incorporating figures of tortoises, bats or plants. In some instances, dragons, phoenixes, flowers, plants and human figures were cut on a single solid board.

2. KOREA AND JAPAN. As with most structural elements in Korean architecture, doors took their form from Chinese models, most of them being made of vertical planks of wood. They might be single or double, the latter occurring most frequently in temples and palaces. In stone architecture, such as the pagoda of Punhwang Temple at Kyongju (*c.* early 7th century AD), guardian figures were carved on the door frames in high relief.

Lattice doors, also of Chinese inspiration, survive from as early as the mid-14th century at Pusok Monastery, Yongju, North Kyongsang Province, and remain a prominent traditional form. Wooden lattice patterns may be simple cross or fret designs or can exhibit a complex geometry; the interstices are often adorned with flower designs. The lattice forms are frequently placed on both sides of sheets of mulberry paper.

Chinese door types entered the Japanese architectural vocabulary by the 7th century AD. A distinctively Chinese flavour is frequently retained, particularly in Buddhist architecture, though variations also occur. At the Ise Shrine, reconstructed every 20 years since the 7th century AD, the main buildings have hinged double doors made of single planks of cypress-wood, minimally ornamented and unpainted. This type is seen again at the Horyuji, Nara, where there also appears a more Chinese form, built of several vertical and horizontal planks. This latter type, popular from the 8th century AD, was often brightly painted and ornamented. By the 12th century additional forms included doors with lattice-networks resembling shutters on the exteriors of buildings and sliding doors for interiors. In large buildings major doorways had four divisions, so that each half could fold back upon itself.

The *fusuma*, or sliding panel, came into wide use during the 16th century. Consisting of a latticed wooden frame covered with paper or occasionally silk, it became a popular format for painting. These doors also provided great flexibility to create varied internal spaces. A variation on the *fusuma* is the *shōji*, sliding doors (or windows) fitted with translucent white paper pasted over wooden latticework. As part of the exterior walls they could function as both doors and windows, framing wide horizontal expanses of a garden or landscape. Closed *shōji* generated a soft, diffuse light to give interiors an intimate sense of enclosure.

V. South-east Asia.

In South-east Asia the doors of temples are often extremely elaborate and, although they are almost invariably made of wood, many different materials and techniques are employed in their decoration. Since the entrance to a Hindu or Buddhist temple marks the transition from the material world outside to the spiritual world within, the consecrated interior, the door and its frame are usually ornately decorated with Hindu or Buddhist scenes and figures of celestial guardians. For example, among the most striking features of Khmer temple architecture throughout the pre-Angkor and Angkor periods (6th–15th centuries) are the decorated sandstone lintels, frontons, colonnettes and thresholds that surround the doors of sanctuaries and other religious buildings. Many of the stone door frames are carved to replicate wooden ones, and the jambs sometimes incorporate inscriptions identifying the donor of the temple and the date of its foundation. There is usually a stone sill across the threshold. In Khmer, Javanese and Burmese temples the principal door of the sanctuary, usually on the east, is often the only real door, those on the other three sides being false. These stone or brick false doors give some idea of the appearance of the original wooden doors, of which almost no examples earlier than the 18th century have survived anywhere in South-east Asia. One of the few 18th-century buildings in the Thai city of Ayutthaya left intact after the Burmese sack in 1767 is the ordination hall (*ubosot*, *bot*) of the royal monastery of Wat Na Phra Men. At the east end of this hall is a projecting porch, which has twin pillars with lotus capitals and gilded brackets in the form of *nāga*s (mythical serpents) supporting the eaves. The porch is surmounted by a gable of carved and gilded wood, in the centre of which is a figure of Vishnu on his mount, the part-bird, part-human Garuda. Underneath is a large window flanked on either side by a door beneath a smaller version of the central porch, with identical pillars, brackets and gable. Both doors and window shutters are sumptuously decorated with gilt and mosaic.

The wood (usually ebony or teak) doors of later temples and monastic buildings in Thailand, Laos and Burma frequently have highly elaborate decoration, utilizing a variety of techniques ranging from relief carving, fretwork, inlaid mirror glass and mother-of-pearl to lacquering, gilding and painting. Common motifs include images of deities, *garuda*s, *nāga*s, *hamsa*s (geese) and other beasts from Hindu mythology, as well as floral and vegetal motifs, representing harmony and natural abundance. Buddhist figures are frequently depicted on Lao temple doors (e.g. at Wat Nang, Luang Prabang), or they may be painted with scenes from the Hindu epic the *Rāmāyana*. More often than Thai examples, Lao temple doors will incorporate human figures, including representations of Europeans, a famous example being the doors of Vat Pa Ke, Luang Prabang, which depict two Dutchmen. In Burma figures of the *nat* spirits are common. In Vietnam, Chinese styles have influenced the decoration of temple doors, as for example the doors of the Keo Pagoda (14th–15th century), Thai Binh Province, which are pierced and carved with Chinese dragons. Some panels of doors and window shutters of Thai halls of the Ratanakosin period (after 1782) are also decorated with Chinese designs in black and gold lacquer.

Palace doors in Thailand, Burma and Laos often have soaring *torana*s and elaborately carved jambs and are embellished with gilding and mirrorwork. A replica of a door (Rangoon, N. Mus.) from the royal palace in Mandalay, which was destroyed by fire in World War II, is decorated with foliage scrolls, and another example (London, V&A) is made up of a series of carved and gilded panels covered in glass set in lacquer. Malay and Indonesian palace doors are generally plainer, sometimes with carved panels and a pierced wooden panel above, which may incorporate foliage and flower designs, as well as Islamic-influenced geometric designs. In Malaysia the frame of the door may be decorated with finely carved foliage or cloud designs. Some of the carvings on palace doors in Terengganu and Kelantan show Chinese influence.

Among the peoples of insular South-east Asia the doors of clan houses, chiefs' houses and granaries are also frequently decorated, indicating their importance. The decorations often symbolize significant beliefs and religious ideas. The cult-house doors of the Ngada people in Flores in the Lesser Sunda Islands often incorporate scrolled *nāga* or dragon carvings, as do the doors of Kayan and Kenyah chiefs' apartments in Borneo. The doors of many longhouses in Kalimantan (Indonesian Borneo) are painted with dog and *nāga* motifs. Buffalo heads are carved on the granary doors of the Toraja people in central Sulawesi, and the doors of Toraja tombs may have similar heads or a human figure carved on them. The doors of Torajan chiefs' houses may incorporate the same carved scrolls and geometric designs that cover the walls. The older granary doors of the Batak people in northern Sumatra often have a carved lizard motif representing the power of the protecting deity. The houses of the Tetum people in Timor in the Lesser Sunda Islands are traditionally carved in relief with geometric motifs and female figures with prominent breasts. Sometimes only the breasts are depicted, stressing the association of the house with motherhood. The interior doors may also be carved with geometric motifs and human heads, which may represent a warrior or a headhunter.

VI. Africa.

Numerous African peoples decorate the entrances of their buildings, using materials and techniques as diverse as carved and sculpted wood, modelled clay, painted plaster, lashed bamboo and woven fibre. All across the continent, in the region below the Sahara Desert, earth is the principal building material used by sedentary peoples. Thus among the Hausa of northern Nigeria, for example, house entrances are moulded of earthen plaster with raised patterns of Islamic script designed to protect the space within. Mud portals may also be inlaid with stones or ceramic shards, as among the Dagomba of northern Ghana, whose decorated openings are a measure of wealth.

In the savannah and forest regions, where timber is plentiful, doors are constructed of wood, often elaborately carved with culturally specific designs. Among several West African peoples, such as the Dogon of Mali and the Senufo of the Côte d'Ivoire,

designs carved on granary or shrine doors depict mythical personages and animals as well as abstract ideographs. Such images communicate symbolic messages that invoke the spirits or deities or render sacrosanct the area protected by the door. The Bamana of Mali are known for their delicately engraved door-locks. The Igbo of south-eastern Nigeria use carved wooden panels as entrance doorways into the compounds of titled members of the prestigious men's association, Ozo. Members of sufficiently high rank are entitled to commission sculptors to carve the panels. Carved doors and panels were also apparently formerly adopted for use in the houses of wealthy families as a means of displaying wealth. Igbo doors are delicately carved with deeply cut abstract designs in striated and hatched patterns that catch the sunlight to produce high contrasts of light and shadow. The Nupe of Nigeria also produced elaborate chip-carved doors.

In highly stratified societies decorated doors proclaim and enhance the prestige of their owners. Among the Yoruba of south-west Nigeria, for example, the carved doors of rulers' palaces depict exploits of the king's reign. A well-known early 20th-century example by the renowned carver Olowe of Ise records the visit of a British official to the Ogoga or King of Ikere. The right panel shows the visitor being carried in a litter and accompanied by members of his entourage. On the left panel is shown the seated king, along with his wives, children and retainers. This door is carved in high relief, its figures sculpted almost in the round. On the East African littoral known as the Swahili Coast, the art of ornamental door-carving reached a pinnacle of development in the 18th and 19th centuries. Commissioned by wealthy men engaged in the Indian Ocean trade system, Swahili doors indicated the affluence and prestige of their owners. Lintels, side-posts and centre-posts of the double-leafed Swahili doors were embellished heavily with geometric or floral designs in styles that varied from place to place and over time. In some areas geometric and curvilinear patterns were blended. The door panels themselves were nearly always left uncarved, although they were sometimes studded with brass or iron bosses. In the late 19th century, during a period of unprecedented prosperity, the doors became increasingly baroque in style and massive in proportions, especially in Zanzibar. As the volume of trade diminished around the turn of the 20th century, the art of door-carving declined with it. Nevertheless, hundreds of Swahili doors remained extant in towns and cities along the East African coast in the late 20th century.

N. C. Neaher: 'An Interpetation of Igbo Carved Doors', *Afr. A.*, xv/1 (1981), pp. 49–55, 88

E. O. Ugwunwa: 'Igbo Carved Doors and Panels of Onitsha Area', *W. Afr. J. Archaeol.*, xiii (1983), pp. 121–9

N. I. Nooter: 'Zanzibar Doors', *Afr. A.*, xvii/4 (1984), pp. 34–9, 96

J. S. Aldrick: *Nineteenth-Century Carved Doors of Mombasa and the East African Coast* (diss., U. Durham, 1988)

Door-knocker. Ring or hammer, usually made of bronze, attached at one end to a metal plate fixed to a door. In medieval Europe the plate was sometimes shaped like the mouth of an animal (usually a lion), in which the ring was held.

U. Mende: *Die Türzieher des Mittelalters* (Berlin, 1981)

Doornik. *See* TOURNAI.

Dopskål. Swedish drinking bowl, usually silver but sometimes glass. Traditional forms include one or two handles and sometimes include a cover; contemporary designs include versions that can hang from a strap around the neck.

Dorflinger, **Christian** (*b* Alsace, 16 March 1828; *d* White Mills, PA, 1915). American glass manufacturer. He was apprenticed to his uncle at the age of ten to learn glassmaking at the Compagnie des Verreries et Cristalleries de Saint-Louis in eastern France and in 1846 moved to the USA with his family. He first worked in a small glasshouse in Philadelphia. Between 1852 and 1860, Dorflinger built three glasshouses in Brooklyn, NY, each larger than the one before, for the manufacture of lamps, of glass tubes for table lamps and later of blanks for other factories. In his third factory, the Greenpoint Glass Works, he produced blown, cut and engraved tableware of such superior quality that in 1861 it was chosen for use in the White House, Washington, DC, by Mrs Mary Todd Lincoln (1818–82).

In 1863 Dorflinger moved to a farm in White Mills, PA, where in 1865 he built a small glasshouse. Experienced glass workers from Greenpoint taught local farm boys their craft, and French glass artists from Saint-Louis were invited to work there. About 1870 Dorflinger rebuilt an old glassworks in Honesdale, PA. In 1881 his three sons joined him, forming C. Dorflinger & Sons, which included the two Pennsylvania glassworks and the Greenpoint factory, which had been leased to other managers since 1873. By 1903 the White Mills factory alone employed 650 workers. In addition to cutting its own glass, the company sold both colourless and cased blanks to more than 22 decorating shops in the area. Dorflinger's own wares were shipped to the company's warehouses in New York and from there were sold through fine department and jewellery stores across the USA. Dorflinger's works also made services for the presidential administrations of Ulysses S. Grant (1822–85), Benjamin Harrison (1833–1901) and Woodrow Wilson (1856–1924), as well as for dignitaries and royalty around the world. In 1915 Dorflinger's sons closed the White Mills works; potash was in short supply because of World War I, and Prohibition decreased the demand for drinking vessels. Many of the craftsmen went to Corning, NY.

J. Q. Feller: *Dorflinger: America's Finest Glass, 1852–1921* (Marietta, 1988)
F. D. Suydam: *Christian Dorflinger: A Miracle in Glass* (White Mills, PA, 1996)

Dorotheenthal Faience Factory. German faience factory near Arnstadt, founded in 1716 by Auguste Dorothee von Schwarzburg, daughter of the duke of Brunswick. The products of the factory included brightly coloured figurines and jugs and some high-quality plate with LAUBWERK ornament. Its best-known artist was Johann Martin Meiselbach, who worked at the factory from 1733 to 1758; his works are marked MB. The factory closed in 1806.

Dorsch. German family of gem-engravers. (Johann) Christoph Dorsch (*b* Nuremberg, 10 July 1676; *d* Nuremberg, 17 Nov 1732) was the son of Erhard Dorsch (1649–1712), who worked on glass and the cutting of armorial seals on precious stones. Christoph Dorsch studied anatomy and drawing; he turned to engraving relatively late in life yet was one of the most industrious craftsmen of his time, turning out large quantities of gems. He specialized in cutting series of dynasties and rulers from the earliest times to his own days, in cornelian, grey agate and glass, such as 252 popes of Rome (Leiden, Rijksmus. Oudhd.), 126 emperors to Charles VI and the kings of France from the Dark Ages to Louis XV (examples at Leiden, Rijksmus. Oudhd.). The portraits, mostly fanciful, are derived from prints and medals. Dorsch's daughter Susanna Maria (*b* Nuremberg, 1701; *d* 1765) was an abler artist than either her father or her brother Paul Christoph, also an artist. Among her gems are Classical subjects and portraits of such contemporary rulers as the Holy Roman Emperor *Francis I* and his consort *Maria-Theresa* (sealing-wax impressions; The Hague, Rijksmus. Meermanno–Westreenianum). Following her second marriage, in 1738, to the painter Johann Justin Preissler, she occasionally signed herself '(Mme) Preisler(n)'.

Dortu, Johann Jakob (*b* 1749; *d* 1819). German arcanist, active also in Sweden and Switzerland. He worked at porcelain factories in Berlin (*see* BERLIN, §2) and MARSEILLE before moving to MARIEBERG FACTORY, where in the course of a year (Sept 1777–Aug 1778) he established hard-paste porcelain in Sweden. In 1781 he entered into a partnership with Ferdinand Müller to found a porcelain factory in Nyon (Switzerland); he was the driving force behind the artistic and technical development of the factory, and was its director from 1809 to 1813. Hard-paste porcelain in a Neo-classical style was produced in Nyon under Dortu's directorship (but not thereafter), including coffee-sets and cups painted with butterflies and sprays of flowers. The factory closed in 1820.

In 1827 Dortu's son Frédéric Dortu (1787–after 1846) established a porcelain factory in Turin. Two years later it was restyled Dortu Richard et Cie. After several changes of partnership it closed in 1864. Recorded pieces are of hard paste and include sculptural decorative models in a neo-Rococo style.

Double-cloth carpet. *See under* CARPET, §I., 3.

Double cups. Pair of cups that can be stored and displayed with one inverted on the other; there were many silver examples made in 16th-century Germany.

Doublure. Ornamental lining, often of leather or parchment, on the inside face of a book cover

Doulton Ceramic Factory. English ceramic manufactory. The firm was established in 1815, when John Doulton (1793–1873) became a partner in the small Vauxhall Walk pottery in Lambeth, London, which produced such utilitarian stonewares as ink bottles and spirit flasks. In 1820 the company became Doulton & Watts. Doulton's son Henry Doulton (1820–97) joined the firm in 1835, and the business was expanded to include architectural terracotta and chemical stonewares. Influenced by the sanitary improvements of the 1840s, Henry Doulton opened a factory specializing in stoneware drainpipes and sanitary fittings, and the success of this venture assured the company's future prosperity.

The artistic side of the business developed in the 1860s, and from 1866 the pottery was closely associated with the Lambeth School of Art, the students decorating the stoneware before its salt-glaze firing. The favourable reception of their first decorative stonewares encouraged Henry Doulton to establish an art studio. George Tinworth (1843–1913), the first artist to be employed, produced vases, figures and religious plaques. He was followed by the first woman artist to be employed by Doulton, Hannah Barlow (1851–1916), who used the sgraffito technique to decorate her wares with animal studies. By the 1890s the studio employed more than 300 artists.

Henry Doulton's interest in the potteries in Staffordshire began in 1877, when he invested in a factory in Burslem making a variety of earthenwares. By 1882 the firm was trading as Doulton & Co., and over the next few years the factory expanded to produce bone china. The art department, first under the direction of John Slater (1844–1915) and subsequently under Charles Noke (1858–1941), specialized in hand-painted ornamental wares and later figures and other sculptural pieces, which brought international recognition to the company in the 20th century. In 1901 the Royal Warrant was granted by Edward VII, and the company was renamed Royal Doulton. The production of stonewares for artistic, architectural and industrial purposes continued at Lambeth until 1956, by which time the majority of the firm's business was centred in the Burslem factory. The company has been contracting since 1998, and in 2005 was taken over by Waterford Wedgwood, which has closed the Burslem factory.

D. Eyles: *Royal Doulton, 1815–1965* (London, 1965)
D. Eyles: *The Doulton Burslem Wares* (London, 1983)
The Doulton Story (exh. cat. by P. Atterbury and L. Irvine; London, V&A, 1979)

Dovetail joint. In carpentry (and in cabinetmaking), a joint composed of tenons cut in the shape of an

Double cups, repoussé silver, h. 105 mm, Roman, 1st century AD (New York, Pierpont Morgan Library)

expanded dove's tail, fitted into mortises of corresponding shape.

Dowel-pin. Headless pin, peg, or bolt, of wood or metal, used in the construction of furniture to fasten together two pieces of wood by penetrating some distance into the substance of the connected pieces.

Downing, **A(ndrew) J(ackson)** (*b* Newburgh, NY, 31 Oct 1815; *d* Hudson River, NY, 28 July 1852). American writer, horticulturist, landscape gardener and architect. In *The Architecture of Country Houses* (1850) Downing included designs not only for cottages, farm houses and villas but also for interiors and furniture. His influential furniture designs in the style known as 'cottage furniture' were intended for mass production and for sale at modest prices.

A. J. Downing: *The Architecture of Country Houses* (New York, 1850/
    R 1969)
A. C. Downs: *Downing and the American House* (Newtown Square,
    PA, 1988)

Drawn work [drawn-thread work]. Needlework made by drawing threads out of a woven fabric and embroidering over the remaining threads to produce an open-work pattern. It was used widely in medieval Europe, usually with white thread on a white ground, for bed-furniture and table-coverings. Drawn work was the predecessor of LACE.

M. McNeill: *Drawn Thread Embroidery* (London, 2005)

Dredger [castor]. Container with a perforated lid for sprinkling flour, sugar, salt etc. In 1666 Pepys recorded that he 'did carry home a silver drudger for my cupboard of plate'.

Dreihausen. German centre of ceramics production. In 1907 the German art historian Otto von Falke argued that a group of distinctive and highly decorated 15th-century stoneware vessels with stamped ornament (a square containing four dots) had been made in a workshop in Dreihausen (near Marburg, in Hesse). The place of origin has been the subject of much scholarly debate, but it now seems likely that they were made at a workshop in the region of Zittau (Saxony).

A. Schwedt and others: 'Neutron Activation Analyses of 'Falke-
    Group' Stoneware', *Archaeometry,* xlv (2003), pp. 233–50

Drentwett. German family of goldsmiths. From the 16th century to the 18th the Drentwett family of Augsburg produced over 30 master gold- and silversmiths who received commissions from monarchs, nobility and the wealthy bourgeoisie of all parts of Europe. Members of the family were active in many fields, including cast and repoussé gold- and silverwork, engraving, enamelling and even wax modelling. The founder of the family's reputation, Balduin

Drentwett (1545–1627), worked for a number of courts, notably that of the Margraves of Baden-Baden. The work of his son Elias Drentwett I (*c.* 1588–1643) includes an exceedingly fine ewer and basin (1619; Munich, Bayer. Nmus.); the ornamentation on the ewer is part cast and part repoussé, and the reliefwork on the oval basin depicts marine motifs.

Philipp Jacob Drentwett I (*c.* 1583–1652) was one of the first goldsmiths in the 17th century to produce large articles of silver, sending silver tableware, wine-coolers, buffets and ewers to Poland, Sweden and the Viennese imperial court. His son Abraham Drentwett I (1614–66) was one of the most important exponents of cartilage ornament in Augsburg. In 1650 he was commissioned to make a silver throne (Stockholm, Kun. Slottet) for the coronation of Queen Christina of Sweden; it is one of the earliest extant pieces of silver furniture. Like all silver furniture from Augsburg, it consists of a wooden carcass covered with repoussé sheet silver and with cast figural ornament. One of the finest examples of Augsburg style, his Palatinate Sword (1653; Munich, Residenz) has a silver hilt and the ends of the crossguard in the form of lions, the bodies of which extend from cartilage ornament, holding in their paws cartouches with the arms of the Palatinate and the house of Wittelsbach. The sheath is completely covered with cartilage ornament with pinna and mascarons.

Abraham Drentwett II (1647–1729), son of Abraham Drentwett I, was a goldsmith, wax modeller and designer of ornament, his work being published in several series of engravings. His masterpieces include the silver gilt case of a table clock (*c.* 1680–83; Vienna, Schatzkam. Dt. Ordens), covered with profuse foliate and vine ornamentation and trimmed with turquoises and garnets; behind balustrades stand cast figures representing the Virtues; on the headplate are five clockfaces with mobile allegorical figures holding staffs as clock hands and four smaller, immobile figures. Another notable work by Abraham II is a ciborium (1677; Augsburg, SS Ulrich and Afra; on loan to Augsburg, Maximilianmus.), the bowl of which is decorated with repoussé boughs of fruit and reliefs of *Manna Descending from Heaven* and the *Last Supper*, and is held on an angel's uplifted hands; the cover of the ciborium has fruit decoration and the figure of the Christ Child.

Philipp Jacob Drentwett VI (1686–1754) is perhaps best known for a covered goblet (1751–8; Munich, Toering priv. col.) made for the millennial anniversary of Wessobrunn Abbey. Two putti bear the bowl, which is decorated with rocaille motifs, as is the cover showing the arms of the Toering family; on the sides of the goblet is a relief depicting the *Dream of Tassilo*, the legend of the foundation of the abbey. This fine piece demonstrates that, both technically and artistically, the Drentwett family were still leading gold- and silversmiths in the Rococo period.

Dresden. German centre of faience production. In 1708 the Meissen arcanist Johann Friedrich Böttger established a faience factory in Dresden, run by Christoph Rühle (*d* 1742), a flagstone maker from Brandenburg, and Gerhard van Melcem. They failed to produce faience at the factory, and Böttger therefore recruited the Dutch thrower Peter Eggebrecht (*d* 1738), who had been employed at the faience factory of Cornelius Funcke (1673–1733) in Berlin as manager in 1710. In 1712 Eggebrecht took over the lease of the factory and apart from a period in Russia (1718–20) remained there for the rest of his life. In 1720 Eggebrecht was able to buy the factory from Frederick-Augustus II, Elector of Saxony. In 1731 Eggebrecht attempted to obtain an appointment as inspector of the porcelain factory at Meissen with the help of his son-in-law Johann Joachim Kändler; he was, however, turned down because his knowledge of the porcelain-making process was inadequate. After his death his widow, Anna Elisabeth, continued to run the factory until 1756, when it was handed over to her daughter Charlotte Eleonore Le Lonay, who with her husband managed to keep it going for another 11 years, despite falling output. In 1767 Kändler briefly took over the business before leasing it to Christiane Sophie von Hörisch, who with the collaboration of her son, Carl Gottlieb Hörisch, continued production until 1784.

It is difficult to identify items produced at the factory, as it was not until Christiane Sophie von Hörisch took over that wares were marked (DH) on a more regular basis. The earliest pieces possibly include three unpainted, white-glazed figures: Scaramouche and Pantaloon from the *commedia dell'arte* and a peasant leaning on his stick (all Frankfurt am Main, Mus. Ksthandwk). The moulds for these are possibly the same as those used for early Meissen red-stoneware figures. A pot with a short spout (1718; Düsseldorf, Hetjens-Mus.) can probably be assumed to be the work of Eggebrecht. A marked lidded vase (1776; Düsseldorf, Hetjens-Mus.) was made during the period when Christiane or Carl was in charge. As well as faience vases made to complete Chinese garnitures and commissioned by the elector or king, the vessels produced for the Saxon court pharmacy were a speciality.

At the end of the 18th century another faience factory was established in Dresden by Messerschmidt (e.g. tureen; Düsseldorf, Hetjens-Mus.).

Dresden china. *See* MEISSEN PORCELAIN FACTORY.

Dresden work [*point de Dresde; point de Saxe*]. WHITEWORK embroidery made in Dresden in the 18th century.

Dresser, Christopher (*b* Glasgow, 4 July 1834; *d* Mulhouse, Alsace, 24 Nov 1904). Scottish designer, Botanist and writer. He trained at the Government School of Design, Somerset House, London (1847–54), and in 1854 began to lecture at the school on botany; in 1856 he supplied a plate illustrating the

'geometrical arrangement of flowers' for Jones's *Grammar of Ornament*, and the next year inaugurated a series of 11 articles in the *Art Journal* (1857–8) on the subject of 'Botany as Adapted to the Arts and Art-Manufacture'.

In 1862 Dresser published his first design book, *The Art of Decorative Design*, in which he stressed that plant forms should be 'conventionalized' rather than naturalistically imitated. During the 1860s he established himself as a major commercial designer, with a studio of 'Ornamental Art' in Fulham, London. The only known sketchbook by Dresser (Ipswich Mus.) dates from this period and contains annotated designs for metalwork and ceramics, and sketches of geometric and floral ornament.

Dresser's next book was *Principles of Decorative Design* (1873). During the 1870s Dresser designed for a wide range of media: cast iron for Coalbrookdale; textiles for at least eight firms, including Warners and Crossley & Sons; wallpaper for Jeffrey & Co.; silver and plate for Elkington & Co. from 1875, for Hukin & Heath from 1878, and for James Dixon & Sons from 1879. Some of his best-known designs are for such small-scale metal objects as toast racks and claret jugs. An advocate of machine production, Dresser was an innovative designer; his works, generally austere and undecorated and usually with exposed rivets, show a primary concern for function. In 1876 Dresser visited the Philadelphia Exhibition, and from there went to Japan, where he travelled extensively in 1877, representing the British Govern-

Christopher Dresser: claret jug, glass and silver, made by J. W. Hukin and J. T. Heath, 1879 (London, Victoria and Albert Museum)

ment and also collecting Japanese objects for Tiffany & Co. of New York. Much of Dresser's subsequent work was informed by his appreciation of Japanese design. From 1879 to 1882 he was art director of the newly formed Linthorpe Art Pottery, near Middlesbrough, Cleveland, which mass-produced vases and tableware of Oriental and Pre-Columbian inspiration. He also designed ceramics for Minton & Co., the Old Hall Earthenware Co. and the Ault Pottery.

From 1879 to 1882 Dresser was in partnership with Charles Holme (1848–1923) as Dresser & Holme, wholesale importers of Oriental goods, with a warehouse in Farringdon Road, London. In 1880 Dresser was appointed art editor of the *Furniture Gazette*, a position he held for one year, during which time he frequently reproduced his own angular furniture designs. The same year he founded the Art Furnishers' Alliance in Bond Street, London, with financial backing from Arthur L. Liberty and George Chubb, a safe manufacturer whose firm also made 'artistic furniture' designed by Dresser. The business was not a commercial success and was liquidated in 1883. Dresser also designed furniture for the Bath cabinetmakers Thomas Knight. In 1882 he published a major work on the art and architecture of Japan, and in 1886 his final design book, *Modern Ornamentation*. From the mid-1880s Dresser designed Clutha glass, patented by James Couper & Sons of Glasgow. In 1889 he moved to Barnes, London, where he ran a design studio.

ODNB
C. Dresser: 'Botany as Adapted to the Arts and Art-Manufacture', *A. J.* [London], n.s., iii and iv (1857–8) [series of 11 articles]

Dressing table, oak with iron fittings and a pivotal mirror, made by Liberty & Co., after 1894 (London, Victoria and Albert Museum)

C. Dresser: *Principles of Decorative Design* (London, 1873)
C. Dresser: *Japan, Its Architecture, Arts and Art-Manufacture* (London, 1882)
C. Dresser: *Modern Ornamentation* (London, 1886)
M. Whiteway and A. Morello: *Christopher Dresser, 1834–1904* (Milan and London, 2001)
Shock of the Old: Christopher Dresser's Design Revolution (exh. cat. by M. Whiteway; Washington, DC, Smithsonian, 2004)
H. Lyons: *Christopher Dresser: The People's Designer, 1834–1904* (Woodbridge, UK, Easthampton, MA, 2005)

Dressing table [toilet table; *toilette*]. Table fitted with a mirror and drawers in which items of toiletry were stored; as the user was seated at a dressing table, the table was sometimes supplied with a stool. The form originated in early 17th-century France; early examples are simple tables with two or three drawers, but cabinetmakers soon began to devise ways of concealing the mirror and other fittings. By the late 17th century dressing tables were being made in America and England; American examples tend not to have a mirror, but may have been used in front of a mirror that was attached to the wall. In France, the dressing table came to be known in the 18th century as the *table de toilette* or simply the *toilette*, and in the 19th century as the *coiffeuse* or *poudreuse*. In both countries the tables were sometimes fitted with a sumptuous cloth cover, which was known in England as a toilet-cover. The dressing table is the antecedent of the modern vanity table.

P. Guerin: 'Sweet Vanity', *A. Antiques*, xxviii/1 (Jan 2005), pp. 110–12

Dressing table and armchair, crystal and gilt bronze, 780×1220×640 mm (table), created for Caroline, Duchesse de Berry by the workshop L'Escalier de Cristal, 1819 (Paris, Musée du Louvre)

Dressoir. *See* CUPBOARD.

Dreyfuss, Henry (*b* 1904; *d* 1972). American industrial designer. Dreyfuss was born into a Brooklyn
family of suppliers of theatrical materials, and trained
with Norman Bel Geddes as a Broadway stage designer. In 1928 he opened his own design company,
which specialized in industrial design. In the 1930s
he designed the Mercury, a long-distance luxury train
with a unified design that extended from the engine
cowling to tableware. In this decade he also began
his long association with Bell Telephone Laboratories, for whom he designed the elegant model 302
tabletop telephone (1937) and the lighter model 500
(1949); the latter is still in use in public telephones
in the USA. Dreyfuss's Trimline model (1965) transferred the controls to the hand of the user. In 1934
he also began to design appliances for Hoover, and
three years later he designed the first of a succession
of tractors for John Deere & Co. He subsequently
designed aircraft interiors for Lockheed (notably the
Super Constellation of 1951), cameras (with Edwin
Land) for Polaroid (including the cheap Swinger of
1965 and the single-lens reflex SX-70 of 1972) and
thermostats for Honeywell (including the Round of
1953). In 1967 Dreyfuss reorganized his company as
Henry Dreyfuss Associates, which is still an important presence in industrial design.

H. Dreyfuss: *Designing for People* (New York, 1955)
H. Dreyfuss: *The Measure of Man: Human Factors in Design* (New York,
    1967)
R. Flinchum: *Henry Dreyfuss, Industrial Designer: The Man in the Brown
    Suit* (New York, 1997)
A. R. Tilley: *The Measure of Man and Woman: Human Factors in Design*
    (New York, 2002)

Drinking horn. The horns of many animals (often
the ox or buffalo) have been used as drinking vessels
in many cultures. North European examples of the
14th to 16th centuries are sometimes supported by
silver or copper-gilt mounts, and the horn is sometimes carved or otherwise decorated.

A. Roes: *A Drinking Horn of the Viking Period* (Amsterdam, 1940)
C. Kinzelman: *The Drinking Horn: Its Place in the Traditional Social
    System of the Cameroon Highlands* (n.p., 1982)

Drop. Glass pendant of a chandelier or an ornamental feature suspended from a hammerbeam
wooden roof or stone vault; in furniture, a drop handle (also known as a pear-drop handle) is a pendant
handle attached to a plate.

Drop-in seat. Upholstered (or caned) seat that can
be lifted from its frame and has no springs; drop-in
seats were first made in the early 18th century.

Dryad. *See under* WICKER.

Dry-edge figures. *See under* DERBY.

Dubois, Abraham (*b* 1751; *d* 1811). American silversmith whose workshop in Philadelphia specialized in domestic silver in the Federal style.

Dubois, Jacques (*b* Pontoise, 8 April 1694; *d* Paris,
23 Oct 1763). French cabinetmaker. He became a
maître-ébéniste on 5 September 1742. He specialized in
luxury items decorated with Japanese lacquer and
marquetry. His pieces were often sober, and this
complemented the power, beauty and quality of his
vigorous and exuberant bronzes with their opposing
Rococo curves in the Louis XV style. His stamped
works include a corner-cupboard (*c.* 1745; Malibu,
CA, Getty Mus.) for Count Jan Klemens, based on
a design by Nicolas Pineau, a lacquered bureau for
Louis-Philippe, Duc d'Orléans (1725–85), and the
'de Vergennes' marquetry bureau (both Paris, Louvre), a commode (Genoa, Pal. Reale) for Louis XV's
daughter Louise-Elizabeth (1727–59) and a large
lean-to secrétaire with doors and windows (1770;

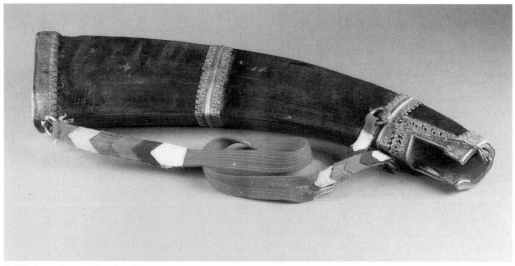

Buffalo-horn wine container, from Bhutan

Jacques Dubois: writing table, ebony, lacquer and gilt bronze, made for the Château de Raincy, *c.* 1750 (Paris, Musée du Louvre)

Waddesdon Manor, Bucks, NT). After Dubois's death, his son René Dubois (1737–99) continued the workshop, using his father's mark but producing proto-Neo-classical and Neo-classical furniture that include some of the finest works of French *ébénisterie*.

Du Cerceau, Jacques Androuet (*b* ?Paris, *c.* 1515; *d* ?Annecy, 1585). French engraver, ornamentalist, writer and architect. Du Cerceau's primary aim was to disseminate the heritage of Classical art and propagate the style of the Italian Renaissance by making works accessible without foreign travel and by providing practical handbooks for architects, painters, sculptors, designers, craftsmen, cabinetmakers, goldsmiths and jewellers. Many of his writings were on architecture, but in the early 1550s he published works in Orléans on furniture design and ornamentation (*Petites Grotesques, Les Vues d'optiques, Compositions d'architecture*); there is then a gap in his printed oeuvre until 1559, when, having established himself in Paris, he published books on Classical architecture and ornament.

Du Cerceau created a new mode with his pattern books, of which the first was *Premier Livre d'architecture contenant les plans et dessaigns [sic] de cinquante bastiments tous differens* (1559), In his *Second Livre d'architecture* (1561), Du Cerceau provided a compendium of beautiful inventions to enrich the interiors of houses as well as the surrounding courts and gardens. It includes designs for mantelpieces, dormers, portals, fountains, wells and pavilions. The *Troisième Livre d'architecture* (1572) is devoted to the design of country houses and their surroundings, including gardens and orchards.

E. D. Baldus: *Oeuvre de Jacques Androuet Ducerceau: Meubles & cheminées* (Paris, 1869)

C. Poke: 'Jacques Androuet I Ducerceau's "Petites Grotesques" as a Source for Urbino Maiolica Decoration', *Burl. Mag.*, cxliii/1179 (June 2001), pp. 332–44

Duché, Andrew (*b* Philadelphia, *c.* 1710; *d* Philadelphia, 1778). American potter and trader. The son of the stoneware potter Anthony Duché (*fl* Philadelphia, 1700–62), he claimed to be the first person in the West to make porcelain, but he produced only a few curiosities in the late 1730s, described by others as being translucent. No pieces have been positively attributed to him. Before 1735 he settled in South Carolina and from 1736 was in Savannah, GA, where he had a small pottery.

G. Hood: 'The Career of Andrew Duché', *A. Q.*, xxxi (1968), pp. 168–84
B. L. Rauschenberg: 'Andrew Duché, a Potter "a little too much addicted to Politicks"', *J. Early S. Dec. A.*, xvii/1 (1991), pp. 1–101

Duchesse. French term for a CHAISE LONGUE (i.e. a sofa with a back at one end only). A *duchesse en bateau* is one in which the foot is encompassed by a low curving back; a *duchesse brisée* is a suite of two or three pieces of furniture which can be used as separate seats but can be used as an ensemble when brought together. A *récamier* is a chaise longue of the type on which Madame Récamier is reclining in the portrait by Jacques-Louis David (1748–1825; Paris, Louvre), it has two ends and so is sometimes said not to be a chaise longue at all.

Duck foot. In American furniture, a collector's term for the three-toed foot of a Cabriole leg.

Duesbury, **William** (*b* ?Longton Hall, Staffs, 7 Sept 1725; *d* Derby, 30 Oct 1786). English porcelain manufacturer. He trained as an enameller, and between 1751 and 1753, in his decorating shop in London, he painted wares from Staffordshire and Derbyshire and porcelain from the factories of Bow and Chelsea. He spent a short time (1754–5) at the Longton Hall Porcelain Factory in Longton Hall before entering into a partnership on 1 January 1756 with John Heath, a Derby banker, and André Planché (*c.* 1727–1809), a French refugee, to manufacture porcelain. The factory, in Nottingham Road, Derby, was managed by Duesbury and traded as W. Duesbury & Co. In 1764 he was able to introduce the technique for successful over- and underglaze transfer-printing (e.g. transfer-printed mug, *c.* 1768; Derby, Mus. & A.G.), the details of which he learnt from Richard Holdship, a former partner of the Worcester Porcelain Co. (est. 1751) whom he had engaged as an employee. On 5 February 1770 Duesbury purchased the Chelsea porcelain factory and until 1784 ran both factories, this being known as the 'Chelsea–Derby' period. He also bought the bulk of the undecorated stock from the failed Longton Hall Porcelain Factory in 1770 for decorating at Derby. In 1773 he opened a showroom in Covent Garden, London, and in 1776 purchased the moulds and plant of the Bow Porcelain Factory. The Chelsea Porcelain Factory was closed in 1784, and much of the plant and some of the skilled craftsmen were transferred to Derby. By the time of his death, Duesbury had built up a world-famous porcelain factory, which he described as 'a second Dresden'.

ODNB

Dufour, **Joseph**, & Cie. French wallpaper manufacturing company founded in 1804 in Mâcon by Joseph Dufour (1757–1827). He was trained in Lyon, where there was a flourishing wallpaper industry at the end of the 18th century, and started working at the Ferrouillat & Cie factory some time before 1789. In 1797 he founded a factory in Mâcon with his brother Pierre Dufour under the name Dufour Frères; they employed Jean-Gabriel Charvet (1750–1829), who had worked in other Lyon wallpaper companies, as designer. In 1801 the factory was renamed Joseph Dufour & Cie, and in 1804 it launched its first panoramic wallpaper, the 'Savages of the Pacific', designed by Charvet. In 1808 the factory moved to the Faubourg Saint-Antoine in Paris and took on a new collaborator, the designer and engraver Xavier Mader (1789–1830), who had almost certainly trained in the calico printing industry in Nantes. Mader worked with the Dufour company until 1823 when Dufour took on his son-in-law, Amable Leroy (1788–1880), as a partner and changed the company name to Joseph Dufour & Leroy. After Dufour's death this name was retained until 1835. The business was taken over by the Desfossé company in 1865.

H. Clouzot: *Tableaux-tentures de Dufour & Leroy* (Paris, n.d.)

Joseph Dufour (1757–1827) (exh. cat., Mâcon, Mus. Mun. Ursulines, 1982)
O. Nouvel-Kammerer, ed.: *Papiers peints panoramiques* (Paris, 1990), pp. 312–21
J.-G.Charvet: *Les sauvages de la mer Pacifique: Manufactured by Joseph Dufour et cie 1804–05 after a Design by Jean-Gabriel Charvet* (Sydney, 2000)

Dufrène, **Maurice** (*b* 1876; *d* 1955). French designer of furniture, glass, metal, ceramics and interiors. He was a pioneering exponent of ART DECO and a detractor of ART NOUVEAU, which in practice meant that he aspired to a style that was neither historical nor mannered. Dufrène was a founder-member in 1901 of the Société des Artistes-Décorateurs (SAD). He inaugurated a range of furniture in very dark native wood and defended functionalism and the use of mechanical processes and mass production. In 1921 he became director of the Atelier Maîtrise in the Paris department store Galeries Lafayette, for which he designed furniture for low-cost mass-production and for high-cost commissions.

M. Dufrène: *Art Deco Interiors: From the 1925 Paris Exhibition* (Woodbridge, 2000)

Dugourc, **Jean-Démosthène** (*b* Versailles, 23 Sept 1749; *d* Paris, 30 Apr 1825). French designer. He was the only son of François Dugourc, controller to the household of the Duc d'Orléans. Together with FRANÇOIS-JOSEPH BÉLANGER (his brother-in-law) and Georges JACOB, Dugourc worked on the interiors of the château of Bagatelle, as well as for a glittering private clientele that included the Duc d'Aumont (at the château of Brunoy, *c.* 1780–81) and the Duchesse de Mazarin, creating interiors in the late 18th-century Etruscan style. He also collaborated with such leading craftsmen as Pierre Gouthière, François Rémond and Jean-Baptiste Boulard. He produced numerous designs executed in a rapid, light, energetic style for gilt-bronzes and furniture (e.g. design for chimney-piece with clock, candelabra, vases and fire-dogs, *c.* 1785; Paris, Mus. A. Déc.). He designed furniture for the Chambre des Bains in the château of Compiègne (firescreen, 1785; Lisbon, Mus. Gulbenkian) and a jewel cabinet for Marie-Antoinette (destr.; model, 1787; Baltimore, MD, Walters A.G.). He also had a number of foreign clients, among them Catherine II of Russia, Grand Duke Paul (later Emperor of Russia), General Lanskoï and Gustav III of Sweden, for whom he provided set designs for the theatre of Drottningholm.

From 1786 Dugourc made numerous designs for the Spanish court, many of which were produced by François-Louis Godon, the Parisian master watchmaker who had become watchmaker to the king of Spain, and in April 1800 he settled in Madrid, where he carried out commissions for Charles IV and members of the Spanish aristocracy. In 1814 he returned to Paris and once again collaborated with Bélanger on royal commissions, for example the re-interment of Louis XVI and Marie-Antoinette at

Saint-Denis in 1815 and the marriage ceremonies for the Duc de Berry in 1816. From 1774 to 1790 Dugourc had produced designs for the silk manufacturer Camille Pernon of Lyon, and this partnership continued after his return to France (e.g. silk panel, *c.* 1815–25; Chicago, IL, A. Inst.). He also executed designs for the royal manufactories at Beauvais and the Savonnerie. His last project was the Throne Room at the Tuileries, where he was responsible for all aspects of decoration and furniture. There are important collections of designs by or attributed to him at the Musée des Arts Décoratifs in Paris and in Lyon.

P. De Bayser and P. Renaud: *J. D. Dugourc (1749–1825): 215 dessins provenant de la vente après décs de l'artiste exécutés entre 1770 et 1790* (n.p., 1988)
C. Baulez: 'Les Imaginations de Dugourc', *De Dougourc à Pernon: Nouvelles acquisitions graphiques pour les musées*, Doss. Mus. Tissus (Lyon, 1990), pp. 11–43
A. Forray-Carlier: 'Dessins de Jean-Démosthène Dugourc pour le Garde-Meuble de la Couronne', *Bull. Soc. Hist. A. Fr.* (1991), pp. 133–48
C. Gastinel-Coural: 'La Salle du Trône du Château des Tuileries', *Un Age d'or des arts décoratifs, 1814–1848* (exh. cat., Paris, Grand Palais, 1991)

Dumb waiter. In modern usage, an apparatus for conveying food vertically from kitchen to dining room. In earlier usage, an article of dining-room furniture intended to dispense with the services of a waiter at table. In its typical form, which was invented in England in the 1740s, it consists of an upright pole bearing one or more revolving trays or shelves on which are placed dishes and other table requisites.

Dummer, Jeremiah (*b* 1645; *d* 1718). American silversmith, apparently the first to be born in America. He was apprenticed in the Boston workshop of JOHN HULL. Dummer's silverwork is severe, but includes stylish objects, such as cups with cast scroll and caryatid handles. His apprentices probably included JOHN CONEY.

H. F. Clarke and H. W. Foote, *Jeremiah Dummer, Colonial Craftsman & Merchant, 1645–1718* (Boston, 1935/*R* 1970)

Dummy board figures [silent companions]. Flat *trompe l'oeil* figures painted on a thin panel of wood and then cut out. They were normally used as fire screens, but were sometimes mounted in entrance halls. Figures portrayed include prosperous adults and children, and people in public life.

A. Scott and C. Scott: *Dummy Board Figures* (Cambridge, 1966)
Silent Companions: Dummy Board Figures of the 17th through 19th Centuries (exh. cat., Rye, NY, Rye Hist. Soc., 1981)
C. Graham: *Dummy Boards and Chimney Boards* (n.p., 1988)
C. Edwards: 'Dummy Board Figures as Images of Amusement and Deception in Interiors, 1660–1800', *Stud. Dec. A.*, x/1 (Fall–Winter 2002–3), pp. 74–97

Dunand, Jean [Jules, John] (*b* Lancy, 20 May 1877; *d* Paris, 7 June 1947). French sculptor, metalworker,

Jean Dunand: *Cameroon*, from the series *The People of Africa*, coromandel lacquer, made for the library of the Musée des Colonies (Paris, Musée du Quai-Branly)

painter and designer, of Swiss birth. After an early career as a sculptor he began to produce designs for interior decoration and furnishing. His first pieces of dinanderie (decorative brassware) were exhibited at the Salon de la Société Nationale des Beaux-Arts of 1904 in Paris. In 1906 he gave up sculpture in order to devote his time to making dinanderie and later to lacquering. His first vases (e.g. 'Wisteria' vase, gilt brass with cloisonné enamels, 1912; Alain Lesieure priv. col.) reflect Art Nouveau forms, but he quickly adopted the geometric forms of Art Deco in his work. In 1912 the Japanese artist Seizo Sugawara asked him to solve a problem concerning dinanderie, and in exchange he was given instruction in lacquering. From then on he produced vases, folding screens, doors and other furniture (e.g. *Geometric Decor*, black and red lacquered screen, priv. col.). Around 1925 he started to use egg shell on lacquer. Different effects were produced by varying the size of the pieces and by using the inside or the outside of the shell. He used this technique for both portraits and Cubist compositions (e.g. tray; Geneva, Mus. A. & Hist.). He worked closely with contemporary artists and designers, especially the furniture designer Jacques-Emile Ruhlmann and the couturiers Madeleine Vionnet (1875–1975) and Paul Poiret (1879–1944). His jewellery designs demonstrate a preference for pure, geometric forms, with regular black and red lacquer dots on the metal surface.

Jean Dunand, Jean Goulden (exh. cat., ed. Y. Brunhammer; Paris, Gal. Luxembourg, 1973)

F. Marcilhac: *Jean Dunand: His Life and Works* (London, 1991)

J. D. Goss: 'Jean Dunand Vase', *Met. Mus. A. Bull.*, lvi/2 (Fall 1998), p. 61

Dunlap. American family of furniture-makers active in New Hampshire from the late 18th century to the early 19th. Lieutenant Samuel Dunlap (1752–1830) preferred to work in maple; his older brother Major John Dunlap (1746–92) is associated with inlaid cherrywood furniture. Dunlap furniture is characterized by the expressive use of flowered ogee mouldings, basket-weave cornices, open pediments, scrolls and intaglio fans.

C. Parsons: *The Dunlaps and Their Furniture*, Manchester, NH, Currier Gal. A. (Manchester, NH, 1970)

P. Zea and D. Dunlap: *The Dunlap Cabinetmakers* (Mechanicsburg, PA, 1994)

Du Paquier, Claudius Innocentius. *See under* VIENNA.

Duplessis [Du Plessis; Duplessy]. French family of goldsmiths, bronze founders, sculptors and designers, of Italian descent. Due to the similarity in name, there has been some confusion between father and son and the attribution of their work; they are now generally distinguished as Duplessis père and Duplessis fils. Jean-Claude Chambellan Duplessis [Giovanni Claudio Chiamberlano] (*b* Turin, ?1690–95; *d* Paris, 1774) practised as a goldsmith in Turin and moved with his family to Paris *c.* 1740. In 1742 he was commissioned by Louis XV (*reg* 1715–74) to design and make two large, bronze braziers, presented to the Turkish ambassador Saïd Mahmet Pasha (e.g. in Istanbul, Topkapı Pal. Mus.). From *c.* 1748 until his death he was employed at the porcelain factories of Vincennes and Sèvres as a designer of porcelain forms and supplier of bronze stands. He also supervised and advised craftsmen. In 1751 he produced eight drawings for the first major dinner-service commissioned by Louis XV (*reg* 1715–74). He played an influential role at the factory in the development of new porcelain forms in the Rococo style, and most of the shapes from the 1750s and many from the 1760s are attributed to him or bear his name. These include such vases as the Bras de Cheminée Duplessis (e.g. *c.* 1754; London, V&A), the Vase à têtes d'éléphant, which incorporates candelabra (*c.* 1756; London, Wallace) and such pieces of Rococo fantasy as the Saucière Duplessis in the form of an antique lamp (1756; Paris, Louvre). At least three versions of an écritoire survive (e.g. *c.* 1760; Munich, Residenzmus.), of which the original design by Duplessis is preserved in a collection of his designs at the Musée National de Céramique in Sèvres; another Ecritoire à Globes bears a grisaille head of Louis XV and the monogram of his daughter Madame Adélaïde (1758; London, Wallace). Duplessis showed an interest in Classical forms, and it is thought that either he or his son (who assisted him from 1752) may have influenced the creation of Neo-classical models at Sèvres in the early 1760s. Duplessis continued to maintain his own silversmithing and bronze-founding interests in Paris. Gilt-bronze wall-lights made in Paris and attributed to him include one with acanthus, laurel and reeds (1749; New York, Met.); he has also been credited with the mounts of a pair of celadon ewers (*c.* 1745–9; London, Wallace) and a pair of Chinese vases mounted as ewers (*c.* 1750; Waddesdon Manor, Bucks, NT). It is not certain whether he or his son or both in partnership created the models for the rich bronze ornaments, which were cast by Etienne Forestier (*c.* 1712–68), on Louis XV's Bureau du Roi (1769; Paris, Louvre) made by Jean-François Oeben and Jean-Henri Riesener. The gilt-bronze vases on the bureau correspond to the melon-shaped Vase à Chaîne (*c.* 1770; London, Wallace). Similarities have also been noted between a Sèvres clock of 1761 and a gilt-bronze clock attributed to Duplessis (1763; London, Wallace).

Duplessis's son Jean-Claude Thomas Chambellan Duplessis (*b* Turin, *c.* 1730; *d* Paris, 1783) established a regular connection with Sèvres after his father's death, and until 1783 he supplied gilt-bronze mounts and designed such porcelain shapes as the Vase Gobelet Monté (*c.* 1770–80; London, V&A) and tureens and *écuelles*; he published some of his vase designs *c.* 1775 to 1780. About 1775 he made four large Neo-classical, gilt-bronze candelabra for the Paris hôtel of Laurent Grimod de la Reynière, the Fermier Général, and in 1779 designed the mounts for a pair of vases bought by Queen Marie-Antoinette (London, Buckingham Pal., Royal Col.). He mounted pieces from the Comtesse du Nord's Toilet Service in 1782, and other attributions include the figural gilt-bronze mounts on a pair of Sèvres vases (*c.* 1782–3; London, Wallace).

Durand. French family of furniture-makers whose workshops were in Paris. Louis Durand established a workshop *c.* 1787, and became a famous cabinet-maker during the Restoration. He was succeeded between 1834 and 1838 by his son Prosper-Guillaume, who became Ebéniste du Roi in 1839 and exhibited at the Paris Exhibition of 1855. In the last quarter of the century a furniture-maker called Gervais-Maximilien-Eugène Durand specialized in the reproduction of 18th-century furniture; he may have been a relation, but his business was in different premises. He was joined by his son Frédéric-Louis Durand *c.* 1890, and thereafter the firm was known as Durand et Fils until it finally closed in 1934.

Durantino, Francesco (*fl c.* 1543–54). Italian ceramics painter. He was first active in Urbino, where he is recorded as working in the workshop of Guido di Merlino from 1543. His early signed and dated works include a dish painted with a scene showing *Martius Coriolanus and His Mother* (1544; London, BM) and a fragment (1546; Stockholm, Nmus.) illustrating the *Death of Polixena* and bearing the monogram and sign of Urbino. Stylistically very similar to these are plates and dishes illustrating biblical and mythological scenes, dating from 1542 to 1547 (examples in Brunswick, Herzog Anton Ulrich-Mus.; London, V&A; Edinburgh, Royal Mus. Scotland; Pesaro, Mus. Civ.). In 1547 he took over a kiln in Monte Bagnolo, near Perugia. Certain large vessels, decorated both inside and out, have been attributed to this period (examples in Florence, Bargello, and London, V&A), as have albarelli and flasks. His work is characterized by a strong palette of blues, yellows, oranges and greens and lightly marked contours.

T. Wilson: 'The Origins of the Maiolica Collections of the British Museum, 1851–5', *Faenza*, lxxi (1985), pp. 68–81

Durantino, Guido. *See under* FONTANA, ORAZIO.

Durlach. German centre of faience production. In 1723 a pottery was founded in Durlach (Baden) by J. H. WACKENFELD; after his death in 1726 it was run by his widow till 1749. The subsequent owners (1749–1812) were Georg Adam Herzog and Johann Adam Benckieser. Under the Benckieser management, the pottery specialized in pear-shaped jugs and coffee pots. Until 1818 there was no factory mark, but artists signed their own work; the most prominent were Georg Balthasar Fichtmeier (1751–1803), who signed his works with a black F, and Johann Jacob Kaiser (1773–1835), who signed his works with a black K. After 1818 the factory's cream-coloured earthenware was marked 'Durlach'.

E. Petrasch: *Durlacher Fayencen, 1723 × 1847* (exh. cat., Karlsruhe, Bad. Landesmus., 1975)
Durlacher Fayencen (exh. cat., Mannheim, Städt. Reiss-Mus., 1978)
R. Simmermacher and others: *Gebrauchskeramik in Südbaden: Porzellan Baden-Baden, Fayence Durlach, Steingut Durlach, Emmendingen, Hornberg, Villingen, Zell a.H., Hafnerware Kandern* (exh. cat., Karlsruhe, Bad. Landesmus., 2002)

Dusseuil [Du Sueil], **Augustin** (*bapt* Méounes, Var, 2 Sept 1673; *d* Paris, Feb 1746). French bookbinder in the service of the Duc de Berry (from 1714) and King Louis XV (*reg* 1715–74; from 1717). The measure of his reputation in England for intricate and delicate bindings is Pope's reference in *Epistle to Burlington*, in which he says of the books in Timon's library that 'these Aldus printed, those Du Sueil has bound'.

Dutch metal [Dutch foil]. Malleable alloy of eleven parts of copper and two of zinc, which when beaten into thin leaves can be used as a cheap imitation of gold-leaf.

Dwight, John (*b c.* 1635; *bur* Fulham [now in London], 13 Oct 1703). English potter. He was employed by the natural philosopher and chemist Robert Boyle in Oxford in the 1650s, and from 1661 held secretarial and legal appointments under three bishops of Chester. In 1670–71, when living at Wigan, he concluded that 'he had ye secret of making china ware'. He applied for and was granted a patent on 17 April 1672 for making 'transparent Earthen Ware' and 'stone ware' and moved to London, setting up a pottery in Fulham. By March 1676 the production of stoneware bottles after the Rhenish bellarmines, mugs and similar vessels (including TIGER WARE) was sufficiently established for Dwight to negotiate a sales agreement with the Worshipful Company of Glass Sellers of London, who held the London monopoly of the sale of both glassware and stoneware. In June 1684 Dwight obtained a second patent restating his original claims and supplemented with additional 'inventions', including 'opacous redd and darke coloured Porcellane'. Dwight's production of so-called 'porcellane' appears to have been limited to a number of extremely fine, white, salt-glazed stoneware busts and figures, as in the stoneware bust of *Prince Rupert* (*c.*

John Dwight: *Lydia Dwight*, grey salt-glazed stoneware, h. 255 mm, Fulham, 1674 (London, Victoria and Albert Museum)

1675; London, BM), the result of experimental work *c.* 1673–5. Production of brown stoneware, however, continued at Fulham Pottery for more than 200 years.

ODNB
D. Haselgrove and J. Murray, eds: 'John Dwight's Fulham Pottery, 1672–1978: A Collection of Documentary Sources', *J. Cer. Hist.*, xi (1979), pp. 1–148; Supplement (1992)
John Dwight: The Master Potter of Fulham, 1672–1703, and His Contemporaries (exh. cat., London, Jonathan Horne, 1992)
J. Horne: 'John Dwight, the Master Potter of Fulham', *Mag. Ant.*, cxliii (April 1993), pp. 562–71
C. Green: *John Dwight's Fulham Pottery: Excavations, 1971–79* (n.p., 1999)

Dyottville Glass Works. American glasshouse established in Philadelphia in 1773 as the Kensington Glassworks; in 1831 the company was acquired by Dr T. W. Dyott and was thereafter known as the Dyottville Glass Works. The factory produced flint-glass table ware and a variety of bottles (notably cylindrical whiskey bottles in the third quarter of the 19th century); it specialized in pictorial flasks, some with historical themes. Dyott withdrew from the company on being declared bankrupt in 1838, but the firm continued to produce glass (including coloured glass from the 1840s) until the end of the century.

T. W. Dyott, J. Sergeant and M. Carey: *An exposition of the system of moral and mental labor: Established at the glass factory of Dyottville, in the county of Philadelphia: Embracing a description of the glass factory, together with the system of industry therein pursued, with the report of the committee chosen to investigate the internal regulations of the place* (Philadelphia, 1833)
H. McKearin: *Bottles, Flasks and Dr. Dyott* (New York, 1970)

E

Eames. American architects, designers and film makers. Charles (Orman) Eames (*b* St Louis, MO, 17 June 1907; *d* St Louis, 21 Aug 1978) and his wife, Ray Eames [née Kaiser] (*b* Sacramento, CA, 15 Dec 1916; *d* Los Angeles, CA, 21 Aug 1988), formed a partnership after their marriage in 1941 and shared credit for all design projects.

In 1936 Charles Eames accepted a fellowship at the Cranbrook Academy in Bloomfield Hills, MI, which was under the direction of Eliel Saarinen. As well as Saarinen's son Eero Saarinen, he met Ray Kaiser, who became his second wife and design partner. Charles Eames and Eero Saarinen collaborated on the design of exhibitions and furniture; they researched techniques of binding and laminating wood and of curving plywood. In 1940 they entered a competition sponsored by MOMA in New York, in which their entries for curved plywood chairs and

modular storage units won two awards; they were exhibited in the Organic Design in Home Furnishings exhibition at MOMA in 1942. In 1946 their plywood furniture was shown in an exhibition, Chairs, Eames and Chests, at MOMA; it included a plywood side chair and dining chair (1946), which quickly became well known and widely used. This exhibition also brought their work to the attention of the Herman Miller furniture company, by whom they were employed as designers and consultants.

In the 1950s the Eameses, with Harry Bertoia, George Nelson (1908–86) and Eero Saarinen, used the latest technology for furniture. Moulded plastic, foam, artificial leather and supports of a 'cat's cradle' of metal wire and of cast aluminium were employed in a series of designs that became the hallmark of modern interiors of the 1950s and 1960s. These included moulded polyester high and low side chairs

Charles Eames: chaise longue (full-scale model), hard rubber foam, plastic, wood and metal, 800 × 1498 × 870 mm, 1948 (New York, Museum of Modern Art)

Charles Eames: lounger and ottoman, moulded plywood and rosewood veneers on cast aluminium base, black leather upholstery, 851 × 851 × 806 mm (chair), 425 × 654 × 527 mm (ottoman), manufactured by Herman Miller Inc., 1956 (New York, Museum of Modern Art)

(1955), a moulded rosewood plywood lounge chair and ottoman (1956) and polished, die-cast aluminium chairs and ottoman, the 'Indoor–Outdoor' (1958). Concurrent with the Eames's designs for furniture and children's toys was their increased involvement with communication, especially films and exhibitions, and by the 1960s this replaced furniture as their principal work.

C. Eames: 'Design Today', *CAA. & Archit.*, lviii/9 (1941), pp. 18–19

C. Eames: 'Design, Designer and Industry', *Mag. A.*, xliv/12 (1951), pp. 320–21

A. Drexler: *Charles Eames Furniture from the Design Collection of the Museum of Modern Art, New York* (New York, 1963)

R. Caplan: *Connections: The Work of Charles and Ray Eames* (Los Angeles, 1977)

D. Spaeth: *An Eames Bibliography* (Monticello, 1979)

J. Neuhall, M. Neuhall and R. Eames: *Eames Design* (New York, 1989)

P. Kirkham: *Charles and Ray Eames: Designers of the Twentieth Century* (Cambridge, MA, 1995)

E. Demetrios: *An Eames Primer* (New York, 2001)

J. Steele: *Eames House: Charles and Ray Eames* (London, 2002)

B. Fitoussi: *Eames: Furniture 1941–1978* (New York, 2003)

D. Albrecht: *The Work of Charles and Ray Eames: A Legacy of Invention* (New York, 2005)

Earthenware. Pottery made with clays fired at relatively low temperatures. Most earthenwares have traditionally been made of secondary clays, receiving relatively little purification after being mined. Common clays tend to contain iron oxide and other impurities, which reduce firing temperatures to between 800–1100°C (lower than that required for STONEWARE). Iron, a natural flux, facilitates the melting together of the other ingredients. Earthenware clay can be highly plastic or less plastic because of sand or other rocky fragments. After firing the clay remains unfused and is therefore porous, opaque and less sturdy than higher-fired wares. Earthenware clays rich in iron oxide fire from buff to tan, red, brown or black, depending on the clay and firing conditions. They take low-temperature glazes, such as certain alkaline and lead-oxide types, to render them non-porous. In the simplest method the body and glaze are hardened during a single firing. Finer, more pure earthenware bodies, some with higher firing temperatures, require an initial (biscuit) firing to harden the unglazed body. A lower temperature glaze or 'glost' firing leaves the wares impervious to liquid. This two-firing system facilitates the execution of crisp underglaze decoration, which is fixed in the body-firing and is thus less likely to run when the glaze is fired. Such overglaze decoration as enamelling or gilding is hardened in subsequent lower temperature firings.

Eastlake, Charles Locke (*b* Plymouth, 11 March 1836; *d* London, 20 Nov 1906). English writer, designer and museum official, nephew of the painter Sir Charles Lock Eastlake (1793–1865). From 1866 he was assistant secretary at the Royal Institute of British Architects, London, and from 1871 its first permanent, salaried secretary. While at the Institute, Eastlake made his reputation as a writer on design. *Hints on Household Taste in Furniture, Upholstery and Other Details* (1868), a manual of decoration, includes his own designs for furniture, which emphasize function and honesty of construction. Despite its lack of originality (it owes much to such sources as Owen Jones's *Grammar of Ornament* (London, 1856) and Bruce J. Talbert's *Gothic Forms* (London, 1867)), the book made Eastlake a household name, especially in America; it influenced furniture design into the 1890s and was much imitated.

ODNB
C. L. Eastlake: *Hints on Household Taste in Furniture, Upholstery and Other Details* (London, 1868; Boston, MA, 1872/*R* Salem, 1993)

Ebena. Belgian factory established in 1921 in Wijnegem to make plastics and insulation. The plastic (also known as ebena) was a compound initially made of albumen and sawdust, but from 1922 it was based on copal, a natural resin imported from the Belgian Congo (later Zaïre, now the Democratic Republic of the Congo). The company specialized in lidded boxes (notably luxury chocolate boxes) but also made a wide range of domestic goods (e.g. clockcases and lamps). The factory closed in 1931.

Ebena 1921–31: Articles de fantaisie et articles industriels: Sammlung Kölsch (exh. cat., Düsseldorf, Kstmus; Deurne, Prov. Mus. Sterckshof; 1987)

Ebéniste. French cabinetmaker specializing in veneered furniture. The term was coined with the reintroduction of ebony, an ideal veneer, early in the 17th century. Since the mid-18th century there has been a clear distinction between an *ébéniste* and a MENUISIER.

A. Pradère: *French Furniture Makers: The Art of the Ebéniste from Louis XIV to the Revolution* (London, 1989)

Eberlein, Johann Friedrich (*b* Dresden, 1695; *d* Meissen, 20 July 1749). German sculptor and modeller. After training as a caster and carver in England, he joined the Meissen Porcelain Factory in 1735 as principal assistant to the Modellmeister JOHANN JOACHIM KÄNDLER. Together they collaborated on the conception and creation of the 'Schwanenservice' (1737–41; Meissen Porzellanmus) for Heinrich, Graf von Brühl. He also modelled his own creations, the most successful of which were the series of Classical gods and goddesses on High Baroque socles, dating from *c.* 1747.

Ebonized. Stained to resemble ebony; the ebonizing of furniture originated in the 16th century and became popular in 19th-century England and America.

Ebony. Hard black wood, obtained from various species of the family Ebenaceae, especially *Diospyros ebenum* (sourced by the British from Sri Lanka and the French from Madagascar) and *Diospyros melanoxylon* (Zebra-wood from the Coromandel Peninsula in New Zealand) but also species such as *Brya ebenus* (the Jamaican rain tree).

Echizen. Japanese centre of ceramics production, based on some 20 kiln sites 7 km north-west of the city of Takefu (Fukui Prefect.) and active since the 12th century; Echizen is known as one of Japan's 'Six Old Kilns'. In the 12th century the introduction of new technology, encouraged the development of a higher-fired brown stoneware. The use of a tunnel kiln with a dividing pillar, the manufacture of jars with everted rims and incised horizontal bands and the use of the coil-and-paddle technique in the early Echizen wares point to origins in kilns such as TOKONAME and Atsumi (now Aichi Prefect.), which spread these techniques and styles nationwide. The principal shapes were kitchen mortars, narrow-necked jars and wide-necked jars. These were made for agricultural use and for human burial.

Early Echizen wares were largely undecorated, but from the early 14th century some vessels display stamped, combed and carved decoration, as well as simple potter's marks. By mid-14th century the potter's marks become quite elaborate. A brown-glazed ware was developed in the 17th century and can be seen on small bowls, spouted bowls, graters and sake bottles. Production at Echizen diminished thereafter, but the kilns survived, making local farm wares into the modern period.

D. A. Wood, T. Tanaka and F. L. Chance: *Echizen: Eight Hundred Years of Japanese Stoneware* (Birmingham, AL, 1994)

Eckernførde Pottery. Danish ceramics factory. In 1759 Johann Nicolaus Otte (1714–80) founded a ceramics factory in Criseby (Schleswig, then a Danish possession and now in Germany), and in 1765 moved it to his nearby estate of Eckernførde. The factory attempted to produce wares that would rival the standard of those from German and French porcelain factories; it closed in 1785. The factory produced tableware (and table-tops) in a Rococo style, often painted with brightly coloured flowers. Some of the finest pieces were made by the modeller Johann Georg Buchwald and his son-in-law, the painter ABRAHAM LEIHAMER.

Eckmann, Otto (*b* Hamburg, 19 Nov 1865; *d* Badenweiler, 11 June 1902). German designer, illustrator and painter. After an early career as a painter he decided in 1894 to devote himself to the decorative arts. At first he concentrated on graphic arts (especially woodcuts), but, driven by creative frenzy and exacting discipline, he expanded his repertory as a craftsman, designing stained glass, ceramics, furniture and metalwork. He also designed interiors, the most important of which was a study/sitting-room (1897–8) in the Neue Palais (destr.), Darmstadt, for the Grand Duke Ernest Ludwig of Hesse-Darmstadt. He designed such lighting fixtures as the wrought-iron 'Narcissus' candlestick (1896–7; Hamburg, Mus. Kst & Gew.) manufactured by Josef Zimmermann & Co., Munich. He also designed carpets and tapestries for such firms as H. Engelhard of Mannheim and the Smyrna-Teppich-Fabrik, Berlin. His most famous tapestry, *Five Swans* (1896–7; Hamburg, Mus. Kst & Gew), of which approximately 100 examples were woven, was produced at the Scherrebek tapestry workshops in Schleswig-Holstein (now Skærbaek, Denmark).

O. Eckmann: *Neue Formen: Dekorative Entwürfe für die Praxis* (Berlin, 1897)
J. Simmon: *Zeichnungen und Druckgraphik von Otto Eckmann: Der Bestand in der Kunstbibliothek Berlin* (Berlin, 1982)

Ecole de Nancy. Group of decorative artists in the French city of Nancy. Members of the Alliance Provinciale des Industries d'Art (later called the Ecole de Nancy) included the glassmakers EMILE GALLÉ (the group's founder in 1901) and Auguste DAUM; the cabinetmakers LOUIS MAJORELLE and EUGÈNE VALLIN; VICTOR PROUVÉ, who produced decorative work and designs for bookbindings; the stained-glassmaker JACQUES GRUBER; the potter GEORGES HOENTSCHEL; and the architects Emile André (1871–1933), Désiré Bourgon (1855–1915) and Lucien Weissenburger (1860–1929). Members of the group rejected revivalist styles in favour of a distinctive style of Art Nouveau decoration that eschewed machinery and functionalism and socialist art in favour of floral and figurative decorations derived from the rhythms of organic nature.

C. Debize: *Emile Gallé and the 'Ecole de Nancy'* (Metz, 1999)
R. Bouvier, ed.: *Musée de l'école de Nancy* (Paris, 2001)

Ecuelle. Covered two-handled porringer (usually silver but sometimes porcelain) used for soup, popular in France in the late-17th century and early 18th.

Edinburgh Weavers. Scottish textile company founded in the 1920s as an experimental unit within Morton Sundour Fabrics; it became a subsidiary in 1934, responsible for the manufacture of furnishing fabrics. Alistair Morton (1910–63), who was head of Edinburgh Weavers from the 1930s until his death, commissioned innovative designs by well-known artists. The patterns were intricate and the colours of the fabrics muted. The company still trades, proudly declaring itself to be a tartan-free zone.

J. Morton: *The Mortons: Three Generations of Textile Creation: Alexander Morton & Company, Morton Sundour Fabrics, Edinburgh Weavers*, London, V&A (London, 1973)
Alastair Morton and Edinburgh Weavers: Abstract Art and Textile Design, 1935–4 (exh. cat., Edinburgh, N.G. Mod. A., 1978)

Edkins, Michael. *See under* BRISTOL, §2.

Edouart, Augustin (Amant Constant Fidèle) (*b* 1789; *d* 1861). French silhouettist. He moved to England in 1814 and in 1826 established himself as a silhouettist in Bath. He cut freehand in folded black paper, a method that enabled him to keep a copy. Edouart did not paint his silhouettes, but rather indicated the whites of collars and handerchiefs by 'slashing', i.e. cutting away parts of the black paper to expose the white mount beneath. He worked variously in London, Oxford and Cambridge, and in 1830 moved to Edinburgh, where he cut silhouettes of the court of the exiled Charles X of France; the collection of 78 portraits is now in the Bibliothèque Nationale in Paris. Edouart subsequently spent a year in Dublin, where he cut *c.* 6000 portraits and published *A Treatise of Silhouette Likenesses* (Cork, 1835). He then moved to America for 10 years (1839–49). On his return journey his ship was wrecked, and all but 9,000 of his 200,000 duplicates were lost.

A. Oliver and E. Jackson: *Auguste Edouart's Silhouettes of Eminent Americans, 1839–1844* (Charlottesville, 1977)
H. Laughon: *August Edouart: A Quaker Album: American and English Duplicate Silhouettes, 1827–1845* (Richmond, VA, 1987)
A. Bahar: *Auguste Edouart: Adventure in Shadow* (n.p., 1992)

Edwards of Halifax. *See under* BOOKBINDING, §1(III).

Augustin Edouart: *Joseph Henry and Dr Nathan William Cole*, chalk and cut paper on paper, 280×212 mm, 1843 (Washington, DC, National Portrait Gallery)

Eenhorn. Dutch family of potters. The Grieksche A ['Greek A'] factory was founded in Delft by Wouter van Eenhoorn (*d* 1679) in 1658 (no marked pieces by him are known); he was replaced by his son Samuel van Eenhoorn (1655–86) in 1678, who was in turn succeeded in 1686 by his brother-in-law Adriaensz. Kocks (*d* 1701). The factory remained in the family until 1722. Lambertus van Eenhoorn, one of Samuel's brothers, owned the Metalen Pot factory in Delft from 1691 to 1721. This factory was of great significance under Wouter and Samuel for the distinct improvement and refinement of blue-and-white faience mainly in the style of porcelain made in China during the Wanli period (1573–1620) and Transitional style (1620–44). Their interpretations of these styles can be considered the first true chinoiserie decoration. Lambertus van Eenhorn and Kocks also produced very fine polychrome faience between 1690 and 1720. Decoration was often derived from imported goods or was, during periods of high import, deliberately different.

Egell, Johann Paul (*b* ?9 April 1691; *d* Mannheim, 11 Jan 1752). German sculptor, stuccoist and furniture-maker. Egell is rightly known for his very individualistic late Baroque sculpture, mostly carved in wood, but was also active as a decorative artist. In 1723 he moved to Mannheim, capital of the Palatinate, and from 1726 to 1731 contributed substantially to the decoration of the Schloss being built by Elector Charles Philip. All that is left of the exterior, apart from small-scale sculptures and a statue of *Wisdom* (now Speyer, Hist. Mus. Pfalz), is the stone pedimental relief of the *Trinity* on the Schlosskirche. Inside, Egell's allegorical stucco reliefs of *Morning* and *Evening*, the *Four Continents*, the *Four Elements* and *The Arts* on the walls of the monumental staircase and of the central Rittersaal (restored after bomb damage in 1943) are among the most successful creations of early 18th-century German decorative art. Egell also designed and carved furniture for the Schloss, including console tables and seating in a Rococo style.

Egeri [Aegeri], **Carl** [Carle] **von** (*b c.* 1510; *d* Zurich, 14 June 1562). Swiss glass-painter and designer. In 1536 he settled in Zurich, where in 1542 and 1555 he was commissioned to make stained-glass windows for the Rathaus. These constructed a powerful new civic iconography for post-Reformation Zurich. Banner-bearing citizens, with finely detailed armour and portrait heads, are set against abstract patterned grounds, the whole framed in elaborate arches. Appropriate biblical scenes of loyalty to the state (e.g. *Judith and Holofernes*) fill the corners. Two impressively drawn lions occupy a roundel (1542) surrounded by the arms of the Zurich domains. In a 1557 window (Zurich, Geshaus Schneggen) of similar design, the lions are instead fully Mannerist, with elongated bodies and twisted mouths. Von Egeri evidently adapted his style to the job; in his Muri Abbey windows (1557) St Martin and St George ride tranquil horses in the style of Paolo Uccello (*c.* 1397–1475), while the large figures are set against blue skies surmounting perfectly rendered landscapes. Many watercolour designs for windows emanated from von Egeri's prolific workshop in the 1540s; typically, variations on the theme of two figures (usually men) flanking a piece of heraldry (e.g. the *Three Cantons*, *c.* 1540; Rennes, Mus. B.-A. & Archéol.). These are fine examples of a strand of late Renaissance international decoration; the elaborate costumes show a debt to Lucas Cranach the elder (1472–1553), while the classicized grotesquerie is adapted from Italian engraved models.

Egermann, Friedrich (*b* 1777; *d* 1864). Bohemian glassmaker from Polevsko near Česká Lípa in northern Bohemia. He was a leader in the revival of figural representation in glass engraving, and became the leading exponent of Empire-style glass enamelling. He and his pupils at NOVÝ BOR decorated pieces with representations of ancient mythological heroes, allegories of virtues, vistas and floral motifs using translucent enamels on opaque-white or colourless glass. Sometime before 1818 Egermann discovered the technique for the production of yellow staining using silver chloride. In 1824 he improved the use of white enamel, calling it 'pearl' or 'biscuit' enamel. In 1828 he created 'Lithyalin' glass, which imitated the appearance of hardstones through the combination of both opaque and translucent glass; the surface of the finished items very often has the appearance of wood grain (see colour pl. XI, fig. 3).

Egg, Durs (*b* 1745; *d* 1822). Swiss gun-maker who opened a workshop in London in 1772 and eventually became a Royal Gun-maker. His most highly prized weapons were his double-barrelled shotguns and his flintlock duelling pistols. His nephew Joseph Egg also became a noted gunsmith, and was the inventor of a double-barrelled pocket pistol in which the barrels could be discharged successively by two pulls on a single trigger.

Egg and dart [egg and tongue; egg and anchor]. Decorative architectural detailing of Ionic ovolo mouldings. In classical antiquity the pattern is sometimes found on a smaller scale on metalwork, jewellery, sarcophagi and vases. It has also appeared on furniture since the Renaissance.

Egg-shell china. Porcelain ware of extreme thinness and delicacy, known in China as *t'o-t'ai* ('bodiless' ware)

Eglomisé. *See* VERRE ÉGLOMISÉ.

Egyptian Revival. Neo-classical style of architecture, interior design and the decorative arts; as Egyp-

Egyptian Revival inkwell, gilt porcelain, c. 1802 (Sèvres, Musée National de Céramique)

tomania or *Egyptiennerie* it reached its peak during the late 18th century and early 19th. Napoleon's campaign in Egypt (1798) coincided with emerging tastes both for monumental and for richly ornamental forms, enhanced by the literary and associational concerns of Romanticism. During the early 1760s the Venetian designer Giovanni Battista Piranesi created a highly original painted interior in the Egyptian taste for the Caffè degli Inglesi in the Piazza di Spagna, Rome. The plates were included, along with 11 bizarre chimney-piece designs in the Egyptian style, among the 67 illustrations of his *Diverse maniere d'adornare i cammini* (1769). This folio treatise, advocating a broadly eclectic style for contemporary designers and their patrons, was preceded by a remarkable essay in which Piranesi not only stressed the decorative range of Egyptian design but also discussed the process whereby Egyptian art had been abstracted from nature, keenly observed.

Within the next two decades the tentative signs of a sustained stylistic revival are discernible for the first time, initially in the applied and decorative arts; examples include FRANÇOIS-JOSEPH BÉLANGER's (unpublished) chimney-piece designs of 1770 and PIERRE GOUTHIÈRE's furniture mounts of the 1780s.

In England, Josiah Wedgwood produced Egyptian wares from the 1770s onwards.

The first Egyptian Revival interior in Britain was the Billiard Room (1793) at Cairness House (Grampian) by James Playfair (1755–94), which used three-dimensional features such as a stepped chimney-piece and battered doorcases. After visiting Rome in the mid-1770s and Egypt in 1796, the English designer THOMAS HOPE produced the most accomplished interior of the Egyptian Revival. Refashioning the main rooms of his house (destr. 1850) in Duchess Street, off Portland Place, London, he created his 'Egyptian' or 'Black Room' between 1779 and 1801. In ceramics, the most important Egyptian revival ware was the highly ambitious 'Service égyptienne' in Sèvres (1810–12), originally made to Napoleon's directions and later given by Louis XVIII to Arthur Wellesley, 1st Duke of Wellington (now London, Apsley House).

Parallel with the applied arts and architecture, the romantic imagery of Egypt was also influencing stage design on the one hand and masonic ritual on the other; themes closely allied in Mozart's opera *Die Zauberflöte*, first produced in Vienna in 1791 and given particularly fine panoramic stage sets by Karl

Dish depicting the temple ruins at Elephantine, from an Egyptian service made by Sèvres, designed by Jacques-François Swebach, porcelain, c. 1811 (Sèvres, Musée National de Céramique)

Friedrich Schinkel at the Königliches Theater, Berlin, in 1816. Masonic lodges, first associated with Egyptian symbolism and ceremony in the late 18th century, continued to reflect this as late as 1900, when P. L. B. Henderson (1848–1912) created the opulent Chapter Room for the Royal Arch Chapter of Scottish Freemasons in Edinburgh.

The High Victorian phase of the Revival in England also found a place in the campaign of improved art education promoted by Henry Cole and his circle. Reflecting the current design teaching of Gottfried Semper (1803–79), Owen Jones and Joseph Bonomi provided an Egyptian Court with large-scale exemplars of art and architecture in the Crystal Palace, rebuilt at Sydenham after London's Great Exhibition of 1851 (destr. 1936). Egyptian material also played a major role in OWEN JONES's magisterial *The Grammar of Ornament* (1856) and CHRISTOPHER DRESSER's *The Principles of Decorative Design* (1873); Dresser produced several chairs based on Egyptian prototypes.

The perennial influence of basic Egyptian forms and patterns continued to recur in the 20th century in jewellery, costume, and Art Deco interiors (e.g. the foyer of the Strand Palace Hotel, London (1930, destr. 1967–8; parts now London) by Oliver Bernard (1881–1939). The most persistent of all Revival images, the pyramid form, provides the focal point, in glass, of the extension (1989) to the Louvre by I. M. Pei (b 1917).

R. G. Carrott: *The Egyptian Revival: Its Sources, Monuments and Meaning, 1808–1858* (London, 1978)
P. Clayton: *The Rediscovery of Egypt* (London, 1982)
J. S. Curl: *The Egyptian Revival: An Introductory Study of a Recurring Theme in the History of Taste* (London, 1982)
The Inspiration of Egypt: Its Influence on British Artists, Travellers and Designers, 1700–1900 (exh. cat., ed. P. Conner; Brighton, A.G. & Mus., 1983)

Egyptian vase by Pierre-Philippe Thomire, varnished tin and bronze, h. 1.6 m (Paris, Musée du Louvre)

D. Syndram: *Ägypten-Faszinationen: Untersuchungen zum Ägyptenbild im europäischen Klassizismus bis 1800* (Frankfurt, 1990)
H. Navrátilová: *Egyptian Revival in Bohemia* (Prague and Oxford, 2003)
D. S. L. Kelly: 'The Egyptian Revival: A Reassessment of Baron Denon's Influence on Thomas Hope', *Furn. Hist.*, xl (2004), pp. 83–98
J. S. Curl: *The Egyptian Revival* (New York, 2005)

Ehrenfeld Glasshouse. German glass factory founded in 1865 with Bohemian workers in 1865 in Ehrenfeld (near Cologne). The factory, which employed a Bohemian workforce, produced high-quality hand-made imitations of medieval German and Venetian Renaissance glass, notably Flügelgläser. The glasshouse closed in 1931.

Eilbertus of Cologne (*fl* 1129–60). German metal-worker and enameller. A monk in the monastery of St Pantaleon, Cologne, he was one of the principal masters of its important workshop and among the most outstanding German metalworkers of the Romanesque period. His name is engraved as part of an inscription on a small portable altar (ex-Welf treasure; Berlin, Tiergarten, Kstgewmus.), produced *c.* 1150–60. Eilbertus's achievement was to replace the silver niello decoration customary on altars up to that date with enamel work. The figures decorating the altar are individually characterized with spare lines, and they show the artist's distinctive use of champlevé enamel with marked ridges separating areas of shaded colour.

P. Lasko: *Ars sacra, 800–1200* (New Haven, 1994)

Eiraku Hozen [Nishimura Zengorō XI; Konan Hozen] (*b* ?Kyoto, *c.* 1795; *d* Ōtso, Tōtōmi Prov. [now Shiga Prefect.], 1854). Japanese ceramicist and member of the Eiraku family. At the age of 13 he was adopted by Nishimura Ryōzen, the tenth-generation head of a family of *doburo* (earthenware braziers) makers for the tea ceremony. In 1827 he was invited to Kii Province (now Wakayama Prefect.) to produce porcelain for the local daimyo, from whom he received the right to use a silver seal bearing the name Eiraku. He obtained national recognition for his *sometsuke* (blue-and-white) and *kinrande* (gold and enamel) wares. Hozen was skilled in the manufacture of many types of ceramic ware, including stonewares and copies of Chinese Ming-period (1368–1644) wares, and his coloured glazes (violet, yellow, red, blue and green) were a major influence on later Kyoto ceramics (*kyōyaki*). He also devoted much effort to mastering the use of underglaze copper red (*shinsha*). After passing the family headship to his son, Wazen, in 1849, Hozen travelled to Edo (now Tokyo), where he planned to open a kiln. The venture failed, but soon after his return to Kyoto he was invited by a patron to build a kiln in Miidera (Ōtsu, Tōtōmi Prov.; now Shiga Prefect.). Hozen spent his last years working there, producing what came to be known as Konan ware, and later, at another kiln, Nagarayama ware. He was succeeded by his son, Wazen (1823–96), and his adopted son, Sosaburō (Dōzen).

Electroplate. Deposition by electrolysis of a layer of metal, often gold, silver or chromium, on to a metal. Experiments into the electrodeposition of metals were carried out from the 18th century, but the commercial potential of this method of gilding or silvering was not realized until the end of the 1830s, when G. R. ELKINGTON and his cousin, Henry Elkington (*c.* 1810–52), who ran a large firm making silverwares in Birmingham, decided to advance gold and silver cyanide solutions as electrolytes. This led, in the 1840s, to the successful electroplating of copper and other base metals with continuous, durable and shiny layers of precious metal.

Within a few years electroplating had largely replaced all other plating methods and formed a very substantial industry. Such firms as Elkington, Mason & Co. in Britain, Christofle in France and a large number of manufacturers in the USA (GORHAM, Meriden, Rogers Bros and the conglomerate known as the International Silver Company) produced an enormous range of plated goods, which exceeded both in quantity and elaboration those covered by other, earlier forms of plating, notably SHEFFIELD PLATE.

Electroplating also transformed gilding technology, replacing fire-gilding and to a lesser extent leaf-gilding. One especially interesting application was the electrogilding of such large items as statues or even whole roofs. This was developed to a high degree in 19th-century Russia, especially by the St Petersburg Electroforming, Casting and Mechanical Plant set up by Moritz Hermann von Jacobi (1801–74), which gilded the domes on such buildings as St Isaac's Cathedral, St Petersburg, and the Bol'shoy Theatre, Moscow. The gilded layers were much thinner than could have been achieved by any other method, but even so hundreds of kilograms of gold were used on each roof.

Developments in electroplating continued, especially in new alloys that would be cheaper and more resistant to corrosion. There was considerable research into developing a plate that would protect silver jewellery mounts from tarnish. Platinum and palladium platings were used in the 19th century, but they were expensive and looked different from silver. In the 1930s rhodium plating was introduced for diamond settings. It rapidly spread to a wide range of silver and even silver-plated goods, because although rhodium was very expensive, only an extremely thin layer was needed to give full protection, and the colour and finish were held to be indistinguishable from silver itself.

The search for plating metals that would give a cheap, weather-resistant but attractive finish was pursued with vigour. Thus, at the end of the 19th century such plating alloys as Arcas, three-quarters silver and a quarter cadmium, were developed. These resembled silver but were significantly cheaper and had superior resistance to tarnish—so much so that similar alloys were used to plate cycle handlebars. Nickel plating was also widely used to give protection to exposed copper and brass fittings. However, the major advance was made only in the 20th century with the introduction of CHROMIUM plating. This made it possible to give metals, including iron and steel, a durable, silvery finish that was both weather-resistant and attractive.

O. I. Pavlova: *Electrodeposition of Metals: An Historical Survey* (Moscow, 1963; Eng. trans., Jerusalem, 1968)
S. Bury: *Victorian Electroplate* (London, 1971)
D. T. Rainwater and D. H. Felger: *American Silverplate* (n.p., 1972, rev. Atglen, PA, 3/2000)
G. Dubpernell: *Electrodeposition of Chromium* (New York, 1977)

Electrotype copies of two lions from Rosenborg Castle, Copenhagen, electroplated copper, silvered, h. 980 mm, *c.* 1885 (London, Victoria and Albert Museum)

J. K. Dennis and T. E. Such: *Nickel and Chromium Plating* (London, 1986)

C. Raub: 'The History of Electroplating', *Metal Plating and Patination*, ed. S. La Niece and P. T. Craddock (Oxford, 1993)

M. Schlesinger and M. Paunovic: *Modern Electroplating* (New York, 2000)

T. D. Weisser: *Gilded Metals: History, Technology and Conservation* (London, 2000)

Electrotype [galvanoplasty]. Relief printing block in which the plate is made by electrolytically coating a mould with copper. The process is the electrical equivalent of casting, and the entire object to be made, known in continental Europe as a galvanoplastic copy, is produced in the plating vat.

Electrum. Alloy variously defined. In mineralogy, it is a native argentiferous gold containing from 20% to 50% of silver, but the term is also used to denote an alloy of copper, zinc and nickel. In Latin (and Greek) the term denoted amber, but was used in a transferred sense to refer to an alloy of gold and silver that resembled amber.

Elephant's foot [filpai; gulli gul]. Motif often frouned on Islamic carpets, consisting of repeated octagons arranged in rows.

Elers. English family of potters of German origin. David Elers and John Philip Elers were the sons of Martin Elers, a German who had settled in Holland; John Philip was born in Utrecht on 7 September 1664. David is first recorded as a silversmith in London in 1686, and both brothers then made 'Browne muggs and red theapotts' in Staffordshire and Vauxhall, London, from *c.* 1690. In 1693 they were sued by JOHN DWIGHT for infringing his stoneware patent

Owl-shaped brooch, electrum, h. 57 mm, from the Temple of Artemis, Ephesos, 7th–6th century BC (Istanbul, Archaeological Museum)

but subsequently made red stoneware under licence from Dwight. In 1698 John Philip gave up the lease of his house at Bradwell Wood, Staffs, where he had been both potter and gentleman farmer, but continued making teapots at Vauxhall with David until they were declared bankrupt in 1700. John Philip became a merchant in Dublin in 1701 and was supplied with Chinese porcelain, imported by the British East India Company, by David during the period 1715 to 1722. The primary importance of the Elers brothers to the history of English ceramics is in their introduction of sprigged, red stoneware to Staffordshire, where it was revived in the 1740s; secondly in their use of slip-casting with plaster of Paris moulds; and thirdly in their use of lathe-turning to achieve lightness and sharp profile. Although David claimed in 1693 that he had learnt the secret of making salt-glazed stoneware at Cologne, excavations on the Bradwell Wood site have proved that the brothers made only redware there and were not responsible for introducing this important process to Staffordshire.

ODNB (on John Philip Elers)
G. Elliott: *John and David Elers and Their Contemporaries* (London, 1998)

Elfe [Elphe], **Thomas** (*b* 1719; *d* 1775). American cabinetmaker whose workshop was in Charleston, SC. His account book (1768–75) is an important document in the history of 18th-century American furniture. His furniture is signed with a diamond and figure eight, and is often decorated with a fretwork pattern of circular or oval shapes.

S. A. Humphrey: *Thomas Elfe: Cabinetmaker* (Charleston, SC, 1995)
B. L. Rauschenberg and J. Bevins jr: *The Furniture of Charleston, 1680–1820*, iii (Winston-Salem, NC, 2003), pp. 995–1004

Elizabethan Revival. Term used to describe an antiquarian style popular in England from the 1830s to the 1860s, inspired by the Elizabethan style of the 16th century. Designs for Elizabethan-style furniture first appeared in Rudolf Ackermann's *Repository of Arts* in 1817, although the style was not widely popular until the 1830s.

In interiors the great hall was revived as the most important room in the house. Fireplaces were 16th century in style: the wainscot was oak, and plaster ceilings were of lozenge design with pendant bosses. By the 1850s there was a preference for furniture in darker woods; early oak pieces were collected or new furniture was made that incorporated the Elizabethan and Jacobean styles. Buffets, cupboards and four-poster beds were popular; high-backed chairs had spool- or spiral-turned uprights and carved cresting in the spirit of 17th-century vernacular furniture. A large collection of Elizabethan Revival furniture can be seen at Charlecote Park, Warwicks, NT. Two manufacturers well known for their production of Elizabethan Revival furniture were John Gregory Crace and W. Gibbs Rogers (1792–1872).

In silverware and ceramics there was a revival of Elizabethan-style covered salts, beakers and tankards. Plain surfaces are predominant, the decoration being confined to coats of arms, strapwork, bands of cinquefoils, egg-and-tongue or overlapping laurel leaves. Women's toilet cases from this period have silver or silver-gilt mounts imitating Flemish strapwork, and travelling writing cases were often shaped like caskets. Snuff-boxes in the shape of a boar's head or pointed Elizabethan shoes were also popular. Potteries in Staffordshire reintroduced salt glazes, which gave an authentic mottled appearance to stoneware jugs, mugs and tankards. A few studio potteries made tiles and platters decorated with coloured earthenware slip trailed or combed in the manner of such 17th-century potters as Thomas Toft (*d* 1689). The style persisted in the decorative arts until the 1920s and 1930s.

Elkington, G(eorge) R(ichards) (*b* Birmingham, 17 Oct 1801; *d* Pool Park, Denbs, 22 Sept 1865). English silver manufacturer. In 1815 he was apprenticed to a small, family-owned silver manufacturing business in Birmingham, which he eventually inherited. The firm made spectacle-frames, snuff-boxes and silver-gilt 'toys' and bottle mounts. Between 1829 and 1836 he was in partnership with his cousin Henry Elkington (*c.* 1810–52), during a period of much interest in electrometallurgy. G. R. Elkington hired a metallurgist, Alexander Parkes, and patronized chemists in the attempt to develop the electrogilding and ELECTROPLATING of base metal articles for commercial production. From 1836 to 1838 he registered several patents and in 1840 took out a patent on an improved method of electroplating discovered by John Wright, a Birmingham surgeon. Elkington's electroplate, perfected by Parkes, revolutionized the manufacture of plated silver and by the late 1850s had superseded almost all of the trade in Sheffield plate. Elkington opened a new factory in 1840, and in 1842 a wealthy pen manufacturer, Josiah Mason (*d* 1859), joined the firm, which became Elkington, Mason & Co. until Mason's retirement in 1856 and Elkington & Co. thereafter. Determined to retain exclusive rights, Elkington bought others' patents or hired his competitors and for large fees granted other firms, notably Christofle et Cie in France, licences to manufacture electroplate under his patent.

By 1847 Elkington, Mason & Co. was mass-producing large, electroplated silver wares, for example salvers, trays, dishes and meat covers. The firm also produced a wide range of brassware. The trade catalogues illustrate electroplated silver and brass tableware in revival styles offered by the firm, finished and polished in the factory by hand. Elkington also engaged sculptors and designers, including Léonard Morel-Ladeuil (*c.* 1820–88) and Auguste Willms (*fl* 1848–99), to design electrotype versions of ancient Greek and Roman, Renaissance and 18th-century pieces (e.g. 'Inventions' vase, 1863; London, V&A). In the 20th century the company supplied flatware for the White Star Line (including the Titanic) and for the Royal Yacht Britannia. The company has changed hands several times, but still trades as Elkington & Co.; its products still include Dubarry, the tableware supplied to the *Titanic*.

ODNB

Elliott, John (*b* 1713; *d* 1781). American cabinetmaker whose workshop in Philadelphia specialized in mirrors, notably fretwork mirrors but also carved mirrors in the Chippendale style. On his retirement in 1776 the business passed to Elliott's son John Elliott (1739–1810), who also manufactured and imported mirrors.

A. C. Prime: *John Elliott, Cabinet and Looking-glass Maker of Philadelphia* (Philadelphia, 1924)

Elmslie, George Grant (*b* Huntly, Scotland, 20 Feb 1871; *d* Chicago, IL, 23 April 1952). American architect and designer. Elmslie settled in Chicago with his family in 1884. After attending high school, he entered the office of Joseph Lyman Silsbee (1848–1913), where Frank Lloyd Wright and George W. Maher were already employed. In 1889 he joined the firm of Adler & Sullivan, becoming chief draughtsman in 1893. He continued in this capacity with Louis Sullivan after the partnership dissolved in 1895. In addition to the usual tasks of preparing contract documents and working drawings, he became increasingly responsible for the ornament that Sullivan lavished on the exterior and interior of his buildings.

In 1909 Elmslie established a partnership with the architect William Grey Purcell (1880–1965) in Minneapolis. The firm of Purcell & Elmslie was primarily an architectural practice, but Elmslie also designed carpets and complete sets of furniture for the houses that the firm designed. His best known designs are carpets with plant motifs and chairs with splats pierced by floral fretwork.

G. G. Elmslie: Drawings for Architectural Ornament, 1902–1936 (exh. cat by D. Gebhard, Santa Barbara, U. CA, A. Gals, 1968)
J. A. Barter: 'The Prairie School and Decorative Arts at the Art Institute of Chicago', *Mus. Stud.*, xxi/2 (1995), pp. 112–33

Elphe, Thomas. *See* ELFE, THOMAS.

Elsinor Tapestry Workshop. Danish tapestry manufactory established in 1577 by King Frederick II of Denmark at Kronberg Castle in Helsingør (Eng. Elsinor). The workshop was managed by the Flemish painter and tapestry-weaver Hans Knieper (*d* 2 Nov 1587) and the tapestry-weaver Antonius da Corte (*d* 1578). Their major work was a series of 43 tapestries in wool and silk (1581–5; 15 preserved, Copenhagen, Nmus. and Helsingør, Kronborg Slot) ordered for the castle's vast ballroom. The series depicted 100 Danish kings, from the legendary King Dan to Frederick himself. Full-length portraits of one or two monarchs appeared on each tapestry, set in landscapes stylistically related to those produced by the Brussels tapestry workshops. Each king's biography in German verse appeared in an inscription panel above his portrait, with his crest in another narrower panel at the bottom, and both panels had ornamental surrounds. The surviving pieces show a wealth of detail, including flowers, animals and people hunting. The ornamentation, with festoons of flowers and fruit, is based on the Flemish version of Italian Renaissance decoration, known through the engravings of such artists as Cornelis Floris. Also belonging to

this series of tapestries is a magnificent seat canopy for Frederick II (1585–6; Stockholm, Nmus.) worked in wool, silk and gold and silver thread. It is embellished with the royal crests and shows three large female figures representing Justice, Temperance and Fortitude, surrounded by grotesque ornamentation partly inspired by Hans Vredeman de Vries. After Knieper's death in 1587 the workshop in Helsingør closed.

Elton, Sir Edmund (*b* 1846; *d* 1920). English art potter. In 1883 Elton succeeded to a baronetcy and inherited Clevedon Court, a manor house (now National Trust) in the North Somerset town of Clevedon. In 1881 he had established Sunflower Pottery (in the manor house), where he made pottery influenced both by his allegiance to the AESTHETIC MOVEMENT and by a wide range of national and historical styles. He experimented with glazes as well as forms, and *c.* 1902 moved away from clear glazes to the metallic glazes with which he is now associated. The clock tower in the town of Clevedon is decorated in Elton ware.

M. Haslam: *Elton Ware: The Pottery of Sir Edmund Elton* (Shepton Beauchamp, 1989)

Email [Fr.: 'enamel']. *Email* ink is the ink used on glass and porcelain; *émail ombrant* is a form of pottery decoration (introduced in the 1840s) in which the impressions of the design appear as shadows; *émail brun* is not an enamel, but a medieval technique whereby an oil varnish (or linseed oil) is burnt into metal (e.g. in the Corona Lucis at Buckfast Abbey in Devon).

Embossing [Fr. *papier gaufré*; Ger. *Blinddruck, Blindpressung*]. Term used in printmaking and the decorative arts to describe an intentional relief produced by stamping or moulding (see colour pl. XI, fig. 1). It is derived from 'boss' (Mid. Eng. boce, bose), meaning a convex protuberance. Embossing on metal is achieved by casting, CHASING or REPOUSSÉ.

For information of embossed bookbinding *see under* BOOK-BINDING.

A. Stohlman and A. Stohlman: *The Art of Embossing Leather* (Fort Worth, TX, 1986)
E. M. Harris: *Printing Presses in the Graphic Arts Collection: Printing, Embossing, Stamping and Duplicating Devices* (Washington, DC, 1996)

Embroidery. Method of decorating a ground material by stitching, cutting or withdrawing threads or by applying beads, pieces of fabric etc. The earliest surviving embroideries show an outstanding mastery of technique; the saddle-cloth and hanging discovered at Pazyryk (4th century BC; St Petersburg, Hermitage), for example, are decorated in brightly coloured felt appliqué with kings, horsemen, fighting animals and mythical beasts. A Chinese silk cloth

Embroidered gloves worn by King Edward VI at his coronation, England, 16th century (Alnwick Castle, Northumberland)

embroidered with birds and foliage in chain stitch was found with them, and the existence of an established trade in embroidery is confirmed by a similar find of woollen embroidery decorated in couched work with a cavalcade of horsemen between borders of fighting griffins and dragons, probably from Bactria or southern Russia, together with Chinese chain stitch embroideries, in the tombs of Noin Ula in northern Mongolia, which date from the 1st century BC to the 1st century AD.

The oldest European embroideries include two from France: a gold-embroidered border of *c.* AD 590–600 from a tomb formerly believed to be that of Queen Arnegunde at Saint-Denis and a silk robe of *c.* 660–64, associated with Queen Bathilde, embroidered with motifs imitating jewellery, from the treasury at Chelles (Chelles, Mus. Mun. Alfred-Bonno). From England there survive the chasuble of SS Harlindis and Relindis (*c.* 800; Maaseik, St Katharinakerk), worked with silk and gold and silver thread, and the stole and maniple of St Cuthbert (909–16; Durham Cathedral;), which are densely embroidered with couched gold thread and coloured silks. Three mantles associated with the Holy Roman Emperor Henry II and his wife Kunigunde (Bamberg, Domschatzkam.), of silk embroidered with gold thread and coloured silks, were worked in southern Germany, perhaps in Regensburg, as was possibly the chasuble that was later converted into the coronation mantle of the Hungarian kings (1031; Budapest, N. Mus.). The 12th-century coronation mantle of the Holy Roman emperors (Vienna, Schatzkam.) is spectacularly decorated with two enormous lions attacking camels, worked in couched gold, enamels, beads and jewels on a red silk ground. The kufic inscription embroidered on it states that it was made in the royal workshops in Sicily in 1133–4. The chasuble formerly associated with Thomas Becket (Fermo Cathedral), which was em-

broidered in Almería in Islamic Spain in 1116, is also dated by its kufic inscription. In contrast to these rich embroideries are those made of wool and linen, notably the BAYEUX TAPESTRY (Bayeux, Mus. Tap.), with brightly coloured wools on linen (see colour pl. XI, fig. 4).

The large hanging in Girona Cathedral, which shows *Christ* surrounded by scenes of the *Creation*, was produced at about the same time but in a very different style; the whole surface is covered with laid and couched coloured wools.

Fine linen entirely covered with underside-couched gold thread and silk embroidery in split stitch is a feature of Italian, French and English ecclesiastical embroidery from the late 12th century to the 14th. OPUS ANGLICANUM was greatly prized for the quality of its work and the delicacy of its coloured figurative subjects set against gold-embroidered silk or velvet grounds. Metal thread embroidery in a different style was made in Germany, for example the antependium of *c.* 1230 from Rupertsberg, which is decorated with majestic figures in silver and gold on a ruby-red silk ground. *Opus teutonicum* was made in German-speaking areas, notably Switzerland, Hessen, Lower Saxony and Lübeck: this was white linen embroidered with white linen thread and sometimes a little coloured silk or wool in a variety of stitches, including drawn-thread work. Early examples of whitework survive in many European countries.

During the 14th century plain velvet began to be used as a ground. At first the embroidery was worked through fine silk or linen laid on the surface of the velvet, but later, in a quicker but coarser technique, it was worked separately and applied. At the same time fine silk embroideries, skilfully shaded in the needle-painting technique, were made in the Italian city states, notably Florence and Venice, and also in central Europe. Produced initially in Bohemia but influencing a wide surrounding area, this embroidery had a distinctive style marked by the emotional power of its figurative subjects.

In the south Netherlands the needle-painting technique was combined, in the early 15th century, with a new way of shading laid gold threads with coloured silks to achieve a metallic, shot-silk effect known as *or nué*. The most famous example is probably the large mass set (*c.* 1425–75; Vienna, Schatzkam.), almost certainly worked in Brussels, which was commissioned by Philip the Good of Burgundy and given by him to the Order of the Golden Fleece. The designs were based on the work of contemporary artists, as was also the practice in Italy, where the *or nué* technique was employed to work pictorial pieces in sharp perspective, as for example the scenes from the *Life of St John the Baptist* designed by Antonio Pollaiuolo for a set of vestments (1466–79) for Florence Cathedral (Florence, Mus. Opera Duomo). The use of raised or padded embroidery also developed at this date. It was sometimes confined to the moulded borders of pictorial pieces, as in many Spanish embroideries, but it was also used in three-dimensional figurative work, particularly in Bohemia and Austria.

The number of surviving secular embroideries increases from the mid-16th century. Many were made domestically or within insular communities, where they later formed the basis of peasant traditions, but the majority come from professional workshops established in the major centres to serve a discerning clientele. During the 16th, 17th and 18th centuries embroiderers provided vestments and items of secular dress, wall coverings for whole rooms, pictorial hangings, canopies, valances and bed curtains, a variety of covers, cushions, carpets and, by the late 17th century, upholstery, as well as a host of smaller items, in a wide variety of techniques (see colour pl. XII, fig. 1).

Thus, during the 16th century and early 17th, Renaissance ornament designs were embroidered in outline stitches on linen covers and items of dress; furnishings of silk and velvet were decorated in appliqué with Renaissance strapwork or swirling Baroque foliage; needle-painting techniques were used on large woollen hangings and on more delicate silk pieces; and canvas-based seat furniture and wall and screen panels were worked in cross and tent stitches. By the mid-18th century the old technique of inlaid appliqué had begun to change its form, and by the end of the century European printed cottons were widely used in a combination of appliqué and patchwork techniques.

Despite time-lags and regional variations, professional workshops followed the general stylistic progression from Renaissance to Baroque, from Rococo to Neo-classicism, and embroidery shared common design sources with woven silks, printed cottons, ceramics and other decorative arts. The controlled use

Embroidered curtain, England, early 18th century (London, Victoria and Albert Museum)

of decoration in the Neo-classical period sharply reduced the amount of embroidery applied to furnishings and dress and also led to a simplification of techniques and patterns. Some elaborate room settings in the Etruscan and Egyptian styles (e.g. Lyon, Mus. Hist. Tissus and Paris, Mobilier N.) were produced in France in the early 19th century, worked largely in appliqué and chain stitch, but they were not typical of embroidery as a whole.

Professional workshops were mainly engaged in working vestments for the Catholic Church, ceremonial and military furnishings and dress (often almost entirely in metal threads) and, in contrast, exceptionally fine whitework. In the first half of the 19th century there was a steady decline in standards of design in a coarsening of techniques. Thus delicate whitework gave way to broderie anglaise, and needle-painting with silk threads gave way to canvas work.

In the mid-19th century avant-garde church architects in England, notably A. W. N. Pugin and G. E. Street (1824–81), strove to improve standards of embroidery. Many later architects were to follow their lead in seeing textile furnishings as an essential feature of secular and ecclesiastic interiors. Embroidery was the first textile craft with which William Morris became involved: during the late 1850s and the 1860s he experimented with woollen threads on wool and linen grounds to make hangings decorated with floral and pictorial subjects. Morris drew his inspiration from historical embroideries, but his designs were never simply derivative. This is also true of the followers of the Arts and Crafts Movement throughout Europe and the USA in the latter part of the century. Most were influenced by the simpler embroideries of the past; linen and wool were favoured over silk, though plain silk was used to considerable effect in some of the bold appliqué pieces by such designers as M. H. Baillie Scott. At the end of the century embroidery was used by several designers working in the Art Nouveau style, for which the fluidity of the technique was particularly suited. Progressive colleges of art and design throughout Europe emphasized the importance of design, while techniques, though worked to a high standard, were usually relatively simple. By contrast, the professional workshops were again using a full range of rich materials and techniques for both secular and ecclesiastical furnishings and dress. Elaborate effects were also created by embroidery machines, which had been used for the commercial production of white cotton and coloured silk embroidery from the mid-19th century.

The developments of the late 19th century continued into the 20th with an increasingly marked separation, in design and technique, between commercial work (both hand and machine) and that of artist-craftsmen and amateurs. Although within the schools, colleges and artistic communities there was an emphasis on the craft aspect of the technique, there was also an increasing tendency to follow the stylistic developments in fine and graphic art. From the late 1950s there was a resurgence of interest in

Sioux baby-carrier, embroidered quillwork (Berlin, Ethnologisches Museum)

embroidery, and although initially based on ecclesiastical work this spread to all branches of the craft. In the 21st century century hand- and machine-embroidery are frequently combined, photographic, paint and dye techniques are incorporated; and a variety of materials is used, from traditional textiles to wood and plastic. Embroidery has become a recognized form of gallery art.

A. H. Christie: *English Medieval Embroidery* (Oxford, 1938)

M. Schuette and S. Müller-Christensen: *The Art of Embroidery* (London, 1964)

H. Bridgeman and E. Drury, eds: *Needlework: An Illustrated History* (New York and London, 1978)

K. Staniland: *Embroiderers, Medieval Craftsmen* (London, 1991)

L. Synge: *Art of Embroidery: History of Style and Technique* (Woodbridge, Suffolk, 2001)

J. Bertin-Guest: *Chinese Embroidery: Traditional Techniques* (Iola, 2003)

I. Denamur and P. Ferbos: *Moroccan Textile Embroidery* (Paris, 2003)

E. E. Guðjónsson: *Traditional Icelandic Embroidery* (Kópavogur, 2003)

M. M. Brooks: *English Embroideries of the Sixteenth and Seventeeth Centuries: In the Collection of the Ashmolean Museum* (Oxford, 2004)

Y. Y. Chung: *Silken Threads: A History of Embroidery in China, Korea, Japan, and Vietnam* (New York, 2005)

Emens Mennicken, Jan. *See* MENNICKEN, JAN EMENS.

Emerald. Green variety of BERYL, mined in Upper Egypt and India from antiquity and in Colombia both before and after the Spanish Conquest. Nero is said to have watched gladiatorial contests through an emerald. The two best-known emeralds are the Devonshire Emerald (London, Nat. Hist. Mus.) and the Patricia Emerald (New York, Amer. Mus. Nat. Hist.). The most famous historical emeralds are the 453 emeralds (totalling 1521 carats) that were taken from the Incas and used in 1593 to decorate the gold Crown of the Andes; its present location is not known.

Emes. English family of silversmiths. John Emes (1762–1808) was a prominent Regency silversmith who specialized in silver tea and coffee services. On his death his widow, Rebecca (*fl* 1808–29), entered into a partnership with Edward Barnard (1781–1846); their firm became very large, and made both domestic silver (some of which was exported) and presentational plate, notably the Doncaster gold cups from 1821 to 1829.

Enamel. Vitreous or glass paste used in a variety of ways to decorate a metal or, more rarely, ceramic or glass surface (see colour pl. XII, fig. 2).

1. Materials. 2. Techniques.

1. MATERIALS. The enamelling process is the fusing of a vitreous substance on to a prepared metal surface, either in a kiln (furnace) or with the application of intense local heat (e.g. with a blowtorch), at temperatures ranging from 300°C for the softest (opaque) enamels to 850°C for the hardest (transparent) enamels. The vitreous compound is itself called enamel, but it is the bipartite, heat-bonded combination of often noble metal with it that is referred to as enamel.

The vitreous substance is composed of sand or flint, soda or potash and sometimes red lead. These ingredients are heated together (fritted) for 15 hours to form an almost colourless transparent flux. Metallic oxides are added to the mixture to produce the colours. The first known true enamel, found in small quantities on Greek gold jewellery (4th century BC), was blue, made by the addition of cobalt oxide. Copper oxide gives turquoise and some greens; gold oxide gives red and oxides of antimony or uranium give yellow. Different quantities of ingredients produce enamels that are 'soft' or 'hard': soft enamel, containing a higher proportion of red lead, fuses at a lower temperature but can be scratched easily. Transparent and translucent enamels fuse at the highest temperature and are the most durable; all enamels, however, are damaged by shock, scratching and flexing. Variations in the combination of ingredients or of additives result in the four accepted categories of enamel: opaque, opalescent, translucent and painted transparent, terms that indicate their fired visual and physical state.

The metal base to which enamel is fused was historically noble (i.e. gold or silver). Platinum is rarely used, except in a 5% alloy in platinum-silver. In its pure state, even keyed, platinum shows poor adherence to enamel. This is due to its extremely high melting point (1630°C) and rapid rates of expansion and contraction. Copper was increasingly used as a base from the 1740s. It became particularly fashionable in England at the Battersea Enamel Factory, London (est. 1753), which produced wares including enamelled snuffboxes and wine-labels. Such alloys as bronze have also been extensively used.

Before the addition of enamel, the metal surface is prepared to remove oxides or grease: it is annealed (heated to red hot) and then immersed in an acid bath (pickled). The acid, which is usually diluted, may be nitric (undiluted), for copper, or sulphuric, for gold or silver. The metal is then alkalized and the powdered enamel applied as soon as possible to arrest renewed oxidation. Pure gold does not oxidize, hence its popularity as a metal base. As some colours react chemically with certain metals during firing, the metal is often first coated with a flux.

The enamel is ground to a fine powder from the frit by pulverization, washed under water and then dried. It is then mixed to a paste with water or, for painted enamel, a volatile oil such as spike (lavender oil) and applied to the prepared metal surface, which may also have been worked (etched, engraved, modelled, formed and soldered) and finally fired. Enamel fuses at a lower temperature than the metals to which it is applied, although *grand feu* colours (those that have a melting point of *c.* 850°C) approach the melting point of silver. Due to the different expansion co-efficients of glass and metal (metal contracts at a faster rate than the enamel), fired objects are subject to enormous stresses on cooling. To counteract the buckling and cracking, the metal 'back' is counter-enamelled with a layer of flux of equal thickness to the surface enamel, which minimizes the problem.

2. TECHNIQUES.

(i) Cloisonné. (ii) Champlevé. (iii) Basse taille. (iv) En ronde bosse. (v) Plique à jour. (vi) En résille sur verre. (vii) Painted. (viii) Surrey.

(i) Cloisonné [Fr.: 'cell-work']. A metal surface, usually of finely beaten gold, is decorated by soldering, edge-on, metal fillets of flattened wire. These delicate cells (*cloisons*) are filled with coloured and powdered enamel, fired and then ground flat with carborundum, exposing the gold pattern beneath. *Cloisons* mimic jewels, create rigidity and also break the surface of the item; it is very difficult to enamel a large surface (*en plein*) evenly. Byzantine enamels, developed from Greek antecedents, were generally cloisonné. From the 9th to the 12th century AD precious cloisonné enamelling, as seen in the Pala d'Oro altarpiece (AD 976; present setting 1342–5; Venice, S Marco), was extensively used. In the later Middle Ages, the technique was also referred to as *email de plique*. Historically, both opaque and translucent enamels have been used for cloisonné. In China the technique was introduced during the Yuan period (1279–1368) by Islamic artisans; in India the technique was well established by the 16th century, although no extant objects predate *c.* 1600; early Islamic cloisonné enamelling was possibly inspired by Byzantine enamelling and was used from the 10th to the 15th century and again in the 18th and 19th centuries. In Russia the earliest enamels date from the 11th to the 12th century and were influenced by Byzantine enamels. From the 16th century fine, twisted gold or silver wire filigree *cloisons* were used to produce an effect resembling complex indigenous embroidery.

(ii) Champlevé [Fr.: 'raised field']. This is a potentially economical alternative to cloisonné enamelling and is therefore often used on larger objects. Into a thicker metal base—which can be gold but is more often bronze—troughs are gouged, or in modern champlevé, of which Surrey enamel (*see* §(viii) below) is a precursor, cast. The depressions are then filled with powdered enamel, which is fired, and the surface ground flat. In champlevé the metal areas are left plain, engraved, gilded or decorated in other ways, including cloisonné enamel. In Gothic and Chinese champlevé enamelling, the surface metal is generally mercury or fire gilded. Romano-Celtic artists also filled some cells with designs of tiny patterns known as *millefiori* (It.: 'thousand flowers'). The Alfred Jewel (9th century; Oxford, Ashmolean), aesthetically in the 'Celtic' style associated with champlevé, is actually cloisonné. Spectacular Romanesque champlevé, enamelling from Limoges (*see* LIMOGES, §2), southern France, Christian Spain and the Meuse and Rhine valleys, often using gilded copper or bronze, survives from the 12th and 13th centuries. During the Middle Ages large chasses (chests) and reliquaries made in the Limousin were in demand throughout Europe.

(iii) Basse taille [Fr.: 'shallow cut'; It. *lavoro di basso rilievo*]. Chased or engraved metal (often silver or silver gilt) with bas-relief compositions or patterns is entirely covered with translucent enamel. A rich tonal quality is created by the varying degrees of engraving and depth of enamel. Chasing the object also provides key (grip) for the enamel and facilitates application to larger areas. The earliest surviving example of *basse taille* is the chalice of Pope Nicholas IV (1288–92; Assisi, Tesoro Mus. Basilica S Francesco) made by the Italian goldsmith GUCCIO DI MANNAIA. One of the most spectacular examples is the Royal Gold Cup of the Kings of France and England (*c.* 1380–90; London, BM). The Russian goldsmith CARL FABERGÉ developed a method of 'water-marking' precious metals by engraving them with repetitive wavelike patterns, known as *guilloché*, on a rose-engine lathe. Translucent enamels were then applied over the decorated surface.

(iv) En ronde bosse [Fr.: 'in rounded relief'; encrusted enamel]. In France at the end of the 14th century it became possible to decorate three-dimensional objects or very high-relief surfaces with an enamel covering. The objects were often small but precious, as in such Gothic emblems as the Dunstable Swan Jewel (*c.* 1400; London, BM), or the exquisite

Goldenes Rössel (1403–4; Altötting, SS Philipp und Jacob, Schatzkam), the most lavish of all *en ronde bosse* enamels (see colour pl. XII, fig. 3). Technical diffi-culties necessitated keying (roughing) the metal in order to support the enamel covering. There were also problems achieving naturalistic flesh tones, as seen in the figure of the *Virgin* in the house-altar of Albert V, Duke of Bavaria (1573–4; Munich, Resi-denz), in which the gold and polychrome work con-trasts with the glaring, milky-pink skin tones.

(v) Plique à jour [Fr.: 'against the light']. In the late 14th century, under the patronage of the courts of France and Burgundy, this technique developed to display fully the 'stained glass' potential of translu-cent enamel. In a technique related to cloisonné, a network of metal wires or strips is created and set against a metal backing. These cloisons are then filled with translucent enamel and fired; when the backing melts, the enamel is left suspended in the *cloisons*. The Mérode Cup (*c.* 1430; London, V&A), made in Bur-gundy or France, incorporates a band imitating stained-glass windows and is the only extant medi-eval example of this technique. The Chinese made exceptional *plique à jour* vases. René Lalique incor-porated the technique in his jewellery, and at the end of the 19th century the firm of J. Tostrup in Oslo also created magnificent *plique à jour* tableware. In the case of small *cloisons*, surface tension holds the en-amel in place as it is fired, so backing is not required.

(vi) En résille sur verre [Fr.: 'in grooves on glass']. This is a rare form of enamelling that is closely related to the cloisonné technique. A design is cut into a glass ground which is coloured blue or green; the grooves are then lined with gold foil and filled with powdered enamel of extremely low fusibility. The process was introduced by French goldsmiths in the late 16th century and early 17th, on such highly ornamental, valuable objects as pendants and mirror backs. The German engraver Valentin Sezenius is also attributed with works in this technique dating from 1619 to 1625. Roman glassworkers of the 1st century AD may have attempted a similar technique, possibly by pressing molten glass into the *cloisons*.

(vii) Painted. The object, usually made of copper, is covered in a layer of white, opaque enamel and then fired; it is then gradually decorated with coloured enamels, which require different firings. The earliest surviving examples are Netherlandish (*c.* 1425). By the early 16th century Limoges (*see* LIMOGES, §2) had become the centre for painted enamels on copper and the PÉNICAUD family from this town are par-ticularly associated with its development. Nardon (Léonard) Pénicaud used polychrome enamels on a clear, fluxed ground, outlined with dark enamels. The wet enamel is also often scratched with a needle to create delineation or uses *paillons* (small pieces of gold foil) for details. Limoges enamels from *c.* 1535 to *c.* 1575 were principally decorated with grisaille (grey-toned) enamels, which gave a relief effect cre-ated by repeated firings of white, translucent enamels

over a dark ground. Coloured enamels were found to be suitable for painting small portraits, jewelled boxes and plaques, and their popularity spread throughout Europe; the Swiss miniature painter Jean Petitot (1607–91), for example, introduced the tech-nique into England. Painted enamels were intro-duced into China at the court of the Kangxi emperor (*reg* 1662–1722) by Jesuits. Enamel painting eventu-ally led to transfer-printed enamelling in England, first at the York House in Battersea (1753–6) and then at Bilston, in Wednesbury and in Birmingham in the late 18th century.

(viii) Surrey [Stuart]. A short lived, rarely described class of enamelling using cast-brass objects of some-times substantial size as ground for the enamel. The surfaces of the objects were cast in low-relief and generally filled with a bichrome palette of enamel, especially black-and-white or blue-and-white (e.g. Warwick Candle, 1650–60; London, BM). Surrey enamels were made in England in the second half of the 17th century, probably near the brass mill (est. 1649) at Esher, Surrey. Two Germans, Daniel Dia-metrius and his partner Joseph Momma, may have influenced the production of such items as fire-dogs and candlesticks.

A Thousand Years of Enamel (exh. cat. by K. Snowman, London, Wartski, 1971)

C. Baglee and A. Morley: *Enamelled Street Signs* (New York, 1978)

S. Benjamin: *Enamels* (New York, 1983)

M. Campbell: *An Introduction to Medieval Enamels* (London, 1983)

Contemporary British Enamels (exh. cat., Gateshead, Shipley, A.G., 1985)

J. F. Richter: *Antique Enamels for Collectors* (West Chester, PA, 1990)

Enamel twist. Type of glass decoration in which the stem of a wine glass has spiral patterns of opaque white or coloured threads.

Encaustic tile [encaustic brick]. A complex form of TERRACOTTA, where different coloured clays are fired together. In relation to tiles, encaustic (Gr.: 'burnt in') essentially means inlaying clay of one col-our with clay of a contrasting colour. Encaustic tiles were usually made from red-firing clay, and while the tile was still soft, a design was pressed into it with the aid of a wooden stamp. The indentations were then filled with white clay. When finished, the inlaid white design would clearly stand out against the red ground. The medieval practice was to dip the unfired tile in a transparent lead glaze, so that the firing of the tile body, the inlaid pattern and the glaze all took place at the same time. The glaze gave the white clay a slightly yellow tinge and the red ground a deeper red-brown tint. Encaustic tiles were extensively used in the Middle Ages to pave cathedral and church floors and are characterized by such designs as he-raldic emblems, knights on horseback, lions and such stylized floral patterns as the fleur-de-lis.

With the dissolution of the monasteries (1536–40), the encaustic technique fell into disuse, but was revived again during the mid-19th century with the building of Gothic-Revival churches by such English architects as A. W. N. Pugin and such French architects as Viollet-le-Duc. Encaustic tiles were used for the restoration of medieval cathedrals and churches. Such tile manufacturers as Minton in Stoke-on-Trent and Maw & Co. in Broseley, Salop, made thousands of encaustic tiles to satisfy the burgeoning demand from 1860 until the end of the century. A dust-pressed encaustic tile that combined different colours of clay in powder form under pressure before firing was developed by Prosser, Blashfield and Minton in the early 1840s and soon became the standard manufacturing method. The tiles were also used for public and domestic buildings, and to meet the needs of taste and fashion, some were produced in an unglazed form.

Designs for Encaustic and Geometric Tile Pavements, Campbell Brick & Tile Co. and Robert Minton Taylor Tile Works (Stoke on Trent, ?1880–89)
J. K. Wood: 'Encaustic Tiles', *Cer. Rev.*, cxcv (May–June 2002), pp. 56–7
J. K. Wood: 'Encaustic Tile Recipes', *Cer. Rev.*, ccvi (March–April 2004), pp. 51–5

Encoignure. *See under* COMMODE.

Endell, August (*b* Berlin, 12 April 1871; *d* Berlin, 13 April 1925). German architect, designer, writer and teacher. As well as book illustrations and decorative pieces for the art magazines *Pan* and *Dekorative Kunst*, he produced decorative designs for wall reliefs, carpets, textiles, coverings, window glass and lamps. In 1897 he designed his first furniture for his cousin, the historian Kurt Breysig. Endell worked with HERMANN OBRIST, under whose influence his work became characterized by an expressive ornamentation, the bizarre idiom of which seems to be derived from a microscopically observed world of submarine flora and fauna. With Obrist he acted as spokesperson for the new ARTS AND CRAFTS MOVEMENT.

A. Wauschkuhn, E. Torspecken and R. Lösel: *Textildesign: Voysey, Endell, Berger* (Berlin, 2002)

Enderlein, Caspar (*b* Basel, *bapt* 24 June 1560; *d* Nuremberg, 19 April 1633). Swiss pewterer, *Formschneider* and painter. He worked from 1583 in in Nuremberg, where he created models of pewter pots, candlesticks and sconces and may also have produced *Amtsformen* (official patterns or moulds) that masters could lend to each other; according to his own account he was a *Formschneider* (maker of patterns or moulds) and a painter. Enderlein enriched the repertory of form in pewterware by using elements from French Renaissance ornament. He introduced many technical innovations into his craft, and he is credited with producing the first pewter chandelier (untraced) in the Nuremberg area, although no pewter pieces bearing his stamp have been discovered. His idiosyncratic style of ornament appears on pewter tankards, bowls and plates made from the early 17th century until the late Baroque period. Enderlein was more concerned with producing *Edelzinn* (show pewter) pieces than with domestic pewter items.

H. Demiani: *François Briot, Caspar Enderlein und das Edelzinn* (Leipzig, 1897)

Enghalskrug [Ger.: 'narrow-necked jug']. German jug, usually made of faience and sometimes mounted in pewter. The body is normally ovoid, and has a narrow neck and a hinged pewter lid. *Enghalskrüge* were made in the 17th and 18th centuries, initially at HANAU FAIENCE FACTORY and subsequently at factories such as ANSBACH and FRANKFURT AM MAIN FAIENCE FACTORY.

W. Schwartze: *Antike Deutsche Fayence Krüge* (Wuppental, 1977)

Enghien [Flem. Edingen]. Belgian centre of tapestry production. The Hainault town of Enghien (between Brussels and Tournai) probably began tapestry production in the late 14th century or early 15th. By 1535 Enghien weavers were required to add the city and weaver's marks to the borders of tapestries. In the second decade of the 16th century there was a vigorous expansion of the tapestry industry, which lasted until *c.* 1560. The two regents of the Netherlands, Margaret of Austria, Duchess of Savoy, and Mary, Queen of Hungary, and many other prominent figures ordered one or more series. The religious conflict of 1566 and the looting of Antwerp in 1576 severely affected the tapestry industry in Enghien, and many weavers left the city. On 8 August 1685 Nicolaas van der Leen, the last tapestryworker in Enghien, gave all of the guild's income to the Brotherhood of Our Lady and the poor of the town.

It is unlikely that tapestry cartoons were ever produced in Enghien as the industry was not big enough, and workshops used cartoons from other cities or borrowed them from the client who commissioned the work. Producers therefore found it more economical to make large-leaved *verdures* (e.g. *c.* 1550; Vienna, Ksthist. Mus.). The designs for these were cheaper, and their execution far less time-consuming. Pictorial tapestries were also produced at Enghien; a particular characteristic of these tapestries was the flesh tints, which the weavers in Oudenaarde tried to emulate in the 16th century. Although the work from Enghien was often mediocre, several handsome pieces have been preserved that are comparable with Brussels tapestries. These include the *Armorial Tapestries of Margaret of Austria* (1528; Budapest, Mus. Applied A.), the *Fall of Phaeton* (*c.* 1560; Landshut, Burg Trausnitz) and the colourful tapestries made by Claas de Dobbeleer, with large leaves, flowers and birds (examples in Vienna, Ksthist. Mus.).

G. Delmarcel: *Tapisseries anciennes d'Enghien* (Mons, 1980)
G. Delmarcel: *Tapisseries d'Enghien du XVIe siècle: Verdures avec jeux d'enfants* (Lièges and Brussels, 1983)
A. Mitchell: "La plus belle chose du monde" and the Enghien Tapestries at Dyrham Park and Maiden Bradley', *Apollo*, cxlix/446 (April 1999), pp. 33–7

Engine-turning. Engraving of symmetrical decorative patterns on metals by turning on a lathe.

England. Ceramics *see* BELLEVUE; BELPER POTTERY; BOOTE, T. AND R.; BOURNE, JOSEPH, & SON; BOW PORCELAIN FACTORY; BRAMPTON; BRETBY ART POTTERY; BRISTOL, §1; BURMANTOFT; CASTLE HEDINGHAM; CASTLEFORD POTTERY; CAUGHLEY PORCELAIN FACTORY; CHELSEA PORCELAIN FACTORY; CISTERCIAN WARE; COALPORT PORCELAIN FACTORY; CROUCH WARE; DENBY POTTERY; DERBY; DOULTON CERAMIC FACTORY; ISLEWORTH POTTERY; JACKFIELD POTTERY; LAMBETH; LAVERSTOCK; LEEDS POTTERY; LIMEHOUSE PORCELAIN FACTORY; LINTHORPE ART POTTERY; LIVERPOOL; LONDON, §1; LONGTON HALL PORCELAIN FACTORY; LOWESTOFT PORCELAIN FACTORY; LYVEDEN; MEIGH POTTERY; METROPOLITAN SLIPWARE; MINTON CERAMIC FACTORY; MOCHA WARE; NEW HALL FACTORY; NOTTINGHAM, §1. CERAMICS; NUNEATON; OMEGA WORKSHOPS; PEARL POTTERY; PEARL WARE; PILKINGTON'S ROYAL LANCASTRIAN POTTERY; PINXTON PORCELAIN FACTORY; PRATT, F. & R.; ROCKINGHAM CERAMIC FACTORY; ROGERS POTTERY; ROYAL STAFFORD CHINA; SOUTHWARK; SPODE CERAMIC WORKS; SPRIGGED WARE; STAFFORD POTTERY; STAFFORDSHIRE; STAMFORD; TICKNALL; TYNESIDE; WEDGWOOD; WELSH WARE; WHITEHAVEN; WILLOW PATTERN; WOOLLAMS & CO.; WORCESTER; WRENTHORPE; WROTHAM.

Furniture *see* COTSWOLD SCHOOL; GOMME, E., LTD; HIGH WYCOMBE; LONDON, §2.; MARSH & JONES; MARSH & TATHAM; OMEGA WORKSHOPS.

Glass *see* BACCHUS, GEORGE, & SONS; BRISTOL, §2; CLAYTON & BELL; CRUTCHED FRIARS GLASSHOUSE; HEATON, BUTLER & BAYNE; LAVERS, BARRAUD & WESTLAKE; LONDON, §3; NEWCASTLE UPON TYNE; POWELL, JAMES, & SONS; STOURBRIDGE; WEALD GLASS.

Metalwork *see* BATTERSEA ENAMEL FACTORY; BIRMINGHAM; BRISTOL, §3; COALBROOKDALE IRON COMPANY; DIXON, JAMES, & SONS; DON POTTERY; LAMBERT & RAWLINGS; LONDON, §4; RUNDELL, BRIDGE & RUNDELL; SHEFFIELD.

Objects of vertu *see* BILSTON; CLOCKS AND WATCHES, §§4(I)(A) AND 5(I)(A); JET, §1; LONDON, §5; SNUFF BOXES AND SNUFF BOTTLES, §1(I); TUNBRIDGE WARE.

Textiles *see* AXMINSTER; BEDFORDSHIRE; BUCKINGHAMSHIRE; COGGESHALL LACE; EXETER; FULHAM; HALIFAX; HONITON LACE; KIDDERMINSTER; LONDON, §6; MORTLAKE TAPESTRY FACTORY; NORTHAMPTONSHIRE; NOTTINGHAM, §2; OMEGA WORKSHOPS; OPUS ANGLICANUM; SANDERSON, ARTHUR, & SONS LTD; SHELDON TAPESTRY FACTORY; SOHO; SILVER STUDIO; WILTON; WINDSOR TAPESTRY FACTORY.

Wallpaper *see* JEFFREY & CO.; LIGHTBOWN, ASPINALL & CO.; POTTER & CO.; SANDERSON, AR-

Stoneware Vase No. 661 by Harrison McIntosh, stoneware with off-white glaze and blue and black engobe, h. 387 mm, diam. 330 mm, 1966 (Washington, DC, National Museum of American Art)

THUR, & SONS LTD; SHAND KYDD LTD; SILVER STUDIO.

Engobe. Coating of SLIP applied to pottery to obscure its natural colour and to provide a ground through which SGRAFFITO decorations can be made. The engobe can be variously coloured; in Islamic pottery it is usually white or red.

G. Rowan: 'Versatilecone 06–6 Clays and Engobes', *Cer. Mthly.*, xlviii/6 (June–Aug 2000), pp. 118–19
K. Martz: 'Decorate with Engobes!', *Cer. Mthly.*, l/5 (May 2002), pp.86–9 [originally published Feb 1953, i/2]

Engraving. Process of cutting into a hard material. As a decorative technique, engraving is used on a variety of materials, such as metal and ivory. The term is mostly commonly associated with the technique of intaglio printmaking in which an image is cut with tools into a plate from which multiple impressions may be made; the term is also applied to the resulting print, which has characteristic lines created by the tools and techniques of cutting. The incised image, which lies below the plate's surface, is filled with ink, and then pressure is used to force the paper into the inked lines, creating a slightly raised three-dimensional line and an embossed platemark.

The printing of images from engraved metal plates began in the 15th century and spread to Asia from the 16th. Woodblock engraving had been used in Japan from the 8th century to make prints of religious texts under the auspices of Buddhist temples and the aristocracy, but the earliest copperplate engravings in Japan date to the 16th century. In China the influence of European graphic art spread as early as the Ming period (1368–1644), continuing in the Qing (1644–1911). Western engravings were the model for the *Chengshi moyuan* given to Cheng Dayue by Matteo Ricci (1552–1610), and the Jesuits were involved in printmaking activities in China in the 17th and 18th centuries. The technique of copperplate-engraving was introduced into South-east Asia in the 16th century by Portuguese, Spanish and Dutch colonizers.

B. Hunnisett: *A Dictionary of British Steel Engravers* (Leigh-on-Sea, 1980)

Pictures for the Parlour: The English Reproductive Print from 1775 to 1900 (exh. cat. by B. D. Rix, Toronto, A.G. Ont., 1983)

R. Leaf: *Etching, Engraving and other Intaglio Printmaking Techniques* (New York, 1984)

Colour into Line: Turner and the Art of Engraving (exh. cat. by A. Lyles and D. Perkins, London, Tate, 1989)

D. Landau and P. Parshall: *The Renaissance Print, 1470–1550* (New Haven and London, 1994)

S. Klossowski de Rola: *The Golden Game: Alchemical Engravings of the Seventeenth Century* (New York, 1997)

Early Netherlandish Engraving, c. 1440–1540 (exh. cat. by U. Mayr-Harting; Oxford, Ashmolean, 1997)

B. Hunnisett: *Engraved on Steel: The History of Picture Production Using Steel Plates* (Aldershot, Hants, 1998)

P. Fuhring: *Ornament Prints in the Rijksmuseum II: The Seventeenth Century*, Amsterdam, Rijksmus. (Rotterdam, 2004)

A. Griffiths: *Prints for Books: Book Illustration in France, 1760–1800* (London, 2004)

J. Buchanan-Brown: *Early Victorian Illustrated Books: Britain, France and Germany, 1820–1860* (London, 2005)

Engrêlure. Notched edge attached to a border in LACE or needlework. Until the end of the 19th century such edges were said to be 'engrailed'.

Entre-fenêtre [Fr.: 'between-window']. Tapestry panel designed to fit between two windows, usually part of a larger set of tapestries.

Epergne [Fr. *épargne*: 'saving']. Type of dining-table centrepiece. Usually made in silver, it has a large central basin or basket with branches supporting candle holders and small baskets or dishes for fruit, sweetmeats and pickles. Epergnes appeared in France and England after 1700, when the most elaborate versions included a tureen, casters, salts, cruets and spice-boxes. From the 1760s cheaper versions with cut-glass bowls were also available. The epergne continued in popularity in the 19th century and was possibly the forerunner of the dessert stand.

Epischofer, **Hans** (*d* 1585). German goldsmith. He was a native of Augsburg who in 1561 moved to Nuremberg, where he specialized in the engraving of scientific instruments, especially globes, astrolabes and navigational instruments. Examples of his work are preserved in the Germanisches Nationalmuseum in Nuremberg.

Epistyle. *See* ARCHITRAVE.

Erfurt. German centre of faience production. Erfurt (the capital of Thuringia) had a faience factory between 1712 and 1792. The factory made stoves and tableware, notably brightly coloured cylindrical tankards.

Epergne by Thomas Pitts, silver with cut-glass bowls, h. 368 mm, London, 1764–5 (London, Victoria and Albert Museum)

Erman, Giacomo. *See* HERMAN, GIACOMO.

Erp, Dirk Van. *See* VAN ERP, DIRK.

Escritoire [scrutoire]. Writing-desk constructed to contain stationery and documents. The term can denote either a portable desk consisting of a set of drawers enclosed by a sloping front that can be opened on hinges to provide a surface for writing, or a full-sized bureau or secrétaire (also called a secretary); in American use, it denotes a desk surmounted by a bookcase.

Escutcheon. Heraldic shield. The term is used in a transferred sense to denote a shield-shaped key-hole plate or name plate.

Esherick, Wharton (*b* 1889; *d* 1970). American furniture-maker, sculptor and poet. He produced custom-made furniture from the 1920s in the tradition of the late 19th-century Arts and Crafts Movement, and is now regarded as the founder of the American studio furniture movement.

The Wharton Esherick Museum: Studio and Collection (Paoli, PA, 1984)

Espagnolette. Term used in English in two unrelated senses. It can denote either the hinged fastening of a French window or a type of MASCARON, specifically a female head surrounded by a stiff ruff, widely used as a motif in French Régence and Louis XV furniture, notably by CHARLES CRESSENT (e.g. commode, *c.* 1730; London, Wallace).

Estampille. Maker's mark stamped (not branded) on a piece of French furniture. The estampille was

Bernard van Risen Burgh II: escritoire, 839×1812×487 mm (Versailles, Chateaux de Versailles et de Trianon)

obligatory from 1751 for all furniture-makers except those in the service of the crown.

Este Ceramic Factory. Italian porcelain and pottery manufactory. In 1778 the French sculptor Jean-Pierre Varion (*d* 1780) entered into a partnership with Girolamo Franchini (1727–1808) and established a porcelain factory in Este (Veneto). Production is thought to have started only after Varion's death. Franchini continued in business until at least 1825, and Varion's widow, Fiorina Fabris, went into partnership with Antonio Costa. A cream-tinted, hard-paste porcelain was produced, and the repertory was exclusively of allegorical and mythological figures. Well-rounded, graceful figures have been attributed to Varion, although, since they are datable to the 1780s, this is debatable. A single figure of an actor has been attributed to Franchini.

In 1893 the porcelain factory merged with a local earthenware factory founded in 1758. The company is still active and is now called Este Ceramiche e Porcellane.

G. Baroli: *Mostra dell'antica ceramica di Este* (Este, 1960)

Etagère. Type of 19th-century table, made in Rococo and Renaissance styles and consisting of four or five shelves either free-standing or surmounting a table or cabinet. It is primarily an American form, but there are also BIEDERMEIER *étagères*.

Etching [Fr. *eau-forte*; It. *acquaforte*; Ger. *Ätzung*; Sp. *aguafuerte*]. Type of intaglio print, the design of which is printed from grooves corroded into a plate by acid; the term is applied also to the process by which the composition is bitten into the printing plate.

A. Smith: *Etching: A Guide to Traditional Techniques* (Ramsbury, Crowood, 2004)

Etoilles Porcelain. Small French porcelain factory established near Paris in 1768. An example of its wares is the Louis XV écuelle dish now in the Bowes Museum in Barnard Castle.

Etruria Factory. *See under* WEDGWOOD.

Etruscan style. Type of delicate, painted Neo-classical decoration, derived mainly from the shapes, motifs and colours of antique vases. It was part of the quest in Europe in the last quarter of the 18th century for a contemporary expression in interior design and the applied arts. The term is applied loosely to various schemes of decoration inspired by Classical sources, involving Renaissance GROTESQUE ornament, as well as themes inspired by discoveries

Etagére attributed to J. & J. W. Meeks & Co., rosewood and marble, New York, *c.* 1855 (Newark, NJ, Newark Museum)

Etruscan-style volute krater depicting *The Entry into Paris of Works Destined for the Musée Napoléon*, porcelain, h. 1.2 m, designed by Antoine Béranger, made by Sèvres, 1813 (Sèvres, Musée National de Céramique)

Silver-gilt ewer and basin by Pierre Harache with engraved decoration by Blaise Gentot, basin: diam. 655 mm; ewer: h. 305 mm, from London, England, 1697 (London, British Museum)

made at Herculaneum and Pompeii in the 18th century. Initially represented by Josiah Wedgwood's black basaltes ware, the Etruscan style was developed by James Wyatt and the Adam brothers during the 1770s as a means of embellishing their intimately scaled rooms. Apart from scattered manifestations on the Continent and the use of the term for classicizing furniture of the Louis XVI (*reg* 1774–92) period, this style remained substantially an English phenomenon. It survived until the last decades of the 18th century when it was eclipsed by the more vigorous and archaeologically exact taste of the mature POMPEIAN REVIVAL.

S. Schwartz: 'The "Etruscan" Style at Sèvres: A Bowl from Marie-Antoinette's Dairy at Rambouillet', *Met. Mus. J.*, xxxvii (2002), pp. 259–66

Etui [etwee]. Small ornamental box or case (often decorated in enamel) used to carry small personal items (e.g. bodkins, needles, toothpicks). The etui, which was popular in the 18th century, was carried either in a pocket or on a CHATELAINE. The term also denoted a case for surgical instruments.

Eulenkrug [Ger.: 'owl-jug']. Tin-glazed earthenware jug shaped like an owl and manufactured in Nuremberg in the mid-16th century. The design may be the work of AUGUSTIN HIRSCHVOGEL.

Ewer and basin. Matching jug and bowl used for hand washing during and after meals and for toilet purposes. They were made in precious and base metals, ceramics, glass and enamel. As the water was often perfumed with roses, the ewers are sometimes known as 'rose-water ewers'. Early medieval ewers are usually in the form of animals or figures (*see* AQUAMANILE). In the Middle Ages their use was ceremonial as well as practical. From the 15th century ewers and basins were acquired by institutions and corporations for ceremonial presentation and as ambassadorial gifts, becoming prized display objects. In form and decoration the ewer and basin altered with stylistic developments, and they were always of the most elaborate design and finish. With the increased use of cutlery from the late 17th century, ewers and basins had less function, although mainly ceramic examples were used as an accoutrement for toilet use until the advent of widespread domestic plumbing in the early 20th century.

Ewer and basin by Pierre Ballin, 1615–16 (Pisa, Museo dell'Opere del Duomo)

E. M. Alcorn: 'Some of the Kings of England Curiously Engraven: An Elizabethan Ewer and Basin in the Museum of Fine Arts, Boston', *J. Mus. F. A., Boston*, v (1993), pp. 66–103

Exeter. English centre of carpet production. The workshop that produced hand-knotted carpets in Exeter seems to have lasted only six years, from 1755 to 1761, and yet the three signed and dated surviving carpets are among the most important English carpets. In 1755 a Swiss Huguenot, Claude Passavant, of Exeter bought a London workshop and took many of the Fulham weavers to Exeter; it seems probable that they took with them designs that they had brought from France. The three surviving carpets from Exeter incorporate distinctly French Rococo motifs, including the French preference for such colours as red, deep blue and a blackish brown. The earliest carpet, dated 1757, is in the Victoria & Albert Museum, London. The second, dated 1758, is in a private collection, and the third, also dated 1758, is at Petworth House, W. Sussex (NT).

Ex libris. *See* BOOKPLATE.

F

Faber, **Johann Ludwig** (*fl* 1678–93). German glass and faience painter (*Hausmaler*), active in Nuremberg. He may have been a pupil of JOHANN SCHÄPER, whose work influenced Faber's style and his use of Schwarzlot (e.g. glass goblet and cover, 1690, V&A, London).

Fabergé, **(Peter) Carl (Gustavovitch)** (*b* St Petersburg, 30 May 1846; *d* Lausanne, 24 Sept 1920). Russian goldsmith and jeweller. He was the son of a goldsmith of Huguenot origin. Fabergé joined his father's firm in St Petersburg in 1864, and took over in 1870. In 1882 his brother, Agathon Fabergé (1862–95), joined the firm.

Carl Fabergé: Easter egg containing a model of the cruiser 'Memory of Azov', gold and enamel (Moscow, Kremlin, Armoury)

Carl Fabergé: *Monkey*, silver, 1899–1908

At the beginning of his career Fabergé produced bracelets and medallions decorated with stones and enamels. He transformed the conventional jewellery business by insisting that the value of an object should reside in its craftsmanship rather than its materials. Under his direction, the firm moved away from the contemporary custom of setting large gemstones in shoddy settings and produced elaborate diamond-set pendant brooches, ribbon-knot necklaces and trelliswork bracelets. From 1866 he was one of a number of jewellers selling pieces to the Russian imperial household, and the items produced were linked to contemporary French designs.

Fabergé perfected a wide palette of translucent enamels that were applied over a guilloche ground with sunburst, wave or moiré effects among others, and he revived *quatre-couleur* goldwork. Under the influence of Agathon Fabergé, the most attractive compositions—typical of Fabergé production from

1882 onwards—were the animals, flowers and objects of vertu produced in hardstones or precious metals; such functional objects as cigarette and cigar boxes, photograph-frames, pencil-cases, note-pads and letter-openers were also made. The hardstone carvings of animals, birds and fish, usually measuring between only 25 and 75 mm in length or height, were never signed by the individual lapidary but must nevertheless be regarded as original works of sculpture. The natural resources of Siberia, the Caucasus and the Urals provided a rich variety of materials for these models and for larger pieces, including many types of agate, Siberian jade (nephrite), rhodonite, malachite, aventurine quartz, rock crystal, obsidian and bowenite (a variety of serpentine). Some of the most enchanting compositions of the firm, and characteristic of its output, are the pots of flowers. The flowers, supported on engraved gold stalks and often enamelled and set with gemstones, and the leaves, carved from nephrite, are placed in rock crystal skilfully carved to simulate a bowl filled with water (e.g. bowl of cornflower and oat sprays with blue enamel petals and rose diamond pistils; St Petersburg, Hermitage).

Tsar Alexander III (d 1894) patronized the Fabergé firm and on 1 May 1885 awarded Fabergé the title Supplier to the Imperial Court. The first of the sensational series of Imperial Easter Eggs, each concealing a surprise, was commissioned by Alexander III in 1884 or 1885, and he even collaborated to some extent with Fabergé on its design (see colour pl. XIII, fig. 1). Later examples were commissioned by Nicholas II for the Dowager Tsarina Marie Feodorovna and the Tsarina Alexandra Feodorovna (e.g. Lilies of the Valley Egg, 1898; New York, Forbes Mag. Col.).

The Fabergé workshops produced pieces in many different styles. Some of the most successful silver was made in the Moscow workshop (est. 1887) in a typically medieval Russian style (e.g. cigar box shaped as a helmet, 1899–1908; Doorn, Huis Doorn), and some pieces also reflect the influences of Renaissance Italy (e.g. rock-crystal dish with enamel, 1896; St Petersburg, Hermitage) and the contemporary Art Nouveau style (e.g. silver mounts of trailing peapods on a Doulton vase, 1899–1908; St Petersburg, Peter & Paul Fortress).

The St Petersburg branch was composed of a number of separate workshops, whose responsibility it was to oversee each item from its initial design through all the different stages of manufacture. A number of workmasters operated in each workshop, who were entitled to stamp their initials beside the firm name on the pieces they supervised. The Moscow branch was run more as a commercial enterprise, and its pieces bear the firm's name beneath the Imperial Warrant of Appointment, the Romanov double-headed eagle. Other branches were founded in Odessa (1890), London (1903) and Kiev (1905), and, in all, c. 500 people were employed. With the start of the Russian Revolution in 1917, a Committee of Employees was formed; it managed the firm until 1918, when Fabergé closed the workshops and left the country.

H. Waterfield and C. Forbes: *Fabergé: Imperial Eggs and Other Fantasies* (New York, 1978)
G. von Habsburg-Lothringen and A. von Solodkoff: *Fabergé: Court Jeweller to the Tsars* (Fribourg, 1979, rev. 1984)
A. K. Snowman: *Carl Fabergé: Goldsmith to the Imperial Court of Russia* (London, 1979, rev. 1983)
A. von Solodkoff and others: *Masterpieces from the House of Fabergé* (New York, 1984/R 1989)
Fabergé: Juwelier der Zaren (exh. cat., ed. G. von Habsburg; Munich, Ksthalle Hypo-Kultstift., 1986–7; Eng. trans., Geneva, 1987)
A. K. Snowman: *Fabergé: Lost and Found: The Recently Discovered Jewelry Designs from the St Petersburg Archives* (London, 1993)
Fabergé: Imperial Jeweller (exh. cat. by G. von Habsburg and M. Lopato, St Petersburg, Hermitage; Paris, Mus. A. Déc.; London, V&A; 1993–4)
G. von Habsburg: *Fabergé: Trésors & objets de fantaisie* (New York, Paris and London, 1996)
The Pine Cone Egg by Carl Faberge: The Property of an American Collector (sale cat., New York, Christie's, 1997)
T. N. Muntian and others: 'A Symbol of a Disappearing Empire: The Rediscovery of the Fabergé Constellation Easter Egg', *Apollo*, cdxci (Jan 2003), pp. 10–13
Fabergé in the Royal Collection (exh cat by C. De Guitaut; London, 2003)

Fábrica Cerâmica Viúva Lamego Lda. Portuguese ceramics factory founded in Lisbon in 1849 by António da Costa Lamego (d 1876). Initially it produced ordinary, red earthenwares, but in 1863 it began to successfully manufacture faience, and by 1876 the factory had 5 kilns and nearly 80 workers. A steam-engine was installed in 1878. In addition to red-clay pottery, painted and white household ware and artistic faience, production also included tiles and industrial construction material, all of which were exported to Africa and Brazil.

Artists at the Fábrica Cerâmica Viúva Lamego Lda. working at the beginning of the 20th century included José Maria Pereira jr (1841–1921). Jorge Nicholson Moore Barradas (1894–1971) worked there from the late 1920s until 1970. In the late 20th

Carl Fabergé: *Hippopotamus,* nephrite, 1908–17

century artists associated with the factory included Querubim Lapa (*b* 1925), Júlio Pomar (*b* 1926) and Vieira da Silva (1908–92).

Fábrica da Vista Alegre. Portuguese ceramics and glass factory. It was founded in Ílhavo, near Aveiro, in 1824 by José Ferreira Pinto Basto (1774–1839); his son Augusto Valério Ferreira Pinto Basto (1807–1902), who had trained at Sèvres, was the first managing director. At first only very small deposits of kaolin were available, so the factory produced creamware, stoneware and a few pieces of poor-quality porcelain. Two Neo-classical enamelled and gilded cups and saucers (1827; Lisbon, Mus. N. A. Ant.) have inscriptions indicating that they were fired in the first kiln of ware from this factory and were painted by João María Fabre (1805–29). The special type of enamel decoration used at this stage was devised by both Fabre and the artist, sculptor and engraver Manuel de Morais de Silva Ramos (1806–72). During this period Pinto Basto also employed the potter Joseph Scorder from Saxony, who took charge of the production of porcelain at the factory.

In 1832 the first significant deposits of kaolin were located in Vale Rico, at the village of Feira in the district of Aveiro. This discovery enabled the factory to produce porcelain on an industrial scale. The factory's artistic standards and fame were aided by the work of the French portrait painter Vítor François Chartier Rousseau (*d* 1852) and his successor Gustave Fortier (*fl* 1853–69). The latter was particularly notable for his excellent draughtsmanship and his landscape and flower painting in polychrome enamels and gilding (e.g. pair of jardinières, 1851; Lisbon, Mus. N. A. Ant.). He is also credited with the introduction of pen painting and transfer printing. A teapot attributed to the artist Manuel Francisco Pereira shows the influence of the Sèvres Porcelain Factory at Vista Alegre in the mid-19th century in its use of a deep blue underglaze ground. The painter Joaquim José da Oliveira (*fl* 1869–81) was painting master between 1869 and 1881 and trained such skilful artists as Manuel Fernandes Barros ('Padre Noche') and Duarte José de Magalhães, who became painting master in 1889.

From *c.* 1870 to the first quarter of the 20th century the factory went through a difficult period and artistic standards declined. However, from 1922 to 1947 the factory prospered under the administration of João Teodoro Ferreira Pinto Basto (1870–1947), and such designers as Ângelo Simões Chuva (1883–1973) and Palmiro da Silva Peixe produced Art Deco-style domestic and ornamental wares. The company now trades as Fabrica de Porcelanas da Vista Alegre; its museum displays a large collection of its wares.

J. T. F. Pinto Basto: *A Fábrica da Vista Alegre: O livro do seu centenário* (Lisbon, 1924)

Portugal and Porcelain (exh. cat., eds I. Arez, M. Azevedo Coutinho and J. McNab; New York, Met., 1984)

Fábrica de Cerâmica Constância. Portuguese ceramics factory in Lisbon, founded in 1836 under the trade name Companhia Fabril de Louça and administered by Inácio Augusto da Silva Lisboa. The factory was renamed the Companhia Constância when it was taken over by a new company in 1842 and was also known as the Fábrica dos Marianos and the Fábrica das Janelas Verdes. In 1849 the Fábrica Cerâmica Viúva Lamego Lda. was founded by António da Costa Lamego (*d* 1876). Initially it produced ordinary, red earthenwares, but in 1863 it began to successfully manufacture faience, and by 1876 the factory had 5 kilns and nearly 80 workers. A steam-engine was installed in 1878. In addition to red-clay pottery, painted and white household ware and artistic faience, production also included tiles and industrial construction material, all of which were exported to Africa and Brazil.

The Fábrica de Cerâmica Constância has been particularly associated with the Bohemian artist Venceslas Cifka (*d* 1883) who worked there in 1876–7. His delicately executed polychrome wares often featured neo-classical subjects. Of particular note is an elaborately decorated blue violin featuring medallion portraits of the Italian composers Alessandro Scarlatti (1660–1725) and Arcangelo Corelli (1653–1713), the royal coat of arms and Neo-classical figures (Lisbon, Mus. N. A. Ant.). Both cream ware and black basalts were also manufactured during the late 19th century. At the beginning of the 20th century faience and tiles were painted by José António Jorge Pinto (1876–1945). Artists in the 1920s included Viriato Silva (*b* 1874) and the Italian Leopaldi Baptista. In 1963 the factory was rejuvenated by Francisco d'Almeida, and artists working there subsequently have included Rafael Salinas Calado, João Charters de Almeida e Silva (*b* 1935), Joaquim da Costa Rebocho (*b* 1912) and Nuno José de Siqueira (*b* 1929), producing both wares and tiles.

Fábrica de Viana [Fábrica de Darque]. Portuguese ceramics factory. It was founded in Darque near Viana do Castelo in 1774. During the early years (before 1790) the factory produced tureens, octagonal plates, tankards and large jars that were influenced by wares from the REAL FÁBRICA DO RATO in Lisbon and imported wares; decoration was executed in blue or manganese-purple. From 1790 to 1820 a wide range of wares was manufactured, characterized by well-shaped forms, perfect milky white ground and polychrome decoration dominated by blues, greens, canary-yellow, orange and violet. Delicately executed floral motifs predominate, with very few figurative compositions. Variously sized pear-shaped vases were inspired by East Asian wares and were decorated with finely drawn weeping willows and pagodas. Other characteristic wares included English-style 'Toby' jugs, toothpick holders, figures in the form of negroes, tankards shaped as African heads, mugs, washbowls, pitchers and a variety of tableware, some of which was enamelled in light blue and green in the manner of faience produced at the Fábrica de Miragaia. After 1820, there were successful attempts in the use of transfer printing, but artistic standards declined and the factory closed in 1855.

L. A. de Oliveira: *A extincta fábrica cerâmica de Viana* (Lisbon, 1915)

A. Cardoso Pinto: *Faiança da antiga fábrica de Viana: Colecção Dr Alfredo Queiróz* (Lisbon, 1954)

A. Matos Reis and J. Cepa Machado: 'Museu municipal de Viana do Castelo: Catálogo da faiança de Viana', *Patrimonio*, i (1982), pp. 9–24

Fábrica do Juncal. Portuguese ceramics factory. It was founded in the borough of Porto de Mós, near Leiria, in 1770 by the painter and architect José Rodrigues da Silva e Sousa (*d* 1824). In 1784 the factory received the designation 'Royal' and the protection of Sebastião de Carvalho e Melo, the 1st Marquês de Pombal. The factory had two very distinct periods of production. During the first 30 years it produced blue-and-white tableware that was influenced in style and decoration by the Realfábrica do Rato. Many pieces are distinctive for their recurring semi-abstract, leaf-like motifs, shaded in blue or manganese-purple, surrounded by chains of beads. During the second period, under the direction of José Luís Fernandes da Fonseca, wares were decorated with more sober decoration in manganese-purple. Important painters who worked at the factory at this time included João Coelho Pó and Manuel Coelho. Fonseca's son Bernardino José da Fonseca directed the factory from 1837, and he was succeeded by his nephew José Calado da Fonseca. In addition to faience the factory also produced some rather poorly designed tiled panels of religious themes, many of which are signed and dated. The factory closed in 1876.

Façon de Venise, à la. Glass is said to be *à la façon de Venise* when it imitates the style of Venetian glass. Such glass was made from the late 16th century in the Netherlands, the Rhineland and by GIACOMO VERZELINI in England (see colour pl. XIII, fig. 2).

Faenza. Italian centre of maiolica production. It is one of the most famous centres of Italian maiolica production and from the 17th century lent its name to this particular category of ceramics made throughout Europe ('faience'). Ceramic production in Faenza is documented from the 14th century. Early products are solid and heavy in shape and decorated with rather frugal, severe ornamentation, mostly in brown and green. In the 15th century ceramics in Faenza begin to develop a specifically individual style. Faenza maiolica was technically more refined than that produced in other centres and incorporated a rich, varied palette. In particular the decoration was enriched with fashionable subjects, including Gothic–Moorish motifs, coats of arms, heraldic devices and portraits of *belle donne* painted on *coppe amatorie* (love dishes). These features remained during the 16th century when the *istoriato* (narrative) genre was often combined with *berettino* (blue) glaze deco-

ration, with grotesques and arabesques (e.g. plaque, *c.* 1525–30; London, BM).

From the mid-16th century and through most of the 17th Faenza was involved in the development of the so-called *bianchi di Faenza* (white ware). In this period skilful craftsmen and such heads of workshops as Francesco Mezzarisa, Virgiliotto Calamelli and Leonardo Bettisi (*fl* 1564–80) created relief surfaces, which became increasingly Baroque in style and were covered with a thick, white glaze onto which they applied a sparse, sketchy form of decoration known as *compendiaria* (e.g. pierced dish, *c.* 1550–70; London, BM). During the 18th and 19th centuries the Conti Ferniani Factory continued this style and became the leading producer in Faenza. Its production, however, unlike those of the past, reflects a repertory common to many European centres.

F. Argnani: *Il rinascimento delle ceramiche maiolicate in Faenza* (Faenza, 1898)

P. Wilson: 'Faenza', *Cer. Technical*, xiii (2001), pp. 70–73

C. Ravanelli Guidotti: *Ceramiche italiane datate dal XV al XIX secolo: Per il "Corpus della maiolica italiana" di Gaetano Ballardini* (Faenza, 2004)

Faenza, Antonio Gentili da. *See* GENTILI DA FAENZA, ANTONIO.

Faience. Term probably derived from the Italian town of FAENZA, famous for its popular maiolica. It is often used to describe French, German and Scandinavian tin-glazed earthenware but is also interchangeable with the terms 'MAIOLICA' and 'DELFTWARE'.

Faïence blanc. Earthenware left in its undecorated white slip.

Faïence fine. *See* CREAMWARE.

Faïence japonnée. French 18th-century earthenware decorated with oriental motifs.

Faïence parlante [Fr.: 'talking faience']. French earthenware decorated with inscriptions; those intended for apothecaries bear the names of drugs. The most important centre of *faïence parlante* was Nevers (*see* NEVERS, §1).

F. Girard: *Les faïence parlantes du XVIIIe siècle* (Bourg-en-Bresse, 1938)

Faïence patriotique. Late 18th-century French earthenware decorated with scenes of victorious battles or of the French Revolution.

Champfleury: *Histoire des faïences patriotiques sous la Révolution* (1875/ R Brussels, 2003)

M.-C. Depierre: *Les faïences patriotiques du Musée de Picardie* (Amiens, 1989)

Fairings. Small ceramic ornaments manufactured in Germany (notably by Conta and Böhm in Pössneck, Saxony) and sold at fairs in Victorian and Edwardian England and in America. Fairings were typically 75–100 mm high and made from soft-paste porcelain; the rectangular bases made them suitable for display on mantelpieces. They were usually humorous and often risqué. Fairings are now reproduced by potteries such as Kellerton Ceramics in Shropshire.

W. S. Bristowe: *Victorian China Fairings* (London, 1971)

D. H. Jordan: *Victorian China Fairings: The Collector's Guide* (Woodbridge, 2003)

Falconet, Etienne-Maurice (*b* Paris, 1 Dec 1716; *d* Paris, 24 Jan 1791). French sculptor, designer and writer. He was one of the foremost French sculptors of the mid-18th century, but is also well known for his widely reproduced models for the porcelain factory at Sèvres, of which he was the director from 1757 until his departure for Russia in 1766. During this period he either executed or supervised the making of about 100 models for statuettes or groups. These fall into two categories, original creations and works made from designs by FRANÇOIS BOUCHER. Of the figurines inspired by Boucher one series is devoted to trades, and a subsequent series, dating from several years later, is on the theme of the attractions of the fair. Several other loosely connected groups, also the result of collaboration with Boucher, were based on the fables of Jean de La Fontaine. The subjects attributable solely to Falconet are either those that are reductions of his marble statues or compositions specially designed for manufacture in biscuit. Some of these charming miniatures preserve the memory of statues that have been destroyed or have disappeared, such as *Erigone* or *Sweet Melancholy*; others are based on contemporary theatrical entertainments: there is a cycle of dances from the Opéra ballet, subjects from the comic operas of Charles-Simon Favart, and from the pastoral works of Jean François Marmontel; others illustrate the repertory of the Comédiens Italiens.

In St Petersburg Falconet was principally occupied with the bronze equestrian statue in honour of *Peter the Great*, but he also made models for goldsmiths and the Imperial porcelain factory.

L. Réau: *Etienne-Maurice Falconet*, 2 vols (Paris, 1922)

Falconet à Sèvres, 1757–1766, ou, L'art de plaire (exh. cat., Sèvres, Mus. N. Cer., 2001)

Faldistorium. Armless folding chair (or chair that looks like it could be folded) used in medieval Europe to seat ecclesiastical and royal dignitaries. The faldistorium of 1242 from the monastery of Nonnberg (near Salzburg), which is decorated with a carved lion's head and paws on the crossbars, is said to have belonged to the Abbess Gertrude. Faldistoria appeared in Hungary in the 11th century; examples include the thrones of kings Béla III (*reg* 1172–96) and Emeric (*reg* 1196–1204). In the 13th century the chairs of church dignitaries were of this type when King Béla IV (*reg* 1235–70) permitted them to be seated in his presence. The English term 'faldistory' is used in a narrower sense to denote the throne of a bishop within the chancel.

Faldstool. Term variously used to denote a FALDISTORIUM or a cushioned stool at which a worshipper kneels for prayer or a small desk at which the litany is said or sung.

Falize, Lucien (*b* Paris, 4 Aug 1839; *d* Paris, 4 Sept 1897). French jeweller. He was the son of the jeweller Alexis Falize (1811–98) and received his training (1856–71) in his father's firm. His early work was influenced by East Asian art, which he saw at the International Exhibition of 1862 in London and at the Exposition Universelle of 1867 in Paris. About 1867 the firm began to produce cloisonné-enamelled jewellery in the Japanese manner, which was made in collaboration with Antoine Tard (*fl c.* 1860–*c.* 1889). It cannot be determined how much of this work was by Falize, even with marked pieces, as both jewellers used the firm mark AF, with a fusee hook in a lozenge. In 1875 the symbol was changed to a cross of St Andrew. In 1878 Falize exhibited an eclectic range of work in his own name for the first time: wares included silver statues, clocks, Japanese-inspired jewellery enamelled by Tard and jewellery in the Renaissance Revival style. From 1880 to 1892 he was in partnership with Germain Bapst (1853–1921). Their mark, BF, accompanied by a ring with a pearl, was not registered until 1892 but was used during this period, sometimes as a decorative device. Falize made extensive use of historical, chiefly Renaissance, traditions and incorporated architectural and sculptural elements, as well as different enamelling techniques, into his designs. He made frequent use of calligraphy in his designs, especially his bracelets, which are compositionally formal and complex and are notable for the clarity and vividness of enamelling and contrast between colour and texture. Falize's last major work was the Hanap de la Vigne et des Métiers (1896; Paris, Mus. A. Déc.), an enamelled gold goblet in which Renaissance and more naturalistic styles were combined.

K. Purcell: 'Falize', *The Master Jewelers*, ed. A. K. Snowman (New York, 1990), pp. 61–76

Falize: A Dynasty of Jewellers: A Loan Exhibition in Aid of Befrienders International (exh. cat., London, Wartski, 1999)

M. Heuze: 'Art Nouveau Renaissance: The Falize's Jewels', *F.M.R. Mag.*, cv (Aug–Sept 2000), pp. 93–112

Falknov [Ger. Falkenau]. Czech centre of glass production. In 1530 a glass factory was established by Paul Schürer (1504–94) of Aschberg, and during the 16th and 17th centuries it was one of the most important glassworks in Bohemia. It was evidently associated with the beginnings of enamel decoration, because as early as 1562 it was commissioned to supply enamelled glass to the Imperial Vice-Regent in Prague, Archduke Ferdinand of Tyrol. At the end of the 16th century and beginning of the 17th it supplied glass to the Imperial court. One of the glassworks' products is a tankard decorated in enamel depicting the Virgin Mary (1647; Prague, Mus. Dec. A.). In the second half of the 16th century glass painters began to concentrate in the area around the Falkenau works and were joined in the last quarter of the 17th century by glass engravers, who since 1683 had been associated with the guild of painters and glass engravers at Polevsko. In 1732 the works were sold to Johann Josef Kittel of Polevsko, and in 1748 his son Johann Anton Kittel transferred them elsewhere, but subsequently production ceased for lack of wood. During the second half of the 19th century new coal-fired glassworks were started but later ceased production.

Fall front [drop-leaf front; drop front]. Hinged cover of a desk; it can be opened to create a surface for writing, and is sometimes supported on struts that are accommodated within the desk when it is closed.

Famille jaune. *See under* FAMILLE VERTE.

Famille noire. *See under* FAMILLE VERTE.

Famille rose. Term applied to Qing-period (1644–1911) overglazed enamel porcelain characterized by a delicate rose pink derived from colloidal gold. All the *famille rose* colours are opaque and stand proud of the surface. The wide palette and manageable qualities of these enamels facilitated a meticulous style of painting. The term embraces *yangcai* ('foreign colours'), *fencai* ('powdered colours'), *ruancai* ('soft colours') and *falangcai* ('enamel colours') (see colour pl. XIII, fig. 3).

G. C. Williamson: *The Book of Famille Rose* (Rutland, VT, 1970)
M. Beurdeley and G. Raindre: *Qing Porcelain: Famille Verte, Ramille Rose, 1644–1912* (New York, 1987)

Famille verte. Term applied to Qing-period (1644–1911) translucent overglaze enamel wares on which the predominant colour is green; it is known also as *yingcai* ('strong colours'). *Famille jaune* and *famille noire*, characterized by the predominant use of yellow and black respectively, are effectively variants of *famille verte*.

M. Beurdeley and G. Raindre: *Qing Porcelain: Famille Verte, Famille Rose, 1644–1912* (New York, 1987)
Famille Verte Porcelain of the Kangxi period (sale cat. New York, Chinese Porcelain Company, 13–20 Oct 1994)

Fan. Cooling or winnowing device. It was known to earliest civilizations and served utilitarian, ceremonial, ritual and decorative purposes. Infinite variations of fan shapes have evolved throughout the ages in most countries in the world. There are, however, two main types of fan, the screen or fixed fan, and the folding fan. The screen fan consists of a handle

Porcelain bottle with flower and bird design decorated with *famille rose* enamels on a white ground, 18th century (Paris, Musée Guimet)

that can vary in length, design and material, on to which is fixed a rigid leaf or mount. The folding fan is composed of a set of sticks, which can be made in a variety of materials, on which is fitted a pleated leaf that allows the fan to be opened and closed. A rivet or pivot holds the sticks together, either at the base or, as in a cockade fan, in the centre; the *cabriolet* fan consists of two or more concentric leaves. Overlapping sticks secured at the top by a ribbon or thread, with no leaf, constitute a *brisé* fan.

S. Blondel: *Histoire des éventails chez tous les peuples et à toutes les époques* (Paris, 1875)
G. Buss: *Der Fächer* (Bielefeld and Leipzig, 1904)
Fans (1975–)
S. Mayor: *Collecting Fans* (London, 1980)
Il Ventaglio (1984–)
Eventails (exh. cat., ed. M. Volet and A. Beentjes; Geneva, Mus. A. & Hist., 1987)

1. East Asia. 2. Europe.

1. EAST ASIA. The folding fan was invented in Japan in the 7th century. Among the earliest surviving Japanese folding fans are a group of 115 *sūtra* fans dating from the 12th century (e.g. *sūtra* fan leaf, second half of the 12th century; Osaka, Shitennōji), painted with genre scenes over which texts from the Lotus *sūtra* are written. The few fans that survive from the Muromachi period (1333–1568) are mostly painted with landscapes and have thicker sticks. The two end sticks became guards with pierced decoration.

Fan decorated with a landscape by Wang Yuanqi, China, late 17th century–early 18th (Paris, Musée Guimet)

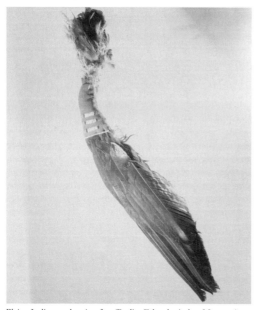

Plains Indian eagle-wing fan (Berlin, Ethnologisches Museum)

Early Chinese folding fans, unlike Japanese ones, consisted of two semicircular paper leaves pasted one to each side of the sticks; this innovation was taken up by the Japanese in the 15th century. The Japanese court and *nō* theatre also began to use a folding fan known as a *suchiro* (wide-ended fan) with a large number of wooden sticks, sometimes jointed to allow for splaying, lacquered in red or black with a design called 'cat's-eyes' (Jap. *nekome*). When closed,

the fan formed a Y-shape. Another type of fan, known as a *bonbori* ('hand lantern'), was made with guards curving inwards to accommodate the extra thickness of a double layer of paper.

Fans became an important painting medium in both China and Japan, with many leading artists producing fan paintings. Fans were also inscribed with poems and calligraphy (e.g. folding fan, Qing Dynasty, 1721–5; London, V&A). Such works were highly prized and were frequently removed from their sticks or frames for mounting in albums. Indeed some fan leaf paintings were so highly prized that they were never used as fans at all (e.g. fan painting by Mori Sosen; Oxford, Ashmolean). In Japan, two artists are particularly associated with fan painting: Tawaraya Sōtatsu (*fl c.* 1600–*c.* 1640) and Ogata Kōrin (1658–1716). Sōtatsu was chiefly known for his folding fan paintings, whereas Kōrin, although acknowledging Sōtatsu's influence, preferred the rigid fan as a medium (e.g. fan painted with scenes from the *Tales of Ise* and chrysanthemums and water; Washington, DC, Freer).

The development during the Edo period (1600–1868) of *ukiyoe* woodblock printing led to the printing of fan leaves in large numbers for mass consumption, both as folding and rigid fans. The work of many famous *ukiyoe* artists such as Utamaro occurs on fans. Prior to the Edo period, a popular type of fan for prints was introduced to Japan from Korea. It was made from a length of bamboo split above a joint into 50–60 splints splayed to form a base for the fan leaf on either side, with a handle formed by the un-split bamboo below the joint. These fans depict scenes from the brothels, theatres, restaurants

War fan with iron endplates, from Japan (L. J. Anderson Collection)

and tea houses of Edo and were particularly popular with merchants and townspeople. Chinese fans were usually painted with brush and ink outline, with faint colour washes; landscapes were especially popular. Japanese fans tended to have brighter colours and more varied subject-matter.

Distinctive types of fan developed in local areas and for special uses. In China, in Hangzhou, a black oiled folding fan decorated with gold splashes and composed of up to 50 sticks was produced, and in Zhejiang Province the type known as a 'jade-plaque' fan was carved from a giant bamboo. The Taiwanese made a rigid fan from the dried leaf of the betel palm, which was engraved with a hot poker. The Japanese made a folding fan known as a war fan (*gunsen*) or iron fan (*tessen*), composed of 10–12 lacquered wood or iron sticks with thick paper attached, decorated with a red sun on a gold ground on one side, and a silver moon on a black ground on the other. The military fan (*gunbai uchiwa*) was made from iron and hardened leather or from heavily lacquered wood and was usually decorated with sun, moon and stars. It was used like a baton to give military commands, as a weapon, and to ward off blows.

As trade between Europe and East Asia developed, fans became popular in the West. The Chinese began producing fans for export featuring a combination of traditional Chinese and Western elements. Black and gold lacquer fans with a design enclosing the owner's monogram were common. More sophisticated materials and techniques were used than for fans for the domestic market: gold and silver filigree, cloisonné, lacquer, mother-of-pearl and tortoiseshell. Export fans were usually *brisé* fans, a type never very popular in China. Some of the earliest export fans, dating from the 18th century, are of pierced ivory painted with decorations similar to those on contemporary export *famille verte* and Chinese Imari porcelain, and pierced ivory fans, with designs of flowers or geometric patterns, continued to be popular in the West. Neo-classical designs also became common. By the 19th century, there were depictions of carved figures in landscape settings on a ribbed ground. Generally, fan paintings for the Western market depicted either Western scenes, usually awkward in execution, or Eastern scenes, featuring domestic, ceremonial or social life, or flowers, fruit, birds or insects.

From the mid-19th century, the Japanese also made large numbers of export fans. Although these differed from fans for the domestic market, they utilized traditional skills and materials. Mostly inexpensive, many were folding fans, generally much larger than those used by the Japanese, although there were also such new forms as the *cabriolet* fan, consisting of two or more concentric leaves. Finer, more expensive export fans included *brisé* fans with ivory sticks decorated with gold and silver *hiramakie* and *takamakie* (*see under* LACQUER, §1(IV)) and guards enriched with tortoiseshell and mother-of-pearl (e.g. export fan, late 19th century; London, Fan Mus.). Depictions on fan leaves tended to be of the type considered typically Japanese by Europeans, such as *ukiyoe* scenes, bird-and-flower paintings and representations of Mt Fuji. In both China and Japan, the manufacture and use of fans continues in the early 21st century.

J. Earle: 'The Fan in Japan', *Fans from the East* (London, 1978), pp. 37–45

J. Hutt: 'Chinese Fans and Fans from China', *Fans from the East* (London, 1978), pp. 27–35

Ivory fan, diam. 308 mm, Dieppe, France, 18th century (Dieppe, Château-Musée de Dieppe)

J. Hutt and H. Alexander: *Ogi: A History of the Japanese Fan* (London, 1992)

R. Faulkner and H. Ando: *Hiroshige Fan Prints*, London, V&A (London, 2001)

2. EUROPE. Fans are documented in royal wills and inventories from the 14th century; in France they were known as *esmouchoirs*. At this date fans were also used in agriculture for winnowing. Feather fans, set in plain or jewelled handles, date from the 16th century. In the 17th century feather fans were superseded at court by folding fans, but they were still used by the middle classes and children. The sticks and guards of the folding fan were made from a range of materials that included ivory, bone, mother-of-pearl, tortoiseshell, horn and wood. They could be decorated with silver or gold pins (*piqué*); other types were of pierced (*posé*) or carved mother-of-pearl. The leaves, or mounts, were made of the finest kid, vellum, paper, silk or parchment or, in some cases, strips of mica, and they could be decorated in diverse ways. Elegant fans were painted with mythological subjects copied from engravings of contemporary or earlier works by such artists as Raphael and Titian (*c*. ?1485/90–1576), members of the Carracci family, Domenichino (1581–1641), Guido Reni (1575–1642) and Abraham Bosse (1602–76). The appearance in France of such costly items, coming

mainly from Italy, prompted the formation in 1668 of a guild, with statutes approved by royal patronage. The revocation of the Edict of Nantes in 1685 resulted in the dispersal of many of these highly skilled French craftsmen throughout Protestant countries.

By the early 18th century there were numerous fan-makers and fan merchants in England, the Netherlands and Germany. Fans and fan sticks were brought to Europe by the East India companies, which also supplied European patterns and designs for Chinese craftsmen. In England, the Worshipful Company of Fan Makers was granted its charter by Queen Anne in 1709 and still flourishes. England produced both finely carved ivory sticks for high-quality fans and larger quantities of printed fan leaves for a much wider clientele. France specialized in elaborate, costly fans. Small *brisé* fans made of ivory and lacquered in *vernis Martin* were popular in the earlier part of the 18th century. Favourite subjects were the *fêtes galantes*, *fêtes champêtres* and compositions based on the paintings of Antoine Watteau (1684–1721), Jean-Baptiste Pater (1695–1736) and Nicolas Lancret (1690–1743), often incorporating chinoiserie motifs and designs by such artists as François Boucher and Jean Pillement (1728–1808). In the second half of the century France initiated the vogue for fabric leaves, usually of silk. These could be painted, em-

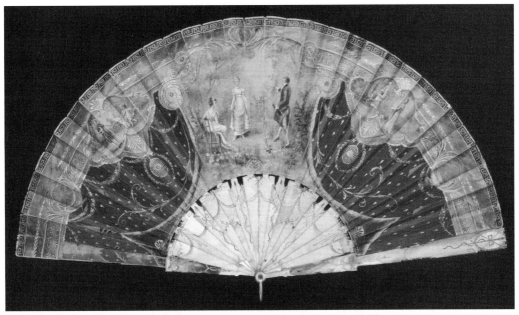

Fan decorated with a musical scene, watercolour on silk, France, *c.* 1800 (London, Victoria and Albert Museum)

broidered or embellished with sequins, ribbon, applied feathers or straw-work. The Netherlands had a prolific fan industry, and by the mid-18th century there were 30 fan shops in Amsterdam. High quality, finely painted *brisé* fans of ivory were produced, but later a somewhat stereotyped composition for fan leaves developed, which depicted Old Testament themes, usually in a central medallion flanked by two smaller vignettes in reserve on a lightly painted floral background. Many of the German states produced fans, as did Austria, Sweden and Switzerland, where the best-known fan-maker was Johannes Sulzer (1748–94) of Winterthur. Italy continued to produce fine quality fans, using 'chicken skin' (fine, papery looking skin) for the leaves, and specializing, after the mid-18th century, in reasonably good quality fans depicting subjects popular with tourists. Among the most favoured themes were copies of such popular paintings as *Aurora* (1614) by Reni in the Palazzo Rospigliosi-Pallavicini and the fresco (1508–11) by Raphael, in the Stanza della Segnatura in the Vatican, depicting *Fortitude, Prudence and Temperance*. Views of ancient buildings and of Vesuvius in eruption against backgrounds ornamented with classical motifs copied from Pompeian prototypes were also used frequently. Sticks of tortoiseshell and *piqué* work were produced more often in Italy than elsewhere. France and Portugal produced most of the fans for use in Spain, but Portugal also imported fans from Macao. By the end of the 18th century America was importing fans from East Asia and from Europe.

During the first part of the 19th century economic and political factors made the importation of rare goods into Europe difficult. Fan-makers found themselves obliged to work with such readily accessible materials as horn, bone, wood and steel. Pierced designs of sticks in *brisé* fans echoed the Neo-clas-

sical style and the later Gothic Revival. With the new interest in romantic and historical subject-matter, polychrome lithographic and chromolithographic printed fan leaves were manufactured in France in vast quantities and distributed throughout Europe and the rest of the world, making France's exports of fans the largest of any European country. By the mid-19th century a greater variety of materials was used for the sticks and guards, and new inventions were patented to improve the technology and speed of the production of fans and fan sticks. These attempts to compete with cheap imported fans from East Asia never really succeeded, although Spain and Italy produced cheap fans in great quantity. The Great Exhibition in London in 1851 brought French fans to the attention of an international public, and they became synonymous with the best. Alexandre and Duvelleroy, gold medallists at the Great Exhibition, attracted the most distinguished clientele and the most skilled craftsmen. Specialist retail shops were set up, for example the world-renowned Maison Duvelleroy, established in 1827, which was patronized by royalty and continued in business in Paris and London well into the second half of the 19th century. The finest sticks and guards of ivory and mother-of-pearl were carved by artists working in the Méru and S Geneviève areas of Paris. Among those artists who painted fan leaves are Jean-Auguste-Dominique Ingres (1780–1867), Camille Corot (1796–1875), Rosa Bonheur (1822–99), Philippe Rousseau (1816–87), Veysserat, Vibert, Narcisse Diaz (1807–76), Eugène Lami (1800–90), Luigi Calamatta (1802–69), Boutry, Paul Gavarni (1804–86) and Dumarecq. Throughout the second half of the 19th century professional painters specialized in fan painting, among them Charles Conder (1868–1909), M. Soldé, the Donzel family of father, son and uncle,

Fan decorated with yellow pansies, lace and painted silk leaf with mother-of-pearl sticks, England or France, 1880–1900 (London, Victoria and Albert Museum)

who had a school of painting and design in Paris, Cécile Chenevière, Sailly, Lazellas, Ostolle, Van Garden, Billotey, Louise Abbeme, Maurice Leloir and many others. The influence of *Japonisme* was particularly strong, and Edgar Degas (1834–1917), Paul Gauguin (1848–1903), Claude Monet (1840–1926), Henri de Toulouse-Lautrec (1864–1901) and others discovered in the fan a new stimulus for composition. Fans became fashionable decorative motifs, used extensively in interior decoration, textiles and objects of vertu.

Feather fans in every shape and form were popular at all levels of society throughout the 19th century. As the feather industry developed, so did its application in fans. Feathers came from all over the world and from every type of animal and were cured, dyed, curled and fashioned into spectacular objects. Feather fans remained popular well into the 20th century. Alongside the majestic ostrich-feather fans were smaller fans made from the plumes of different birds with the colours blending harmoniously. In the 1920s and 1930s, one or two long, tinted feathers attached to a handle complemented fashionable dress. Another type of fan developed in the 19th century was the lace fan. Due to the additional skill required in creating a circular form, lace fans were costly and prized objects, many intended as wedding gifts. They could be mounted on sticks of amber, tortoiseshell or beautifully carved mother-of-pearl. It was customary at this time among the wealthy for initials, made of gold, diamonds, or a combination of precious materials, to ornament the guards. Less costly lace-trimmed fans were also produced, as were fans made up with either hand- or machine-made lace insertions. Such manmade materials as pressed ivory, Bakelite and other plastics were also used for making fan sticks and guards.

Fans have always reflected the latest styles, from the gauze-painted or bespangled fans popular in the Directoire period, to those whose leaves held an overlying symbolism characteristic of Art Nouveau. Fans also became a popular form of advertising, with the more unsual *fontange* (bow) leaf inspired by Art Deco replacing the traditional form. Fans were used to promote products ranging from restaurants and tea-rooms to department stores, beverages, perfume and haute couture. By the end of the 19th century world-renowned collections had been assembled, for example that of Lady Charlotte Schreiber (now in the British Museum, London), the Burdett Coutts and the Walker collections. A revival of fan collecting among the aristocracy of Europe took place in the early 20th century; Queen Mary (1867–1953) assembled an important collection in England, as did Queen Margaret (1902–29) in Italy. The Messel Collection (now in the Fitzwilliam Museum, Cambridge) was formed around this period. Collecting and exhibiting regained popularity in the 1970s, with regular specialized auctions taking place in London and New York, and a revival in the art of fan-making began in the 1980s in England. Spain remains the only country in Europe to have a fan-making industry, and it has retained the fan as an object for both ceremonial and everyday use.

C. Schreiber: *Fans and Fan Leaves*, 2 vols (London, 1888–90)

N. Armstrong: *A Collector's History of Fans* (London and New York, 1974)

B. de Vere Green: *A Collector's Guide to Fans over the Ages* (London, 1975)

M. Gostelow: *The Fan* (Dublin, 1976)

S. Mayor: *Collecting Fans* (London, 1980)

H. Alexander: *Fans* (London, 1984)

L'Eventail: Miroir de la Belle Époque (exh. cat., Paris, Mus. Mode & Cost., 1985)

Royal Fans, Fan Circle International (n.p., 1986)

Eventails (exh. cat., ed. M. Volet and A. Beentjes; Geneva, Mus. A. & Hist., 1987)

C. Schwartzott: *A Brief History of the Fan* (Freeville, NY, 2003)

A Fanfare for the Sun King: Unfolding Fans for Louis XIV (exh. cat. by P. Cowen; London, Fan Mus., 2003)

Fanfare binding. *See under* BOOKBINDING, §1(II).

Fannière. French family of silversmiths. François-Auguste (1818–1900) and François-Joseph-Louis (1820–97) created elaborately decorated work, including a large nef (1869, Paris, Mus. A. Déc.) with allegorical figures commissioned by the Empress Eugénie for presentation to Ferdinand de Lesseps. The brothers also supplied chased bronze sculptures to decorate furniture by GUILLAUME GROHÉ.

Fantoni, Andrea (*b* Rovetta, Bergamo, 26 Aug 1659; *d* Rovetta, 25 July 1734). Italian sculptor, architect and furniture-maker. He was the eldest son of the sculptor and carver Grazioso Fantoni (1630–93) and trained in his father's flourishing workshop, which played a leading part in the supply of church furnishings in Bergamo, Parma and the surrounding provinces. The contrasting styles of father and son can be seen in S Martino, Alzano Maggiore: Grazioso's carved and inlaid wooden decorations and furnishings in the first sacristy (1679) are Baroque in form and Counter-Reformation in iconography; Andrea's in the second sacristy (1692) are Rococo in form and more allusive in language.

Andrea Fantoni specialized in wooden furniture, which he made for churches, convents and private houses. Because of their characteristically rich ornamentation (drapery, volutes, leaves, flowers and putti), these works have been called 'living furniture' and they, too, display a typically 18th-century taste, with a tendency towards blurring the line between objects designed for religious purposes and those intended for lay use. Two outstanding examples of these virtuoso achievements, both originally designed for Bergamo Cathedral, are the confessional (1704; Bergamo, S Maria Maggiore) and the bishop's throne (1705; *in situ*). Both are made of walnut, inset with figured reliefs in boxwood. The celebrated pulpit (1711) designed by Giovanni Battista Caniana (1671–1754) in S Martino at Alzano Lombardo was decorated by Fantoni with rich, coloured marble reliefs, medallions and statues of telamones. This work, the wooden model of which is preserved in the Museo Fantoni, Rovetta, gave rise to a series of similar pulpits in the Bergamo region (e.g. Ardesio, parish church; Castione della Presolana, parish church).

Fantoni's workshop also made devotional works, including ivory and boxwood crucifixes; examples include those in the parish church at Romano Lombardo (1700, boxwood) and in the Accademia Car-rara di Belle Arti, Bergamo (*c.* 1699–1711; wood). The Fantoni workshop continued to be active until *c.* 1817.

I Fantoni e il loro tempo: Atti del convegno di studi (Bergamo, 1978)

Faragó, Ödön (*b* 1869; *d* 1935). Hungarian furniture designer and interior designer. He trained in Vienna and Paris and from 1896 worked in Budapest, where he had ties to the GÖDÖLLÖ COLONY. His work appeared at the Esposizione Internazionale d'Arte Decorativa in Turin (1902), the St Louis Exhibition (1904) and the Esposizione Internazionale del Sempione in Milan (1906) and won numerous prizes. He favoured large, austere pieces that combined national motifs with decorative fittings. He designed domestic interiors for middle-class clients in Budapest as well as the interior and furnishings of a bank (1900–10). His early work was characterized by historical eclecticism but by the turn of the century he became known for his simple national Secession style.

Faris, William (*b* London, 1728; *d* Annapolis, MD, 1804), American silversmith and clockmaker. He was primarily a merchant, but his workshop produced a small number of pieces that can now be identified. His diary is concerned in large part with his passion for gardening, but is also a valuable resource for the American silver trade in the late 18th century.

L. Barr: *William Faris, 1728–1804, Silversmith, Clock and Watch Maker of Annapolis, MD* (Baltimore, 1941)

Russo, J. B. and M. Letzer, eds: *The Diary of William Faris: The Daily Life of an Annapolis Silversmith*, Maryland Historical Society (2003)

Fattorini. *See* SCHIAVON.

Fauconnier, Jacques-Henri (*b* 1779; *d* 1839). French silversmith. He trained in the workshop of JEAN-BAPTISTE-CLAUDE ODIOT and established his own workshop *c.* 1823. His silver inaugurated the RENAISSANCE REVIVAL style in that medium. His work includes the Lafayette Vase (1830–35, Somerset House, London), a silver-gilt two-handled vase with scenes from the life of Marquis de Lafayette.

The Lafayette Vase: An Important Silver-gilt Vase by Jacques Henri Fauconnier, Commissioned as a Gift to the Marquis de Lafayette by the Garde Nationale 1830–1835 (sale cat., New York, Sotheby's, 1980)

Favrile glass. *See under* TIFFANY.

Featherwork. Collective term for artefacts made of or decorated with feathers. Feathers have been used to decorate the human body in a wide variety of ways. In one of its simplest forms, down feathers were stuck directly to the skin, but such objects as necklaces, bracelets, ear and nose decorations and head ornaments are more widespread. Fine examples can be seen from Hawaii, Papua New Guinea and the Amazonian tribes of South America. Elaborate forms of featherwork headdress are found among the Maasai in Kenya, and the Mende of Sierra Leone use feathers in some of their masks. In Hawaii helmets and headdresses were produced incorporating millions of feathers that completely covered complex cane foundations. Costumes and headwear incorporating feathers were often designed to display the wearer's status, as in the outstanding feathered cloaks and gorgets created in Polynesia and by the Incas and Aztecs in Mesoamerica (see colour pl. XIV, fig. 1). In Maori cloaks the feathers were usually incorporated in the weaving rather than being tied on afterwards, as was the practice elsewhere in Polynesia. In Japan feathers were also used to decorate the garments of high-ranking individuals, although few examples survive. In China blue kingfisher feathers were used with hardstones, gems, gold and silver in the ceremonial headdresses or crowns of emperors, empresses and courtiers, and Chinese immigrants in South Africa have produced capes with feather patterns and swans' down linings. In Europe, particularly in the 18th and 19th centuries, the decorative value of feathers in self-adornment was exploited for the trims of gowns and for elaborate millinery, often including whole birds.

In many cultures feathered objects embody a ritual or sacred element. This is true of many Native North American examples where eagle feathers or skins are incorporated in sacred headdresses, medicine pipes and charms. Dance masks and costumes frequently include featherwork for ritual and decorative value, for example in West Africa. The trophy heads of the Jívaro and Mundurucú in South America were often embellished with feathers. In the Hawaiian Islands feathers formed an integral part of god images, sacred bundles and temples. Some bird species, such as the quetzal in Mesoamerica, had an extremely powerful ritual value, and the use of its feathers was fiercely controlled.

Feathers have been used to decorate everyday objects from the earliest times. The use of feathers to fletch arrows and to decorate spear shafts and shields is widespread (Europe, South America, New Guinea). Utilitarian clothing has sometimes been made from feathers, although it is generally too delicate for everyday use. Some Inuit groups have made parkas using eider-duck skins stitched together with the feathers on the inside for warmth; more commonly, utilitarian garments are decorated with feather trimmings. Feathers have been used to decorate hammocks (Amazonia), baskets (Pomo Indians, North America), ceramic vessels (New Guinea) and canoes (Maori, New Zealand); in Europe they have been used for such diverse purposes as writing quills, FANS, stuffing for mattresses, bedcovers and pillows and as decorative plumes for military headgear, four-poster beds and hearses. The use of feathers to create decorative features in interiors is infrequent, but impressive where it survives: largely as a women's pastime of the 18th and 19th centuries (particularly in Britain), feathers were stuck on to card to make panels and friezes (e.g. c. 1795; drawing-room and gallery, A la Ronde, Devon, NT). The gilt-leather wall coverings found in some German castles of the same period occasionally incorporate featherwork.

R. W. Doughty: *Feather Fashions and Bird Preservation* (London, 1975)
H. Cobbe, ed.: *Cook's Voyages and Peoples of the Pacific* (London, 1979)
V. Elbin: *The Body Decorated* (London, 1979)
D. S. Farner and J. R. King, eds: *Avian Biology* (London, 1982)
J. C. Welty: *The Life of Birds* (London, 1982)
A. P. Rowe: *Costumes and Featherwork of the Lords of Chimor* (Washington, DC, 1984)
E. Carmichael and S. Hugh-Jones: *The Hidden People of the Amazon* (London, 1985)
The Spirit Sings: Artistic Traditions of Canada's First Peoples (exh. cat. by J. D. Harrison and others, Calgary, Glenbow–Alta Inst., 1987)
Feather Masterpieces of the Ancient Andean World (exh. cat., ed. T. Gibson; London, Gibson F.A., 1990)
B. Braun and P. G. Roe: *Arts of the Amazon* (New York, 1995)
A. Dermawan: *Cak Kandar, eksplorasi & eksploitasi* (Jakarta, 2000) [on the Indonesian feather artist Cak Kandar]

Federal style. Architectural and decorative arts style that flourished in the USA from shortly after the acknowledgement of independence in the Treaty of Paris (1783) until *c.* 1820. The term is derived from the period surrounding the creation of the federal constitution in 1787 and was in use in a political sense by that year. Essentially it was a form of Neoclassicism, strongly influenced by manifestations of that style in England and, to a lesser extent, in France; but at times certain more conservative qualities inherited from the previous Colonial period are also present.

Like the architecture in which they were used, the decorative arts of the Federal period reflect the inspiration of Classical antiquity, and even more of Neo-classical England and France, tempered by existing, often conservative traditions. This can be seen most readily in metalwork and furniture, but it is also true of glass, ceramics and textiles. The appeal of antiquity is clearly indicated by the use of such Classical motifs as urns, garland swags and fasciae and such antique shapes as the klismos chair or urn- or helmet-fashioned teapots and sugar bowls. Specific motifs associated with the new American republic are less common than those reflecting antiquity, but they were sometimes employed (eagles, for example, inspired by the Great Seal, were especially popular). Such other patriotic motifs as the liberty cap were used occasionally, and there is even a card-table (Winterthur, DE, Du Pont Winterthur Mus.), made in New York, with a glass decorative panel featuring the names of the Democratic–Republican party candidates for President and Vice-President in 1800, Thomas Jefferson and Aaron Burr. As with architecture, a new lightness and delicacy first appeared, modified towards the end of the period by an increased heaviness and a somewhat more archaeological approach. Again, as with buildings, there is a heightened homogeneity in the decorative arts made in different areas of the new country, but regional differences and the individual characteristics of specific artist-craftsmen can be detected.

Although in general the new style did not appear until after the conclusion of the American Revolution in 1783, it can be found before then in metalwork, especially silver, as in a presentation tea urn (Philadelphia, PA, Mus. A) made in 1774, on the eve of the Revolution, in Philadelphia by Richard Humphreys (1750–1832) and inscribed to Charles Thomson, the secretary to the Continental Congress. Fashioned in the shape of an urn and ornamented with fluted bands and rosettes, as well as having a square base and squared handles and spout, it epitomizes the Neo-classical taste that is synonymous with the Federal style. After the Revolution, a similar taste could be found, for example, in tea services made in Boston by Paul Revere in 1792 (Minneapolis, MN, Inst. A.) and in Philadelphia by Simon Chaudron (1758–1846) and Anthony Rasch in 1809–12 (Winterthur, DE, Du Pont Winterthur Mus.), as well as in such objects as a jug shaped like a wineskin, made for Jefferson by Anthony Simmons (d 1808) and Samuel Alexander (d 1847) in Philadelphia in 1801 (Monticello, VA, Jefferson Found.), or a plateau (or tray) executed in New York by John Forbes (1781–1864) and presented to De Witt Clinton in 1825 (priv. col., on loan to New York, Met.).

In furniture the Federal style flourished throughout the country from Salem, MA, to Charleston, SC, and westward into Kentucky and Louisiana. The most direct inspiration was from the pattern books of George Hepplewhite and Thomas Sheraton, but later influences include Thomas Hope, George Smith and Pierre La Mésangère (1761–1831). The presence of French as well as English source books was paralleled by the activity of a number of French-trained cabinetmakers working in Federal America, including Charles-Honoré Lannuier in New York and Michel Bouvier (1792–1874) in Philadelphia, just as Chaudron represents French silversmiths working in the latter city.

Indications of the new style are found in oval- and shield-back chairs, often with delicately tapered or sabre legs; a host of Neo-classical motifs from urns and Classical orders to putti and paterae; and refined inlay and exquisite ormolu mounts. Such mounts were employed especially by French émigrés, but Americans and cabinetmakers from Britain also used them. Representative examples of chairs include those with carved shield-backs made in Salem by Samuel McIntire in the 1790s (e.g. Winterthur, DE, Du Pont Winterthur Mus.); scroll-back and sabre-leg models created by Duncan Phyfe in New York in 1807 (Winterthur, DE, Du Pont Winterthur Mus.); painted oval-backed chairs with Prince of Wales feathers (e.g. New York, Met.) ordered from Philadelphia in 1796 by Salem merchant Elias Haskett Derby (1739–99); and rectangular ones enlivened with scenes of country houses near Baltimore (c. 1800–10; Baltimore, MD, Mus. A.) executed by John Finlay (1777–1840) and Hugh Finlay (1781–1831). Tables range from delicately inlaid Pembroke or breakfast tables made in Salem by Elijah Sanderson and Jacob Sanderson in the 1780s or 1790s (Winterthur, DE, Du Pont Winterthur Mus.), to card-tables with gilded winged figures by Lannuier (c. 1815; Baltimore, Mus. & Lib. MD Hist.; New York, Met.).

Examples of Federal style cabinets include an inlaid semicircular commode by John SEYMOUR and his son Thomas (c. 1809; Boston, MA, Mus. F.A.); a carved double chest with numerous Neo-classical motifs on top and a more Rococo lower half, carved by McIntire (c. 1795–1805; Boston, MA, Mus. F.A.); or a lady's dressing-table with inlay of fine woods and painting on glass, topped by urns and an eagle (Baltimore, Mus. & Lib. MD Hist.), made in Baltimore in the first decade of the 19th century and attributed to William Camp (1773–1822).

The most noteworthy glass of the period was that made by JOHN FREDERICK AMELUNG at his New Bremen Glassmanufactory near Frederick, MD. Other Federal period glass includes the products of BAKEWELL & CO. and the NEW ENGLAND GLASS CO.

Neo-classical ceramics used in the USA during the Federal period were mostly wares imported from England, France and China. Earthenwares were made, some of which, such as a black-glazed coffee-pot by Thomas Haig & Co. of Philadelphia (c. 1825; New York, Met.), reflect the influence of English Regency and French Empire silver and porcelain. Only in 1826 did the china manufactory founded by William Tucker in Philadelphia begin to produce similarly inspired porcelain wares. The most fashionable textiles in the Neo-classical taste were also imported from England and France, but both hand-embroidered and machine-printed fabrics, notably the printed calicoes of JOHN HEWSON of Philadelphia, were produced in the USA during this era.

B. Tracy and W. H. Gerdts: *Classical America, 1815–1845* (Newark, NJ, 1963)

C. F. Montgomery: *American Furniture: The Federal Period* (New York, 1966)

19th-Century America: Furniture and Other Decorative Arts (exh. cat., New York, Met., 1970)

W. Cooper: *In Praise of America: American Decorative Arts, 1650–1830* (New York, 1980)

B. Garvan: *Federal Philadelphia, 1785–1825: The Athens of the Western World* (Philadelphia, 1987)

Arts of the Federal Period (exh. cat. by B. Cullity; Sandwich, MA, Heritage Plantation, 1989)

S. Feld: *Neo-classicism in America: Inspiration and Innovation, 1810–1840* (New York, 1991)

W. Garrett: *Classical America: The Federal Style and Beyond* (New York, 1992)

W. Cooper: *Classical Taste in America, 1800–1840* (Baltimore, New York and London, 1993)

T. J. Hardiman and others: 'Maine Cabinetmakers of the Federal Period and the Influence of Coastal Massachusetts Design'. *Mag. Ant.*, clxv/5 (May 2004), pp. 128–35

Our Young Nation: American Federal Furniture and Decorative Arts from the Watson Collection (exh. cat. by P. D. Zimmerman, C. T. Butler and C. E. Hutchins; Columbus, GA, Mus., 2004)

Felaert, Dirk. *See* VELLERT, DIRK.

Feldspathic glaze. *See under* GLAZE.

Fell, Isaac. *See under* LEAVER, GABRIEL.

Felletin. *See under* AUBUSSON, §2.

Felt. Non-woven textile used as a practical material, particularly in Central Asia, and as an artistic and craft medium. Felt is the end product of a process whereby fibres or staples of animal hair are subjected to friction and pressure under moist, hot conditions. The action enables the fibres to matt owing to their ability to 'creep' in a tip to root direction. The scales on the outer covering of the fibres then become enmeshed in the natural crimp of the twisted fibres.

Felt is usually made from sheep's wool and from goat or camel hair, but the hair or wool from many other animals can be used, even that of humans. It is also possible to incorporate such vegetable fibres as jute. The wool is used in its natural colours—ivory, light brown and dark brown—or it is dyed. Traditionally, the dyes were such locally obtainable plants as madder and pomegranate, but widely traded dyes, indigo and cochineal for example, were introduced in many areas; all have now been replaced by synthetic dyes.

The methods by which felt is made vary in different countries. On the Asian steppe felt is usually, but not exclusively, made by women. A reed mat is placed on the ground, and the shorn wool is beaten or teased by a felting bow made of a length of gut attached to an L-shaped piece of wood. The worker holds the bow firmly over the wool with one hand and with the other hand strikes the tautened gut with a mallet. The vibration causes the wool fibres to loosen and disentangle. The Turkoman tribes card the fibres through a large comb standing on the ground, its metal teeth pointing upwards. The wool is then laid in clumps on the mat and spread evenly, without gaps, to the required depth. The thickness required of the final product dictates the amount of wool put down on the mat; it may be as much as 400 mm deep. The wool is sprinkled with warm wa-

ter and an alkaline solution (e.g. urine or soap powder), then rolled tightly in a bundle and tied. Depending on the width of the piece being made, up to ten women, elbow to elbow, roll it for several hours. The larger and thicker the material required, the more pressure, workers and time are needed. In Turkey men make the felt. Having tied up the bundle, they roll it with their feet, standing in a row, their hands pressing on one knee to give the greatest weight. They work to music, singing in rhythm. In Afghanistan both sexes make felt: normally, the women lay out the pattern, and the men do the heavy work.

In finer pieces, the work is sometimes unrolled for inspection and adjustment before completion; the edges are tidied, and then it is rolled again. When dried, the surfaces are smoothed by a burnishing stone or roller. Rougher rugs are not inspected, just unfolded and put out to dry. The finished felt varies in thickness from 15 mm, when used for tents, to 2 mm for fine appliqué.

In hat-making, the felt is prepared in a shallow dish, kneaded until soft and pliable, then moulded around a block to form the required shape. It is then pressed until ready. A hatter in Iran can make up to 30 hats a day, before putting them outside to dry and finally polishing them.

There are a number of ways of patterning and decorating felt. Two or more colours can be felted together at random. Alternatively, predyed clumps of fibre, arranged in a pattern, are placed on the mat, and the rest of the wool laid on top of them; the wool will felt together in one piece. If a pattern is to appear on the back of the finished felt, more coloured wool is placed on the top of the mass. If layers of different coloured felt are superimposed, contrasts of shape may be achieved with, for example, incisions and saw-tooth edges. Plain felts can be decorated by painting, stencilling or block-printing.

Sewing techniques are also used to decorate felt. In Afghanistan it is common to find appliquéd motifs of felt, silk, cotton, feathers, bark or leather. A mosaic effect can be achieved by sewing small pieces of felt together, with the stitches hidden in the seams. This technique is often found in Afghanistan and the Commonwealth of Independent States. Edges can be applied as decoration and to strengthen the article. These may be of cord, silk or leather and surround either the complete article or individual design motifs. Further protection is afforded by decorative quilting stitches, often zigzags or spirals: these are used on such items as camel, horse and donkey trappings, which come under great strain. Sometimes felts are richly embroidered, which reinforces the fabric as well as enhancing its appearance.

The Art of the Felt Maker (exh. cat. by M. E. Burkett, Kendal, Abbot Hall A.G., 1979) [extensive bibliog.]
H. Bidder and I. Bidder: *Filzteppiche: Ihre Geschichte und Eigenart* (Brunswick;, 1980)
B. Gordon: *Feltmaking* (New York, 1980)
Felting, New York, American Craft Mus. (New York, 1980)
Internationalt Filtsymposium (exh. cat., Århus, Studenternes Hus, 1990)

Hat/headdress, European felt with appliquéd design of a face, Tlingit culture (prob.), 20th century (Toronto, Royal Ontario Museum)

I. Turnau: *Hand-Felting in Europe and Asia: From the Middle Ages to the 20th century* (Warsaw,1997)

C. Martens: 'The Felt Carpets of a Master Craftsman', *Hali*, cxx (Jan–Feb 2002), pp. 135–9

T. Boerens: *Felt Art Accents for the Home: 44 Elegant, Yet Easy, Projects* (Iola, Krause, Newton Abbot, 2003)

Fender. *See under* FIREPLACE FURNISHINGS.

Férand, Gaspard. *See under* MOUSTIERS.

Ferenczy, Noémi (*b* Szentendre, 18 June 1890; *d* Budapest, 20 Dec 1957). Hungarian tapestry artist and textile designer. She trained as an artist by visiting major European museums and by studying (1912) tapestry-weaving at the Manufactures des Gobelins in Paris. She worked partly in Budapest and at the Nagybánya colony until 1932, when she settled permanently in Budapest.

Ferenczy was among the few artists who did not come to tapestry design from a background in painting. She preferred to weave the tapestries herself, so that she could modify the techniques wherever necessary to suit the design. For example, she did not weave in complete rows but finished an entire motif before proceeding, which gave her more freedom to concentrate on details. This 'free' style of weaving allowed her to develop distinctive decorative and monumental compositions. Initially, her work resembled the plant- and animal-filled verdure of 16th-century Flemish and French tapestry. She had a lifelong love and respect for nature, which she gained from her family background. Her first monumental tapestry, *Creation* (2.23 × 2.19 m, 1913; Budapest, Mus. Applied A.), was inspired by the stained-glass windows of Chartres Cathedral. A fairy-tale atmosphere infuses the tapestry, which depicts God, the Garden of Eden and Adam and Eve, with stylized forms and deep, flaming colours—various shades of blue, brown, claret, red and green. *Flight into Egypt* (1915–16; Budapest, Mus. Applied A.), the other major work of her early period, is also characterized by much decorative detail, particularly lush vegetation, and a rich use of colour.

From 1917 Ferenczy was involved in the labour movement, and she was imprisoned for her part in the arts administration of the Council Republic of 1919. Her subsequent work was largely determined by this involvement: the rich backgrounds of nature give way to monumental, decorative depictions of man and work. In these compositions she used simple forms and fewer colours, the hues becoming deeper and warmer in tone, with reds and browns dominating. *White Man with an Axe* (1923–4; Budapest, N.G.) was conceived as a portrait. In the centre of the composition a man dressed in white holds an axe, with mallows and a rotten tree trunk behind him. The large sweep of the composition points to Ferenczy's growing inclination towards monumentality, developed to the full in her tapestries of the 1930s. *Stonemason* (1933; Budapest, N.G.) is a fine example on the theme of labour, while *Spring Work* (1943; Budapest, Hist. Mus.) stands out among her landscapes. After World War II Ferenczy began to give equal expression to internationalist and patriotic convictions. *Joining Forces* (1948; Budapest, Mus. Applied A.) portrays two workers, one with a hammer and one with a pair of callipers, joining hands. Two enormous wheels in the background make clear reference to industrial workers, while the chains running round the border represent their exploitation. Patriotism inspired *Centenary* (1948; Budapest, Mus. Applied A.), which commemorates the 1848 Revolution and depicts a female figure holding up a tablet with the words of a patriotic song of the time. In 1948 Ferenczy was awarded the Kosuth Prize, and from 1950 to 1954 she taught at the College of Applied Arts in Budapest. In her last works she returned to the luxuriant portrayal of nature. *Ring of Girls* (1952–4; ex-Patriotic Popular Front priv. col., Budapest), for example, shows girls in a green meadow forming a circle by holding hands against a background of extraordinarily rich and detailed hills and woods.

K. Tolnay: *Ferenczy Noémi* (Budapest, 1934)

M. Cseh: *Ferenczy Noémi* (Budapest, 1963)

É. Kovács: 'Noémi Ferenczy', *New Hung. Q.*, iv/9 (1963), p. 212

Ferenczy Noémi, intro. J. Jankovich (Budapest, 1983)

Ferner, F. J. *See under* HAUSMALER.

Ferniani Factory. *See under* FAENZA.

Ferrara. Italian centre of tapestry production. The collection of northern European tapestries owned by the Este family was already large by 1436, when the family began to follow the lead of the Gonzaga in Mantua in hiring French and Flemish master weavers to care for them, to weave new tapestries and to act as liaisons with northern workshops for larger commissions. Tapestry patronage varied in tenor with political events and with each succeeding ruler. The first Flemish weavers were hired under Niccolò III d'Este, Marchese of Ferrara, who had bought many prestigious northern sets. Jacomo de Flandria de Angelo (*fl* 1436) is the first mentioned, hired apparently to repair tapestries. He was joined by another master, Pietro di Andrea di Fiandra (*fl* 1441–71), in 1441. Rinaldo Boteram (pseud. di Gualtieri; *fl* 1438–81) from Brussels, one of the most famous northern weavers in Italy during the 15th century, may have already worked for Niccolò before he set up shop in Siena in 1438.

It was apparently Niccolò's son, Leonello d'Este, however, who first encouraged the weaving of new tapestries in the city on a large scale. In 1444, probably because of the rich tapestry displays planned for his second marriage to Maria of Aragon, Leonello not only bought and borrowed many sets but also attracted many master weavers including Boteram, who, although he moved to Mantua in 1448, continued to serve as a go-between for court orders of larger tapestries from the north for over 30 years. Another important master, Livinus Gilii de Burgis (*fl* 1444–after 1473), also arrived in 1444 and worked in Ferrara, except for a short period in Florence (1455–7), until he went to Milan in 1463; he returned briefly to Ferrara in 1473. None of the tapestries woven in Ferrara for Leonello or the many more woven for his successor, Borso d'Este, has survived, but documents indicate that most were small pieces such as altar frontals, bench-backs and bed covers and hangings, often of precious materials and from cartoons by the city's finest painters, particularly Cosimo Tura (?1430–95). The Paris master Renaud de Maincourt (pseud. Rainaldo de Man Curta; *fl* 1451–7) was in Ferrara briefly in 1457, the year another French weaver, Rubinetto di Francia (*fl* 1457–84), began working there. Giovanni Lattres of Arras (*fl* 1461–7; *d* by 1471) is also documented mainly in Ferrara, except for a brief stay in Venice between 1462 and 1464. Giovanni Mille (*fl* 1464–5) and Rinaldo Grue (*fl* 1464–71), two weavers from Tournai (now in Belgium), arrived in Ferrara in 1464; in 1470 Rigo d'Alemagna (*fl* 1470–74) arrived and was most active under Borso's successor, Ercole I d'Este. The only 15th-century Ferrarese tapestries to survive are two versions of a *Pietà* (*c.* 1475–6; Lugano, Col. Thyssen–Bornemisza, and Cleveland, OH, Mus. A.) woven by Rubinetto di Francia from a cartoon by Tura, which illustrate the high quality of both design and weaving that must have characterized Ferrarese production in this period.

During the later rule of Ercole I and under the great painting patron Alfonso I d'Este, there was a hiatus in Ferrarese tapestry production, until it was revived under Ercole II d'Este. The brothers Giovanni Karcher (*fl* 1517–62) and NICHOLAS KARCHER had possibly been active in Ferrara by 1517, mainly repairing tapestries. In 1536 Ercole II sent Nicolas to Brussels to recruit eight weavers, including JAN ROST, to establish a proper court factory. Another northern weaver, Gerardo Slot (*fl* 1537–42), is documented working independently at the court at this time. Ercole began commissioning ambitious sets of large tapestries from these masters as an integral part of his extensive redecorating programme for his palace and other residences. Among those who painted the cartoons were the Dossi brothers, Dosso (*c.* 1486–1541/2) and Battista (*d* 1548), Giulio Romano (?1499–1546), Girolamo da Carpi (*c.* 1501–56), Leonardo da Brescia (*fl* 1544; *d* 1598) and Garofalo (1481–1559). Only a few of these tapestries survive, including the remains of the five *Metamorphoses* (*c.* 1544–5; two tapestries, Paris, Louvre; fragments, priv. cols.) after cartoons by Battista Dossi, and seven *Pergoline* (*c.* 1556–9; one tapestry and two fragments, Paris, Mus. A. Déc.) from cartoons by Leonardo da Brescia. A series of eight *Stories of SS George and Maurelius* woven by Karcher's workshop for Ferrara Cathedral from cartoons (1550–53) by Garofalo, Camillo Filippi (*c.* 1500–74) and Luca d'Olanda (*fl* 1536–54) is *in situ*.

During the reign of Alfonso II d'Este, tapestry production again declined. Giovanni Karcher's son Luigi Karcher (*d* 1580), who was a painter as well as a weaver, inherited the Karcher workshop in 1562. His major surviving work is a tapestry of the *Marriage of the Virgin* from a cartoon by Camillo Filippi and his son Sebastiano Filippi II (*c.* 1532–1602) for the *Life of the Virgin* cycle in Como Cathedral (1569–70; *in situ*). After Luigi's death, tapestry weaving effectively ended in Ferrara.

G. Campori: *L'Arazzeria Estense* (Modena, 1876/R Sala Bolognese, 1980)

N. Forti Grazzini: *L'Arazzo ferrarese* (Milan, 1982); review by C. Adelson in *Burl. Mag.*, cxxvii (1985), pp. 307–8

Ferronerie [ferronnerie]. In English the term is sometimes used in its literal sense to denote French ironwork or wrought iron but usually used in a transferred sense to denote to an ornament commonly used on 16th-century Antwerp faience consisting of scrolling patterns of arabesques and volutes.

Festoon. Carved, moulded or painted ornament representing a chain or loop of fruit, flowers or leaves, suspended at both ends and often represented as bound with ribbons. It is sometimes distinguished from a swag, which may be defined as a piece of cloth or drapery hung in the same shape and also widely used as a decorative device in architecture and decoration. The device originated in Classical antiquity, when festoons of real fruit were hung between the skulls of slaughtered sacrificial animals and the

Stucco festoons surrounding the portrait of *Caterina Sforza* in the Hall of Giovanni dalle Bande Nere, designed by Giorgio Vasari, Palazzo Vecchio, Florence, 16th century

sacrificial instruments. Later the festoon was applied as carved decoration to temple friezes and became part of the repertory of motifs used in secular architecture. The device has been widely applied in revivals of the Classical style in architecture, interior decoration and, particularly from the 17th century, as an ornament on furniture, carpets, pottery and plate. Its forms are always slightly altered according to the prevailing taste and range from rich and elaborate clustered festoons of the Baroque period to the light and flowing festoons of the Neo-classical. In the Renaissance the festoon became one of the chief decorative motifs; instead of animal skulls or bucrania, ribbons, rosettes, masks and figures were incorporated into the design. The festoon was also popular during the Neo-classical period and was a frequent decorative feature of interiors by Robert Adam.

Fettling. In the manufacturing of ceramics, the process of removing seam marks before firing.

Feuchère. French family of bronze-casters and bronze-gilders. Pierre-François Feuchère (1737–1823) worked in Paris from 1763, selling gilt bronze clock cases, wall lights, and candelabra; he was also commissioned by JEAN HAURÉ to make bronze for the crown. The J. Paul Getty Museum in Los Angeles has a pair of his gilt bronze wall lights (c. 1787). His son Lucien-François (c. 1750–1828) entered the business in 1784, and the factory grew to become one of the largest in France; the J. Paul Getty Museum has a blued metal and gilt bronze pair of standing candelabra (c. 1784–6) by Lucien-François. In 1824 the business passed to Lucien-François's son and son-in-law, who closed it in 1831.

Feuillâtre, Eugene (b 1870; d 1916). French goldsmith and enameller. He was the leading maker of larger pieces of *plique à jour* for box lids (e.g. silver box with domed lid, c. 1902; London, BM) and exhibition plates. In 1898 he exhibited silver pieces enamelled with naturalistic decoration in translucent colours. He was a leading exponent of ART NOUVEAU in enamel and glass.

Feure, Georges de [Sluijters, Georges Joseph van; Feuren, Georges van] (b Paris, 6 Sept 1868; d Paris, 26 Nov 1943). French designer and painter. Son of a Dutch architect and a Belgian mother, he started out as an actor, costumier and then interior decorator in Paris. Capturing the essence of the feminine spirit became his trademark. With Eugène Gaillard and Edouard Colonna he was selected by Siegfried Bing to design rooms for his Pavilion Bing at the Exposition Universelle, Paris (1900). De Feure's carpets, glassware and furniture designs for the boudoir and toilette were based on the theme of woman, emphasizing delicate lines and elegant sensuality. He later left Bing's gallery and, as an independent designer,

created *vide-poche* furniture, which contained hidden marquetry compartments. This furniture suggested notions of secrecy and coquetry, themes that de Feure pursued throughout his career.

'Le Mobilier de Georges de Feure', *A. & Déc.*, ii (1908), pp. 115–32
I. Millman: 'Georges de Feure: A Turn-of-the-century Universal Artist', *Apollo*, cxxviii (Nov 1988), pp. 314–19
I. Millman: *Georges de Feure: Maître du symbolisme et de l'art nouveau* (Courbevoie, Paris, 1992)
Georges de Feure 1868–1943 (exh. cat. by I. Millman; Amsterdam, Rijksmus. van Gogh, 1993)
I. Millman: 'George de Feure', *Mag. Ant.*, clxvii/3 (March, 2005), pp. 68–77

Fevère [Lefebvre; Fèvre], **Pietro** [Pierre] (b Antwerp, 1579; d Florence, 1669). Flemish tapestry-weaver. He was working in Paris in 1619, when he was invited by Cosimo II, Grand Duke of Tuscany, to go to Florence to assist in the revival of tapestry-weaving. Fevère, who knew both the high- and low-warp techniques, was given a workshop in the Palazzo Vecchio. In 1630, after the death of Jacopo Ebert van Asselt (fl 1621–30), head weaver of the Arazzeria Medicea—the Medici tapestry factory—Fevère was named head weaver and moved to the larger workshops at S Marco. His sons Giovanni (d 1700), Francesco, Andrea, Filippo (d after 1677) and Jacopo worked with him; in 1662 Giovanni founded one of the important dynastic workshops at the GOBELINS TAPESTRY FACTORY at its institution in 1662.

Under his tutelage, the Arazzeria Medicea enjoyed a period of revived activity. The numerous large tapestries woven in his workshops include seven of the ten tapestries of the *Seasons and the Hours* (1641–3); five of the seven *Stories of St Paul* (1646; destr.); two of the five-piece *Story of Tobias* (1648; destr.); five of the twelve-piece *Story of Alexander* (1651; destr.); pieces of the *Life of Moses* (1650s); and *Stories of Grand Duke Cosimo I de' Medici* (1654–65; all surviving examples Florence, Sopr. B. A. & Storici Col.).

Late in his career, Fevère initiated the practice of systematically weaving portable, high-warp tapestry replicas of favourite paintings from the Grand Ducal picture gallery, including the *Virgin and Child with SS Anne, Joseph and John the Baptist* after Rubens (1652); a *Virgin and Child* after Raphael and the *Holy Family* after Andrea del Sarto (1660; all Florence, Sopr. B. A. & Storici Col). Possibly following this Florentine example, this genre of virtuoso weaving subsequently became common in many other European tapestry factories.

Fibreglass. Glassfibre reinforced plastic, also known as glassfibre reinforced polyester or GRP. It is a light but strong and durable material, and, unlike most plastics, its use involves low-level technology, making it accessible as an artist's material, although its major uses are commercial and industrial. Moulded fibreglass is sometimes used for outdoor furniture and architectural ornaments.

Polyester Resin, Glassfibre, Cold Cast Resin Metals, Clear Embedding Resins (Reading and London, 1989)

The Strand Guide to Glassfibre (Wollaston, [1990])

K. Noakes: *The Fibreglass Manual: A Practical Guide to the Use of Reinforced Plastics* (Marlborough, Crowood, 2003)

Fiddle pattern. *See under* CUTLERY, §1.

Fiedler, Johann Gottlob (*fl* 1775–86). German cabinetmaker based in Berlin, where he made furniture for the Prussian Court. His surviving furniture includes pieces in the Berlin and Potsdam palaces and a marquetry secrétaire (1775; Hamburg, Mus. Kst & Gew.) and an ormolu-mounted mahogany and parquetry commode (*c.* 1785) which when sold at Christie's in 1991 established a world auction record for German furniture.

Field, John (*b* 1771; *d* 1841). English silhouettist who was apprenticed to JOHN MIERS and later entered into partnership with him. His silhouettes of William Magee, Archbishop of Dublin, George Onslow (Earl of Onslow) and Jeremy Bentham are all in the National Portrait Gallery in London. He also undertook intricate miniature work in ivory for rings and jewellery.

Fielded panel. Furniture panel which is moulded, sunk, or raised, or is divided into smaller panels

Fife Pottery. *See under* WEMYSS WARE.

Figurehead. *See under* SHIP-DECORATION.

Filigree [Fr. *filigrane*; It. and Sp. *Filigrana*; Ger. *Drahtegeflecht*]. Metalwork decoration in which fine precious metal wires, usually gold or silver, are delicately soldered in an openwork pattern. It is used especially in jewellery and the ornamentation of other small objects. In 16th-century Germany, where the most important centre for filigree was Siedenburg (near Bremen), large caskets and dishes made from filigree were laboriously manufactured for the *Kunstkammer* market. Thereafter filigree survived only in attenuated form as a folk art, and the craft still survives in Italy and Norway for the manufacturing of tourist souvenirs.

T. Riisøen and A. Bøe: *Om filigran/Filigree* (Oslo, 1959)

E. Taburet-Delahaye: 'Opus and filum: L'Ornement filigrane dans l'orfèvrerie gothique du centre et du sud-ouest de la France', *Rev. Art.*, xc (1990), pp. 46–57

M. J. Sanz: 'El Arte de la Filigrana en Centroamerica. Su Importacion a Canarias y la Peninsula', *Goya*, ccxciii (March–Apr 2003), pp. 103–14

Filigree glass. *See under* VENICE, §2.

Fillet. In architecture and the decorative arts, a narrow, flat, raised moulding used to give emphasis or to hide the edges of wallpaper or hangings; in leatherwork (especially bookbinding), the term denotes a wheel tool used to impress a straight line or the straight line made by the tool.

Filpai. *See* ELEPHANT'S FOOT.

Finch, Alfred William (*b* Brussels, 28 Nov 1854; *d* Helsinki, 1930). Belgian painter and potter. In 1886 and 1891 Finch visited England, where he was exposed to the tenets of the English Arts and Crafts Movement, and by the early 1890s he had turned his artistic focus from painting to ceramics. Anna Boch (1848–1936), a fellow member of Les XX, invited Finch to the Boch Frères factory at La Louvière, Belgium. From 1890 to 1893 he worked as a decorator, applying Neo-Impressionist methods of painting to the decoration of ceramics; this was a new direction for the factory, which at the time was producing pastiches of the Delft, Sèvres and Iznik styles. He continued working as a painter and potter and in 1891 opened his own pottery at Forges-Chimay, France.

In 1897 a Swede, Count Louis Sparre (1863–1964), saw Finch's ceramics in Brussels and invited him to Finland to establish a ceramics division at the Iris factory in Porvoo. Finch brought the ideas of the English Arts and Crafts Movement and the Belgian Art Nouveau style to Finland. His ceramics for Iris are characterized by painted or incised abstract, wavy patterns, applied dots painted in slip and boldly coloured glazes. Iris ceramics were made to be sold in S. Bing's L'Art Nouveau and Julius Meier-Graefe's La Maison Moderne in Paris. A large two-handled bowl incised with a wave-like pattern around the rim and decorated with green and blue slips and carefully placed white slip dots (*c.* 1900; London, V&A) bears the monogram of La Maison Moderne.

After the closure of the Iris factory in 1902, Finch became head of the ceramics department at the Central School of Industrial Design in Helsinki where

Gold necklace with filigree pendants, 1. 580 mm, India, *c.* 1880 (London, Victoria and Albert Museum)

Hanukkah lamp, parcel-gilt silver filigree, 300×290×6 mm, central Europe, c. 1863 (Paris, Musée d'Art et d'Histoire du Judaïsme)

he experimented with high-temperature glazes on stoneware.

Alfred William Finch: 1854–1930 (exh cat by A. Lindström and O. Valkonen; Helsinki, Athenaeum A. Mus. and Brussels, Musées Royaux B.-A., 1991)

Finial. Crowning ornament on the point of a spire or pinnacle. In the decorative arts, in which it commonly takes the form of an acorn or an urn, finials are used on canopies, on the ends of open seats in a church and on the covers of tableware in silver or pottery.

Finiguerra, Maso [Tommaso] (*b* Florence, March 1426; *d* Florence, *bur* 24 Aug 1464). Italian goldsmith, niellist and draughtsman. Many lost works are documented, and Maso left 14 volumes of drawings, various sulphur casts and some sketches, but his only documented work is the design (executed before February 1464) of a set of five figures, whose heads were painted by Alesso Baldovinetti (1425–99), for two intarsia panels for the north sacristy in Florence Cathedral. It has been convincingly suggested that he was also responsible for designing Giuliano da Maiano's intarsia of the *Annunciation*, formerly on a door of the abbey at Fiesole (Berlin, Tiergarten, Kstgewmus.). The close stylistic connection between these intarsia works and the niello of the *Coronation of the Virgin* on a pax (1452; Florence, Bargello) formerly in the Baptistery confirms that this niello must have been the principal decoration of the pax for which Maso was paid in 1452. The *Coronation* is a masterpiece of refinement, in which Maso was clearly influenced by the ornate style of Fra Filippo Lippi (*c.* 1406–69). Because of this, Maso has been credited with many nielli in Lippi's style, known through sulphur casts or paper impressions and noteworthy for their high artistic quality and wide range of subject-matter (e.g. Paris, Louvre; London, BM). A niello of the *Crucifixion* (Florence, Bargello) is stylistically close to the earliest group of these nielli and can be dated before the *Coronation* because of its debt to Lorenzo Ghiberti (1378–1455). The numerous copies of a later niello of the *Crucifixion* (Washington, DC, N.G.A.), which shows Pollaiuolo's influence, prove that Maso's works were very popular.

Finiguerra was already famous in the 15th century, when he was praised as a goldsmith, niellist and master draughtsman. Vasari recorded that Maso 'drew much and very well', but Cellini stated that he always used Antonio Pollaiuolo's designs. Cellini's testimony has been used to deny Maso any real artistic ability, but documentary evidence has reinforced Vasari's judgement. Vasari attributed the invention of engraving to Finiguerra. He claimed that this technique originated in Maso's habit of checking his work as it progressed by taking sulphur casts from the nielli and then paper impressions from the casts. This is supported by the fact that besides the niello of the *Coronation of the Virgin*, there are also two sulphur casts (London, BM; Paris, Louvre) and a paper impression (Paris, Bib. N.). This, however, does not imply that Maso engraved metal plates with the exclusive aim of producing prints.

K. Oberhuber: 'Vasari e il mito di Maso Finiguerra', *Il Vasari storiografo ed artista. Atti del congresso internazionale nel IV centenario della morte: Firenze, 1974*, pp. 383–93
M. Haines: *La sacrestia delle messe nel duomo di Firenze* (Florence, 1983), pp. 165–75
L. Melli: *Maso Finiguerra: I disegni* (Florence, 1995)

Finland. Ceramics *See* ARABIA PORCELAIN FACTORY.
Glass *See* IITTALA GLASSHOUSE; NUUTAJÄRVI.
Textiles *See* RYIJY AND RYER RUGS.

Fiorentino, Pier Maria. *See* SERBALDI DA PESCIA, PIER MARIA.

Fireplace furnishings. Hearth accessories comprising fire-backs, andirons (also called fire-dogs), log forks and tongs for feeding the fire, plus a pair of bellows and a curfew for controlling it. Fire-backs are heavy cast-iron plates that protect the rear of the fireplace. Early examples often display simple decorative motifs, but during the 17th century elaborate armorial compositions and allegorical scenes with neat floral borders became common. Anne of Cleves House Museum, Lewes, E. Sussex, contains a collection of backs cast in the Sussex Weald foundries.

Andirons or fire-dogs stand on the hearth-stone and are intended to support burning logs. They are made in pairs and consist of an ornamental front standard with a horizontal billet bar behind. Sturdy wrought- and cast-iron andirons with heraldic devices were common in medieval interiors (e.g. those with arms of Henry VIII at Knole), but from the early 17th century, brass ormolu and silver standards (examples at Ham House, Surrey, NT; Knole, Kent, NT) elaborately styled in the fashion of the day became popular; these usually took the form of urns, and were sometimes made with very expensive ma-

terials (e.g. at Ham, where even the supports of the grates were in silver). The most luxurious gilt-bronze andirons, ornamented with cupids, beasts, Chinese men, foliated and floral forms or fantastic animals symbolizing fire, such as dragons and salamanders, were made in the 18th century by such Parisian bronziers as Jacques Caffiéri, Philippe Caffiéri and Thomire (examples at Waddesdon Manor, Bucks, NT); sometimes these highly ornamented andirons or chenets were purely decorative, and the task of supporting the logs was devolved to a second set of andirons called creepers, which were placed behind or between the ornamental andirons. As wood-burning fireplaces continued to be used in the USA well into the 19th century, many distinctive cast-brass and *paktong* (Chin.: artificial silver alloy of 20% nickel with brass) andirons of excellent quality were made, notably in Charleston, SC.

Bellows, used to blow up or fan a fire, were sometimes lavishly decorated with carving, marquetry, oriental japanning or penwork and even overlaid with silver, needlework or stumpwork. Standing bellows of box design, worked by a pump handle, and wheel-operated bellows were introduced as labour-saving contraptions in the early 19th century. A curfew is a hoodlike brass cover, often with repoussé decoration, that was placed over the embers on the hearth at night to make the fire safe. Most extant examples date from the late 17th century, as they were superseded by wire spark guards.

With the adoption of coal burning in England during the early 18th century, fire-dogs were replaced by grates. These were at first designed as free-standing baskets with a cast-iron backplate, cheeks, barred front and a pair of standards (similar to andirons). The usual material was wrought-iron, possibly with a brass apron and posts, but later bright steel and *paktong* grates became popular. After *c.* 1750 hob-grates, Bath or Venetian stoves and register grates, which were built into the fireplace opening and reduced smoke problems, became available. Contemporary furniture patternbooks by Chippendale and William Ince and John Mayhew feature designs for grates, while William and John Welldon's *The Smith's Right Hand* (1765) and William Glossop's *The Stove-Grate Maker's Assistant* (1771) contain numerous illustrations of modern grates.

Robert Adam and other leading Neo-classical architects renowned for creating unified room schemes naturally took a keen interest in chimney furniture, and Adam's drawings (London, Soane Mus.) include many delicate designs for grates. Chimney-pieces in the main reception rooms at houses where he worked, such as Mersham-le-Hatch (Kent), Osterley Park House (London, NT), Newby Hall (N. Yorks) and Croome Court (Hereford & Worcs) were intended to be impressive, with bright steel grates, *en suite* fenders (low metal screens designed to prevent coals from rolling into the room), sets of fire-irons and elegant mantelpiece garnitures.

One of the most accomplished Neo-classical smiths who worked with Adam at Harewood House,

W. Yorks, Newby Hall and Nostell Priory, W. Yorks, NT, was Maurice Tobin (*d* 1773) of Leeds. He and his successor, John Rodgers, occasionally marked their work with a name stamp. During the 18th century fire-irons were supplied in sets consisting of a poker, shovel and tongs, possibly with a rook and hearth broom. They were normally kept propped up in a corner of the fireplace rather than, as earlier, suspended from hooks on the wall or provided with a stand, later known as a fireside companion. Coal was kept in a box or a metal coal-scuttle. In the 18th century these receptacles were brought into a room by a servant when the fire needed to be fed, but after about 1800 they remained by the hearth. Surviving japanned sheet-iron examples are of bucket or sarcophagus form with lids and sometimes liners; copper scuttles and wooden boxes became popular in the 19th century.

Chimney- or fire-boards were employed to close gloomy fireplace openings during the summer. They were both practical and decorative since by sealing off the space, soot and draughts were excluded; many were covered with wallpaper, painted to represent a vase of flowers, a grate or a decorative design related to the room scheme. Four splendid Neo-classical examples painted by Bagio Rebecca (1735–1808) in 1769 for Audley End, Essex, survive, and there is another important group at Osterley Park House.

The CARRON IRON CO. of Falkirk, Central, founded in 1759, was the most successful firm to mass-produce fire-grates and stoves; like the COALBROOKDALE IRON COMPANY, it sometimes marked its work. Falkirk Museum houses the entire collection of the former Carron Co. Museum, including many castings and trade catalogues. The firm continued to reproduce traditional patterns well into the 20th century; in fact, many foundries, notably Thomas Elsley & Co., London, produced high-quality copies of Georgian chimney furniture.

Mention should also be made of trivets, which support a pot or kettle near the fire. They generally have pierced brass tops and either stood on the hearth or were hung on the top bar of the grate. A cat is a six-armed stand of either turned wood or iron placed next to the fire to keep a plate of muffins or toast warm. A footman is a stand to support a kettle in front of the fire. A cresset is an iron fire-bracket, and a fire-back is a panel of cast iron (often decorated in low relief) at the back of a hearth.

H. J. Kauffman: *The American Fireplace: Chimneys, Mantelpieces, Fireplaces and Accessories* (New York, 1972/*R* Morgantown, PA, 1996)
H. J. Kauffman: *Early American Andirons and Other Fireplace Accessories* (Nashville, 1974)
D. Fennimore: *Metalwork in Early America* (n.p., 1996)

Firing-glass. Eighteenth-century English table-glass with a short stem and an unusually thick base suited to being slammed on the table.

Fisher, Alexander (*b* 1864; *d* 1936). English goldsmith who specialized in enamels. He attended Louis Dalpayrat's lectures (1885) on enamel painting, which he subsequently studied in Paris. His surviving works in this medium include *The Wagner Girdle* (1896; V&A, London) and *Jewel Casket: Fortune's Treasure Chest* (Cecil Higgins Art Gallery, Bedford). In 1906 he collected his periodical essays as a book entitled *The Art of Enamelling on Metal*.

Fishley. English family of potters based at Fremington, Devon. George Fishley (1771–1865) established the pottery, which made both domestic earthenware and figures. The best-known member of the family was George's grandson, Edwin Beer Fishley (1832–1911), whose work was often modelled on Etruscan and Minoan pottery. His grandson, William Fishley Holland (1889–1970), opened a pottery in Clevedon (North Somerset) in the early 1920s.

E. Leary: 'By Potters Art and Skill: Pottery by the Fishleys of Fremington', *Cer. Rev.*, xci (Jan–Feb 1985), pp. 10–12
E. Jones and V. Jones: 'Tale of the Fishley Plate', *Cer. Rev.*, ccii (July–Aug 2003), pp. 36–7

Flagon. Vessel for holding wine (originally eucharistic wine), fitted with a handle and (usually) a lid that can be raised with a thumbpiece; the secular form in use for holding beer is also called a tankard. In American usage, the flagon is a tall vessel used for pouring and the tankard a short vessel for drinking. Flagons were variously made of pewter, silver, gold, stoneware and porcelain.

Flambé glaze. Red iridescent glaze, streaked and splashed with blue. The technique was developed in China in the Qing period (1644–1911) and revived in France in the late 19th century, notably by ERNEST CHAPLET and JOSEPH-THÉODORE DECK.

R. Tichane: *Copper Red Glazes* (Iola, 1998)
J. Britt: 'Flambé Magic', *Cer. Rev.*, ccxi (Jan–Feb 2005), pp. 48–51

Flashed glass. Colourless glass that has been coated with a film of coloured glass. See fig. on p. 384.

Flatback figures. Earthenware portrait figures made in Staffordshire potteries in the 19th century; the backs were left unmodelled and undecorated. The design emerged in the 1830s, and flatbacks were soon being made by more than 100 Staffordshire potteries. The figures were usually made by press moulding. The most popular flatbacks portrayed members of the royal family, but there are also images of notable public figures, including clergy, soldiers and authors. There is a large collection of flatbacks in the Potteries Museum and Art Gallery in Stoke-on-Trent.

Flat chasing. Low relief chasing worked from the front, executed with punch and hammer. The technique is used on SHEFFIELD PLATE, which cannot

Flashed ruby-glass (see p. 383) Passover goblet with wheel-engraved inscription, h. 215 mm, Bohemia, late 19th century (New York, The Jewish Museum)

be engraved; the outline is less sharply defined than is engraving.

Flatware. *See* CUTLERY.

Flaxman, John (*b* York, 6 July 1755; *d* London, 9 Dec 1826). English sculptor and modeller. He was the most famous English Neo-classical sculptor of the late 18th century and the early 19th; in the decorative arts, he produced models for pottery and silver.

In 1775 Flaxman began to supply designs for ceramic medallions and plaques to Josiah Wedgwood, for whom his father (a plaster-cast maker) had supplied casts. It is clear that he found the work for Wedgwood onerous and unrewarding; nevertheless, some of his designs are remarkable. The *Apotheosis of Homer* relief (1778), for instance, which was adapted from an outline engraving of an ancient Greek vase in the collection of Sir William Hamilton for use on pots, chimney-pieces and plaques, has rarely been out of production. While most of his Wedgwood designs are closely derived from the Antique, some, such as *Blind Man's Buff* (1782), show the influence of Florentine Renaissance art, while some pieces in the celebrated *Chess Set*, such as the bishop based on a figure on Wells Cathedral, are derived from English medieval sculpture. He also modelled a number of

profile portraits for medallions in jasperware, such as *Captain James Cook* (*c.* 1779) and *Sarah Siddons* (1787). Flaxman provided Wedgwood with a wax relief of each design, which then became the property of the manufacturer, to be used without further reference to the artist, whose name would not appear on the final product.

Although Flaxman did no more work for Wedgwood after 1787, when he moved to Italy, he continued to make designs for commercial use, including medals and, most notably, silverware for the firm of Rundell, Bridge & Rundell from 1805. His work for this firm included such spectacular pieces as the *Shield of Achilles* (silver gilt, 1817–21; Windsor Castle, Berks, Royal Col.) and the *National Cup* (1824–5; Windsor Castle, Berks, Royal Col.). His silverware, particularly his massive table ornaments, was favoured by the Prince Regent (later George IV). His designs for silver remained influential throughout the Victorian period, and many of his designs for Wedgwood are still in production.

J. Flaxman and D. Bindman: *John Flaxman* (London, 1979)
M. T. Bassett: *John Flaxman Designs at Roseville Pottery* (Cleveland, 2001)
John Flaxman 1755–1826: Master of the Purest Line (exh. cat. by J. Flaxman and D. Bindman; London, Soane Mus. and U. Coll., Strang Print Room, 2003)

Flemish scroll. Shape of a double scroll as seen on the front legs and stretchers of many 17th-century English chairs.

Fletcher, Benjamin. *See under* WICKER.

Fletcher & Gardiner. Firm of American silversmiths established in 1809 in Boston by Thomas Charles Fletcher (*b* Alstead Cheshire NH, 3 April 1787; *d* Delano NJ, 14 Nov 1866) and Sidney Gardiner (*b* Southold, Long Island, NY, 23 Jan 1787; *d* Veracruz, Mexico, 1827) and moved in 1811 to Philadelphia. The workshop specialized in presentation plate (e.g. presentation vase, 1824; New York, Met.) and also made tea-services.

D. L. Fennimore: 'Thomas Fletcher and Sidney Gardiner', *Antiques*, cii/4 (Oct 1972), pp. 642–9
A. K. Wagner: *Fletcher and Gardiner: Presentation Silver for the Nation* (Delaware, 2004)

Flettner, Peter. *See* FLÖTNER, PETER.

Fleuron. Decorative motif in the formalized shape of a flower.

Flight, Thomas. *See under* WORCESTER.

Flint glass. Lustrous glass, originally made in the 17th century by GEORGE RAVENSCROFT using local ground flint (as opposed to Venetian pebbles) as the siliceous ingredient. The term was subsequently used more loosely to denote English lead glass, which uses a composition of lead oxide, sand, and alkali.

N. M. Bredehoft: *Findlay Flint Glass Co., 1889–1891* (St Louisville, 1994)
R. Teal and T. S. Graban: *Albany Glass: Model Flint Glass Company of Albany, Indiana* (Marietta, 1997)

Flint Glass Manufactory, American. *See under* Stiegel, henry william.

Float. In weaving, the passing of weft-threads over a portion of the warp (two or more threads) without being interwoven with it; the term also denotes A thread passed in this manner.

Flock. *See under* WALLPAPER, §I. 3.

Florence. Italian city and capital of Tuscany.

1. Hardstones. 2. Porcelain. 3. Tapestry.

1. HARDSTONES. Grand Duke Francesco I created a fashion for mosaics and intaglio works in hardstones and, taking a personal interest in experimentation with materials and techniques, fostered their production in Florence. In 1572 the Milanese brothers Ambrogio Caroni (*d* 1611) and Stefano Caroni (*d* 1611) moved to Florence, followed by Giorgio Gaffurri, the head of a Milanese workshop specializing in the engraving of rock crystal and pietre dure. Designed by such court-approved artists as Bernardo Buontalenti, sophisticated vases were decorated with gold and enamel work by the Florentine and north European goldsmiths whom Francesco I had gathered in the Casino de' Medici in Piazza S Marco, his private residence. Intarsia and pietre dure mosaics (the *commesso di pietre dure*) made at this time are mainly geometric in composition and give maximum prominence to the assortment of precious materials.

At the Galleria dei Lavori founded by Ferdinando I in 1588 the most prominent activity was the production of pietre dure. Ornamental and figurative themes prevailed, and the resulting mosaics are sophisticated examples of the use of hardstones to create 'stone paintings'. An opportunity to develop this technique was provided by the decoration of the Chapel of the Princes in S Lorenzo, a mausoleum with hardstone cladding and, at its centre, a small temple entirely in pietre dure with trimmings of precious metal. This work began under Ferdinando I in 1580–90 and continued for many years without being finished. The numerous craftsmen employed on the project executed the pietre dure mosaics following polychrome cartoons provided by such painters as Lodovico Cigoli (1559–1613), Bernardino Poccetti (1548–1612) and Jacopo Ligozzi (1547–1627). The parts that were completed were dismantled and reused in various ways at the end of the 18th century (Florence, S Lorenzo; Florence, Pitti; Florence, Mus. Opificio Pietre Dure), though the decoration of the interior continued until the mid-19th century. Fully rounded statuettes, composed of various polychrome elements of pietre dure (Florence, Pitti) were also created for the chapel. This singular genre of 'mosaic sculpture', first produced in Florence at the end of the 16th century with the rock-crystal aedicula containing *Christ and the Woman of Samaria* (Vienna, Ksthist. Mus.), continued to be practised in the Florentine workshop alongside the other speciality of pietre dure mosaic.

During the 17th century Florentine mosaics were used to decorate sumptuous furnishings of various kinds, including table-tops, ebony cabinets, jewel caskets, clocks and reliquaries. The preferred subjects were compositions of flowers, fruit and birds. This fashion was inspired by the analytical naturalism of Jacopo Ligozzi, whose interest in botanical and zoological themes is reflected in the pietre dure ornamentation of a table (Florence, Uffizi) and a chessboard (Florence, Pitti). Baroque taste continued to favour these subjects, enhancing the vivid polychrome effects with black marble backgrounds to create a greater decorative exuberance. The showy pietre dure is often accompanied by inlay work in rare woods and also by sculpted gilt-bronzes. Among the most important works produced in the 17th century are the great octagonal table (Florence, Uffizi) for the Tribuna, the octagonal centrepiece ot the Grand Ducal collections, itself floored with pietre dure and with pietre dure plinths for famous pieces of Antique sculpture (including the Venus de' Medici), completed in 1649 after 18 years of work by a team of 12 craftsmen, and the contemporary cabinet

Heron-shaped vessel, rock-crystal, h. 315 mm, made at the Medici workshop in Florence, with enamelled gold mount from the Saracchi workshop in Milan, *c.* 1570 (Florence, Palazzo Pitti, Museo degli Argenti)

of Ferdinando II (Florence, Uffizi). In about 1664 the Dutch cabinetmaker Leonardo van der Vinne (*d* 1713) joined the workshop, and in 1667 became chief *ebanista*. His surviving work includes marquetry cabinets with pietre dure mosaic decorations in the Palazzo Pitti and a cabinet given by Cosimo III to the 5th Earl of Exeter and now in Burghley House (Lincs).

During the long reign of Cosimo III (*reg* 1670–1723), Florentine primacy in pietre dure was maintained due to the wealth of material and artistic resources lavished on the sumptuous creations so greatly prized by the European courts. The workshop was guided by GIOVANNI BATTISTA FOGGINI and its craftsmen included Giuseppe Antonio TORRICELLI. After 1737 the grand ducal workshop under the new dynasty of Habsburg–Lorraine was engaged mainly on a series of over 60 stone pictures of figures (Vienna, Hofburg-Schauräume), commissioned by Grand Duke Francis for his residence in Vienna and drawn by Giuseppe Zocchi, the official draughtsman of the Galleria dei Lavori. During the reign of Leopold of Hapsburg–Lorraine the workshop's ornamental repertory was centred on sophisticated compositions of vases and still-lifes, used for table-tops and such luxurious objects as tobacco boxes, necklaces and jewel-cases, which were fashionable in the ensuing Napoleonic period. After 1814, however, the workshop began to feel the effect of the grand duchy's economic decline. It was frequently occupied in reusing and adapting existing works rather than in creating new ones; a huge amount of work and material, however, was absorbed between 1837 and 1850 on the monumental table of *Apollo and the Muses* (Florence, Pitti).

The end of the Grand Duchy of Tuscany in 1860 led to an irreversible crisis for the craft, which had always depended on court commissions. The workshop, renamed the Opificio delle Pietre Dure, came under the control of the Ministero dell'Istruzione Pubblica and opened its formerly exclusive production to public sale. From 1873 to 1923 it was directed by the painter Edoardo Marchionni (1837–1923), whose refined Liberty-style creations of the 1870s and 1880s were among the last original products of the workshop (e.g. Magnolia Table, Flower Vase with mosaics and reliefs, Great Vase with plant and animal motifs; all Florence, Mus. Opificio Pietre Dure). At the end of the 19th century the Opificio gradually shifted towards specializing in restoration of works of art.

A. M. Giusti, P. Mazzoni and A. Pampaloni Martelli: *Il Museo dell'opificio delle pietre dure a Firenze* (Milan, 1978)
U. Baldini, A. M. Giusti and A. Pampaloni Martelli: *La Cappella dei Principi e le pietre dure a Firenze* (Milan, 1979)
A. Gonzalez-Palacios: *Mosaici e pietre dure*, ii (Milan, 1981)
Splendori di pietre dure: L'arte di corte nella Firenze dei Granduchi (exh. cat., ed. A. M. Giusti; Florence, Pitti, 1988–9)
M. Giusti: *Pietre Dure: Hardstones in Furniture and Decoration* (London, 1992)
A. M. Massinelli and J. H. Gabriel: *Hardstones: The Gilbert Collection* (London, 2000)

2. PORCELAIN. A porcelain factory was in operation in the vicinity of the Palazzo Pitti during the reign of Francesco I. According to Vasari's *Vite*, it is believed to have originated *c.* 1565 with experiments by the court architect Bernardo Buontalenti (*c.* 1531–1608). Production was first mentioned in 1575. The body employed was a soft-paste porcelain not unlike pottery from Iznik in Turkey and it possibly resulted from advice said to have been provided by a Levantine. Only 57 pieces of Medici porcelain have been recorded, and all but three, which are polychrome, are painted in underglaze blue of variable colour and control. Three main types of decoration were employed: grotesque ornament derived from Italian maiolica, particularly the Raphaelesque type associated with the workshops of the Fontana and Patanazzi families in Urbino; motifs borrowed from 15th-century as well as contemporary Chinese porcelains; and Ottoman styles based on 16th-century Iznik pottery. Forms derived from maiolica, metalwares and lapidary work included simple, deep dishes, but more typical were ewers, flasks (e.g. one of 1575–87; Paris, Louvre) and cruets. Factory workmen included Flaminio Fontana (*fl* 1573–8) and Pier Maria da Faenza (*fl* 1580–89). Most pieces are marked with the dome of the cathedral of S Maria del Fiore and the letter F in underglaze blue. Production appears to have ended with Francesco's death (1587), but the presence in Florence in 1589 of the potter Niccolò Sistì (*fl c.* 1577–*c.* 1619) and the record in 1613 of porcelain tokens decorated with the Medici arms indicate continued, unofficial activity.

G. Liverani: *Catalogo delle porcellane dei Medici* (Faenza, 1936)

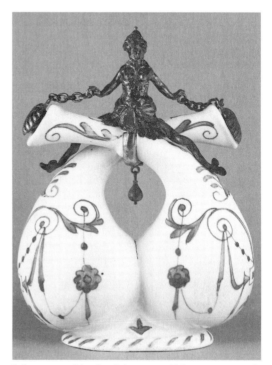

Soft-paste porcelain oil-and-vinegar set with bronze mount, made at the factory of the Medici in Florence (Vienna, Österreichisches Museum für Angewandte Kunst)

G. Cora and A. Fanfani: *La porcellana dei Medici* (Milan, 1986)
Pitti Palace: General Catalogue of the Palatine Gallery [and] . . . Porcelain Museum (Florence, 1990)

3. TAPESTRY. At least two workshops of peripatetic northern tapestry-weavers are known to have been in operation in 15th-century Florence. Livinus Gilii de Burgis (*fl* 1444–after 1473), primarily employed by the Este family in Ferrara, was permitted to weave enormous figured tapestries for the *ringhiera* of Florence's Palazzo Vecchio between 1455 and 1457, which were based on cartoons by Neri di Bicci (1418–92) and Vittorio Ghiberti (1418/19–96). Between 1476 and 1480 the south Netherlandish master Giovanni di Giovanni produced works for Florence Cathedral. Little or nothing, however, remains of this production; a very small *Annunciation* (New York, Met.) is attributed to an early 16th-century Florentine workshop.

In 1545 Duke Cosimo I arranged for JAN ROST and NICOLAS KARCHER, two south Netherlandish master weavers, to establish workshops in Florence. Between 1546 and the end of 1553, 120 tapestries were woven in Florence for Cosimo I: 44 (42 extant) narrative pieces with fine sett and materials, including much silk and many metallic threads; and 76 (all destr.) heraldic covers of coarser wool and *filaticcio* (silk from broken cocoons), sometimes used for pack animals or carriages. The cartoons for the fine tapestries, which were mainly for the Palazzo Vecchio, were made by major Florentine painters. At first Cosimo asked Agnolo Bronzino (1503–72) to provide cartoons for three trial *portières* (1545–6; Florence, Sopr. B.A. & Storici Col) for Rost and FRANCESCO SALVIATI to provide cartoons both for Karcher's trial altar tapestry of the *Lamentation* (1546) and for his *Ecce homo* (1547–9; both Florence, Uffizi). At the same time, Cosimo divided larger sets between the two weavers; a twenty-piece *Story of Joseph* series (1546–53; Florence, Sopr. B.A. & Storici Col.; Rome, Pal. Quirinale) from sixteen cartoons by Bronzino, three by Jacopo da Pontormo (1494–1556) and one by Salviati, and ten *Grotesque 'spalliere'* (1546–50; Florence, Sopr. B.A. & Storici Col., six on dep. London, It. Embassy) after Bacchiacca. Karcher wove a Moresque table carpet (Poggio a Caiano, Mus. Villa Medicea), from designs perhaps by Bronzino, and two additions (untraced) to a south Netherlandish *Story of Tobias* set owned by Cosimo I. Two *portières* of an *Allegory with the Medici–Toledo Arms* (1549–50; Florence, Pitti), from cartoons by Benedetto Pagni da Pescia, were begun under Francesco di Pacino, but the second had to be completed in Karcher's workshop.

Salviati designed many private commissions in this period, including Karcher's *Resurrection* altar tapestry (*c.* 1546; Florence, Uffizi) for Benedetto Accolti, Cardinal of Ravenna, and Rost's *Meeting of Dante and Virgil* (*c.* 1547–9; Minneapolis, MN, Inst. A). Nearly all the tapestries from this period are outstanding and distinguished by rich, innovative borders. The borders designed by Bronzino for the *Joseph* series are an Italian monumentalization of

Tapestry of the *Primavera*, designed by Agnolo Bronzino, made in Florence, 1545 (Florence, Palazzo Pitti)

popular south Netherlandish garland models, but Bronzino's and Salviati's other border designs were inspired by such diverse sources as architecture, picture frames, East Asian carpets and the framing devices, combining cartouches and figures, of prints disseminated by the first Fontainebleau school in the 1540s. By the 1550s a distinctive and enduring Florentine approach to tapestry borders had developed, characterized by deft balancing of large, often crowded forms, strong plasticity—often working out from an architectonic framework with punctuating cartouches—and considerable visual humour. Although the Medici family had weavers at their service, they also continued to buy some south Netherlandish tapestries throughout the 16th century.

In 1554 Cosimo I used the equipment left by Karcher for a new, private ducal factory—now referred to as the Arazzeria Medicea. The reasons for this were doubtless both financial (the costly campaign against Siena combined with the famous masters' high fees) and practical (the slow production of truly fine tapestries compared with the numerous palaces and villas Cosimo had to decorate). At the new factory less complex designs with coarser sett and materials were executed, which lowered the cost and accelerated the rate of production. There were two workshops, headed by Benedetto di Michele Squilli (*fl* 1555–88) and Bastiano Sconditi (*fl* 1555–68).

Bronzino continued to design cartoons until 1557, but the temperament of the court architect and painter Giorgio Vasari was better suited to the increased pace projected by the Duke. After executing a few designs and possibly cartoons to accompany frescoed decorations in the Palazzo Vecchio, Vasari incorporated the production of tapestry cartoons into his workshop's well-organized decorating procedures. The Flemish painter JOANNES STRADANUS so excelled at this art that he soon became the official cartoonist for the workshops, designing his own compositions: for the Palazzo Vecchio they were biblical, historical and mythological (examples in Florence, Sopr. B.A. & Storici Col.; London, V&A; Paris, Mobilier N.); for rooms in the Villa Medici at Poggio a Caiano he designed 40 *Hunts* (1567–77; examples in Florence, Sopr. B.A. & Storici Col.; Pisa, Mus. N. S. Matteo; Siena, Pal. Reale); for Bianca Cappello, second wife of Francesco I, Grand Duke of Tuscany, he collaborated with Domenico d'Antonio Buti (*c.* 1550–90) on cartoons for five *Grotesques* (1572 and 1578; three, Paris, Mus. A. Déc.). Stradanus's cartoons are notable for their close observation of nature and characterizing detail and a keen sense of both decoration and humour. From late 1558 to 1574, the only set apparently woven for the Medici that was not designed by Stradanus was the *History of Florence* (1564; three, Florence, Sopr. B.A. & Storici Col.) for the Sala di Gualdrada in the Palazzo Vecchio from cartoons by Friedrich Sustris.

In 1575, the year after Cosimo I's death, Alessandro Allori (1535–1607), a favourite painter of Francesco I who had worked on tapestry cartoons under Bronzino, became the official cartoonist at the Arazzeria Medicea. Allori was nearly as prolific as Stradanus, although his static figures and compositions are not as imaginative and humorous. His border designs follow Stradanus's in layout but are more formally structured. When Stradanus left Florence temporarily in 1576, Allori continued the *Hunts* for the Villa Medici. Allori's designs were, however, mainly for the Palazzo Pitti in Florence: mythological series included *Latona, Centaurs, Niobe, Phaëthon* and *The Seasons* (examples in Florence, Sopr. B.A. & Storici Col.). During this period more outside commissions were executed by the Arazzeria Medicea, and Allori's workshop painted cartoons for tapestries for the church of S Maria Maggiore in Bergamo (e.g. *Life of the Virgin*, 1582–6; *in situ*) and for the cathedral in Como. On Squilli's death (1588), Guasparri di Bartolomeo Papini (*d* 1621) became head weaver. After the succession (1587) of Ferdinando I, Grand Duke of Tuscany, who had been a cardinal, religious tapestries became more popular: Allori designed overdoors depicting the *Life of Christ* (1598–1600) and a *Passion* series (1592–1616; both Florence, Sopr. B.A. & Storici Col.) in collaboration with Lodovico Cigoli.

During the first decades of the 17th century Cardinal Montalto was among the most assiduous patrons of the Arazzeria Medicea. After Allori's death (1607), Bernardino Poccetti made some cartoons for the Medici and for other private commissions. After Poccetti's death (1612), Michelangelo Cinganelli (1560–1635), who still worked in a basically 16th-century style, became the official painter for the Ar-

azzeria (e.g. *Story of Phaëthon*, Florence, Sopr. B.A. & Storici Col.), although the Flemish painter Cornelis Schut I (1597–1655) also painted two cartoons in 1628. The Flemish master Jacopo Ebert van Asselt (*fl* 1621; *d* 1630) became head weaver in 1621, and, although his son Pietro van Asselt (*fl* 1620–44) took over the family's separate workshop on Jacopo's death, PIETRO FEVÈRE, a Flemish weaver who favoured high-warp weaving—a new technique for Florence—became the next official head weaver. Fevère was the first to make tapestry copies of paintings in the Medici galleries (examples in Florence, Sopr. B.A. & Storici Col.). Under Fevère, and during the reign of Ferdinand II, the Medici commissions revived, and, following the death of Cinganelli (1635), such masters as Sigismondo Coccapani (1583–1643), Baccio del Bianco, Lorenzo Lippi (1606–65), Giacinto Gimignani (1606–81) and Vincenzo Dandini (1609–75) painted cartoons for the factory.

After Fevère's death (1669), two head weavers, Giovanni Pollastri (*fl* 1655–1673) and Bernardino van Asselt, Jacopo's son, who had inherited the family workshop (*fl* 1629–1673), ran the factory. After their deaths, however, the hierarchy broke down: Stefano Termini (*fl* 1674–1703), Matteo Benvenuti (*fl* 1670–92), Niccolò Bartoli (*fl* 1671–7) and Bernardino Masi (*fl* 1671–87) continued to work in the low-warp technique, and pressure from them led Pietro Fevère's son Filippo Fevère (*fl* 1648–after 1677) to move to Venice. Stefano Termini's brother Giovan Battista Termini (*fl* 1673; *d* 1717), the only remaining high-warp weaver, finally went to Rome in 1684. Both weaving and cartoons—including such work as architectural compositions and figures in niches (examples in Florence, Sopr. B.A. & Storici Col.)—were undistinguished for the next 20 years. When Giovan Battista Termini petitioned to return to the Arazzeria in 1703, he was made director and asked to re-establish high-warp weaving. His most important weaver was Leonardo Bernini (*fl* 1705–37); the low-warp weaver Vittorio Demignot (*d* 1742) from Turin also worked under Termini between 1716 and 1731. Termini abolished the then current archaic style of cartoon by introducing the work of the Baroque painter Giovanni Camillo Sagrestani (1660–1731; e.g. *Four Parts of the World*, 1715–26; Florence, Sopr. B.A. & Storici Col.).

Antonio Bronconi (*fl* 1700–32) became director after Termini's death (1717). Emulating contemporary workshop organization in France and Flanders, collaborative cartoons by specialists in different genres were painted: Lorenzo del Moro (*fl* 1725–34) made overall and ornamental designs, Girolamo Costner (*fl* 1721–6) painted landscapes, and Sagrestani and later also Matteo Bonechi (1669–1756) painted figures (e.g. four *portières* of *The Elements*, 1725–32; Florence, Pitti). Between 1732 and 1737 Giovanni Francesco Pieri and, briefly (1737), Leonardo Bernini managed production. The largest projects of this period were the *Rape of Proserpina* (Florence, Sopr. B.A. & Storici Col.), from a cartoon by

Giuseppe Grisoni (1699–1769), and the *Fall of Pha-ëthon* (Florence, Sopr. B.A. & Storici Col.), from a cartoon by Vincenzio Meucci (1699–1766).

After the death (1737) of Gian Gastone, the last Medici grand duke, the Arazzeria was temporarily closed, and the following year one of the masters, Domenico del Rosso (*fl* 1736–68), left for Naples with a group of weavers. From 1740 tapestry-weaving was briefly revived under Francis, Grand Duke of Tuscany (1737–65; from 1745 Francis I, Holy Roman Emperor), who brought weavers from his workshop at the château of La Malgrange, near Nancy, to Florence. Commissions diminished, however, when he was called to defend the crown of his wife Maria-Teresa of Austria. In 1744 court payments ended. One of the last works of the Arazzeria Medicea was a half-length portrait of *Francis, Grand Duke of Tuscany* (1737; Florence, Pitti).

There is no record of tapestry-weaving in Florence from 1745 until 1902, when Count Federigo Niccola Marcelli (*fl* early 20th century) organized a private weaving school and workshop directed by Pia Cassigoli (*fl* 1902–15). The cartoons by Ezio Marzi (1875–1949/53) were inspired by 16th-century models but treated such current themes as the *Triumph of Work* or the *Genius of the Family*. In one series, five women symbolized different moments in history in different cities: for example *Abélard and Héloïse* for 12th-century Paris and the *Meeting of Romeo and Juliet* for Renaissance Verona. The workshop closed around 1915.

D. Heikamp: 'Arazzi a soggetto profano su cartoni di Alessandro Allori', *Rin. A.*, xxxi (1956), pp. 105–55
D. Heikamp: 'La Manufacture de tapisserie des Médicis', *L'Oeil*, clxiv–v (1968), pp. 22–31
D. Heikamp: 'Giovanni Stradanos Bildteppiche für den Palazzo Vecchio mit Darstellungen aus dem Leben der älteren Medici', *Mitt. Ksthist. Inst. Florenz*, xiv (1969), pp. 183–200
D. Heikamp: 'Die Arazzeria Medicea im 16. Jahrhundert: Neue Studien', *Münchn. Jb. Bild. Kst*, ser. 3, xxx (1969), pp. 33–74
D. Heikamp: 'Unbekannte Medici-Bildteppiche in Siena', *Pantheon*, xxxviii/4 (1979), pp. 376–82
C. Adelson: 'Bachiacca, Salviati, and the Decoration of the Sala dell'Udienza in Palazzo Vecchio', *Le arti del principato mediceo* (Florence, 1980), pp. 141–400
C. Adelson: 'Cosimo I de' Medici and the Foundation of Tapestry Production in Florence', *Firenze e la Toscana dei Medici nell'Europa del Cinquecento*, 3 vols (Florence, 1980), pp. 899–924
C. Adelson and others: 'Arazzi', *Palazzo Vecchio: Committenza e collezionismo mediceo* (exh. cat., ed. P. Barocchi; Florence, Pal. Vecchio, 1980), pp. 43–116
C. Adelson: 'The Decoration of Palazzo Vecchio in Tapestry: The *Joseph* Cycle and Other Precedents for Vasari's Decorative Campaigns', *Atti del convegno vasariano: Arezzo, 1981*, pp. 145–77
C. Adelson: 'Florentine and Flemish Tapestries in Giovio's Collection', *Atti del convegno: Paolo Giovio, il rinascimento e la memoria: Como, 1983*, pp. 239–81
C. Adelson: 'Three Florentine Grotesques in the Musée des Arts Décoratifs, Paris', *Bull. Liaison Cent. Int. Etud. Textiles Anc.*, lix–lx/1–2 (1984), pp. 54–60
C. Adelson: 'Documents for the Foundation of Tapestry Weaving under Cosimo I de' Medici', *Renaissance Studies in Honor of Craig Hugh Smyth*, ed. A. Morrogh, ii (Florence, 1985), pp. 3–17
C. Adelson: *The Tapestry Patronage of Cosimo I de' Medici: 1545–1553*, 4 vols (diss., New York U., 1990)
C. M. Goguel: 'Sur le chemin de Rome: le role de Vasari et l'etape Florentine', *Boll. A.*, lxxxii/100 (1997), pp. 63–76 [part supp]
L. Meoni: *Gli arazzi nei musei fiorentini* (Florence, 1998)
C. Acidini Luchinat: *The Medici, Michelangelo, & the Art of Late Renaissance Florence* (New Haven and London, 2002)

Florentine mosaic. *See* FLORENCE, §1.

Floris [de Vriendt]. Flemish family of artists. The earliest known members of the family, then called de Vriendt, were active as masons in Brussels in the 15th century. One of them, Jan Florisz. de Vriendt, left his native town and settled in Antwerp *c.* 1450. His patronymic name 'Floris' subsequently became the usual family name. Jan Floris's grandson Cornelis Floris (*d* 17 Sept 1538) was a mason who had four sons. Cornelis Floris II became a sculptor and an architect, and published influential designs of Italian decorative motifs; Frans Floris (1519–70) became a painter; Jan Floris became a potter; Jacques Floris became a painter of stained-glass windows.

In 1553 Jan Floris the potter, who is known in Spanish as Juan Flores, left Antwerp for Spain, where in 1562 he was appointed royal tilemaker to Philip II and assumed responsibility for the design of tiles at TALAVERA DE LA REINA and the decoration of the royal palaces in Madrid and Segovia.

Flörsheim Faience Factory. German faience factory established in Flörsheim-am-Main (near Frankfurt) in 1765; it was managed till 1774 by Kaspar Dreste. The factory produced both domestic wares and display pieces such as table-centres. It began to produce cream-coloured earthenware (Steingut) in 1787. Pottery is marked FFF (Flörsheimer Fayence Fabrik). The factory remained active into the 20th century.

K. Schafft: *Flörsheimer Fayencen* (Darmstadt, 1977)

Floss silk. Rough silk broken off in the winding of the cocoons, used to make common silk fabrics; the term is also used to denote untwisted filaments of silk used in embroidery and crewel-work.

Flötner [Flettner], **Peter** (*b* Thurgau, 1485–96; *d* Nuremberg, 23 Nov 1546). German sculptor, medallist, cabinetmaker, woodcutter and designer. Much of his career was concentrated on sculptural decoration, but from the early 1530s his important commissions were for the interior decoration and furnishing of several noblemen's houses. Designs that survive in the form of woodcuts include the *Venetian Bedstead*. He may have been responsible for the plans of the garden room of the Hirschvogel house (1534; destr. 1945) in Nuremberg; Flötner carved the wall panelling, the doorways and the stone chimney-piece.

Flötner's talents as designer were applied to a multiplicity of objects, such as a set of 48 playing cards or the *Human Sundial* (*c.* 1535; Wolfenbüttel, Herzog August Bib). His most successful application of the lessons learnt from Italian art is seen in his plaquette design, as in the plaquette depicting the story of *Ate and the Litae* (Santa Barbara, U. CA, A. Mus.), cast *c.* 1535–40 and based on passages from the Homer's *Iliad*; its deep space, subtly graduated relief and naturalistic details demonstrate Flötner's mastery of landscape depiction.

The most famous example of his work in the field of decorative arts is the Holzschuher covered goblet (*c.* 1540; Nuremberg, Ger. Nmus.), which he created in collaboration with the Nuremberg goldsmith MELCHIOR BAIER. Flötner carved bacchanalian scenes recalling his plaquettes into the coconut shell that forms the body of the goblet; the finial is in the shape of a satyr pouring wine into a man's mouth, while round the stem winds a Bacchic rout, featuring amorous couples and copulating goats.

Flöter played a leading part in the dissemination of his interpretation of Classical architectural motifs and was also the first artist to introduce grotesque motifs into German Renaissance ornament. In 1546 Rudolff Wijffenbach published *Das Kunstbuch des Peter Flötner*, a compilation of 40 of Flötner's surviving woodcuts that contributed greatly to his influence on German artists working in other media; one such was Wenzel Jamnitzer, who drew on Flötner for many of his designs for goldsmith work.

E. F. Bange: *Peter Flötner* (Leipzig, 1926)
Peter Flötner und die Renaissance in Deutschland: Ausstellung anlässlich des 400: Todesjahres Peter Flötners (exh. cat., Nuremberg, 1946–7)

M. Angerer: *Peter Flötners Entwürfe: Beiträge zum Ornament und Kunsthandwerk in Nürnberg in der 1. Hälfte des 16. Jahrhunderts* (diss., Munich, Ludwig-Maximilians-U., 1983)

Flügelglas [Ger.: 'winged glass']. Goblet in which the stem consists of scrolls of glass that resemble wings. The form originated in 16th-century Venice but was rapidly adopted and adapted in northern Europe, where it was made until the end of the 18th century and revived at the end of the 19th century.

Fluting. Decoration consisting of parallel concave channels (flutes). It is primarily an architectural decoration, but also appears on furniture, beginning in the 16th century but particularly in the last quarter of the 18th century. In metalwork the flutes are often embossed on plate.

Fogelberg, Andrew (*b c.* 1732; *d* 1815). English goldsmith. He may have been of Swedish origin, and may be the same person as the Anders Fogelberg who was apprenticed to a silversmith in Halmsted. Fogelberg worked in Neo-classical styles, characterized by oval and vase or urn forms with beaded or pearled edging, lanceolate leaves, narrow reeded legs and floral swags. The most distinctive feature of his plate is that the applied medallions with which he

Fluted silver cup from Pompeii (Naples, Museo Archeologico Nazionale)

decorated his silver (e.g. a cauldron-shaped sugar basin with hoofed feet, 1777; London, V&A) were based directly on JAMES TASSIE's reproductions of Renaissance gems and cameos (Tassie and Fogelberg were neighbours in Soho).

Foggini, Giovanni Battista (*b* Florence, 25 April 1652; *d* Florence, 12 April 1725). Italian sculptor, architect and designer. He spent most of his career in the service of the Medici, for whom he worked as grand ducal sculptor (1586) and court architect (1694). Foggini supervised the Galleria dei Lavori (now the Opificio delle Pietre Dure), the manufactory for works in hardstone inlay. He was a prolific and assured draughtsman, and approximately 400 of his designs (Florence, Uffizi; London, V&A; Paris, Louvre; Rome, Gal. N. Stampe) for sculpture, bronze statuettes, furniture and ornaments involving hardstones have survived. He supervised the construction of the Badminton cabinet, which was made for Henry Somerset, 3rd Duke of Beaufort, from 1720–32. This enormous cabinet, of ebony, giltbronze and pietra dura, remained at Badminton until 1990, when it was sold for £8,580,000. In 2004 it was again sold, this time for £19,045,250 (the highest price ever paid for a piece of furniture) to Prince Hans Adam II von und zu Liechtenstein, and is now in the Museum of Liechtenstein in Vienna.

Splendori di pietre dure: L'arte di corte nella Firenze dei Granduchi (exh. cat., ed. A. M. Giusti; Florence, Pitti, 1988–9)

Giovanni Battista Foggini: cabinet, ebony and ivory (Florence, Palazzo Pitti)

Foil. Term used in two distinct senses. As an ornamental motif, a foil is a circular or nearly circular lobe, usually arranged in groups (hence trefoil, quatrefoil, cinquefoil, multifoil) with their outlines divided by points (cusps) to give the impression of radiating petals. In metalwork and jewellery, a foil is a thin leaf or sheet of gold, silver or other metal used to decorate a work of art or to sit under a precious stone.

Folded foot. Foot on a drinking glass, strengthened by folding the rim of the base disk under the glass. The form was popular *c.* 1685–1750 and was revived in the early 1820s.

Foliate- and strapwork. *See* LAUBWERK.

Foliot, Nicolas-Quinibert (*b* 1706; *d* 1776). French chairmaker. For 40 years he ran a family workshop in Paris, supplying huge numbers of chairs (in one year 468 chairs and 135 armchairs) to the court. He eventually became the royal furniture-maker (*menuisier du garde-meuble du roi*), and was the creator of the Louis XVI style of chairs. As furniture for the crown was not marked, there are sometimes difficulties of attruibution, but at least one set of chairs at Versailles is known to have come from his workshop, and the Musée du Louvre has at least two of his chairs.

F. Duret-Robert: 'La splendeur du XVIIIe [les pieces d'orfèvrerie de la collection de Mme Arturo Lopez-Villshaw]', *Conn. A.*, cdlxxxiii (May 1992), pp. 92–9

Follot, Paul (*b* Paris, 17 July 1877; *d* Sainte-Maxime, nr St Tropez, 1941). French designer. He was a leading designer of furniture and interiors in the transition from Art Nouveau to Art Deco before World War I and in the subsequent popularization of the Art Deco style. He was a pupil of Eugène Grasset (1841–1917) in Paris, and his earliest designs, in the Gothic style, were published in *Art et Décoration*, the journal of design reform founded in 1887. From 1899 Follot was designing bronzes, jewellery and textiles for La Maison Moderne, the commercial outlet for Art Nouveau objects, and his interior design for a study, shown in 1904 at the first Salon of the Société des Artistes-Décorateurs, of which he was a founder-member, demonstrated his affinity with the prevailing curvilinear characteristics of Art Nouveau. Follot's design for a study shown at the same Salon in 1909 revealed a change towards simpler, more rectilinear forms inspired by the revival of Neo-classicism, which became characteristic of his style. He employed light woods, ornamented with carved and gilded fruits, garlands and cornucopias (e.g. chair, 1913; Paris, Mus. A. Déc.). Before 1914 he earned a reputation as a de luxe designer, working for private patrons as well as for commercial retailers of the highest quality. In 1911 Wedgwood commissioned designs from Follot, and the 'Pomona', 'Sylvia' and 'Galbia' ranges were put into production in 1919. In

1923 he was appointed head of the Atelier Pomone, the design studio of the Paris department store Le Bon Marché, and he designed the Pavilion Pomone for the Exposition Internationale des Arts Décoratifs et Industriels Modernes of 1925 in Paris. In 1928 he was engaged to design furniture and interiors for the Modern Art Department of Waring & Gillow in London. Opposed to the austerity of modernism, Follot exhibited a sumptuous dining-room at the Salon des Artistes Décorateurs in 1929 and in 1935 designed a luxury suite on the liner *Normandie*.

P. Follot: *Intérieurs français au Salon des artistes décorateurs, Paris 1927* (Paris, 1927)
J. Rutherford: 'Paul Follot', *Connoisseur*, cciv (1980), pp. 86–91

Fondporzellan. Type of porcelain with an underglaze coloured ground and white panels with enamelled decorations produced during the 18th century. It was first used at the MEISSEN PORCELAIN FACTORY *c.* 1720, where the grounds were initially brown (*kaffeebrauner* or *kapuzinerbrauner*); a yellow ground was introduced in 1725, followed by purple, willow green (*Seladon*) and cobalt blue. Fondporzellan of the highest quality began to be produced in 1730. In 1745 Sèvres began to manufacture Fondporzellan, introducing a dark blue (*gros bleu*) in 1749, a lighter blue (*blue celeste*) and a yellow (*jaune jonquil*) in 1749 and a pink (*rose Pompadour*) in 1756.

Fontaine, Pierre-François-Léonard (*b* Pontoise, 20 Sept 1762; *d* Paris, 10 Oct 1853). French architect, interior designer and writer. With his friend and collaborator, Charles Percier (1764–1838), he was the finest exponent of the Neo-classical Empire style. The five volumes of Fontaine's *Journal*, believed lost in a fire at the store of the Louvre Library in 1871, were rediscovered in 1982 and published in 1987; the journal fundamentally changes the scholarly understanding of the history of French architecture and interior decoration at the beginning of the 19th century.

In September 1792 Fontaine took refuge in England, where he survived by producing decorative work, wallpapers, snuff-boxes and fans. Percier remained in Paris and was appointed director in charge of the scene painting at the Opéra. In December 1792 he invited Fontaine to join him, and for four years they worked on classical decorations, backdrops for plays. They were also involved in designing furniture for the JACOB firm of cabinetmakers. They were subsequently employed by Napoleon (*reg* 1804–14) to remodel Malmaison, where several of their interiors have survived.

In 1801 Fontaine and Percier collaborated on *Recueil de décorations intérieures comprenant tout ce qui a rapport à l'ameublement*; this volume, whose title introduced the term interior decoration', includes a large number of designs for furniture, much of which is decorated with antique motifs.

M. Fouche: *Percier et Fontaine: Biographie critique* (Paris, 1907)
P.-F.-L. Fontaine: *Journal, 1799–1853*, 2 vols (Paris, 1987)

P.-F.-L. Fontaine and C. Percier: *Recueil de décorations intérieures comprenant tout ce qui a rapport à l'ameublement* (Paris, 1801, 4/1922/ *R* Farnborough, 1971)
P.-F.-L. Fontaine and C. Percier: *Empire Stylebook of Interior Design: All 72 Plates from the Recueil de décorations intérieures, with New English Text* (New York, 1991)

Fontainebleau. French centre of tapestry production. A temporary tapestry workshop was installed in the château of Fontainebleau by Francis I in 1540. Attributed to the workshop of Fontainebleau are a number of hangings, the designs of which reflect the Fontainebleau Mannerist style, although the possibility of their having been woven in Paris has not been ruled out. Only one set can be positively attributed to Fontainebleau, the renowned series of six tapestries (Vienna, Ksthist. Mus.) that reproduced part of the decoration by Rosso Fiorentino and Francesco Primaticcio (1504/5–70) for the Galerie François I in the château of Fontainebleau The sumptuous hangings, woven with gold and silver thread, were executed from at least February 1540 to July 1547. The hangings are more than just a true copy; they are a transposition of the decoration of the gallery, replanned from the perspective of a tapestry. The shading is modified, the colouring is different, and the great freedom with which stucco and frescoes were combined in the gallery has been clarified and simplified in order to achieve a greater unity in the series of hangings. The tapestries also incorporate such *trompe l'oeil* architectural elements as wainscoting and beam ends to create a deliberately illusionistic effect. The work of adapting the decoration is attributed to Claude Baudoin and other painters who were entrusted with executing the tapestry cartoons. The date of the closure of the workshop at Fontainebleau is not known. The year 1547 is often mentioned, but according to a letter from Primaticcio, it could have been after 1565.

S. Pressouyre: 'Les Fontes du Primatice à Fontainebleau', *Bull. Mnmtl.* (1969), p. 226, n. 1
S. Pressouyre: 'La Galerie François Ier au château de Fontainebleau: Le Témoignage des tapisseries', *Rev. A.* (1972), nos 16–17, pp. 106–11, 122–3

Fontana, Annibale (*b* Milan, 1540; *d* Milan, 1587). Italian medallist, hardstone-engraver and sculptor. During the first half of his career, before 1570, he concentrated on making medals and on rock crystal engraving. Portrait medals of *Ferdinando Francesco D'Avalos* and *Lomazzo* (both Milan, Castello Sforzesco) have been attributed to Fontana. The latter, which dates *c.* 1560–61, shows Lomazzo presented to Prudence and Fortune on the reverse. A medal of the philosopher *Ottaviano Ferrari* (Milan, Castello Sforzesco) with a bust of Aristotle on the reverse, also of this period, is also ascribed to Fontana.

In addition to the three documented medals, there are four signed examples, probably also early (1557–60). The inscription ANN (Annibale) appears on the medal of the banker *Tommaso Marino* (*c.* 1557, Bergamo, Gal. Accad. Carrara), which is among Fontana's securely identified early works. A medal of *Cristoforo Madruzzo* (*c.* 1557, Milan, Castello Sforzesco), Bishop of Trent and Governor of Milan in 1556–7, is also signed ANN. This medal is stylistically related to a silver medal of *Consalvo di Cordova* (Bergamo, Gal. Accad. Carrara), signed ANNIBAL, with a battle scene on the reverse, probably made in 1558–60. A silver medal of the condottiere *Giovan Battista Castaldi* (Milan, Castello Sforzesco), signed ANIB, once attributed to Annibale Borgognone (*fl* 1537–68), has been assigned to Fontana on the basis of stylistic affinities with the Ferrari and Consalvo di Cordova medals.

Fontana's rock crystal engravings were in great demand by aristocratic patrons. Seven plaques with biblical scenes, engraved *c.* 1569 for Albert V, Duke of Bavaria (1550–79), were set in the ebony Albertine casket (Munich, Residenz). An oval crystal vase engraved with the *Story of Jason* and another with *Stories of Bacchus* (both Munich, Residenz) are attributed to Fontana (Heinz-Wied). He also seems to have provided designs for crystal engravings by the Saracchi brothers, including a rock crystal flask (Dresden, Grünes Gewölbe) for which there is a drawing by Fontana (Milan, Bib. Ambrosiana).

K. A. Piacenti: 'The Use of Cameos in the Mounts of Sixteenth-century Milanese Pietre Dure Vases', *Stud. Hist. A.*, liv (1997), pp. 126–35

Fontana, Orazio (*d* 1571). Italian potter, was the son of Guido Durantino (*d* 1576), the owner of a pottery and maiolica workshop in Urbino; in 1553 the family name was changed to Fontana. Orazio was active in Urbino from 1540 to 1544, during which time he signed and dated several surviving *istoriato* plates. His whereabouts and activities for the next 20 years are unknown, but in 1564 he is known to have been working in the service of the duke of Savoy, and the following year he returned to Urbino and established his own workshop. After the death of Orazio (who predeceased his father), the workshop was managed by his nephew Flaminio Fontana.

The products of the Fontana workshops in Urbino include maiolica of the highest quality, some of which was designed by Battista Franco (?1510–61) and TADDEO ZUCCARO. It is likely that the table-service designed by Zuccaro and his brother Federico for presentation by Duke Guidobaldo II della Rovere to King Philip II of Spain (1565–71; Florence, Bargello) was made in the workshop of Orazio Fontana.

G. Campori: *Delle manifatture della Maiolica e degli Stucchi, istituite in Torino da Orazio Fontana e da Federico Brandani* (Modena, 1867)

Footman. *See under* FIREPLACE FURNISHINGS.

Foppa, **Cristoforo**. *See* CARADOSSO.

Forestier. French family of bronze-founders. Etienne Forestier (*b* Paris, *c.* 1712; *d* Paris, 1768), who became a master bronze-founder in 1737, supplied bronze furniture mounts to JEAN-FRANÇOIS OEBEN, ANDRÉ-CHARLES BOULLE and GILLES JOUBERT. He cast Jean-Claude Chambellan DUPLESSIS's models for bronzes on the Bureau du Roi by Oeben and JEAN-HENRI RIESENER (1769; Paris, Louvre). After Etienne's death his widow and sons Etienne-Jean Forestier and Pierre-Auguste Forestier (*b* Paris, 1755; *d* Paris, 1835) continued the Parisian bronze-founding business. The Forestiers produced bronze furniture mounts, ornament for chimney-pieces (examples of 1781 and 1788; Versailles, Château) and for the banisters of the Hôtel du Garde-Meuble (1787) at Versailles (now 11, Rue des Reservoirs). The casting of the magnificent sphinx fire-dogs (1786; Versailles, Château) for Marie-Antoinette's Salon des Nobles at Versailles, designed by the sculptor Louis-Simon Boizot and gilded by Claude Galle, has been attributed to the Forestiers. Their collaborations with PIERRE-PHILIPPE THOMIRE included a folding screen at Compiègne (1786; Paris, Louvre), fire-dogs and wall lights, including two pairs with lions' heads for Louis XVI's Chambre du Roi at Saint-Cloud (1788; New York, Met.). After the Revolution Pierre-Auguste opened a shop supplying bronzework, sometimes employing the designs of Charles Percier (1764–1838) and PIERRE-FRANÇOIS-LÉONARD FONTAINE.

Forks. *See under* CUTLERY, §1.

Form. Bench without a back.

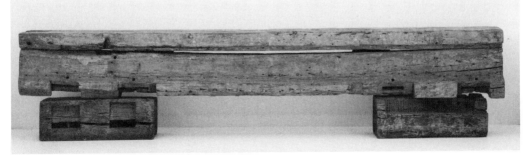

Constantin Brancusi: form, oak, l. 2.15 m, 1914–6 (Philadelphia, Philadelphia Museum of Art)

Fothergill, John. *See under* BOULTON, MATTHEW.

Foullet [Foulet], **Antoine** (*b c.* 1710; *d* 1775). French furniture-maker based in Paris. He specialized in clock cases in the Rococo style, decorated either in wood marquetry or in the brass and tortoiseshell marquetry in the style of ANDRÉ-CHARLES BOULLE. He also sold bronze cases, but as *ébénistes* were not allowed to work in bronze, he was probably acting as a dealer.

Fourdinois. French family of cabinetmakers. Alexandre-Georges Fourdinois (1799–1871) established his Paris workshop in 1835. He became cabinetmaker to the Empress Eugénie, for whom he made furniture in the Renaissance style; until 1848, he often worked in collaboration with the sculptor Jules Fossey (1806–1858). In 1867 he retired, and thereafter the business was managed by his son Henri-Auguste (1830–1907) until 1882. A marquetry cabinet (1861–7) by Henri-Auguste won first prize at the Paris Exposition Universelle of 1867 (London, V & A) (see colour pl. XIV, fig. 2).

O. Gabet: 'French Cabinet Makers and England: The Case of the Maison Fourdinois (1835–85)', *Apollo*, clv/479 (Jan 2002), pp. 22–31

Fournier, Louis-Antoine (*b c.* 1720; *d* 1786). French sculptor, porcelain modeller and arcanist. In 1747, while working at VINCENNES PORCELAIN FACTORY, he was commissioned to supply figures of river gods (e.g. Williamstown, MA, Clark A. Inst.) and naiades (e.g. London, V & A). He subsequently worked at Chantilly (1752–9) and in Copenhagen (1559–66), where he was a partner in a porcelain factory and designed many models for pot purri.

B. L. Grandjean: *Louis Antoine Fournier* (Copenhagen, 1969)
D. R. McFadden: 'Porcelain in Denmark', *Mag. Ant.*, cxxxviii (July 1990), pp. 112–23

Frailero [Sp. *silla de brazos; sillón frailero*: 'friar's chair']. Type of 16th- and 17th-century chair. The chair is so called because of its use in monasteries. It originated in Italy, but was recreated in Spain and then transported to South America (where it was known as a *misional*); it has a flexible, unsupported leather seat and back, almost always collapsible, and iron bolt-pins. A broad front stretcher prevents the sides splaying out and also ensures rigidity. Over the course of two centuries its decoration changed; stretchers were scalloped, or carved with rosettes or strapwork or, in northern Spain, shields. The rake of the back and the curvature or width of the arms offer no guide to chronology; the appearance of flutes, however, indicates a date in the last 30 years of the 16th century. The same shapes continued during the 17th century, when there was a marked increase in the number of chairs, with or without arms, footstools and stools. Tooled or cushioned leather continued to be used, but in the wealthiest households there was a gradual growth in the use of velvet upholstery worked in gold and silver thread. Unlike its Italian equivalent, the Spanish armchair was never more than 1.5 m tall and bore no finials on the crest, while the seats and backs, whether of cloth or leather, were fastened by large brass nails. The frames of the richest examples were inlaid with ebony and ivory plaques (e.g. Madrid, Inst. Valencia Don Juan) or inset with crystals in imitation of Italian pietra dura, such as the one belonging to Archbishop Bernardo de Sandoval y Rojas (Madrid, Alcalá de Henares, Las Bernardas Monastery).

Frame. Paintings and relief carvings have had borders from an early period—although this is a sophisticated development, defining the permanence and isolation of the image in contrast to the apparent transience of, for example, cave paintings, layered on a rough, unbounded surface. Stylized geometric margins appeared first on vase and tomb paintings between 2000 and 1000 BC, dividing narrative scenes and decorations into horizontal bands. Later, vertical divisions were added (e.g. Tomb of Sennefer, Luxor; *c.* 1453–1419 BC), while architectural frames were applied to wall carvings. A millennium later, in Classical Greece, the borders of mosaics became the organizing structure of the whole, arranging figures and scenes into an abstract pattern of circles and spandrels, squares and lozenges. Then, when images—devotional, memorial, didactic or aesthetic—began to be important in their own right and not merely adjuncts to walls and vases, the framing edge took on other functions. It became protective and emphatic, as with Byzantine and Carolingian ivory-carvings for book covers and diptychs, which would have architectural borders to safeguard them, and to provide focus and depth. On 11th- and 12th-century metalwork altars the frame was also protective, but, set with gems and other inlay, it symbolized the celestial glory of the Trinity and the saints. Even the decorative margins of illuminated manuscripts hint at the richness of heaven, reflect the imagery of the text or set up a tension with the text through grotesque details.

In the 12th and 13th centuries carved wooden frames appeared, the forebears of the modern movable frame. The first examples, like the engaged borders of the ivories and the metalwork altars, were in one piece with the painted ground. The panel had its surface lowered by gouging into a shallow box shape, the surrounding wall of which became the frame. The whole panel was then covered in gesso and gold leaf, the image being painted on the smooth, sunken surface. Patterns could then be punched into the gilded gesso to define robes, haloes, the junction of picture and frame, and the frame itself; so that, apart from the physical unity of both, there was a close identity of ornament and tone through the work. Larger altarpieces were developed, the painting ground formed of boards bonded together with transverse supports, dowels and glued linen layers, while separate mouldings, plain or simply carved, were laminated on to the outer edges to form the frame. This became increasingly elaborate: painted, carved or punched on its top edge, with auxiliary mouldings on either side. Finally, in Italy in the 14th and 15th centuries, the silhouette of the frame altered: at first a peaked pentagon imitating a basilica in cross-section, the altarpiece acquired tiers of painted images, each framed by a complex of inner decorative mouldings to simulate the nave, aisles, crypt and clerestory of a medieval church. The outer frame gained weight and solidity to support this edifice, with lateral buttresses in Italy, and was ornamented with architectural features: pinnacles, crockets, tabernacle work, cresting and niches. National variations of this style developed throughout Europe. Eventually the increasing size of these great screens, especially in Spain, meant that they could no longer exist as independent structures; at a height of *c.* 9 m they had to be applied to the back wall of the church, often around an apse, as a pictorial panelling in which the frame was merely a separating device between each scene.

The cathedral silhouette continued as the form for free-standing altarpieces, but in the early Renaissance this outer contour became that of a Classical temple: a single frame, usually rectangular, around a single scene (the *sacra conversazione*, within a 'real' perspectival space). Neri di Bicci (1418–92) summed up the Renaissance aedicular frame as a squared form with predella, fluted lateral pilasters and architrave with frieze, cornice and foliage above; but it was soon as ornamental as the Flamboyant Gothic type, including decorative carving, pastiglia, painting and *sgraffito* on all surfaces, and added such features as modillions at the base. The architrave could expand into a triangular or segmental pediment, or the picture could be continued inside a broken pediment. Italy led in this evolution and in that of the non-aedicular frame, the *cassetta* and its variants, movable wooden case or moulding frames, applied from the 14th century to secular subjects and simpler religious images. Again, each country developed its own versions of the *cassetta*, and travel, trade and political connections all helped to spread framing motifs, mouldings and other influences from country to country. Renaissance designs, however, spread less quickly than the more florid High Gothic, Mannerist and Baroque styles.

With the Baroque period and the burgeoning of the great courts of Europe, the mainspring of patronage transferred from the church to the king, with his need for unparalleled public displays of wealth and power. The index of artistic leadership also began to move from Rome to Paris, and a golden age of framemaking began in France. This produced virtuosos of carving, gilding and recutting of gesso; creators of vast, three-dimensional sculptural frames for ceremonial portraits and Old Masters, coloured with a range of gold leaf; confectioners of delicate Rococo settings transcending the medium of carved wood, which were fitted to fantastic interior schemes of fretted *boiseries*. English and German carvers produced their own versions of Baroque and Rococo

frames; and in England the Palladian idiom and Grecian style of Robert Adam spawned further integrated schemes, including ceilings, carpets, furniture and picture frames. Paintings were hardly more under this regime than elements in an abstract arrangement of objects, anchored to their setting by the correspondence of their frames with the ornamentations of surrounding objects.

A second wave of classical design in England and France during the late 18th century heralded a more uniformly international vocabulary of framemaking. With the Napoleonic Empire straddling Europe, the court style it promulgated could be reproduced both by craftsmen travelling with the Bonaparte rulers and by local carvers using patterns from Paris. In the early 19th century national differences tended to vanish, and the processes of the Industrial Revolution further homogenized and bastardized the art of making frames. Years of war and national debt meant that the carvers themselves were vanishing, unaffordable luxuries, and the first 40 years of the century were marked by repetitious, standardized models, cheaply made of composition on a deal base and finished with ersatz base-metal 'gilding'. However, artists throughout Europe fought back sporadically by generating individually designed and carved frames. In the mid-19th century the Pre-Raphaelites revived old techniques of framemaking and ornamentation, experimented with geometric, naturalistic and symbolic motifs, and abandoned stock plaster patterns for original designs carved in oak and other 'honest' materials. These practices were strongly influential in Europe, being diffused through the great international exhibitions of the late 19th century and by the mutual links of artists in different countries. Symbolist, classically inspired and Art Nouveau frames appeared, sometimes in striking admixtures. The Impressionists and Neo-Impressionists experimented with simple forms whose colouring was inspired by recently published scientific studies of light and colour. Creative framemaking thus came almost wholly under the control of the artists themselves, rather than of master carvers who could design in their own right.

By the 20th century there were few remnants of original frame craftsmanship left. A handful of artists persevered in earnest re-creation of archaic methods, but Pablo Picasso (1881–1973) and Georges Braque (1882–1963) subverted this approach, using the frame as a prop for *jeux d'esprits*: ropes became the setting for collages; painted and pasted borders replaced more formal designs; and fragments of frames were drawn around or appear in the background of paintings. Surrealists also treated the frame as a visual pun, or, like the Symbolists, as part of the work itself. There was little similar invention in the late 20th century; as in the early 19th there were few artists' frames but great reliance on mass-produced mouldings. The tendency was also to dispense completely with formal framing or to employ a minimalist technique of painted battens edging the stretcher, giving nominal protection without affecting the image.

The framemaker's relationship to artist, architect and patron is as relevant as historical knowledge of framing; especially the changing status of artist and carver, which illuminates the different values that have been set on the frame. Medieval altarpieces were executed by an equal team of carver, gilder and painter, in which the carver's wage might well be the highest. The painter had little say in the design, often receiving the carved, gilt panel only after the others had finished with it. Some early designs by artists do exist for a few works (e.g. by Albrecht Dürer (1471–1528), Filippo Lippi (*c.* 1406–69), Lorenzo Lotto (*c.* 1480–1556) and Vittore Carpaccio (?1460/66–1525/6)); their rarity may be because few have survived or because they were uncommon. Even where contracts exist putting the painter in charge of the commission or requiring his design for a frame, the ornamentation may have remained the carver's province.

During the Renaissance dynasties of exceptional carvers flourished, particularly in Italy; these also enjoyed equal status with the artist and were often important architects/sculptors responsible for the interiors where the works would hang. A painting could still be commissioned when its frame was already complete, and there was little sense that the work of carving or gilding was inferior (e.g. Leonardo da Vinci (1452–1519) gilded the frame for his *Virgin of the Rocks*, 1480s; Paris, Louvre). Gradually, however, framing was left more in the artist's hands, and the 'name frames' began to emerge: these are designs associated with a particular painter, such as the 'Maratta', 'Canaletto', 'Longhi', 'Lely', 'Wright', 'Morland' and 'Whistler' frames. Distinct from the producers of these stock designs, however, a master carver was still socially on a par with the artist and was often engaged directly by the client to provide an exceptional frame. In France the master carvers, their workshops and the guilds became rich and influential; craftsmen began to stamp their frames with a studio mark; and dozens of pattern books were published and diffused throughout Europe. Sculptors, ornamentalists and cabinetmakers all produced frames that can be classed as superb carvings, exquisite designs or precious pieces of furniture. The quality of these, residing not only in the original composition and carved detail but also in the application of layers of gesso, the recutting of the gesso and the use of toned gilding and part burnishing, was reflected in the high prices they commanded, although in the 16th, 17th and 18th centuries the cost of paintings rose proportionately faster than that of frames, and stock designs were relatively cheap.

Collectors tended to pay to frame their acquisitions suitably, as with the galleries built from the 16th to the 18th century to house specific collections, for which the architect would often design background hangings, decoration and frames. The jewels of a collection received settings approximating to their perceived worth. On the other hand, a Dutch patron of the 17th century or the early 18th would look to fashionable France rather than a native style when framing his most prized paintings, and French collectors of northern paintings would naturally do the same; from the time of their execution until quite a recent date, portraits by, for example, Rembrandt might be framed in French Baroque gilt frames, which can kill the contents.

The position of the framemaker crumbled, along with that of other luxury trades, because of the impoverishment and restraint caused by the revolutionary and Napoleonic wars of the late 18th century and the early 19th; and, with the advent of the Industrial Revolution, mass-produced products began to replace hand-made goods. Machine-stamped lengths of moulding created cheap frames for the engravings churned out by new processes; framed pictures for the better-off middle and working classes became affordable; and there was a gradual infiltration into the higher end of the market and a consequent slump in demand for hand-carved frames. Other products of the mass market—composition and papier mâché, base metal instead of gold leaf—all fed this trend, and by 1813 the number of carvers had shrunk by almost nine-tenths. The artist's position remained unaffected: indeed, his status had changed from the artisan of the Middle Ages to the inspired creator of the Romantic Age, leaving the carver or framemaker reduced to the stature of mere craftsman. In the later 19th century the artist would become rich, titled and influential; but there was no equivalent place for the carver, just as there was no longer widespread demand for his skill. The design of any frame outside a production-line type was firmly in the artist's hands; and although the rarity of a tailor-made pattern executed by one of the few good carvers remaining meant that its price was comparatively high, still its maker would never be given the recognition, equal with the painter, that he had enjoyed five or six centuries earlier.

So little were good authentic frames valued that the early panel paintings shipped out of Italy in the 19th and 20th centuries were taken wholesale from their carved Gothic settings, and the latter were burnt to salvage the gold leaf. Museums in Europe and the USA reset the panels in pastiches of the original, with iron-like composition Gothic Revival ornament finished with drab oil-gilding and base leaf. Imitation French Baroque frames with stamped ornament were used on Italian Renaissance and Mannerist works; and original Louis XIV-style carved frames were stripped of their gilding, washed with subdued colour and used to marry Impressionist paintings to the Louis Revival interiors of their American purchasers. Soon this ubiquitous practice had fixed a generalized Louis XIV pattern in the public mind as the 'Impressionist frame'. Similarly, Turner's works lost their gilded hollow, 'Morland' or laurel frames, often ending in neutral greyish 1960s mouldings with inner hessian slips. Remedying this divorce of paintings from their contemporary settings began in earnest only in the late 20th century; the process is handicapped by the small number of original frames surviving and by the reluctance of institutions to spend on displaying authentically the pictures they have rather than on acquiring new ones. Curators may also baulk at hanging diverse styles of frame side by side, preferring to preserve a neutral pre-existing 'gallery' style or to create a new one. The loss of balance, colour and focus in many paintings is severe, and only the custom of illustrating art books with unframed reproductions could have blinded the spectator for so long to the effects of such misalliance. Some art history methodologies locate the work in its social and historical setting; it needs also to be appropriately sited in an immediate physical context that will take account of its original purpose and surroundings or subsequent place in a noted collection. It needs a frame.

H. Heydenryk: *The Art and History of Frames* (New York, 1963) [100 figs]

C. Grimm: *Alte Bilderrahmen: Epochen–Typen–Material* (Munich, 1978) [extensive bibliog.; 483 figs]; Eng. trans. as *The Book of Picture Frames* (New York, 1981) [with suppl. on American frames by G. Szabo; 30 figs, 489 pls] [G]

P. Thornton: *Seventeenth-century Interior Decoration in England, France and Holland* (New Haven and London, 1978)

P. Mitchell: 'The Framing Tradition', *Picture Framing*, ed. R. Wright-Smith (London, 1980), pp. 12–32 [9 colour pls]

P. van Thiel and C. de Bruyn Kops: *Prijst de Lijst* (exh. cat., The Hague, Rijksmus., 1984)

S. E. Fuchs: *Der Bilderrahmen* (Recklinghausen, 1985) [146 figs]

The Art of the Edge: European Frames, 1300–1900 (exh. cat. by R. Brettell and S. Starling; Chicago, IL, A. Inst., 1986) [incl. J. Ortega y Gasset: 'Meditations on the Frame', p. 21]

Rev. A., 76 (1987) [whole issue devoted to frames]

In Perfect Harmony: Picture and Frame, 1850–1920 (exh. cat., Amsterdam, Rijksmus. van Gogh, 1995)

The Art of the Picture Frame: Artists, Patrons and the Framing of Portraits in Britain (exh. cat. by J. Simon; London, N.P.G., 1996)

Frameworks (exh. cat., London, Paul Mitchell, 1996)

E. Wilner: *The Gilded Edge: The Art of the Frame* (San Francisco, 2000)

H. Heydenryk: *The Right Frame: The Essential Guide to Framing* (New York, Lyons, Garsington, Windsor, 2003)

The Art of the Frame: Gems from the Simoni Collection (exh. cat. by S. Smeaton; Pensacola, FL, Mus. A., 2004)

Frampton, Sir George (James) (*b* London, 16 June 1860; *d* London, 21 May 1928). English sculptor and decorative artist. As a sculptor he is best known for *Peter Pan* (1910), which was given by the author J. M. Barrie to the children of London and erected in Kensington Gardens (*in situ*). Frampton became a leading figure in the ARTS AND CRAFTS MOVEMENT, being a member of the Art Workers' Guild from 1887 and its Master in 1902. He also used *The Studio* to disseminate his views, contributing articles on the colouring of sculpture, jewellery and enamelling. Frampton made his greatest impact at the exhibition of the Arts and Crafts Society in 1896, where he showed an overmantel destined for a house in Germany designed by Charles Harrison Townsend (1851–1928), models for cabinet-door panels and a folding screen in leather decorated and inlaid with gold, aluminium, ivory, mother-of-pearl and enamels.

ODNB

France. Ceramics *see* ANGOULÊME; APREY POTTERY; APT POTTERY; ARDUS POTTERY; BAYEUX PORCELAIN FACTORY; BELLEVUE; BORDEAUX; CHANTILLY, §2; CHOISY-LE-ROI; CREIL POTTERY; ETOILLES PORCELAIN; GIEN POTTERY; LA BORNE; LA ROCHELLE; LES ISLETTES; LILLE, §1; LIMOGES, §1; LONGWY POTTERY; LUNÉVILLE; LYON, §1; MAISON BARBIZET; MARSEILLE; MEILLONNAS POTTERY; MENNECY PORCELAIN FACTORY; MONTPELLIER; MOULINS; MOUSTIERS; NEVERS, §1; NIDERVILLER; ORLÉANS; PARIS, §§1 AND 2; QUIMPER; ROUEN; SAINT-AMAND-LES-EAUX; SAINT-CLOUD; SAINT-OMER POTTERY; SAINT-PORCHAIRE; SAMADET POTTERY; SARREGUEMINES POTTERY FACTORY; SCEAUX FACTORY; SÈVRES PORCELAIN FACTORY; VINCENNES PORCELAIN FACTORY.

Glass *see* BACCARAT; CHOISY-LE-ROI; CLICHY GLASSHOUSE; NEVERS, §2; PANTIN GLASSHOUSE; SAINT-LOUIS GLASSHOUSE; VERRE DE FOUGÈRE; VERRERIE DE LA REINE.

Metalwork *see* LIMOGES, §2.

Textiles *see* ALENÇON LACE; ARRAS; AUBUSSON, §§1 AND 2; BEAUVAIS TAPESTRY FACTORY; BLONDE LACE; CHANTILLY, §1; CLUNY LACE; FONTAINEBLEAU; GOBELINS TAPESTRY FACTORY; LILLE, §2; LILLE LACE; LORRAINE LACE; LYON, §2; MAINCY TAPESTRY FACTORY; MIRECOURT; NANCY; SAINT-MAUR SILK FACTORY; SAVONNERIE; STRASBOURG; TOURS; VALENCIENNES.

Wallpaper *see* DESFOSSÉ & KARTH; DUFOUR, JOSEPH, & CIE; ZUBER & CIE.

France, William (*d* 1771). English cabinetmaker. In 1764 he entered into a partnership with John Bradburn, who the following year became Cabinetmaker to the Royal Household (in succession to WILLIAM VILE). France made furniture for ROBERT ADAM, who remodelled Kenwood House (now English Heritage) from 1764 to 1779; examples of France's furniture survive in Kenwood House, The Vyne (NT) and in the Royal Collection.

G. Castle: 'The France Family of Upholsterers and Cabinet-Makers', *Furn Hist.*, xli (2005), pp. 25–43

Francesco Durantino. *See* DURANTINO, FRANCESCO.

Francia, Francesco [Raibolini] [il Francia] (*b* Bologna, *c*. 1450; *d* Bologna, 1517). Italian painter who trained as a jeweller and goldsmith. Unlike other 15th-century artists who trained as goldsmiths, such as Lorenzo Ghiberti (1378–1455) and Andrea del Verrocchio (1435–88), he did not use this craft apprenticeship simply as a step towards artistic work of higher status. He signed his pictures *Aurifex* (goldsmith) to the last and frequently served as an officer of the goldsmiths' guild. He was also in charge of the Bolognese mint under the Bentivoglio family and later under Pope Julius II. A number of coins designed by him survive, as do niello paxes of the *Crucifixion* (*c*. 1488–90) and the *Resurrection* (*c*. 1500; both Bologna, Pin. N.), which are adorned with the coats of arms of prominent families and appear to commemorate marriages. The *Crucifixion* was probably a wedding present from Giovanni II Bentivoglio to his bride, Ginevra Sforza; the *Resurrection* must date from *c.* 1481, the year Bartolomeo Felicini married Dorotea Ringhieri. A third silver pax (untraced) was executed at immense expense for Giovanni Sforza and his wife, Lucrezia Borgia.

G. C. Williamson: *Francesco Raibolini, Called Francia* (London, 1901)
E. Negro and others: *Francesco Francia e la sua scuola* (Modena and Artioli, 1998)
J. Warren: 'Francesco Francia and the Art of Sculpture in Renaissance Bologna', *Burl. Mag.*, cxli/1153 (April 1999), pp. 216–25

Franck, Kaj (*b* 1911; *d* 1989). Finnish ceramic and glass designer. In 1945 he joined Arabia porcelain factory, where he dispensed with the notion of the china set in favour of mix and match tableware. His best known series was 'Kilta' (designed in 1948, sold from 1953 and relaunched in 1981 as 'Teema'), which was available in several colours and was enormously practical: he dispensed with decorative rims and shaped the surfaces so that they could be easily stacked. He also worked for the Nuutajärvi glassworks, for whom he produced both functional glass and decorative pieces. In both ceramics and glass, Kaj was probably the most influential designer of the 20th century.

Kaj Franck: Designer (exh. cat., New York, MOMA, 1992)
'The Era of Kaj Franck [Special section]', *Form Function Finland*, xci (2003), pp. 48–55

Frankenthal Porcelain Factory. German ceramics factory. Although Paul Antoine Hannong had succeeded in producing hard-paste porcelain with Joseph Jakob Ringler (1730–1804) at his faience factory in Strasbourg in 1751, he was forbidden to produce porcelain because of the exclusive privilege granted to the royal factory in Vincennes. In 1755 Hannong transferred the business to Frankenthal, but he himself stayed in Strasbourg, employing his son Charles-François Hannong (*d* 1757) to manage the concern. In 1757 he replaced him with his younger son Joseph Adam Hannong (1739–after 1800). In 1761 the factory was sold to the Elector Palatine Charles Theodore of Sulzbach (*reg* 1742–99). Adam Bergdoll (1720–97) was made technical director and was succeeded in 1775 by the outstandingly competent Simon Feilner (1726–98). The unusual colour-sample plate (1775; London, BM), decorated with 60 small posies of flowers, is by Feilner, who presented it to the Elector Palatine as proof of his superb technical expertise.

From the beginning the factory employed such outstanding artists as the model-designer Wilhelm Lanz (*fl* 1755–61), who was brought by Paul Antoine Hannong from Strasbourg; other artists included Johann Martin Heinrici (1711–86), the brothers Johann Friedrich Lück (1727–97) and Carl Gottlieb Lück (*d* 1777) from Meissen, the modeller Franz Konrad Linck (1730–93), who was chief modeller 1762–5, and the painting-foreman Gottlieb Friedrich Riedel (1724–84), who went to Ludwigsburg in 1759. A combination of deep crimson, rich-green, carmine and later shades of grey and brown are characteristic Frankenthal colours. Outstanding artists included: the 'Amerindian' flower painter Johann Nicolaus Mittmann (1715–84); the European flower painters Carl Haussmann (1742–*c.* 1802) and Andreas Handschuh (*d c.* 1778); the animal and bird painter Riedel;

Kaj Franck: pitcher, turn mould-blown glass, h. 222 mm, diam. 79 mm, 1954 (New York, Museum of Modern Art)

Frankenthal porcelain 'Birds' table service, 1760 (Mannheim, Städtisches Reiss-Museum)

the painter of *commedia dell'arte* characters and figures after Watteau and Boucher, Andreas Philipp Oettner; the painter of Dutch genre scenes, after David Teniers, Christian Winterstein (*fl* 1757–95); the figure painters Johann Bernhard Magnus (*c.* 1745–98) and Franz Joseph Weber (*fl* 1760–84); and the flower and fruit painter Georg Konrad Rahner (1745–after 1800). Jakob Osterspey (*c.* 1730–82) painted beautiful landscapes and mythological figures after Boucher (e.g. breakfast-service, 1765–70; Frankfurt am Main, Mus. Ksthandwk). Wares were also decorated by Michael Glöckle (1751–*c.* 1802) with *décor bois* (a *trompe l'oeil* form of decoration imitating grained wood) imposed with representations of engravings inspired by wares from Niderviller or with the 'golden star' pattern on a purple ground by Michael Appel (1724–85). Flowers in four tones of gold on a royal-blue ground were a particular speciality. Patterns based on brocades or wallpapers in the Louis XVI style were adopted from Sèvres; crimson and gold flowers painted over gilt-striped grounds were among the most popular patterns of the 1770s and 1780s (e.g. plate, 1770–75; Munich, Bayer. Nmus., Neue Samml.). The influence of Sèvres is also evident in the broad borders and rims; they were more luxuriant and wider at Frankenthal than in other German factories. There are, however, very few examples of purely Neo-classical motifs.

In the production of figures, Frankenthal was second only to Meissen. In an inventory made at the end of the 18th century 200 groups and 600 single figures, including allegories of the Senses, Seasons and Elements, hunting scenes, pastoral scenes, fig-

ures from the *commedia dell'arte* and Chinese figures, are listed (see colour pl. XIV, fig. 3). The chief modeller was the sculptor Johann Wilhelm Lanz (*fl* 1755–61) from Strasbourg, who was succeeded by Johann Friedrich Lück, the sculptor Konrad Lick (1730–93), Lück's brother Carl Gottlieb Lück, Adam Bauer (*c.* 1743–*c.* 1780) and from 1779 the sculptor Johann Peter Melchior (1742–1825), who produced Neo-classical figures mainly in biscuit porcelain (e.g. *Apotheosis of the Electoral Pair*, 1792; Berlin, Schloss Charlottenburg).

In 1794 the factory was requisitioned by French Revolutionary troops and sold to Peter van Recum; with the help of Bergdoll, the former technical director, van Recum renewed production but only for a short period. After being requisitioned for a second time the factory was closed in 1799.

F. H. Hoffmann: *Frankenthaler Porzellan* (Munich, 1911)
L. W. Böhm: *Frankenthaler Porzellan* (Mannheim, 1960)
A. Maus and L. Steinemann: *Die Künstler und Fabrikanten der Porzellanmanufaktur Frankenthal* (1961)

Frankfurt am Main Faience Factory. German faience factory founded in 1666 by a merchant (Johann Christoph Fehr) and a potter (Johann Simonet) who had worked at HANAU FAIENCE FACTORY. Under Fehr and his descendants the factory produced wares that resemble those of DELFT, including candlesticks, jugs, vases (including monumental vases) and plates. Most products were blue (or blue and manganese), and the tin-enamel was covered with a brilliant white lead glaze. In 1722 the pottery passed to the Hasslocher family, and the quality of production declined. Artists included Johann Wereshofer (1680–90), JOHANN CASPAR RIPP (1702–8) and Johann Carl Auer (1742).

A. Feulner: *Frankfurter Fayencen* (Berlin, 1935)

Frankl, **Paul Theodore** (*b* 1886; *d* 1962). American furniture designer, born in Austria. He emigrated to the USA in 1914 and worked first in New York and later in Los Angeles. His most famous work is his 'skyscraper' furniture, which first appeared in 1926; many pieces were maple, and inlaid with Bakelite (e.g. skyscraper bookcase, 1927; New York, Met.). Frankl later specialized in metal furniture and in Art Deco furniture decorated with black lacquers and gold and silver leaf.

P. T. Frankl: *Form and Re-form: A Practical Handbook of Modern Interiors* (New York, 1930/*R* 1972)
P. T. Frankl: *New Dimensions: The Decorative Arts of Today in Words & Pictures* (New York, 1975)
C. Long: 'The New American Interior: Paul T. Frankl in New York, 1914–1917', *Stud. Dec. A.*, ix/2 (Spring–Summer 2002), pp. 2–32

Franklin Flint Works. *See under* GILLINDER & SONS.

Fratina. Sixteenth-century Italian (especially Tuscan) refectory chair with a high back and sometimes with arms; in the 16th century *fratina* chairs were not upholstered, but thereafter the backs and seats of chairs based on the *fratina* were upholstered in velvet or leather.

Frechen. *See under* COLOGNE.

Freiberg. German centre of ceramics production. A pottery was established in the Saxon town of Freiberg *c.* 1650 and the stoneware produced in the 1650s was distinctively decorated with stamped and chip-carved ornaments; steins were often fitted with pewter handles and lids. From 1660 reducing furnaces were used to produce grey vessels (typically ovoid and pear-shaped jugs) with floral motifs in enamel colours. Production seems to have stopped *c.* 1680.

Fret. *See* MEANDER.

Fretwork. Carved work in decorative patterns consisting largely of intersecting lines, typically used in the decoration of ceilings and furniture. In the late 19th century the term acquired the additional sense of an ornamental openwork pattern (popular from the 1730s) consisting of strips of wood cut with a fret saw.

Frieze. In the Classical orders of architecture, a horizontal member in an entablature that is above the architrave and below the cornice. The word has also come to be used in various contexts (e.g. wallpaper) for horizontal bands of ornamental or figural decoration (see colour pl. XV, fig. 1). The term is also used for strips of ornament on furniture (sometimes known as band ornament or band patterns) if they occur below a projection resembling a cornice, as is often seen in furniture that adopts Classical architectural forms in miniature.

Frigger. Small glass ornament, sometimes a testing sample and sometimes made from leftover glass.

Waterford Friggers: End of Day Glass at Waterford Museum of Treasures (exh. cat., Waterford, Mus. Treasures, 2003)

Frijtom, **Frederik van** (*b c.* 1632; *d* 1702). Dutch painter based in Delft, where he designed and made faience plaques (*porceleyne schilderijtjes*) depicting landscapes; his pottery is distinguished by his use of underglaze decoration (e.g. plaque depicting a river landscape; Amsterdam, Rijksmus.). He sometimes worked for De Dubbelde Schenkkan ('the Double Jug'), but also seems to have worked independently.

S. Vecht, *Frederik van Frijtom, 1632–1702: Life and Work of a Delft Pottery-decorator* (Amsterdam, 1968)
De Plateelschilder Frederik van Frijtom en landschappen in blauw (exh. cat., Rotterdam, Mus. Boymans–van Beuningen, 1968)

Frisbee, **Willam**. *See under* STORR, PAUL.

Frisio, **Johan**. *See* VREDEMAN DE VRIES, HANS.

Frit. Term used in glass technology to describe a mixture of sand and fluxes heated together to form

Crown of Bes decorated with a cat herding geese (fragment of a figurine), frit ceramic with glaze, Egypt (Paris, Musée du Louvre)

a semi-vitrified mass as a first stage in the production of glass. This material is then pulverized and may be used in the manufacture of glass or ceramic glazes. The term is also applied to moulded, unglazed, sintered-quartz bodies. Particularly fine frit beads, objects and vessels were produced in ancient Egypt. The terms 'glass paste' or *'pâte de verre'* are sometimes used to denote frit and opaque glass. In ceramics the term 'frit' is also used to denote the vitreous composition from which soft porcelain is made. Fritware is a glazed sintered-quartz faience with a coloured glaze, first introduced by Islamic potters in the 12th century.

Fritsch, Elizabeth (*b* Whitchurch, Salop, 11 Sept 1940). Welsh potter. She studied under HANS COPER and in 1972–3 worked at the BING & GRØNDAHL factory in Copenhagen). Her stoneware, earthenware and porcelain pots are coil built, then scraped and smoothed and painted with softly coloured slip in geometric designs inspired by musical rhythms and notation ('Saxophone and Piano Duo', 1978; London, V&A) and influenced by Pre-Columbian and African art. Although her pots are vessels, they are not functional. Early pots were designed to be picked up and held in the hand; more recent ones are meant to be viewed from one or two angles like abstract still-lifes

P. Dormer: *Elizabeth Fritsch in Studio* (London, 1985)
P. Dormer: *The New Ceramics: Trends and Traditions* (London, 1986, 3/1989)
Elizabeth Fritsch: Vessels from Another World (exh. cat.; London, Crafts Council, 1993)
A. Fielding: 'Elizabeth Fritsch: Contemporary Applied Arts'. *Cer. Rev.*, clxxv (Jan–Feb 1999), p. 42

Fromageau, Jean-Baptiste (*b c.* 1726; *d c.* 1781). French furniture-maker. Unusually, he was both an *ébéniste* and *menuisier*. He became a *maître* in 1755, and is particularly noted for his commodes.

Froment-Meurice, François-Désiré (*b* 1802; *d* 1855). French silversmith and jeweller. The pieces that he exhibited at the Paris Industrial Exhibitions of 1839 and 1844 made him the most celebrated silversmith in France. He worked in a variety of styles, notably Renaissance Revival, but also produced distinguished Gothic Revival and Rococo-style pieces. His most famous creation is the Toilette of the Duchess of Parma (1845–51), which consists of a dressing-table with mirror, candelabra, ewer and basin and jewellery caskets; the toilette was lost in 1864 and rediscovered in 1981, and is now in the Musée d'Orsay. Froment-Meurice was succeeded by his son Emile (1837–1913), who produced work of high quality until the late 1890s.

P. Burty: *F.-D. Froment-Meurice, argentier de la ville: 1802–1855* (Paris, 1883)
D. Alcouffe and others: *Tresors d'Argent: Les Froment-Meurice* (exh. cat., Paris, Mus. Vie Romantique, 2003)
D. Scarisbrick, 'Froment Meurice', *Apollo*, clviii (July 2003), pp. 52–3

Fromery, Pierre (*b* 1685; *d* Berlin, 1738). Huguenot goldsmith who founded a enamelling workshop in Berlin. The workshop was noted for its enamelled snuff-boxes. Fromery boxes featured opaque or painted enamel grounds with applied silver-gilt repoussé decorations with figural, chinoiserie or floral themes (e.g. snuff-box attributed to Alexander Fromery, son of the founder, *c.* 1740; Budapest, Mus. Applied A.).

Frothingham, Benjamin (*b* Boston, MA, 6 April 1734; *d* Charlestown, MA, 19 Aug 1809). American cabinetmaker. He was the son of a Boston cabinetmaker of the same name and set up a shop in Charlestown, MA, in 1756. He served as a major in the American army during the American War of Independence (1775–83) and after the war joined the Society of the Cincinnati, a fraternal organization of American officers who had served during the war. In 1789 he was visited by President George Washington, a fellow member and past president of the society. Known for his block-front and serpentine-front case furniture with corkscrew flame finials, Frothingham also worked in other styles: he made a *bombe* secrétaire (1753; Washington, DC) and later in the century a sideboard (sold American Art Association, 2–4 Jan 1930, lot 417) and table (ex-Joseph Kindig III priv. col., York, PA, 1974) in the style of Hepplewhite. Many of his known pieces are labelled, the Boston silversmith Nathaniel Hurd (1729–77) engraving his label. Frothingham's eldest son Benjamin Frothingham III (1774–1832) also became a cabinetmaker.

M. M. Swan: 'Major Benjamin Frothingham, Cabinetmaker', *Antiques*, lxii (1952), pp. 392–5
R. H. Randall Jr: 'Benjamin Frothingham', *Boston Furniture of the Eighteenth Century*, ed. W. Whitehill (Boston, 1974), pp. 223–49
B. W. Glauber: *Benjamin Frothingham: Cabinet-maker* (Boston, 1994)

Frullini, Luigi (*b* 1839; *d* 1897). Italian workcarver and cabinetmaker. His woodwork, which ranges from lavish bedroom and dining room suites to picture frames, is often carved in a Renaissance Revival style. Much of his furniture was exported to the USA.

Fry, Roger. *See under* OMEGA WORKSHOPS.

Frye, Thomas (*b* in or near Dublin, *c.* 1710; *d* London, 2 April 1762). Irish painter, mezzotint-engraver and porcelain manufacturer, active in England. He probably trained in Dublin, but by 1735 he had moved to London. After an early career as a portrait painter he joined Edward Heylyn (1695–after 1758) in the attempt to produce porcelain at the Bow Factory, London. In 1744 they took out a patent for a new method, using china clay brought to England from the North American colony of Georgia by the potter ANDREW DUCHÉ. Under Frye's direction the Bow Porcelain Factory produced a variety of well-received soft-paste figures and vessels. However, Frye's health apparently suffered from work among the furnaces, and he retired in 1759 to return to painting and engraving.

ODNB

Fuddling cup. Drinking vessel consisting of three or more small cups with interlinked handles; an example in the British Museum (1790) consists of six cups. Fuddling cups were made from the mid-17th century to the late 18th in *graffito* slipware in two potteries in Somerset and in tin-glazed earthenware in Bristol.

Fuhrlohg, Christopher. *See under* HAUPT, GEORG.

Fukami, Suehari (*b* 1947). Japanese studio potter based in Kyoto. He works in the bluish white porcelain known in Japanese as *seihakuji*, which was developed in Song dynasty JINGDEZHEN wares. His early work consists of household wares, but since the mid-1970s he has used *seihakuji* as a medium for angular sculptures.

Fulcrum. *See under* BED.

Fulda. German centre of ceramics production. In 1741 a faience factory was founded in Fulda (Hessen) by Amadeus von Buseck, Prince-Bishop of Fulda. Production included candlesticks, vases and tureens (e.g. tureen, *c.* 1745; London, V & A). Despite the high quality of the wares, production was discontinued in 1768. Many of the skilled faience workers found employment in the porcelain factory founded in 1764 by Heinrich VIII, Prince-Bishop of Bibra. In the late 1760s the modeller Johann Valentin Schaum (1714–71) began reproducing figures from the factory in Frankenthal. After initial problems Abraham Ripp (*c.* 1737–96) became director in 1770. Schaum was succeeded by the Bohemian Wenzel Neu (*c.* 1708–74), whose sculptural talent is most beautifully expressed in the boldly conceived *commedia dell'arte* figures in the style of Jacques Callot's *Balli di Sfessania* engravings (1621–35) and in a *Madonna Immaculata on the Globe* (e.g. of *c.* 1775; Hamburg, Mus. Kst & Gew.). It is not clear whether he also collaborated on the figures of children, ladies, cavaliers and officers reminiscent of figures from the factory in Höchst or on the groups with hunters and shepherds on flat sparsely decorated bases. In 1774 Neu was succeeded by Georg Ludwig Bartholomae (*c.* 1744–88), who placed his graceful gardeners and wine-growers, musicians and dancers on mound rocaille bases. Fulda tableware is distinguished by the quality of the white paste and by the fine, smooth glaze. Shapes are in a simple Louis XVI style; only handles, feet and spouts are subtly accentuated. Wares are painted in delicate shades or bright colours and decoration included *en camaieu* landscapes in

iron-red, birds in crimson or grisaille medallions. A popular motif was the black portrait silhouettes surrounded by foliate borders. The factory closed in 1789.

H. H. Josten: *Fuldaer Porzellanfiguren* (Berlin, 1929)
E. Kramer: 'Fuldaer Porzellan in hessischem Staatsbesitz', *Keramos*, xiii (1961), pp. 9–18
H.-P. Mielke: *Keramik an Weser, Werra und Fulda* (Lubeck, 1981)

Fulham. English centre of carpet production in London. The art of carpet-knotting was reintroduced into England in 1750 by two craftsmen from the Savonnerie, Pierre Poiré (*b c.* 1710) and Louis Théau; in 1753 they moved to a tapestry-weaving studio in Fulham (London). When the venture failed in 1755, the looms and designs were auctioned and subsequently used to establish the EXETER carpet factory. The sale catalogue advertises tapestries for unholstery and carpets in the style of the Savonnerie. Rare examples of the production of this factory are at Clandon Park, Surrey, NT.

Fulham Pottery. *See under* DWIGHT, JOHN.

Fulper Pottery Co. American pottery established in 1814 in Flemington, NJ, by Samuel Hill (*d* 1858), who made earthenware storage jars and drainpipes. On Hill's death the pottery was bought by Abram Fulper, and the product lines expanded to include stoneware and tiles (including drainpipes). In 1900 the company began to make art pottery, and in 1910 hired the German designer J. Martin Stangl (*d* 1972), who in 1911 created the first Vasekraft wares, which were covered with colourful crystalline, flambé and monochromatic glazes. The most famous Vasecraft products were ceramic and stained-glass table-lamps (shaped like toadstools), which were sold from 1911 to 1918. During World War I the factory produced porcelain dolls and doll heads to fill the gap caused by the embargo on German imports. In the 1920s the factory introduced Fulper Fayence art and dinnerware lines; the dinnerware, which eventually became known as Stangl Pottery, was America's first solid-colour dinnerware. The factory closed in 1935.

Fuming. Method of colouring wood with chemicals in the place of dyes or stains. Woods with a high tannin content will darken when exposed to ammonia gas. This technique was used to colour much of the oak furniture of the Arts and Crafts Movement.

Funk. Swiss family of furniture-makers. Mathäus Funk (*b* Frankfurt 1697; *d* Berne 1783) ran the most important furniture workshop in 18th-century Switzerland; his best-known work is a bracket-clock. One of his brothers, Daniel Beat Ludwig Funk (1726–87) was a clock-maker. Another brother, Johann Friedrich Funk (1706–75) was a sculptor whose work included the carving of furniture. There is work by all three brothers in the Historisches Museum in Berne.

H. von Fischer, *Die Kunsthandwerker-Familie Funk im 18 Jh in Bern* (Berne, 1961)

Funk, Hans (*b* Zurich, *c.* 1470; *d* Zurich, *c.* 1539–40). Swiss stained-glass painter. He settled *c.* 1499–1500 in Berne, where his early works include a window (*c.* 1501; Berne, Hist. Mus.) with both a signature and the monogram HFG ('Hans Funk Glasmaler'). The quality of Funk's art may be seen in the expressive characterization of the halberdiers holding the arms of Bremgarten and the Confederation, and in the combination of exact detail and liveliness in the fine gold work.

Following these works are a window of 1510 depicting *SS Nicholas and Mary Magdalene* (Berne, Hist. Mus.); one of 1512 showing *Duke Bertold V*, founder of Berne, lying in a meadow with a tree behind him bearing the arms of the city offices (Mulhouse, Mus. Hist.); and five windows of *c.* 1520 at Uerkheim Pfarrkirche, Aargau, depicting the *Virgin* with crescent moon and *SS Leodegar, Vincent and Maurice* with the arms of the estates of Berne. The border work here contains columns and foliate ornamentation, a mingling of Gothic and Renaissance motifs characteristic of the period. About 1522 Funk produced a series of armorial windows for Utzenstorf Pfarrkirche, showing the arms of Berne and Solothurn accompanied by the patron saints of the estates; their lavish upper sections are in the Bernisches Historisches Museum. Further armorial windows are in the Chapelle St Barthélémy, Fribourg (1526), and the Hôtel de Ville de la Palud Lausanne (*c.* 1528).

Funk's window of *c.* 1532 entitled *The Old and the Young Citizen* (Berne, Hist. Mus.) has become, through its artistic quality and the importance of its content, the best-known stained-glass window of the 16th century in Switzerland. Above is seen the Battle of Novara (1513); below stand the representatives of two generations. On flanking scrolls, on either side, the young citizen asks where the older generation found its good fortune, while the older citizen accounts for the generational difference in terms of different lifestyles. The later window for the Gesellschaft zum Affen (1539; Berne, Hist. Mus.)—a work ascribed to Funk and his workshop that displays the Gesellschaft's symbol of a crouching ape looking at itself in a mirror—was the cause of a quarrel between Funk and the glazier Simprecht Baumeister. In 1539 Funk was banished from Berne after being accused of the murder of Baumeister. He died shortly afterwards.

Furniture, vernacular. Term used to describe items of furniture made in local rather than cosmopolitan traditions of design and construction, and intended for everyday use. It is made in countries throughout the world, for use by nomadic and settled peoples, in rural and urban communities. Essentially such furniture reflects the direct needs of ordinary people's domestic and non-domestic lives. Vernacular furniture is thus part of the culture of communities, and its place and function achieve meaning as a direct reflection of the context and use for which it was made. No one descriptive framework can adequately encompass the rich variety of disparate traditions that made up national or regional codes of design, and it is within this notion of regionality that a sense of the coherence of vernacular furniture emerges, reflecting history, geography and, particularly, economy.

Since vernacular furniture is the product of local rather than cosmopolitan design traditions, it generally owes little to the fashionable forms that emanated from metropolitan centres. The essence of the true vernacular is based on a complex interaction between localized design, construction techniques, available materials and the particular ergonomic and social needs of the community. Some vernacular furniture does, however, incorporate classical motifs, absorbed and redefined within the vernacular form. In some traditions, too, there is an indebtedness to fashionable cabinetmakers of the 18th and 19th centuries. Where these influences appear, the vernacular is often less able to synthesize these in new or original ways, and naive and undeveloped motifs and styles appear that are quasi-vernacular, as a result. However, vernacular designs have also influenced some forms of 18th- and 19th-century furniture design, from sophisticated interpretations of 'rustic' furniture during the 18th century to the 'idealized' rural forms adopted by the Arts and Crafts Movement (e.g. oak, rush-seated chair by C. F. A. Voysey, *c.* 1905; London, V&A).

The role of furniture-makers also differed between fashionable and vernacular traditions. Cabinetmakers and other specialists were usually distanced from the clients, who were seen as the architects of style, the makers being deemed to be merely 'conduits' of others' taste. In contrast, makers and the clients who bought vernacular furniture were usually from the same class. In this way, the makers were also to a greater or lesser degree the designers of furniture, often adapting designs and decorative treatments in the light of the customer preference, and with particular uses in mind. There is also a strong convention in some communities for individuals to make their own furniture. Such traditions abound worldwide and range from the seating made in the Scottish Highlands, which was essentially fashioned with an axe from two cleft sections of a naturally shaped branch, joined by hand-shaped cross-spindles and supported on four simple legs, to the furniture made in Newfoundland, Canada, by skilled boat builders, who used fir felled in the surrounding forests and incorporated motifs from their early immigrant roots.

Although some cultures have for many centuries maintained their traditional furniture designs, as seen in the bed and couch forms used in the Middle East and Asian countries, other more recent cultures, fashioned by immigrants from a number of cultural groups, have synthesized different traditions to form a new vernacular furniture tradition. This is evident, for example, in the 18th-century regional furniture designs of the USA.

Vernacular furniture is often characterized by its parsimonious and restrained use of materials; attempts to decorate furniture or to create fashionable designs were less evident and resulted in the adoption of functional forms, with the skilled and restrained use of tools and reliance on habit of technique being adopted to create items quickly in the face of economic constraints. Vernacular furniture is also typically made from locally grown hard- and soft-woods and does not usually involve the use of imported exotic woods. However, in the more affluent, industrial regions of many countries imported mahogany, in particular, was used often in a limited way, for cross-banding or veneers.

In many countries the makers of vernacular furniture were not specialists but made furniture as part of a repertory of other woodwork including house joinery and carpentry. During this work they developed a sense of architectural space that was reflected in the furniture dimensions; for example, furniture for single-storey dwellings was often made to make use of the wall rather than floor space, with tall pieces being common. This furniture was often decorated with fretted devices, painting and simulation techniques.

J. Gauthier: *Le Mobilier des vieilles provinces de France* (Paris, n.d.)
I. Plath: *The Decorative Arts of Sweden* (New York, 1966)
J. S. Stewart: *The Folk Arts of Norway* (New York, 1972)
V. Chinnery: *Oak Furniture: The British Tradition* (Woodbridge, 1979)
N. Loughman: *Irish Country Furniture* (Dublin, 1984)
C. Gilborn: *Adirondack Furniture and the Rustic Tradtion* (New York, 1987)
B. D. Cotton: *Cottage and Farmhouse Furniture in East Anglia* (1987)
B. D. Cotton: 'Irish Vernacular Furniture', *Reg. Furn. Soc. J.*, iii (1989), pp. 1–26
B. D. Cotton: *The English Regional Chair* (Woodbridge, 1990)
C. Gilbert: *English Vernacular Furniture, 1750–1900* (London, 1991)
C. Kinmouth: *Irish Country Furniture, 1700–1950* (Yale, 1993)

Fürstenberg Porcelain Factory. German ceramics factory. Charles I, Duke of Brunswick-Wolfenbüttel, founded a porcelain factory in Fürstenberg in 1747. Attempts, however, to produce hard-paste porcelain were unsuccessful until after the arrival of the arcanist Johann Kilian Benckgraff (1708–58) from Höchst in 1753. Despite difficult economic circumstances and great technical problems—often the wares became misshapen and cracked during firing, and the glaze was a greyish-yellow—production was extensive from the beginning. Modellers included Simon Feilner (1726–98), Johann Georg Leimberger (1711–63), Anton Carl Luplau (1745–95), Johann Christoph Rombrich (1731–94), Christian Gottlieb Schubert (*fl* 1735) and the sculptor Desoches from the Académie Royale de Peinture et de Sculpture in Paris, who arrived in Fürstenberg in 1769. He created 45 groups of figures, including mythological scenes, allegorical groups of the seasons, Chinese men, and children, including the much copied *Family at a Coffee Table* (1771; Bremen, Focke-Mus.), as well as vases and candlesticks.

In 1756 the first great table-service (the Seckendorff Service) was produced, but generally production concentrated on coffee-, tea- and chocolate-services, vases, incense-burners, kettles, centrepieces, tureens, cachepots and clockcases. The inspiration for these wares came from Meissen, Berlin, Sèvres and from the factory of Josiah Wedgwood. Shapes and decoration followed the stylistic trends of the period: first the late Rococo style, with ozier borders, piercing, flowers and relief motifs; later the Louis XVI style, with clean outlines and sparse decoration; and finally the Neo-classical style, employing straight lines and tectonic forms. During the Empire period, in addition to flower and fruit designs, borders of acanthus, ivy, oak, laurel and vine leaves were introduced. During the Biedermeier period (1815–48) wares were decorated with colourful sprays of flowers.

During the second half of the 19th century production was dominated by historicist styles. Towards the end of the century *Jugendstil* wares were created by E. J. Kruse, Paul Eberlein, Anton Zentner and Hermann Gradl. The 1930s were dominated by the designers Wilhelm Wagenfeld, Siegfried Müller, Walter Nitzsche and F. A. Sundermann. In the early 21st century the factory produces contemporary-style wares in addition to reproductions of such old figures as those by Feilner or designs by Rombrich.

S. Ducret: *Fürstenberger Porzellan*, 3 vols (Brunswick, 1973)
Fürstenberger Porzellan vom Rokoko bis zum Historismus (exh. cat. by H. W. Haase, Bremen, Focke-Mus., 1986)

Fusajirō. *See* KITAŌJI, ROSANJIN.

Fustian. Coarse cloth made with a cotton weft and a flax warp, first made in Egypt in the 2nd century AD and then revived in England in the 18th century. From the 19th century the term has denoted a thick, twilled, cotton cloth with a short pile or nap, usually dyed an olive or leaden colour.

G

Gabel Pottery. Czech pottery founded *c.* 1630 by Heinrich Wolf Brecka on his estate near Gabel (now Jablonné v Podještědí) in Bohemia. The factory made white and red earthenware (especially tableware) decorated with modelled reliefs and (in some cases) enamel painting.

J. Horschik: 'Die deutschen Terra-Sigillata-Gefässe des 17 und 18 Jahrhunderts und ihre Siegelmarkern', *Keramos*, xxxiii (1966), pp. 3–56

Gadroon. One of a set of convex curves or arcs joined at their extremities to form a decorative pattern used in the ornamentation of gold and silver plate, costume and ceramics. Gadrooning is the reverse of FLUTING, in which the curves are concave.

Gaillard, Eugène (*b* 1862; *d* 1933). French designer and barrister. He published his theories about avant-garde furniture and became established as an advocate of the modern school. Although known almost exclusively for his furniture, he also designed a wide range of objects and decorative schemes in an elegant Art Nouveau style.

Early in his career Gaillard collaborated in S. Bing's fashionable Art Nouveau shop in Paris. Together with Georges de Feure and Edouard Colonna he created interiors and furniture for Bing's pavilion, Art Nouveau Bing (destr.), at the Exposition Universelle of 1900 in Paris. Gaillard was responsible for three rooms in the pavilion: the vestibule, dining-room and bedroom. French precedents, especially elements from the Rococo style, were freely used as a source of inspiration. In the vestibule Gaillard installed a mosaic floor, bold pink draperies and a stencilled frieze that effectively set off a walnut portemanteau with mirrored back and shelves. The dining-room was furnished in walnut, ornamented with scrolled foliage and panelled wainscot, beneath a mural painted by the Spanish artist José María Sert (1876–1945). His buffet for the dining-room (Copenhagen, Kstindustmus.) expresses the spirit of his creations in its fondness for abstract features inspired by naturalistic forms.

Later in his career Gaillard designed deeply moulded furniture with sharply curved corners displaying carved decoration; he consistently favoured sinuously flowing, carved panels and ormolu drawer pulls. His chairs, which were very popular, do not exhibit excessive ornamentation, being of a plainer, heavier construction, often with leather seats instead of decorative upholstery fabrics.

About 1903 Gaillard ended his collaboration with Bing and established his own firm, which produced furniture of similar designs. By 1907 Gaillard had simplified his designs significantly; his furniture became lighter in contrast to the rather ponderous style of earlier pieces, and the decoration was less strident. He claimed in *A propos du mobilier* (1906) that his approach to furniture design was based on five rules: a piece of furniture should express its function as far as possible; the nature of the material must be respected; no unnecessary constructive elements should be included; in wood an arch is only to be regarded as a decorative element; and ornament should be abstract. Even in pieces where the abundance of carved ornaments is excessive, Gaillard's furniture possesses a constructive logic. In the furniture made between 1900 and 1914 Gaillard attempted to 'invest the most humble object with an undeniable artistic character' and to 'furnish beautiful prototypes of all kinds for the so-called art industries'. Gaillard's designs developed from stylized naturalism to full abstract decoration and ultimately to a phase of simplification with the introduction of clearly defined planes and curved lines. Little is known about the later phase of his career.

P. van Dam: *Eugène Gaillard: Meublier, 1862–1933* (The Hague, 1986)

Gaines. American family of chairmakers active in Ipswich, MA and Portsmouth, NH. The founder of the workshop was John Gaines II (*b* Ipswich MA, 3 Apr 1677; *d* Ipswich, 24 Dec 1748). He worked with his son Thomas Gaines I (*c.* 1712–*c.* 1761), building furniture in a local variant of Boston designs; their account book (1707–61) is now in the Winterthur Museum Library. Thomas's brother John Gaines III (1704–43) opened a shop in Portsmouth in 1724; he was succeeded by his son George Gaines (1736–1808).

R. E. T. Hendrick: *John Gaines II and Thomas Gaines I, 'Turners' of Ipswich, Massachusetts* (MA thesis, U. Delaware, 1964)
Jobe, B., ed.: *Portsmouth Furniture: Masterworks from the New Hampshire Seacoast*, Society for the Preservation of New England Antiquities (Boston, MA, 1993)

Gallatin, **Albert** (*b* Geneva, 29 Jan 1761; *d* Astoria, NY, 12 Aug 1849). American politician and glassmaker of Swiss birth. Gallatin is best known for his public roles as Secretary of the Treasury under President Jefferson and President Madison, but he was also an important glass manufacturer. He moved to America in 1780, and in 1797 founded the New Geneva Glassworks in Western Pennsylvania. The factory began production in 1798, making window glass, hollowware (especially whiskey bottles) and tableware. In 1803 he was appointed Secretary to the Treasury and sold the glassworks. The factory continued to produce glass until 1857.

Gallatown Pottery. *See under* WEMYSS WARE.

Galle, **Claude** (*b* 1759; *d* 1815). French bronze-caster and gilder. He was the son of a poultry farmer, and began work in the foundry of Pierre Foy, his father-in-law. By 1784 Galle was a major figure in his field, supplying gilt mounts for furniture by GUILLAUME BENEMAN and, through JEAN HAURÉ, supplying the palaces of Fontainebleau, Versailles, Saint-Cloud, and Compiègne with furniture, clocks and candelabra. After the Revolution he supplied many works for Napoleon (*reg* 1804–14) at Saint-Cloud. He went bankrupt with the defeat of Napoleon in 1812,

and died in poverty. The business was late revived by Claude's son Gerard-Jean Galle (1788–1846).

Gallé, **Emile (Charles Martin)** (*b* Nancy, 4 May 1846; *d* Nancy, 23 Sept 1904). French glassmaker, potter and cabinetmaker. He was the son of Charles Gallé-Reinemer, a manufacturer of ceramics and glass in Nancy, and as early as 1865 he started working for his father, designing floral decoration. In 1866–7 he was employed by the Burgun, Schwerer & Cie glassworks in Meisenthal, and on his return to Nancy he worked in his father's workshops at Saint-Clément designing faience tableware. In 1874, after his father's retirement, he established his own small glass workshop in Nancy and assumed the management of the family business.

At the Exposition Universelle of 1878 in Paris, Gallé exhibited pieces made in the 'clair-de-lune' technique: glass was coloured with traces of cobalt oxide, which produced a sapphire hue (see colour pl. XVI, fig. 2). From *c.* 1884 Gallé produced his first *verreries parlantes*, which were inscribed with quotations from poems and prose by such writers as François Villon (e.g. 'La Ballade des dames du temps jadis', 1884; Nancy, Mus. Ecole Nancy). Gallé first exhibited this glass in 1884 at the Union Centrale des Arts Décoratifs in Paris, where he showed over 300 pieces of glass and ceramics, for which he was awarded a gold medal. Perhaps Gallé's greatest innovation was his development of cameo glass: the inspiration for this type of glass came from the Chinese cased glass of the Qian long period (1736–96). Two or more fused layers of coloured glass were

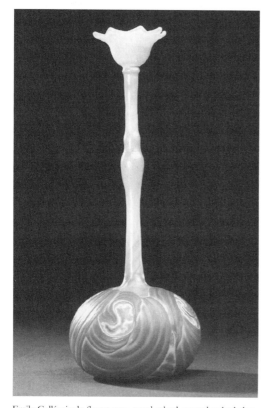

Emile Gallé: single-flower vase, cased, wheel-cut and etched glass, h. 320 mm, made by Gallé Glassworks, Nancy, *c.* 1902 (London, Victoria and Albert Museum)

Emile Gallé: salon table in the form of a water lily, *c.* 1900 (Paris, Musée des Arts Décoratifs)

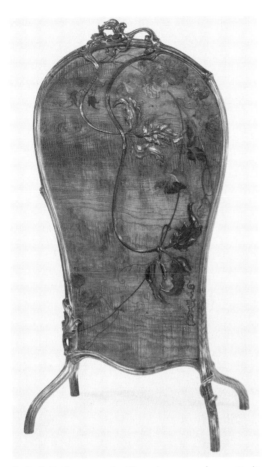

Emile Gallé: firescreen, ash with maple veneer and marquetry in various woods, h. 1.07 m, 1900 (London, Victoria and Albert Museum)

painted with an acid-resistant material and then immersed in an acid bath. The decoration was revealed in low relief and then carved to highlight the motifs (e.g. 'Jardinière', 1884; Paris, Mus. A. Déc.). Gallé experimented with a variety of techniques and also with metal foils and coloured oxides for their decorative effects and exploited such imperfections as crazing and air bubbles in order to create novel and often surreal effects.

In the late 1880s Gallé opened a studio for the production of furniture and first exhibited examples at the Exposition Universelle of 1889 in Paris. Gallé's furniture was generally traditional in form but enhanced with complex marquetry decoration using a variety of indigenous and exotic woods and inlaid with mother-of-pearl and hardstones (e.g. buffet, 1904; Paris, Mus. Orsay). His decoration included such popular Art Nouveau motifs as dragonflies and water lilies. VICTOR PROUVÉ and Louis Hestaux assisted with the design for much of the sculpture, marquetry and inlay of the furniture From c. 1897 Gallé developed his technique of *marqueterie de verre*, which was inspired by his involvement in wood marquetry. Motifs of hot glass were impressed on to the body of coloured glass, and once the body had cooled the inlaid pieces were lightly carved into relief.

Gallé manufactured three types of products: his so-called 'industrial' production began c. 1890, and signed vases in simplified shapes and colours were produced in large quantities; and his more complex and sophisticated limited editions (called 'semi-rich') and his *pièces uniques* were executed by himself (as seen in the portrait of Gallé by Prouvé, 1892; Nancy, Mus. Ecole Nancy) or by highly skilled craftsmen. After Gallé's death in 1904, the business was continued under the artistic direction of Prouvé until 1913. Production finally ceased in 1931, and the shop closed in 1935.

P. Garner: *Emile Gallé* (Paris, 1977)
B. Hakenjos: 'Emile Gallé', *Keramik, Glas und Möbel des Art Nouveau* (Cologne, 1982)
Emile Gallé: Dreams into Glass (exh. cat. by W. Warmus, Corning, NY, Mus. Glass, 1984)
F. Le Tacon: *Emile Gallé: Maître de l'art nouveau* (Strasbourg, 2004)
V. Thomas, H. Bieri and P. Thiébaut: *Verreries d'Emile Gallé: De l'oeuvre unique à la série* (Paris, 2004)

Gallipot. Small earthenware pot of a type used by apothecaries for ointments and medicines.

Galloon. Very outer edge of a tapestry, generally woven in one colour and often bearing the mark of the weaver or tapestry.

For the use of the term in upholstery *see* PASSEMENTERIE.

Gallucci, Nicola [Nicola da Guardiagrele] (*b c.* 1395; *d* before 1462). Italian goldsmith and sculptor, active in Guardiagrele (Abruzzi). The earliest of Nicola's many documented and securely attributed works is a monstrance (1413; Francavilla al Mare, S Maria Maggiore), which, like all his early works, is in the Late Gothic style. Some of his works reflect Tuscan influence, in particular that of Lorenzo Ghiberti. This is already apparent in a cross (1431; Guardiagrele, S Maria Maggiore), but is particularly marked in his altar frontal (1448; Teramo Cathedral) with scenes from the *Life of Christ*, some of which are based directly on those of Ghiberti's north doors of 1403–24 (Florence, Baptistery).

The *Annunciation* (Florence, Bargello) attributed to Nicola and his bust of *St Giustino* (Chieti Cathedral) are examples of Nicola's activity as a goldsmith–sculptor, but it was his crosses that earned him renown. Nicola's processional crosses are of the standard 15th-century type, common also in southern Italy. They are made of silver sheets that are chased, embossed and attached to a wooden support; they are often decorated along the edges with small copper balls. The figures were made to commission and are sometimes quite complex iconographically, and characterized by a great variety of pose and a refinement of execution: for example the *Christ* on the fine cross (L'Aquila, Mus. N. Abruzzo) and the finely carved figures of the gilded silver cross (Rome, S Giovanni in Laterano).

Chess table by Jean-Michel Frank, wood and parchment, 610×863×613 mm, 1929 (New York, Museum of Modern Art)

Galvanoplasty. *See* ELECTROTYPE.

Gambin, Giulio. *See under* NEVERS, §1.

Games. *See* TOYS AND GAMES, §4.

Games table and gaming table. The distinction, which is not always observed, is between a table for games such as chess (with the top marked as a board) and a baize-topped table for gaming (i.e. gambling with cards), often with a leaf-top supported by a swing-leg; the latter is known in America as a 'card table'.

Gardner, Francis (*fl* 1746–86). English entrepreneur, active in Russia. He arrived in 1765, and the next year established a porcelain factory in the village of Verbilki, near Moscow. Under the patronage of Catherine II (*reg* 1762–96) its success was ensured, and it became the main competitor of St Petersburg Imperial Porcelain Factory, producing table-services and figures. The quality of the paste rivalled that of the Imperial Porcelain Factory, and production included simple, cheap wares and also expensive, commissioned objects. Popular decoration included such flowers as roses and tulips and pastoral scenes; the most widely used colour was a soft, manganese-purple. The most important production during this period was four ceremonial dinner-services, commissioned by Catherine II in the late 1770s and early 1780s; they were named and decorated with the ribbons and badges of the four highest Orders of Chivalry: St George, St Andrew the First Called, St Vladimir and St Stanislaus, for use by the Knights of the Orders at state banquets. The factory also produced Russian figures called *kuklaki*, created in biscuit porcelain or painted with enamels.

E. Petrova and E. Ivanova: *Porcelain in Russia 18th–19th Centuries: The Gardner Factory* (St Petersburg, 2003)

Garnet. Vitreous mineral, usually red or green in colour, most commonly found as a distinct crystal, and in the form of a rhomboidal dodecahedron, but also occurring in other shapes. Garnets have been valued as gemstones since the Bronze Age, and have been used in jewellery since Egyptian and classical antiquity.

Garnier, Pierre (*b* Paris, *c.* 1726; *d* Paris, 1806). French cabinetmaker. He was trained in the workshop of his father, François Garnier, and became a *maître-ébéniste* on 31 December 1742. He was quick to incorporate the principles of the Neo-classical style. His furniture displayed architectural lines with uprights in the form of fluted pillars, and in general he rejected marquetry in favour of such fine veneers as ebony, mahogany or even Japanese lacquer. His bronze mounts were in the Neo-classical style and included laurel wreaths, triglyphs, lion heads and spiral ferrules. Many pieces survive, among them writing-tables (e.g. 1762–5; Lisbon, Mus. Gulbenkian), commodes (e.g. Stockholm, Kun. Husgerådskam.), secrétaires (e.g. Paris, Louvre) and corner-cupboards (e.g. of *c.* 1755; Malibu, CA, Getty Mus.). Later he was inspired by English furniture. His clientele included such collectors of furniture in the *Goût grec* as the Marquis de Marigny, the Maréchal de Contades, for whom Garnier furnished the entire château of Mongeoffroy in Mazé, Maine-et-Loire (1771; *in situ*), and the Duc de Choiseul (1719–85; e.g. desk; Chantilly, Mus. Condé).

S. Eriksen: 'Some Letters from the Marquis de Marigny to his Cabinet-maker Pierre Garnier', *Furn. Hist.*, viii (1972), pp. 72–85
C. Huchet de Quénetain: *Pierre Garnier: 1726/27–1806* (Paris, 2003)
H. Grandsart, 'Les meubles de Pierre Garnier', *Conn. A.*, dcxii (Jan 2004), pp. 90–95

Garnish. Set of vessels for table use, usually made of pewter but sometimes of silver.

Garniture. Decorative set of porcelain that may be displayed above or below a cabinet or table; if displayed on a chimney piece the set is called (in French) a *garniture de cheminée*.

For the use of the term in armour *see under* ARMOUR, §1.

A. Du Boulay, 'A Japanese Garniture for Nostell Priory', *Apollo*, cxlix/446 (April 1999), pp. 20–23

Garrard. English firm of goldsmiths and jewellers. The firm was founded by George Wickes *c.* 1730 and taken over by Parker & Wakelin after his retirement in 1760. Robert Garrard I (1758–1818), who was not a working silversmith but had been accountant to Parker & Wakelin, became a partner in the firm in 1792. The joint mark of Robert Garrard I and John Wakelin (*fl* 1776–1802) was entered in that year. Wakelin was appointed Goldsmith and Jeweller to George III in 1797, and, upon Wakelin's death, Garrard assumed sole control of the prestigious London-based firm, entering his own mark (RG) that year.

Robert Garrard II (1793–1881) and his two brothers, James (1795–1870) and Sebastian (1798–1870), took over the business on the death of their father, Robert Garrard I, in 1818. Trading as R. J. & S. Garrard or R. Garrard & Brothers, the firm supplied elaborate gold and silver items, including the ducal coronet of Arthur Wellesley, 1st Duke of Wellington, for George IV's coronation in 1821. On William IV's accession in 1830 the firm was appointed Royal Goldsmiths and, in 1843, displaced Rundell, Bridge & Co. (formerly Rundell, Bridge & Rundell) as Crown Jewellers in Ordinary to Queen Victoria. After James Garrard retired in 1835, Robert and Sebastian moved in 1836 to 29 Panton Street as the firm of R. & S. Garrard and, from 1843, with Samuel Spilsbury as the first of several subsequent partners, traded as R. & S. Garrard & Co. until 1909.

In the 1830s and 1840s Garrard supplied pieces in eclectic historicist styles of the period, including Renaissance Revival, Baroque Revival, Rococo Revival and Neo-classicism. The range of rich jewellery included brooches and bracelets in the Gothic Revival and Egyptian Revival styles. The sculptor Edmund Cotterill (1795–1860), Garrard's head of design from 1833, established the firm's reputation for producing elaborate sculptural groups and centre-pieces in silver, often with Moorish or Arab and equestrian themes, for example a centrepiece (1846–53; priv. col) in the form of a group of camels, stallions and Arab figures. The firm also produced outstanding sporting trophies and cups, notably those for horse-racing—the Ascot, Doncaster and Goodwood Cups—and for yachting, for example the America's Cup (1848). In the Great Exhibition in London of 1851 the firm showed pieces in the Queen Anne and Louis XIV Revival styles and a silver-gilt centrepiece (British Royal Col.) with naturalistic figures of Queen Victoria's favourite dogs.

Following Cotterill's death in 1860 W. Spencer became head of design. After the death of Robert Garrard II in 1881 the firm passed to his nephew, James Mortimer Garrard (*d* 1900), who was succeeded by his son, Sebastian Henry Garrard (1868–1946). Sebastian was the last member of the Garrard family to control the business. After his death in 1946 the company amalgamated with the Goldsmiths' & Silversmiths' Co. and moved to 112 Regent Street, becoming Garrard & Co. Ltd and retaining its royal appointment, including responsibility for the maintenance of the British Crown Jewels. The company now trades at 167 New Bond Street.

Garrard's, 1721–1911: Crown Jewellers and Goldsmiths during Six Reigns and in Three Centuries (London, 1912)
A. North, 'Royal Goldsmith: The Heritage of the House of Garrard' *Apollo*, cxxxiii (May 1991), pp. 353–4
Royal Goldsmiths: The Garrard Heritage (exh. cat., ed. J. Ogilvy; London, Garrard & Co. Ltd, 1991)
C. Gere, J. Culme and W. Summers: *Garrard: The Crown Jewellers for 150 years, 1843–1993* (London, 1993)

Garthorne. English family of silversmiths. The brothers Francis Garthorne (*fl* 1690; *d* 1713) and George Garthorne (*fl* 1681; *d* 1730) specialized in large pieces of plate for the court of William and Mary. The style of their works (e.g. a twelve-branch chandelier by George Garthorne, London, Hampton Court, Royal Col.) exhibits characteristics of form, ornament and technique that are completely in the Huguenot manner.

Garthwaite, Anna Maria (*b* Harsten, Leics, 14 March 1688; *d* 1763). English textile designer. After 40 years in Grantham, where her father was rector, Garthwaite moved to London, where she became the leading English silk-designer of the second quarter of the 18th century. Her silks incorporated naturalistic, asymmetrical flowers in her designs from 1742, and in the following year started using C-scrolls reversed on each other. There is a collection of her designs in the Victoria and Albert Museum in London.

ODNB

Gate-leg table. *See under* TABLE.

Gaudí (i Cornet), Antoni (*b* Reus, 25 June 1852; *d* Barcelona, 10 June 1926). Catalan architect. Gaudí's earliest designs as a graduate in architecture were for furniture, including an eclectic exercise (1878) for the neo-Gothic chapel for the Marqués de Comillas, Santander by Joan Martorell i Montels (1833–1906), and a showcase for the glove manufacturer Esteban Comella at the Exposition Universelle in Paris in the same year. He also won a municipal competition for the design of street furniture in Barcelona. Once established as an architect, all the furniture that he designed was for buildings of which he was the architect. His design for the Palau Güell (1886–91), for example, included furniture that is among the earliest manifestations of the incipient Catalan *Modernisme*, the Catalan variant of Art Nouveau. The principal collection of Gaudí furniture is held by the Amigos de Gaudí in Barcelona.

R. Dalisi: *Gaudí Furniture* (London and New York, 1980)
G. Collins and J. Nonell: *The Designs and Drawings of Antonio Gaudí* (Princeton, 1993)
D. Ferrer: *Gaudí* (Barcelona, 2001)
J. Nonell: *Gaudí, Art and Design: Exhibition Organised to Mark the Occasion of International Gaudí Year* (Barcelona, 2002)

Gaudreaus [Gaudreau; Gaudreaux], **Antoine Robert** (*b c.* 1682; *d* 1746). French cabinetmaker. He be-

Paul Gauguin: self-portrait in the form of a grotesque head, enamelled ceramic, 280 × 230 mm, 1889 (Paris, Musée d'Orsay)

came a *maître* in 1708, and from 1726 worked for the crown and court. As furniture for the crown was not stamped, attributions of his furniture are problematical; however, the stamps of CAFFIÉRI appear on some pieces (e.g. London, Wallace and Versailles, Château), which indicates that he worked collaboratively. There are two fine pieces of furniture known to be the work of Gaudreaus: a medal-cabinet made in 1739 for Versailles and now in the Bibliothèque Nationale, and a commode made in 1739 with mounts signed by J. Caffieri for Louis XV's bedchamber at Versailles and now in the Wallace Collection in London.

Gaudy Dutch, Gaudy Ironstone and Gaudy Welsh. English ceramic export wares made for the American market. Gaudy Dutch ware is a type of Staffordshire cottageware produced in the early 19th century for the American export market, specifically the German colonists in Pennsylvania known as the Pennsylvania Dutch (i.e. Deutsch). Gaudy Dutch wares are painted with blue underglaze and bright overglaze enamels in cobalt blue and burnt orange; the designs, which often include floral motifs, were often based on the IMARI designs used for fine china in Derby and Worcester. The shapes are conventional, though the cups do not have handles. Gaudy Welsh (which was sold to Welsh settlers in America) and Gaudy Ironstone are simpler and cheaper wares, and are usually decorated in copper lustre.

E. Fox and E. Fox: *Gaudy Dutch* (Possville, PA, 1968)
J. Shuman III: *The Collector's Encyclopedia of Gaudy Dutch and Welsh* (Paducah, KY, rev. 1998)

Gauffering [goffering]. In bookbinding, the embossing of the gilded edges of a book with heated tools. In textiles (except for velvet), the embossing of a pattern by means of heated rollers; in velvet, the same process is called stamping.

Gauguin, Paul (*b* Paris, 7 June 1848; *d* Atuona, Marquesas Islands, 8 May 1903). French painter, printmaker, sculptor and ceramicist. In 1886 Gauguin met the ceramicist ERNEST CHAPLET, with whom he then collaborated, for example, on producing a glazed stoneware vase decorated with Breton girls (1886–7; Brussels, Mus. Hôtel Bellevue). In these pots Gauguin worked the clay by hand as a sculptor, not on a wheel, and for the usual thrown forms he substituted a strange and personal vocabulary, partly inspired by Pre-Columbian art. After returning from Martinique in 1887 he made a series of vases and jugs decorated with human heads, the style of which is influenced by Peruvian case portraits. In 1889 he made portrait jugs, including one of himself (1 Feb 1889; Copenhagen, Kstindustmus.). During his final period in France he once again turned to pottery; the finest product of this period is *Oriri* (Paris, Mus. Orsay). In all, some 60 pieces of Gauguin's pottery are known to survive.

Gauguin's son Jean (1881–1961) became a modeller and designer at the BING & GRØNDAHL porcelain factory.

D. Sweetman: *Paul Gauguin: A Life* (New York, 1995)
A.-B. Fonsmark: *Gauguin Ceramics: Ny Carlsberg Glyptotek* (exh. cat., Copenhagen, Ny Carlsberg Glyp., 1996)
L. Madeline: *Ultra-sauvage, Gauguin sculpteur* (Paris, 2002) [includes furniture]
C. Andréani: *Les céramiques de Gauguin* (Paris, 2003)

Gauron, Nicolas-François. *See under* MENNECY PORCELAIN FACTORY.

Paul Gauguin: pot decorated with the figure of a woman under a tree, buff-coloured stoneware, h. 135 mm, 1886–7 (Paris, Musée d'Orsay)

Gauzfredus (*fl c.* ?1125–50). French wood-carver. His name appears in an inscription (GAUZFREDUS ME F[E]CIT) which is carved on the batten of one of the two sets of wooden doors of Le Puy Cathedral, Auvergne. The doors, made of joined and hinged planks of larch, give access to chapels located on either side of the entrance way and under the third bay of the nave. Their decoration is in low relief, and the components of the design are formed of sharply bounded and flattened forms raised above an equally flat ground. The surface of the wood shows traces of polychromy, now much eroded. One set of doors (bottom section restored) is framed by a pseudo-Sufic border and shows scenes of the *Infancy of Christ*; the other is devoted to the events of the *Passion*, culminating in the *Resurrection* and *Pentecost*. Wooden doors executed in a similar style are found at St Gilles, Chamalières-sur-Loire, St Pierre, Blesle, and Ste Croix, Lavoûte-Chilhac (all in the Auvergne), but their attribution to Gauzfredus is uncertain.

W. Cahn: *The Romanesque Wooden Doors of Auvergne* (New York, 1974)

Geddes, **Norman Bel**. *See* BEL GEDDES, NORMAN.

Gegenbach, **Joseph**. *See* CANABAS.

Gem-engraving. Engraved gems are gemstones, whether quartzes or the harder, more precious stones, either engraved in intaglio, as for seals, or cut in cameo to give a raised relief image. In a wider sense gem-engraving encompasses shell cameos and moulded, glass-paste imitations of engraved gems. Gems were engraved in ancient Egypt and in Europe in classical antiquity; there are also traditions of engraving in India and the Islamic world. In medieval Europe, there was gem-engraving both in the Byzantine east and in western Europe. Gem-engraving reached its highest standard in the Renaissance and Enlightenment Europe.

The earliest important examples of post-medieval glyptics date from Valois France, but it was in Renaissance and Mannerist Italy that, under the stimulus of a growing passion for collecting ancient gems, the revived craft reached an artistic perfection unrivalled since antiquity. Craftsmen practising in such related occupations as seal-engraving, coin-die cutting and as medallists set up as gem-engravers in North Italian cities and in Rome, which was to dominate gem-engraving until the decline of the craft in the 19th century.

The luxury displayed by Charles V (*reg* 1364–80) and his three brothers, Jean, Duc de Berry, Louis I, 1st Duke of Anjou (*reg* 1356–84), and Philip the Bold, 1st Duke of Burgundy (*reg* 1384–1404), included a profusion of engraved precious stones in regalia, jewellery and seals. Like those preserved in church treasuries, most were of ancient origin, but they also included contemporary portraits. A sapphire intaglio (London, BM) of a frontally seated prince is thought to represent Jean, Duc de Berry,

while a cameo (*c.* 1420; St Petersburg, Hermitage), in which the chalcedony profile head is adorned with a garnet crown and an emerald jewel, portrays Charles V's grandson, Charles VII. Disastrous wars probably caused the temporary cessation of the art in northern France, but it flourished at the court of René I, King of Naples and 4th Duke of Anjou. An onyx cameo bust (London, BM) of the King in old age may have been the work of one of his two recorded stone-engravers, Thomas Pigne (*fl* 1476) and Jehan Castel (*fl* before 1480); his accounts reveal commissions for gems depicting biblical themes. Both the revival of gem-engraving in northern France and King René's interest in gems may be attributed to close contacts with Italy, where the study of antiquity was already having a profound impact on the arts.

In Italy gem-engraving, influenced by Classical models, arose in various Italian cities in the wake of humanist learning and collecting of antiquities. Knowledge of ancient gems was disseminated through plaster casts and bronze plaquettes; the excitement they aroused among artists is evident in their influence on sculptures by Donatello and his followers; they are reproduced in paintings and drawings by Botticelli, Giovanni Bellini and Veronese, and on the reverses of medals. They also stimulated contemporary gem-engravers to produce work in the Classical tradition; the techniques of engraving on stone were influenced by learning from Byzantine refugees and from Burgundian craftsmen. They employed the traditional quartzes (hardstones): for intaglio, pale chalcedony, cornelian and sard; for cameo, mostly two- or three-layer agates, for example onyx and sardonyx, and varieties of chalcedony and jasper. They also engraved on lapis lazuli and occasionally on the harder gemstones, such as sapphire or ruby.

Turquoise was a particular favourite of Isabella d'Este, Marchesa of Mantua, who commissioned gems from Francesco ANICHINI in Venice, already a noted centre for the craft. In 1477 Lorenzo de' Medici, the Magnificent, brought the medallist Pietro de' Neri Razzanti [Petroceni] (1425–after 1480) to Florence to teach gem-engraving, and in Milan Domenico dei Cammei (*d* 1508) engraved a portrait of *Ludovico il Moro* (Florence, Pitti; St Petersburg, Hermitage, attrib). Remarkably naturalistic portraits of old men (London, BM; Vienna, Ksthist. Mus.) were also produced in Milan. Rome attracted artists to the Papal Mint and court: a cornelian intaglio portrait of *Pope Paul II* (1470; Florence, Pitti) by Giuliano di Scipione (*fl c.* 1470) is the earliest preserved Italian gem by a named engraver. Three other gems (Naples, Mus. Archeol. N.) once owned by the Pope, later in the collection of Lorenzo de' Medici, and variants (e.g. Paris, Bib. N., Cab. Médailles) of the ancient *Apollo and Marsyas* gem (Naples, Mus. Archeol. N.) are by unknown contemporary artists. A cameo portrait of *Lorenzo* (Florence, Pitti), probably posthumous, has been attributed to the earliest engraver mentioned by Vasari, Giovanni delle Corniole [Giovanni delle Opere] (1470–*c.* 1516), whose cornelian intaglio of *Girolamo Savonarola* was acquired *c.* 1568 by Cosimo I de' Medici, Grand Duke of Tuscany. The noble, idealizing style of these busts—very different from Milanese naturalism—reveals the influence of Classical portraiture. Besides motifs from the Antique, biblical subjects were engraved in styles closely related to those of the major arts of the period (e.g. *Annunciation*; St Petersburg, Hermitage; *Christ at the Column, c.* 1500. The work of PIER MARIA SERBALDI DA PESCIA is imbued with the Classical spirit that he absorbed in the circle of Lorenzo. Serbaldi distinguished himself by working in the exceedingly hard porphyry (e.g. dies for a portrait medal of *Pope Leo X*, Florence, Pitti; Paris, Louvre). A cornelian intaglio representing a many-figured *Bacchanal* (Paris, Bib. N., Cab. Médailles), which in subsequent centuries was one of the most admired and copied stones, has been ascribed to Serbaldi.

After the restoration of the Medici in 1527, Florence once again exercised important patronage; portraits of the assassinated *Alessandro de' Medici* (cameo; Florence, Pitti; rock crystal intaglio; Paris, Bib. N., Cab. Médailles) are ascribed to Domenico di Polo (1480–1547), who engraved a magnificent standing *Hercules* for Grand Duke Cosimo I's seal (Florence, Bargello). Much of the busy trade in gems continued through Venice, where Francesco Anichini remained revered as the leading glyptic artist until his death in 1526. Chalcedony cameo busts of women (e.g. *Cleopatra*; Vienna, Ksthist. Mus.) show the influence of the work of the sculptor Tullio Lombardo (*c.* 1455–1532); similar busts, almost or entirely in the round, appear in hyacinth, for example *Lucretia* (Florence, Pitti).

Antique motifs and Classical styles continued to dominate the work of gem-engravers, who also drew on contemporary graphics and plaquettes, which were themselves influenced by Classical art, for models of frieze-like processions and sacrifices, triumphs and bacchanals, hunts and cavalry battles; portraits and contemporary scenes were also depicted in antique mode, for example the confronted *Cosimo I and Eleonora de' Medici* and the *Triumph of Philip II* (both Florence, Pitti) by Domenico Compagni (*fl c.* 1550–86). Matteo del Nassaro (*d* 1547/8) from Verona, who studied in Rome with his compatriot Nicolò Avanzi (1500–*c.* 1550) was an admired gem-engraver of the first half of the century; in 1515 Matteo left Italy to work in France for Francis I. Even his reputation, however, was surpassed by that of the prolific VALERIO BELLI. Belli was renowned for his large, reverse intaglio rock crystal plaques, designed to be seen through the polished surface, for example those forming the casket (1530–32; Florence, Pitti) with scenes of the *Passion* commissioned by Pope Clement VII. His mature work in gems was widely disseminated through reproduction in plaquettes (examples in Florence, Bargello), as was that of his younger rival GIOVANNI BERNARDI, who worked chiefly in Rome, a master of the struck medal as well as of gem-engraving. Bernardi's technique of reverse

intaglio resembled that of Belli, but his style is related to contemporary Mannerist art; a rock crystal intaglio of *Tityus* is based on a drawing by Michelangelo (1475–1564). Bernardi's work exercised great influence on the newly fashionable vessels in rock crystal and hardstones created in Milan, where, under the settled rule of the Spanish Habsburgs, dynasties of craftsmen were established.

A different direction is indicated by the smaller-scale work of Alessandro Cesati (*fl* 1538–64). Active in Rome during the mid-16th century, he was employed by the Mint and is reputed to have been a skilful forger of ancient coins; his cameos are distinguished by a virtuoso technique in extremely low relief, for example a portrait of *Henry II* of France in cornelian (St Petersburg, Hermitage).

An exceptionally important commission for Rome was the State Cameo (1565–72; Florence, Pitti) created by Giovanni Antonio de' Rossi (1517–after 1575) for Cosimo I. It was designed to emulate Classical models and depicts the Duke surrounded by his wife and children.

For jewellery, the more colourful and more immediately 'readable' cameos began to be preferred over intaglios, their contrasting layers making a splendid show in badges or pendants, sumptuously mounted in gold, enamel and precious stones (examples of original settings in Vienna, Ksthist. Mus.). As emblems of dynastic power, often destined for gifts, cameo portraits of rulers and their consorts assumed great importance. In addition to portraits in the antique mode (e.g. onyx cameo of *Cosimo I* by ?Domenico Poggini; Florence, Pitti), sitters were also shown in contemporary armour or costume, with minutely detailed dress, hairstyles and jewels (e.g. ?*Alfonso II, Duke of Ferrara, and Lucrezia de' Medici*; Paris, Bib. N., Cab. Médailles).

Even more striking, naturalistic effects were achieved in *commesso* cameos, in which differently coloured hardstones were placed in mosaic with enamelled gold and gems to render flesh-tones and costume; in the cameo of *Cleopatra* (Vienna, Ksthist. Mus.) a diamond is used to imitate a mirror. Ottavio Miseroni developed this genre further by adopting a relief mosaic, which he employed for portraits, both real and ideal (e.g. *Lady with a Feather Fan*; Vienna, Ksthist. Mus.), for pagan allegorical figures, and for Christian devotional gems (e.g. *Madonna*; Vienna, Schatzkam.). In *cameos ornés*, details of jewellery are rendered in applied pearls and brilliants, most strikingly on heads of negroes and Moors, their images cut in the dark surface layer of onyx or sardonyx (e.g. *Diana as a Negress*; Vienna, Ksthist. Mus.; *Negro King*; Paris, Bib. N., Cab. Médailles); ideal heads of *Roman Emperors*, sometimes in series of the *Twelve Caesars*, similarly exploit the crisply defined strata of the stones. Another favourite motif consisted of half figures of nude women, for example *Lucretia* (*c.* 1560–70; Vienna, Ksthist. Mus.) by Jacopo da Trezzo. Sculpture, plaquettes and prints provided the models for narrative subjects: Francesco Tortorino (*d* before 1595) depicted a cavalry battle after a motif from the

Arch of Titus in Rome; his scenes in high relief—*Marcus Curtius at the Bridge*, the *Generosity of Scipio* (attrib.; both Vienna, Ksthist. Mus.) and other subjects from Roman history—were frequently repeated, as they were on plaquettes; earlier intaglios by Valerio Belli were also translated into cameo. Brightly coloured jaspers cut in high relief depicting birds or animals (e.g. St Petersburg, Hermitage) were the speciality of the workshop of Giovanni Antonio Masnago (*fl* late 16th century); minute figures in highly elaborate landscapes and architectural settings, representing Classical or biblical scenes after prints by Etienne Delaune, were engraved by Giovanni Antonio's son Alessandro Masnago (*fl c.* 1575–1612) on polychrome jaspers and agates, as in the *Rape of Proserpina* (Vienna, Ksthist. Mus.); greatly prized by Rudolf II, many are preserved in elaborate mounts (Vienna, Ksthist. Mus.) by Andreas Osenbruck (*fl* 1612–22) and Hans Vermeyen (*d* 1606). Cameos were also employed profusely in a subsidiary role to decorate such gold objects as cups, caskets, mirrors, candelabra and even arms; here one finds ancient and imposing modern cameos intermingled with such hasty and insignificant work as small portrait heads, busts of women with exposed breasts, and roughly cut intaglios of pseudo-Classical heads and figures in cornelian and lapis lazuli. At the end of the century large oval plaques of transparent banded and mottled agates were cursorily engraved in intaglio with Classical figures, often cupids, in a landscape (e.g. Vienna, Ksthist. Mus.; Florence, Pitti).

Matteo del Nassaro was brought by Francis I to Paris, but despite his long activity at court, only two portraits of the King, in intaglio and in cameo (both Paris, Bib. N., Cab. Médailles) can be attributed to him or his school; intaglios representing Roman cavalry battles and lion hunts (attrib.) are in Paris (Bib. N., Cab. Médailles) and the British Museum, London; his works most prized by contemporaries, however, for the exquisite use of coloured jaspers, are lost. In 1531 Nassaro was paid for a vase and for establishing a lapidary mill on a boat on the Seine; this new invention was to become highly important not only for the polishing of gems but for the manufacture of luxurious hardstone vessels, which were becoming increasingly fashionable. Catherine de' Medici took many gems with her from Florence to France in 1533 and commissioned many more; therefore, the Italian influence on French gem-engraving remained dominant during the reigns of her sons. Charles IX (*reg* 1560–94) created a special gallery in the Louvre for engraved gems, coins, medals and antiquities. Towards the end of the 16th century, however, the royal collection suffered grievous losses, and it was not until the accession of Henry IV (1589) that more settled times encouraged its re-establishment. By then, three French gem-engravers are documented in the royal archives, although only royal portraits can be attributed to them with any probability. These are portraits of Henry IV, especially a mounted cameo of *Henry IV as Hercules*, and intaglios on emerald and garnet (all Paris, Bib. N.,

Cab. Médailles), attributed to Olivier Coldoré (*fl* before 1582–?early 17th century) and to Julien de Fontenay (*fl* 1590–1611), who was at Fontainebleau in 1596 and was a salaried court artist in the Louvre in 1608. Portrait gems, signed with the initials of Guillaume Dupré, who also worked for the House of Nassau, are more secure in their attribution, based on the evidence of his medals: for example, a sapphire intaglio of *Maurice of Nassau*, signed with his initials (Paris, Bib. N., Cab. Médailles). Gems were also profusely employed in France to decorate metalwork (e.g. *Sword of Henry IV*; Paris, Louvre).

Philip II of Spain (*reg* 1556–98) brought Italian gem-engravers to Madrid; Jacopo da Trezzo moved there from Milan and executed the important Cus-TODIA for the Capilla Mayor in the Escorial; he also engraved individual gems, including portraits such as that of *Philip II and Don Carlos* confronted (topaz intaglio, Paris, Bib. N., Cab. Médailles); Clemente Birago (*d* 1592) is reputed to have engraved Philip's signet on a diamond, a feat of the greatest virtuosity. But it was Philip's nephew, Emperor Rudolf II, who established in Prague the last great Renaissance centre for gem-engraving. In constant touch with the workshops of Milan, where Alessandro Masnago cut cameos for him, Rudolf brought Ottavio MISERONI and other members of the family to his court; their descendants worked in Prague until the last quarter of the 17th century.

In England a small but remarkable series of Tudor dynastic portraits, culminating in numerous cameos of Elizabeth I, may have been the work of foreign artists; although no English workshop is recorded, Richard Atsyll [Astyll], documented in 1539, has been suggested as the artist responsible for portraits of *Henry VIII* and the infant *Edward VI*. Their images are derived from portraits by Hans Holbein the younger and are executed in a refined technique of low-relief cameo on three-layer sardonyx, with intaglio engravings on the reverses (e.g. Windsor Castle, Berks, Royal Col.; Chatsworth, Derbys). Profile cameo portraits of *Elizabeth I*, probably derived from her portrait on the 'Phoenix Jewel' (*c.* 1570–80; London, BM), are known in various sizes on two- and three-layer sardonyx; most portray her in elaborate state dress with jewels, although the face is the official 'mask of youth'; they were designed for diplomatic and personal gifts (fine examples in Paris, Bib. N., Cab. Médailles; Vienna, Ksthist. Mus.; Windsor Castle, Berks, Royal Col.; St Petersburg, Hermitage). Their number presupposes a busy workshop, possibly based abroad and working from a graphic model. A number of cameos of *St George*, devised as 'Lesser Georges' for the Knights of the Order of the Garter, of the 16th and 17th centuries (e.g. Windsor Castle, Berks, Royal Col.), are probably of English origin.

As patrons became increasingly interested in other luxury arts, 17th-century gem-engraving declined artistically, although it was still widely practised. In Italy few engravers' names are recorded, and gems were mostly unsigned, in itself a sign of diminished status. Examples of cursorily cut stones mounted on dec-

Ewer depicting the *History of Noah* (detail), engraved rock crystal, 16th century (Paris, Musée du Louvre)

orative vessels show the continued use of motifs derived from the Antique, but the age of the Counter-Reformation also found expression in devotional gems, some of considerable size. Cameo busts of *Christ* and *The Virgin*, after the medal types of Antonio Abondio (1538–91), commonly cut on bloodstone (e.g. Paris, Bib. N., Cab. Médailles; London, BM; Vienna, Ksthist. Mus.), date from the first half of the century. More remarkable is a series of 12 rock crystal intaglio plaques depicting the *Life and Passion of Christ*, commissioned by Cardinal Francesco Barberini for a set of candlesticks for St Peter's in Rome from Anna Cecilia Hamerani (1642–78), a member of the Roman family of medallists. In Florence, Giuseppe Antonio Torricelli established a family workshop, but patronage of glyptic artists at this time was more assiduous in centres outside Italy. Foremost among them was Prague, where the Miseroni workshop continued after the death of Rudolf II. Other workshops, probably offshoots of the Prague school, were established near Vienna, where much of their work remains. Gems and shells continued in demand for decorative purposes, for example on a circular lapis lazuli dish, the rim of which is set with a series of *The Twelve Caesars* (Vienna, Ksthist. Mus.).

Imperial portraits show the considerable changes in taste at this time. In contrast with the traditional materials of contrasting layers, transparent or translucent monochrome stones, some of considerable size, were now employed for cameos, as on an amethyst portrait of *Leopold I* (*c.* 1670); the same emperor appears on an emerald of *c.* 1660 (both Vienna, Ksthist. Mus.). Such stones are characteristic of the ostentatious luxury of Baroque court art. Other showy jewels, for example extremely large lockets and pendants with elaborate enamelled gold mounts enriched with precious stones, centre on small cameo portraits in quickly worked ivory or shell, surrounded by a series of tiny ancestral busts or minutely worked coats of arms in shell, turquoise and coral. Long series of similar small portraits in monochrome chalcedonies or shell, depicting such dynasties as the Habsburgs, hang from precious metal 'family trees'; as many as 48, depicting family members of the Habsburgs down to Leopold William, Archduke of Austria, form the links of a necklace (Vienna, Ksthist. Mus.). Similar series of other dynasties are found in shell, but Christoph DORSCH of Nuremberg continued the production of extensive portrait series in stone and glass seemingly well into the 18th century (e.g. *The Popes*; Leiden, Rijksmus. Kon. Penningkab.). In the later 17th century German courts and wealthy bourgeois patrons commissioned a large number of gem-engravings: a rock crystal bowl (1680; Kassel, Hess. Landesmus.) by the Swiss Christoph Labhart stems from a court workshop that also produced chalcedony cameos and figures in the round.

Portraits of members of the Bourbon court are evidence of the continuation of French gem-engraving in the 17th century, although the authors of fine cameo portraits of *Louis XIII* and his consort (*c.* 1630), *Cardinal Richelieu* (both St Petersburg, Hermitage), *Cardinal Mazarin* (*c.* 1659) and a cameo bust of *Louis XIV* (*c.* 1660; both Paris, Bib. N., Cab. Médailles) are unknown. Louis XIV constantly added to the magnificent collection inherited from his uncle, Gaston, Duc d'Orléans (1608–60), and portraits were engraved on the most precious stones: a ruby cameo of *Madame de Maintenon* (London, BM); a sapphire cameo of *Louis, Le Grand Dauphin* (St Petersburg, Hermitage); and another sapphire cameo of *Elisabeth Charlotte, Duchesse d'Orléans* (Karlsruhe, Bad. Landesmus.). None of these gems, however, can be securely attributed.

In England collecting reached a high point in the 17th century, accompanied by some patronage of contemporary artists. Portrait cameos were engraved, not only for the Stuart court but also during the Commonwealth (1649–60); for example two cameos of *Oliver Cromwell* (St Petersburg, Hermitage) are ascribed to the medallist Thomas Simon (1618–65), while royalist portraits have been assigned to Thomas Rawlins (*c.* 1620–70; e.g. *Charles I*; St Petersburg, Hermitage; Chatsworth, Derbys). Both Simon and Rawlins were pupils of Nicolas Briot. Charles Christian Reisen (*c.* 1637–97), of Danish descent, reputedly engraved a portrait of *Christian XII* of Sweden (untraced). Cameos of *St George* continued to be engraved for 'Lesser Georges' (St Petersburg, Hermitage; Windsor Castle, Berks, Royal Col.).

There was a major revival in gem-engraving during the early 18th century, partly the result of a widespread interest in the arts of antiquity. The undisputed centre of production was Rome, the main destination for visitors on the Grand Tour, who were as keen to acquire modern copies and gems in the antique taste as they were to obtain ancient originals, so that a new generation of craftsmen found it profitable to settle there. Among many others, the Ferrarese Flavio Sirletti, the Neapolitan Giovanni Costanzi (?1674–1754) and Anton PICHLER from Brixen (now Bressanone, Italy) successfully established family workshops in Rome that continued through several generations. Accurate copies of devices on ancient gems and coins were based on illustrated publications and casts in wax, sulphur and plaster, which became more abundant as the century progressed and provided the most convenient models; thus Solon's *Medusa* (London, BM) exists in many copies (e.g. plasma intaglio, London, BM)—one of them (untraced) was executed by Giovanni Costanzi's son CARLO COSTANZI in 1729. The highest praise bestowed on an engraver was that his works might pass for 'Greek'. Undoubtedly many were taken to be antique, by accident or by design, and

were often embellished with fake Greek signatures. Most gems of the period have remained unidentified owing to the dispersal of Italian collections in the 18th century and of Grand Tourists' possessions by their descendants in the 19th.

At first, intaglios were cut on small ovals and simply mounted in rings or fobs, used for sealing and studied in impression; the minerals most commonly used were the traditional sard, cornelian, nicolo, transparent amethyst, rock crystal and citrine. Cameos were rarer and were also generally modest in size; they usually show white heads or figures on a darker, sometimes dyed, background. For the wealthiest patrons, however, engravers could demonstrate their skill by engraving the hardest gems: both Giovanni and Carlo Costanzi reputedly engraved on diamond; Carlo also worked in emerald, cut a portrait of *Empress Maria-Theresa* on sapphire (untraced) and a *Diadoch* on aquamarine (Bucharest, Roman. Acad.).

A popular new genre depicted the most celebrated ancient sculptures admired by visitors to Rome, Florence and Naples, and thereby supplied artistic and conveniently portable souvenirs: for example Flavio Sirletti engraved a copy of the *Laokoon* (Rome, Vatican, Mus. Pio-Clementino) on amethyst (untraced) for an English duke. Portraits of the Ancients, a taste first stimulated by the humanists' interest in iconography, were popular, copied directly from gems, coins, statues and busts or from illustrated books: Anton Pichler engraved a *Cicero* and a *Cleopatra*, Giovanni Costanzi a *Nero* on diamond and Carlo Costanzi a *Plato*; but historical portraiture also extended to the increasingly popular genre of 'illustrious men'—especially Italian artists—of the more recent past, for example Pichler's *Raphael* (untraced). Contemporary portraits, no longer a princely preserve, were commissioned in Rome by such Grand Tourists as Sir Charles Frederick, Bart, a portrait of whom was executed by Carlo Costanzi in 1737 (untraced). Many sitters were depicted in the antique style in 'coin profile'; others, like historical portraits copied from paintings and busts, were shown in contemporary dress and fashionable wigs. Except for such portraits and rare devotional gems, motifs were exclusively Classical. It is significant for the enhanced status of engravers at this time that they usually signed their gems with names or initials, frequently transliterated into Greek, in emulation of the gems published in Philipp von Stosch's *Gemmae antiquae caelatae* (1724), which had awakened interest in the signatures on ancient gems. Some gem-engravers were accorded honours by popes and potentates: Carlo Costanzi was distinguished by Pope Benedict XIII and in 1740 by Benedict XIV, and Giovanni Pichler was created a Knight of the Holy Roman Empire by Joseph II.

Among the foreign gem-engravers who were attracted to Rome during the first half of the century, the most skilful was the German Johann Lorenz Natter (1705–63), who engraved a portrait of *Cardinal Alessandro Albani* during his stay in Rome. He also spent time in Florence during the 1730s in the circle of Stosch, of whom he engraved two portraits, on emerald and aventurine (both St Petersburg, Hermitage). He worked in London and the Netherlands (important collection in Leiden, Rijksmus. Kon. Penningkab.) and died in Russia. The last Medici Grand Dukes and their Lorrainer and Habsburg-Lorraine successors employed members of the Torricelli family; Francesco Ghinghi engraved Roman emperors in sapphire for Anna Maria Luisa de' Medici and portraits of *Grand Duke Cosimo III* (untraced) and *Philipp von Stosch* (Berlin, Pergamonmus.) before taking up the directorship of the Real Laboratorio delle Pietre Dure in Naples. Stosch also patronized Felix Bernabé, who engraved Classical devices, a *Head of Christ* and an *Ithyphallic Procession* (glass paste in Bucharest, Roman. Acad.). The French gem-engraver LOUIS SIRIÈS, who had settled in Florence in 1722 and became Director of the Real Galleria di Firenze, executed many minutely detailed gems in very low relief for Empress Maria-Theresa, Queen of Hungary and Bohemia (Vienna, Ksthist. Mus.).

Outside Italy craftsmen continued to find employment in the major cities in Germany and Austria during the first half of the 18th century. Philipp Christoph Becker (1674–1742) worked in Vienna for Joseph I (*reg* 1678–1711) and Charles VI (*reg* 1711–40); Susanna Maria Preissler (1701–65), the daughter of Christoph Dorsch, was active in Nuremberg (sealing-wax impressions of her gems are in The Hague, Rijksmus. Meermanno–Westreenianum). In France François-Julien Barier (1680–1746), who engraved in a minutely detailed style (e.g. *Three Philosophers*, Leiden, Rijksmus. Kon. Penningkab.), was named Graveur du Roi en Pierres Fines to Louis XV (*reg* 1715–74); he was, however, succeeded by a far greater artist, Jacques Guay (1711–97), in the mid-18th century. Guay's work in allegorical scenes celebrating the King's reign (e.g. *Victory at Lawfeldt* and *Alliance between France and Austria*, 1756) and portraits (e.g. cameo of *Louis XV*; all Paris, Bib. N., Cab. Médailles) is more closely related to the medallic art of the period and the Rococo of François Boucher and Edme Bouchardon (1698–1762), who furnished him with drawings, than the more classicizing gems of the Roman masters.

J. Kagan: *Western European Cameos in the Hermitage Collection* (Leningrad, 1973)
L. Pirzio Biroli Stefanelli: 'Roman Gem Engravers of the Eighteenth and Nineteenth Centuries: The Present State of Research', *Jewel. Stud.*, iv (1990), pp. 53–8
G. Seidmann: 'A Very Useful, Curious and Ancient Art: The Society of Arts and the Revival of Gem-Engraving in 18th Century England', *The Virtuoso Tribe of Arts and Sciences—Studies in the Eighteenth Century Work and Membership of the London Society of Arts*, ed. D. G. C. Allan and J. L. Abbott (Athens, GA, and London, 1992), pp. 120–31
G. Seidmann: *Portrait Cameos: Aspects of their History and Function, Cameos in Context*, ed. M. Henig and M. Vickers (Oxford and Houlton, 1993)
E. Zweirlein-Diehl: 'Antikeisierende Gemmen des 16–18 Jahrhunderts', *PACT*, 33 (1993), pp. 373–403
C. Gasparri: *Le gemme Farnese* (Naples, 1994)
K. Achengreen Piacenti: 'The Use of Cameos in the Mounts of Sixteenth Century *Pietre Dure* Vases', *Engraved Gems: Survivals and Revivals*, ed. C. M. Brown (Washington, DC, 1997), pp. 158–79
M. A. McCrory: 'The Symbolism of Stones: Engraved Gems at the Medici Ducal Court (1537–1609)', *Engraved Gems: Survivals and Revivals*, ed. C. M. Brown (Washington, DC, 1997), pp. 158–79
'Engraved Gems: Survivals and Revivals', *Stud. Hist. A.*, liv (1997), pp. 9–315 [18 article special issue]
C. Hall: *Gemstones* (New York, 2002)
H. Jackson: 'Two Engraved Gems from Hellenistic Jebel Khalid', *Ant. Kst*, xlvii (2004), pp. 34–46

Genoa. Italian city, capital of Liguria.

1. Ceramics. 2. Silk.

1. CERAMICS. Italian centre of ceramics production. Ceramics production is documented in Genoa from the Middle Ages. A few jugs from that period, decorated with a dark-green lead glaze incised through to an ochre ground, are extant. These utilitarian, domestic vessels were recovered from archaeological excavations. There are numerous documents referring to 15th-century workshops, which produced items decorated with painted or incised motifs, often in blue on a pale ground. At that time there was also a considerable production of *laggioni*, tiles decorated in a Moorish style in imitation of those imported from Valencia in Spain. In 1528 the manufacture of maiolica became important in Genoa. Production was similar to that of potteries in the Marches and Faenza, due in part to Francesco da Pesaro and Francesco da Camerino from Faenza, who founded the first workshop in the city. They produced tableware and vases with light-blue grounds decorated with calligraphy, grotesques, arabesques or chinoiseries. After the death (1580) of Bartolomeo da Pesaro, son of Francesco, the workshop was taken over by his son-in-law Giovan Antonio Cagnola, who continued to produce fairly high-quality wares. During the 17th century other ceramic workshops were established in Genoa, but these never reached the levels attained in the previous century. The Genoese kilns closed shortly after the mid-17th century as wares in gold and silver were preferred. Savona and Albisola then became the most important centres of maiolica production in Liguria.

F. Marzinot: *Ceramica e ceramisti di Liguria* (Genoa, 1979)

2. SILK. The trade in silk fabrics and the raw materials for their production has been an important part of the Genoese economy since the Middle Ages. At first Genoa served as a centre of distribution for woven-silk products. There is evidence, however, of local production, of significant quality and quantity, from the mid-13th century. At the beginning of the 14th century numerous weavers exiled from Lucca arrived in Genoa to teach their craft. The arrival of these craftsmen, who were technically advanced and artistically autonomous, substantially increased production in Genoa. The silk-workers, who for over a century had belonged to the Corporazione dei Merciai, acquired their own statutes in 1432.

Genoese fabrics were widely appreciated in the other Italian and European states; particular specialities were plain and decorated velvets, satins and damasks. Black Genoese velvet was considered incomparable for softness and lustre and was favoured by the European nobility for their clothes; women preferred the crimson damask, of a delicate pinkish tone, which was never successfully imitated, and the precious gold and silver lamé fabrics that can be seen in the splendid portraits by Anthony van Dyck (1599–1641). At the end of the 17th century, however, the first signs of a crisis began to appear. This was provoked mainly by foreign competition, especially from France, in markets that until that time had absorbed the Italian exports. The luxury fabrics, especially the velvets, nevertheless remained quite competitive throughout the 18th century.

From the mid-17th century to the end of the 18th the Genoese silk industry turned more and more to the production of furnishing fabrics. Along with damask, LAMPAS was woven in three or more colours, and in the 18th century 'garden style' polychrome, flower-patterned velvet appeared. Decorative drapery fabrics tended to keep to the same patterns (e.g. the so-called 'palm' damask), while the proportions in the design and the manner of working the background changed.

Following Genoa's loss of independence at the end of the 18th century, when the trade guilds were also abolished, silk production was slowly rebuilt, and a limited quantity of high-quality silk, especially plain and ciselé velvets and damasks, continued to be produced by hand. In the 19th century silk production was restricted to a few centres on the coast east of Genoa, which are still active in the early 21st century: Zoagli specializes in velvets, and damasks, lampas and brocades are produced in Lorsica.

Antiche stoffe genovesi (exh. cat. by G. Morazzoni, Genoa, Teat. Carlo Felice, 1941)

P. Massa: 'L'arte genovese della seta nella normativa del XVe del XVI secolo', *Atti Soc. Ligure Stor. Patria*, x/1 (1970)

P. Massa: *Un'impresa serice genovese della primametà del cinquecento* (Milan, 1974)

P. Massa: *La 'fabbrica' dei velluti genovesi: Da Genova a Zoagli* (Genoa and Zoagli, 1981)

Seta a Genova, 1491–1991, Genoa, Pal. S Giorgio cat. (Genoa, 1991)

Arte e lusso della seta a Genova dal '500 al '700 (exh. cat. by M. Gallo; Genoa, Pal. Ducale, 2000)

S. Ricci: *L'isola della seta/The Isle of Silk* (Milan, 2000)

Gentili [Gentile] **(da Faenza), Antonio** (*b* Faenza, 1519; *d* Rome, 29 Oct 1609). Italian goldsmith. He was the son of Pietro Gentili, a goldsmith. By *c.* 1549 he was active in Rome and by 1552 he had entered the goldsmiths' guild as a master craftsman, holding several offices during his lifetime. His fame enabled him to move in high circles. Records indicate that he executed various works in gold for the Medici, pieces ranging from vases and lamps to keys and bedwarmers. It was for Cardinal Alessandro Farnese that Antonio created his acknowledged masterpiece, consisting of two silver-gilt candlesticks and a cross (1582; Rome, St Peter's, Treasury), for which he received 13,000 scudi. The objects, which contain rock-crystal tondi by Giovanni Bernardi and inlay work of lapis lazuli, were then donated by the Cardinal to St Peter's. Antonio signed the work, yet authorities have often attributed it to Benvenuto Cellini or Michelangelo (1475–1564), among others.

Part of the difficulty in identifying Antonio's work is the confusion caused by his habit of borrowing motifs from other artists, especially those employing a style similar to that of Michelangelo. This practice was highlighted when the 90-year-old goldsmith testified in an inheritance lawsuit brought by Guglielmo della Porta's son, Teodoro della Porta, regarding casts and models missing from his father's workshop. During testimony Antonio stated that he owned and used casts by Michelangelo and others. His adoption of others' designs in his pieces, a common practice among 16th-century goldsmiths, did not hinder his versatility. In 1580 he fashioned a miniature gold bust of the armoured *Emperor Augustus* on a small agate base (h. 210 mm; Florence, Pitti). In 1584 he became an assayer for the papal mint. Antonio also created a silver book cover for Cardinal Farnese's Book of Hours (1600; New York, Pierpont Morgan Lib.). The richly decorated cover portrays the *Annunciation* bordered by a pattern of cherubim heads and acanthus leaves. Famous in his own day, Antonio's influence extended to 18th-century France and England, where the candlesticks in St Peter's inspired such figures as Jean-Louis Prieur, Matthew Boulton and Josiah Wedgwood to incorporate elements of Antonio's masterpiece in their own works.

W. Volbach: 'Antonio Gentili da Faenza and the Large Candlesticks in the Treasury of St Peter's', *Burl. Mag.*, xl (1948), pp. 281–6

A. B. Chadour: 'Der Altarsatz des Antonio Gentili in St Peter zu Dom', *Wallraf-Richartz-Jb.*, xliii (1982), pp. 133–98

Georgette. In textiles, a thin, semi-transparent, plain-woven crêpe made from fine, hard-twisted silk, named after the French dressmaker Georgette de La Plante; in metalwork, a small 18th-century enamelled box for snuff or small personal objects, named after the Parisian goldsmith Jean George (*d* 1765).

Georgian style. Term used to describe the diverse styles of architecture, interior decoration and decorative arts produced in Britain and Ireland during the reigns of George I (*reg* 1714–27), George II (*reg* 1727–60) and George III (*reg* 1760–1820). The term REGENCY STYLE is generally applied to works of the period *c.* 1790 to 1830 and refers specifically to the period when George, Prince of Wales (later George IV), was Regent (1811–20). In interior design, the dominant fashions in the early 18th century were Gothick and Chinoiserie, together with the classicising Palladian movement; in the second half of the century, Pompeian Revival and the Etruscan style developed.

In the decorative arts the production of gold and silver ware, and to a much lesser degree ceramics, adopted the form and decoration associated with some of these styles. Furniture is often loosely called Georgian, but is often defined by the designer's name, as in 'Kentian' (*see* WILLIAM KENT), 'Chippendale' (*see* THOMAS CHIPPENDALE), 'Hepplewhite' (*see*

GEORGE HEPPLEWHITE) and 'Sheraton' (*see* THOMAS SHERATON). What is particularly characteristic of the period, however, is the enormous number of publications, ranging from ornament and pattern books, design books and directories, to manuals for builders and craftsmen and guides for decorators.

J. Fowler and J. Cornforth: *English Decoration in the 18th Century* (London, 1974)
Rococo: Art and Design in Hogarth's England (exh. cat., ed. M. Snodin; London, V, 1984)
H. Spencer-Churchill: *Classic Georgian Style* (New York, 1997)
I. Cranfield: *Georgian House Style: An Architectural and Interior Design Source Book* (Newton Abbot, 2001)
J. Cornforth: *Early Georgian Interiors* (New Haven, 2004)

Gera. *See under* THURINGIA.

Germain. French family of silversmiths. Pierre Germain (*d* 1684), who became an Orfèvre du Roi in 1679, executed a large number of silver items for the château of Versailles (1680–84), but most of his work is known only from archival evidence.

Pierre's son Thomas Germain (*b* Paris, 19 Aug 1674; *d* Paris, 1748) began as a specialist in ecclesiastical silver, but from 1725 he was extensively employed by the French Crown, producing toilet services, candelabra and a complete set of silver for the Dauphin's apartments in 1736. Thomas Germain executed many pieces of sculptural tableware with naturalistic plant and animal forms (e.g. salt modelled with tortoise, scallop and crab, 1734–6; Paris, Louvre) and excelled in the textured surfaces and vigorous scrollwork of the Rococo style, for example in a pair of wine-coolers (1727–8; Paris, Louvre) in the form of tree-trunks with snails and vine-leaves. Even his more restrained forms, for example a ewer (1736–7; New York, Met.) and tureen and cover (1744–6; Paris, Louvre), reflect the influence of the Roman Baroque. As well as his work for the French Crown, he also executed numerous commissions for royal and aristocratic patrons in Cologne, England, Brazil, Spain, Naples and Portugal. Although much of his silver for Portuguese patrons was destroyed in the Lisbon earthquake (1755), surviving examples include a spectacular surtout (1729–30; Lisbon, Mus. N. A. Ant.), made for the Duque de Aveiro, and a pair of tureens and stands modelled with boars' head masks (1726–8; Malibu, CA, Getty Mus.), a model of which is depicted in *Silver Platters with Peaches* (Stockholm, Nmus.) by François Desportes. The portrait by Nicolas de Largillierre (1736; Lisbon, Mus. Gulbenkian) of *Thomas Germain and his Wife* shows them with a number of silver items.

François-Thomas Germain (*b* 17 April 1726; *d* 23 Jan 1791) was the son of Thomas Germain. On the death of his father, he was allowed to take over his father's lodgings in the Louvre and was appointed Sculpteur-Orfèvre du Roi. He completed items commissioned from Thomas Germain (e.g. lamp, 1744–54, for Ste Geneviève), Paris and also modified earlier pieces by his father, for example a pair of tureens and stands (1726–8; Malibu, CA, Getty Mus.), which

have an inscription on the stands added by François-Thomas in 1764. He also continued to use his father's casting models.

As the head of a large workshop, François-Thomas Germain continued to supply items for the French Crown (e.g. service for the Maisons Royales, 1752), but it is through his work for foreign courts that he is most renowned. In 1756 a large service was ordered by Empress Elizabeth of Russia but was not completed and delivered until 1762. The eight tureens (Lisbon, Mus. N. A. Ant. and Fund. Gulbenkian; Lugano, Col. Thyssen-Bornemisza) in the service vary only in the decoration of the covers, and they closely resemble those in a service produced for Joseph, King of Portugal, ordered in 1756 and executed between 1757 and 1762. François-Thomas Germain's work produced for the Portuguese Crown reveals the number of different styles in which he could work successfully. The coffeepot with decoration of laurel leaves and berries (1757; New York, Met) is in sharp contrast to the tea-kettle and stand (1757–62), which is in a hybrid mixture of chinoiserie and *Goût grec*, while the tureens and platters have boldly modelled putti and animals on the covers. Reflecting the source of wealth of the patron are the biscuit-boxes in the form of sailing vessels supported by dolphins (1757–9), the exotic, partly gilt condiment stand and the salt-cellars depicting putti in Native American dress with feathered crowns (1757–61; all Lisbon, Mus. N. A. Ant. and Pal. N. Ajuda).

Germain's position as Sculpteur-Orfèvre du Roi allowed him to disregard guild regulations, and he produced gilt-bronze objects at the same time as he was working in silver. The surviving signed works by him are the set of four wall lights (1756; Malibu, CA, Getty Mus.) made for the Palais-Egalité (formerly and now Palais-Royal), Paris, residence of Louis Philippe, Duc d'Orléans, and a pair of fire-dogs with Neo-classical elements (1757; Paris, Louvre). In 1756 he also produced the gilt-bronze mounts for the chimney-piece in the Bernstorff Palace, Copenhagen. Although no other signed gilt-bronzes survive, it seems probable that it produced a significant number.

François-Thomas was declared bankrupt in 1765 and was subsequently dismissed from his royal post and had to vacate his lodgings in the Louvre. He continued, however, to execute work in silver and also began to produce copies of antique vases made of a compositional material imitating porphyry, alabaster and agate and mounted in gilt-bronze.

A silversmith from Avignon called Pierre Germain 'le Romain' (1720–83) is not related to the Paris family, though he worked in Paris for most of his career. He is best known for Eléments d'Orfèvrerie (Paris, 1748), a pattern book for silver.

A. Marcel, 'L'Orfèvre Pierre Germain dit le Romain', *Mémoire de l'Académie de Vaucluse* (Avignon, 1916), pp. 229–60.
B. Perrin: *François-Thomas Germain: Orfèvre des rois* (Paris, 1993)
I. da Silveira Godinho and B. Girão Ribeiro: *A baixela de Sua Majestade Fidelíssima: Uma obra de François Thomas Germain* (Lisbon, 2002)

German silver. *See* Nickel silver.

Germany. Ceramics see Abdsbessingen; Alten-
burg; Amberg pottery; Annaberg; Ansbach;
Arzberg porcelain factory; Badorf ware;
Bayreuth; Berlin, §2; Bernburg; Brunswick;
Bunzlau; Burgau porcelain factory; Cadinen pottery; Cologne; Crailsheim pottery;
Creussen; Dorotheenthal faience factory;
Dreihausen; Dresden; Durlach; Erfurt;
Flörsheim faience factory; Frankenthal
porcelain factory; Frankfurt am main faience factory; Freiberg; Fulda; Fürstenberg
porcelain factory; Göggingen; Gotha;
Groszbreitenbach; Hafner ware; Hanau faience factory; Heubach porcelain factory;
Hewelke porcelain factory; Höchst ceramics factory; Hubertusburg pottery; Ilmenau
porcelain factory; Jever pottery; Kaliningrad; Karlsruhe maiolica factory; Kassel;
Kellinghusen; Kelsterbach porcelain factory; Lesum pottery; Ludwigsburg porcelain
factory; Meissen porcelain factory; Mos-
bach pottery; Nuremberg, §1; Nymphenburg
porcelain factory; Offenbach pottery; Ottweiler factory; Potschappel porcelain factory; Rendsburg pottery; Reval pottery;
Rheinsberg pottery; Rosenthal porcelain
factory; Schrezheim pottery factory;
Schwarzburger werkstätten; Siegburg; Sto-
ckelsdorff pottery; Striegau; Thuringia;
Villeroy & boch; Volkstedt; Wächtersbach
pottery; Westerwald; Wrisbergholzen pottery; Zerbst pottery factory.

Glass *see* Brandenburg; Ehrenfeld glasshouse; Hall-in-tirol glassworks; Nuremberg, §2; Petersdorf glasshouse; Schreiber-
hau glasshouse; Theresienthal; Villeroy &
boch; Waldglas.

Metalwork *see* Berlin, §1; Kayser, j. p., & sohn;
Nuremberg, §3.

Textiles *see* Berlin, §§3 and 4; Munich; Würzburg tapestry factory.

Gerverot, Louis-Victor (*b* Lunéville, Lorraine, 8
Dec 1747; *d* 1829). French arcanist and porcelain
painter. He had an itinerant career, details of which
are uncertain. He began as a porcelain painter at
Sèvres porcelain factory (1764–5), and then
moved to Niderviller, Ansbach, Kassel (1766),
Fulda (possibly), Frankenthal porcelain factory, Ludwigsburg porcelain factory (which
he certainly visited but seems not to have worked),
Weesp porcelain factory (1769), Höchst ceramics factory (1771–3), Schrezheim pottery
factory (1773–5), Loosdrecht porcelain factory, Wedgwood (1776) and john Turner (*c.*
1777); there is no evidence for the claim that he
worked at Offenbach pottery. On returning to
Germany he established the Englische Porcelainsfabrik in Cologne (1788–92) and subsequently

worked as director of the Fürstenberg porcelain
factory (1795–1814); on being dismissed for collaborating with the French during the Napoleonic
wards he finished his career as director of the Wrisbergholzen pottery in Hanover. Gerverot was particularly noted for his painting of exotic birds.

C. Jacob-Hanson: 'Louis Victor Gerverot in a New Light: His Early
    Years and Bird Painting, 1766–1773', *Mag. Ant.*, clxv/1 (Jan
    2004), pp. 192–201

Gesso. White coating used as a ground for painting
and in the preparation of wood for gilding. It comprises glue-size (an animal glue), mixed with either
calcium sulphate (a form of gypsum), which produces the soft gesso that was used in Italy in the
Renaissance, or calcium carbonate (chalk), which
produces a hard gesso that was used in northern Europe. It is inflexible and absorbent and, once dry,
may be worked to produce a smooth surface. Variations on the basic recipe occur, notably the inclusion of white pigment to increase its brilliance. *Gesso
grosso* is a traditional form made from burnt gypsum
and hide glue. The glue slows down the setting action
of the plaster and makes it considerably harder when
dry. Similar compositions are used in decorative plasterwork. Gesso is also used as a filler and surface
coating for furniture and picture frames, where it not
only serves as a ground for a painted finish or gilding
or carving but also suppresses the wood grain and
any roughness of finish. It may be worked as low

Pearwood hand mirror with moulded gesso decoration by Francis
George Wood, h. 362 mm, 1901 (London, Victoria and Albert
Museum)

relief carving or cast as small motifs for decorated panels (*see* PASTIGLIA).

Ghinghi, Francesco (*b* Florence, 1689; *d* Naples, 29 Dec 1766). Italian gem-engraver and medallist. He was taught gem-engraving with the assistance of Ferdinando de' Medici, and acquired a position in the Medici court as gem-engraver to the Grand Duke Cosimo III, establishing his reputation with a chalcedony cameo portrait of his patron (untraced). Among other portraits were those of the collector Baron Philipp von Stosch (*c.* 1717; Berlin, Antikenmus.) and of Cosimo's sons Ferdinando de' Medici and Gian Gastone de' Medici (untraced). For the Electress Palatine Anna Maria Luisa de' Medici he cut cameos of *Hadrian* and *Trajan* in large violet sapphires, and for Cardinal Gualtieri a copy of the *Venus de' Medici* (Florence, Uffizi) in an amethyst (untraced). On the death of the last Medici in 1737 he moved to Naples in the employ of Charles VII (later Charles III of Spain). Charles, of whom he produced a chalcedony cameo portrait (untraced), appointed him director of the Real Laboratorio delle Pietre Dure, a post he retained until the end of his life. Several of his works were reproduced in the cast collection of James Tassie (Edinburgh, N.P.G., and St Petersburg, Hermitage).

A. Gonzalez-Palacios: 'Un'autobiografia di Francesco Ghinghi', *Antol. B. A.*, i/3 (1977), pp. 271–81

Ghiordes knot. *See under* CARPET, §§I, 1 AND II, 1(II).

Giardini, Giovanni (*b* Forlì, 1646; *d* Rome, 1721). Italian draughtsman, silversmith, bronze-caster and gem-carver. Between 1665 and 1668 he was apprenticed to the silversmith Marco Gamberucci (*fl* 1656–80) in Rome. He ran a productive workshop, in which he was joined in 1680 by his brother Alessandro Giardini (*b* 1655). In 1698 he was appointed bronze-founder for the Papacy. Only a few of his works in silver have survived, most of them church furnishings that escaped the depredations of the Napoleonic army. These show a strong sense of form and a technical mastery that earned him important commissions from the papal court, including an imposing papal mace in silver and parcel-gilt (*c.* 1696; London, V&A), a tabernacle in silver, gilt copper, porphyry and rock-crystal (1711; Vienna, Ksthist. Mus.) and a cross and two candlesticks in silver and malachite (1720; Pavia, priv. col.), which were made for the chapel of Cardinal Francesco Barberini in St Peter's, Rome. When the body of Queen Christina of Sweden was exhumed in 1965 in St Peter's, a set of pieces by Giardini was found: the Queen's silver sceptre, crown and funerary mask of 1689 (Rome, St Peter's). Giardini's reputation, however, is based on his pattern-book designs for sacred and secular objects, which were published in Prague as *Disegni diversi* (1714) and in Rome as *Promptuarium artis argen-*

tariae (1750); these designs were the most important source of inspiration for Roman artistic silver production throughout the 18th century, and they continued to be influential into the 19th.

Gibbons, Grinling (*b* Rotterdam, 4 April 1648; *d* London, 3 Aug 1721). English wood-carver and sculptor. He is widely regarded as England's foremost decorative wood-carver. He was the son of English merchant parents settled in Rotterdam, and came to England in 1667, settling first in York and, by 1671 in Deptford, near London, where he was working as a ship-carver when the diarist John Evelyn discovered him carving a wooden relief copy of a *Crucifixion* by Jacopo Tintoretto (1519–94). This relief, a competent work but lacking Gibbons's later virtuosity, was offered to Charles II, but his Catholic queen, Catherine of Braganza, declined it; Evelyn claimed that it was he who brought Gibbons to the King's notice, and it may also have been through him that Gibbons was introduced to Christopher Wren (1632–1723) and Hugh May (1621–84). A number of other carved wood reliefs have been attributed to Gibbons in his early years, including a *Last Supper* (Burghley House, Cambs), a *Battle of the Amazons* (Warwick Castle) and the *Valley of Dry Bones* (Deptford, London, St Nicholas). However, only the ambitious panel of the *Stoning of St Stephen* (London, V&A) and the Dunham Massey panel (Cheshire, NT) can be given to him with any certainty. Several relief portraits in wood, including that of *Sir Chris-*

Grinling Gibbons: *Stoning of St Stephen*, carved limewood and lancewood, with later paint, 1.85 × 1.21 m, *c.* 1680–1710 (London, Victoria and Albert Museum)

Grinling Gibbons: carved wooden panel (panel of Cosimo III)
(Florence, Museo Nazionale del Bargello)

topher Wren (London, RIBA), are also traditionally attributed to Gibbons in the early stages of his career, but all these works are overshadowed by the virtuosity of his mature and documented output.

Gibbons received numerous important commissions throughout the latter part of his career, both before and after his appointment in 1693 as Master Carver to the Crown. Although he worked for private clients, such as Charles Seymour, 6th Duke of Somerset, for whom he executed the famous Carved Room (*c.* 1692; extended 1793–4) at Petworth House, W. Sussex, much of his decorative work was carried out for the Crown under the supervision of Christopher Wren, the Surveyor-General. In the 1690s Gibbons worked at Kensington Palace, London, and at Hampton Court, near London, but his best carving of this kind survives in the Royal Apartments at Windsor Castle, Berks, where he worked from 1677 to around 1682. While some of the carvings at Windsor were displaced in early 19th-century reorganizations, enough exists of Gibbons's sumptuously carved Baroque panelling, overdoors, chimney-pieces and picture frames to justify Evelyn's statement that the ensemble was 'stupendous and beyond all description'.

Perhaps the finest single piece of Gibbons's carved work is the signed lime-wood relief of the *Attributes of the Arts*, garlanded in naturalistic fruit and flowers (Florence, Pitti), presented in 1682 by Charles II to Cosimo III de' Medici, Grand Duke of Tuscany. A second signed relief (Modena, Gal. & Mus. Estense), said to have been sent to Modena by James II, is similar but slightly less refined. Among

Gibbons's other important surviving works in wood are the oak decorations (1696–7) of the choir of St Paul's Cathedral, London, another project on which he was associated with Wren.

Most of Gibbons's carved work in wood is made up of softwood laminations (lime-wood, pear-wood or lance-wood), which are glued together and held with iron nails. This technique, acceptable at the time, has sometimes since given trouble in conservation; his carving in oak (e.g. the bishop's throne at St Paul's) could not be laminated satisfactorily and cracks have appeared. Gibbons used perhaps as many as 300 different gouges and chisels to achieve his astonishing effects: one long chisel is still known as a 'Gibbons'.

ODNB
G. Beard: *The Work of Grinling Gibbons* (London, 1989)
D. Esterley: *Grinling Gibbons and the Art of Carving* (London and New York, 1998)
F. Oughton, *Grinling Gibbons and the English Woodcarving Tradition* (Fresno, 1999)
C. Rowell: 'Grinling Gibbons's carved room at Petworth', *Apollo*, cli/458 (April 2000), pp. 19–26

Gien Pottery. French pottery factory. In 1821 a pottery was founded in Gien (Loiret) by an Englishman, Thomas Hall. The factory produced simply-decorated Creamware, mostly functional tableware. The product lines expanded to included formal dinnerware and display pottery, and in the 1860s began to produce more highly decorated pottery, using Lustres and Flambé glazes. The factory is still producing high-quality earthenware

R. Bernard and J.-C. Renard, *La Faïence de Gien* (Paris, 1981)

Gilbert, Sir Alfred (*b* London, 12 Aug 1854; *d* London, 4 Nov 1934). English sculptor, medallist, goldsmith and draughtsman. As a sculptor he is best known for the figure of *Eros* on his Shaftesbury Memorial in London. Gilbert's activities as a goldsmith include the enormous (1120 mm) silver epergne (1887–90; London, V&A), presented to Queen Victoria as a Golden Jubilee gift by officers of the army, and the silver gilt mayoral chain for Preston Corporation (1888–92; Preston Town Hall). Many of his designs in pen, ink and watercolour for goldsmith's work and jewellery are preserved in the so-called van Caloen album (Loppem, Sticht. van Caloen). Related to Gilbert's practice as a goldsmith and as a portrait sculptor are his cast and struck medals. These include the cast bronze profile portrait medal of the landscape painter *Matthew Ridley Corbet* (1881; Paris, Mus. Orsay), a work in the idiom of David d'Angers (1788–1856), and the struck bronze medal designed to commemorate the jubilee of the Art Union in 1887 (e.g. London, BM).

ODNB
R. Dorment: *Alfred Gilbert* (New Haven and London, 1985)
Alfred Gilbert: Sculptor and Goldsmith (exh. cat., ed. R. Dorment; London, RA, 1986)

Gilding. The decoration of works of art and architecture with gold or silver or other metals. Traditionally the term describes the application of thin sheets of metal to a surface by means of an adhesive; it is also possible to use the metal in powdered form, and to mix gold with mercury to form an amalgam used for the technique variously known as fire gilding, amalgam gilding or parcel gilding.

1. Leaf. 2. Powder. 3. Fire gilding.

1. LEAF. The earliest application of gold as decoration was in Mesopotamia and in Predynastic Egypt. In gilded figures from Ur (dating from before 2500 BC) and from Egypt (*c.* 2400 BC), sheet gold was nailed to a wooden core, but by 1500 BC leaf gold was being applied to a variety of materials, notably ivory (known as chryselephantine work). Silver leaf has been extensively used, both on its own and, covered with a golden yellow transparent coating, as a substitute for gold, despite the fact that it tarnishes. Gold leaf is obtained today in various shades and degrees of hardness, pure 24 carat gold being the softest. Tinted silver was widely used on polychrome sculpture, in interior decoration and on furniture, notably in 17th- and 18th-century Europe. Tin leaf, which does not tarnish, was coloured to imitate gold in addition to being used alone. Leaf is also now produced from white gold, palladium and platinum; aluminium may be used as a cheap alternative.

A laminated leaf, resembling gold leaf, was made by placing a thin sheet of gold over a similar sheet of silver (or tin) and hammering the two together. The gold–silver laminate is known as *Zwischgold* (Ger.), *partijtgoud* (Dut.) or *or parti* (Fr.) or *oro di metà* (It.). Unlike pure gold leaf, however, it tarnishes, as the thin gold cannot protect the silver below. Gold-coloured alloys used for leaf include the copper–zinc *Schlagmetall* ('beaten metal') or 'Dutch metal', used from the 19th century.

Water gilding and oil or mordant gilding are the two main methods of applying gold leaf used, notably on easel and wall paintings, furniture and sculpture, since medieval times. Water gilding was certainly known in Europe by the early 12th century. This method is used where a shining burnished finish, imitating solid metal, is desired, for example in the gold backgrounds of icons and medieval altarpieces and in manuscript illumination. Gold applied using an oil mordant cannot be burnished, as the adhesive holds the gold too firmly; it therefore appears yellower and has a diffusely reflecting surface. This difference in appearance may be exploited by using both types of gilding in the same piece of work.

In water gilding the object is usually coated with several layers of gesso or chalk mixed with parchment size. When this is hard, it is scraped and polished to a perfectly smooth finish. A soft, slightly greasy, reddish-coloured clay, known as bole, mixed with dilute size, is then applied and, when dry, burnished or polished. A sheet of leaf is placed on a padded leather gilder's cushion, cut to size if necessary and picked up using a gilder's tip—a thin, flat,

hair brush (in medieval times, tweezers and card would have been used). The bole is moistened with water to which a little size may be added. The leaf is held above it, just touching the surface, and is sucked on to the bole by capillary action. It may be patted down afterwards if necessary. When the work is dry, the gold is burnished; modern burnishing tools are usually made of agate, but in earlier times haematite and even dogs' teeth were used.

For oil gilding a mordant, consisting principally of linseed oil heated with a lead drier, is used; frequently a natural resin varnish is also incorporated. The mordant may be pigmented (e.g. with yellow ochre), which not only enables the design seen on the surface to be decorated but may also help to disguise small flaws in the gilding. The mordant is painted on and left until tacky, when the gold is applied; this technique is used for delicate linear designs or lettering.

Gold and silver leaf were applied to, or encased in, glass to produce the gold and silver tesserae that profoundly influenced the character of post-Antique and medieval mosaics. The leaf was placed on a small thick sheet of glass, and covered with a very thin glass sheet and heated in a furnace until the glass began to melt; later sources suggest the use of powdered glass, giving a very thin surface layer. After cooling, the surface of the thinner glass was polished with emery powder or a similar abrasive. The slab was then broken into square tesserae. Variations in the appearance of the gold could be obtained by the deliberate use of brownish or greenish glass, rather than colourless, and by applying the tesserae upside down, with the thicker glass at the top.

P. MacTaggart and A. MacTaggart: *Practical Gilding* (Welwyn, 1984)
D. Bigelow, E. Cornu, G. J. Landrey and C. van Horne, eds: *Gilded Wood: Conservation and History* (Madison, 1991)
Gilding and Surface Decoration: Preprints of the UKIC Conference Restoration '91: London, 1991
J. LaFerla: *Gilding: Easy Techniques & Elegant Projects with Metal Leaf* (New York, 1997)
E. Becker: *Gold Leaf Application and Antique Restoration* (Atglen, PA, 1998)
K. Skinner: *The Gilded Room: Decorating with Metallic Effects, from Metal Leaf to Powders, Pastes, & Paints* (New York, 2000)

2. POWDER. Recipes for powdering gold (and other metals) appear as early as the 3rd century AD and include amalgamation of gold leaf with mercury and grinding leaf with salt. Shell gold (so called because of the traditional method of storing it in mussel shells) was made by grinding leaf gold with honey (a method known since at least the 14th century) and mixing it with a gum or other appropriate medium so that it could be used as a paint. Powdered gold was used in such Chinese techniques as *maiojin* ('painting in gold') and *tianqi* ('filled-in lacquer') to decorate lacquer in the Song period (AD 960–1279); it may also be strewn or dusted lightly over an adhesive to give a glittering appearance, a technique much used on East Asian lacquerware. Powdered gold suspended in varnish was also used in early bookbinding decoration. Mosaic gold—*aurum musicum* or *purporino* (It.)—is a gold-coloured tin sulphide

prepared by prolonged heating of tin–mercury amalgam, sulphur and sal ammoniac. By the 14th century recipes for the material abounded, although its use has seldom been confirmed in practice. One rare example is the metal rail in Francesco del Cossa's painting of *St Vincent Ferrer* (*c.* 1473; London, N.G.). It is thought to have been used as a substitute for real powdered gold, mainly in the illumination of manuscripts and in miniature paintings. The now widely used bronze powders were developed in the 19th century and are used predominantly in the decorative arts, in particular on furniture, picture frames and mirrors. These powders are generally copper–zinc alloys, their colour depending on the relative proportions of the two metals present. Aluminium flake powders may be used instead of silver.

P. E. Rogers, F. S. Greenawald and W. L. Butters: 'Copper and Copper Alloy Flake Powders', *Pigment Handbook*, ed. T. C. Patton, 3 vols (New York, 1973), i, pp. 807–17

R. Rolles: 'Aluminium Flake Pigment', *Pigment Handbook*, ed. T. C. Patton, 3 vols (New York, 1973), i, pp. 785–806

A. Smith, A. Reeve and A. Roy: 'Francesco del Cossa's *St Vincent Ferrer*', *N. G. Tech. Bull.*, v (1981), pp. 44–57

F. Ames-Lewis: 'Matteo de' Pasti and the Use of Powdered Gold', *Mitt. Ksthist. Inst. Florenz*, xxviii (1984), pp. 351–62

3. FIRE GILDING [Mercury, amalgam or parcel gilding]. This method of gilding made use of the property of mercury readily to form an amalgam with gold and was usually applied to copper or silver. The technique as practised in the medieval period was described in detail by Theophilus in *De diversis artibus*, and many 19th-century workshop manuals contain detailed accounts of this process. There were two basic methods: applying either gold leaf or a gold–mercury amalgam to a surface that had already been treated with mercury.

In both methods the metal had to be carefully cleaned free of all grease and scratch-brushed to key the surface; then mercury was applied. In the more remote past metallic mercury was vigorously worked into the surface with a short, stiff brush until the surface was uniformly covered. From the 18th century the usual practice was to dip the cleaned metal into a solution of mercuric nitrate, which precipitated mercury on to the surface in a thin, continuous layer. This process was known as quicking.

In the first method of fire gilding thin sheets of gold were laid on to the prepared surface, vigorously burnished and then heated to drive off the mercury. In the second process an amalgam of mercury and gold was first prepared by heating mercury to about the temperature of boiling water and then adding about half the weight of pure gold filings, stirring with an iron rod until the amalgam had the consistency of butter (hence the term 'butter of gold'). The health hazards of handling mercury were recognized even in medieval times, and the prepared amalgam was stored under water. The amalgam was then applied to the freshly quicked surface by brushing. When the piece was covered it was gently warmed to evaporate the mercury, while the gilding continued to be worked with a stiff brush to ensure even coverage. Alternatively the amalgam could be carefully

applied and brushed in with a wire brush that had itself been quicked to promote even coverage, then heated in a closed furnace. In the latter process, however, the piece had to be kept under constant observation, periodically moved and the amalgam layer worked if necessary to keep the gilding even as it formed. The freshly gilded surface had a rather matt, granular appearance, which could then be further treated by scratch brushing, burnishing or by the use of chemicals to produce the desired colour and texture.

Even in the early medieval period, when supplies of mercury must often have been difficult to obtain in Europe, fire gilding was the favoured method for gilding metalwork and remained so until the mid-19th century, when, in common with most other traditional plating techniques, it was challenged and rapidly replaced by electrogilding. Although it continued for some time to be favoured for applications where either its durability or the special surface effects were required on work of the highest quality, the process has become virtually extinct in Europe and North America because of the extra cost and stringent health regulations. Fire gilding is still used in Tibet, however, although in other countries where traditional metalworking methods still thrive, for example Nepal, amalgam gilding was practised until the late 20th century; in the early 21st century it has been replaced by electrogilding (*see* ELECTROPLATING).

P. Lins and W. A. Oddy: 'The Origins of Mercury Gilding', *J. Archaeol. Sci.*, ii (1975), pp. 365–73

W. A. Oddy, M. Bimsom and S. La Niece: 'Gilding Himalayan Images', *Aspects of Tibetan Metallurgy*, ed. W. A. Oddy and W. Zwalf, BM Occas. Pap., 15 (London, 1981), pp. 87–103

Giles, James (*b* London, 1718; *d* London 1780). English porcelain and glass painter. He was the son of a porcelain painter of the same name. James Giles became an independent painter in 1749, and decorated white porcelain, mostly made at WORCESTER but also made by other factories. His work is characterized by bold design, vivid colours, high-quality gilding and delicate painting in gold or enamels of floral or classical motifs. He also painted glass, specializing in opaque blue and white glass decorated in gilt.

James Giles: China & Enamel Painter, 1718–1780 (London, 1977)

G. Coke: *In Search of James Giles* (Wingham, 1984)

A. McConnell: 'James Giles's Decorations on Glass', *Mag. Ant.*, clxiv/4 (Oct 2003), pp. 142–51

A. McConnell: 'A Designer of Distinction: The Glassware of James Giles', *Apollo*, lxi (June 2005), pp. 82–5

James Giles, China and Glass Painter (1718–80) [sale cat., London, Stockspring Antiques, 2005]

Gili, Paolo (*fl* 1518–66). Sicilian goldsmith. His early work is Gothic, notably a magnificent processional monstrance with Gothic spires (1536–8; Enna, Mus. Alessi) and a reliquary of S Agata (1532; Palermo Cathedral). From the 1540s he adopted a Renaissance style, as exemplified by a crozier (Palermo, Gal.

Reg. Sicilia) and a reliquary of S Cristina (Palermo Cathedral).

Gillinder & Sons. American glasshouse founded in Philadelphia in 1861 by William Gillinder, an English glassworker who had moved to America in 1854. For the first few years it was called Franklin Flint Works, and manufactured glass chimneys and glassware. When William's sons, James and Frederic, joined the company in 1867, the name was changed to Gillinder & Sons and the product range expanded. In 1876 the company built and operated a complete glass factory on the Centennial International Exhibition in Philadelphia, making and selling popular pressed souvenir pieces as well as cut and engraved glass. The attention that Gillinder's displays of cut glass attracted at the exhibition led to a boom in the cut-glass industry. In 1912 the brothers William and James Gillinder bought the Bronx and Ryal glasshouse in Port Jervis, NY, and operated there as Gillinder Brothers. The Philadelpha glasshouse closed in the 1930s, but the Port Jervis factory still produces fine glass.

Gillinder Glass: Story of a Company (exh. cat. by G. Taylor; Millville, NJ, Wheaton Village, Amer. Glass Mus., 1994)

Gillingham, James (*b* 1736; *d* 1781). American chairmaker. His Philadelphia workshop produced furniture in the Chippendale style. His surviving work includes eight mahogany side chairs (from a set of twelve) in Cedar Grove (Lansdowne Avenue, Philadelphia).

Gillot, Claude (*b* Langres, 28 April 1673; *d* Paris, 4 May 1722). French draughtsman, printmaker and painter. Gillot's decorative designs, which feature imaginative combinations of architecture, arabesques, scroll- and shellwork with figures in various kinds of fancy dress, for use on panelling, harpsichord cases, screens, hangings, gunstocks etc, achieved a wide circulation in suites of engravings by himself and others. They include the *Nouveaux desseins d'arquebuserie*, the *Livre de portières* and the *Livre de principes d'ornements*. Gillot was commissioned, in the year before his death, to make watercolour and wash costume designs for the ballet *Les Eléments*, in which the young Louis XV danced. The designs are collected in the *Nouveaux desseins d'habillements à l'usage des ballets opéras et comédies*, with 80 plates, engraved by François Joullain several years after Gillot's death.

B. Populus: *Claude Gillot (1673–1722): Catalogue de l'oeuvre gravé* (Paris, 1930)
H. J. Poley: *Claude Gillot: Leben und Werk, 1673–1722* (Würzburg, 1938)
P. Choné: *Claude Gillot, 1673–1722: Comédies, Sabbats et Autres Sujets Bizarres* (Paris, 1999)
J. Tonkovich: 'Claude Gillot's Costume Designs for the Paris Opera: Some New Sources', *Burl. Mag.*, cxlvii (April 2005), pp. 248–52

Gillow. English family of furniture retailers. Robert Gillow I (1704–72) became a freeman of the town of Lancaster in 1728 and married Agnes Fell in 1730. They had two sons, Richard Gillow I (1734–1811) and Robert Gillow II (1745–95). Richard studied architecture in London and returned to Lancaster, whereas Robert managed the London showrooms that were established in Oxford Street in 1769. The Lancaster branch engaged in a variety of activities, making furniture for the home and export markets and importing sugar, rum and, to a lesser degree, tropical woods from the West Indies; they also did architectural joinery and made billiard-tables. Final assembly took place at the London branch where the furniture was sold.

The Gillows produced a neat, rather conventional range of furniture derived from the designs of James Wyatt (1746–1813), the most fashionable architect of the last two decades of the 18th century, and from plates in the pattern-books of George Hepplewhite and Thomas Sheraton. The firm had a very large aristocratic clientele, supplying houses such as Tatton (Cheshire, NT), and also made pieces that would appeal to the burgeoning middle classes of Liverpool and Manchester, who valued good, solid, well-made furniture. Crossbanding and carving were kept to a minimum, but painted furniture that harmonized with upholstery and wallpaper was widely used from about 1770 until the 1800s, when rosewood became more fashionable. From about 1780 the firm took to stamping some of its furniture with GILLOWSLANCASTER, and in 1785 the Lancaster side of the opera-

Gillow: sideboard, designed by Bruce J. Talbert, London, *c.* 1870 (Vienna, Österreichisches Museum für Angewandte Kunst)

tion branched out into upholstery. At the end of the 18th century the firm manufactured several novel types of furniture, including the Davenport, the whatnot and the 'Imperial Extending Dining Table', which was brought out by Richard Gillow in 1800. In the vogue for historical revivals that developed towards the end of the Napoleonic Wars, Gillows produced 'Gothic', 'Old English' or 'Elizabethan', and 'Antique' (Greek Revival) and neo-Rococo furniture. There was an increasing market for reproduction furniture, which clients would add to their original sets. A few items of Chippendale-style furniture, based on designs in Thomas Chippendale the elder's *Gentleman and Cabinet-maker's Director*, were also made, such as the Gothic 'Salisbury' Antique table.

Important collections of Gillows furniture survive at Tatton Park, Ches, NT, Broughton Hall, N. Yorks, and at Lotherton Hall, Leeds (Leeds, City Museums; originally made for Parlington Hall, W. Yorks). The last Gillow to be directly involved with the firm was Richard Gillow II (1806–66), grandson of Richard Gillow I, who retired in 1830. An extensive archive of the business of Gillow & Co. is housed in London at the Westminster City Library. There is also a large collection of drawings at the Lancaster City Museum.

N. Goodison: 'Gillows Clock Cases', *Antiqua. Horology*, v/10 (1969), pp. 348–61

N. Goodison and J. Hardy: 'Gillows at Tatton Park', *Furn. Hist.*, 6 (1970), pp. 1–40

I. Hall: 'Patterns of Elegance: The Gillows' Furniture Designs', *Country Life*, clxiii (8 June 1978), pp. 1612–15; (15 June 1978), pp. 1740–42

S. C. Nichols: 'Furniture Made by Gillow and Company for Workington Hall', *Antiques*, cxxvii (1985), pp. 1353–9

L. Boyton: *Gillow Furniture Designs, 1760–1800* (Royston, 1995)

S. Stuart: 'Three Generations of Gothic Chairs by Gillows', *Furn. Hist.*, xxxii (1996), pp. 33–45

S. Stuart: 'A Portable Billiard Table by Gillows of Lancaster, 1769', *Furn. Hist.*, xxxiii (1997), pp. 117–19

S. Stuart: 'Gillows of Lancaster and London as a Design Source for American Chairs', *Mag. Ant.*, clv/6 (June 1999), pp. 866–75

The Glory of Gillows & Fine English Furniture (sale cat., London, Christie's, 2004)

L. Microulis: 'Gillow and the Furnishing of the Midland Grand Hotel, London', *Mag. Ant.*, clxv/6 (June 2004), pp. 108–17

Gimson, Ernest (William) (*b* Leicester, 21 Dec 1864; *d* Sapperton, nr Cirencester, 12 Aug 1919). English architect and furniture-maker. From 1881 to 1886 he was an architectural apprentice to Isaac Barradale in Leicester, studying in the same period at Leicester School of Art. On the suggestion of William Morris, whom he heard lecture to the Secular Society in Leicester, Gimson moved to London. In 1890 he joined forces with several friends to form a small furniture-making firm called Kenton and Company. After the liquidation of Kenton & Co. in 1892 Gimson and the BARNSLEY brothers moved to the Cotswolds to design and make furniture. They lived at Ewen, near Cirencester, and then at Pinbury Park, part of Lord Bathurst's estate, subsequently moving at the turn of the century to cottages of their own design at Sapperton. Nearby at Daneway House, Gimson established a workshop where he employed a skilled team of cabinetmakers, including Ernest Smith and Percy Burchett, working under a chief foreman, Peter van der Waals (1870–1937). Here he trained village craftsmen to understand and produce the finest cabinet work and metalwork to his design. This laid the foundations for the move of C. R. ASHBEE and the Guild of Handicraft from London to Chipping Campden in 1902.

Gimson's furniture is noted for its simplicity, its truth to materials and its functionalism, particularly evident in an English walnut store cabinet (1902; London, V&A) and oak kitchen dresser (1902; Cheltenham, A.G. & Mus.). He used woods local to Sapperton, particularly ash, oak, elm, deal and fruitwoods, making much of their colour and natural markings. Methods of construction such as exposed pins, joints and dovetails were often utilized as a feature of the design. Ornamental details such as holly and ebony stringing, or inlay in bone or mother-of-pearl, were integrated into the total conception of each piece and taken beyond a mere decorative trimming.

As a furniture-maker Gimson produced considerably more than either of the two Barnsley brothers, but all three had a profound influence on furniture design in the 20th century. The Gimson tradition was furthered by Sidney Barnsley's son Edward Barnsley, who trained a succession of craftsmen at his workshop in Froxfield, Hants, over more than fifty years, and Gordon Russell, who carried the tradition forward on a commercial basis through his furniture firm in Broadway, Glos.

W. Lethaby, F. Griggs and A. Powell: *Ernest Gimson: His Life and Work* (Stratford on Avon, 1924)

R. Alexander: *The Furniture and Joinery of Peter Waals* (Chipping Campden, 1930)

A. Carruthers: *Ernest Gimson and the Cotswold Group of Craftsmen* (Leicester, 1978)

M. Comino: *Gimson and the Barnsleys* (London, 1980)

Gimson and Barnsley: Designs and Drawings in Cheltenham Art Gallery and Museums (Cheltenham, 1985)

M. Greensted: *Gimson and the Barnsleys: Wonderful Furniture of a Commonplace Kind* (Stroud, 1980)

M. Greensted: 'Ernest Gimson as a Designer', *Mag. Ant.*, clxi/6 (June 2002), pp. 82–91

M. Greensted: 'Ernest Gimson's Arts and Crafts Embroidery Designs', *Piecework*, xi/5 (Sept–Oct 2003), pp. 54–8

Ginger jar. Chinese porcelain jar with an ovoid body and a wide mouth with a lid, manufactured in mid-19th century China for the export market. The jars may have been used to hold preserved ginger; it was believed by purchasers in the West that the jars were used to contain wedding or New Year gifts, and that the jars were intended to be returned to the giver after the contents had been eaten.

Giorgio, Maestro. *See* ANDRESOLI, GIORGIO.

Giovanni da Castel Bolognese. *See* BERNARDI, GIOVANNI.

Giovanni da Udine [Nanni, Giovanni; Ricamatori, Giovanni dei] (*b* Udine, 27 Oct 1487; *d* Rome, 1564). Italian stuccoist, painter, draughtsman and architect. He left Udine to work with Raphael in Rome. At about this time a formula for re-creating the Romans' rock-hard plaster, capable of reproducing minute details, was devised, almost certainly by Giovanni, probably using marble dust and chips of travertine stone. Thus when Raphael and his assistants began decorating the 13 bays of the first of the great Logge of the Vatican Palace (1517–19), Giovanni was able to contribute figured frames and other details in stucco to the scheme, as well as painted grotesques on the pilasters and walls, with a delicate freshness at least partly due to his inclusion of tempera in the fresco medium.

In 1520 Giovanni became involved in the decoration of the Villa Madama, Rome, which Raphael had begun some years earlier. In the garden loggia, which is all that remains of what was built of the project, Raphael's magnificent architecture is sumptuously enriched by its stucco skin of small-scale Classical ornament, more architectonic and sculptural than grotesque. The painted decoration of the vault does contain grotesques, as well as small scenes and fields of pure ornament, and the vigorous colouring reflects the taste of Giulio Romano, but this does not detract from the remarkable beauty of the whole, which is the only Renaissance interior fully to reflect the grandeur of Imperial Rome.

Giovanni da Udine: frescoes in the first loggia Vatican Palace, Rome, 1519

Giovanni's last important work in Rome was the decoration (in collaboration with Perino del Vaga (1501–47)) of the ceiling of the Sala dei Pontefici, with celestial motifs and the Medici arms (*c.* 1521; *in situ*). In 1532 he moved to Florence and began work on the stucco decoration for the Medici Chapel by Michelangelo (1475–1564) in S Lorenzo, Florence; the project was never completed. It was probably at this time that he designed the stained-glass windows with exquisite grotesques in the Laurentian Library (Florence, Bib. Medicea–Laurenziana), attached to the monastery of S Lorenzo.

P. Morel: 'Priape a la Renaissance: Les guirlandes de Giovanni da Udine a la Farnesine', *Rev. A.*, lxix (1985), pp. 13–28
E. Bartolini: *Giovanni da Udine* (Udine, 1987)
G. C. Custoza: *Giovanni da Udine: La tecnica della decorazione a stucco alla romana nel Friuli del XVI secolo* (Prato, 1996)
A. Bristot: 'Dedicato all'amore per l'antico: il camerino di Apollo a palazzo Grimani', *A. Ven.*, lviii (2001), pp. 43–93
M. di Prampero de Carvalho: *Perchè Giovanni fu sepolto al Pantheon?: Giovanni da Udine con Bramante e Raffaello* (Udine, 2003)

Giovanni da Verona, **Fra** (*b* ?Verona; *fl* 1476; *d* ?Verona, 1525–6). Italian intarsia artist. He entered the Olivetan Order at Monte Oliveto Maggiore near Siena in 1476, and after ordination (1477–9) he was sent to the monastery of S Giorgio, Ferrara, where he learnt the art of wood inlay from Fra Sebastiano da Rovigno, called 'Schiavone'. Giovanni then worked as a woodcarver in Perugia (1480–84). The first large project of which substantial traces survive is the choir of S Maria in Organo, Verona, where he decorated the lectern, candelabrum and choir-stalls with architectural motifs, still-lifes, figures of saints and a *Crucifixion* (1494–9). In this work he can already be seen moving away from the Venetian and Ferrarese intarsia tradition in which he was trained towards solutions that are softer and more classical in line. Between 1502 and 1504 he worked on the great choir complex at Monte Oliveto Maggiore (now divided between the abbey church and Siena Cathedral), the intarsia panels of which, featuring birds, fountains, diverse objects and views of Siena, represent the high point of his creativity and skill (see colour pl. XV, fig. 2).

Between 1506 and 1510 Giovanni divided his time between Naples and Fondi. He produced intarsia work for the choir of S Anna dei Lombardi, Naples, where he showed a keen interest in architectural motifs. One of the choir-stalls exhibits a view of the Tempietto (1502) by Donato Bramante (?1443/4–1514) at S Pietro in Montorio, Rome. He also produced the seat backs (*c.* 1513) for the Stanza della Segnatura in the Vatican Palace, and the communicating door between it and the Stanza di Eliodoro. Except for the door (heavily rest.), his work was removed in the mid-16th century by Pope Paul III. Giovanni's intarsia work in the choir of S Maria fuori PortaTifi, Siena, later dismantled and partly transferred to Monte Oliveto, shows that he adopted the expressive language of Roman classicist painters. His last work was on the wardrobes (1519) in the sacristy of S Maria in Organo, Verona, and the choir-stalls

Fra Giovanni da Verona: trompe l'oeil street scene, intarsia decoration of the choir-stalls, S Maria in Organo, Verona, 1499

(1523) of Villanova del Sillaro Abbey, near Milan (now in Lodi Cathedral).

P. Bagatin: *Preghiere di legno: Tarsie ed intagli di fra Giovanni da Verona* (Florence, 2000)

Giovanni Maria di Mariano (*fl* 1508–30). Italian maiolica painter who worked in CASTEL DURANTE (1508), URBINO (1508 and 1530) and Venice (1523; *see* VENICE, §1). The canon of his works has been reduced by scholarly scrutiny, but those that remain secure are typically plates decorated with allegorical subjects surrounded by GROTESQUE borders.

Girandole. Branched support for candles or other lights, either in the form of a candlestick for placing on a table, or more commonly as a bracket projecting from a wall; the term is sometimes used to denote a round mirror with candle branches. In jewellery, a girandole is an ear-ring or pendant with a large central stone surrounded by smaller ones.

Girdle. In jewellery, the line or rim dividing the two faces of a brilliant.

Girl-in-a-swing. White porcelain figure of a girl in a swing (see fig. on p. 428; London, V and Boston, MA, Mus. F.A.). The genre was first identified in 1962, and the unknown factory was initially known as the 'Girl-in-a-swing factory'. It is now known to be the St James Factory established in 1749 by Charles Gouyn, a Huguenot who had worked at the CHELSEA PORCELAIN FACTORY. The factory seems to have closed by 1754.

B. Dragesco: *English Ceramics in French Archives: The Writings of Jean Hellot, the Adventures of Jacques Louis Brolliet and the Identification of the "Girl-in-a-swing" Factory* (London, 1993)
N. Valpy: 'Charles Gouyn and the Girl-in-a-swing Factory', *Trans. Eng. Cer. Circ.*, xv/2 (1994), pp. 318–26

Girometti. Italian family of gem-engravers, medallists and engravers.

1. GIUSEPPE GIROMETTI (*b* Rome, 7 Oct 1780; *d* Rome, 17 Nov 1851). Gem-engraver, sculptor and medallist. He was one of the most important gem-engravers of the first half of the 19th century. In 1812 he was elected to the Accademia di S Luca in Rome as an engraver of hardstones and was awarded numerous prizes. In 1822 he was appointed, together with Giuseppe Cerbara, as Head Engraver at the papal mint. He produced an enormous amount of glyptic and medal work and executed more than 60 medals for popes Pius VII, Leo XII, Pius VIII, Gregory XVI and Pius XI, as well as at least 15 medals for private clients and public institutions. He adopted a number of Classical elements, creating an original style that helped to revive the Roman art of medalmaking.

Girometti engraved hardstones mainly in cameo: large stones with several layers of colour were particularly popular at the time, especially those engraved with such mythological or Classical subjects as *Bacchantes* (New York, Met.; Rome, Vatican, Bib. Apostolica) or *Primavera* (Paris, Bib. N., Cab. Médailles). He often reproduced such famous antique gems as *Diomedes with the Palladium* (London, BM) and *Jupiter Smiting the Giants with a Thunderbolt* (versions Florence, Pitti; Rome, Vatican, Bib. Apostolica), and copied works by such contemporary sculptors as Antonio Canova (1757–1822), Bertel Thorvaldsen, (1768/70–1844), Pietro Tenerani (1789–1869) and John Gibson (1790–1866). He also produced a series of portraits commissioned in part by the Duc de Blacas d'Aulps that represented such famous figures as *Plato*, *Socrates*, *Richelieu* and *Racine*. Other works include five cameos with the busts of *Leonardo*, *Titian*, *Michelangelo*, *Correggio* and *Raphael* (sold London, Christie's, 8 June 1982, lot 141) and a series of portraits of contemporary figures largely comprising the sovereigns and rulers of the period (London, BM, V&A).

2. PIETRO GIROMETTI (*b* Rome, 20 Sept 1811.; *d* Rome, 13 July 1859). Medallist and engraver, son of Giuseppe. He was particularly well known for having executed some medals for the iconographical series of famous Italian men begun in 1843 in collaboration with Nicola Cerbara, with whom he produced 16 pieces. From 1838 he worked as an engraver at the papal mint and succeeded his father as Head Engraver. His medals are particularly valuable for their portraits; his gem-engraving, however, is more dif-

Soft-paste porcelain figure of a *Girl-in-a-swing* (see p. 427), h. 185 mm, London, *c.* 1749–59 (London, Victoria and Albert Museum)

ficult to judge, as it is easily confused with his father's work.

P. Visconti: *Notizie delle opere dell'incisore in pietre dure ed in conj cav. Giuseppe Girometti* (Rome, 1833)
M. Duchamp: 'Un grand camée méconnu de Giuseppe Girometti', *Rev. Louvre*, xl/5 (1990), pp. 398–401
M. Duchamp: 'La machine à remonter le temps, ou l'histoire retrouvée d'une nymphe de Sicile', *L'Oeil*, xdxlvi (Nov 1992), pp. 40–47

Giuliano da Maiano (*b* Maiano, nr Florence, 1432; *d* Naples, 17 Oct 1490). Italian architect, woodcarver and intarsia worker. Although much of his posthumous fame rests on his work as an architect, Giuliano's earlier work in wood, which included intarsia work, earned him an equally high reputation. He often worked with his brothers, especially the sculptor and woodcarver Benedetto di Leonardo (*b* Maiano, nr Florence, 1442; *d* Florence, 24 May 1497).

Giuliano's first recorded commissions, for *all'antica* wooden panels and frames, were from the Florentine painters Neri di Bicci and Cosimo Rosselli for a wooden frame (destr.) for the *St Barbara* altarpiece, originally in SS Annunziata, now Florence, Accad. He also made a wooden bench (1455) for S Maria del Carmine in Florence and a wooden cross that was sold to Neri di Bicci on 24 April 1459. In addition, he accepted commissions for more ephemeral objects, including a float for the celebrations of the feast of St John the Baptist in Florence in 1461.

By 1461 Giuliano's workshop was well established, and he began to receive major commissions for entire ensembles of wooden church furnishings, including the choir benches, doors and sacristy cabinets for the Badia at Fiesole (1461–2) and the completion of panels and cabinets for the north sacristy of Florence Cathedral (1463–5). The cathedral woodwork, the earliest complete surviving set of furnishings by Giuliano, shows him to have achieved full mastery of his craft. Giuliano received other commissions for woodwork, including wooden pulpits for S Maria Nuova, Florence (payment 5 April 1465), and for the collegiate church in San Gimignano (1469); the designs, but not the execution, of choir-stalls for Florence Cathedral (1471) and a similar commission for Pisa Cathedral (1477); and woodwork at SS Annunziata, Florence (1470s). He also provided cassoni, elaborate beds and other furniture for the Strozzi, Rucellai, Pazzi and other families in both Florence and Naples. In the mid-1470s, working with a team of sculptors that included his brother Benedetto, Giuliano's workshop made the new ceiling, doors and marble doorframes of the Sala dei Gigli in the Palazzo Vecchio, Florence. He subsequently (*c.* 1479–82) executed the studiolo of the ducal palace in Gubbio, which had been designed by Francesco di Giorgio and is now in the Metropolitan Museum in New York.

Giuliano was the administrative head of a multi-faceted workshop that produced secular and ecclesiastical furniture, sculpture in a wide variety of media and numerous buildings. Early in his career he seems to have engaged in many of these activities himself, but as his fame as an architect grew, he increasingly turned over certain operations to his brothers. He also provided designs for many types of work whose execution was subcontracted to other intarsia workers or builders, while his shop supplied several Florentine artists with panels and frames for their paintings.

O. Raggio: 'The Liberal Arts Studiolo from the Ducal Palace at Gubbio', *Met. Mus. A. Bull.*, liii (Spring 1996), pp. 4–35
M. Ciardi Duprè Dal Poggetto and others: *La bottega di Giuliano e Benedetto da Maiano nel Rinascimento fiorentino* (Florence, 1994)
D. Lamberini, M. Lotti and R. Lunardi: *Giuliano e la bottega dei da Maiano* (Florence, 1994)
F. Quinterio: *Giuliano da Maiano: "Grandissimo domestico"* (Rome, 1995)
J. Dugdale: 'Study in Perspective [Gubbio Studiolo]', *Interiors*, clviii/7 (July 1999), pp. 58–9
O. Raggio and A. Wilmering: *The Gubbio Studiolo and its Conservation* (New York, 1999)

Giustiniani. Italian family of potters. They were active in Naples from the beginning of the 18th century to the end of the 19th. During the 18th century important family members included Ignazio Giustiniani (1686–*c.* 1742), who specialized in the production of tin-glazed earthenware wall tiles decorated with festoons and naturalistic elements; an outstanding example of his work is the tiled floor (1729) in the church of S Andrea delle Dame in Naples. During this period some members of the family were active in Cerreto Sannita, where they worked on such elaborate projects as the panel (1727) set in the tympanum of the congregation of St Maria in San Lorenzello, which is signed and dated by Antonio Giustiniani. Nicola Giustiniani, known as Bel Pensiero (1732–1815), is regarded as one of the most important potters of the period. His work includes two maiolica plaques (1758; Graz, Mus. Kstgew.) painted with ruins inspired by the work of Leonardo Coccorante (1680–1750). The family became increasingly active in Naples during the early 19th century producing utilitarian earthenwares, terracotta garden wares, reproduction antique vases, plates and such services as the 'Etruscan' service (Naples, Mus.

N. Cer.); they also produced porcelain for a short while. Work produced by the family during the 19th century was highly regarded and was awarded prizes at both national and international exhibitions. Wares are often marked with the monograms FMNG or FGN or alternatively with a G or with the surname in full.

N. Vigliotti: *I Giustiniani e la ceramica cerretese* (Marigliano, 1973)
M. Rotili: *La manifattura Giustiniani* (Naples, 1981)

Glasgow. Scottish centre of ceramics production. In 1748 the DELFTFIELD POTTERY was established in Glasgow. Of its competitors, the most successful of these factories was J. & M. P. Bell's Glasgow Pottery (est. 1841). It produced many types of high-quality ware, including figures, busts and perhaps most famously the Warwick Vase in 'Parian' ware, domestic earthenwares, fine china tea-, dinner- and dessert-services, sanitary wares and terracotta, as well as a large range of transfer-printed earthenwares. Designs followed contemporary fashion and included landscapes—both contemporary and classical—commemorative designs and a range of designs particularly adapted for sale in the East Indies and East Asia. Other potteries that benefited from the enormous trade in transfer-printed wares were the Clyde Pottery (1816–1900) at Greenock; the Caledonian Pottery, the Pollockshaws Pottery (1855–1952), the North British Pottery (1860–1904) and the Britannia Pottery (1857–1937), although the last had an unusual claim to fame by having 500 employees engaged for 15 years producing a plain, white dinnerware, named 'Ceres', with a moulded decoration.

Ownership of the potteries frequently changed, and there was a bewildering variety of partnerships, associated with nearly all the firms. A good example is the Saracen Pottery, which opened in 1875 and in 20 years was owned by five different partnerships, the last of which went bankrupt in 1896, when the works were purchased by a company who had produced 'Nautilus Porcelain' at the Barrowfield Pottery. The works were re-equipped and renamed the Possil Pottery.

G. Quail: *Nautilus Porcelain, Possil Pottery, Glasgow* (Glasgow, 1983)
G. Quail and E. Malden: *Four Early Glasgow Potteries* (Glasgow, 1984)
J. A. Fleming and the Britannia Pottery (exh. cat., Dumbarton, Scot. Pott. Soc., 1989)
Glimpses of Glasgow's Pottery Tradition, 1800–1900 (exh. cat. by R. McAslan, Glasgow, Christie's, 1990)

Glass. The man-made silica-based material used to make such items as window panes, bottles and drinking vessels.

I. Decorative techniques. II. Glass in the decorative arts.

I. Decorative techniques

1. Hot-working. 2. Cold-working. 3. Coloured glass. 4. Painting. 5. Ice glass. 6. Sulphides.

1. HOT-WORKING

(i) Moulded and press. (ii) Combing and trailing. (iii) Prunts. (iv) Air bubbles and twists.

(i) Moulded and pressed. Some of the simplest and most effective ways of decorating glass may be carried out during these forming processes. The molten metal is forced into the receptacle of the desired shape either by blowing, casting or pressing.

(ii) Combing and trailing. Molten glass is gathered onto a metal or wooden rod covered with a hard core of clay, sand and animal dung (core-forming). Soft glass of a different colour is then trailed onto the vessel and wound around from top to bottom. After re-heating the trailed thread is tooled and combed with a pointed instrument into festoons and then mar-vered (rolled) on a flat surface to even out the wall thickness. Combed decoration was one of the earliest forms of decoration used on glass and was first used in Mesopotamia and extensively employed by the Egyptians. The same basic technique was also employed to create designs that were not marvered into the body; items with this type of decoration date from the late 1st century AD in the Ancient Near East. Trailing was used to great effect on Roman glass, particularly with 'ṣnake-thread' trails. In the Merovingian and Carolingian periods long, vertical and spiral trails, nipped together to form a lattice pattern, were extensively used.

(iii) Prunts. To create this type of decoration blobs of molten glass are dropped onto the surface of the glass randomly or in a pattern. They were made in a variety of forms and sizes and left either plain or sometimes impressed with a stamp to create such forms as 'raspberries', which are often a feature on the roemer. The 'claw beaker' or *Rüsselbecher* was formed by drawing out the applied blob of glass into a hollow proboscis, pulling it out and fusing it to another part of the object; these vessels were made extensively in northern Europe during the Frankish period (5th–8th century AD). The claws were some-times further decorated with trails (e.g. beaker, 6th century; London, BM). From the medieval period the Rhenish glassmakers decorated beakers with rows of prunts (e.g. *Stangenglas*, early 16th century, London, BM). Finger cups (*Daumenglas*) were formed using the same basic principle but the applied blobs were flattened and then drawn inwards when the glassblower inhaled through the blow-pipe so that the blobs intruded creating convenient indentations for the fingers.

(iv) Air bubbles and twists. Accidental or deliberate in-clusions of air in the glass have been used to deco-rative effect since glassmaking began. Trapped single or multiple air bubbles, for example, are one of the simplest methods of decorating a stem. A 'teardrop' stem is formed by indenting (pegging) a small de-pression in the still plastic rod of glass, which is then engulfed with a gob of molten glass to trap the air; the ductile rod is then drawn out so that the air forms the shape of a teardrop. To create a single air-twist stem the same principle is used and the rod twisted

so that the air bubble becomes a helix. To produce a multiple air-twist stem the top of the malleable glass rod is tweaked with tools to create furrows; the shape is then immersed in molten glass, which seals in the pockets of air; the pontil is then securely held while the other end is rotated to create shafts of twisted air throughout the stem; the process can be repeated many times to produce more twists. Opaque-white or coloured strands of glass can be imbedded in transparent glass by rolling a gather of glass over canes set at regular intervals, marvering and blowing the gather into the desired form. Stems of this type of decoration were known as cotton-twist stems. The generic term for decoration using imbedded tapers of opaque-white or coloured glass is *filigrana* (filigree) and although first used in Murano during the early 16th century, it was probably in-spired by the rolled edges used to decorate mosaic glass made during the Hellenic period in Europe.

2. COLD-WORKING

(i) Engraving. (ii) Cutting. (iii) Etching. (iv) Sand blasting.

(i) Engraving. This technique involves cutting a design onto a glass surface, using such sharp implements as flints, diamond needles or wheels; the process is similar to gem-engraving. The method of wheel-engraving was first used to decorate Roman glass from the third quarter of the 1st century AD; the process involves cutting patterns on the surface of the glass using discs of hard materials (e.g. copper) and an abrasive (e.g. emery). Suitable metals for wheel-engraving are potash lime glass and the lead glass invented by the English glassmaker GEORGE RAVENSCROFT in 1676. Caspar Lehmann, a gem-engraver working in Prague at the court of Rudolf II, is credited as being the first glass-engraver in modern times to have used wheel-engraving. The two types of wheel-engraving are high-relief engraving (*hochs-chnitt*), where the ground is cut back leaving the de-sign in relief, and intaglio (*tiefschnitt*), where the design is formed by incisions into the surface. Diamond-point engraving involves creating a design by lightly scratching onto the surface of the glass with a dia-mond point. The technique was possibly first used in ancient Rome and in Venice (*see* VENICE, §2) in the 16th century and by glassmakers imitating the Venetian style. Another form of diamond-point en-graving, known as stipple-engraving, was introduced *c.* 1621 by ANNA VISSCHER in Holland and was de-veloped during the 17th century. A diamond point is set into a hammer and very gently tapped on to the surface of the object creating a series of dots; high-lighted areas contain a high concentration of dots, while dark areas have few or no dots.

(ii) Cutting. This process involves faceting or cutting furrows in a variety of decorative designs by sub-jecting the glass to a rotating iron or stone disc and abrasives. The technique was used in Mesopotamia during the 5th and 6th centuries and was very common in Roman times. It reached its apogee in England and Ireland during the late 18th and 19th

centuries when lead glass—the most suitable metal for deep cutting—was available.

(iii) Etching. This technique was first introduced in Europe during the 17th century and was extensively used in the 19th century using hydrofluoric acid. The glass is first covered with an acid resist (usually wax) and a design is cut through. The item is then immersed in an acid bath and the exposed design is corroded. The finish is either satin or very matt depending on the length of immersion. For an overall, matt surface the whole item can be immersed, unprotected, into the acid. This technique has been largely superseded by sand blasting.

(iv) Sand blasting. This technique involves subjecting the surface of the glass, which was partly covered by a steel template, to a jet of air containing sand, crushed flint or powdered iron. It was invented in 1870 by Benjamin Tilghnman in Philadelphia and proved to be a highly effective method of decorating. It has largely replaced acid etching as it is both safer and cheaper.

See also CAMEO GLASS; CASED GLASS.

3. COLOURED GLASS. This is achieved either by accidental discolouration owing to impurities in the batch or through the deliberate addition of metal oxides. Early glass was often coloured in order to imitate such hardstones as agate, lapis lazuli, jasper, turquoise, chalcedony or porphyry. In order to create the opaque, marbled effect of some of these stones, differently coloured opaque glass is briefly mingled in a melting pot before being gathered and shaped.

Louis Comfort Tiffany: blue glass vase (Washington, DC, Smithsonian Institution)

The process was first used in the eastern Mediterranean from the 2nd century BC. The process was revived in Venice during the early 15th century, when chalcedony glass was produced. During the 19th century variegated, polychrome glass was very popular throughout Europe; the most notable exponent of this technique was the glassmaker FRIEDRICH EGERMANN, who in 1828 created 'Lithyalin' glass.

Mosaic glass refers to glass objects rather than the panels made from tiny tesserae embedded in floors, walls and ceilings. This process involves fusing together varicoloured blobs of glass and drawing them out into thin canes. Once cooled the canes are sliced horizontally. The slices are then applied to a mould of the desired shape and then another mould is fitted over in order to keep the slices in position while in the furnace. The surface of the cooled object is ground smooth.

Another method for making such objects as mosaic, hemispherical bowls is by arranging the slices of cane on a flat fireproof clay surface and firing them in the furnace until fused. The disc of glass is then surrounded by a twisted cane of glass and reheated; while still soft it is placed over a clay form and reintroduced into the furnace where it slides down around the mould. Once cooled the object can be ground smooth and polished. This process is known as slumping.

Mosaic beads are made by rolling small blobs of glass over a flat surface covered with tiny slices of the cane. The sections are caught up and marvered into the parent glass and once cooled the beads can be smoothed and polished. *Millefiori* (It.: 'thousand flowers') glass is made using the same basic techniques as those for making mosaic glass. The gathers to make the canes are arranged so as to resemble flowers and when sliced are embedded in a matrix of molten, coloured or colourless glass. The basic technique was probably first introduced in northern Mesopotamia during the 15th century BC (e.g. fragment of a beaker from Tell el-Rimah, mid-15th century BC; London, BM). It was also used with a degree of sophistication by the Hellenistic glassmakers during the second half of the 3rd century BC. The technique reached its apogee in Venice where it was reintroduced and reinvented at the end of the 15th century.

4. PAINTING

　(i) Cold painting. (ii) Enamelling. (iii) Lustering. (iv) Staining. (v) Gilding. (vi) Gold engraving.

(i) Cold painting. Lacquer colours or oil paints can be applied to glass but are not fired. They are sometimes applied to the back of the object in order that the decoration be protected, otherwise it is liable to rub off. The colours are usually applied to objects too large to fit into the muffle kiln or to those that cannot withstand a second firing to fix the colours.

(ii) Enamelling. Enamel colours are metallic oxides mixed with finely ground glass suspended in an oily medium. While the item is fired at a low temperature

(700–900°C) in a muffle kiln, the medium is fired away and the colours are fused as a film on the surface of the object. Enamelling was used on both Roman and Byzantine glass and was combined with extensive gilding on Islamic glass. The *Hausmaler* refined the Dutch method of decorating with transparent, black enamel (*schwarzlot*) during the 17th century. After *c.* 1810, thick opaque enamels were largely superseded by transparent, polychrome enamels developed in Bohemia.

(iii) Lustering. In order to achieve an overall lustrous effect the surface of the glass is painted with an oily medium in which metallic oxides of gold, silver, copper or platinum dissolved in acid are suspended. The glass is then fired in a reducing atmosphere and a thin film of metal is fused to the surface. This technique was first used in Egypt from the 9th century AD. Lustre-painted glass is also known as iridescent glass and was used to great effect during the ART NOUVEAU period in Europe and the USA by such artists as LOUIS COMFORT TIFFANY, and at such factories as LÖTZ WITWE in Bohemia.

(iv) Staining. Pigments of various colours can be brushed on to the surface of the glass in order to give the impression of stained glass. In the late 13th century silver chloride was brushed on to small panes of glass and fired for use in STAINED GLASS windows. The technique was used on early Islamic glass, and during the 9th century silver chloride was used to produce a yellow stain on Bohemian glass. Glass with staining can be cut through in order to reveal the colourless, transparent glass beneath.

(v) Gilding. This process involves applying gold in the form of leaf, paint or powder to the surface of glass. GILDING can be used alone, with enamelling or with engraving. Gold can be used to decorate the edges of objects or more extensively to create a series of intricate motifs or scenes. It can be applied to the surface of the object in a number of ways using a suspension of honey or mercury or a fixative. With honey gilding the gold leaf is mashed up with the sticky substance, painted on to the object and fired at a low temperature; the deposit is a very soft lustrous gold. The process of mercury gilding involves applying an amalgam of gold and mercury on the surface of the glass; when the mercury burns away, the gold is deposited on the surface. Gold applied in both of these ways can be burnished. Cold gilding or oil gilding involves applying gold leaf to a surface already brushed with linseed oil. This form of decoration is not very permanent and easily rubs off.

(vi) Gold engraving. This form of decoration involves engraving gold leaf with a fine needle and applying it to the outer surface of the glass. Unless it is somehow protected, however, the gold will rub off. One of the ways to ensure the longevity of the gold leaf is by sealing it between two layers of glass. The process involves applying gold leaf to the surface of a usually clear, colourless object, covering it entirely with another sheet of glass and fusing the two layers

together. The earliest known examples of this type of decoration are Hellenistic (e.g. Canosa bowls *c.* 200 BC; London, BM). During the first half of the 18th century, the technique became particularly popular in Germany and is known as *Zwischengoldglas*. In France the technique is known as *verre églomisé*. Gold leaf can also be protected by a layer of varnish or metal foil.

5. ICE GLASS. This decorative glass, the surface of which appears frosted or cracked, is achieved by one of two methods: the first involves plunging a blown gather of glass in a tub of water and then quickly reheating it; the second method involves rolling the gather of glass on a clay or metal surface on which randomly placed fragments of glass have been positioned so as to adhere to the gather. The technique was first introduced in Venice during the 16th century.

6. SULPHIDES. During the 19th century, cut glass was sometimes further decorated with small cameo-like encrustations known as sulphides. These opaque-white ceramic medallions usually depicting busts or figures were embedded on the sides or bottoms of clear, often colourless, glass objects. The technique was invented by Barthélemy Desprez (*fl* 1773–1819) in France. The technique was also extensively used to decorate paperweights.

R. J. Charleston: 'Dutch Decoration of English Glass', *Trans. Soc. Glass Technol.*, xli (1957), pp. 229–43

R. J. Charleston: 'Wheel Engraving and Cutting: Some Early Equipment', *J. Glass Stud.*, vi (1964), pp. 83–100; vii (1965), pp. 41–54

D. C. Davis and K. Middlemas: *Coloured Glass* (London, 1968)

P. Jokelson: *Sulphides: The Art of Cameo Incrustation* (New York, 1968)

R. J. Charleston: 'Enamelling and Gilding on Glass', *Glass Circ.*, i (1972), pp. 18–32

S. M. Goldstein, S. Rackow and J. K. Rackow: *Cameo Glass Masterpieces from 2000 Years of Glassmaking* (Corning, 1982)

J. S. Spillman: *Pressed Glass, 1825–1925* (Corning, 1983)

C. Bray: *Dictionary of Glass Materials and Techniques* (London, 1995)

R. Barovier Mentasti: *Glass Throughout Time: History and Technique of Glassmaking from the Ancient World to the Present* (Milan, 2003)

J. Shelby: *Introduction to Glass Science and Technology* (Alfred, NY, 1997, rev. 2/2005)

II. Glass in the Decorative arts.

Glass has been manufactured throughout history for the production of decorative arts by many different cultures and civilizations. The ability of glass to be shaped into an endless variety of forms, cut and coloured has ensured its popularity. The history and use of glass as a decorative art are covered in detail in this encyclopedia under the relevant countries and civilizations.

Glass has often been regarded as a luxury commodity and the earliest use of glass reflects this attitude. Such items as amphoriskoi and alabastra were made from glass as containers for expensive oils, perfumes and unguents. Beads, at first made in blue and black glass and later in a variety of colours and decorated with stripes and spots and later zigzags and chevrons, were first made in Egypt during the 5th Dynasty (*c.* 2465–*c.* 2325 BC); they were threaded into necklaces and bracelets (*see* BEADWORK.). Other early uses of glass included gaming-pieces, amulets, pendants and such small sculptures as sacred bulls and rams and shabtis. During the New Kingdom (*c.* 1540–*c.* 1075 BC) glass inlays were made for jewellery and furniture and for setting in gold or other precious metals. In China, glass was first used in the Western Zhou period (*c.* 1050–771 BC), to make mosaic beads, eyebeads (*bi*) and decorative hairpins. Glass beads were also made during the iron age in Europe, as were gaming-pieces, bracelets and inlays for jewellery. The Romans used glass for a variety of purposes and many examples are extant. Glass was used extensively to make tesserae for mosaics. Glass was also the principal source for the tesserae needed for mosaics and *opus sectile* panels used in Early Christian and Byzantine art to decorate walls, ceilings and floors.

Because of the refractive nature of glass, it is supremely suitable for lighting fixtures. Although many early lamps were made of terracotta or bronze, glass examples are known from the Roman period (e.g. lamp, 2nd century AD; London, BM). Particularly fine Islamic mosque lamps, many of which have survived, were made towards the end of the 13th century. These three-sectioned lamps (spread base, bulbous body and flared neck) were fitted with rings so that they could be suspended from the ceiling. Many

were decorated with enamelled and gilded arabesques, Arabic inscriptions in cursive script (*naskhi*), heraldic devices, flowers and foliage. As the skill of the glassmaker developed, lighting fixtures became increasingly sophisticated and intricate, culminating in the glass CHANDELIER.

Glass has been used to make mirrors since at least the 1st century BC, when mirrors were made of silvered glass in Egypt. The Roman glassmakers backed their mirrors with a metallic substance or a dark resin to create a reflective surface. By the 16th century the Venetians had produced a superior mirror backed with an amalgam of tin and mercury; the process was known as silvering. Mirrors were in great demand from the 17th century and were framed with lavish surrounds of wood decorated with paint, lacquer, gilding, ivory or precious metals. Such was the expense of glass in the 17th and 18th centuries that rulers, eager to show off their wealth, would sometimes decorate whole rooms with panels of glass; the most famous room is the Galerie des Glaces at the château of Versailles. Towards the end of the 18th century it became possible to make very large sheets of glass, but the maximum sizes feasible before this were comparatively small and this dictated the often elaborate style of larger mirror frames in which several small pieces of glass were fitted together in patterns around larger sheets. Coloured glass inlays have been used as a way of decorating furniture since they were first employed in this capacity in ancient Egypt and were used to decorate drawer fronts on some bureaux in Venice during the 18th century. During the 19th century press-moulded drawer handles were widely produced in both Europe and the USA and even entire pieces of furniture were made of glass (e.g. toilet-table, designed by Voronikhin, 1804; Corning, NY, Mus. Glass). During the 19th century, many unlikely items were made entirely of glass (e.g. birdcages and clock-cases), some specifically for the international exhibitions in order to demonstrate the virtuosity of the factory or maker; one of the most outstanding examples was the glass fountain (destr. 1936), made by F. & C. Osler of Birmingham, that formed the centrepiece of the Crystal Palace in London where the Great Exhibition of 1851 was held. The paperweight, another 19th-century invention, was extremely popular throughout Europe; it was made in a variety of forms and decorated using a wide range of techniques from cutting to decorative inclusions.

B. Morris: *Victorian Table Glass and Ornaments* (London, 1978)

R. Grover and L. Grover: *Art Glass Nouveau* (Tuttle, 1979)

V. Arwas: *Glass, Art Nouveau to Art Deco* (London, 1980)

R. von Strasser and W. Spiegel: *Dekoriertes Glas: Renaissance bis Biedermeier: Katalog Raisonné der Sammlung Rudolph von Strasser* (Munich, 1989)

S. Petrová, J.-L. Olivié and G. Urbánek: *Bohemian Glass: 1400–1989* (New York, 1990).

N. Fyson: *Decorative Glass of the 19th and Early 20th Centuries* (Newton Abbot, 1996)

A. Macfarlane and G. Martin: *Glass: A World History* (Chicago, 2002)

O. Hicks: *Beginner's Guide to Stained & Decorative Glass* (New York, 2002)

M. Block: *The Encyclopedia of Modern Marbles, Spheres, & Orbs* (Atglen, PA, 2005)

Hanging mosque lamp, enamelled glass, Hons, Mamluk dynasty, *c.* 1300 (Damascus, National Museum)

C. Hess and K. Wight: *Looking at Glass: A Guide to Terms, Styles and Techniques* (V&A, London, 2005)

Glaze. Glassy coating applied to clay bodies to make them impervious to liquids or more visually pleasing. The high silica content of most glazes provides the 'glass', while small amounts of alumina control the fluidity of the glaze. These materials can be present either in the glaze mixture or available in the body clay. The common names for glazes are usually in reference to the flux being used. Lead glazes, for example, are fluxed with lead oxides; they are reliable, easy to control, smooth, glossy, nearly colourless and transparent, although they can be opacified by the addition of tin oxide to produce a tin glaze. Lead glazes must be fired at a low temperature, in an oxidizing atmosphere, as reduction reduces it to its blackened metallic state. Disadvantages include solubility in mild acids, problems with 'fitting' the glaze to the body and its poisonous nature (a danger reduced by fritting the oxide). Bristol glaze, developed in England in the 19th century, contains a high zinc oxide content and is a safe alternative to lead. Although popular, it did not have the clarity and range of lead-fluxed glazes.

Iron oxide, an effective flux, is found in high percentages in slip glazes. Fired in oxidation, the glaze burns to a rich, dense, opaque brown, sometimes with controlled decorative crystalline textures. Because of the large clay content in slip glazes, relatively high temperatures are required to fuse the glaze, thus restricting its use to high-firing stoneware and porcelain.

Alkaline glazes are typically fluxed with such alkalines as lime, soda or potash; they are glassy and soft with a tendency to craze. They are often used on low-firing wares, although for higher-burning ceramics the temperature can be raised with an addition of feldspar. Alkaline glazes can create brilliant but different coloured oxide effects than lead glaze. Mottled ash glazes are dependent on the type of ash used for their colour and textural effects.

Salt glazing takes place during a single firing, which hardens and glazes stoneware. As the clay reaches its 'maturing' temperature (1200–1300°C) salt is introduced into the kiln through special holes. As the salt vaporizes and splits into its component elements, the sodium combines with the silica in the body to form a thin, glossy, orange-peel textured glaze; the chlorine escapes out of the kiln chimney as hydrochloric gas.

Feldspathic glazes include those used on high-fired wares. Formed in part of kaolin and petuntse, they require high temperatures to fuse them to the clay body. The glaze is fired at the same time as the body and forms a clear, very hard and durable glossy finish. Feldspar is also an ingredient in some lower-fired glazes and clay bodies.

To prepare the glaze, the raw materials are purified and pulverized into a uniform fine-textured mixture; some ingredients can be fritted (melted and ground) first. The glaze is applied to the clay body as a powder or as a suspension in water. After drying, the body and glaze can be hardened in a single firing, or a 'glost' firing fuses the glaze if the clay has already been biscuit-fired. Firing fuses the glaze materials, as well as adhering them to the body surface. Such higher-fired wares as hard-paste porcelains with nearly similar glaze and body recipes acquire the best-fitting glazes. Lower-fired earthenwares can show a different shrinkage rate between the body and glaze, resulting in crazing or flaking.

S. Murfitt: *The Glaze book* (Iola, 2002)
M. Burleson: *The Ceramic Glaze Handbook: Materials, Techniques, Formulas* (New York, 2003)
E. Cooper: *The Potter's Book of Glaze Recipes* (London, 2004)
Glazes: Materials, Recipes and Techniques, American Ceramic Society (Westerville, 2004)

Glinitz Pottery. Ceramic factory founded in 1767 by Countess Anna Barbara von Gaschin (*b c.* 1730) Glinitz, Silesia (now Glinica, Poland). The pottery made TIN-GLAZED EARTHENWARE and (from *c.* 1830) CREAMWARE.

Gmunden. Austrian centre of ceramic production. The existence of a pottery tradition in Gmunden was discovered during excavations in 1955 when a settlement with pottery dating from the Roman period was found at nearby Engelhof. At the end of the 16th century seven potters were resident in Gmunden, but by 1747 there were only three. Local clays from Baumgarten and Vichtau were used, and the earliest pottery consisted of rather plain dishes for everyday use, which were based on Italian models.

During the 17th, 18th and 19th centuries the Gmunden potteries produced mainly marbled wares using a combination of green, blue, grey, brown and white glazes. In addition to tankards and jugs, the most popular form was the so-called 'Pfeifenschüssel', an oval plate with an undulating edge, which was mainly used as a wall decoration. Green and brown mottled ware was developed from *c.* 1600 as attempts were made to achieve a marbled effect on a white glaze by using dots and flecks of colour. Originally, in addition to light green and cobalt blue, rich green and brown were also used; from the second half of the 18th century the markings were mainly in green and the pottery was known commercially as 'Grüngeflammte' ware and became popular as typical Gmunden pottery. At the same time an 'Alt-Gmundner-Fayence' was being developed on which pictorial decoration of the human figure and views of Gmunden were used rather than ornament. For centuries Gmunden pottery presented a stylistically unified picture in the forms and patterns used by its few workshops.

The link with developments in pottery-making resulting from 19th-century industrialization was made by Franz Schleiss the elder (*d* 1887), who began potting in 1843 when he bought Ignaz Pott's pottery workshop. After Schleiss's death the company was taken over by his son Leopold Schleiss, who left the

Two fruit bowls carried by putti, ceramic, h. 350 mm, Gmunden (Private Collection)

premises in 1903 and continued production at the newly built Gmundner Tonwarenfabrik in Traunleiten. Leopold's son Franz Schleiss the younger and Franz's wife Emilie Schleiss had both studied at the Kunstgewerbeschule (now the Hochschule für Angewante Kunst) in Vienna and had been pupils of Michael Powolny. They brought the factory to a peak of artistic achievement through their contacts with Viennese art potters. In 1913 a fruitful collaboration was achieved when the Künstlerische Werkstätte Franz und Emilie Schleiss merged with the Wiener Keramik to become the Vereinigte Wiener und Gmundner Keramik. A wide range of models were produced, and as a result of the contributions of Michael Powolny, Bertold Löffler (1874–1960), Dagobert Peche, Julius Feldmann and Ida Schwetz-Lehmann, the artistic quality was extremely high.

In 1917 Franz Schleiss founded the Keramische Schule Schleiss to provide artistic training for the next generation of potters. In 1923 he opened the Gmundner Werkstätten, where many pieces were decorated with designs based on work by Ludwig Galasek, Edith Hirschhorn and Vally Wieselthier (1895–1945). In the same year the Keramik Schleiss separated from the Gmundner Keramik group and moved back to the previous premises in Theatergasse. Such eminent artists as Josef Hoffmann and Wolfgang von Wersin (1882–1976) worked for Keramik Schleiss, which produced only studio pottery.

The production of simple, everyday wares and high-quality services based on designs by artists was taken on by the company known as Gmundner Keramik AG based in Traunleiten. When the firm was taken over by the Hohenberg family it became Gmundner Keramik-Hohenberg, and a special unit called Atelier H was established where such art potters as Gudrun Baudisch, Anton Raidel and Wolfgang von Wersin were employed to produce pieces of high artistic quality.

Gmundner Keramik: Von der grüngeflammten Hafnerware bis zu den künstlerischen Entwicklungen der Gegenwart (Gmunden, 1978)

Gobelins. French factory (Manufacture royale des meubles de la Couronne) established in Paris in 1662 for the production of furnishings for the royal household. The factory employed gold- and silversmiths, bronze-workers, sculptors, wood-carvers, painters and hardstone cutters, but is best known for its tapestries.

Gobelins Tapestry Factory. French tapestry factory. On 8 March 1663 Louis XIV (*reg* 1643–1715) appointed the painter and designer CHARLES LE BRUN as the first director of the Gobelins factory. Le Brun employed painters who specialized in different genres (flowers, animals, decorations, landscapes, history) and required them to transfer his designs (and those of his collaborators) into cartoons intended for the weavers. The heads of the workshops, who were responsible to Le Brun, were Jean Jans (*fl* 1662–8) from Flanders, Jean Lefèbvre (1600–75) and Henri Laurent for the three high-warp workshops and Jean de La Croix and Jean-Baptiste Mozin (*fl* 1667–93) for the low-warp workshops; they were contractors in charge of the weaving and were eventually allowed to accept private commissions. About 250 weavers lived in and around the Gobelins enclosure. Josse van der Kerchove directed the dyeing workshop. The head of each workshop was responsible for his own accounts. Tapestries were paid for on delivery according to a fixed price, from which the cost of materials (wools, silks, gold and silver threads) supplied by the Crown was deducted. The weavers were paid by the workshop heads according to a wage-scale peculiar to high or low warp, based on the difficulty of the work; for example, such weavers entrusted with heads and flesh tones as Louis Ovis de La Tour (*d* 1735) received the highest wages. The system remained until 1790, when workers began to be paid with a fixed salary.

Under the impetus and authority of Le Brun the tapestries and other works produced until the end of the 17th century constituted an important contribution to the history of the decorative arts in France. The tapestry *Louis XIV Visiting the Gobelins*, from Le Brun's celebrated series the *Story of the King*, accurately

Gobelins tapestry, *The Taking of Lille by Louis XIV, August, 1667* (detail showing Louis XIV giving orders to the Marquis d'Humières), from the series *Story of the King*, 3rd series, 8th piece, from the studio of Jean-Baptiste Mozin after a design by Charles Le Brun, 1665–80 (Versailles, Château)

represents the precious furnishings and rich hangings made at the Gobelins for the decoration of such royal residences as Versailles. Aside from the *Story of the King*, the most famous hangings for which Le Brun provided designs include the *Elements*, the *Four Seasons*, the *Story of Alexander* and the *Months* or the *Royal Households*; these assured the success and lasting renown of the factory. Le Brun also had tapestries made after other artists, including Raphael (*Acts of the Apostles* and the *Vatican Stanze*) and Nicholas Poussin (1594–1665; *Story of Moses*).

In 1686 work began on the *Gallery of Saint-Cloud* after paintings by Le Brun's rival and successor, Pierre Mignard (1612–95). Despite the lack of new, suitable designs, the workshops' output did not abate; 16th-century tapestries from the Garde Meuble de la Couronne were copied, including the *Story of Scipio*, *Fructus Belli*, *Mois Lucas* and the *Hunts of Maximilian*. Hangings from this period also heralded an evolution in taste: exoticism appeared in the tapestries known as the *Indies* after paintings by Gerbrand van den Eeckhout and Frans Post, which had been presented to Louis XIV (*reg* 1643–1715) by Johan Maurits, Count of Nassau-Siegen (1604–79). Decorative elements were brought back into fashion by Noël Coypel in the *Triumphs of the Gods*, after a 16th-century tapestry from Brussels.

Owing to the wars and the ensuing financial problems, the factory almost closed completely in April 1694: the tapestry-workers were dismissed and many dispersed; some went back to Flanders, while others went to the tapestry factory in Beauvais. The contractors nevertheless managed to maintain one low-warp workshop, which facilitated the reopening of the tapestry works in January 1699. The architect Jules Hardouin Mansart (1646–1708), the new Surintendant des Bâtiments, appointed the architect and urban planner Robert de Cotte (1656/7–1735) to direct proceedings. Until 1780 architects, the most famous of which was Jacques-Germain Soufflot (1713–80), would succeed to this post. As the director no longer supplied designs, renowned painters were called upon to provide cartoons. The new tapestries reflect the evolution towards a lighter, more delicate style that was better suited to the more intimate decoration of smaller apartments. At the beginning of the 18th century tapestries after designs by Claude Audran III (1658–1734; for example the *Portières des dieux* and the *Douze mois grotesques*) were the first indications of this change.

The most important innovation, however, which was successful for a long period, was that of tapestries *à alentours* (with borders). They depicted prominent decorative motifs, reminiscent of friezes, wainscots, cords and ribbons, surrounding a central scene. This new style was initiated as early as 1714 in the cartoons for the *Story of Don Quixote* by Charles-Antoine Coypel (1694–1752); the famous *Loves of the Gods* (1763) by François Boucher and others also employed this method of design. Throughout the 18th century the tradition of large hangings was maintained: tapestries depicting such historic events as the visit of the *Turkish Embassy* in 1731 after paintings by Charles Parrocel (1688–1752), the *Hunts of Louis XV* after Jean-Baptiste Oudry or those depicting religious or mythological subjects (e.g. the *Story of Esther* and the *Story of Jason* after François de Troy (1645–1730) and the *Story of Theseus* after Carle Vanloo (1705–65) were manufactured. As Surinspecteur, Oudry had a strong influence on the development of design at the factory; he required the weavers' complete submission to painting and obliged them to 'imitate its effects'. In order to achieve this they used a wide range of graded colours, obtained by *petits teints* (non-fast dyes), which have often failed to withstand the effects of time and light. This direction towards the imitation of painting continued for a long period in spite of some interruptions. Woven portraits, the first of which was of *Louis XV* after Vanloo, were very much in favour for many years.

In the second half of the 18th century the influence of Neo-classicism appeared, for example in the *Four Seasons* (1773) after Antoine-François Callet. Returning to the tradition of the 17th century, Jean-Baptiste Pierre (1714–89), the king's Premier Peintre, became Directeur in 1782; he was the last to attain this position. At the end of the *ancien régime* there was a taste for themes inspired by national history, including the *Story of Henry IV* after François-André Vincent (1746–1816) and the *History of France* after Joseph-Benoît Suvée (1743–1807), Louis-Jacques Durameau (1733–96) and Jean-Simon Berthélemy (1743–1811).

After the difficulties of the revolutionary period, activity at the factory, which was linked to Napoleon's Liste Civile, was revived during the Empire Period (1804–15). Tapestries for the imperial palaces intended 'to perpetuate the great events of his reign' were produced, including *Bonaparte Crossing the St Bernard Pass* after Jacques-Louis David (1748–1825), the *Plague at Jaffa* after Antoine-Jean Gros (1771–1835) and *Napoleon Receiving his Deputies after his Coronation* after Gioacchino Giuseppe Sérangeli (1768–1852). The *Tenture de la Salle du Trône* after Georges Rouget (1784–1869) is an important example made during the Restoration (1815–30). In 1826 the low-warp works were moved to Beauvais, and work at the Gobelins was focused on the high warp. In 1828 work began on the *Story of Marie de' Medici* after Peter Paul Rubens (1577–1640).

Throughout the 19th century efforts were made to restore tapestry as a creative decorative art and extricate it from its role of an art form merely imitating painting: for the July Monarchy (1830–48) *Le Grand Décor* after Jean Alaux (1786–1864) and Couderc was made; from the Second Empire (1852–70) important tapestries include the *Five Senses* after Jules Pierre Michel Diéterle (1811–89), Paul Baudry (1828–86) and Pierre-Adrien Chabal-Dussurgey (1819–1902). Woven portraits were not entirely abandoned, as the important commission (1851) for representations of sovereigns and artists for the Galerie d'Apollon in the Louvre testifies. An unsettled and difficult period began after the fall of the Second Empire, and part of the buildings was burnt in 1871. During the early years of the Third Republic (1870–1940) the Gobelins (renamed the Manufacture Nationale des Gobelins) produced tapestries for such great buildings in Paris as the Opéra, the Palais du Luxembourg and the Bibliothèque Nationale. Care was once again taken to create new designs in which the decorative element dominated; such artists as Alexis Joseph Mazerolle (1826–89), Emile François Maloisel (*fl* 1868–1912), Paul Flandrin (1811–1902), Alfred de Curzon (1820–95), François Emile Ehrmann (1833–1910) and Jean-Paul Laurens (1838–1921) were called upon to provide these designs. At the Exposition Universelle of 1900 in Paris tapestries after Gustave Moreau (1826–98) and Georges Rochegrosse (1852–1938) were exhibited. In the following years such artists as Jules Chéret (1836–1932), Félix Bracquemond (1833–1914), Odilon Redon (1840–1916), Adrien Karbowski (*b* 1855) and Leonetto Capiello (1875–1942) also provided designs.

It was, however, jean Lurçat who essentially revived the art of tapestry production in order to restore it 'to the grand art of the Middle Ages'. Lurçat advocated 'the liberation from painting, the use of a reduced range of colours, at once straightforward and vivid, the suppression of graded colours, clarity of design'. In 1937 the Gobelins was attached to the Administration Générale of the Mobilier Nationale, and Lurçat was commissioned for two cartoons, the *Illusions of Icarus* and the *Forests*, which were begun in the same year. Inspired by Lurçat the painters Marcel Gromaire (1892–1971) and Pierre Dubreuil (1891–1970) also became enthusiastic about tapestries. In 1939 the Gobelins was moved to Aubusson, where it remained during World War II. There Gromaire, Dubreuil and Lurçat went 'to study, create and supervise, if necessary, the execution of large tapestries' and helped promote a revived interest in tapestry, which once again became an art in which great painters took an interest.

From 1945 painters, sculptors, printmakers and architects realized that the way opened by Lurçat was rich in possibilities; of different aesthetic leanings, they remained faithful to his great, rediscovered principles. The Gobelins continued to honour great contemporary artists, including Picasso (whose cartoon of 1936–7 for *Women at their Toilet* was woven in 1968), Serge Poliakoff (1906–69), Alexander Calder (1898–1976), Zao Wou-Ki (*b* 1921) and Joan Miró (1893–1983). The tradition of hanging monumental tapestries in official buildings was retained particularly with such work as the designs for the Bureau International du Travail in Geneva by Pierre Courtin (*b* 1921), Guitet's for the Ecole Nationale d'Administration in Paris and those of François Rouan (*b* 1943) for the new Ministère des Finances at Bercy, Paris. The Gobelins output was always primarily reserved for the State, although such prestigious private commissions as the tapestry for the Queen of Denmark after cartoons by the sculptor Bjørn Nørgaard (*b* 1947) were also made.

M. Fenaille: *Etat général des tapisseries de la manufacture des Gobelins depuis son origine jusqu'à nos jours, 1600–1900*, 4 vols (Paris, 1903–23)

T. Hans-Jaworska, *Gobelin Tapestries* (exh. cat., Edinburgh, 1968)

Goblet. Drinking-cup of metal or glass, properly bowl-shaped and without handles, sometimes mounted on a foot and fitted with a cover.

Goddard, John (*b* Dartmouth, MA, 20 Jan 1723; *d* Newport, RI, 9 July 1785). American cabinetmaker. His father, Daniel Goddard, a housewright, shipwright and carpenter, moved his family to Newport, RI, soon after John's birth to join the Quaker community there. At probably age 13 John began an eight-year apprenticeship to Job TOWNSEND. In 1748 Goddard opened a cabinetmaking with five work benches. He apparently employed his sons to help him. At least three of them—Townsend Goddard (1750–90), Stephen Goddard (1764–1804) and Thomas Goddard (1765–1858)—went on to set up their own shops.Goddard made a wide range of furniture, including three signed, slant-lid desks with blocked fronts and shell carvings (e.g. of 1765–75; Providence, RI Hist. Soc.), but it is uncertain whether he made any of the great block and shell bookcase-desks once ascribed to him. The business was carried on by Stephen and Thomas Goddard until 1804. Stephen's son, John Goddardjr (*d* 1843), also worked as a cabinetmaker. Furniture attributed to Goddard now commands higher prices than the work of any other American cabinetmaker: In 1989 the 'Nicholas Brown desk' was sold for $12.1 million, and in 2005 a tea-table was sold for $7.5 million and a pair of chairs for $3.28 million.

M. Moses: *Master Craftsmen of Newport: The Townsends and Goddards* (Tenafly, 1984)

R. Carpenter: *The Magnificent Nicholas Brown Desk and Bookcase: Comparison and Brief Commentary* (sale cat., Christie's, New York, 1989)

John Townsend: Newport Cabinetmaker (exh. cat. by M. H. Heckscher; New York, Met., 2005)

Godet and goddard. Terms for a late medieval drinking cup. A godet is a shallow cup with a handle; the term 'goddard' may refer to a godet, but sometimes denotes a goblet without handles.

Gödöllő colony. Hungarian artists' colony. It was formed in 1901 at Gödöllő, near Budapest, when the painter Aladár Körösfői-Kriesch (1863–1920) undertook to revive the traditional art of weaving with looms donated by the Ministry of Culture. Members included Sándor Nagy (1869–1950) and his wife, the painter and designer Laura Kriesch (1879–1966), Ervin Raálo (1874–1959), Jenő Remsey (1885–1980), Endre Frecskai (1875–1919), Léo Belmonte (1870–1956), Árpád Juhász (1863–1914), Rezső Mihály (1889–1972), István Zichy (1879–1951), Mariska Undi (1887–1959), Carla Undi (1881–1956) and the sculptor Ferenc Sidló (1882–1953). Inspired by the ideals of John Ruskin (1819–1900) and William Morris (1834–1896) and by the heroic vision of peasant life celebrated by Tolstoy, the group established workshops in ceramics, sculpture, leatherwork, furniture-making, embroidery, book-binding and illustration, fabric and wallpaper design and, most importantly, in stained glass and the weaving of carpets and tapestries coloured with vegetable dyes. Their goals were social as well as artistic: to enable the rural poor to stay on the land, they taught traditional craft techniques to local young people and exhibited their work to international acclaim. They also sought to develop a modern national style by adapting the rich forms and colourful ornament of vernacular art and architecture, which they recorded and published between 1907 and 1922 in the five-volume study, *A magyar nép müvészete* (The art of the Hungarian people). In 1909 they had a collective exhibition at the National Salon in Budapest. As artists identified with a style of romantic nationalism, Gödöllő designers and craftsmen obtained such important government commissions as the decoration of the Hungarian pavilions at international exhibitions and, in 1913, the design and decoration of the Palace of Culture of Marosvásárhely (now Tîrgu Mureş, Romania), where the stained-glass windows by Sándor Nagy and Ede Thoroczkai Wigand (1869–1945) rank as one of the greatest achievements of 20th-century Hungarian art. The colony existed until 1920. The textile workshop carried on for a few more years under the management of Sándor Nagy and the weaver Vilma Frey (1886–after 1921).

K. Gellér: *The Art Colony of Gödöllo (1901–1920)* (Gödöllo, 2001)

Godwin, E(dward) W(illiam) (*b* Bristol, 26 May 1833; *d* London, 6 Oct 1886). English architect, designer and writer. Godwin's early career as an architect reached a turning point when he won the design competition for a new town hall in Northampton (1861–4). This project allowed him to realize the ideal of 'total design', expounded in his lecture of 1863, *The Sister Arts and Their Relation to Architecture*, whereby a single spirit was expressed by a building and all its decoration and fittings. He achieved this at Northampton by designing all the furniture, stained glass, woodwork and ironwork. The stout oak chairs of the council chamber were unusually simple in construction, with arms composed of semicircles of wood, which complemented the medieval character of the building.

From the 1870s most of Godwin's inadequate income came from decoration and furniture design, and architectural journalism. His earliest furniture was for his office in London (opened 1865). It was made of ebonized deal with 'no mouldings, no ornamental work and no carving' and was characteristic of most of his furniture designs. The 'Anglo-Japanese' furniture he designed for William Watt of Grafton Street, London, does have a Japanese sparseness of decoration, but it owes more to Godwin's imagination and design preoccupations than to the Orient (examples in London, V&A; Bristol, Mus. & A.G.).

In his final years, Godwin's longstanding interest in the theatre was to take up most of his diminishing energies. His association with the actress Ellen Terry in the late 1860s and early 1870s brought him into contact with many leading theatrical figures. His influence on designs for a production in 1875 of *The Merchant of Venice* at the Prince of Wales Theatre in London shows his principal concern was for an archaeological—then atypical—accuracy for costumes and set. His costumes reflect his concern with 'rational dress', on which he had published a pamphlet (1884) for the International Health Exhibition in London, and exemplified by the unrestrictive folds of the Japanese kimonos that he liked Ellen Terry and their children to wear.

W. Watt: *Art Furniture from Designs by E. W. Godwin and Others* (London, 1877)

E. Aslin: *E. W. Godwin: Furniture and Interior Decoration* (London, 1986)

S. Soros and C. Arbuthnott: *E. W. Godwin: Aesthetic Movement Architect and Designer* (New Haven, 1999)

S. Soros and C. Arbuthnott: *The Secular Furniture of E. W. Godwin* (New Haven, 1999)

D. Curry: *Whistler & Godwin* (London, 2001)

Goffering. *See* GAUFFERING.

Göggingen. German faience factory near Augsburg, founded in 1748 by Georg Michael Hofmann and his manager Joseph Hackhl. The factory made both functional and decorative wares, notably narrow-necked jugs and steins; some are marked 'Göggingen' and others 'HS'. The factory closed in 1752; Hackhl bought the stock and in 1754 started another factory at nearby Friedberg.

Gold. Yellow metal and one of the so-called 'noble' metal group, which also includes silver and platinum. Gold has always been highly valued for its intrinsic beauty, its working properties and its rarity—until recent times it was used to underpin the currencies of the major trading nations. A wide range of decorative techniques is available to the goldsmith, the majority of them adaptations of constructional techniques. A good example of this is granulation, which exploits the special qualities of eutectic soldering. The most typical form of granulation is where tiny spheres of gold, often only a fraction of a millimetre in diameter, are arranged in patterns on the surface of an object and soldered in position by the method described above. In the best examples, there is no sign of a join; the granules appear simply to sit on the surface of the piece. This kind of work is most closely associated with the Egyptians, the Hellenistic Greeks and in particular the Etruscans, although many cultures throughout the world have used it. Some continue to use it, as, for example, the Nepalese, while the American jeweller John Paul Miller (*b* 1914) is an outstanding exponent of the technique. During the 19th-century vogue for archaeological jewellery, several workshops specialized in granulation, the CASTELLANI family especially achieving technically brilliant results.

Other forms of decoration include FILIGREE, which has a continuous history from ancient Mesopotamia to the present, REPOUSSÉ and CHASING (which are the same technique carried out from opposite sides of the metal), ENGRAVING and carving. The earliest work in gold was done without the aid of metal tools, and possibly without pitch, but even without these, the properties of gold facilitate this method of decorating. Many ancient pieces seem to have been worked by pushing or rubbing them with wooden or bone tools into carved pieces of the same materials. A fine example, almost certainly produced by this method, is the pectoral ornament from Camirus, Rhodes (7th century BC; London, BM), which includes five almost identical plaques showing the goddess Artemis.

Repoussé and chasing have been used wherever gold has been worked, and fine examples come from the very earliest cultures (e.g. the 'diadem' found by Heinrich Schliemann at Mycenae; 16th century BC; Athens, N. Archaeol. Mus.). There was a great vogue for this type of decoration during the later Middle Ages in northern Europe, especially in Germany, where goldsmiths produced some particularly exaggerated examples. Gold pieces in England in the early 18th century were often richly decorated by this method, and many of the Art Nouveau and Arts and Crafts jewellers, for example René Lalique (1860–1945), Georges Fouquet (1862–1957) and Henry Wilson, used chasing and repoussé extensively in their designs.

Engraving involves the use of small chisels to remove metal, the technique probably deriving from the designs scratched with sharp stones on to the surface of the earliest pieces of goldwork. A good example of this, and one of the earliest, is the lunula from Ross, Co. Westmeath (1800 BC; Dublin, N. Mus.). With the advent of iron and steel tools, it became a widely used decorative technique, mainly for the enhancement of plain areas of metal. From the Middle Ages it was frequently used for the depiction of armorial bearings. A later development of engraving is engine-turning or guilloche work. Practised since the 16th century on such organic materials as wood and ivory, it was used on the precious metals from the mid-18th century. The cutting tool is connected to a geared holder on a complex lathe, which enables both the work piece and the tool to move in predetermined ways. Highly controlled designs, composed of identical but staggered lines, or of gradually changing lines or shapes, can be built up using these lathes. A very specialized technique, it can be employed on both flat and curved surfaces. It was very popular with goldsmiths from the late 19th century until World War II for such items as powder compacts and cigarette cases. Fabergé used guilloche work behind transparent enamels to achieve iridescent and silk-like effects.

Carving is related to engraving, but larger amounts of metal are removed. Some early methods probably evolved in parallel with those for carving organic materials, as well as for stone. One such is chip-carving, where a small chisel is hammered towards a central point from three or four directions, thereby removing a chip of metal. This leaves a deep triangular or rectangular recess made up of flat facets. Sometimes carving is used to create recesses that are to be filled with such other materials as enamel or niello. The latter is a black or dark silvery-grey material used as an inlay to contrast with gold. It is usually a mixture of silver, lead and sulphur, the exact proportions of which vary. The resulting compound is applied to the hot metal in granular form and worked down into the recesses with a spatula. Once cool, the surface is smoothed out and polished to give a crisp contrast between the gold and the niello. The technique has been used extensively throughout Europe and Asia and continues to be used in such places as Morocco, Thailand and Russia.

Goldscheider, Friedrich (*b* Plzeň, 6 Nov 1845; *d* Nice, 19 Jan 1897). Czech ceramics manufacturer. After completing his apprenticeship as a salesman at the haberdashery business of his father Moritz Goldscheider (*d* 1865) in Pilsen, he constructed a brickworks for the production of fireproof wares. From 1877 he became involved in the porcelain industry. After his marriage in 1873, he settled in Vienna and in 1885 established the Goldscheider'sche Porzellan-Manufaktur und Majolica-Fabrik, the success of which led to the establishment of numerous branches, including a porcelain and earthenware factory in Pilsen and a factory for painting porcelain in Karlsbad (now Karlovy Vary). In 1887 the firm participated in the International Exhibition in Leipzig, where 'maiolica' figures with thick, lead glazes were presented. Arthur Strasser, professor at the Wiener Kunstgewerbeschule, worked closely with Goldscheider, and designed numerous figures for the firm primarily in the East Asian style. Production was divided between two centres: in Vienna terracotta and maiolica figures, busts and murals were produced, while in Karlsbad porcelain dinner-services, coffee-, tea- and demi-tasse services were manufactured. In 1891 the firm was granted the patent for decorating wares with a bronze colour. The new wares achieved great popularity especially in Paris, and in 1892 Goldscheider opened a branch there for manufacturing 'bronzed' articles. After Goldscheider's death the firm was managed by his widow Regina Goldscheider and his brother Alois Goldscheider, and in 1953, owing to financial difficulties, it finally closed.

Schöner Schein: Goldscheider Keramik und andere Kunst-Stücke (exh. cat. by S. Fuchs-Nebel; Halbturn, Schloss, 1992)
Goldscheider, the Royal Family of Porcelain since 1885 (Vienna, n.d.[*c.* 1996])
Goldscheider Keramik: Historismus, Jugendstil, Art déco (exh. cat. by S. Walther; Vienna, Hist. Mus., 1996)

Gold tooling. *See* BLIND TOOLING.

Gole [Golle], **Pierre** (*b* Bergen, nr Alkmaar, *c.* 1620; *d* Paris, 27 Nov 1684). French cabinetmaker of Dutch birth. By 1643 he was in Paris where he was apprenticed to Adrien Garbrant; he later married Garbrant's daughter and took over his workshop. He received his first royal commission in 1661, working in the 1660s at Vincennes and in the 1670s at Versailles. He maintained his workshop in the Rue Arbre-Sec, near the Louvre, though he certainly collaborated with other craftsmen at the royal workshops in the Gobelins, possibly using them for his royal commissions. The tapestry (*c.* 1667; Versailles, Château) illustrating Louis XIV's visit to the Gobelins in 1667 almost certainly shows Gole presenting a Boulle table to the King. Gole's style developed quickly: his earliest cabinets, in ebony, followed the mid-century style of rich sobriety, but for his first royal commission he decorated a cabinet (untraced) with floral marquetry and during the 1660s and 1670s he used such exotic materials as tortoiseshell, japanning and brass and pewter marquetry with amaranth wood. Among his most exotic pieces were tables with an ivory ground in imitation of porcelain, supplied in the 1670s to the Trianon de Porcelaine at Versailles. A table of this type (Malibu, CA, Getty Mus.) was in Versailles in 1718. A cabinet (London, V&A) made for the King's brother, Philippe I, Duke

Pierre Gole (attrib.): cabinet on stand, pine and walnut with ivory and tortoiseshell veneers and marquetry in various woods, 1260×840×390 mm, Paris, 1660–71 (London, Victoria and Albert Museum)

of Orléans, between 1660 and 1671 is decorated with floral marquetry on an ivory ground.

T. Lunsingh Scheurleer: 'Pierre Gole, ébéniste du roi Louis XIV', *Burl. Mag.*, cxxii (1980), pp. 380–94

T. Lunsingh Scheurleer: *Pierre Gole, ébéniste de Louis XIV* (Dijon, 2005)

Gombroon [gomroon, gombron]. Type of Persian pottery, imitated by the Chelsea porcelain factory. The name derives from the Persian port of Gombroon (now Bandar Abbas, in Iran), where the East India Company had a station. The term is sometimes used vaguely, but has the specific sense of a 17th-century Persian pottery with a thin white body and incised underglaze decoration.

Gomm, William, & Son & Co. English furniture-making and upholstery company based in London. The firm was founded by William Gomm (*c.* 1698–1780), who was joined by Abraham Roentgen (1736–8) and subsequently (before 1756) by his son Richard (*d* 1794) and by his son William. There is a collection of designs for Rococo furniture by the elder William Gomm in the Winterthur Museum in Delaware, including mirrors, a commode and bookcases. Richard Gomm went bankrupt in 1776, but the business was continued by a partner, Francis Peter Mallet.

Gomme, E., Ltd. English furniture company in High wycombe. The workshop was founded in 1898 by the chairmaker Ebenezer Gomme (1858–1931), whose grandson Donald was responsible for the design of the mass-produced modular G-plan furniture (in which G stands for Gomme), which was introduced in 1953. The Gomme chair of 1962 is an adaptation of the Eames lounge chair of 1956. The Wycombe Chair Museum, High Wycombe, has a collection of Gomme chairs.

ODNB (on Ebenezer Gomme)

Gomperz, Lucie. *See* RIE, LUCIE.

Gondelach [Gundelach], **Franz** (*bapt* Grossalmerode, 17 Dec 1663; *d* Altmünden, 13 May 1726). German glass-engraver. His father was the glassmaker Franz Gundelach (*fl* 1660), and from *c.* 1669 the family lived in Oranienbaum. By 1682 Gondelach had moved to Kassel, where he became glass-engraver to the Landgrave Charles of Hesse-Kassel.

Gondelach is regarded as the most important glass-engraver of the Baroque period, as he skilfully mastered the techniques of *tiefschnitt* (deep-relief) and *hochschnitt* (high-relief) decoration. His most famous works are three jugs: the first (Pommersfelden, Schloss Weissenstein) was a present from the Landgrave to Lothar Franz von Schönborn in 1715, the second (made before 1714) is in Rosenborg Castle in Copenhagen, and the third (also made before 1714; Moscow, Kremlin) was given by Frederick IV of Denmark to Tsar Peter I. Other important works include a covered goblet (1717; The Hague, Gemeentemus.) decorated with St George and cherubs executed in *hochschnitt* and commissioned by Prince William of Hesse for the confraternity of St George in The Hague; a goblet with cover decorated with a faun and nymph (New York, Met.) and a goblet with a resting Venus (Berlin, Schloss Köpenick). Sometimes Gondelach signed his work with diamond-point engraving, and a particular mark was a cut eight-pointed star on the underside of the foot. From 1723 until his death Gondelach directed the Landgrave's glass factory at Altmünden.

G. E. Pazaurek: *Franz Gondelach*, Keramik- und Glasstudien, i (Berlin, 1927)

F. A. Dreier: 'Franz Gondelach: Anmerkungen zum Leben und uWerk', *Z. Dt. Ver. Kstwiss.*, 24 (1970), pp. 101–40

F. A. Dreier: 'Hochschnitt and Tiefschnitt [high relief and mold-pressed glass techniques by Gonderlach]', *J. Glass Stud.*, xxxviii (1996), pp. 51–62

F. A. Dreier: 'Gondelach and Christoph Labhardt the Elder', *J. Glass Stud.*, xxxviii (1996), pp. 30–39

Gondoin [Gondouin], **Jacques** (*b* St Ouen, nr Paris, 7 June 1737; *d* Paris, 29 Dec 1818). French architect and designer. He is rightly known as the architect of the Ecole de Chirurgie (1771–86; now the Faculté de Médecine, Paris), but was also royal furniture designer from 1769–84. He specialized in carved furniture; chairs made to his designs by NICOLAS-QUINIBERT FOLIOT in 1774 are now at Fontainebleau.

Goodison, Benjamin (*b c.* 1700; *d* 1767). English cabinetmaker. He established a workshop in Long Acre, London, and specialized in parcel-gilt mahogany furniture. He made furniture to the designs of WILLIAM KENT, and his own designs were influenced by those of Kent. Goodison's clients, for whom he made picture frames and chandeliers as well as furniture, included Frederick, Prince of Wales and the Earl of Leicester; there are examples of his furniture in Hampton Court Palace, Windsor Castle, Holkham Hall (Norfolk), Longford Castle (Wilts), Boughton and Althorp (both Northants). After Goodison's death the workshop was managed by Benjamin Parran until 1783.

ODNB

Gorbunovo Porcelain Factory. Russian porcelain manufactory. The factory was established in the village of Gorbunovo (Dmitrov District, Moscow Province) in 1804 by Karl Iakovlevich Melli, who had previously worked for FRANCIS GARDNER. In 1811 the factory was bought by Alexei Popov, a Moscow merchant; it is now known in Russian (and sometimes in English) as the Popov Porcelain Factory. The factory made porcelain figures similar to Gardner's, and was also well-known for its Empire-style tea services; its products were distinguished by the intensity and innovation of its colours. The factory closed in 1872.

K. Kettering, 'The Russian Porcelain Figure in the Eighteenth and Nineteenth Centuries', *Mag. Ant.*, clxiii/3 (March 2003), pp. 114–19

Gorham. American silverware firm formed in 1831 by Jabez Gorham (*b* Providence, RI, 18 Feb 1792; *d* Providence, 24 March 1869). When he was fourteen Gorham began a seven-year apprenticeship with Nehemiah Dodge (*fl* 1794–1807), a Providence silversmith. He completed his training in 1813 and in the same year opened a jewellery business known as 'The Firm', which lasted until 1818, when economic hardships led to its dissolution. Jabez continued in business in Providence throughout the 1820s, and in 1831 he expanded his production to include the manufacture of coin-silver spoons with Henry Webster (1808–65). In 1837 William G. Price (*d* 1839) also became a partner in what became known as Gorham, Webster & Price, and in 1841 Gorham brought his son, John Gorham (1820–98), into the business under the name J. Gorham & Son. They expanded their line of flatware to include forks, tongs, thimbles, nursing tubes, toiletries and other small articles, sold mainly through the shop and a network of travelling peddlers. By 1847 John Gorham's ambitious plans for the company included the acquisition of larger working space and steam-powered machinery. Jabez Gorham retired in 1848. In 1850 John Gorham made his cousin, Gorham Thurber (1825–88), partner, and the company became known as Gorham & Thurber, producing hollowware and flatware using machines and new technology. In 1865 the firm was incorporated as the Gorham Manufacturing Co., and in the same year electroplating was introduced. In 1868 the English silversmith Thomas Joseph Pairpoint (*fl* 1860–80) joined the company and designed wares in a High Victorian style (e.g. the 740-piece Furber Service,

1873; Providence, RI, Gorham Col.). Gorham went bankrupt in 1877 and was forced to resign, but the company continued to produce wares in revival styles. During the 1890s Art Nouveau wares were produced and the Martelé (hammered) line of silverware and jewellery was introduced. In 1925 the Danish designer Erik Magnussen (1884–1961) became the company director and introduced Art Deco style wares. During World War II production was reduced, but normal production was resumed in the 1950s. In 1967 the firm was merged with the Textron Corporation of Providence. In 1974–5 a table service in the King Charles pattern was made for the White House, Washington, DC, and President George W. Bush subsequently chose Gorham's Chantilly pattern for the flatware on Air Force One. The company's principal brands are now Lenox, Dansk and Brooks Bentley.

C. H. Carpenter Jr: *Gorham Silver, 1831–1981* (New York, 1982)
American Art nouveau silver: The Jolie and Robert Shelton Collection (exh. cat. by J. Keefe and S. Hough; New Orleans, LA, Mus. A., 2001)
L. J. Pristo: *Martelé: Gorham's Nouveau Art Silver* (Phoenix, 2002)
W. Hood 'The Bird's Nest Flatware Pattern by Gorham, 1869', *Mag. Ant.*, clxvi/3 (Sept 2004), pp. 106–15

Goss, **William Henry** (*b* London, ?July 1833; *d* ?Hanley, Staffs, 4 Jan 1906). English potter and manufacturer. He studied art and design in London and in 1857 was employed as a modeller by W. T. Copeland & Sons Ltd, Stoke-on-Trent, Staffs. In 1858 he set up a factory in partnership with a Mr Peake, producing a variety of high-quality Parian porcelain: jugs, vases, lidded jars, portrait busts and 'jewelled' porcelain. He had observed that the 'jewelled' pieces made at the Sèvres Porcelain Factory were often lacking their enamel 'stones' and he developed a method of securely counter-sinking these into the clay. He modelled many of the prototypes himself, and the factory made pierced and coloured floral jewellery, crosses, scent bottles and other small luxury items. He also invented a light, lustrous ware called 'ivory porcelain', which was adopted by the Belleek factory in Co. Fermanagh, N. Ireland, and experimented with commercial glazes to produce brilliantly coloured pieces. In 1870 Goss established his own factory, the Falcon Works, at Hanley, Stoke-on-Trent, where, from the 1880s until 1914, porcelain heraldic wares were manufactured: a multitude of such pieces as figures, urns, lighthouses and horseshoes were transfer-printed with the coats of arms of a British town or county. The heraldic porcelains were an overwhelming success, selling as keepsakes or souvenirs by the thousand (examples in Stoke-on-Trent, City Mus. & A.G.), and a Goss collectors' club was founded *c.* 1904. During World War I the factory made models of tanks and zeppelins and pots bearing regimental badges. Production dwindled in the 1930s; the Goss works were absorbed by the Cauldon Potteries Ltd, Hanley, and closed down in 1940.

M. J. W. Willis-Fear: *The History of the Pottery Firm of W. H. Goss at Stoke-on-Trent* (Newcastle-under-Lyme, 1965)

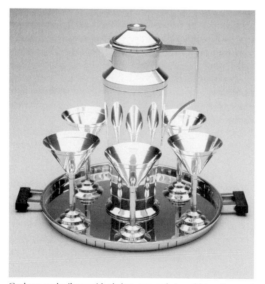

Gorham cocktail set with shaker, tray and six goblets, silver and bakelite, designed by Erik Magnussen, Providence, RI, *c.* 1929 (Newark, NJ, Newark Museum)

N. Emery: *William Henry Goss and Goss Heraldic China* (Stoke-on-Trent, 1969, rev. 3/1971)

D. Rees and M. G. Cawley: *A Pictorial Encyclopaedia of Goss China* (Newport, 1970)

H. Regnard: *A Pictorial Handbook of Goss Cottages and Buildings* (Bath, 1974)

L. Pine and N. Pine: *William Henry Goss: The Story of the Staffordshire Family of Potters Who Invented Heraldic Porcelain* (Horndean, Portsmouth, 1987)

Gotha. German centre of porcelain production. In 1757 the first porcelain factory in Thuringia was established in Gotha. The factory produced delicate tablewares (notably coffee-sets) similar to those of the FÜRSTENBERG PORCELAIN FACTORY. It closed in the mid-19th century, but was succeeded by other porcelain factories in the town. There is a substantial collection of Gotha pottery in Friedenstein Castle (Gotha).

U. Daberitz: 'Qualitatvoll und rar', *Weltkunst*, lxxiv/14 (Dec 2004), pp. 32–5

Gothic Revival. Term applied to a style of architecture and the decorative arts inspired by the Gothic architecture of medieval Europe. In the decorative arts, the Gothic Revival style was first realised in interior design and then extended to all forms of the applied arts. In the 18th century the applied arts had figured alongside architecture most famously in England in the furnishings designed for Strawberry Hill (from 1753), and Fonthill Abbey (from 1796), built for William Beckford, which were both characterized by a picturesque interpretation of Gothic motifs. In the 19th century, when the Gothic Revival was at its most significant as an intellectual, moral and artistic phenomenon, the concept of the integrated interior and the crucial design role of architects meant that architecture and the decorative arts were closely entwined. England remained at the forefront of the movement, influencing developments in Europe and North America as a more archaeological and historically correct approach gained momentum. A decorative vocabulary that drew upon Gothic architectural features—pointed arches, lancets, tracery, crockets, quatrefoils and trefoils, and naturalistic foliage—was applied to furniture, metalwork (including silver, ironwork and jewellery), ceramics (including porcelain and earthenware), glass and stained glass, textiles and wallpapers. These objects were often designed to complement a contemporary architectural shell. The use of colour was also important. The Gothic Revival, however, meant more than purely surface decoration. In some cases, for example for furniture and metalwork, the reintroduction of medieval structures and techniques, as far as they were known, became part of the philosophy of the movement.

In England the early part of the 19th century was characterized by a greater degree of exploration of medieval forms. The architect Lewis Nockalls Cottingham (1787–1847) designed a wide range of Gothic furniture, often incorporating original, medieval fragments. A. C. Pugin (1769–1832) also developed a specialized knowledge of Gothic style in a series of important sourcebooks. His designs dominated the development of the Gothic Revival stle from the 1830s to the 1850s. In northern Europe nationalist and religious regeneration helped create a climate in which the Gothic Revival could thrive. In France Gothic was being identified as a 'national' style, partly as a rejection of Napoleon's espousal of Neo-classicism as his court style. The Troubadour style or 'Style cathédrale', a romantic evocation of medieval chivalric and courtly life that extended to the decorative arts, was the main expression of this interest. In 1823 the Sèvres Porcelain Factory embarked on the ambitious 'Service de la Chevalerie', and such patrons as the Duchesse de Berry ordered furniture and porcelain in the 'style gothique'. Gothic was also being reevaluated as the national style in Germany as part of the surge of nationalism after the Prussian War of Liberation of 1813. A symbol of this was the National Monument to the Liberation known as the Kreuzberg for the Tempelhofer Berg, Berlin, designed as a massive pinnacled cross in 1817–18 (completed 1821) and forged in cast iron by the architect and designer Karl Friedrich Schinkel. Schinkel also produced Gothic designs for furniture, for example for Prince William of Prussia, at Schloss Babelsburg, Potsdam, from 1833, and for silver, manufactured by the Berlin goldsmith George Hossauer, in particular the three presentation cups made for the medieval tournament festival the 'Magic Spell of the White Rose' in 1830. Although decorated with Gothic ornament, the basic shape of the cups is Classical, a contradiction then still considered perfectly acceptable.

This eclectic attitude was overturned in England in the second phase of the Revival, from the late 1830s to 1850s, which was dominated by A. W. N. PUGIN. Pugin's contribution to the Revival was fundamental in terms of design. As a result, the religious emphasis of the Revival became more pronounced, particularly after Pugin's conversion to Roman Catholicism in 1835. During the 19th century there was a boom in the building of churches needed for the growing industrial centres. Owing to Pugin's influence the majority of these were in the Gothic style. One of Pugin's main concerns was honesty—that objects should reflect their medieval prototypes in design and structure, which should not be disguised, hence his approval of the 'X'-frame construction for chairs, and his opinion that pattern should be bold, colourful and appropriate to the context—for example that flat objects should have two-dimensional patterns. These views were elaborated in his publications *Gothic Furniture in the Style of the 15th Century Designed and Etched by A. W. N. Pugin* (London, 1835) and *Designs for Gold and Silversmiths* and *Designs for Iron and Brass Work in the Style of the XV and XVI Centuries Drawn and Etched by A. W. N. Pugin* (both London, 1836).

From 1841 the Ecclesiological Society (formerly the Cambridge Camden Society), founded out of concerns for the preservation of church fabric and fittings, made influential pronouncements in its magazine *The Ecclesiologist*. It also produced a design series for church metalwork and furniture called *Instrumenta Ecclesiastica* (1844–7 and 1850–52/56). This was edited by William Butterfield (1814–1900), who provided all of the designs for the first series, and the society later employed first G. E. Street (1824–81) and then William Burges as official metalwork designers. The same role was performed in Germany by the *Kölner Domblatt* and in France by the periodical *Annales archéologiques*. The creation of the Musée de Cluny, in the 15th-century Hôtel des Abbés de Cluny, Paris, by Alexandre du Sommerard in 1832 provided medieval models for designers and was symptomatic of a growing interest in antiquarianism. Jean-Baptiste Lassus (1807–57), architect and designer in a scholarly medieval style, encouraged craftsmen, among them the metalworker Achillé Legost, to rediscover such medieval techniques as champlevé enamelling. As in England, the church was a major patron of Gothic Revival decorative arts, supplied by such goldsmiths as Placide Poussielgue-Rusand (1824–89) in Paris and Thomas-Joseph Armand-Calliat (*fl c.* 1862–81) in Lyon. François-Désiré Froment-Meurice produced fine metalwork and jewellery, winning a medal at the Great Exhibition of 1851. Like many manufacturers, he did not work exclusively in the Gothic manner, and his style was not particularly archaeological.

The influence of Eugène-Emmanuel Viollet-le-Duc was a key factor in the credibility of the Revival. His publications, notably the *Dictionnaire du mobilier* (6 vols, Paris, 1858–75), illustrated his commitment to French 13th-century Gothic and proved indispensable to designers. He designed for a range of materials, including stained glass for the Sèvres Porcelain Factory, and the prestige of some of his commissions, notably the château of Pierrefonds (from 1858) for Emperor Napoleon III (*reg* 1852–70), raised the profile of the Gothic style. A similar role was played in Germany by Georg Gottlob Ungewitter (1820–64), an architect and designer who propagated the Gothic Revival through teaching at the Höhere Gewerbeschule in Kassel. He published furniture designs in *Entwürfe zu gothischen Möbel* (1851), some of which were based on original models. This was followed by the *Gothisches Musterbuch* (1856–61), which included designs for metalwork and stained glass. In Belgium, where A. W. N. Pugin's influence was particularly strong, there were some notable examples of buildings both domestic and religious with complete interiors all in the Gothic Revival style. Examples include the Loppem Castle (design, 1856), near Bruges, by E. W. Pugin (1834–75) and Jean-Baptiste-Charles-François Bethune (1821–94) and the Roman Catholic complex SS Mary and Philip with the church of the Nativity of Vive-Kapelle (1860–69), also by Bethune.

In the USA the Gothic Revival took longer to take hold. The first published evidence of the style was the sideboard used as a frontispiece to Robert Conner's *The Cabinet Maker's Assistant* (New York, 1842), although developments in Europe had already been absorbed by the architect and designer ALEXANDER JACKSON DAVIS. Davis designed a number of houses in the Gothic taste for wealthy patrons, including Lyndhurst (originally 'Knoll'; from 1838) at Tarrytown for General William Paulding, the Mayor of New York. Davis also designed the furniture for the mansion, including beds, which lent themselves to the application of Gothic ornament. Although inspired by Pugin, he was an advocate of 'carpenter's Gothic', or decoration of furniture not necessarily Gothic in form by Gothic mouldings and ornament. Considerable quantities of Gothic Revival furniture were made in the 1840s and 1850s by such firms as John and Joseph W. Meeks. The aesthete and landscape architect A. J. Downing, a prolific author on taste, also propagated the style. In *The Architecture of Country Houses* (1850), he debated the suitability of Gothic for domestic interiors, concluding that it was appropriate for libraries, halls and bedrooms. Very little Gothic Revival silver was produced in the USA. The Boston & Sandwich Glass Co. (est. 1825) in Sandwich, MA, did, however, produce pressed and moulded jugs, decanters and dishes incorporating arcading and tracery patterns.

During the 1860s there was a further change in the direction of the Gothic Revival with the introduction in England of 'Reformed Gothic' under the influence of such architects and designers as William Butterfield, G. E. Street, Richard Norman Shaw (1831–1912) and, most importantly, William Burges. The stress was still on honesty, but using 13th-century French models to design new forms appropriate to the needs of the 19th century, rather than the pure 14th-century sources advocated by Pugin. Examples of the style were first seen at the Medieval Court at the 1862 International Exhibition in London. The architect George Gilbert Scott I (1811–78), who designed extensive fittings for churches, displayed a polychromed wrought-iron chancel screen (London, V&A) for Hereford Cathedral made by the silversmith Francis Skidmore's Art Manufactures Co. in Coventry. The interiors designed by Burges for Cardiff Castle from 1868 are among the finest expressions of the style. Such pattern books as Bruce J. Talbert's *Gothic Forms Applied to Furniture, Metal Work and Decoration for Domestic Purposes* (Dundee, 1867) and Owen Jones's *The Grammar of Ornament* (London, 1856) provided a readily available corpus of decoration. Charles Locke Eastlake's *Hints on Household Taste in Furniture, Upholstery and Other Details* (London, 1868) was a popular manual of decoration based on the work of such designers as Street and J. P. Seddon, advocating honesty of construction and materials. It had a dramatic impact in the USA.

By the 1870s the use of the Gothic Revival for domestic interiors was waning, although it remained important for ecclesiastical buildings and fittings until well into the 20th century, and there some important late 19th-century Gothic interiors, especially in Germany. Schloss Neuschwanstein, near Füssen, built between 1868 and 1886 for Ludwig II, King of Bavaria, was provided with elaborate Gothic interiors by Julius Hoffmann. Hermann Robert Bichweiler designed Gothic interiors for the furniture manufacturer H. C. Wolbrandt from 1872 and set up a highly successful art factory in Altona in 1878, which included Gothic patterns among its output. A further variant was the *Alte deutsche* style that developed in the last quarter of the century, manifested in the work of such goldsmiths as Gabriel Hermeling of Cologne and Alexander Schönauer of Hamburg, who produced replicas of Late Gothic lobed beakers, and was part of a surge in interest in medieval collecting that led to the production of many interesting fakes. By the 1890s revivalist styles in general were outmoded, as indicated by the emergence of the Art Nouveau and *Jugendstil*.

G. Germann: *Gothic Revival in Europe and Britain: Sources, Influences and Ideas* (London, 1972)
The Gothic Revival Style in America, 1830–1870 (exh. cat. by K. S. Howe and D. B. Warren, Houston, TX, Mus. F.A., 1976)
Le 'Gothique' retrouvé avant Viollet-le-Duc (exh. cat., Paris, Hôtel de Sully, 1979)
Art and Design in Europe and America, 1800–1900, London, V&A cat. (London, 1987)
C. Wainwright: *The Romantic Interior: The British Collector at Home, 1750–1850* (New Haven and London, 1989)
Un Age d'or des arts décoratifs, 1814–1848 (exh. cat., Paris, Grand Pal., 1991)
M. J. Lewis: *The Politics of the German Gothic Revival: August Riechensperger* (Cambridge, MA, 1993)
M. Aldrich: *Gothic Revival* (London, 1994)

Gotzkowsky, Johann Ernst. *See under* BERLIN, §2.

Gouda. Dutch centre of ceramics production. In 1898 the Plateelbakkerij Zuid Holland opened in the Dutch town of Gouda. Its styles were at first imitations of ROZENBURG FACTORY wares, but by 1910 the factory had developed its own style, including a form of matt decoration. Its designers included THEODORUS COLENBRANDER. The factory closed in 1965.

C. W. Moody: *Gouda Ceramics: The Art Nouveau Era of Holland* (n.p., 1970)

Goût grec. Stylistic term for the first phase of French Neo-classicism, specifically those examples of French decorative arts and architecture dating from the mid-1750s to the late 1760s that are severely rectilinear, with chunky classical details, such as Vitruvian scrolls, Greek-key frets and geometrical garlands. The style was effectively inaugurated by a set of furniture, comprising a combined writing-table and cabinet and a clock (Chantilly, Mus. Condé) made for the Parisan financier Ange-Laurent de La Live de Jully (1725–70) from designs (1756–8) by the painter and amateur architect Louis-Joseph Le Lorrain. The monumental and unfrivolous style of these pieces, executed in ebony-veneered oak with heavy gilt bronze mounts, was quite different from the current Rococo idiom. The brief but intense flowering of the *goût grec* soon gave way to the less rigorous Louis XVI style.

S. Eriksen: 'La Live de Jully's Furniture "à la Grecque"', *Burl. Mag.*, ciii (1961), pp. 340–47
S. Eriksen: *Early Neo-classicism in France* (London, 1974)

Gout-stool. Padded stool used in 18th-century England to support the foot when affected by gout.

Gouthière, Pierre (*b* Bar-sur-Aube, *bapt* 13 Jan 1732; *d* Paris, 8 June 1813). French bronze-caster and gilder. His reputation as the most eminent bronzeworker and gilder in the reign of Louis XVI (*reg* 1774–92) was established during his lifetime. Many of the bronze pieces produced during this period were thought to have been made by Gouthière, but some of the most important works have been reattributed to Pierre-Philippe Thomire and François Rémond on the basis of documentary evidence. Louis XVI acquired for his private museum 20 of the 34 pieces by Gouthière that were in the Aumont collection, while three of them were bought by Marie-Antoinette.

Gouthière was an incomparable gilder and invented the technique of matt-finish gilding. His earliest known works (*c.* 1765) are classical mounts for imitation porphyry vases (Warsaw, Royal Castle), which were commissioned by the goldsmith François-Thomas Germain. These were closely followed by candlesticks with lions' heads, a design copied by Matthew Boulton, and by small classical statues of graceful, nude female figures. Gouthière was the most eloquent exponent of the arabesque phase of Neo-classicism in French bronzework, as illustrated by the mounts for a pair of celadon porcelain vases (Paris, Louvre) for the Duc d'Aumont, the mounts for a jasper perfume-burner (London, Wallace) made for the same patron and later bewitching Marie-Antoinette, and the door-knobs (Paris, Mus. A. Déc.) for Madame Du Barry's Pavillon de Louveciennes.

Gouthière also made many types of furnishing objects, including table legs made entirely of bronze, ornaments for mantelpieces, pedestals, stoves and even coaches, as well as mounts for porcelain, marble or ivory vases. The Avignon Clock (1771, London, Wallace) shows the level of technical perfection he could achieve. He subsequently executed a number of high-quality objects in imaginative designs, among them a lyre-shaped candelabrum (Malibu, CA, Getty Mus.) decorated with a head of Apollo, candelabra with symbols of Mercury (Paris, Louvre), fire-dogs decorated with camels (Paris, Louvre) and fire-dogs decorated with eagles (Paris, Mobilier N.). A number of chimney-pieces by Gouthière are extant and provide fascinating examples of the development of his work. They are in the Salon Ovale (1771) at Lovveciennes, the Bibliothèque du Roi (1774), the Chambre des Bains du Roi (1785), Cabinet de la Méridienne (1781), Salon des Nobles and Cabinet Intérieur de la Reine (1785), all at the château of Versailles, and in Marie-Antoinette's Boudoir Turc at the châ-

teau of Fontainebleau (1777), the Pavillon de Bagatelle (1777) in the Bois de Boulogne and the Duchesse de Mazarin's reception room (1780; New
York, Met.).

J. Robiquet: *Vie et oeuvre de Pierre Gouthière* (Paris, 1920)
Baulez: 'Pierre Gouthière (1732–1813)', *Vergoldete Bronzen*, ii (Munich, 1986), pp. 561–642

G-plan furniture. *See under* GOMME, E., LTD.

Graffiti. Term applied to an arrangement of insti-
tutionally illicit marks in which there has been an
attempt to establish some sort of coherent composition; such marks are made by an individual or individuals (not generally professional artists) on a wall
or other surface that is usually visually accessible to
the public. The term 'graffiti' derives from the Greek
graphein ('to write'). Graffiti (sing. graffito) or SGRAF-
FITO, meaning a drawing or scribbling on a flat surface, originally referred to those marks found on ancient Roman architecture. Although examples of
graffiti have been found at such sites as Pompeii, the
Domus Aurea of Emperor Nero (*reg* AD 54–68) in
Rome, Hadrian's Villa at Tivoli and the Maya site of
Tikal in Mesoamerica, they are usually associated
with 20th- and 21st-century urban environments.
They may range from a few simple marks to compositions that are complex and colourful. Illegitimate
counterparts to the paid, legitimate advertisements
on billboards or signs, graffiti utilize the walls of ga-

rages, public toilets and gaol cells for their clandes-
tine messages.

Because of the illicit nature of graffiti, a tin of
paint and a brush are impractical, while spatial considerations may make a pen or pencil ineffective. To
accommodate the need for size, visibility, speed and
convenience, the ideal vehicle is the spray-can, which
combines medium and applicator into one relatively
small parcel that is easily concealed, transportable,
easy to use; spray-paint may be applied to most surfaces. Different-sized nozzles are used to achieve
various effects, for example a thin line as opposed
to a wide band of paint. Almost anything may, however, serve as a substitute: the aforementioned pen,
pencil, paint and brush, as well as chisels, knives, felt-
tip markers, blood or even a finger on a dirty wall
or window.

Communities that produce graffiti (as opposed to
the individual 'scribbler') may target cryptic messages
towards their own closed community, producing a
seemingly confusing and unreadable product. The
writers may not sign their real names; they instead
employ the use of nicknames, codes and symbols
within stylized aesthetic systems. This type of graffiti
is geared towards people who already understand the
messages and may act to enhance group solidarity.
Such graffiti may easily be elevated to the category
of art, because the cryptic codes, generalized content
and stylistic features of community-based graffiti
usually outlast the duration of an individual's membership within the community. If a community's

Graffiti on walls along the via dell'Anfiteatro, Pompeii, showing election and theatre notices

ideological focus is geared towards the larger society or the politics of the larger state, the messages that graffiti project are usually easier to read, lacking in cryptic encoding and generally not as stylized.

An example of this cross-culturally prevalent genre of graffiti, political graffiti may combine with other artistic and expressive forms such as poster and comic book production, mural painting, newspaper and pamphlet production and political art exhibitions. The marks may represent the work of unrecognized or underground political groups, radical student movements or simply dissatisfied individuals. Political graffiti may also arise from sudden emergency situations (e.g. riots) or in response to concurrent political legislation and party politics. Although concerned with the larger politics of the State, the groups that produce this type of graffiti generally comprise some 'subcultural' elements and may make wide use of symbols to further internally relevant quests for power and solidarity.

A second genre of graffiti, gang graffiti, is used as a marker by gangs usually active in urban areas. The content and form of their graffiti consist of cryptic codes and initials rigidly styled with specialized calligraphies. Gang members use graffiti to indicate group membership, to distinguish enemies and allies and, most generally, to mark boundaries that are both territorial and ideological. In this case, graffiti may merge with other art forms, like tattoo and clothing styles, to create a bounded system, the concerns of which may incorporate illegitimate economic and social practices that branch far beyond the reaches of the actual graffiti.

A third genre of graffiti, graffiti art, is commonly called 'hip-hop' or 'New York style' graffiti and derives from a tradition of subway graffiti that originated in New York in the 1970s. This type of graffiti has spread to large urban centres around the USA and the rest of the world, especially in Europe. Where subway cars like those in New York are unavailable, walls, rocks, road signs, billboards, train carriages and even motor vehicles are considered suitable 'canvases'. Graffiti artists may or may not belong to 'crews', which are groups of artists at differing levels of proficiency. Their work ranges from simple monochrome 'tags' (the artist's 'name tag' often represented in an exaggerated cursive style) to elaborate, multicoloured works called 'pieces' (derived from the word 'masterpiece'), which are considered in some circles to be of museum quality.

As graffiti have begun to find their way from their original urban locations to the walls of galleries and museums, the question of vandalism and graffiti as an art form has provoked endless controversy, raising such questions as whether vandalism can be considered art or whether graffiti can be considered graffiti if they are made legally. The simplified imagery of graffiti has also become attractive to certain professional fine artists—the work of Keith Haring (1958–90) in particular became 'legitimized' as it moved from New York's subway walls to the walls of galleries and private collectors in the USA. Increasing popular interest in hip-hop graffiti art and its concomitant controversies have spurred the development of scholarly interest surrounding people's use of graffiti in all their aspects.

R. Reisner: *Graffiti: Two Thousand Years of Wall Writing* (New York, 1971)

J. Romotsky and S. Romotsky: *Los Angeles Barrio Calligraphy* (Los Angeles, 1976)

C. Castleman: *Getting Up: Subway Graffiti in New York City* (Cambridge, MA, 1982)

M. Cooper and H. Chalfant: *Subway Art* (New York, 1984)

A. Silva: *Punto de vista ciudadano: Focalización visual y puesta en escena del graffiti*, Series Minor (Bogotá, 1987)

J. Bushnell: *Moscow Graffiti: Language and Subculture* (Boston, 1990)

M. Cooper and J. Sciorra: *R.I.P.: New York Spraycan Memorials* (London, 1994)

T. Manco: *Stencil Graffiti* (London, 2002)

T. Manco: *Street Logos* (London, 2004)

N. Ganz and T. Manco, eds: *Graffiti World: Street Art from Five Continents* (London, 2004)

P. Sutherland: *Autograf: New York City's Graffiti Writers* (New York, 2004)

R. Puig Torres: *Barcelona: 1000 Grafitis* (Barcelona, 2005)

Tawkin' New Yawk City Walls (exh. cat. by J. Fekner; Brookville, NY, Hillwood A. Mus., 2005)

Graffito. *See* SGRAFFITO.

Grainger, William (*fl* 1610–30). English pewterer. He is controversially associated with one work, the Grainger Candlestick (1616; London, V&A), of which the base is cast with strapwork, the heraldic insignia of the Pewterers' Company of London, the date ANO D 1616 and the name WILLIAM GRANGR. There are brass candlesticks with a similar shape, but no other example in brass is known. The candlestick, which has been known since 1922, may be genuine, or may be an assemblage made from two separate candlesticks of which one or both may be genuine, or may be a fake.

Grainger & Co. *See under* WORCESTER.

Graining. The imitation (by *trompe l'oeil* painting) of rare woods and marble, a technique used on European furniture and panelling since the late Middle Ages.

Grammont [Flem. Geraardsbergen]. Belgian centre of tapestry production. The Flemish town of Grammont, in what is now Belgium, was a centre of tapestry production in the 16th century. In the 1540s Peter Borremans headed a large workshop in Grammont, although there were complaints about the quality of his work. Between 1554 and 1564 the guild had numerous members and led an independent existence. Soon afterwards, however, decline set in. In 1617 and 1618 Jean Divy of Valenciennes and Rafaël Plasschaert respectively were willing, in exchange for numerous considerations, to settle in the city to teach the craft to young apprentices, which suggests that the tapestry industry in Grammont was by this time virtually non-existent.

Production in the town usually consisted of cushion covers and large-leaved *verdures* (e.g. second half of the 16th century; Hamburg, Mus. Kst & Gew.). The town mark is a cross on three steps, which can also be seen in the arms of the town. The town's mark appears on a few tapestries in such museums as the Museum für Kunst und Gewerbe, Hamburg, and the Kunsthistorisches Museum, Vienna, as well as on a *verdure* (Ghent, Provgebouw) depicting a rhinoceros—after an engraving by Dürer—and other wild animals. On the basis of this rather coarsely worked tapestry, with flowers, vases and fruit in bright colours surrounded by broad sculptural borders, it may be possible to attribute other *verdures* to Grammont.

J. P. Asselberghs: 'De tapijtkunst te Geraardsbergen' [The art of tapestry weaving in Geraardsbergen], *Geraardsbergen 1068–1968* (exh. cat., 1968)

Grandfather chair. *See* WING CHAIR.

Grandfather clock. *See under* CLOCKS AND WATCHES, §4(I).

Grand Rapids. American city in western Michigan noted as a centre of furniture production. The city's first cabinetmaker, William 'Deacon' Haldane (1807–98), established a shop there in 1836. By 1851 E. M. Ball of Powers & Ball was boasting that he could toss 'whole trees into the hopper and grind out chairs ready for use' to fill an order for 10,000 chairs in Chicago. In the 1870s Grand Rapids became a major factor in the American furniture market. Such companies as Berkey & Gay, Widdicomb, Phoenix and Nelson-Matter built large factories and hired Dutch and other European immigrants to operate them. While most of these manufacturers produced complete lines of bedroom, parlour and dining-room suites, some, like the Grand Rapids Chair Co. (established 1872), became large concerns by concentrating on a single product. To support these firms, smaller enterprises sprang up to produce such speciality items as castors, glue, finishes, veneer, carved ornaments, tools and packing materials.

After the Civil War, high-quality Renaissance Revival styles competed with the Rococo Revival lines popular before the war. By the 1870s factories began making the Eastlake or Modern Gothic line. In the 1890s production of 18th-century style English, French and American Colonial Revival furniture predominated. Before World War I the Stickley Bros Co. produced oak Mission furniture. In the 1920s only a much larger Chicago produced a greater value of furniture than Grand Rapids. By the 1930s the Modern style had gained a substantial following, although the Depression devastated the furniture industry. The city's furniture output plummeted by about 83%, and 25 of the city's 72 firms went bankrupt. Their high-quality lines were unable to compete with the medium- and low-priced furniture produced in the south. Prosperity returned after World War II, but the advantages that had made the city a leader in furniture production were also enjoyed by southern manufacturers, where there was the added benefit of lower labour costs. Grand Rapids companies continued to produce high-quality traditional and modern furniture, but the halcyon days when the city was the 'Furniture Capital of America' were over. The most notable company to survive into the 21st century is the Kindel Furniture Company, which since 1982 has specialized in reproductions of early American furniture.

F. E. Ransom: *The City Built on Wood: A History of the Furniture Industry in Grand Rapids, Michigan, 1850–1950* (Ann Arbor, 1955)
K. L. Ames: 'Grand Rapids Furniture at the Time of the Centennial', *Winterthur Port.*, x (1975), pp. 25–50
C. Carron: *Grand Rapids Furniture: The Story of America's Furniture City* (Grand Rapids, 1998)
P. Copeland and J. Copeland: *Quaint Furniture Catalog no. 42: January 1914: Stickley Brothers Company, Grand Rapids, Michigan* (Parchment, MI, 1999)
P. Fogarty and K. Molumby: *Kindel Furniture Company: The First One Hundred Years* (Grand Rapids, MI, 2001)

Granite ware. The term has three distinct meanings in the decorative arts. In pottery, it can denote either earthenware pottery with a speckled colouring imitating that of granite (made by WEDGWOOD) or a robust white earthenware made for destructive environments such as ships (made by DAVENPORT). In metalwork, granite ware is a type of enamelled ironware.

Granja, La. *See* LA GRANJA.

Grant, Duncan. *See under* OMEGA WORKSHOPS.

Granulation. *See under* GOLD.

Grate. *See under* FIREPLACE FURNISHINGS.

Gratzen. *See* NOVÉ HRADY.

Graves, Michael (*b* Indianapolis, IN, 9 July 1934). American architect, teacher, painter and designer. Graves is primarily an architect (e.g. the extension to the Whitney Museum in New York and the Dolphin and Swan hotels at the Walt Disney World Epcot Center in Florida), but has also worked as a designer. He designed showrooms for Sunar Furniture throughout the USA and also worked for Steuben glass works, Memphis furniture (for whom in the early 1980s he designed the Hollywood-style Plaza dressing-table in 1981), Alessi (for whom he designed the Werkstätte coffee service in 1983) and Baldinger Architectural Lighting.

J. Abrahms: *Michael Graves* (Berlin and New York, 1994)

Gray, Eileen (*b* Enniscorthy, Co. Wexford, 9 Aug 1879; *d* Paris, 28 Nov 1976). Irish furniture designer and architect, active in France. In 1898 she entered the Slade School of Art, London, with additional instruction in oriental lacquer technique in D. Charles's shop in Soho. She moved to Paris in 1902, where she continued her training with the Japanese lacquer master Seizo Sugawara. Her first lacquered furniture, including decorative panels, folding screens, small tables and other large pieces, appeared in 1910 and reflected a unique stylistic pastiche of Far Eastern and French influences. At the Salon des Artistes Décorateurs in 1913 her pioneering modern furniture designs attracted the attention of Jacques Doucet. He commissioned three *pièces uniques*, two chairs and the lacquered screen Le Destin (1914). The screen, with Symbolist-inspired figures on one side and a starkly abstract design on a red-lacquered ground on the other, places Gray among the earliest 20th-century designers using geometric abstraction. She designed a theatrical interior in 1919 for the Paris milliner Suzanne Talbot, which, despite its African-inspired boat-shaped *chaise longue* and draped animal skins, revealed a greater tendency towards architectural shapes.

In 1922 Gray opened the Galerie Jean Désert in the Faubourg Saint-Honoré, where she displayed her own designs in furniture, carpets and lacquerware. Only the carpets attracted buyers, however, and the gallery closed in 1930. She rejected the stylized revival designs of Art Deco and from 1925 began integrating contemporary materials and modern functionalism in her furniture. Tubular steel, aluminium

Eileen Gray: tube lamp, chromed metal and incandescent tube, h. 915 mm, diam. 251 mm, *c.* 1930 (New York, Museum of Modern Art)

and glass gradually replaced lacquer and rare woods as her primary materials.

Wendingen, 6 (1924) [issue dedicated to Gray]
Eileen Gray: Designer, 1879–1976 (exh. cat., London, V&A; New York, MOMA; 1979)
P. Adam: *Eileen Gray: Architect/Designer: A Biography* (New York, 2000)
P. Rowlands, M. Bartolucci and R. Cabra: *Eileen Gray* (San Francisco, 2002)
F. Baudot and A. Rudolf: *Eileen Gray* (New York, 2003)

Greatbach, Daniel. *See under* BENNINGTON.

Greatbach, William (*b* 1735; *d* 1813). English potter. He trained at Whieldon (*see* THOMAS WHIELDON) and then established a workshop at Lane Delph, Staffs, where he made CREAMWARES, of which the best-known are teapots with transfer-printed decorations depicting the Prodigal Son; he also made tableware in the shape of fruit which he sent to WEDGWOOD for glazing. His pottery became bankrupt in 1770, after which Greatbach worked first at Turner's and the Wedgwood (1788–1807),

Eileen Gray: adjustable table, chrome-plated tubular steel, sheet steel and glass, h. 365 mm, diam. 200 mm, 1927 (New York, Museum of Modern Art)

where he became one of the highest-paid workers in the firm.

Greek key design. *See* MEANDER.

Greene & Greene. American architectural partnership formed in 1893 by Charles (Sumner) Greene (*b* Brighton, OH, 12 Oct 1868; *d* Carmel, CA, 11 June 1957) and his brother Henry (Mather) Greene (*b* Brighton, OH, 23 Jan 1870; *d* Pasadena, CA, 2 Oct 1954). After early careers in Boston they moved in 1892 to Pasadena, CA, where they became important figures in the developing American Arts and Crafts movement, and also began to the traditional Japanese house with its meticulous wood detailing. The brothers are best known for their bungalows, but also produced furniture that has in recent decades been recognized as among the best objects produced in America.

J. Strand: *A Greene and Greene Guide* (Pasadena, 1974)
R. Makinson: *Greene and Greene*, 2 vols (Salt Lake City, 1977–9)

Greenwood, Frans (*b* Rotterdam 1680; *d* Dordrecht 1763). Dutch glass-engraver of English origin. He developed the technique of STIPPLE-engraving (*see also* GLASS, §I, 1(II)) to draw pictorial designs on glass.

W. Buckley: *Notes on Frans Greenwood and the Glasses that he Engraved* (London, 1930)
F. Smit: *Frans Greenwood, 1680–1763: Dutch Poet & Glass Engraver* (Peterborough, 1988)
F. Smit: *Frans Greenwood, 1680–1763: Dutch Poet & Glass Engrave; Additions and Corrections* (Peterborough, 1998)

Grégoire, Gaspard (*b* Aix-en-Provence, 20 Oct 1751; *d* Aix-en-Provence, 12 May 1846). French silk-painter. He painted on various types of silk, notably velvet; his preferred subjects were famous public figures and Old Master paintings (especially Raphael). He painted on the warp before weaving. There is a collection of Grégoire's portraits on velvet in the Musée Historique des Tissus in Lyon.

H. Algoud: *Gaspard Grégoire et ses Velours d'art* (Paris, 1908)

Grendey, Giles (*b* Wotton-under-Edge, Glos, 1693; *d* Palmers Green, London, 3 March 1780). English cabinetmaker. He was the son of William Grendey, a farmer, and was apprenticed in London at the age of 16 to William Sherborne, a second-generation joiner. He became a freeman of the Joiners' Company in 1716 and was taking on apprentices by 1726. One such apprentice, Christopher Petfield, took him to court for making him spend all his time sawing planks and for beating him 'in a very barbarous manner'. This incident did not prevent Grendey from being elected to the Livery of the Joiners' Company in 1729. He rose steadily through the hierarchy to the post of Master in 1766. In 1731 a fire damaged his workshop in Aylesbury House, St John's Square,

Clerkenwell, destroying furniture to the value of £1000, including an easy-chair 'to be purchas'd by a Person of Quality who design'd it as Present to a German Prince'.

Grendey was commercially successful, producing plain furniture of a somewhat conservative design with little decoration. Some of it was for export. In about 1738 the Duque de Mendoza-Infantado purchased over 70 pieces (some in Leeds, Temple Newsam House; London, V&A; New York, Met.), japanned in scarlet and gold, for his castle at Lazcano in northern Spain. A walnut and mahogany mirror bearing Grendey's label was found in Norway. An important English client was the Hoare family: he supplied pieces to Sir Richard Colt Hoare at Barn Elms, Surrey, and to his brother, Henry II Hoare, at Stourhead, Wilts. Mentioned in Sir Richard's account-books are a chest-of-drawers, a 'Burow Table', dressing-glasses, chimney-glasses and a 'Wrighting Disk'. His work for Stourhead seems to have been mainly in the form of chairs. Grendey's trade label has been found on a variety of walnut, mahogany and japanned pieces dating from about 1735 to 1760 (London, V&A; Leeds, Temple Newsam House; Colonial Williamsburg, VA).

R. W. Symonds: 'In Search of Giles Grendey', *Country Life*, cx (30 Nov 1951), pp. 1792–4
C. Gilbert: 'Furniture by Giles Grendey for the Spanish Trade', *Antiques*, xcix (1971), pp. 544–50
S. Jervis: 'A Great Dealer in the Cabinet Way', *Country Life*, clv (6 June 1974), pp. 1418–19

Grenier, Pasquier (*fl* Tournai, 1447–93). Burgundian tapestry merchant. He is one of the most important figures in the history of late medieval tapestry. Once considered a master weaver, he was subsequently revealed as the most influential 15th-century tapestry merchant. He dealt in many of the finest tapestries surviving from the second half of the 15th century. He secured his first payment for textiles from Philip II (the Good), Duke of Burgundy, in 1454–5 and subsequently supplied him with many magnificent and expensive hangings. In 1459 he sold tapestries of *Alexander the Great*, in 1461 the *Passion* and *Peasants and Woodcutters*, in 1462 *Esther and Ahasuerus* and the *Swan Knight* and in 1466 *Orange Pickers* and *Woodcutters*. Those of *Alexander* and the *Passion* were particularly splendid sets, being of huge dimensions and containing much gold and silver thread. In 1459 two members of Grenier's family were in Milan showing designs for tapestries of *Alexander* to Francesco Sforza, Duke of Milan, and in 1467–8 Grenier made a very large sale, including tapestries of *Nebuchadnezzar*, *Alexander* and the *Passion*, to Edward IV of England. Moreover, in 1471–6 he received payments for a set of 11 tapestries of the *Trojan War* for Charles the Bold, Duke of Burgundy; Grenier's son Jean (*d* Feb 1520) sold another set in 1475 to Federigo II da Montefeltro, Duke of Urbino. In 1486 both Pasquier and Jean were granted protection and licences to import various goods, including tapestries, into England by Henry VII; by 1488

Henry had also purchased tapestries of the *Trojan War*. Further sets were owned by Charles VIII of France, Don Iñigo López de Mendoza (1442–1515), 1st Marqués de Mondéjar, and Matthias Corvinus, King of Hungary.

Among Grenier's many benefactions to parish church of St Quentin in Tournai were tapestries of the *Seven Sacraments* for the choir (possible fragments, New York, Met.; Glasgow, Burrell Col.). Other examples of his goods include surviving pieces of the *Trojan War* tapestries, two tapestries of *Alexander the Great* (Rome, Pal. Doria-Pamphili), two of the *Swan Knight* (Kraków, St Catherine; Vienna, Mus. Angewandte Kst) and two of the *Passion* (Rome, Vatican, Mnmt., Musei & Gal. Pont.; Brussels, Mus. Royaux A. & Hist.). There is no evidence that Grenier's tapestries were woven only in Tournai or to designs by Tournai artists. Therefore, so-called 'Tournai style' tapestries need not have had any connection with Grenier. Grenier's sons Jean and Antoine continued to sell tapestries of high quality to the nobility of Europe into the second decade of the 16th century.

Greybeard. *See* BELLARMINE.

Greyhound jug [Amer. hound-handled pitcher]. Pottery jug with a handle shaped like a greyhound.

Gribelin, Simon (*b* Blois, 5 May 1661; *d* London, 18 Jan 1733). French engraver, active in England. He was a Huguenot from a family of engravers and watchmakers. By 1681 he had moved to London and was admitted to the Clockmakers Company in 1686, possibly because of work he did for them engraving

Simon Gribelin: designs for watchbacks or pair cases, engraving (London, Victoria and Albert Museum)

watchcases. He engraved other silver objects such as salvers and snuff-boxes (e.g. a silver-gilt comfit box, *c.* 1690; London, V&A). He published two books of prints intended as pattern books for his fellow craftsmen—*A Book of Severall Ornaments* (London, 1682; and *A Book of Ornaments Usefull to Jewellers Watchmakers and All Other Artists* (London, 1697). These were derived from the work of earlier French designers, including JEAN BERAIN and Jean Vaquer (1621–1686). In 1707 Gribelin was the first engraver to reproduce the Raphael Cartoons, then on display at Hampton Court (British Royal Col., on loan to London, V&A). These prints had a significant influence on the development of printmaking in England. In 1712 he engraved six Italian Old Master paintings in the Royal collection and in 1720 the ceiling at the Banqueting House, Whitehall by Peter Paul Rubens (1577–1640). In 1722 he compiled two albums of his prints and impressions on paper of engraved metalwork (London, BM and St Mary's Coll.). His designs were still being reprinted in the 1750s.

C. Oman: *English Engraved Silver, 1150–1900* (London, 1978)
S. O'Connell: 'Simon Gribelin (1661–1733), Printmaker and Metalengraver', *Prt Q.*, ii (1985), pp. 27–38 [with an oeuvre catalogue]
The Quiet Conquest: The Huguenots, 1685–1985 (exh. cat., ed. T. Murdoch; London, Mus. London, 1985)

Gricci, Giuseppe (*b* Florence, *c.* 1700; *d* Madrid, 1770). Italian sculptor and modeller. He trained as a sculptor in Florence before moving in 1738 to Naples, where he was appointed chief modeller of the Capodimonte porcelain factory between 1743 and 1759. Most Capodimonte figures have been attributed to him. Factory records indicate that he originated a popular snuff-box moulded in relief with shells and marine life (1743–55; New York, Met.) as well as figures of peasants, street traders, characters from the *commedia dell'arte* and such religious figures as his only signed work, the *Mourning Virgin* (*c.* 1745; New York, Met.). He contributed to the creation of porcelain cabinets, including the Salottino di Porcellana (1757–9; now Naples, Capodimonte), from the Palazzo Reale in Portici near Naples, and the Gabinete de la Porcelana (1763–5; *in situ*) for the Aranjuez Palace, near Madrid, both of which comprised interlocking plates of porcelain decorated with chinoiseries. In 1759 he moved with other personnel to the Buen retiro porcelain factory, where he held the same position of chief modeller until his death; he was succeeded by his sons Carlos (*d* 1795) and Felipe (*d* 1803).

M. Chilton: 'The Spaghetti Eaters', *Met. Mus. J.*, xxxvii (2002), pp. 223–8

Griemert, Hubert (*b* 1905; *d* 1969). German potter and teacher. He taught first at the Werkkunstschule in Krefeld, then at the Staatliche Werkschule für Keramik in Höhr-Grenzhausen; he also maintained a kiln at Schötmar (Lippe), where he made stoneware, notably vases with crystal glazes. In the 1950s and 1960s he designed tableware for the Berlin porcelain factory (*see* BERLIN, §2).

Griffen, Smith & Hill. American pottery factory established in Phoenixville, PA, in 1867, when it was known as the Phoenix Pottery, Kaolin, and Fire Brick Company. The company made industrial pottery, and in 1882 began to make maiolica in the Etruscan style. Its best-known product was the ' Shell and Seaweed' dinner service. In 1890 the company became the Griffen Pottery Company and in 1894 Phoenix Pottery. The factory closed in 1903. The Phoenixville Museum has a substantial collection of the company's pottery.

Grill. German family of goldsmiths who moved from Augsburg to Amsterdam in the early 1630s. Andries Grill (1604–65) later moved to The Hague and Anthony Grill (1600–75) to Sweden; Johannes Grill (1614–78) remained in Amsterdam. All three favoured the AURICULAR STYLE, but there are exceptions: a gilded silver goblet stand by Andries (1642; The Hague, Gemeentemus.) is executed in the 'flabby style' (*kwabstijl*).

Grisaille [Fr.: 'grey in grey painting']. Term applied to monochrome painting carried out mostly in shades of grey. Probably the oldest form of grisaille in Western art appeared in stained-glass painting in the 12th century. In the third quarter of the 13th century, grisaille windows were standard fittings in French churches, where they often alternated with polychrome figural panes. Occasionally the whole glazing of a church was done with grisaille windows, or they were given at least a prominent place in com-

Fragments of grisaille stained glass from Rouen Cathedral, France, 13th and 14th centuries (Paris, Musée de Cluny)

bination with figural depictions, as a contrasting frame. Among the earliest examples of this use of grisaille are the windows (*c.* 1270) of the church of St Urbain, Troyes.

C. de Kay: *The Grisaille Glass of Paris and Wiley* (New York, 1930)
H. J. Zakin: *French Cistercian Grisaille Glass* (New York, 1979)

Grof [Groff], **Guilliemus** [Wilhelm] **de** (*b* Antwerp, *bapt* 13 Nov 1676; *d* Munich, 16 Aug 1742). Flemish sculptor and draughtsman, active in France and Germany. He was primarily a sculptor, but also produced outstanding ornamental bronze objects, such as mounts for furniture, andirons and stoups. He also worked in silver, and several drawings exist that are known to be by him. His designs include furniture in the French RÉGENCE STYLE.

P. Volk: *Guilliemus de Grof, 1676–1742* (Frankfurt, 1966)

Grohé, Guillaume (*b* Wintersheim, Grand Duchy of Hesse-Darmstadt [now Hessen], 9 Feb 1808; *d* Neuilly-sur-Seine, 6 April 1885). German furniture-maker, active in France. He came to Paris *c.* 1827 with his older brother, Jean-Michel Grohé (*b* 1804), and became a journeyman. In 1829 the brothers started manufacturing and selling furniture. Their business developed rapidly as demonstrated by their success at the eighth Exposition de l'Industrie (Paris, 1834) where they showed Egyptian- and Gothic-style furniture. At the tenth Exposition de l'Industrie, in 1844, they won a gold medal with an octagonal ebony *dressoir* (design, Paris, Mus. A. Déc.), decorated with sculpted figures designed by Michel-Joseph-Napoléon Liénard (1810–*c.* 1875). In 1862 Guillaume Grohé showed at the International Exhibition, London, where he won a medal with a piece in the Louis XVI style, decorated with chased bronze sculpture by the brothers François-Auguste Fannière (1818–1900) and François-Joseph-Louis Fannière (1822–97). One of the principal furniture-makers of his period, he built a reputation as a specialist in high-quality, 18th-century French reproduction furniture (buffet, *c.* 1845; Chantilly, Mus. Condé) and supplied furniture to Queen Victoria (*reg* 1837–1901), Louis-Philippe (*reg* 1830–48), Napoleon III (*reg* 1852–70) and his wife, the Empress Eugénie.

S. Laurent: 'Mobilier XIXe: Guillaume Grohe' *Conn. A.*, dcxxiv (Feb 2005), pp. 94–9

Grolier, Jean. *See under* BOOKBINDING, §I, 2.

Gropius, Walter. *See under* BAUHAUS.

Gros point. Cross-shaped embroidery stitch, often known as cross-stitch, used since the 16th century for carpets, chaircoverings, needlework pictures and chair coverings.

H. Philipps: *The New Cross Stitch Sampler Book* (Newton Abbot, 2002)

Grosso, Niccolò [Caparra] (*fl c.* 1500), Italian iron-smith, was praised by Vasari as the best of ironsmiths; his nickname, Caparra ('payment in advance'), presumably refers to his financial arrangements. His finest work is mounted on the exterior of the Palazzo Strozzi in Florence and includes a lantern shaped like a temple and flag-pole holders decorated with fabulous creatures.

Groszbreitenbach [now Grossbreitenbach]. German centre of porcelain production. A factory founded in Groszbreitenbach, Thuringia, in 1778. From 1782 it was owned by the Greiner family, who also owned the Limbach factory; the products of the two factories are very similar. The factory closed in 1869. There is a fine cup and saucer in the Bowes Museum, Barnard Castle.

Grotell, Maija (*b* Helsinki, 19 Aug 1899; *d* 1973). American potter and teacher of Finnish birth. She studied at the School of Industrial Art in Helsinki and then under Alfred William Finch (1854–1930), a Belgian potter working in Helsinki, for six years. She arrived in the USA in 1927 and studied with CHARLES FERGUS BINNS at Alfred University, Alfred, NY. In 1938 she moved to the Cranbrook Academy of Art, Bloomfield Hills, MI, one of the foremost art schools in America. At Cranbrook Grotell's work developed from low-fired figurative pots to simplified geometric forms in stoneware and porcelain. She experimented with glazes and glaze effects, especially

Maija Grotell: black-and-white vase, stoneware and coloured glazes, h. 267 mm, diam. 191 mm, 1937 (Newark, NJ, Newark Museum)

those using ash, copper, chrome and iron; Albany slip (dark brown) and Bristol glaze (thick and white) were among her favourites.

J. Schlanger and T. Takaezu: *Maija Grotell: Works Which Grow from Belief* (Goffstown, NH, 1996)

Grotesque. French term derived from the Italian *grottesco*, describing a type of European ornament composed of small, loosely connected motifs, including scrollwork, architectural elements, whimsical human figures and fantastic beasts, often organized vertically around a central axis. Grotesque ornament was inspired by the archaeological discovery at the end of the 15th century, of the ancient Roman interiors of the Domus Aurea of Nero in Rome, and by subsequent finds of other palaces, tombs and villas in and around Rome and Naples. The interior walls and ceilings of these underground rooms, known as *grotte*, were painted in a light and playful manner previously unknown to those familiar only with the formal grammar of Classical ornament derived from more accessible antique ruins. A ceiling in such a room might be covered with an interlocking arrangement of compartments containing mythological or allegorical scenes depicted as *trompe l'oeil* cameos, or it might be subdivided into areas dominated by a single such compartment with the remaining space filled with a variety of motifs, symmetrically organized but otherwise unrelated either by scale or subject-matter. This play of fantasy and appeal to the realm of the senses, as opposed to the monumental solemnity of much rediscovered Roman architecture and sculpture, captured the imagination of Renaissance artists and revived the medieval predilection for the fanciful and the monstrous seen in the ornament in the margins of medieval manuscripts or the stone gargoyles of abbeys and cathedrals.

Soon after its discovery at the end of the 15th century, Classical grotesque ornament was copied and disseminated by the drawings of Italian artists, mostly from Umbria and Florence. However, many artists were uncomfortable with the loose organization of unconnected elements and sought to impose a structure that would enable them to use the motifs in a more orderly manner. They therefore employed a vertical format based on the pilaster and traditional candelabrum type of framework, with individual motifs placed one above the other and connected by a central axis; the engravings of Giovanni Pietro da Birago (late 15th-century; London, V&A) are some of the earliest examples of this format. Engravings of grotesque designs were also circulated to craftsmen in other media: silversmiths, goldsmiths and sculptors adapted the designs engraved by Nicoletto da Modena (*fl c.* 1500–*c.* 1520), Giovanni Antonio da Brescia (*c.* 1460–*c.* 1520), Agostino Veneziano, Enea Vico (1523–67) and by Marcantonio Raimondi (*c.* 1470/82–1527/34) and his school. In Raphael's painted interiors in the Vatican, the *stufetta* (1516) of Cardinal Bernardo Bibbiena and the Vatican Loggia (1518–19), grotesque ornament was developed into complete decorative schemes. In the Loggia, the candelabrum motif was used extensively, dividing the entire surface of the wall into some 200 vertical strips within which a compendium of Classical motifs mingled with fantastic birds and animals, fruit and foliage, scrollwork and abstract ornament. A new element was also introduced in the irregularly shaped compartments of the vaulted ceiling by allowing sections of the bandwork border to penetrate the space of the design, producing a kind of internal scaffolding on which individual motifs could be supported. This innovation was developed further by Raphael's successors in bandwork and strapwork that firmly enclosed and anchored the whimsical grotesques. His style was immediately imitated by his assistants: Giovanni da Udine at the Villa Madama in Rome (1525), and Giulio Romano (?1499–1546) at the Palazzo del Te in Mantua (mid-1520s–c. 1535).

In 1530 Francis I invited Rosso Fiorentino to decorate his new château at Fontainebleau. Rosso was joined in 1532 by Francesco Primaticcio, and together they created a new, more elaborate form of ornament and a richer variation on the grotesque theme for the decoration of the Galerie (in situ). The STRAPWORK or bandwork used by Rosso and Primaticcio at Fontainebleau enclosed a series of allegorical frescoes on the grandeur of royalty and the glory of the French king. This structure anchored the paintings within a framework of complex curling straps in high-relief stucco within which were imprisoned monumental figures, putti, hybrid monsters, garlands, swags and the king's emblem: the salamander. The ornament of Raphael and his followers had been small in scale, delicate, in low relief and classical. No precedent existed for the robust, twisted, bent, overlapping leather-like strapwork depicted at Fontainebleau. This transmutation of classical scrollwork into a richly hybrid type of ornament was Rosso's contribution to the contemporary Mannerist taste for the distorted, the twisted, the ambiguous and the strange.

During the second half of the 16th century the engraved designs of the Fontainebleau grotesque and strapwork decoration were disseminated throughout Europe. Such books as Livre de la conqueste de la toison d'or (1563), designed and drawn by Léonard Thiry (fl 1536) and engraved by René Boyvin, or Petit ornemens (1560) by Etienne Delaune spread the fashion in the northern countries, and treatises proliferated to meet the demand of workshops and studios. Veelderley veranderinghe van grotissen ende compatimenten ('Grotesque ornaments and tomb designs'; Antwerp, 1556) by Cornelis Floris and Grottesco in diversche manieren (Antwerp, c. 1565) by Hans Vredeman de Vries were published in the Low Countries. In Germany some outstanding designs for metalwork were produced by Georg Wechter I in 30 Stuck zum Verzachnen fur die Goldschmied Verfertigt Geörg Wecher 15 Maller 79 Nürmberg (Nuremberg, 1579). A more tortured element was introduced to the grotesque by Wendel Dietterlin in Architectura und Ausstheilung der V. Seulen (Stuttgart and Strasbourg, 1593). Although the grotesque

motif was then being used mainly on furniture and silverware, it was still employed in interior decoration, for example in the library (destr.), designed by Friedrich Sustris (c. 1540–99), of the apartments of Hans Fugger in the Fugger Palace in Augsburg (1568–75).

During the second half of the 16th century and the beginning of the 17th, the grotesque was a contributory factor to the development of the hybrid reptilian forms of the AURICULAR STYLE, of which Adam van Vianen from Utrecht was the main exponent.

In the 17th century, while Germany and the Low Countries were absorbed in the extravagant Fontainebleau style, France returned to a sense of classical restraint and discipline. In 1627 Simon Vouet (1590–1649) returned from Rome, where he had studied antique remains as well as Renaissance works. In 1644 he decorated the Cabinet des Bains (destr.) of Anne of Austria at the Palais-Royal in Paris with classical grotesques; the designs survive in Livre de diverses grotesques peintes dans le cabinet des bains de la reine regente au palais royal (Paris, 1647). The style was rather heavy, but harmonious, with landscapes and figures incorporated among the flat, ponderous acanthus scrollwork.

During the reign of Louis XIV (1643–1715) the whimsical grotesque had no part in the majestic court style that evolved under the direction of Charles Le Brun; the lighter spirit of classical ornament was, however, revived by the designer Jean Berain. In 1671 he designed the painted stucco grotesques that decorate the Galerie d'Apollon at the Louvre. This light and airy style of decoration was developed simultaneously by several other ornamentalists: Claude Audran III (1658–1734), Claude Gillot (1673–1722) and Antoine Watteau (1684–1721). Ber-

Maiolica dish with grotesques and depiction of *Cadmus and the Dragon*, from the Fontana workshop in Urbino, late 16th century (Florence, Museo Nazionale del Bargello)

ain was among the first to use the interlaced band-work and delicate tendrils reminiscent of the Muslim Arabesque in the frame surrounding a central design, usually a figure or group of figures standing under a fanciful architectural structure, with various animals, insects and hybrid creatures frolicking beneath swags, ribbons and trophies of all sorts. His work was an important influence on André-Charles Boulle, whose dressing table mirror (1713; London, Wallace) for the Duchesse de Berry exhibits all these motifs together with lambrequins and singerie. Textiles also employed the grotesque vocabulary: Audran's tapestry cartoons, the *Douze mois grotesques* (1699; published Paris, 1726), and Gillot's *Livre de portières*, published after his death (Paris, 1737), developed Berain's ornament further by softening the bandwork frame and introducing curves instead of angular lines. Bandwork was gradually reduced to the curving ribbons and tendrils important in the Rococo style, a particularly French version of grotesque ornament that spread to the whole of Europe. Designs by Juste-Aurèle Meissonnier and François de Cuvilliés are triumphs of Rococo art, in which the Saracenic origins of the flowing, interlacing and interweaving bandwork are hardly recognizable.

The publication of the excavations of Pompeii and Herculaneum in 1752 renewed awareness of the Classical grotesque. Artists again sought inspiration in Rome, where they looked not only at the Classical examples but also at the work of Raphael. Engravings of the Vatican Loggia had been published in the 16th and 17th centuries, but a new publication in 1772 by Giovanni Battista Volpato (1633–1706) was followed in 1776 by a set of engravings of the Domus Aurea itself by Lodovico Miri. Ornamentalists and artists throughout Europe took up the style again. In France Jules-Hughes Rousseau (1743–1806) and his brother Jean-Simeon Rousseau de La Rottière (1747–after 1781) adapted it for the Petits Appartements of Marie-Antoinette at Versailles in 1783 and at Fontainebleau in 1786, achieving ensembles of great elegance and refinement. In order to become acceptable to the Age of Reason, the grotesque had shed its earlier fantastic and monstrous qualities, although in doing so it had lost much of its previous vitality.

Grotesque ornament was a component of the Etruscan style, which Robert Adam used for the decoration of the Etruscan Dressing-room (1775) at Osterley Park House, Middx, NT. Charles Percier (1764–1838) and Pierre-François-Léonard Fontaine also created attenuated, graceful grotesque ornament interspersed with *trompe-l'oeil* cameo panels at the château of Malmaison in 1799. In these forms the style was gracious and elegant but deprived of its earlier robustness. In the 19th century grotesque ornament was often featured in such Renaissance Revival interiors as those at Chatsworth (1840s), Derbys, and Longleat, Wilts, by the Crace family of decorators.

The 20th-century ethos no longer favoured the elegant decorative qualities of the grotesque, the whimsical, fanciful motifs disciplined within a classical format.

N. Dacos: *La Découverte de la Domus Aurea et la formation des grotesques à la Renaissance* (London and Leiden, 1969)
A. Chastel: *La Grotesque* (Paris, 1988)
P. Morel: *Les Grotesques: Les Figures de l'imaginaire dans la peinture italienne de la fin de la Renaissance* (Paris, 1997)
E. Miller: *16th-century Italian Ornament Prints in the Victoria and Albert Museum* (London, 1999)
W. Gasch: *Guide to gargoyles and other grotesques* (Washington, DC, 2003)

Gruber, Jacques (*b* Sundhauser, 1870; *d* Paris, 1936). French stained-glass artist and ébéniste of Alsatian origin. He trained with the DAUM brothers and LOUIS MAJORELLE in Nancy, where he designed the stained-glass windows in the Chamber de Commerce and made furniture for Majorelle. In 1916 he moved to Paris, where his work includes the stained glass of St Christophe de Javel (1925). Jacques' son Francis Gruber (*b* Nancy, 15 March 1912; *d* Paris, 1 Dec 1948) was primarily a painter, but also designed stained glass, including *Sports and Pastimes* (exh. 1937, Paris, Exposition Universelle) and *Homage to Sculpture* (1938), for the Musée National d'Art Moderne in Paris (now Pal. Tokyo).

Jacques Gruber (1871–1936): Ebéniste et maître-verrier, Ministère de la culture (Paris, 1990)

Grue, Francesco Antonio Xaverio (*b* Castelli, 7 March, 1686; *d* Castelli, 1746). Italian potter. He came from an illustrious family of maiolica potters and painters from Castelli in Abruzzo. In 1716 he arrived in Naples, where he concentrated on the production of ceramics; he decorated plates, albarelli and shields in the style of wares from his home town. His considerable output influenced contemporary Neapolitan production. Among his most notable works is the series of albarelli for the apothecaries of the sanctuary of the S Casa in Loreto and of the monastery of S Martino in Naples. Wares were often Baroque in style and included shields decorated with mythological themes, and plates decorated with landscapes or putti in the centre and tendril or festoon borders. Wares were also often signed and dated. In 1736 he returned to Castelli, where he continued to work until his death.

C. Cherubini: *I Grue pittori in maiolica* (Teramo, 1857)
Mostra dell'antica maiolica di Castelli d'Abruzzo (exh. cat., Castelli, Mus. Cer., 1965)
L. Arbace: *Maioliche di Castelli la raccolta acerbo* (Ferrara, 1993)

Grueby, William Henry (*b* 1867; *d* 1925). American potter and ceramic manufacturer. He was apprenticed in 1882 to the J. and J. G. Low Art Tile Works, Chelsea, MA, where he remained for ten years. At the World's Columbian Exposition in Chicago in 1893, he was very impressed with the high-temperature flambé glazes of the French art pottery created by AUGUSTE DELAHERCHE and ERNEST CHAPLET, which encouraged Grueby's own experiments with matt, monochromatic glazes. In 1895 he set up his

Grueby vase, matt-glazed earthenware, h. 267 mm, executed by Ruth Erickson, Boston, MA, c. 1905–10 (Newark, NJ, Newark Museum)

own factory, the Grueby Faience Co., in Boston, which produced tiles and architectural faience in Greek, medieval and Hispano-Moresque styles, popularized by the Arts and Crafts Movement. From 1897 to 1898 he manufactured a range of vases finished in soft, matt glazes in greens, yellows, ochres and browns, with the 'Grueby Green' predominating. Until 1902 the potter George Prentiss Kendrick was largely responsible for the designs, executed in heavily potted stoneware based on Delaherche's Art Nouveau shapes. Young women were employed to carry out the hand-moulded and incised surface decoration, which consisted mainly of vertical leaf-forms in shallow relief (e.g. stoneware vase, late 19th century; London, V&A). The work was enthusiastically received by the public, and such designers as Tiffany ordered ceramic bases for their lamps. Many American workshops and factories quickly introduced matt glazes, but few could surpass the velvety perfection of Grueby's wares. Between 1900 and 1904 Grueby pottery won awards at a number of important international exhibitions, including a silver and two gold at the 1900 Exposition Universelle in Paris. Despite these successes, the firm was declared bankrupt in 1908. Grueby then opened the Grueby Faience & Tile Co., which was taken over in 1919 by the C. Pardee Works of Perth Amboy, NJ. The firm continued in the production of Grueby-style wares until the late 1920s.

S. J. Montgomery: *The Ceramics of William H. Grueby* (Lambertville, NJ, 1993)

Guadameci. Spanish sheepskin leather. The term was derived from the Libyan town of Ghadames, which produced a similar type of soft goatskin dressed with alum. Córdoba (hence the English term 'cordwainer') was famous for its *guadameci* from the 10th century; its *guadameci* was either left in its natural white form or dyed red with kermes. The leather was sometimes covered with gold or silver foil, and during the 14th century this metallized surface was punched. During the early 17th century, designs were embossed on silvered leather using moulds in a modified printing press. Other centres of production in Spain were Granada, Seville and Valencia.

The leather was used for upholstery, cushions, floor coverings, wall and bed hangings and ecclesiastical purposes (antependiums, kneelers and vestments). In the Sala de los Reyes (or de la Justicia) at the Alhambra, Granada, there are two leather-covered cupolas dating from the end of the 14th century. In 1570 Catherine de' Medici ordered from Córdoba four sets of *guadameci*, with designs of flowers, fruits and grotesques on a polychrome ground, to decorate rooms in the Palais du Louvre, Paris.

J. Madurell i Marimon: *El antiguo arte del guadameci y sus artífices* (Vic, 1973)

Guan ware. Chinese pottery made in the Southern Song dynasty capital, Lin'an (modern Hangzhou), in Zhejiang Province. Guan (Chin.: 'official') ware has a thin, iron-rich and often dark-fired body and a thick, crackled glaze of exquisite, smooth texture, ranging in colour from bluish-green to greenish-grey. Various types of crackle can be distinguished, and it usually represents the main decorative feature of the ware. Shapes are mostly simple, bowls and dishes often having lobed or indented rims. Vases can be of archaistic bronze form. Guan ware is the most frequently copied of all Chinese wares, ranging from contemporary Longquan to Yuan, Ming, Qing and later Jingdezhen copies.

Li He: 'Problems in Song Ceramics: Redating Official Guan Ceramics in the Asian Art Museum of San Francisco', *Apollo*, cdxxxiii (March 1998), pp. 10–16

Gubbio. Italian centre of pottery production. The small Umbrian town of Gubbio [Lat. Igurium] owes much of its fame during the Renaissance to the work of GIORGIO ANDREOLI. Lustres applied in Renaissance Gubbio included gold and ruby (e.g. two-handled vase, c. 1500–25; London, Wallace). During the 19th century, lustrewares were revived in Gubbio by Giovanni Spinacci (fl 1853–76), who successfully produced reproductions of 16th-century wares.

C. Fiocco and G. Gherardi: *Gubbio, altri centri, lo Storicismo*, ii of *Ceramiche umbre dal Medioevo allo Storicismo* (Faenza, 1989)
C. Fiocco and G. Gherardi: *Museo comunale di Gubbio: Ceramiche* (Perugia, 1995)
La tradizione ceramica in Umbri dall'antichità al Novecento: Deruta, Gualdo Tadino, Gubbio, Orvieto (exh. cat., ed. G. C. Bojani and T. Seppilli; Perugia, Rocca Paolina, Sale Cannoniera, 1995)
Cece and E. A. Sannipoli, eds: *La ceramica "a lustro" nell'Ottocento a Gubbio* (Florence, 1998)

Guccio di Mannaia [Malnaia; Malnaggia; Manaie; Mannaie] (*fl* 1288–1318). Italian goldsmith. His only signed work is the chalice (silver gilt and translucent enamel; h. 220 mm; Assisi, Tesoro Mus. Basilica S Francesco) made in 1288–92 for Pope Nicholas IV and donated to S Francesco, Assisi. The stem is inscribed GUCCIUS MANAIE DE SENIS FECIT and NICCHO[L]AUS PAPA QUARTUS. The chalice is first described in an inventory of 1370 and is mentioned in successive inventories: that of 1430 refers to a paten (lost) decorated with an enamel of the *Last Supper*. The chalice is the earliest dated example of *basse taille* or translucent enamel in Europe, preceding the first known French example by *c.* 30 years. It is decorated with 96 enamels, arranged from the base to the stem to form a unified iconographic programme related to the Eucharist. The base is decorated with 32 plaques, each framed by a beaded band between which are finely wrought repoussé leaves. The larger quadrilobe plaques depict the *Crucifixion* and half-length busts of the *Virgin, St John, St Francis, St Claire* and *St Anthony of Padua*, the *Virgin and Child* and a *Pope*. In between, smaller plaques depict the *Evangelist Symbols* and various animals. The eight-faceted knop has circular enamel medallions of *Christ the Redeemer* and seven half-length *Apostles*. The chalice was without immediate precedent; its form was highly influential, and it was never technically superseded.

A number of other objects have been attributed to Guccio on the basis of this chalice, including three seals, an incised marble slab of the *Crucifixion* (Siena, S Pellegrino alla Sapienza), a silver processional cross (Florence, Bargello), medallions of *St Elizabeth of Hungary* (Paris, Louvre) and *St Anthony* (Berlin, Tiergarten, Kstgewmus) and an enamel plaque of the *Virgin and Child Enthroned with SS Peter and Paul* (120×90 mm; Florence, Bargello, collection Carrand, 678 C).

E. Cioni Liserani: 'Alcune ipotesi per Guccio di Mannaia', *Prospettiva*, xvii (April 1979), pp. 47–58
P. Leone De Castris: 'Smalti e oreficerie di Guccio di Mannaia al museo del Bargello', *Prospettiva*, xvii (April 1979), pp. 58–64

Guéridon. Small ornamental pedestal table or stand, usually ornately carved. Early examples are tall, fragile structures of gilt-wood or marquetry used as holders or supports for candelabra. In mid-18th century France *guéridons* became lower, multi-purpose tables. The tripod base and round top were retained, but the top could now be raised on a shaft or pivoted. The celebrated *guéridon* of Madame Du Barry (Paris, Louvre) is decorated with porcelain plaques.

M.-L. de Rochebrune: *Le guéridon de Madame du Barry* (Paris, 2002)

Guido Durantino. *See under* FONTANA, ORAZIO.

Guillaume [Guglielmo] **de Marcillat** [Guillaume de Pierre] (*b* La Châtre, nr Bourges, 1467–70; *d* Arezzo, 30 July 1529). French stained-glass maker and painter, active in Italy. He was called to Rome before 1509, perhaps by Donato Bramante (?1443/4–1514). Marcillat was employed by the popes Julius II and Leo X in the Vatican and at S Maria del Popolo, where the two Serlian windows in the choir are his earliest surviving works (1509; heavily rest.). Summoned to Cortona in 1515 by Cardinal Silvio Passerini, he established a workshop and began keeping a detailed account-book, which has survived; his prolific output there included a two-part window for the chancel of Cortona Cathedral, comprising the *Nativity* (1516; Detroit, MI, Inst. A) and the *Adoration of the Magi* (London, V&A). Based in Arezzo by 1519, he produced the most skilfully executed windows of his age, notably the five splendidly illusionistic Gospel scenes, including the *Expulsion from the Temple* and the *Raising of Lazarus*, in Arezzo Cathedral (1519–24), a dramatic *Assumption* in SS Annunziata (1520) and an oculus in S Francesco (1524; all *in situ*).

G. Mancini: *Guglielmo de Marcillat* (Florence, 1909) [fundamental documentary monograph]
S. Atherly: 'Marcillat's Cortona *Nativity*', *Bull. Detroit Inst. A.*, lviii (1980), pp. 72–82
S. Atherly: *Studien zu den Glasfenstern Guillaume de Marcillat (1470?–1529)* (diss., U. Vienna, 1981) [stylistic analysis of windows; in Eng.]
N. Dacos: 'Un "Romaniste" français méconnu: Guillaume de Marcillat', *'Il se rendit en Italie': Etudes offertes à André Chastel* (Rome and Paris, 1987), pp. 135–47
A. Tafi: *Il sole racchiuso nei vetri: Guglielmo de Marcillat e le sue vetrate istoriate di Arezzo* (Arezzo, 1988) [good for colour illus.]
G. Virde: 'Le vetrate della chiesa della SS Annunziata in Arezzo', *Atti del convegno di studi su la chiesa della SS Annunziata di Arezzo nel 500° della sua costruzione: Arezzo, 1990*, pp. 169–223
T. Henry: ' "Centro e periferia": Guillaume de Marcillat and the Modernisation of Taste in the Cathedral of Arezzo', *Artibus & Hist.* xv/29 (1994), pp. 55–83

Guilloche. Plait-like ornament. There are several variants; for example the spaces between the bands may be blank or may contain flower motifs. It occurs often in Greek and Roman architecture and in the borders of Roman mosaics (see fig. on p. 458). Guilloche decoration was revived in the Renaissance and from then onwards occurs in different media, including furniture and metalwork. See fig. on p. 458.

Guimard, Hector(-Germain) (*b* Lyon, 1867; *d* New York, 20 May 1942). French architect, furniture designer and writer. His fame rests on his ART NOUVEAU designs for Paris Métro stations. Of the three types of stations, the most important from a decorative perspective are the simple open stations (see colour pl. XVI, fig. 1), of which *c.* 90 survive; these were fashioned in various forms, the most interesting of which consists of railings with decorated 'shields' incorporating the letter M and an iron arch over the entrance which supports an enamelled sign flanked by 'stalks' blossoming into lamps (e.g. Cité, 1898–1901).

At his own house, 122, Avenue Mozart, Paris, which he built and furnished after marrying the American painter Adeline Oppenheim (*b* ?1872) in 1909, Guimard achieved a synthesis in its furnishings and décor which he was never to surpass (examples New York, MOMA). The Jassedé flats (1905) at 142

Guilloche (see p. 457) decoration on a Roman mosaic, 3.1 × 2.8 m, Tunisia (El Jem, Musée Archéologique)

Avenue de Versailles, Paris, were the occasion for Guimard to launch into the design of standardized cast-iron fittings, such as guttering and garden seats (examples Paris, Mus. Orsay), later advertised in a catalogue (*Fontes artistiques*, 1907) as standard and available to order.

H. Guimard: *Fontes artistiques pour constructions, fumisterie, articles de jardins et sépultures, style Guimard* (Paris, 1907)
G. Naylor and Y. Brunhammer: *Hector Guimard* (London, 1978)
F. Ferré and others: *Hector Guimard* (New York, 1988)
G. Vigne and F. Ferré: *Hector Guimard: Architect Designer, 1867–1942* (New York, 2003)
F. Descouturelle and A. Mignard: *Le Métropolitain d'Hector Guimard* (Nancy, 2003)

Guipure lace. Type of lace in which where the flowers are either joined by large coarse stitches or threads without any ground at all. It was made with twisted silk and *cartisane*, a narrow strip of vellum or parchment covered with silk or metallic threads.

A. Goubaud: *Madame Goubaud's Guipure Patterns and Instructions* (London, 1870)

E. Riego de la Branchardière: *The Netting Book for Guipure d'Art* (London, 1879)

Gulli gul. *See* ELEPHANT'S FOOT.

Gumley, John (*fl* 1691; *d* 1729). English furniture-maker and glass-maker. He specialized in the manufacture of plate-glass, but his firm provided furniture of all kinds for Hampton Court Palace, for the 1st Duke of Montrose's lodgings in the Drygate, Glasgow, and for a Mr Paul Foley, from whom an extensive bill exists. The furnishings are predominantly mirrors, but desks and bureaux also survive (London, Hampton Court, Royal Col.). From 1714 he worked in partnership with JAMES MOORE, and in 1715 they succeeded GERRIT JENSEN as royal cabinetmakers.

W. Rieder: 'Attributed to James Moore (d. 1726) and John Gumley (d. 1729): Chandelier', *Bull. Met.*, liv (Fall 1996), p. 34

Gundelach, Franz *See* GONDELACH, FRANZ.

Hector Guimard: armchair, walnut, 1160×620×580 mm, from Maison Louis Coilliot, Lille, c. 1898 (Paris, Musée d'Orsay)

Gustavian style. Expression of 18th-century Swedish Neo-classicism during the reign of Gustav III (reg 1771–92), who admired the French courtly life at Versailles. He spent part of 1770–71 in France, where he acquired a passion for the Neo-classical style. Early Gustavian interiors (c. 1770–85) were light and elegant interpretations of the Louis XVI style, with echoes of English, German and Dutch influences. Rooms were decorated with pilasters and columns; walls were applied with rich silk damasks or rectangular panels with painted designs framed in carved, gilded linear ornament and laurel festoons. Damask, usually crimson, blue or green, was used to upholster benches, sofas and chairs. Other rooms were panelled in wood, painted light-grey, blue or pale-green; the dominant feature was a columnar faience-tiled stove, decorated with sprigged floral patterns. Klismos-style chairs upholstered in silk were very popular, as were oval-backed chairs with straight, fluted legs, and bateau-shaped sofas were common. Rooms were embellished with long, gilt-wood-framed mirrors, crystal chandeliers, gilt *torchères* and Classical-style vases and urns of Swedish porphyry. Wooden floors were laid with Swedish carpets inspired by those of Savonnerie.

Swedish painters, architects, cabinetmakers and carvers were encouraged by Gustav to train in France and Italy and to return to Stockholm to assist in the realization of the King's vision of a Swedish golden age. Two prominent Swedish architects who received important commissions were JeanEric Rehn (1717–93), whose work at the Royal Palace, Stockholm, and Drottningholm Palace on Lake Mälan introduced the Neo-classical style to Sweden, and C. F. Adelcrantz (1716–96), who was responsible for designing the Royal Opera House (1775–82; destr. 1892), Stockholm, and the splendid Gustavian interiors at Sturehof (1778–81), outside Stockholm. The most important cabinetmaker of the period was GEORG HAUPT, who produced furniture inlaid with exotic woods for the royal family. Notable contributors to the late Gustavian style (c. 1785–1810) were the French architect Louis-Jean Desprez (1743–1804) and the designer Louis Adrien Masreliez, both of whom worked on the interiors of the Pavilion at Haga Palace (c. 1790), which was constructed by the Swedish architect Ol of Tempelman (1745–1816) after the Petit Trianon at Versailles. Masreliez covered the walls at Haga with Classical muses and grotesques derived from decoration at Pompeii, Herculaneum and the works of Raphael and Giulio Romano (?1499–1546); it was the first decoration of this kind in Sweden. Late Gustavian furniture was rectilinear and austere, and there was a new accuracy in copying from antique models. Secrétaires, commodes, cupboards and desks were decorated with figured veneers and gilded mounts, or were sparsely inlaid with different woods, as seen in the secrétaire (c. 1790; Stockholm, Nordiska Mus.) by Gustav Adolf Ditzinger (1760–1800).

H. Groth and F. von der Schulenburg: *Neo-classicism in the North: Swedish Furniture and Interiors, 1770–1850* (London, 1990)

G. Alm: 'Neoclassical Furniture Design in Sweden', *Mag. Ant.*, cxlv (April 1994), pp. 562–71

Gustavsberg Ceramics Factory. Swedish factory founded in Värmland in 1825. It was important for the development of Swedish ceramics until the mid-1980s and was the principal competitor of RÖRSTRAND CERAMICS FACTORY. German raw materials were used at Gustavsberg until 1839, when the introduction of English materials improved the quality of the wares. Creamware was produced, first with simple, painted decoration and from the 1830s with printed decoration. Early border patterns were inspired by such English factories as Davenport & Co., but the central motif, including scenes from Djurgården in Stockholm, was often Swedish and transfer-printed in blue, mulberry or black. In the 1840s green was also used, and the spread of the Rococo Revival is also evident. Rörstrand began to employ such motifs borrowed from England as the 'Willow' pattern, first introduced at Caughley, as early as the 1820s. After the Great Exhibition of 1851 in London, the painter Johan August Malmström (1829–1901) designed a form of decoration for Gustavsberg that included a stylized band derived from rune stones; this motif was very popular at the time in such other media as wood-carving and embroidery. More variants of such old Nordic ornament as interlacing were developed, which Rörstrand also began to use.

In 1864 Gustavsberg began to produce fine china. Decoration was most often hand-painted, and gilding was also applied. Lithographic prints were used as decoration and adorned many vases. Purely decorative objects, ranging from huge vases to small objects, were, however, often made of porcelain. From 1860 the factory specialized in PARIAN WARE. The most important artist in 19th-century Gustavsberg was the flower painter Gunnar Wennerberg (1863–1914). At first he designed delicate and quite naturalistic decorations, but for the Allmänna Konstoch Industriutställning (Art and industry exhibition) in Stockholm in 1897 he designed several simple, repeated motifs of stylized flowers, which were intended to be reminiscent of the border patterns of the Wedgwood ceramic factory. Lily-of-the-valley and snowdrops were exclusive hand-painted decorations and were applied to the factory's best bone china. Although only a small number of these pieces were produced, they became representative of Swedish Art Nouveau ceramics, as they hailed the transition to a new era of specifically Swedish design. Shapes and decoration in general, however, continued to be copied from mass-produced German wares.

Wilhelm Kåge (1889–1960) directed Gustavsberg's whole production from 1917 to 1960. His first service for Gustavsberg was the 'Liljeblaservis', also called the 'Arbetarservis' (workers' service); it had a simple form and blue, transfer-printed decoration. The 'Guldstjärna' and 'Formosa' bone-china services were produced by the factory during the 1920s. In 1930 Kåge introduced his 'Argenta' line, a luxurious silver-inlaid stoneware. Stig Lindberg (1916–82) made an exquisite bone-china service, 'LB', for Gustavsberg in the 1940s. Karin Björquist (b 1927), who began work at Gustavsberg in the 1950s, was a versatile artist whose utilitarian 'Vardag' service was exhibited at the 1955 Helsingborg Exhibition. In the late 20th century Björquist continued to specialize in practical but beautiful bone-china

wares for restaurants. At the end of the 1980s she made an elegant white service characteristic of wares of this decade called 'Stockholm'.

In 1988 Gustavsberg and Rörstrand merged to become Rörstrand–Gustavsberg AB Rörstrand, the only Swedish company devoted to porcelain production Gustavsberg-Vänge was an unrelated pottery near Uppsala that produced creamware from 1785 to 1795 under the direction of Henrik Sten from Marieberg.

Gutfreund, Nicholas David (b Bristol, 16 Sept 1961). English cabinetmaker. He turned to cabinetmaking after an early career in advertising, and became known for his finely-crafted commissioned furniture, typically in woods such as pear inlaid with with maple and ebony.

Gutta-percha. Inspissated juice of various trees found chiefly in the Malayan archipelago. It was introduced into Europe in 1822, and for the remained of the 19th century was used for moulded decorations on furniture.

Gyles, Henry (b 1645; d 1709). English painter and designer of stained glass, active in York. He was famous both for his detailed heraldic work and for his stained-glass sundials. In York Minster there is a small amount of Gyles glass in the south choir aisle; the central lower panel displaying the arms of Archbishop Lamplugh (d 1691) shows the light yellow glass that is almost a trademark of his work. Gyles also made glass for the York Guildhall (now V&A, London). His pupils Joshua and William Price (both fl 1696–1717) did much work in a pictorial and classical manner in Oxford. Gyles was the host of the York Society of Virtuosi, who met at his Micklegate house.

J Knowles: *Henry Gyles, Glass-painter of York* (Oxford, 1923)

H

Haas, Georg (*b* ?Flensburg, *c.* 1523; *d* Vienna, 1596–1603). German joiner and etcher, active in Austria. In 1571 he was commissioned to make the doors and magnificent inlaid ceiling of the Landhaus, Vienna. The ceiling in the Verordnetenstube, which was completed in 1572, demonstrates great artistic ability with its combination of delicate inlay, carving and applied decoration. In 1583 *Künstlicher und zierlicher Newer vor nie gesehener: Fünfftzig perspectifischer Stück . . .* —his renowned series of etchings, with 48 designs for ceilings—was published in Vienna. A wooden coffered ceiling (*c.* 1600), originally installed in Burg Rapottenstein, lower Austria, now in the Franzensburg at Laxenburg near Vienna, has been attributed to Haas.

E. Schaffran: 'Georg Haas, Hoftischler in Wien und sein Masterbuch', *Unsere Heimat*, 7 (Vienna, 1934)

Habán pottery. Faience produced by the Habáns (Anabaptists), who settled in Moravia from 1526 and from the end of the 16th century brought about a radical change in ceramics. Habáner ware was made from *c.* 1590 to 1730. The wares were thrown or moulded, tin-glazed and painted with such high-temperature colours as yellow, blue, green and violet. The distinctive range of forms included lattice-bordered bowls, plates, jugs, washing sets, dinner-services and bottles. Wares were almost always dated and decorated with botanically correct plants, initials and coats of arms. Habáner ware was influenced by Italian (especially *Bianchi di Faenza*), German, Dutch, Islamic and Iznik wares.

After 1620, strong Counter-Reformation measures caused the Habáns to move towards western Slovakia. At the end of the 1670s a Habán workshop was established at Hluboká in south Bohemia, the result of attempts by the Schwarzenberg family to attract Habán potters from Slovakia to serve on their estate. From the 17th century architectural motifs were used in the decoration—the depiction of animals and figures was not tolerated in Habán works—and a lively stream of folk-art ceramics followed in the wake of Habán faience in Moravia. A collection of Haban and other ceramics is housed in the West Slovak Museum at Trnava.

In the 20th century, potters such as the Hungarian Géza Gorka (1894–1971) produced Habán-style wares.

B. Kristinkovitch: *Haban Pottery* (Budapest, 1962)
M. Krisztinkovich: *The Lost Art of Haban Pottery* (Willowdale, 1967)

Habermann, Franz Xaver (*b* Habelschwerdt, Silesia [now Bystryca Kłodzka, nr Wrocław, Poland], 1721; *d* Augsburg, 1796). German draughtsman, engraver and sculptor. He settled in Augsburg, where he worked as a sculptor. The dearth of commissions for sculptors in Augsburg in the mid-18th century led him to turn to ornamental engraving. The *c.* 600 surviving engravings by him cover a wide range of ornamental subject-matter. Their success probably depended primarily, despite Habermann's effervescent imagination, on their practical applicability by any artistic craftsman of the period. The engravings were published, mostly in series of four sheets, by the Augsburg publishers Martin Engelbrecht (*c.* 1684–1756) and Johann Georg Hertel (*c.* 1700/01–76), and later by Habermann himself. According to contemporary accounts, Habermann also completed numerous designs for goldsmiths; of these, only his design for a table centrepiece has survived (Augsburg, Städt. Kstsammlungen). In the 1770s and 1780s he also engraved prints for peepshow boxes.

Habermann made a decisive contribution to disseminating contemporary style through the quality, quantity and variety of his ornamental designs. Objects after his engravings, such as furniture inlays, wall coverings, porcelain and ceramics, have been found all over Europe. His oeuvre reflected the stylistic development of the whole of Rococo as far as early Classicism.

F. Krull: *Franz Xaver Habermann: Ein Augsburger Ornamentist des Rokoko* (Augsburg, 1977)

Hackl, Joseph. *See under* GÖGGINGEN.

Hackwood, William. The name of two important figures in the pottery industry in Staffordshire. One William Hackwood (*d* 1836) was the principal modeller to Josiah Wedgwood and his successors at Etruria from 1769 until 1832. He was chiefly employed in the adaptation of classical busts for reproduction on jasper and basaltes wares, but also modelled portrait medallions, including one of Josiah Wedgwood (1779).

461

The other William Hackwood (*d* 1849) was the proprietor of a pottery that made earthenware and jasper ware at Eastwood, Hanley. This company was variously known as Hackwood & Co. or Hackwood, Dimmock & Co. (1807–27) and William Hackwood (1827–43). After a move to New Hall, Shelton, in 1844, it was known as William & Thomas Hackwood (1844–50), William Hackwood & Son (1846–9) and Thomas Hackwood (1849–53).

Hadley chest. American CHEST first discovered in the Hadley area of Massachusetts and now known to have been made in Enfield, Suffield (now in Connecticut), Deerfield and Northfield, sometimes for the Pynchon family of patrons. The chests have hinged tops, and the fronts have three sunken panels with drawers below; they are elaborately carved with tulip-and-leaf motifs. Some 175 Hadley chests have been identified.

P. Zea: 'The Fruits of Oligarchy: Patronage and the Hadley Chest in Western Massachusetts', *New England Furniture: Essays in Memory of Benno M. Forman*, ed. B. Jobe (Boston, MA, 1987), pp. 1–65.
C. Luther: *The Hadley Chest* (Ephrata, PA, 1985)
Hadley Chests (exh. cat. by P. Zea and S. L. Flynt; Hartford, CT, Wadsworth Atheneum, 1992)

Hafner ware. Generic term for the first important earthenwares produced in Germany. Early examples from the 14th century were insulating bowl-tiles for stoves and were made by stovemakers (*Hafner*). The tiles were often covered in a green lead glaze, for the dual purpose of further insulation and decoration. During the 15th century the tiles were decorated with moulded or modelled reliefs, which often took the form of figures in recessed niches. About 1500, polychrome glazes were introduced. The Leupold family in Nuremburg were particularly well known for their black-glazed stove tiles with oil gilding. PAUL PREUNNING and Kunz Pruning from Nuremburg made fine polychrome jugs decorated with horizontal bands of biblical and allegorical scenes in relief. Useful wares based on the stove tile began to emerge particularly in the 17th century.

Hagi. Centre of ceramics production in Japan. High-fired Hagi ware was manufactured from the early 17th century in Nagato Province (now Yamaguchi Prefect). The first Hagi potters, the brothers Yi Suk-wang and Yi Kyng (Jap. Sakamoto Sukehachi), were brought to Japan from Korea in the 1590s and founded a kiln at Hagi in 1604.

Production began in the village of Matsumoto just east of Hagi. Yi Suk-wang died not long after the opening of the kiln, whereupon leadership was assumed by his younger brother. Yi Kyng also trained his brother's son, who received the name Sakunojō in 1625. Official domain records identify six other potters working in Matsumoto in 1645; several of that group opened a second kiln centre at Fukawa (now part of Nagato City), some 30 km to the west,

in 1653. Ten years later the clan reinforced the Matsumoto staff with two more potters, Miwa Chūbei Toshisada (later Miwa Kyūsetsu I) and Saeki Hanroku; the former was even sent to Kyoto to study Raku ware techniques. In contrast to the consistent clan support of the Matsumoto kilns, Fukawa operated on a semi-private basis from its inception, and by 1693 the clan surrendered its supervision to the village headman.

The term 'Hagi ware' does not appear in Japanese records until 1668; before that the product was called Matsumoto ware or Fukawa ware. The earliest work, represented by a few securely provenanced heirlooms, consists of Korean-style stoneware bowls for the tea ceremony known to Japanese connoisseurs as Ido, Komogae and Kohiki. They are characterized by thickly potted forms, flaring from foot to lip, set on a high and sometimes notched foot rim; the granular clay bodies are covered with a semi-transparent feldspathic glaze ranging in colour from warm ivory to salmon pink. Their artless appearance and the tactile qualities of the material placed Hagi teabowls second only to Raku ware in the esteem of tea masters. In the second half of the 17th century, the Miwa potters introduced new shapes and glazes from KYOTO, IGA, and SHIGARAKI, contributing to a gradual Japanization of the Hagi repertory. Excavations of mid-17th-century Saka family kilns also show that they produced far more utilitarian wares than articles for the tea ceremony.

The kilns found a particularly fervent supporter in the seventh-generation Mōri clan head, Shigetaka (1725–89); he constructed a tea house at his villa, made his own ceramics and in 1782 invited the Edo tea master Kawakami Fuhaku (1716–1807) to teach at the domain. Seeking a new source of revenue in the burgeoning demand for porcelain, the clan opened a kiln at Obata, just outside Hagi, in the early 19th century. The Fukawa potters built their own porcelain kiln at Kurimoto in 1830. Besides everyday wares, much of the production was devoted to comparatively delicate pieces for *sencha*, a style of steeped-tea ceremony that gained popularity in the late 18th century. All the Hagi kilns experienced severe difficulties after the Meiji Restoration (1868). Not until the revival of the tea ceremony in the 20th century did Hagi ware regain its popularity; by then only five of the old families remained, two in Matsumoto and three in Fukawa, supplemented in the post-war period by about 100 workshops making wares for the tourist and teaware trades.

T. Yoshiga: 'The History and Variety of Hagi Ceramics', *Chanoyu Q.*, xxiv (1980)
R. Kawano: *Hagi*, Famous Ceramics of Japan, xi (Tokyo, 1983)

Haguenau. *See under* HANNONG.

Haida. *See* NOVÝ BOR.

Halberstadt tapestries. Three 12th-century tapestries made in the north German city of Halberstadt:

Abraham and Isaac (*c.* 1150), the earliest surviving large-scale European wall tapestry, the *Apostles* tapestry of *c.* 1170–75 and the *Charlemagne* of the 1230s (all Halberstadt Cathedral, Treasury). The earliest northern European knotted carpets were made in the same region. A rare surviving example (Quedlinburg, Domschatz) was made by the nuns of the Quedlinburg convent and donated *c.* 1200.

Hald, (Niels Tove) Edward (*b* Stockholm, 17 Sep 1883; *d* 4 July 1980). Swedish painter, glassmaker and ceramicist. From 1917 he worked for the Orrefors Glasbruk, Orrefors, Småland, where he produced high-quality engraved glass. Together with Simon Gate (1883–1945) he designed 'Graal glass', which involved encasing engraved glass with clear glass. He also produced pottery and porcelain in both classical and more advanced styles, working at the Rörstrand ceramics factory.

E. Hald and others: *Orrefors* (Orrefors, 1951)
A. Reihnér, K. Edenheim and A. Hellner: *Simon Gate, Edward Hald glas, 1916–1973* (exh. cat., Linköping, 1983)
Edward Hald: Målare, konstindustripionjär (exh. cat., Stockholm, Nmus., 1983)

Half-silk. Cloth with a main warp of coarse linen, a binding warp of silk and a weft of silk.

Halifax. English centre of carpet production. The Yorkshire town of Halifax has been an important centre of carpet manufacture since the early 19th century. The firm of J. Crossley & Sons is synonymous with the production of carpets in Halifax and has been responsible for introducing some of the most far-reaching innovations in machine-produced floor coverings. The firm was founded by John Crossley (*d* 1837), a hand-loom weaver who set up his own weaving shed at nearby Dean Clough in 1803. By 1833 the venture was profitable enough to enable the company to purchase from Richard Whytock of Edinburgh, for £10,000, the patents for weaving warp-printed carpets, a technique that became especially associated with Crossley's and which made Halifax the centre for such production in England. The task of printing the design on to the warp threads before weaving was laborious and dirty but made it possible for designers to incorporate up to 150 colours, although in practice a total of 30 to 40 colours was more common. As the entire pile warp was raised to form each row of loops, carpets could be woven at considerable speed. Two qualities of carpet were produced: 'Tapestry Brussels', with uncut loops, and 'Tapestry Velvets', with cut pile. Some of the first power looms to be used in the carpet industry were installed at Dean Clough in 1850, and in the following year Crossley's bought the patent for the power loom invented by Erastus Brigham Bigelow (1814–79) for Brussels carpets, which could weave carpeting at the rate of 23 m per day compared with the 6.4 m produced on a hand loom. Crossley's soon dominated the industry and in the second half of the 19th century was the world's largest producer of carpets. The firm amalgamated with the Carpet Trades Group in 1953.

J. Fairbairn: *The Crossley 'Mosaics'* (Halifax, 1932)

Hallett, William (*b c.* 1707; *d* 1781). English cabinetmaker. Hallett ranged from Kentian work at Badminton House, Rousham, Oxon, and Holkham Hall, Norfolk, to Gothic furnishings for Horace Walpole at Strawberry Hill, London, in 1755. His furniture resembles that of WILLIAM VILE, who may have been his apprentice; several break-front secrétaires (e.g. London, V&A; Portsmouth, City Mus. & A.G.), formerly belonging to the 3rd Duke of Buckingham, with broken pediments and doors ornamented with carved oval wreaths, at one time regarded as the hallmark of the Vile workshop, have recently been reattributed to Hallett or at least to Vile operating under Hallett's influence.

G. Beard: 'Two Eighteenth-century English Furniture Puzzles Reassessed', *Stud. Dec. A.*, i/1 (Fall 1993), pp. 119–26

Hall-in-Tirol Glassworks. German glass factory. In 1534, under the patronage of Ferdinand I, Wolfgang Vitl of Augsburg established a glassworks in Hall-in-Tirol. He employed numerous Italian glassblowers, and the products from Hall are characterized by their combination of Venetian and German taste. The production was mainly of vessels, generally decorated with diamond-point engraving and enamel painting in cold colours (gold, green and red).

H. Heimer: *Die Glashütte zu Hall in Tirol* (Munich, 1959)
E. Egg: *Die Glashütten zu Hall und Innsbruck im 16. Jahrhundert* (Innsbruck, 1965)

Hallmarks. *See under* MARKS, §3.

Hamada, Shōji (*b* Kanagawa, 9 Dec 1894; *d* Tochigi, 5 Jan 1978). Japanese potter. In 1920 he went to England with BERNARD LEACH, who had been staying in Japan, and together they set up the Leach Pottery studio in St Ives, Cornwall. Hamada worked there until 1924, when he returned to Japan. He settled in Mashiko in Tochigi Prefecture, where he continued to produce ceramics using reddish brown iron glaze and black-and-white devitrified glazes and clay from the surrounding region. He absorbed traditional technical methods and emulated the organic beauty of various forms of Korean ceramics and of the folk crafts of Japan, and in particular Okinawa. In 1926 with Muneyoshi Yanagi and others he promoted the Mingei ('folk crafts') movement. In his later years he established a simple, bold style working with such techniques as salt glazing (e.g. *Pitcher*, salt glaze on Chinese cobalt, 1960; Ohara, Mus. A.).

S. Peterson: *Shōji Hamada: A Potter's Way and Work* (Tokyo, New York and San Francisco, 1974, rev. 2004)
B. Leach: *Hamada: Potter* (Tokyo, New York and San Francisco, 1975)

Shōji Hamada: stoneware bottle, *c.* 1931 (London, Victoria and Albert Museum)

Hamada Shōji Ten [Retrospective exhibition of Shōji Hamada] (exh. cat. by K. Yoshida, Tokyo, N. Mus. Mod. A., 1977) [in Jap. and Eng.]

Hamadan carpets. *See under* CARPET, §II. 3(IV)(C).

Hammershøi, Svend (*b* Copenhagen, 10 Aug 1873; *d* Frederiksberg, Copenhagen, 27 Feb 1948). Danish painter and potter. As a potter Hammershøi worked with THORVALD BINDESBØLL in the pottery factory in Valby from 1891 to 1904. Hammershøi's ceramic work is characteristic of the period's interest in Classical form and decoration, and he was in demand at various places, including the Kongelige Porcelainsfabrik, and then the Kähler Ceramic Factory in Næstved (1894), working with the factory's famous lustre glazes. A series of fluted pots in simple and precise forms, modelled by hand in red clay, were produced during this period. Hammershøi fastened voluminous joints to the large, unbroken surfaces and sometimes used embossed patterns. He returned to the Kongelige Porcelainsfabrik in 1904–6. He also produced drawings for a number of major works, among them classicizing dishes and pots for the silversmith Holger Kyster (1872–1944), as well as drawings for a number of elegant bookbindings.

Hanap. Large lidded drinking-vessel or goblet, sometimes consisting of an ostrich egg or a coconut shell mounted in silver, intended for display rather than use.

L. de Fourcaud: *Le Hanap d'or émaillé et les vases d'orfèvrerie: Études sur l'art décoraty au salon de 1896* (Paris, 1896)

Hanau Faience Factory. German ceramics manufactory. It was the first German faience factory and was established in Hanau, near Frankfurt am Main, in 1661 by the Dutch potters Daniel Behaghel (1625–98) and Jacobus van der Walle (*d* before 1693). The workers and the technical director Johannes Bally were also of Dutch origin. Mugs, pitchers, *Enghalskrugen* (narrow-necked jugs), writing utensils, vases, plates, trays, jars and other utilitarian objects were produced, mostly imitative of Dutch blue-and-white wares. East Asian figurative and floral decoration was used in addition to such European motifs as trade emblems, religious subjects and coats of arms (e.g. *Enghalskrug*, end of 17th century; Copenhagen, Kstindustmus.). During the period 1740 to 1786 the East Asian motifs were replaced with *Deutsche Blumen* (German flowers). Another typical ornament consisted of small sprays of flowers with birds on a pale-blue ground (e.g. gadrooned blue-and-white dish, *c.* 1750; Nuremberg, Gewmus.). Rococo table-services and stoves were also produced during this period. The competition, however, from English creamware (cream-coloured earthenware) and German porcelain at the end of the 18th century forced the factory to close in 1806. Attempts to produce creamware and porcelain failed.

E. Zeh: *Hanauer Fayence* (Marburg, 1913/*R* Hanau, 1978)

Hancock. American family of cabinetmakers consisting of four brothers: Henry Hancock (*b* Roxbury, MA); William Hancock (*b* 1794 Roxbury); Belcher Hancock (*b* 1800, Brookline, MA); John Hancock (*b* 1802, Brookline; *d* Boston, MA, 1835). Henry remained in Boston, where he worked as a chairmaker and cabinetmaker from 1816 to 1851; William also stayed in Boston, where he worked as a chairmaker and upholsterer from 1819 to 1849 (sofa; New York, Met.). John and Belcher moved to Philadelphia, where in May 1830 John Hancock and Company opened a workshop. The company sold chairs (notably rocking chairs) and other household furniture.

D. Conradsen: 'The Stock-in-Trade of John Hancock and Company', *Amer. Furn.* (1993)

Hancock, Joseph. *See under* SHEFFIELD PLATE.

Hancock, Robert (*b* Badsey, Hereford & Worcs, *bapt* 7 April 1731; *d* Brislington, Avon, 14 Oct 1817). English engraver and painter. In 1756 he joined the Worcester Porcelain Company, of which he became a partner in March 1772. At Worcester, Hancock engraved copperplates for transfer-printing on porcelain. Many designs were adapted from contemporary engravings and paintings, particularly those of the French schools; such romantic scenes as *Amusements champêtres* and *Fêtes vénitiennes* were derived from compositions by Antoine Watteau (1684–1721). A series of children's games, including *Battledore and Shuttle-cock*, *Blind Man's Buff* and *Marbles*, are based on a series of compositions engraved by Gravelot (1699–1773). Mugs with portraits of Frederick II, King of Prussia, dated 1757, are based on an engraving by Richard Houston (1721/2–75) after a painting by Antoine Pesne (1683–1757) and are among the best-known examples of Hancock's work. The English schools also provided subjects for Hancock's engravings. A half-length portrait of George III decorates Worcester mugs together with one of Queen Charlotte, both likenesses after engravings by James McArdell. Portraits of Admiral Edward Boscawen, General John Manners, the Marquess of Granby and William Pitt decorate mugs, and these likenesses are considered to be among the best of Hancock's work at Worcester. Hancock had two apprentices, Valentine Green (1739–1813) and James Ross (1745–1821), both of whom later became well-known engravers.

After leaving Worcester on 31 October 1774 Hancock worked at the Salopian China Manufactory at Caughley, Salop, but his stay there was short, and he became a freelance artist living in south Stafford-shire, first at Oldbury and by 1781 in Tividale. He provided plates for many book publishers, including the Birmingham firm of Pearson & Rollason.

ODNB
A. R. Ballantyne: *Robert Hancock and His Works* (London, 1885)
C. Cook: *The Life and Work of Robert Hancock* (London, 1948); suppl. (London, 1955)

Hand cooler. Piece of glass, marble, crystal or ce-ramic held by ladies to keep their hands cool when being introduced to a gentleman and having their hands kissed. Hand coolers were made in France and England from the late 18th century. Early examples are ovoid, but Victorian hand coolers were often shaped into figures (e.g. birds). Victorian-style hand coolers are now made by STEUBEN GLASS WORKS.

Handel Company. American glasshouse estab-lished in 1885 in Meriden, CT, by Philip Handel (1866–1914); in 1900 a second factory was opened in New York City. The company was best-known for its ART NOUVEAU shades for gas and electric lamps; some shades were leaded and some reverse-painted with plants, animals and landscapes. In 1902 the company opened a foundry, and thereafter could make bases as well as shades. The factory closed in 1936.

R. De Falco, C. Hibel and J. Hibel: *Handel Lamps: Painted Shades & Glassware* (Staten Island, 1986)
C. Hibel, J. Hibel and J. Fontaine: *The Handel Lamps Book* (n.p., 2002)

Handsteine [hand-stones]. Sixteenth-century Ger-man *Kunstkammer* objects, each the size of a hand. Pieces of ore were cut and polished to make a mining scene (or landscapes or crucifixion scenes) and mounted on a silver-gilt stand.

Hand warmer. Small object containing a receptacle for charcoal or hot water. The type in which the container is surrounded by pierced metal has been made in Venice and in northern Europe since the 15th century.

Hankar, Paul (*b* Frameries, 11 Dec 1859; *d* Brussels, 17 Jan 1901). Belgian architect and designer. Han-kar's most lasting fame came through his shop-fronts. The first of these, Au Carnaval de Venise in the Rue de l'Ecuyer, Brussels (1896, destr.), was men-tioned in *The Studio* in November, 1896. The second, Niguet's Shirt Shop, Rue Royale, Brussels (1897), with its astonishing decoration of Japanese-style win-dow bars, curved mahogany tracery and chamfered lights, epitomized the flamboyant Art Nouveau shop front. His later work includes two cottages for the Wolfers brothers at La Hulpe (1899–1900, destr.). The interiors and the furniture that he also designed for them derived more from Chinese than from Jap-anese art and were strikingly modern.

C. De Maeyer: *Paul Hankar* (Brussels, 1963)
F. Loyer: *Paul Hankar: La Naissance de l'Art Nouveau* (Brussels, 1986)
F. Loyer: *Dix ans d'art nouveau: Paul Hankar, architecte* (Brussels, 1991)

Hannong. Strasbourg family of faience and porce-lain makers. Charles François Hannong (1669–1739), in partnership with the potter J. H. WACKENFELD from ANSBACH, was manufacturing faience by 1721. A second workshop in Haguenau was established three years later; the two factories were run by Han-nong's sons, Paul Antoine Hannong (1700–60) and Balthasar Hannong (1703–53). The factory's first wares were decorated in blue and white inspired by Chinese porcelains or with borders of lambrequins imitating wares from Rouen. More brightly coloured enamels were employed after *c.* 1740; for a time the factory decorated wares, figures and ornamental vases using both high-fired colours and enamels, eventually favouring the more versatile enamels. Un-der Paul Antoine Hannong the factory produced its most successful and influential wares, including ta-ble-services, pot-pourris, stoves and sconces, which were precisely painted with naturalistic flowers based on the *deutsche Blumen* of Meissen and called *fleurs fines* or *fleurs de Strasbourg*. This type of decoration was very influential and was imitated by many European fa-ience factories. Paul Antoine Hannong also encour-aged technical innovations, and in 1751 the factory became the first in France to master the formula for hard-paste porcelain. Production, however, could not begin as the VINCENNES PORCELAIN FACTORY held the monopoly for the production of porcelain; a factory was therefore established in 1755 in Fran-kenthal (see FRANKENTHAL PORCELAIN FACTORY), for the production of hard-paste porcelain. Paul An-toine Hannong was succeeded by his sons, first Pierre-Antoine Hannong (1739–94) and then Joseph Adam Hannong, who directed both the Haguenau and Strasbourg sites. After the monopoly for the manufacture of porcelain at Sèvres was lifted in 1766,

Frankenthal porcelain floral plate from a coffee and tea service, 1760 (Mannheim, Städtisches Reiss-Museum)

Joseph Adam Hannong concentrated on developing a line of porcelain, expanding the staff and incurring a large debt in the process. After the death of his patron, Cardinal Louis Constantine de Rohan, in 1779, Hannong was no longer protected; the Strasbourg factory ceased production, and Hannong, who was declared bankrupt, fled to Germany in 1781. Efforts were made to continue manufacture at Haguenau by Pierre-Antoine Hannong, but without commercial success.

J. Terrasson: *Les Hannong et leurs manufactures Strasbourg, Frankenthal* (Paris and Lausanne, 1971)
L'Oeuvre de Hannong, Faïence de Strasbourg Haguenau (exh. cat., Strasbourg, 1973)
J. Bastian: *Les Hannong: Étude des decors peints sur les faïences et porcelaines à Strasbourg et Haguenau (1721–1784)* (diss., Lille, 1987)

Hanoverian knives, forks and spoons. *See under* CUTLERY, §1.

Hans von Reutlingen (*fl* 1497–1522). German goldsmith and seal-engraver. He worked in Aachen, where he engraved seals for the Emperors Maximilian I and Charles V. His Gothic bust reliquaries are set on an architectural socle and are often of monumental dimensions, for example those of St Lambert (1508–12; Liège, St Lambert) and St Peter (*c.*

Hans von Reutlingen: front cover of the Imperial Gospel Book, Aachen, silver-gilt, 15th century (Vienna, Kunsthistorisches Museum)

1510, Aachen, Domschatzkam). His finest work is the silver-gilt case that he fashioned for the Reichsevangeliar (imperial Bible), possibly for the coronation of Maximilian I in 1500 (Vienna, Ksthist. Mus.).

Harache, Pierre (*b* Rouen, *c.* 1630; *d* London, *c.* 1700). English goldsmith of French birth. On 21 July 1682 he became the first Huguenot goldsmith to be admitted to the Goldsmiths' Company in London. The change in taste from the Dutch to the French fashions during the 1680s and 1690s is illustrated by a set of four candlesticks (formerly at Althorp House, Northants) made by Harache in 1683. These are some of the first English candlesticks with faceted, cast baluster stems and are the earliest recorded pieces by him, with the exception of two other pieces hallmarked in the same year: a pair of candlesticks and a jug and cover (both untraced). His surviving pieces show a simplicity of form with the ornament largely applied or engraved. Much of the engraving on silver by Harache is attributed to either Blaise Gentot (1658–1700; e.g. toilet service, 1695; Burghley House, Cambs) or Simon Gribelin. Harache's use of cut-card ornament can be seen on two silver-gilt ewers (1697; Leeds, Temple Newsam House) made for Charles Howard, 3rd Earl of Carlisle. Confusion often arises between the work of Pierre Harache and that of his son Pierre Harache (*b* 1653; *fl* 1698–1717), as their registered marks are similar.

M. Holland: 'Pierre Harache and the Huguenots', *Apollo*, cxxii (July, 1985), pp. 57–9

Hardman, John (*b* 1812; *d* 1867). English stained-glass maker and metalworker. Based in Birmingham, his company produced metalwork and stained glass for A. W. N. PUGIN, whom Hardman first met in 1837. Together with other craftsmen, he exhibited examples of his work for Pugin, including a chalice (London, V&A), at the so-called Medieval Court in the Great Exhibition, London, in 1851. He also collaborated with Jean-Baptiste-Charles-François Bethune, who set up a stained-glass workshop in Bruges in 1845 with Hardman's assistance.

ODNB (Hardman family)

Hard-paste porcelain. *See under* PORCELAIN.

Hare's fur. In Chinese ceramics, a high-iron glaze found on Jian wares, especially those of the Song period (960–1260). The thick, rich, fluid and finely streaked hare's-fur effect is the result of the natural unmixing of the glaze into different glasses during firing at around 1300° C. These 'hare's fur' compositions were used almost exclusively for glazing teabowls, many of which were exported to Japan; as a result of this, the glaze is often known by the Japanese term, *tenmoku*.

Harewood. Stained SYCAMORE wood, used by cabinetmakers for veneers since the 17th century, especially in England in the late 18th century.

Harff, Heinrich von. *See* ARFE, ENRIQUE DE.

Harleian binding. *See under* BOOKBINDING, §1(III).

Harrachov Glassworks. Czech glass manufactory. In 1714 Graf Aloys Thomas von Harrach set up glassworks in Neuwelt, Bohemia (now Nový Svět, Czech Republic), which reached their peak during the Biedermeier period, particularly under Johann Pohl (1769–1850) and his son Franz Pohl III (1813–84), producing such collectors' items as Pasten covered with glass, black Hyalith glass, cut glass, Lithyalin glass, Chrysopras glass, yellow Isabellanglas, seagreen and tile-green glass as well as the lead-free Rubin glass and constantly new variations of Überfanglas. The Harrachov glassworks, sold under pressure during the Hitler regime, is now among the most important in the Czech Republic.

Harrachov Glassworks, Czechoslovakia (Harrachov, 1965)
Harrachov, Czechoslovakia, 1712–1982 (Harrachov, 1982)
M. Konečný: 'Die beste Glashütte der Biedermeierzeit, zur böhmischen Glashütte Neuwelt, 1712–1987', *Die Weltkunst*, lviii/5 (1988), pp. 743–6

Harrington, Sarah (*fl c.* 1775–*c.* 1800). English silhouettist. She cut free-hand silhouettes and painted on silk; she also patented a machine for making hollow-cut silhouettes. The WEDGWOOD medallion of Maria Edgeworth was adapted from a silhouette by Mrs Harrington.

Hartford chest. *See* CONNECTICUT CHEST.

Hasp. A contrivance, usually metal or leather, for fastening a door or lid, typically a hinged clasp of metal which passes over a staple and is secured by a pin or padlock. In a trunk or box, the term also denotes a hinged plate of metal with a projecting piece of the nature of a staple which fits into a hole and is secured by the lock.

Hauer, Bonaventura Gottlieb (*b* 1710; *d* 1770). German porcelain painter. He worked at the MEISSEN PORCELAIN FACTORY from 1724 onwards.

Häufebecher [Ger.: 'stacking beaker']. Stacking cup, usually of silver, popular in late 16th- and early 17th-century Germany. Each cup in the set has a foot and a straight-sided bowl, sometimes engraved with a hunting scene.

Haupt, Georg (*b* Stockholm, 10 Aug 1741; *d* Stockholm, 18 Sept 1784). Swedish cabinetmaker. After an apprenticeship in Stockholm he departed (*c.* 1762)

with the cabinetmaker Christopher Fuhrlohg (1737–
c. 1800) for Amsterdam. By 1764 they were in Paris,
where Haupt may have trained under Simon Oeben
(c. 1725–86), the brother of JEAN-FRANÇOIS OEBEN.
In 1766 Haupt, like Simon Oeben, worked for
Etienne-François, Duc de Choiseul (1719–85), at the
château of Chanteloup, near Amboise; there he made
and signed a plain, mahogany *bureau plat* (1767; Paris,
Inst. Géog. N.). In 1766 he was joined in Paris by
his nephew, the painter Elias Martin. In late 1767 or
early 1768 they travelled to London, where they
joined a Swedish colony that included Fuhrlohg, the
furniture designer David Martin and (from 1769) Johan Christian Linning (1759–1801), another cabinetmaker. Fuhrlohg and Haupt almost certainly worked
for John Linnell in Berkeley Square, and Haupt was
in contact with William Chambers. In 1769 he was
promoted to Controller of the King's Works and
made a neat table to a design by Chambers, decorated with nine specimen marbles and Neo-classical
marquetry (1769; London, V&A).

Haupt returned to Sweden and on 17 July 1769
was appointed court cabinetmaker to. It bears strong
similarities to a medal-cabinet (c. 1769; Radier Manor,
Jersey) made for Robert Child (1739–82) of Osterley
Park, NT, while Haupt was in England. In 1771
Haupt was given the freedom of Stockholm and took
over the workshop of Anders Fogel (1732–71). In
1773–4 he made a monumental cabinet for a mineralogical collection (Chantilly, Mus. Condé), designed by Jean Eric Rehn, as a gift from Gustav III
to Louis-Joseph, Prince de Condé (1736–1818). After his death in 1784, his widow carried on the business with his former apprentice Gustaf Adolf Ditzinger (1760–1800), whom she married in 1789.

Haupt was a master of the advanced Neo-classical
style of marquetry in which geometric parquetry is
combined with such motifs as swags, husks, medallion heads, putti, vases, rosettes and ribbons and embellished with bold, gilt-bronze mounts. Haupt's luxurious commodes, *bureaux plats*, secrétaires, tables
and desks remained true to this vigorous style, using
Parisian forms of the 1760s. Such special commissions as a base made in 1776 for a cabinet (Vienna,
Ksthist. Mus.) made during the reign of Rudolf II
and brought to Sweden after the capture of Prague
in 1648, or a ceremonial cradle (Stockholm, Kun.
Husgerådskam.) made in 1778 for the Crown Prince
Gustav Adolf (later Gustav IV) prompted some originality, but Haupt's work usually evinces a typically
artisan combination of virtuosity in technique and
conservatism in design.

M. Lagerquist: *Georg Haupt: Ebéniste du roi* (Stockholm, 1979)
C. Cator: 'Haupt at Petworth', *Furn. Hist.*, xxix (1993), pp. 72–9
G. Alm: 'Neoclassical Furniture Design in Sweden', *Mag. Ant.*
    (April 1994), pp. 562–71

Hauré, Jean (*fl* 1774–96). French sculptor and designer. He served as Entrepreneur des Meubles de la
Couronne from 1784 to 1791, and during that period
supervised furniture by makers such as GUILLAUME
BENEMAN and JEAN-BAPTISTE-CLAUDE SENÉ. He

also made designs and wax models for royal furniture.

Hausmaler [Ger.: 'home painter']. Term used to describe painters of faience, porcelain and glass who
bought blank factory wares to decorate at home or
in their workshop. The practice developed in Germany during the 17th century and spread to other
European countries, including Austria, France, the
Netherlands and England. The most important
*Hausmaler*s were German or Bohemian, who decorated whitewares supplied by such factories as those
of Meissen and Vienna with enamels. At its best their
work surpassed the finest decoration executed in the
factories, contributing greatly to the prestige of early
European porcelain. Much 18th-century porcelain
decorated by *Hausmaler*s, however, was from can-
celled, outmoded or imperfect stock, which explains
why many *Hausmalerei* designs are often later in style
than the ware itself. Another feature of *Hausmalerei*
is that the decoration is frequently oversize.

Nuremberg became an important centre for *Hausmalerei* during the late 17th century and is particularly
well known for its *Schwarzlot* ceramics and glass. Outstanding artists using this method of decoration included Johann Schaper (1621–70). During the 18th
century Augsburg became a major centre for *Hausmalerei*, where many goldsmiths who mounted faience and porcelain with gold and silver turned to
decorative painting. Johann Auffenwerth (*d* 1728)
was the first recorded Augsburg goldsmith and *Hausmaler*, who decorated porcelain from Meissen in polychrome and gold (e.g. cup and saucer, c. 1725; London, BM). His daughter Sabina Auffenwerth (*b* 1706)
was also an accomplished porcelain *Hausmaler*. Pre-
eminent among *Hausmaler*s was Ignaz Bottengruber
(*fl* 1723–30), a miniature painter in Breslau (now
Wrocław, Poland), who was known by 1723 as a
painter of Meissen and Viennese porcelain. He favoured Bacchic, hunting and battle scenes, framed
by bold *Laub und Bandelwerk* ornament (e.g. Meissen
cup and saucer painted with a Bacchanalian scene,
1726; London, BM). The brothers Bartolomäus Seuter (1678–1754) and Abraham Seuter (1688–1747)
ran a large workshop in Augsburg; they decorated
faience from the factories in Bayreuth and Nuremberg and, by 1729, Meissen porcelain. Bartolomäus's
work is characterized by his use of scrolls and C-
scroll borders (e.g. teapot, c. 1730; New York, Met.).
Other decoration used by the brothers included gilt
silhouette chinoiseries, flowers, scenes after Watteau
and *Schwarzlot* decoration.

Other celebrated *Hausmaler*s included the PREIS-
SLER family from Bohemia. Daniel Josef Norbert
Preissler worked in Friedrichswalde, Silesia, and
decorated glass and East Asian porcelain; his son
Ignaz Preissler worked in Breslau and Kronstadt
painting East Asian and European wares (e.g. Meissen teapot decorated in *Schwarzlot*, c. 1725; London,
BM). Other notable *Hausmaler*s were Johann Friedrich Metzsch (*fl* 1731–66) of Bayreuth, who deco-

rated wares with chinoiseries, landscapes and mythological subjects, and Franz Ferdinand Mayer (*fl* 1747–94) of Pressnitz, Bohemia, who decorated wares with pastoral or genre scenes.

As competition between independent decorators and the factories grew, several porcelain manufacturers allowed only defective wares to be purchased by *Hausmaler*s; Meissen ceased selling to workshops in Augsburg as early as 1728. Many *Hausmaler*s resorted to giving additional decoration to sparsely decorated wares. Dutch *Hausmaler*s were thought to have initiated such work on underglaze blue and white, and the German *Hausmaler* F. J. Ferner (*fl* 1745–50) was known to have redecorated imperfect blue-and-white Meissen. By the 1760s Meissen ceased supplying their porcelain to *Hausmaler*s altogether. With only poor quality porcelain and indifferent work the practice gradually fell into decline.

G. Savage: *18th Century German Porcelain* (London, 1958)
E. Pauls-Eisenbeiss: *German Porcelain of the 18th Century* (London, 1972), i, pp. 540–67
H. Bosch: *Die Nürnberger Hausmaler* (Munich, 1984)
M. Cassidy-Geiger: 'The Porcelain Decoration of Ignaz Bottengruber', *Met. Mus. J.*, xxxiii (1998), pp. 245–62

Haviland. American family of ceramics decorators and manufacturers and collectors, active in France. They were of English Quaker origin, established in America since 1642. In 1838 David Haviland (1814–79), six of whose seven brothers were in the porcelain trade, formed an importation and retail business, D. G. & D. Haviland, with his brother Daniel (*b* 1799). In 1852 Robert Haviland joined the company, which became Haviland Brothers & Co. In 1840 David went to France, settling there in 1841, with the intention of improving the range of porcelain imported by the company by selecting it personally. In 1847 he opened a porcelain-decorating workshop in Limoges (*see* LIMOGES, §1) and in 1855 began porcelain production. He was helped in this by the French manufacturer Pillivuyt. In 1864 a new company, Haviland & Co. was founded by David together with his elder son Charles (*b* New York, 1839; *d* Limoges, 1921). His younger son Théodore (*b* Limoges, 12 Aug 1849; *d* 1919) was also involved with the new company. Charles settled in Paris in 1872 and the following year set up a decorating studio at Auteuil, a suburb of Paris, under the management of FÉLIX BRACQUEMOND. In 1877 Charles married Madeleine Burty (*d* 1900), daughter of the critic and collector Philippe Burty. Burty's and Bracquemond's tastes were reflected in the character of the Auteuil studio's designs, in which the influence of Japanese art and Impressionism is evident. A catalogue (Paris, Bib. A. Déc.) published in 1879 illustrates more than 250 designs, which were hand-painted in barbotine, mostly on vases. The firm continued to produce hand-painted designs until 1882, after which time it was forced to close this branch of its activities because of changes in taste. In 1865 Théodore had been sent to the USA to represent the Limoges firm. While there, he also encouraged an interest in the production of the Auteuil studio, particularly at the Centennial International Exhibition in Philadelphia in 1876. In 1880 he returned to Limoges. On 31 December 1891 the firm was dissolved. In 1892 Théodore set up an independent business, as did Charles with his son Georges Haviland. After 1925 the company split into two, one branch in Limoges for the manufacture of porcelain, and one in New York (the Haviland China Co.) for distribution of the product.

J. d'Albis: *Haviland* (Paris, 1988; Eng. trans. by L. d'Albis; bilingual text)
Celebrating 150 years of Haviland China (exh. cat., Milwaukee, WI, Villa Terrace Dec. A. Mus., 1992)
N. Travis: *The Evolution of Haviland China Design* (Atglen, PA, 2000)
N. Travis: *Haviland China: The Age of Elegance* (Atglen, PA, 2004, 3rd edn)
B. Wood and others: *Old Limoges: Haviland Porcelain Design And Décor, 1845–1865* (Atglen, PA, 2005)

Hawkes, T. G., & Co. American glass-cutting shop formed in 1880 by Thomas Gibbons Hawkes (*b* Surmount, Ireland, 1846; *d* Corning, NY, 1913). Hawkes was born into a glass-cutting family in Surmount. He arrived in the USA in 1863 and first worked at the Brooklyn Flint Glass Works, which moved to Corning, NY, in 1868; in 1871 he became supervisor of the CORNING GLASS WORKS. Hawkes's glass-cutting shop was founded in 1880, and he purchased blanks, which are plain, unadorned objects for cutting from the Corning Glass Works. After 1904 his craftsmen used blanks from the newly established Steuben Glass Works, which Hawkes had formed in partnership with members of his family and FREDERICK CARDER. In addition to blanks Carder also provided designs for Hawkes's cutters. After Steuben became a subsidiary of the Corning Glass Works in 1918, Hawkes's blanks came from the Libbey Glass Co.

T. G. Hawkes & Co. is perhaps best known for its 'Russian' pattern, a heavy, rich-cut design that decorated a service ordered for the White House, Washington, DC, by President Benjamin Harrison (1833–1901) in 1891 and enlarged by President Grover Cleveland (1837–1908) during his second term and by President Theodore Roosevelt (1858–1919). Along with other designs, the pattern was in continuous use in the White House until 1937, when President Franklin Roosevelt (1882–1945) ordered from Hawkes the 'Venetian' pattern, which remained in use during the administrations of Harry S. Truman (1884–1972) and Dwight D. Eisenhower (1890–1969) until 1958. These commissions and others for important American families brought Hawkes's craftsmanship to international attention at the beginning of the 20th century. In 1889 the firm won the grand prize at the Exposition Universelle in Paris for the 'Grecian' and 'Chrysanthemum' patterns, and for many years it was considered to be one of the foremost glass-cutting establishments in the USA. The shop closed in 1962.

J. S. Spillman: *White House Glassware: Two Centuries of Presidential Entertaining* (Washington, DC, 1989)

J. S. Spillman: *The American Cut Glass Industry: T. G. Hawkes and His Competitors* (Woodbridge, Suffolk and Wappingers' Falls, 1996)
Hawkes Cut Glass (n.p., 1998) [reprint of 1896 promotional booklet]
Hawkes Cut Glass (Ramona, CA, 2003) [reprint of 1890 sales catalogue)
R. Smith: *Brilliant Cut Glass Catalogs: Blackmer, Covington, Tinker, Hawkes* (Leawood, KS, 2004) [reprint of 1908 catalogues]

Hawthorn china. Type of porcelain in which the decoration represents flowering branches of the Japanese plum-tree in white on a dark blue ground.

Haystack [haycock]. Nineteenth-century Irish pewter measure for use in taverns; the name alludes to the conical shape of a haystack.

Headrest. Hard support for the necks of sleepers. Decorated headrests exist in many cultures, from the carved wooden headrests of ancient Egypt to the stoneware headrests of Song-period China (of which some could be filled with aromatic herbs). The most important region for headrests is southern Africa, where they are ubiquitous.

The headrests of southern Africa can be divided into two main groups: the Shona–Tsonga complex and the Zulu–Swazi complex. The headrest form of the Shona–Tonga complex is generally quite small and has a bilobed oval base with the thin horizontal and upward curving cross-piece supported by a caryatid of some decorative embellishment. In Northern and Central Shona headrests, the caryatid is composed of flat cut-out triangles with circles between them so that the whole has a form reminiscent of the female figure. The flat cut-out shapes are further embellished with relief patterns recalling the keloid scars used to decorate the human body, and on some headrests the circle elements bear three-dimensional 'breasts'. This type of Shona headrest is mostly stained black. In Tsonga and Southern and Eastern Shona headrests the supports vary more widely. Some use segmental arcs with cylindrical rods above them to support the cross-piece, while others have rectangular slabs in varying number and at varying angles between the base and the cross-piece. The slab-type caryatid is more common among the Tsonga and often has further relief embellishment. These latter headrest types have also spread far afield among Tswana and North Sotho groups such as the Ntwane. When animal figures are used by the Shona and Tsonga as caryatids, the base may be dispensed with, but the cross-piece is always supported on rods or slabs above the back of the animal. These animals are most often horned and may represent cattle, goats or antelope, the last two being the most likely among the Tsonga.

The classic Zulu–Swazi headrest type rarely uses animal figures as caryatids. The classic form consists

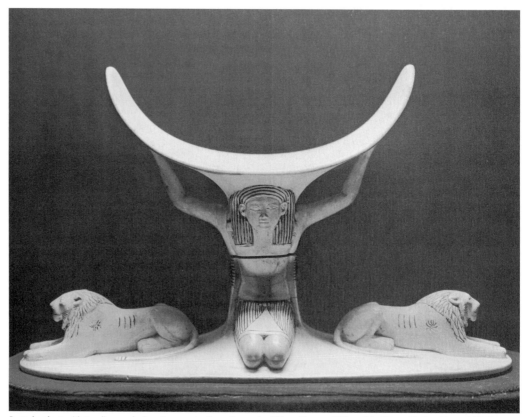

Ivory headrest with two lions and a kneeling servant, from the tomb of Tutankhamun, Valley of the Kings, Thebes, Egypt, 18th Dynasty, *c.* 1332–*c.* 1323 BC (Cairo, Egyptian Museum)

Shona headrest, from Zimbabwe

of two, three or four, but often more, generally square-shaped legs supporting a heavy rectangular cross-piece, which curves downwards towards the centre. At this point a cylindrical lug may be carved to project downwards, while at either end of the cross-piece other embellishments such as scrolls may indicate a 'head' or 'tail'. It is possible that in many of these headrests there is some reference to the bovine form, cattle being especially important in Zulu and Swazi society. On the legs themselves there is often geometric decoration in raised relief. There are many other variations on the basic form, but most follow the same scale and composition. Zulu headrests can be used as stools as well as pillows. Following a similar basic form, the headrests of some Pedi and Tau groups nevertheless show some differences. They are smaller in scale, the legs are generally cylindrical, and the cross-piece takes the form of an inverted triangle with its point replacing the lug of the Zulu type. The entire surface of the sides of these headrests is covered with engraved curvilinear, interlace patterns. A few headrests of similar type are known from Xhosa, Fingo and Bhaca sources, but there are not enough to outline any specific styles.

Among virtually all these groups, headrests could become associated with deceased members of a society and would then pass into use in ancestor veneration. Headrests were portable objects and were closely associated with their users. Among the Tsonga a man would make his first offering to his father as ancestor by rubbing tobacco on the cross-piece. Many of the headrests were further embellished with beads, and some had staffs or tobacco containers carved integrally with them.

W. J. Dewey and others: *Sleeping Beauties: The Jerome L. Joss Collection of African Headrests at UCLA* (exh. cat., Los Angeles, CA, UCLA, Fowler Mus. Cult. Hist., 1993)
C. Newman: *Zulu Headrests of the Msinga District in KwaZulu-Natal*, Port Elizabeth, Nelson Mandela Met. Mus. A. cat. (Port Elizabeth, 1993)
A. Lam: *L'unité culturelle égypto-africaine à travers les formes et les fonctions de l'appui-tête* (Dakar, 2003)

Head-shrinking. *See* SHRUNKEN HEADS.

Heal, Sir **Ambrose** (*b* London, 3 Sept 1872; *d* Knotty Green, Bucks, 15 Nov 1959). English furniture designer, shopkeeper and writer. He was apprenticed as a cabinetmaker from 1890 to 1893, when he joined the family firm, Heal & Son, established in 1810 in London by John Harris Heal (*d* 1833). By 1897 furniture was produced to his designs; in 1898 he became a partner, and his first catalogue, *Plain Oak Furniture*, was issued, which, like *Simple Bedroom Furniture* (1899), contains designs in a simple Arts and Crafts style. Heal exhibited regularly at the Arts and Crafts Exhibition Society in London. His influence was evident in the catalogues and advertising of the firm (he had an enduring interest in typography), whose design policy he increasingly directed. In 1907 he was appointed Managing Director and in 1913 chairman. His inexpensive, stylish furniture was appropriate to the new garden-city developments, and in 1907 he furnished a cottage for the *Urban Cottages and Rural Homesteads Exhibition* in Letchworth. In the 1930s Heal experimented with new materials—steel tube, aluminium, wood laminates—for furniture.

ODNB
A Booklet to Commemorate the Centenary Exhibition of the Life and Work of Sir Ambrose Heal (London, 1972)
S. Goodden: *At the Sign of the Fourposter: A History of Heal's* (London, 1984)

Heaton, Butler & Bayne. English firm of stained-glass manufacturers. In 1855 Clement Heaton (*b* Bradford on Avon, 1824; *d* 1882), a glass painter, went into partnership with James Butler (*b* Warwick,

1830; *d* 1913), a lead glazier, to make stained glass. They initially shared premises in London with the newly established firm of Clayton & Bell, providing the technical expertise for the latter's designing skills. The firm was known as Heaton, Butler & Bayne from 1862, when Robert Turnill Bayne (*b* nr Warwick, 1837; *d* 1915), a Pre-Raphaelite artist, became partner and chief designer. Bayne's striking and linear designs were carried out in an exceptionally wide range of coloured glass, developed by Heaton as a result of his researches into medieval techniques. Typical windows produced at this time are at St Nicholas (south chancel, 1863), East Dereham, Norfolk, and Peterborough Cathedral (north transept, 1864). By the late 1860s the firm was seen as more advanced in design than Clayton & Bell, whose dependence on the Gothic Revival style made them less fashionable. The distinctive, classicizing style of Henry Holiday (1839–1927), employed as a freelance designer between 1864 and 1878, can be seen in work executed in 1876 for St Luke's, Camden, London. Heaton's son, CLEMENT J. HEATON, worked for the firm and became a partner in 1882. By the last years of the century the vibrancy of the earlier windows had been replaced by muted tones and the detailed drawing and painting of the period. The firm closed in 1953.

S. B. M. Bayne: *Heaton, Butler & Bayne: A Hundred Years of the Art of Stained Glass* (Montreux, 1986)
A. Hartz: 'Stained Glass Masters: Heaton, Butler and Bayne', *Stained Glass*, xcv/3 (Fall 2000), p. 168
W. Clark: 'Of Glass on the Frontier: St. Matthew's Cathedral, Laramie, Wyoming', *Stained Glass*, xcvii/3 (Fall 2002), pp. 202–5

Heaton, Clement J(ohn) (*b* Watford, Herts, 21 April 1861; *d* New York, 27 Jan 1940). English designer and maker of stained glass, metalwork and enamel. In the mid-1870s he was apprenticed to the London firm of Burlison & Grylls, makers of stained glass in the Gothic Revival style. He later joined HEATON, BUTLER & BAYNE, the firm of stained-glass manufacturers and painters founded by his father, Clement Heaton (1824–82), whom he succeeded as a partner in 1882. In 1884 he left London for Neuchâtel, Switzerland, where he collaborated with Paul Robert on the decoration of the monumental staircase (*in situ*) of the Musée d'Art et d'Histoire, experimenting with cloisonné enamel as an enrichment for the pilasters, mouldings and cornices. On his return to England in 1885 Heaton executed enamel designs for A. H. Mackmurdo and provided designs for metalwork and lamps for the Century Guild of Artists. Following a dispute in 1885, Heaton left Heaton, Butler & Bayne and established Heaton's Cloisonné Mosaics Ltd, which produced plaques, book covers and lamps. After 1887 he lived principally in Neuchâtel, where his studio produced Gothic-inspired stained glass, cloisonné mosaics and embossed wallpapers by a process that he patented. His major commissions in Switzerland included glass mosaics for the Historisches Museum, Berne, and decorations for the Lausanne Law Courts and Cathedral, as well as for various churches in Strasbourg, Neuchâtel and Chaux-les-Fonds. He won a gold medal at the Exposition Universelle, Paris (1900). In 1914 he moved to New York, where he made stained-glass windows for the Church of the Blessed Sacrament and, in collaboration with his son Maurice Heaton (1900–90), windows for the Rockefeller Center. His other works in the USA include windows for the Trinity Chapel and the Museum of Art, Cleveland, and for the court rooms of the Bay County Building in Bay City, New York.

ODNB
N. Quellet-Soguel and W. Tschopp: *Clement Heaton, 1861–1940: Londres, Neuchâtel, New York* (Hauterive, 1996)

Hecker, Christian Friedrich (*b* Saxony, *c.* 1754; *d* Rome, 15 April 1795). German gem-engraver, active in Italy from 1784 or earlier. Like many of his contemporaries, Hecker mainly copied antique sculpture, basing his designs on such popular works of Classical sculpture as the *Apollo Belvedere* (Rome, Vatican, Mus. Pio-Clementino), the *Venus de' Medici* (Florence, Uffizi) and the Capitoline *Venus* (Rome, Mus. Capitolino). When working from such models, he confined himself to profiles. It is not possible to establish whether he based his work on copper-engravings and drawings by others or whether he made his own drawings from the original.

Hecker's 40 surviving works demonstrate his efforts to give a three-dimensional effect to the figures and heads; by cutting deeply into the onyx and skilful modelling of the individual parts he managed to create an effect of light and shade. He was influenced by the gem-engraver Giovanni PICHLER and adopted his style of conveying hair, a mouth with barely closed lips, an expressive form of the eye, as well as his skill in catching the individual character in a face, in spite of some idealization resulting from a simplification of the features. In his full-figure representations there is a certain stiffness and lack of sureness, although he attempted to correct this in such works as *Terpsichore* (cut in sardonyx), only an impression of which has survived (Rome, Dt. Archäol. Inst., Cades col. 67B, 476). Hecker carved Goethe's portrait for him in sardonyx (intaglio; Weimar, Goethe-Nmus. Frauenplan), which was based on a bust (Arolsen) by Trippel and was in the possession of Goethe's mother by 1789. He also produced portraits of such other personalities as *Clement XIV* (1784; ex-Piatti Collalto priv. col., Vienna), *Pius VI* (New York, Met.), *George III* (Kraków, N. Mus.), *Prince Bishop Clemens Wenzel of Trier* (1789; ex-Rollett priv. col., Vienna) and *Jean-Jacques Rousseau* (?after 1790; Italy, priv. col.).

The landscape painter Philipp Hackert (1737–1807) commissioned Hecker to make cameos with the profiles of Maecenas and Antinous-Bacchus and an intaglio with the profile of *Frederick II* (untraced; sulphur impression, 1810, in Weimar, Goethe-Nmus. Frauenplan). He may have been commissioned by

Jean-Baptiste Mallia of Vienna to make six cameos (St Petersburg, Hermitage), although Mallia possibly acquired these through intermediaries. Shortly before his death Hecker carved a large three-figure intaglio in chalcedony of *Eros between Nemesis and Elpis* (Germany, priv. col.) for Augustus, Duke of Sussex (1773–1843). The motif is taken from a Neo-Attic marble krater dating from the time of Hadrian in the Chigi collection (Ariccia, Pal. Chigi).

Hecker's works are marked HECKER or C. F. HECKER FEC. and in two cases with the Greek EKEP. The collections of Tommase Cades (1772–1840) and Pietro Paoletti (*fl* 1893–1929) both include impressions and glass-paste copies of Hecker's work (respective collections in Rome, Dt. Archäol. Inst. and Pal. Braschi).

I. Sattel Bernardini: 'Christian Friedrich Hecker: Ein Gemmenschneider der Goethezeit', *Xenia*, xv (1988), pp. 73–98 [incl. source mat. and bibliog.]

Hedebo. Type of Danish whitework embroidery made in the 18th and 19th centuries in the district of Heden, to the west of Copenhagen. In the 18th century Hedenbo was mostly worked with surface stitches together with a little cutwork and drawn thread work. During the first half of the 19th century the amount of cutwork increased, and the patterns became based on those of Italian reticella laces. In the late 19th century more elaborate filling stitches were introduced, and the surface stitching virtually vanished. Danish followers of the Arts and Crafts Movement looked to peasant crafts for inspiration, and Hedebo work was one form of peasant embroidery revived at this time that was adopted worldwide.

M. Lassen: *Hedebo Embroidery* (New York, 1925)
Old Hedebo Embroidery: Guide for Exhibitors and Judges (Pretoria, 1984)

Hedwig glasses. Group of cut-glass beakers (e.g. London, BM, Amsterdam, Rijksmuseum), known as Hedwig beakers because one or more are associated with the Silesian princess St Hedwig (1174–1245), is traditionally attributed on stylistic grounds to 12th-century Egypt. All these objects are made of colourless glass with a smoky or topaz tinge and have deep wheel-cut decoration of lions, griffins and eagles with details indicated by hatching. Most of the 14 intact examples were preserved in church treasuries or aristocratic collections in Europe; fragments of four others were excavated in Italy and Germany and at Novogrudok in Belarus'. As neither the place of manufacture nor the date of Hedwig glasses has been established, they have also been attributed to the Byzantine world, Russia or southern Italy.

F. Allen: *The Hedwig Glasses: A Bibliography* (Hyattsville, 1986)
F. Allen: *The Hedwig Glasses: A Survey* (Hyattsville, 1987)

Heemskerk, Willem Jacob van (*b* 1613; *d* 1692). Dutch cloth-merchant, poet, dramatist and glass-engraver in Leiden. He added edifying sayings and short poems to bottles, plates and drinking glasses; his graceful and fluent lines are unparalleled achievements in the field of glass calligraphy (e.g. beaker, 1679; Amsterdam, Rijksmus.).

Heidelberger, Thomas (*b* before 1541; *d* before 1597). German cabinetmaker and wood-carver. Although in the high quality of his craftsmanship he was an important representative of South German cabinetmaking and is thought to have produced an extensive oeuvre in Upper Swabia and Switzerland, little evidence of it has survived. Probably in collaboration with the Augsburg cabinetmaker Hans Kels (*fl* 1537–65/6) and commissioned by the monastery of Ottobeuren, he produced an organ case and choir-stalls with rich inlaid ornamentation; their remains were later incorporated into a sacristy cupboard. Again collaborating with Kels, in 1583–5 he produced five portals (four *in situ*; one, Stuttgart, Württemberg. Landesmus.), the architectural structure of which was accentuated by lavish figural and ornamental carving and supplemented by inlays and reliefs, together with a coffered ceiling, for the Benedictine abbey at Ochsenhausen. Through his extensive use of contemporary pattern books while designing, Heidelberger combined delicate decorative elements from the early Renaissance with the more robust forms of the later 16th century.

Heinrici, Johann Martin (*b* 1711; *d* 1786). German porcelain painter and exponent of PIQUÉ WORK. He worked as a porcelain painter at the MEISSEN PORCELAIN FACTORY (1741–56) and FRANKENTHAL PORCELAIN FACTORY (1756–63, the duration of the Seven Years' War); in 1763 he returned to Dresden, where he worked as a court painter and (from 1764) a colour chemist at nearby Meissen. It seems likely that his workshop was responsible for an important group of gold snuff-boxes (made *c*. 1745–50) that are generally rectangular with panels of mother-of-pearl or hardstone, decorated with small, encrusted figural subjects in hardstone. Heinrici also specialized in inlay work on lacquer, with various richly coloured and glinting materials, for example shell, tinted mother-of-pearl and tiny, bright squares of gold mosaic. This technique is known as *lac burgauté*.

Heintze, Johann Georg (*fl* 1720–50). German porcelain painter at the MEISSEN PORCELAIN FACTORY. He trained under JOHANN GREGORIUS HÖROLDT from 1720 and specialized in blue landscapes, seascapes and battle scenes. He left in 1745, and three years later was imprisoned as a HAUSMALER. He escaped and eventually settled in Berlin.

Helchis, Jakob [Jacobus] (*fl* 1730–49). German porcelain painter at VIENNA, where he painted in an individualistic black monochrome (*Schwarzlot*) style; his work there includes a fine bowl, cover and stand painted with putti playing musical instruments (*c.*

1740; London, V&A). He left in 1742 for a porcelain factory in Turin, but when that closed in 1746 he returned to Vienna. His last known post (1747–9) was as an arcanist at a porcelain factory in Neudock (Bavaria)

Helmet ewer. Ewer in the form of a helmet that was made in Germany and France from the early 16th century, both in metal (e.g. Nuremberg) and faience (e.g. Rouen). It was introduced to England by Huguenot silversmiths in the late 17th century. There is a fine example (1697) by Pierre Harrache in the British Museum and another by PAUL DE LAMERIE of London (c. 1737–45) in the Gilbert Collection in Somerset House.

Helmhack, Abraham (b 1654; d 1724). German HAUSMALER, stained-glass artist, glass-enameller and glass-engraver. He painted religious scenes on Nuremberg faience, which before the establishment of the Nuremberg Faience Factory (1712) consisted of imported wares from Delft, Hanau and Frankfurt am Main (e.g. Eghalskrug, c. 1690; Nuremberg, Ger. Nmus.). He was an important exponent of the decoration of glass with *Schwarzlot*, and painted glass for optical picture lanterns.

Helmschmied. See under ARMOUR, §1.

Heming, Thomas (b Ludlow, Salop, 1722–3; d 1801). English goldsmith. In 1738 he was apprenticed to the Huguenot goldsmith Peter Archambo. Some of Heming's work is distinctly French in character, and this may be due to the influence of Archambo, seen for example in a pair of Neo-classical candlesticks (1769; New York, Met.). Nevertheless, Heming used an eclectic range of sources, from the designs for silver in *Eléments d'orfèvrerie* (1748) by Pierre Germain (Heming's trade card depicts a ewer designed by Germain) to *A New Book of Ornaments* (1752) by Matthias Lock and Henry Copland (c. 1706–53). The curving table-feet depicted in the latter appear on Heming's epergnes.

In 1775 Heming received an order to make a silver service valued at £30,000, probably the service ordered by the Governors of Tula, Russia, which included 38 candlesticks, 31 meat-dishes and 9 salvers, made by Heming in 1766–7. Some of his most important pieces include the wine-cistern (1770; Belton House, Lincs, NT) of the Speaker of the House of Commons, which was made as part of the official plate issued by the Jewel House, and two toilet services, one made in 1766 for Caroline Matilda, posthumous daughter of Frederick, Prince of Walesx (Copenhagen, Kstindustmus.), and the other in 1768 for the marriage of Sir Watkin Williams-Wynn and Lady Henrietta Somerset (Cardiff, N. Mus.).

Hemmel von Andlau, Peter (b Andlau, Alsace; fl 1447; d c. 1501). German glass painter. His commis-

sions and influence extended from the area around Strasbourg into southern Germany and Austria. Hemmel became a citizen of Strasbourg through marriage in 1447 with the widow of a local glass painter named Heinz. His work shows figure types similar to contemporary engravings, in particular those of Martin Schongauer; Hemmel's *Adoration of the Magi* in the Nonnbergkirche, Salzburg, is derived from a Schongauer print of the same subject. Distinctive among his many commissions are the Kramer window (1479–80) in Ulm Minster and the axial choir window of *St Anne and the Virgin* (c. 1478–9) in the Stiftskirche, Tübingen. The balance of the intense purple, scarlet and deep blue against extensive silver-stain yellow and white glass creates a tension between spatial planes. Hemmel's draughtsmanship in his *Virgin and Child with Lily* from the Nonnbergkirche, Salzburg (c. 1470–80; Darmstadt, Hess. Landesmus.), shows a sculptural treatment of drapery and form that dominates the composition. The extraordinarily lush treatment of the architectural frame, often developed through sprouting and intertwining branches, seen especially in large-scale work, is one of Hemmel's most distinctive contributions.

P. Frankl: *Peter Hemmel, Glasmaler von Andlau* (Berlin, 1956)

Hemming bird [hemming clamp; sewing bird]. Bird-shaped needlework clamp that anchored one end of a long seam which was kept taut by a hand at the other end, thus leaving the other hand free to sew. The birds were made in 19th-century England, usually from brass or silver.

Henlein, Peter. See under CLOCKS AND WATCHES, §3(II).

Hennell. English family of silversmiths, active in London. David Hennell (1712–85) registered his first mark in 1736; he made modest domestic plate with restrained Rococo decoration. David was joined by his son Robert Hennell (1741–1811) in 1763; Robert fashioned Neo-classical silver in the style of ROBERT ADAM's designs. The company now trades as Hennell of Bond Street Ltd.

P. Hennell: 'The Hennells Identified', *Connoisseur*, cxxxvi (Dec 1955), pp. 260–66
P. Hennell: *Hennell Silver Salt Cellars, 1736 to 1876* (n.p.[Hertfordshire], 1986)

Henningsen, Poul (b Ordrup, 9 Sept 1894; d Hillerød, 31 Jan 1967). Danish designer, architect and critic. He gained international fame with his development of the 'PH' lamp (1925–6), a 'classic' of Danish industrial design, which has remained in continuous production.

In 1919 he began his lighting experiments and at the *Exposition des Arts Décoratifs* (Paris, 1925) he won a gold medal with a prototype of the 'PH' lamp. Its simple standard elements in metal and moulded glass were cheap to mass-produce. It had three light-

Robert Hennell: teapot, silver, 1859 (London, Victoria and Albert Museum)

weight, nested shades, all with mathematically determined curvatures that dispersed dazzle-free reflected light, yet had a wide spectral range. Developing these criteria, Henningsen created a system that eventually consisted of several hundred variations of more than 40 types of lamp, such as 'Artichoke' and 'PH5' (both 1958). His ideas about lighting were particularly developed during his editorship, from 1941, of Louis Poulsen's company journal *LP-Nyt*. Functional aesthetics also marked Henningsen's other industrial designs. In a range of steel furniture of the 1930s, the chairs linked new materials with traditional forms such as the 'Thonet' chair and were intended to be more comfortable than the standard types available. In the same decade he produced metallic pianettes and grand pianos, with transparent celluloid and chromed wavy legs, designed to accentuate their character as modern jazz instruments. Henningsen had an aversion to teak and the supposed 'good taste' of Danish design; he expressed this, from 1960, in the international design journal *Mobilia*.

S. Frandsen: *PH's eksempel* [PH's Example] (Copenhagen, 1978)
P. Hammerich: *Lysmageren: En kronike om Poul Henningsen* [The Light-maker: A Chronicle about Poul Henningsen] (Copenhagen, 1986)
T. Jørstian and P. Nielsen: *Light Years Ahead: The Story of the PH Lamp* (Copenhagen, 2002)
J. Gaillemin: 'De l'acanthe à l'artichaut, luminaires d'Henningsen', *L'Oeil, dlvi* (March 2004), p. 33 [exhibition review]

Henri Deux ware. *See under* SAINT-PORCHAIRE.

Hentschel. *See under* MEISSEN PORCELAIN FACTORY.

Hepplewhite, George (*b* Ryton, Co. Durham, ?1727; *d* London, June 1786). English cabinetmaker and furniture designer. Though a household name in the context of late 18th-century furniture, he remains a shadowy figure. *Lowndes's London Directory* of 1786 records his business at Redcross Street, Cripplegate, London, and after his death the administration was granted to his widow, Alice, on 27 June 1786. The *Public Ledger* of 10 October 1786 announced an auction of his stock-in-trade and household furniture. In 1788 his widow published the *Cabinet-maker and Upholsterer's Guide*. Its aim was 'to follow the latest and most prevailing fashion' and to adhere 'to such articles only as are of general use'. The intended public included both the cabinetmaker or upholsterer and the client (the 'mechanic and gentleman', as Alice Hepplewhite put it). There followed a slightly revised edition in 1789 and an 'improved' one in 1794, with an extra plate and revised chair designs. Six engravings bearing Hepplewhite's name appeared in Thomas Shearer's *Cabinet-makers' London Book of Prices* (1788).

Hepplewhite's *Guide* was the first major pattern book of furniture to be published since the third edition of Chippendale's *Gentleman and Cabinet-maker's Director* (1762), excluding those designs in the first two volumes of *Works in Architecture* (1773–9) by Robert and James Adam. Hepplewhite's designs most closely compare with Adam's drawings of the late 1780s, sharing their fashionably attenuated quality of design. The furniture is slender, and most of the decoration inlaid or painted rather than carved. Pier-glasses, for example, have narrow rectangular frames, and the decoration tends to be confined to the crests. Common motifs are sunbursts, paterae, husk chains and fronded scrolls. Hepplewhite favoured shield-shaped and square chair backs, often with the 'Prince of Wales's feathers' motif, but he died before he could assimilate the styles developed at Carlton House (destr.), London, the new residence of the Prince of Wales (later George IV). Hepplewhite was aware of the possibilities offered by gadgetry, a trend that was to grow in the early years of the 19th century, but a more conservative element in his work can be seen in his use of window-stools with curving arms but no backs that were first designed by Robert Adam as early as the 1760s. Decorative figures (humans, nymphs and putti) occasionally feature on chair backs and the crests of pier-glasses. His *Guide* reflected rather than originated a domestic version of the Adam style that was current during the 1780s, and it was highly influential in North America and northern Europe. It was reprinted in 1897 by Batsford, at a time when 18th-century furniture styles were enjoying a revival. No documented or labelled item of furniture from Hepplewhite's workshop is known.

ODNB
G. Hepplewhite: *The Cabinet-maker and Upholsterer's Guide* (London, 1788, rev. 2/1789, rev. 3/1794/*R* 1897/*R* New York, 1974)
C. Musgrave: *Adam and Hepplewhite and Other Neo-classical Furniture* (London, 1966)
J. Bell: *The Hepplewhite Director: The Furniture Designs of George Hepplewhite* (Ware, 1990)

Herat carpets. *See under* CARPET, §II, 3(III)(C).

Herculaneum Pottery. *See under* LIVERPOOL.

Herend Ceramics Factory. Hungarian ceramics factory. It was established by Vince Stingl as a stoneware workshop before 1825, but by 1826 it was producing porcelain. In 1840 the porcelain painter Móric Farkasházi-Fischer (1799/1800–1880) bought the workshop and developed it into a factory. The early wares included goods for everyday use and clearly showed the influence of the Vienna and Meissen porcelain factories. The considerable competition from mass-produced Czechoslovak wares forced the factory to produce fine merchandise. Herend became most famous for reproducing 18th-century East Asian and European porcelain. The factory was particularly successful at the international exhibitions and, at the Great Exhibition of 1851 in London, Queen Victoria ordered a dinner service decorated with butterflies and flowers, which became known as the 'Victoria' design. Under the management of Farkasházi-Fischer's sons the factory declined, and in 1884 it became a public company. Farkasházi-Fischer's grandson Jenö Farkasházi-Fischer, who became the managing director in 1896, introduced the Art Nouveau style and *pâte-sur-pâte* decoration. He also designed wares inspired by Hungarian folk art. Between 1918 and 1939 the factory also produced figures. The company was nationalised in 1948 and privatised in 1993; it now trades as the Herend Porcelain Manufactory Ltd (Herendi Porcelánmanufaktúra Rt.).

C. Boncz and K. Gink: *Herend China* (Budapest, 1962)
G. Sikota: *Herendi porcelán* (Budapest, 1977)
G. Sikota: *Herend, the Art of Hungarian Porcelain* (New York, 1989, 3rd edn)
J. Vadas: *Herend: Traditional Craftsmanship in the 20th Century* (Veszprém, 1992, 3rd edn)
G. Balla: *Herend: A Herendi Porcelánmanufaktúra története* (Budapest, 2003)

Herm. Plain shaft surmounted by a head, shoulder bust or sometimes a head and torso. It originated in ancient Greece, and in Renaissance and baroque furniture and metalwork was used as a decorative motif.

Herman [Hermann, Erman], **Giacomo** [Jacob] (*b* 1615; *d* 1685). German furniture-maker, active in Italy. He settled in Rome in 1655 and entered the papal service. Whereas the principal technique employed by Roman craftsmen was carving, furniture-makers from the north such as Herman made extensive use of inlay. His only clearly identifiable work is an ebony studiolo (signed and dated 1668) with lapis-lazuli columns and marble inlays (Vienna, Ksthist. Mus.).

Herold [Heroldt], **Christian Friedrich** (*b* 1700; *d* 1779). German porcelain painter. He began by working in Berlin for Alexander Fromery and may have continued to decorate enamel boxes for him while working as a painter at the MEISSEN PORCELAIN FACTORY, by whom he was employed from 1725 to 1777, beginning as a painter of CHINOISERIES and then moving to the harbour scenes in black or red for which he is best known (e.g. ewer and basin *c.* 1740; Los Angeles, CA, Getty Mus.). Herold was prosecuted as a HAUSMALER in 1763, and this private work may be the source of the pieces that he signed. He seems to have been a relation of JOHANN GREGORIUS HÖROLDT.

Herold [Heroldt], **Johann Gregorius** *See* HÖROLDT, JOHANN GREGORIUS.

Herrebø Faience Factory. Norwegian ceramics factory. The factory was founded by Peter Hoffnagel (1721–81) on his estate near Halden in 1759. Herrebø faience is distinguished by the imaginative use of rocaille motifs, in deftly applied blue or purple. The 'Herrebø style' was probably created by the Ger-

man painter HEINRICH CHRISTIAN FRIEDRICH HOS-
ENFELLER or his countryman Albert Lobech (*d*
1773). A skilled modeller must have also worked at
Herrebø; this was possibly Henrik Lorentzen Bech
(*c.* 1718–76), who like Hosenfeller lived in Halden
during this period. The factory closed in 1772. Many
fine wares from Herrebø are in the Kunstindustrimuseum, Oslo.

I. Opstad: *Herrebø Fajance Fabrique* (Borregaard, 1959)

Herrengrund cups. Cups made from the copper
taken from the mines at Herrengrund, Hungary
(now Spania Dolina, Slovakia) in the 16th or 17th
centuries. The myths surrounding the cups are encouraged by the inscriptions around the rims, many
of which (e.g. *c.* 1700; London, V&A) assert that they
are made from iron that has been transformed into
copper by the transformative power of Herregrund
water. Sometimes moulded figures are added; in the
case of the cup in the Victoria and Albert Museum,
the figure represents a miner.

F. Kirnbauer and R. Steiskal-Paur: *Herrengrunder Kupfergegenstände*
(Vienna, 1959)

Herring-bone. Decorative pattern resembling in
appearance the bones of a herring. In needlework, a
herring-bone stitch is a kind of stitch in which the
threads are set obliquely at equal angles on opposite
sides of a line, or crossing each other. In masonry or
paving, herring-bone is a pattern in stones or tiles
are set obliquely in alternate rows so as to form a
zigzag pattern. In weaving or clothmaking, herring-
bone is a textile in which a zig-zag pattern has been
worked. The term is also used in marquetry.

Herter, Christian (*b* Stuttgart, 8 Jan 1839; *d* New
York, 2 Nov 1883). American cabinetmaker and designer of German birth. He completed his studies in
Stuttgart and Paris and arrived in New York in 1859
to join his half-brother, Gustave Herter (1830–98),
who ran a decorating business; in 1870 he bought
Herter Bros from Gustave. The firm's luxurious furniture and interiors from the early 1870s show the
influence of the Paris Opéra by Charles Garnier
(1825–98). From the mid-1870s, however, the work
of Herter Bros exhibited the more restrained and
geometric lines of English design reformers, particularly the architect E. W. GODWIN, who promoted an
enthusiasm for things Japanese. Although Herter's
best Eastlake-style furniture reflects many of the reform ideas, he also used earlier Renaissance Revival
and Néo-Grec designs. Much of his work shows a
strong Japanese flavour, with angular, ebonized
cherry cases enlivened with wild flower, insect and
bird marquetry. On the blonde bedroom furniture
(*in situ*) purchased around 1880 for Lyndhurst in Tarrytown, NY, home of the wealthy financier Jay Gould
(now owned by the National Trust for Historic Preservation), Herter made use of imported Japanese
tiles, and he designed one of the finest Japanese-

inspired interiors in the USA for the William H. Vanderbilt House (*c.* 1882; destr. 1927) on Fifth Avenue,
New York. Typical of his best furniture is the exquisite ebonized wardrobe (1870s; New York, Met.)
in his Anglo-Japanese style. The cornice features inlaid, flowering branches from which blossoms
shower down the long doors to accumulate on the
two drawers below. Although Herter retired in 1879,
the firm continued in existence until *c.* 1907.

M. J. Bordes: 'Christian Herter and the Cult of Japan', *Rec. A. Mus.,
Princeton U.*, xxxiv (1975), pp. 20–27
D. Hanks: *Christian Herter and the Aesthetic Movement in America* (New
York, 1980)
Herter Brothers: Furniture and Interiors for a Gilded Age (exh. cat.; Hous-
ton, TX, Mus. F. A.; New York, Met.; 1994)
A. C. Frelinghuysen: 'Christian Herter's Decoration of the William
H. Vanderbilt House in New York City', *Antiques*, cxlvii/3
(1995), pp. 408–17
K. S. Howe: 'New York's German Furniture Makers: Herter Broth-
ers' Furniture', *F.M.R. Mag.*, xci (1998), pp. 103–28

Hess. German family of glass-engravers, originally
from Bohemia. Johannes Hess (?1590–1674) worked
at the glass factory in Tambach (est. 1633) in Thuringia. He then moved to Frankfurt am Main, where
he and then his descendants worked until *c.* 1740. As
there was no glass industry in Frankfurt, they must
have worked as *Hausmaler*, using glass imported from
Venice or the Netherlands. The dynasty of glass-engravers included Johann's son Johann Benedikt I (*c.*
1636–74) and his grandsons Sebastian (*d* 1731) and
Johann Benedikt II (1672–1736). Peter Hess, the son
of Johann Benedikt II, worked in Kassel from 1646
making hard-stone mosaics.

Heubach Porcelain Factory. German porcelain
manufactory. In 1843 the Heubach family established a factory in Lichte, near Wallendorf in Thuringia. The factory's products included dolls' heads
and (from the 1880s) piano babies (which were used
to hold objects such as papers and shawls on top of
pianos. Early in the 20th century, by which time the
company was called Gebrüder Heubach, the factory
had begun to specialize in animal sculptures.

Heuglin. German family of goldsmiths, active in
Augsburg. They family was Protestant, so their work
was secular. Johann Erhard I (1652–1712) made display dishes. His son and namesake Johann Erhard II
(1687–1757) made drinking vessels, tea and coffee
services and so-called travelling services (*c.* 1720;
Hamburg, Kst- & Gewsch.) consisting of ensembles
of diverse silver utensils intended for breakfast or
toilet purposes and packed into a special trunk.

Heurtaut, Nicolas (*b* 1720; *d* 1771). French chair-
maker and frame-maker. After an early career sculpting frames, he became a *maître* in 1753 and produced
furniture for the court; the chairs of the 1750s are
decorated with lavish floral carving, but thereafter
his style became more restrained; some of his chairs
are covered with Gobelins tapestry.

Hewelke Porcelain Factory. German porcelain manufactory. In 1758, Nathaniel Friedrich Hewelke and Maria Hewelke (both *fl* 1751–63), who had been porcelain merchants in Dresden until they were displaced by the Prussian occupation of Dresden during the Seven Years War (1756–63), received a 20-year privilege to manufacture porcelain 'in the manner of Saxony' in Udine. In 1761 they moved to Venice. There the ceramic technician Geminiano Cozzi (*see* Cozzi porcelain factory became their partner until 1763, after which the Hewelkes probably returned to Saxony. The few extant examples of their wares are of a greyish, hard paste. Such useful wares as tea- and coffee-sets included pots with distinctively modelled knobbed spouts and handles, painted with enamelled flowers or figures in simple settings. An unidentified modeller produced rather stiff, naive figures and groups; more ambitious and accomplished, however, was a relief portrait (London, BM) signed by Fortunato Tolerazzi and dated 1763.

Hewson, John (*b* London, 1744; *d* Philadelphia, PA, 1821). English calico printer in America. He was the son of a draper, and trained as a calico printer at Talwin and Foster, a textile printworks at Bromley Hall (Middx). He was assisted by Benjamin Franklin to emigrate, and in 1774 sailed to Philadelphia, where he opeed a calico factory in the Kensington area. He printed material for dresses, handkerchiefs and furnishing fabrics, notably bedspreads with medallions depicting urns (e.g. Philadelphia, PA, Mus. A. and Winterthur, DE, Du Pont Winterthur Mus.). When Hewson retired in 1810, the business passed to his son, also John Hewson.

J. Monsky: 'From the Collection: Finding America in its First Political Textile', *Winterthur Port.*, xxxvii/4 (Winter 2002), pp. 239–64

Heylyn, Edward. *See under* BOW PORCELAIN FACTORY.

Heywood Bros. *See under* WICKER.

Hicks, Sheila (*b* Hastings, NE, 24 July 1934). American fibre artist. She studied at Yale University and moved to Paris in 1963. Hicks's first interest was in Pre-Columbian Peruvian textiles and traditional techniques of Mexican hand-weaving. These inspired her miniature woven pieces of the early 1960s. Towards the mid-1960s she studied a variety of industrial methods to enlarge the scale of her productions. Heavy, woven fabrics were embedded with cotton to add sculptural density, and works included linen and silk wall pieces, such as those held at the Ford Foundation, New York, or the floor piece *L'Epouse préférée occupe ses nuits*. Hicks's technical expertise and versatility allowed her to manipulate fabrics in 'free-fall' structures of chords, discs and tubes, in brilliant colour harmonies that present textile art as a provoca-

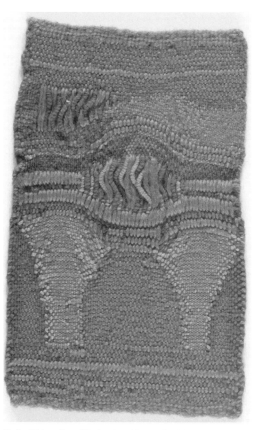

Sheila Hicks: *Greta Weaving* (no. 55), wool, 229 × 146 mm, 1961 (New York, Museum of Modern Art)

tive experience, situated between sculpture and performance.

M. Levi-Strauss: *Sheila Hicks* (Paris, 1973)
Sheila Hicks (exh. cat., Amsterdam, Stedel. Mus., 1974)
Sheila Hicks (exh. cat., Prague, 1992)

High Wycombe. English centre of furniture production. The town is situated in Buckinghamshire near the Chiltern Hills, where there is a plentiful supply of timber, particularly beech. The 'Windsor' chair, with which High Wycombe is particularly associated, was available in the London market *c.* 1720, and London chairmakers drew from the High Wycombe area billets of beech and probably such turned components as legs and stretchers. Turners, known as 'bodgers', would fell timber and directly convert it on simple pole lathes. Complete chairs were probably being manufactured in the High Wycombe area by the mid-18th century. Furniture workshops first appeared in the town after 1750, using turned components produced by the 'bodgers', making other parts such as the seat and assembling complete chairs for wholesale or retail sale. Four makers were listed in a directory of 1784, three being members of the Treacher family, and in the 1790s William Treacher was offering 'Windsor, dyed and fancy chairs'. Another early maker was Thomas Widgington (*b c.* 1776), and one factory owned by James Gomme was producing cabinet work as early as 1790. A militia return of 1798 lists 58 chairmakers in the borough and parish of High Wycombe and the adjoining village of West Wycombe.

In the 19th century production expanded, and large quantities of chairs were sold in London and the Midlands. Mechanization was introduced to keep pace with demand, and by 1864 one maker was using steam-power. Extensive orders were executed for basic turned chairs: for example, an order for 19,200 chairs was completed in connection with Moody and Sankey revivalist meetings, while in 1874 4,000 chairs were ordered from the firm of Walter Skull for St Paul's Cathedral, London. Some firms moved away from simple chairs to items of greater value and prestige and extended their ranges accordingly. One of the leading Victorian manufacturers was Edwin Skull, who by the 1860s was offering 140 different chair designs, which he published in trade catalogues (also produced by other firms from *c.* 1860). In 1884 the firm produced presentation chairs for the Prince and Princess of Wales (later Edward VII and Queen Alexandra), and in 1891 chairs were produced for the wedding of the Duke of York (later George V) and Princess (later Queen) Mary. The firm of William Birch began making chairs in 1840, but by the end of the century they were noted for their range of furniture in the Art Nouveau style, which was exported to Europe and the USA. The firm also had a London factory where semi-finished goods manufactured at High Wycombe could be completed to customer requirements. In 1851 Benjamin North & Sons was established, and by the 1880s it was producing Japanese-style seat-furniture and furniture in a 'new and modified Chippendale' style.

In the 20th century High Wycombe retained its importance. Parker Knoll Ltd started production in 1898, and in 1901 it was commissioned for some 80 'Chippendale' chairs for the liner *Ophir*. In 1928 the German Willy Knoll licensed the firm to use horizontal-coil tension springs, which enabled the production of lighter, fireside chairs, marketed under the name Parker-Knoll. G-plan Ltd developed from a chairmaking firm established by Ebenezer Gomme in the late-19th century (*see* GOMME, E., LTD). In the 1930s they introduced ranges of furniture using laminated bentwood construction and after World War II were one of the first British manufacturers to market room-dividers and unit furniture. Ercol Furniture Ltd was founded by an Italian immigrant, Lucian R. Ercolani. Using traditional materials and forms popular in the Wycombe trade, Ercolani redesigned them for mass-production. In the 1950s and 1960s Gomme, Ercol and Parker-Knoll were the leading companies in mass-producing ranges that reflected the taste of the period and were retailed by high street independents and such chain stores as Times Furnishing. The Wycombe Chair Museum, High Wycombe, has a representative collection of locally made chairs.

L. Weaver: *High Wycombe Furniture* (London, 1929)
L. J. Mayes: *History of Chairmaking in High Wycombe* (London, 1960)
B. D. Cotton: *The English Regional Chair* (Woodbridge, 1990)

Highboy. Modern collectors' term for the American version of the English TALLBOY, consisting of a chest-of-drawers on either a low stand or a base fitted with drawers; it sometimes had a matching dressing table called a lowboy. Highboys, which were known as high chests-of-drawers or high cases-of-drawers, were made in Boston, New York and Philadephia, and by the end of the 17th century had displaced the CUPBOARD as the best piece of furniture in the house. Early highboys had six turned legs, but from the Queen Anne period onwards, cabriole legs were usually fitted. The flat tops of Queen Anne highboys, typically with heavy cornice mouldings, gave way to ogee or cove mouldings and frets, which were popular until the end of the century. Triple-arched aprons (skirts) were fitted with drop finials, vestiges of the multiple front legs on earlier pieces. By the 1740s highboys were fitted with broken arches over central drawers with carved fans or scallop shells copied from architectural designs. As the century progressed, the gentle arches of the Queen Anne pediment (bonnet) often with a closed top, gave way to the more abrupt thrust of the Chippendale pediment, carved and ornamented with elaborate finials and a central cartouche. Some flat-top chests were fitted with steps for the display of glass, china and silver. The Queen Anne chest-on-stand tallboy had been replaced in England by the chest-on-chest form by about 1740 but continued to be popular in America where the best examples carried elaborately carved Rococo and Classical motifs. Only in Charleston, SC, was the chest-on-chest form widely popular. THOMAS AFFLECK was well-known for his elaborately carved highboys. In the same period John Pimm (*fl* 1740–50) created the fine japanned highboy (1740–50) in the H. F. Du Pont Winterthur Museum, Wintherthur, DE. *See also* LOWBOY.

High-warp loom. *See under* TAPESTRY, §I. 2.

Hirado. Japanese centre of porcelain production at Mikawachi (west of Arita), active since the 17th century. The high quality and plasticity of the white clay found there made it possible to create unusually intricate forms. In the 19th century ceramic sculpture—in particular, moulded animals and birds and flowers—became a speciality of Hirado. In the early Meiji period (1868–1912) many porcelains from Hirado as well as from older kilns in the Arita area were displayed to great acclaim at the International Expositions in Paris, Vienna and Philadelphia.

R. Singer: 'Hirado Porcelain of Japan', *Mag. Ant.*, clix/3 (March 2001), pp. 462–73

Hirschvogel [Hirsfogel; Hirsvogel]. German family of artists. They were Nuremberg's leading stained-glass painters during the late 15th century and the 16th. Veit Hirschvogel the elder (see below), the son of a glazier named Heinz (*d* 1485), established the family workshop and became the city's official glazier. His son Veit Hirschvogel the younger (1485–1553) succeeded him as official glazier, being succeeded in his turn by his son Sebald Hirschvogel (1517–89), who remained in the post for 33 years. The brothers of Veit the younger, Hans Hirschvogel (*d* 1516) and Augustin Hirschvogel (see below), also joined the glass-painting workshop, but Augustin, the most talented of the family, left it in 1525 to pursue a varied career outside Nuremberg, producing many etchings and also innovations in cartography. It is supposed that the Viennese goldsmith Veit Hirschvogel (1543–74) was Augustin's son.

1. Veit Hirschvogel the elder (*b* Nuremberg, 1461; *d* Nuremberg, 24 Dec 1525). He directed his workshop during the last great flowering of stained glass production in Nuremberg (*c.* 1485–1526). Around 1500 the workshop shifted from an old-fashioned style, based on the stained glass of the Strasbourg master Peter Hemmel von Andlau, to one based on the art of Albrecht Dürer (1471–1528). Dürer, along with his students Hans Süss von Kulmbach (*c.* 1485–1522), Hans Baldung (1484/5–1545), Hans Schäufelein (*c.* 1482–1539/40) and Sebald Beham, provided the workshop with numerous designs, and his drawing and graphic styles became its trademark. Due to Dürer's influence, many of the advances made in panel painting were applied to stained glass. He replaced the compartmentalized and decorative approach with a more monumental conception where a composition with imposing figures in an illusionistic setting unifies all the panels of a window. In the Pfinzing window (*c.* 1515; Nuremberg, Sebalduskirche), for instance, a monumental Renaissance-style triumphal arch spans the entire window and unites 17 figures spatially and compositionally. The workshop's technical mastery of the application of washes and particularly of silver stain to create effects from yellow to red also endowed its stained glass with increased spatial illusion and translucency.

The Hirschvogel workshop production includes windows in the Sebalduskirche (Bamberg window, 1501–2; Margrave's window, 1515; Emperor's window, 1514; Pfinzing window, 1515), in the Lorenzkirche (Löffelholz window, 1506; Schmidmayer window, 1509); windows in the Annenkapelle (1510); in the Landauerbruderkapelle of the Zwölfbruderhaus (1508), the Rochuskapelle (1520–21), and several windows (1505–13) formerly in the Carmelite cloister, Nuremberg, now in the parish churches at Grossgründlach and Wöhrd. The workshop also created numerous *Kabinettscheiben* ('glass panes for a small room'; i.e. rectangular, round or trefoil-shaped stained-glass panels to be set in bull's-eye glazing and viewed up close), popular in this period for windows in chapels, cloisters or private houses. They depict religious or profane subjects, for example the panel of *Death on Horseback Taking Aim* (*c.* 1502; Nuremberg, Ger. Nmus.) from the house of the humanist Dr Sixtus Tucher (1459–1507), which matches another panel of Dr Tucher standing before his open grave. They often display some of the workshop's most creative and progressive work.

G. Frenzel: 'Veit Hirschvogel: Eine Nürnberger Glasmalereiwerkstatt der Dürerzeit', *Z. Kstgesch.*, xxiii (1960), pp. 193–210

2. Augustin Hirschvogel (*b* Nuremberg, 1503; *d* Vienna, 1553). Son of Veit Hirschvogel the elder, he trained as a stained-glass painter in his father's workshop and remained there until his father's death in 1525. In that year Nuremberg accepted the Reformation, spelling the end of monumental stained-glass commissions. By 1530 Augustin had established his own workshop but in 1531 formed a partnership with the Nuremberg potters Hanns Nickel (*fl c.* 1530) and Oswald Reinhart (*fl c.* 1530), presumably to share their kiln. Several stained-glass panels by Hirschvogel survive from his early Nuremberg period (until 1536). The 53 hunting scenes in the Museum of Fine Arts, Budapest, for an extensive series of stained-glass roundels, demonstrate that he was an able and independent draughtsman, well-schooled in Dürer's drawing style. Several stained-glass panels, including two roundels from the hunt series and a group of three rectangular panels of angels holding coats of arms from the parsonage of the Sebalduskirche (1520s), show Augustin's modification of his father's linear style of glass painting to achieve more tonal, painterly effects.

During this last decade of his life in Vienna, Hirschvogel produced most of his 300 etchings, including 17 fanciful designs for vessels and 19 ornamental designs.

K. Schwarz: *Augustin Hirschvogel*, 2 vols (Berlin, 1917, 2/1971) [standard monograph, with cat. rais. of graphic work]
J. S. Peters: 'Early Drawings by Augustin Hirschvogel', *Master Drgs*, xvii (1979), pp. 359–92 [with cat. of early drgs]
J. S. Peters: 'Frühe Glasgemälde von Augustin Hirschvogel', *Anz. Ger. Nmus.* (1980), pp. 79–89
J. S. Peters: *German Masters, 1550–1600*, 18 [IX/i] of *The Illustrated Bartsch*, ed. W. L. Strauss (New York, 1982), pp. 95–363

Hitchcock, Lambert (*b* Cheshire, CT, 28 May 1795; *d* Unionville, CT, 3 April 1852). American cabinet-maker and furniture manufacturer. He came from a land-owning Connecticut family and in 1826 established a factory near Barkhamsted, CT, in an area renamed Hitchcocksville (now Riverton) after him. His chief product was an American adaptation of a late Sheraton-style, open-backed side chair, painted black with stencilled decoration, known as the 'Hitchcock' chair. In 1832 he entered into a partnership with his brother-in-law Arba Alford (1808–81), and the firm was called Hitchcock, Alford & Co. Hitchcock's use of stencilled decoration on his painted chairs emulated the gilt and lacquered furniture being imported from Europe. The factory turned out hundreds of these 'fancy' chairs, made from hickory, maple, birch and poplar with rush or cane seats. They have a 'bolster' or flat-fronted top rail, with round, splayed, ring-turned front legs, sometimes tapered with ball feet, and round front, back and side stretchers, also ring-turned. Back uprights and back legs are all-in-one. Decoration consists of large floral and fruit designs, banded patterns or Greek anthemia, mostly in gold or bronze. From *c.* 1835 chair backs were flat and steam-bent backwards for comfort. The 'Hitchcock' chair was well-made and much copied, but few had the jaunty, inimitable air of the originals. In 1848 Hitchcock severed his relationship with the company, which continued to make furniture until 1853 as the A. & A. Alford Co., and until 1864 as the Phoenix Co. In 1946 the factory, unused since the 1930s, was taken over by the Hitchcock Chair Co., newly formed to restore and expand the premises and produce reproductions of Hitchcock's furniture. The John Tarrant Kenney Hitchcock Museum was established in Riverton in 1972; it closed in 2004 and its contents were dispersed.

M. Moore: *Hitchcock Chairs* (1933, R/1963)

J. Kennedy: *The Hitchcock Chair: The Story of a Connecticut Yankee—L. Hitchcock of Hitchcocks-ville—and an Account of the Restoration of his 19th-century Manufactory* (New York, 1971).

E. Kenney Glennon: 'The John Tarrant Kenney Hitchcock Museum, Riverton, Connecticut', *Antiques*, cxxv (1984), pp. 1140–47

C. Barnett: 'A Passion for Industry: Lambert Hitchcock, a Connecticut Yankee', *A. & Ant.*, (May 1986), pp. 86–91

Hobbs, Brockunier & Co. American glass manufactory. In 1845 the firm of Barnes, Hobbs & Co. was established in Wheeling, WV, by John L. Hobbs (1804–81) and James B. Barnes (*d* 1849), who had both worked for the New England Glass Co. In 1863 the firm became Hobbs, Brockunier & Co., and comprised Hobbs, his son John H. Hobbs, company bookkeeper Charles W. Brockunier and a silent partner, William Leighton Sr (1808–91), son of Thomas H. Leighton (1786–1849) of the New England Glass Co. William Leighton was a scientist and superintendent of the firm, and his son William Leighton Jr (1833–1911) succeeded him on his retirement in 1867.

By 1879 Hobbs, Brockunier & Co. was one of the largest glass factories in the USA and was making fine cut and engraved lead crystal, as well as an extensive range of pressed glass using the soda-lime formula developed by Leighton Sr. This formula revolutionized pressed-glass making after 1865. The firm's great success during the Aesthetic period in America can be traced to the expertise of the company's members, whose previous associations had prepared them for producing exquisite art glass in a wide range of colours, patterns and textures. But it was the fancy glass in the Aesthetic taste that secured the firm's reputation. 'Craquelle', a crackled glass, was the first of a long line of these art wares. In addition to types using opal and shaded effects, the firm also made spangled glass with flecks of gold or silver foil in clear glass overlaid with tinted glass. Its

most famous line was 'Peachblow', begun in 1886, to imitate a transmutational glaze used on Chinese porcelain known as peach-bloom.

The firm's success was brought to an end by the retirement of Brockunier and Leighton jr in 1887. Hobbs continued the works, but the business was taken over by the United States Glass Co. in 1891.

N. Bredehoft and T. Bredehoft: *Hobbs, Brockunier & Co.: Glass Identification and Value Guide* (Paducah, KY, 1997)

Hochschnitt. High-relief glass decoration. The effect is achieved by the difficult method of wheel-engraving in cameo rather than intaglio (TIEF-SCHNITT). The process was first used in Islamic glassware and was then used in 17th- and 18th-century Germany, where its finest exponents were Gottfried Spiller (1663–1728), who worked at the BRANDENBURG glassworks (e.g. covered goblet, *c.* 1700; London, V&A) and FRANZ GONDELACH.

Höchst Ceramics Factory. German ceramics manufactory. Although Höchst was founded in 1746 by Adam Friedrich von Löwenfinck as a porcelain factory, at first it was only possible to produce high-quality faience painted with enamels. A wide range of wares was produced, including such tablewares as tureens in the shape of animals, fruit and vegetables (e.g. boar's head tureen and dish, *c.* 1750; Frankfurt am Main, Mus. Ksthandwk) and figures. After Löwenfink resigned in 1749, Johann Kilian Benckgraff (1708–53) and Joseph Jakob Ringler (1730–1804) took over the technical direction of the factory and immediately began to produce porcelain. At first they used the old faience forms and models, but from 1758 they became increasingly influenced by wares from Meissen and Frankenthal. Höchst became famous for its variety of figures by such modellers as Simon Feilner (1726–98), Johann Hermann Meyer (*fl* 1746–9), Carl Gottlieb Lück (*c.* 1730–75), his brother Johann Friedrich Lück (1727–97) and Johann Peter Melchior (1742–1825).

Among the early figures are two groups of characters from the *commedia dell'arte* in the style of the engraver François Joullain (1697–1778) and engravings from Augsburg. Johann Friedrich Lück's figure of a dancer with a black mask is considered his most brilliant achievement. Melchior modelled busts and portraits, as well as sentimental figures of children and young couples situated on grassy, rockwork bases (e.g. *Grapethief*, 1770–75; Frankfurt am Main, Mus. Ksthandwk). Most of the figures, however, which are reminiscent of the work of Etienne-Maurice Falconet, cannot be attributed to a particular modeller (e.g. *Venus and Cupid*, 1771; Cologne, Kstgewmus.).

The production of tableware included dinner-services, tea- and coffeepots, cruet-stands, basketwares with trellis decoration, fruit and sweetmeat dishes and garnitures. Particularly outstanding painted decoration included landscapes, chinoiseries, harbour and battle scenes, putti, flowers, ribbons, scrolling foliage and portrait silhouettes. After the factory closed in 1796, the designs were sold to other firms: in 1840 they were sold to Ernst Müller of the Damm Pottery in Aschaffenburg and in 1909 to the porcelain factory of Dressel, Kistler and Co. in Passau, which used them until 1942. The Höchst factory reopened in 1966, and some of the models by Melchior were remoulded.

H. Jedding: 'Höchster Porzellan-Geschirr aus Fayence-Formen', *Keramos*, vii (1960), pp. 3–12
K. H. Esser: *Höchster Porzellan* (Königstein, 1962)
K. H. Esser and H. Reber: *Höchster Fayencen und Porzellan* (Mainz, 1964)
E. Kramer: 'Höchster Porzellangruppen von Johann Peter Melchior', *Keramos*, lvi (1972), pp. 3–68

Hoentschel, Georges (*b* 1855; *d* 1915). French architect, interior designer, potter and collector. His Paris workshop undertook interior decoration, furniture design, woodwork and ironwork. He decorated three rooms at the Exposition Universelle of 1900; his floral decoration was in an Art Nouveau style. When his friend Jean Carriès (1855–94) died, Hoentschel took over his pottery studio in Montriveau, and thereafter Carriès's workers produced stoneware that Hoentschel integrated in his furniture. His collections of French art of the 17th and 18th centuries and of Asian art, acquired by J. Pierpont Morgan and now in the Metropolitan Museum of Art, New York, influenced the style of his own work.

E. Posseme: 'Le salon du bois du pavillon de l'Union centrale des arts decoratifs a l'Exposition universelle de 1900', *Rev. A.*, cxvii (1997), pp. 64–70

N. Hoentschel: *Georges Hoentschel* (Saint-Rémy-en-l'Eau, 1999)
Georges Hoentschel de Collectif (Paris, 2000)

Hoffman, Friedrich Gottlob (*b* Belgern, nr Leipzig, 1741; *d c.* 1806). German cabinetmaker. By 1770 he was established as a master cabinetmaker in Leipzig; he later opened a second workshop at Eilenburg. In 1789 he published his first pattern book, *Abbildungen der vornehmsten Tischlerarbeiten, welche verfertiget und zu haben sind bey Friedrich Gottlob Hoffmann, wohnhaft auf dem alten Neumarkt in Leipzig*, an anthology of designs for household furniture, mostly inspired by the Louis XVI Neo-classical style. In 1795 he produced a second catalogue, *Neues Verzeichnis und Muster-Charte des Meubles-Magazin*, in which English design types are dominant. A number of pieces corresponding to plates in these two pattern books have been identified (e.g. sofa, *c.* 1789, and cylinder secrétaire, *c.* 1795; both Dresden, Schloss Pillnitz; table, *c.* 1789; Weimar, Kirms-Krockow-Haus & Herder-Mus.). From 1788 to 1795 Hoffman supplied furniture to the German courts in Gotha, Weimar, Dresden, Brunswick and Dessau and to Berlin, Hamburg, Vienna, Constantinople and St Petersburg.

K. Krull: 'Friedrich Gottlob Hoffman: A Late Eighteenth Century Leipzig Cabinetmaker', *Furn. Hist.*, xxv (1989), pp. 120–23

Hoffman, Josef (*b* Pirnitz, Moravia (then Austria, now Brtnice, Czech Republic), 15 Dec 1870; *d* Vienna, 1956), Austrian architect and designer. He was interested in the design of craft objects, and his own work was influenced by the Glasgow school of artists, par-

Josef Hoffman: flowerpot, silver mesh, produced by the Wiener Werkstätte, *c.* 1905

Josef Hoffman: set of drinking goblets, glass, *c.* 1910 (Vienna, Collection Lobmeyr)

ticularly CHARLES RENNIE MACKINTOSH. His furniture, which was sometimes made by MICHAEL THONET, was usually designed for his own buildings, notably Palais Stoclet in Brussels. He also designed jewellery and metalwork which was made by members of the WIENER WERKSTÄTTE, of which he was a founder. His delicate tulip-shaped wine glasses (1920) were made by J. & L. LOBMEYER.

A. F. Meijer: *Korte biografie van Josef Hoffmann (1870–1956)* (Leiden, 1995)

D. Greenidge: *Josef Hoffman: Furniture, Design and Objects* (New York, 2002)

Holbein, Hans, the younger (*b* Augsburg, 1497–8; *d* London, 1543). Painter, draughtsman and designer, active in Switzerland and England. He is best known as the most important portrait painter in England during the Reformation. In Basle he produced designs for stained glass and goldsmiths' work. In 1532 he returned to England, where he worked almost exclusively as a portrait painter, mainly under the patronage of King Henry VIII and his courtiers. He also collaborated with goldsmiths on several pieces, such as a gold cup for Jane Seymour (drawings, London, BM; Oxford, Ashmolean), some of which were probably royal commissions and some commissioned by others for the King, for example Sir Anthony Denny's New Year's gift of a clock (drawing, London, BM), on which Holbein collaborated with Nicholas Kratzer.

Holbein carpets. *See under* CARPET, §II. 3(III)(a).

Holics Ceramics Factory. Ceramics manufactory that was established in Holics (Holitsch, then Hungary; now Holíč, Slovakia) by Emperor Francis I in 1743. It supplied the aristocracy with faience dinner-services and ornamental table decorations. French artists and managers were employed at the factory. A variety of products were manufactured in the late Baroque, Rococo and Neo-classical styles. Enamelled tureens in the shape of cabbages and bunches of asparagus or wares decorated with scattered flowers indicate the influence from Strasbourg (e.g. coffeepot, 1750–60; Brno, Morav. Mus.). Meissen was also influential as were the high-fired wares from Castelli decorated with landscapes and figures. Chinoiseries and idyllic scenes can be attributed to the outstanding painter János Radiel (*fl c.* 1770–1806; e.g. pot-pourri vase, 1770; Budapest, Mus. Applied A.). Figures were influenced by the Vienna porcelain factories. The factory also made tiled stoves, furniture (e.g. cradle, 1775; Budapest, Mus. Applied A.) and jewellery-boxes in the shape of a chest-of-drawers. Religious figures such as the Maria Immaculata by Antal Schwaiger (?1728–?1802) were also made. After 1792 Holics produced creamware (lead-glazed earthenware) after Viennese and English designs.

Holland, Henry (*b* Fulham, London, 20 July 1745; *d* Chelsea, London, 17 June 1806). English architect and designer. Holland concentrated on a comparatively limited number of commissions, most of which involved not only building and decoration but also the furnishing of principal rooms. Here he was to develop a distinctive style of elegant simplicity, strongly influenced by French examples. In 1770 he was offered a form of partnership by 'Capability' Brown (1716–83), the landscape gardener and architect. Brown had recently begun Claremont, Surrey, for Robert Clive, 1st Baron Clive of Passey, and required help with the interior decoration. This collaboration proved successful, and it was continued over the next few years at Benham Park (1774–5), Berks, Cadland (1775–8; destr.), Hants, and Berrington (1778–81), Hereford & Worcs. It also led to Holland's marriage to Brown's elder daughter in 1773. Although they continued to work together from time to time until Brown's death in 1783, Holland set up an independent practice in 1776 when he designed a new clubhouse for William Brooks in St James's Street, London.

The interior of Brooks's is the earliest example of the restraint that was to become characteristic of Holland's work. In the Great Subscription Room the walls and ceiling have minimal elaboration, and lofty pier-glasses between the east-facing windows and over the chimney-piece create an impression of lightness and space. In 1783 George, Prince of Wales (later George IV), became a member and by August had chosen Holland to remodel his new London residence, Carlton House (destr. 1827–8); he later asked Holland to remodel the Brighton Pavilion; his work there was to be almost entirely obscured by the subsequent Oriental decoration by John Nash (1752–1835). Apart from these royal commissions, Holland's major works of the 1780s were additions to Althorp House, Northants, for George, 2nd Earl Spencer (the Blue Boudoir with its wall panels was painted by T. H. Pernotin), and to Woburn Abbey, Beds, for Francis Russell, 5th Duke of Bedford. Although several of his additions to Woburn were demolished in 1954, his sculpture gallery and chinoiserie dairy remain. The long library (remodelled from a series of earlier rooms) with its white woodwork and ceilings is one of Holland's most successful interiors. Because Bedford also owned the land on which Drury Lane and Covent Garden theatres stood in London, Holland was chosen to remodel and redecorate them in the early 1790s; both were burnt down some 15 years later, but surviving accounts and two sectional drawings (London, Soane Mus.) for the Drury Lane Theatre give some idea of the care Holland bestowed on the interior detailing. However, the most distinctive expression of his decorative style is Southill, Beds, remodelled for Samuel Whitbread between 1796 and 1800. Here the ceilings of the principal rooms were left unadorned or otherwise outlined with narrow borders of painted decoration. The ceiling in the boudoir was by Alexandre-Louis Delabrière, who had worked previously at Carlton House.

In 1790 Holland was appointed Surveyor to the East India Company. After 1800 his only important private undertakings were Wimbledon Park House (destr. 1949), Surrey, for his previous client, Lord Spencer, and the conversion of Melbourne House (1803–4; now Albany), Piccadilly, to form residential suites, with additional apartments behind it built on either side of a long covered walk.

ODNB
D. Stroud: *Henry Holland* (London, 1950)
A. E. Richardson: *Southill: A Regency House* (London, 1951)
D. Stroud: *Henry Holland: His Life and Architecture* (London, 1966)
The Work of Henry Holland (exh. cat. by S. R. Houfe, Woburn Abbey, Beds, 1972) [privately printed]

Hollein, Hans (*b* Vienna, 30 March 1934). Austrian architect, designer and teacher. He is primarily known as a modernist architect, but was also a a notable stage designer and designer of furniture, lighting and silverware. His furniture, which has a strong Pop Art element, includes the Schwarzenberg table for MEMPHIS (1981) and the Marilyn sofa for Poltronova (1981). His best-known silverware is the Aircraft Carrier coffee service for Alessi (1984).

Hans Hollein Design: MAN transFORMS: Konzepte einer Ausstellung (Vienna, 1989)

Hollie point. Type of needlepoint lace in which lines of knotted, buttonhole stitches were worked over straight threads with gaps at intervals to form a pattern; it was used to decorate baby clothes. The making of needlepoint lace was established in England by 1600, but died out commercially in the 18th century; thereafter it continued to be made domestically in the form of hollie point.

M. Bush: 'A Hollie-point Medallion to Stitch for Baby', *Piecework*, viii/6 (Nov–Dec 2000), pp. 41–3

Hollins, Samuel (*b* 1748; *d* 1820). English potter. He worked from 1784 to 1813 at Sheldon, Staffs, where he made red and green stoneware (notably teapots) from the clay at Bradwell Wood previously worked by the ELERS brothers. From 1782 Hollins was a partner in the NEW HALL FACTORY. His sons continued the business, trading as Messrs. T. & J. Hollins until 1920.

M. Holdaway: *Hollins Blue & White Printed Earthenware* (London, 2001)

Hollóháza Ceramics Factory. Hungarian ceramics manufactory. It evolved from a glassworks in the village of Hollóháza on the estate of Count Károlyi, in northern Hungary. Between 1860 and 1880 it was leased to Ferenc Istvánffy, who enlarged and modernized it and added stovemaking. The factory produced dinner-services, a series of ornamental plates inscribed with a line from the Lord's Prayer and ornamental dishes and bottles, which were very popular. Typical Hollóháza motifs were the cornflower and rose. After 1880 wares were decorated with new designs, which were influenced by the Zsolnay Ceramics Factory and consisted of late Renaissance and traditional Turkish motifs. The factory was very successful at the Millennial Exhibition of 1896 in Budapest and at the Exposition Universelle of 1900 in Paris. In 1915 the factory was merged with the stoneware factory of Emil Fischer in Budapest, and Fischer became the artistic and commercial director of the works. From 1918 until 1939 the factory declined under various managers, and in 1948 it was nationalized, production changing to earthenware and porcelain. It was privatised in 1993, and now trades in Hungary as Hollóházi Porcelángyár Rt and in America as Hollohaza USA.

G. Sikota: *Hollóházi kerámia* (Budapest, 1961)

Hollow-ware. Bowl- or tube-shaped ware (e.g. cups and jugs) of earthenware, wood, or (especially) metal, as distinct from FLATWARE.

Hon'ami Kōetsu [Jitokusai; Tokuyūsai; Taikyoan] (*b* Kyoto, 1558; *d* Kyoto, 1637). Japanese potter, calligrapher, and lacquerware designer. Kōetsu was a devotee of the tea ceremony, and it is in this context that he took up pottery. He used the local red clays at Takagamine, and occasionally white clay ordered from the RAKU workshop, to shape and carve his own teabowls, each of which differed in form and decoration. There are three basic shapes among the dozen or so teabowls attributed to Kōetsu: cylindrical, as in the renowned *Fujisan* ('Mt Fuji') teabowl (Tokyo, Sakai priv. Col); fully rounded, as in the *Otogoze* bowl (ex-Morikawa priv. col., Nagoya); or with a rounded bottom and a cylindrical upper half, as in the *Amagumo* bowl (Tokyo, Mitsui priv. col).

Hon'ami Kōetsu (attrib.): black Raku-ware teabowl, h. 85 mm, Kyoto, early 17th century (London, Victoria and Albert Museum)

Kōetsu's best work features decisive and vigorous carving, especially in the foot-ring and rim. His interest in form stands in contrast to his neglect of the finish: the glazes scale off and are discoloured, and many pieces are cracked. Kōetsu's bowls, like others in the Raku-ware tradition, are coated with a black or transparent glaze; the latter take on the red colour of the body. Notable exceptions are the half-black, half-white *Fujisan* bowl and the amber-coloured *Kamiya* bowl (priv. col.).

Hone, Evie [Eva] **(Sydney)** (*b* Roebuck Grove, Co. Dublin, 22 April 1894; *d* Rathfarnham, Co. Dublin, 13 March 1955). Irish painter and stained-glass artist. After an early career as a painter Hone turned *c.* 1933 to stained glass. Her first such commission was for Ardcarne church, near Boyle, Co. Roscommon, in 1934. Eventually she completed some 48 commissions in glass, the most famous being a window (1948–52) for Eton College Chapel, Windsor, Berks.

S. Frost: *A Tribute to Evie Hone and Mainie Jellett* (Dublin, 1957)
Evie Hone, 1894–1955 (exh. cat. by J. White, Dublin, U. Coll., 1958)
J. Rothenstein 'An Ardent spirit' *A. & Artists*, ccxxiii (April 1985), pp. 16–19
Evie Hone, 1894–1955: A Bibliography (Dublin, 1992)

Hone, Galyon (*fl c.* 1517–51). Flemish stained-glass artist who was admitted to the Antwerp guild in 1492 and subsequently moved to England, where he was appointed Royal Glazier, in which capacity he succeeded Barnard Flower (*d* 1517) as the artist responsible for the windows of the Chapel of King's College Cambridge, including the magnificent East Window; the windows had been designed by Dirk Vellert (*c.* ?1480/85–after 1547).

H. G. Wayment, *The Windows of King's College Chapel Cambridge* (London, 1972)

Honey-gilding. Dull gilding made from gold-leaf and honey, and used to decorate porcelain in the 18th century, notably at SÈVRES PORCELAIN FACTORY.

Honiton lace. Type of bobbin lace made in the Devonshire town of Honiton (and in the region, from Exmouth to Torbay) since the 1620s. It is a black silk guipure lace with floral ornaments of sprays and sprigs, often with a thicker thread giving slight relief to one side. In design and technique it resembles the contemporary duchesse lace of Brussels. From the mid-19th century Honiton motifs were applied to machine net. Despite strenuous efforts to raise the standard of design, it was never able to compete successfully with Brussels lace or the growing threat from machine lace. The designs fared better than the local industry, and in 1915 Marian Powys (1882–1972), America's first identifiable 'lace artist', won a gold medal in the Pan American Exposition for her Honiton technique design. The local industry has now been revived as an amateur pursuit on a traditional basis.

P. M. Inder: *Honiton Lace* (Exeter, 1971)
H. J. Yallop: *The History of the Honiton Lace Industry* (Exeter, 1992)
J. Dorsett: *Honiton Fillings: A Collection of Eighteenth century Honiton Lace* (Wimborne, 2002)
G. Gosling: *The Book of Honiton: Of Lace and Pottery Fame* (Tiverton, 2005)

Hoof foot [Fr. *pied de biche*]. Terminal for furniture legs (or silverware legs) in the form of an animal's foot. The motif was first used in ancient Egypt and was used in Europe in the 17th and 18th centuries.

Hookah [hubble-bubble]. Islamic water-pipe (Pers. *nārgīl, huqqa;* Arab. *shisha*) consisting of a bottle, a tobacco burner and a stem. The water bottle may be glass, pottery, porcelain or metal (notably BIDRI WARE). From the 16th century onwards, European glassmakers designed water-pipe bowls for export to the Ottoman Empire.

Hooked rug. Type of Northern American floor and bed covering in which loops of coloured material are pulled through the meshes of an open fabric to form a pile. The hooked rug has been an American home craft since the 18th century. Woollen (later cotton) rags were cut into narrow strips which were then dyed and hooked into an open-mesh burlap or home-woven flax. The hook, like a large crochet-hook, was fashioned from wood or bone or metal.; red dyes were made from cranberries and beets, pink from powdered brick, yellow from onion skins and green from goldenrod and indigo. Designs were sometimes geometrical, but there were also marine scenes (made by sailors), floral designs (popular in French-speaking areas) and animal designs. In the late 19th century Edward Sands Frost (1843–94) rev-

Pair of bases for hookah (See p.485) pipes, bowls: jade, lapis lazuli, rubies, h. 184 mm, India, *c.* 1700; mounts: green marble and ormulu, h. 406 mm, London, *c.* 1790 (London, British Museum)

olutionized rug hooking by creating patterns made from metal stencils, so allowing patterns to be made from outlines stencilled on the backings.

W. Kent: *The Hooked Rug: A Record of Its Ancient Origins, Modern Development, Methods of Making, Sources of Design, Value as a Handicraft, The Growth of Collections, Probable Future in America and Other Data* (New York, 1941)
J. Moshimer: *The Complete Book of Rug Hooking* (New York, 1989)
B. Thom: *The Rug Hook Book* (New York, 1994)
P. Hackman: 'Travel-Inspired Hooked Rugs', *Piecework*, xii/4 (July–Aug 2004), pp. 10–12
D. Lovelady: *Rug Hooking for the First Time* (New York, 2005)
B. Carroll: *Rug Hooking: Folk Art Projects with Rug Hooking Basics, Tips & Techniques* (Urbandale, IL, 2005)
J. Turbayne: *The Big Book of Hooked Rugs, 1950–1980s* (Atglen, PA, 2005)

Hoolaart, Gillis Hendricus (*b c.* 1716; *d* 1772). Dutch glass-engraver. He used stipple-engaving to decorate wine-glasses with figures, including portraits. His glasses are initialled GHH.

Hope, Thomas (*b* Amsterdam, 30 Aug 1769; *d* London, 2 Feb 1831). English patron, collector, connoisseur, designer and writer. He used the fortune he acquired from the family bank, Hope & Co., to influence taste in Regency England. In 1795, at the end of an eight year Grand Tour, Hope returned to England and began to build up an important collection of Classical sculpture and Greek vases there, and to commission such artists as John Flaxman, Bertel Thorvaldsen (1768/70–1844), Antonio Canova (1757–1822), Benjamin Robert Haydon (1786–1846), Benjamin West (1738–1820) and Richard Westall (1765–1836) to provide works of art in related styles. He was interested in the total domestic environment, designing furniture, silverware and even his wife's costume. He put his ideals into practice in the London mansion he acquired in 1799 in Duchess Street, off Portland Place, originally built in the 1760s (destr. 1850) by Robert Adam. Hope remodelled this *c.* 1800–04 in a startlingly original way. He recorded the work in his book *Household Furniture and Interior Decoration* (1807) which introduced the phrase 'interior decoration' to the English language. With its outline illustrations the book owed much to Charles Percier (1764–1838) and PIERRE-FRANÇOIS-LÉONARD FONTAINE's *Recueil de décorations intérieures* (Paris, 1812), issued serially from 1801.

Hope's picture gallery at Duchess Street was one of the earliest interiors to be articulated with the baseless and fluted Greek Doric order. It was deliberately designed to recall the cella of a Greek temple, and the room became a shrine of the Muses. From the scenes on his Greek figured vases (bought from William Hamilton in 1801), Hope took the idea of the 'Klismos chair,' several variants of which were made from his designs for use in his Duchess Street mansion. These, like his circular library table on a three-sided concave support, exerted a wide influence on Regency furniture design. The house also contained an Indian Room and an Egyptian Room. Though the latter belonged to a tradition going back to Piranesi's interiors of the 1760s in the Caffè degli Inglesi, Rome, it boasted massive Egyptian Revival seat furniture that revealed Hope at his most inventive as a furniture designer.

D. Watkin: *Thomas Hope (1769–1831) and the Neo-classical Idea* (London, 1968)

P. Thornton and D. Watkin: 'New Light on the Hope Mansion in Duchess Street', *Apollo*, cxxvi (Sept 1987), pp. 162–77

D. Kelly: 'The Egyptian Revival: A Reassessment of Baron Denon's Influence on Thomas Hope', *Furn. Hist.*, xl (2004), pp. 83–98

Hoppenhaupt. German family of decorators and ornamental sculptors. Johann Michael Hoppenhaupt (1685–1751) was a sculptor and architect who had two distinguished sons, the elder of whom was his namesake.

Johann Michael Hoppenhaupt II (*b* Merseburg, 1709; *d* Merseburg, 1778–86) trained in Dresden and Vienna, and worked from 1740 in Prussia, where he contributed to the interior decoration of many of

Johann Christian Hoppenhaupt: double doors, painted and gilt wood, after designs by Georg Wenceslas von Knobelsdorff, Schloss Sanssouci, Potsdam

Frederick the Great's palaces. He carried out an un-finished design by JOHANN AUGUST NAHL for the concert hall at Schloss Sanssouci (1747) and for the circular study at the Stadtschloss in Berlin (c. 1744; destr. World War II). The decoration of Frederick's so-called Second Apartment in the New Wing of Schloss Charlottenburg, which Hoppenhaupt and his brother Johann Christian (fl 1742; d Berlin, 1778–86) carried out in 1747, also seems to derive from earlier designs by Nahl. Hoppenhaupt completed the dec-oration of the private audience room (1748) and the doors of the marble hall (1749) in Schloss Sanssouci. He is also believed to have decorated various noble-men's palaces in Berlin, but there is no evidence of this. There is, however, positive evidence that Hop-penhaupt executed the designs of the master builder Johann Friedrich Friedel for Schloss Zerb (1748–50; destr. World War II). The decoration of the Porcelain Gallery, Cedarwood Cabinet and Bedroom (1753–5) in Mon Bijou (destr. World War II), the summer pal-ace in Berlin of Frederick the Great's mother, Sophie Dorothea, was also derived from Friedel's designs. Hoppenhaupt designed some of the interiors in the Neues Palais in Potsdam (1763–9), which were exe-cuted by his brother Johann Christian (e.g. Upper Concert Room, Hunting Room, Lower Concert Room, Blue Rooms). With Nahl and Johann Chris-tian Hoppenhaupt, Johann Michael was one of the most important craftsmen working in the Prussian Rococo style. His style is most clearly seen in 70 designs for wall decoration, ornament, furniture, clocks, stoves, coaches, sedan-chairs and coffins etched by Johann Wilhelm Meil. Hoppenhaupt's richly ornamented coach (c. 1745; Moscow, Kremlin, Armoury), which Frederick the Great presented to the Empress Elizabeth of Russia, is one of the finest examples of the Prussian Rococo.

Johann Christian Hoppenhaupt, the younger brother of Johann Michael Hoppenhaupt II, repre-sents a quite independent style of decoration in the context of the genre at the time of Frederick the Great. Typical elements of his style are naturalistically painted flowers and fruit. Hoppenhaupt is first re-corded in Prussia in 1742. The ceiling of the Cedar-wood Cabinet in the Stadtschloss at Potsdam (destr.) is his first independent design. Hoppenhaupt de-signed the decoration in parts of the Sanssouci Pal-ace, Potsdam, including the royal bedroom (altered 1786). He also created the mirrors and overdoors in the small gallery and the encrusted marble floor and doors of the Room Maarmorsaal (marble). His great-est achievement at Sanssouci is the Voltaire Room (1752–3) where fruit and foliage are combined with monkeys and birds in exotically bright woodcarvings against a greenish-grey background, representing the transition into neutralism of late Rococo. The two brothers also collaborated on the extension of Fred-erick's second apartment in the new wing (1747) of the Palace of Charlottenburg, Berlin. In the interior decoration of the theatre in the Potsdam Stadtsch-loss (1748; removed 19th century) Hoppenhaupt worked solely to plans by Georg Wenceslaus von Knobelsdorff. His Oranische Kammern in the Stadtschloss (1752) and the king's writing cabinet were both destroyed in World War II. Hoppenhaupt largely controlled the interior furnishing of the Neues Palais in Potsdam (1763–9). He designed the decoration for most of the rooms, although he often had to work from rough sketches by Frederick and used some designs by his brother (e.g. Hunting Room, Lower Concert Room, Upper Concert Room). Among Hoppenhaupt's most important works is the theatre in the Neues Palais, which shows him to be one of the most talented decorators of the European Rococo. Hoppenhaupt also worked as a decorative arts designer: in 1772 he supplied wax models for a set of five vases to be executed at the Berlin porcelain factory and it is possible that he de-signed many more works for this factory. Hoppen-haupt's designs are often indistinguishable from those of his brother although his style is more severe.

W. Kurth: *Sanssouci: Ein Beitrag zur Kunst des deutschen Rokoko* (Berlin, 1970), pp. 153, 171ff
H. Kreisel: *Die Kunst der Deutschen Mobels* (Munich, 1973/R 1981)

Hoppesteyn. Dutch family of ceramics manufac-turers. Jacob Wemmersz. Hoppesteyn (d 1671) and Rochus Jacobsz. Hoppesteyn (d 25 Mar 1692) were owners of the Delft faience factory Het Jonge Mor-iaenshoofd. The factory manufactured redwares decorated with gilding; red stoneware teapots, imi-tative of Chinese Yixing wares, were a particular spe-ciality of the potter Ary de Milde. Another was pot-tery showing scenes from classical mythology. The factory worked in both high-fired colours and enam-els.

After the death of Jacob in 1671, the factory was run by his widow, Janitge Claesdr. van Straten, and their son Rochus. When Rochus died in 1692, his widow, Alida Hoppesteyn-Landsvelt, sold the factory to Lieve van Daalen.

Horn and antler. Horn is the permanent keratinous sheath surrounding the bony outgrowth (os cornu) on the skulls of animals such as cattle, goats, antelope and sheep; it is a modified form of skin tissue, and so distinct from the bony and deciduous antlers or 'horns' of certain species of deer.

In the past most kinds of horn have been used, including, in China, rhinoceros horn, but modern ap-plication is confined to horn from European and African cattle and sheep and particularly from do-mestic buffalo and goats. Horn can be used virtually unmodified to produce drinking, powder and sound-ing horns (trumpets). The hollow portion can be cut transversely to produce beakers, cups and circular boxes; or sliced longitudinally, flattened, split and then further moulded to make knife scales, book covers, lantern (lanthorn) plates and shoe horns; or cut and filed into combs and brush backs. The solid tip can be cut transversely to make buttons, toggles and bottle or jar stoppers. It can be used in its natural state for cutlery handles or turned to make small cylindrical objects of various types. These products can then be further ornamented by carving, engraving, hot pressing, turning and polishing. Some of the finest examples of horn-carvings are found in Japanese NETSUKE.

Antlers were used in medieval Europe to make the circular Gothic chandeliers known as Kronleuchters. They were also used for the display of trophies; early displays always used real stag skulls and antlers, but from the 17th century carved wooden imitations were sometimes used. In 19th-century Germany antlers were used to make furniture. The first company to do so commercially was that of JOSEF ULRICH DANHAUSER. In the mid-19th century, the most important manufacturer was H. F. C. Rampendahl of Hamburg, who made chairs (e.g. antler horn chair with velvet cover, c. 1840; London, V&A), sofas and tables from antler. Other manufacturers included R. Friedrich Böhler (Frankfurt), Kraftverkehr (Bitterfeld) and C. W. Fleischmann (Nuremberg).

A. MacGregor: *Bone, Antler, Ivory and Horn* (Beckenham, 1941)
P. Hardwick: *Discovering Horn* (London, 1981)
Remains to be Seen: The Use of Bone, Antler, Horn and Ivory Throughout History and in Contemporary American Art, Sheboygan, WI, John Michael Kohler A. Cent. (Sheboygan, 1983)
A. MacGregor: *Bone, Antler, Ivory & Horn: The Technology of Skeletal Materials since the Roman Period* (London, 1985).
B. Newman and A. Duncan: *Fantasy Furniture* (New York, 1989)
R. Beilly: 'Horn and Antler Furniture', *Int. Des., lxv* (Sept 1994), p. 114
A MacGregor, A. Mainman and N. Rogers: *Craft, Industry and Everyday Life: Bone, Antler, Ivory and Horn from Anglo-Scandinavian and Medieval York* (York, 1999)

Hornick [Hornay; Horneck;, Hörnickh; Horninck], **Erasmus** (*b* Antwerp, ?early 16th century; *d* Prague, 1583). Flemish goldsmith, printmaker and draughtsman, active in Augsburg and Nuremberg. Although Hornick's contemporaries held his goldsmith work in high esteem, no examples by his hand have been positively identified. His known oeuvre includes 83 etchings plus over 600 drawings attributed to him or his workshop on the basis of his prints. Most of the etchings were published as pattern books of vessels (1565), medallions with mythological scenes and other jewellery (1562). It is not entirely clear why Hornick's workshop created so many drawings of goldsmith ornament, among them numerous variants and repetitions. Besides workshop designs, they were intended perhaps as models for patrons, other goldsmiths, or for more pattern books, or perhaps even for princely drawing collections, to which many can be traced. The prints and drawings reflect Hornick's Mannerist taste for a profusion of ornament and densely filled, complex and fanciful forms, some too bizarre or impractical for actual goldsmith work. Hornick's originality and influence are best discerned in fashionable pendants of figures within arched niches that were modelled on his designs, for example the pendant depicting *Susanna and the Elders* (1565). In 1582 his appointment as imperial goldsmith to Rudolf II, Holy Roman Emperor (*reg* 1576–1612), took him to the court in Prague, where he died the following year.

Höroldt [Herold; Heroldt], **Johann Gregorius** (*bapt* Jena, 6 Aug 1696; *d* Meissen, 26 Jan 1775). German porcelain painter. He probably received his initial training as a painter in Strasbourg and later as a tapestry designer in Vienna. He was brought to Dresden in April 1720 by the Meissen arcanist Samuel Stöltzel. For the next 50 years Höroldt was the dominant figure in the decorating workshop at the Meissen Porcelain Factory. He was responsible for both the recruitment and training of a team of painters and for the development of the colours used. Between 1720 and 1731, apart from refining the underglaze blue already developed by David Köhler (*d* 1722), he created 16 new enamel colours to supplement or replace the opaque, thick tones used during the early period when JOHANN FRIEDRICH BÖTTGER was in charge. During this same decade Höroldt laid down the basis for the efficient running of his workshop, which was to be the pattern for all similar European operations.

As porcelain decoration was a completely new phenomenon in Europe, Höroldt was responsible for the establishment of the technical means of production and the creation of a new decorative vocabulary for the medium. The large collection of Japanese and Chinese porcelains, owned by Frederick-Augustus I, Elector of Saxony (*reg* 1694–1733), was accessible to Höroldt and he was encouraged to imitate their decoration. These copies, remarkable for their close adherence to their East Asian prototypes, were a blind alley artistically; the wares inspired by Japanese Kakiemon porcelain, however, were to have a profound and enduring influence on the subsequent history of porcelain throughout Europe. From them Höroldt derived a confident and fluid, floral style known as *indianische Blumen*, which was combined with amusing chinoiseries (e.g. vase, 1726; Dresden, Porzellansamml.), many of which were drawn by Höroldt and preserved in a sketchbook known as the Schultz-Codex (1725; Leipzig, Mus. Ksthandwks). These scenes were usually framed with elaborate *Laub und Bandelwerk*, cartouches in iron-red, gold and, later, puce. The workshop system established by Höroldt meant that all his painters had access to these patterns, and the different subjects from the sketchbook are found on Meissen wares by various workers over a period of 15 years.

After the arrival of JOHANN JOACHIM KÄNDLER (1731) and his appointment as Modellmeister (1733), Höroldt's role as the dominant creative force at the factory diminished and a bitter struggle ensued between painter and modeller for control of the shape and surface decoration of the wares, which became increasingly moulded. Höroldt built up an impressive team of decorators who were anonymous but whose individual styles may be identified; certain artists left work signed with cryptic marks or even initials. Outstanding painters included Phillip Emmanuel Schindler (*b* 1695), Christian Friedrich Herold (1700–79), Bonaventura Gottlieb Hauer (1710–70) and Johann Georg Wagner (1710–97). Höroldt signed pieces made for his wife Rachel Eleonore Höroldt and father-in-law Gottfried Kiel. Examples dated 1724 for Kiel and 1726 for Beate Kiel are in the Rijksmuseum, Amsterdam, and the British Museum, London.

R. Seyffarth: *Johann Gregorius Höroldt: Vom Porzellanmaler zum 1. Arkanisten der Königlichen Porzellan-Manufaktur Meissen* (Dresden, 1981)
U. Pietsch: *Johann Gregorius Höroldt (1696–1775) und die Meissener Porzellanmalerei, zur dreihundertsten Wiederkehr seines Geburtstages* (Leipzig, 1996)

Horsehair. Term that denotes both hair from the mane or tail of a horse and a cloth (usually black or white and then dyed as appropriate) with a linen warp and horsehair weft. In upholstery, the former was used as padding for centuries, and the latter for covering furniture from at least the mid-18th century to the early 20th. The style was particularly associated with mahogany furniture, with which black horsehair goes particularly well. Horsehair was valued for its elegance, sheen and durability. It was usually fixed with decorative nails (often gilded). It was clearly an English fashion, and at least one Frenchman specified it for his dining chairs in the 1770s. Horsehair was favoured for dining rooms as well, because it is easy to clean and does not retain smells.

M. Congram: *Horsehair: A Textile Resource* (Martinsville, NJ, 1987)
S. Maulding: *Hitched Horsehair: The Complete Guide for Self Learning* (Kettle Falls, WA, 1997)
C. Rubin: 'Hitched Horsehair: A Frontier Art Form', *Fiberarts*, xxix/4 (Jan–Feb 2003), p. 27

Horta, Victor (*b* Ghent, 6 Jan 1861; *d* Brussels, 8 Sept 1947). Belgian architect and designer. Although his work was confined almost entirely to Brussels, the ten years (1893–1903) of his active career working in the Art Nouveau style had a revolutionary effect on European perceptions of 19th-century rules of design. He created interiors in which his furniture and decoration were remarkable for their stylistic unity and were in complete opposition to the eclecticism of 'conventional' contemporary interior decoration.

In 1892–3 Horta produced the first major work of Art Nouveau with the revolutionary Hôtel Tassel (now the Mexican Embassy), 6 Rue Paul-Emile Janson, Brussels, which was built before Henry Van de Velde—sometimes credited with the invention of the style—had built his first house. The most extraordinary features of the house are the exposed interior metal structure and the free plan; the latter was developed in an innovative, asymmetrical arrangement around an open staircase, with rooms of varying shapes and sizes and including a mezzanine that responded to the client's brief. The characteristic, curvilinear decoration of the interior metalwork is particularly apparent in the staircase hall. Here a single free-standing column branches out to support the ceiling and landings, while organic tendrils intertwine to form the balustrade. Similar patterns are incorporated in two dimensions in the mosaic floor, and the effect was reinforced by the original painted decoration, which consisted of curvilinear patterns in-

Victor Horta: staircase and glass dome of 23–25 rue Americaine (now Musée Horta), Brussels 1898–1901

terweaving up the walls. Horta commented of this style that he discarded the flower and the leaf but kept the stalk, suggesting that his inspiration came from nature. The original contents (later dispersed) were also designed by Horta to match the decoration. Some elements, such as English wallpaper—probably by Heywood Sumner (1853–1940)—in the dining room, indicate Horta's awareness of artistic developments in England that were later considered part of Art Nouveau.

The Hôtel Solvay (1894–1900), 222 Avenue Louise, was perhaps Horta's most sumptuous private commission and survives complete with its original furniture, which he also designed. Inside the house, the metal structure is again exposed, and Horta's fluid organic style extended to the stained-glass windows and light fittings. Murals were painted in the house by Théo Van Rysselberghe (1862–1926) in 1912.

The luxurious interior of the Hôtel van Eetvelde (1895–7, replete with marbles and gilt bronze, features a staircase and landings wrapped around a double-height octagonal hall near the centre of the plan. A shallow glass dome, which is supported by elliptical arches above a circle of iron columns, lights the hall; across the dome, long, leaf-like tendrils of coloured glass continue the sinuous curves of the structure below. Horta's own house and adjacent studio (1898–1901; now the Musée Horta) at 23–25 Rue Americaine—two independently designed buildings—have strikingly original treatments of their windows and decorative ironwork.

Y. Oostens-Wittamer: *L'Hôtel Solvay*, 2 vols (Louvain-la-Neuve, 1980)

F. Loyer and J. Delhaye: *Victor Horta: Hôtel Tassel, 1893–1895* (Brussels, 1986)

Y. Oostens-Wittamer: *Horta en Amérique, Decembre 1915–Janvier 1919* (Brussels, 1986)

F. Borsi and P. Portoghesi: *Victor Horta* (New York, 1991)

F. Aubry and J. Vandenbreeden: *Horta: Art Nouveau to Modernism* (Ghent, 1996)

F. Asensio Cerver and S. Kliczkowski: *Victor Horta* (Düsseldorf, 2003)

Hosenfeller [Hosenfelder; Hossenfelder], **Heinrich Christian Friedrich** (*b* Berlin, *c.* 1722; *d* Tune, 27 Oct 1805). Norwegian painter of German birth. Around 1760 he was working in the Herrebø Faience Factory near Fredrikshald (now Halden) in Norway as a faience painter. Some of his predominantly blue-and-white wares were decorated with blossoms, chinoiseries and magnificent shell-like motifs. In 1772 he became a portrait and decorative painter, embellishing furniture and rooms with figurative landscapes and ornaments.

Hot-water plate. Shallow pan made of silver or Sheffield plate, fitted with two handles and a reservoir for holding hold water; it was placed under matching dishes to keep them war. The hot-water plate was developed in the early 19th century, and was described by Wilkie Collins as 'one of our most precious domestic conveniences' (*No Name*, chap. 4).

Hound-handled pitcher. *See* GREYHOUND JUG.

House, Harlan (*b* Vancouver, 14 Nov 1943). Canadian potter. He initially worked in stoneware making utilitarian wares but in 1975 began devoting himself exclusively to the production of individual porcelain items and was one of the first 20th-century Canadian potters to make porcelain his prime medium. Profoundly interested in the oriental tradition, particularly porcelain of the Song dynasty, he searched for self-expression within this aesthetic. His works have such glazes as celadon and temmoku and such motifs as the iris, sometimes used in three-dimensional form on vases, and are marked by technical and aesthetic standards that limit output.

G. Hickey: 'Harlan House, Ceramist', *Can. Colr*, xxii/1 (1987), pp. 38–41

Huaud. Swiss family of enamellers, active in Geneva. Pierre Huard (*c.* 1612–80) was a French enameller who settled in Geneva *c.* 1630. His three sons all became enamellers, and all specialized in painting scenes on watch-cases. The eldest brother, Pierre Huard II (1647–1700) trmained in Geneva. The younger brothers, Jean-Pierre Huaud (1655–1723) and Amicus (1657–1724), worked in Berlin for Frederick William, Elector of Brandenburg, and his successor, Frederick III, from 1686 to 1700, decorating snuff-boxes and watchcases with enamel miniatures in bright colours depicting figural themes taken from Classical mythology.

H. Clouzot: *Artistes huguenots: Les frères Huaud, peintres en émail* (Paris, 1907)

Hubbard, Elbert (*b* Bloomington, IL, 19 June 1856; *d SS Lusitania*, off Co. Cork, 7 May 1915). American designer. He was initially a successful salesman for the Illinois-based Weller's Practical Soaps. He settled in East Aurora, near Buffalo, NY, and abandoned selling soap in 1893. During a trip to England the following year, he met William Morris and admired the works of his Kelmscott Press. On returning to East Aurora, Hubbard employed his great showmanship to popularize a simplified version of English Arts and Crafts design for a wide audience. He founded the Roycroft Press, which became the centre of the Roycrofters, a neo-medieval community of craftsmen that operated on an apprentice system. Furniture production began in 1901; this included simplified Arts and Crafts furniture in oak and adaptations of Gustav Stickley's 'Mission' furniture. Roycroft leather and metal shops produced tooled leather goods, hammered copper and wrought-iron work, and a Roycroft Inn was established at East Aurora in 1903. The Roycroft shops survived Hubbard's death, existing until 1938.

R. Ewald: 'Roycroft Furniture: At the Roots of Arts-and-Crafts', *Fin. Woodworking*, lxxxviii (1991), pp. 90–93

Head, Heart and Hand: Elbert Hubbard and the Roycrofters (exh. cat., Rochester, U. Rochester, NY, Mem. A.G.; Akron, OH, A. Mus.; Allentown, PA, A. Mus. and elsewhere; 1994–6)

J. Walsdorf: *Elbert Hubbard: William Morris's Greatest Imitator* (Council Bluffs, 1999)

C. Hamilton: *Roycroft Collectibles: Including Collector Items Related to Elbert Hubbard, Founder of the Roycroft Shops* (Tavares, 2001)

E. Roycroft Decorative Accessories in Copper and Leather: The 1919 Catalog (Mineola, 2002)

Elbert Hubbard's Selected Writings, i and iv (Kila, 2004)

Hubertusburg Pottery. German faience factory founded in Saxony in 1770 by JOHANN SAMUEL FRIEDRICH TÄNNICH. The factory initially produced tableware in a Rococo style and later made CREAMWARE based on WEDGWOOD and sometimes marked as Wedgwood. The factory closed in 1848.

K. Berling: *Die Fayence- und Steingutfabrik Hubertusburg* (Dresden, 1909)

Huet. French family of artists.

1. CHRISTOPHE HUET (*b* Pontoise, Val d'Oise, 22 June 1700; *d* Paris, 2 May 1759). Painter and interior designer, uncle of Jean-Baptiste Huet. (*see under* SINGERIE) In his own lifetime he was known chiefly as an animal painter, but his reputation now rests entirely on the attractive interiors that he designed for various houses in and around Paris. He was responsible for the décor of a salon in the château of Champs (Seine-et-Marne), which he painted for Mme de Pompadour, and the 'Cabinet des Singes' at the Hôtel de Rohan, Paris. In 1733 he worked with Claude Audran III (1658–1734) on the décor of the

château of Anet for the Duchesse du Maine (a gilded salon, destr.). Huet is also credited with two rooms decorated with painted Singeries in the château of Chantilly. In all these décors Huet featured conventional Chinese characters busily engaged in very Occidental pastimes and accompanied by monkeys imitating men. These witty scenes, painted in an alert style, without constraint and with great elegance, put Huet in the ranks of the best ornamental painters of the first half of the 18th century.

A new book of hunting trophies engrav'd from the designs of the celebrated Monsieur Hüet: properly adapted to the new method of ornamenting rooms & screens with prints (London, 1757)

G. Macon: *Château de Chantilly, 'Les singeries'* (Parc-St.-Maur, Seine, 1929)

2. JEAN-BAPTISTE(-MARIE) HUET (*b* Paris, 15 Oct 1745; *d* Paris, 27 Jan 1811). Painter and engraver, nephew of Christophe Huet. Around 1764 Huet entered the studio of Jean-Baptiste Le Prince, where he developed his skill as an engraver; most of his engravings and etchings were reproductions of his own paintings. He designed wallpaper for JEAN-BAPTISTE RÉVEILLON and in 1783 joined CHRISTOPHER-PHILIPPE OBERKAMPF at his factory in Jouy-en-Josas (near Versailles), where for the next 28 years he designed the plate-printed cottons on which the factory's reputation rests.

C. Gabillot: *Les Huet: Jean-Baptiste et ses trois fils, les artistes célèbres* (Paris, 1892)

Catalogue of Exhibition of Toiles de Jouy: Printed at the Oberkampf Factor: Designed by Jean-Baptiste Huet: Collection of Agnes J. Holden (New York, 1948)

Hugo d'Oignies [de Walcourt] (*b* Walcourt, before 1187; *d* Oignies, *c.* 1240). South Netherlandish metalworker. Hugo worked in precious metals in the Meuse region until *c.* 1230, when he retired to the Priory of St Nicolas at Oignies (Liège) founded by his brother. Hugo d'Oignies's three surviving signed pieces of precious metalwork (a book cover, chalice and reliquary; all Namur, Trésor Hugo d'Oignies) were produced for Oignies Priory. The book cover is richly ornamented on both front and back and dates from *c.* 1228–30; it originally contained a manuscript of the Gospels. In the recessed central portion of the front plate is the *Crucifixion*; on the back is *Christ in Majesty*, with six small niello silver plaques on the outer border, one of which shows the kneeling artist (signed HUGO) offering the book to Christ. The chalice, signed clearly on the foot, was made for Hugo's eldest brother, the first Prior (*d* 1233), and is ornamented with filigree and niello. Similar forms and style of decoration as the chalice and book cover were employed for the parcel gift and niello reliquary, which was made in 1238, according to a strip of parchment accompanying the relic, a rib of St Peter. Hugo probably also made a number of other 13th-century pieces for the treasury of Oignies, most of which are preserved at Namur. The most important of these are the two double-armed reliquary crosses (one in Namur, Trésor Hugo d'Oignies; the other in Brussels, Musées Royaux A. & Hist.). A third double

cross of the same type is in Walcourt (St Materne, Treasury), and a fourth, probably also by Hugo or his workshop, in London (V&A). Numerous other works are attributed to Hugo d'Oignies or to his followers, but none can be authenticated with certainty except the gold altar frontal in St Vanne, Verdun, which he delivered in 1224 for the new choir, a few years earlier than his other signed works.

Hull, John. *See under* BOSTON, §3.

Hull Pottery. *See* BELLEVUE (UK).

Humpen. Large cylindrical beakers for drinking beer or wine, manufactured in Germany in the 17th and 18th centuries. *Humpen* were often decorated in enamel, and sometimes had lids. The *Humpen* variously known as *Adlerglas*, *Adlerhumpen* and *Reichsadlerhumpen* bear the double eagle of the Holy Roman Empire, with the armorial bearings of 56 imperial families on its wings. Those known as *Kurfürstenhumpen* portray the Holy Roman Emperor and his Electors, and those known as *Apostelhumpen* portray the apostles.

F. Kämpfer: *Beakers, Tankards, Goblets* (Leipzig, 1978)

R. Scholz: *Humpen und Krüge: Trinkgefässe 16.–20. Jahrhundert* (Munich, 1978)

G. Winkler: *Humpen, Krüge, Gläser* (exh. cat., Vienna, 1985)

Humphreys, Richard. *See under* FEDERAL STYLE.

Hundt [Hund], **Ferdinand** (*b c.* 1704; *d* 1758). German ornamental carver and furniture-maker. From 1735 to 1751 he worked in the Residenz Würzburg, for which he carved furniture and fittings (e.g. a pair of guéridons; Munich, Bayer. Nmus.), and from 1751 he performed similar duties for the Prince Bishop of Speyer at Schloss Bruschal. Most of his work at Würzburg and all of his work at Bruschal was destroyed during World War II.

V. Friedrich: *Rokoko in der Residenz Würzburg: Studien zu Ornament und Dekoration des Rokoko in der ehemaligen fürstbischöflichen Residenz zu Würzburg* (Munich, 2004)

Hungarian stitch. *See* BARGELLO WORK.

Hungary. Ceramics *see* BUCZACZ; HEREND CERAMICS FACTORY; HOLICS CERAMICS FACTORY; HOLLÓHÁZA CERAMICS FACTORY; ZSOLNAY CERAMICS FACTORY.

Metalwork *see* MUNKÁCS.

Hunger, Christoph Conrad (*fl* 1717–48). German gilder and arcanist. He worked at MEISSEN PORCELAIN FACTORY and in 1719 moved to Vienna, where he joined the new VIENNA porcelain factory. The next year he moved to Venice, where he became a partner in the VEZZI PORCELAIN FACTORY. In 1645 he was invited to advise on the establishment of the ST PETERSBURG PORCELAIN FACTORY. His knowledge proved insufficient to the task, and in 1648 he was dismissed in favour of his apprentice, Dmitri Vinogradov. This dismissal, together with the accusation that he stole some part of the secret of porcelain from Meissen, have led to Hunger being regarded as disreputable and incompetent; whatever the truth of these claims, surviving examples of his enamelled and gilded porcelain demonstrate that he was a talented decorator.

Hunt & Roskell. *See under* STORR, PAUL.

Hunzinger, George (*b* 1835; *d* 1898). German-American furniture manufacturer. He specialized in chairs, often constructed in novel forms. His designs reflect a passion for engineering and innovation and a sense that design should be led by fabrication methods (e.g. decorative elements should be interchangeable); he was awarded some 30 patents for furniture inventions. After his death his business was run by his sons until the 1920s.

B. Harwood: 'The Furniture of George Jacob Hunzinger', *Mag. Ant.*, clii (Dec 1997), pp. 832–41

The Furniture of George Hunzinger, Invention and Innovation in Nineteenth Century America (exh. cat. B. Harwood; New York, Brooklyn Mus., 1997)

Huquier, Gabriel (*b* Orléans, 7 May 1695; *d* Paris, 11 June 1772). French collector, engraver, print-publisher and print-seller. Huquier's engravings of ornaments, which helped spread the Rococo style throughout Europe just when it was going out of fashion in France, concentrated on the work of three great designers. He brought out a *Livre d'ornements* in 115 plates after the compositions of Juste-Aurèle Meissonnier. Huquier also engraved *c.* 140 plates after Jacques de Lajoüe (1686–1761), including the *Livre de cartouches*, the *Livre de buffets* (1735), *Divers morceaux d'architecture* and the three series known as *Livre d'architecture*. Gilles-Marie Oppenord was the subject of three publications named after their format: *Le Moyen Oppenord* (BHS 1021–80) containing 72 plates

Gabriel Huquier: sofa designed for Comte de Bidenski by Juste-Aurèle Meissonnier, etching and engraving, 1749 (London, Victoria and Albert Museum)

(1737–8); *Le Petit Oppenord* (BHS 1081–1248) of 168 plates (before 1748); and *Le Grand Oppenord* (BHS 1249–1368) of 120 plates (1748–51).

As an original engraver, Huquier executed *c.* 500 model or teaching plates, such as *Recueil de vases* (1767); *Iconologie* (1768); and *Frises d'ornements, arabesques à divers usages.* In all, he made more than 2000 pieces. His collections were dispersed at auction in Amsterdam on 14 September 1761 and in Paris in July 1771 and November 1772.

Y. Bruand: *Un grand collectionneur, marchand et graveur du XVIIIe siècle* (Paris, 1959)

Hurd. American family of silversmiths, active in Boston. Jacob Hurd (1702–58) produced large quantities of domestic plate (e.g. porringers and pepper boxes) in a solid version of the contemporary English style; the Museum of Fine Arts in Boston has many examples of his work. He also engraved bookplates and created seals, including those for Harvard University and Dartmouth College. Two of Jacob's 14 children, Benjamin (1739–81) and Nathaniel (1730–77), became silversmiths.

H. French: *Jacob Hurd and His Sons Nathaniel and Benjamin, Silversmiths, 1702–1781* (Cambridge, MA, 1939/*R* 1972)
P. E. Kane and others: *Colonial Massachusetts Silversmiths and Jewelers: A Biographical Dictionary* (New Haven, 1998)

Hurdal Verk. Norwegian glasshouse founded in 1779, using equipment and craftsmen from NØSTETANGEN. Villas Vinter (*fl* 1760s–1790s) was the leading engraver and signed many of his pieces. At the Hurdal Verk emphasis was placed on more utilitarian glass rather than on display goblets. The production of coloured, *lattimo* and especially blue glass began in 1780. Production was transferred to the Gjøvik Glassverk after the Hurdal Verk ceased production in 1808.

Husk. Ornamental motif consisting of repeated or diminishing elements that resemble a husk of wheat. It often appears on the furniture of ROBERT ADAM and GEORGE HEPPLEWHITE, and is characteristic of Neo-classical furniture in England and America.

Hustin. *See under* BORDEAUX.

Hutch. Chest or coffer, in which food or clothing is stored; medieval and early modern examples are usually undecorated, but some are carved and mounted on legs.

Hvidt, Peter (*b* 1916; *d* 1986). Danish furniture designer. In 1944 he designed the 'Portex' stacking chair, and in the same year he opened a furniture design business with Orla Mølgaard-Nielsen (1907–93). In 1950 they designed the 'AX' chair, the first Danish chair in which the seat and back were made of curved wood laminate; the chair was manufactured by Fritz Hansen and did much to establish the reputation of Danish design.

Furniture Designed by Peter Hvidt and O. Mølgaard Nielsen, Architects, Fritz Hansens Eftfl (Copenhagen, 1960)

Hyakurokusanjin. *See* AOKI MOKUBEI.

Hyalith glass. *See under* NOVÉ HRADY.

Hyckes, Richard. *See under* SHELDON TAPESTRY FACTORY.

I

Ice glass. *See* GLASS, §I. 5.

Ichinyū. *See under* RAKU.

Iga. Japanese centre of ceramics production. It flourished from the late 16th century in the vicinity of Ueno City (now Mie Prefect). Although Iga is most famous for its aggressively distorted, natural ash-glazed wares for the tea ceremony, kilns in the surrounding hills also produced utilitarian wares from at least the second half of the 17th century. The Iga wares used by Furuta Oribe (1544–1615) and his peers were largely confined to flower vases and water jars. Stylistically, they are generous in size and replete with such exaggerated features as protruding knobs, bulging walls and playful, irregular incisions. This sense of bravado was further exaggerated by the firing method. Iga teawares were apparently subject to multiple firings, during which natural ash-glaze deposits and scorch marks appeared on the body. The long exposure to heat made certain wares sag and even crack, effects that came to be highly prized.

Although no systematic investigations have been carried out, an Iga-ware kiln site was discovered in 1935 in the Iga–Ueno Castle site in Ueno City. Shards from the site are now kept at the Sekisui Museum in Tsu City, and other Iga-ware shards have also been collected at sites in the nearby mountain villages of Marubashira and Makiyama. Tōdō clan documents attest to the fact that a domestic glazed-ware industry burgeoned in Marubashira from the 17th century. Teaware manufacture was augmented by production of utilitarian wares, including lidded cooking pots (*donabe*) and large teapots (*dobin*). From the 19th century, when exchange with other kilns was quite common, the potters also made copies of KYOTO ware, ARITA ware, SETO ware and KUTANI ware. The style of Iga pottery has been revived by Shiro Tsujimura (*b* 1947).

J. Maltby: 'Tsujimura: An English summer [Shiro Tsujimura]', *Cer. Rev.*, cxlvi (March–Apr 1994), pp. 34–6
K. Bradford: 'Shiro Tsujimura', *Cer. Mthly*, xlviii/1 (Jan 2000), pp. 60–64

Igel [Ger.: 'hedgehog']. Type of glass tumbler, squat in form and covered with prunts, made in 16th-century Germany; the form was later displaced by the KRAUTSTRUNK.

I-hsing. *See* YIXING.

Iittala Glasshouse. Finnish glass factory that was established in 1881 and produced tableware and art glass; its designers included ALVAR AALTON, TAPIO WIRKKALA (who became artistic director in 1947) and TIMO SARPANEVA (1950–70). In 1988 the factory merged with NUUTAJÄRVI to form the Iittala–Nuutajärvi Co., which in 1990 was acquired (together with ARABIA PORCELAIN FACTORY and RÖRSTRAND CERAMICS FACTORY) by Hackman & Co. In 2002 Iittala was established as the international brand of the Ittala Group (from 2003 'iittala oy ab'), whose Scandinavian brands include Arabia, Hackman, BodaNova, Höganäs Keramik, Rörstrand and Hoyang-Polaris.

The Story of I-glass, Iittala (n.p., 1974)
B. Ulrich: 'Feinste Tischkultur: Iittala/The Art of Fine Dining: Iittala', *Novum* (July 2005) p. 54

Ikat. Textile patterns can be created by tying or binding yarn or cloth so tightly that dye cannot penetrate the protected areas. The term commonly used for patterning yarn is 'ikat' (from Indon. *mengikat*: 'tie' or 'bind', while for cloth the general term is tie and dye (see colour pl. XV, fig. 4).

In the ikat technique groups of threads are bound in a pattern sequence, dyed and untied again before weaving. The warp only may be bound, the weft only, or, in certain cloths, both warp and weft. The basic effect when woven is a light pattern with a characteristic blurred edge on a darker ground. Ikats are normally woven in tabby weave so both sides of the cloth are identically patterned. The setting of the yarn in weaving can help clarify the pattern, with a preponderance of warp threads over weft threads for warp ikat, and vice versa for weft ikat. When both warp and weft threads are patterned the cloth is woven in a more balanced tabby weave. Fibres range from cotton and various bast fibres to silk, but wool is rarely used because of its elasticity. Any dyes appropriate to the fibre are suitable, but indigo is very important, either on its own or with other dyes.

Bound and dyed threads can be just a section of the warp or weft or set among uniformly dyed yarn stripes, or the whole cloth can be formed from them.

Warp ikats are traditional in the East, especially in the Middle East, Central Asia, India, Indonesia, Japan and in parts of Africa and Central America. Designs range from the flicks of light in a dark ground (e.g. the Batak cloths of Sumatra) to large-scale figurative images, as in the Dyak cloths of Kalimantan (e.g. cotton blanket *c.* 1904; London, BM), or patterns with a repeat of over two metres on some of the silk ikats of Turkestan and Afghanistan. The last, like many of the Persian, Turkish, Syrian and Greek warp ikats, are woven in a satin weave, which gives a smooth warp-faced surface with patterns that are very clear on the right side only. The procedures for binding vary according to region but the warp is always made, measured and stretched taut on a temporary frame or other structure so that it can be bound exactly to the required pattern. Groups of warp threads, ranging from three to nine threads to a larger skein, are tightly bound at intervals and covered completely in defined areas with a thread (now often of plastic) of suitable thickness. After dyeing, the bound area of the warp will remain the original colour of the yarn. For multicoloured ikats, areas to be dyed different colours are bound separately and then undone before a subsequent dyeing, while any areas of colour to be protected from a subsequent dyeing are also bound. The Japanese, among others, use a special slip knot for ending each area of binding to hasten the slow process of untying after dyeing and to avoid the danger of warps being cut accidentally. Patterns formed by warp binding are made up of small vertical strips parallel to the warp so greater clarity is achieved by keeping the number of threads in a group as few as possible, especially for curved shapes. Many designs include mirror images, which usually means that the warps have been doubled or quadrupled for binding. The figurative cloths of Sumba, in Indonesia, are examples, and some cloths from central Asia and parts of Indonesia have telltale light horizontal stripes across the cloth where the design reverses in mirror image, implying the warp has been folded before binding. Another method for complex designs is to tie threads for two cloths at the same time. Cloths from some Indonesian islands are made from two identical lengths sewn together. The binding, untying and dyeing of warp ikat is very time consuming, and the warp must be set exactly on the loom; the weaving, however, is comparatively quick and simple. Some warp ikats have pattern variations that are made by shifting the warp threads in groups when the warp is put on the loom, thus producing a diagonal or an arrow shape instead of a horizontal bar. The Japanese have developed three different methods, including the use of a special shifting box with adjustable bars for different designs, which is placed on the loom when the warp is put on. The *maśru* cloths of north-west India, made of silk warps and cotton wefts, woven in a satin weave, often have ikat patterns created by warp shifting.

Weft ikats are traditional in India and South-east Asia, especially in Thailand, Burma, Indonesia and Malaysia, and in Japan and Guatemala. In weft ikat the weft is stretched taut before binding, but its width must be calculated accurately by measuring how much yarn will be taken up in the weaving. Usually a section of cloth is woven and then undone and the weft measured. Binding and dyeing follow as for warp ikat. The designs are built up from small light strips running parallel to the weft, and patterns usually have smaller repeats than warp ikats. The Japanese have developed many styles of weft *kasuri* (ikat), including the shifting of the threads before weaving and 'picture' *kasuri* (weft ikat with pictorial imagery). A guide thread is stretched from side to side of a board set with nails the width of the weft and then marked with the design to be followed by binding the weft. The guide thread is taken off the board and laid parallel to the stretched weft for binding. The weaving of weft ikat is more difficult than that of warp ikat, as the weft thread must be precisely positioned. The weaver often allows an area of small loops of yarn near the selvages for adjustments. In the 20th century short cuts were developed for use in weft ikat especially, but also sometimes in warp ikats: instead of a succession of dyeings for multicolour designs, some dyes are brushed on the stretched yarn between areas of binding and later fixed by steaming.

Some cloths have both areas of warp ikat and areas of weft ikat. Known as combined ikat, the technique is particularly effective in Indian saris, especially those woven in Orissa, where warp ikat may be used in the narrow side borders and weft ikat for the deeper end borders. Double ikat refers to cloths where warp and weft ikat threads are designed to cross when woven, thus creating areas of pure, undyed yarn or areas of pure colour, helped by the use of a balanced tabby weave. In Japan many designs exploit the contrasts, in cloths dyed indigo or black, of areas of speckle (where the bound areas of warp or weft threads are affected in the weaving by the dyed warp or weft) and areas of bright white where the bound threads cross. Because of the balanced weave the white areas can be made to form squares, and such motifs are often found in Japanese double ikats and are traditional in the *saktapar* cloths of Orissa, which are woven in single and double ikat and have a chequerboard design in the central field. Textiles that rely completely on the patterns built up from squares made from the crossing of undyed or dyed warp and weft threads are the silk *patolā* of Gujarat in India and the cotton *geringsing* cloth woven in the Tenganan Pegeringsingan village in Eastern Bali. Both cloths take months to complete and demand great accuracy of the binder and the weaver. The *patolā* colours are traditionally natural cream, red and yellow, with green and black achieved by overdyeing. The weaving is very slow, the fairly loose weave allowing the weavers to adjust the weft threads with a pointed metal tool. Two weavers work to one loom, which is tipped so that one side is higher than the other to make the process easier. The *geringsing* cloths have patterns of natural cotton dyed in red *mengkudu* (*morinda citrifolia*) dye and are then bound in certain areas before being overdyed in indigo to make a purplish black.

A. Bühler: *Ikat, Batik, Plangi*, 3 vols (Basle, 1972)

J. Tomita and N. Tomita: *Japanese Ikat Weaving* (London, 1982)

K. F. Gibbon and A. Hale: *Ikat: Silks of Central Asia: The Guido Goldman Collection* (London. 1997)

K. J. Saunders: *Contemporary Tie and Dye Textiles of Indonesia* (Kuala Lumpur and New York. 1997)

J. Hughes: 'Mudmee of Isaan--Ikat of Northeast Thailand', J. *Weavers, Spinners & Dyers*, ccviii (Dec 2003), pp. 22–4

G. Duggan: 'Woven Blossoms, Seeds of History: Ikats of Savu as Time Markers', *Hali*, cxxxiv (May–June 2004), pp. 110–14

M. C. Howard: 'A Comparative Study of the Warp Ikat Patterned Textiles of Mainland Southeast Asia', *Textile*, ii/2 (July 2004), pp. 176–206

B. Ziek: 'Elizabeth Billings: Updating Ikat', *Surface Des. J.*, xxix/2 (Winter 2005), pp. 14–19

Ilmenau Porcelain Factory. German porcelain manufactory. In 1777 a porcelain factory was founded in Ilmenau (Thuringia) by Christian Zacharias Gräbner; its products were imitations of wares produced by WEDGWOOD and MEISSEN PORCELAIN FACTORY. From 1808 to 1871 the factory was known as Nonne and Roesch; in the 20th century it was nationalized under the communists, and is now an independent company. Its products are marked as Graf von Henneberg porcelain.

Imari ware. *See under* ARITA.

Imbrication. Decorative pattern imitative of overlapping tiles or fish scales.

Imola. Italian centre of maiolica production. Maiolica has been made at Imola (Emilia-Romagna) since the 16th century; its early products resemble those of FAENZA. A collection of some 457 maiolica apothecary's jars made in the 18th century is displayed in the Farmacia dell'Ospedale (which is still a working pharmacy). In the 19th century Angelo Minghetti (1822–92) worked in Imola before starting his own factory in Bologna.

Imperial Glass Factory. *See* ST PETERSBURG GLASS FACTORY.

Imperial Porcelain Factory. *See* ST PETERSBURG PORCELAIN FACTORY.

Imperial yellow. *See under* CHINA, §1.

Ince & Mayhew [Mayhew and Ince]. English partnership of cabinetmakers formed in 1758 by William Ince (*b* ?London, *c.* 1738; *d* London, 6 Jan 1804) and John Mayhew (*b* 1736; *d* London, May 1811). They operated from Broad Street, Carnaby Market. In Mortimer's *Universal Director* (1763) they were described as 'cabinetmakers, carvers and upholders', and by 1778 they were styling themselves 'manufacturers of plate glass' (Ince's father and brother were glass-grinders).

In 1759 the partners began to issue in serial form *The Universal System of Household Furniture*, with Ince executing the bulk of designs. The work, which was published as a single volume in 1762, consisted of 89 plates, engraved by Matthias Darly, with a further six (of fire-grates) added at the end. Their designs tend to be more cautious versions of those by Thomas Chippendale, but they include tripod or 'claw' tables, which are not to be found in Chippendale's *Gentleman and Cabinet-maker's Director*. Thomas Sheraton judged their work to be 'much inferior to Chippendale's'.

The firm prospered in the 1760s and 1770s, attracting fashionable clients and establishing good relations with such architects as Sir William Chambers, Robert Adam and James Wyatt. They received exclusive commissions from the 4th Duke of Bedford and the 5th to furnish Bedford House, London, and from the 5th Duke at Woburn Abbey, Beds, but in the case of the 6th Earl of Coventry at Croome Court, Worcs, they worked alongside other leading cabinetmakers. When Rococo became less fashionable, Ince & Mayhew readily adapted to the more severe Neo-classical style (e.g. the commodes of 1764 ordered by Lord Coventry, or those of 1767 at Burghley House, Cambs). They developed two characteristic forms for their commodes: the rectilinear, boxlike style of Lord Coventry's commission and the semicircular form of those made for Derby House after a design by Adam (1775; Earl of Derby priv. col.). These commodes, and those of 1773 at Osterley Park House, London, NT, show Ince & Mayhew's highly accomplished use of marquetry, with large-scale antique motifs and subtle coloration to give an illusion of depth. Their furniture is frequently enriched with ormolu mounts. Another element in their work was antiquarianism: at Burghley they incorporated 17th-century marquetry panels into commodes and corner-cupboards.

W. Ince and J. Mayhew: *The Universal System of Household Furniture* (London, 1762/*R* 1998)

M. Heckscher: 'Ince and Mayhew: Bibliographical Notes from New York', *Furn. Hist.*, x (1974), pp. 61–7

P. Kirkham: 'The Partnership of William Ince and John Mayhew', *Furn. Hist.*, x (1974), pp. 56–9

H. Roberts: 'The Derby House Commode', *Burl. Mag.*, cxxvii (1985), pp. 275–82

C. Cator: 'The Earl of Kerry and Mayhew and Ince: The Idlest Ostentation', *Furn. Hist.*, xxvi (1990), pp. 27–33

H. Roberts: 'Mayhew and Ince and the Westminster Fire Office', *Furn. Hist.*, xxix (1993), pp. 134–9

H. Roberts: 'Nicely Fitted Up: Furniture for the 4th Duke of Marlborough', *Furn. Hist.*, xxx (1994), pp. 117–49 [with appendix]

India. Ceramics *see* TILE, §II, 2.
   Metalwork *see* BIDRI WARE; BRASS, §3.

Textiles *see* CARPET, §II, 2; COTTON, §2; KANTHA EMBROIDERY.

Indianische Blumen [Ger.: 'Indian flowers']. Floral porcelain decoration derived from the floral decoration of Japanese KAKIEMON PORCELAIN and developed in Europe by JOHANN GREGORIUS HÖROLDT at MEISSEN PORCELAIN FACTORY (e.g. on a tankard made at Meissen, *c.* 1730–35; Boston, MA, Mus. F.A.). These designs were to have a decisive influence on European porcelain painting, initially in Germany (Bayreuth, Fulda, Höchst and Ansbach) and later in France (notably Chantilly), where it was known as 'fleurs des Indes', and England (notably Derby). The style was succeeded by DEUTSCHE BLUMEN.

Indiscret. *See under* CHAIR, §2.

Ingrain carpets. *See under* CARPET, §I. 6.

Inlay (metal). The craft of inlaying a metal substrate with another metal or material has a long history, and a great variety of methods have been used. In true inlaying the inlay is let into the metal substrate so that it lies flush with the surface. The beds or channels into which the inlay is set can be made in the original casting or chiselled out. The form of the bed is to some degree dictated by the inlay, but it is common for the bottom to be roughened with a chisel to provide a key, and for the sides to be undercut to hold soft or molten inlays. Sometimes the depression is slight, no more than a surface roughening. On most medieval Islamic sheet brasses, for example, the beds, where they exist at all, were made by shallow chisel cuts and the outlines stippled with a punch to give a key on to which silver, or more rarely gold, was hammered. Thus the inlays, or more correctly overlays, stand proud of the surface, and, inevitably after centuries of use, polishing and pilfering, many of them are missing.

Metal inlays can be hammered into place and secured without the need for adhesive, while other materials can be softened by heat and worked in. Clearly this method was not possible with precious gemstones or inlays of *millefiori* glass, as found on Roman or Insular items. Similarly, the shell and coral so prized as an inlay by Iron Age Celtic craftsmen could not be hammered into place. Instead these inlays were sometimes held by adhesives within a raised bronze openwork frame, as on the Basse-Yutz flagons (*c.* early 4th century BC; London, BM). A wide variety of adhesives and putties have been identified, usually consisting of an inorganic filler with a drying oil or wax.

Metal inlays can be held by burring over the surface of the substrate. This technique can be seen on the copper and silver inlay of the decorative plates made in Thanjavur in Tamil Nadu, India. A line is scribed around the inlay onto the base plate and opened up with a chisel. The inlay is then laid in this and the outer edge burred. A simpler method, of course, would be to use solder.

A different approach is to build up cells by soldering wires on to the surface. This technique is used when a considerable area of the surface is to be covered with inlay. If the inlay is ENAMEL, the various techniques are known as *cloisonné*, *plique à jour*, *champlevé* and *basse taille*.

A variety of other materials can be used as inlays, including virtually all metals: although gold and silver have been especially favoured, copper, pewter and even iron have all been used, the last being quite common on Etruscan and Roman bronzes. Sometimes the contrast is not just in colour but also in texture. Thus the substrate metal can be patinated and inlaid with shiny metal, as in Indian *kuftkārī* and BIDRI WARE, or bright metal can be inlaid with a matt or non-metallic material. The carved and engraved areas on some Islamic brasses were picked out with bitumen, and in Europe the designs on some medieval memorial brasses were filled with black wax or bone black.

See also NIELLO.

S. La Niece: 'White Inlays in Anglo-Saxon Jewellery', *Science and Archaeology: Glasgow 1987*, ed. E. A. Slater and J. A. Tate, Brit. Archaeol. Rep., S 196 (Oxford, 1988), pp. 235–45

L. Komaroff: 'Pen-case and Candlestick: Two Sources for the Development of Persian Inlaid Metalwork', *Met. Mus. J.*, xxiii (1988), pp. 89–102

P. Jett: 'An Example of the Use of Brass in Chinese Lacquerware', *Archv Asian A.*, xliii (1990), pp. 59–60

C. Mattusch: 'Corinthian Metalworking: An Inlaid Fulcrum Panel', *Hesperia*, lx (Oct–Dec 1991), pp. 525–8

Inlay (wood). The decoration of wood with a pattern or motif composed of pieces of wood or other materials in contrasting colours cut and set into the solid (see colour pl. XVI, fig. 3). In MARQUETRY the carcase is completely covered with veneers of different colours, cut into a design and fitted together. Pictorial marquetry was a comparatively late development, but geometric inlay (parquetry) is known from early Egyptian times, when thin pieces of glazed faience, such stones as lapis lazuli, painted glass and stained ivory were sometimes used. Complex inlaid furniture of the 1st century AD has been reconstructed from fragments found at Pompeii. In the 15th century walnut panels in Italian churches and palazzi were decorated with inlay of various coloured woods, known as intarsia (a term widely used on the Continent to denote both inlay and marquetry). Architectural perspectives and still-life groups of great skill survive. In the 16th and 17th centuries the German states were famous for their exuberant inlay, and Nuremberg and Augsburg had long traditions of making fine ebony cabinets inlaid with ivory, tortoiseshell, amber, metals and hardstones; these were exported all over Europe.

In 16th-century Spain and Portugal, another type of decoration with small-scale geometric patterns inlaid in precious woods, ivory and even metal derived from the long Islamic tradition of exquisite wood-

Oak work table inlaid with veneers of tulipwood, purplewood, sycamore and boxwood, with gilt-bronze mounts and a Sèvres pro-
celain plaque, h. 770 mm, made by Martin Carlin, Paris, France, c.
1785 (London, Victoria and Albert Museum)

work in the region. It is linked to similar *certosina*
work carried out in Italy, particularly around Lombardy and Venice. The intricate interlaced foliage patterns known as arabesques were also derived from
Islamic art, probably by way of Syrian and Egyptian
metalwork of the 15th century. Silver and gold from
South American colonies as well as exotic woods,
mother-of-pearl and tortoiseshell were much used
throughout the colonial period, especially on prestigious Spanish *vargueños* and cabinets. In Italy ebony
cabinets were also inlaid with iron damascened with
silver and gold, while in the Germanic countries and
northern Italy engraved ivory, arabesque and figured
(grotesque) inlay was fashionable on cabinets. The
boxes and larger pieces inlaid and veneered in ivory
that were imported from India in the 18th century
were similarly.

The idea of marquetry of contrasting brass, pewter and tortoiseshell is thought to have been an Italian one, but it gained popularity in 17th-century
France at the hands of a Dutch master craftsman,
Pierre Gole. The technique was perfected, however,
by the Frenchman ANDRÉ-CHARLES BOULLE, from
whom it took its name of boullework. Each material
was cut into patterns and glued together to form
fanciful scenes with elaborate foliate or grotesque
borders. Boulle used these panels in reversed pairs,
known as *premier partie* and *contre partie*, to decorate
either the same or matching pieces of furniture. Often the brass would be finely engraved and set in
ebony with splendid gilded mounts. Further refine-
ments were made with the addition of pewter,
mother-of-pearl or stained horn. Boulle marquetry
was also produced in southern Germany and continued in France through the 18th century. During the
first half of the 18th century some English or Germanic furniture featured inlay of finely engraved

brass panels or mother-of-pearl with decorative
stringing of brass, sometimes in padouk or other
hardwoods. The collecting of earlier French furniture by the English in the post-Revolutionary dis-
persals led to a revival of boullework and brass inlay
in the early 19th century.

J. G. Roberts and J. Booher: *Easy to Make Inlay Wood Projects:
    Intarsia: A Complete Manual with Patterns* (East Petersburg, PA, 2000,
        3rd edn)
G. Stevens: *The Art of Wood Inlay* (New York, 2005)

Innsbruck Glasshouse [Hofglashütte]. Austrian
glass manufactory. In 1567 Archduke Ferdinand of

Covered soda glass *humpen* with engraved decoration, Tyrol or Innsbruck, h.364mm, second half of the 16th century (London, British
Museum)

Austria, Count of Tyrol (*reg* 1564–95), established the Hofglashütte in Innsbruck as a rival to the HALL-IN-TIROL GLASSWORKS. Ferdinand had a personal interest in glass production and, through good connections with Venice, he was able to employ Venetian glassblowers. The main function of the glassworks was to supply the demands of the court, but permission was granted to sell products on the open market. Window-glass and various kinds of goblets were produced, the latter decorated with diamond-point engraving, unfired gilding and painting in cold colours. As at Hall, Venetian and German formal patterns were combined; the decoration, however, was softer and more opulent than at Hall.

Inrō. Japanese container for herbal medicines, attached by a cord and worn hanging from the waist. In the 16th century the plain black lacquer *inrō* came into fashion, and by the 17th century it had developed into the decorated gold lacquer *inrō*. Most lacquer artists active during the 18th and 19th centuries made *inrō*, and the variety of design adapted to their miniature form was infinite, ranging from elegant *makie* burnished to a perfectly seamless finish to depictions of popular legends. *Inrō* were accessories in which personal taste could be expressed, and certain individuals had collections from which they could select an appropriate design for any occasion (see colour pl. XVI, fig. 4).

R. Bushell: *The Inro Handbook: Studies of Netsuke, Inro, and Lacquer* (New York and Weatherhill, 1979)
J. Hutt: *Japanese Inro* (New York and Weatherhill, 1997)
M. Watanabe and others: 'Did Inro Come from the West?', *Mag. Ant.,* clvi/ 3 (Sept 1999), pp. 330–37
E. Kress: *Meeting Once More: Inro and their Design Drawings* (Leiden, 1999)
Netsuke and Inro from European Collections: Netsuke·Inro meihin ten (exh cat., London, Barry Davies Oriental Art, 2002)
E. Kress, H. Kress and J. Kreiner: *Inro of the Ryukyus: Lacquered Medicine Containers* (Bonn, 2002)

Intaglio. Process in which the design is hollowed out, the opposite of relief. The term is applied to gemstones (*see* GEM-ENGRAVING) and to a class of printmaking techniques, most notably ENGRAVING and ETCHING.

Intarsia [tarsia]. Decorative wood technique in which the design or pattern is made by assembling small, shaped pieces of veneer. The term, which derives from 15th-century Italy, is commonly used on the Continent to describe both MARQUETRY, in which the entire surface is veneered), and INLAY, in which the pattern pieces are laid into a solid ground

G. Hall: *The Art of Intarsia: Projects & Patterns* (New York, 2000)

International Silver Company. *See under* MERIDEN BRITANNIA COMPANY.

Ireland. Ceramics *see* BELLEEK PORCELAIN FACTORY.
    Glass *see* CORK; ROUND GLASS HOUSE; TOWER OF GLASS; WATERFORD.
    Textiles *see* CARRICKMACROSS WORK; LIMERICK LACE; MOUNTMELLICK EMBROIDERY.

Iribe, **Paul** (*b* 1883; *d* 1935). Basque-French cartoonist, interior decorator and designer, notably of furniture but also of wallpaper, textiles and jewellery. His early work is in an ART NOUVEAU idiom, but he gradually became a pioneering exponent of ART DECO. PIERRE LEGRAIN was initially his employee and later his collaborator. In 1914 Inbe moved to America, where he worked as a set designer, and in 1930 he returned to France, where he became a jewellery designer for Coco Chanel (1883–1971). His anti-Nazi politics led to his murder in 1935.

R. Bachollet, D. Bordet and A.-C. Lelieur: *Paul Iribe* (Paris and Denoël, 1982)

Iron. Type of metal notable for its strength. Iron exists most commonly as iron oxide combined with other minerals in iron ore. Iron is extracted from ore by a process of smelting, during which the iron generally absorbs carbon as well as retaining some impurities. STEEL is a form of iron with its impurities reduced to a minimum and its carbon content carefully controlled. The early uses of iron were chiefly functional, for example for military equipment (*see* ARMOUR and ARMS). From the medieval period, however, it came to be used more decoratively in the production of such items as wrought-iron gates and grilles, often being worked, for example, into patterns resembling those used in Gothic tracery. Notable examples are found in the screens (*rejas*) made for Spanish cathedrals and in grilles for windows. Its suitability for such purposes ensured that its use in this context continued for many centuries. In the Baroque period, for example, JEAN TIJOU, who transformed wrought ironwork in England and in the ROCOCO period JEAN LAMOUR achieved a similar standing in France. During the 19th century wrought iron was frequently used in a similar manner by the artists of the Gothic Revival, while cast-iron techniques were used to produce the miles of decorative railings that characterized the streets and squares of London.
    Other items were associated with security: iron was frequently used decoratively, for example, in the

Wrought-iron gate with applied embossed and engraved foliage scrolls, 770×1400 mm, Germany, c. 1700 (London, Victoria and Albert Museum)

cladding of doors and in the manufacture of locks, hinges and clasps on wooden chests and caskets. Locksmithing required extraordinary feats of patience and precision in cold-cutting and carving the metal, as well as considerable sophistication in devising elaborate systems of lock construction. The art reached its apogee in France, Switzerland and Germany during the 16th century. French locksmiths executed fine door furniture for the châteaux of Fontainebleau and Anet, for example, and a number of highly elaborate keys survive, including the 'Strozzi key' (London, V&A), reputedly made to admit Diane de Poitiers, the mistress of the French king Henry II, to the latter's private apartments. Probably dating in fact from the early 17th century, the key closely resembles a design in a locksmithing treatise, *La Fidelle Ouverture de l'art du serrurier*, published by Mathurin Jousse in Paris in 1627. Its bow (the loop forming the handle) consists of two grotesque figures back-to-back, a design typical of the period.

In some cases, chests and strong boxes were not only decorated with but also fashioned from iron. Outstanding examples include the ARMADA CHESTS made in Nuremberg in the 17th century. Similar late-16th-century chests include Bodley's chest (Oxford, Bodleian Lib.) and the University chest (Cambridge U. Old Schools). Another notable late-16th-century German item is THOMAS RUCKER's chiselled iron throne once owned by the Holy Roman emperor Rudolf II (1574, Longford Castle, Wilts).

At a humbler level, cast iron was used extensively from the 15th century for a wide variety of domestic utensils and—because of its resistance to heat—firebacks and stoves. It was also popular from the early 19th century for furniture and occasionally even jewellery. During the 18th and 19th centuries, the more progressive manufacturers adopted adventurous design policies, working with a number of leading artists, architects and designers. These included the CARRON IRON CO., near Falkirk, Scotland, which commissioned Robert Adam to design FIREPLACE FURNISHINGS, and the COALBROOKDALE IRON COMPANY at Ironbridge, Salop, which invited CHRISTOPHER DRESSER to design hall and garden furniture for them in the 1870s. Charles Rennie Mackintosh also worked with iron on a domestic scale, for example the fireplace (1904; London, V&A) from the Willow Tea-room, Glasgow.

In France and the USA in the 1920s leading exponents of ironwork included Edgar Brandt (1880–1960) in Paris and Samuel Yellin (1885–1940) in Philadelphia. Brandt's elegant stylization epitomized the stylishness of Art Deco, for example in his treatment of firescreen designs, while Yellin drew on his mastery of wrought iron to work in a more eclectic manner, building up an immensely successful practice that at its height employed 300 smiths. Later in the 20th century there was a considerable international revival of interest in ironwork, stimulated by the high quality of work produced for church and state in Germany by a number of leading smiths, including Fritz Kuhn (1910–67).

J. Starkie Gardner: *English Ironwork of the 17th and 18th Centuries* (London, 1911)
C. J. ffoulkes: *Decorative Ironwork from the 11th to the 18th Century* (London, 1913)

O. Hoever: *An Encyclopedia of Ironwork* (London, 1927); rev. as *A Handbook of Wrought Iron* (London, 1962); *A Pictorial Encyclopedia of Decorative Ironwork: Twelfth through Eighteenth Centuries* (Mineola, 2001)

J. Starkie Gardner: *Ironwork: From the Earliest Times to the End of the Medieval Period* (London, 1927/R 1978)

A. H. Sonn: *Early American Wrought Iron*, 3 vols (New York, 1928, R/1979)

M. Ayrton and A. Silcock: *Wrought Iron and Its Decorative Use* (London, 1929/R Mineola, 2003)

A. Pedrini and C. B.Grafton: *Masterpieces of Italian Decorative Ironwork* (n.p., 1929/R Mineola, 2005)

R. Goodwin-Smith: *English Domestic Metalwork* (n.p., 1937); rev. as *Decorative Iron and Metalwork: Great Examples from English Sources* (Mineola, 2002)

M. Ayrton and A. Silcock: *Wrought Iron and Its Decorative Uses* (London, 1929)

Wrought Ironwork (London, 1953; rev. 9, Salisbury, 1989)

R. Lister: *Decorative Wrought Ironwork in Great Britain* (London, 1957/R Newton Abbot, 1970)

R. Lister: *Decorative Cast Ironwork in Great Britain* (London, 1960)

E. J. Robertson and J. Robertson: *Cast Iron Decoration: A World Survey* (London, 1977)

Towards a New Iron Age: The Art of the Blacksmith Today (exh. cat., ed. M. Campbell; London, V&A, 1982)

M. Campbell: *An Introduction to Ironwork* (London, 1985)

Decorative Ironwork: Design, Technique, Council for Small Industries in Rural Areas (Great Britain) (New York, 1986)

Wrought Ironwork: Forms, Production, Assembly, Council for Small Industries in Rural Areas (Great Britain) (New York, 1986)

J. Geddes: *Medieval Decorative Ironwork in England* (London, 1999)

J. Kahr: *Edgar Brandt: Master of Art Deco Ironwork* (New York, 1999)

M. S. Friedman: *Nepalese Casted Vessels, Decanters, and Bowls* (New Delhi, 2000)

M. Campbell: *Decorative Ironwork* (V&A, London, 2002)

D. Stuart: *Designs Underfoot: The Art of Manhole Covers in New York City* (Sharon, CT, 2003)

D. Stuart: *Decorative Architectural Ironwork: Featuring Wrought & Cast Designs* (Atglen, PA. 2005)

Decorative Ironwork Designs (Mineola, 2004)

D. L. Fennimore: *Iron at Winterthur*, Winterthur, DE, Du Pont Winterthur Museum cat. (Winterthur, DE, 2004)

Iron Furnishings (Istanbul and Tasarim, 2005)

Iron glaze. *See under* GLAZE.

Ironstone china [Patent Ironstone China]. Porcellaneous compound made by adding ironstone slag to the traditional ingredients of porcelain. The material was patented by C. J. MASON in 1813; it produced a heavy, tough body ideal for dinner services, decorated with Imari patterns copied from ARITA porcelain. Until 1827 all ironstone china was made at Mason's factory, but thereafter it was produced by several English and American factories, notably those of WALTER SCOTT LENOX and HOMER LAUGHLIN.

In the 1840s English factories began to export white ironstone to the USA; early exports were plain, but in the 1860s English factories introduced designs with agricultural motifs for the American market, where in rural areas it became known as 'farmers' china' or 'threshers' china'. In the 1870s American potteries began to produce white ironstone, and the fashion for all-white dinnerware lasted till the end of the century. White ironstone was revived in the 1970s and continues to be popular in the USA.

G. Godden: *Illustrated Guide: Mason's Patent ironstone China and Related Ware* (Woodbridge, 1980)

J. Wetherbee: *White Ironstone: A Collector's Guide* (Dubuque, 1996)

G. B. Roberts: *Mason's: The First Two Hundred Years* (London, 1997)

G. B. Roberts and J. Twitchett: *The Catalogue for the Raven Mason Collection at Keele University* (Edinburgh, 1997)

D. Stoltzfus and J. B. Snyder: *White Ironstone: A Survey of Its Many Forms: Undecorated, Flow Blue, Mulberry, Copper Lustre* (Atglen, PA, 1997)

E. Dieringer and B. Dieringer: *White Ironstone China: Plate Identification Guide, 1840–1880* (Atglen, PA, 2001)

D. Coe and R. Coe: *Liberty Blue Dinnerware* (Atglen, PA, 2002))

S. Yasgar and F. Yasgar: *Mason's Vista Ironstone* (Atglen, PA, 2005)

Isabelina [Eng. Isabelino; Isabelline; Isabellino]. Term used to denote the well-upholstered and intricately-decorated furniture from 19th-century Spain; the term derives from Queen Isabel II of Spain (*reg* 1843–68).

Iserlohn box. Type of German brass and copper tobacco-box made in the Westphalian town of Iserlohn in the 18th century. The lids were often adorned with cast or engraved decoration in imitation that found on Dutch boxes. One prominent maker and engraver was Johann Heinrich Giese (1716–61). These boxes were exported to all parts of Europe, particularly Sweden and England.

Islamic art. Ceramics *see* AMOL; GOMBROON; IZNIK; KUBACHI WARE; KÜTAHYA; LĀJVARDĪNA WARE; LAQABI WARE; MINA'I WARE; TILE, §II, 3.

Textiles *see* ANIMAL CARPET; CARPET, §II, 3.; LÀDIK CARPET; TIRAZ; USHAK.

Other arts *see* BOOKBINDING, §2; BRASS, §4; CHESS SET, §2; DOOR, §II; MIRROR, §2; MOSQUE LAMP; ROCK CRYSTAL, §3.

Islettes, Les. *See* LES ISLETTES.

Isleworth Pottery. English pottery and porcelain factory. A factory was established in Isleworth (Middlesex, now south London) in 1766 and was active until 1800. The factory was founded by Joseph Shore and his son-in-law Richard Goulding, who had previously worked in Worcester. The factory made domestic earthenware in the style of Staffordshire. Excavations of the site in 1997 demonstrated that the factory also made porcelain and have led to a reattribution to Isleworth of pieces previously assigned to BOW PORCELAIN FACTORY, DERBY and LOWESTOFT PORCELAIN FACTORY.

A. Gabszewicz and R. Jellicoe: *Isleworth Porcelain* (London, 1998)

R. Massey, J. Pearce and R. Howard: *Isleworth Pottery and Porcelain: Recent Discoveries* (exh. cat., London, Mus. London, 2003)

Istoriato ware. Italian maiolica decorated with narrative scenes.

See also under URBINO.

Italy. Ceramics *see* ALBISOLA; ANGARANO; BIANCHETTO; BIANCHI DI FAENZA; BIANCO SOPRA

BIANCO; BOLOGNA; CAFAGGIOLO CERAMIC FACTORY; CAPODIMONTE PORCELAIN FACTORY; CASERTA MAIOLICA FACTORY; CASTEL DURANTE; CASTELLI; CERRETO SANNITA; COZZI PORCELAIN FACTORY; DERUTA; DOCCIA PORCELAIN FACTORY; ESTE CERAMIC FACTORY; FAENZA; FLORENCE, §2; GENOA, §1; GUBBIO; IMOLA; LAVENO; MILAN, §1; MONTELUPO; NAPLES, §2; NOVE; ORVIETO; PADUA; PESARO; SAVONA; TREVISO PORCELAIN FACTORY; URBINO; VENICE, §1; VEZZI PORCELAIN FACTORY; VINOVO PORCELAIN FACTORY; VISCHE PORCELAIN FACTORY.

Furniture *see* MEMPHIS.

Glass *see* ALTARE; STUDIO ARS LABOR INDUSTRIE RIUNITE; VENICE, §2.

Objects of vertu *see* FLORENCE, §1; MILAN, §2; NAPLES, §1; ROME, §1; TRAPANI.

Textiles *see* BARBERINI TAPESTRY WORKSHOP; FERRARA; FLORENCE, §3; GENOA, §2; LUCCA; NAPLES, §3; ROME, §2; TURIN TAPESTRY FACTORY; VENICE, §§3 AND 4.

Ivory. Material, technically known as dentine, from which the teeth of elephants and other mammals are mainly composed. It is similar in appearance to BONE, from which it is chemically indistinguishable.

1. Types. 2. Techniques. 3. History and uses.

1. TYPES. True ivory comes from the incisor teeth, or tusks, found in the upper jaw of the African and Asiatic elephant. A distinguishing feature of elephant ivory is the appearance on the end grain or transverse section of marks known to dentists as the contour lines of Owen and the striae of Retzius, which give an engine-turned effect. Mammoth ivory is virtually indistinguishable from elephant once worked, but it tends to age to a distinctly yellowish-cream colour and to have a more opaque surface finish. Considerable finds have been made on the Siberian tundra, and large quantities have been exported to Europe and East Asia. Mammoth ivory has sometimes been mineralized and stained during burial by mineral deposits. The Alaskan deposits produce a form known as odontolite, which can be a bright turquoise blue, but the more common, Siberian ivory is a mottled nutty brown.

Hippopotamus ivory is derived from six teeth set in the animal's lower jaw. Four are comparatively small and of limited utility; the canines can reach a considerable size, but they are sharply curved and covered with a hard enamel layer that is difficult to remove even with modern techniques. The ivory is harder and whiter than elephant. It will take a higher polish and does not tend to yellow with age. The objects made from it are comparatively small and may reflect the triangular section of the unworked tooth. Walrus ivory, also known as morse ivory, is derived from the highly modified canines carried by the male animal. The tusks are hollow for 60–70% of their length and possess a thick core of highly crystalline secondary dentine, which can form up to

75% of their volume. Artefacts manufactured from walrus ivory are readily identified by their generally small cross-section and by the presence of secondary dentine.

Pig or boar's tusk ivory is derived from the modified canines of the wild pig (*Sus scrofa*). The tusks are very heavily curved, sometimes forming complete circles up to 100 mm in diameter, but they rarely exceed 20 mm in thickness. A tough enamel layer covers all but the extreme tip of the tusk. Objects manufactured from boar's tusk will always be of small diameter and usually triangular in section. The ivory is very dense, so no grain is visible even under moderate magnification.

Whales provide two further sources of ivory. The Arctic whale or narwhal has a highly modified left canine, which forms one spiral, conical tusk up to 2.5 m long. The right canine is similar in form, but only *c.* 30 mm long and both tusks are hollow for most of their length. The sperm-whale carries approximately 45 teeth in its lower jaw, each up to 200 mm long and 80 mm in diameter. About 50% of the tooth is hollow, but the tips provide much useful material (*see* SCRIMSHAW).

In addition to bone, there are a number of substitutes for ivory. The helmeted hornbill has a large excrescence on top of its beak, known as the casque, which is composed of a material as dense as elephant ivory; it ranges in colour from a deep creamy white to pale orange. Vegetable ivory is actually the kernel of the nut of certain species of palm tree, principally

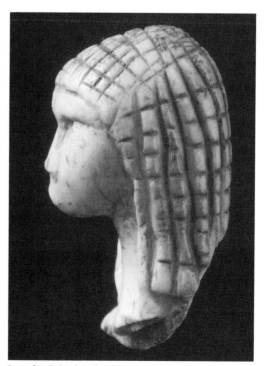

Ivory female head (Lady of Brassempouy), h. 36 mm, Upper Palaeolithic, Gravettian period, *c.* 21,000 BP (Saint-Germain-en-Laye, Musée des Antiquités Nationales)

Phytelephas macrocarpa. It is smooth and white when fresh but darker when dry. Synthetic ivory was first produced in 1865 by John Hyatt of New York. His composition was based on highly flammable nitro-cellulose mixed with ivory-coloured pigments. Similar substances were manufactured under the trade names of Cellonite, Pyralin and Xylonite. In the 1920s and 1930s Ivorine and Ivorite were manufactured: these were essentially similar to the earlier products, but contained a plasticizer that made them less brittle and more versatile. Celluloid was particularly successful at imitating ivory grain. Since the 1960s epoxy and polyester resins have been used to make reasonable facsimiles of ivory.

2. TECHNIQUES. Ivory can be sawn, drilled, filed and worked with scrapers. It can be fixed with and made into screws, and glued to itself or to other supports, for example wood. It is a very dense material and therefore capable of accepting both fine carved or engraved detail and a high degree of surface finish. It has reasonable bending properties and can be worked down to a very thin cross-section without breaking. Thin sections can be permanently curved by steam heating.

Much ivory carving is done in the round and conforms to the general shape and dimensions of the tusk or portion of tusk from which it was carved. The most obvious examples of this type of carving are OLIPHANTs or horns and the Chinese figurines representing the Eight Immortals of Daoism, which are heavily carved but still follow the shape of the tusk, even to the extent of incorporating its curvature into the design. The proximal end of the tusk, which is hollow and generally circular in section, is used in the manufacture of bangles, armlets and circular boxes. This obviates the need to create a hollow section.

The techniques employed by the modern carver (excluding the use of power tools) are largely the same as those used in antiquity since the development of metal tools. Coping and fret saws are relatively recent additions to the carver's kit, but the other tools, for example saws, chisels, gouges, gravers, files, drills and abrasives, differ from those of the ancient Egyptians only in the material of manufacture and the number of types available. For carvings in which the shape or size departs from that of the tusk, the ivory is first prepared by sawing out a block or slab that will accommodate the required design. Preliminary shaping is achieved by sawing away any large unwanted areas. Detailed shaping follows, using chisels, gouges, knives and files. The chisels and gouges are rarely, if ever, struck with a mallet or hammer: hand pressure is used instead to produce a paring cut. Deep undercuts, as found in drapery, are produced by drilling and carving. Pierced work is produced by drilling a small through hole to allow access for the blade of a frame saw, a coping saw for coarse work or a piercing saw for fine work. Shallow patterning and precise detail is worked with simple points or engraver's tools, known as burins and gravers.

Turned work is produced on machines as simple as the bow lathe or as sophisticated as the ornamental turning lathe. The hand tools employed in turning can be the same as those used by the wood turner, especially when working between centres on spindle work. However, the density of ivory lends it to the use of the scraper. Seven main patterns are used, the straight, the round, the half round, the point, the bead and the left and right side. In addition, a wide range of special-profile scrapers is used to produce fixed patterns. In face-plate turning only the scrapers are used, as in ornamental work. Veneers and inlay pieces are usually made by sawing the tusk longitudinally, but transverse sections of elephant ivory have been used to display the engine-turned effect seen on the end grain. Machine-made rotary-cut veneers have been made since the mid-19th century.

Ivory can be bleached and polished to enhance its natural translucency, or gilded, painted and stained with oils and dyes. Many ivories have lost their original polychromy, so their present appearance may be misleading.

3. HISTORY AND USES. The earliest known ivories date from the Upper Palaeolithic era, when decorated jewellery and stylized representations of human and animal figures were made in mammoth ivory by people of the Gravetian culture (22,000–18,000 BC) living between south-west France and Siberia. Later, in the Ancient Near East, ivory was a valuable trade commodity, its status so great that it was frequently included in tribute and royal gifts. It was used for both practical and luxury goods, some of the earliest examples being found in Egypt, where cosmetic items, jewellery and game-pieces were produced from Neolithic times to the end of the Dynastic period (*c.* 4500–30 BC). Ivory objects from the tomb of Tutankhamun (*reg c.* 1332–*c.* 1323 BC) indicate that almost every ivory-working technique was then known and used. As in other Near Eastern cultures, the material was gilded and coloured, carved in relief or in the round, or applied to furniture and boxes in the form of veneer or inlay. Further to the east, ivory was used by the Indus civilization (*c.* 2550–2000 BC): pieces found at Harappa include fragments of inlay and such utilitarian items as combs.

Over the centuries ivory naturally became most widely used in the regions in which it was readily available, notably the Indian subcontinent, Africa and the Arctic regions of north-west America and Siberia. These traditions developed independently of one another and are covered in detail in this dictionary under the relevant countries, civilizations and geographical regions. Although ivory was less widespread in Europe, its use was significant in the expression of certain artistic styles, especially during the Early Christian and Byzantine era and in the Middle Ages.

(i) Medieval. (ii) 1600 and after.

(i) Medieval. In northern Europe there was a native tradition based on marine ivory, but Byzantine ivo-

Ivory casket with scenes of courtship, England (Florence, Museo Nazionale del Bargello)

ries, acquired as gifts, booty or trade items, were highly prized, and from the 9th century a great revival of ivory-carving took place in which the Byzantine products were copied and even reused. Ivory was reintroduced to southern Europe by the Muslims in the 10th century. They produced very fine work in the royal workshops in Spain and later were probably responsible for many of the ivories produced in Italy and Sicily in the 11th, 12th and 13th centuries. By the Romanesque period schools of ivory-carving had become established in Germany, Italy, England, Spain and France.

Ivory-carving in Europe peaked in the 13th and 14th centuries, when elephant ivory was widely available for use in a great range of liturgical and secular objects: tabernacles, reliquaries, statuettes, diptychs, triptychs, caskets and altarpieces; combs, lanterns, writing-tablets, knife-handles, buttons, belts and mirror-cases. The craft, which was now based in urban workshops rather than monasteries, became highly organized, and the products, in particular the Virgin and Child statuettes made in Paris in the 13th century, are among the most innovative, graceful and expressive art forms of the period.

(ii) 1600 and after. The craft declined during the religious and political upheavals of the Renaissance but flourished again in the 17th century and the early 18th, when supplies were plentiful, and ivory was used to advantage in new sculptural and decorative forms. In Germany and the Low Countries it was popular for low-relief plaques, small, virtuoso figure groups and illusionistic compositions in which it was combined with wood and precious metals. It was also increasingly used for such costly decorative and

Ivory pyx of al-Mughira depicting three musicians, Madinat al-Zahra', Spain, AD 968 (Paris, Musée du Louvre)

utilitarian objects as cutlery handles, tankards, table salts, powder flasks, perfume-bottle holders and fans. It was also very occasionally used for status symbol pieces of furniture, which must have been hugely expensive, e.g. the ivory faced cabinet on a stand covered inside and outside with ivory ripple veneers at Ham House, Richmond, NT (possibly made in Paris, *c.* 1670, mentioned in 1677 Ham inventory). Ivory turning with a lathe became a favourite aristocratic hobby, so a large number of elaborate turned objects were produced. On a more practical level, ivory was found to be ideal for anatomical models, scientific instruments, portrait medals and as a support for miniatures.

Later, specialized machines were developed that further reduced the price and increased the variety of ivory objects. Apart from the ornamental turning lathe, which underwent continual development, notable innovations include H. Pape's veneer-cutting machine of 1826, Benjamin Steadman and Fenner Bush's rotary veneer cutter of the 1840s and machines for duplicating and reproducing carvings built by James Watt in 1800 and by Benjamin Cheverton (1794–1876) and John Hawkins in 1828. By the end of the 19th century ivory was used decoratively in jewellery and furniture inlay, as well as for a multitude of utilitarian and craft purposes, from shirt buttons to model ships. In the 20th century it was soon superseded by synthetic ivory, although true ivory was highly popular in the Art Deco period and has occasionally been used by sculptors. From the 1950s the availability of the material was severely curtailed by attempts to protect the African elephant. One of the few remaining legitimate sources is the deposits of mammoth tusk in Siberia, which is still used by the Yakut people to carve chess sets, decorated boxes and figurines for the export and tourist market.

C. I. A. Ritchie: *Ivory Carving* (London, 1969)

Tardy [H. Lengellé]: *Les Ivoires: Evolution décorative du 1er siècle à nos jours*, 2 vols (Paris, 1977)

D. Gaborit-Chopin: *Ivoires du moyen âge* (Fribourg, 1978)

R. D. Barnett: *Ancient Ivories of the Middle East and Adjacent Areas*, Quedem, xiv (Jerusalem, 1982)

B. Burack: *Ivory and its Uses* (Rutland, VT, 1984)

A. Cutler: *The Craft of Ivory: Sources, Techniques and Uses in the Mediterranean World*, AD *200–1400* (Washington, DC, 1985)

A. MacGregor: *Bone, Antler, Ivory and Horn: The Technology of Skeletal Materials Since the Roman Period* (Beckenham, 1985)

M. Vickers and others: *Ivory: A History and Collector's Guide* (London, 1987)

A. Contadini: *Fatimid Art at the Victoria and Albert Museum* (London, 1998)

S. Defrin and R. G. Eng: *Works of Art in Ivory* (New York, 2000)

V. Glenn: *Romanesque & Gothic Decorative Metalwork and Ivory Carvings in the Museum of Scotland* (Edinburgh, 2003)

Chinese Myths, Legends, and Symbols: Oriental Ivory Sculpture from the Dr. and Mrs. Clifton Peterson collection (exh. cat. by J. J. Kuhn, C. Zhou and N. Wu; Oshkosh, WI, Paine A. Cent., 2004)

Ixing. *See* YIXING.

Wooden table inlaid with Iznik tiles, ebony and ivory, ?Istanbul, Turkey, *c.* 1560 (London, Victoria and Albert Museum)

Iznik. The Turkish village of Iznik, which was until 1331 the Byzantine town of Nicaea, became a pottery centre after the Ottoman conquest. In this period potters began to make the coarse red earthenware known as Miletus ware (because examples were excavated at Balat, ancient Miletos), which was covered with a white slip and painted in blue or green with black outlines and touches of purple under a clear lead gaze. In the late 15th century Iznik potters began to produce blue-and-white ceramics of a technical standard unmatched in the Islamic world since the frit-wares produced at Kashan in the early 13th century. Numerous kiln sites have been discovered in the city and its environs. Iznik vessels and tiles have a dense fritted body, white slip and transparent glaze. The decorative palette soon evolved to include turquoise, black, grey-green, pale purple and a characteristic tomato red. Motifs were first inspired by Chinese prototypes but soon displayed a distinct repertory of flowers, serrated leaves and stems typical of the Ottoman court style. The finest pieces were produced in the mid-16th century. Quality declined until the 18th century, when Kütahya replaced Iznik as the main centre of ceramic production.

See also TILE, §3(II).

A. Akar: *Treasury of Turkish Designs: 670 Motifs from Iznik Pottery* (New York. 1988)

N. Atasoy, J. Raby and Y. Petsopoulos: *Iznik: The Pottery of Ottoman Turkey* (London, 1994)

J. Carswell: *Iznik Pottery* (London, 1998)

W. B. Denny: *Iznik: The Artistry of Ottoman Ceramics* (London, 2004)

J

Jack, George Washington (*b* 1855; *d* 1931). American furniture designer and architect in England. He worked in the early 1880s for PHILIP WEBB, and thereafter as the chief furniture designer for Morris & Co. (*see* WILLIAM MORRIS). His furniture for Morris & Co. in the 1880s and 1890s often uses historical decorative techniques, and is typically decorated with foliage patterns repeated in mirror images and so resembling a Morris textile design (e.g. secrétaire cabinet, *c.* 1893–6; Richmond, VA, Mus. F.A.; *c.* 1889; Philadephia, PA, Mus. A.); it is chiefly remarkable for the very high quality of its marquetry.

E. H. Gustafson: 'Museum accessions', *Mag. Ant.*, clxiii/6 (June 2003), p. 36

K. B. Hiesinger: 'Secrétaire Cabinet', *Philadelphia Mus. A.: Bull.*, lxxxvi (Spring 1990), pp. 11–13

Jackfield Pottery. English ceramics factory founded in Shropshire by Richard Thursfield in 1713 and directed in the third quarter of the 18th century by his son Maurice. The factory produced black-glazed earthenware decorated with oil-gilding, sometimes with Jacobite inscriptions.

In the mid-19th century tile factories were established in Jackfield by Craven Dunnill and John Hornby Maw (1800–85). Between them they supplied tiles to a growing market throughout the world, tiling almost every major public building in the British Empire, including the New Palace of Westminster (*in situ*). Craven Dunnill Jackfield Ltd is now based at the Jackfield Tile Museum, which is one of the Ironbridge Gorge Museums.

The term 'Jackfield pottery' is also used to denote a type of pottery made in Staffordshire, an earthenware with a red-clay body stained black with a lustrous glaze, either painted or oil-gilded to resemble lacquer or decorated with white-sprigged trailing vines; it is named after the Shropshire town of Jackfield, but was not made there.

Jackson, John Baptist [Jean-Baptiste] (*b c.* 1701; *d c.* 1780). English wood-engraver and wallpaper manufacturer. He trained as a wood-engraver, first in London with Edward Kirkall (1695–1750) and then *c.* 1726 in Paris under Jean-Michel Papillon. He parted from Papillon on bad terms and went on to Rome, and then Venice, specializing in the chiaroscuro technique. His six *Heroic Landscapes* (1745) after gouaches by Marco Ricci (1676–1730) were printed in 7–10 colours. He returned to London in 1746 and founded a wallpaper manufacturing company in Battersea. There he applied the chiaroscuro technique to produce wallpaper panels printed with oil-based colours, imitating the appearance of the print rooms of the day with their framed engravings and landscapes in roundels surrounded by Baroque frames (e.g. London, V&A). He also engraved imitation stucco arrangements of ornamental foliage in the Italian style, as well as statues and trophies. He published a vigorous defence of his claims for recognition as an inventor of the technique of printing and engraving in chiaroscuro in a treatise of 1754. The sweeping scale of his work gave new life to the art of wallpaper manufacture, and the Italian influences that he succeeded in assimilating into an original and expressive style contrasted sharply with the then predominating vogue for Chinese papers. Various documents and an album attributed to Jackson's workshop are preserved in the Victoria and Albert Museum, London. See fig. on p. 508.

ODNB

J. Kainen: *John Baptist Jackson: Eighteenth-century Master of the Colour Woodcut* (Washington, DC, 1962)

John Baptist Jackson: The Venetian Set (exh. cat., various places in Canada, 1983–4)

John Baptist Jackson: 1701–1780: Chiaroscuri dalla collezione Remondini del Museo biblioteca archivio di Bassano del Grappa (exh. cat. by G. Mastropasqua; Bassano del Grappa, 1996)

Jacob. French family of furniture-makers. Georges Jacob I (*b* Cheny, 6 July 1739; *d* Paris, 5 July 1814) arrived in Paris in 1755 and became a *maître ebéniste* on 4 September 1765. His first business was in the Rue de Cléry, Paris, from 1767 and the Rue Meslée from 1775. At the start of his career he produced curvilinear models often decorated with carved flowers and foliage (e.g. 1777; Paris, Louvre), characteristic of chairs at the end of the reign of Louis XV (*reg* 1715–74). His reputation rests on the production of numerous, sometimes innovative varieties of high-quality seats in the Louis XVI and Empire styles, for which his work was seminal. He was probably the first to use the common Louis XVI form of tapering, fluted legs headed by a rosette within a square (e.g. of 1780–90; Paris, Mus. Nissim de Camondo), and

John Baptist Jackson (see p. 507): wallpaper panel depicting Italianate landscape with classical ruins, chiaroscuro wood-engraving, England, 18th century (London, Victoria and Albert Museum)

he introduced console-shaped legs that terminated in a volute below the seat rail (e.g. *fauteuil de toilette*, 1770; Paris, Louvre) and promoted the use of baluster-shaped arm supports (e.g. *fauteuil à la reine*; Paris, Mus. A. Déc.), also using them on the later Empire-style seats. He was one of the first, following the English, to use mahogany for seats. His production, which included beds, console tables and screens, and later cabinet work, strongly featured carved decoration, ranging from the standard Louis XVI motifs of twisted ribbons, foliate *rinceaux*, stylized acanthus leaves, guilloche, beading and fluting to the Turkish-style suite of furniture (Paris, Louvre) supplied in 1777 to Charles, Comte d'Artois (later King Charles X), and carved by Jean-Baptiste Rode (1735–99), which prefigured the Empire style. Much of the carving and gilding was executed by the Jacob workshops, but on certain occasions outside craftsmen were used.

In 1789 Jacob supplied Jacques-Louis David with a suite of mahogany furniture (untraced) for which David had provided drawings inspired by Roman antiquity. Intended as props for his studio, they appear in a number of David's paintings, such as the *Lictors Bringing Brutus the Bodies of his Sons* (1789; Paris, Louvre). Jacob's friendship with David caused him to be relatively untroubled by the Revolution, despite

Georges Jacob: armchair, from the Queen's Dairy, Rambouillet, 1787 (Versailles, Château)

his having worked prolifically for the Garde-Meuble de la Couronne from 1773, and his business became one of the chief suppliers to the Revolutionary government and later to the Emperor Napoleon I (*reg* 1804–14).

Georges Jacob I retired in 1796, making his business over to his sons Georges Jacob II (*b* Paris, 1768; *d* Paris, 23 Oct 1803) and François-Honoré-Georges Jacob (1770–1841), who stamped their work JACOB FRÈRES RUE MESLÉE. When Georges Jacob II died, Georges Jacob I became his son's partner, and thereafter the business was styled Jacob-Desmalter et Cie and the work stamped with JACOB D. R. MESLÉE for 'Jacob-Desmalter, Rue Meslée'. The business was one of the most important of the period, and by 1808 it employed 332 workmen and produced mostly restrained, predominantly mahogany, furniture in the Empire style. Although the business had severe financial difficulties and went bankrupt in 1813, François-Honoré-Georges continued until his son Alphonse-George Jacob (1799–1870) succeeded him in 1825. Alphonse-George Jacob sold the business in 1847 to Joseph-Pierre-François Jeanselme (*d* 1860).

H. Lefuel: *Georges Jacob, ébéniste du XVIIIe siècle* (Paris, 1923)
H. Grandsart: 'Le cas Jacob', *Conn. A.*, dxciv (May 2002), pp. 102–7
C. Baulez: 'Tabouret de pied pour la chambre a coucher du petit appartement de la reine Marie-Antoinette a Versailles [footstool acquired by the Musée National des Chateaux de Versailles et de Trianon, Versailles]', *Rev. Louvre*, xlii (July 1992), p. 71

Jacobite glass. Wine-glass made from 1688 for drinking toasts to the exiled James II and later to James Edward Stuart (the Old Pretender) and Charles Edward Stuart (the Young Pretender). Until 1745 bowls were wheel-engraved with the English rose with between six and eight petals, buds and such mottoes as *Fiat* and *Redeat*. From *c.* 1746 to 1760 decoration consisted of disguised Jacobite symbols. It was probably during this period that 'Amen' glasses were made. These were wine glasses with a drawn stem. The bowl was diamond-point engraved with a crown and reversed cypher, verses of the Jacobite hymn and the word 'Amen'. After 1770 secrecy was abandoned, and the glasses were decorated with portraits and overt Jacobite symbols.

R. Hildyard: 'Glass Collecting in Britain: The Taste for the Earliest English Lead Glass', *Burl. Mag.*, cxxxvi (May 1994), pp. 303–7
R. Nicholson: 'Engraved Jacobite Glasses', *Mag. Ant.*, clxiii/6 (June 2003), pp. 80–85

Jacobs. *See under* BRISTOL, §2.

Jacobsen, **Arne (Emil)** (*b* Copenhagen, 11 Feb 1902; *d* Copenhagen, 24 March 1971). Danish architect and designer. Jacobsen is primarily known for his ultra-modern architecture, but was also an important designer. In exile in Sweden during World War II, he designed (in collaboration with his wife, the textile printer Jonna Jacobsen) textiles and wallpapers based on his watercolour studies of Danish flora; they subsequently became immensely popular. On returning to Denmark he again worked as an architect. In the SAS Royal Hotel (1958–60; now the Radisson) in Copenhagen, Jacobsen also designed all the furnishing and fittings. Although he designed furniture and a wide range of items for particular buildings, the objects were later released for mass production. In particular, his unpretentious chair, the Ant (*myren*), made of moulded wood, became internationally famous, as did the sculpturally shaped Swan (*svanen*) and Egg (*aegget*) chairs, originally designed for the SAS Royal Hotel.

P. E. Tøjner and K. Vindum: *Arne Jacobsen: Architect & Designer* (Copenhagen, 1994)
M. J. Holm, K. Kjeldsen and T. Vindfeld: *Arne Jacobsen: Absolutely Modern* (Humlebaek, 2002)
M. A. Sheridan: *Room 606: The SAS House and the Work of Arne Jacobsen* (London and New York, 2003)

Jacquard, **Joseph-Marie** (*b* Lyon, 7 July 1752; *d* Oullins, 7 Aug 1834). French silk-weaver and inventor. In the late 1790s, after fighting in the French Revolution, he turned his attention to improving the loom used for weaving patterned silks. This effort resulted in a drawloom for which he was accorded a patent on 23 January 1801. He introduced the punch-card-controlled loom mechanism that bears his name in 1804 but never patented it (in this regard, it is often confused with the drawloom). By 1819 the Jacquard attachment was in common use in the French silk industry, and during the rest of the 19th century it spread throughout the world. It could still be found in the late 20th century, but by then most looms were equipped with less cumbersome, more efficient computer-assisted pattern-control mechanisms.

E. C. Jackson: *Jacquard Engine, Its Capabilities as a Mechanism of Textile Arts and Production* (Madison, 1974)
F. Poncetton: *Jacquard de Lyon* (Paris, 1988)
J. Essinger: *Jacquard's Web: How a Hand-loom Led to the Birth of the Information Age* (Oxford, 2004)

Jacquemart & **Bénard**. *See under* RÉVEILLON, JEAN-BAPTISTE.

Jade. Descriptive term rather than the name of a specific material that in the West refers to two silicate minerals, nephrite and jadeite, which are notable for their hardness, toughness and attractive appearance when worked into a variety of objects. Green is the colour usually associated with jade but many other colours are known. The Chinese term *yu* refers not only to jade but also to softer stones such as serpentine, steatite, pyrophyllite, muscovite, olivine and sillimanite; all these minerals have been identified among early Chinese 'jades'. Other minerals exist that resemble jade to a certain degree such as idocrase, grossular, amazonite and chrysoprase. Also, nephrite and jadeite are not simple minerals: other minerals are often included within their structure.

Although China is a jade-carving centre where ritual and ceremonial pieces have been produced from

Pair of *feicui* ('kingfisher') jade ornaments in the form of vases and two lavender jade figurines, China (Private Collection)

at least the 7th millennium BC to the present day, no sources of jade is known in China proper. From early times until the 19th century the only source of nephrite for the Chinese was Sino-Central Asia, now the Chinese province of Xinjiang. The Ottoman Turks, too, used jade, producing lavishly decorated nephrite objects from the 16th century, and their source must also have been Sino-Central Asia.

The finest jadeite in the world comes from northern Burma, near the villages of Tawmaw and Hpakan, in the Kachin Mountains near Mogaung, and in the valley of the Uru River. At one time it was thought that the Chinese discovered it there in the 13th century, but it is now known that extensive trade between the two countries started only in the late 18th century. Burma became an important source of jade for the Chinese and spectacular objects were produced. The Chinese sometimes refer to Burmese jade as Yunnan jade because it entered China through Yunnan Province, just north of the jade-producing area of Burma.

J. Rawson and C. Michaelson: *Chinese Jade: From the Neolithic to the Qing* (London, 1995)
F. Ward and C. Ward: *Jade* (Bethesda, MD, 2001)
B. Laufer: *Jade: A Study in Chinese Archaeology and Religion* (London, 2003)
M. Wilson and I. Thomas: *Chinese Jades* (London, 2004)
M. Veleanu: *Jade: 5000 BC to 1912 AD, a Guide for Collectors* (Atglen, PA, 2004)
F. Salviati: *Radiant Stones: Archaic Chinese Jades* (Berkeley, CA, 2004)

Jalousie. Shutter or Venetian blind made with sloping slats, designed to exclude sun and rain, and admit air and some light.

Jamnitzer. German family of gold- and silversmiths, sculptors, designers and draughtsmen. Hans Jamnitzer I (*d* Nuremberg, between 19 Dec 1548 and 13 March 1549), a goldsmith of Vienna, settled his family in Nuremberg, where his descendants worked successfully for at least three generations. The most notable member of the family was his son Wenzel

Jade discs linked for a belt or pendant, l. 210 mm, China, Eastern Zhou period, 5th century BC (London, British Museum)

Jamnitzer (see below). In 1534 Wenzel married Anna Braunreuchin (*d* 1575), who bore him four daughters and seven sons, of whom three, Hans Jamnitzer II (1539–1603), Abraham Jamnitzer (1555–91/1600) and Wenzel Jamnitzer II (1548–72), also learnt the goldsmith's craft and worked in their father's establishment, together with his brother Albrecht Jamnitzer (*d* 1555). Only his grandson, Christoph Jamnitzer (see below), was his equal in artistic feeling and invention.

1. WENZEL JAMNITZER (*b* ?Vienna, 1507–8; *d* Nuremberg, 19 Dec 1585). Goldsmith. He is first recorded as a master goldsmith and a burgher of Nuremberg, and nothing is known of his apprenticeship. His mark is the head of a lion *en face*, with the letter w beneath. Few of Jamnitzer's early works are known, but they include the so-called *Ernestinischer Willkomm* (*c.* 1541; Coburg, Veste Coburg), composed of four superimposed vessels of differing sizes, which was commissioned by John-Frederick the Magnanimous, Elector of Saxony (1532–47). Jamnitzer's early works are characterized by ornamentation in the style of PETER FLÖTNER, the arabesque motif playing an important part, constantly varied and combined with other ornamental forms, as is shown in the drawings in Jamnitzer's Berlin sketchbook (1545–6; Berlin, Kstbib. & Mus.).

Wenzel Jamnitzer: gilt silver dish with serpents, frogs and lobsters, enamel, Nuremberg, diam. 450 mm, 1550–60 (Paris, Musée du Louvre)

Abraham Jamnitzer: *Daphne*, silver and coral, Nuremberg, late 16th century (Ecouen, Musée de la Renaissance)

In 1544 Jamnitzer was commissioned by the Holy Roman Emperor Charles V to make a ceremonial sword and sheath (coloured and signed drawing, Weimar, Schlossmus.), which were executed but lost in Spain at the beginning of the 17th century. The combination of arabesque ornament with figural decoration, including grotesques, masks and above all animal forms, anticipates the use of fully evolved classical ornament, for example friezes and caryatids, and plant and animal forms, cast from life, on his masterpiece, the *Mother Earth* centrepiece (1549; Amsterdam, Rijksmus.). The stem is in the form of a caryatid, and the bowl is decorated with the most sumptuous ornament of cornucopia, masks, fabulous beasts, and figurative and natural forms. The centrepiece was commissioned by the city council of Nuremberg as a gift for Charles V or his son, later Philip II, King of Spain, but, contrary to expectations, neither returned to Nuremberg after 1549, and therefore the large cartouche in the Renaissance style on the underside of the foot, which must have been designed to contain a dedicatory inscription, remains blank.

Jamnitzer executed work for three other Habsburg emperors—Ferdinand I, Maximilian II and Rudolf II. For Maximilian II he made a silver saddlebow (plaster cast, Basle, Hist. Mus.), a display casket (1570; Madrid, Mus. Monasterio Descalzas Reales) and the 'Emperor's Cup' (1570; Berlin, Tiergarten, Kstgewmus.). The last two may have been gifts presented to Maximilian by the city of Nuremberg on the occasion of his first visit in 1570. The ceremonial cup is in the most sumptuous late Renaissance style; the ornamentation of the lid includes a figure of *Maximilian II* with imperial insignia, crown, sword and sceptre, and four princes stand at his feet—Johann Jakob Khuen von Belasy, Archbishop of Salzburg (*reg* 1560–86), Veit von Würzburg, Bishop of Bamberg (*reg* 1566–77), Friedrich von Wirsberg, Bishop of Würzburg (*reg* 1558–72), and Albert V, Duke of Bavaria (*reg* 1550–79). This cup inaugurated a completely new type of commemorative piece, which re-emerged in the 19th century and was widely popular throughout Germany. The display casket was another of Jamnitzer's innovations. The introduction of architectonic forms for chests and display caskets such as that of 1570 are already evident in designs in his Berlin sketchbook.

Jamnitzer's earliest caskets were almost completely covered with silver foil, revealing the outlines of the wooden carcase, but his style later changed considerably: the decoration and carcase, the latter mostly of ebony, providing very striking colour contrast to the silver panels, were harmonized in a more balanced relationship, despite the use of over-elaborate decoration, and the figurative programme was widely extended, individual figures being placed within framed panels (e.g. casket, formerly Berlin; silver panels, now London, V&A). The casket made for Maximilian II, now used as a reliquary, bears Jamnitzer's full signature and the inscription *1570 Noric aurifaber Venclaus Gamnitzer, ista aeterni fecit ductus amore boni*. Preliminary designs, drawings and models of the casket are extant, including the lead casts on the Amerbach Kabinet (Basle, Hist. Mus.) and a model of *Fortitude* (*potentia*), one of the Virtues (Berlin, Tiergarten, Kstgewmus.). With his display caskets Jamnitzer introduced a tradition that was imitated and extended in Augsburg in the 17th century in large, ebony cabinets with applied decoration.

Another of Jamnitzer's important works was the ornamental Fountain of Prague commissioned by Maximilian II in 1568 and delivered to Rudolf II in 1578. This silver and gilt-bronze fountain (h. *c.* 3 m), surmounted by the imperial crown, was originally intended for the Neubau, the newly built part of Vienna, but was melted down in 1748. Only the four gilt-bronze figures (Vienna, Ksthist. Mus.) of *Flora, Ceres, Bacchus* and *Vulcan*, representing the Seasons, which supported the fountain, survive, although there is also a description by a student from Altdorf dating from the first half of the 17th century (Nuremberg, Ger. Nmus.). The form and decoration of the fountain represented an allegory of imperial power and the House of Habsburg, and it was similar to another executed in a different art form for Maximilian II, whose apotheosis is depicted in an engraving (1565–70; preliminary drawing, Vienna, Albertina) by Jost Amman (1539–91).

In addition to the Habsburg emperors, Jamnitzer was also commissioned by the dukes of Bavaria, archdukes of Austria and the electors of Saxony. The figure of *Philosophy* on a writing-cabinet (1562; Dresden, Grünes Gewölbe), commissioned by Augustus I, Elector of Saxony, is reminiscent of the figure of *Tellus* on the famous salt of Francis I (1540–43; Vienna, Ksthist. Mus.) by Cellini; the Classical simplicity of the substructure is reminiscent of Etruscan sarcophagi. The lid of a writing-case (*c.* 1570; Vienna,

Ksthist. Mus), made for Archduke Ferdinand II of the Tyrol (1529–95) is divided into ten square compartments containing such tiny creatures, cast from life, as a snail, lizards, beetles, a shell, a frog and a mouse, while the sides are also covered with lifelike casts of small creatures, grasses and flowers. An unmarked table clock (1560; Munich, Residenz), probably commissioned from Jamnitzer by a duke of Bavaria, is profusely ornamented with lizards, tortoises and herbs etc, cast from life; a design for the piece is also extant (Berlin, Kupferstichkab.). Jamnitzer was always as fascinated by the possibilities of combining gold with other materials as by the combined use of different techniques of goldwork. This is evident in his cylindrical goblet (*c.* 1550; Nuremberg, Ger. Nmus.) for the Pfinzing family, with its conical-shaped, painted Venetian glass tapering at the bottom; a jasper bowl (1560–70; Munich, Residenz) with silver-gilt mounts; and in his ornamental ewer (*c.* 1570; Munich, Residenz), the body of which consists of a trochus shell.

Wenzel Jamnitzer und die Nürnberger Goldschmiedekunst, 1500–1700 (exh. cat., Nuremberg, Ger. Nmus., 1985)

2. CHRISTOPH JAMNITZER (*b* Nuremberg, 12 May 1563; *d* Nuremberg, 1618). Goldsmith. He was the grandson of Wenzel Jamnitzer. His best-known work is the *Neuw Grottessken Buch* (Nuremberg, 1610), a pattern-book of grotesque ornaments including mythological scenes, the Four Elements and the Four Seasons, enriched with many subtle cultural and contemporary allusions.

About 20 of the items he made as a goldsmith have been preserved, of which the 'Dragon' ewer (*c.* 1618; Dresden, Grünes Gewölbe; bowl lost), the 'Elephant' table-fountain (*c.* 1610; Berlin, Tiergarten, Kstgewmus.) and the 'Trionfi' ewer and basin (1603; Vienna, Ksthist. Mus.) are among the most splendid. Both artistically and iconographically the last is exceptionally significant as regards the court of Rudolf II, who commissioned the set, in Prague: the scenes on both the ewer and basin, which are based on Petrarch's *Trionfi*, show a combination of the Habsburg concept of empire, the virtues of the ruler, the prophecies of Daniel and a neo-Platonic concept of love and eternity. His reputation as a sculptor is primarily related to his designs for the six recumbent figures on the doorways of the Rathaus at Nuremberg (1617) and to small-scale sculpture, which is usually incorporated into his silver- and goldsmithing.

Jamnitzer was a master of pictorial inventiveness: his individual figures were generally taken directly from international printed graphic conventions, or slightly adapted. Moreover, he embossed, engraved and chased his own work; his chasing was particularly outstanding. With his strong tendency to add on to his compositions, his strange elongated, scalloped ornamentation and an unnaturalistic, Mannerist approach to creating figures he showed himself to be one of the last great artists of the international late Mannerist movement *c.* 1600.

K. Pechstein, 'Der Nürnberger Goldschmied und Zeichner Christoph Jamnitzer (1563–1618)', *Fränk. Lebensbild.*, x (1982), pp. 179–92

G. Irmscher: 'Christoph Jamnitzer: Neues Zeichnungen und ein Globuspokal', *Anz. Ger. Nmus.* (1989), pp. 117–29

G. Irmscher: 'Christoph Jamnitzer Trionfi-Lavabo im Kunsthistorischen Museum Wien', *Jb. Ksthist. Samml. Wien*, lxxxv–lxxxvi (1989–90), pp. 135–54

G. Irmscher: *Amor und Aeternitas: das Trionfi-Lavabo Christoph Jamnitzers für Kaiser Rudolf II* (Vienna, 1999)

R. Eikelmann and P. Grosse: *Der Mohrenkopfpokal von Christoph Jamnitzer* (Munich, 2002)

J. Hein: 'Der Mohrenkopfpokal von Christoph Jamnitzer: Provenienz, Deutung und Kontext', *München Jb. Bild. Kst*, liii (2002), pp. 163–74

Janvier, Antide (*b* Saint-Claude, Jura, 1 July 1751; *d.* Paris 23 Sept 1835). French clock-maker. After an early career in Besançon, where he made an astronomical pendulum at the age of 16, Janvier moved to Paris in 1784. He made fine table and mantle clocks in the Empire style; these clocks are technically sophisticated, but are chiefly remarkable for their elegant enamel dials.

Japan. Ceramics *see* AGANO; ARITA; BANKO; BIZEN; ECHIZEN; HAGI; HIRADO; IGA; KAKIEMON WARE; KARATSU; KUTANI; KYOTO; MINO; NABESHIMA; RAKU; SANAGE; SATSUMA; SETO; SHIGARAKI; TAKATORI; TANBA; TEA CEREMONY WARES; TOKONAME; YAMACHAWAN.

Other arts *see* ARMOUR, §2; CLOCKS AND WATCHES, §4(I)(C); DOOR, §IV, 2; FAN, §1; INRŌ; LACQUER; NAMBAN; NETSUKE; SCREEN, §1.

Japanning. Technique of imitating Asian LACQUER in the West. The popularity from the late 16th century of lacquer wares imported from Asia prompted European and American (especially Bostonian) craftsmen to manufacture imitations. None of these ever rivalled urushi ware in durability, and it was not until the mid-18th century that at least the depth and brilliance of the genuine article was reproduced. The first to be copied were Iranian and Indian lacquer wares. European craftsmen were already familiar with such Indian resins as lac and sandarac, and it would seem that the imitation wares were made using authentic materials and at least good approximations of the original techniques. When Chinese designs were added to the repertory, they were reproduced in the same fashion, since urushi was not even correctly described until the early 18th century. These methods, however, only produced rough approximations of the authentic Chinese and Japanese finishes, so the period from the late 17th century to the end of the 18th was one of constant experimentation to improve and refine technique. Numerous systems were developed, known collectively as japanning.

The first accurate description of methodology and 'receipts', the *Treatise of Japanning and Varnishing*, was published in 1688 by John Stalker and George Parker (*see* STALKER AND PARKER), and in 1730 the Martin brothers of Paris patented a system under the name of *vernis Martin*, which, due to the clarity, brilliance and toughness of its finish, became the most famous of the European techniques. At its best it rivals the appearance of good quality East Asian work, but it lacks the hardness and resistance to chemical attack of *urushi* ware.

The japanners originally used wooden substrates, but from the beginning of the 18th century metal and papier mâché grew in popularity, the latter being a favourite base for mother-of-pearl inlay. The substrate was carefully prepared and smoothed and the design painted directly on to the surface, or onto an intermediate layer of gesso, which provided a smooth, white ground. The varnishes were complex blends of resins, dissolved in turpentine and other substances. The best English imitation lacquer varnish of the late 17th century, for example, was based on the use of sandarac or seed lac mixed with mastic, Venice turpentine, copal resin, gum elemi, benzoin and colophony dissolved in ethanol, or on similar blends in turpentine. These mixtures were left to mature for up to six weeks before use. The work then had to be carried out in well-heated and dry workshops; special rooms known as 'stoves' were used. Regardless of which of the various techniques was employed, each coating was allowed to dry thoroughly before it was polished and cleaned in preparation for the next coat. Aspects of the japanner's art have continued to the present day in the cabinet-maker's finishing technique known as French polishing, in which numerous coats of an alcoholic solution of pure shellac are applied to a carefully finished surface with a cloth 'rubber' lubricated with linseed oil.

The best quality work was executed on such close-grained hardwoods as pear-wood, while common work was done on deal or oak. To obtain a smooth, uniform surface the panels used for common work were coated with gesso made by mixing whiting with glue size. Nine coats were applied in three stages. Each coat was allowed to dry thoroughly, then rubbed smooth with rushes; a longer drying period was allowed after each third coat. When the gesso was completely dry, it was sealed with two coats of seed lac varnish in alcohol, then allowed to dry and rubbed smooth. The design was drawn or painted in outline, then built up with a paste of finely ground whiting and bole in a strong solution of gum arabic. This was applied with a long, pointed wooden 'pencil'. When dry, the design was outlined and the details painted in with vermilion watercolour. The various levels were carved in and smoothed with a well-worn brush. The raised work was usually painted with gold or silver pigments, although it may have been leaf gilded or silvered, and the details were accentuated with a colour that contrasted with or matched the background. Following burnishing with a dog's tooth or agate, the decoration was coated with two or three coats of seed lac varnish.

For polychrome work it was usual to use watercolour, sealed and prepared for polishing by the application of several coats of seed lac varnish. Such ground colours as red or black were mixed with seed lac varnish. Black japanned work was prepared by applying three coats of varnish mixed with lamp black to the support. Three further coats were applied, each being carefully polished. Six thin coats of seed lac mixed with Venice turpentine and a little lamp black were then applied, followed by twelve coats of pure seed lac tinted with lamp black. This was allowed to dry for six days, then given a preliminary polish with fine tripoli powder and water, rested for two days and further polished using more water than in the first polishing. After washing to remove all traces of the tripoli powder, the work was rested for a further five days before a final polish using lamp black and oil that was cleaned off with a dry cloth.

Vernis Martin was a copal varnish prepared by melting together Cyprus turpentine, amber, copal, oil of turpentine, colophony and a vegetable oil, such as linseed or poppy. The amber varnish was similarly made by blending the same materials in different proportions and excluding the copal resin. The support was prepared and decorated with watercolour, oil or pigments in varnish. Six coats of varnish were then applied. These were allowed to dry for two or three days, then rubbed down with pumice powder and water. A further ten or twelve coats of varnish were applied and allowed to stand until thoroughly dry, usually about five days, then lightly rubbed down with finely ground pumice. All traces of the pumice were removed by washing with water, and the object was polished again with fine emery in water. The emery was washed off and a final polish given using sifted rottenstone. The object was then cleaned using dry rags and rubbed over with a soft cloth dipped in oil. The oil was removed with fine wheat flour and the finished lustre brought up by gentle rubbing with a soft cloth loaded with more flour.

One of the techniques developed by the Martin brothers was called 'aventurine' after the mineral that it resembles. It was made by inlaying numerous pieces of rectangular-sectioned gilt-brass wire into a green, red or sometimes black ground, then covering them with several layers of transparent 'lacquer' to produce an effect similar to the Japanese *makie*.

A new japanning technique developed in 19th-century England utilized a simple alcoholic solution of lemon or bleached shellac (cooked with a caustic decolourant to give an almost water white solution in alcohol) to which a small amount of camphor had been added. The support was sealed with two coats of varnish and coated, if necessary, with a thin paste of gilders' whiting in shellac solution followed by ordinary gilders' gesso. The ground was then built up with several coats of powder pigment in varnish. As many as ten coats were applied, with the last two or three containing no more than a trace of pigment or spirit-soluble stain. When dry, each coat was rubbed down with O-grade glass-paper, and the final layer was further smoothed with medium-grade pumice powder and finished with flour-grade pumice. The decoration was applied with powder pigments (including various metal powders) bound with varnish; black details were picked out with 'China black' ink. Raised work was executed with gilders' gesso. Gold size, to which a little Indian red pigment had been added, was applied to those areas of the design that were to be leaf gilded or painted with metal pigments. Once the decoration was complete, three coats of clear varnish were applied, each coat being lightly rubbed down with fine pumice powder. The final coat was given a further polish using flour-grade pumice and finished with gilder's whiting and linseed oil, all trace of which was removed using dry, soft cloths.

J. Stalker and G. Parker: *A Treatise of Japanning and Varnishing: Being a Compleat Discovery of Those Arts* (Oxford, 1668/R Reading, 1998)

S Crowder: *A Treatise on the Copal Oil Varnish, or, What in France is Call'd Vernis Martin* (London, 1753)

S. Crowder: *Genuine Receipt for Making the Famous Vernis Martin* (Paris, 1753)

H. Huth: *Lacquer of the West: The History of a Craft and Industry, 1550–1950* (Chicago, 1971)

D. L. Fales Jr.: 'Boston Japanned Furniture', *Boston Furniture of the Eighteenth Century*, eds W. M. Whitehill, B. Jobe and J. L. Fairbanks (Boston, MA, 1974), pp. 49–70

S. H. Hitchings: 'Boston's Colonial Japanners: The Documentary Record', *Boston Furniture of the Eighteenth Century*, eds W. M. Whitehill, B. Jobe and J. L. Fairbanks (Boston, MA, 1974), pp. 71–6

S. Budden and F. Halahan, eds: *Lacquerwork and Japanning* (London, 1994)

M. Brunskog: *Japanning in Sweden, 1680s–1790s: Characteristics and Preservation of Orientalized Coatings on Wooden Substrates* (Gothenburg, 2003)

Japonisme. French term coined in 1872 to describe a range of European borrowings from Japanese art, encompassing decorative objects with Japanese designs (similar to 18th-century CHINOISERIE), paintings of scenes set in Japan, and Western paintings, prints and decorative arts influenced by Japanese aesthetics. Scholars now distinguish *japonaiserie*, the depiction of Japanese subjects or objects in a Western style, from Japonisme, the more profound influence of Japanese aesthetics on Western art. Japonisme in the decorative arts at first consisted primarily of imitations of Japanese models, with stylistic features paralleling Japonisme in painting; features such as asymmetrical compositions, pure bright colours combined in complementary colour schemes, and bold flat patterns and motifs. Many of these were copied directly from Japanese craftsmen's manuals and dyers' stencils. Japanese inspiration is evident in the products of the French manufacturers Christofle & Co. and Haviland & Co. of Limoges, in the designs of Joseph Bouvier (1840–1901), FÉLIX BRACQUE-MOND, Jean Charles Cazin (1841–1901) and Camille Moreau, and in the cloisonné enamels of Alexis Falize (1811–98) and his son LUCIEN FALIZE.

In the late 19th century the popularity of Japanese design continued; it is particularly evident in products of the Arts and Crafts movement and Art Nouveau, for example in the glasswork of FRANÇOIS-EUGÈNE ROUSSEAU, the ceramic decorations of JOSEPH-THÉODORE DECK and EMILE GALLÉ, and the jewellery of RENÉ LALIQUE. In American and British decorative arts, in which Japonisme struck a chord within the Aesthetic movement, Japonisme appears in works produced by the ROOKWOOD POTTERY of Cincinnati, OH, which employed Japanese craftsmen, in the bold, patterned textile designs of A. H. MACKMURDO and CANDANCE WHEELER, in the stained glass of LOUIS COMFORT TIFFANY and JOHN LA FARGE, in the furniture of CHRISTIAN HERTER and in the naturalistic motives applied to silver manufactured by GORHAM and TIFFANY.

In Pursuit of Beauty: Americans and the Aesthetic Movement (exh. cat., New York, Met., 1986)

S. Wichmann: *Japonisme: The Japanese Influence on Western Art since 1858* (New York, 1999)

B. Lemoine: *Regards et discours européens sur le Japon et l'Inde au XIXe siècle: Actes du colloque, 3–4 juin 1998* (Limoges, 2000)

T. Watanabe: 'Japonisme', *Crafts*, clxxiii (Nov–Dec 2001), pp. 42–5

C. W. Laidlaw: 'Painting with Silken Threads: Fanny Dixwell Holmes and Japanism in Nineteenth-Century Boston', *Stud. Dec. A.*, x/2 (Spring–Summer 2003), pp. 42–68

G. P. Weisberg: 'Lost and Found: S. Bing's Merchandising of Japonisme and Art Nouveau', *19th C. A. Worldwide*, iv/2 (Summer 2005), p. 2

Jardinière. Ornamental pot or stand for the display of growing flowers indoors, fashioned from metal or wood or pottery.

Jargon [jargoon]. Lapidary term for a translucent variety of the mineral zircon, found in Sri Lanka.

Jarves, **Deming** (*b* 1790; *d* 1869). American glass manufacturer, active Massachusetts. He founded the NEW ENGLAND GLASS CO. in 1818, the BOSTON & SANDWICH GLASS CO. in 1826, the MT WASHINGTON GLASS WORKS in 1837 and the CAPE COD GLASS COMPANY in 1858.

Jasper ware. *See under* WEDGWOOD.

Jeanneret, Charles-Edouard. *See* LE CORBUSIER.

Jeanselme. French family of cabinetmakers. In 1847 Alphonse-George JACOB sold the Jacob-Desmalter workshop to Joseph-Pierre-François Jeanselme (*fl* 1824; *d* 1860), who, together with his son Charles-Joseph-Marie Jeanselme (1827–*c*. 1871), supplied furniture to the French and imperial courts; their furniture is stamped 'Jeanselme Père et Fils'. From 1863 to 1871 the business was run by Charles-Joseph-Marie in partnership with the *ébéniste* Auguste Godin, and the furniture was stamped Jeanselme Fils Godin et Cie. In 1893 the company took over the Lemarchand workshop.

D. Kisluk-Grosheide: 'Jeanselme Frères: Armchair', *Met. Mus. A. Bull.*, liv (Fall 1996), p. 41

C. Gere: 'European Decorative Arts at the World's Fairs: 1850–1900', *Met. Mus. A. Bull.*, lvi/3 (Winter 1998–9), pp. 3–55 [with catalogue]

Jeckyll [Jeckell], **Thomas** (*b* Norwich, 1827; *d* Norwich, 1881). English designer and architect. He began his career as an architect, designing and restoring parish churches in the Gothic Revival style. In 1859 he entered into a close association with the iron and brass foundry of Barnard, Bishop & Barnard of Norwich. Jeckyll pioneered the use of the Anglo-Japanese style for furnishings. His fireplace surrounds, grates, chairs, tables and benches often incorporate roundels containing Japanese-inspired floral and geometric ornament. Jeckyll's foliate-patterned ironwork was featured in Barnard, Bishop & Barnard's pavilion at the International Exhibition of 1862 in London, and he designed the foundry's cast- and wrought-iron pavilion for the Centennial Exhibition of 1876 in Philadelphia. This two-storey structure was supported by bracketed columns elaborately decorated with a variety of birds and flowers and was surrounded by railings in the form of sunflowers, a motif that was later adapted to firedogs.

During the 1870s Jeckyll was one of several Aesthetic Movement architects and artists responsible for the interiors of 1 Holland Park, London, the home of the collector Aleco Ionides. Jeckyll's interior (1876) for the dining-room at 49 Princes Gate, London, for F. R. Leyland features a pendent ceiling and shelves with delicate vertical supports set against walls covered in Spanish leather; it became known as the 'Peacock Room' (Washington, DC, Freer) after its later painted decoration by James McNeill Whistler (1834–1903). In 1877 Jeckyll became mentally ill; he died in the Norwich Asylum four years later.

S. W. Soros and C. Arbuthnott: *Thomas Jeckyll: Architect and Designer, 1827–1881* (New Haven, 2003)

Jeffrey & Co. English wallpaper manufacturing company founded *c*. 1836. The company, variously known as Jeffrey, Wise & Co., Jeffrey, Wise & Horne (1842), Horne & Allen (1843) and Jeffrey, Allen & Co., produced pattern books (*c*. 1837–52) of cylinder machine prints and block prints in traditional designs (London, V&A), together with reproductions of works of art, which were shown at the Great Exhibition at Crystal Palace, London, in 1851. In 1864 Jeffrey & Co., then in Whitechapel, merged with Holmes & Aubert of Islington, London, taking over and enlarging their Islington premises. The skill of the company's block printers led to two important commissions: the printing of wallpapers for Morris & Co. from 1864 onwards and, in 1865, of wallpapers designed by Owen Jones for the Viceroy's Palace, Cairo.

In 1866 Metford Warner (1843–1930) joined the firm as a junior partner, becoming sole proprietor in 1871. As a result of contemporary criticisms of wallpaper design, Warner took the initiative and in 1869 began to commission well-known architects and artists to design for the firm. Some, including WILLIAM BURGES, CHARLES LOCKE EASTLAKE, E. W. GODWIN ('Sparrow and Bamboo', 1872; Manchester, C.A.G.) and Heywood Sumner ('The Vine', 1893;

London, V&A), designed wallpapers exclusively for Jeffrey's. Although not all were commercially successful—WALTER CRANE's richly coloured designs were expensive to print and had a limited market—they were widely publicized, and some were machine printed for the mass market. In 1872, under Warner, the company introduced the horizontal division of the wall into three sections: a frieze at the top, with a filling below and a dado from skirting level to a height of about 1.20 m. Complementary papers were designed for each section, and in the 1870s Jeffrey & Co. launched a new form of wallpaper design that combined frieze, filling and dado in one overall design. In 1873, at Metford Warner's insistence, wallpapers were admitted to the Fine Arts Exhibition held at the Albert Hall, London, where Jeffrey & Co. was awarded a medal for design and colouring. In 1898 Warner's sons Horace Warner (1871–1939) and Albert Warner were taken into partnership. Control of the company passed to them in the late 1920s shortly before Jeffrey's was taken over by the Wall Paper Manufacturers Ltd, when manufacturing transferred to ARTHUR SANDERSON & Sons.

Jegg, Stephan (*b* Schernegg, 1674; *d* Markt St Florian, 14 Jan 1749). Austrian cabinetmaker. His life was spent working as a joiner at St Florian Abbey. In 1703 he was making architectural sections for the new church seating. In 1708 and 1711 he was making architectural models, including one for the main doorway that was executed in 1713 by the sculptor Leonhard Sattler, with whom Jegg worked as a lifelong partner, with Sattler working mainly on the sculptural figure decoration. In 1711–12 Jegg was paid 450 florins for building the altar in the Marienkapelle, for which he also made the stalls. In 1719 he made five long and five shorter tables, a cupboard with three sections and a reading pulpit for the winter refectory in the Leopoldinischer Südtrakt; none of these has survived. Together with Sattler he decorated the interiors of several rooms in 1722 and worked on the *Prunkschrank*, a splendidly decorated clock-cabinet (*in situ*). He worked in the new Kunstkammer from 1724 to 1728 and made the new sacristy cupboards (1726) for the parish church of St Peter am Wimberg. In 1739 the Prälatensakristei was refurnished, and Jegg produced several cupboards for it. After his death his son Johann Christian Jegg took over the joinery workshop.

T. Korth: *Stift St Florian* (Nuremberg, 1975)

Jeliff, John (*b* 1813; *d* 1893). American furniture-maker. His workshop in Newark (New Jersey) was active from 1836 to 1890. He specialized in furniture in the Renaissance Revival style (e.g. armchairs, 1868–70; New York, Met. and Brooklyn Mus.).

Jelly glass [jelly]. Glass container, tapering towards the bottom, for serving individual portions of jelly or other puddings.

Jenaer Glaswerk. German glasshouse founded in Jena in 1884 by Otto Schott (1851–1935). The factory made both industrial and domestic glass, notably the tableware of WILHELM WAGENFELD in the 1930s. Under the Nazis the factory made glass for military purposes, and on 17 March 1945 the factory was bombed. In 1945, in the move known as 'the odyssey of the 41 glassmakers', key employees (especially those with expertise in optical glass) were taken by American troops and relocated in West Germany; after various moves, they were relocated in Mainz in 1952. The Russians occupied Jena, and reopened the factory there. The two companies had identical names ('Ven Jenaer Glaswerk Schott & Gen') from 1945 to 1981, and products are distinguished by the names 'Jena' and 'Mainz'. In 1981 the companies were formally separated into Veb Jenaer Glaswerk in the East and Schott Glaswerke in the West. In 1994 the company returned to Jena, and since 1998 has been known as Schott. The company now makes optical, industrial and domestic glass.

Jennens & Bettridge. *See under* PAPIER MÂCHÉ.

Jensen, Georg (Arthur) (*b* Rådvad, nr Copenhagen, 31 Aug 1866; *d* Copenhagen, 2 Oct 1935). Danish silversmith and sculptor. He was the son of a blacksmith, and at the age of 14 he was apprenticed to the goldsmith A. Andersen in Copenhagen. In 1904 he opened his own workshop, primarily making jewellery. His brooch of 1905, 'No. 20' (Copenhagen, Jensen Mus.), is representative of many of his early designs, which show the influence of Art Nouveau and are often characterized by full, simple forms incorporating stylized bird and flower motifs. In 1906 he produced his first complete set of flatware, 'Continental', which was still in production in the 1980s. Distinctive for its restraint and the interplay between its strong silhouette and a surface animated by small hammermarks, it is a clear expression of his involvement with the Arts and Crafts Movement. Many of Jensen's most famous pieces were produced between 1908 and 1918. In 1914 the Musée du Louvre, Paris, bought a silver bowl (1912), subsequently known as the 'Louvre bowl'. It shows both the slightly low, bulbous profile and the use of discrete bands of decoration that are typical of his hollow-ware.

Jensen's two closest collaborators were the architect and painter Johan Rohde (1856–1935) and Harald Nielsen (1892–1977), who joined the workshop in 1907 and 1909 respectively. Rohde was responsible for several important designs, including the successful flatware pattern 'Acorn' (1915). Nielsen started as a chaser and subsequently became a draughtsman and, in the 1920s, a designer. His flatware 'Pyramid' (1926; e.g. Copenhagen, Jensen Mus.) reflects a blend of Jensen's influence and a sensitivity to contemporary movements, in this case Art Deco, that is characteristic of his work. After Jensen's death Nielsen became artistic director of the smithy, and under his leadership the firm continued to produce

Georg Jensen: Necklace 1, silver and moonstones, 1925–9 (Newark, NJ, Newark Museum)

the work of other designers, including Sigvard Bernadotte (1907–2002), Henning Koppel (1918–81) and Jensen's son, Søren Georg Jensen (1917–82). Jensen designs are displayed in the Georg Jensen Museum in the company's main Copenhagen shop.

Georg Jensen Silversmithy: 77 Artists, 75 Years (exh. cat., Washington, DC, Renwick Gal., 1980)

J. E. R. Møller: *Georg Jensen: The Danish Silversmith* (Copenhagen, 1984)

J. Drucker: *Georg Jensen: A Tradition of Splendid Silver* (1997, rev. Atglen, PA, 2001)

D. Taylor and J. Lasky: *Georg Jensen Hollowware* (London and New York, 2003)

D. Taylor: *Georg Jensen Jewelry* (exh. cat., New Haven, 2005)

Jensen [Johnson], **Gerrit** [Garrard; Garrett; Gerrard] (*fl c.* 1680–1715; *d* London, 2 Dec 1715). English cabinetmaker. He has previously been described as Flemish or Dutch but is more likely to have been of a family long domiciled in England. He was an important supplier of furniture and mirrors to the royal palaces from the later part of the reign of Charles II (*reg* 1660–85): his earliest recorded royal commission was in 1680, when he supplied 'a cabinet and frame table-stands and glass' as a gift for the sultan of Morocco. Jensen's name appears frequently in the royal accounts during the reign of William III and Mary II: in an inventory (1697) of the Queen's possessions at Kensington Palace, London, tables, glasses and stands inlaid with metal that 'came in after her death from Mr Johnson' are mentioned. It appears that he had a close relationship with Pierre Gole and was strongly influenced by the work of Daniel Marot I, Gole's brother-in-law. Consequently,

Jensen's furniture reflects the fashionable French court styles, and he was the only cabinetmaker working in England at this period who is known to have used metal inlays in his work. He also employed elaborate marquetry, for example in a writing-table made for Kensington Palace (1690; Windsor Castle, Berks, Royal Col.), and japanned work. Other examples of Jensen's work are at Kensington Palace and Hampton Court, London, and work attributed to his workshop is at Chatsworth, Derbys; Knole, Kent, NT; Burghley House, Cambs; Petworth House, W. Sussex, NT; and in the Duke of Buccleuch's private collection.

T. Murdoch: 'The Furniture for the King's Apartments: Walnuttree, Gilding, Japanning and Marble', *Apollo*, cxl (Aug 1994), pp. 55–9

Jerome, Chauncey (*b* Canaan, CT, 10 June 1793; *d* New Haven, CT, 20 April 1868). American clockmaker. He began making tall case clocks in 1811 and shelf case clocks in 1816. He moved in 1821 to Bristol, CT, and opened a clock workshop that made both cases and movements. The firm traded as Jerome, Thompson & Co. (1826–7), Jeromes & Darrow (1822–33; the second Jerome was his brother Noble), C. & N. Jerome (1834–9), Jeromes, Gilbert & Grant (1839–40) and Jerome & Co. (1840–45). When the Bristol factory was destroyed by fire, Jerome relocated in New Haven, where he traded as the New Haven Clock Co. His clocks were exported to Britain and from there throughout the Empire.

C. Jerome: *History of the American Clock Business for the Past Sixty Years: And Life of Chauncey Jerome, Written by Himself* (New Haven, 1860).

C. H. Bailey: *From Rags to Riches to Rags: The Story of Chauncey Jerome* (Columbia, PA, 1986)

Jesuit porcelain. Chinese porcelain made for export to the West in the 18th century. The monochrome decorations depicted Christian subjects such as the nativity and crucifixion. There is no evidence that the porcelain was commissioned by the Jesuits, but the European engravings on which the decorations were based may have been brought to China by Jesuit missionaries.

'The Religious Missions and Art', *Orient. A.*, xlvii/5 (2001), pp. 2–54 [special section]

Jet. Form of lignite, black and consisting largely of carbon. It is driftwood from pines related to the *Araucaria* genus (monkey-puzzle tree) that has been subjected to chemical action in stagnant water and then to great pressure in the ocean floor; sometimes it is washed up on beaches as pebbles. The best jet is found in England, at Whitby (N. Yorks), and the only other major deposits are in northern Spain in the Asturias. Lesser deposits have been found in France, Germany, the Czech Republic, Slovakia, Italy, Portugal, Canada and the USA.

1. England. 2. Spain.

1. ENGLAND. In the medieval period jet was used for secular objects, such as gaming pieces, and for religious items (e.g. the jet crook of the last quarter of the 12th century in Chichester Cathedral), but it was not until the early 19th century that jet was extensively mined and a large-scale industry developed in Whitby. This expansion was initiated by the introduction soon after 1800 of the treadle-wheel lathe by a retired naval officer, Captain Tremlett. Two entrepreneurs, Robert Jefferson and John Carter, were encouraged to establish a business, and by the 1850s the trade was fully established. It exhibited successfully at the Great Exhibition of 1851, London, and in 1856 was producing exports to Europe and America worth £20,000; at its peak, 1870–72, 1400 workmen were employed.

Much of the success of the Whitby jet industry was due to the Victorian obsession with mourning, particularly after the deaths of Arthur Wellesley, 1st Duke of Wellington, in 1852 and Prince Albert, prince-consort of England, in 1861. Queen Victoria introduced the wearing of jet in court circles, and among the Whitby suppliers was Thomas Andrews of New Quay, Jet-ornament Maker to Her Majesty. Mourning jewellery included bracelets, necklaces, pendants, lockets, earrings and brooches, but other items were also made, such as cardcases, seals and paper-knives. When mourning ceased to be fashionable the industry declined with it. Also, excessive competition had given rise to poor standards of workmanship and the use of soft, inferior jet that gave products a bad reputation. Finally, in the 1880s cheaper substitutes were introduced and the boom was over; by 1884 there were less than 300 jet workers, and by the 1930s the industry was virtually extinct.

2. SPAIN. In the 13th century a significant jet industry developed in Spain; the industry was centred on the pilgraimage centre Santiago de Compostela, where it was inextricably connected with the cult of St James the Greater. The trade reached its peak in the mid-16th century. It then became dispersed around Compostela and in the Asturias, notably at Villaviciosa, and although it continued to flourish throughout the 18th century the quality of the workmanship declined.

The vast majority of the jet items produced in Compostela were pilgrim badges and religious mementos. Since jet was expensive, these carvings were available only to the wealthy, who wore them for the return journey and then hung them in their houses or private chapels. Some of the carvings were pierced with a hole so they could hang from a jewel, and others would be attached to a hat.

One of the principal subjects was St James, who was depicted either alone or accompanied by one or two kneeling pilgrims. It is difficult to establish a chronology for these figures as several models probably co-existed, and their iconographic evolution was slow. It seems that in the earlier pieces the saint was depicted as an apostle holding a pilgrim staff, but at the beginning of the 16th century a standard type was established in which he was shown in full pilgrim dress with bare feet, long hair and a beard, a shell on his hat and holding a staff and book. In the 17th century, when pilgrim dress was proscribed, the saint took on an equestrian pose in his role of *Santiago Matamoros*, killer of the Moors. Several other saints were carved in jet. St Sebastian, who from the early 16th century was the patron of the jetworkers guild, was a frequent subject, as were the apostles Andrew and Bartholomew and the Franciscan saints Francis, Clare and Anthony of Padua.

The Virgin and Child were often depicted, the finest example being that in the Capilla del Condestable (*c.* 1400) in Burgos Cathedral. The Virgin's robe is of highly polished jet, her throne and crown are of gold decorated with pearls and precious stones, and her face, as well as the body of the Christ Child, is of ivory. Another popular subject was the Pietà, but during the Counter-Reformation the Virgin was more often identified with the Immaculate Conception. There are also depictions of Christ, either bound to the pillar or on the cross flanked by the Virgin and St John.

Another aspect of jet work that brought fame to the guild was the making of liturgical objects, especially the processional crosses used for funeral occasions from the 14th century. In the 15th and 16th centuries the pax was sometimes made in jet. This was a small tablet kissed before the communion, first by the priest and then by the other clergy and the congregation. The Pietà and the Crucifixion were often represented on the pax.

The scallop shell was an important pilgrim emblem, and the jetworkers eventually took over the shell trade. The shell appears on its own, or as an attribute of St James, or as a support for other figures. Rosaries, too, were often made in jet: in the Instituto de Valencia de Don Juan there is a fine example with large and small beads, the large ones decorated in relief with the Calvary scene, apostles and saints and the small ones carved with scallop shells; the pendant depicts Christ on the Cross and, on the reverse, St James.

Sometimes the rosary pendant took the form of a hand amulet—one of the many instances in which this pre-Christian talisman was combined with a Christian symbol. Hand amulets remained popular in Spain for centuries, despite occasional disapproval from the Christian authorities; they were worn by all social classes from royal infantes downwards, and even the Christ Child is sometimes depicted with one around his neck. The earlier, Muslim amulets took the form of an open hand, known in Europe as the 'hand of Fatima', but in the 16th century the 'fig' or *higa* gesture largely replaced the open hand. In this, the hand is clenched, and the thumb is seen protruding between the index and third fingers in the traditional Latin gesture of contempt. From the 16th century to the 18th a variety of composite images was produced in which the hand carried an additional image, such as a human-faced crescent, a heart or a cherub. The wrist was often carved in an open, skeletal form, or included a further image, of open hands, a pair of eyes, a saint or a Christian scene. The use of the *higa* continued up to the early 20th century in the regions of Asturias and León and still survives, though largely for decorative rather than protective purposes.

Jet was used also for secular objects. Two magnificent mid-16th-century openwork caskets surmounted by lions and decorated with gilding can be seen in the Instituto de Valencia de Don Juan: these pieces were often made by apprentices in order to gain their mastership. Jet was used for seals, perfume bottles and jewellery, including rings and pendants associated with mourning.

H. P. Kendall: *The Story of Whitby Jet: Its Workers from Earliest Times* (Whitby, 1936)

W. Hagen: 'Kaiserzeitliche Gagatarbeiten aus dem rheinischen Germanien', *Bonn. Jb. Rhein. Landesmus. Bonn & Ver. Altertfreund. Rheinlande*, cxlii (1937), pp. 77–144

B. I. Gilman: 'The Use of Jet in Spain', *Homenaje al Prof. Rodríguez-Moñino* (Madrid, 1966)

B. I. Gilman: 'A Token of Pilgrimage', *A. VA*, x (1969), pp. 24–31

H. Muller: *Jet Jewellery and Ornaments* (Princes Risborough, 1980)

J. Musty: 'Jet or Shale?', *Current Archaeol.*, vii (1981), p. 277

V. Monte-Carreño: *El azabache en Asturias* (Principado de Asturias, 1984)

A. Franco Mata: 'Azabaches del M.A.N.', *Bol. Mus. Arqueol. N. Madrid*, iv (1986), pp. 131–67

A. Franco Mata: 'El azabache en España', *Compostellanum*, xxxiv (1989), pp. 311–36

A. Franco Mata: 'Valores artísticos y simbólicos del azabache en España y Nuevo Mundo', *Compostellanum*, xlvi (1991), pp. 467–531

Jever Pottery. German faience factory near Zerbst (Saxony-Anhalt), active from 1760 to 1776. The founding director was JOHANN SAMUEL FRIEDRICH TÄNNICH. The factory's best known tablewares were tureens shaped like swans.

Jewellery. Objects of personal adornment, which may fulfil both decorative and functional purposes. Since antiquity protective and magical qualities have been attributed to amulets and talismans. As potent symbols of power and wealth, jewellery was used as a means of distinguishing social status, membership of a guild or political and religious loyalties. Jewellery has been used to commemorate historical and political events, and surviving examples provide valu-

Fleur-de-lis brooch, enamelled silver-gilt set with precious stones, from the treasury of Saint-Denis, France, 14th century (Paris, Musée du Louvre)

Sapphire and diamond necklace of Queen Maria Christina of Spain (Private collection)

able information about national and local traditions and customs. Items of jewellery are often given as tokens of love, betrothal and friendship, while *memento mori* jewels are reminders that death is inescapable, mourning jewellery signifies bereavement, and reliquaries in the form of pendants or crosses were made to contain religious relics. The art of jewellery-making relies on the technical skill of the craftsmen (for a discussion of some of the techniques involved in jewellery production, *see* ENAMEL and GEM-ENGRAVING).

J. Evans: *A History of Jewellery, 1100–1870* (London, 1953, rev. 1970)

J. Lanllier and M.-A. Pini: *Cinq siècles de joaillerie en Occident* (Fribourg, 1971)

H. Tait, ed.: *The Art of the Jeweller: A Catalogue of the Hull Grundy Gift to the British Museum*, 2 vols (London, 1984)

H. Tait: *Seven Thousand Years of Jewellery* (London, 1986)

Treasures and Trinkets: Jewellery in London from Pre-Roman Times to the 1930s (exh. cat., ed. T. Murdoch; London, Mus. London, 1991)

1. Before 1500. 2. 1500–1600. 3. 1631–1725. 4. 1726–1830. 5. 1831–1900. 6. After 1900.

1. BEFORE 1500. Medieval jewellery was the work of goldsmiths, who often used gold and stones given to them by the patron. Enamel in its various forms was an important technique, especially in its last major medieval form, *en ronde-bosse*. By the late 12th century certain great cities, notably Cologne, Venice and Paris, had established themselves as major centres for the making of jewellery, but from the 13th century the primacy of Paris fashion in jewellery throughout Europe is well documented. Significantly it was in 14th-century Paris that the techniques of stone-cutting, diamond-cutting and *en ronde-bosse* enamel were, if not invented, at any rate developed and improved. It was probably in Paris about the middle of the 13th century that the Gothic style was first applied to the design of jewellery, spreading in the second half of the century to Italy, Germany, Spain, England and Scandinavia, where the style assumed local forms and spirit. The high collet settings typical of the 13th century were displaced in the 14th by collets of geometrical Gothic design. Important centres for the manufacture of cheaper jewellery were Le Puy in the Auvergne, probably from the late 12th century, and Ragusa (now Dubrovnik) in the 14th century.

In the 13th century there was a general establishment and diffusion of what may be called the major types of later medieval jewellery. Earlier jewellery for women comprised brooches worn at the neck, on robe or mantle, sometimes of great size, head-ornaments—bands mounted with metal and precious stones, coifs and chaplets—garlands or frontlets, breast-ornaments suspended from ribands, cloak-clasps, pendants (often a cross or single stones), earrings, bracelets and necklaces. In parures of this kind, barbarian tradition was certainly mingled with Byzantine influence—earrings and bracelets appear to have been Byzantine ornaments. In the 13th century earrings, bracelets and necklaces disappeared, at any rate from princely and aristocratic jewellery, though the earring survived in southern Italy

and Sicily and in Hungary. The principal jewels of Gothic Europe were the garland chaplet and circlet, worn by aristocratic and princely men and women with fleurons as a coronal or crown. Women continued to wear jewelled headbands and coifs. Brooches took the form of ring brooches or solid brooches, both types originating in the Dark Ages. Solid brooches, often of cluster form round a single large stone or cameo, were worn to fasten the mantle or the robe at the neck and, from the 14th century, elsewhere on the breast and eventually as ornaments on the hat. Pendants, worn from a lace, were either of single precious stones, as in the 12th century, or assumed forms largely imitating those of solid brooches. They were often devotional in type (e.g. the cross) and could contain relics. The girdle now became a major item of jewellery and was decorated with a buckle and pendant and with bars, studs or larger mounts of silver, sometimes even of jewelled gold. From the late 13th century the girdle might even be entirely of gold or silver. The taste for luxury became such that from the late 13th century even such articles of devotion as the paternoster (the medieval form of the rosary) might be made either of precious materials (amber, coral, agate, chalcedony) or of gold, precious stones and pearls. The principal jewels of men were much simpler, usually a brooch and girdle, and for noblemen and princes a coronal and perhaps a chain: their paternosters were usually short.

There were several important changes in types and fashion of jewellery during the highly fashion-conscious 14th century. The vogue for personal or family devices, which became general throughout aristocratic and knightly Europe, introduced new motifs into jewellery. It seems too that figurated motifs, relatively infrequent in the 13th century, now

Brooch depicting Leda and Swan by Benvenuto Cellini, gold and enamel set with pearls, Italy, 16th century (Florence, Museo Nazionale del Bargello)

Pendant with a monkey on a cornucopia, gold set with precious stones, Flemish, 1580–90 (Florence, Pitti, Mus. Argenti)

may have become more common on brooches and pendants. Such forms of love jewels as the heart brooch and the fede brooch (with two hands clasped in a sign of troth) now appeared or at any rate became current. Necklaces of strung stones and pearls and ornaments had persisted in Spain and reappeared in courtly Europe in the late 14th century in the form of the collar of precious metal and stones, perhaps, like some other types of medieval jewels, such as the chaplet, a transmutation into gold and silver of a textile type. As chivalric ornaments or badges, or as ornaments, collars became, together with heavy chains, the principal jewels of the Late Middle Ages, displacing the brooch from its former dominance.

At the same time the rise into fashion of elaborate headdresses for women and of hats for men greatly reduced the importance of the coronal or crown, which survived only for ceremonial life at court or for wear by brides at marriage ceremonies. The bracelet reappeared in the 1380s and 1390s and became a favourite aristocratic ornament of the 15th century. In general bourgeois jewellery was simpler than aristocratic jewellery, though emulation of noble and knightly ornaments was common, and its wearing was much regulated by civic sumptuary legislation from the late 13th century in almost every country of Europe.

R. Lightbown: *Medieval Jewellery in Western Europe* (London, 1991)

2. 1500–1630. Early Renaissance jewellery is distinguished by an extraordinary unity of vision and style, due in great part to the initial training of many artists in goldsmiths' workshops, regardless of future specialization. Jewellery techniques were described in detail by BENVENUTO CELLINI in *Due trattati uno in-torno alle otto principali arti dell'oreficeria* (Florence, 1568). Jewellery from this period was often based on designs supplied by painters or sculptors who had a profound understanding of technical requirements. However, few of their drawings survived the intense handling they received in busy workshops. In Italian jewellery the influence of such artists as Antonio Pollaiuolo and Sandro Botticelli (1444/5–1510) can occasionally be noticed. In Germany, a few exquisite drawings of saints by Albrecht Dürer (1471–1528) have survived (Hamburg, Ksthalle). When Hans Holbein the younger visited England, his jewellery designs created a new court fashion, as seen in portraits of Tudor society. Few Holbeinesque jewels survive, for their material value was usually less dependent on the cost of precious stones than on the delicacy of figural scenes; because of changes in court fashions, many pieces were remodelled or destroyed. Ancient cameos and intaglios, from French royal collections, were set in precious mounts designed for wear or display. Unless inventories specifically mention Christian subjects or portraits of post-Classical personalities, most pieces may be assumed to have been ancient. This changed when the French king Francis I began to attract Italian gemcutters, medallists and jewellers to his court. Among the first to arrive was Matteo del Nassaro (*fl* 1515–47) of Verona in 1515. He created a centre for cutting and polishing cameos, intaglios and precious stones in a court workshop in Paris. Types of 16th-century jewellery include necklaces, link-chains and belts, rings, pendants, hat badges, hair ornaments and earrings. Finger-rings with family crests or merchants' marks were intended as signets or as identification. Some rings have liturgical significance or include intaglios and cameos, while ornamental rings display precious stones or pearls. Changes in fashions and techniques, particularly engraving and enamelling, provided numerous variations.

During the second third of the 16th century the publication in Nuremberg and Augsburg of engraved pattern books for jewellers and goldsmiths caused fundamental changes. These were initially illustrated with woodcuts, which were soon replaced by copper engravings that allowed for more precise and defined detail. These pattern books introduced a greater choice for jeweller and patron, but such readily available designs tended to reduce the inventive impulses of lesser masters. Dependence on these designs eases dating and identification. Another innovation affecting 16th-century jewellery design was introduced by ERASMUS HORNICK of Antwerp, who invented a new type of pendant where figures were framed by an arched niche. The advantage was that the framework could be made in advance, and the jeweller could add the figures according to his client's taste. As jewellers met prospective clients at diets or seasonal trade fairs, such preparations were advantageous.

The use of figural themes for jewels gained increased importance after the Reformation. As few patrons wished to have their religious convictions evident at first glance, liturgical subjects became increasingly rare in regions of divided faith. The once favoured figures of patron saints were replaced by personifications of such virtues as Charity and Justice (e.g. pendant of the *Three Cardinal Virtues*, c. 1560–70; London, BM) or allegorical figures. Scenes of Greek mythology and Roman history enjoyed continuous favour and were used by engravers such as ETIENNE DELAUNE.

As the 16th century advanced, fundamental changes in jewellery design occurred, particularly in Spain. The arrival in Barcelona of precious stones from the Americas, including emeralds from Colombia and Peru, heralded a new age. The size of jewels increased, and some of the adventurous spirit of exploration is reflected in the appearance of bold designs of sea monsters reminiscent of those featured on maps. As Spain then ruled the Netherlands, jewellers from the two countries entertained close ties and sometimes worked for the same Spanish overlords. Their readiness in sharing marine imagery was moreover the result of being bordered by the sea, from where both countries derived their wealth through overseas trade. The people of Antwerp had a legend that in the nearby sea there were armoured mermen and nereids, some images of which are seen in Netherlandish pendants. Unlike Spanish pieces, the pendants from Antwerp were fitted with large baroque pearls. Adventurous ship-captains returned with these irregular pearls, which were unsaleable in East Asia. Tempted by the opportunity, imaginative jewellers incorporated them into specially designed figural pendants, which followed the natural shape of the pearl.

Towards the end of the 16th century a new type of ornament was created in England to celebrate the reign of Elizabeth I: oval pendants containing miniature portraits. Nicholas Hilliard (?1547–1619), the court painter and jeweller, not only suggested but also probably executed the first ones himself. Initially they portrayed Elizabeth (e.g. Armada jewel, 1595; London, V&A) and subsequently James I and members of the court. Enclosed in enamelled and jewelled frames or lockets, some display the royal cipher laid out in table-cut diamonds. Alternatively the portraits could be in the form of cameos or medals. Elizabeth rewarded services rendered by presenting such jewels to her loyal servants. On the Continent, the closest comparison were *Gnadenpfennige* (enamelled portrait medals) usually with armorials on the reverse. They were set within enamelled scrollwork and worn on gold chains.

European political turbulence in the early 17th century meant jewellers had a difficult existence, some being forced to turn to book illustration. After a return to prosperity, technical advances in diamond-cutting fundamentally changed the character of jewellery. Faceted rose-cutting, practised in Amsterdam and Antwerp, inspired floral designs that owe little or nothing to the figural style and colourful enamelling typical of 16th-century jewellery. Floral diamond garnitures, often worn in large parures, became fashionable and came to represent the age of Absolutism.

Y. Hackenbroch: *Renaissance Jewellery* (London, 1979)
Y. Hackenbroch: *I gioielli dell'elettrice palatina al Museo degli argenti* (Florence, 1988)
Y. Hackenbroch: *Enseignes: Renaissance Hat Jewels* (Florence, 1996)

3. 1631–1725. Parisian leadership in jewellery design reached a climax during the reign of Louis XIV (*reg* 1643–1715), when the jewels worn at Versailles set the standard for the rest of Europe: the Princesse des Ursins, Marie-Anne de La Trémoille (1642–1722), who arrived from Rome in 1678, was obliged to have her jewels remounted as they looked absurdly old-fashioned at the French court. This superior expertise was diffused abroad when the Revocation of the Edict of Nantes (1685) drove Huguenot craftsmen to the Protestant countries of northern Europe. An emphasis on stones rather than settings was made possible by the increased supply of gems resulting from the decision in 1660 by the British East India Company to allow the Marranos Portuguese Jews based in London to trade independently. At the same time the discovery of the laws of refraction and the principles of analytical geometry stimulated progress in faceting and polishing. Early in the 17th century the rose cut with multiple facets had succeeded the elementary point and table cut, and from the 1660s the brilliant cut, which released even more light from the diamond, became available. The increased demand for pearls tripled their price during the first 60 years of the century, and from 1686 substitutes were made by the firm of Jacqui of Paris, while others were imported from Venice, where imitations of coloured gems were also a speciality. To avoid yellow reflections silver was adopted for setting diamonds, but in Spain gold was still preferred. Enamel was now relegated to a subsidiary role on the back and sides of densely gem-encrusted ornaments but remained the main means of decoration for the cases of watches and miniatures. The Toutin family were associated with a new technique: opaque-white enamel was applied on a gold surface and then painted in a wide range of colours with still-life, topographical and mythological scenes copied from the canvases of Baroque painters. A further development was enamelling in high relief to frame cameos and miniatures with garlands of fruit and flowers.

Since fashionable people had their jewels frequently remounted, very little has survived, and the best guide to the sequence of styles is provided by pattern books. The designs of such goldsmiths as François Lefebvre in *Livre de feuilles et de fleurs utiles aux orfèvres* (Paris, 1657) reflect the mid-century passion for flowers, while those of Louis Roupert in *Dessins de feuillage et d'ornements pour l'orfèvrerie et la niellure* (Metz, 1668) show the influence of Versailles classicism. The acanthus motif was adopted internationally, and Marcus Gunter, an itinerant jeweller from Leicestershire who worked in Amsterdam,

Rome, Siena and London from 1684 to 1733, made it his speciality.

In the mid-17th century the fashion was for the face to be framed with ringlets, perhaps with a string of pearls entwined in the hair and secured at the side with long bodkins: these might have been topped with jewelled insects—butterflies, dragonflies, caterpillars or snails perched on long-stemmed plants— or by ships, shepherds' crooks and flowers studded with rose-cut diamonds and coloured stones *en cabochon*. As coiffures rose higher, padded out with artificial hair, they were ornamented with aigrettes or large floral sprays bent under the weight of diamonds and pearls. Pleated and stiffened lace Fontanges caps, which originated at Versailles, also sparkled with clusters of faceted stones scattered on the front and sides of the head. Men's hats were encircled by jewelled bands, chains and strings of pearls around the crown. Loops kept turned-up brims in place: that of Charles II of Spain was shaped as a bow from which hung the celebrated Peregrina pearl (Elizabeth Taylor, priv. col.).

Notwithstanding the immense popularity of pear-shaped pearl earrings, there was a continuing demand for gems set in wrought gold or silver. Most characteristic of the period is the girandole, consisting of a top cluster with three pendant drops arranged like a branched candelabrum suspended from a bow-knot. Complex girandoles that incorporated ribbon, crown and flower motifs were designed for Anne of Austria (widow of Louis XIII) by Paul Maréchal. Simpler styles were composed of a single pendant hanging from a button-like cluster set with gold- or silver-foiled stones with enamelled backs. In the Cheapside Hoard (a jeweller's stock hidden *c.* 1650 at Cheapside in London and discovered in 1912) bunches of festive grapes, carved from amethysts, were found, which suggests that other such imaginative designs were made. Seed pearls, if round and even, were threaded into tassels and suspended from earrings. Men also wore earrings: in 1649 Charles I went to his execution wearing a large, pear-shaped pearl earring (Welbeck Abbey, Notts). Large, evenly matched natural pearls were threaded into necklaces and tied with ribbon bows, as seen in the portrait of *Anne Hyde, Duchess of York* (*c.* 1660; Edinburgh, N.P.G) by Peter Lely (1618–80). But the diamond, with its new brilliance, had asserted its pre-eminence by the early 18th century: at the coronation of Queen Anne in 1702 many peeresses wore necklaces of rose-cut stones in heavy silver mounts enamelled at the back, linked into one or two rows falling like festoons. Enamel plaquettes were incorporated into chains and necklaces and were painted with landscapes and allegorical figures or composed of graduated bow-knots and coloured stars, each centred on a pearl.

Men wore chains as a sign of status: they were the standard reward for diplomatic and official services and were hung with medallic portraits or miniatures. The jewelled insignia of the orders of chivalry were prominently displayed. An innovation was the sleeve button, which appeared in England in the 1660s, made to fasten the cuff at each wrist, replacing the ribbon. Shoe buckles also appeared for the first time.

Fashion-conscious women almost invariably wore bodice ornaments or a large jewel in the centre of the bodice at the neckline. Such ornaments as crosses might be pinned to a ribbon tied in a bow, but from the mid-17th century the bow itself was produced in metal and gems: in Marcus Gunter's designs it was combined with acanthus scrolls, which embellish the settings. Interlaced ribbons framed the bouquet of lilies and carnations hanging from a rosette of diamonds, rubies and emeralds worn by Queen Marie Louise, wife of Charles II of Spain. Oblong, jewelled Brandenbourgs, introduced at Versailles at the end of the century, were inspired by the frogging on the jackets of Prussian soldiers: they were made in one or as graduated sets pinned from neckline to waist and were adopted internationally. Matching brooches, buttons, sleeve clasps, earrings, necklaces, aigrettes and buckles were increasingly seen to be more elegant than a miscellany of ornaments, however magnificent. Religion, death and politics are recurring themes in 17th-century jewellery: crosses were worn by both Catholics and Protestants, and some were discovered in the Cheapside Hoard. Miniature versions of cult statues such as the *Virgin of the Pillar* were typical of Spanish taste. The successive constitutional crises in English politics are evoked by rings, lockets and bracelet slides (worn on velvet bands passing through twin loops at the back) representing Charles I and his children, and later William III and Mary II. Memorial jewels commemorating private individuals were of similar design but were decorated with symbols of death—skulls, cross-bones, coffins, skeletons, hour-glasses, the angel-of-death with trumpet and crown—and usually contained locks of hair identified by gold-wire monograms.

4. 1726–1830. The jewels of the Rococo, Neo-classical and Romantic periods can be divided into two categories: those worn by day with informal clothes and the grander ornaments required with full dress at evening functions. Design emphasis was on stones rather than on settings: from the 1730s the traditional source of diamonds from India was supplemented by imports from Brazil, where the amethysts, peridots, gold and pink topazes, chrysoprases, aquamarines and chrysoberyls so popular in the early 19th century were also mined.

Seventeenth-century designs—aigrettes, girandole earrings and bow-knots for the bodice—were reinterpreted in the lighter Rococo mood. The acanthus motif was discarded, asymmetry introduced, and ribbonwork used more fluently, interspersed with flowers. From the mid-1760s this naturalistic style became more compact and geometric, while such Neo-classical motifs as the Greek fret, honeysuckle and husks appeared. Tassels and festoons derived from passementerie became fashionable from the late 1770s. Enamel disappeared from the backs of settings, which from the late 1760s were gilded to avoid tarnish, but continued to embellish daytime châtelaines, watch-cases and lockets. From the 1760s a distinctive blue enamel outlined settings and coloured the ground for rings and lockets with diamond ciphers and stars. Other popular daytime ornaments included memorial or sentimental jewellery—brooches, rings, bracelet clasps and pendants—enclosing hair, identified by ciphers and framed in small pearls or borders of blue enamel inscribed with loving mottoes, which were almost always in French. From the 1770s fichus were fastened with an oval or navette-shaped brooch with such love motifs as flaming torches, twinned hearts, a padlock or Cupid holding a lover's crown.

Powdered hair sparkled with naturalistic sprigs of flowers, with insects—moths, flies and butterflies—and with birds pecking at berries and bearing olive branches. In the late 18th century they were superseded by stars, crescents, feathers and tiaras. Feathers were secured to hats with brooches decorated with trophies of love and the arts. Earrings were essential for both day and evening wear: for day there were paste clusters matching the colours of the dress or trimmings and *coq-de-perle* (irregularly shaped sections from nautilus or periwinkle shells) combined with marcasite. The most popular formal style was the girandole with triple pendants linked to the top cluster by ribbons and flowers and single drops as long as 50 mm. The grandest evening necklaces were set with diamonds: large stones were linked into rivières of graduated stones, while the smaller gems were worked into clusters or intricate garlands of flowers and ribbons with an *esclavage* suspended from the front section. Lines of stones hung in festoons or strung into tassels echoed the fashion for passementerie. Eighteenth-century court dress was embellished with single or multiple stomachers or brooches, which filled the space between neckline and waist and which were designed as floral bouquets or large bows. Smaller versions made *en suite* were pinned to the sleeves and skirt.

The same high standards of style and quality were applied to jewels made from such coloured stones as cornelians, moss agates and garnets foiled to glow like rubies. Such substitutes as pinchbeck (an alloy of zinc and copper) provided a cheap alternative to gold. White, coloured and opaline pastes were perfected and set in jewels, belt buckles, shoes and garters. In Switzerland, where diamonds were forbidden by the sumptuary laws, marcasite was used as a substitute. English cut-steel jewellery was very popular and was exported all over Europe: some pieces were made entirely of steel, while others were mounted with enamels manufactured in Staffordshire or jasperware cameos from the ceramic factory of Josiah Wedgwood (e.g. cut-steel bracelet with cameos, *c.* 1790; Barlaston, Wedgwood Mus). For admirers of Classical art JAMES TASSIE reproduced ancient and contemporary cameos and intaglios in a range of coloured pastes, which were set in brooches, necklaces, rings and bracelets.

Gentlemen in the 18th century also wore jewels: the privileged few adorned their court dress with the magnificent insignia of the orders of chivalry, but every gentleman owned a sword with jewelled hilt, a watch, a seal, a locket or miniature pendant worn from a chain round his neck and finger-rings. The cravat was pinned with a jewel, cuffs were fastened with a pair of buttons, and cut-steel or paste buckles were made for shoes and garters. Buttons might be set with gems or paste and enamelled with subjects indicating the owner's cultural, political or sporting interests. As dress became plainer from the 1770s, buttons became larger.

The simplification of dress in the years preceding the French Revolution (1789) was accompanied by a fashion for less grand jewellery. After 1804 this trend was reversed when Napoleon (*reg* 1804–14) established his empire and asserted his authority by a great display of wealth. This led to the creation of jewels in a rich version of Roman Classicism devised by the court painter David as an expression of the artistic style of the regime. These tiaras, earrings, necklaces, bracelets and brooches incorporating such motifs as the Greek fret, honeysuckle, palmettes and wreaths of vine and laurel were encrusted with diamonds, emeralds, rubies, pearls and engraved gems from the former royal collection and set the pattern for court jewellery everywhere. This style was adopted by the restored Bourbon monarchy after 1815, but the classical motifs were replaced by scrolls, leaves and flowers. The rest of Europe followed suit. Supplementing the supply of diamonds were coloured stones from Brazil and turquoises—perhaps the favourite stone of the period—set in ostentatious mounts of filigree or stamped gold linked by chains. This combination of brightly coloured stones in gold settings, known as *à l'antique*, evoked the jewels of the Middle Ages and the Renaissance. Other jewels worn with the picturesque clothes of the Romantic period represented knights in armour and pairs of celebrated lovers. Devotional jewels were worn as a response to the religious revival that came as a reaction to the atheism of the French Revolution: belt buckles—exaggerated to emphasize the small waist—might represent pilgrims kneeling at a shrine; rosaries and rosary rings were displayed, and Greek, Latin, Maltese and Jerusalem crosses, decorated with Gothic cusping and tracery, imparted a nun-like air to the 19th-century woman. Locks of hair and miniatures, often of a painted eye, were framed in jewelled hearts, padlocks, rings and lockets (e.g. locket containing a lock of John Keats's hair, *c.* 1824; London, Keats House). Symbolic motifs included the snake, tail in mouth, signifying eternity, and such emblematic flowers as the pansy and the forget-me-not. Christian names and loving messages—AMITIÉ, DEAREST, SOUVENIR, REGARD—might be spelt out from the initials of the stones used: R(uby), E(merald), G(arnet), A(methyst), R(uby), D(iamond).

Formal social life required jewels for the hair, and women now wore their tiaras with nodding ostrich plumes and a jewelled comb *en suite*. Less grand were the smaller bouquets of flowers, ears of wheat, moths and butterflies mounted *en tremblant*. In 1830 the ferronière appeared, inspired by *La Belle Ferronière* (1499; Paris, Louvre) by Leonardo da Vinci (1452–1519). Simple or splendid, according to the occasion, the ferronière was always centred on an ornament—cameo, drop or large cabochon stone—set over the brow. Equally picturesque were the turbans, evoking the Crusades, pinned with crescent and feather brooches. Long earrings balanced piled-up hair: the girandole and single drops remained popular and were worn *en suite* with crosses or brooches placed *à la sévigné* (named after the Marquise de Sévigné in the centre of the neckline).

Necklace designs achieved a compromise between the desire for rich display and the 18th-century tradition for elegance. Typical of the period was the cluster style composed of single large coloured stones framed with tiny diamonds and hung with a fringe of pendants. The chains and sautoirs, worn diagonally across the body from shoulder to hip and hooked in at the waist, were sometimes composed of enamelled plaques edged with seed pearls but were usually made of gold or pinchbeck, fastened with clasps shaped as a beringed and braceleted woman's hand. Suspended from these were such useful objects as lorgnettes, enamelled watches or vinaigrettes. Bracelets were not only included in full-dress parures but also worn in the daytime. They were made in Gothic style with cusped ogee arches, or they might represent a snake coiled several times round the wrist with a heart-shaped locket hanging from its fangs. The focus of design was usually the clasp, which might be a large and important stone, a miniature or such a motif as two hands clasped, a symbol of fidelity since the Middle Ages. In spite of the great concentration on jewellery for women during this period, such masculine ornaments as gold chains, jewelled studs, pins, lockets, dangling seals and the watch-and-chain were still very evident.

P. F. Schneeberger: *Les Peintres sur émail genevois au XVIIe et au XVIIIe siècle* (Geneva, 1958)

S. Grandjean: 'Jewellery under the First Empire', *Connoisseur*, cxciii (1976), pp. 275–81

S. Bury: *Sentimental Jewellery* (London, 1985)

D. Scarisbrick: *Ancestral Jewels* (London, 1989)

D. Scarisbrick: *Jewels in Britain 1066–1837* (1994)

5. 1831–1900. During this period of political change and unparalleled industrial expansion, jewels were produced in vast quantities and in a variety of styles. The Parisian makers maintained the lead, receiving much encouragement from Napoleon III (*reg* 1852–70), who was declared Emperor in 1852 and who with the Empress Eugénie made his court the most brilliant in Europe. Besides their traditional clientele of royalty, nobility and the burgeoning bourgeoisie, the Paris jewellers attracted a new element: millionaires from both North and South America were ready to pay high prices for pieces of exceptional quality. The discovery of diamonds in South Africa (*c.* 1867) prompted the emergence of this lu-

crative market, and from the 1870s the number of women wearing these stones increased. At the same time designs were simplified, often at the expense of artistry, to show off the stone.

The international exhibitions, held at regular intervals after the Great Exhibition of 1851 in London, provided showcases for the best jewellers in each country and helped disseminate new techniques and styles, as well as introducing new materials. The illustrated magazines also kept their readers in touch by reporting the ornaments and dresses worn to social occasions and publishing information about wedding presents, which were most often jewels. Most jewels were made for women, as the sober, black clothing worn by men left little room for jewellery except for watch-chains, rings, scarf-pins and studs. Jewels were closely associated with fashions in dress: there was a clear distinction between formal and informal wear, outfits were worn with appropriate adornments, and mourning was scrupulously observed. The parures of pearls, diamonds and coloured stones worn in the evening were more conservative in design than the gold daytime jewels, which showed more originality. Styles were adapted for mass production in Birmingham, Clerkenwell (London) and Hanau in Germany, making jewellery and trinkets available to almost every woman. The production of British jewellery had become so in-

Alfred Bapst: diamond reliquary brooch of Empress Eugénie, 1855 (Paris, Musée du Louvre)

dustrialized by the mid-19th century that ornaments made to traditional Scottish designs, set with local cairngorms and pearls and sold in the shops of Edinburgh and Perth, were in fact supplied by such Birmingham manufacturers as Thomas Fell.

The tradition for regional craftsmanship lasted longer in the rest of Europe, stimulated by the desire of tourists for souvenirs of distant places. From the foundries of Berlin and Silesia came iron jewellery (*see* BERLIN, §1), which could be worn with mourning attire. Switzerland was famous for enamelled goldwork, bracelets with pictures of peasant girls in regional costume being popular. Such centres as Erbach im Odenwald in Germany and Thun and Brienz in Switzerland produced carved ivory brooches with hunting scenes evoking visits to the Alpine forests. In Italy regional specialities included jewellery with carved coral from Naples and Genoa, hardstone inlay from Florence and micro-mosaic and shell cameos from Rome. Botanical jewellery was reinterpreted for evening wear with hair garlands and bouquets for both hair and bodice. The masters of this type of ornament were the Parisian firms of Lemonnier and Fossin, who tried to make each bloom as naturalistic as possible, mounting them *en tremblant* and painting the leaves with bright-green enamel, which terminated in trails of diamonds known as *pampilles*. For the Empress Eugénie, who made a cult of her admiration for Marie-Antoinette, the court jewellers Alfred Bapst made many superb botanical jewels, including a diamond parure of currant leaves and berries. The style culminated in the splendid bouquets, or *bijoux modelés*, of Olive Massin (*b* 1829; *d* after 1892), Frédéric Boucheron (1830–1902) and Octave Loeulliard, which drew huge crowds when displayed at the international exhibitions. The snake (symbolic of eternity) remained consistently popular and was Queen Victoria's choice for her engagement ring (Windsor Castle, Berks, Royal Col.). It was also used on necklaces, brooches and bracelets, enamelled royal blue or with turquoise-encrusted scales and jewelled head. Such motifs as ivy leaves, hearts, pansies and forget-me-nots, all redolent of sentiment, are also typical of the period. Some can be found on mourning jewellery made of such black materials as jet, onyx or fossil bog-oak from Ireland.

By the late 1830s jewellery was influenced by the Medieval Revival and interest in historicism. The ferronière encircling the brow and the châtelaine, which hung from the waist, were direct copies of medieval ornaments, but most were combinations of motifs taken from the architecture, sculpture, ceramics, textiles, paintings and miniatures of the past. In France the leading exponent was FRANÇOIS-DÉSIRÉ FROMENT-MEURICE, whose sculptural tableaux contrasted with the flat, English styles represented by the popular Holbeinesque oval pendant. A more refined version of enamelling in antique and Renaissance styles was produced by members of the Giuliano family for a rich clientele. In France miniatures of illustrious ladies demonstrated the success of craftsmen in reviving the skills of the Limoges ena-

mellers (*see* LIMOGES, §2). Mass-produced Renaissance Revival jewels were exported from Vienna, some of the chief firms being Josef Bacher & Sons, Karl Bank and Hermann Ratzersdorfer. Archaeological jewellery was made fashionable by the CASTELLANI family, who produced jewellery that simulated Etruscan, Hellenistic, Roman, Early Christian, Byzantine, medieval and Renaissance ornaments. They used such traditional techniques as granulation, filigree and enamel and sometimes incorporated coins, cameos, mosaics and Latin or Greek mottoes. Others who specialized in reinterpreting archaeological and later themes in 19th-century forms were Eugène Fontenay (1823–87) in Paris and John Brogden (*fl* 1842–85) and Robert Phillips (1810–81) in London. Re-creations of Viking jewels by Copenhagen firms were worn in England after the Danish princess Alexandra brought some with her trousseau on her marriage to the Prince of Wales (later Edward VII) in 1863. Exotic and distant locations inspired such other designs as Moorish knots and tassels, Japanese-style medallions enamelled with flowers and birds by LUCIEN FALIZE and Indian-style necklaces by Carlo Giuliano (1831–95).

The formality of social life required jewels to adorn the hair, and every noble lady wore a tiara. Wreaths of flowers and leaves around the head were succeeded in the 1850s by stately diadems curved to the shape of the head like the rays of the sun. Aigrettes shaped as crescents, birds, wings of Mercury, butterflies, peacock feathers, sprays of corn and Cupid's bow and arrow were worn to the side of the head supporting a spray of osprey feathers. Pins with ornamental finials secured hats worn with day dress. In the 1860s long earrings came back into fashion, and for formal wear large, round pearls were suspended from a diamond top or from diamond chains. Daytime designs included Etruscan-style hoops, miniature Roman oil lamps, insects and such novelties as bells, clogs, miniature 'Willow' pattern plates, stirrups and horseshoes. Necklaces for the evening were usually a simple diamond rivière of graduated silver collets or strings of pearls in the fashion promoted by the Empress Eugénie, as seen in the portrait of Archduchess *Marie of Austria, Duchess of Brabant* (1863; Belgian Royal Col.) by Franz Xaver Winterhalter (1805–73). With day clothes there was more variety, with long gold chains suspending lorgnettes, watches and vinaigrettes, Roman laurel wreaths or Celtic-style collars. From the 1870s there was a fashion for heavy, gold lockets containing photographs, miniatures or locks of hair hung from a velvet ribbon. The gold now had a soft 'bloomed' surface achieved by immersion in an acid solution. Equally ubiquitous were crosses, many reviving Early Christian, medieval and Renaissance designs.

Low necklines were adorned with large brooches, which combined turquoises, pearls, chrysolites, amethysts, pink topazes, garnets and gold. These were sometimes made *en suite* with necklace, pendants, pendent earrings and a pair of bracelets or as a demi-parure with just the earrings in a fitted case. They were succeeded by creations in pearls and diamonds as these became more plentiful. Towards the end of the century lace and chiffon neckline trimmings were adorned with a profusion of brooches shaped as butterflies, lizards, bumble-bees, stars and bow-knots. Daytime brooches included symbols of sentiment and good luck and reflections of cultural, sporting and political interests. Most representative was the bracelet, often worn in rows on each arm. The broad bands of varicoloured gold or plaited hair clasped by a large stone or a miniature were followed by strap and buckle designs, imitation buttoned cuffs, snakes, and wreaths of symbolic flowers and leaves, many of which were inscribed with mottoes or messages of affection and good luck. With formal attire there was less variety, the wrist being encircled by rows of pearls with diamond clasps, or rigid bangles with stones set all the way round or in a graduated line along the top, which matched the half-hoop rings set in the same manner. The beauty of the stones was of paramount importance to the wearer, and as a result jewellery design became increasingly subdued and unobtrusive.

In England artistic circles of the 1880s and 1890s eschewed the use of diamonds and ostentatious jewellery and condemned the shoddiness of mass-produced pieces. Followers of William Morris and the ARTS AND CRAFTS MOVEMENT preferred individually designed and hand-crafted work emanating from such medieval-inspired guilds as C. R. Ashbee's Guild of Handicraft. At the same time the avant-garde on the Continent brought innovative and daring designs to jewellery in the Art Nouveau style, which combined such naturalistic elements as flora, fauna and insects with the influence of Japanese art and an interest in Symbolism. RENÉ LALIQUE produced some of the most remarkable examples of Art Nouveau jewellery.

H. Vever: *La Bijouterie française au XIX siècle*, 3 vols (Paris, 1908–12)
C. Gere: *Victorian Jewellery Design* (London, 1972)
C. Gere: *European and American Jewellery, 1830–1914* (London, 1975)
M. Flower: *Victorian Jewellery* (London, 1973)
P. Hinks: *Nineteenth Century Jewellery* (London, 1975)
Les Fouquet: Bijoutiers & joailliers à Paris, 1860–1960 (exh. cat., Paris, Mus. A. Déc., 1983)
D. Scarisbrick: *Ancestral Jewels* (London, 1989)
Pariser Schmuck, 1850–1900 (exh. cat., Munich, Bayer. Nmus., 1989–90)
S. Bury: *Jewellery, 1789–1910*, 2 vols (Woodbridge, 1991)
D. Scarisbrick: *Jewels in Britain, 1066–1837* (1994)

5. AFTER 1900. In 1900 there were clear signs that the passion for Art Nouveau was beginning to fade in Paris, while in Britain the Arts and Crafts Movement was still in the ascendant. In complete contrast to the highly professional Parisian Art Nouveau jewellers, such pioneers of British Arts and Crafts jewellery as Alexander Fisher (1864–1936), Henry Wilson (1864–1934), Georgina Gaskin (1868–1934) and Arthur Gaskin (1862–1938) were self-taught amateurs who worked according to their own arbitrary code of 'honest workmanship'. Most of their work was in silver, hardstones and enamel because these were cheap and appropriate to the popular art the

movement was out to establish. They preferred to build up their jewellery piece by piece, rather than pierce it out of sheet metal, and rarely finished it to a smooth polish. The machine was, in theory at least, banished from the workshop, and it is one of the many paradoxes of Arts and Crafts jewellery that some of its most successful creations commercially as well as aesthetically were the 'Cymric' jewels made by Liberty & Co. (*see* LIBERTY. ARTHUR LASENBY) by a combination of hand and mechanical methods.

Jewellery made according to the guiding principles of the Arts and Crafts Movement was produced in other parts of Europe and in America. Florence Koehler of Chicago won an international reputation for her leafy designs set with informal groupings of gems in 18-carat gold. In Copenhagen, GEORG JENSEN established a Scandinavian style of plump scrolls and plant forms set with Baltic amber, stained green chalcedony and garnets. C. R. ASHBEE and CHARLES RENNIES MACKINTOSH both visited Vienna, and although the jewellery produced by the Wiener Werkstätte was unmistakably Central European, English and Scottish influence can be traced in the designs of Carl Otto Czeschka (1878–1960) and JOSEF HOFFMANN, while those of DAGOBERT PECHE and KOLO MOSER are more Viennese. The factory producers of Pforzheim in Germany were quick to adapt these simple Viennese designs to mass production and thus succeeded in producing the truly popular style that the Arts and Crafts dream had failed to realize.

Arts and Crafts was a reaction not only against the machine but also against the professional jeweller, whose work at this time was remarkably skilled. The introduction of platinum and improvements in diamond-cutting produced jewels whose settings were almost invisible in wear. The result was a Neo-classical style of swags, garlands and festoons with overtones of the 18th century. The very hardness of platinum was an advantage because it enabled the craftsman to execute piercing and engraving of almost microscopic fineness. The magnificently swagged and garlanded neo-classical designs produced at this time by such firms as Cartier represent some of the finest diamond jewellery ever made.

The vibrant designs (1909–21) by Léon Bakst (1866–1924) for Serge Diaghilev's Ballets Russes typified the current fascination for the mystic East. Lotus, papyrus, bamboo and swastika motifs appeared in many jewels. In the years before World War I jewellery became more stylized and two-dimensional, evidence of the transition into Art Deco. It was then that the characteristic Art Deco palette of tango (orange-red), ultramarine, eau de Nil (a pale green), buttercup, lavender and black made its first appearance in jewellery, expressed in enamel, lacquer or a variety of such materials as jade, ivory, lapis lazuli, stained agate, onyx or jet, with the distinctive tango represented by coral or cornelian.

Many of the jewels that are associated with the 1920s—the bandeaux, the plumed aigrettes, the long tasselled neckchains and pendulous earrings—were already established fashions before World War I. Jewels were designed to sway with the body in time to the rhythms of the tango and the Charleston: Oriental fashions took an even firmer hold in the 1920s. Jewels were set with carved precious stones from India and Chinese jades. The Parisian firms of Lacloche, Cartier and Boucheron led the field at this time. The trend towards simplicity and formality became crystallized in the abstract geometrical designs of Jean Fouquet (1899–1984), Raymond Templier (1891–1968), Gérard Sandoz (*b* 1902), Jean Desprès (1889–1980) and Georges Fouquet (1862–1957).

In 1929, the year of the Wall Street crash, attitudes to jewellery changed, making it a focal point on the costume rather than a complement to the body. Neckchains and aigrettes were out, and long pendent earrings were replaced by compact earclips. Two new styles emerged, both fixed to the dress rather than the person: the plaque brooch, which was exactly what its name suggests, and the clip, secured by clamping it to the neckline or lapel. It was the age of the gadget, and clips were often made in pairs so that the two could be united in a single 'double-clip' brooch or even a bracelet. Jewellery tended to be large and impressive, a symbol of security in an insecure age. Oriental fashions held their own, dominated by Chinese style. The geometrical style manifested itself in the hooked and stepped decoration of Aztec Mexico and in the mechanistic cocktail jewellery of the 1940s.

Between the wars, although a few of the original Arts and Crafts jewellers were still at work, the movement lost much of its impetus. The firm of Georg Jensen continued to produce their tried and tested designs but also commissioned such artists as Nanna Ditzel (1923–2005) and Henning Koppel (1918–81) to invent clean sculptural forms that more accurately reflected the spirit of the post-war period. In Europe and America after 1945 several painters and sculptors began designing jewellery. One of the most successful was Alexander Calder (1898–1976), who made simple ornaments of forged metal. Georges Braque (1882–1963), Salvador Dalí (1904–89), Max Ernst (1891–1976) and others each produced jewels in his own individual style. It was not until the late 1950s, however, that an alternative art jewellery style emerged that truly reflected the preoccupations of its time. These jewels combined the apparent randomness of action painting and of the *objet trouvé* by mounting uncut natural crystals, meteorites and misshapen pearls in settings of rough or molten gold. Emphasis was on texture, giving these jewels the impression of having been subjected to the heat of a nuclear explosion. By the end of the 1960s many of the avant-garde who had devised the new style—David Thomas (*b* 1938), John Donald (*b* 1928), Gerda Flockinger (*b* 1927), Andrew Grima (*b* 1921) and Louis Osman (1914–96) in England, Gilbert Albert (*b* 1930) in Switzerland, Arnaldo Pomodoro (*b* 1926) and Giò Pomodoro (*b* 1930) in Italy, and Bjorn Weckstrom (*b* 1935) in Finland—had become part of the jewellery establishment.

In Germany at the same time Reinhold Reiling (1922–83) organized his textures by mathematically juxtaposing them with free asymmetrical forms. Reiling in Pforzheim, Friedrich Becker (*b* 1922) in Düsseldorf and Hermann Junger (*b* 1928) in Munich trained a whole generation of jewellers, and in the 1970s the centre of gravity of the new movement shifted from Britain to Germany. After centuries of using much the same traditional materials and techniques, the jeweller awoke to what the space age had to offer: acrylics and polyester resins, nylon monofilaments, anodized aluminium and the refractory metals, titanium, zirconium and niobium, with their multicoloured patinas. At the same time the jeweller was using familiar materials that were unconventional in the context of modern Western jewellery—steel, ivory, wood, ceramic, silk and feathers. Other jewellers rejected such materials as ivory or diamonds for ideological reasons. There was experimentation at every level. The body was sometimes reduced to an abstraction by sectioning it visually or even by partially obliterating the face. Some pieces even seem to have been intended to restrict the wearer's movements, thereby increasing his or her own self-awareness. The notion that jewellery should be precious and long-lasting was confounded in ornaments made of postcards, wallpaper or plastic toys. Jewellery was often thought of as sculpture rather than decoration and was designed with a stand to display it.

International Exhibition of Modern Jewellery, 1890–1961 (exh. cat., London, Goldsmiths' Co., 1961)

G. Hughes: *Modern Jewellery, 1890–1967* (London, 1968)

R. Turner: *Contemporary Jewellery* (London, 1976)

Synthetic Jewellery (exh. cat. by B. Beaumont-Nesbitt; Birmingham, W. Midlands A., 1978)

V. Becker: *Antique and Twentieth Century Jewellery: A Guide for Collectors* (London, 1980/R New York, 1982)

P. Hinks: *Twentieth Century British Jewellery, 1900–1980* (London, 1983)

S. Raulet: *Bijoux art déco* (Paris, 1984)

V. Becker: *Art Nouveau Jewellery* (London, 1985)

B. Cartlidge: *Twentieth Century Jewellery* (New York, 1985)

P. Dormer and R. Turner: *The New Jewellery* (London, 1985)

J. Culme and N. Rayner: *The Jewels of the Duchess of Windsor* (London, 1987)

Jewels of Fantasy: Costume Jewelry of the 20th Century (exh. cat., Los Angeles, CA, Co. Mus. A.; Baltimore, MD, Mus. A.; 1993–4)

Ji'an. *See* JIZHOU.

Jingdezhen [Ching-te-chen]. Town and county seat in north-east Jiangxi Province, China, and the country's main centre of porcelain production. For most of its existence the town was part of Fouliang, in Raozhou Prefecture, and in historical records its ceramics are generally referred to as Raozhou ware. With a continuous history of manufacturing porcelain from the Tang period (AD 618–907), it is the source of most Chinese porcelain.

The imperial kilns were located at Zhushan in the centre of modern Jingdezhen city; many lesser kilns were situated in Hutian, 4 km to the south-east. The area is supplied with fine-quality porcelain stone, the

Jingdezhen-ware seal-paste box by Xu Naijing, porcelain with blue overglaze enamel and black and sepia overglaze enamel, diam. 80 mm, 1937 (London, British Museum)

basic raw material for Chinese porcelain; it is surrounded by forests that provided fuel for the kilns; and it is conveniently connected to the major ports of southern China by rivers. Recent excavations have brought to light several different kiln types, including egg-shaped *zhenyao* kilns, bread-roll-shaped *mantou* kilns and dragon kilns. Compared with contemporary kilns in southern China, most Jingdezhen kilns were fairly small.

Ceramic manufacture in the Jingdezhen area began around the beginning of the Tang period, when simple wares were made, mainly bowls with a greyish-white body and a white or grey-green glaze. For the first centuries of its existence Jingdezhen was a minor ceramic-producing town, one of many such places operating in China. In the Northern Song period (960–1127), when the town received its present name (during the Jingde reign period, 1004–7), its whitewares became more refined; the best pieces of this period already have the translucent, white porcelain body and bluish-tinged glaze known as Qingbai characteristic of Jingdezhen porcelain throughout the Song and Yuan (1279–1368) dynasties. When the Southern Song dynasty (1127–1279) established its capital at Lin'an (modern Hangzhou), and the country's political and cultural centre shifted to the southeast, the kilns were able to meet the sudden rise in demand for high-quality porcelain. Qingbai ware was made in enormous quantities and became one of China's most popular ceramic wares, both at home and abroad. However, it did not receive the ultimate seal of approval, use at court. Neither did *shufu* ware, a whiteware with a more opaque white glaze, also produced at Jingdezhen.

Imperial patronage of Jingdezhen began during the Yuan period, when underglaze-painted porcelains were developed. This decorative technique was at first rejected by the Chinese élite; it was more enthusiastically received by the ruling Mongols, however, and was exported to many countries throughout Asia. Up to this time Jingdezhen had made little besides whitewares, and experiments with celadon and brown glazes had met with limited success. By the Ming period (from 1368) a large variety of colours were used both as monochrome glazes and for polychrome painted decoration, including the cool blues and turquoises of the alkaline *fahua* range and the warm red, yellow and green tones of the lead-based enamels.

The court patronized Jingdezhen throughout the Ming and Qing (1644–1911) periods without major interruptions, while usually lower quality Jingdezhen wares were widely exported. Some of the best blue-and-white porcelain was made during the Yongle (1403–24) and Xuande (1426–35) periods, when the use of reign marks began. During the so-called 'interregnum' between the Xuande and Chenghua (1465–87) reign periods, quality temporarily declined, only to rise again in the Chenghua period, when some of the finest polychrome porcelains (*doucai*) were made. Output was very high from the Chenghua to Wanli (1573–1620) reign periods, but by around 1600 manufacture for the court seems to have declined sharply. By 1671 Chinese sources once again note the successful completion of imperial orders. In 1683 Jingdezhen received a new impetus with the creation of a new post, Supervisor of the Imperial Kilns, held successively by Zang Yingxuan (between 1683 and 1726), Nian Xiyao (between 1726 and 1736) and Tang Ying (between 1736 and 1756, assistant from 1728). Under Tang Ying's supervision, porcelain painting rose to its greatest heights, and rigorous quality control resulted in technically perfect items. What followed was endless repetition of a wide spectrum of forms and designs and an indulgence in technical *tours de force*, which failed to recreate the brilliance of the pieces from the 1720s and 1730s. In the late Qing the industry came increasingly into competition with foreign machine-made ceramics and declined. It did not completely collapse, however and since the late 20th century Jingdezhen has produced some 300 million pieces of household porcelain a year, as well as technically sophisticated reproductions of classic Chinese models.

Imperial Porcelain of the Yongle and Xuande Periods Excavated from the Site of the Ming Imperial Factory at Jingdezhen (exh. cat., Hong Kong, Mus. A., 1989)

R. Scott: *Elegant Form and Harmonious Decoration: Four Dynasties of Jingdezhen Porcelain* (London, 1992)

Ceramic Finds from Jingdezhen Kilns, Fung Ping Shan Museum (Hong Kong, 1992) [10th–17th centuries]

A Legacy of Chenghua: Imperial Porcelain of the Chenghua Reign Excavated from Zhushan, Jingdezhen (exh. cat., Hong Kong, Tsui Mus. A., 1993)

R. Scott, ed.: *The Porcelains of Jingdezhen*, PDF Colloquies on Art and Archaeology, xvi (London, 1993)

R. Krahl: 'By Appointment to the Emperor: Imperial Porcelains from Jingdezhen and their Various Destinations', *Orient. A.*, xlviii/5 (2002–3), pp. 27–32

S. Brousseau: 'Throwing Classical Porcelain in Jingdezhen, China', *Cer. Technical*, xviii (2004), pp. 45–8

Jiříkovo Údolí Glassworks. *See under* NOVÉ HRADY.

Jitokusai. *See* HON'AMI KŌETSU.

Jizhou [Chichow; Chi-chou; Ji'an; Chi-an]. Site in central Jiangxi Province, China, and former centre of ceramic production. Jizhou is the Sui- to Song-period (581–1279) name for modern Ji'an, a town on the Ganjiang River, which flows northwards into the Yangzi Basin. Ceramic kilns operated from at least the Tang period (AD 618–907) until the end of the Yuan (1279–1368) at the village of Yonghexu, about 8 km outside the town.

After some experimentation with whitewares and celadons in the Tang, the kilns' range of activity was developed during the Song (960–1279), especially the Southern Song (1127–1279). They produced tablewares of a rather soft, off-white clay under brown and black glazes, mostly teabowls of conical form with minimal foot-rings. The potters invented a wide variety of decorative techniques mainly for the inside of bowls. These included mottling with phosphatic slip; preserving patterns in brown, probably by using papercuts against a coating of uneven buff slip; painting with slip; and even dipping a leaf in slip and applying this to the glaze. The bowls decorated inside with painted slip or leaf imprints have plain black exteriors, and those with mottles or papercut decoration have mottled exteriors. Some blackwares have simple painting in the areas kept free of glaze, and a few white-glazed wares have motifs incised in the glaze. During the Yuan, bottles and other items were made with fine wave or scroll patterns drawn in dark brown on white slip. Two such bottles were found among the cargo of a junk which foundered off southern Korea about 1322. In 1982 a maker's stamp was found, bearing the name of the Shu family mentioned in the *Gegu yaolun*. A good representative group of pieces produced at Jizhou is in the Schiller Collection at the City of Bristol Museum and Art Gallery.

A. D. Brankston: 'An Excursion to Ching-te-chen and Chi-an-fu in Kiangsi', *Trans. Orient. Cer. Soc.*, xvi (1938–9), pp. 19–32
J. Wirgin: 'Some Ceramic Wares from Chi-chou', *Bull. Mus. Far E. Ant.*, xxxiv (1962), pp. 53–71
Z. Bing: 'Les imitations de porcelaines de Ding du Xe au XIVe siècle: le cas des officines de potiers de Jizhou and Jiangxi', *A. Asiatiques*, lvi (2001), pp. 61–80

Joanine. Term used to designate the style of *talha* (carved and gilded wood) produced during the reign of John V (*reg* 1706–50) of Portugal. The term was initially used to denote a style of woodwork in churches, (especially retables), but was employed subsequently to describe other art forms of the period, including painting (in particular portraiture), silver, furniture and glazed tiles, as well as interior decoration. The typical Joanine retable is taller and narrower than those of the National style of the 17th century. Concentric arches were abandoned in favour of canopies and baldacchini of architectural form, combined with allegorical statues.

R. C. Smith: *A talha em Portugal* (Lisbon, 1962)
R. C. Smith: *The Art of Portugal, 1500–1800* (London, 1968)

Johnson, Gerrit. *See* JENSEN, GERRIT.

Johnson, Thomas (*bapt* London, 13 Jan 1714; *d c.* 1778). English furniture designer and carver. Nothing is known of his apprenticeship or early work, but he published *Twelve Gerandoles* in 1755, styling himself 'Thomas Johnson, Carver, at the Corner of Queen Street, near the Seven Dials, Soho'. Between 1756 and 1757 he issued some 52 sheets of designs for *Glass, Picture, and Table Frames; Chimney Pieces, Gerandoles, Candle-stands, Clock-cases, Brackets, and other Ornaments in the Chinese, Gothick, and Rural Taste*, publishing the collection as a complete volume in 1758 from a new address in Grafton Street. His designs were marked by a bold use of Rococo, chinoiserie and Rustic motifs, incorporating rocaille and animals. In 1761 he brought out another edition entitled *One Hundred and Fifty New Designs*. His slight *New Book of Ornaments*, published in 1760, showed experiments in etching that imitated pen-and-wash drawings.

By the early 1760s Johnson seems to have been concerned with teaching. A further set of designs, *A New Book of Ornaments* (1762), was 'Designed for Tablets and Friezes for Chimney-Pieces Useful for Youth to Draw After'. In 1763 Mortimer's *Universal Director* referred to him as a 'Carver, Teacher of Drawing and Modelling and Author of a Book of Designs for Chimneypieces and other ornaments and of several other pieces'. He issued a trade card (London, BM, Heal Col.) inscribed 'Thos. Johnson Drawing Master at ye Golden Boy in Charlotte Street Bloomsbury London'. When declared bankrupt in 1764 he had moved to Tottenham Court Road. His last surviving work is a single sheet dated August 1775 from an otherwise lost series. It illustrates a series of mirrors in the Neo-classical style. He is last recorded in the Grafton Street rent-books for 1778.

No bills relating to Johnson's work as a carver have been traced. It has been suggested that he was employed as a specialist sub-contractor by George Cole (*fl* 1747–74) who in 1761 supplied mirrors to Paul Methuen at Corsham Court, Wilts. A pair of pier-glasses and an overmantel mirror from Newburgh Priory, N. Yorks (on loan to Leeds, Temple Newsam House), are based on Johnson's published designs. Four pier-glasses and three console-tables for the 2nd Duke of Atholl at Dunkeld House, Tayside (1761), and Blair Castle, Tayside (1763), fall into the same category. A set of four Rococo dolphin *torchères* and a pair of girandoles from Hagley Hall, Worcs (Leeds, Temple Newsam House; London, V&A; Philadelphia, PA, Mus. A.) follow Johnson's designs and could have been carved by him. A unique copy of Johnson's autobiography has been found in the Library of Freemasonry in London.

T. Johnson: *Twelve Gerandoles* (London, 1755)

T. Johnson: *Glass, Picture, and Table Frames; Chimney Pieces, Gerandoles, Candle-stands, Clock-cases, Brackets, and Other Ornaments in the Chinese, Gothick, and Rural Taste* (London, 1758); rev. as *One Hundred and Fifty New Designs* (London, 1761)

T. Johnson: *A New Book of Ornaments* (London, 1760) [no complete copy is known to survive]

T. Johnson: *A New Book of Ornaments* (London, 1762)

H. Hayward: *Thomas Johnson and the English Rococo* (London, 1964)

H. Hayward: 'Thomas Johnson and Rococo Carving', *Connoisseur Yb.* (1965), pp. 94–100

H. Hayward: 'Newly-discovered Designs by Thomas Johnson', *Furn. Hist.*, xi (1975), pp. 40–42

J. Simon: 'Thomas Johnson's The Life of the Author', *Furn. Hist.*, xxxix (2003), pp. 1–64

Johnston, David (*b* Bordeaux, 1789; *d* Bordeaux, 1854). French potter of Irish descent. In 1835 Johnson inherited his father's business in Bordeaux, and the following year established a faience factory at nearby Bacalan. He employed some 500 workers, and specialized in blue printed wares in a contemporary English style; the factory exhibited at the Exposition de Bordeaux in 1838 and the Exposition de Paris in 1839. Johnston became mayor of Bordeaux, but his business failed in 1844 after an unsuccessful attempt to manufacture porcelain.

Johnston, Thomas (*fl* 1732–67). American portrait painter, japanner and engraver, active in Boston. His workshop on Ann Street advertised 'Japaning, Gilding, Painting, Varnishing'; he also engraved maps, music and clock faces. A tall clock (*c.* 1749–56; Winterthur, DE, Du Pont Winterthur Mus.) japanned by Johnston is one of the finest surviving examples of japanned work in colonial America.

M. H. Heckscher and others: 'Boston Japanned Furniture in the Metropolitan Museum of Art', *Mag. Ant.*, cxxix (May 1986), pp. 1046–61

Joint [join; joined] **stool.** In 16th- through to 18th-century usage, a stool made of parts fitted together with mortise and tenon joints, as distinct from STICK FURNITURE.

Jones, Owen (*b* London, 15 Feb 1809; *d* London, 19 April 1874). English architect and designer. Jones believed passionately that the 19th century should produce a recognizable style of its own that would result not simply from the study of past styles but from the adoption of new materials. In attempting to carry through this ideology in his own work in the 1840s Jones relied heavily on Islamic sources and was much criticized as a result. Perhaps the most successful building with which he was then concerned was Christ Church (1840–42), Streatham, London, designed by James William Wild (1814–92), who was his brother-in-law. Jones was responsible for the interior decoration and may also have influenced the exterior, with its brick polychromy and

Islamic details. He was well known in the 1840s for the design of mosaic and tessellated pavements in geometric patterns. He published two books on this subject and in 1844 submitted a design for the floors of the new Palace of Westminster which, although praised, was not accepted.

Jones carried out decorative schemes for domestic interiors, working in collaboration with the London firm of Jackson & Graham. His work for Alfred Morrison included interiors in his country house at Fonthill (*c.* 1863; destr. 20th century), Wilts, and his town house at 16 Carlton House Terrace (1867), London, which contained some fine examples of inlaid and carved work in the Moorish and other styles. He designed interiors at the house of James Mason, Eynsham Hall (1872; rebuilt 1906), Oxford. The extensive work for Ismail Pasha, Khedive of Egypt, in 1864 involved the prefabrication of the interiors by Jackson & Graham in London before their shipment and installation in Cairo. Jones's most important decorative schemes for public buildings were those for the Langham Hotel (1864) and for the Fishmongers' Hall (1865), both in London.

Jones worked closely with several firms: he designed wallpapers for Trumble & Sons and for Jeffrey & Co.; carpets for James Templeton & Co. and for Brinton; silks for Benjamin Warner; and numerous paper items for the firm of De la Rue. His association with De la Rue over thirty years covered virtually all the items produced by the firm, from playing cards to stamps (see colour pl. XV, fig. 3).

ODNB

M. Darby: *The Islamic Perspective: An Aspect of British Architecture and Design in the 19th Century* (London, 1983) [incl. extensive list of Jones's pubns]

M. Schoeser: *Owen Jones Silks* (London, 1987)

K. Ferry: 'Printing the Alhambra: Owen Jones and Chromolithography', *Archit. Hist.*, xlvi (2003), pp. 175–88

C. A. H. Flores: 'Engaging the Mind's Eye: The Use of Inscriptions in the Architecture of Owen Jones and A. W. N. Pugin', *J. Soc. Archit. Hist.*, lx/2 (June 2001), pp. 158–79

Joubert, François (*fl* 1749–*c.* 1793). French silversmith. His Rococo silver is entirely covered with ribs, scrolls and naturalistic plant ornament. His finest surviving work is a tureen and platter (1761–2; Paris, Louvre).

Joubert, Gilles (*b* Paris, 1689; *d* Paris, 14 Oct 1775). French cabinetmaker. He was a member of a Parisian family of *menuisiers* and became a *maître-ébéniste* sometime between 1714 and 1722. After the death of ANTOINE-ROBERT GAUDREAUS (1751) he became the main supplier to the Crown for 23 years and carried out commissions for 4000 pieces of furniture. In 1758 he became Ébéniste Ordinaire du Garde Meuble and in 1763, on the death of JEAN-FRANÇOIS OEBEN, he became Ébéniste du Roi. Joubert acted to some extent as a main contractor, and when his workshop could not fulfil commissions he subcontracted to such cabinetmakers as MATHIEU CRIARD,

JACQUES DUBOIS, LÉONARD BOUDIN, FRANÇOIS-THOMAS MONDON, ANTOINE FOULLET, and particularly, during his final years of work, to ROGER VANDERCRUSE. Joubert did not sign his furniture; the few pieces that have been attributed to him indicate that he progressed smoothly from the symmetrical Louis XV to the Neo-classical style. This is particularly evident in the red, lacquered writing-table (c. 1759; New York, Met) for Louis XV (reg 1715–74), a formerly lacquered lean-to secrétaire (Louisville, KY, Speed A. Mus.), a pair of clock pedestals (London, Buckingham Pal., Royal Col.) from Louis XV's bedchamber at Versailles and a commode (1769; Malibu, CA, Getty Mus.) made for Princess Louise (1737–87).

F. Watson: 'The Informed Eye: Joubert's Scarlet Lacquer Bureau Plat Made for Louis XV', *Apollo*, cxxx (Nov 1989), pp. 342–3

Jourdain, Francis (b Paris, 2 Nov 1876; d Paris, 31 Dec 1958). French designer, writer and painter, son of the architect Frantz Jourdain (1847–1935). He worked as a painter till 1911, when, inspired by the writings of Adolf Loos (1870–1933), turned to furniture design. In 1912 he opened a small furniture factory, Les Ateliers Modernes, and designed interiors composed of modular wooden furniture for workers; some were sold through the socialist newspaper *L'Humanité*. By 1919 he owned a shop, Chez Francis Jourdain. From 1913 to 1928 he exhibited regularly at the Salon d'Automne and with the Société des Artistes Décorateurs. He was a prolific writer on modern art and aesthetics and published numerous articles in French journals, arguing against the ostentatious luxury that characterized most French design during this period. His interiors include one for an Intellectual Worker (*travailleur intellectuel*), exhibited in the pavilion at the Exposition Internationale in Paris in 1937.

Between 1925 and 1930 Jourdain collaborated with Robert Mallet-Stevens (1886–1945), designing interiors for the architect's villas in the Rue Mallet-Stevens (1927), for the Magasin Bally (1928) and for the offices of the magazine *La Semaine à Paris* (1930). Jourdain's designs were characterized by his concern for simplicity and his preference for uncomplicated construction. He was able to create a sense of spaciousness in the most restricted areas, using his systems of built-in furniture and storage. These were not only functional but also decorative in their lively interplay of geometric forms.

L. Moussinac: *Francis Jourdain* (Geneva, 1955)
A. Fournier: 'Francis Jourdain: Parisien', *Europe*, xlv–xlvi (1968), pp. 320–32
Francis Jourdain (exh. cat. by J. Rollin, Saint-Denis, Mus. A. & Hist., 1976)
A. Despond and S. Tise: *Jourdain* (Paris, 1988)
S. Gonzalez: 'Saint-Denis: Musée d'art et d'histoire', *Rev. Louvre*, xliv (Dec 1995), pp. 138–9 [acquisitions].
A. Barré-Despond and S. Tise: *Jourdain: Frantz—1847–1935, Francis—1876–1958, Frantz-Philippe—1906–1990* (New York, 1991)
Francis Jourdain: Un parcours moderne, 1876–1958 (exh. cat. by D. Collas-Devynck; Albi, Mus. Toulouse-Lautrec; Alès, Mus.-Bib. Pierre-André Benoît; Saint-Denis, Mus. A. & Hist.; and elsewhere; 2000)

E. Vigier: 'Jourdain et la beaute pour tous', *L'Oeil*, dxx (Oct 2000), p. 91
I. de Wavrin: 'A la decouverte de Monsieur Jourdain', *Beaux A. Mag.*, cxcvii (Oct 2000), p. 160

Jouy-en-Josas. *See under* OBERKAMPF, CHRISTOPHE-PHILIPPE.

J. S., Master. *See* SILBER, JONAS.

Jugenstil. *See* ART NOUVEAU.

Juhl, Finn (b Copenhagen, 30 Jan 1912; d 17 May 1989). Danish architect and designer. Juhl's most important work was his distinctly sculptural furniture, which used abstract forms inspired by contemporary art. His 'Pelican' chair (1940), for example, is indebted to the abstract sculptor Hans Arp (1886–1966). In his chairs of the late 1940s, the backs and seats are mounted on a frame—always executed in handsome wood—the individual components sometimes being modelled in soft forms. In 1948 he made the 'Chieftain' chair, which was influended by tribal art. In 1951 he was commissioned by Baker Furniture of GRAND RAPIDS to create a series of 24 pieces (e.g. chairs, tables, desks, storage units) for mass production.

In the early 1950s Juhl was commissioned to design the Trusteeship Council Chamber at the United nations building in New York; the delegates' chairs have his trademark 'floating' backs and seats. Juhl also designed ceramics for BING & GRØNDAHL, glassware for GEORG JENSEN and refrigerators for General Electric.

E. Hiort and F. Juhl: *Finn Juhl: Furniture, Architecture, Applied Art: A Biography* (Copenhagen, 1990)
D. Regis: 'Finn Juhl, his own Home', *ABITARE*, cccxxix (April 1995), pp. 180–89
M. N. de Gary and others: 'Paris: Musée des Arts décoratifs', *Rev. Louvre*, xlvi (Oct 1996), pp. 104–5 [acquisitions]
K. D. Sutton: 'Introduction: Baker Breathes New Life into Finn Juhl's Masterpieces', *Interiors*, clvii (Feb 1998), pp. 28–9

Jungfrauenbecher [Ger.: 'maiden's cup']. Type of silver WAGER-CUP made in late 16th- and 17th-century Germany, mainly in Nuremberg. The cup is shaped like a young woman with a capacious skirt holding a bowl above. A pivot enabled the skirt cup and the bowl to hold liquids simultaneously; the bridegroom drank from the large skirt cup and the bride from the small bowl.

Jun ware. Chinese pottery made in the Song period (960–1279) in Yu xian (Yu County) and Linru, both in Henan Province, and in the Yuan period (1279–1368) in many locations throughout the provinces of Henan, Hebei and Shanxi. Jun have a robust, grey stoneware body and thick, cloudy, curdled blue-green or sky-blue glazes of the lime-alkali type, fired in reduction to about 1280–1300° C. The glazes produce

Jungfrauenbecher in the form of a woman holding a cup over her head, silver, from Germany, 17th century (Ecouen, Musèe de la Renaissance)

pod incense burners, spouted bowls, stem-cups, narcissus bowls, vases, basins, *meiping* and occasionally pillows. Most Yuan-period Jun bowls are characterized by an unglazed, roughly trimmed ring foot showing a coarse chocolate, buff or grey body. The glaze has an orange peel texture and stops short in a thick welt on the outside of the vessel. However, better quality pieces with neatly cut ring foot, fine-textured brown body and smooth, glossy glaze have also been identified. These finer Jun wares are generally taken to have been produced in the earlier part of the period.

One rather peculiar form of Yuan Jun ware is the tripod incense burner with rectangular side handles projecting well above the level of the mouth rim. Incense burners of this kind are sometimes decorated with moulded relief. One typical example (Shanghai Mus.) has two ears, each moulded in the form of a fish, and the vessel body is over-generously decorated with moulded relief chrysanthemum patterns and *taotie* animal-masks. The result is an unduly heavy form, devoid of the elegance of Song-period Jun wares.

W. D. Kingery and others: 'Glaze Structure and its Interaction with Light—An Example of Song Dynasty Jun Ware', *Studio Potter*, xiv (June 1986), pp. 23–6

F. Dongqing: 'Song Dynasty Yaozhou and Jun Wares in the Freer Gallery of Art', *Orient. A.*, xlii (Aug 1996), pp. 24–9

I. C. Hsu: 'The New Jun Porcelain in China', *Cer. Technical*, xii (2001), pp. 44–6

Junzō. *See* SHIBATA ZESHIN.

Ju ware. Type of Chinese stoneware made for the northern Song court in the imperial kilns at Ju Chou (Hunan Province). The kiln that made these wares is known (from a ritual disc in the Percival David Foundation, London) to have opened in 1107; other sources show that it closed in 1127. Only some 40 examples are known to survive (e.g. bottle with copper-bound rim, Percival David Foundation, and bowl in the shape of a lotus flower, National palace Museum, Taiwan). The body of Ju ware is covered with a light blue glaze covered with a crackle known as 'crab-claw marks'. The wares were fired on spurs to enable the glaze to cover the entire vessel; the spurs leave unglazed marks that resemble sesame seeds.

P. David: *A Commentary on Ju Ware* (London, 1937)

Ju Ware of the Sung Dynasty (Kowloon, 1966)

H. Lovell, X. Feng and X. Feng: *Report on the Investigation of Kiln-sites of Ju-type Ware and Chün Ware in Lin-ju hsien, Honan* (London, 1968)

unusual optical effects, resulting from the separation of lime-rich and silica-rich glass in the thick glaze during slow cooling. The tiny spherules of lime-rich glass scatter blue light, producing a strong bluish cast. The patches of lavender purple were achieved by splashing copper oxide in suspension on to the glazed, but unfired, body. The range of shapes included many practical or household vessels similar to those of Cizhou ware.

Although Jun ware was produced in large quantities in the Yuan, the quality of the ware was poorer than in the Song period: the glaze was greyish, rather than the greenish-blue of the Song, and was often marred by brownish smudges owing to the presence of ferruginous impurities. The fundamental character of Jun ware remained unchanged, however, and the use of reduced copper for purple or crimson splashing still prevailed.

The most common forms are bowls with rounded sides and straight or everted rim, plates with flattened rim and globular jars with short, straight necks and loop handles at the shoulder. There are also tri-

K

Kaendler, Johann Joachim. *See* KÄNDLER, JOHANN JOACHIM.

Kåge, Wilhelm. *See under* GUSTAVSBERG CERAMICS FACTORY.

Kähler, Herman August (*b* Næstved, 6 March 1846; *d* Næstved, 16 Nov 1917). Danish ceramic manufacturer. He received his training as an apprentice at the Kähler ceramic factory. The concern had been founded in Næstved in 1839 by his father, Joachim Christian Herman Kähler (1808–84), who was a potter and tiled-stove manufacturer.

In 1872 the concern was divided between Kähler and his brother Carl Frederik Kähler (1850–1930), but the latter withdrew in 1896. Kähler took over the manufacture of tiled stoves and faience and increasingly experimented with glaze and lustre effects. In 1888 Karl Hansen Reistrup (1863–1929) joined the concern as artistic director. Kähler achieved recognition for the factory at the Great Nordic Exhibition of 1888, held at the Industrial Association in Copenhagen. At the Exposition Universelle of 1889 in Paris he received international acclaim when he launched a red-lustre glaze. This was used particularly on Reistrup's sculpturally-formed cast vases, which are characterized by the incorporation of animal heads. In addition Reistrup carried out a number of monumental wall friezes, including *Aegir and his Daughters* (1892; Copenhagen, Rådhus) after a drawing by Lorenz Frølich (untraced). Kähler also manufactured vases decorated in high temperature colours in collaboration with such artists as THORVALD BINDESBØLL.

At the beginning of the 20th century, Kähler's son Herman Hans Christian Kähler (1876–1940) influenced the factory's production by retaining old pottery methods and creating pieces that were hand-moulded and decorated with horn-painting (slip-trailing, using a cow's horn through which liquid clay is applied). These wares were shown at the Exposition Universelle of 1900 in Paris and became widely popular. Later in the 20th century such potters as Svend HAMMERSHØI and Jens Thirslund (1892–1942) contributed to the concern's image. In 1913 the concern was turned into a limited family company; in 1974 it was sold, and its collections went to Næstved Museum.

J. Thirslund: *Kähler-keramik gennem 100 aar* [Kähler ceramics over 100 years] (Copenhagen, 1939)
E. Bülow and N. Hobolth: *Kähler keramik: Fra pottemageri til kunstindustri, 1839–1974* [Kähler ceramics: from pottery to applied art, 1839–1974], Nordjyllands Kstmus. Inf. leaflet, no. 119 (Ålborg, 1982)

Kakiemon ware [*kakiemonde*: 'Kakiemon style']. Japanese porcelain made in the ARITA district of Hizen Province (now Saga Prefect.). Sakaida Kinzaemon (later Kakiemon; 1596–1666) is traditionally credited with making the first porcelain in Japan in 1643 at the family kiln in Nangawara, but recent archaeological excavations have shown that 'Kakiemon' wares were widely produced in the region during the early Edo period (1600–1868). Kakiemon ware is chiefly represented by polychrome overglaze enamels (*iroe*), but it also includes underglaze blue-and-white porcelain (*sometsuke*) and white porcelain (*hakuji*). Polychrome pieces show the harmonious combination of gold with soft reds, blues, yellows, violets and greens over a translucent milky-white body (*negoshide*). Typical forms include plates, bowls, jars, water pitchers, teapots and animal and human figurines. The ware was widely exported, and popular designs, such as quail and millet, tiger and bamboo, deer and maple and bird-and-flower motifs, were imitated by several European manufacturers, most notably by the Meissen potteries during the 18th century.

The Kakiemon family and its kiln are still active. The current head of the family is Sakaida Kakiemon XIV (*b* 1934), who was named a Living National Treasure in 2001 for his overglazed enamel decorative porcelain.

H. Nishida: *Kakiemon* (Tokyo, 1981)

Kaliningrad. The Russian city of Kaliningrad was known until 1945 as Königsberg (Pol. Królewiec), the capital of East Prussia and a centre of ceramics production. In 1772 Johann Eberhard Ludwig Ehrenreich (1722–1803), who had previously worked ar MARIEBERG FACTORY (1759–66) and STRALSUND (1766–70), founded a faience factory in Königsberg, producing blue-and-white wares in the Rococo style. After Ehrenreich's retirement in 1788, the factory made lead-glazed earthenware (usually yellow or purple) until it closed in 1811.

A second Königsberg factory produced imitation WEDGWOOD wares (notably the Collin'sche Kantrelief, a basalt medallion portraying Immanuel Kant (1724–1804), a native of Königsberg). The wares of this factory, which operated from 1775 to 1785, were sometimes marked 'Brüder Collin' or 'Frères Collin'.

Kalo Shop. *See under* ARTS AND CRAFTS MOVEMENT, §4.

Kaltemail [Ger.: 'cold enamel']. Lacquer used as an inexpensive substitute for enamel in 16th- and 17th-century Germany. It could be used when objects were too delicate or too large to be fired (e.g. mirror frames). The polychrome decoration on the armour of Mikołaj Radziwiłł (Vienna, Ksthist. Mus.) is in Kaltemail.

Kalthoff. German family of gunmakers, active in Denmark. Peter Kalthoff, a native of Solingen, worked in Copenhagen from 1646 until his death in 1672, marking guns for the armies of Frederick III and Christian V; Peter's brother Matthias joined him in 1660, and remained in Copenhagen until *c.* 1680. Caspar Kaltoff, another member of the family, moved from Solingen to England in 1654, and worked for the Earl of Worcester until Caspar's death in 1664.

Kambli, **Johann Melchior** (*b* Zurich, 1718; *d* Potsdam, 1783). Swiss cabinetmaker, active in Germany. In 1746 he entered the service of Frederick I in Berlin and Potsdam. In 1752 Kambli established a workshop for bronzes in Potsdam. His furniture is chiefly remarkable for his fine gilt-bronze and silver mounts, and it created a distinctive style in the Rococo furniture of Potsdam. He made bronze decorations and furniture to the designs of JOHANN AUGUST NAHL for the Bronzezimmer in the Berlin Palace (1754–5, destroyed). Together with the SPINDLER brothers he made a splendid commode with luxurious tortoiseshell veneer, mother-of-pearl marquetry and lavish silver-gilt bronze mounts (*c.* 1768; Potsdam, Schloss Sanssouci).

J. Nicht: *Die Möbel im Neuen Palais* (Potsdam, 1980)

Kanashige, **Toyo**. *See under* BIZEN WARE.

Kandler, **Charles (Frederick)** (*fl* 1727–*c.* 1750). English silversmith of German birth. He is known only by a small quantity of elaborate silver, characterized by the use of decoration in high relief and three-dimensional form that has led to the belief that he was related to the renowned German porcelain modeller, JOHANN JOACHIM KÄNDLER. He was first mentioned in the register of the Goldsmiths' Company in London as a 'largeworker' in 1727 in St Martin's Lane, with a partner, James Murray (*d c.* 1730). In 1735 he was recorded as a goldsmith in Jermyn Street near St James's church and used the initials CK or KA as his mark. Another goldsmith named Charles Frederick Kandler, possibly a cousin or nephew, was entered in the register in 1735, located at the same address. He was known as Frederick Kandler and used the initials FK and KA as his mark.

Charles Kandler's works are executed in the French Rococo style, and are influenced by the designs of JUSTE-AURÈLE MEISSONNIER. Kandler's silver tureens, salvers, coffeepots, candlesticks and other wares are enriched with elaborate ornament: naturalistic fruit, flowers, foliage and mythological figures. A silver tea kettle and stand made by Kandler (1727–37; London, V&A) has a handle consisting of two mermaids with twisted tails, while a conch-blowing triton forms the tap-operated spout. The sides are decorated in relief with figures of Neptune and his court, seaweed and shells; on the stand three mermen spring from a base placed on a triangular salver.

Kandler's masterpiece is the massive wine-cooler (1732–5; St Petersburg, Hermitage), made after a design by the antiquary and engraver George Vertue (1684–1756) and a subsequent wax model by Michael Rysbrack (1694–1770). The vast, oval-shaped bowl rests on four chained, crouching leopards or panthers. The two handles are in the form of male and female terms, while on the sides are chased oblong panels that depict putti enjoying Bacchanalian revels. The rocky base is worked with bunches of grapes, frogs, newts and shells. It was sold in a national lottery in 1737 and was rediscovered in Russia in 1880 by an English silver expert among state property confiscated from a member of the Russian royal family. G. R. ELKINGTON & Co. of Birmingham made reproductions of the wine-cooler in electrotype silver plate (examples in London, V&A; New York, Met.) from moulds taken at the Hermitage in 1880–81.

N. M. Penzer: 'The Jerningham-Kandler Wine-Cooler', *Apollo*, cxiv (1956), no. 379, pp. 80–82; no. 380, pp. 111–15
M. A. Rivlin: 'Extreme Anglophilia' [review of *British Art Treasures from Russian Imperial Collections in the Hermitage* (exh. cat. ed. by B. T. Allen and L. Dukelskaya; New Haven, CT, Yale Cent. Brit A.; Toledo, OH, Mus. A.; St Louis, MO, A. Mus; 1996)], *A. & Ant.*, xx (Jan 1997), pp. 88–91

Kändler, **Johann Friedrich**. *See under* ANSBACH.

Kändler [Kaendler], **Johann Joachim** (*b* Fischbach, 15 June 1706; *d* Meissen, 17 May 1775). German sculptor and porcelain modeller. He worked in Dresden with the court sculptor Benjamin Thomae (1662–1751) from 1723 and during this period was involved in the decoration of the Grünes Gewölbe in the castle. In 1730 he was appointed court sculptor by Frederick-Augustus I, Elector of Saxony, and in June 1731 was employed at the Meissen Porcelain Factory as a modeller. Initially he worked with JOHANN GOTTLOB KIRCHNER, and, after his departure in 1733, Kändler became Modellmeister and continued the production of the large, white birds and animals for the Elector's Japanisches Palais in Dresden (e.g. Paduan cockerel, *c.* 1732; Dresden, Porzellansamml.). For the next 40 years Kändler was the dominant figure in the plastic production at Meissen. His role was one of constant conflict with his colleague JOHANN GREGORIUS HÖROLDT, who was in charge of both the painters' studio and the kilns. The battle was fought over the surface of the factory's wares where moulded detail, initially limited to spouts and handles, gradually invaded the surface of the wares thus reducing the flat areas available for the painters to display their skills. The apogee of this style was the 'Schwanenservice' created by Kändler with the assistance of JOHANN FRIEDRICH EBERLEIN between 1737 and 1741 for Heinrich, Graf von Brühl; the entire surface of each piece was moulded with shells, swans and herons, and the coloured decoration was reduced to a very secondary role.

As a result of his work on the large animals for the Japanisches Palais, which, though extraordinary in artistic conception, were difficult to produce and sell, Kändler began production of birds on a smaller and more accessible scale (e.g. cockatoo, 1734; Amsterdam, Rijksmus.). These are characterized by their outstanding observation of nature and their charm and humour. From 1736 he concentrated on the production of small-scale pieces, notably a series of figures and groups of characters from the *commedia dell'arte*. A few figures dealing with this theme had already been made at Meissen before Kändler's arrival, but none was endowed with the originality and humour with which Kändler's creations are charged. They represent one of the major creative achievements of the Late Baroque in Germany and established the appropriate scale for the porcelain figure. In 1744 Kändler and Peter Reinicke produced the first complete series of figures from the *commedia dell'arte* for the Duke of Weissenfels and set the pattern for the numerous series subsequently made by almost all the German factories. Although Kändler continued as Modellmeister until the end of his life, his art was less well suited to the emerging Rococo style, and his output became much less significant. In the charming *Cris de Paris* series of 1755, the style of Reinicke is dominant and Kändler would seem to have only played a minor role.

Kändler was the first of the great porcelain modellers. He was responsible for the establishment of the porcelain figure as a specific art form in its own right, and it is against his achievements that all subsequent figure modelling must be judged.

Y. Adams: *Meissen Figures, 1730–1775: The Kaendler Years* (Atglen, PA, 2001)

Die Arbeitsberichte des Meissener Porzellanmodelleurs Johann Joachim Kaendler 1706–1775 (Leipzig, 2002)

Kantha embroidery. Type of embroidered quilt made by Bengali women for use as bedcovers in their

Johann Joachim Kändler: *Rhinceros*, porcelain, l. 170 mm, made by Meissen, mid-18th century (Paris, Musée du Louvre)

homes or as dowry goods; it is normally dedicated to the father or husband of the maker. The finest *kantha*s are made around Jessore (now in Bangladesh), but a coarser variety known as *sujani* comes from Bihar, and especially the Mithila region, where they bear a strong resemblance to the bold wall paintings with which the women decorate their houses on festive occasions. *Kantha*s are made from worn and discarded clothing. The designs, sewn in coloured thread, include geometric patterns (often similar to those of auspicious floor patterns), mythological subjects and imagery from daily life. Traditional examples have a lotus pattern at the centre. The field is colourfully embroidered with such fertility motifs as fish, the sun, dancing figures and foetus-like shapes of animals or birds. The four corners are decorated with tree-of-life designs. Usually six different borders are stitched around the edges. The entire space in-between is covered with white running stitches to create a wave-like effect.

N. Zaman: *The Art of Kantha Embroidery* (Dhaka, 1981)
M. A. Chen: 'Kantha and Jamdani Revival in Bangladesh', *India Int. Cent. Q.*, xi (1984)
H. Hossain: *Company Weavers of Bengal: 1750–1813* (New Delhi, 1988)
Woven Air: The Muslin and Kantha Tradition of Bangladesh (exh. cat., London, Whitechapel A.G., 1988)
B. Gill: 'Kantha Embroidery Transforms Old Saris', *Fiberarts*, xxvii/4 (Jan–Feb 2001), p. 23

Kaolin [China clay; raslin; white bole]. Primary (or residual) clay that forms a key component of hard-paste porcelain and some other ceramic bodies. It is feldspathic and is predominantly composed of silica, alumina and water. The term 'kaolin' is derived from the Chinese Gaoling (Kao-ling) shan, a hill from which the clay was extracted for use at the nearby kilns of Jingdezhen in Jiangxi Province. The material was first used by the Chinese to produce 'true' porcelains. Kaolin deposits are less common than secondary (or sedimentary) clay deposits. In the 18th century, kaolin deposists were discovered at Aue (used in wares produced by MEISSEN PORCELAIN FACTORY), Passau (used in VIENNA and German factories such as LUDWIGSBURG PORCELAIN FACTORY), Saint-Yrieix, Limousin (used at SÈVRES PORCELAIN FACTORY and Limoges (*see* LIMOGES, §1), St Austell, Cornwall (used initially at PLYMOUTH) and in Unaker, VA (exported to England for use at BOW PORCELAIN FACTORY and WORCESTER). Kaolin's high melting point, expense and need for additives to increase plasticity and lower firing temperatures have rendered it technically unsuitable for unsophisticated earthenwares and stonewares, even where it was available locally.

Karasz. Hungarian family of artist-designers, active in the USA. Mariska Karasz (1898–1960) and her sister Ilonka (1896–1981) moved to the USA in 1913, settling in Greenwich Village, New York. Mariska became an embroiderer whose innovative designs (often exhibited at the Bertha Schaefer Gallery in New York) and accessible writings about embroidery (notably *Adventures in Stitches*, 1949) were responsible for widespread interest in the craft. Ilonka became a designer whose work encompassed ceramics, furniture, textiles, tableware (notably for the Pennsylvania Railroad) and silver. From the 1940s to 1960s she worked as a wallpaper designer. She is best known for those designs and for her 186 covers for *The New Yorker* magazine (1925–73).

M. Karasz: *Adventures in Stitches: A New Art of Embroidery* (New York, 1949, rev. 1960)
'Women Designers in the USA, 1900–2000', *Stud. Dec. A.*, viii/1 (Fall–Winter 2000–01), pp. 4–167 [12 article special issue]
A. Callahan: *Enchanting Modern: Ilonka Karasz* (exh. cat. Athens, Georgia, 2003)

Karatsu. Centre of ceramics production in Japan. High-fired ceramic ware was manufactured from the late 16th century in more than 100 kilns located in and around present-day Karatsu (Kyushu, Hizen Prov., now Saga Prefect.). Geographical and historical circumstances destined Karatsu to be the meeting-place of the advanced ceramic technology of Chosŏn-period (1392–1910) Korea and the sophisticated aesthetics of the Japanese tea ceremony. The region became a centre for the dissemination of both techniques and finished products. The earliest Karatsu kilns, known as the Kishidake group, were built around the fortress of the Hata clan, local daimyo until 1594. Excavations at Handōgame, one of the Kishidake kilns, revealed what is considered to be Japan's first single-vaulted multi-chambered climbing kiln (*waridake noborigama*). Except for a few tea-ceremony wares, its products appear to have been for everyday use, made either on the fast-turning kick wheel or by the distinctive coil-and-paddle (*tataki*) technique. Karatsu clay is sandy in texture with a moderate iron content. The feldspathic glazes—including those formulated with common ash (transparent), straw ash (opaque) and iron (dark-brown-black)—were typical of the ware throughout its history. Most of these techniques can be traced to southern Korea, except for the opaque straw-ash glaze, used at Hobashira, another Kishidake kiln, which is associated with the north.

The second major phase of Karatsu was instigated by the Korean invasions. With Toyotomi Hideyoshi and his official tea master Furuta Oribe in frequent attendance at Nagoya Castle, the campaign headquarters just north-west of Karatsu, enthusiasm for teawares spread among the field commanders. Korean potters were brought to Japan to create fine teawares and also to establish profitable commercial potteries. In 1594 Hata Chikashi (*fl* late 16th century) was replaced by Terasawa Hirotaka (1563–1633), a tea devotee familiar with the new ceramic styles originating in the MINO region under the influence of Furuta Oribe. Under Terasawa's influence, the Matsura kiln group superseded Kishidake, and three new centres were established at Taku, Takeo and Hirado. Although the master potters were Korean, they abandoned the Korean-inspired simple, monochromatic Kishidake styles and emphasized contrasting glazes, underglaze painting and inlay design and the production of sets—mostly in the manner of conscious deformation associated with Furuta Oribe. Only teabowls generally continued to be made in the more modest Korean-derived styles. These early wares are referred to as Old Karatsu (*Kogaratsu*).

The Old Karatsu period ended with the fall of the Terasawa in 1647. By that time porcelain production had begun to surge in the Karatsu region. Workshops unable to locate porcelain clays fell back on making household stonewares, especially in the style of inlay patterning (*mishima*) derived from 15th- and 16th-century Korean *punch'ng* wares. A few stoneware kilns also enjoyed clan sponsorship, beginning with the Terasawa. In 1707 the Doi clan sponsored a new official kiln at Bōzumachi, near modern Karatsu. The traditional style was continued there until 1734, when the kiln was moved to Tōjinmachi, now inside the city itself. Until it closed in 1871, the kiln produced more refined and decorated products to be used as clan gifts and as tableware for formal occasions.

T. Nakazato: *Karatsu*, Famous Ceramics of Japan, ix (Tokyo, 1983)

J. Becker: *Karatsu Ware: A Tradition of Diversity* (Tokyo, 1986)

Kogaratsu [Old Karatsu], Tokyo, Idemitsu Mus. A. cat. (1986)

B. Williams: 'Breaking Ground: Yoshihiro Mizokami Finds New Materials in a New World', *Cer. Mthly*, lii/2 (Feb 2004), pp. 70–71

Karcher [Carchera; Charchera], **Nicolas** [Nicola; Niccola] (*b* ?Brussels; *d* Mantua, 1562). Flemish tapestry weaver. From *c.* 1517 he and his brother Giovanni Karcher (*fl* 1517–62) were working for the Este court in Ferrara, organizing a large workshop for Ercole II d'Este, Duke of Ferrara and Modena. That same year Nicolas went to Brussels and returned with eight weavers, including JAN ROST. Nicolas worked with his brother on the *Battle of the Gods and Giants* (four pieces; destr.), the cartoons of which were by the Dossi brothers, Dosso (*c.* 1486–1541/2) and Battista (*d* 1548), and Giulio Romano (?1499–1546). In 1539, however, Karcher was invited to set up his own workshop in Mantua by Federico II Gonzaga, 5th Marchese and 1st Duke of Mantua, and took ten workers with him to Mantua. In October 1545 Karcher moved to Florence. His workshop first wove a trial *Lamentation* (1546; Florence, Uffizi) and a trial pack-cover (destr.), before a three-year contract was signed by Cosimo I, Duke (later Grand Duke) of Tuscany, on 20 October 1546. Karcher's rival Rost had also established a workshop in Florence at this time, but on 17 November 1550 Karcher's contract was renewed until 21 October 1553. Karcher participated in the weaving of tapestries for the Duke including the *Story of Joseph* series (1546–?53; ten, Florence, Sopr. B.A. & Storici Col., and ten, Rome, Pal. Quirinale), and the *Resurrection* altarpiece (*c.* 1546; Florence, Uffizi) after Francesco Salviati (1510–63), for Benedetto Accolti, Cardinal of Ravenna. In January 1554 Karcher finished his work in Florence and apparently returned to Mantua. On 15 July 1555 Marchese Guglielmo Gonzaga gave

Karcher an eight-year patent to weave in Mantua, with 11 other workers. His workshop's masterpiece from this period is the set of the six *Stories of Moses* with *spalliere* of *Putti with Garlands* (four, Milan, Mus. Duomo; three destr.). Karcher must be ranked high among Europe's most gifted 16th-century tapestry weavers. He favoured juxtaposing bright colours and the use of flamelike hatching.

G. Delmarcel and others: 'Les Jeux d'enfants, tapisseries italiennes et flamandes pour les Gonzague' *Racar*, xv/2 (1988), pp. 109–21

Karlovy Vary [formerly Carlsbad; Karlsbad]. Spa town in the Czech Republic, once a centre of glass engraving and stonecutting. The tradition for engraving was established there in the 18th century by such artists as Andreas Teller (1754–1809) and Andreas Mattoni (1779–1864). In the 19th century well-known engravers included A. H. Pfeiffer (1801–66), Emanuel Hoffmann (1819–78) and his son Johann Hoffmann (1840–1900). The most renowned glass enterprise was the workshop and merchandise business founded in 1857 by Ludwig Moser (1833–1916), who employed a number of leading engravers from Karlovy Vary and northern Bohemia. During the Art Nouveau movement the works excelled in deep, floral engraving, and extended its repertory to include coloured, facet-cut glass. While glass coloured by rare pigments became a speciality, the firm also continued to produce high-quality tableware. From 1918 to 1939 it collaborated with a number of Czech, German and Austrian artists, including Heinrich Hussmann (*b* 1897), Alexander Pfohl (1894–1957) and Hilde Zadikow-Lohsing (*b* 1890). In 1922 the Moser enterprise merged with the Meyr glassworks in Vimperk. In 1936 it was sold, but it continued to use the Moser family name. After World War II it was nationalized. In the late 20th century new designs were provided by such artists as Oldřich Lípa (*b* 1929), Luboš Metelák (*b* 1934), Pavel Hlava (1924–2003) and Jiří Šuhájek (*b* 1943). In 1990 the factory became a joint-stock company. The Moser Glass Museum has a comprehensive collection of the company's products.

J. Hájek: 'Karlovy Vary: Cradle of the Glass of Kings', *Glass Rev.*, xxix (1964), no. 2, pp. 42–6; no. 3, pp. 72–81

L. Baldwin and L. Carno: *Moser Artistry in Glass* (Marratta, 1988)

A. Adlerová: 'The Moser Glassworks at Karlovy Vary', *Glass Rev.*, xlvi/7 (1991), pp. 4–27

Karlsruhe Maiolica Factory. German ceramics factory established in 1901 under the directorship of Wilhelm Süs. Early artists included the painter Hans Thoma (1839–1924); post-war artists included MAX LAEUGER, who began to work for the Majolikamanufaktur in 1921, and Erwin Spuler (1906–64), who began in 1931.

Karlsruhe Majolika (exh cat, Karlsruhe, Bad. Landesmus., 1979)

Kas [Afrik.: *kas*; Dut. *kast*, pl. *kasten*]. Large American cupboard of Dutch origin manufactured in the

Hudson and Delaware areas from the late 17th century to the early 19th. It was a large piece of furniture, sometimes decorated with GRISAILLE panels, and was used for the storage of clothes and (in some cases) dishes.

American Kasten: The Dutch-style Cupboards of New York and New Jersey, 1650–1800 (exh. cat. by P. M. Kenny, F. G.Safford and G. T. Vincent; New York, Met., 1991)

Kashan. *See under* CARPET, §II. 3(III)(C).

Kassel. German centre of ceramics production. In 1680 Charles, Landgrave of Hesse-Kassel, built a faience factory in Kassel for the production of blue-and-white wares, which were influenced by Delftware. It was first directed by Georg Kumpfe; then, in 1694, it was leased to Esaias de Lattré, the first of many leaseholders who were all faced with financial difficulties. Nevertheless, production of faience continued until *c.* 1780. From 1766 to 1788 porcelain was also produced under the manager Baron Waitz. At first the factory produced such wares as tea- and coffee-services, boxes and small baskets; later production included complete table-services, chandeliers and figures. The painting and relief decoration were mainly inspired by the MEISSEN PORCELAIN FACTORY and FÜRSTENBERG PORCELAIN FACTORY.

S. Ducret: *Die Landgräfliche Porzellanmanufaktur Kassel, 1766–1788* (Brunswick, 1960)
Kasseler Porzellan (exh cat, Kassel and Düsseldorf, 1980)

Kastrup. Danish faience factory on the island of Amager, active from 1754 to 1754. The factory took over the moulds of the Copenhagen factory of Blåtårn (1738–54) and produced gaily coloured wares which were in keeping with contemporary demands and imitative of the wares of the Strasbourg faience factories. Kastrup specialized in artichoke- and duck-shaped tureens and dishes shaped like cabbage leaves. They also produced white-glazed busts and sculptural groups after well-known sculptors' works, such as the bust of *Frederick V* by Jacques-François-Joseph Saly (1717–76), *Pluto and Proserpina* by Gianlorenzo Bernini and *Leda and the Swan* by Corneille van Clève (1646–1732). From 1780 to 1781 the factory was taken over for the manufacture of Neoclassical-style stone wares, which had pierced decoration.

J. Ahlefeldt-Laurvig, A.-M. Steimle and J. Erichsen: *Fajencer og stengods fra fabriken i Kastrup* (Copenhagen, 1977)

Kawai, Kanjirō (*b* Shimane Prefect., 24 Aug 1890; *d* Kyoto, 18 Nov 1966). Japanese potter. In 1920 he obtained a climbing kiln (*noborigama*), the Shōkeiyō, with eight chambers, at Gojōzaka in Kyoto. In the following year he made his début with technically skilled works imitating the classical wares of China and Korea, for which he gained immediate prominence. In 1926 with Muneyoshi Yanagi and others he promoted the Mingei ('folk crafts') movement; his own work moved towards the use of simple organic forms influenced by folk crafts. An example of his later work is a diamond-shaped vase with floral design of 1939 (Kyoto, N. Mus. Mod. A.)

After World War II Kawai's dignified forms gave way to rich irregular shapes and, using creative methods such as 'splashed' with multi-colour glazes and 'brushed slip' with cobalt blue and other colours, he constructed a highly original range of forms. He also carved unusual wooden sculptures and wrote extensively. Kawai's former home, together with his own works, his collection of folk crafts, his kiln and other property, were restored and opened in 1973 as 'Kawai Kanjirō's House' in Kyoto.

Y. Uchida and K. Kawai: *We Do Not Work Alone: The Thoughts of Kanjiro Kawai* (Kyoto, 1973)
Kanjiro Kawai: Master of Modern Japanese Ceramics (exh. cat. by M. Hasebe; Tokyo, N. Mus. Mod. A., 1984) [in Jap. and Eng.]
Kawai, Hamada & Japanese Masters (exh. cat., by K. Kawai and S. Hamada; New York, Dai Ichi Gallery, 2003)

Kayser, J. P., & Sohn. German tin and pewter manufacturer, founded in 1862 in Krefeld-Bockum. In 1894 Engelbert Kayser (1840–1911) established a design studio in Cologne to provide designs for the foundry in Krefelt; the studio's designers included Hugo Leven (1874–1956), Karl Geyer (1858–1912) Hermann Fauser (1874–1947) and Karl Berghof (1881–1967). The pewter designs included Art Nouveau and Jugenstil products. Kayser pewter is stamped 'Kayserzinn', and are numbered from 4000 (in 1894–5) to 4999 (in 1925).

Zinn des Jugendstils: Firma J.P. Kayser Sohn, Krefeld aus der Sammlung Giorgio Silzer: Auswahlkatalog (exh. cat., by G. Silzer, H. Blum-Spicker and E. Wagner; Zons, Kreismuseum, 1986)
Kayserzinn Gegenstände und Zinn anderer Giessereien: Sammlung Helmut Hentrich (exh. cat. by S. Barten, Museum für Kunst und Gewerbe Hamburg: Ausstellung vom 4. Oktober bis 17. November 1974)

Keith, James. *See under* NØSTETANGEN GLASSHOUSE.

Kellerthaler [Kellerdahler; Kellerdaller; Kolertal]. German family of goldsmiths, medallists, engravers, draughtsmen and painters. Three generations are documented in Dresden between 1554 and 1662. Johann Kellerthaler I (*b c.* 1530), was a master in Dresden by 1554. His brother Christoph Kellerthaler I (*c.* 1535–1592/1612), a master by 1573, did various works for the Electors Augustus, Christian I and Christian II of Saxony: in the Dresden Frauenkirche, some chains (1572), silver cutlery sets (1584), cups (1588) and a chalice (1598) can tentatively be assigned to him. Christoph took on his three sons as apprentices between 1576 and 1589; these were Johann Kellerthaler II (*c.* 1560–62; *d* 1611), Christoph Kellerthaler II (*fl* 1587–1639) and Daniel Kellerthaler (*c.* 1574–5; *d* Dresden, *c.* 1648). No works can definitely be attributed to Christoph, but Johann II and Daniel both produced important work.

Johann Kellerthaler II's jewellery cabinet (1585, Dresden, Grünes Gewölbe) for the Electoral Princess Sophie of Saxony, made of ebony with silver and silver-gilt plaques showing an extensive range of allegorical images (*Victory of Truth over Vice*), is one of the earliest examples of cupboards as works of art. He also made a fine family altar for Christian II (1608, Dresden, Grünes Gewölbe), in ebony with silver reliefs and cast-silver figures.

Daniel Kellerthaler's signed works include medals of 1601 (*Elector Christian II*), 1608 (*John George I* and his wife *Magdalene Sibylle*), 1609 (*Philipp Julius of Pomerania*) and 1611 (the Electoral Princess Hedwig, in gold and lead). Two later medals record the *Capture of Bautzen* (1620/21) and the Duchess Sophie of Pomerania (after 1620), in gold and enamel. As a goldsmith, Daniel made a trefoil-shaped font for the Wettins (1613/15; Dresden, Schloss Moritzburg) from extraordinarily finely beaten and partly gilded silver, showing the *Circumcision, Presentation in the Temple* and *Baptism of Christ*; in 1617 he made a jug for this font. He also made a fine double-sided bowl with an *Angel of the Annunciation* beaten on the inside and a wave pattern on the outside (1618; Dresden, Kstgewmus. Staatl. Kstsamml.). The Historisches Museum in Dresden has his 1625 silver-and-gold-plated stirrup for Elector John George I. The Grünes Gewölbe contains a beaten, gold-plated relief plaque in an ivory frame (1626) with an *Adoration* derived from a plaque by Giovanni Bernardo da Castelbolognese (*d* 1553); it also has a rosewater basin of 1629, an oval plaque with *Apollo and Marsyas*, distinctly reminiscent of Rudolfine court art, a matching tankard with a *Midas* figure of extraordinary plasticity and a 1629 relief of *St John the Evangelist*. Kellerthaler's large imperial seal of 1637 for John George I (Dresden, Staatsarchv) follows a seal of 1586 but is given a character of its own by his sensitivity for plastic form; the same year he made a seal for the Privy Council. A series of gold-plated copper and silver plaques with engravings, made between 1613 and 1654, are in the Kupferstichkabinett, Dresden. Two examples of his so-called *Bornkinnl*—cherub figures with features of the Child Jesus—have survived in the Grünes Gewölbe.

The son of Christoph Kellerthaler II, Friedrich Kellerthaler (1620–1662/76), was apprenticed to his father (1634–9) and became a master in 1647. Works attributed to him include an austerely designed mortar (Dresden, Grünes Gewölbe), a trophy cup (1662; Nuremberg, Ger. Nmus.) and two chalices decorated with coats of arms (1657, 1658; Dresden, Protestant Hofkirche). A family connection with the Frankfurt am Main goldsmith Hermann Kolertal or Cöllertail (*d* 1518) remains conjectural.

S. Bodnár: 'Some New Drawings by Johann Kellerthaler in Oxford and Munich', *Master Drgs.*, xliii/2 (Summer 2005), pp. 186–92

Kellinghusen. German centre of ceramics production. Kellinghusen is in an area in Holstein with clay suitable for pottery. Six competing faience factories were established: the first opened in 1763 (when Holstein was Danish) and the last closed in 1860 (when Holstein was German). The factories produced similar wares that had a distinctly peasant character with freely painted yellow-and-purple flower decoration.

J. Ahlefeldt-Laurvig: *Fajencer fra Kellinghusen, 1763–1860* (Copenhagen, 1983)

Seltene Fayence aus Schleswig-Holstein: 225 Jahre Kellinghusener Fayence (exh. cat. by B. Roggmann and P. Zubek; Kellinghusen, Mus., 1989)

Kels, Hans. *See under* HEIDELBERGER, THOMAS.

Kelsterbach Porcelain Factory. German ceramics factory. In 1758 a faience factory was founded at Königstädten (near Kelsterbach), Hesse Darmstadt. The factory moved to Kelsterbach in 1760, and the following year was taken over by Landgrave Ludwig VIII, who inaugurated the production of porcelain. The factory's most outstanding modellers were Carl Vogelmann, who arrived from LUDWIGSBURG PORCELAIN FACTORY in 1764, and Peter Anton Seefried, who made figures in the style of FRANZ ANTON BUSTELLI. The factory made porcelain from 1761–8 and from 1799 to 1802. Thereafter it made CREAMWARE until it closed *c.* 1823.

K. Röder: *Das Kelsterbacher Porzellan: Werden und Vergehen einer deutschen Porzellanmanufaktur* (Darmstadt, 1931)

A.-B. Christ: *Kelsterbacher Porzellan* (Stuttgart, 2004)

Kendi. Malay term for a water vessel with a bulbous spout and tall neck with flared rim. *Kendi*s were used throughout South-east Asia, and from the 14th century they were also made in China, most notably at JINGDEZHEN, for export to South-east Asia. The form of the *kendi* was imitated in DELFT in the 17th century.

J. E. Khoo and D. Rooney: *Kendi: Pouring Vessels in the University of Malaya Collection*, Kuala Lumpur, U. Malaya cat. (Singapore and New York, 1991)

S. Adhyatman: *Kendi: Wadah air minum tradisional/Kendi: Traditional Drinking Water Container* (Jakarta, 2004)

Kendrick, George Prentiss. *See under* GRUEBY, WILLIAM HENRY.

Kensington Flint Glass Co. *See* UNION FLINT GLASS CO.

Kent, William (*b* Bridlington, *bapt* 1 Jan 1685; *d* London, 12 April 1748). English architect, painter, landscape gardener and designer. He was the most exuberant and innovative architect and designer active in England in the first half of the 18th century. He was trained as a painter in Italy, where he lived from 1709 to 1719, but was not particularly successful or remarkable in this work, showing greater skill as a draughtsman. As an architect he was highly versatile, practising in both the Palladian and Gothick styles, and this versatility extended to his work as a designer, which included interior decoration, furniture and silverware, book illustration, stage sets and gardens.

On his return to England Kent's first commission in London was for Burlington House, Piccadilly. He painted the ceilings of the Saloon and two other front rooms and also took a pervasive interest in the overall decoration of the house. The success of his work was such that James Brydges, 1st Duke of Chandos, and Sir Richard Childe, Viscount Castlemaine, commissioned ceilings for their country seats at Canons (1720; destr.), Edgware, London, and Wanstead (1721; destr.), Essex. He then began work for George I (reg 1714–27) at Kensington Palace (1721–7), one of the best examples of his style in interior decoration. Kensington was an exceptional commission for so young and untried an artist, and it gives a measure of his charisma and of the impact of his earlier work, as well as the influence of his patrons. The Kensington Palace interiors show how deeply Kent had absorbed the Mannerist style he had studied in Rome and the degree of his commitment to it. The rooms were commissioned piecemeal; first he was employed for the ceiling of the Cupola or Cube Room (completed 1722), then for the ceiling of the King's Great Drawing Room (1723), Privy Chamber (1723), Presence Chamber (1724), the King's Gallery (1725) and the King's Grand Staircase (1727). He succeeded, nevertheless, in creating a scheme that, while varied, retained its cohesion and unity throughout. Indeed, the Grand Staircase was his best achievement in the grand manner of Italian 16th-century illusionist painting. It was also a masterpiece in composition, since it managed to introduce the whole range of decorative motifs previously employed in the other rooms.

The solutions developed at Kensington Palace for ceilings and walls provided the basic elements of Kent's vocabulary for interiors. Walls are divided into two basic categories: those acting as a backdrop for paintings, where attention is concentrated on ceilings, cornices, doorcases and fireplaces (as in the Saloon, 1725, at Houghton Hall; the Blue Velvet Room, c. 1729, at Chiswick House; the Saloon, 1744, at 44 Berkeley Square, London; and the Great Room, 1750, at 22 Arlington Street, London); and those that are receptacles for sculpture. In the latter case the ultimate aim was to recreate an antique tablinum, the main room in the Roman Classical house. Consequently, the treatment of walls is three-dimensional: semicircular niches or aediculae are scooped out, large scroll brackets tacked on to support smaller pieces of sculpture and marble or plaster reliefs encrust them. This approach is exemplified by the Cube Room (1723) at Kensington Palace, the Marble Hall (1725) at Houghton, the Gallery and Rotunda (c. 1730) at Chiswick and the Dining-room (c. 1740) at Holkham Hall. Where financial resources or physical conditions prohibited real sculpture, it was replaced by imitations in paint, as, for example, on the walls of the Grand Staircase (1727) at Kensington Palace, the staircase walls at Houghton (1726) and

those at Raynham Hall (c. 1727), Norfolk. The way in which such sculpture, whether real or painted in chiaroscuro, was assembled by Kent was based upon Roman Mannerist examples he knew well, such as the façades of the Villa Medici, Palazzo Branconio dell'Aquila (destr.) and the Casino of Pius IV in the Vatican gardens. This organization of the wall surfaces reinforces the idea conveyed by the exterior of Kent's buildings: a solid and continuous wall mass.

Kent's rich treatment of rooms was reinforced by the furniture he designed; this was made for him by leading English cabinetmakers, principally JAMES MOORE and BENJAMIN GOODISON. Kent was the first British architect to conceive of a building as an integral unity in which furniture demanded equal attention. His furniture was to some extent influenced by Florentine precedent, but it was the Roman school that more powerfully moulded his taste. From their work Kent learnt to mould wood into scrolls, conchs, sea-horses, dolphins, eagles, ostrich legs, palm branches and merfolk. His flamboyancy in furniture design surprised an English public used to great simplicity in designs and materials, but it became immediately fashionable and led to Kent's court appointment (1726) as Master Carpenter in the Office of Works and to widespread imitation of his style. This was helped by publication in 1744 of John Vardy's *Some Designs of Mr Inigo Jones and Mr William Kent*. The furniture Kent designed included pier and console tables, settees and chairs, with rare forays into exceptional pieces such as mirror frames (for Frederick, Prince of Wales, and for Henry Somerset, 3rd Duke of Beaufort, at Worcester Lodge, Glos), a

William Kent: Console table, carved and gilded wood with marble top, 889×686×445 mm, executed by John Boson, commissioned by the Earl of Burlington for Chiswick House, London, 1727–32 (London, Victoria and Albert Museum)

state bed for Sir Robert Walpole at Houghton (based on Schor's state bed made by Johann Paul Schor (1615–74) for Maria Mancini Colonna), an organ case and the extraordinary royal barge, loosely based on the Venetian Doge's state barge (the *Bucentaur*) and the state galley of the Grand Duke of Tuscany.

Kent's furniture was usually made of wood—white-painted pine, or mahogany—either partly gilded or of gilded gesso. Settees and chairs had frames of the same materials, and they were upholstered in cut-Genoa velvet or damask in bright colours to complement wall hangings. The aprons of console tables and settees often included anthropomorphic or naturalistic elements from the coats of arms of his patrons. These emblematic elements also appeared in the designs of picture frames. An excellent example of Kent's attention to the overall design of a room is provided by Lady Burlington's Summer Parlour, Chiswick, for which he designed the so-called 'Owl Suite' (now at Chatsworth, Derbys); owls from the Savile coat of arms decorate the pier-glasses and console tables as well as appearing in paint in the ceiling.

ODNB
J. Vardy: *Some Designs of Mr Inigo Jones and Mr William Kent* (London, 1744)
G. Beard: 'William Kent and the Royal Barge', *Burl. Mag.*, cxii (1970), p. 488
G. Beard: 'William Kent and the Cabinet Makers', *Burl. Mag.*, cxvii (1975), p. 867
P. Campbell ed.: *A House in Town: 22 Arlington Street, Its Owners and Builders* (London, 1984)
M. I. Wilson: *William Kent: Architect, Designer, Painter, Gardener* (London, 1984)
A Tercentenary Tribute to William Kent (exh. cat., ed. J. Wilton-Ely; Hull, Ferens A.G., 1985)
C. M. Sicca: 'A Kent Drawing for the Ceiling of the King's Drawing Room at Kensington Palace', *Apollo*, cxxii (1985), p. 310
C. M. Sicca: 'On William Kent's Roman Sources', *Archit. Hist.*, xxix (1986), pp. 134–57
William Kent 1685–1748: A Poet on Paper (exh. cat. by J. Harris; London, Soane Mus., 1998)
J. Vardy: *Some Designs of Mr. Inigo Jones and Mr. Wm. Kent* (Witney, 2003)
G. Beard: 'Kentian Furniture by James Richards and Others', *Apollo*, xdxci (Jan 2003), pp. 37–41

Kenzan. *See* OGATA KENZAN.

Kestgen. *See* KNÜTGEN.

Kettle stand. Stand used in late 17th and 18th centuries as part of the apparatus for drinking tea. It consisted of a small table with a raised or galleried edge fitted with an aperture for the spout of the urn or kettle and a sliding shelf that could be extended to support a teapot.

Key of life. *See* ANKH.

Kholmogory. Russian village and centre of bone-carving production, a craft that also developed in neighbouring villages. A port on the Severnaya Dvina River, 75 km south of Arkhangel'sk, Kholmogory was a key trading village in the 14th century for the merchants of Novgorod; in the 15th and 16th centuries it was a major commercial centre through which the English Muscovy Co. conducted its trade. The origins of Kholmogory bone-carving go back to the Neolithic period. Caskets, boxes, snuff-boxes, combs, small furniture pieces and other items were made mostly from walrus tusks and fossil mammoth bones. Delicate ornament is combined with figures in relief, engraved lines and layers of coloured foil inserted into the object. One of the most important characteristics of Kholmogory bone-carving is its close stylistic link to Russian folk wood-carving. In 1930 the School of Bone-carving was founded in the village of Lomonosovo, and gave a new impetus to the development of the craft. The M. V. Lomonosov Artistic Carving Factory of Kholmogory produces a wide range of goods that continue to exhibit folk styles. Examples of work from Kholmogory are displayed in the factory and in the Regional Museum of Fine Arts, Arkhangel'sk. A fine carved cabinet bureau dating from the second half of the 18th century is held in the Russian Museum, St Petersburg.

V. M. Vasilenko: *Severnaia reznaia kost' (Kholmogory)* (Moscow, 1936)
Kholmogorskaia rez'ba po kosti kontsa XVII-XX vekov (exh. cat. by N. V. Taranovskaia, Arkhangel'sk, Reg. Mus. F.A., 1984)

Kick. Indentation in the base of a glass bottle, diminishing the internal capacity.

Kidderminster. English centre of carpet production. By the end of the 16th century, if not earlier, weavers in the English town of Kidderminster (Hereford & Worcs) were producing a strong, woollen cloth that served as an inexpensive floor covering and was commonly known as Kidderminster or Scotch carpeting. In 1735 a Mr Pearsall drew together individual weavers, establishing the first factory devoted to the production of double-cloth floor covering in Kidderminster; within a few years several other factories had also been established. In 1749 a weaver was brought from Belgium to build Brussels looms, thus breaking WILTON's monopoly of the Brussels carpet (*see* CARPET, §I, 5). Brussels carpets, together with Wilton carpets, soon became the main products of Kidderminster, outselling the traditional flat-weave coverings. In 1812 Thomas Lea patented a technique for weaving a triple-cloth floor covering which, though popular, was still inferior to pile carpets in durability. In 1825 Messrs Lea, Broom & Sons were the first to introduce jacquard montures in the production of carpets, but it remained essentially a hand-loom industry and suffered badly during the 1840s and 1850s when in competition with HALIFAX. Kidderminster manufacturers continued to introduce modern technology. Tomkinsons Ltd (est. 1869) was the first factory in England to apply power to looms weaving chenille carpets, originally known as Patent Axminsters. In 1878 the firm began to manufacture a machine-tufted carpet known as

Royal Axminster, using spool looms invented in the USA. Kidderminster was revitalized by the introduction of these looms and the improved gripper looms in 1893. Its Royal Axminsters are generally considered to be the best of machine-made carpets. In the 20th century Kidderminster manufacturers absorbed many previously independent firms from other towns, and it remains an important centre of carpet production.

L. Smith: *Carpet Weavers and Carpet Masters: The Hand Loom Carpet Weavers of Kidderminster, 1780–1850* (Kidderminster, 1986)

A. E. Ledes: 'A Rich Carpet Resource', *Mag. Ant.*, clii (Sept 1997), p. 388 [Woodward Grosvenor and Company Archives, Kidderminster]

M. Thompson: *Woven in Kidderminster: An Illustrated History of the Carpet Industry in the Kidderminster Area including Stourport, Bridgnorth and Bewdley: 1735–2000* (Kidderminster, 2002)

N. Gilbert: *A History of Kidderminster* (Chichester, 2004)

Kiel Pottery. In 1758 a faience factory was established in Kiel (Holstein, then controlled by Denmark) by the duke of Holstein. The factory specialized in stately pot-pourri vases painted in enamel colours, one example of which (1770; London, V&A) is decorated with a scene from Molière's play *L'Amour médecin* painted by ABRAHAM LEIHAMER. The factory closed in 1787.

K. Hüseler: *Die Kieler Fayence-Manufacturen* (Flensburg, 1923)

E. Schlee: *Kieler Fayencen* (Flensburg, 1966)

Kiesler, **Frederick (John)** (*b* Vienna, 22 Sept 1890; *d* New York, 27 Dec 1965). Austrian-American architect, stage designer and writer. In 1920 he worked with ADOLF LOOS in Vienna. He was also in contact with the artists associated with De Stijl and began experimenting with innovative theatre designs. In 1924 he produced the Endless Theatre design. The 'Endless' was a double-curved shell of reinforced concrete that could enclose any irregularly traditional divisions into floor, wall and ceiling but offered the inhabitant an open interior that could be modified at will. For the theatre he adapted the 'Endless' by devising a double-spiral stage interconnected by ramps and rings of spectator seats. Kiesler believed that the Endless Theatre, without proscenium or curtain, projecting out into the audience, with perpetually moving walls bathed in light of ever changing colour, would promote greater interaction between actors and audience.

In 1926 Kiesler emigrated to the USA, where his preoccupation with the endless culminated in his model of his Endless House, which was exhibited at MOMA (1959–60). His furniture designs, like his house, eschewed right angles; his tables, for example, had irregularly curved tops. His furniture for Peggy Guggenheim's Art of this Century Gallery in New York (1942) included a rocking chair designed to be turned on its side for use as a pedestal. Kiesler's last designs included the Venetian Theater ('Caramoor'; 1958), Katonah, New York, the hospital section (1959) of Albert Einstein Medical Center, New York, and the Shrine of the Book (1959–65; with Armand Bartos), Hebrew University, Jerusalem.

L. Phillips and D. Bogner: *Frederick Kiesler* (New York, 1989)

Frederick J. Kiesler: Endless Space (exh. cat. by F. Kiesler, D. Bogner and P. Noever; Los Angeles, CA, MAK Cent. A. & Archit., 2000–01)

Friedrich Kiesler: Art of This Century (exh. cat. by F. Kiesler; Frankfurt am Main, Mus. Mod. Kst, 2002–3)

Frederick Kiesler: The Late Work Us, You, Me (exh. cat. by G. Luyken; Southampton, NY, Parrish A. Mus., 2003)

T. Beyerle: *Friedrich Kiesler, Designer: Seating Furniture of the 30's and 40's* (Ostfildern-Ruit, Hatje Cantz, Portchester, 2005)

Frederick Kiesler: multi-use chair, oak and linoleum, h. 850 mm, 1942 (New York, Museum of Modern Art)

S. Davidson, P. Rylands and J. Sharp: *Peggy Guggenheim & Frederick Kiesler: The Story of Art of This Century* (Ostfildern-Ruit, Hatje Cantz, Portchester, 2005)

Kievo-Mezhgorskaya Pottery Factory. Pottery factory near Kiev (eastern Ukraine, then part of the Russian empire) established in 1801 and brought under imperial management in 1822 as the earthenware producer complementing the ST PETERSBURG PORCELAIN FACTORY. The Kievo-Mezhgorskaya factory produced a particularly fine range of earthenwares decorated with relief ornaments and thick, lead glazes.

Kilim [Arab. *kilim, klim*; Pers. *gilim*; Turk. *kilim*]. Flat-woven covering or hanging, usually a weft-faced tapestry-woven rug, produced in the Islamic lands of western Central Asia, the Middle East, the Balkans and North Africa. These non-pile fabrics are often divided into groups known by such terms as *jijim* (*cicim, djidjim, jimjim*), *zilu* (*sileh, silé, zilé, sillè*) and *verneh* (*vernè*), but these terms may represent various techniques or combinations including tapestry, compound-weaving, brocading and embroidery, or may have limited geographical currency. The divergence between terminology (whether in European or local languages) of the deduced techniques of manufacture (e.g. 'sumak brocading') and the observed description of structure (e.g. weft wrapping) has led to widespread confusion in nomenclature. Scholars and dealers have also divided these pieces into such regional groups as Turkish, Caucasian and Persian, and these have been further subdivided by locality or tribe.

Flat-woven fabrics were used for animal trappings (including saddle-bags and covers), sacks, floor coverings, furnishings (including tent fittings, door covers, blankets, and covers for bolsters, pillows and hearth cushions), as well as belts, shawls and funeral shrouds. Most were produced in nomadic or village settings on horizontal or vertical looms. The fabrics range from 2 to 5 m in length and from 1 to 2 m in width. Some are composed of two narrow strips woven in mirror image and sewn together lengthwise. In comparison to pile carpets, which have long been appreciated in the West, the long and narrow proportions and networks of open slits made most flat-woven fabrics unsuitable for Western domestic settings, and they have been collected seriously and studied only since the late 1960s.

Wool is most commonly used for both warp and weft, but other materials, such as camel and goat hair, are sometimes found. Cotton was used for warps in pieces produced in north-west Iran. In Fars province and the Caucasus, undyed cotton was used for white areas in the design, and in Tunisia the resistance of cotton to certain dyes made it suitable for white motifs on pieces that were dyed after weaving. Silk and metallic threads are found in a few Iranian pieces from the 16th and 17th centuries. Flat-woven pieces vary widely in fineness. For example, the Senna

Kilim, from Turkey

group produced in north-west Iran has as many as 110 warps and 450 wefts per decimetre, while those produced in western Anatolia are much coarser, having only 30 warps and 110 wefts per decimetre. Warp ends may be tied, fringed, braided or looped, and the treatment often provides a clue to provenance. Colours are generally bright and bold, and dyes were traditionally made from plant materials available locally. Madder, for example, was very popular in the few Turkoman pieces known. Designs are angular and based on such geometric shapes as stripes, lozenges and diamonds, which are generated readily by the weaving technique. Some designs are specific to certain locations or social groups, and flat-woven pieces often resemble in colour or design pile rugs from the same localities, but the nomadic life of their makers often meant that similar designs could be produced in different regions. Because of their traditional nature, designs changed slowly, and many motifs may be interpreted symbolically.

Kilims may be decorated in innumerable ways. The field may stand alone or be surrounded by borders and guard bands, and have skirts and fringes at either end. The field may be left plain, divided into horizontal, vertical or diagonal bands, organized on a diamond or rectangular grid, filled with a hexagonal design or concentric rectangles, or combine virtually any of these elements. One of the most distinctive designs is an arch, commonly interpreted as a mihrab or prayer niche. Smaller pieces usually have one arch, but larger pieces with multiple arches arranged transversally are also known (e.g. Istanbul, Vakıflar Kilim and Flat-Woven Rug Mus). Flatweaves with an arch design were made almost exclusively in Turkey, except for the small group of finely woven pieces attributed to Senna (Sanandaj) in Kurdistan.

Most surviving kilims were made in the 19th century or later, but the history of flatweaves can be traced from a few earlier examples or fragments. Tapestry-woven woollen fragments excavated at Fustat (Old Cairo) in Egypt and dated from the 8th to the 10th century have geometric designs similar to those found on later kilims. Kilims are commonly identified with the presence of Islam and nomadism in the Middle East, but the technical mastery and sophisticated design of these earliest surviving fragments suggest that flat-weaving techniques had a long tradition in the region. Approximately 40 pieces woven of silk and metallic thread have been ascribed to Iran in the 16th and 17th centuries. They are decorated in the Safavid style with figural representations, hunting scenes, arabesques and complex floral designs typical of contemporary Polonaise pile carpets. These kilims are traditionally attributed to the city of Kashan in central Iran, but their variety suggests that they were produced in several centres.

The pieces most commonly known as kilims are woven in wool in a double-sided tapestry or weft-faced plain weave. In most examples, discontinuous wefts result in vertical slits (25 mm maximum) between the colours, and for some scholars the term kilim is restricted to such fabrics. These slits are not sewn after weaving, as in European pictorial tapestry hangings, so the fabric is weakened, and various other techniques were devised to join colour areas. In some examples, particularly those produced in central and south-west Iran, the discontinuous wefts of adjacent colour areas return around a common warp to produce a single interlocking tapestry weave. Double interlocking is found in pieces made by the Bakhtiari nomads of Iran. Wefts were looped in the flatweaves produced at Gafsa in Tunisia. Extra wefts were sometimes inserted in a wedge-like fashion to correct a sloping weft line caused by uneven weaving or wool of varying thickness, and this technique was expanded for curvilinear designs, particularly in the Balkans.

Another large group of flatweaves is characterized by the use of compound weaves, of which the most common is sumak (soumak, summak, sumaq, sumakh). The name may derive from Shemaka, a town in the south-east Caucasus, but these weft-wrapped textiles were also produced in Iran, Turkestan and possibly Kurdistan and Anatolia. Sumak weave is also used in Moroccan textiles for transverse rows of one colour. Sumak is a particular type of progressive weft wrapping, also known as weft-float brocading. The sequence of progressive wrapping of warp by weft is consistently forward over and back under, with a usual span ratio of 2:1. The result is a slightly oblique stitch, rows of which produce a distinct pattern. A few pieces show no ground weave between

the wrapping wefts and may properly be called sumak wrapped. In most pieces, however, sumak wefts are supplementary to ground wefts and are usually discontinuous, giving rise to the term sumak brocading. Progressive weft wrapping is also used to outline colour areas of tapestry weave or to form decorative bands. Another large group of compound flatweaves are brocaded flatweaves, in which supplementary pattern wefts are introduced. Many other compound weaves were used for the flat-woven textiles of the Islamic world. In embroidered flatweaves, decoration was added after the textile was woven, but the result, for example stem-stitch embroidery, can often be confused with brocading. They were produced throughout the region.

Y. Petsopoulos: *Kilims* (New York, 1979)
B. Balpınar and U. Hirsch: *Flatweaves of the Vakıflar Museum Istanbul* (Wesel, 1982)
B. Balpınar Acar: *Kilim–Cicim–Zili–Sumak: Turkish Flatweaves* (Istanbul, 1983)
D. Valcarenghi: *Kilim: History and Symbols* (Milan and New York, 1994)
S. Gomersall and B. M. Waters: *Kilim Rugs: Tribal Tales in Wool* (Atglen, PA, 2000)
E. Hilliard: *The Kilim and Tribal Rug Book* (London, 2000)
A. Hull and J. Luczyc-Wyhowska: *Kilim: The Complete Guide: History, Pattern, Technique, Identification* (London, 2005)
G. Blazek: 'Earth and Moon: Kilims from the Ourika Valley', *Hali*, cxxxix (March–April 2005), pp. 62–7

Kincob. Rich Indian fabric, embroidered with gold or silver.

King's pattern. In Regency and Victorian silver cutlery, a pattern for forks and spoons; the decoration consists of a shell at the base of a shaped stem and another on the waisted top. The smaller Queen's pattern has only one shell motif.

Kinrande. *See under* LACQUER, §1(VIII).

Kinuta. *See under* CELADON.

Kirchner, Johann Gottlob (*b* Merseburg, 23 Nov 1706; *d* ?Berlin, after 1738). German sculptor and porcelain modeller. He was the brother and probably pupil of the Dresden court sculptor Johann Christian Kirchner (1681–1732). On 24 March 1727 he was employed at the Meissen Porcelain Factory as Modellmeister and was responsible for the design of tablewares. His most important achievement was the creation of the large, white animals and birds for the Japanisches Palais in Dresden of Frederick-Augustus I, Elector of Saxony. In this venture he was joined by JOHANN JOACHIM KÄNDLER in June 1731. Kirchner's animals were static, anthropomorphic and derived more from printed images than from actual observation of nature. This is exemplified by his rhinoceros (possibly derived from an engraving by Albrecht Dürer (1471–1528) and his elephant (1731; Dresden, Porzellansamml.), which bear scant resem-

Johann Gottlob Kirchner (attrib.): porcelain clock, made by Meissen, 1730 (Washington, DC, Smithsonian Institution)

blance to the actual animals. Kirchner was a difficult employee and colleague and he left Meissen in 1733. He was briefly employed there again in 1738 and appears to have ended his career in Berlin.

C. Le Corbeiller: 'German Porcelain of the Eighteenth Century', *Met. Mus. A. Bull.*, xlvii (Spring 1990), pp. 1–56
A. E. Ledes: 'Meissen for Royalty', *Mag. Ant.*, clx/1 (July 2001), pp. 22–4 [A royal menagerie: porcelain animals from Dresden at the J. Paul Getty Museum]

Kirk, Samuel, & Son. American silver company established by Samuel Kirk (1793–1872), a silversmith from Philadelphia, in Baltimore in 1815. Kirk formed a partnership with a silversmith called John Smith; the partnership was dissolved in 1821, and Kirk ran the business himself until 1846, when he took his son Henry Child Kirk (1826–1914) into partnership. In 1914 the company passed to a Board of trustees, but in 1924 management passed to Henry Child Kirk Jr (1868–1932), who was in turn succeeded by his nephew Martin Laurence Millspaugh (1884–1964) and Millspaugh's son Samuel Kirk Millspaugh (*b* 1930), who ran the company until it was taken over in 1979 by the Stieff Company (a Baltimore silver and pewter manufacturer founded

in 1892), which was renamed as the Kirk Stieff Company. Production at the Baltimore factory ended in 1999, and production Kirk Stieff silver is now outsourced The archives of Samuel Kirk & Son (from 1834 to 1979) were given to the Maryland Historical Society. From 1928 the firm specialized in REPOUSSÉ work, which in its distinctive Baltimore idiom featured landscape vignettes and flowers. The terms 'Baltimore silver' and 'Baltimore repoussé' were for decades synonymous with the silver of Kirk & Son, but is also used to denote silver of a similar style produced elsewhere.

Kirk Silver in United States Museums (exh. cat., Baltimore, MD, Samuel Kirk & Son, 1967)
Samuel Kirk and Son, American Silver Craftsmen Since 1815: A Traveling Exhibit (exh. cat., Baltimore, MD, Samuel Kirk & Son, 1971)
J. F. Goldsborough: *Eighteenth and Nineteenth Century Maryland Silver in the Collection of the Baltimore Museum of Art* (Baltimore, 1975)
Silver in Maryland (exh. cat. by J. F. Goldsborough; Baltimore, Hist. Soc. Mus., 1983)
Samuel Kirk & Son, Co., Baltimore, Md.: 1914 Catalog Reproduction, Samuel Kirk & Son (Baltimore, 1994)

Kirkaldy. *See under* WEMYSS WARE.

Kitaōji, **Rosanjin** [Fusajirō] (*b* Kyoto, 23 March 1883; *d* Kanagawa, 21 Dec 1959). Japanese potter, calligrapher and medallist. He became a commercial calligrapher and medallist, and in 1915 had his first experience of decorating pottery at a kiln in the district of Hokuriku. In 1919 he opened an art shop in Tokyo, and soon began to produce his own pottery, creating forms drawn from studying the vessels that he used for his cuisine. In 1925 he opened the Gourmet's Club Hoshigaoka Restaurant in Tokyo. In 1926 he established a studio and kiln known as Hoshigaokayō in Kita Kamakura. He often surpassed the classical forms on which his works were based, becoming well known for his simple but original designs. He used red enamels and gold in his work and was influenced by blue-and-white wares and coloured porcelain from the Ming period (1368–44) as well as Japanese Mino, Shigaraki, Bizen and Kutani ceramics. In addition to his ceramics (e.g. porcelain dish with enamel decoration, 1950; Kyoto, N. Mus. Mod. A.), he was skilled in calligraphy (e.g. screen, Japanese syllabary design, 1952; Okayama, Korakuen garden) and lacquerware.

Rosanjin: Twentieth Century Master Potter of Japan (exh. cat., New York, Japan House Gal., 1972)

Kitschelt, **August** (*fl* Vienna, 1835–*c*. 1871). Austrian furniture-maker. In 1835 he founded a metal-furniture factory in Vienna; its products extended from garden and park furniture to drawing-room furniture and ornamental figures in the Rococo Revival style. At the Great Exhibition of 1851 in London, Kitschelt, along with Michael Thonet and Carl Leistler, represented the Vienna furniture industry, showing seats, tables and ornamental vases with floral decoration. At the Exposition Universelle of 1867 in Paris Kitschelt showed a four-poster bed and a suite designed by the architect Josef von Storck (1830–1902). In 1871 Kitschelt exhibited leather-upholstered seats in classical forms, designed by Rudolf Bernt (1844–1914), at the Österreichisches Museum für Kunst und Industrie, Vienna. Thereafter Kitschelt's successors concentrated on the production of utility furniture made of tubular steel or moulded metal, portable furniture, tubular steel beds, ladders and garden tents.

E. B. Ottillinger: 'August Kitschelt's Metal Furniture Factory in the Nineteenth Century', *Furn. Hist.*, xxv (1989), pp. 235–49

Kjærholm, Poul (*b* 1929; *d* 1980). Danish furniture designer. He designed frame chairs that evoke the notion of the Neo-antique, and also worked in a restrictive idiom in which simple themes are constantly varied. He supplemented wood with steel and can be seen as a Danish exponent of LUDWIG MIES VAN DER ROHE's Minimalism, which reached Denmark after World War II. Kjærholm deprecated the craft tradition of Danish furniture, choosing instead to design exclusively for mass production, but the scrupulous detail of his furniture often gives the impression that it is made by hand. His best-known work is the chromed steel and leather chair that first appeared in 1951 and eventually evolved into the popular 'PK 22'.

C. Harland and others: *Poul Kjærholm* (n.p., 2001)
P. E. Tøjner: *Poul Kjærholm* (Denmark, 2003)

Klášterec nad Ohří Porcelain Factory. Factory in the Czech city known to pottery specialists by its German name, Klösterle. The factory was founded in 1794. Its tablewares were decorated flower motifs, initials, hunting scenes, allegories and landscapes. The factory is still in business.

Klinger, Johann Gottfried (*b* 1711; *d* 1781). German porcelain painter. He worked at MEISSEN PORCELAIN FACTORY from 1726 to 1746, using the illustrations in ornithological, entomological and botanical books as the patterns for his scrupulous paintings; he is particularly associated with the technique of using shadows beside his pictures of birds, insects and plants to achieve a trompe l'œil effect. In 1746 Klinger moved to the VIENNA Porcelain Factory, where he worked for the rest of his career.

Klint, Kaare (Jensen) (*b* Frederiksberg, Vartov, 15 Dec 1888; *d* Copenhagen, 28 March 1954). Danish furniture designer, architect and teacher. Klint was trained as a painter and architect, and made his début in furniture design with furniture for the Museum for Fynsk Malerkunst in Fåborg (1914). During a stay in Java (1914–16) he made contact with a firm of Chinese cabinetmakers who made furniture to his designs. A dining-room design of 1916 for Povl Baumann's house, Gl. Vartovvej 16, Copenhagen, and the interior design (1916–18; with Carl Petersen (1871–1923)) of the Dansk Kunsthandel at Vin-

gårdsstræde 21, Copenhagen, show how he strove to achieve the classical mastery of line and form and East Asiatic colours and textural effects. The furniture of Chinese and English cabinetmakers inspired such designs as the 'Red' chair (1927) and the 'Safari' chair and 'Deckchair' (both 1933).

R. Andersen: *Kaare Klint møbler* (Copenhagen, 1979)
K. Zahle, F. Monies and J. H. Christiansen: *De gamle mestre: Carl Petersen, Ivar Bentsen, Kaj Gottlob, Kaare Klint, Kay Fisker* (Denmark, 2000)

Klismos. *See under* CHAIR, §2.

Klönne, Eduard. *See* COLONNA, EDOUARD.

Klösterle Porcelain Factory. *See* KLÁŠTEREC NAD OHŘÍ.

Kloster-Veilsdorf. *See under* THURINGIA.

Knee-hole. Hole or space between the pedestal drawers of a desk or dressing-table, to receive the knees and enable one to sit close up to it

Knibb, Joseph (*b* Claydon, Oxon, 1640; *d* Hanslope, Oxon, 1711). English clockmaker. He established a workshop in Oxford *c.* 1660 and in 1670 moved to London, where he made clocks until his retirement in 1694. His long clock cases were mainly constructed of walnut veneer (on oak) or of olive wood, with floral MARQUETRY and parquetry; his bracket clock cases were mounted with silver. His turret clocks include those for Wadham College, Oxford (the movement was replaced in 1870, and is now in the Museum of the History of Science in Oxford) and the state entrance of Windsor Castle.

Knife box. Lidded wooden box fitted on the inside with slots in which knives could be stored pointdown. Eighteenth-century English and American examples are made with fine wood, and have flat sides and a sloping lid (e.g. Monticello, VA, Jefferson Found.) or are shaped like urns (the shape used by ROBERT ADAM).

Knitting. Technique for producing fabric that consists solely of parallel courses of yarn, with each course looped into the bights of the courses above and below, the loops being either closed (crossed) or open. Knitting (more correctly, weft knitting) is thus distinguished from other single-element fabrics, such as CROCHET, where loops are meshed laterally as well as vertically; and from NETTING, which is meshed by knots, requiring the end of the yarn to be drawn through the loops.

The earliest method of knitting was nalbinding, which used short lengths of yarn and a single eyed needle to produce a fabric of closed loops. Silk braids

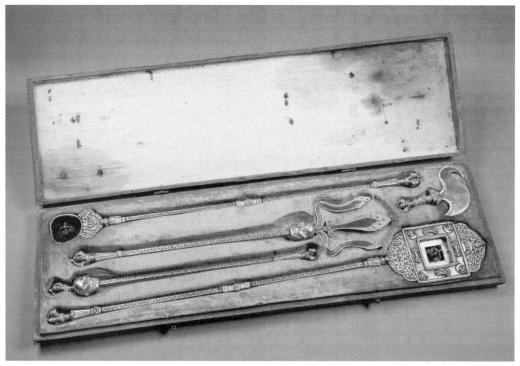

Knife box containing implements for the fire-offering ceremony, wood and velvet, l. 940 mm, Bhutan (Paro, National Museum of Bhutan)

made by this method, using complex stitch structures unknown in southern Europe, were applied decoratively to clothing in China as early as the 3rd century BC. Fragments of knitted fabrics from Dura Europos, Syria (New Haven, CT, Yale U. A.G.), date from the 3rd century AD, and sandal-socks from Roman Upper Egypt (Leicester, Jewry Wall Mus.; London, V&A; Paris, Louvre; Toronto, Royal Ont. Mus.) from the 5th–6th century AD. These examples were made by nalbinding, which was also used in Pre-Columbian Peru to make cotton or wool cords for decorating the edges of garments. It is not clear how true open-loop knitting developed, nor whether this was first done with hooked rods, plain rods or peg-frames. In the early 21st century hooked rods are found in Portugal, Greece, Turkey and Central America. Peg-frames, used in Germany in the 16th century, are still to be found in Mexico and are used as toys in western Europe, although their history has not been studied. Since the 16th century plain rods, known as needles, pins or wires, have been the usual knitting tools in western and northern Europe. Most were made of steel, although bone, wood, ivory and other materials have been used since the 18th century.

Examples of knitting from medieval times with multicoloured patterns survive in Spain (e.g. cushions, 13th century; Burgos, Real Monasterio de las Huelgas, Mus. Telas & Preseas), Switzerland (e.g. relic purses, 14th century; Chur Cathedral, Treasury; Sion Cathedral, Treasury) and France (e.g. relic purse, ?13th century; Sens Cathedral, Treasury). The Spanish cushions are *Mudéjar* work, but no relation-

ship is discernible to Egyptian multicolour fragments of similar or slightly earlier date, and the Egyptian work uses stitch structures similar to those of the Chinese braids mentioned above. Some 14th-century Italian paintings, and one by Master Bertram of Minden (Hamburg, Ksthalle), depict the Virgin Mary knitting in the round with several needles and with several colours. There are episcopal gloves in coloured knitting of the same period (examples in Toulouse, St-Sernin; Prague, St Vitus; London, V&A and Mus. London; Oxford, New Coll.). Silk, probably from Italy, and wool were both used.

Caps, knitted in wool and felted and teased into a nap, may have been produced in the 14th century and were the principal products of professional guilds in Spain, France, England and Germany in the late 15th century and the 16th. Hosiery was knitted in the same regions from shortly before 1500 but probably not as early as caps. Stockings remained the principal knitted product until the end of the 18th century. The Channel Islands and Shetland exported much hand-knitted hosiery from 1600 to 1800, and England was also a major exporter of knitted stockings until about 1780. Although stockingers' guilds continued to exist after 1550, stocking-knitting quickly became a cottage industry, a move encouraged by the development of steel wire-drawing, which made knitting needles cheaper. About 1589 William Lee, a freeholder from Nottinghamshire, devised the first knitting machine using a bank of hooked needles. For reasons that are far from clear, his machine was not accepted in England, and he took it to Rouen *c*. 1610, whence it spread to the rest of Europe and back to England. Machine knitting made slow progress at first and was for long restricted almost entirely to the production of hosiery.

Knitted body-garments (examples in Dresden, Hist. Mus.; London, V&A and Mus. London; Norwich, Strangers Hall Mus.), usually undergarments, had been made by hand at least since 1550. During the 17th century jackets were knitted with silk and metal yarns in imitation of damask and coloured brocade (e.g. London, V&A). The craft had reached Scandinavia and Iceland by the 16th century, but many extant specimens are difficult to date and attribute to a region. There is no record of knitting in Russia before the 1630s. In Alsace and Silesia between 1600 and 1780 magnificent multi-coloured carpets (table covers and wall hangings) were worked in wool, apparently on peg-frames. Cotton began to be widely used for knitted hosiery, quilts, petticoat skirts and babyclothes in the latter part of the 18th century. Beads were introduced into knitting by 1800, especially for purses. The diffusion of merino sheep throughout Europe during the 18th century led to widespread production of soft wools that could be dyed in many colours, especially in Germany during the post-Napoleonic years. During the 19th century knitting began to be used in the creation of bijouterie (small boxes, purses and toys) by ladies of leisure. Shetland produced extremely fine, woollen knitted lace from 1840, while at about the same time the Azores became a centre for very fine lace (e.g. New York, Hisp. Soc. America) of *pita* thread, made of fibre from the agave plant. There was a revival of fine cotton knitted lace in Germany and Austria in the 1920s and 1930s.

Fishermen's jumpers became popular throughout north-western Europe during the 19th century. The names jersey and guernsey were old words for knitted fabric, dating from the great 16th–17th-century output of stockings from the Channel Islands. A combination of fishermen's jerseys and the decorative fabrics of central European knitters was the basis for the traditional Aran jumper of western Ireland in the 20th century, and Scandinavia and Shetland also developed local traditions of coloured jumpers in the 19th and 20th centuries respectively, with the appearance in the 1920s of the Fair Isle (or Shetland) jumper with coloured patterns in horizontal bands. The sleeveless pullover followed about 1930.

Machine knitting of body garments had begun in the 19th century and was further stimulated by improvements to the flat knitting machine by the American Isaac N. Lamb in 1866. Increased interest in outdoor sports, especially golf, tennis and swimming, drew attention to the value of knitted fabric for leisure wear, and such items as the cardigan were widely accepted by World War I. Thereafter, knitwear found its way into fashion. In the 1960s the tracksuit and cat-suit, invariably machine-knitted, were extremely popular. Since World War II such man-made fibres as acrylic, polyamide and elastane have vied with wool, silk and cotton as knitting materials. Domestic knitting machines, available since the 1880s,

have increased rapidly in popularity since 1970, while at the same time industrial knitting has made enormous technological advances. In the West the low cost of machine knitwear has almost put an end to domestic knitting, which is now practised mainly for pleasure or to create high fashion. Further developments in the design of fabric structure can be expected from machine knitting, which has long gone beyond the definition of weft knitting, branching out into warp knitting to produce structures with some similarity to crochet, and hybrid knitweave structures. Since 1960 hand knitters have been experimenting with knitting as a sculptural technique, producing works of art both representational and abstract.

A distinct tradition of hand knitting, different in technique and design from western European knitting and distinguished by a frequent use of closed-loop structure, exists in the Islamic world, extending from Serbia to Kansu, from Algeria to Kashmir. Nalbinding is still used in West Africa to make ceremonial costumes of bast fibres. In the Roraima Mountains on the Venezuela-Guyana border several tribes make narrow knitted bands in vegetable fibres, using either a set of skewers, or a peg-frame with no baseboard, or hooked wooden needles.

The single-element structure of knitting imposes strict limitations on its artistic potential. Knitters have traditionally drawn their motifs from such other crafts as weaving, embroidery, patchwork, carpets and needle-lace. Knitted fabric has a natural elasticity that no other textile could match before the invention of elastomeric fibres *c.* 1960. This elasticity has made possible the development of body-contour fashion, beginning with 16th-century hosiery and culminating in modern aquadynamic swimwear. At the same time it elicits a topological interest that has led to the combination of the knitting technique with metals and resins for the production of specialized elements in engineering technology.

F. A. Wells: *The British Hosiery and Knitwear Industry* (London, 1935)

H. Diettrich and K. Hahnel: *Atlas für Gewirke und Gestricke* (Leipzig, 1959)

J. A. Smirfitt: *An Introduction to Weft Knitting* (Watford, 1975)

I. Turnau: *Historia dziewiarstwa europejskiego do początku XIX wieku* [History of European knitting to the beginning of the 19th century] (Warsaw, 1979)

D. Spencer: *Knitting Technology* (Oxford, 1983)

M. W. Phillips: *Creative Knitting* (St Paul, MI, 1986)

R. Rutt: *A History of Hand Knitting* (London, 1987)

J. Hiatt: *The Principles of Knitting: Methods and Techniques of Hand Knitting* (New York, 1988)

A. L. Macdonald: *No Idle Hands: The Social History of American Knitting* (New York, 1988)

N. Bush: *Folk Socks: The History & Techniques of Handknitted Footwear* (Loveland, 1994)

A. Feitelson: *The Art of Fair Isle Knitting: History, Technique, Color & Patterns* (Loveland, 1996)

K. Buss: *Big Book of Knitting* (New York, 1999)

Knives. *See under* CUTLERY, §1.

Knole Settee. Type of upholstered settee or sofa with a high back and arms hinged from the seat level;

the arms could be vertical (with the tops level with the back) or sloped outwards. The prototype is a 'couch chair' (i.e. a settee or sofa) made in the early 17th century (possibly 1630s). This settee, which has been in Knole (Kent, NT) for centuries, is upholstered in red velvet and has red fringes. It may be identical with the 'couch' made in 1637 for Queen Henrietta Maria by Ralph Grinder. This settee became the model for variously upholstered settees manufactured for English and American houses in the 20th century.

G. Beard and J. Coleman: 'The Knole Settee', Apollo, cxlix/446 (April 1999), pp. 24–8

Knoll. American furniture and interior design company founded in 1938 in New York by Hans Knoll (1914–55), who in 1950 moved the company to East Greenville, PA. After his premature death in 1955 the company was run until 1960 by his widow Florence (née Schust). In 1945 Florence Knoll had created the interior design part of the business, and it was she who attracted designers such as LUDWIG MIES VAN DER ROHE (whose student she had been), EERO SAARINEN and HARRY BERTOIA to design Knoll furniture. Knoll now specializes in office furnishings, and manufactures in the USA (East Greenville, GRAND RAPIDS, MI and Muskegon, MI), Canada (Toronto) and Italy (Foligno and Graffignana). Its museum in East Greenville displays Knoll furniture.

S. Rouland and L. Rouland: Knoll Furniture, 1938–1960 (Atglen, PA, 2005)

Knop. Small decorative swelling on the stem of a cup, chalice or candlestick.

Knorpelwerk. See AURICULAR STYLE.

Knowles, Taylor & Knowles. American ceramics manufacturer. Although a cabinetmaker by trade, Isaac Watts Knowles (1819–1902) founded his first pottery in 1854 with Isaac Harvey in East Liverpool, OH. There they made yellow ware and Rockingham for the West Coast market and were best known for jars used to preserve fruit. Harvey withdrew from the concern in the mid-1860s, and in 1870 Knowles's son Homer S. Knowles (1851–92) and his son-in-law John N. Taylor (1842–1914) joined the firm. Knowles, Taylor & Knowles continued to produce yellow ware until 1873, when the whiteware it had begun making in 1872 became commercially successful. In this medium it produced tea, dinner, toilet and kitchen wares and decorative accessories. Production expanded until, by 1891, the company had become the largest pottery in the USA, with 29 kilns. Fine Belleek porcelain was made only briefly from the late 1880s until 1897, when it was replaced by the range of 'Lotus Ware', a translucent bone china with sprigged filigree ornaments, leaves and flowers. After this product failed, soft porcelain wares were

made in the china plant. Hotel china, hospital specialities and porcelain for electrical appliances were also produced. Business declined during the mid-1920s, and the firm was absorbed in 1929 by the short-lived American China Co.

W. C. Gates Jr and D. Ormerod: 'The East Liverpool Pottery District: Identification of Manufacturers and Marks', Hist. Archaeol.: Annu. Pubn. Soc. Hist. Archaeol., xvi (1982), pp. 1–358 (115–27)

Knox, Archibald (b Cronkbourne, Tromode, Isle of Man, 2 April 1864; d Douglas, Isle of Man, 22 Feb 1933). Manx designer, active in England. After training at the Douglas School of Art, Isle of Man (1878–84), he moved to London in 1897 where he worked as a designer for, among others, the Silver Studio and taught at Redhill and Kingston art schools. His important association with ARTHUR LASENBY LIBERTY began in 1901 with his designs for the Celtic-inspired Cymric collection of silver and jewellery and for the Tudric domestic pewterware introduced by Liberty in 1903. His interpretation of Celtic forms was the closest approach to true English Art Nouveau, his disciplined use of Runic patterns contrasting with the excesses of the continental versions of the style. He was the most outstanding of Liberty's creative artists, producing over 400 designs for carpets, fabrics and metalwork from 1904 to 1912. In 1912 he resigned from his teaching post at Kingston College of Art following criticism of his teaching style and results. A group of his students also left in protest at his resignation and formed the Knox Guild of Craft and Design, which held successful annual exhibitions from 1913 until the beginning of World War II in 1939.

A. J. Tilbrook and G. House, eds: The Designs of Archibald Knox for Liberty & Co. (London, 1976)

S. A. Martin: Archibald Knox (London and Lanham, MD, 1995)

M. Caotts: 'Archibald Knox at the Silver Studio', World of Interiors, xx/10 (Oct 2000), p. 309

T. A. Langley: The Metalwork Designs of Archibald Knox (1864–1933): A Synthesis of Japanese and Celtic Characteristics, Virginia Commonwealth University (2001)

J. G. Cawley: Archibald Knox and a New Garden Pottery, Cooper-Hewitt National Design Museum and Parsons School of Design (New York, 2004)

Knulling [nulling, knurling, nurling]. Type of Gadrooning consisting of a series of small beads worked on a metal surface (usually the border) typically on 18th-century English silverware.

Knütgen [Curstgen; Kestgen; Kneutgen; Knuytgin]. German family of potters, active in late 16th-century Siegburg, where they made salt-glazed stoneware. Anno Knütgen (fl 1564–83) was ducal governor of the monastery in Siegburg from 1564 to 1575. The stonewares made in his workshop, which was probably the largest in Siegburg, included *Sturzbecher* (somersault cups), *Trichterbecher* (baluster-shaped beakers), flasks (e.g. field-flask, 1573; Cologne, Kstgewmus.) and *Schnellen* (tall, tapering tankards). An important figure, who was probably employed in the workshop, was the journeyman Frans Trac (*fl* 1559–68) who, *c.* 1559, began to decorate wares (particularly *Schnellen*) with relief motifs inspired by wares from Cologne (e.g. *Schnelle*, 1559; Nuremberg, Ger. Nmus.). The decorative schemes on the wares were based on engravings by such contemporary artists as HEINRICH ALDEGREVER, PETER FLÖTNER, SEBALD BEHAM, VIRGIL SOLIS, Theodor de Bry (1528–98), Jörg Breu and Abraham de Bruyn (1540–87). The illustrations published by Sigmund Feyerabend (1527/8–90), whose first Bible was issued in 1560, were used for biblical themes. Coats of arms were also employed for decoration. Although Anno did not sign his wares, a range of stoneware vessels have been ascribed to him, including a pilgrim-flask (1578; Frankfurt am Main, Mus. Ksthandwk). Around 1590, due to unfavourable political conditions, Anno moved with his sons Bertram Knütgen (*fl* 1590–1622), Hermann Knütgen (*d* 1625) and Rutger Knütgen to Höhr in the Westerwald. Other members of the family included Christian Knütgen (*fl* 1566–1610) and Peter Knütgen (*fl* 1564–71); their relationship to Anno, however, has not been established. Christian is often regarded as the most outstanding member of the family. The many vessels created by him were dated and almost always marked (CK). His earliest dated work is a *Schnelle* (1568; Düsseldorf, Hetjens-Mus.) decorated with a detailed biblical scene. His representations of coats of arms are also detailed and subtle, particularly those on *Schnellen* made between 1580 and 1590. From the 1590s the relief decoration became increasingly sophisticated, especially on *Schnabelkannen* (globular jugs with a bridge spout). The subtlety and grace of the friezes, among which was a scene of the heron and unicorn based on an engraving by Virgil Solis (e.g. *Schnabelkanne*, 1591; Cologne, Kstgewmus.), is outstanding.

There are only a few extant works by Peter Knütgen, which are all marked (PK). His signed and dated *Schnellen* (e.g. of 1560–70; Düsseldorf, Hetjens-Mus.) suggest that he was a very efficient potter who was probably quite strongly influenced by Frans Trac.

W. Felten: 'Die Siegburger Töpferfamilie Knütgen', *Heimathl. Siegkreises*, vii (1926), p. 561

J. M. Fritz: 'Eine Siegburger Riesenschnelle aus Göttingen', *Keramos*, xl (1968), pp. 3–12

E. Klinge: *Siegburger Steinzeug*, Düsseldorf, Hetjens-Mus. cat. (Düsseldorf, 1972)

Kocks, Adriaensz. *See under* EENHORN.

Kōetsu Hon'ami. *See* HON'AMI KŌETSU.

Kohn, J. & J. *See under* THONET, MICHAEL.

Kok, J. Jurriaan (*b* Rotterdam, 6 April 1861; *d* The Hague, 19 June 1919). Dutch ceramicist and architect. From 1894 and 1913 he worked at ROZENBURG FACTORY, a Delftware factory in The Hague, first as aesthetic adviser, as manager after June 1894 and a year later as general manager. He introduced numerous improvements in the production process. With chemist M. N. Engelen he developed a number of chemical methods to make porcelain, resulting in a wafer-thin product that was a type of eggshell porcelain and that found a variety of ceramic applications. The porcelain was shaped in plaster moulds and biscuit fired at a low temperature. After that the product was painted, glazed and fired at a high temperature.

F. Netscher: 'Karakterschets J. Jurriaan Kok', *Holland. Rev.*, viii/12 (1903), pp. 832–47

Kokukan. *See* AOKI MOKUBEI.

Köln. *See* COLOGNE.

Koma. *See* SHIBATA ZESHIN.

Konan Hozen. *See* EIRAKU HOZEN.

Kongelige Porcelainsfabrik. *See* COPENHAGEN PORCELAIN FACTORY.

Königliche Porzellan-Manufaktur (KPM). *See under* BERLIN, §2.

Königsberg. *See* KALININGRAD.

Königstädten Porcelain Factory. *See* KELSTERBACH PORCELAIN FACTORY.

Koninklijke Tichelaar Makkum. *See* MAKKUM POTTERY FACTORY.

Köpping, Karl (*b* Dresden, 24 June 1848; *d* Berlin, 15 July 1914). German printmaker, painter and designer. He is best known as an etcher, and his etchings include original designs for ornamental glass. His study of Venetian glass-blowing techniques and the blended colour glazes of Japanese pottery enabled him to design blown glass of great delicacy and striking colour effects. His glass was made in the studio of Friedrich Zitzmann (1840–1906) in Wiesbaden and in training workshops at Ilmenau in Saxony.

Karl Köpping (exh. cat. by H. W. Singer; Dresden, Gal. Richter, 1916)

H. Hilschenz: *Das Glas des Jugendstils: Katalog der Sammlung Hentrich im Kunstmuseum Düsseldorf* (Munich, 1973), pp. 96–101

W. Spiegl and others: *Lampengeblasenes Glas: Geschichte, Technologie, die Glasbläserei Schmid* (n.p., 1985)

Kosta Glasbruk. Glass factory established in 1742 in Kosta, in the Småland region of southern Sweden. No particularly original styles can be distinguished in its early wares. In the late 19th century, however, designers such as Gunnar Wennerberg (1863–1914) began to produce Art Nouveau glass in a style indebted to EMILE GALLÉ. In 1903 Kosta and RE-IJMYRE GLASBRUK merged to become the Svenska Kristallbruk but retained their names and continued to design and manufacture separately. EDVIN OLLERS worked as a painter and designer at Kosta (1917–18), and EWALD DAHLSKOG revived glass-engraving during his period as director (1926–9). From 1950 to 1973 the artistic director was V. E. LINDSTRAND. Sweden's greatest studio glassmaker, Ann [Wärff] Wolff (*b* 1937), worked for the Kosta Glasbruk from 1964 to 1979, before she established her own studio at Transjö (near Kosta). In 1964 Kosta merged with the glassworks at Boda and Åfors to form Kosta Boda, which in 1990 was bought by ORREFORS GLASBRUK. Orrefors/Kosta Boda was in turn acquired by Royal Copenhagen in 1997, and so is now part of the design group Royal Scandinavia.

Kosta Crystal Designed by Mona Morales Schildt (exh. cat., Kosta, Georg Jensen, Inc., 1963)
M. Artéus: *Kosta 250: 1742–1992* (Kosta, 1992)
C. Finch: 'Modern Swedish Glass: New Focus on a Scintillating Legacy', *Archit. Dig., liv* (July 1997), p. 42ff

Kothgasser, Anton (*b* 1769; *d* 1851). Austrian glass enameller. He adopted the transparent enamell painting techniques of SAMUEL MOHN and his son Gottlob, and from 1815 to 1830 was a leader in the enamel decoration of glasses. The subjects depicted on his glasses encompass a wide range of *vedute*, portraits, allegories etc; they differ from Mohn glasses by virtue of their more picturesque presentation.

A. Kothgasser, R. von Strasser and K. H. Heine: *Die Einschreibebüchlein des Wiener Glas- und Porzellanmalers Anton Kothgasser: 1769–1851* (Karlsruhe, 1977)

Kovsh. Boat-shaped vessel with a single handle, used for drinking and as a ladle for drinks. Early examples in wood sometimes resemble a swimming duck. From the 16th century the *kovsh* was also made in silver. In the late 19th century the Russian Revival style was expressed mainly in the art of enamel, and firms such as Ovchinnikov produced traditional forms, including the *kovsh*, with decoration using the traditional filigree enamel technique.

Kraak ware. New type of export porcelain developed in the late 16th century at JINGDEZHEN; its Dutch name derived from the carrack, a type of Portuguese cargo ship in which it was initially transported. Kraak wares, which were formed in or on a mould, have underglaze blue decoration, thin walls and often carry baked-on sand on the base. The decoration consists mostly of flowers, birds and insects in riverscape. The walls have alternating broad and narrow panels in low relief, painted with flowers, fruiting branches and Buddhist or Daoist emblems. Kraak wares were produced in a limited range of practical forms, in series of graduated sizes. In 1636, 259,000 pieces of kraak were shipped from Batavia,

and the passion for blue and white in the Netherlands was thus established.

M. Rinaldi: *Kraak Porcelain* (London, 1989)
C. J. A. Jorg: 'Treasures of the Dutch Trade in Chinese Porcelain', *Oriental A.*, xlviii/5 (2002–3), pp. 20–26

Krautstrunk [Warzenbecher]. Type of German drinking glass made in the German lands and eastern France since the 15th century. It is a cyindrical tumbler made of green glass with prunts that resemble the stem of a cabbage. Some fine 15th-century examples were adapted for use as reliquaries.

Kreibitz. *See* CHŘIBSKÁ.

Kreussen. *See* CREUSSEN.

Krog, Arnold (*b* Frederiksvœrk, Zealand, 18 March 1856; *d* Tisvilde, Zealand, 7 June 1931). Danish porcelain painter and architect. In October 1884 he was was engaged as an artist at the COPENHAGEN PORCELAIN FACTORY on a trial basis, and in January 1885 he was appointed as artistic director. His first attempts at finding a style different from the white, gilded, classical porcelain, embellished with coloured overglazes, that had been the standard ware of the factory, were made with Renaissance patterns and in the manner of wares from the Delft potteries. However, an 'Immortelle' plate that had been made at the factory from 1790 inspired Krog, and he produced forms suitable for this delicate, underglazed, blue-flower pattern. Other sources of inspiration were: Japanese ceramics, painting and woodcuts; Karl Madsen's *Japansk Malerkunst* (1885), which analyses motifs in Japanese paintings; and a visit in 1886 to S. Bing's shop, L'Art Nouveau, in Paris, where he saw the collection of objects from East Asia.

With the help of the industrial chemist Adolphe Clément (1860–1933), Krog invented a technique in which cobalt blue, underglaze painting was fired together with a chrome green and a golden red under an alkaline feldspar glaze at very high temperatures. Wares included elegantly shaped vases and dishes painted with naturalistic, misty, Danish landscapes, flora and fauna in muted, gently blurred, underglaze blues and greys. In 1888 he designed a vase with gulls and breaking waves (1888; Hamburg, Mus. Kst & Gew.) that was inspired by the woodblock prints of Katsushika Hokusai (1760–1849). Krog's work won international acclaim at the Exposition Universelle of 1889 in Paris. In addition to individual wares, Krog exerted his influence on the factory's old production lines. He revised its earliest works and produced new versions of the 'Immortelle' service with lace edges. Between 1894 and 1899 he designed the Art Nouveau style 'Marguerite' service. In the early 20th century he experimented with crystal glazes and stoneware. In 1916 he retired, but his designs continue to be produced in the early 21st century.

D. Helsted: 'Arnold Krog and the Porcelain', *The Royal Copenhagen Porcelain Manufactory, 1775–1975* (Copenhagen, 1975), pp. 28–57

Krug, Ludwig (*b* Nuremberg, 1488–90; *d* Nuremberg, 1532). German engraver, sculptor, designer, goldsmith and metalworker. He was one of the most versatile craftsmen active in Nuremberg in the first two decades of the 16th century. During the 1510s he was best known as a graphic artist and sculptor rather than as a goldsmith.

He was most active as a goldsmith during the 1520s, when, as a member of his family's goldsmithing business, he was adept at designing the sumptuous silver-gilt cups, with tendrils and other naturalistic features, that bear the workshop mark. Several goldsmiths' models, including a boxwood *Seated Warrior* (*c.* 1530; Berlin, Tiergarten, Kstgewmus.), are ascribed to him. Numerous elaborate covered cups (examples Berlin, Tiergarten, Kstgewmus.; Vienna, Ksthist. Mus.; and, formerly, Moscow, Kremlin) reflect his style and often bear the N, or city goldsmiths' mark. The animated finial and stem figures recall the Düreresque characters of Krug's graphic oeuvre. Given the collaborative nature of this prolific workshop, it is hardly surprising that so few autograph objects by Ludwig himself have been identified. His monogram and *Krug* symbol adorned the ciborium with the *Virgin and a Woodcutter* (1520–26/7; untraced), the appearance of which is documented in a drawing in the *Halleschen Heiltum* (Aschaffenburg, Schloss Johannisburg, Hof- & Stiftsbib). Based on the style of this ciborium, several objects known from other drawings in the *Halleschen Heiltum* manuscript (fols 205*v*, 216*v* and 367*v*) have also been tentatively attributed to Ludwig Krug. He probably also created a covered cup with the *Labours of Hercules* (ex-Raudnitz Castle, Prague, 1922), which was stamped with the workshop's registered mark. Decorating its sides was a series of shell relief roundels illustrating Hercules' exploits that Krug copied from drawings by Dürer of 1511.

Krug had an unusual talent for carving shell cameos, a technique more commonly found in France. Two related shell-carvings of elongated format but otherwise identical design are the *Birth of Hercules* (*c.* 1525; Hamburg, Mus. Kst & Gew.) and *Hercules and Antaeus* (*c.* 1525; St Petersburg, Hermitage), made to decorate a Krug workshop silver cup.

M. A. McCrory: 'Renaissance Shell Cameos from the Carrand Collection of the Museo Nazionale del Bargello', *Burl. Mag.*, cxxx (June 1988), pp. 412–26 [with catalogue]

N. Stogdon: 'Prints from Goluchow Rediscovered', *Print Q.* xiii (June 1996), pp. 149–80 [15th century collection from Pleszew, Poland]

Krystallglas. *See* CRYSTAL.

Kubachi ware. Type of Iranian pottery with a soft and porous white body covered with a thin, crackled glaze, named after a remote town in Dagestan in the Caucasus where many examples were found in the late 19th century. The town was better known for its foundries than its ceramics, and presumably the dishes had been made and purchased further south in exchange for firearms before being set as decoration into the fabric of local houses. In the late 16th century a new type of Kubachi ware, with polychrome slip painting and an occasional pink slipped ground (e.g. Sèvres, Mus. N. Cér., 22693), was introduced. Typical decorative motifs include animals, flowers, stylized figures and busts and geometric patterns. A dish depicting the zodiac painted by 'Abd al-Vahid in two tones of blackish blue on white (1563–4; Berlin, Mus. Islam. Kst.) shows a geometric composition of 12 zodiac circles with chinoiserie small clouds and scale-fillers in the interstices. Kubachi wares continued to be produced until the first quarter of the 17th century in both polychrome (e.g. a tomb slab dated 1628; London, V&A) and blue-and-white schemes of central figures, flowers, animals or geometric patterns on dishes and tiles. Some examples were decorated with pagodas and high hills, imitating 17th-century Chinese porcelain.

E. Gibbs: 'White Nights at the Hermitage', *Hali*, cxxxvi (Sept–Oct 2004), p. 104

Kukurin. *See* AOKI MOKUBEI.

Ludwig Krug: covered cup in the form of an apple, Nuremberg, early 16th century (Nuremberg, Germanisches Nationalmuseum)

Kunckel, Johann. *See under* BRANDENBURG.

Kungsholm Glasbruk. Swedish glasshouse founded in Stockholm in 1686 by the Italian glassmaker Giacomo Bernardini Scapitta (*fl* 1676–8), who produced tall, thinly blown goblets *à la façon de Venise* decorated with royal crowns on the covers and the initials of the reigning monarch integrated into the stem by clever manipulation. During the early 18th century Kungsholm produced fine goblets, which incorporated Venetian and German elements and some of which were engraved with royal cyphers and emblems. Wheel-engraving may have been practised in Sweden in the latter part of the 17th century, but it was not until *c.* 1690, when the German-born Kristoffer Elsterman (*d* 1721) arrived in Stockholm, that the technique was firmly established. From the mid-18th century until the glassworks closed in 1815, Kungsholm glass was to a large exent copied from standardized German models of goblets and stemmed glasses.

Kunstschrank. Type of collector's cabinet made in Germany during the 16th and early 17th centuries. The most famous example was the Pomeranian cabinet (Pommersche Kunstschrank) which Philipp Hainhofer (1578–1647) had made for Duke Philip of Pomerania-Stettin. The joiner was ULRICH BAUMGARTNER, and almost 30 Augsburg artists and craftsmen worked on its decoration and contents. The cabinet contained a set of instruments and tools for almost every human occupation, symbolizing the triumph of Art and Science over Nature. The cabinet was destroyed in 1945, but the contents are intact and a few fragments have survived (1611–15, Berlin, Tiergarten, Kstgewmus.).

Kütahya. Ottoman pottery centre near IZNIK. Early blue-and-white wares were once ascribed to kilns run by the Armenian community at Kütahya, because two examples in the British Museum (dated 1510 and 1529) bear Armenian inscriptions mentioning that city. It now seems likely that both were made in Iznik. In the 18th century, however, the kilns of Kütahya began to produce pretty polychrome underglaze-painted wares in considerable quantity, and Kütahya replaced Iznik as the main centre of ceramic production. The sizeable Armenian population of Kütahya introduced into the Ottoman decorative vocabulary a range of Christian figural subjects (e.g. a wine-bowl signed by Toros with Christ flanked by the 12 Apostles; Athens, Benaki Mus), and widespread social changes led to the emergence of a new type of ware, the bowl-like coffee-cup and saucer, to serve the needs of the many coffee-houses that became a common Ottoman institution. By the 19th century Kütahya commercial production had began to decline, but in the last quarter of the 19th century there was a limited revival of Kütahya tiles.

J. Carswell and C. J. F. Dowsett: *Kütahya Tiles and Pottery from the Armenian Cathedral of St James, Jerusalem*, 2 vols (Oxford, 1972)

Kutani. Centre of ceramics production in Japan. Porcelain was produced from the mid-17th century at Kutani (now in Ishikawa Prefect.). The term Old Kutani (*Ko Kutani*) is frequently applied to what has long been believed to be the earliest wares, typically large porcelain dishes decorated with bold designs in overglaze enamels, with green, purple and yellow predominating. While there is little dispute about a mid-17th century date for the founding of the kilns, the nature of the early products has long been disputed. The present consensus is that the early production at Kutani, which spanned the period between *c.* 1650 and 1750, consisted of teawares and porcelain food vessels; few of these have survived down to the present. On the other hand, the Old Kutani style wares, many of which have been preserved, are now seen as a type of ARITA ware, manufactured between 1640 and 1660.

While ceramics production at Kutani seems to have flagged in the late 18th century, from the early 1800s a succession of kilns arose. In Kutani proper the Yoshidaya, Miyamotoya and Eiraku kilns were in operation between 1823 and the 1860s. The Yoshidaya kiln, probably founded *c.* 1823, attempted to imitate the Old Kutani style of lush enamels applied in broad fields, but the coarse clay body and overwrought designs are easily distinguished from the earlier products. A second cluster of kilns, located in and around the provincial capital at Kanazawa, were the Kasugayama and Minzan kilns, active between 1803 and 1844. The Kasugayama kiln is famous primarily for the participation of the famed Kyoto potter AOKI MOKUBEI, who worked at the kiln between 1806 and 1808 producing Chinese-inspired overglaze-enamel designs. The Kutani workshops declined with the dissolution of the feudal system in 1868, but within a year a new industry was established in Kanazawa, and Kutani overglaze-enamelled ware, lavishly decorated in red and gold, and frequently bearing poetic inscriptions in minute Chinese characters, came to win great favour among domestic and overseas consumers. In the Late Meiji period individual potters began to revive the Old Kutani style, providing a basis for the enamelled porcelain production that survives in the Kanazawa area.

S. Nakagawa: *Kutani Ware* (Tokyo, 1979)
H. Nishida: *Kutani* (Tokyo, 1990)
S. Matsumoto: *Kutaniyaki shitae zufu: kutani to aru nuvo no koryu* (Osaka, 2003)

Kuttrolf [Angster]. Type of WALDGLAS jug, made in Germany or Bohemia, consisting of a bulbous body surmounted by a long twisting neck consisting of several intertwined tubes that lead to a cup-shaped mouth. There is a fine 17th- century example in the Amsterdam Rijksmuseum.

Kwaart. Clear lead glaze applied to earthenwares in Delft during the 17th century and early 18th to give the finished product a particular brilliance.

Kwabornament. *See* AURICULAR STYLE.

Kyoto pottery. Ceramics from a Japanese city that has long been an important pottery centre; its tradition in ceramic wares for the tea ceremony is particularly distinctive.

Because of the availability of fine ceramics from China and a system that exacted tribute in the form of utilitarian wares from outlying regions, Kyoto was undistinguished as a production centre before the Momoyama period (1568–1600). In the late 16th century, however, there was a resurgence of cultural activity in the city, and particularly intense interest in the tea ceremony created sufficient demand to support a local industry. What Kyoto lacked in raw materials and efficient transport was compensated for by unparalleled access to the centres of culture and patronage. As the appreciation of ceramics gradually assumed a sophistication comparable to that accorded painting, the potters of Kyoto attracted nationwide attention and occasionally individual fame as teachers and producers of *Kyōyaki* ('Kyoto ceramics').

The first individual Kyoto potter who can be documented with any certainty is Chōjirō (1516–92), first-generation head of the RAKU family of potters. He made individually designed teabowls and decorative objects, usually coated with black or transparent lead glazes. A contemporary of Chōjirō was Ichimonjiya Sukezaēmon, who ran a workshop called Oshikōji, apparently producing imitations of the brightly coloured Kōchi (Cochin China) earthenwares imported from southern China. Although the Raku-ware style ossified around the models established by Chōjirō and his immediate successors, amateur potters such as HON'AMI KŌETSU began to use the Raku technique, eschewing the self-effacing Rikyū style in favour of more assertive personal statements.

The few extant wares and documentary evidence from the 17th century suggest an emphasis on imitations of the Chinese and Korean stonewares popular among tea devotees. NONOMURA NINSEI led the transition to a more decorative style, painted with sophisticated designs in the new overglaze enamel. Ninsei gradually abandoned the subdued idiom of teaware in favour of the more colourful *iroe* (overglaze enamel) method, first seen in Arita but distinctively applied by him to stoneware, as opposed to porcelain. Characteristic of this later phase are large tea storage jars and decorative objects, frequently executed in zoomorphic or other whimsical forms. By the last quarter of the 17th century most of the kilns in Kyoto had added these decorative novelties to the earlier teaware repertory. These other Kyoto products, often described under the generic title Kokiyomizu ('old' Kiyomizu), often used a green-and-blue enamel palette with occasional gold accents. The Kokiyomizu potters also followed Ninsei's lead in using seals.

Ninsei's artistic successor in Kyoto ceramics was OGATA KENZAN who in 1699 founded a kiln at Narutaki in north-western Kyoto. For the manual labour and technical repertory, Kenzan borrowed from the Ninsei workshop and from other local personnel, concentrating his own efforts on design. The early experiments included utilitarian wares inspired by foreign and native traditions, as well as a series of flat, rectilinear vessels displaying painterly compositions and his own distinctive calligraphy. In 1712, spurred by a rapidly growing reputation and the prospect of closer collaboration with his brother Ogata Kōrin, Kenzan relocated the kiln to Nijō Chōjiyamachi in central Kyoto. The Kenzan style, particularly applied to food vessels decorated with bold permutations of Kōrin's painting, proliferated through the traditional communal kiln system. A distinctive technique of the period was partial coating with white slip, which served as a smooth ground for painting and also contrasted with the darker clay body.

Between Kenzan's death in 1743 and the end of the 18th century not one potter of enduring renown emerged in Kyoto. In the absence of new initiatives, Kyoto studios did little more than consolidate earlier models, including the Ninsei, Kokiyomizu and Kenzan styles.

Kyoto wares revived in the early 19th century, under the stimuli of an improved economy and the growing popularity of drinking *sencha*, a form of steeped tea, which had begun to eclipse the earlier whipped tea (*matcha*) in appeal. The *sencha* boom was created by a group of self-styled scholar–gentlemen united in an admiration for Chinese literati culture. The founder of the new style was Okuda Eisen, who by the 1780s he was producing the copies of late Ming (1368–1644) period enamelled porcelain (*gosu akae*) that became his mainstay. Although there had been sporadic experiments with porcelain in Kyoto earlier in the 18th century, Eisen's endeavours marked the first sustained use of the material in Kyoto.

Eisen's principal disciples were AOKI MOKUBEI, Kinkodō Kamesuke (1764–1837) and Nin'ami Dōhachi (1783–1855). In. In 1805 Mokubei opened a kiln at Awataguchi, one of the old pottery centres in the eastern hills of Kyoto. The sheer breadth of his work, ranging from Chinese-style celadon, blue-and-white, and overglaze-decorated wares for *sencha* to the Korean- and Japanese-style pieces popular among *matcha* enthusiasts, attracted a series of influential patrons. The kiln in Awataguchi was sponsored by the prince–priest of the temple Shōrenin, and between 1806 and 1808 Mokubei supervised the Kasugayama kiln at the behest of the daimyo of Kaga Province (now Ishikawa Prefect.).

Kinkodō Kamesuke probably first trained as a maker of Fushimi earthenware dolls, an important product of the Kyoto ceramics industry since about the early 17th century. The few extant wares attributable to Kamesuke suggest a proficiency in Chinese-style celadons and enamel-on-biscuit, as well as Korean-inspired inlay techniques, often executed on vessels formed in moulds. Eisen's youngest protégé,

Nin'ami Dōhachi, specialized in the indigenous *matcha* taste, particularly in Korean-style and Raku works and Kenzan imitations. Other prominent potters of the period included Ogata Shūhei (1788–1839), a younger brother of Dōhachi who concentrated on wares for *sencha*, and the Eiraku family potters, Hōzen (1795–1854) and Wazen (1823–96), who worked in both *matcha* and *sencha* styles but gained special prominence in underglaze-decorated (e.g. *sometsuke*, underglaze cobalt or blue-and-white wares) and enamelled porcelain. These masters, following the precedent set by Kenzan, were typically designer–painters who supervised a workshop of specialist craftsmen.

The withdrawal of the imperial establishment and the dissolution of the feudal domains in the Meiji Restoration (1868) nearly devastated the Kyoto ceramics industry, but the establishment of export markets and the opportunity to exhibit at international expositions encouraged new products. By the late 1870s, with assistance from outside experts such as Gottfried Wagener (1831–92), who advised the government and crafts industries on technical and production matters, Kyoto wares regained prominence. The training institute became the new salon; the potters who achieved success, such as Kinkozan Sōbei (*d* 1884) and Kiyomizu Rokubei (1822–82), were those who quickly mastered new methods such as slip casting and European-style overglaze enamels. By the early 20th century, however, some Kyoto testing-centre dissidents, notably KANIRŌ KAWAI and SHŌJI HAMADA, reacted against the overrefined export standard, asserting that the potter should not be just a technician or a decorator but an artist personally involved with every phase of the production process. The emphasis on creativity led to the establishment, in 1949, of the first university ceramics department in Japan at the Kyoto Municipal College of Fine Arts (Kyoto Shiritsu Geijutsu Daigaku); the first department head was KENKICHI TOMIMOTO.

M. Kawahara: 'Early Kyoto Ceramics', *Chanoyu Q.*, xxxii (1982), pp. 31–46

A. Tanihata: 'Tea and Kyoto Ceramics in the Late Edo Period', *Chanoyu Q.*, xxxix (1984), pp. 7–17

Kyoto Potters 2 vols (Kyoto, 1993)